Lecture Notes in Artificial Intelligence **11012**

Subseries of Lecture Notes in Computer Science

More information about this series at http://www.springer.com/series/1244

Xin Geng · Byeong-Ho Kang (Eds.)

PRICAI 2018: Trends in Artificial Intelligence

15th Pacific Rim
International Conference on Artificial Intelligence
Nanjing, China, August 28–31, 2018
Proceedings, Part I

Editors
Xin Geng
Southeast University
Nanjing
China

Byeong-Ho Kang
University of Tasmania
Hobart, TAS
Australia

ISSN 0302-9743 ISSN 1611-3349 (electronic)
Lecture Notes in Artificial Intelligence
ISBN 978-3-319-97303-6 ISBN 978-3-319-97304-3 (eBook)
https://doi.org/10.1007/978-3-319-97304-3

Library of Congress Control Number: 2018949307

LNCS Sublibrary: SL7 – Artificial Intelligence

This Springer imprint is published by the registered company Springer Nature Switzerland AG
The registered company address is: Gewerbestrasse 11, 6330 Cham, Switzerland

Preface

This volume contains the papers presented at the 15th Pacific Rim International Conference on Artificial Intelligence (PRICAI 2018) held during August 28–31, 2018, in Nanjing, China. PRICAI is a biennial conference inaugurated in Tokyo in 1990. It provides a common forum for researchers and practitioners in various branches of artificial intelligence (AI) to exchange new ideas and share experience and expertise. Over the past 28 years, the conference has grown, both in participation and scope, to be a premier international AI event for all major Pacific Rim nations as well as countries from further afield. This year, PRICAI 2018 featured two special tracks in addition to the main track, "Reinforcement Learning" and "Smart Modelling and Simulation," both of which accentuated emerging hot topics in recent years of AI research.

This year, we received 382 high-quality submissions from 24 countries to both the main and special tracks. The submission number set a record over the last ten years (six PRICAIs in a row), reflecting the growing boom of artificial intelligence all over the world. The paper selection process was very competitive. From these submissions, 82 (21%) were accepted as regular papers, with a further 58 (15%) accepted as short papers. Each submitted paper was considered by the Program Committee (PC) members and external reviewers, and evaluated against criteria such as relevance, significance, technical soundness, novelty, and clarity. Every paper received at least two reviews, in most cases three, and in some cases up to five. Finally, the program co-chairs read the reviews, the original papers, and called for additional reviews if necessary to make final decisions. The entire review team (PC members, external reviewers, and co-chairs) expended tremendous effort to ensure fairness and consistency in the paper selection process.

The technical program consisted of workshops and tutorials and the three-day main conference program. There were four tutorials and six workshops coving thriving and important topics in artificial intelligence. The workshops included the Pacific Rim Knowledge Acquisition Workshop (PKAW), co-chaired by Kenichi Yoshida (University of Tsukuba, Japan) and Maria R. Lee (Shih Chien University, Taiwan, China), which has long enjoyed a successful co-location with PRICAI. All regular papers were orally presented over the three days in the topical program sessions and special sessions. The authors of short papers presented their results during the poster sessions, and were also offered the opportunity to give shortened talks to introduce their work. It was our great honor to have three outstanding keynote/invited speakers, whose contributions have pushed boundaries of artificial intelligence across various aspects: Professor Stephen Muggleton (Imperial College London, UK), Professor Qiang Yang (Hong Kong University of Science and Technology, China), and Dr. Kun Zhang (Carnegie Mellon University, USA). We are grateful to them for sharing their insights on their latest research with us.

The success of PRICAI 2018 would not have been possible without the effort and support of numerous people from all over the world. First of all, we would like to thank the Program Committee members and external reviewers for their engagements in providing rigorous and timely reviews. It was because of them that the quality of the papers in this volume is maintained at a high level. We wish to express our gratitude to the general co-chairs, Zhi-Hua Zhou (Nanjing University, China) and Geoff Webb (Monash University, Australia) for their continued support and guidance. We are also thankful to the workshop co-chairs, Yang Yu (Nanjing University, China) and Tsuyoshi Murata (Tokyo Institute of Technology, Japan), the tutorial co-chairs, Mengjie Zhang (Victoria University of Wellington, New Zealand) and Tru Hoang Cao (Ho Chi Minh City University of Technology, Vietnam), the publication chair, Min-Ling Zhang (Southeast University, China), the sponsorship chair, Xiang Bai (Huazhong University of Science and Technology, China), the local organizing co-chairs, Feng Xu (Hohai University, China) and Deyu Zhou (Southeast University, China), and the publicity co-chairs, Chuan-Kang Ting (National Chung Cheng University, Taiwan, China) and Sheng-Jun Huang (Nanjing University of Aeronautics and Astronautics, China).

We gratefully acknowledge the support of the organizing institutions Southeast University, Jiangsu Association of Artificial Intelligence, Nanjing University, Nanjing University of Aeronautics and Astronautics, and Hohai University, as well as the financial support from Nanjing Future Sci-Tech City, Alibaba Group, Baidu Inc., Huatai Securities Co., Ltd., Huawei Technologies Co., Ltd., iHome Technologies Co., Ltd., Key Laboratory of IntelliSense Technology, CETC, Springer Publishing, and Jiangsu Zhitu Education Technology Co., Ltd. Special thanks to EasyChair, whose paper submission platform we used to organize reviews and collate the files for these proceedings. We are also grateful to Alfred Hofmann and Anna Kramer from Springer for their assistance in publishing the PRICAI 2018 proceedings as a volume in its *Lecture Notes in Artificial Intelligence* series.

Last but not least, we also want to thank all authors and all conference participants for their contribution and support. We hope all the participants took this valuable opportunity to share and exchange their ideas and thoughts with one another and enjoyed their time at PRICAI 2018.

August 2018

Xin Geng
Byeong-Ho Kang

Organization

Steering Committee

Tru Hoang Cao	Ho Chi Minh City University of Technology, Vietnam
Aditya Ghose	University of Wollongong, Australia
Byeong-Ho Kang	University of Tasmania, Australia
Dickson Lukose	GCS Agile Pty. Ltd., Australia
Hideyuki Nakashima (Chair)	Future University Hakodate, Japan
Seong-Bae Park	Kyungpook National University, South Korea
Duc Nghia Pham	Griffith University, Australia
Abdul Sattar (Treasurer)	Griffith University, Australia
Ito Takayuki	Nagoya Institute of Technology, Japan
Thanaruk Theeramunkong	Sirindhorn International Institute of Technology, Thailand
Toby Walsh	NICTA, Australia
Zhi-Hua Zhou (Co-chair)	Nanjing University, China

Organizing Committee

General Co-chairs

Zhi-Hua Zhou	Nanjing University, China
Geoff Webb	Monash University, Australia

Program Co-chairs

Xin Geng	Southeast University, China
Byeong-Ho Kang	University of Tasmania, Australia

Workshop Co-chairs

Yang Yu	Nanjing University, China
Tsuyoshi Murata	Tokyo Institute of Technology, Japan

Tutorial Co-chairs

Mengjie Zhang	Victoria University of Wellington, New Zealand
Tru Hoang Cao	Ho Chi Minh City University of Technology, Vietnam

Publication Chair

Min-Ling Zhang	Southeast University, China

Sponsorship Chair

Xiang Bai	Huazhong University of Science and Technology, China

Local Organizing Co-chairs

Feng Xu	Hohai University, China
Deyu Zhou	Southeast University, China

Publicity Co-chairs

Chuan-Kang Ting	National Chung Cheng University, Taiwan, China
Sheng-Jun Huang	Nanjing University of Aeronautics and Astronautics, China

Program Committee

Eriko Aiba	The University of Electro-Communications, Japan
David Albrecht	Monash University, Australia
Patricia Anthony	Lincoln University, New Zealand
Quan Bai	Auckland University of Technology, New Zealand
Daan Bloembergen	Centrum Wiskunde and Informatica, New Zealand
Richard Booth	Cardiff University, UK
Patrice Boursier	University of La Rochelle, France
Marut Buranarach	NECTEC, Thailand
Rafael Cabredo	De La Salle University, Philippines
Tru Hoang Cao	Ho Chi Minh City University of Technology, Vietnam
Gang Chen	Victoria University of Wellington, New Zealand
Hao Chen	Fortiss GmbH, Germany
Lei Chen	Nanjing University of Posts and Telecommunications, China
Shikai Chen	Southeast University, China
Siqi Chen	Southwest University, China
Songcan Chen	Nanjing University of Aeronautics and Astronautics, China
Wu Chen	Southwest University, China
Yingke Chen	Sichuan University, China
Wai Khuen Cheng	Member of TC, Malaysia
Krisana Chinnasarn	Burapha University, Thailand
Phatthanaphong Chomphuwiset	Mahasarakham University, Thailand
Jen Jen Chung	ETH Zurich, Switzerland
Jirapun Daengdej	Assumption University, Thailand
Enrique De-La-Hoz	UAH, Spain
Andreas Dengel	German Research Center for Artificial Intelligence, Germany
Shyamala Doraisamy	University Putra Malaysia, Malaysia

Vlad Estivill-Castro	Griffith University, Australia
Christian Freksa	University of Bremen, Germany
Qiming Fu	Suzhou University of Science and Technology, China
Katsuhide Fujita	Tokyo University of Agriculture and Technology, Japan
Naoki Fukuta	Shizuoka University, Japan
Dragan Gamberger	Rudjer Boskovic Institute, Croatia
Wei Gao	Nanjing University, China
Xiaoying Gao	Victoria University of Wellington, New Zealand
Yang Gao	Nanjing University, China
Saurabh Kumar Garg	University of Tasmania, Australia
Xin Geng	Southeast University, China
Michael Granitzer	University of Passau, Germany
Fikret Gurgen	Bosphorus University, Turkey
Peter Haddawy	Mahidol University, Thailand
Bing Han	Xidian University, China
Soyeon Han	University of Tasmania, Australia
Choochart Haruechaiyasak	National Electronics and Computer Technology Center, Thailand
Kiyota Hashimoto	Prince of Songkla University, Thailand
Tessai Hayama	Nagaoka University of Technology, Japan
David Herbert	University of Tasmania, Australia
Chenping Hou	National University of Defense Technology, China
Juhua Hu	Simon Fraser University, Canada
Biwei Huang	Carnegie Mellon University, USA
Di Huang	Beihang University, China
Ko-Wei Huang	National Kaohsiung University of Science and Technology, Taiwan, China
Sheng-Jun Huang	Nanjing University of Aeronautics and Astronautics, China
Van Nam Huynh	JAIST, Japan
Masashi Inoue	Tohoku Institute of Technology, Japan
Sanjay Jain	National University of Singapore, Singapore
Jianmin Ji	University of Science and Technology of China, China
Binbin Jia	Southeast University, China
Liangxiao Jiang	China University of Geosciences, China
Mingmin Jiang	Southeast University, China
Yichuan Jiang	Southeast University, China
Yuan Jiang	Nanjing University, China
Hideaki Kanai	Japan Advanced Institute of Science and Technology, Japan
Ryo Kanamori	Nagoya University, Japan
Byeong-Ho Kang	University of Tasmania, Australia
Alfred Krzywicki	The University of New South Wales, Australia
Satoshi Kurihara	The University of Electro-Communications, Japan
Young-Bin Kwon	Chung-Ang University, South Korea

Weng Kin Lai	TARC, Malaysia
Ho-Pun Lam	CSIRO, Australia
Wee Sun Lee	National University of Singapore, Singapore
Roberto Legaspi	Research Organization of Information and Systems, The Institute of Statistical Mathematics, Japan
Gang Li	Deakin University, Australia
Guangliang Li	University of Amsterdam, The Netherlands
Li Li	Southwest University, China
Ming Li	Nanjing University, China
Nan Li	Alibaba Group, China
Tianrui Li	Southwest Jiaotong University, China
Wu-Jun Li	Nanjing University, China
Yu-Feng Li	Nanjing University, China
Beishui Liao	Zhejiang University, China
Miaogen Ling	Southeast University, China
Jiamou Liu	The University of Auckland, New Zealand
Liping Liu	Columbia University, USA
Mingxia Liu	The University of North Carolina at Chapel Hill, USA
Qing Liu	CSIRO, Australia
Ping Luo	Institute of Computing Technology, CAS; University of Chinese Academy of Sciences, China
Xudong Luo	Guangxi Normal University, China
Jiaqi Lv	Southeast University, China
Michael Maher	Reasoning Research Institute, Canberra, Australia
Xinjun Mao	National University of Defense Technology, China
Eric Martin	The University of New South Wales, Australia
Sanparith Marukatat	NECTEC, Thailand
James Montgomery	University of Tasmania, Australia
Koichi Moriyama	Nagoya Institute of Technology, Japan
Muhammad Marwan Muhammad Fuad	Technical University of Denmark, Denmark
Ekawit Nantajeewarawat	Thammasat University, Thailand
M. A. Hakim Newton	IIIS, Griffith University, Australia
Su Nguyen	Victoria University of Wellington, New Zealand
Shahrul Azman Noah	Universiti Kebangsaan Malaysia, Malaysia
Masayuki Numao	Osaka University, Japan
Kouzou Ohara	Aoyama Gakuin University, Japan
Hayato Ohwada	Tokyo University of Science, Japan
Noriko Otani	Tokyo City University, Japan
Takanobu Otsuka	Nagoya Institute of Technology, Japan
Maurice Pagnucco	The University of New South Wales, Australia
Hye-Young Paik	The University of New South Wales, Australia
Jantima Polpinij	Mahasarakham University, Thailand
Chao Qian	University of Science and Technology of China, China
Yuhua Qian	Shanxi University, China
Joel Quinqueton	LIRMM, France

Ali Raza	University of Tasmania, Australia
Fenghui Ren	University of Wollongong, Australia
Yi Ren	Southeast University, China
Deborah Richards	Macquarie University, Australia
Kazumi Saito	University of Shizuoka, Japan
Chiaki Sakama	Wakayama University, Japan
Nicolas Schwind	Tokyo Institute of Technology, Japan
Rolf Schwitter	Macquarie University, Australia
Nazha Selmaoui-Folcher	University of New Caledonia, New Caledonia
Zhiqi Shen	Nanyang Technological University, Singapore
Chuan Shi	Beijing University of Posts and Telecommunications, China
Zhenwei Shi	Beihang University, China
Soo-Yong Shin	Kyung Hee University, South Korea
Shun Shiramatsu	Nagoya Institute of Technology, Japan
Yanfeng Shu	CSIRO, Australia
Waralak V. Siricharoen	Silpakorn University, Thailand
Tony Smith	University of Waikato, New Zealand
Chattrakul Sombattheera	Mahasarakham University, Thailand
Safeeullah Soomro	AMA International University, Bahrain
Markus Stumptner	University of South Australia, Australia
Hang Su	Tsinghua University, China
Xing Su	Beijing University of Technology, China
Merlin Teodosia Suarez	Center for Empathic Human-Computer Interactions, Philippines
Shiliang Sun	East China Normal University, China
Yanan Sun	Sichuan University, China
Boontawee Suntisrivaraporn	dtac, Thailand
Thepchai Supnithi	NECTEC, Thailand
Chang Wei Tan	Monash University, Australia
David Taniar	Monash University, Australia
Qing Tian	Nanjing University of Information Science and Technology, China
Binh Tran	Victoria University of Wellington, New Zealand
Shikui Tu	Shanghai Jiao Tong University, China
Miroslav Velev	Aries Design Automation, USA
Toby Walsh	The University of New South Wales, Australia
Dayong Wang	Nanyang Technological University, Singapore
Di Wang	Nanyang Technological University, Singapore
Jing Wang	Southeast University, China
Ke Wang	Southeast University, China
Kewen Wang	Griffith University, Australia
Qi Wang	Northwestern Polytechnical University, China
Rui Wang	Southeast University, China
Wei Wang	Nanjing University, China

Zhe Wang	East China University of Science and Technology, China
Yu-Wei Wen	National Chung Cheng University, Taiwan, China
Paul Weng	UM-SJTU Joint Institute, China
Yang Wenli	University of Tasmania, Australia
Wayne Wobcke	The University of New South Wales, Australia
Feng Wu	University of Science and Technology of China, China
Jiansheng Wu	Nanjing University of Posts and Telecommunications, China
Chang Xu	The University of Sydney, Australia
Guandong Xu	University of Technology Sydney, Australia
Ming Xu	Xi'an Jiaotong-Liverpool University, China
Ning Xu	Southeast University, China
Shuxiang Xu	University of Tasmania, Australia
Xin-Shun Xu	Shandong University, China
Hui Xue	Southeast University, China
Kong Yan	Nanjing University of Information, Science and Technology, China
Bo Yang	Jilin University, China
Meimei Yang	Southeast University, China
Ming Yang	Nanjing Normal University, China
Wanqi Yang	Nanjing Normal University, China
Roland Yap	National University of Singapore, Singapore
Dayong Ye	University of Wollongong, Australia
Kenichi Yoshida	University of Tsukuba, Japan
Chao Yu	University of Wollongong, Australia
Guoxian Yu	Southwest University, China
Han Yu	Nanyang Technological University, Singapore
Yang Yu	Nanjing University, China
Nanqi Yuan	University of Tasmania, Australia
Takaya Yuizono	Japan Advanced Institute of Science and Technology, Japan
Yifeng Zeng	Teesside University, UK
De-Chuan Zhan	Nanjing University, China
Chengqi Zhang	University of Technology Sydney, Australia
Daoqiang Zhang	Nanjing University of Aeronautics and Astronautics, China
Du Zhang	California State University, USA
Junping Zhang	Fudan University, China
Min-Ling Zhang	Southeast University, China
Minjie Zhang	University of Wollongong, Australia
Qieshi Zhang	Shenzhen Institutes of Advanced Technology, Chinese Academy of Sciences, China
Shichao Zhang	Guangxi Normal University, China
Wen Zhang	Beijing University of Chemical Technology, China

Yu Zhang	The Hong Kong University of Science and Technology, China
Zhao Zhang	Soochow University, China
Zhaoxiang Zhang	Institute of Automation, Chinese Academy of Sciences, China
Zongzhang Zhang	Soochow University, China
Dengji Zhao	University of Southampton, UK
Li Zhao	Microsoft, China
Xiang Zhao	National University of Defense Technology, China
Yanchang Zhao	CSIRO, Australia
Shuigeng Zhou	Fudan University, China
Zhi-Hua Zhou	Nanjing University, China
Xiaofeng Zhu	Guangxi Normal University, China
Xingquan Zhu	Florida Atlantic University, USA
Fuzhen Zhuang	Institute of Computing Technology, Chinese Academy of Sciences, China
Quan Zou	Tianjin University, China

Additional Reviewers

Ahmed Loai Ali
Komate Amphawan
Mohammad Dawud Ansari
Molood Barati
Ying Bi
Sebastian Binnewies
Alan Blair
Weiling Cai
Xinyuan Chen
Zixuan Chen
Honghong Cheng
Zhanzhan Cheng
Zhi Cheng
Yao-Xiang Ding
Duy Tai Dinh
Shaokang Dong
Yinpeng Dong
Alan Downes
Suhendry Effendy
Sara Elkasrawi
Ji Feng
Zeyu Feng
Anna Förster
Longwen Gao
Chuanxing Geng
Mingming Gong
Alircza Goudarzi
Ryan Green
Qian Guo
Yuze Guo
Anasthasia Agnes Haryanto
Shaojie He
Paramate Horkeaw
Yi-Qi Hu
Kai Huang
Paul Salvador Inventado
Saichon Jaiyen
Chong Jiang
Johannes Jurgovsky
Abdul Karim
Bojana Kodric
Longteng Kong
Andre Kostenko
Bin Li
Chaoqun Li
Feijiang Li
Weihua Li
Yuyu Li
Xinyan Liang
Jiahao Lin
Aiden Liu
Chong Liu
Mengyu Liu
Mingxia Liu
Shaowu Liu
Songtao Liu
Yong Liu
Alex Long
Guoshuai Ma
Huifang Ma
Zhongchen Ma
Arturo Magana-Mora
Wolfgang Mayer
Koichi Moriyama
Guodong Mu
Mohsin Munir
Courtney Ngo
Hung Ba Nguyen
Lei Niu
Sebastian Palacio
Jianhui Pang
Ming Pang
Manna Philip

Harun Pirim
Chen Qiu
Muhammad Imran Razzak
Adrien Rougny
Seung Ryu
Zafar Saeed
Fatemeh Salehi Rizi
Jörg Schlötterer
Matt Selway
Syed Wajid Ali Shah
Yang Shangdong
Xiang-Rong Sheng
John Shepherd
Leslie Sikos
Thanongchai Siriapisith
Fengyi Song
Kexiu Song
Sirawit Sopchoke
Changzhi Sun
Danyang Sun
Jia Sun
Jiahua Tang
Yanni Tang
Amit Thombre
Yanling Tian
Jannai Tokotoko
Tina Vajsbaher
Tina Vajsbaher-Kelc
Jasper van de Ven
Narumol Vannaprathip
Maria Vasardani
Nhi N. Y. Vo
Chaoyue Wang
Dengbao Wang
Hui Wang
Jieting Wang
Lu Wang
Xueping Wang
Yishen Wang
Yong Wang
Yuchen Wang
Yulong Wang
Zhiwei Wang
Fan Wu
Maonian Wu
Mingda Wu
Shiqing Wu
Song Wu
Xi-Zhu Wu
Yi-Feng Wu
Wei Xia
Peng Xiao
Zhang Xiaoyu
Qingsong Xie
Zhihao Xing
Junping Xu
Ziqi Yan
Fang Yang
Haote Yang
Yang Yang
Yi Yang
Haochao Ying
Vithya Yogarajan
Shan You
Liangjun Yu
Sicong Zang
Chenyu Zhang
Jihang Zhang
Weitong Zhang
Xiao Zhang
Xiaowei Zhao
Yao Zhou
Zili Zhou
Yunkai Zhuang
Zhiqiang Zhuang

Organized by

Sponsored by

南京未来科技城

Contents – Part I

Contents – Part II

HAVAE: Learning Prosodic-Enhanced Representations of Rap Lyrics

Hongru Liang[1], Qian Li[1], Haozheng Wang[1], Hang Li[1], Jun Wang[2], Zhe Sun[3], Jin-Mao Wei[1], and Zhenglu Yang[1](✉)

[1] College of Computer and Control Engineering, Nankai University, Tianjin, China
{lianghr,liqian515,hzwang,hangl}@mail.nankai.edu.cn,
{weijm,yangzl}@nankai.edu.cn

[2] College of Mathematics and Statistics Science, Ludong University, Yantai, China
junwang@mail.nankai.edu.cn

[3] RIKEN Head Office for Information Systems and Cybersecurity Computational Engineering Applications Unit, Saitama, Japan
zhe.sun.vk@riken.jp

Abstract. Learning and analyzing rap lyrics is a significant basis for many applications, such as music recommendation, automatic music categorization, and music information retrieval. Although numerous studies have explored the topic, knowledge in this field is far from satisfactory, because critical issues, such as prosodic information and its effective representation, as well as appropriate integration of various features are usually ignored. In this paper, we propose a hierarchical attention variational autoencoder framework (HAVAE), which simultaneously consider semantic and prosodic features for rap lyrics representation learning. Specifically, the representation of the prosodic features is encoded by phonetic transcriptions with a novel and effective strategy (i.e., rhyme2vec). Moreover, a feature aggregation strategy is proposed to appropriately integrate various features and generate prosodic-enhanced representation. A comprehensive empirical evaluation demonstrates that the proposed framework outperforms the state-of-the-art approaches under various metrics in both NextLine prediction task and rap genre classification task.

Keywords: Representation learning · Variational autoencoder
Hierarchical attention mechanism

1 Introduction

Rap music is one of the most popular types of music genres [19], and worth exploring statistically. Learning rap lyrics is an important task that has attracted growing interest from academic researchers, as it is a basis of many real-world applications, such as music generation [18,21], music information retrieval [18], and scheme identification [1,12]. A complicated issue for the task of learning rap

X. Geng and B.-H. Kang (Eds.): PRICAI 2018, LNAI 11012, pp. 1–15, 2018.
https://doi.org/10.1007/978-3-319-97304-3_1

lyrics is that rap lyrics are unstructured, thereby hampering the direct use of the off-the-shelf natural language processing techniques in phonological analysis [28].

Recent studies have analyzed rap lyrics by plain text analysis [21], rhyme scheme detection [1,12], rap lyrics generation [21,28], and evaluation methodology development [14,18,22]. However, the strategies of manipulating features in existing studies are flawed, which dramatically deteriorate the performance of learning rap lyrics. Either partial features (such as the semantic features obtained from raw lyrics) rather than the complete ones are captured, or ineffective representations of features (e.g., statistical representations) are employed. The comprehensive and general representations of rap lyrics involving both semantic and prosodic information are urgently required.

We notice that variational autoencoder (VAE) [17] empirically demonstrates strong power for density modeling and generation studies [15], including its successful applications in music information retrieval area [2,10]. Nonetheless, these studies are interested in small pitches of music melodies and thereby simply utilize VAEs to reduce the dimensionality of acoustic features.

To tackle the aforementioned issues, we scrutinize both semantic and prosodic features in a unified framework specific to representation learning, that is, a prosodic-enhanced representation of rap lyrics is well constructed. Concretely, the semantic information is encoded into vectors through the popular paragraph embedding technology (i.e., doc2vec) [23]. The prosodic features are represented through our newly proposed strategy, dubbed rhyme2vec, in an effective fashion of incorporating various rhyme schemes. Consequently, the prosodic-enhanced representation of rap lyrics is accomplished, in which the VAE-based feature aggregation approach is designed to seamlessly combine the semantic and prosodic information, as well as the attention mechanism is employed to appropriately balance their importance. All of these strategies are integrated into a general representation learning framework named as hierarchical attention VAE network (HAVAE). The main contributions of this study are as follows:

- We propose a hierarchical attention VAE-based framework, called HAVAE, to effectively address the issue of representation learning for rap lyrics. The framework can represent rap lyrics both prosodically and semantically.
- A novel strategy, called rhyme2vec, is proposed to accomplish the prosodic representation learning. This method involves two models, namely, continuous lines and skip-line, to appropriately cope with rhyme schemes with distinct characteristics. To effectively integrate various features, we deliberately design a feature aggregation module via VAE network and introduce the hierarchical attention mechanism for seamless fusion of diverse types of information.
- We extensively evaluate the proposed framework on benchmark datasets and fulfill two tasks. Results demonstrate that our framework is remarkably better than the state-of-the-art approaches under various evaluation metrics.

2 Related Work

The most relevant task to learn rap lyrics representation is poetry analysis. Poetry is a highly varied genre, and each poetry type has its distinct structural, rhythmical, and tonal patterns. Rule-based and template-based approaches [20] were mainstays in the early days. Subsequently, generic algorithm [24], summarization framework [29], and statistical machine translation models [11] were developed. Recent work illustrated that poetry analysis eliminated man-made constraints and professional silo restrictions with the aid of neural networks [27].

Rap lyrics analysis is generally more challenging than poetry analysis, because it is more free-form structurally. Hirjee and Brown [12] proposed a probabilistic scoring model based on phoneme frequencies in rap lyrics. Although their model identified internal and line-final rhymes automatically, it requires additional manually annotated rap lyrics and rhyming pairs. Wu et al. [28] explored a generation task in rap battle improvisation. They presented improvisation as a quasi-translation task, in which any given challenge was "translated" into a response. However, a "translation lexicon" is required before training and the correlation relationship between challenge and response lines are strictly limited to one-to-one correspondence. As such, it is nearly inapplicable in practice. Potash et al. [21] applied long short-term memory network in generating lyrics that were similar in style to that of a certain rapper, and they presented computational and quantitative evaluation methods. An inevitable drawback is that this system requires sufficient training data to capture the rhythmic style, and thus, rhyming pairs must appear frequently enough in the corpus.

DopeLearning, which was proposed by Malmi et al. [18], has been proven to be able to generate powerful features. The authors introduced three kinds of prosodic features, a structural feature, and four kinds of semantic features. DopeLearning has shown desirable performance in rap lyrics learning due to its comprehensive consideration of various features, but it still suffers from a major issue that hampers its effective utilization in practice, that is, a unified representation of rap lyrics has not been generated. Different types of features are separately extracted to measure different similarity/distance scores for specific tasks. A crucial issue for rap lyrics representation, i.e., the non-linear relationship among features, is neglected. Furthermore, three prosodic features are extracted simply in statistical views by merely considering vowel phonemes, and apparently, these features cannot represent the entire prosodic information in rap lyrics.

As for feature aggregation, VAE has been discussed extensively in computer vision [7] and nature language processing [30]. For example, in music information retrieval area, several VAE-based frameworks have been proposed to solve specific problems. Fabius and Amersfoort [9] proposed a variational recurrent autoencoder (VRAE) to generate video game melodies. The work of Alexey and Ivan [2] explored a history supported VRAE to generate monotonic music. Hadjeres *et al.* [10] introduced a refined regularization function for VAE to generate chorales polyphony. The aforementioned works focused on music melodies bypassing music lyrics, and correspondingly, VAE is only deployed to model plain audio features. Furthermore, the VAE method is constrained to be a generative tool in the conventional sense.

As such, we propose an effective VAE-based framework that embeds both the semantic and prosodic information. Intuitively, we expect to extract the representative prosodic information and model the relationships between the semantic and prosodic features. The prosodic features are generated by an effective strategy (i.e., rhyme2vec). Specifically, we use the VAE network to integrate both prosodic features and semantic features, which are generated via rhyme2vec and doc2vec, respectively. The final representation of rap lyrics is prosodic aware in addition to semantic awareness.

3 Model Description

The architecture of the proposed framework is illustrated in Fig. 1. It consists of two main modules, namely, feature extraction and feature aggregation. The feature extraction module encodes the input materials, which involve the phonetic transcriptions and the raw lyrics, into distributed prosodic and semantic vectors. The feature aggregation module fuses both information and learn the prosodic-enhanced representation vectors. The learned vectors can be used to represent the rap lyrics in various tasks, such as NextLine prediction and genre classification. The entire structure is a hierarchical attention variational network, and we name it as HAVAE.

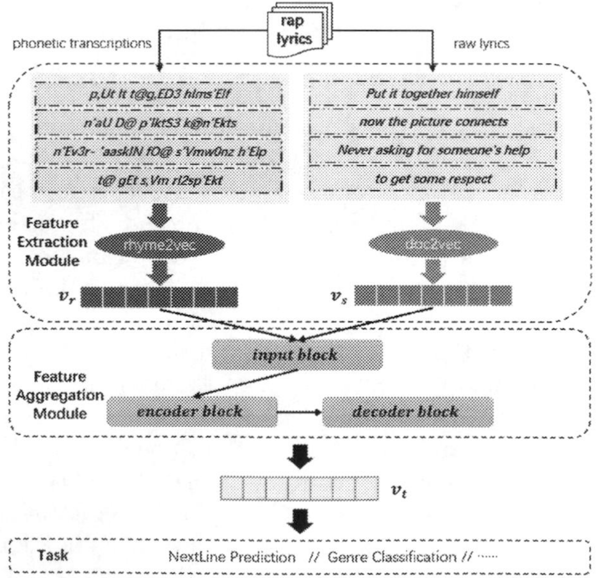

Fig. 1. Architecture of HAVAE

3.1 Preliminary

Table 1 presents an overview of useful notations in this paper. Vectors, matrices, and sets are highlighted in bold. Assume that $\boldsymbol{S}$ indicates a rap song, which consists of k rap lines. Let $\boldsymbol{L} = \{l_i\}_{i=1}^{k}$ denote the raw lyrics of $\boldsymbol{S}$, and $\boldsymbol{P} = \{p_i\}_{i=1}^{k}$ denote the corresponding phonetic transcriptions of $\boldsymbol{S}$, respectively. For ease of exposition, we present a concrete example in Table 2 (i.e., four consecutive rap lines from Fort Minor's *Remember the Name*) to illustrate the intuitive idea and explain the proposed techniques. We use $\boldsymbol{v_s}$ to represent the semantic vector encoded from $\boldsymbol{L}$, and $\boldsymbol{v_r}$ to represent the prosodic vector encoded from $\boldsymbol{P}$. $\boldsymbol{v_t}$ denotes the target unified representation of $\boldsymbol{S}$ learned by the proposed feature aggregation method.

Table 1. Overview of useful notations

Symbols	Descriptions
$\boldsymbol{S}, \boldsymbol{L}, \boldsymbol{P}$	A rap song, and its raw lyrics and corresponding phonetic transcriptions
k	Number of lines in $\boldsymbol{S}$
l_i, p_i	*i-th* line of $\boldsymbol{L}$ and $\boldsymbol{P}$
$\boldsymbol{v_s}, \boldsymbol{v_r}, \boldsymbol{v_t}$	Semantic vector of $\boldsymbol{L}$, prosodic vector of $\boldsymbol{P}$, and target representation of $\boldsymbol{S}$
$\boldsymbol{B}$	Prosodic block
$\boldsymbol{\rho}$	Prosodic vector of $\boldsymbol{B}$
$\boldsymbol{\psi}$	Dense vector of a phoneme
$\boldsymbol{\xi}$	Scheme vector of a prosodic block
n	Number of phonemes in a prosodic block
w	Size of the sliding window over prosodic blocks
N	Number of samples

Table 2. Rap lyrics with their phonetic transcriptions

raw lyrics (L)	**phonetic transcription** (P)
[l_1] Put it together himself	[p_1] p,Ut It t@g,ED3 hIms'Elf
[l_2] Now the picture connects	[p_2] n'aU D@ p'IktS3 k@n'Ekts
[l_3] Never asking for someone's help	[p_3] n'Ev3ɪ- 'aaskIN fO@ s'VmwOnz h'Elp
[l_4] to get some respect	[p_4] t@ gEt s,Vm rI2sp'Ekt

The English language is known to have 48 International Phonetic Alphabets [4]. We treat affricates (e.g., [ʧ]) and diphthongs (e.g., [ɔɪ]) as two separate phonemes, and translate the rap lyrics into phoneme codes using the eSpeak tool [8]. The final phonetic transcription file is a sequence of characters from a token-level alphabet and each token acts as an individual member. The alphabet is defined as follow:

$$pbtTdDsSzZkgfvhmnNljwr2Y3L5aAeEiI0VuUoO.$$

Based on the transcription files with phoneme codes, we can perform examinations w.r.t. an important factor (i.e., rhyme) in rap lyrics learning. A rhyme is a repetition of similar sounds (or the same sound) in two or more words [6] appearing in a single rap line or cross lines, and it can be classified into two mainstream rhyme schemes, namely, monorhyme[1] and alternate rhyme[2]. Monorhyme, alternate rhyme, and other schemes are random throughout an entire rap song, exhibiting various levels of importance.

We assume that the rap lines have both monorhyme and alternate rhymes. For monorhyme, we unify all consecutive lines as one prosodic block ($\boldsymbol{B_m}$). Regarding alternate rhyme, we split rap lines into two prosodic blocks. One block includes all of the odd lines ($\boldsymbol{B_o}$, i.e., the red lines in Table 2), the other block includes all of the even lines ($\boldsymbol{B_e}$, i.e., the blue lines in Table 2). The number

[1] Monorhyme is a rhyme scheme in which each line has an identical rhyme.

[2] In alternate rhyme, the rhyme is on alternate lines.

of prosodic blocks is triple of the number of samples (i.e., $3N$). We define the problem of learning prosodic representation of rap lyrics as follows:

Problem 1. *Given a sequence of k rap lines* $\boldsymbol{S}$, $\boldsymbol{P}$ *is its phonetic transcription. Let* $\boldsymbol{\rho_m}$ *denote the monorhyme representation vector generated from* $\boldsymbol{B_m}$, *and* $\boldsymbol{\rho_a}$ *denote the alternate rhyme representation vector generated from* $\boldsymbol{B_o}$ *and* $\boldsymbol{B_e}$. *The goal of learning the prosodic representation of rap lyrics is to generate the prosodic vector* $\boldsymbol{v_r}$ *of* $\boldsymbol{P}$ *by combining* $\boldsymbol{\rho_m}$ *and* $\boldsymbol{\rho_a}$.

To solve Problem 1, we propose a novel and robust model in Sect. 3.2, called rhyme2vec. This model involves two submodels: the continuous lines model handles the monorhyme involving $\boldsymbol{B_m}$, and the skip-line model handles the alternate rhymes involving $\boldsymbol{B_o}$ and $\boldsymbol{B_e}$.

On the basis of analyzing the prosodic representation of rap lyrics, we further discuss the task of learning its complete representation. A good rap song possesses an outstanding topic and maintains catchy rhymes. Thus, an appropriate representation of rap lyrics needs to involve both semantic and prosodic information. Here, we provide the definition of the task for rap lyrics representation learning as follows:

Problem 2. *Given a rap song* $\boldsymbol{S}$ *with k rap lines, and assuming that its prosodic vector* $\boldsymbol{v_r}$ *and semantic vector* $\boldsymbol{v_s}$ *are known, the goal of learning the representation of rap lyrics is to generate* $\boldsymbol{v_t}$ *by combining the useful information of* $\boldsymbol{v_r}$ *and* $\boldsymbol{v_s}$.

An attentive VAE-based feature aggregation module is proposed in Sect. 3.3 to combine $\boldsymbol{v_s}$ and $\boldsymbol{v_r}$ seamlessly. In addition, the attention mechanism is introduced to model the mutual relationship between $\boldsymbol{v_s}$ and $\boldsymbol{v_r}$. Consequently, the target representation $\boldsymbol{v_t}$ is learned by sampling on a latent Gaussian distribution, and it is expected to be utilized in various rap lyrics-based tasks, as demonstrated in Sect. 4.

3.2 Feature Extraction Module

The feature extraction module (illustrated as the first dotted box in Fig. 1) is utilized to generate fine-grained features . This module consists of prosodic and semantic sections.

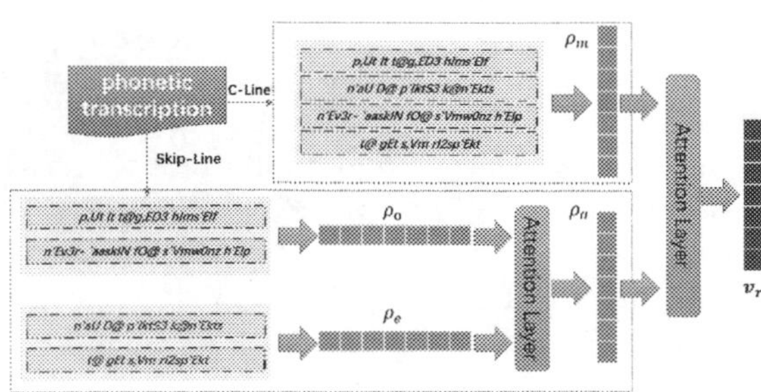

Fig. 2. The architecture of rhyme2vec

Prosodic Section. In the prosodic section, we introduce a novel method to tackle Problem 1. Figure 2 illustrates the process to obtain the prosodic representation $\boldsymbol{v_r}$ of given rap lyrics. We call it rhyme2vec.

Inspired by the idea of modeling document [23], for each prosodic block, we import a scheme vector, which is denoted as $\boldsymbol{\xi}$. As aforementioned, each rap song possesses three prosodic blocks. We first map each phoneme into a unique vector, denoted as $\boldsymbol{\psi}$. All phonemes in the same prosodic block share the same $\boldsymbol{\xi}$. The embedding of a prosodic block is denoted as $\boldsymbol{\rho}$. $\boldsymbol{\rho}$ is defined as the sum of the phoneme vectors and the scheme vector, formulated as $\boldsymbol{\rho} = \sum_{i=1}^{n} \boldsymbol{\psi}_i + \boldsymbol{\xi}$. Given a piece of $\boldsymbol{P}$ with a set of phoneme vectors $\boldsymbol{\psi}$ and scheme vectors $\boldsymbol{\xi}$, we maximize its log probability and the objective function of extracting $\boldsymbol{P}$ is written as

$$\max_{\boldsymbol{\psi},\boldsymbol{\xi}} \mathcal{F}_r, F_r = \frac{1}{3N} \times \sum_{i=1}^{3N} \sum_{j=w}^{n_i - w} \frac{1}{n_i - 2w} \log p(\boldsymbol{\psi}_{ij} | \boldsymbol{\psi}_{i,j-w} : \boldsymbol{\psi}_{i,j+w}, \boldsymbol{\xi}_i). \tag{1}$$

The negative sampling strategy is deployed for effective training. Let $\boldsymbol{P_0}$ denote the negative sample set, and $\boldsymbol{P_1}$ denote the positive set, which is the same as the original set. For each sample $(\boldsymbol{\psi}_{ij}, \boldsymbol{c}_{ij}) \in \boldsymbol{P_1}$, where $\boldsymbol{c}_{ij} = \{\boldsymbol{\psi}_{i,j-w} : \boldsymbol{\psi}_{i,j+w}, \boldsymbol{\xi}_i\}$, we randomly sample ζ fake samples $(\boldsymbol{\psi}_{ij}, \boldsymbol{c}') \in \boldsymbol{P_0}$. $\boldsymbol{P_0}$ is ζ times larger than $\boldsymbol{P_1}$, and $\boldsymbol{P_0} \cap \boldsymbol{P_1} = \varnothing$. We use $\boldsymbol{P_1} \cup \boldsymbol{P_0}$ as the entire corpus, the objective function is rewritten as

$$\max_{\boldsymbol{\psi},\boldsymbol{\xi}} [\mathcal{F}_r(\boldsymbol{P_1}) - \mathcal{F}_r(\boldsymbol{P_0})]. \tag{2}$$

The first term refers to the log probability of the positive set ($\boldsymbol{P_1}$), and the second term refers to the log probability of the negative set ($\boldsymbol{P_0}$).

Specifically, to describe the monorhyme, we propose the continuous lines model, which is denoted as C-Line for short. In C-Line (illustrated as the upper part in Fig. 2), we regard the input consecutive lines (i.e., $\boldsymbol{B_m}$) as a content, and generate a distributed vector $\boldsymbol{\rho_m}$ from the corresponding phoneme vectors and prosodic block vector using the abovementioned method.

As to the alternate rhyme, we use $\boldsymbol{\rho_a}$ to indicate its dense representation. Seeing that monorhyme and alternate rhyme have different degrees of importance in rap lyrics, we introduce the Attention Layer to assign appropriate weights for $\boldsymbol{\rho_m}$ and $\boldsymbol{\rho_a}$, respectively. The Attention Layer is defined as $\boldsymbol{AttL} : \boldsymbol{\mathcal{H}} := [\boldsymbol{h}_i]_{i=1}^{m} \in \mathbb{R}^{d \times m} \rightarrow \boldsymbol{t} \in \mathbb{R}^d$, detailedly expressed as follows:

$$\boldsymbol{t} = \sum_{i=1}^{m} \alpha_i \boldsymbol{h}_i, \quad \alpha_i = \frac{exp\left(\hat{\boldsymbol{h}}_i{}^{\top} \hat{\boldsymbol{h}}_c\right)}{\sum_{j=1}^{m} exp\left(\hat{\boldsymbol{h}}_j{}^{\top} \hat{\boldsymbol{h}}_c\right)}, \quad \hat{\boldsymbol{h}}_i = tanh(\boldsymbol{W}\boldsymbol{h}_i + \boldsymbol{b}), \tag{3}$$

where $\boldsymbol{\mathcal{H}}$ is the input matrix and built by a stack of m vectors $\boldsymbol{h}_i$, $\boldsymbol{t}$ is the target vector learned by $\boldsymbol{AttL}$, α_i is the attention weight scalar of $\boldsymbol{AttL}$ and evaluated by the latent vector $\hat{\boldsymbol{h}}_i$ of $\boldsymbol{h}_i$ along with the randomly initialized context vector $\hat{\boldsymbol{h}}_c$, and W and b are hyper-parameters involved in the $tanh$ function to compute $\hat{\boldsymbol{h}}_i$. Hence, we formulate the prosodic vector as $\boldsymbol{v_r} = \boldsymbol{AttL}\ (\boldsymbol{\mathcal{H}} := [\boldsymbol{\rho_m}; \boldsymbol{\rho_a}])$.

Specifically, to describe the alternate rhyme comprehensively, we propose the skip-line model, which is denoted as Skip-Line for short. Unlike in C-Line, we first split the phonetic transcription into the odd (with all the odd lines, i.e., $\boldsymbol{B_o}$) and even prosodic blocks (with all the even lines, i.e., $\boldsymbol{B}_e$) in Skip-Line (illustrated as the lower part in Fig. 2). $\boldsymbol{\rho}_o$ and $\boldsymbol{\rho}_e$ are encoded from $\boldsymbol{B}_o$ and $\boldsymbol{B}_e$ as $\boldsymbol{\rho}_m$. In addition, similar to aggregating monorhyme and alternate rhyme vectors, we employ the Attention Layer on $\boldsymbol{\rho}_o$ and $\boldsymbol{\rho}_e$, that is, $\boldsymbol{\rho}_a = \boldsymbol{AttL}(\boldsymbol{\mathcal{H}} := [\boldsymbol{\rho}_o; \boldsymbol{\rho}_e])$.

The final prosodic representation of $\boldsymbol{P}$ is obtained through the proposed rhyme2vec method and reformulated as $\boldsymbol{v}_r = \boldsymbol{AttL}\ (\boldsymbol{\mathcal{H}} := [\boldsymbol{\rho}_m; \boldsymbol{AttL}\ (\boldsymbol{\mathcal{H}} := [\boldsymbol{\rho}_o; \boldsymbol{\rho}_e])])$.

Semantic Section. To extract semantic features, we employ the doc2vec approach [23]. Doc2vec is a state-of-the-art sentence embedding technique, which stems from the distributed memory model of paragraph vectors (PV-DM) and the distributed bag-of-words version of paragraph vectors (PV-DBOW). The empirical analysis has shown that PV-DM usually works better than PV-DBOW [23]. In this paper, we deploy PV-DM to generate the semantic vector of $\boldsymbol{L}$, i.e., $\boldsymbol{v}_s$. At line level, we regard consecutive lines as a paragraph. At song level, we regard each rap song as a document.

3.3 Feature Aggregation Module

The feature aggregation module is designed to solve Problem 2, and is an essential part of our model (illustrated as the second dotted box in Fig. 1). In this section, we design a VAE network to produce representation of rap lyrics by combining prosodic and semantic information. We also introduce attention mechanism to balance their importance. Figure 3 illustrates the structure, which consists of three main stages, namely, INPUT, ENCODER, and DECODER.

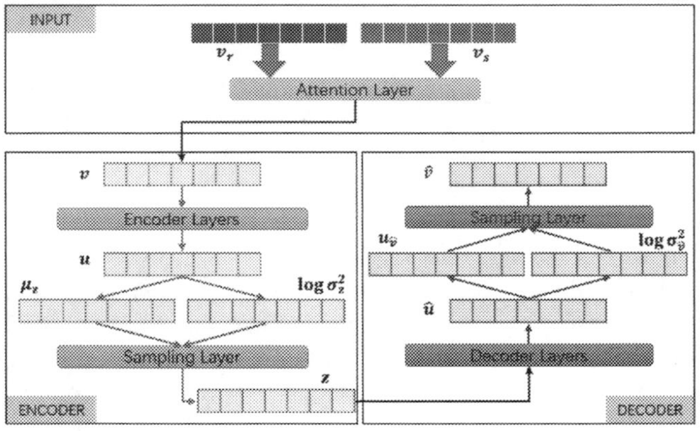

Fig. 3. Architecture of the feature aggregation module

In the INPUT stage (see upper part in Fig. 3), we use the aforementioned Attention Layer to handle the input variables. $\boldsymbol{v}_r$ and $\boldsymbol{v}_s$ are the fine-grained features of prosodic and semantic information, and have already been learned through the feature extraction module. The output vector $\boldsymbol{v}$ of the Attention Layer in this stage is utilized as the input of the following stage. We formulate this procedure as $\boldsymbol{v} = \boldsymbol{AttL}(\boldsymbol{\mathcal{H}} := [\boldsymbol{v}_r; \boldsymbol{v}_s])$.

In the ENCODER stage, we deploy the Encoder Layers over the input vector ($\boldsymbol{v}$). The Encoder Layers are a sequence of densely-connected layers, and the *i-th* densely-connected layer is formulated as $\boldsymbol{v}_i = \boldsymbol{\delta}(W\boldsymbol{v}_{i-1} + b)_{i=2}^{\chi}$, where

χ is the number of the layers, $\boldsymbol{\delta}$ is an activation function, and $\boldsymbol{v_1} := \boldsymbol{v}$. The Encoder Layers generate a latent representation of $\boldsymbol{v}$. The VAE network generates latent variable $\boldsymbol{z}$ on the basis of $\boldsymbol{v}$, and $\boldsymbol{z}$ is expected to be most representative for $\boldsymbol{v}$. Suppose $\boldsymbol{z}$ follows the Gaussian distribution $\mathcal{N}(\boldsymbol{\mu_z}, \boldsymbol{\sigma_z^2})$, where $\boldsymbol{\mu_z}$ indicates the mean vector, and $\log \boldsymbol{\sigma_z^2}$ indicates the log-covariance vector ($\boldsymbol{\sigma_z}$ indicates the standard deviation vector). For telesis, we use the latent representation (denoted as $\boldsymbol{u}$), to generate the mean vector and log-covariance vector of $\boldsymbol{z}$ through fully-connected layers. For ease of calculating the gradient, "reparameterization trick" [17] is adopted. Mathematically, the Sampling Layer is formulated as

$$\boldsymbol{z} = \boldsymbol{\mu_z} + \boldsymbol{\sigma_z} \odot \boldsymbol{\epsilon}, \quad \boldsymbol{\epsilon} \sim \mathcal{N}(\mathbf{0}, \mathbf{1}); \tag{4}$$

where $\boldsymbol{\epsilon}$ is the noise variable following the normal distribution, and $\odot$ represents the element-wise product.

The DECODER stage accomplishes an inverse manipulation of the ENCODER stage. $\boldsymbol{z}$ is utilized as the input of this stage. We then use the Decoder Layers, which are a sequence of densely-connected layers with reversed order of the Encoder Layers, to decode $\boldsymbol{z}$ to $\hat{\boldsymbol{u}}$[3]. On the basis of $\hat{\boldsymbol{u}}$, we can obtain the mean vector $\boldsymbol{\mu_{\hat{v}}}$ and the standard deviation vector $\boldsymbol{\sigma_{\hat{v}}}$ of $\hat{\boldsymbol{v}}$ with the normal distribution $\mathcal{N}(\boldsymbol{\mu_{\hat{v}}}, \boldsymbol{\sigma_{\hat{v}}^2})$. $\hat{\boldsymbol{v}}$ can be considered as the reconstructed vector of $\boldsymbol{v}$.

We use $\boldsymbol{\mu_z}$ as the target representation of the rap lyrics, that is, $\boldsymbol{\mu_z} = \boldsymbol{v_t}$.

Loss Function. Inspired by [16], we incorporate the label information. We construct a latent variable $\hat{\boldsymbol{y}}$ on the basis of $\boldsymbol{v_t}$ to represnt the true label set $\boldsymbol{y}$. The operation can be expressed as $\hat{\boldsymbol{y}} = sigmoid\,(\boldsymbol{v_t})$. $\hat{\boldsymbol{y}}$ and $\boldsymbol{y}$ possess the same dimenssion.

Based on the above analysis, the eventual objective function of our feature aggregation module is given as

$$\min_{\hat{\boldsymbol{v}}, \hat{\boldsymbol{y}}} (\mathcal{F}_{vae} + \alpha \mathcal{F}_{label}), \tag{5}$$

where $\mathcal{F}_{vae}$ is the loss of the VAE-based feature aggregation network, $\mathcal{F}_{label}$ is the loss between the latent variable $\hat{\boldsymbol{y}}$ and the true label set $\boldsymbol{y}$, and α is a hyper parameter to balance the importance of $\mathcal{F}_{vae}$ and $\mathcal{F}_{label}$.

$\mathcal{F}_{vae}$ can be divided into two parts, and formulated as $\mathcal{F}_{vae} = \mathcal{F}_{GL} + \mathcal{F}_{RL}$. The first term describes the generative loss, which evaluates the similarity between the latent variable ($\boldsymbol{z}$) and the original data ($\boldsymbol{v_r}$ and $\boldsymbol{v_s}$). The second term represents the reconstructed loss, which estimates the loss between the latent variable ($\boldsymbol{z}$) and the reconstruction vector ($\hat{\boldsymbol{v}}$).

Let $\mathcal{Q}(\boldsymbol{z}|\boldsymbol{v})$ denote an approximate posterior distribution of $\boldsymbol{z}$ and $\mathcal{P}(\boldsymbol{z})$ denote the prior distribution. Intuitively, we expect to train our VAE network by minimizing the difference between $\mathcal{Q}(\boldsymbol{z}|\boldsymbol{v})$ and $\mathcal{P}(\boldsymbol{z})$. In doing so, we can capture the most representative vector $\boldsymbol{z}$ for $\boldsymbol{v}$ with minimal difference between both variables. We introduce the Kullback-Leibler ($\mathcal{KL}$) divergence metric to evaluate the difference between $\boldsymbol{z}$ and $\boldsymbol{v}$, and mathematically expressed as follows:

[3] The dimension of $\hat{\boldsymbol{u}}$ is equal to that of $\boldsymbol{u}$.

$$\mathcal{KL}[\mathcal{Q}(\boldsymbol{z}|\boldsymbol{v}_r,\boldsymbol{v}_s)||\mathcal{P}(\boldsymbol{z})] = \sum_{i=1}^{N} \mathcal{Q}(\boldsymbol{z}_i|\boldsymbol{v}_i) \times \log\left[\frac{\mathcal{Q}(\boldsymbol{z}_i|\boldsymbol{v}_i)}{\mathcal{P}(\boldsymbol{z}_i)}\right]. \tag{6}$$

Suppose both the prior and posterior approximations are Gaussian distributed. The following equation holds:

$$\mathcal{F}_{GL} = -\mathcal{KL}[\mathcal{Q}(\boldsymbol{z}|\boldsymbol{v}_r,\boldsymbol{v}_s)||\mathcal{P}(\boldsymbol{z})] = \frac{1}{2}\sum_{i=1}^{N}[1+\log(\boldsymbol{\sigma}_z)_i^2 - (\boldsymbol{\mu}_z)_i^2 - (\boldsymbol{\sigma}_z)_i^2]. \tag{7}$$

The reconstructed loss describes the loss between the latent variable and the reconstruction of the input. Seeing that the decoder is a multivariate Gaussian with a diagonal covariance structure, we introduce the reconstructed loss, which is defined as $\mathcal{F}_{RL} = \log\mathcal{P}(\boldsymbol{v}|\boldsymbol{z}) = log\mathcal{N}(\boldsymbol{v};\boldsymbol{\mu}_{\hat{\boldsymbol{v}}},\boldsymbol{\sigma}^{\boldsymbol{2}}_{\hat{\boldsymbol{v}}})$.

In conclusion, the loss function of the VAE network is formulated as

$$\mathcal{F}_{vae} = -\mathcal{KL}[\mathcal{Q}(\boldsymbol{z}|\boldsymbol{v})||\mathcal{P}(\boldsymbol{z})] + \log\mathcal{P}(\boldsymbol{v}|\boldsymbol{z}). \tag{8}$$

Moreover, $\mathcal{F}_{label}$ can be estimated through the binary cross entropy as follows:

$$\mathcal{F}_{label} = -\frac{1}{NM}\sum_{i=1}^{N}\sum_{j=1}^{M}[y_{ij}\log\hat{y}_{ij} + (1-y_{ij})\log(1-\hat{y}_{ij})], \tag{9}$$

where M is the dimension of the label set.

4 Experiments and Results

The performance of our model (HAVAE) is evaluated with NextLine prediction and rap genre classification tasks under various metrics. Considering the reality that few online sources provide rap lyrics, we obtain a corpus of rap lyrics crawled from Internet[4]. This corpus involves 65730 songs from 3154 rappers[5].

4.1 NextLine Prediction

The NextLine prediction task is developed in [18]. Given a rap song with a sequence of k rap lines, we assume that the first κ ($\kappa < k$) lines, denoted by $\boldsymbol{Q} = \{s_i\}_{i=1}^{\kappa}$, are available. Let $\boldsymbol{C} = \{c_i\}_{i=1}^{\pi}$ indicate a set of candidate lines. The task is to predict the following $(\kappa+1)^{th}$ line, i.e., $s_{\kappa+1}$, from $\boldsymbol{C}$. The closest rap line $c_i \in \boldsymbol{C}$ will be chosen as the matching object.

Dataset. We break up rap songs into lines, and obtain a corpus consisting of 810567 lines from 16697 songs. We divide the dataset by songs into the train set (50%), validation set (25%), and test set (25%).

[4] http://ohhla.com/.

[5] The source code and dataset are available at https://github.com/mengshor/HAVAE.

Baseline Methods. We compare the proposed HAVAE with the followings: **EndRhyme** [18]: consider the number of matching vowel phonemes at the end of candidate line c_i and the last line s_κ. **Rhyme2vec**: our novel rhyme embedding method that is proposed in Sect. 3.2. **NN5** [18]: a character-level neural network for rap lines encoding by taking five previous lines, i.e.,$\{s_{\kappa-i}\}_{i=0}^{4}$, as query. **Doc2vec** [23]: the most popular sentence embedding method, wherein we treat $\{s_\kappa; c_i\}$ as a unified paragraph. **DopeLearning** [18][6]: the most representative rap lyrics representation learning method concatenating a series of statistical characteristics, including EndRhyme, EndRhyme-1 (the number of matching vowel phonemes at the end of c_i and $s_{\kappa-1}$), OtherRhyme (the average number of matching vowel phonemes per word), LineLength (the line similarity of c_i and s_κ), BOW (the Jaccard similarity between the corresponding bags of words of c_i and s_κ), BOW5 (the Jaccard similarity between the corresponding bags of words of five previous lines and c_i), LSA (the latent semantic analysis similarity of c_i and s_κ), and NN5 (a confidence value generated from the NN5 network) features. **Early fusion** [3]: a widely used multi-modal aggregation method, in which all features are concatenated as the unified representation (i.e., $\boldsymbol{v}_t := [\boldsymbol{v}_r, \boldsymbol{v}_s]$). **EF-AE**: a variant of HAVAE that adopts the same learning manipulations with HAVAE, bypassing the sampling strategy and taking $[\boldsymbol{v}_r, \boldsymbol{v}_s]$ as the input of the network. **EF-VAE**: another variant of HAVAE method that takes $[\boldsymbol{v}_r, \boldsymbol{v}_s]$ as the input of the VAE network instead of the INPUT stage.

The comparison approaches can be categorized into three types based on the involved information, i.e., prosodic, semantic, and both (prosodic and semantic) types.

Experiment Setting. In the training phase, every query line s_κ has two candidate lines. One line is the true next line of the given line, which is the ground truth and serves as a positive example. The other line is a randomly selected line from the corpus, which serves as a negative example. In the testing phase, every query line has a candidate set that contains the true next line and 299 randomly chosen lines.

We combine each query line with a candidate line as a pair. Unlike BOW5 and NN5, which consider the five previous lines when extracting semantic features, we only utilize s_κ as materials. Following [18], the representation obtained by [18] is fed into the SVM^{rank} [25] tool for ranking. A complicated issue is that the representations generated by other methods are high dimensional; thus, the SVM^{rank} tool is infeasible. To tackle this issue, we design a Rank Layer, which is defined as $score = sigmoid(W\boldsymbol{v}_t + b)$, where $score \in [0, 1]$ is a confidence value indicating the relevancy between the candidate and query lines. The higher the *score*, the better the performance.

Evaluation Results. The performance of the compared approaches is evaluated under the metrics of mean rank, mean reciprocal rank (MRR), and recall at $*$ ($* = 1$, 5, 30, 150), which is denoted as Rec@$*$. Let $rank_i$ denote the rank

[6] In the current paper, we report the results in the original work, and reproduce it on the crawled dataset.

Table 3. Results of the proposed method and the baseline methods

Information	Methods	Mean rank	MRR	Rec@1	Rec@5	Rec@30	Rec@150
prosodic	EndRhyme	103.2*	0.140*	0.077*	0.181*	0.344*	0.480*
	rhyme2vec	17.7	0.463	0.347	0.592	0.841	0.981
semantic	NN5	84.7*	0.067*	0.020*	0.083*	0.319*	0.793*
	doc2vec	15.5	0.430	0.293	0.588	0.870	0.985
both	DopeLearning	60.8*/79.9	0.243*/0.168	0.169*/0.102	0.304*/0.220	0.527*/0.446	0.855*/0.775
	early fusion	9.6	0.588	0.464	0.738	0.926	0.991
	EF-AE	5.3	0.771	0.683	0.879	0.966	0.995
	EF-VAE	2.3	0.941	0.914	0.973	0.990	0.997
	HAVAE	**1.2**	**0.982**	**0.973**	**0.993**	**0.999**	**1.000**

*denotes the reported results from the original paper [18]

position of the correct next line in the candidate set for the *i-th* query. Mean rank is the average value of $\sum_{i=1}^{N} rank_i$. The value of mean rank is between 1 and 300, and a lower value is better. MRR is the average score of $\sum_{i=1}^{N} \frac{1}{rank_i}$, and a higher value is better. Rec@$*$ is the probability of $rank_i \leq *$, and higher values are better.

Table 3 reports the results. The proposed HAVAE outstrips all baseline methods and achieves the state-of-the-art performance. We also note the following observations:

Effectiveness of HAVAE. Among all of the evaluated methods, our proposed HAVAE achieves superior performance. The mean rank is **1.2**, which outperforms the most advanced approaches by a substantial margin. The mean rank of DopeLearning is 60.8 in the original paper, and 79.9 with settings in our paper; both are more than 60. For MRR, HAVAE achieves **0.982**, which beats DopeLearning at 73.9*/81.4% points. The performance under the evaluation of Rec@$*$ illustrates a similar observation that HAVAE has the ability to yield better results. In summary, HAVAE exceeds the state-of-the-art approaches under various evaluation metrics, due to its effective technology of combining fine-grained prosodic and semantic features (distributed representation learning instead of simple statistical characteristics) and appropriate feature aggregation strategy (attentive VAE-based framework instead of early fusion).

Effectiveness of rhyme2vec. Compared with EndRhyme, rhyme2vec exhibits more promising performance under all evaluation metrics. This outcome demonstrates that the prosodic vector representation learned by our rhyme embedding method, which comprehensively considers various rhyme schemes, is far more effective than the state-of-the-art prosodic features-based approach.

Effectiveness of the Prosodic-Enhanced Representation. We observe that when utilizing the semantic representations (doc2vec) or prosodic representations (rhyme2vec) solely, the value of mean rank is more than 15, and the MRR score is below 0.5. By contrast, the performance is significantly improved after fusing both representations. Consistently, DopeLearning performs better than EndRhyme and NN5. This result demonstrates that taking prosodic information together with semantic information is more consummate than taking the prosodic or semantic information solely, and our prosodic-enhanced vector is more representative than the traditional semantic vectors.

Effectiveness of the Feature Aggregation Module. The early fusion method takes the concatenation of all features as the unified representation (the same manner as DopeLearning), and obtains a 9.6 mean rank score and a 0.588 MRR score. Taking the early fusion approach as the baseline, the EF-AE method prevails. The reason is that the EF-AE employs the autoencoder network, which can learn useful information from the inner relationship of the input [5]. Moreover, EF-VAE performs superior to EF-AE, revealing from another aspect that VAE is more powerful than AE in generating the representations of rap lyrics. Conclusively, the superiority of HAVAE over EF-VAE indicates that the attention mechanism, which amplifies mutual relationship between semantic and prosodic information, can bring substantial benefits.

Remarks. Doc2vec is comparably good as rhyme2vec under some evaluation metrics. Similarly, NN5 works better than EndRhyme in terms of the mean rank and Rec@150 scores. The persuasive reason is that rappers commonly image the topic of a song at first to present the semantic information. However, different rhymes may be used to realize the idea. For instance, "mommy[mɒmɪ]" and "daddy[dædɪ]" can be replaced with "mother[mʌðə]" and "father[fa: ðə]" without changing the fundamental semantics.

4.2 Rap Genre Classification

To demonstrate the generalizability of our method, we design a rap genre classification task at song level complementally. Given a set of rap songs and a set of genre labels, our aim is to predict a proper set of labels for every song. In essence, this experiment is a multi-label classification task.

Dataset. We create a dataset from the rap song corpus. The dataset consisting of 10167 songs from nine genres (including Alternative rap, Christian rap, East Coast rap, Grime rap, Hardcore rap, Horrorcore rap, Midwest rap, Southern rap, and West Coast rap), and these genres are regarded as labels of songs.

Baseline Models. RhymeAPP [13]: a lyrical analysis tool that calculates statistical features of rap songs. **Rhyme2vec**: our rhyme embedding approach, merely including prosodic information. **Doc2vec**: the widely used paragraph embedding approach, merely including semantic information. **HAN** [26]: a state-of-the-art approach for genre classification of intact lyrics.

Experiment Setting. We feed the features generated by the comparison models into a classification network and obtain a genre prediction vector $\boldsymbol{y}$ for each song, indicating the probability of nine labels to be tagged to a given song. We construct a threshold t to determine whether the given song should be categorized into the corresponding genre, that is, if $y_i \leq t$, $y'_i = 0$, otherwise $y'_i = 1$, where y_i the *i-th* element of $\boldsymbol{y}$. We use $\boldsymbol{y'} = \{y'_i\}_{i=1}^{9}$ as the predicted label set. Specifically, we attach the *i-th* genre label with a rap song only when $y'_i = 1$.

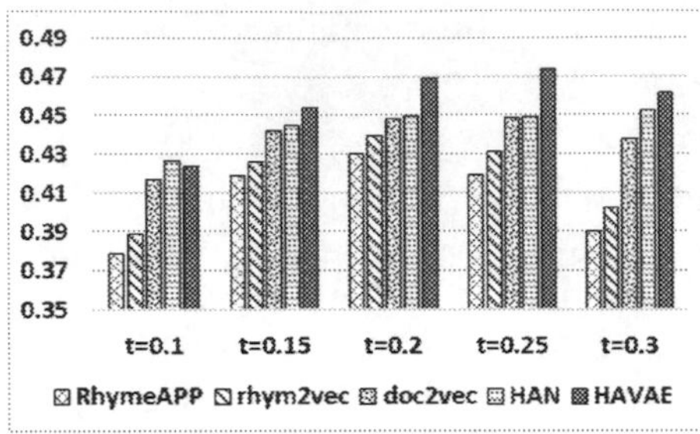

Fig. 4. The micro-F1 scores

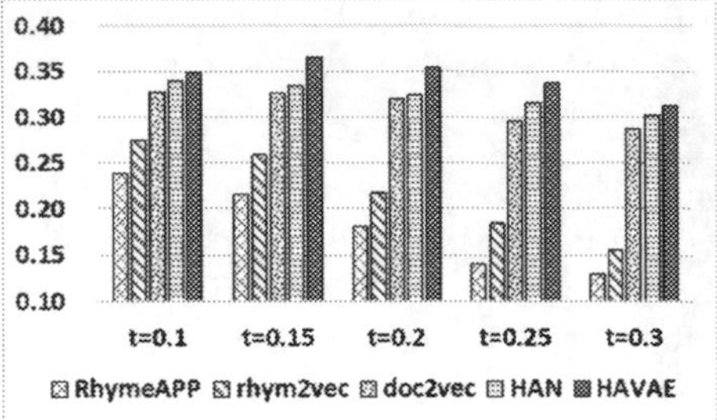

Fig. 5. The macro-F1 scores

Evaluation and Results. The micro-F1 and macro-F1 scores are illustrated in Figs. 4 and 5, respectively. Overall, HAVAE significantly outperforms the other methods, especially when $t = 0.25$ (the micro-F1 score is 0.474) and when $t = 0.15$ (the macro-F1 score is 0.365). This situation indicates that HAVAE can be applied in various cases, and it is perfectly competent to capture prosodic and semantic information in rap lyrics.

5 Conclusions

We have proposed a general framework to learn rap lyrics (HAVAE), taking into account the semantic and prosodic features. Several effective strategies have been introduced (rhyme2vec), VAE-based feature aggregation module, and hierarchical attention mechanism. The effectiveness of the framework has been experimentally demonstrated by comparing it with state-of-the-art approaches on benchmark datasets in both tasks.

Acknowledgements. This work was supported in part by the National Natural Science Foundation of China under Grant No. U1636116, 11431006, 61772288, the Research Fund for International Young Scientists under Grant No. 61650110510 and 61750110530, and the Ministry of education of Humanities and Social Science project under grant 16YJC790123.

References

1. Addanki, K., Wu, D.: Unsupervised rhyme scheme identification in hip hop lyrics using hidden Markov models. In: ISMIR (2013)
2. Alexey, T., Ivan, P.Y.: Music generation with variational recurrent autoencoder supported by history. In: CMMR (2017)
3. Ashman, R., Baird, A., Allard, R., et al.: Effect of spinal construct stiffness on early fusion mass incorporation. Experimental study. Spine **15**(9), 908–912 (1990)
4. Association, I.P.: Handbook of the International Phonetic Association: A guide to the use of the International Phonetic Alphabet. Cambridge University Press, Cambridge (1999)
5. Bengio, Y.: Learning deep architectures for AI. Mach. Learn. **2**(1), 1–127 (2009)

6. Bryant, P.E., MacLean, M., Bradley, L.L., Crossland, J.: Rhyme and alliteration, phoneme detection, and learning to read. Dev. Psychol. **26**(3), 429–438 (1990)
7. Dosovitskiy, A., Brox, T.: Generating images with perceptual similarity metrics based on deep networks. In: NIPS (2016)
8. Duddington, J.: eSpeak text to speech (2012)
9. Fabius, O., van Amersfoort, J.R.: Variational recurrent auto-encoders. arXiv preprint arXiv:1412.6581 (2014)
10. Hadjeres, G., Nielsen, F., Pachet, F.: GLSR-VAE: geodesic latent space regularization for variational autoencoder architectures. In: SSCI (2017)
11. He, J., Zhou, M., Jiang, L.: Generating Chinese classical poems with statistical machine translation models. In: AAAI (2012)
12. Hirjee, H., Brown, D.G.: Automatic detection of internal and imperfect rhymes in rap lyrics. In: ISMIR (2009)
13. Hirjee, H., Brown, D.G.: Rhyme analyzer: an analysis tool for rap lyrics. In: ISMIR (2010)
14. Hirjee, H., Brown, D.G.: Using automated rhyme detection to characterize rhyming style in rap music. Empirical Musicology Rev. **5**(4), 121–145 (2010)
15. Hou, X., Shen, L., Sun, K., Qiu, G.: Deep feature consistent variational autoencoder. In: WACV (2017)
16. Kingma, D.P., Rezende, D.J., Mohamed, S., Welling, M.: Semi-supervised learning with deep generative models. In: NIPS (2014)
17. Kingma, D.P., Welling, M.: Auto-encoding variational bayes. In: ICLR (2014)
18. Malmi, E., Takala, P., Toivonen, H., Raiko, T., Gionis, A.: DopeLearning: a computational approach to rap lyrics generation. In: SIGKDD (2016)
19. Mauch, M., MacCallum, R.M., Levy, M., Leroi, A.M.: The evolution of popular music: USA 1960–2010. Royal Soc. Open Sci. **2**(5), 150081 (2015)
20. Oliveira, H.G.: PoeTryMe: a versatile platform for poetry generation. In: ECAI (2012)
21. Potash, P., Romanov, A., Rumshisky, A.: GhostWriter: using an LSTM for automatic rap lyric generation. In: EMNLP (2015)
22. Potash, P., Romanov, A., Rumshisky, A.: Evaluating creative language generation: the case of rap lyric ghostwriting. arXiv preprint arXiv:1612.03205 (2016)
23. Quoc, L., Tomas, M.: Distributed representations of sentences and documents. In: ICML (2014)
24. Ruli, M., Graeme, R., Henry, S.T.: Using genetic algorithms to create meaningful poetic text. J. Exp. Theor. Artif. Intell. **24**(1), 43–64 (2012)
25. Thorsten, J.: Training linear SVMs in linear time. In: SIGKDD (2006)
26. Tsaptsinos, A.: Lyrics-based music genre classification using a hierarchical attention network. In: ISMIR (2017)
27. Wang, Q., Luo, T., Wang, D., Xing, C.: Chinese song iambics generation with neural attention-based model. In: IJCAI (2016)
28. Wu, D., Addanki, V.S.K., Saers, M.S., Beloucif, M.: Learning to freestyle: hip hop challenge-response induction via transduction rule segmentation. In: EMNLP (2013)
29. Yan, R., Jiang, H., Lapata, M., Lin, S.D., Lv, X., Li, X.: i, Poet: automatic Chinese poetry composition through a generative summarization framework under constrained optimization. In: IJCAI (2013)
30. Yu, C., Mohammed, J.Z.: KATE: K-competitive autoencoder for text. In: SIGKDD (2017)

DKE-RLS: A Manifold Reconstruction Algorithm in Label Spaces with Double Kernel Embedding-Regularized Least Square

Chao Tan(✉) and Genlin Ji

School of Computer Science and Technology, Nanjing Normal University, Nanjing, China
{chaotan,glji}@njnu.edu.cn

Abstract. Dimension reduction is an important preprocess for multi-label classification, such as feature extraction. This paper attempts to explore multi-label learning in the label space. Our approach works using machine learning's smoothness assumption, where nearby points are more likely to share the same label and the feature manifold and label manifold can share the local topology structure. Thus, here we propose a new multi-label feature-extraction algorithm with a new method for embedding regression, i.e., manifold regularization learning in the subspace formed by multi-labels to reconstruct and use the label manifold. We integrate two least-squares formulas by linear combination, and establish the regression estimation for multi-label manifold learning. To test our approach, we conduct multiple experiments and compare our algorithm against four other multi-label learning algorithms. Results show that our approach significantly improves the performance of label manifold learning.

Keywords: Multi-label learning · Smoothness assumption
Manifold regularization learning

1 Introduction

Multi-label learning is a hot research topic in machine learning and data mining. The learning process, essentially, is to create a mapping from examples to labels. The task of traditional multi-label learning is to discover the predictor that maps samples from the eigenvector space to the label vector space. Each label vector element y_i is a logical indicator that the corresponding label is either related to or irrelevant with an example x_i. Over the past decade, multi-label learning has been applied successfully to learn from rich semantic data, such as text [1,2], image [3,4], and audio [5,6]. The traditional label space is logical, where the manifold does not exist. To explore the manifold with labels, we should extend the labeled space to a Euclidean space [7]. However, the label manifold has not been provided explicitly in training examples.

X. Geng and B.-H. Kang (Eds.): PRICAI 2018, LNAI 11012, pp. 16–28, 2018.
https://doi.org/10.1007/978-3-319-97304-3_2

Fortunately, according to the smoothness assumption in machine learning [8], data points within close proximity are more likely to share one label, and the local topology can be shared between the feature manifold and label manifold. Hou et al. [9] proposed a new learning method, by extending from a logical label space to a Euclidean label space. This method allows us to induce the local topological structure naturally from the smooth hypothesis, and transform from the feature space to label space (i.e., multi-label manifold learning), to reconstruct and use the label manifold. Hou et al. denoted that this method is the first to explore the manifold structure of label space in multi-label learning.

To reconstruct the label manifold, the key issue is the topology structure. Although the eigenspace and label space share a similar local topological structure, often the global manifolds in these two spaces differ. In the past, researchers mostly studied mapping from the feature space to the traditional logical label space-that is, determining how to predict the adjacent logical label vectors in the label space from the manifold structure in the feature space. However, recent research on manifold structure in the Euclidean label space is sparse. In response, here we discuss how the local topological structure, which is transformed from feature space to label space, will be guided by the vectors in the feature manifold structure and the logical label space.

We also approximate the feature manifold (during big data streams' feature extraction) via the alignment of overlapping local linear neighborhoods. We obtain each neighborhood's weight using the least-squares optimization method. Then we use the transformation of the feature manifold and existing logical labels to reconstruct the label manifolds from the local topological structure. As we detail in this paper, we realize the reconstruction process using a quadratic programming approach, using the numerical label symbols to indicate whether the label is related to the sample. Exploiting the label manifolds, we effectively find the mapping from the feature manifolds to the label manifolds via a regression process.

We should note that label manifolds have three advantages. First, according to the smoothness hypothesis, a label manifold helps exploit the correlation between the label and transformation from feature space to topological structure. Second, it extends the traditional logical label to a numerical label to describe the samples in more detail, thereby making it possible to improve performance. Third, it helps the classification system make more complex decisions based on numerical labels, because the value of the numerical labels is indicative of the relative importance to corresponding labels. However, the relationship between the feature manifold and label manifold is not embedded and it does not reduce dimension. The manifolds are in two different spaces, but they share a local topological structure based on the smoothness assumption. This leads to two related problems. The first is how to use nonlinear manifold learning methods to guide the label manifolds' reconstruction and preserve the neighborhood's structure information between them. The second is determining which kind of regularized least-squares programming to adopt to realize the reconstruction process, so that the optimal function reaches the optimal solution.

To solve these problems, here we use a feature-extraction method with an adaptive-alignment character, to direct the label manifold's reconstruction and keep the neighborhood structural information between them. Then, we reconstruct the local topological structure obtained from the feature manifold and existing logic label transformation to obtain a label manifold. We use a regularized least-squares method to reconstruct and make the optimal function reach the optimal solution.

The contributions of this paper are as follows:

1. In this paper, we use the feature extraction method with a tangent space-alignment property to reconstruct the label manifold and keep their neighborhood structure information, to better understand the space structure relationship of high-dimensional samples.
2. We propose a double kernel-embedding regularized least-squares (DKE-RLS) optimization model to realize the reconstruction process. The model has a simple kernel transformation form, which can extract the manifold structure's features. It only needs to compute the sparse inverse matrix and has high computational efficiency.
3. Then we propose a regularized form of manifold learning and embed the manifold regularization terms derived by the feature-extraction method introduced in the previous steps into the subspace spanned by the eigenvectors of the two-kernel matrix, which reflect the local and global structures, respectively. That can better reflect the data manifold and speed up the computational efficiency.

2 Related Work

The existing multi-label methods can be divided into three categories, based on the idea of label relevance [10]. The simplest type is the first-order methods that assume the independence between class labels [11,12]. Then multi-label classifications become a series of binary classification problems. In contrast, the second-order methods take into account the correlation between each pair of class labels [13,14], and the high-order methods consider the correlation between the label subsets or all the class labels [15]. The common modeling strategy for all the approaches is to process each label in a clear way, i.e., whether it is related to the sample.

Some existing multi-label research works transform the logical label space into the Euclidean mark space. In contrast, Hou et al. [9] proposed a method named Multi-label Manifold Learning (ML^2), which explored manifolds in label spaces and treated them as numbers. In this case, the label set contains more semantic information, which is beneficial to the learning process.

Another related work is Label Distribution Learning (LDL) [16], which is a new paradigm of machine learning where each example is annotated by a label distribution. What merits attention is the difference between manifold learning and ML^2. Manifold learning assumes that the data of interest are actually located on an embedded nonlinear manifold located in a higher dimensional space, so manifold learning is mainly used for dimensionality reduction and visualization. Three well-known local methods in manifold learning are Local Linear Embedding (LLE) [17], Laplacian Eigenmaps (LE) [18], and Locality Preserving Projection (LPP) [19]. The reconstruction of the label manifold in ML^2 is similar to LLE. However, the relationship between the feature manifold and label manifold is not embedding or dimensionality reduction. They are located in two different spaces, and they only share the local topological structure according to the smoothness assumption. ML^2 moves the local topological structure from feature space to label space.

However, ML^2 has no dimensionality reduction. In addition, both of the first two methods generate new space projected from the original label space. ML^2 extends the original logical label space into a Euclidean space, where the meaning of each dimension still exists.

A Semi-Supervised local multi-manifold Isomap by linear embedding is proposed in Zhang et al's work [20]. Their model can use labeled and unlabeled data to deliver manifold features. To enhance the performance of nonlinear manifold feature learning, the authors also incorporate the neighborhood reconstruction error to preserve the local topology structures between both labeled and unlabeled samples.

Belkin et al. [21] proposed a new form of regularization learning algorithm framework, using edge-distribution geometry, where a regularized least-squares method was used in this algorithm framework. They used the regenerative kernel Hilbert space's property to provide the theoretical foundation for an algorithmic proof.

Belkin et al. [22] proposed two regularization algorithms: Laplacian Regularized Least Squares (LapRLS) and Laplacian Support Vector Machines (LapSVM). We can extend these algorithms to new samples, and the semisupervised algorithm effectively uses unlabeled data. This is suitable for unsupervised and semisupervised cases, and works well to solve the out-of-sample extension problem.

Chen et al. [23] indicated that the Laplacian Support Vector Machine (LapSVM) and Laplacian Regularized Least Squares (LapRLS) laid a solid foundation for a manifold regularization framework. However, because of matrix computation's high cost, most of these optimization algorithms are limited to small-scale problems. Chen proposed a new framework called Laplace embedding regression, which introduced the regression of intermediate decision variables into a manifold regularization framework and proposed a Laplacian Embedded Support Vector Regression algorithm (LapESVR) and Laplacian Embedded Regularized Least Squares (LapERLS) [23]. Based on Kernel PCA, in this paper we introduce decision variables into the subspaces spanned by several eigenvectors of the manifold matrix, to better reflect the data manifold.

More regularized least-squares approaches for optimization can be found in [24–26].

In summary, we come to the following conclusions:

1. For manifold structure research in the Euclidean label space, many key theoretical and practical issues require further study to be resolved. In the past,

the mapping relationship from the study of the feature space to the traditional logical label space was mostly studied, i.e., how to predict the adjacent logical label vectors from the manifold structure in the feature space. Thus, the first problem we tackle in this paper is how to transform the local topology structure from a feature space to label space using nonlinear manifold learning methods.

2. The second issue we tackle is how to combine the local topological structure converted from the feature manifold and logical labels. The label manifold is reconstructed to design the regularized least-squares program function to realize this reconstruction process, so that the optimization function reaches the optimal solution and improves learning efficiency.

3 A Double Kernel Embedding-Regularized Least Square Method (DKE-RLS) Algorithm

3.1 Transformation of Local Topologies from Feature Space to Label Space

When we extract big data streams' features, we obtain the feature manifold by aligning the learning method via overlapping local linear neighborhoods [27]. So in this paper, we use the feature-extraction method with a tangent space-alignment property to reconstruct the label manifold and keep the neighborhood structure information between them. In the Euclidean label space, we study the manifold structure and transform the local topological structure from feature space to label space under the guidance of nonlinear manifold learning methods, to better understand the space structure relationship of high-dimensional samples, and to direct the label manifold's reconstruction while preserving the neighbor structure information.

According to the smoothness hypothesis, we can transfer the feature space's topological structure locally to the numerical label space. To preserve the locality, we need to construct the topological structure using the local neighborhood information of each point [9]. Based on Zhang and Zha hypothesis [27], each data point can be optimally reconstructed using a linear combination of its neighbors. Then the approximation of the feature manifold is the induction of reconstruction error minimization, which we use to construct the loss function:

$$\min ||E|| = \min_{c,U,T} ||X - (ce^T + UT)||_F, \tag{1}$$

where $||\cdot||_F$ is the Frobenius form of matrix E, $c = Xe/N$ is the mean value of a set of data points $X = [x_1, \cdots, x_N]$ sampled from the nonlinear manifold $\Re^m$, and e is an N-dimensional unit column vector. Matrix U is an orthonormal basis of the affine subspace, $U \in \Re^{m\times d}$, while T is the low-dimensional eigenvector of X in space $\Re^d$. The reconstruction of the label manifold can be inferred as the minimization of the following equation:

$$E_i = T_i(I - \frac{1}{k}ee^T)(I - U_i^T U_i). \tag{2}$$

The matrix $T_i = [t_{i_1}, \cdots, t_{i_k}]$ is composed by the optimal embedding coordinates.

Set $R_i = (I - \frac{1}{k}ee^T)(I - U_i^T U_i)$, Eq. (2) can be converted to solve the approximate standard least-squares programming problem.

$$\min_{T_i} ||E_i||_F^2 = \min_{T_i} ||T_i R_i||_F^2 = Tr(T_i R_i R_i^T T_i^T).s.t.TT^T = I \tag{3}$$

To minimize $||E_i||_F^2$, the eigenvectors corresponding to the first d smallest eigenvalues of $R_i R_i^T$ should be chosen, i.e., $T_i = [t_{i_1}, \cdots, t_{i_d}]$. So the optimal solution of Eq. (3) is given by the eigenvectors corresponding to the first d smallest eigenvalues of $R_i R_i^T$.

Through the topology transformation, we express the label manifold's reconstruction as a constrained quadratic programming process, which is actually a multioutput regression problem in the case of multi-labels. Tuia et al. [28] proposed a multioutput support vector regression (M-SVR) method to solve the problem of regression estimation for multiple variables. In M-SVR, The regression estimation problem is regarded as finding the mapping between an incoming vector $x \in \Re^d$ and an observable output $y \in \Re$, $\{(x_i, y_i)\}_{i=1}^l$. The problem is solved in M-SVR by finding regressors w and b to minimize the loss function:

$$L(w, b) = \frac{1}{2}\sum_{j=1}^{Q} ||w^j||^2 + C\sum_{i=1}^{l} L_1(u_i), \tag{4}$$

where $u_i = ||e_i|| = \sqrt{c_i^T e_i}$, $e_i^T = y_i^T - \varphi(x_i)^T W - b^T$, $W = [w^1, \cdots, w^Q]$, $b = [b^1, \cdots, b^Q]^T$.

Here $\varphi(\cdot)$ is a nonlinear transformation to a dimensional space H, also known as the feature space. In this paper, we intend to use the optimal alignment matrix U in Eq. (2) to replace $\varphi(\cdot)$ to minimize the loss function L, to reconstruct the multi-label manifold through the regression estimation by Eq. (4).

In Hou's work [9], they generalized the 1-D SVR to solve the multidimensional case, which is similar to the MSVR. In addition, they proposed a regressor based on the MSVR and set a $L2$ loss function,

$$L(w, b) = \frac{1}{2}\sum_{j=1}^{Q} ||w^j||^2 + C_1\sum_{i=1}^{l} L_1(u_i) + C_2\sum_{i=1}^{l}\sum_{j=1}^{Q} L_2(t_i^j), \tag{5}$$

where $t_i^j = y_i^j(\varphi(x_i)^T w^j + b^j)$.

Here, we will use the optimal alignment matrix U in (2) to replace $\varphi(x)$ in the loss function (5), which is the innovation point in this paper. To yield a single support vector for all dimensions, the L_1 loss function in (5) is set as:

$$L_1(u) = \begin{cases} 0, u < \varepsilon; \\ (u - \varepsilon)^2, u \geq \varepsilon. \end{cases} \tag{6}$$

To make the signs of the numerical label and logical label the same as much as possible, the L_2 loss function in (5) is set as:

$$L_2(t) = -t\sigma(-t) = \begin{cases} 0, t > 0; \\ -t, t \leq 0, \end{cases} \tag{7}$$

where $\sigma(t)$ is an activation function with the value 0 if t is negative; otherwise, the value will be 1. Hou et al. [9] used an iterative quasi-Newton method called Iterative Re-Weighted Least Square (IRWLS) [29] to minimize $L(w, b)$.

After two orders of Taylor expansion, a quadratic approximation of $L(w, b)$ can be constructed as

$$L^{''}(w, b) = \frac{1}{2}\sum_{j=1}^{Q} ||w^j||^2 + \frac{1}{2}C_1 \sum_{i=1}^{l} a_i u_i^2 - C_2 \sum_{i=1}^{l}\sum_{j=1}^{Q} t_i^j \sigma(-t_i^j) + \tau. \tag{8}$$

To get the optimal solution of (5), we solve the least-squares problem in (8), and obtain the optimal solution w and b.

w and b can be obtained via setting the derivatives of L with respect to $L^{''}(w, b)$ to be zero, i.e.,

$$\frac{\partial L^{''}(w,b)}{\partial w} = \begin{cases} w^j - C_1 \sum\limits_i \varphi(x_i) a_i (y_i^j - \varphi(x_i)^T w^j - b^j) = 0, \\ t_i^j = y_i^j(\varphi(x_i)^T w^j + b^j) > 0 \\ w^j - C_1 \sum\limits_i \varphi(x_i) a_i (y_i^j - \varphi(x_i)^T w^j - b^j) - \\ C_2 \sum\limits_{i=1}^{l} \sum\limits_{j=1}^{Q} (y_i^j \varphi(x_i)^T + y_i^j b^j) = 0, t_i^j \leq 0. \end{cases} \tag{9}$$

$$\frac{\partial L^{''}(w,b)}{\partial b} = \begin{cases} -C_1 \sum\limits_i a_i (y_i^j - \varphi(x_i)^T w^j - b^j) = 0, t_i^j = y_i^j(\varphi(x_i)^T w^j + b^j) > 0 \\ -C_1 \sum\limits_i a_i (y_i^j - \varphi(x_i)^T w^j - b^j) - C_2 \sum\limits_{i=1}^{l} \sum\limits_{j=1}^{Q} y_i^j = 0, t_i^j \leq 0. \end{cases} \tag{10}$$

Under fairly general conditions, a learning problem can be expressed as a linear combination of the training examples in the feature space [9,24]. The linear system of (9) and (10) can be expressed as follows:

$$\begin{bmatrix} C_1 \varphi^T D_a \varphi + I & C_1 \varphi^T a \\ C_1 a^T \varphi & C_1 I^T a \end{bmatrix} \begin{bmatrix} w^j \\ b^j \end{bmatrix} = \begin{bmatrix} C_1 \varphi^T D_a y^j + C_2 \varphi^T D_j y^j \\ C_1 a^T y^j + C_2 (\sigma^j)^T y^j \end{bmatrix}. \tag{11}$$

3.2 Using a Kernel Matrix in the Feature Space

To use the kernels to express the nonlinear mapping in feature space, the learning problem in (11) can be expressed as follows:

$$\begin{bmatrix} C_1 (K + D_a^{-1}) & C_1 I \\ C_1 a^T K & C_1 I^T a \end{bmatrix} \begin{bmatrix} w^j \\ b^j \end{bmatrix} = \begin{bmatrix} C_1 y^j + C_2 y^j \\ C_1 a^T y^j + C_2 (\sigma^j)^T y^j \end{bmatrix}, \tag{12}$$

where $K = k(x_i, x_j)$ is the kernel matrix, $(D_a)_i^j = a_i \delta_i^j$, δ_i^j is the Kronecker's delta function, $I = [1, ..., 1]^T$ is a unit column vector, $a = [a_1, ..., a_N]^T$, $(D_j)_i^k = \sigma(-t_i^j)\delta_i^j$, and $y^j = [y_1^j, ..., y_N^j]^T$.

In this paper, we reconstruct the local manifold from the feature manifold and the existing logical labels. We prepare to use a double kernel-embedding regularized least-squares (DKE-RLS) algorithm to realize the reconstruction process. The proposed optimization model has a simple kernel-transformation form, which can extract the manifold structure's features. It only needs to compute the sparse inverse matrix and has high computational efficiency.

Then we propose a regularized form of manifold learning. We embed the manifold regularization terms derived by the feature-extraction method introduced in the previous section into the subspace spanned by the eigenvectors of the two-kernel matrix, which reflect the local and global structures, respectively. These can better reflect the data manifold and speed up the computational efficiency.

According to the smoothness assumption, data close to each other are more likely to have the same labels. The regularization term in the objective function can be constructed as follows:

$$\arg\min f = \arg\min L + (1-\alpha)||f_1||^2 + \alpha||f_2||^2. \tag{13}$$

We replace L in the objective function (13) with the loss function $L(w, b)$ in (5). $||f_1||^2$ and $||f_2||^2$ are the manifold kernel matrix defined in Zhang et al.'s work [26].

$$||f_1||^2 = f^T K f, \tag{14}$$

$$||f_2||^2 = f^T W f, \tag{15}$$

where $K = \lambda_{\max} I - M$ is the kernel matrix of algorithm LLE [17] in kernel form, and $W = -\frac{1}{2}HSH$ is the kernel matrix of algorithm ISOMAP [31]. $(1-\alpha)$ and α are balancing parameters that can adjust the relationship between the neighborhood's construction and preserving the global distance (as we presented in Tan's work [30]).

The matrix M is a symmetric, semipositive definite matrix, and $\lambda_{\max}$ is the largest eigenvalue of M. $I = [1, ..., 1]^T$. S is obtained by taking the squared elements in matrix D, which is constructed by the distances between each data point and its neighbors, to preserve the geodesic distances between all data points. $H = I - ee^T/n$, $e = [1, ..., 1]^T$, and n is the number of samples.

In summary, we represent the optimal problem of (13) as the following function:

$$\arg\min f = \arg\min_{w,b} L(w, b) + (1-\alpha) f^T K f + \alpha f^T W f. \tag{16}$$

The loss function $L(w, b)$ in (16) is given by (5), and the regressors w and b are searched to minimize the loss function. In $L(w, b)$, $t_i^j = y_i^j(\varphi(x_i)^T w^j + b^j)$, where $\varphi(\cdot)$ is a nonlinear transformation in the feature space. Here, we use the optimal alignment matrix U in (2) to replace $\varphi(\cdot)$.

4 Experiments

To test our algorithm, we carried out experiments on 10 real-world, multi-label datasets. The proposed algorithm DKE-RLS is compared with four recent, well-established multi-label learning algorithms.

4.1 Experimental Setup

Dataset. Table 1 shows the real multi-label datasets' detailed characteristics, collected from the Mulan website [32], in which S is the number of training samples, T is the number of testing samples, $dim(S)$ denotes the feature dimensions, $L(S)$ represents the number of class labels, and $LCard(S)$ is the label cardinality. More multi-label statistics include the label cardinality $LCard(S)$, label density $LDen(S)$, distinct label sets $DL(S)$, and domain of datasets. As Table 1 shows, half of the datasets belong to the regular-sized, and half of them belong to the large-sized (with more than 1,000 samples, both in the training sets and in the testing sets).

Table 1. Characteristics of multi-label datasets

Dataset	S	T	$dim(S)$	$L(S)$	$LCard(S)$	$LDen(S)$	$DL(S)$	Domain
Yeast	1200	1217	103	14	4.237	0.303	198	Biology
Emotions	415	178	72	6	1.869	0.311	27	Music
Medical	645	333	1449	45	1.245	0.028	94	Text
Cal500	250	252	68	174	26.044	0.150	502	Music
Birds	320	325	260	19	1.014	0.053	133	Audio
Image	1000	1000	294	5	1.236	0.247	20	Images
Scene	1211	1196	294	6	1.074	0.179	15	Images
Enron	1123	579	1001	53	3.378	0.064	753	Text
Corel5k	2500	2500	499	374	3.522	0.009	3175	Images
Bibtex	3700	3695	1836	159	2.402	0.015	2856	Text

Comparing Algorithms and Parameter Sets. In this experiment, we compare our algorithm with four other multi-label learning algorithms, which were well-established recently: Multi-Label Manifold Learning (ML^2) [9], Multi-label lazy learning approach ($ML-kNN$) [12], Multi-Label Naive Bayes classifier ($MLNB$) [33], and Multi-label Learning with Feature-induced labeling information Enrichment ($MLFE$) [34]. The number of neighbors K for ML^2 is set to $q+1$, because it is necessary for K to be larger than q to generate a q-dimensional space using K vectors [9]. The penalty parameters C_1 and C_2 are set to 1 and 10 and balance parameter $\lambda = 1$ according to Hou's work [9]. For $MLFE$, parameters β_1, β_2 and β_3 are chosen among $\{1, 2, ..., 10\}$, $\{1, 10, 15\}$ and $\{1, 10\}$ respectively with cross-validation on the training set. The balancing parameters in (16) are consistent with Tan's work [30]. And the model parameters in (12) are set as: $\sigma = \{10^{-1}, ..., 10\}$, $C = \{1, ..., 100\}$, and $\varepsilon = \{10^{-6}, 10^{-3}\}$.

Evaluation Metrics. In this experiment, we use five evaluation metrics widely used in multi-label learning algorithms, such as Hamming Loss, Ranking Loss, One-Error, Coverage, and Macro-averaging AUC [10]. In a typical scenario, the larger the values, the better the performance for Average Precision, while the smaller the values, the better the performance for the other metrics.

Table 2. Predictive performance of each compared algorithm (mean value) on the regular- and large-sized datasets

Compared algorithms	Hamming loss↓									
	Yeast	Emotions	Medical	Cal500	Birds	Image	Scene	Enron	Corel5k	Bibtex
$DKE-RLS$	0.2040	**0.2285**	**0.0112**	0.1631	0.0619	0.1662	**0.0844**	**0.0541**	0.0097	0.0125
ML^2	0.2073	0.2388	0.0114	0.1578	0.0636	0.1642	0.0847	0.0546	0.0098	0.0126
$ML-kNN$	**0.1980**	0.2706	0.0153	0.1416	0.0546	0.1862	0.0989	0.0620	**0.0094**	0.0136
$MLNB$	0.2166	0.2804	0.0339	**0.1395**	0.0779	0.2300	0.1299	0.1145	0.0145	0.0824
$MLFE$	0.2038	0.2434	0.0112	0.1549	**0.0615**	**0.1616**	0.0903	0.0543	0.0101	**0.0124**
Compared algorithms	Ranking loss↓									
	Yeast	Emotions	Medical	Cal500	Birds	Image	Scene	Enron	Corel5k	Bibtex
$DKE-RLS$	0.3004	**0.1916**	0.1426	0.4642	0.2943	**0.1443**	**0.0574**	0.3179	0.4373	**0.0857**
ML^2	0.3022	0.2228	0.1084	0.4721	0.3288	0.1467	0.0580	0.3210	0.4177	0.0897
$ML-kNN$	**0.1715**	0.2724	0.0540	0.1928	0.3070	0.1927	0.0931	0.1220	0.2663	0.2234
$MLNB$	0.2323	0.2150	0.0599	**0.1927**	**0.2157**	0.2420	0.1124	0.1768	**0.1267**	0.1584
$MLFE$	0.1777	0.2061	**0.0209**	0.2089	0.3210	0.1443	0.0713	**0.0958**	0.3156	0.0914
Compared algorithms	One-Error↓									
	Yeast	Emotions	Medical	Cal500	Birds	Image	Scene	Enron	Corel5k	Bibtex
$DKE-RLS$	**0.2143**	0.3820	0.3947	**0.0793**	0.6609	**0**	**0**	0.6923	0.9157	**0.3522**
ML^2	0.2857	0.5000	0.3421	0.0805	0.7895	0.20000	0	0.6731	0.9360	0.3899
$ML-kNN$	0.2345	0.4213	0.2492	0.1190	0.7356	0.3600	0.2425	0.3921	0.7892	0.6225
$MLNB$	0.4170	0.4848	0.4234	0.1190	**0.5517**	0.4390	0.2851	0.5233	0.8804	0.5876
$MLFE$	0.2356	**0.3708**	**0.1471**	0.1984	0.7471	0.2680	0.2157	**0.2608**	**0.7832**	0.3710
Compared algorithms	Coverage↓									
	Yeast	Emotions	Medical	Cal500	Birds	Image	Scene	Enron	Corel5k	Bibtex
$DKE-RLS$	0.8728	**0.1545**	0.5967	0.2280	**0.2694**	0.9602	0.9438	0.4492	**0.1746**	**0.2455**
ML^2	0.8749	0.160	0.5236	0.2302	0.2836	0.9510	0.9282	0.4523	0.1813	0.2472
$ML-kNN$	0.6414	0.2247	0.3441	**0.1319**	0.3606	1.0420	0.5686	0.1631	0.1978	0.5723
$MLNB$	**0.2499**	0.2871	0.1925	0.1346	0.2695	1.2450	0.6564	0.2313	0.2102	0.3819
$MLFE$	0.6503	0.1887	**0.1475**	0.1354	0.3763	**0.8410**	**0.4582**	**0.1495**	0.2238	0.2586
Compared algorithms	Macro-averaging AUC ↑									
	Yeast	Emotions	Medical	Cal500	Birds	Image	Scene	Enron	Corel5k	Bibtex
$DKE-RLS$	**0.8234**	**0.8023**	**0.9808**	**0.7897**	0.6891	0.8556	0.9349	0.9050	**0.7129**	0.9247
ML^2	0.8228	0.7764	0.9806	0.7758	0.6430	0.8555	0.9329	**0.9056**	0.7059	**0.9261**
$ML-kNN$	0.6642	0.7142	0.7695	0.5054	0.6173	0.8187	0.9108	0.5512	0.5233	0.6528
$MLNB$	0.6936	0.6807	0.5227	0.5120	0.6955	0.7788	0.8993	0.5569	0.3559	0.8209
$MLFE$	0.6996	0.7901	0.8745	0.5377	**0.7047**	**0.8617**	**0.9385**	0.6581	0.5549	0.8672
Compared algorithms	Time↓									
	Yeast	Emotions	Medical	Cal500	Birds	Image	Scene	Enron	Corel5k	Bibtex
$DKE-RLS$	**0.2496**	**0.0001**	**0.1248**	**0.1404**	**0.0001**	0.1250	0.1719	**0.1248**	**1.2948**	4.6020
ML^2	0.2808	0.0625	0.2496	0.1404	0.0001	**0.1248**	**0.1404**	0.1716	1.3260	**4.5864**
$ML-kNN$	0.5148	0.0312	0.2184	0.2028	0.0468	0.2808	0.5928	0.4992	4.1028	10.1869
$MLNB$	0.4108	0.8899	0.5269	0.2186	0.7372	0.4365	0.6040	0.8964	7.0152	9.3436
$MLFE$	0.4680	0.0312	0.2652	1.0452	0.1560	0.6084	0.4056	0.5148	12.4957	12.3397

4.2 Experiment Results

Table 2 shows the detailed experimental results of five comparing algorithms on the regular-scale and large-scale data sets respectively, where the best performance among the comparing algorithms is shown in boldface. The average performance on each dataset has been recorded. For each evaluation metric, ↑ indicates the larger the better, while ↓ indicates the smaller the better. The table shows the best performance among the five compared algorithms in boldface.

From the experiment results, we can see that $DKE-RLS$ ranks first in more than half of the cases across all the evaluation metrics on the regular- and large-sized datasets. Thus $DKE-RLS$ achieves competitive performance against the well-established multi-label learning algorithms across extensive data sets and diverse evaluation metrics, which validate the effectiveness of the multi-label manifold learning.

4.3 Time Complexity

From Table 2, we also find that $DKE - RLS$ receives the advantage of performance in time complexity. Thus, our algorithm reduces computational cost in the optimization problem.

5 Conclusion

In this paper, we propose a new multi-label feature-extraction algorithm, which uses a new embedded regression method in subspace formed by a multi-label. First, we transform the local topology from the feature space to the label space under the guidance of a nonlinear manifold learning method. Second, we reconstruct the label manifold by combining the local topological structure converted from the feature manifold and the logical labels. We designed the regularized least-squares program function to realize this reconstruction process, to make the optimization function find the optimal solution, and to improve learning efficiency. Experiments confirm that the computational cost is reduced during the optimization problem; this validates $DKE - RLS$'s learning effectiveness for the multi-label manifold. In future work, we plan to extend the proposed regularization form to large-scale learning problems.

Acknowledgements. This work is supported by National Natural Science Foundation of China (41471371, 61702270), the Project funded by China Postdoctoral Science Foundation under Grant. 2017M621592 and the open project foundation of Shanghai Key Laboratory of Intelligent Information Processing, Fudan University, Grant No. IIPL-2016-009.

References

1. Rubin, T.N., Chambers, A., Smyth, P., Steyvers, M.: Statistical topic models for multi-label document classification. Mach. Learn. **88**(1–2), 157–208 (2012)
2. Yang, B., Sun, J., Wang, T., Chen, Z.: Effective multilabel active learning for text classification. In: Proceedings of the 15th ACM SIGKDD International Conference on Knowledge Discovery and Data Mining, pp. 917–926 (2009)
3. Cabral, R.S., Torre, F., Costeira, J.P., Bernardino, A.: Matrix completion for multi-label image classification. In: Advances in Neural Information Processing Systems, pp. 190–198 (2011)
4. Wang, H., Huang, H., Ding, C.: Image annotation using multi-label correlated green's function. In: 12th International Conference on Computer Vision, pp. 2029–2034 (2009)
5. Lo, H., Wang, J., Wang, H., Lin, S.: Costsensitive multi-label learning for audio tag annotation and retrieval. IEEE Trans. Multimedia **13**(3), 518–529 (2011)
6. Sanden, C., Zhang, J.: Enhancing multi-label music genre classification through ensemble techniques. In: Proceedings of the 34th International ACM SIGIR Conference on Research and Development in Information Retrieval, pp. 705–714 (2011)
7. Geng, X., Ji, R.: Label distribution learning. In: Proceedings of the International Conference on Data Mining Workshops, Dallas, TA, pp. 377–383 (2013)
8. Zhu, X., Lafferty, J., Rosenfeld, R.: Semi-supervised learning with graphs. In: International Joint Conference on Natural Language Processing, vol. 6493, no. 10, pp. 2465–2472 (2005)
9. Hou, P., Geng, X., Zhang, M.: Multi-label manifold learning. In: Proceedings of the Thirtieth AAAI Conference on Artificial Intelligence, pp. 1680–1686 (2016)
10. Zhang, M., Zhou, Z.: A review on multi-label learning algorithms. IEEE Trans. Knowl. Data Eng. **26**(8), 1819–1837 (2014)
11. Boutell, M., Luo, J., Shen, X., Brown, C.: Learning multi-label scene classification. Pattern Recogn. **37**(9), 1757–1771 (2004)
12. Zhang, M., Zhou, Z.: ML-KNN: a lazy learning approach to multi-label learning. Pattern Recogn. **40**(7), 2038–2048 (2007)
13. Elisseeff, A., Weston, J.: A kernel method for multilabelled classification. In: Proceedings of the 14th International Conference on Neural Information Processing Systems: Natural and Synthetic, pp. 681–687 (2001)
14. Frnkranz, J., Hllermeier, E., Menca, E., Brinker, K.: Multilabel classification via calibrated label ranking. Mach. Learn. **73**(2), 133–153 (2008)
15. Tsoumakas, G., Katakis, I., Vlahavas, I.: Random k-labelsets for multilabel classification. IEEE Trans. Knowl. Data Eng. **23**(7), 1079–1089 (2011)
16. Geng, X.: Label distribution learning. IEEE Trans. Knowl. Data Eng. **28**(7), 1734–1748 (2016)
17. Roweis, S., Saul, L.: Nonlinear dimensionality reduction by locally linear embedding. Science **290**(5500), 2323–2326 (2000)
18. Belkin, M., Niyogi, P.: Laplacian eigenmaps for dimensionality reduction and data representation. Neural Comput. **15**(6), 1373–1396 (2003)
19. He, X., Niyogi, P.: Locality preserving projections. Adv. Neural Inf. Process. Syst. **16**(1), 86–197 (2004)
20. Zhang, Y., Zhang, Z., Qin, J., Li, F.: Semi-supervised local multi-manifold Isomap by linear embedding for feature extraction. Pattern Recogn. **76**, 662–678 (2018)
21. Belkin, M., Niyogi, P., Sindhwani, V.: Manifold regularization: a geometric framework for learning from labeled and unlabeled examples. J. Mach. Learn. Res. **7**(1), 2399–2434 (2006)

22. Belkin, M., Niyogi, P.: On manifold regularization. Neurocomputing **73**(10–12), 2203–2216 (2010)
23. Chen, L., Tsang, I., Xu, D.: Laplacian embedded regression for scalable manifold regularization. IEEE Trans. Neural Netw. Learn. Syst. **23**(6), 902–915 (2012)
24. Zhang, Z., Li, F., Zhao, M., Zhang, L., Yan, S.: Robust neighborhood preserving projection by nuclear/L2,1-norm regularization for image feature extraction. IEEE Trans. Image Process. **26**(4), 1607–1622 (2017)
25. Pahikkala, T., Airola, A.: RLscore: regularized least-squares learners. J. Mach. Learn. Res. **17**, 1–5 (2016)
26. Zhang, Z., Chow, T., Zhao, M.: Trace ratio optimization-based semi-supervised nonlinear dimensionality reduction for marginal manifold visualization. IEEE Trans. Knowl. Data Eng. **25**(5), 1148–1161 (2013)
27. Zhang, Z., Zha, H.: Principal manifolds and nonlinear dimensionality reduction via tangent space alignment. SIAM J. Sci. Comput. **26**(1), 313–338 (2004)
28. Tuia, D., Verrelst, J., Alonso, L., Prez-Cruz, F., Camps-Valls, G.: Multioutput support vector regression for remote sensing biophysical parameter estimation. IEEE Geosci. Remote Sens. Lett. **8**(4), 804–808 (2011)
29. Prez-Cruz, F., Navia-Vazquez, A., Alarcon-Diana, P., Artes-Rodriguez, A.: An IRWLS procedure for SVR. In: European Signal Processing Conference, pp. 1–4 (2000)
30. Tan, C., Chen, C., Guan, J.: A nonlinear dimension reduction method with both distance and neighborhood preservation. In: Wang, M. (ed.) KSEM 2013. LNCS (LNAI), vol. 8041, pp. 48–63. Springer, Heidelberg (2013). https://doi.org/10.1007/978-3-642-39787-5_5
31. Tenenbaum, J., De Silva, V., Langford, J.: A global geometric framework for nonlinear dimensionality reduction. Science **290**(5500), 2319–2323 (2000)
32. Mulan: Multi-label datasets for Multi-Label Learning[EB/OL]. http://mulan.sourceforge.net/datasets-mlc.html. Accessed 01 Feb 2018
33. Zhang, M., Peña, J., Robles, V.: Feature selection for multi-label naive Bayes classification. Inf. Sci. **179**(19), 3218–3229 (2009)
34. Zhang, Q., Zhong, Y., Zhang, M.: Feature-induced labeling information enrichment for multi-label learning. In: Proceedings of the 32nd AAAI Conference on Artificial Intelligence (2018)

Learning Relations from Social Tagging Data

Hang Dong[1,2], Wei Wang[2(✉)], and Frans Coenen[1]

[1] Department of Computer Science, University of Liverpool, Liverpool, UK
{HangDong,Coenen}@liverpool.ac.uk
[2] Department of Computer Science and Software Engineering,
Xi'an Jiaotong-Liverpool University, Suzhou, China
Wei.Wang03@xjtlu.edu.cn

Abstract. An interesting research direction is to discover structured knowledge from user generated data. Our work aims to find relations among social tags and organise them into hierarchies so as to better support discovery and search for online users. We cast relation discovery in this context to a binary classification problem in supervised learning. This approach takes as input features of two tags extracted using probabilistic topic modelling, and predicts whether a broader-narrower relation holds between them. Experiments were conducted using two large, real-world datasets, the Bibsonomy dataset which is used to extract tags and their features, and the DBpedia dataset which is used as the ground truth. Three sets of features were designed and extracted based on topic distributions, similarity and probabilistic associations. Evaluation results with respect to the ground truth demonstrate that our method outperforms existing ones based on various features and heuristics. Future studies are suggested to study the Knowledge Base Enrichment from folksonomies and deep neural network approaches to process tagging data.

1 Introduction

Many social media platforms allow users to annotate online data and resources with tags. The accumulated social tags, contributed by millions of online users (folks) collaboratively, are referred to as folksonomies [26]. The original idea was that such folksonomies can provide efficient content organisation mechanisms to support searching of online resources. However, over the years these folksonomies have become a dormant collection of unstructured, noisy and often ambiguous "keywords", which has shown little usefulness.

To address this issue an interesting line of research is to extract "useful" tags and organise them into some forms of structured knowledge, e.g., concept hierarchies or lightweight terminological ontologies [14,19,28]. This task is quite different from ontology learning from textual corpora [7] in which it is usually assumed that enough textual data covering specific domains is available. There are several reasons that make learning from tagging data challenging: (i) the

X. Geng and B.-H. Kang (Eds.): PRICAI 2018, LNAI 11012, pp. 29–41, 2018.
https://doi.org/10.1007/978-3-319-97304-3_3

difficulties in capturing the intrinsic semantic relations among tags, (ii) sparsity of the tagging data and (iii) the significant amount of noise (e.g. syntactical variations, typos and spam) and ambiguity (e.g. polysemy and synonymy).

Current methods rely heavily on exploiting co-occurrences of data or external lexical resources to infer tag pair relations [9]. For example, by using heuristics based on set inclusion [18,19] or graph centrality analysis [14], it is possible to derive the relations, but it is difficult to interpret their meanings explicitly. The co-occurrence based methods typically need to re-compute the whole model when new data is available and therefore do not scale well. In the case of methods based on external lexical resources [8,12], relations can be explicitly defined; however, a limitation of this class is the low coverage of social tags and their senses typically found in such lexical resources.

We chose academic research as the domain of study because the structured knowledge that can be derived from academic resources is of particular interests to the research community. Learning relations from tagging data in academic domains is also more challenging than learning from general domains, as in the former case many tags are phrases which have complex meanings. To address the limitations of existing work, we propose a new approach to automatically learn relations between tag pairs. The objective is to create knowledge hierarchies by organising tags according to subsumption relations; more specifically, the "broader" and "narrower" relations in the SKOS vocabulary [17] were adopted.

The main contributions of the work include:

- A method to extract domain independent feature sets for articulating the meaning of tags based on probabilistic association analysis, which addresses the aforementioned challenges associated with learning from tagging data;
- A supervised learning method to detect subsumption relations between tags based on their features; the idea being that model trained in one domain can be used in other domains; and
- Extensive experiments and evaluation using two large real world datasets (Bibsonomy[1] and DBpedia[2]) to demonstrate the effectiveness of the proposed approach.

The rest of the paper is organised as follows. Related work on learning subsumption relations and probabilistic topic analysis are presented in Sect. 2. The proposed approach to learn subsumption relations from social tagging data is described in Sect. 3. Experiment and evaluation results are demonstrated in Sect. 4. Finally, conclusion and future works are presented in Sect. 5.

2 Related Work

There are three broad categories of method that are used to learn relations from social tagging data: (i) heuristic/rules, (ii) external lexical resource and (iii)

[1] https://www.bibsonomy.org/.
[2] http://dbpedia.org/.

machine learning. Heuristic/rules based methods make use of various heuristics or rules to define and consequently infer relations. Some well-known examples include the use of generality measures based on set inclusion [18,19] and popularity-generality measures using graph centrality [1,4,14]. However, it is known that this category of method cannot formally define the semantic relations among social tags [11,22]. Another problem is that it is difficult to establish meaningful relations if tagging data are sparse. In other words, two tags may co-relate to each other even though they do not co-occur. Furthermore, this category of methods needs to re-compute the whole model whenever new data becomes available and is thus not likely to scale well.

The second category of method is to ground social tags to external lexical resources to find relations, for example, using WordNet[3] [8], DBpedia and other resources in the Linked Open Data Cloud[4] [12]. However, the methods suffer from the limited coverage of the external resources. The relatively static (or slow-evolving) lexical resources or domain ontologies in general cannot effectively capture data evolution in social media data. It has been found in [2,3] that WordNet can only represent less than half (48.7%) of the tags in the popular general social tagging dataset del.icio.us [29]; moreover, for many of those that are actually present in WordNet, no intended senses can be found.

The third category of method is to use either unsupervised or supervised machine learning techniques to discover desired hierarchical patterns. The study in [30] proposed an unsupervised divisive clustering algorithm based on Deterministic Annealing to generate a reasonable tag hierarchy; however, it could not discriminate among subordinate, related and parallel relations. By casting relation learning as a supervised classification problem, the work in [22] proposed to detect subsumption relations using association rule mining, set-based tag inclusion measures and graph searching measures. One advantage is that various heuristics or metrics can be used to learn relations. It is also shown in [22] that when using supervised learning with a combination of feature sets, higher F-measures can be achieved compared to any individual approach in the heuristic/rule based category. However, these methods only extract features based on co-occurrence and therefore have similar disadvantages as heuristic/rule based methods. We adapt the idea of supervise learning, but with distinct feature sets to detect semantic relations between tags.

To address the problem of data sparsity, it is necessary to reduce the dimensionality of tagging data. A more effective method is also required to capture the intrinsic semantic meanings of social tags, in different contexts, to disambiguate their meanings. The study in [28] applied probabilistic topic analysis, e.g. Latent Dirichlet Allocation (LDA) [5,23], to a collection of abstracts of scientific publications from which subsumption relations could be derived. The study in [25] also defined several metrics based on the distribution of topics for concepts to learn ontologies from folksonomies. However, they only suggest how different two tags are, not how they are associated or co-related. Our work addresses this

[3] http://wordnet.princeton.edu/.
[4] http://lod-cloud.net/.

problem by extracting domain independent features from tag pairs according to similarity, topic distributions and probabilistic associations. These features are subsequently used for supervised learning.

Similar to probabilistic topic analysis, word embedding approaches can also be used to represent tags in the form of a low dimensional space and consequently better capture the similarity between tags than co-occurrence representation [20]. However, a key disadvantage is that dimensions in word embeddings are not probabilistically and semantically interpretable as probabilistic topic representations (*cf.* [6]). Therefore in this study we chose probabilistic topic analysis as the data representation technique and leave word embedding approaches for a further study.

3 A Supervised Model for Learning Tag Relations

In social tagging platforms, *users* create *tags* to annotate *resources*. Thus, a folksonomy can be formally represented using tuples of the form $\mathbb{F} := \langle U, T, R, Y \rangle$ where U, T and R are finite sets representing *users*, *tags* and *resources* respectively; Y is a ternary relation between them, $Y \subseteq U \times T \times R$ [15]. Due to the noisy nature of tagging data (e.g. special characters, typos, and spam), data cleaning is necessary. Variants of tags (e.g. ontology/ontologies, machine_leaning/machine-leaning) also need to be handled using morphological analysis. Once cleaned the folksonomy is transformed to $\mathbb{F}^{clean} := \langle U, C, R, Y \rangle$, where T is replaced by the new finite set C, whose elements are *tag concepts* or *tag groups*.

We cast the problem of deriving relations among social tags into a supervised learning problem. The input is a pair of tag concepts, C_a and C_b, represented as two probabilistic distributions in the latent space. The output is the relationship between them: a positive value means that C_a is a narrow concept of C_b. We aim to find these broader-narrower relations (including both direct and indirect ones) and optimise the sensitivity or recall [24] of the classification model.

As shown in Fig. 1, the architecture for the proposed method consists of four main components: (i) **Data Cleaning:** cleaning of noisy tagging dataset and transforming it into a cleaned Folksonomy $\mathbb{F}^{clean}$; (ii) **Data Representation:** representing each tag as a distribution of topics in a low dimensional semantic space based on probabilistic topic analysis; (iii) **Feature Set Generation:** generation of feature sets based on topic distributions, similarity and probabilistic associations; and (iv) **Classification:** training and testing of classification models by optimising sensitivity to detect subsumption relations.

3.1 Probabilistic Topic Analysis of Tagging Data

Analogous to "bag-of-words", each resource from a tagging dataset can be represented as a "bag-of-tags". Using probabilistic topic analysis, we can infer the topic structure of tags in an unsupervised manner. One advantage of doing this is that it allows us to obtain the topic distributions in a low dimensional space which captures the meanings of tags under different contexts. This representation

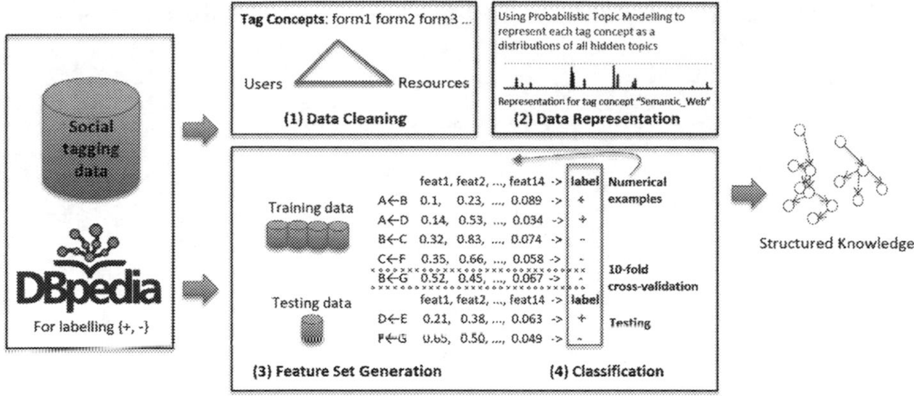

Fig. 1. Architecture of the supervised method to learn relations between tag pairs

is also semantically interpretable: the value of an entry in the latent topic vector reflects its relatedness to that particular topic. With probabilistic topic analysis we can obtain a clear view on the semantic structure of the underlying data, with tag-topic distributions $p(C|\mathbf{z})$ and topic-resource distributions $p(\mathbf{z}|R)$.

Based on $p(C|\mathbf{z})$ and the the Bayes' rule, we represent each tag concept as a probability distribution, $p(z|C_a)$, computed as $p(z|C_a) \propto p(C_a|z) * p(z)$. The prior probability $p(z)$ is usually treated as uniform in the literature [23]. However, the prior distributions of the latent topics are certainly not uniform. We use a non-uniform prior $p(z)$ which respects the underlying dataset, computed as the ratio of the number of tokens sampled to a topic z, N_z, to the number of tokens in the whole dataset, N, $p(z) = \frac{N_z}{N}$. This can be obtained after approximation in probabilistic topic analysis [23]. Usually a tag concept is only closely related to few topics. As such, we introduce the notion of a *significant topic set* $\mathbf{z}_a^{sig}$ for a tag concept, which is specified as $\mathbf{z}_a^{sig} = \{z \mid z \in \mathbf{z} \text{ and } p(z|C_a) \geqslant p\}$, where p is a pre-defined threshold (0.1 in this work).

3.2 Assumptions for Feature Set Generation

We define three assumptions for extracting features in order to discover broader-narrower relations. They are proposed based on the human understanding of a subsumption relation and the cognitive processing of such a relation with respect to three aspects: (i) similarity (the two concepts should be similar), (ii) topic distribution (a more general concept should relate to more topics than a more specific one), and (iii) probabilistic association (given a concept in a certain context, one would be able to derive associated concepts).

Assumption 1. *(Similarity) For two tag concepts C_a and C_b to have a broader-narrower relation, they must be similar to each other to some extent or they must not diverge greatly.*

Table 1. Feature sets **S1**, **S2** and **S3** corresponding to the three assumptions

Features	Description
	S1: Similarity Measure Features
Cos_sim	The cosine similarity of two topic distribution vectors
KL_Div1	The Kullback-Leibler Divergence from C_a to C_b
KL_Div2	The Kullback-Leibler Divergence from C_b to C_a
Gen_Jaccard	The generalised Jaccard Index of two topic distribution vectors
	S2: Topic Distribution Related Features
overlapping	Number of overlapping significant topics
diff_num_sig	Difference of the number of significant topics
diff_max	Difference of the maximum elements in two tag vectors
diff_aver_sig	Difference of the average probability of significant topics
	S3: Probabilistic Association Features
$p(C_a\|C_b)$	The probabilistic association of C_a given C_b
$p(C_b\|C_a)$	The probabilistic association of C_b given C_a
$p(C_a\|C_b, R_{a,b})$	The local probabilistic association of C_a given C_b and a common root concept $R_{a,b}$
$p(C_b\|C_a, R_{a,b})$	The local probabilistic association of C_b given C_a and $R_{a,b}$
$p(C_a, C_b)$	The joint probabilistic association of C_a and C_b
$p(C_a, C_b\|R_{a,b})$	The local joint probabilistic association of C_a and C_b given $R_{a,b}$

Assumption 2. *(Topic distribution) A broader concept should have a topic distribution spanning over more dimensions; while the narrower concept should span over less dimensions within those of the broader concept. This reflects that the narrower concept tends to have a focus on less topics but with higher probabilities than the broader one.*

Assumption 3. *(Probabilistic association) For two tag concepts C_a and C_b to have a broader-narrower relation, they should have a strong association with each other. In a certain context, given one concept, one should be able to associate the other. This can be modelled using the conditional and joint probability of latent topics in a probabilistic framework.*

3.3 Feature Set Generation

The three assumptions are translated into three feature sets, as listed in Table 1. For Assumption 1, we extract features based on a number of similarity/divergence measures, i.e., Cosine similarity, Kullback-Leibler (KL) Divergence and Generalised Jaccard Index, together denoted as the feature set **S1**. (KL) Divergence is an asymmetric measure of the divergence of two probability distributions, which is also the relative entropy of one distribution with respect to another. Since it is asymmetric, we generate two features, denoted as *KL_Div1* and *KL_Div2* as in Table 1. In [28], the difference between KL Divergences was used to discover relations; however, we found that it is difficult to determine a suitable noise threshold.

Topic Distribution Based Features. The intuition behind Assumption 2 is that the significant topic sets $\mathbf{z}^{sig}$ for two tag concepts C_a and C_b that have a broader-narrower relation tend to be similar or significantly overlapped. While the probability distribution for $\mathbf{z}^{sig}$ of C_a tends to be more uniform, the distribution for C_b tends to be more imbalanced. This reflects the fact that the meaning of a narrower tag concept is more specific and is concentrated on fewer topics. This is translated into the features on number of overlapped significant topics, difference of the number of significant topics, difference of maximum probability, and difference of the average probability of significant topics. They are referred to as feature set **S2** (see Table 1).

Probabilistic Association Based Features. The idea of probabilistic association between two words has its root in cognitive psychology and was first introduced in [13]. It measures the associative relations between words, which can be computed as a conditional probability over a response word given a cue word. The probabilistic association between two tag concepts can also be computed based on this idea.

We model the associations using both conditional and joint probabilities in the latent semantic space. While the conditional probability measures how a tag concept would be associated given another one as a cue, the joint probability measures how two tag concepts would be associated together.

We further propose to compute these two types of probability associations with reference to a specific context. This is done by computing the probabilistic associations conditioned on a third tag concept, which is usually the root concept of a specific domain or sub-domain under consideration. This allows us to learn relations and build a tag concept hierarchy in a progressive, top-down manner. As an example, if machine learning is the domain of consideration, then the concept "Machine Learning" is used as the root concept or context. As the features are extracted by considering a particular context, they are referred to as local associations. The relevant features are together denoted as **S3** (see Table 1) and explained below.

- **Probabilistic Association.** The probabilistic association between two tag concepts is computed as the probability of one tag concept given another as a cue in a global context. By the global context we mean that the conditional probability is computed not conditioned on any other concepts. As this measure is asymmetric, we generate two features, $p(C_a|C_b)$, and $p(C_b|C_a)$; the higher the probability, the stronger the association and the more likely that a tag concept can be associated by another. We adopt the method proposed in [13] to compute the two features.
- **Joint Probabilistic Association.** The joint probabilistic association captures the likelihood of associating two tag concepts together without references to any specific context. It is a symmetric measure, denoted as $p(C_a, C_b)$, which is computed as $p(C_a, C_b) = p(C_a|C_b) \sum_{z \in \mathbf{z}} p(C_b|z)p(z)$.
- **Local Probabilistic Association.** To better capture the association between two tag concepts under a particular context, we propose the idea of local probabilistic association, conditioned on the common root, $R_{a,b}$,

of both tag C_a and tag C_b. Since the association is asymmetric, we generate two features denoted as $p(C_a|C_b, R_{a,b})$ and $p(C_b|C_a, R_{a,b})$, respectively. The feature is computed as $p(C_a|C_b, R_{a,b}) = \sum_{z \in \mathbf{z}} p(C_a|z)p(z|C_b, R_{a,b}) = \sum_{z \in \mathbf{z}} \frac{p(C_a|z)p(C_b|z)p(R_{a,b}|z)p(z)}{p(C_b, R_{a,b})}$, where $p(C_a|z)$, $p(C_b|z)$, and $p(R_{a,b}|z)$ can be obtained from the LDA analysis, $p(C_b, R_{a,b})$ can be computed using the joint probabilistic association.

- **Local Joint Probabilistic Association.** The local joint probabilistic association is calculated conditioned on the root concept $R_{a,b}$ for both tag C_a and tag C_b. It measures how the two tags are jointly generated within a particular context. It is also a symmetric measure, denoted as $p(C_a, C_b|R_{a,b})$. Similarly, it is computed as $p(C_a, C_b|R_{a,b}) = p(C_a|C_b, R_{a,b})p(C_b|R_{a,b})$, where $p(C_a|C_b, R_{a,b})$ can be obtained using local probabilistic association.

4 Experimental Results and Evaluation

To evaluate the proposed mechanism for learning the relations from social tagging data, a series of experiments were conducted using two large, real-world datasets: Bibsonomy and DBpedia. The tagging data from Bibsonomy was cleaned and only the quality, frequently occurred tags were kept and matched to the terms in DBpedia, which had been organised in a hierarchy. The features were extracted by using the proposed method and used for training and testing different classification models. We also re-implemented and compared to (i) the features proposed in [22] denoted as **S4** with different feature sets and (ii) the "Information Theory Principle for Concept Relationship" in [28] related to our feature set **S1**. The evaluation results demonstrated that our method achieved the highest recall, precision and F_1.

Dataset and Feature Extraction. We used the open dataset from Bibsonomy[5], which contains 3,794,882 annotations, 868,015 distinct resources and 283,858 distinct tags contributed by 11,103 users, accumulated from 2005 to July 2015. We cleaned the dataset using morphological and statistical methods, following the four steps in [10]: (i) specific character handling, (ii) multiword and single tag group extraction, (iii) tag selection using selected metrics and (iv) tag selection by language. After these, We selected the tag groups and annotations only for academic publication resources. Each resource was represented as a "bag-of-tags", including all tags used by different users to annotate the resource. We further removed the resources which have less than 3 tag tokens. Finally, we obtained a cleaned, potentially high quality dataset, comprising 7,458 tag concepts and 128,782 publication resources.

To infer latent topics from social tags, we ran the LDA and Gibbs sampling based on the MALLET Machine Learning Library[6]. The topic-word hyperparameter α was set to $50/|\mathbf{z}|$, where $|\mathbf{z}|$ is the number of latent topics, and the

[5] https://www.kde.cs.uni-kassel.de/bibsonomy/dumps, the "2015-07-01" version.

[6] http://mallet.cs.umass.edu/.

document-topic hyperparameter β was set to 0.01. We held out 10% of the data to optimise the perplexity of the LDA model and set $|\mathbf{z}|$ as 600.

For tag grounding and instance labelling, we used DBpedia[7] through querying two ontological relations, *skos:broader* and *dct:subject*. Six categories with which we are familiar were chosen (i.e., Machine learning, Semantic Web, Data mining, Natural language processing, Social information processing and Internet of Things). The extracted concepts were matched to the tag concepts in Bibsonomy. In total, we extracted 355 tag pairs with direct broader relations grounded to all the six DBpedia categories, which were used as positive instances. It should be noted that an instance in our method represents features extracted with respect to a pair of tag concepts and a common root of the two tags. Negative instances were created by reversing the broader relations in the positive instances, and generating some random negative relations under each category. We finally obtained 1,065 instances for both training and testing. For each of the instances, we extracted all the 14 features proposed in Sect. 3.3.

Classification Evaluation. 80% of the data was randomly selected for training and 20% for testing. In both the training and testing data, the ratio of the number of positive to negative instances was around 1:2. For the current work we aimed to train classification models with high sensitivity. The evaluated metrics used include precision, recall, F_1 score, accuracy and the Area Under the receiver operating characteristic Curve (AUC). For imbalanced data, as in the case of our experiments, precision, recall, F_1 score and AUC are more suitable evaluation metrics than accuracy [24].

We trained a number of classifiers, Logistic Regression (LR) and Support Vector Machine (SVM), on the data described above. For parameter tuning, 10-fold cross validation was used. For the SVM model, we used the standard radial basis (RBF) kernel and tuned two parameters C and γ [16] to optimise the sensitivity. In addition, the weighted-SVM [21,27] was used to boost the recall. Weighted-SVM specifies two different misclassification cost parameters for the two classes: C^+ for positive observations and C^- for negative observations. The ratio of the misclassification cost parameters was set to 2, i.e., $\frac{C^+}{C^-} = 2$.

The evaluation and comparison results are presented in Table 2. From the table, it can be seen that in all experiments, SVM performed better than LR in terms of recall, precision, F_1 score, accuracy and AUROC. A sensitivity of 73.2% was obtained using the standard SVM with RBF kernel. This setting also produced the highest precision, F_1, accuracy and AUROC values. By heavily penalising the misclassification cost on positive instances, the weighted-SVM achieved 100% recall. However, this setting produced a very high false positive rate and therefore, the precision and accuracy were lower than the best results obtained using the standard SVM.

Compared to the feature set **S4**, proposed in [22], which was mainly based on tag co-occurrences, our proposed mechanism performed significantly better. This

[7] http://downloads.dbpedia.org/2015-10/core/, the "2015-10" version.

Table 2. Classification results using different feature set combinations

		Recall	Precision	F_1 score	Accuracy	AUC
S1 + S2 + S3 (Full features in our approach)	LR	54.9%	60.0%	57.4%	72.8%	0.808
	SVM	**73.2%**	65.0%	68.9%	77.9%	0.814
	weighed-SVM	**100.0%**	42.0%	59.2%	54.0%	0.792
Wang et al. [28](**S1**)	LR	12.7%	47.4%	20.0%	66.2%	0.585
	SVM	38.0%	58.7%	46.2%	70.4%	0.648
Rêgo et al. [22] (**S4**)	LR	16.9%	63.2%	26.7%	69.0%	0.657
	SVM	22.5%	57.1%	32.3%	68.6%	0.563
S1 + S2 + S3 + S4	LR	56.3%	62.5%	59.3%	74.2%	0.808
	SVM	71.8%	64.6%	68.0%	77.5%	0.818
S2	LR	22.5%	59.3%	32.7%	69.0%	0.752
	SVM	59.2%	55.3%	57.1%	70.4%	0.688
S3	LR	4.2%	37.5%	7.6%	65.7%	0.769
	SVM	5.6%	50.0%	10.1%	66.7%	0.794
S1 + S2	LR	42.3%	61.2%	50.0%	71.8%	0.761
	SVM	63.4%	57.0%	60.0%	71.8%	0.699
S1 + S3	LR	32.4%	54.8%	40.7%	68.5%	0.700
	SVM	62.0%	64.7%	63.3%	76.1%	0.776
S2 + S3	LR	33.8%	60.0%	43.2%	70.4%	0.787
	SVM	59.2%	60.9%	60.0%	73.7%	0.743

* **S1** denotes Similarity and Divergence Based Features; **S2**, Topic distribution Based Features; **S3**, Probabilistic Association Features; **S4**, the baseline feature set in [22] including support, confidence, cosine similarity, inclusion and generalisation degree, mutual overlapping and taxonomy search

is attributed to the well-founded assumptions based on the semantically interpretable latent topics. Also, the recall and precision were not improved when we combined our features with the baseline features (**S1 + S2 + S3 + S4**), 71.8% recall, 55.0% precision compared to 73.2% and 55.0% when only **S1 + S2 + S3** was used, showing that the co-occurrence based features do not provide any further contribution to the results.

Table 2 also shows the results obtained when different combinations of the feature sets were used. With all three feature sets both LR and SVM produced the best recall, F_1, accuracy and AUC values. When only one feature set was considered, as can be seen from from the table, using the topic distribution related features (**S2** founded on Assumption 2) generated the best results when using SVM (59.2% recall and 57.1% F_1). Both topic distribution related features and similarity/divergence features significantly outperforms the baseline **S4**. When two sets of features were considered, the similarity/divergence (Assumption 1) and topic distribution related (Assumption 3) features produced the best results in all cases. If the similarity/divergence based feature set **S1** alone were used, then the method corresponds to the method on learning ontologies from publication abstracts as described in [28]. Surprisingly, the result produced from

Table 3. Examples of learned relations from Bibsonomy tags using the three feature sets **S1+S2+S3** with SVM

narrower → broader concept	narrower → broader concept
social_graphs → social_networks	semantic_analysis → machine_learning
mixture_model → data_mining	unsupervised_learning → machine_learning
folksonomy → collective_intelligence	latent_variables → bayesian_networks
semantic_search → semantic_web	sentiment_analysis → natural_language_processing
delicious →social_bookmarking	word_sense_disambiguation → natural_language_processing

tagging data was not useful, which shows that the feature set **S1** alone is not sufficient for capturing the meaning of tag concepts. This can be attributed to the fact that publication abstracts contain much richer information than tags. Another notable finding is that, although probabilistic association based features **S3** alone led to low recall (5.6% by SVM and 4.2% by LR), it boosted the recall significantly (increasing it by 15.5% from 63.4% to 73.2%) when combined with the other two feature sets. Some example hierarchical relations predicted on the test set using SVM and the three feature sets are shown in Table 3.

5 Conclusion and Future Work

Social tagging data represent a potential source for extracting structured knowledge, which is of particular interests and importance to the research communities. In this on-going work, we have presented a novel method to derive domain independent features and learn broader-narrower relations among tag concepts in constructing such structured knowledge. Based on our understanding and perception of concept relations, three assumptions are proposed to determine if a broader-narrower relations holds between any two given tag concepts. These assumptions are then translated into a number of effective feature sets for the learning task, in particular, the probabilistic association based one, which helps capture tag relations based on human cognitive processing of information. The experiment and evaluation results confirmed the effectiveness of the method and showed that the proposed method significantly outperforms existing work in terms of recall, the primary focus, precision and the F_1 measure. The combination of feature sets is an effective strategy for detecting relations among tags. For future study, we plan to further fine-tune this approach to built knowledge hierarchies iteratively and progressively. We will extend our experiments, using DBpedia only, to several heterogeneous Knowledge Bases covering all domains for tag grounding and instance labelling. We also plan to evaluate the performance of our method to see if it can be used for the purpose of enriching existing Knowledge Bases with new concepts and relations. Deep neural network approaches, leveraging both probabilistic topic representation and word embeddings, are also to be explored.

Acknowledgment. This research is funded by the Research Development Fund at Xi'an Jiaotong-Liverpool University, contract number RDF-10-2015.

References

1. Almoqhim, F., Millard, D.E., Shadbolt, N.: Improving on popularity as a proxy for generality when building tag hierarchies from folksonomies. In: Aiello, L.M., McFarland, D. (eds.) SocInfo 2014. LNCS, vol. 8851, pp. 95–111. Springer, Cham (2014). https://doi.org/10.1007/978-3-319-13734-6_7
2. Andrews, P., Pane, J.: Sense induction in folksonomies: a review. Artif. Intell. Rev. **40**(2), 147–174 (2013)
3. Andrews, P., Pane, J., Zaihrayeu, I.: Semantic disambiguation in folksonomy: a case study. In: Bernardi, R., Chambers, S., Gottfried, B., Segond, F., Zaihrayeu, I. (eds.) AT4DL/NLP4DL -2009. LNCS, vol. 6699, pp. 114–134. Springer, Heidelberg (2011). https://doi.org/10.1007/978-3-642-23160-5_8
4. Benz, D., Hotho, A., Stumme, G., Stützer, S.: Semantics made by you and me: Self-emerging ontologies can capture the diversity of shared knowledge. In: Proceedings of the 2nd Web Science Conference (WebSci 2010) (2010)
5. Blei, D.M., Ng, A.Y., Jordan, M.I.: Latent dirichlet allocation. J. Mach. Learn. Res. **3**(Jan), 993–1022 (2003)
6. Chang, J., Gerrish, S., Wang, C., Boyd-Graber, J.L., Blei, D.M.: Reading tea leaves: how humans interpret topic models. In: Advances in Neural Information Processing Systems, pp. 288–296 (2009)
7. Cimiano, P.: Ontology Learning and Population from Text: Algorithms, Evaluation and Applications. Springer, New York Inc., Secaucus (2006). https://doi.org/10.1007/978-0-387-39252-3
8. Djuana, E., Xu, Y., Li, Y.: Learning personalized tag ontology from user tagging information. In: Proceedings of the Tenth Australasian Data Mining Conference - Volume 134 (AusDM 2012), pp. 183–189. Australian Computer Society, Inc. (2012)
9. Dong, H., Wang, W., Liang, H.N.: Learning structured knowledge from social tagging data: a critical review of methods and techniques. In: 2015 IEEE International Conference on Smart City/SocialCom/SustainCom (SmartCity), pp. 307–314, December 2015
10. Dong, H., Wang, W., Frans, C.: Deriving dynamic knowledge from academic social tagging data: a novel research direction. In: iConference 2017 Proceedings. iSchools (2017)
11. García-Silva, A., Corcho, O., Alani, H., Gómez-Pérez, A.: Review of the state of the art: discovering and associating semantics to tags in folksonomies. Knowl. Eng. Rev. **27**(1), 57–85 (2012)
12. García-Silva, A., García-Castro, L.J., García, A., Corcho, O.: Social tags and linked data for ontology development: A case study in the financial domain. In: The 4th International Conference on Web Intelligence, Mining and Semantics, pp. 1–10. ACM (2014)
13. Griffiths, T.L., Steyvers, M., Tenenbaum, J.B.: Topics in semantic representation. Psychol. Rev. **114**(2), 211 (2007)
14. Heymann, P., Garcia-Molina, H.: Collaborative creation of communal hierarchical taxonomies in social tagging systems. Technical report, Stanford (2006)
15. Hotho, A., Jäschke, R., Schmitz, C., Stumme, G.: Information retrieval in folksonomies: search and ranking. In: Sure, Y., Domingue, J. (eds.) ESWC 2006. LNCS, vol. 4011, pp. 411–426. Springer, Heidelberg (2006). https://doi.org/10.1007/11762256_31
16. Hsu, C.W., Chang, C.C., Lin, C.J.: A practical guide to support vector classification. Technical report, Department of Computer Science, National Taiwan University (2003)

17. Isaac, A., Summers, E.: SKOS simple knowledge organization system primer. W3C Working Group Note. World Wide Web Consortium (W3C) (2009). https://www.w3.org/TR/skos-primer/. Accessed 10 July 2018
18. Meo, P.D., Quattrone, G., Ursino, D.: Exploitation of semantic relationships and hierarchical data structures to support a user in his annotation and browsing activities in folksonomies. Inf. Syst. **34**(6), 511–535 (2009)
19. Mika, P.: Ontologies are us: a unified model of social networks and semantics. Web Semant.: Sci. Serv. Agents World Wide Web **5**(1), 5–15 (2007)
20. Niebler, T., Hahn, L., Hotho, A.: Learning word embeddings from tagging data: a methodological comparison. In: Lernen, Wissen, Daten, Analysen (LWDA) Conference Proceedings, pp. 229–240 (2017)
21. Osuna, E., Freund, R., Girosi, F.: Support vector machines: training and applications. Technical report, AI Memo 1602, Massachusetts Institute of Technology (1997)
22. Rêgo, A.S.C., Marinho, L.B., Pires, C.E.S.: A supervised learning approach to detect subsumption relations between tags in folksonomies. In: Proceedings of the 30th Annual ACM Symposium on Applied Computing (SAC 2015), pp. 409–415. ACM (2015)
23. Steyvers, M., Griffiths, T.: Probabilistic topic models. Handb. Latent Semant. Anal. **427**(7), 424–440 (2007)
24. Tan, P.N., Steinbach, M., Kumar, V.: Introduction to Data Mining, 1st edn. Addison-Wesley Longman Publishing Co. Inc., Boston (2005)
25. Tang, J., Leung, H.f., Luo, Q., Chen, D., Gong, J.: Towards ontology learning from folksonomies. In: Proceedings of the IJCAI, vol. 9, pp. 2089–2094 (2009)
26. Vander Wal, T.: Folksonomy (2007). http://vanderwal.net/folksonomy.html. Accessed 07 June 2018
27. Veropoulos, K., Campbell, C., Cristianini, N., et al.: Controlling the sensitivity of support vector machines. In: Proceedings of the IJCAI, pp. 55–60 (1999)
28. Wang, W., Barnaghi, P.M., Bargiela, A.: Probabilistic topic models for learning terminological ontologies. IEEE Trans. Knowl. Data Eng. **22**(7), 1028–1040 (2010)
29. Wetzker, R., Zimmermann, C., Bauckhage, C.: Analyzing social bookmarking systems: A del.icio.us cookbook. In: Proceedings of the ECAI 2008 Mining Social Data Workshop, pp. 26–30 (2008)
30. Zhou, M., Bao, S., Wu, X., Yu, Y.: An unsupervised model for exploring hierarchical semantics from social annotations. In: Aberer, K., et al. (eds.) ASWC/ISWC -2007. LNCS, vol. 4825, pp. 680–693. Springer, Heidelberg (2007). https://doi.org/10.1007/978-3-540-76298-0_49

Selecting Optimal Source for Transfer Learning in Bayesian Optimisation

Anil Ramachandran(✉), Sunil Gupta, Santu Rana, and Svetha Venkatesh

Centre for Pattern Recognition and Data Analytics (PRaDA),
Deakin University, Geelong, Australia
{aramac,sunil.gupta,santu.rana,svetha.venkatesh}@deakin.edu.au

Abstract. Bayesian optimisation offers an efficient solution to optimise black box functions. When coupled with transfer learning methods, Bayesian optimisation can leverage data from other function optimisations. A crucial requirement of transfer learning, however, is to restrict the transfer of knowledge only from related functions. Since the relatedness is not known a priori, selection of useful sources is an important problem. To address this problem, we propose a new method for optimal source selection for transfer learning in Bayesian optimisation. Using multi-armed bandits for source selection, we construct a new technique for identifying the optimal source and then use it for transfer learning in Bayesian optimisation. We show theoretically that the proposed technique is guaranteed to select the most related source and thus helps to improve the optimisation efficiency. We demonstrate the effectiveness of our method for several tasks: synthetic function optimisation, the hyper-parameter tuning of support vector machines, and optimisation of short polymer fiber synthesis in an industrial environment.

1 Introduction

One of the problems in determining the relation between control variables and a stipulated product target through experimental optimisation is that experiments are both costly and time consuming. It is thus imperative to often find the target goal through fewest experiments. When a new product or process is designed, the experimenter has to perform a new optimisation (*target* experiment). As the experimental process are expensive, knowledge from past data (*source*) can be helpful in kick-starting the optimisation provided the new set up is similar. Such knowledge transfer addresses three key questions: what knowledge to transfer, when to transfer and how to transfer [1]. "What" estimates the common elements to transfer between the source and target, "when" limits transfer to related tasks, and the "how" handles the transfer mechanics. This paper examines the "when" aspect. We present a method for judicious source selection to address the challenge that previous experimental setups may have varying degree of relatedness (low to high) to the current experimental set up. This degree of relatedness, of course, is unknown. A careful choice of the source is *required* to

X. Geng and B.-H. Kang (Eds.): PRICAI 2018, LNAI 11012, pp. 42–56, 2018.
https://doi.org/10.1007/978-3-319-97304-3_4

fully utilize the potential of transfer learning and achieve the optimal efficiency for the target optimisation.

Bayesian optimisation provides a powerful stochastic approach to experimental optimisation, efficiently finding the optima of black box functions with minimum function evaluations [2]. This approach has been applied successfully in diverse areas like automatic algorithm configuration [3], sensor selection [4] and robotics [5]. The unknown function is modeled through a Gaussian process whose mean and posterior are updated as observations from experiments come in sequentially. To make a recommendation for the next experimental setting, Bayesian optimisation circumvents sampling the expensive function by using a surrogate acquisition function [2] that is inexpensive to sample. The acquisition function balances the trade-off between only selecting points where the function is expected to be high (*exploitation*) with only selecting points where there is maximum uncertainty about the function estimate (*exploration*).

Prior art in transfer learning for Bayesian optimisation has used given sources without checking their relatedness with the target. Different heuristics have been used for knowledge transfer e.g. function ranking across parameter settings [6] or deviations of a function from its mean [7] are transferable. Multi-task Bayesian optimisation in [8] can utilize sources as per their relatedness to the target, as it assumes that task relationships are known apriori. The belief that task relationships are known or that the processes are highly related is not valid in most real world cases. To avoid the *performance degradation* when an unrelated source is used, Joy et al. [9] model the source data as noisy observations of the target function. However, none of the previous works has actively selected the source to optimise transfer learning. Thus selecting the optimal source in transfer learning for Bayesian optimisation *remains an open problem.*

Our approach to the optimal source selection for transfer learning is based on using a Multi-arm bandit (MAB) and then coupling it with transfer learning in Bayesian optimisation. At each iteration, MAB selects a source, and within the Bayesian optimisation process this source is used to recommend an experimental point in a transfer learning setting. This point is then used to update the reward function of MAB. The reward function is defined such that the reward due to each source in the MAB models the relatedness of the source to the target. Since MAB is an established framework to maximize reward, it ensures that the source closest to the target is eventually selected at convergence. We use this reward function to develop an algorithm that couples MAB with transfer learning in Bayesian optimisation. We provide a theoretical analysis to show that the proposed algorithm is guaranteed to select the optimal source from the set of available source functions. We validate our algorithm through application to optimisation of synthetic functions, hyperparameter tuning of SVM classifier and optimisation of short polymer fiber synthesis. We show that in all cases our algorithm outperforms several baselines performing transfer learning with either a single source or all sources.

2 Preliminaries

2.1 Gaussian Process

Gaussian process (GP) is a common and powerful prior distribution over smooth functions and are completely specified by a mean function, μ and covariance function, k. Using a Gaussian process, a function $f(\mathbf{x})$ can be modeled as $f(\mathbf{x}) \sim GP(\mu(\mathbf{x}), k(\mathbf{x}, \mathbf{x}^{'}))$ where $\mathbf{x}, \mathbf{x}'$ are points from the function domain. Without loss in generality, the mean function $\mu(\mathbf{x})$ can be set to zero thus making the Gaussian process fully specified by the covariance matrix alone [10]. There are many popular covariance functions e.g. Matérn kernel, linear kernel, squared exponential kernel.

We assume the function evaluations are noisy, *i.e.* $\mathbf{y} = f(\mathbf{x}) + \epsilon$. Given any t observations, we can collectively denote them as $\mathcal{D}_t = \{\mathbf{x}_{1:t}, \mathbf{y}_{1:t}\}$. The function values $f(\mathbf{x}_{1:t})$ follow a multivariate Gaussian distribution $\mathcal{N}(0, \mathbf{K})$, where $\mathbf{K}(i, i') = k(\mathbf{x}_i, \mathbf{x}_{i'})$. Given a new point $\mathbf{x}_{t+1}$, $\mathbf{y}_{1:t}$ and $f(\mathbf{x}_{t+1})$ are jointly Gaussian, which leads to the predictive distribution $p(y_{t+1} \mid \mathcal{D}_t, \mathbf{x}_{t+1}) = \mathcal{N}(\mu_t(\mathbf{x}_{t+1}), \sigma_t^2(\mathbf{x}_{t+1}))$ where $\mathbf{k} = [k(\mathbf{x}_{t+1}, \mathbf{x}_1)\, k(\mathbf{x}_{t+2}, \mathbf{x}_2)\, \ldots\, k(\mathbf{x}_{t+1}, \mathbf{x}_t)]$ and we have the predictive mean $\mu_t(\mathbf{x}_{t+1}) = \mathbf{k}^{\mathbf{T}}\mathbf{K}^{-\mathbf{1}}\mathbf{y}_{1:t}$ and variance $\sigma_t^2(\mathbf{x}_{t+1}) = k(\mathbf{x}_{t+1}, \mathbf{x}_{t+1}) - \mathbf{k}^{\mathbf{T}}\mathbf{K}^{-\mathbf{1}}\mathbf{k}$.

2.2 Bayesian Optimisation

Bayesian optimisation is an efficient framework for finding global optima of expensive functions where we cannot express the function in closed-form (black box functions). Since the function form is unknown and its evaluations are noisy, Bayesian optimisation builds a probabilistic model of the function by setting a prior over it. Usually a Gaussian process prior is used because of its tractability and robustness. However, other possibilities have been explored [3,11]. Evidence is then gathered by evaluating the function at some points and combined with the prior to derive a posterior distribution. Bayesian optimisation gains its efficiency by carefully deciding in a sequential manner at what points to evaluate the function next. This decision is made by maximizing an acquisition function, which is constructed by combining the function estimate so far along with uncertainty in the estimate. This combination is motivated by the need to keep a balance between two strategies: exploitation and exploration [2,12]. Several combination of the predictive mean $(\mu_t(\mathbf{x}))$ and predictive variance $(\sigma_t^2(\mathbf{x}))$ lead to different acquisition functions e.g. improvement based acquisition functions, namely probability of improvement [13], expected improvement [14], and upper confidence bound based acquisition function GP-UCB [15]. In this paper, we use GP-UCB mainly due to its well analyzed theoretical properties.

2.3 Multi-armed Bandit Problem

The multi-armed bandit (MAB) problem [16] is a sequential decision making task in which an agent has to make a decision sequentially at each iteration $t = 1, \ldots, T$ where $T > 1$. In this setting, the agent is faced with M actions or arms (indexed as $m = 1, \ldots, M$). By taking m^{th} action (or pulling the mth arm) at iteration t, the agent receives some reward $r_{t,m}$. The aim is to maximize the cumulative sum of rewards by optimally exploring different actions (or arms) as well as exploiting the seemingly most rewarding arms. The Adversarial MAB is the one of the strongest generalizations of the bandit problem as it removes most of the assumptions on the generation of rewards including *i.i.d.* assumption. A well known algorithm for the adversarial MAB is EXP3 (Exponential-weight algorithm for Exploration and Exploitation). The algorithm maintains a list of weights for each arm, which is used to decide the next arm to be played. The weight for an arm increases when the reward for the arm is good and vice versa. Also, a factor $\gamma \in (0, 1]$ is used to ensure uniform random selection for each arm [17].

2.4 Transfer Learning for Bayesian Optimisation

Standard Bayesian optimisation algorithms may recommend several points with low function values before reaching a high function value region. Transfer learning can be used as a remedy to this "cold start" problem. Transfer learning methods utilize the knowledge acquired in previous function (source) optimisations to achieve faster optimisation for a new related function (target). However, when the source functions are significantly different from the target function, transfer learning may degrade the optimisation efficiency. Therefore, using the right source function is crucial to the efficiency of the optimisation.

Most of the previous research in transfer learning for Bayesian optimisation has made assumptions regarding the source similarity. For example, Bardenet et al. [6] propose a method assuming that the function ranking is transferable from any source to target. In an another approach, Yogatama and Mann [7] use deviations of a function from its mean scaled by its standard deviation. These transfer learning assumptions often do not hold in real world scenarios. Since there is no care taken as to whether a source is useful for the target, these methods do not reach the true potential of transfer learning. To handle different levels of relatedness between source and target, Joy et al. [9] proposed an alternate transfer learning method by modeling source data as noisy observations of the target function. This method is known as envelope-stretching Bayesian optimisation or simply Env-GP. Although this method protects against an unrelated source, it does not actively select the best source. In this paper, using Env-GP as base, we propose a method to select the best source for transfer learning.

Env-GP models the source observations, y_i^s as noisy measurements from the target function, i.e

$$y_i^s = f^t(\mathbf{x}_i^s) + \epsilon_i^s, \forall i = 1, \ldots, N^s$$

where $f^t(\cdot)$ denotes the target function, $\mathbf{x}_i^s$ is the training data, N^s is the size of source data and $\epsilon_i^s \sim \mathcal{N}(0, \sigma_s^2)$ is a random noise. This source data is then combined with the target and a new GP is built over this combined data. The updated kernel matrix of this combined data that incorporate the source noise can be written as:

$$\mathbf{K} = \mathbf{K} + \begin{bmatrix} \sigma_s^2 I_{N^s \times N^s} & 0 \\ 0 & \sigma_t^2 I_{N^t \times N^t} \end{bmatrix}$$

where σ_s^2 models the source/target relatedness, σ_t^2 is the target measurement noise and N^t is the size of target observations so far. The noise variance, σ_s^2 from source data is estimated in a Bayesian setting by placing an inverse gamma distribution. Then its posterior distribution is updated using the output values of source and target with parameters, $\alpha_n = \alpha_0 + n/2$ and $\beta_n = \beta_0 + \frac{\sum_{i=1}^{N^t} (y_i^t - \hat{y}_i^s)^2}{2}$, where α_0 and β_0 are the parameters of the prior gamma distribution, y_i^t is the target function value and $\hat{y}_i^s$ is the predicted source function value. Then source variance can be written as the mode of the posterior distribution. i.e. $\sigma_s^2 = \frac{\beta_n}{\alpha_n + 1}$. For further details, we refer the reader to [9,18].

3 Proposed Method

We propose a framework to select source functions that can help a transfer learning method to achieve its true potential and thus optimise the target function in most sample-efficient manner. Our framework is built on the theory of multi-arm bandits (MAB). We first define a measure of relatedness between target and source functions. Next we derive a crucial result to characterize the benefits of transfer learning in terms of source-target relatedness. Finally, we present a multi-arm bandit based source selection algorithm that theoretically guarantees the selection of the best source.

3.1 Source/Target Relatedness

Definition. (*Source/Target Relatedness*): Given a target and source function $f(\mathbf{x})$ and $f^s(\mathbf{x})$, their relatedness is defined by the norm of their difference function. Let $b^s(\mathbf{x}) = f(\mathbf{x}) - f^s(\mathbf{x})$, then the source/target relatedness is expressed using $||b^s(\mathbf{x})||^2$. The lower the value of the $||b^s(\mathbf{x})||^2$, the more related are the target and source functions.

When we do not have precise knowledge of a source function $f^s(\mathbf{x})$, we can estimate it using its observations. In this paper we use GP model for such estimation.

Impact of the Source/Target Relatedness on Transfer Learning. Transfer learning algorithms typically use the observations from both target and the source functions to model the target function. We provide a theoretical result that formally states the impact of source/target relatedness on transfer learning for Bayesian optimisation of the target function.

Let $\{\mathbf{x}_i^s, y_i^s\}_{i=1}^{Ns}$ be source observations from source s generated as $y_i^s = f^s(\mathbf{x}_i^s) + \epsilon_i^s$, where $\epsilon_i^s \sim \mathcal{N}(0, \sigma^2)$. Similarly, let $\{\mathbf{x}_j, y_j\}_{j=1}^t$ be the target observations generated as $y_j = f(\mathbf{x}_j) + \epsilon_j$ up to iteration t, where

$\epsilon_j \sim \mathcal{N}(0, \sigma^2)$. Using a Gaussian process model on the augmented observations set $A_t = \{\mathbf{x}_i^s, y_i^s\}_{i=1}^{N_s} \cup \{\mathbf{x}_j, y_j\}_{j=1}^t$, the posterior distribution of target function estimate at a point $\mathbf{x}$ is given as $f(\mathbf{x}) | \{\mathbf{x}_i^s, y_i^s\} \cup \{\mathbf{x}_j, y_j\} \sim \mathcal{N}(\tilde{\mu}_t(\mathbf{x}), \tilde{\sigma}_t^2(\mathbf{x}))$ where $\tilde{\mu}_t(\mathbf{x}) = \mathbf{k}'^T \mathbf{Q}_{s,t}^{-1} \mathbf{y}'$, $\tilde{\sigma}_t^2(\mathbf{x}) = k(\mathbf{x}, \mathbf{x}) - \mathbf{k}'^T \mathbf{Q}_{s,t}^{-1} \mathbf{k}'$. In the above expression, we have $\mathbf{Q}_{s,t} = \begin{bmatrix} \mathbf{K}^s & \mathbf{K}' \\ \mathbf{K}'^T & \mathbf{K}_t + \sigma^2 \boldsymbol{I} \end{bmatrix}$, $\mathbf{k}' = [k(\mathbf{x}, \mathbf{x}_1^s), \ldots, k(\mathbf{x}, \mathbf{x}_{N_s}^s), k(\mathbf{x}, \mathbf{x}_1), \ldots, k(\mathbf{x}, \mathbf{x}_t)]$, $\mathbf{K}'(i,j) = \text{Cov}(f^s(\mathbf{x}_i^s), f(\mathbf{x}_j))$, $\mathbf{K}_t = [k(\mathbf{x}_j, \mathbf{x}_{j'})]_{\forall j,j'}$, $\mathbf{K}^s(i,i') = \text{Cov}(f^s(\mathbf{x}_i), f^s(\mathbf{x}_{i'}))$ and $\mathbf{y}' = [\{y_i^s\}, \{y_j\}]$. Using the definition of source/target relatedness measure, we write $\mathbf{K}^s(i,i')$ as below

$$\begin{aligned}\mathbf{K}^s(i,i') &= \text{Cov}(f^s(\mathbf{x}_i^s), f^s(\mathbf{x}_{i'}^s)) = \text{Cov}(f(\mathbf{x}_i^s) - b^s(\mathbf{x}_i^s), f(\mathbf{x}_{i'}^s) - b^s(\mathbf{x}_{i'}^s)) \\ &= \text{Cov}(f(\mathbf{x}_i^s), f(\mathbf{x}_{i'}^s)) + \text{Cov}(b^s(\mathbf{x}_i^s), b^s(\mathbf{x}_{i'}^s)) = k(\mathbf{x}_i^s, \mathbf{x}_{i'}^s) + k^b(\mathbf{x}_i^s, \mathbf{x}_{i'}^s)\end{aligned}$$

where we have assumed that the difference function $b^s(\mathbf{x})$ is independent of the target function $f(\mathbf{x})$, and $k^b(\mathbf{x}_i^s, \mathbf{x}_{i'}^s)$ is a covariance function modeling the structure of the function $b^s(\mathbf{x})$. Collectively, we use the notation $\mathbf{K}^s = \mathbf{K}_{Ns} + \mathbf{K}_{Ns}^b$ where $\mathbf{K}_{Ns}^b = [k^b(\mathbf{x}_i^s, \mathbf{x}_{i'}^s)]_{\forall i,i'}$ and $\mathbf{K}_{Ns} = [k(\mathbf{x}_i^s, \mathbf{x}_{i'}^s)]_{\forall i,i'}$. Similarly, we can write $\mathbf{K}'(i,j) = \text{Cov}(f^s(\mathbf{x}_i^s), f(\mathbf{x}_j)) = \text{Cov}(f(\mathbf{x}_i^s) - b^s(\mathbf{x}_i^s), f(\mathbf{x}_j)) = k(\mathbf{x}_i^s, \mathbf{x}_j)$. A popular measure to determine the optimisation efficiency of the Bayesian optimisation is the regret bound. When using the GP-UCB [15], the upper bound on the regret after T iterations is given as

$$Pr\left\{R_T \leq \sqrt{C_1 \beta_T \gamma_T T} + C_2 \; \forall T \geq 1\right\} \geq 1 - \delta \tag{1}$$

where the sequence $\beta_0, \beta_1, \ldots$ is a specified sequence that ensures convergence, C_1 is a constant dependent on observation noise σ^2, γ_T is the maximum information gain brought by points $\{\mathbf{x}_j\}_{j=1}^T$ and C_2 is a constant.

When there is no source and we are using the observations from the target alone, the information gain $\mathbb{I}_t = \frac{1}{2}\log|\boldsymbol{I} + \sigma^{-2}\mathbf{K}_t|$. In Lemma 1 (adopted from Shilton et al. [18]) and Lemma 2, we show that in presence of observations from a related source, the information gain by the target reduces depending on the source/target relatedness.

Lemma 1. *Using the augmented observations set A_t, the information gain $\tilde{\mathbb{I}}_t = \frac{1}{2}log|\boldsymbol{I} + \sigma^{-2}\mathbf{K}_t - \sigma^{-2}\mathbf{K}'^T\left(\mathbf{K}_{Ns} + \mathbf{K}_{Ns}^b\right)^{-1}\mathbf{K}'|$.*

Proof. The proof is adopted from Shilton et al. [18].

Next, we want to establish that the higher the source/target relatedness, the higher the *reduction* in the information gain. We will relate the reduction with the term $|\mathbf{K}'^T\left(\mathbf{K}_{Ns} + \mathbf{K}_{Ns}^b\right)^{-1}\mathbf{K}'|$. To proceed further, we assume that for transfer learning purpose we use the Env-GP model in [9], which models the function $b^s(\mathbf{x})$ via a noisy Gaussian process, meaning $\mathbf{K}_{Ns}^b = \sigma_s^2 I$. This is mainly done to simplify our proof. When using Env-GP, lower σ_s^2 implies higher average source/target relatedness and vice versa (see equations (15) and (16) on Joy et al. [9]). To see this relationship, consider $b^s(\mathbf{x})$ as a draw from a

Gaussian process with zero mean and then $\mathbb{E}[(b^s(\mathbf{x}))^2] = \text{var}(b^s(\mathbf{x})) = \sigma_s^2 I$. The last equality follows from the noise process assumption of Env-GP. Lemma 2 establishes a relationship which is then used with Lemma 1 to prove our main result for transfer learning (see Theorem 1).

Lemma 2. *Under the assumptions of Env-GP transfer learning model, the higher the source/target relatedness, the higher the value of the gap term* $|\mathbf{K}'^T \left(\mathbf{K}_{Ns} + \sigma_s^2 I\right)^{-1} \mathbf{K}'|$.

Proof. Let us consider sources s_1 and s_2 having observations at *identical* points in the input space and without loss in generality assume that s_1 is more related to the target than s_2 (i.e. $\mathbb{E}[(b^{s_1}(\mathbf{x}))^2] < \mathbb{E}[(b^{s_2}(\mathbf{x}))^2]$ or $\sigma_{s_1}^2 < \sigma_{s_2}^2$). Then for source s_1, consider $\left(\mathbf{K}_{Ns} + \sigma_{s_1}^2 I\right)^{-1} = C_1$ and factorize $\mathbf{K}'$ using Singular Value Decomposition (SVD), we can write

$$
\begin{aligned}
|\mathbf{K}'^T \left(\mathbf{K}_{Ns} + \sigma_{s_1}^2 I\right)^{-1} \mathbf{K}'| &= |\mathbf{K}'^T C_1 \mathbf{K}'| = |VSU^T C_1 USV^T| \\
&= \prod_{k=1}^{t} \lambda_k \left(VSU^T C_1 USV^T\right) = \prod_{k=1}^{t} \lambda_k \left(C_1\right) \left(\alpha_k \left(\mathbf{K}'\right)\right)^2
\end{aligned}
$$

where $\alpha_k(\mathbf{K}')$ are the singular values therein, and $\lambda_k(C_1)$ are the eigenvalues of the matrix, C_1. Similarly for source s_2,

$$
|\mathbf{K}'^T \left(\mathbf{K}_{Ns} + \sigma_{s_2}^2 I\right)^{-1} \mathbf{K}'| = |\mathbf{K}'^T C_2 \mathbf{K}'| = \prod_{k=1}^{t} \lambda_k \left(C_2\right) \left(\alpha_k \left(\mathbf{K}'\right)\right)^2
$$

where $C_2 = \left(\mathbf{K}_{Ns} + \sigma_{s_2}^2 I\right)^{-1}$. Due to identical input points, the matrices $\mathbf{K}'$ and $\mathbf{K}_{Ns}$ are same for both s_1 and s_2. Therefore, the value of $|\mathbf{K}'^T \left(\mathbf{K}_{Ns} + \sigma_s^2 I\right)^{-1} \mathbf{K}'|$ is dictated by how big is the term σ_s^2. Since $\sigma_{s_1}^2 < \sigma_{s_2}^2$, we have $\lambda_k(C_1) > \lambda_k(C_2)$, which implies

$$
|\mathbf{K}'^T \left(\mathbf{K}_{Ns} + \sigma_{s_1}^2 I\right)^{-1} \mathbf{K}'| > |\mathbf{K}'^T \left(\mathbf{K}_{Ns} + \sigma_{s_2}^2 I\right)^{-1} \mathbf{K}'|
$$

Therefore, if source s_1 is more related to the target compared to source s_2 (i.e. $\sigma_{s_1}^2 < \sigma_{s_2}^2$), the gap term for source s_1 is higher than that for source s_2.

Using the results of Lemmas 1 and 2, the following theorem formally states the impact of source/target relatedness on the benefits of transfer learning.

Theorem 1. *Under the assumptions of Env-GP transfer learning model, the reduction in the maximum information gain when using additional observations from a source function depends on the source/target relatedness. The higher the average source/target relatedness, the higher is the reduction in the maximum information gain and therefore, the higher is the reduction in the regret bound of transfer learning for Bayesian optimisation.*

Proof. Let γ_T denote the maximum information gain when using only the target observations. Further, let $\tilde{\gamma}_T$ denote the maximum information gain when using the augmented observations set, $A_t = \{\mathbf{x}_i^s, y_i^s\} \cup \{\mathbf{x}_j, y_j\}$. We can write $\tilde{\gamma}_T = \max_{\{\mathbf{x}_j\}:|\{\mathbf{x}_j\}|=T} \tilde{\mathbb{I}}(\{y_j\} \cup \{y_i^s\}, \{f(\mathbf{x}_j)\} \cup \{f(\mathbf{x}_i^s)\})$. By Lemma 1, we have $\tilde{\gamma}_T = \max_{\{\mathbf{x}_j\}:|\{\mathbf{x}_j\}|=T} \frac{1}{2}\log|\boldsymbol{I} + \sigma^{-2}\mathbf{K}_t - \sigma^{-2}\mathbf{K}'^T\left(\mathbf{K}_{Ns} + \sigma_s^2 I\right)^{-1}\mathbf{K}'|$. Using the Minkowski inequality on determinants of two positive definite matrices A and B, we have $|A + B| \geq |A| + |B| > |A|$. Assuming $A = \boldsymbol{I} + \sigma^{-2}\mathbf{K}_t - \sigma^{-2}\mathbf{K}'^T\left(\mathbf{K}_{Ns} + \sigma_s^2 I\right)^{-1}\mathbf{K}'$ and $B = \sigma^{-2}\mathbf{K}'^T\left(\mathbf{K}_{Ns} + \sigma_s^2 I\right)^{-1}\mathbf{K}'$, we can write $\log|\boldsymbol{I} + \sigma^{-2}\mathbf{K}_t - \sigma^{-2}\mathbf{K}'^T\left(\mathbf{K}_{Ns} + \sigma_s^2 I\right)^{-1}\mathbf{K}'| < \log|\boldsymbol{I} + \sigma^{-2}\mathbf{K}_t|$. From the above, we can conclude that $\tilde{\gamma}_T < \gamma_T$ [18] and the difference is dictated by how big is the gap term, $|\mathbf{K}'^T\left(\mathbf{K}_{Ns} + \sigma_s^2 I\right)^{-1}\mathbf{K}'|$ (see Lemma 2). A source with high average relatedness with the target will be able to use smaller σ_s^2 [9] and therefore, will have bigger gap term $|\mathbf{K}'^T\left(\mathbf{K}_{Ns} + \sigma_s^2 I\right)^{-1}\mathbf{K}'|$ for the information gain and hence a higher reduction in the regret bound of transfer learning for Bayesian optimisation (see (1)).

3.2 Source Selection Strategy

Theorem 1 suggests that the regret bound of Bayesian optimisation is reduced when using a source with high relatedness to the target. Next, we propose a method that selects a source that has the highest relatedness to the target. Our approach is based on a combination of exploration-exploitation strategies commonly used in reinforcement learning community. In particular, we use MAB formulation with an analogy where each *source* can be thought of an *arm* of a bandit. Different sources may offer different levels of benefit for modeling the target function. The level of benefit is linked to the reward when a particular source (arm) is selected (pulled). We design a reward function such that MAB based source selection strategy leads to maximizing the reward and hence selects the source that brings the maximum benefit for target function optimisation.

Assuming M sources, indexed as $m = 1, \ldots, M$, we have M-armed bandit problem defined by random variables $\{r_{t,m}\}$ for $1 \leq m \leq M$ and $t \geq 1$. The random variable $r_{t,m}$ denotes the reward when the mth source is selected at iteration t. Rewards in our case have a fixed distribution for each source, however, they become increasingly dependent with iterations as Bayesian optimisation approaches convergence and samples points from the region around the function optimum. So, although for a large part, the rewards are *i.i.d.*, they become fairly non-*i.i.d.* after some iterations. Due to the non-*i.i.d.* nature of reward, we use EXP3 algorithm for MAB to converge to the arm.

The following theorem provides a reward function, which is maximum for a source that has the highest relatedness with the target. Since MAB selects the arm with the highest reward, it converges to the best source for transfer learning.

Algorithm 1. The proposed transfer learning algorithm

1. **Input:** Source observations: $\{\mathbf{x}_i^s, y_i^s\}_{s=1}^M$, Target observations: $\{\mathbf{x}_j, y_j\}_{j=1}^{n_0}$.
2. **Initial Settings:** Set $\gamma \in (0, 1]$ and initial weights, $w_s(1) = 1, \forall s$.
3. **Output:** $\{\mathbf{x}_t, y_t\}_{t=1}^T$
4. Fit a GP for each source using $\{\mathbf{x}_i^s, y_i^s\}_{s=1}^M$and define predictive mean $\mu^s(\mathbf{x})$, $\forall s$.
5. **for** $t = n_0, \ldots, T$ **do**
   (a) Set $p_{t,m} = (1-\gamma)\frac{w_m(t)}{\sum_{i=1}^M w_i(t)} + \frac{\gamma}{M}$, $m = 1, \ldots M$.
   (b) Select a source s_t by maximizing $\underset{m=1,\ldots,M}{\text{argmax}}\, p_{t,m}$.
   (c) Augment the target observations to the selected source observations, $A_t = \left\{\{\mathbf{x}_i^{s_t}, y_i^{s_t}\} \cup \{\mathbf{x}_j, y_j\}_{j=1}^{t-1}\right\}$.
   (d) Fit a GP using set A_t following the transfer learning algorithm (Env-GP) in [9] and maximize the acquisition function to recommend a new point $\mathbf{x}_t$.
   (e) Evaluate the target function: $y_t = f(\mathbf{x}_t) + \epsilon_t$.
   (f) Compute the reward as $r_{t,s_t} = -\left(y_t - \mu^{s_t}(\mathbf{x}_t)\right)^2$ utilizing the source GP.
   (g) **for** $m = 1, \ldots, M$ **set**
      i. $\hat{r}_{t,m} = \begin{cases} \frac{r_{t,m}}{p_{t,m}} & \text{if}\, m = s_t \\ 0 & \text{otherwise,} \end{cases}$
      ii. $w_m(t+1) = w_m(t)\exp(\frac{\gamma \hat{r}_{t,m}}{M})$
   (h) **end for**
6. **end for**

Theorem 2. *Given sufficiently large number of source observations, if the reward for m^{th} source at iteration t is defined as $r_{t,m} = -\left(f(\mathbf{x}_t) - \mu^m(\mathbf{x}_t)\right)^2$, then source selection strategy based on MAB converges to the optimal source for transfer learning.*

Proof. The goal of MAB (EXP3) algorithm is to identify the source which minimizes the pseudo-regret, which after T iterations is given by $\mathbb{E}\left[\sum_{t=1}^T r_{t,m^*} - \sum_{t=1}^T r_{t,s_t}\right]$ where m^* is the source returning the highest reward and s_t is the source selected using Bayesian optimisation policy at time t. Here the expectation is with respect to the distribution of both reward and the source selection of Bayesian optimisation policy. As T increases, the EXP3 algorithm increasingly converges towards identifying the best source $m*$ that has the largest cumulative reward. We show that the cumulative reward has a direct connection with the source/target relatedness. Consider the cumulative reward up to iteration T, i.e. $\sum_{t=1}^T r_{t,s_t}$. We can write $\sum_{t=1}^T r_{t,s_t} = -\sum_{t=1}^T \left(f(\mathbf{x}_t) - \mu^{s_t}(\mathbf{x}_t)\right)^2 = -\sum_{t=1}^T \left(f(\mathbf{x}_t) - \mathbb{E}[f^{s_t}(\mathbf{x}_t)]\right)^2$. Given sufficiently large number of source observations, we have $\mathbb{E}[f^{s_t}(\mathbf{x}_t)] \approxeq f^{s_t}(\mathbf{x}_t)$, which implies $\sum_{t=1}^T r_{t,s_t} = -\sum_{t=1}^T \left(b^{s_t}(\mathbf{x}_t)\right)^2$, which is an estimate of the source/target relatedness using target observations. Therefore, with increasing T, EXP3 algorithm is guaranteed to converge to the best source for the transfer learning. Our proposed method is summarized in Algorithm 1.

4 Experiments

We perform experiments with both synthetic and real datasets. Through synthetic data, we illustrate the behavior of our source selection technique in a controlled setting. In this experiment, the task is to reach the peak of a target function in an efficient manner utilizing the observations from several related sources with varying degree of relatedness. We demonstrate that our technique can accurately identify the best source. For real data experiments, we perform hyperparameter tuning for support vector machine and optimisation of short polymer fiber synthesis. We demonstrate the efficiency of our algorithm by comparing it with following baseline methods: (1) **Transfer with Fixed Source:** A fixed source is chosen randomly and used in transfer learning algorithm [9], (2) **Transfer with Merged Source:** All sources are merged, that is their observations are pooled to create a single source which is then used in transfer learning algorithm [9], (3) **No Transfer:** This baseline is the standard Bayesian optimisation algorithm that does not use any source data, (4) **SMBO:** Transfer learning algorithm [7] that transfers deviation of a function from its mean scaled by its standard deviation is used, (5) **SCoT:** Transfer learning algorithm [6] that transfers some function ranking from source to target is used. The baselines (4) and (5) are two well known transfer learning methods and is used for the comparison with our method.

4.1 Experimental Setting

For Gaussian process modeling, we use the square exponential kernel. The kernel length scale is set to 0.1 after normalizing the input space along each dimension to $[0, 1]$. All the results are averaged over 10 runs with random initialization. We use DIRECT [19] to optimise the acquisition function.

4.2 Synthetic Experiments

We consider three different scenarios: (1) there is only one related source, (2) there are multiple related sources, and (3) there are no related sources. For each case we created 4 different sources and a common target function. The target is a 2-dimensional bimodal Gaussian function with one peak at $[0.7, 0.7]$ and the other peak at $[2.7, 2.7]$. The covariance matrices for these peaks are $\boldsymbol{I}_{2\times 2}$ and $[0.25 \times \boldsymbol{I}_{2\times 2}]$ respectively. Our source selection method can select any of the 4 sources. We also added a 5th option 'No source' to handle the scenario when none of the sources are useful (perform optimisation using only the target data without selecting any of the sources). In each case, we generate bimodal Gaussian source functions with modes at different locations and for the two modes, the covariance matrices are taken as $\boldsymbol{I}_{2\times 2}$ and $[0.25 \times \boldsymbol{I}_{2\times 2}]$ respectively.

Case 1 (Single Related Source): We generate 4 bimodal Gaussian source functions in 2-dimensions with their first peaks at $[-5, -5]$, $[\mathbf{0.8}, \mathbf{0.8}]$, $[5, 5]$, $[6, 6]$ and the second peaks at $[-3, -3]$, $[\mathbf{2.8}, \mathbf{2.8}]$, $[3, 3]$, $[4, 4]$ respectively. As seen from peak locations, only the 2nd source is closely related to the target.

For each source, 100 data points are sampled randomly from $[-4, 5]$ along each dimension. Figure 1a shows the maximum function value obtained with respect to iterations. Each method starts with the same two random observations. Our method outperforms the baselines by achieving 90% of the maximum value by the 7th iteration and reaches the maximum by the 10th iteration. On the other hand, all the three baselines are only able to gain 80% of the maximum until the final iteration. The histograms of the source selections at different stages are shown in Fig. 1b. The source with peaks at $\mathbf{[0.8, 0.8]}$ and $\mathbf{[2.8, 2.8]}$ has correctly been used the most number of times for transfer learning. Comparison of our method with other two transfer learning methods and simple Bayesian optimisation algorithm is presented in Fig. 1c. Our method outperforms the baselines using the knowledge from the related source.

Case 2 (Two Related Sources): We generate 4 bimodal Gaussian source functions in 2-dimensions with their first peaks at $[-5, -5]$, $\mathbf{[0.8, 0.8]}$, $\mathbf{[0.4, 0.4]}$, $[6, 6]$ and the second peaks at $[-3, -3]$, $\mathbf{[2.8, 2.8]}$, $\mathbf{[2.4, 2.4]}$, $[4, 4]$. In this case, both source-2 and 3 are related to the target function. This case is generated to illustrate that our source selection scheme is capable of identifying multiple related sources if applicable. For each source, 100 data points are sampled randomly from $[-4, 5]$ along each dimension. Maximum value obtained with respect to iterations is illustrated in Fig. 2a. When compared to the baselines, our method is able to reach 90% of the maximum value by the 10th iteration and reaches the maximum by 15th iteration. The Maximum value reached by the baselines at the final iteration is only 80%. The histograms of the source selections are shown in Fig. 2b. At the final iteration, the most related source with peaks at $\mathbf{[0.8, 0.8]}$ and $\mathbf{[2.8, 2.8]}$ is chosen the most number of times followed by the second most related source with peaks at $\mathbf{[0.4, 0.4]}$ and $\mathbf{[2.4, 2.4]}$. This shows that our method has a tendency to select the sources in order of their relatedness to the target function. Figure 2c shows the comparison of our method with other three baselines.

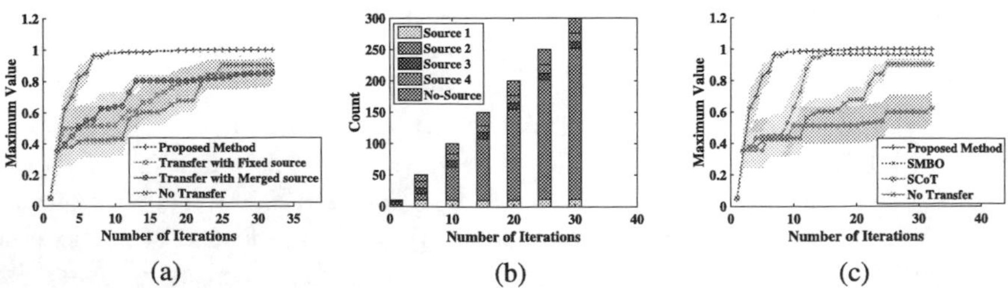

Fig. 1. Synthetic data (Case 1): (a) Maximum value vs iterations (b) Selection count of each source with iterations (source 2 count is prominent) (c) Comparison with other transfer learning methods.

Case 3 (No Related Source): We generate 4 bimodal Gaussian source functions in 2-dimensions with their first peaks at $[-5, -5]$, $[4.5, 4.5]$ $[5, 5]$, $[6, 6]$ and

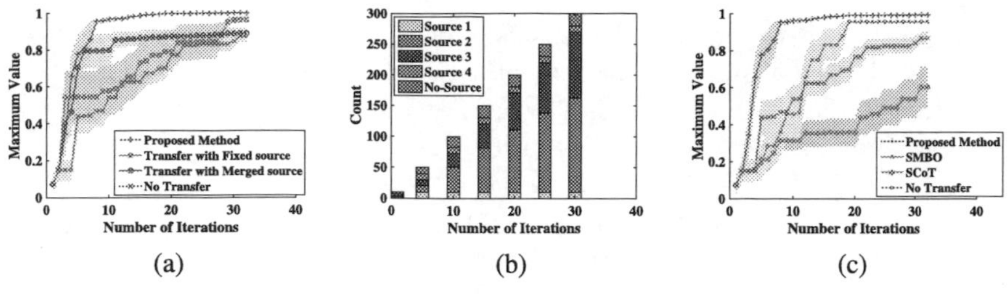

Fig. 2. Synthetic data (Case 2): (a) Maximum value vs iterations (b) Selection count of each source with iterations (source 2 count is prominent followed by source 3) (c) Comparison with other transfer learning methods.

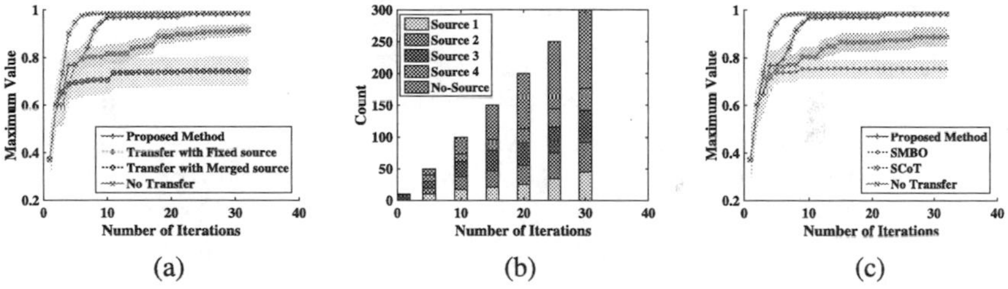

Fig. 3. Synthetic data (Case 3) (created to illustrate that our method is capable **to prevent negative transfer**): (a) Maximum value vs iterations (b) Selection count of each source with iterations (c) Comparison with other transfer learning methods.

the second peaks at $[-3, -3]$, $[6.5, 6.5]$ $[3, 3]$, $[4, 4]$. In this case, no source is related to the target function. For each source, 100 data points are sampled randomly from $[-1.5, 1.5]$ along each dimension. Figure 3*a* plots the maximum value obtained with respect to iterations. Since there is no related source to the target, the baseline *No-Transfer* outperforms the proposed method in the initial run but because of using the 'No source' option our method is still able to perform reasonably well unlike other transfer learning baselines that force learning from unrelated sources. The histograms of the source selections are shown at different stages in Fig. 3*b*. As may be seen, 'No source' option is correctly chosen most number of times until the final iteration. Using the 'No source' option, our algorithm outperforms the other two transfer learning methods in the comparison plot shown in Fig. 3*c*.

4.3 Hyperparameter Tuning

The experiments are performed on a real world dataset [20] for tuning hyperparameters of Support Vector Machine (SVM) with sigmoid kernel. The dataset is Landsat Satellite dataset, which is a multi-class classification dataset consisting of six classes: Two hyperparameters are tuned for SVM with sigmoid kernel: cost parameter (C) and kernel parameter (γ). The ranges for both C and γ are chosen to be within $\left[10^{-3}, 10^{3}\right]$. The multi-class classifier is realized by training pairwise binary classifiers. To demonstrate our source selection technique, we use AUC vs hyperparameter functions of some class-pairs to represent a set of sources (here 5 pairs) and one class pair as target. We also added the 'No source' option to handle no useful source scenario.

The AUC performance on a held-out validation set is shown in Fig. 4*a*. The proposed method outperforms all three baselines. In this case, the baselines *Transfer with Fixed source* and *Transfer with Merged source* do better than *No transfer* and are only able to catch up with the proposed method at the 25th iteration. The histograms of the source selections at various stages are shown in Fig. 4*b*. The comparison graph is presented in Fig. 4*c*.

4.4 Short Polymer Fiber Synthesis

Short polymer fiber is produced by injecting a semi-crystalline polymer into a high-speed coagulant liquid. The fiber production includes three geometric variables namely 'device position', 'constriction angle' and 'channel width' which highly effect on the geometrical features of the produced fibers. Two other parameters which control the fiber production are 'polymer flow' and 'coagulant speed'. The goal is to achieve a short polymer with stipulated length and diameter [21].

To demonstrate our source selection method, we created source functions corresponding to different combinations of parameters: 'channel width' and 'coagulant speed'. Five settings were selected as sources and one as target. The utility

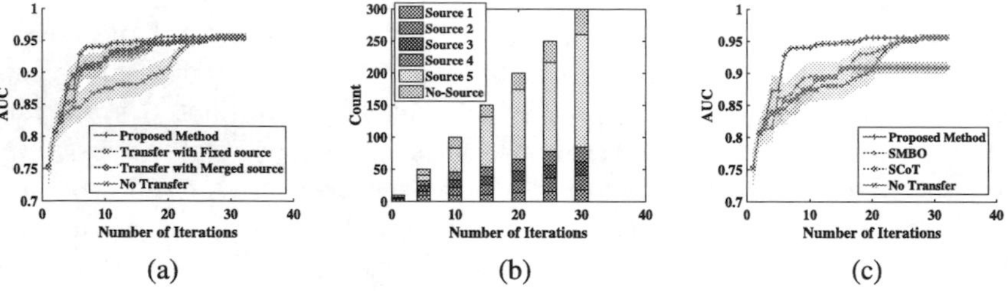

Fig. 4. Hyperparameter tuning: (a) AUC vs iterations (b) Selection count of each source with iterations (c) Comparison with other transfer learning methods.

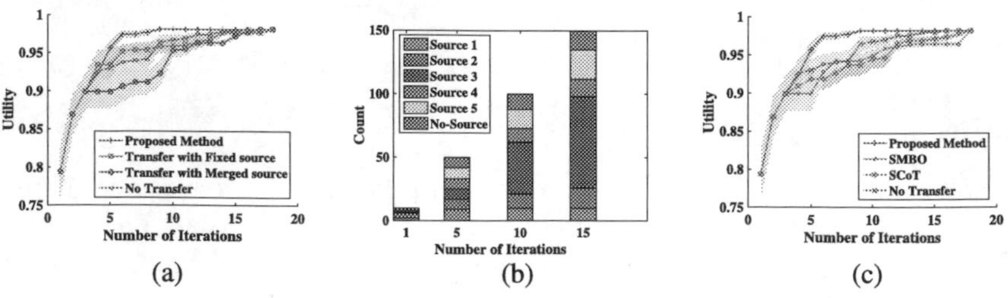

Fig. 5. Short polymer fiber: (a) Utility vs iterations (b) Selection count of each source with iterations (c) Comparison with other transfer learning methods.

score with respect to iterations is plotted in Fig. 5*a*. Our method outperforms all other baselines. As seen from the histogram in Fig. 5*b*, source-3 is most related to the stipulated target experiment. The performance of our method in Fig. 5*c* shows that our method outperforms all other baselines.

5 Conclusion

We proposed a novel algorithm for optimal source selection for transfer learning in Bayesian optimisation. Our algorithm being based on MAB uses a reward function which is aligned with the goal of estimating target function. We theoretically analyze our algorithm and prove that it is guaranteed to select the best source for target function modeling. Our experiments with diverse optimisation tasks demonstrate the effectiveness of our method.

Acknowledgment. This research was partially funded by the Australian Government through the Australian Research Council (ARC) and the Telstra-Deakin Centre of Excellence in Big Data and Machine Learning. Professor Venkatesh is the recipient of an ARC Australian Laureate Fellowship (FL170100006). The authors thank Dr Alessandra Sutti and her team for providing short polymer fiber data and several useful discussions.

References

1. Pan, S.J., Yang, Q.: A survey on transfer learning. IEEE Trans. Know. Data Eng. **22**, 1345–1359 (2010)
2. Brochu, E., Cora, V.M., De Freitas, N.: A tutorial on Bayesian optimization of expensive cost functions, with application to active user modeling and hierarchical reinforcement learning. arXiv preprint arXiv:1012.2599 (2010)
3. Hutter, F., Hoos, H.H., Leyton-Brown, K.: Sequential model-based optimization for general algorithm configuration. In: Coello, C.A.C. (ed.) LION 2011. LNCS, vol. 6683, pp. 507–523. Springer, Heidelberg (2011). https://doi.org/10.1007/978-3-642-25566-3_40
4. Garnett, R., Osborne, M.A., Roberts, S.J.: Bayesian optimization for sensor set selection. In: Proceedings of the 9th ACM/IEEE International Conference on Information Processing in Sensor Networks, pp. 209–219. ACM (2010)
5. Lizotte, D.J., Wang, T., Bowling, M.H., Schuurmans, D.: Automatic gait optimization with Gaussian process regression. In: IJCAI, vol. 7, pp. 944–949 (2007)
6. Bardenet, R., Brendel, M., Kégl, B., Sebag, M.: Collaborative hyperparameter tuning. In: ICML, vol. 2, pp. 199–207 (2013)
7. Yogatama, D., Mann, G.: Efficient transfer learning method for automatic hyperparameter tuning. Transfer **1**, 1 (2014)
8. Swersky, K., Snoek, J., Adams, R.P.: Multi-task Bayesian optimization. In: Advances in neural information processing systems, pp. 2004–2012 (2013)
9. Joy, T.T., Rana, S., Gupta, S.K., Venkatesh, S.: Flexible transfer learning framework for Bayesian optimisation. In: Bailey, J., Khan, L., Washio, T., Dobbie, G., Huang, J.Z., Wang, R. (eds.) PAKDD 2016. LNCS (LNAI), vol. 9651, pp. 102–114. Springer, Cham (2016). https://doi.org/10.1007/978-3-319-31753-3_9

10. Rasmussen, C.E.: Gaussian processes in machine learning. In: Bousquet, O., von Luxburg, U., Rätsch, G. (eds.) ML 2003. LNCS (LNAI), vol. 3176, pp. 63–71. Springer, Heidelberg (2004). https://doi.org/10.1007/978-3-540-28650-9_4
11. Snoek, J., et al.: Scalable Bayesian optimization using deep neural networks. In: International Conference on Machine Learning, pp. 2171–2180 (2015)
12. Shahriari, B., Swersky, K., Wang, Z., Adams, R.P., de Freitas, N.: Taking the human out of the loop: a review of Bayesian optimization. Proc. IEEE **104**, 148–175 (2016)
13. Kushner, H.J.: A new method of locating the maximum point of an arbitrary multipeak curve in the presence of noise. J. Basic Eng. **86**, 97–106 (1964)
14. Močkus, J., Tiesis, V., Žilinskas, A.: The application of Bayesian methods for seeking the extremum. In: Toward Global Optimization, vol. 2, pp. 117–128. Elsevier (1978)
15. Srinivas, N., Krause, A., Kakade, S.M., Seeger, M.W.: Information-theoretic regret bounds for Gaussian process optimization in the bandit setting. IEEE Trans. Inf. Theory **58**, 3250–3265 (2012)
16. Robbins, H.: Some aspects of the sequential design of experiments. Bull. Am. Math. Soc. **58**(5), 527–535 (1952). https://projecteuclid.org/euclid.bams/1183517370
17. Auer, P., Cesa-Bianchi, N., Freund, Y., Schapire, R.E.: The nonstochastic multiarmed bandit problem. SIAM J. Comput. **32**, 48–77 (2002)
18. Shilton, A., Gupta, S., Rana, S., Venkatesh, S.: Regret bounds for transfer learning in Bayesian optimisation. In: Artificial Intelligence and Statistics, pp. 307–315 (2017)
19. Jones, D.R., Perttunen, C.D., Stuckman, B.E.: Lipschitzian optimization without the Lipschitz constant. J. Optim. Theory Appl. **79**, 157–181 (1993)
20. Lichman, M.: UCI machine learning repository (2013)
21. Sutti, A., Lin, T., Wang, X.: Shear-enhanced solution precipitation: a simple process to produce short polymeric nanofibers. J. Nanosci. Nanotechnol. **11**, 8947–8952 (2011)

Fast Spatially-Regularized Correlation Filters for Visual Object Tracking

Pengyu Zhang[1,2], Qing Guo[1,2], and Wei Feng[1,2(✉)]

[1] School of Computer Science and Technology, Tianjin University, Tianjin, China
wfeng@tju.edu.cn

[2] Key Research Center for Surface Monitoring and Analysis of Cultural Relics, SACH, Beijing, China

Abstract. Spatially-regularized correlation filters have achieved great successes in visual object tracking, with excellent tracking accuracy and robustness to various interferences. The performance improvement mainly attributes to spatial regularization (SR), which is a powerful tool to alleviate the boundary effects of correlation filters (CF) based tracking, but on the other hand, also severely harms the efficiency. In this paper, we propose an effective fast spatial regularization model that can be learned within the joint frequency and spatial domain. Extensive experiments on OTB-100 validate the effectiveness and generality of our model in helping state-of-the-art CF trackers to achieve much faster (near 5 times) frame rate and even better tracking accuracy.

Keywords: Visual object tracking · Correlation filters
Fast spatial regularization · Single-layer CNN

1 Introduction

Single object tracking estimates the coordinates and scales of a given target throughout a whole video sequence, which is an important problem in computer vision and has far-reaching applications, such as smart surveillance, autonomous driving, human-computer interaction. High accuracy and real-time speed are two requirements for a practical tracker. To this end, a number of tracking frameworks have been proposed, including SVM [16], compressive sensing [12], correlation filters [17], CNN [13,29]. Among them, correlation filters (CF) [17] is one of notable tracking schemes, that has great successes on various tracking benchmarks [21,33] with high accuracy and beyond real-time speed. Specifically, CF obtains training samples by circularly shifting a base sample centering at the target, thus realizes dense sampling and efficient learning in frequency domain. However, those training samples are not the real representations of negative samples, which leads to the boundary effects [11] and significantly jeopardizes the discriminative power of learned filters. Several improved CF trackers are then

P. Zhang and Q. Guo—Both authors contributed equally to this work.

W. Feng—This work is supported by NSFC 61671325, 61572354, 61672376.

X. Geng and B.-H. Kang (Eds.): PRICAI 2018, LNAI 11012, pp. 57–70, 2018.
https://doi.org/10.1007/978-3-319-97304-3_5

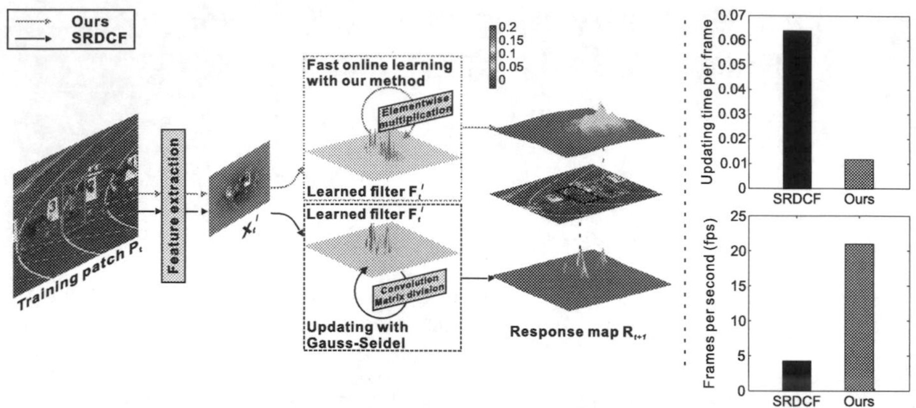

Fig. 1. A comparison between our method (red) and SRDCF [7] (black). We propose to fast online learn spatially-regularized correlation filters. The left subfigure shows that our method gets a discriminative response map and locates target accurately. SRDCF, however, generates a multi-peaks response map whose maximum is in the background region, thus misses the target. The right subfigure shows that our method runs near 5X faster than SRDCF according to average fps and updating time per frame on OTB-100. (Color figure online)

proposed by using more discriminative features, such as color [1,19,23], pre-trained CNN [25], context information [2,15,28,34], etc. However, the boundary effects, being an essential drawback of CF tracking framework, cannot be completely solved in these ways.

Recently, it has been shown that spatial regularization (SR), e.g. SRDCF [7], CCOT [8] and ECO [5], can significantly suppress the negative influence of boundary effects. SRDCF introduces a spatially variant weight map into the CF model and helps to online learn a group of more discriminative filters from a larger training patch with boundary effects caused by synthetic samples being reduced. Hence, spatial regularization within CF is a satisfying framework that can significantly boost the accuracy of CF trackers. However, the SR term leads to high computing complexity due to breaking of elementwise multiplication and division when we solve correlation filters in Fourier domain [17]. As a compromise, SRDCF uses an iterative way, e.g. Gauss-Seidel method, to solve the filters instead of a close-form solution. It, however, still leads over 10 times deceleration due to the operations of convolution and matrix division at each iteration. Hence, spatial regularization, being a powerful tool to improve tracking accuracy of CF, is incompatible with a fast tracker and cannot be used in real-time tracking. Therefore, it is highly desirable to find a way to accelerate spatial regularization within the CF tracking scheme without harming the accuracy.

In this paper, we propose to solve spatially-regularized correlation filters jointly within frequency and spatial domain. We specifically treat the optimization of correlation filters as learning a single-layer CNN that includes only one circular convolution layer. Then, the SR weight map becomes a spatially variant decay term. As a result, the correlation filters per frame can be efficiently online learned without performing convolution and matrix division at each iteration, which significantly speeds up SR based CF trackers. As shown in Fig. 1, our tracker can run near 5 times faster than SRDCF and locate the target accurately with a discriminative response map, while SRDCF misses the target in this case. Since avoiding the convolution and matrix division in the filters learning process, our tracker reduces 80% of updating time, which accounts for the most part of complexity of SRDCF tracking scheme. Extensive experiments on OTB-100 validate that our method outperforms the original spatial regularization in both speed and accuracy. In addition, our method is also capable of significantly improving the accuracy of many state-of-the-art CF trackers, with comparable or only slightly lower speed.

2 Background

SRDCF applies spatial regularization term to traditional CF formulation. The objective function for learning filters in a single frame can be expressed as,

$$\mathrm{E}(\mathbf{F}) = ||\sum_{l=1}^{D} \mathbf{X}^l * \mathbf{F}^l - \mathbf{Y}||^2 + \sum_{l=1}^{D} ||\mathbf{W} \odot \mathbf{F}^l||^2. \tag{1}$$

Here, '$*$' denotes circular convolution and '$\odot$' represents elementwise multiplication. $\mathbf{X} \in \mathcal{R}^{M \times N \times D}$ are features of a patch. $\mathbf{F} \in \mathcal{R}^{M \times N \times D}$ are online learned filters obtained by minimizing Eq. (1). The superscript $l \in \{1, 2, ...D\}$ of each variable denotes the index of dimension. $\mathbf{Y} \in \mathcal{R}^{M \times N}$ is the desired response map which is a 2D Gaussian map whose peak is located at the center of target. In SRDCF, the role of SR is reflected in the second term of Eq. (1) by a spatial regularization weight map to penalize the filters. The SR weight map $\mathbf{W} \in \mathcal{R}^{M \times N}$ is set as

$$\mathbf{W}(x, y) = a * ((\frac{x - x_0}{w})^n + (\frac{y - y_0}{h})^n) + w_{\min}, \tag{2}$$

where (x, y) is the corresponding coordinate in $\mathbf{W}$ and (x_0, y_0) is the coordinate of target center. w and h represent the width and height of the target, respectively. a, $w_{\min}$ and n are preset scalars. $\mathbf{W}$ determines the confidence of each coordinate in filters $\mathbf{F}$. The value of each coefficient in $\mathbf{W}$ depends on the distance to the target center. High constraints are added to the background region of $\mathbf{F}$ and vice versa.

For fast training and detection, SRDCF can be solved in Fourier domain by rewriting Eq. (1) as follow,

$$\mathrm{E}(\widehat{\mathbf{F}}) = ||\sum_{l=1}^{D} \widehat{\mathbf{X}}^l \odot \widehat{\mathbf{F}}^l - \widehat{\mathbf{Y}}||^2 + \sum_{l=1}^{D} ||\widehat{\mathbf{W}} * \widehat{\mathbf{F}}^l||^2, \tag{3}$$

where $\widehat{\cdot}$ denotes Discrete Fourier Transform (DFT) of a signal. Although Eq. (1) is transformed in the Fourier domain, convolution operation still exists, which

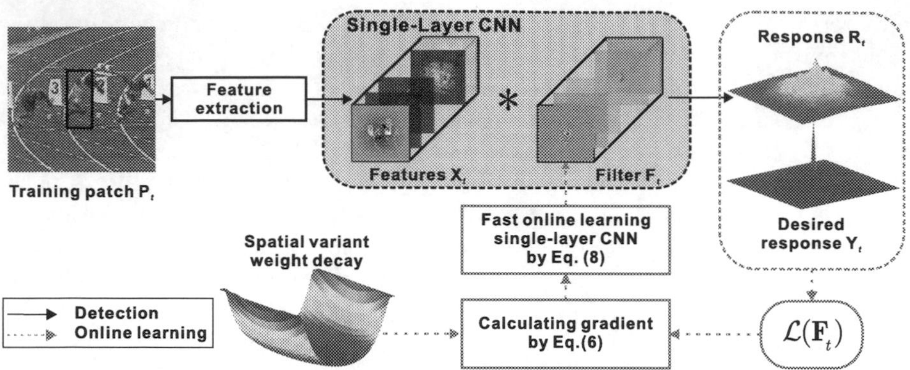

Fig. 2. Pipeline of SRCFNet, '$*$' denotes the circular convolution operation, $\mathrm{L}(\mathbf{F}_t)$ is the loss value defined in Eq. (1). The subscript t of each variable denotes the index of frame.

leads a heavy computing burden in training stage. In spite of applying an iterative Gauss-Seidel method to solve Eq. (3), the computation complexity of $\mathcal{O}(M^3N^3D^3)$ in each iteration cannot meet the satisfaction of real-time tracking scenarios.

SRDCF obtains the tracking response $\mathbf{R} \in \mathcal{R}^{M\times N}$ through the optimized filters. Let $\mathbf{X} \in \mathcal{R}^{M\times N\times D}$ denote features exacted from a patch used for detection or training. The tracking response $\mathbf{R}$ can be computed as following,

$$\mathbf{R} = \sum_{l=1}^{D} \mathbf{X}^l * \mathbf{F}^l = \mathcal{F}^{-1}(\sum_{l=1}^{D} \widehat{\mathbf{X}}^l \odot \widehat{\mathbf{F}}^l). \tag{4}$$

Here, $\mathcal{F}^{-1}(\cdot)$ denotes inverse Discrete Fourier Transformation operation. Owing to the property of convolution in Fourier domain, the cost of detection is reduced to $\mathcal{O}(DMN\log(MN))$ instead of $\mathcal{O}(DM^2N^2)$.

3 The Method

3.1 Fast Spatial Regularization for CF

Given a patch $\mathbf{P} \in \mathcal{R}^{U\times V\times 3}$ and its features $\mathbf{X} \in \mathcal{R}^{M\times N\times D}$, we obtain a response map by filtering $\mathbf{X}$ with filters $\mathbf{F}$, i.e. $\mathbf{R} = \sum_{l=1}^{D} \mathbf{X}^l * \mathbf{F}^l$. The circular convolution used in CF can be regarded as a convolution layer. As introduced in [27], circular convolution can be used to replace the traditional convolution layer to accelerate the CNN, which can be effectively online trained by a number of few-shot learning or truncated iteration techniques. For this reason, the single-layer CNN[1] denoted

[1] The term single-layer convolution network has been used in feature learning [4,20]. With the single-layer CNN, we can jointly learn the deep feature representation and filters to get better tracking accuracy by back propagating the loss to feature network in the future.

as SRCFNet is proposed for fast spatial regularization. The pipeline of SRCFNet is shown in Fig. 2. Note that we remove the subscript t in the paper, which denotes the index of the frame for clarity. Given the desired response $\mathbf{Y}$, we can define a loss function $\mathrm{L}(\mathbf{F})$ for the filters $\mathbf{F}$ by transforming Eq. (1) to

$$\mathrm{L}(\mathbf{F}) = ||\sum_{l=1}^{D} \widehat{\mathbf{X}}^l \odot \mathcal{F}(\mathbf{F}^l) - \widehat{\mathbf{Y}}||^2 + \sum_{l=1}^{D} ||\mathbf{W} \odot \mathbf{F}^l||^2, \tag{5}$$

where $\mathcal{F}(\cdot)$ denotes the DFT operation. With SRCFNet and $\mathrm{L}(\mathbf{F})$, we can online learn $\mathbf{F}$ with technologies of training CNN instead of using iterative optimizing methods, e.g. Gauss-Seidel method, for solving large scale linear system. In particular, two terms of $\mathrm{L}(\mathbf{F})$ are formulated in frequency and spatial domain, respectively. The second term corresponds to the weight decay in a CNN as discussed in [22], which is an important parameter for regularization and plays a key role to avoid overfitting. It, however, is usually set to a fixed value for all parameters when we train CNN [22]. In Eq. (5), SR term actually defines spatial variant weight decays for parameters of correlation filters according to their coordinates. The values of weight decays are determined by the SR weight map $\mathbf{W}$. Besides, Eq. (5) avoids the convolution operation of SR term in frequency domain, as defined in Eq. (3), which can lead to a more efficient iterative process. Please refer to Sect. 3.2 for more details.

Above all, compared with SRDCF, fast spatial regularization is achieved by SRCFNet, which removes the convolution operation in Eq. (3). On the other hand, compared with other deep learning based trackers [29], SRCFNet contains only one layer. It does not need offline training process which costs too much time. Furthermore, due to the single-layer framework, SRCFNet is more efficient in tracking speed.

3.2 Fast Online Learning of SRCFNet

With the loss function defined in Eq. (5), we can efficiently learn filters $\mathbf{F}$ through back-propagation and gradient descent. In the back-propagation stage, we can calculate the gradient of L to each channel $\mathbf{F}^l$ via by chain rule,

$$\frac{\partial \mathrm{L}}{\partial \mathbf{F}^l} = \mathcal{F}^{-1}(\frac{\partial \mathrm{L}}{\partial \widehat{\mathbf{F}}^l}) + 2\mathbf{W} \odot \mathbf{W} \odot \mathbf{F}^l \tag{6}$$

with

$$\frac{\partial \mathrm{L}}{\partial \widehat{\mathbf{F}}^l} = 2(\sum_{l=1}^{D} \widehat{\mathbf{X}}^l \odot \widehat{\mathbf{F}}^l - \widehat{\mathbf{Y}}) \odot \mathrm{conj}(\widehat{\mathbf{X}}^l), \tag{7}$$

where $\mathrm{conj}(\cdot)$ denotes complex conjugate of the variable. Then we can iteratively update $\mathbf{F}^l$ with gradient descent by

$$\mathbf{F}^l_{i+1} = \mathbf{F}^l_i - \eta \frac{\partial \mathrm{L}}{\partial \mathbf{F}^l_i}, \tag{8}$$

Algorithm 1. SRCFNet boosted CF tracker.

Input: Bounding box of the object in the first frame $\mathbf{b}_1 \in \mathcal{R}^4$.
Output: Bounding box of the object in all frames $\{\mathbf{b}_t | t = 1, 2, ..., \text{nFrames}\}$.

Initialize filters $\mathbf{F}_1$ and $t = 1$;
for $t = 1 : \text{nFrames}$ **do**
  if $t > 1$ **then**
    // **Detection stage:**
    Obtain $\mathbf{X}_t^G$ from detection region $\mathbf{G}_t$.
    Obtain $\widehat{\mathbf{X}}_t^G$, $\widehat{\mathbf{F}}_{t-1}$ by applying DFT.
    Calculate response $\widehat{\mathbf{R}}$ with $\widehat{\mathbf{R}}_t = \widehat{\mathbf{X}}_t^G \odot \widehat{\mathbf{F}}_{t-1}$.
    Get $\mathbf{b}_t$ by $\max(\mathcal{F}^{-1}(\widehat{\mathbf{R}}_t))$.
  // **Training stage:**
  Obtain $\mathbf{X}_t$ from $\mathbf{P}_t$ and $\mathbf{X}_{t-1}$.
  for $i = 1 : \text{maxit}$ **do**
    Calculate $\frac{\partial \text{L}}{\partial \widehat{\mathbf{F}}_i^l}$ with Eq. (7).
    Train $\mathbf{F}_i$ by using Eq. (9) in the t-th frame.
  Get the optimized filters $\mathbf{F}_t$.

where η is learning rate of $\mathbf{F}^l$ and the subscript i denotes the i-th iteration. The updating formulation can be described as

$$\mathbf{F}_{i+1}^l = (1 - 2\eta \mathbf{W} \odot \mathbf{W}) \odot \mathbf{F}_i^l - \eta \mathcal{F}^{-1}(\frac{\partial \text{L}}{\partial \widehat{\mathbf{F}}_i^l}). \tag{9}$$

By regarding the SR term as weight decays, convolution operation introduced by SR is removed. We obtain the optimized filters only using elementwise multiplication and DFT instead of matrix multiplication and division. The computing complexity of our learning method is $\mathcal{O}(MND\log(MN))$, being much lower than that of Gauss-Seidel method being $\mathcal{O}(M^3N^3D^3)$. SRCFNet thus achieves a real-time learning in tracking assignment. In addition, we find that changing the coefficients of $\mathbf{W}$ may cause significant change on tracking performance, which verifies that it is important for SRCFNet to set a proper $\mathbf{W}$ for object tracking. The influence of $\mathbf{W}$ will be discussed in Sect. 4.4.

3.3 SRCFNet Boosted CF Tracking

In the first frame, We initialize the filters by solving Eq. (3) using Gauss-Seidel method to give a reliable guidance for learning. As described in [7], we adopt an online updating method for $\mathbf{X}$ which the previous frames are taken into account. In the t-th frame, we extract the features of the training patch $\mathbf{P}_t$ centered at the target and update the features $\mathbf{X}_t$ with a learning rate γ.

In the detection stage, forward process is used to detect the target in the next frame. We extract multi-scale patch $\mathbf{G} \in \mathcal{R}^{U \times V \times 3 \times S}$ where $S \in \{s_1, s_2, ..., s_k\}$ denotes the number of scales. The scale estimation method is borrowed from [7], we use various scales to control the size of target. The scale is decided by the size of target in previous frame. Tracking algorithm is shown in Algorithm 1.

Excluding the cost of feature extraction, the computation complexity of SRCFNet boosted SRDCF sums up to $O(TMNDlog(MN)) + O(SMNDlog(MN))$, while the complexity of SRDCF is $O(TMND(D+K^2))+O(SMNDlog(MN))$, where K is the number of non-zero Fourier coefficients in SR map; T denotes the number of iterations in learning filters; S is the number of scales. The first term in the complexity of each tracker is brought by filters learning, in which SRCFNet boosted SRDCF is much more efficient than SRDCF.

4 Experimental Results

4.1 Setup

Baselines. SRCFNet can be theoretically used to improve not only SR based CF trackers but CF trackers. Although various trackers can be improved by our SRCFNet, for validating SRCFNet, we choose parts of them as our baselines on the basis of distinguishing features and scale estimation methods among them. The introduction of our baseline trackers is shown in Table 1. To ensure a fair comparison with baseline CF trackers, we first improve these selected CF trackers with traditional SR method (if available) and refer them to SAMF_{SR} and DSST_{SR}. Also, we improved all baseline trackers with our SRCFNet and call them $\text{SRDCF}_{\text{SRCFNet}}$, $\text{SAMF}_{\text{SRCFNet}}$ and $\text{DSST}_{\text{SRCFNet}}$. Note, all the trackers in Fig. 3 run on the same workstation (Intel Xeon CPU E5-2687w @3.10 GHz, 128 GB RAM) using MATLAB.

Table 1. Introduction of our baseline trackers

Trackers	Features	Published
DSST [6]	HOG [9]	2014 (BMVC)
SAMF [23]	HOG & color name [19] & intensity	2014 (ECCV-W)
SRDCF [7]	HOG & color name & intensity	2015 (ICCV)

Datasets and Metrics. All the trackers are evaluated on the OTB-100 dataset. Two metrics defined in OTB-100 are success plot and precision plot. Precision plot measures the center error, which computes average Euclidean distance between the center location of bounding box and ground truth in all frames. Success plot is defined as Intersection over Union (IoU) of bounding box and ground truth. The area under curve (AUC) of success plot and precision plot at 20 pixels threshold are used for evaluation. We also involve average fps (frames per second) to evaluate the speed of trackers, which is obtained by averaging the fps in whole 100 sequences.

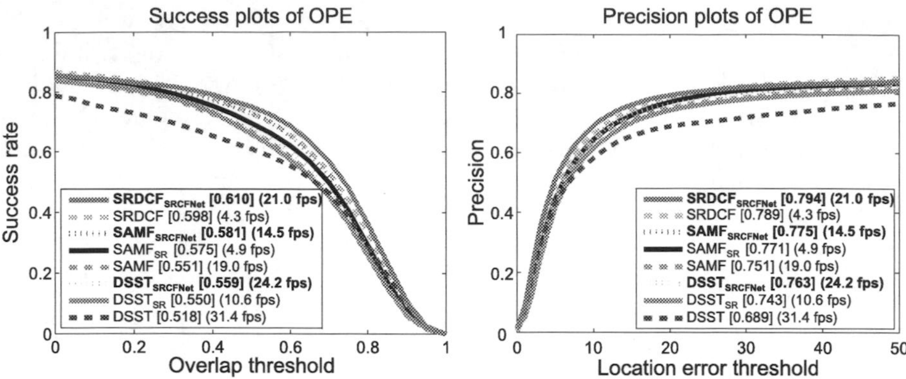

Fig. 3. Comparing baseline trackers, i.e. SRDCF, SAMF and DSST with their SRCFNet and SR boosted versions on OTB-100 in the AUC for success plots and precision at 20 pixels for precision plot. SRCFNet boosted CF trackers outperform all SR boosted ones and baseline trackers on both success and precision plot. Furthermore, all SRCFNet boosted trackers slightly harm speed of baseline trackers and run significantly faster than SR boosted versions.

Parameter Setting. For fair comparison, source codes of all baseline trackers are provided by the authors. With regard to SR and SRCFNet boosted trackers, all the parameters irrelevant to SR are inherited from corresponding baseline trackers. We set γ and η to 0.025 and 0.00015. The iterations of SRCFNet, maxit, are set to 5 and the number of scale S is set to 7 for our trackers.

4.2 SRCFNet Based CF Trackers

Overall Results. Figure 3 shows tracking results of baseline trackers and their SR and SRCFNet improved trackers. Compared with baseline CF trackers containing SAMF and DSST, $\mathrm{SAMF}_{\mathrm{SR}}$ and $\mathrm{DSST}_{\mathrm{SR}}$ have performance development of 4.4% and 6.2% in success plot but reduce the speed to 25.8% and 33.8%. By applying SRCFNet to SAMF and DSST, $\mathrm{SAMF}_{\mathrm{SRCFNet}}$ and $\mathrm{DSST}_{\mathrm{SRCFNet}}$ maintain their strengths in speed. More importantly, the significant improvement of success plot is 5.4% and 7.9% respectively. For SR based tracker, $\mathrm{SRDCF}_{\mathrm{SRCFNet}}$ get 2.0% improvement in success plot and 4.9 times speed development in comparison to SRDCF. With 1.0% and 1.6% respective development in success plot and 3.0 and 2.3 times promotion in speed, $\mathrm{SAMF}_{\mathrm{SRCFNet}}$ and $\mathrm{DSST}_{\mathrm{SRCFNet}}$ show their advantages compared to corresponding SR improved trackers in speed and tracking accuracy.

Qualitative Results. As shown in Fig. 4, some challenging scenarios are illustrated to validate our method. Compared with baseline trackers and SR improved trackers, trackers with SRCFNet have convincing tracking results in most cases. In the first row of Fig. 4, the tracking target suffers a complete occlusion by a pedestrian. $\mathrm{SRDCF}_{\mathrm{SRCFNet}}$ can track the correct target with a tight bounding

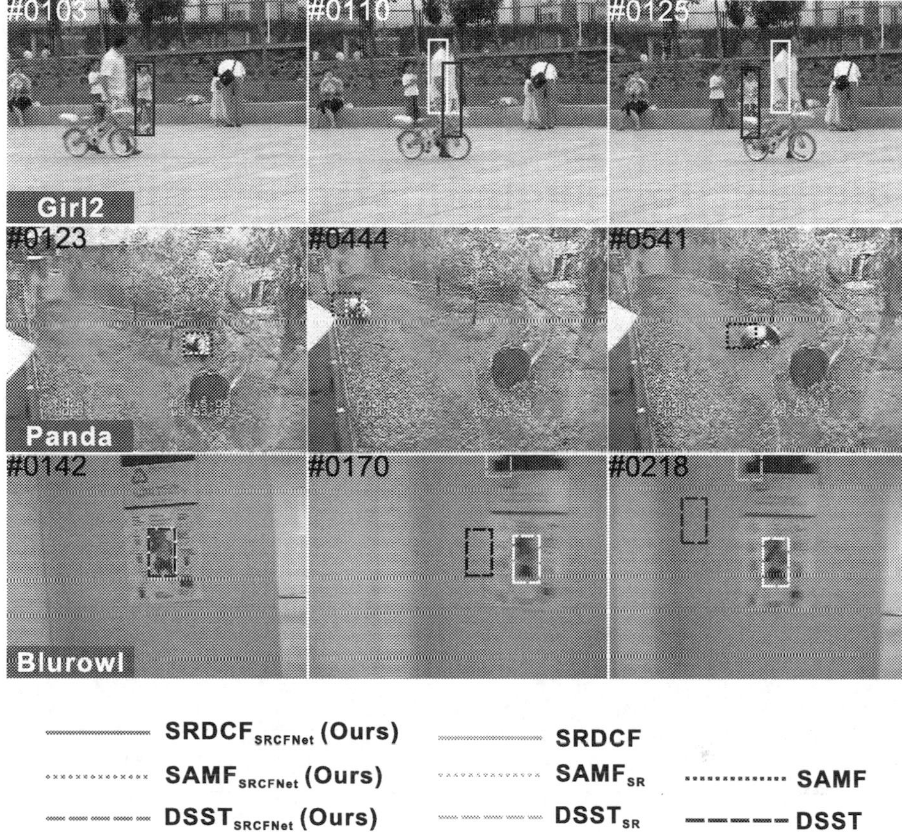

Fig. 4. Qualitative comparison between baseline trackers, i.e. SRDCF, SAMF and DSST, and their SR and SRCFNet boosted versions on sequences: girl2, panda, blurowl, respectively.

box. In the sequence 'panda', panda walks around in the scene with obvious scale changes and object deformation occurs. SAMF and $\mathrm{SAMF}_{\mathrm{SR}}$ appear scale and position inaccuracy in varying degrees. The corresponding SRCFNet improved tracker, $\mathrm{SAMF}_{\mathrm{SRCFNet}}$, captures the panda tightly and has an accurate scale estimation. In 'blurowl' sequence, the target is difficult to track due to the irregular, fast moving and serious motion blur. $\mathrm{DSST}_{\mathrm{SR}}$ and DSST miss the target completely and get meaningless bounding boxes, while the strength of $\mathrm{DSST}_{\mathrm{SRCFNet}}$ is stood out in dealing with fast motion and motion blur.

4.3 Comparison with State-of-the-Art Trackers

Overall Results. We compare the best performing SRCFNet improved tracker ($\mathrm{SRDCF}_{\mathrm{SRCFNet}}$) with the most recent state-of-the-art trackers ($\mathrm{STAPLE}_{\mathrm{CA}}$ [28], DSiamM [13], CFNet [31], LMCF [32], CSR-DCF [24], LCT [26], DLSSVM

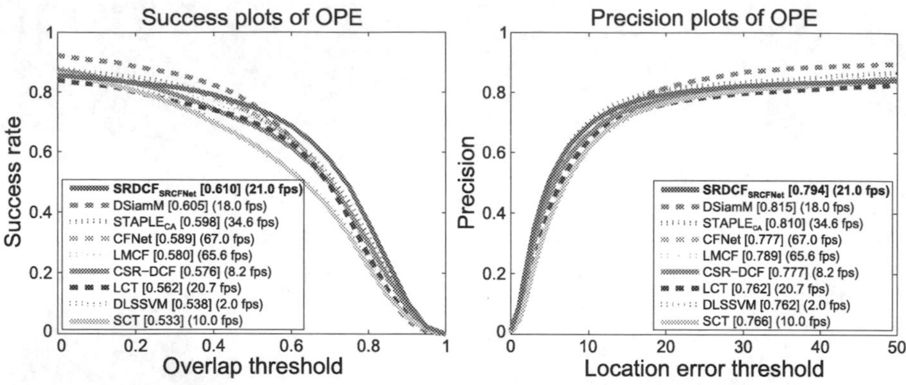

Fig. 5. Comparison results of state-of-art trackers on OTB-100. $\text{SRDCF}_{\text{SRCFNet}}$ outperforms all other trackers on success plot AUC and is slightly worse than DSiamM and $\text{STAPLE}_{\text{CA}}$ on the precision at 20 pixels. Note, $\text{SRDCF}_{\text{SRCFNet}}$ does much better than CSR-DCF, another improved SRDCF, on both accuracy and speed.

[30], SCT [3]). These trackers are not necessarily CF based. As shown in Fig. 5, our tracker, with a near real-time speed, outperforms all other reported trackers in success plot on OTB-100 benchmark. Compared with some trackers in CF framework such as $\text{STAPLE}_{\text{CA}}$, LMCF, CSR-DCF, LCT and SCT, $\text{SRDCF}_{\text{SRCFNet}}$ achieves 2.0%, 5.2%, 5.9%, 8.5% and 14.4% improvement respectively in success plot. Two popular trackers (DSiamM, CFNet), which are not based on CF, are considered. Although DSiamM and CFNet adopt more discriminative deep features, $\text{SRDCF}_{\text{SRCFNet}}$ simply using traditional features outperforms DSiamM and CFNet with 0.8% and 3.6% respective improvement in success plot. DLSSVM, a tracker based on SVM, is also introduced to validate our method. Compared with DLSSVM, $\text{SRDCF}_{\text{SRCFNet}}$ obtains 13.3% improvement in success plot and 10.5 times speed boosting. In regard of precision plot, $\text{SRDCF}_{\text{SRCFNet}}$ is slightly worse than DSiamM and $\text{STAPLE}_{\text{CA}}$ but has a better performance than other trackers. Note that results of DSiamM, $\text{STAPLE}_{\text{CA}}$ and CSR-DCF run on our computer by using open source code provided by authors. Results of other trackers are downloaded from the home page of authors.

Attribute Based Comparison. We evaluate tracking accuracy in different cases sorted by attributes which are provided by OTB-100. Our tracker achieves performance boosting in most challenging cases especially in four attributes (occlusion, scale variation, fast motion and motion blur) shown in Fig. 6. Compared with recent CF based tracker, $\text{STAPLE}_{\text{CA}}$, which also uses context information to improve CF based tracker, $\text{SRDCF}_{\text{SRCFNet}}$ outperforms $\text{STAPLE}_{\text{CA}}$ with 5.6%, 9.0%, 3.6% and 9.4% corresponding development for each attribute.

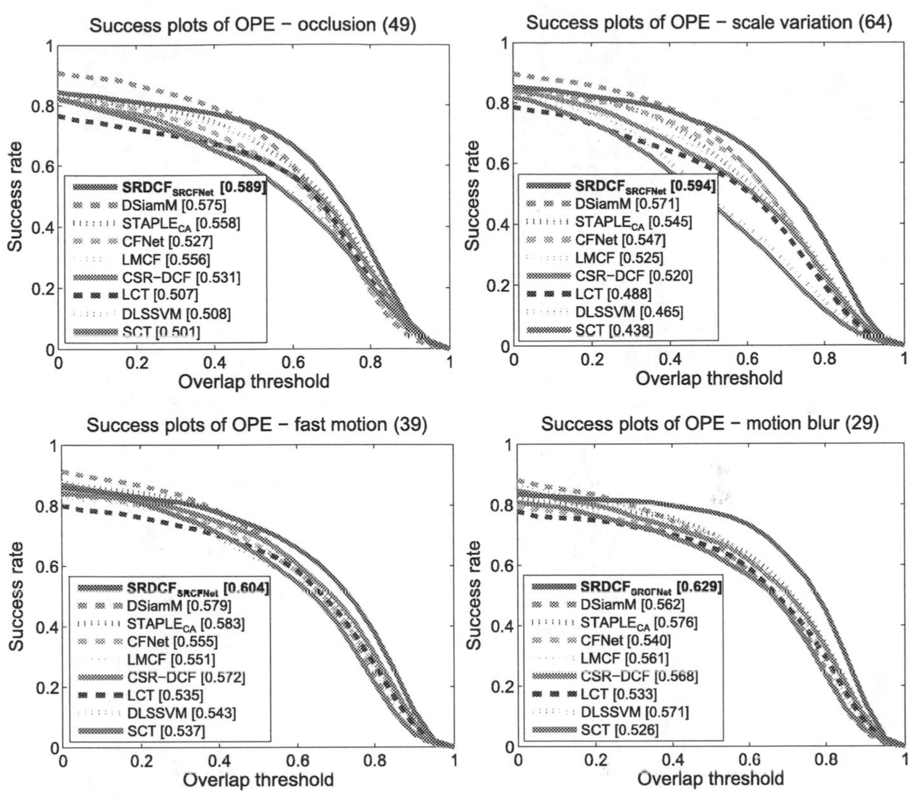

Fig. 6. Comparison results of state-of-art trackers on four subsets of OTB-100 corresponding to four attributes, i.e. occlusion, scale variation, fast motion and motion blur. Our method outperforms all other trackers on the four subsets, which demonstrates the excellent performance of our method on addressing above kinds of challenges.

4.4 Discussion About SR Weight Map W

In practice, different shapes of $\mathbf{W}$ can lead significantly discriminative tracking performances. In this section, we discuss the importance of choosing $\mathbf{W}$ by setting different n. Figure 7(a) shows the cross section shapes of different $\mathbf{W}$. Note that we set a threshold for $\mathbf{W}$ in order to avoid unpractical weight decays and the threshold is set to 100 for preferable results. It is shown that power value n obviously affects the coefficients of $\mathbf{W}$ which locate at the background region while the coefficients of $\mathbf{W}$ in target region scarcely change. In Fig. 7(b), we further discuss the relationship between tracking performance on OTB-100 and the confining ability of SR by setting different values of n. The 2-norm of $\mathbf{F}_{bg}$ is introduced to represent the confining ability of SR. Note that $\mathbf{F}_{bg}$ denotes the filters whose coordinates belong to the background. We calculate $\mathbf{F}_{bg}$ by setting the coefficient of $\mathbf{F}$, which belongs to target region, to zero. With the increasing confining ability of SR, tracking performance becomes better in a

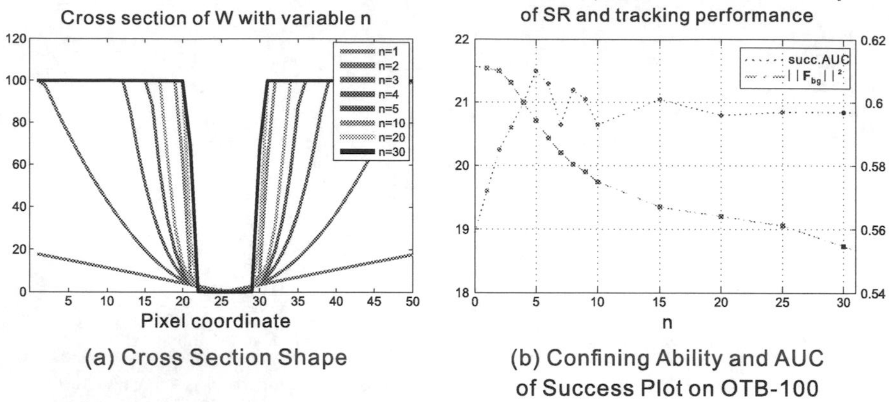

(a) Cross Section Shape

(b) Confining Ability and AUC of Success Plot on OTB-100

Fig. 7. Influence of **W**. (a) Shows the cross section shapes of **W** by setting different power values n in Eq. (2). (b) Illustrates the relationship between n and the effectiveness of SR as well as tracking performance. We use the 2-norm of $\mathbf{F}_{bg}$ (green) defined in Sect. 4.4 and success plot AUC of $\mathrm{SRDCF}_{\mathrm{SRCFNet}}$ on OTB-100 (blue) to represent effectiveness of SR and tracking performance, respectively. 2-norm of $\mathbf{F}_{bg}$ corresponds to the left y-axis and AUC for success plot corresponds to the right y-axis. (Color figure online)

certain range (n from 1 to 5) and stays stable when $n > 10$. When n is set to 1, the coefficient of filters in the background is not much penalized, which too much background information interferes tracking performance. When $n > 10$, little background information is considered in the process of learning **F** and lead to missing the optimal solution. Above all, it is necessary to introduce proper background information in training more discriminative filters.

5 Conclusion

In this paper, we proposed an effective and much faster model for spatially-regularized correlation filters. By regarding correlation filtering as a single-layer CNN denoted as SRCFNet, we can efficiently online learn the filters with the spatial regularization (SR) weight map being spatial variant weight decays. The time-consuming operations of classical SR at each iteration, i.e. matrix division and convolution, can thus be avoided. As a result, SRCFNet significantly accelerates SRDCF [7] with near 5 times speedup while getting even better tracking accuracy on OTB-100. Furthermore, our method, being an alternative to classical SR, has significantly improved the tracking accuracy of two mainstream CF trackers while maintaining their near real-time speed.

In the future, we plan to extend our model by jointly learning deep feature representation and the correlation filters by back propagating the loss to feature network, thus could achieve higher tracking accuracy. Furthermore, segmentation

[10,14] and saliency information [18] can be introduced in our method to achieve higher tracking accuracy.

References

1. Bertinetto, L., Valmadre, J., Golodetz, S., Miksik, O., Torr, P.H.S.: Staple: complementary learners for real-time tracking. In: CVPR (2016)
2. Chen, Z., Guo, Q., Wan, L., Feng, W.: Background-suppressed correlation filters for visual tracking. In: ICME (2018)
3. Choi, J., Chang, H., Jeong, J., Demiris, Y., Jin, Y.: Visual tracking using attention-modulated disintegration and integration. In: CVPR (2016)
4. Coates, A., Lee, H., Ng, A.: An analysis of single-layer networks in unsupervised feature learning. In: AISTATS (2011)
5. Danelljan, M., Bhat, G., Khan, F., Felsberg, M.: ECO: efficient convolution operators for tracking. In: CVPR (2017)
6. Danelljan, M., Häger, G., Khan, F.S., Felsberg, M.: Accurate scale estimation for robust visual tracking. In: BMVC (2014)
7. Danelljan, M., Häger, G., Khan, F.S., Felsberg, M.: Learning spatially regularized correlation filters for visual tracking. In: ICCV (2015)
8. Danelljan, M., Robinson, A., Khan, F., Felsberg, M.: Beyond correlation filters: learning continuous convolution operators for visual tracking. In: ECCV (2016)
9. Dollar, P.: Piotr's computer vision matlab toolbox: histogram of oriented gradients
10. Feng, W., Jia, J., Liu, Z.Q.: Self-validated labeling of Markov random fields for image segmentation. IEEE TPAMI **32**(10), 1871–1887 (2010)
11. Galoogahi, H.K., Sim, T., Lucey, S.: Correlation filters with limited boundaries. In: CVPR (2015)
12. Guo, Q., Feng, W., Zhou, C.: Structure-regularized compressive tracking with online data-driven sampling. IEEE TIP **26**(12), 5692–5705 (2017)
13. Guo, Q., Feng, W., Zhou, C., Huang, R., Wan, L., Wang, S.: Learning dynamic Siamese network for visual object tracking. In: ICCV (2017)
14. Guo, Q., Sun, S., Ren, X., Dong, F., Gao, B., Feng, W.: Frequency-tuned active contour model. Neurocomputing **275**, 2307–2316 (2018)
15. Han, R.Z., Guo, Q., Feng, W.: Content-related spatial regularization for visual object tracking. In: ICME (2018)
16. Hare, S., Saffari, A., Torr, P.H.S.: Struck: structured output tracking with kernels. In: ICCV (2011)
17. Henriques, J.F., Caseiro, R., Martins, P., Batista, J.: High-speed tracking with kernelized correlation filters. IEEE TPAMI (2015)
18. Huang, R., Feng, W., Sun, J.: Color feature reinforcement for co-saliency detection without single saliency residuals. IEEE SPL **24**(5), 569–573 (2017)
19. Van De Weijer, J., Schmid, C., Verbeek, J., Larlus, D.: Learning color names for real-world applications. IEEE TIP **18**(7), 1512–1523 (2009)
20. Knerr, S., Personnaz, L., Dreyfus, G.: Handwritten digit recognition by neural networks with single-layer training. IEEE TNN **3**(6), 962–968 (1992)
21. Kristan, M., Matas, J., Leonardis, A., Vojir, T., Pflugfelder, R., Fernandez, G., Nebehay, G., Porikli, F., Cehovin, L.: A novel performance evaluation methodology for single-target trackers. IEEE TPAMI **38**(11), 2137–2155 (2016)
22. Krizhevsky, A., Sutskever, I., Hinton, G.E.: Imagenet classification with deep convolutional neural networks. In: NIPS (2012)

23. Li, Y., Zhu, J.: A scale adaptive kernel correlation filter tracker with feature integration. In: ECCVW (2014)
24. Lukezic, A., Vojir, T., Cehovin, L., Matas, J., Kristan, M.: Discriminative correlation filter with channel and spatial reliability. In: CVPR (2017)
25. Ma, C., Huang, J.B., Yang, X., Yang, M.H.: Hierarchical convolutional features for visual tracking. In: ICCV (2015)
26. Ma, C., Yang, X., Zhang, C., Yang, M.H.: Long-term correlation tracking. In: CVPR (2015)
27. Mathieu, M., Henaff, M., Lecun, Y.: Fast training of convolutional networks through FFTs. In: ICLR (2014)
28. Mueller, M., Smith, N., Ghanem, B.: Context-aware correlation filter tracking. In: CVPR (2017)
29. Nam, H., Han, B.: Learning multi-domain convolutional neural networks for visual tracking. In: CVPR (2016)
30. Ning, J., Yang, J., Jiang, S., Zhang, L., Yang, M.: Object tracking via dual linear structured SVM and explicit feature map. In: CVPR (2016)
31. Valmadre, J., Bertinetto, L., Henriques, J.F., Vedaldi, A., Torr, P.H.S.: End-to-end representation learning for correlation filter based tracking. In: CVPR (2017)
32. Wang, M., Liu, Y., Huang, Z.: Large margin object tracking with circulant feature maps. In: CVPR (2017)
33. Wu, Y., Lim, J., Yang, M.H.: Online object tracking: a benchmark. In: CVPR (2013)
34. Zhou, C., Guo, Q., Wan, L., Feng, W.: Selective object and context tracking. In: ICASSP (2017)

Similarity-Adaptive Latent Low-Rank Representation for Robust Data Representation

Lei Wang[1], Zhao Zhang[1(✉)], Sheng Li[2], Guangcan Liu[3], Chenping Hou[4], and Jie Qin[5]

[1] School of Computer Science and Technology, Soochow University, Suzhou 215006, China
cszhang@gmail.com
[2] Adobe Research, Adobe Systems Inc, San Jose, CA 95110, USA
[3] School of Information and Control, Nanjing University of Information Science and Technology, Nanjing, China
[4] College of Science, National University of Defense Technology, Changsha, China
[5] Computer Vision Laboratory, ETH Zürich, 8092 Zürich, Switzerland

Abstract. We propose a novel Similarity-Adaptive Latent Low-Rank Representation (SA-LatLRR) model for the robust representation and subspace recovery. SA-LatLRR inherits all merits of recent LatLRR, and further improves it by enhancing the representations. SA-LatLRR aims at decomposing given data into a principal feature part encoded by the Frobenius-norm based coefficients, a similarity-adaptive salient feature part and a sparse error part. Specifically, our SA-LatLRR incorporates a reconstructive error minimization term over coefficients and salient features, which can clearly preserve the neighborhood information of salient features adaptively. The added regularization can also encourage the coefficients to be block-diagonal and discriminative, as the shared coefficients could minimize the reconstruction errors over both original data and salient features at the same time, where the embedded salient features contain less noise and unfavorable features than the original data. Moreover, to make salient features more informative and robust to noise, SA-LatLRR imposes the sparse L2,1-norm and low-rank constraints on the projection jointly so that the features are more notable and discriminative. The Frobenius-norm based principal feature part can also make the coefficients coding process very efficient. Extensive comparison results demonstrate the validity of our SA-LatLRR.

Keywords: Similarity-adaptive latent LRR · Robust data representation Salient feature extraction · Classification

1 Introduction

With the increasing volume and complicated contents (e.g., high-dimensional attributes, corruptions, unfavorable features) of data in the areas of pattern recognition and data mining, how to represent data by learning compact and robust expressions is still

X. Geng and B.-H. Kang (Eds.): PRICAI 2018, LNAI 11012, pp. 71–84, 2018.
https://doi.org/10.1007/978-3-319-97304-3_6

an important topic. Towards dealing with this problem to extract useful information from data, several feasible approaches can be used, e.g., dimension reduction [1–3], sparse representation [17, 18] and low-rank recovery [5, 7–11]. In this study, the data representation issue by low-rank subspace recovery is discussed, which is motivated by the fact that low-rank matrices can be observed in various applications and real high-dimensional data usually lie in or lie near a low-rank subspace [1–4, 6–14].

Two representative low-rank representation models are Robust Principal Component Analysis (RPCA) [5] and Low-Rank Representation (LRR) [10, 11]. RPCA and LRR aim at decomposing given data into a low-rank component and a sparse error part, where the low-rank part corresponds to the compact representations of data. Due to the low-rank coding, RPCA and LRR can well handle the corruptions and correct errors. Compared with RPCA, LRR considers a more general case that the data are approximately drawn from several low-rank subspaces [10, 11]. Thus, LRR can handle the mixed data well. Note that both RPCA and LRR are essentially transductive models, i.e., they cannot handle new data efficiently. Specifically, when given a new data, RPCA and LRR have to recalculate over all data again, which usually leads to high cost and restricts them to the applications needing fast online computations. In recent years, several efforts have been made to improve RPCA and LRR for handling the recovery and error correction issues by extending them to the inductive scenario. One enhanced version of RPCA is Inductive Robust Principal Component Analysis (IRPCA) [9] that learns a nuclear norm minimization based low-rank projection to process the new datum by embedding samples into their respective underlying subspaces [9]. Another popular method is Latent Low-Rank Representation (LatLRR) [19] that is an enhanced version of LRR by recovering the hidden effects and integrating certain latent observations for low-rank basis estimation. As a result, the insufficient sampling issue suffered by LRR can be solved and the robustness to noise can also be enhanced. Compared with LRR, the modeling of LatLRR seamlessly integrates the subspace segmentation and feature extraction into a unified model, i.e., it decomposes given data into a low-rank principal feature part, a low-rank salient feature part and a sparse error. Moreover, the representation process of LatLRR can preserve both row and column information of given data, compared with LRR and IRPCA [21]. Thus, the representation of LatLRR may be more informative than those of LRR and IRPCA in reality, but note that LatLRR did not correlate the representation coefficients and salient features during the low-rank decomposition process explicitly, which may potentially result in the degraded representations.

It is worth noting that existing low-rank coding methods usually cannot preserve the local geometry structures of learnt coefficients or the salient features in an adaptive manner. Although several efforts have been made to preserve local information of learnt coefficients or low-rank representations in the processes of LRR and LatLRR [15, 16], they still suffer from two drawbacks. First, existing local low-rank coding models usually pre-calculate the weights to measure the pairwise similarities of data prior to the low-rank coding step, but such operation cannot ensure the pre-computed weights to be optimal for subsequent low-rank coding. Second, the pre-calculated weights usually use the k-neighborhood or ε-neighborhood to find the neighbors of each sample, but the optimal determination of parameter k and ε which usually needs the transcendental knowledge to choose remains an open problem to date.

In this paper, we therefore propose a similarity-adaptive strategy to address the above drawbacks, i.e., preserving neighborhood information adaptively among salient features without the requirement to specify the choices of k and ε. The main contributions of this paper are summarized as follows:

- We propose a novel Similarity-Adaptive Latent Low-Rank Representation framework called SA-LatLRR technically for robust representation and subspace recovery. SA-LatLRR is based on the formulation of LatLRR, so it inherits all merits of LatLRR. More importantly, our SA-LatLRR further improves LatLRR by correlating the representation coefficients and salient features during the low-rank decomposition process to preserve the local neighborhood information. Specifically, our SA-LatLRR aims at decomposing given data matrix into a principal feature part encoded using a set of Frobenius-norm based coefficients, a similarity-adaptive salient feature part and a sparse component part. For similarity-adaptive salient feature extraction, SA-LatLRR incorporates a reconstructive error minimization term over coefficients and salient features jointly, which preserves the neighborhood information among salient features adaptively.
- The included reconstructive error minimization term can also encourage the learnt coefficients to be block-diagonal and discriminative, which can be observed from the example in Fig. 1, because the shared coefficients could jointly minimize the reconstruction errors over original data and salient features at the same time, Note that the salient features by the neighborhood preserving low-rank embedding of SA-LatLRR usually contain less noise and unfavorable features than original data.
- To make the learnt salient features more informative and robust to noise, our SA-LatLRR imposes the sparse L2,1-norm and low-rank constraints jointly on the projection so that the notable and discriminative salient features can be predicted in the latent sparse and low-rank subspaces [22–24, 29]. In addition, the Frobenius-norm is used to encode the principal features. Although the Frobenius-norm is just an approximation to Nuclear-norm, we still experimentally find that block-diagonal structures can also be delivered as can be observed from Fig. 1, where we can also find that less wrong intra-class connections and better intra-class connectivity are obtained. Besides, the Frobenius-norm can also make the coefficients coding process efficient, since it avoids the eigen-decomposition process in LatLRR.

The outline of this paper is organized as follows. In Sect. 2, we briefly review LatLRR. In Sect. 3, we introduce our SA-LatLRR, and also discuss the relations to other related low-rank algorithms. Section 4 shows the experimental results and analysis. Section 5 draws the conclusion of this paper.

2 Related Work: LatLRR

Given a set of samples in $X = [x_1, \ldots x_N] \in \mathbb{R}^{d \times N}$, where d denotes the original dimension and N is the number of samples, LatLRR improves LRR using the unobserved hidden data to extend the dictionary and thus overcome the insufficient data sampling issue. To recover the hidden data, LatLRR considers the following minimization problem:

$$\min_{Z} \|Z\|_*, \quad s.t.\ X_O = [X_O, X_H]Z, \tag{1}$$

where $\|Z\|_*$ denotes the nuclear-norm [9–11, 19], i.e., the sum of the singular values, X_O is the observed data and X_H denotes unobserved hidden data. Suppose $Z_{O,H} = [Z_{O|H}, Z_{H|O}]$ is the solution to this problem, where $Z_{O|H}$ and $Z_{H|O}$ respectively correspond to X_O and X_H, and let X_H be the skinny SVD of $[X_O, X_H]$ and partition V as $V = [V_O, V_H]$ such that $X_O = U\Sigma V_O^{\mathrm{T}}$ and $X_H = U\Sigma V_H^{\mathrm{T}}$, the above constraint can be simplified as $X_O = X_O Z_{O|H} + L_{H|O}X_O$, where $L_{H|O} = U\Sigma V_H^{\mathrm{T}} V_H \Sigma^{-1} U^{\mathrm{T}}$, which has been improved in LatLRR. Since both $Z_{O|H}$ and $L_{H|O}$ should be low-ranked, one can let Z and P represent $Z_{O|H}$ and $L_{H|O}$ simply. As the sparse L1-norm is used on E, LatLRR recovers the hidden effects by minimizing the following problem:

$$\min_{Z,P,E} \|Z\|_* + \|P\|_* + \lambda\|E\|_1, \quad s.t.\ X = XZ + PX + E, \tag{2}$$

where XZ, PX and E are principal features, salient features and sparse error respectively, and $\lambda > 0$ is a parameter depending on the noise level [9–11]. No adjustable parameter is used between Z and P since they can be balanced automatically [9].

3 Similarity-Adaptive Latent Low-Rank Representation (SA-LatLRR) for Robust Data Representation

3.1 Proposed Formulation

We present the objective function of SA-LatLRR in this section. Note that our SA-LatLRR improves the performances of LatLRR in two aspects. First, to build the connection between principal features XZ and the salient features PX for enhancing the data representations, we add a reconstructive error minimization term $\|PX - PXZ\|_F^2$ over the coefficients Z and salient features PX into the objective function of LatLRR, which can also keep the neighborhood information among salient features adaptively. We also regularize the Frobenius-norm on the coefficients to make the process efficient. These lead to the following initial optimization problem:

$$\min_{Z,P} \frac{1}{2}\|Z\|_F^2 + \|P\|_* + \frac{\beta}{2}\|PX - PXZ\|_F^2 + \lambda\|X - XZ - PX\|_1. \tag{3}$$

Clearly, the shared coefficients Z can minimize the reconstruction errors over both original data and salient features at the same time, where the encoded salient features by embedding usually contain less noise and unfavorable features than original data, so the incorporated regularization $\|PX - PXZ\|_F^2$ with the Frobenius-norm based coefficients can encourage learnt coding coefficients to be block-diagonal and discriminative implicitly, as can be observed from Fig. 1. The Frobenius-norm based principal feature part can also make the coefficients coding process very efficient.

The nuclear-norm based projection P can ensure salient features PX hold the low-rank properties, but it cannot ensure the extracted features hold the sparse and discriminating abilities explicitly. To make the learnt salient features more informative and robust to noise, our SA-LatLRR imposes the L2,1-norm constraints on the projection in addition. Since $X - XZ - PX = E$, the objective function can be reformulated as

$$\min_{Z,P,E} \frac{1}{2}\|Z\|_F^2 + (1-\alpha)\|P\|_* + \alpha\|P\|_{2,1} + \frac{\beta}{2}\|PX - PXZ\|_F^2 + \lambda\|E\|_1, \quad s.t.\ X = XZ + PX + E, \tag{4}$$

where α balances the low-rank and sparse effects on P, and β trades-off the contributions of the adaptive neighborhood reconstruction error in minimizing the objective function value. Note that the unified formulation of our SA-LatLRR has three major variables (i.e., Z, P and E), so the optimization of the SA-LatLRR formulation can be performed alternately between the following two steps:

(1) ***Adaptive neighborhood preserving low-rank and sparse projection learning:*** When the coefficients matrix Z is known, we focus on learning the joint low-rank and sparse projection P for neighborhood preserving salient feature extraction. Since Z is fixed in this step, $\|Z\|_F^2$ is a constant. Thus, the reduced problem can be defined as

$$\min_{P,E} (1-\alpha)\|P\|_* + \alpha\|P\|_{2,1} + \frac{\beta}{2}\|PX - PXZ\|_F^2 + \lambda\|E\|_1, \quad s.t.\ (X - XZ) = PX + E. \tag{5}$$

Clearly, the joint low-rank and sparse projection learning is based on data $X - XZ$, and the representation coefficients matrix Z is applied as the adaptive reconstruction weight matrix for measuring the similarities of salient features PX. As a result, the neighborhood information of salient features can be effectively preserved due to the regularization $\|PX - PXZ\|_F^2$. In other words, the above problem forces the weight matrix Z to simultaneously minimize the reconstruction error over PX, which can enhance the learning result potentially. After P is obtained, we can update the coefficients matrix Z alternately by the following representation learning process.

(2) ***The Frobenius-norm based representation coefficients learning:*** When the joint low-rank and sparse projection P is obtained, we focus on learning the coefficients matrix Z by the following Frobenius-norm based problem:

$$\min_{Z,E} \frac{1}{2}\|Z\|_F^2 + \frac{\beta}{2}\|PX - PXZ\|_F^2 + \lambda\|E\|_1, \quad s.t.\ (X - PX) = XZ + E, \tag{6}$$

from which we can see that the coefficients learning process of Z depends on the original data and salient features PX as the same time. By substituting the error back into the above problem, we can have the following equivalent formulation:

$$\min_{Z,E} \frac{1}{2}\|Z\|_F^2 + \frac{\beta}{2}\|PX - PXZ\|_F^2 + \lambda\|(X - PX) - XZ\|_1. \quad (7)$$

It is clear that the shared representation coefficients Z aims at minimizing the reconstruction errors over both original data and salient features, while the salient feature learning process by joint low-rank and sparse embedding can remove noise and unfavorable features, so the joint minimization of $\|PX - PXZ\|_F^2$ and $\|(X - PX) - XZ\|_1$ can guarantee the learnt coefficients to be more informative for representation.

3.2 Optimization

We describe the optimization procedures of our new approach. Similar to LatLRR, we also employ the inexact Augmented Lagrange Multiplier (Inexact ALM) [20, 25] method for efficiency. Following the common optimization procedures [9–11, 19], we also introduce two auxiliary variables J and F to make the objective function easily solvable. The augmented Lagrangian function $\wp$ can be constructed as

$$\begin{aligned} \wp(Z,P,E,J,F,Y_1,Y_2,Y_3,\mu) &= \frac{1}{2}\|Z\|_F^2 + (1-\alpha)\|J\|_* + \alpha\|F\|_{2,1} + \lambda\|E\|_1 \\ &+ \frac{\beta}{2}\|PX - PXZ\|_F^2 + \langle Y_1, X - XZ - PX - E\rangle + \langle Y_2, P - J\rangle + \langle Y_3, P - F\rangle \\ &+ \frac{\mu}{2}\left(\|X - XZ - PX - E\|_F^2 + \|P - J\|_F^2 + \|P - F\|_F^2\right), \end{aligned} \quad (8)$$

where Y_1, Y_2 and Y_3 denote the Lagrangian multipliers, μ is a weighting factor and $\langle A, B\rangle = trace(A^T B)$. It should be noticed that the involved several variables in our framework cannot be solved directly, since they depend on each other. Therefore, we follow the common procedures and use an alternative updating strategy, i.e., updating one variable by fixing the others at each time. Using the inexact ALM, the variables can be updated by solving the augmented Lagrangian function $\wp$:

$$(Z_{k+1}, P_{k+1}, E_{k+1}, J_{k+1}, F_{k+1}) = \arg\min_{Z,P,E,J,F} \wp_k(Z,P,E,J,F). \quad (9)$$

Thus, the optimization of our proposed SA-LatLRR framework can be detailed as:

- **Fix others, update J, F and E:**
  When Z and P are fixed, we first describe how to update the auxiliary variable J. For the optimization of J, other variables are fixed as constants. By removing terms irrelevant to J, we can update J_{k+1} at the *(k + 1)*-th iteration from the following problem:

$$J_{k+1} = \arg\min_{J} \left((1-\alpha)/\mu_k\right)\|J\|_* + \frac{1}{2}\left\|J - \left(P_k - Y_2^k/\mu_k\right)\right\|_F^2. \quad (10)$$

  Following the common optimization of Nuclear-norm based problem [9–11], one can similarly update J by SVD. Note that the updating procedures of F and E are also similar to solve J. Specifically, we can update F_{k+1} and E_{k+1} by [9]:

$$F_{k+1} = \arg\min_{F} (\alpha/\mu_k)\|F\|_{2,1} + \frac{1}{2}\left\|F - \left(P_k + Y_3^k/\mu_k\right)\right\|_F^2, \quad (11)$$

$$E_{k+1} = \arg\min_{E} (\lambda/\mu_k)\|E\|_1 + \frac{1}{2}\left\|E - \left(X - XZ_k - P_kX + Y_1^k/\mu_k\right)\right\|_F^2. \quad (12)$$

- **Fix others, update the coefficients *Z* and projection *P***:
  With the other variables updated, we are ready to compute Z and P. We first update Z. By dropping terms independent of Z from the Lagrangian function, taking the derivative with respect to Z and zeroing the derivative, we can easily infer Z_{k+1} as

$$Z_{k+1} = \left(\left(I + \beta X^{\mathrm{T}} P_k^{\mathrm{T}} P_k X\right)/\mu_k + X^{\mathrm{T}} X\right)^{-1} X^{\mathrm{T}}\left(\left(\beta P_k^{\mathrm{T}} P_k X + Y_1^k\right)/\mu_k + X - P_k X - E_{k+1}\right), \quad (13)$$

where I is an identity matrix. By dropping the terms independent of P, taking the derivative with respect to variable P and zeroing it, we can similarly update P_{k+1} as

$$\begin{aligned} P_{k+1} = & \left[\left(Y_1^k X^{\mathrm{T}} - Y_2^k - Y_3^k\right)/\mu_k + (X - XZ_{k+1} - E_{k+1})X^{\mathrm{T}} + J_{k+1} + F_{k+1}\right] \\ & \times \left[2\beta(X - XZ_{k+1})(X - XZ_{k+1})^{\mathrm{T}}/\mu_k\right]^{-1}. \end{aligned} \quad (14)$$

For complete presentation of our approach, we summarize the optimization procedures below. The major computational cost of SA-LatLRR is computing the SVD of matrix. Thus, the problem of our SA-LatLRR is also calculated with the complexity of $O(d^2N + d^3)$, which is the same as that of the existing LRR and IRPCA, etc.

Inputs: Training data matrix $X = [x_1, x_2, \ldots, x_N] \in \mathbb{R}^{n\times N}$, parameters α, β and λ;
Initialization: $k = 0$, $J_k = 0$, $F_k = 0$, $E_k = 0$, $Z_k = 0$, $P_k = 0$, $Y_1^k = 0$, $Y_2^k = 0$, $Y_3^k = 0$, $\max_\mu = 10^{10}$, $\mu_k = 10^{-6}$, $\eta = 1.12$, $\varepsilon = 10^{-6}$;
While not converged do

1. Fix others to update the low-rank matrix J_{k+1} by Eq.(10);
2. Fix others to update the sparse matrix F_{k+1} by Eq.(11);
3. Fix others to update the sparse error matrix E_{k+1} by Eq.(12);
4. Fix others to update the representation coefficients Z_{k+1} by Eq.(13);
5. Fix others to update the projection matrix P_{k+1} by Eq.(14);
6. Update the Lagrange multipliers Y_1, Y_2 and Y_3 by $Y_1^{k+1} = Y_1^k + \mu_k(X - XZ_{k+1} - P_{k+1}X - E_{k+1})$, $Y_2^{k+1} = Y_2^k + \mu_k(P_{k+1} - J_{k+1})$, $Y_3^{k+1} = Y_3^k + \mu_k(P_{k+1} - F_{k+1})$;
7. Update the parameter μ with $\mu_{k+1} = \min(\eta\mu_k, \max_\mu)$;
8. Check for convergence: if $\max(\|P_{k+1} - J_{k+1}\|_\infty, \|P_{k+1} - F_{k+1}\|_\infty, \|X - XZ_{k+1} - P_{k+1}X - E_{k+1}\|_\infty)$ $< \varepsilon$, stop; else $k=k+1$.

End while
Output: $P^* \leftarrow P^{k+1}$, $Z^* \leftarrow Z^{k+1}$ and $E^* \leftarrow E^{k+1}$.

3.3 Discussion: Relationship Analysis

We mainly discuss the connection and differences among LatLRR, Regularized LRR (rLRR) [16], and our SA-LatLRR. Note that both rLRR and SA-LatLRR are formulated based on LatLRR, and improve the representation power by preserving local neighborhood information of salient features. But note that SA-LatLRR offers attractive properties over both LatLRR and rLRR in three aspects. First, LatLRR, rLRR and our SA-LatLRR all aim at decomposing the given matrix X into a principal component XZ, a salient feature part PX and a sparse error E, but the decomposition process LatLRR and rLRR did not take the intrinsic relations between XZ and PX into account clearly, i.e. the coefficients matrix Z and the underlying projection P are not explicitly correlated. In contrast, our SA-LatLRR incorporates a reconstructive error minimization term over the coefficients and salient features clearly, which can clearly correlate the coefficients with salient features. Second, rLRR preserve the neighborhood information of salient features by pre-calculating the Laplacian matrix from the original data [16], but the original data usually contains noise, outliers and unfavorable features, so the pre-defined Laplacian may be inaccurate for similarity measure and the subsequent low-rank coding. On the contrary, SA-LatLRR performs the joint reconstruction weight learning and the learning process is based on the joint sparse and low-rank salient features rather than based on the original data. Third, the robust L2,1-norm is also regularized on the projection P, so that joint sparse and low-rank salient features can be obtained by our SA-LatLRR, but rLRR and LatLRR only consider the low-rank property. Thus, our SA-LatLRR can outperform rLRR potentially for representation, as can be observed clearly from the visualization results of the learnt coefficients Z, the quantitative evaluations of image de-noising by reconstructing with Z and embedding by P, and the quantitative evaluations image recognition.

4 Experimental Results and Analysis

We perform experiments to illustrate the effectiveness of our SA-LatLRR, along with illustrating the comparison results with several closely related models. The data representation power of our SA-LatLRR is mainly compared with those of LRR, IRPCA, LatLRR and rLRR. For linear feature extraction and classification, our SA-LatLRR is mainly compared with PCA, IRPCA, Locality Preserving Projections (LPP) [26], Neighborhood Preserving Embedding (NPE) [27], Isoprojection (IsoP) [28], rLRR and LatLRR. For the quantitative evaluations, the result of each method is averaged over 10 times random splits of training and testing samples for fair comparison. Besides, we follow the common strategy to select the parameters of our method by using grid search, i.e., fixing one and tune on the other two. The experiments are carried out on a personal computer with Intel(R) Core (TM) i5-4590 @ 3.30 Hz 8.00 GB.

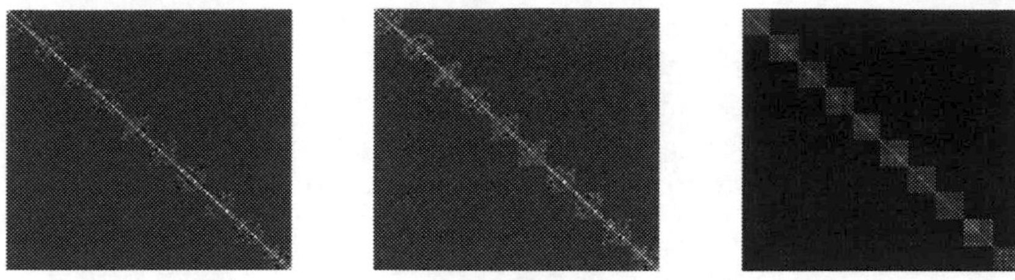

Fig. 1. Coefficients matrix Z of LRR (left), LatLRR (middle) and our SA-LatLRR (right).

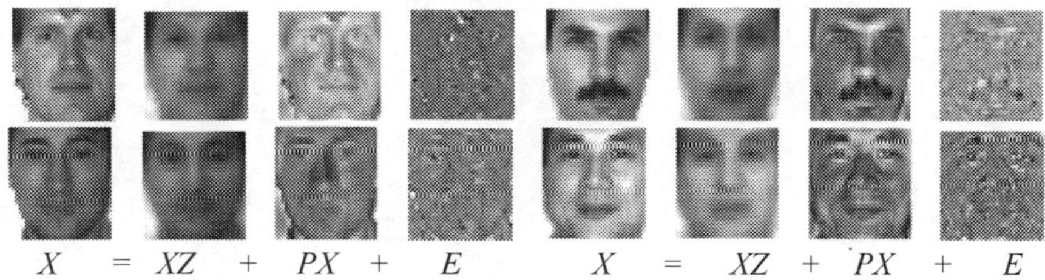

Fig. 2. Given a face image data, our method can decompose it into a principal component part *XZ*, a low-rank and sparse part *PX* and a sparse error part *E* fitting noise.

4.1 Visualization of Learnt Representation Coefficients *Z*

For efficient representations, the learnt coefficients should have a powerful discriminating power for various classes, i.e., it should hold the exact or nearly block-diagonal structures, where each block is the coefficients for certain class so that each sample can be reconstructed using the samples of the same class as much as possible. Thus, we would like to evaluate the ability by visualizing the coefficients in this simulation.

We follow the evaluation procedures in [9] by generating 10 independent subspaces $\{S_i\}_{i=1}^{10}$ whose basis $\{B_i\}_{i=1}^{10}$ are computed by applying $B_{i+1} = RB_i$, $1 \leq i \leq 9$, where R is a random rotation and B_i is a random column orthogonal matrix whose dimension is 200×10. Thus, each subspace has a fixed rank of 10. Then, we can easily construct a data matrix $X = [X_1, X_2, \ldots, X_{10}] \times \mathbb{R}^{200\times 90}$ by sampling 9 (that is smaller than the rank of subspace) data vectors from each subspace by $X_i = B_i C_i$, $1 \leq i \leq 9$, where C_i is a 10×9 i.i.d. $N(0, 1)$ data matrix. At last, we use this artificial data matrix for low-rank coding by LRR, LatLRR and SA-LatLRR. The visualizations of the coefficients matrix Z of each method are shown in Fig. 1. We can observe that our SA-LatLRR can obtain a clear block-diagonal structure compared with LRR and LatLRR, i.e., less inter-class connections and better intra-class connectivity are obtained by SA-LatLRR, which can enhance the subspace representations by reducing the reconstruction error.

4.2 Image Representation by Decomposition

We also evaluate SA-LatLRR for decomposing face images. Yale face database [30] that contains 165 face images of 15 persons is involved. We resize all images into

32 × 32 pixels and normalize the pixel values to [0, 1]. Some original images and the decomposable images are reported in Fig. 2. We find that the low-rank salient features mainly reflect some key local parts of face images, e.g., eyes, nose and mouth, etc. Note that for face recognition the salient features including the key body parts, such as eyes and nose, etc., would be important for enhancing the performance.

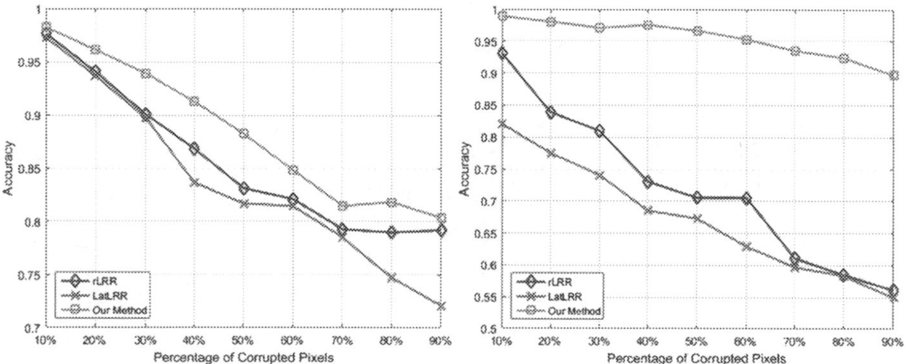

Fig. 3. Evaluation results of image de-noising by reconstruction with Z (left) and P (right).

4.3 Quantitative Evaluation of Image De-Noising

We evaluate the performance of each method of recovering the noisy face images. AR face database [31] that contains 2600 face images of males and females is tested. We corrupt a percentage of randomly selected pixels from the testing images by replacing the original gray values with random Gaussian noise with the variance 20. Then, we vary the percentage of corrupted level from 10% to 90% and record the change of results. Specifically, we quantify the image de-noising result of each low-rank method by the reconstruction: $Acc(Z) = \exp(-\left\| XZ - X\hat{Z} \right\|_F / \|XZ\|_F)$ and $Acc(P) = exp(-\left\| PX - \hat{P}X \right\|_F / \|PX\|_F)$, where XZ and PX are the reconstructions to the original face images without extra pixel corruptions. Figure 3 illustrate the quantitative results of our model and its competitors as a function of the level of random pixel corruptions, from which we can find that: (1) the result of each method decreases with the level of corrupted pixels increases; (2) our SA-LatLRR outperforms both LatLRR and rLRR for recovering the corrupted pixels. We also note that the superiority of our algorithm over the other two is more obvious for the recovery result by embedding with P which can be attributed to the fact that the optimization of the coefficients Z is explicitly correlated with the joint projection learning.

4.4 Face Recognition by Feature Extraction

We evaluate PCA, LPP, NPE, IsoP, IRPCA, LatLRR, rLRR and our SA-LatLRR for face recognition. In this experiment, four widely-used face database, i.e., Extended

YaleB [30], MIT CBCL face recognition database (available from http://cbcl.mit.edu/softwaredatasets/heisele/facerecognitiondatabase.html), AR [31] and UMIST [32], are evaluated. In this simulation, we choose 30, 100, 10 and 20 face images from each individual class in the YaleB, MIT and AR datasets as the training samples and test on the rest. To evaluate the robustness property against noise, we add random noise *i.i.d.* Gaussian distribution into the training data of each dataset for investigating the effects of added noise on the face recognition results of each method. Specifically, the noise level of the corrupted pixels is set from 0% to 90%. The recognition results of each algorithm over the four databases are shown in Fig. 4, where the horizontal axis denotes the levels of noise and the vertical axis denotes the face recognition accuracy. Note that IRPCA, LatLRR and SA-LatLRR can extract salient features from samples by using low-rank coding without reducing the dimensionality of data, compared with PCA, LPP, NPE, IsoP that perform the feature extraction by dimension reduction. But determining an optimal number of reduced dimensions is never easy in reality, so we follow the common evaluation procedures to set the number of reduced dimension to be the number of persons simply.

Then, we discuss how to use the proposed SA-LatLRR for handling the inductive classification task of outside new data efficiently. Note that our SA-LatLRR computes an optimal low-rank and sparse salient feature extractor P^* jointly, and the learnt P^* can extract the salient features from each sample x efficiently by embedding the data x onto P^* directly using the form of P^*x. Motivated by the efficient effects due to embedding, we also propose to learn a linear projection classifier W for performing classification based on embedded features P^*X of the training data X. Denote by $H = [l(x_1), l(x_2), \ldots, l(x_N)] \in \mathbb{R}^{C \times N}$ the initial labels, where C is the number of classes and N is the number of data, where $l(x_i) = [0, \ldots, 1, \ldots, 0]^{\mathrm{T}}$ shows the label information of sample x_i. The resulted formulation can be defined as

$$W = \arg\min_{W} \left\| W^{\mathrm{T}} P^* X - H \right\|_F^2 + \psi \left\| W^{\mathrm{T}} \right\|_F^2 \tag{15}$$

where H is the label matrix of all training samples and ψ is a small positive number that is set to 0.01 in this paper. The term associated with is mainly included to make the computations stable by avoiding the singularity issue.

We can see from the results that our proposed SA-LatLRR method delivers better results than the others and the results decrease slowly than the others with the increasing noise levels, i.e., our method is more robust to the included noise in data, which can be contributed to the data de-noising effect by using the L2,1-norm regularization on the projection in our model. rLRR also performs well in most cases by delivering slightly low accuracies than our SA-LatLRR. IRPCA and LatLRR can deliver better results than others in most cases. NPE, IsoP and LPP are comparative with each other in most cases and cannot perform well because of the included noise. We also observe that PCA has a better de-noising ability than NPE, IsoP and LPP.

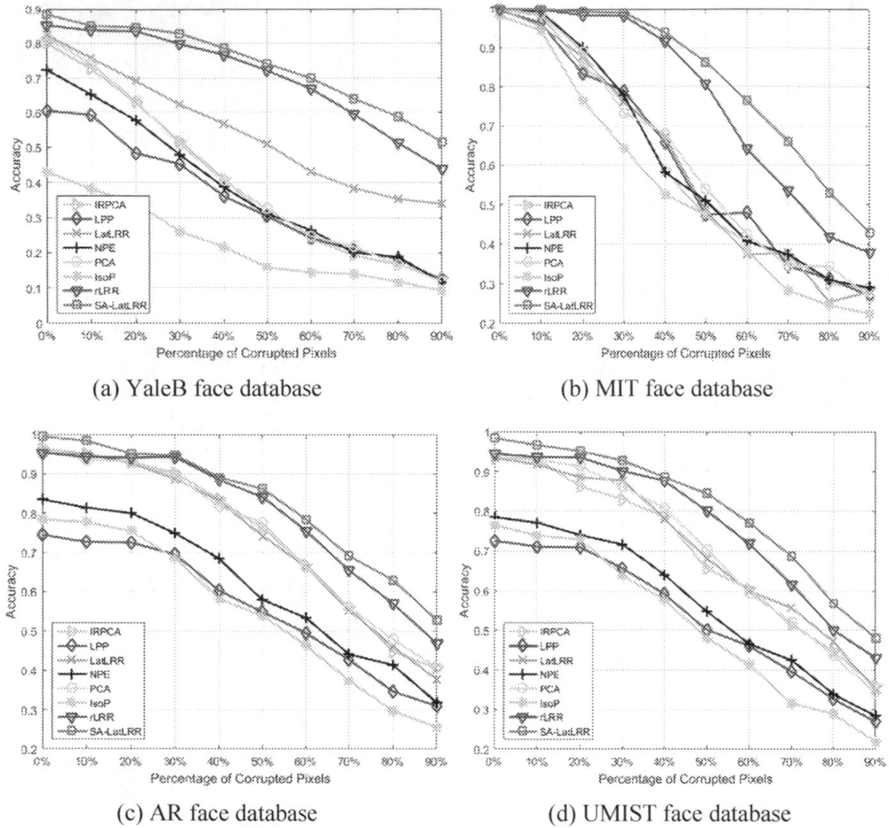

(a) YaleB face database

(b) MIT face database

(c) AR face database

(d) UMIST face database

Fig. 4. Recognition comparison of each algorithm over the four face image databases.

5 Conclusion Remarks

In this paper, we have proposed a similarity-adaptive latent low-rank representation model that can decompose given data explicitly into a principal feature part, a similarity-adaptive low-rank and sparse salient feature part and a sparse error. Our approach can simultaneously learn an adaptive reconstruction weight matrix and a low-rank & sparse projection for robust representation and discriminative salient feature extraction. One contribution of our similarity-adaptive coding algorithm is to incorporate a reconstructive error minimization term over the representation coefficients and salient features jointly so that the data representation power can be enhanced by forcing the coefficients matrix to be block-diagonal and discriminating, boosting the discriminating power of learnt projection, and meanwhile preserving neighborhood information of the salient features jointly. The detailed computations are also shown.

We have evaluated our approach by the visualizations of learnt representation coefficients, and the quantitative comparison of face recognition. Classification on several image databases show that remarkable results are delivered by our method. In future, we will investigate how to extend the proposed formulation into the semi-supervised representation scenario by learning with both labeled and unlabeled data. The parameter selection issue and convergence analysis should also be well studied.

Acknowledgment. This work is partially supported by the National Natural Science Foundation of China (61672365, 61432019, 61772171, 61622305, 61502238, 61672364), Major Program of Natural Science Foundation of Jiangsu Higher Education Institutions of China (15KJA520002) and "Six Talent Peak" Project of Jiangsu Province (XYDXX-055).

References

1. Bruce, L.M., Koger, C.H., Li, J.: Dimensionality reduction of hyperspectral data using discrete wavelet transform feature extraction. IEEE Trans. Geosci. Remote Sens. **40**(10), 2331–2338 (2002)
2. Wang, X., Paliwal, K.: Feature extraction and dimensionality reduction algorithms and their applications in vowel recognition. Pattern Recogn. **36**(10), 2429–2439 (2003)
3. Zhang, Z., Zhao, M.B., Chow, T.: Binary and multi-class group sparse canonical correlation analysis for feature extraction and classification. IEEE Trans. Knowl. Data Eng. **25**(10), 2192–2205 (2013)
4. Zhan, M., Cao, S., Qian, B., Chang, S., Wei, J.: Low-rank sparse feature selection for patient similarity learning. In: Proceedings of the International Conference on Data Mining, Barcelona, Spain (2016)
5. Cand, S., Li, X., Ma, Y., Wright, J.: Robust principal component analysis? J. ACM **58**(3), 11 (2009)
6. Li, T., Cheng, B., Ni, B.B., Liu, G.C., Yan, S.C.: Multitask low-rank affinity graph for image segmentation and image annotation. ACM Trans. Intell. Syst. Technol. **7**(4), 1–18 (2016)
7. Wright, J., Ganes, A., Rao, S.: Robust principal component analysis: exact recovery of corrupted low-rank matrices. J. ACM. **58**(3) (2009)
8. Hubert, M., Rousseeuw, P.J.: ROBPCA: a new approach to robust principal component analysis. Technometrics **47**(1), 64–79 (2005)
9. Bao, B.K., Liu, G.C., Xu, C.: Inductive robust principal component analysis. IEEE Trans. Image Process. **21**(8), 3794–3800 (2012)
10. Liu, G.C., Lin, Z., Yu, Y.: Robust subspace segmentation by low-rank representation. In: Proceedings of International Conference on Machine Learning, pp. 663–670 (2010)
11. Liu, G.C., Lin, Z.C., Yan, S.C.: Robust recovery of subspace structures by low-rank representation. IEEE Trans. Pattern Anal. Mach. Intell. **35**(1), 171–184 (2013)
12. Mairal, J., Bach, F., Ponce, J., Sapiro, G., Zisserman, A.: Discriminative learned dictionaries for local image analysis. In: Proceedings of the IEEE Conference on Computer Vision and Pattern Recognition, Anchorage, pp. 1–8 (2008)
13. Liu, G.C., Xu, H., Tang, J.H., Liu, Q.S., Yan, S.C.: A deterministic analysis for LRR. IEEE Trans. Pattern Anal. Mach. Intell. **38**(3), 417–430 (2016)
14. Balasubramanian, K., Yu, K., Lebanon, G.: Smooth sparse coding via marginal regression for learning sparse representations. Artif. Intell. **238**, 83–95 (2016)
15. Lu, X., Wang, Y., Yuan, Y.: Graph-regularized low-rank representation for destriping of hyperspectral images. IEEE Trans. Geosci. Remote Sens. **51**(7), 4009–4018 (2013)

16. Zhang, Z., Yan, S.C., Zhao, M.B.: Similarity preserving low-rank representation for enhanced data representation and effective subspace learning. Neural Netw. **53**, 81–94 (2014)
17. Wright, J., Ma, Y., Mairal, J.: Sparse representation for computer vision and pattern recognition. Proc. IEEE **98**(6), 1031–1044 (2010)
18. Zhang, L., Zhou, W., Chang, P.: Kernel sparse representation based classifier. IEEE Trans. Signal Process. **60**(4), 1684–1695 (2012)
19. Liu, G.C., Yan, S.C.: Latent low-rank representation for subspace segmentation and feature extraction. In: Proceedings of IEEE International Conference on Computer Vision, pp. 1615–1622 (2011)
20. Lin, Z., Chen, M., Ma, Y.: The Augmented Lagrange Multiplier Method for Exact Recovery of Corrupted Low-Rank Matrices. Eprint Arxiv, vol. 9 (2009)
21. Zhang, Z., Yan, S.C., Zhao, M.B., Li, F.Z.: Bilinear low-rank coding framework and extension for robust image recovery and feature representation. Knowl.-Based Syst. **86**, 143–157 (2015)
22. Hou, C.P., Nie, F.P., Li, X.L., Yi, D.Y., Wu, Y.: Joint embedding learning and sparse regression: a framework for unsupervised feature selection. IEEE Trans. Cybern. **44**(6), 793–804 (2014)
23. Nie, F., Huang, H., Cai, X., Ding, C.: Efficient and robust feature selection via joint L2,1-norms minimization. In: Proceedings of Neural Information Processing Systems, British Columbia, Canada, pp. 1813–1821 (2010)
24. Zhang, Z., Zhang, Y., Li, F., Zhao, M.B., Zhang, L., Yan, S.C.: Discriminative sparse flexible manifold embedding with novel graph for robust visual representation and label propagation. Pattern Recogn. **61**, 492–510 (2017)
25. Wang, P., Zhang, C., Cai, S.: Accelerated matrix recovery via random projection based on inexact augmented lagrange multiplier method. Trans. Tianjin Univ. **19**(4), 293–299 (2013)
26. He, X., Niyogi, P.: Locality preserving projections. In: Proceedings of Neural Information Processing Systems (NIPS), vol. 16 (2003)
27. Schmidhuber, J.: Deep learning in neural networks: an overview. Neural Netw. **61**, 85–117 (2015)
28. Cai, D., He, X., Han, J.: Isometric projection. In: Proceedings of the National Conference on Artificial Intelligence, Vancouver, Canada (2007)
29. Zhang, Z., Li, F., Zhao, M., Zhang, L., Yan, S.: Joint low-rank and sparse principal feature coding for enhanced robust representation and visual classification. IEEE Trans. Image Process. **25**(6), 2429–2443 (2016)
30. Sim, T., Kanade, T.: Combining models and exemplars for face recognition: an illuminating example. In: Proceedings of the CVPR Workshop on Models versus Exemplars in Computer Vision, vol. 1 (2001)
31. Bergstra, J., Yamins, D., Cox, D.: Making a science of model search: hyperparameter optimization in hundreds of dimensions for vision architectures. In: Proceedings of the International Conference on Machine Learning, pp. 115–123 (2013)
32. Graham, D.B., Allinson, N.M.: Characterising virtual Eigensignatures for general purpose face recognition. In: Wechsler, H., Phillips, P.J., Bruce, V., Soulié, F.F., Huang, T.S. (eds.) Face Recognition. NATO ASI Series, vol. 163, pp. 446–456. Springer, Berlin (1998). https://doi.org/10.1007/978-3-642-72201-1_25

Adaptively Shaping Reinforcement Learning Agents via Human Reward

Chao Yu(✉), Dongxu Wang, Tianpei Yang, Wenxuan Zhu, Yuchen Li, Hongwei Ge, and Jiankang Ren

School of Computer Science and Technology, Dalian University of Technology, Dalian 116024, Liaoning, China
{cy496,wdx}@mail.dlut.edu.cn, 1164439923@qq.com, 654424653@qq.com, 842087989@qq.com, {hwge,rjk}@dlut.edu.cn

Abstract. The computational complexity of reinforcement learning algorithms increases exponentially with the size of the problem. An effective solution to this problem is to provide reinforcement learning agents with informationally rich human knowledge, so as to expedite the learning process. Various integration methods have been proposed to combine human reward with agent reward in reinforcement learning. However, the essential distinction of these combination methods and their respective advantages and disadvantages are still unclear. In this paper, we propose an adaptive learning algorithm that is capable of selecting the most suitable method from a portfolio of combination methods in an adaptive manner. We show empirically that our algorithm enables better learning performance under various conditions, compared to the approaches using one combination method alone. By analyzing different ways of integrating human knowledge into reinforcement learning, our work provides some important insights into understanding the role and impact of human factors in human-robot collaborative learning.

Keywords: Reinforcement learning · Human reward
Reward Shaping · Human-agent interaction

1 Introduction

Recently, reinforcement learning (RL) has made enormous achievements in dealing with complex sequential decision-making problems in various areas, such as robotics [11,27], games [17,20], healthcare [18,21] and social science [28,29]. However, due to the curse of dimensionality, state-of-the-art RL algorithms [16,17,22] usually cannot converge quickly on real world problems. These algorithms usually require thousands of episodes of experience before convergence, which is impractical in real life applications. For example, in robotic control, collecting the required training data may be time consuming, and repeated trial and error during learning may lead to substantial wear or even damage to the robot.

X. Geng and B.-H. Kang (Eds.): PRICAI 2018, LNAI 11012, pp. 85–97, 2018.
https://doi.org/10.1007/978-3-319-97304-3_7

A remedy to this problem is to provide RL agents with informationally rich human knowledge, so as to expedite the learning process. Using human knowledge to guide the agent can not only effectively reduce the number of learning samples, but also potentially improve the learning performance to human levels. Therefore, plenty of work has proposed RL algorithms based on human knowledge [2,10,12–14,30]. These human-agent RL algorithms transform human instructions into a form that an RL agent can recognize so that the human knowledge can be embedded in the learning process. Various combination methods have been proposed to integrate human knowledge into RL, and to test how different ways of combination can influence the learning performance [14,15].

Although some progress has been made, the essential distinction of these human-agent RL methods and their respective advantages and disadvantages are still unclear. For example, it is generally believed that the methods that human rewards directly affect an RL agent's actions and policies are the most efficient combination methods [14]. However, we found that these methods usually performed worse when human guidance is more error prone, while the methods affecting the agent's reward and value functions can guarantee comparatively stronger robustness. Moreover, various human factors, such as different understanding of the task and capabilities in solving the task, can play a vital role in the final performance using different combination methods. Thus, further investigations are required to reveal the impact of such human factors on the performance of human-agent RL methods.

In this paper, we first summarize and formally define the four different kinds of human-agent RL methods in the literature, by distinguishing how human reward can be explicitly represented and integrated into an agent's RL process. To grasp a better understanding of the roles and advantages of different combination methods, we then propose an adaptive learning algorithm that is capable of selecting the most suitable combination method from a portfolio of different kinds of methods in an adaptive manner. We show empirically that this algorithm performs well in two classic RL problems, i.e. Pac-Man and CartPole. Results demonstrate that our algorithm enables better learning performance under various or even extreme conditions, compared to those approashes using only one combination method alone. By analyzing different ways of integrating human knowledge into an agent's RL process, our work thus provides some important insights into understanding the role and impact of human factors in future human-robot collaborative learning.

Section 2 gives a brief introduction to RL. Section 3 summarizes and formally defines the general human-agent RL methods. Section 4 elaborates on the details of our algorithm. Section 5 provides experimental validation and discussions. Section 6 gives related work, and finally, Sect. 7 concludes the paper.

2 Reinforcement Learning

A Reinforcement Learning (RL) problem [24] is typically modeled as a Markov Decision Process (MDP), which can be defined by the tuple (S, A, T, R), where S

and A are respectively the set of agent's states and actions, $T(s,a,s') = P(s'|s,a)$ gives the probability of jumping to the new state s' given current state s and action a, and $R(s,a)$ is the reward function. An agent's behavior is defined by a policy $\pi(s,a)$ which maps states to a probability distribution over the actions. In this paper, we assume that the policy is stochastic. The aim of RL is to find the best policy $\pi^*(s,a)$ to maximize the cumulative discount reward $G = \sum_t \gamma^t r_t$, where r_t is the reward at time t, and $0 < \gamma < 1$ is a discount factor.

Given an MDP and an agent's policy, we can then define the action-value function $Q^\pi(s,a)$, which represents the cumulative discount reward after taking action a in state s and then using policy π to explore. According to the Bellman equation, the optimal action-value function is given by:

$$Q^*(s,a) = R(s,a) + \gamma \sum_{s'} P(s'|s,a) \max_{a'} Q^*(s',a'), \tag{1}$$

and the optimal policy $\pi^*(s,a) = \arg\max_a Q^*(s,a)$.

3 Human-Agent RL Methods

As can be seen, an RL process is composed of the following main components: the action A, the policy π, the reward R and the value function V. Consequently, to guide an agent's RL process, humans can manipulate the agent's action A [1, 23], policy Π [9,10], reward R [6,7,19], value function V [13] or their various combinations as follows:

$$(A, \Pi, R, V, (A, \Pi), (A, R), (A, V), \ldots, (A, \Pi, R, V)). \tag{2}$$

However, current human-agent RL methods only consider one single component in A, Π, R, V alone. These methods can be generally categorized into the following four types: the *Action-based* methods, the *Policy-based* methods, the *Reward-based* methods, and the *Value-based* methods. For example, a combination method of a policy-based approach with Bayesian Q-learning was proposed in [10]. A theoretical analysis for reward-based methods was provided in [19]. Authors in [13,14] proposed a framework called TAMER+RL to evaluate performance using different combination approaches. Let A_a, Π_a, R_a, V_a denote the function space of an agent's actions, policies, rewards, and value functions, respectively, and A_h, Π_h, R_h, V_h denote the function space of a human's actions, policies, rewards, and value functions, respectively. The above four different types of methods can be formally defined as follows:

1. **Action-Based Methods**
   Action-based methods use human's reward signals to directly affect the agent's action selection process. Let $c(s) \in A_a$ denote the set of an agent's candidate actions, and $H_a(s) \in A_h$ denote the human's suggestion function. Then the combination function $\Phi_a(c, H_a)$ can be defined to map the agent's action function $c(s)$ and human's suggestion function $H_a(s)$ to the agent's next action.

We should emphasize that $c(s)$ is different from the policy function $\pi(s,a)$ in RL, because $c(s)$ can take various forms but $\pi(s,a)$ is one of these forms. Moreover, due to the transformation by Φ, $c(s)$ and $H_a(s)$ may have different output forms.

The *Action Biasing* method [14] is a typical action-based method, which treats the action-value function $Q(s,a)$ as $c(s)$. The action chosen by the agent is determined by $\Phi_a(c,H_a) = argmax_a Q(s,a) + B * H_a(s,a)$, where B represents the weight that the agent tends to believe in humans.

2. **Policy-Based Methods**

   Policy-based methods combine the human's policy with the agent's policy to influence the agent's learning process. Let $\pi(s,a) \in \Pi_a$ denote the agent's policy function, and $H_\pi(s,a) \in \Pi_h$ denote the human's policy function. Then the combination function $\Phi_\pi(\pi, H_\pi) \in \Pi_a$ can be defined to map the agent's policy function $\pi(s,a)$ and human's policy function $H_\pi(s,a)$ to the agent's new policy function.

   The *Control Sharing* method, similar to the *Probabilistic Policy Reuse* (PPR) strategy [9], is one typical policy-based method. Instead of providing an advice directly to the agent, the Control Sharing method controls the agent' policy of choosing actions. So, the agent learns the optimal control policy through observation. The policy is determined by $\Phi_\pi(\pi, H_\pi) = \pi(s,a)^l * H_\pi(s,a)^{1-l}$, in which l is a Bernoulli random variable that controls the probability of choosing human's policy function.

3. **Reward-Based Methods**

   Reward-based methods convert human's reward signals directly into some useful form to be integrated with rewards in RL. Let $r(s,a) \in R_a$ denote the agent's reward function, and $H_r(s,a) \in R_r$ denote the human's reward function. Then the combination function $\Phi_r(r, H_r) \in R_a$ can be defined to map the agent's reward function $r(s,a)$ and human's reward function $H_r(s,a)$ to agent's new reward function to be used by the RL agent.

   The *Reward Shaping* method [2] is a classic reward-based method, in which the combination reward can be determined by $\Phi_r(r, H_r) = r(s,a) + H_r(s,a)$.

4. **Value-Based Methods**

   Value functions, i.e. $V(s)$ and $Q(s,a)$, are fundamental components in RL. Let $v(s,[a]) \in V_a$ denote the state-action-value or state-value function of an RL agent, and $H_v(s,a) \in V_h$ denote the human's value function. The combination function $\Phi_v(v, H_v) \in V_a$ can be defined to map the agent's value function $v(s,[a])$ and human's value function $H_v(s,a)$ to the agent's new value function.

   The *Q Augmentation* method [13] can be considered as one type of value-based methods, in which combination function can be given by $\Phi_v(v, H_v) = Q(s,a) + H_v(s,a)$.

Previous studies have shown that the above human-agent RL methods have distinct advantages for different RL tasks or at different learning stage [14]. It is necessary to investigate how different kinds of combination methods can interact with each other, and how this interplay can impact the final learning performance [2]. This motivates our adaptive shaping algorithm as follows.

4 Adaptively Shaping RL Agents

We here propose an algorithm that is able to adaptively shape an RL agent with human learned knowledge based on the idea of multi-armed bandit. Our algorithm takes several different human-agent RL methods as input, and maintains the cumulative rewards that they can achieve during the current learning phase. Then, it chooses the best method in the current stage to execute. In order to enable exploration, the cumulative reward of each method is converted into a probability, and importance sampling is applied to speed up the update of probability in choosing each method. More specifically, let π^* denote the best policy of an agent and Q_{π^*} be the corresponding Q-value, such that $\pi^*(s) = argmax_a Q_{\pi^*}(s, a)$. The agent receives the reward R_e from the environment and the reinforcement signal H from the human simultaneously (H can be anyone of H_c, H_π, H_r, H_v). There are a set of human-agent RL methods ($M = m_1, m_2, \ldots, m_{|M|}$). Our algorithm adaptively chooses the best method by calculating the probability of how each method can maximize the overall learning performance at the current stage.

Algorithm 1. Adaptively shaping RL agents with human reward

Input: M

1: $w_{m_i} \leftarrow 0, \quad i = 1, 2, \ldots, |M|$

2: **while** not converge **do**

3: $\quad P(m_i) = \frac{e^{\beta(w_{m_i} - min(w_{m_i}))}}{\sum_{j=1}^{|M|} e^{\beta(w_{m_j} - min(w_{m_i}))}}$

$\quad$ sample a method $m_{current}$ from $P(m_i), \quad i = 1, 2, \ldots, |M|$.

4: $\quad sim, R =$ **run_one_episode**$(m_{current})$

5: $\quad$ **for** $i = 0$ to $|M|$ **do**

6: $\quad\quad w_{m_i} = w_{m_i} + \tau * \frac{sim_{m_i}}{\sum_{j=1}^{|M|} sim_{m_j}} (R - w_{m_i})$

7: $\quad$ **end for**

8: **end while**

Algorithm 1 is the main procedure of our algorithm, in which w_{m_i} stands for the weight of method i. Initially, we set all $w_{m_i} = 0$ to indicate an equal probability of choosing every human-agent RL method. (Actually, if we have related domain knowledge, it is possible to achieve better results by manually setting w_{m_i} beforehand). Then, our algorithm runs the chosen method and updates the weights of all the methods based on the reward obtained by that method (Line 2–8). More specifically, in each iteration, the algorithm calculates the probability of each human-agent RL method by using a softmax function according to the current weight vector, and then selects a method $m_{current}$ according to probability (Line 3). Then, function **run_one_episode** applies this human-agent RL method to run one episode, and returns the similarity sim and total reward R. Similarity sim maintains the policy similarity between each method and the current running method. Then the weights of all human-agent RL methods are updated based on sim and R, using a learning rate τ (Line 5, 6).

Algorithm 2. run_one_episode($m_{current}$)

Input: method $m_{current}$
1: $sim_{m_{current}} \leftarrow 1, \quad i = 1, 2, \ldots, |M|$
2: $R \leftarrow 0$
3: $s =$ **init_task**()
4: **while** episode not over **do**
5: get human feedback H
6: $a =$ **get_action**($m_{current}, s, H$)
7: $s, R_e =$ **do_action**(s, a)
8: **update_q**(s, a, R_e, H)
9: $R \leftarrow R + R_e$
10: **for** $i = 0$ to $|M|$ **do**
11: $\pi_{m_i} =$ **get_prob**(m_i, s, a, H)
12: $sim_{m_i} = sim_{m_i} * \pi_{m_i}$
13: **end for**
14: **end while**
15: **return** sim, R

Algorithm 2 is the detail of function **run_one_episode**. At each time step in an episode, the specific human-agent RL method asks for the guidance from human (Line 6), i.e. the human reinforcement signal H (It is possible that the human may not provide guidance at this request), and then determines the next action based on the currently chosen human-agent RL method $m_{current}$, the current state s and human guidance H (Line 6). After taking this action, the next state s and reward from environment R_e are achieved (Line 7). Then the Q-function is updated using the chosen human-agent RL method (Line 8), and the final accumulated reward is added by the RL reward R_e (Line 9). At each time step, our algorithm calculates the similarity between other human-agent RL methods and $m_{current}$, based on the probability that the current action is considered to be optimal by each method (Line 10–12). Function **get_prob**(m_i, s, a, H) outputs a probability of choosing action a in state s using method m_i. Since some methods such as *Control Sharing* and *Action Biasing* can also influence the final policy, the human reward H should also be included in the **get_prob** function. When the whole episode is finished, the algorithm returns the *sim* value of each human-agent RL method and the total environmental return R (Line 15).

5 Experimental Evaluations

We use two benchmark RL tasks: Pac-Man and CartPole to evaluate the performance of our algorithm in different parameter settings. Four typical distinct human-agent RL methods in [13, 14] are chosen as the specific combination methods in our algorithm: the Action Biasing, the Control Sharing, the Reward Shaping and the Q Augmentation. We assume that the human has only two instructions: right or wrong. We set constant r_h as a positive value and $-r_h$ as a negative value given by the human, corresponding to the right and wrong guidance, respectively. A reward vector is used to denote the human's reward function H regarding the action choices. When the human thinks that an action is the best choice, then the corresponding action in the reward vector is denoted as r_h, and other actions are denoted as $-r_h$.

Following [10], we obtained the optimal policy through standard Q-learning in the two experiments to simulate the completely correct human guidance. When the agent requires human guidance, we can then use the largest Q-value as the perfect human guidance in current state. In order to quantitatively study the advantages and disadvantages of different methods in various parameter settings, two extra parameters are introduced as in [10]: L (the likelihood of feedback) which represents the probability that the human provides guidance at each time step, and C (the consistency of feedback) which represents the probability that the human provides the optimal instructions correctly. It should be noted that, although the Q-learning is used to obtain the optimal Q values to model human guidance, in the experiments, no human-agent RL methods can directly access these Q values. An RL agent can only receive the information of optimal actions associated with the maximum Q values by $a^* = argmax_a Q[s, a]$.

5.1 Experimental Setup

Pac-Man is a 2D grid game, which includes food, walls, ghosts and a Pac-Man agent. The goal of the game is to control the agent to get all the food while avoiding colliding with any ghost. Every time the agent gets a food, it gets a reward of 10 points. When the agent gets all the food, it gets 500 points. A collision with a ghost will result in ending the game. The agent will gain a reward of -500 points when game is over. Every step of the game will cost the agent with 1 point. Our experiment uses a $5 * 5$ square, which contains two foods and a ghost. The actions of the agent include four movements: up, down, left, and right. When the agent encounters a wall, it stops moving and stays where it was. The state of the agent includes the agent's current position, the ghost's current position, the ghost's current direction and the presence of foods. The hyper-parameters of each method are kept the same in order to give a fair comparison: the discount factor $\gamma = 0.7$, updated parameter $\alpha = 0.3$ and exploring policy parameter $\epsilon = 0.1, \beta = 5$. The guiding influence parameter in all four methods $B = 1$ and this value decreases by $\frac{1}{30000}$ after each episode. Each method performs 30,000 episodes (this is because ordinary Q-learning needs roughly 30,000 episodes to converge), and the final results are averaged over 20 independent runs.

We use CartPole to test the performance of our algorithm in continuous domains. In CartPole, a small car can move around with a pole standing on the car. The agent needs to choose two movements: moving left or right to control the car, while keeping the pole upright. The agent gains +1 reward by maintaining the pole at each time it interacts with the environment. When the pole is unable to remain vertical, the game ends with a -1 reward. The state of the agent includes the angle and the acceleration of the pole. The hyper-parameters settings are as follows: discount coefficient $\gamma = 0.99$, and exploration parameter $\epsilon = 0.3, \beta = 5$. The parameter $B = 1$ in all methods, and decreases

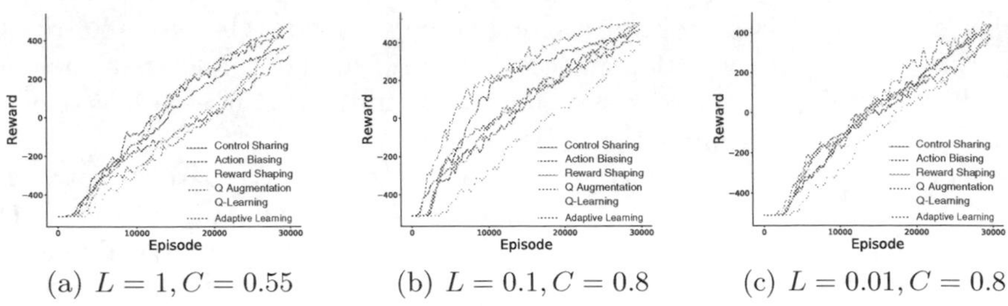

(a) $L = 1, C = 0.55$ (b) $L = 0.1, C = 0.8$ (c) $L = 0.01, C = 0.8$

Fig. 1. The average reward under different parameters of L, C and $r_h = 10$ in the Pac-Man domain. The x-coordinate is the learning episode, and the y-coordinate is the average cumulative reward averaged over 20 independent runs.

by $\frac{1}{2000}$ after each episode. Each of the methods performed 2000 episodes, and the experimental results are averaged over 20 independent runs.

5.2 Experimental Results

Figure 1 shows the average cumulative rewards using the four individual combination methods, the Q-learning method and our adaptive algorithm under different parameter settings in the Pac-Man domain. In case of (a), when the likelihood of feedback $L = 1$ and the consistency of feedback $C = 0.55$, our algorithm behaves slightly better than the Control Sharing and Action Biasing method, while Q Augmentation and Reward Shaping can only achieve similar performance with basic Q-learning. In case of (b), when $L = 0.1$ and $C = 0.8$, our algorithm converges completely faster than the other methods. When $L = 0.01$ and $C = 0.8$, all the methods perform roughly the same as Q-learning, but our algorithm converges faster than the other methods after around 15000 episodes.

Figure 2 compares the learning performance of the four combination methods and our algorithm in different parameter settings in the CartPole domain. In Fig. 2(a), when L is 0.01 and C is 0.8, all the combination methods and our proposed algorithm can achieve similar performance, enabling faster convergence than the basic Q-learning algorithm. This implies that if the human can give correct guidance with high probability ($C = 0.8$), human-agent RL methods can greatly increase the learning performance, even if this guidance occurs only occasionally ($L = 0.01$). In Fig. 2(b), when L is 1 and C is 0.5, which means that the human gives guidance randomly at each time step, the four combination methods all perform poorly. Especially, Control Sharing cannot converge at all, while Action Biasing, Reward Shaping and Q Augmentation all perform far worse than the traditional Q-learning algorithm. This result demonstrates that, to enable good performance of human-agent RL methods, the human must have a good understanding of the RL task, and thus can give guidance correctly.

In order to further reveal the impact of human's error on the learning performance, we slightly increase the correctness probability C to 0.51. As can be seen from Fig. 2(c), a very minor increase in C can cause apparent impact on the

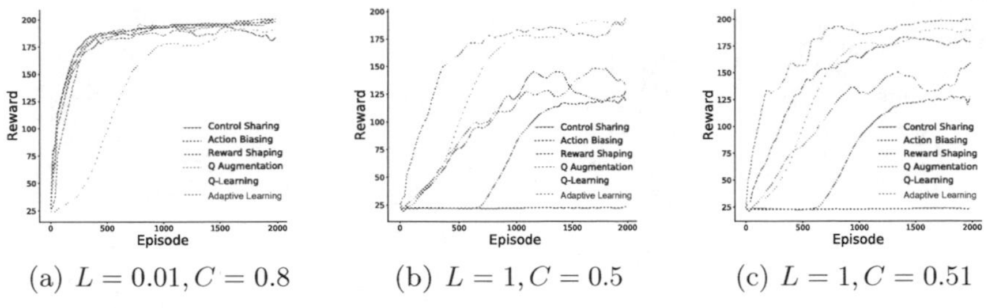

(a) $L = 0.01, C = 0.8$ (b) $L = 1, C = 0.5$ (c) $L = 1, C = 0.51$

Fig. 2. The average reward with different L, C and $r_h = 10$ in the CartPole domain.

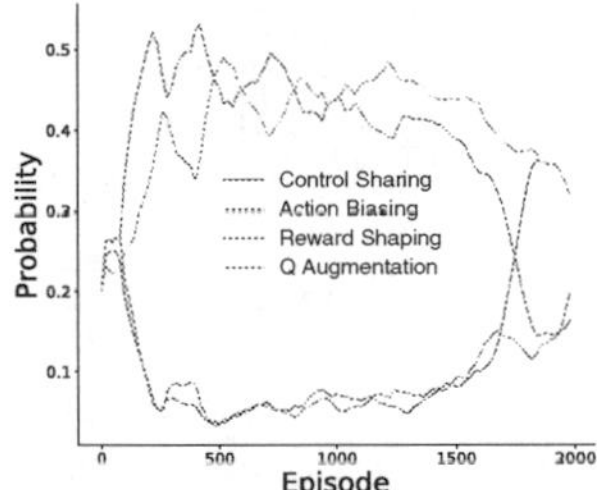

Fig. 3. The dynamics of choosing the four combination methods using our algorithm when $L = 1, C = 0.51$ in the CartPole domain.

Fig. 4. The average reward when $L = 0.01, C = 0.8$ in the CartPole domain when human reward $r_h = 100$.

learning performance, especially for the Reward Shaping method, which can now achieve comparative performance against the Q-learning method. Figure 3 plots the probability of choosing the four methods using our adaptive algorithm. The probability of choosing Reward Shaping and Control Sharing begin to decrease after around 100 episodes, while the probability of choosing the other two methods is on the rise. As time proceeds, the probability of choosing Reward Shaping and Control Sharing declines slowly before a dramatic drop at around 1500 episodes. By dynamically switching among the four different combination methods, our algorithm can achieve better performance though the whole learning process, fully demonstrating the benefits of our algorithm.

It is argued by previous studies that Action Biasing and Control Sharing are more efficient than the other methods in shaping an agent' RL process [14]. However, this phenomenon cannot be observed in our result, as shown in Fig. 2. To reveal this reason, we increase the human reward r_h to 100 in order to raise the influence of human reward. Figure 4 shows that by increasing r_h from 10 to 100, the action-based and policy-based methods indeed outperform the reward-based and value-based approaches. The result indicates that action-based and policy-based methods may be more efficient over other methods only when the human reward is set a comparatively high value over the RL reward.

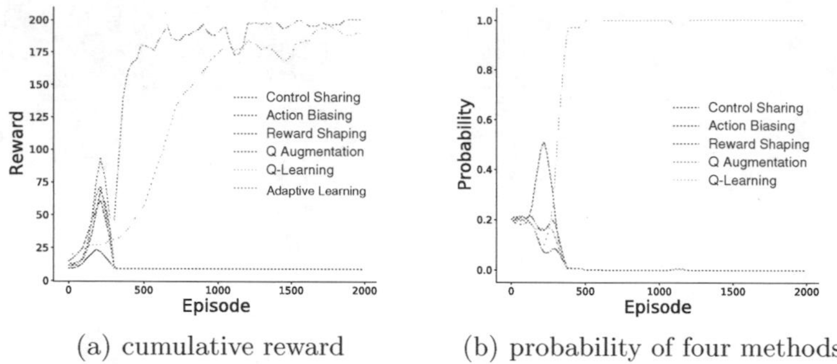

(a) cumulative reward (b) probability of four methods

Fig. 5. The performance of our algorithm and the four individual combination methods when the four methods were disabled at 200 episode). (a) the cumulative reward of four methods and our algorithm. (b) the probability of choosing the four methods and Q-learning using our algorithm.

It is clear that the human-agent RL methods are not robust enough when being applied alone. Various parameter settings can bring about diverse learning performance. Especially, when the consistence of guidance provided by human is not high enough (e.g., when C is close to 0.5 in the above experiments), the individual methods are easy to fail and lead to divergence of value functions. Our algorithm, due to the implementation of an adaptive mechanism, can detect the failed methods and decrease their weights accordingly. In order to illustrate this issue more clearly, we additionally designed a special case to test the robustness of our algorithm. We added the Q-learning method into the portfolio of methods in our algorithm, and then we manually disabled the functions of the other four individual human-agent RL methods in the 200th episode. Figure 5(a) shows that the performance of our algorithm decreases sharply in episode 200, and then increases dramatically afterwards. Figure 5(b) shows that our algorithm can successfully detect the failure of the four methods after 200 episodes, by reducing their probability and increasing the probability of choosing Q-learning.

In all, none of the four individual combinations methods can achieve a parameter-independent performance. For the action-based and policy-based methods to be more efficient, the human reward should be more error free and set a high enough value to entrench its influence. However, by combining different human-agent RL methods in an adaptive manner, our algorithm can take advantage of each method to achieve robust and efficient learning performance.

6 Related Work

There is plenty work in the literature on studying how human reward can help in an agent's RL process. Different ways of human-agent combination methods have been proposed. Knox *et al.* [12] proposed the TAMER framework for designing agents that can be interactively shaped by human trainers who give only positive and negative feedback signals. However, TAMER does not allow human reward to be directly combined with autonomous learning reward. Later, Knox *et al.* proposed eight plausible combination methods for combining a previously learned human reinforcement function with MDP reward in an RL algorithm [13], and studied how human reward and RL reward can be learnt simultaneously [14,15]. However, all these studies focus on analyzing the different ways of integrating human reward into RL reward and their various performance. This is different from our work that aims at selecting dynamically from a portfolio of human-agent combination methods for efficient and stable learning.

There is also tremendous work that uses human demonstrations or advice to facilitate reinforcement learning. For example, the HAT algorithm transfers knowledge directly from human policies [25]. Other following work showed how expert advice or demonstrations can be used to shape rewards in the RL problem [3–5]. Abel *et al.* [2] developed a general agent-agnostic framework for human-agent interaction that can capture a wide range of ways a human can help an RL agent, and Griffith *et al.* [10] introduced an algorithm for estimating a human's Bayes optimal policy and a technique for combining this with the policy formed from the agent's direct experience in the environment. Some studies have also analyzed a teacher agent's action advise on RL under the teacher-student advising framework [8,26,30]. However, all these studies focus more on transferring human/agent knowledge to RL, which differs slightly from our work that focuses on adaptively combining human learning reward with RL reward.

7 Conclusions

Integrating human knowledge into RL is an effective means to facilitate an agent's learning efficiency. In this paper, we first summarized and formally defined the four different kinds of human-agent RL methods in the literature, by distinguishing how human reward can be explicitly represented and integrated into an agent's RL process. We then proposed an adaptive shaping algorithm, which can combine different human-agent RL methods and select the most favorable one from them dynamically during learning. We showed empirically that this algorithm performed better in two classic RL problems, i.e. Pac-Man and CartPole, compared to other approaches using only one human-agent RL method alone. We came to the conclusion that, to ensure good performance of a human-agent RL method, the human must have a good understanding of the RL task, and thus can give guidance correctly. However, if such perfect human knowledge is lacking, our proposed algorithm is a promising candidate to guarantee high-level performance by making the best of each human-agent RL method.

In this paper, following the work [10], we employed an optimal agent with two main parameters, i.e., likelihood and consistency of human guidance, to model the behaviors of humans. This enables us to quantitatively study the advantages and disadvantages of different methods in various parameter settings. However, it is still an interesting issue to design a human-computer interface to implement our algorithm on real humans. This will be left for our future work.

Acknowledgments. This work is supported by the National Natural Science Foundation of China under Grant 61502072, 61572104 and 61403059, Hongkong Scholar Program under Grant XJ2017028, and Dalian High Level Talent Innovation Support Program under Grant 2017RQ008.

References

1. Abel, D., Hershkowitz, D.E., Barth-Maron, G., Brawner, S., O'Farrell, K., MacGlashan, J., Tellex, S.: Goal-based action priors. In: ICAPS2015, pp. 306–314 (2015)
2. Abel, D., Salvatier, J., Stuhlmüller, A., Evans, O.: Agent-agnostic human-in-the-loop reinforcement learning. arXiv preprint arXiv:1701.04079 (2017)
3. Brys, T., Harutyunyan, A., Suay, H.B., Chernova, S., Taylor, M.E.: Reinforcement learning from demonstration through shaping. In: IJCAI2015, pp. 3352–3358 (2015)
4. Cederborg, T., Grover, I., Isbell, C.L., Thomaz, A.L.: Policy shaping with human teachers. In: IJCAI2015, pp. 3366–3372 (2015)
5. Suay, H.B., Brys, T., Taylor, M.E., Chernova, S.: Learning from demonstration for shaping through inverse reinforcement learning. In: AAMAS2016, pp. 429–437 (2016)
6. Devlin, S., Kudenko, D.: Dynamic potential-based reward shaping. In: AAMAS2012, pp. 433–440 (2012)
7. Devlin, S., Yliniemi, L., Kudenko, D., Tumer, K.: Potential-based difference rewards for multiagent reinforcement learning. In: AAMAS2014, pp. 165–172 (2014)
8. Fachantidis, A., Taylor, M.E., Vlahavas, I.: Learning to teach reinforcement learning agents. Mach. Learn. Knowl. Extr. **1**(1), 2 (2017)
9. Fernández, F., Veloso, M.: Probabilistic policy reuse in a reinforcement learning agent. In: AAMAS2006, pp. 720–727. ACM (2006)
10. Griffith, S., Subramanian, K., Scholz, J., Isbell, C.L., Thomaz, A.L.: Policy shaping: integrating human feedback with reinforcement learning. In: NIPS2013, pp. 2625–2633 (2013)
11. Gu, S., Holly, E., Lillicrap, T., Levine, S.: Deep reinforcement learning for robotic manipulation with asynchronous off-policy updates. In: 2017 IEEE ICRA, pp. 3389–3396. IEEE (2017)
12. Knox, W.B., Stone, P.: Tamer: training an agent manually via evaluative reinforcement. In: 7th IEEE ICDL, pp. 292–297. IEEE (2008)
13. Knox, W.B., Stone, P.: Combining manual feedback with subsequent MDP reward signals for reinforcement learning. In: AAMAS2010, pp. 5–12 (2010)
14. Knox, W.B., Stone, P.: Reinforcement learning from simultaneous human and MDP reward. In: AAMAS2012, pp. 475–482 (2012)
15. Knox, W.B., Stone, P.: Framing reinforcement learning from human reward: reward positivity, temporal discounting, episodicity, and performance. Artif. Intell. **225**(C), 24–50 (2015)
16. Lillicrap, T.P., et al.: Continuous control with deep reinforcement learning. arXiv preprint arXiv:1509.02971 (2015)
17. Mnih, V., et al.: Playing atari with deep reinforcement learning. arXiv preprint arXiv:1312.5602 (2013)

18. Moodie, E.E., Chakraborty, B., Kramer, M.S.: Q-learning for estimating optimal dynamic treatment rules from observational data. Can. J. Stat. **40**(4), 629–645 (2012)
19. Ng, A.Y., Harada, D., Russell, S.: Policy invariance under reward transformations: theory and application to reward shaping. In: ICML1999, vol. 99, pp. 278–287 (1999)
20. Peng, P., et al.: Multiagent bidirectionally-coordinated nets for learning to play starcraft combat games. arXiv preprint arXiv:1703.10069 (2017)
21. Prasad, N., Cheng, L.F., Chivers, C., Draugelis, M., Engelhardt, B.E.: A reinforcement learning approach to weaning of mechanical ventilation in intensive care units. arXiv preprint arXiv:1704.06300 (2017)
22. Schulman, J., Levine, S., Abbeel, P., Jordan, M., Moritz, P.: Trust region policy optimization. In: ICML2015, pp. 1889–1897 (2015)
23. Sherstov, A.A., Stone, P.: Improving action selection in MDP's via knowledge transfer. In: AAAI2005, vol. 5, pp. 1024–1029 (2005)
24. Sutton, R., Barto, A.: Reinforcement Learning: An Introduction. The MIT press, Cambridge (1998)
25. Taylor, M.E., Suay, H.B., Chernova, S.: Integrating reinforcement learning with human demonstrations of varying ability. In: AAMAS2011, pp. 617–624 (2011)
26. Torrey, L., Taylor, M.: Teaching on a budget: agents advising agents in reinforcement learning. In: AAMAS2013, pp. 1053–1060 (2013)
27. Yu, C., Zhang, M., Ren, F., Tan, G.: Multiagent learning of coordination in loosely coupled multiagent systems. IEEE Trans. Cybern. **45**(12), 2853–2867 (2015)
28. Yu, C., Zhang, M., Ren, F.: Collective learning for the emergence of social norms in networked multiagent systems. IEEE Trans. Cybern. **44**(12), 2342–2355 (2014)
29. Yu, C., Zhang, M., Ren, F., Tan, G.: Emotional multiagent reinforcement learning in spatial social dilemmas. IEEE Trans. Neural Netw. Learn. Syst. **26**(12), 3083–3096 (2015)
30. Zhan, Y., Fachantidis, A., Vlahavas, I., Taylor, M.E.: Agents teaching humans in reinforcement learning tasks. In: Proceedings of the Adaptive and Learning Agents Workshop (AAMAS) (2014)

Incomplete Multi-view Clustering via Structured Graph Learning

Jie Wu[1], Wenzhang Zhuge[1], Hong Tao[1], Chenping Hou[1](✉), and Zhao Zhang[2]

[1] National University of Defense Technology, No. 47, Yanwachi Street, Changsha 410073, China
wujienudt@yahoo.com, zgwznudt@yeah.net, taohong.nudt@hotmail.com, hcpnudt@hotmail.com

[2] School of Computer Science and Technology, Soochow University, No. 1, Shi-zi Street, Suzhou 215006, People's Republic of China
cszzhang@gmail.com

Abstract. In real applications, multi-view clustering with incomplete data has played an important role in the data mining field. How to design an algorithm to promote the clustering performance is a challenging problem. In this paper, we propose an approach with learned graph to handle the case that each view suffers from some missing information. It combines incomplete multi-view data and clusters it simultaneously by learning the ideal structures. For each view, with an initial input graph, it excavates a clustering structure with the consideration of consistency with the other views. The learned structured graphs have exactly c (the predefined number of clusters) connected components so that the clustering results can be obtained without requiring any post-clustering. An efficient optimization strategy is provided, which can simultaneously handle both the whole and the partial regularization problems. The proposed method exhibits impressive performance in experiments.

Keywords: Incomplete multi-view data · Clustering
Structured graph learning

1 Introduction

In many real applications, data are often coming from multiple sources or with multiple modalities becoming multi-view data, which have attracted extensive attention in the data mining field [1,7,14]. Observing that multiple views usually provide each other with complementary and compatible information, integrating them together to get better performance becomes natural [6,14]. However, in real applications, it is often the case that some or even all of the views suffer from some missing information [12,19]. For example, in speaker grouping, the audio and visual appearances represent two views and some speakers may miss audio or

Supported by the National Natural Science Foundation of China (No. 61473302, 61503396).

X. Geng and B.-H. Kang (Eds.): PRICAI 2018, LNAI 11012, pp. 98–112, 2018.
https://doi.org/10.1007/978-3-319-97304-3_8

visual information. Another example is document clustering, different language versions of a document can be regarded as multiple views, but many documents may not be translated into each language. Therefore, it is necessary to explore how to integrate such incomplete multi-view data. In this paper, we focus on multi-view clustering with incomplete data. Exiting approaches for this task can be divided into two categories: completion methods [2,13] and subspace methods [12,20].

Completion methods are based on matrix completion. For example, singular value decomposition imputation [2] first uses the eigenvalues to apply a regression to the complete attributes of the instance, to obtain an estimation of the missing value itself, and then applies conventional multi-view clustering methods [7,10] to derive the clustering results. The difference among different completion methods [7,9,10] is that they complete the incomplete data according to different principles. Their performances are usually unsatisfactory when the data are missing block-wise [12].

In recent years, some subspace methods to handle this case have been proposed. Partial multi-view clustering (PVC) [12] first divides the partial examples into two blocks and then executes non-negative matrix factorization (NMF) [11] to learn a low-dimensional representation for each multi-view data. Incomplete multi-modal visual data grouping (IMG) [20] can be regarded as a version of PVC, which requires that the low-dimensional representations conform to a self-learning manifold structure. Other methods such as [17,18] can also be classified into this category. Although these methods have achieved good performance, there is still room to improve. Most of them are based on NMF, which is aimed at learning the latent low-dimensional representations of data rather than clustering data. As a result, they must utilize a post-clustering such as K-means and spectral clustering to obtain the clustering results. Besides, they assume that the shared data in different views have exactly the same representation in the latent space, which may lead to a negative effect on the intrinsic inner structure of each individual view.

In this paper, with the goal to learn cluster structures directly, we propose the Structured Graph Learning (SGL) method to manipulate incomplete multi-view data and group them simultaneously. For each view, our SGL excavates a structured graph to combine the partial and the complete examples. To establish interaction between the different views, we naturally constrain the subgraphs corresponding to the shared data (in different views) to be close. Thus to some extent, we maintain the intrinsic structure of each individual view, as well as the consistency between different views. By improving the mechanism of the graph learning, the graph matrixes learned by our method have ideal structures-exactly c connected components, so that the clustering results can be derived from these graphs without requiring any post-clustering. Besides, we propose an efficient optimization strategy to solve our formulated problem. Experimental results on real benchmark data sets validate the advantages of our method.

2 The Proposed SGL

For the convenience of presentation, we take two-view data for illustration. As we can see from following formulations, extension to any number of views is direct. For example, most simply, we can separate the multiple views into pairs and then solve all the two-view problems. For input data, each column is a data and each row is an attribute. The feature dimensions of view 1 and view 2 data are d_1 and d_2, respectively. Input data $[X^{(1)^T}, X^{(2)^T}]^T \in \mathbb{R}^{(d_1+d_2)\times n_3}$, $\hat{X}^{(1)} \in \mathbb{R}^{d_1\times n_1}$ and $\hat{X}^{(2)} \in \mathbb{R}^{d_2\times n_2}$ denote the examples appearing and only appearing in both views, view 1 and view 2, respectively. $X^{(1)} \in \mathbb{R}^{d_1\times n_3}$ denotes the shared data in view 1, and $X^{(2)} \in \mathbb{R}^{d_2\times n_3}$ denotes the shared data in view 2. We assume that $X_1 \in \mathbb{R}^{d_1\times(n_3+n_1)} = [X^{(1)}, \hat{X}^{(1)}]$, $X_2 \in \mathbb{R}^{d_2\times(n_3+n_2)} = [X^{(2)}, \hat{X}^{(2)}]$, so that the n-th ($\forall n \leq n_3$) columns of X_1, X_2 belong to the same example, while the rest columns of them contain no common example. Figure 1 illustrates the notations.

We denote the initial graphs constructed from X_1 and X_2 as $A_1 \in \mathbb{R}^{(n_3+n_1)\times(n_3+n_1)}$ and $A_2 \in \mathbb{R}^{(n_3+n_2)\times(n_3+n_2)}$ respectively. And we denote the learned graphs that best approximate A_1 and A_2 as $S_1 \in \mathbb{R}^{(n_3+n_1)\times(n_3+n_1)}$ and $S_2 \in \mathbb{R}^{(n_3+n_2)\times(n_3+n_2)}$ respectively. We denote the initial graphs that correspond to $X^{(1)}$ and $X^{(2)}$ as $\bar{A}_1 \in \mathbb{R}^{n_3\times n_3}$ and $\bar{A}_2 \in \mathbb{R}^{n_3\times n_3}$ respectively. Thus $\bar{A}_1$ and $\bar{A}_2$ are the subgraphs of A_1 and A_2 respectively. And we denote the learned graphs that correspond to $X^{(1)}$ and $X^{(2)}$ as $\bar{S}_1 \in \mathbb{R}^{n_3\times n_3}$ and $\bar{S}_2 \in \mathbb{R}^{n_3\times n_3}$ respectively. Thus $\bar{S}_1$ and $\bar{S}_2$ are the subgraphs of S_1 and S_2 respectively. Figure 2 illustrates the learned graphs S_1 and S_2.

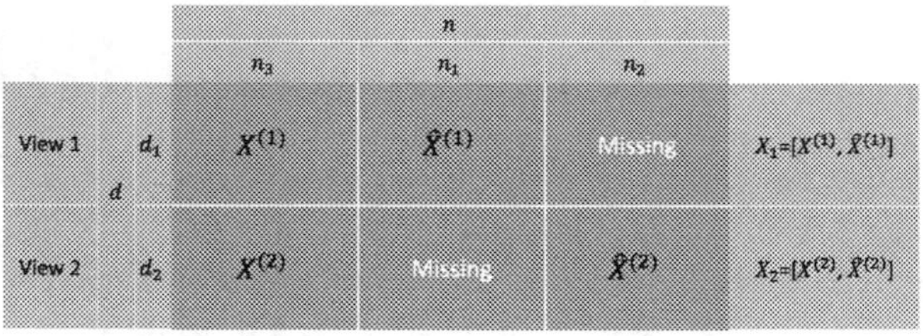

			n			
			n_3	n_1	n_2	
View 1	d	d_1	$X^{(1)}$	$\hat{X}^{(1)}$	Missing	$X_1=[X^{(1)}, \hat{X}^{(1)}]$
View 2		d_2	$X^{(2)}$	Missing	$\hat{X}^{(2)}$	$X_2=[X^{(2)}, \hat{X}^{(2)}]$

Fig. 1. Notations of data.

For each individual view, we aim to excavate its intrinsic clustering structure. Motivated by [16], which is effective in learning clustering structure with complete single-view data, we intend to learn the ideal structured graph from the initial graph. Given initial affinity matrixes A_1 and A_2 constructed from X_1 and X_2 respectively, we can learn the graph matrixes S_1 and S_2 that best approximate A_1 and A_2 respectively. Following are the elementary objectives:

$$\min_{\sum_j s_{1ij}=1, s_{ij}\geq 0} \| S_1 - A_1 \|_F^2, \tag{1}$$

$$\min_{\sum_j s_{2ij}=1, s_{ij}\geq 0} \| S_2 - A_2 \|_F^2. \tag{2}$$

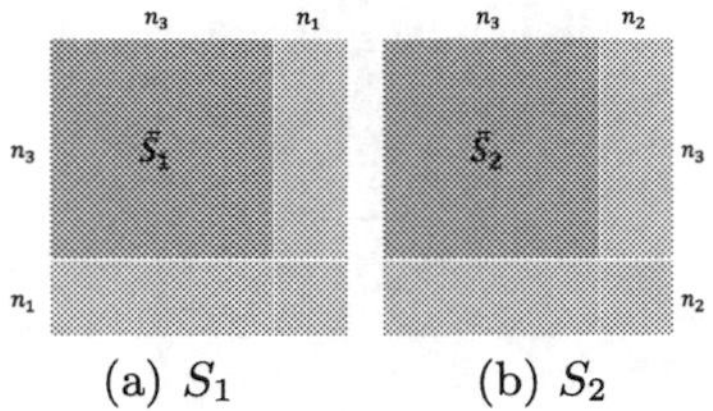

(a) S_1 (b) S_2

Fig. 2. Learned graphs S_1 and S_2. S_1 and S_2 are corresponding to X_1 and X_2 respectively. $\bar{S}_1$ and $\bar{S}_2$ are corresponding to $X^{(1)}$ and $X^{(2)}$ respectively.

Here we append the constraints $\sum_j s_{1ij} = 1$ and $\sum_j s_{2ij} = 1$ $(\forall i)$ to avoid the case that some rows of S_1 or S_2 are all zeros, and to make S_1 and S_2 to be comparable at the same scale.

For each view, according to Eq. (1) (or Eq. (2)), we can learn a graph to explore and maintain the inner structure of each view. Further, we aim to bridge different views, for which it is natural to take into account the consistency between the shared data in different views. For $\bar{S}_1$, we can not only learn from $\bar{A}_1$, but also $\bar{S}_2$. For $\bar{S}_2$, we can not only learn from $\bar{A}_2$, but also $\bar{S}_1$. Thus we have the following objective function:

$$\begin{aligned} \min_{S_1,S_2} \quad & \| S_1 - A_1 \|_F^2 + \| S_2 - A_2 \|_F^2 + \mu \| \bar{S}_1 - \bar{S}_2 \|_F^2 \\ s.t. & \sum_j s_{1ij} = 1, s_{1ij} \geq 0, \sum_j s_{2ij} = 1, s_{2ij} \geq 0, \end{aligned} \tag{3}$$

where $\mu > 0$ is a parameter that balances the first two terms and the last term.

To make the learned graphs have ideal structures directly for clustering tasks, we introduce the following property [4,15]:

Property 1. The number of connected components in the graph with the similarity matrix S is equal to the multiplicity c of the eigenvalue zero of L_S.

$L_S \in \mathbb{R}^{n \times n}$ in Property 1 is the Laplacian matrix of the nonnegative similarity matrix S, i.e. $L_S = D_S - (S^T + S)/2$ (where D_S is the degree matrix defined as a diagonal matrix whose i-th diagonal element is $\sum_j (s_{ij} + s_{ji})/2$).

Given a graph with graph matrix S, Property 1 indicates that if $rank(L_S) = n - c$, then this graph contains c connected components and each component corresponds to a cluster. We can obtain clustering results from the learned graph. Thus the problem (3) can be improved to the following problem:

$$\begin{aligned} \min_{S_1,S_2} \quad & \| S_1 - A_1 \|_F^2 + \| S_2 - A_2 \|_F^2 + \mu \| \bar{S}_1 - \bar{S}_2 \|_F^2 \\ s.t. & \sum_j s_{1ij} = 1, s_{1ij} \geq 0, rank(L_{S_1}) = n_1 + n_3 - c, \\ & \sum_j s_{2ij} = 1, s_{2ij} \geq 0, rank(L_{S_2}) = n_2 + n_3 - c, \end{aligned} \tag{4}$$

which is equivalent to the following optimization problem for large enough values of both λ_1 and λ_2:

$$\begin{aligned}\min_{S_1,S_2} \quad & \| S_1 - A_1 \|_F^2 + 2\lambda_1 \sum_{i=1}^{c} \sigma_{1i}(L_{S_1}) + \| S_2 - A_2 \|_F^2 \\ & + 2\lambda_2 \sum_{i=1}^{c} \sigma_{2i}(L_{S_2}) + \mu \| \bar{S}_1 - \bar{S}_2 \|_F^2 \\ s.t. \; & \sum_j s_{1ij} = 1, s_{1ij} \geq 0, \sum_j s_{2ij} = 1, s_{2ij} \geq 0.\end{aligned} \tag{5}$$

Here, $\sigma_{1i}(L_{S_1})$ and $\sigma_{2i}(L_{S_2})$ denote the i-th smallest eigenvalue of L_{S_1} and L_{S_2} respectively. Noting that $\sigma_{1i}(L_{S_1}) \geq 0 (\forall i)$ and $\sigma_{2i}(L_{S_2}) \geq 0 (\forall i)$, therefore when λ_1 and λ_2 are large enough, $\sum_{i=1}^{c} \sigma_{1i}(L_{S_1}) = 0$ and $\sum_{i=1}^{c} \sigma_{2i}(L_{S_2}) = 0$, so that the constraint $rank(L_{S_1}) = n_1 + n_3 - c$ and $rank(L_{S_2}) = n_2 + n_3 - c$ in the problem (4) will be satisfied. Thus, the problem (5) is equivalent to the problem (4). According to Ky Fan's Theorem [5], we have

$$\begin{aligned}\sum_{i=1}^{c} \sigma_{1i}(L_{S_1}) &= \min_{F_1 \in \mathbb{R}^{(n_1+n_3)\times c}, F_1^T F_1 = I} Tr(F_1^T L_{S_1} F_1), \\ \sum_{i=1}^{c} \sigma_{2i}(L_{S_2}) &= \min_{F_2 \in \mathbb{R}^{(n_2+n_3)\times c}, F_2^T F_2 = I} Tr(F_2^T L_{S_2} F_2),\end{aligned} \tag{6}$$

where F_1 and F_2 are the intermediate variables. Thus the problem (5) is further equivalent to the following problem:

$$\begin{aligned}\min_{S_1,F_1,S_2,F_2} \quad & \| S_1 - A_1 \|_F^2 + 2\lambda_1 Tr(F_1^T L_{S_1} F_1) + \| S_2 - A_2 \|_F^2 \\ & + 2\lambda_2 Tr(F_2^T L_{S_2} F_2) + \mu \| \bar{S}_1 - \bar{S}_2 \|_F^2 \\ s.t. \; & \sum_j s_{1ij} = 1, s_{1ij} \geq 0, \sum_j s_{2ij} = 1, s_{2ij} \geq 0, \\ & F_1 \in \mathbb{R}^{(n_1+n_3)\times c}, F_1^T F_1 = I, F_2 \in \mathbb{R}^{(n_2+n_3)\times c}, F_2^T F_2 = I,\end{aligned} \tag{7}$$

where both parameters λ_1 and λ_1 are large enough to guarantee that the sums of the c smallest eigenvalues of both L_{S_1} and L_{S_1} are equal to zero.

According to Eq. (7), note that different from previous graph-based methods, our graphs are learned, which are learned from both the initial graphs and the consistency between different views. Besides, Eq. (7) is designed to cluster data points directly by learning graphs with structures which are ideal for clustering. From the learned structured graph, we can obtain clustering results of each view directly. Then by making a simple best one-to-one map between the clustering results of $X^{(1)}$ and $X^{(2)}$, the final clustering results can be derived.

Since the problem (7) is not convex and the regularization is added on the partial elements of the graph matrixes, it seems difficult to solve. We propose an efficient algorithm to solve this problem in the next section.

3 Optimization Algorithms

When S_1 and S_2 are fixed, optimizing F_1, F_2, the problem (7) becomes

$$\min_{F_1 \in \mathbb{R}^{(n_1+n_3)\times c}, F_1^T F_1 = I} \quad Tr(F_1^T L_{S_1} F_1), \tag{8}$$

$$\min_{F_2 \in \mathbb{R}^{(n_2+n_3)\times c} F_2^T F_2 = I} \quad Tr(F_2^T L_{S_2} F_2). \tag{9}$$

The optimal solution of F_1 and F_2 is formed by the c eigenvectors of L_{S_1} and L_{S_2} respectively corresponding to their c smallest eigenvalues.

When F_1, F_2 and S_2 are fixed, optimizing S_1, the problem (7) becomes

$$\begin{aligned} &\min_{S_1} \ \| S_1 - A_1 \|_F^2 + 2\lambda_1 Tr(F_1^T L_{S_1} F_1) + \mu \| \bar{S}_1 - \bar{S}_2 \|_F^2 \\ &s.t. \sum_j s_{1ij} = 1, s_{1ij} \geq 0, \end{aligned} \tag{10}$$

where $S_1, A_1 \in \mathbb{R}^{(n_3+n_1)\times(n_3+n_1)}$ and $\bar{S}_1, \bar{S}_2 \in \mathbb{R}^{n_3 \times n_3}$.

The problem (10) is equal to

$$\begin{aligned} \min_{\sum_j s_{1ij}=1, s_{1ij}\geq 0} \ & \sum_{1\leq i,j\leq n_3+n_1} (s_{1ij} - a_{1ij})^2 + \lambda_1 \sum_{1\leq i,j\leq n_3+n_1} s_{1ij}(f_{1i} - f_{1j}) \\ & + \mu \sum_{1\leq i,j\leq n_3+n_1} (\bar{s}_{1ij} - \bar{s}_{2ij})^2. \end{aligned} \tag{11}$$

We can solve the following problems separately for each i since the problem (11) is independent for different i.

Update the first n_3 **rows of** $S_1 (1 \leq i \leq n_3)$. For each i, we denote $v_{1ij} = f_{1i} - f_{1j}$. Then the problem (11) becomes

$$\begin{aligned} \min_{\sum_j s_{1ij}=1, s_{1ij}\geq 0} \ & \sum_{j=1}^{n_3} (s_{1ij} - a_{1ij})^2 + \sum_{j=n_3+1}^{n_3+n_1} (s_{1ij} - a_{1ij})^2 + \lambda_1 \sum_{j=1}^{n_3} s_{1ij} v_{1ij} \\ & + \lambda_1 \sum_{j=n_3+1}^{n_3+n_1} s_{1ij} v_{1ij} + \mu \sum_{j=1}^{n_3} (s_{1ij} - \bar{s}_{2ij})^2. \end{aligned} \tag{12}$$

For each i, we denote $s_{1i} = [\bar{s}_{1i}, \hat{s}_{1i}]$, $v_{1i} = [\bar{v}_{1i}, \hat{v}_{1i}]$ and $a_{1i} = [\bar{a}_{1i}, \hat{a}_{1i}]$. $\bar{s}_{1i}$, $\bar{v}_{1i}$ and $\bar{a}_{1i}$ contains and only contains the first n_3 elements of the vector s_{1i}, v_{1i} and a_{1i} respectively. $\hat{s}_{1i}$, $\hat{v}_{1i}$ and $\hat{a}_{1i}$ contains and only contains the last n_1 elements of the vector s_{1i}, v_{1i} and a_{1i} respectively.

The problem (12) can be written in vector form as

$$\min_{s_{1i}^T \mathbf{1}=1, s_{1i}\geq 0} \| \sqrt{1+\mu}\bar{s}_{1i} - \frac{(\bar{a}_{1i} - \frac{1}{2}\lambda_1 \bar{v}_{1i} + \mu \bar{s}_{2i})}{\sqrt{1+\mu}} \|_2^2 + \| \hat{s}_{1i} - (\hat{a}_{1i} - \frac{1}{2}\lambda_1 \hat{v}_{1i}) \|_2^2 . \tag{13}$$

We denote $c1 = \bar{a}_{1i} - 1/2\lambda_1\bar{v}_{1i} + \mu\bar{s}_{2i}$, $c_2 = \hat{a}_{1i} - 1/2\lambda_1\hat{v}_{1i}, b_1 = [c_1, c_2]$. U_1 is a diagonal matrix whose first n_3 diagonal elements are all $1 + \mu$, and the others are all 1. Then the problem (13) becomes

$$\min_{s_{1i}^T \mathbf{1}=1, s_{1i} \geq 0} \quad s_1 U_1 s_1^T - 2 s_1 b_1. \tag{14}$$

This problem can be solved by algorithm in [16].

Update the last n_1 rows of $S_1 (n_3 < i \leq n_3 + n_1)$. When $n_3 < i \leq n_3 + n_1$, denoting $v_{1ij} = f_{1i} - f_{1j}$, the problem (11) becomes

$$\min_{\sum_j s_{1ij}=1, s_{1ij} \geq 0} \quad \sum_j (s_{1ij} - a_{1ij})^2 + \sum_j s_{1ij} v_{1ij}. \tag{15}$$

The problem (15) can be written in vector form as

$$\min_{s_{1i}^T \mathbf{1}=1, s_{1i} \geq 0} \quad \| \, s_{1i} - (a_{1i} - \frac{1}{2}\lambda_1 v_{1i}) \, \|_2^2 \, . \tag{16}$$

This problem can be solved with an effective iterative algorithm [8], or solved by the solution with a similar form as Eq. (30) in [16]

When F_1, F_2 and S_1 are fixed, optimizing S_2 is similar to optimizing S_1. We omit the detailed process.

Update the first n_3 rows of $S_2 (1 \leq i \leq n_3)$. When $1 \leq i \leq n_3$, the problem (7) becomes

$$\min_{s_{2i}^T \mathbf{1}=1, s_{2i} \geq 0} \quad s_2 U_2 s_2^T - 2 s_2 b_2, \tag{17}$$

where $b_2 = [c_3, c_4]$, U_2 is a diagonal matrix whose first n_3 diagonal elements are all $1+\mu$, and the others are all 1, $c_3 = (\bar{a}_{2i} - 1/2\lambda_2\bar{v}_{2i} + \mu\bar{s}_{1i}), c_4 = \hat{a}_{2i} - 1/2\lambda_2\hat{v}_{2i}$.

Update the last n_2 rows of $S_2 (n_3 < i \leq n_3 + n_2)$. When $n_3 < i \leq n_3 + n_2$, the problem (7) becomes

$$\min_{s_{2i}^T \mathbf{1}=1, s_{2i} \geq 0} \quad \| \, s_{2i} - (a_{2i} - \frac{1}{2}\lambda_2 v_{2i}) \, \|_2^2 \, . \tag{18}$$

The algorithm is provided in Algorithm 1, in which for each data point, we only update the nearest k similarities in S in order to reduce the complexity of updating S, F significantly. This technique makes our method applied on data sets with very large scale.

Algorithm 1. SGL

Input: A_1, A_2, μ, large enough λ_1, large enough λ_2.
Initialize: F_1 formed by the c eigenvectors of L_{A_1} corresponding to the c smallest eigenvalues, F_2 formed by the c eigenvectors of L_{A_2} corresponding to the c smallest eigenvalues.
repeat
  For each i, update the i-th row of S_1 by solving the problems (14)(16).
  Update F_1 by solving the problems (8).
  For each i, update the i-th row of S_2 by solving the problems (17)(18).
  Update F_2 by solving the problems (9).
until convergence
Output: S_1 with c connected components, S_2 with c connected components.

4 Discussion

4.1 Convergence Analysis

Property 2. The Algorithm 1 will monotonically decrease the objective of the problem in each iteration, and converge to a local optimum of the problem.

The brief idea in proving this theorem is summarized as follows. The Algorithm 1 converges because the objective function value of Eq. (7) decreases as iteration round increases. In detail, with fixed S_1 and S_2, optimal F_1 and F_2 can be obtained by solving the problems (8) and (9) respectively, which will reduce the objective function value, and with fixed F_1 and F_2, we can get optimal S_1 and S_2 by solving the problems (14) (16) and (17) (18) respectively, which will also reduce the objective function value. In summary, the Algorithm 1 will converge to a local optimum of the problem (7).

4.2 Computational Time

Since SGL is solved in an alternative way, we calculate their total computational complexity by analyzing the computational complexity in solving corresponding alternative optimization problems. The Algorithm 1 of SGL can be divided into three alternative optimization problems. The problems in Eqs. (8) and (9) updating matrix F_1 and F_2 respectively can be solved by eigen-decomposition, and the computational complexity is $O((n_1 + n_3)^3)$ and $O((n_2 + n_3)^3)$ respectively. Therefore, the total computational complexity of this procedure is $O(\max\{(n_1 + n_3)^3, (n_2 + n_3)^3\})$.

The problems in Eqs. (14) and (16) to update S_1 row by row are the subproblems of (10). The problem in Eq. (14) can be solved by Lagrange Multiplier and Newton's method, of which the computational complexity is $O((n_1 + n_3) \times n_3)$. The problem (16) can be solved by an efficient iterative algorithm [8], and the computational complexity is $O((n_1 + n_3) \times n_1)$. Therefore, the total computational complexity of this step is $O((n_1 + n_3)^2)$.

The problems in Eqs. (17) and (18) to update S_2 are similar to Eqs. (14) and (16) respectively, and the total computational complexity is $O((n_2 + n_3)^2)$.

As a result, the total computational complexity of SGL is $O(T \times \max\{(n_1 + n_3)^3, (n_2 + n_3)^3\})$, where T is the number of iterations. Obviously, cubic time complexity is caused by spectral decompositions. But in our algorithm, the Laplacian matrixes on which we implement spectral decompositions is sparse. Besides, nowadays there are many other novel alternative efficient methods handling spectral decomposition.

5 Experiment

5.1 Data Sets

MSRCv1 is comprised of 240 images in 8 class in total. Two pairs of visual features are extracted: 256 Local Binary Pattern(LBP) and 512 GIST noted as **MSRCv1GC**, 1302 CENTRIST and 200 SIFT noted as **MSRCv1CS**. **Ionosphere** is composed of 351 free electrons in the ionosphere observed by a system in Goose Bay, Labrador. The data can be divided into two classes: "Good" are those showing evidence of some type of structure in the ionosphere. "Bad" returns are those that do not. **Caltech101-7** contains 441 objective images in 7 categories as whole. We extract two features from each image data, including 200 SIFT and 32 Gabor texture. **Handwritten numerals (HW)** contains 2000 images data points for 0 to 9 digit classes and each class has 200 data points. We select 216 profile correlations (FAC) and 76 Fourier coefficients of the character shapes (FOU) for our clustering. **WebKB** is comprised of 1051 pages collected from four universities. Each page has 2 views: 334 citation view, and 2949 content view. Statistics of the data sets are summarized in Table 1.

Table 1. Data sets descriptions

Data sets	Size	View	Cluster Num	Feat1	Feat2
MSRCv1GC	210	2	7	256	512
MSRCv1CS	210	2	7	1302	200
Ionosphere	351	2	2	34	25
Caltech101-7	441	2	7	200	32
HW	2000	2	10	216	76
WebKB	1051	2	2	334	2949

5.2 Comparing Methods

Single-view methods **V1CLR** and **V2CLR**: With the partial example ratio being zero, CLR [16] algorithm is executed separately on view 1 and view 2 noted as V1CLR and V2CLR respectively.

Completion methods **CentroidSC** and **PairwiseSC**: Firstly, the partial examples are completed with the Robust Rank-k Matrix Completion [9] method. Two co-regularization schemes [10] are proposed to accomplish this work: Centroid-Based Co-regularization noted as CentroidSC and Pairwise-Based Co-regularization noted as PairwiseSC.

Subspace methods **PVC** [12] and **IMG** [20].

Other method: **CGC** [3] is aimed to deal with many-to-many instance relationship, which supports the situation of incomplete views.

We construct the sparse affinity matrixes A_1 and A_2 by Eq. (35) in [16]. Following [12], we randomly select a ratio of examples to be partial to simulate the partial view setting, i.e. they only appear in either of the two views while the remaining ones are described by both views. we evenly assign them to the two views to simplify the experiment. Each time we randomly select 10% to 90% examples, with 10% as interval, as partial examples. We repeat such process 10 times and record the average and standard deviation results. For PVC and IMG, the k-means algorithm is performed to get the final clustering result as in the original paper. The other clustering methods may be also feasible. We utilize two standard clustering evaluation metric to measure the multi-view clustering performance, that is, Clustering Accuracy (ACC) and Normalized Mutual Information (NMI). Same as [12], we test all the methods under different Partial Example Ratio (PER) varying from 0.1 to 0.9 with an interval of 0.1.

5.3 Clustering Result Comparison

Table 2 and Fig. 3 report the ACC and NMI values respectively on various data sets with different PER ratio settings. From these figures and the table, we make the following observations and discussions.

In almost all the settings, our method usually outperform both methods executed on single complete view (V1CLR and V2CLR) even when the PER ratio equals 30% , which confirm that our approach synthesizes the information from both views validly and proposed constraint between the subgraphs corresponding to the same samples (from different views) is effective. As the partial example ratio PER varies from 10% to 90%, the proposed method usually performs much better than other multi-view clustering baselines. Particularly, the performance of our approach improves much compared with the baselines when Per is less than 40%. And with more missing examples, the performance of all the methods drops basically.

CentroidSC and PairwiseSC usually perform worst on almost all the data sets, which may be caused by that matrix completion requires the randomness of the missing locations, while the data are missing block-wise for the multi-view incomplete data setting. One may be curious why our method performs much better than other subspace learning methods. This may be caused by that their assumption that shared data in different views have exactly the same representations in the latent space may damage the inner structure of each view and increase the risk of over-fitting. Besides, our graphs are learned from both

Table 2. Experimental ACC (the higher the better) results (mean(std)) on six data sets. The best result is highlighted in boldface. T-Test (statistical significance of T-Test is 5%) results between our and other algorithms, Win (•) means our performs better. Lose (⊗) means other algorithm performs better. Tie (⊙) means that our and other algorithms cannot outperform each other.

Data sets	V1CLR	V2CLR	PER	CentroidSC	PairwiseSC	PVC	IMG	CGC	SGL
			0.1	.6499(.0399)•	.6160(.0598)•	.6879(.0191)•	.6952(.0182)•	.6271(.0487)•	**.8300(.0430)**
			0.2	.6030(.0370)•	.5752(.0382)•	.6510(.0414)•	.6749(.0294)•	.5924(.0349)•	**.8238(.0365)**
			0.3	.5480(.0329)•	.5494(.0223)•	.6482(.0429)•	.6645(.0332)•	.5952(.0435)•	**.8090(.0282)**
			0.4	.4979(.0354)•	.5165(.0296)•	.6403(.0246)•	.6748(.0445)•	.5876(.0664)•	**.7852(.0313)**
MSRCv1GC	.7524	.6619	0.5	.4568(.0246)•	.4619(.0297)•	.6302(.0442)•	.6564(.0381)•	.5986(.0583)•	**.7657(.0279)**
			0.6	.4329(.0371)•	.4339(.0361)•	.5848(.0313)•	.6605(.0438)•	.5848(.0743)•	**.7371(.0413)**
			0.7	.4134(.0296)•	.4199(.0318)•	.5926(.0407)•	.6415(.0470)•	.5771(.0436)•	**.7224(.0440)**
			0.8	.4014(.0347)•	.4043(.0298)•	.5758(.0233)•	.6250(.0593)•	.5652(.0552)•	**.6810(.0341)**
			0.9	.3733(.0243)•	.3830(.0246)•	.4948(.0297)•	.5505(.0711)•	.5152(.0995)•	**.6368(.0310)**
			0.1	.6231(.0269)•	.6193(.0232)•	.6305(.0331)•	.5983(.0270)•	.5286(.0490)•	**.7895(.0071)**
			0.2	.5604(.0328)•	.6125(.0423)•	.6228(.0367)•	.5600(.0244)•	.5000(.0231)•	**.7067(.0415)**
			0.3	.5521(.0209)•	.6036(.0364)•	.5823(.0682)•	.5628(.0468)•	.5667(.0554)•	**.7210(.0568)**
			0.4	.5129(.0423)•	.5757(.0240)•	.5552(.0550)•	.5611(.0341)•	.5562(.0600)⊙	**.6762(.0516)**
MSRCv1CS	.6762	.5667	0.5	.4629(.0352)•	.5175(.0395)•	.5386(.0735)⊙	.5541(.0731)⊙	.5714(.0288)•	**.6381(.0297)**
			0.6	.4525(.0376)•	.4859(.0390)•	.5550(.0460)•	.5570(.0445)⊙	.6067(.0338)⊙	**.6390(.0701)**
			0.7	.4268(.0380)•	.4433(.0277)•	.5294(.0764)⊙	.5171(.0546)•	.5467(.0407)•	**.6143(.0370)**
			0.8	.4149(.0321)•	.4090(.0208)•	.5496(.0269)⊙	.5518(.0550)⊙	.5267(.0605)⊙	**.5981(.0300)**
			0.9	.3972(.0165)•	.4017(.0332)•	.4605(.0218)•	.4890(.0643)•	.4990(.0652)•	**.5848(.0637)**
			0.1	.6407(.0192)•	.6397(.0172)•	.5832(.0044)•	.5983(.0270)•	.5286(.0490)•	**.7179(.0083)**
			0.2	.6270(.0251)•	.6172(.0287)•	.5770(.0125)•	.5600(.0244)•	.5000(.0231)•	**.7179(.0110)**
			0.3	.6227(.0351)•	.6076(.0379)•	.5683(.0075)•	.5628(.0468)•	.5667(.0554)•	**.7179(.0252)**
			0.4	.6101(.0234)•	.6180(.0332)•	.5693(.0085)•	.5611(.0341)•	.5562(.0600)•	**.7174(.0174)**
Ionosphere	.6097	.5726	0.5	.5907(.0354)•	.5960(.0367)•	.5648(.0053)•	.5541(.0731)•	.5714(.0288)•	**.7020(.0162)**
			0.6	.5870(.0331)•	.5887(.0260)•	.5730(.0088)•	.5570(.0445)•	.6067(.0338)•	**.6923(.0225)**
			0.7	.5744(.0174)•	.5855(.0206)•	.5794(.0056)•	.5171(.0546)•	.5467(.0407)•	**.6917(.0219)**
			0.8	.5532(.0188)•	.5670(.0345)•	.5652(.0140)•	.5518(.0550)•	.5267(.0605)•	**.6883(.0235)**
			0.9	.5558(.0351)•	.5554(.0382)•	.5656(.0049)•	.4890(.0643)•	.4990(.0652)•	**.6724(.0309)**
			0.1	.4221(.0339)•	.3976(.0197)•	.5189(.0258)•	.5472(.0118)•	.5757(.0280)⊙	**.5912(.0137)**
			0.2	.4011(.0231)•	.3926(.0189)•	.5128(.0209)•	.5243(.0596)•	.5508(.0769)⊙	**.5821(.0143)**
			0.3	.3891(.0225)•	.3709(.0212)•	.4903(.0366)•	.5365(.0243)•	.5054(.0606)•	**.5653(.0245)**
			0.4	.3639(.0266)•	.3604(.0201)•	.4645(.0241)•	.5060(.0670)⊙	.5279(.0636)⊙	**.5440(.0364)**
CaltechSW	.5578	.4671	0.5	.3506(.0225)•	.3457(.0224)•	.4325(.0175)•	.5033(.0508)⊙	**.5086(.0467)**⊙	.5075(.0291)
			0.6	.3307(.0296)•	.3344(.0303)•	.4226(.0345)•	.4901(.0414)⊙	**.5159(.0324)**⊙	.4912(.0270)
			0.7	.3230(.0262)•	.3194(.0265)•	.3988(.0274)•	.4657(.0530)⊙	**.4968(.0644)**⊙	.4776(.0196)
			0.8	.3205(.0248)•	.3251(.0222)•	.4053(.0405)•	.4546(.0361)•	.4649(.0340)⊙	**.4794(.0186)**
			0.9	.3098(.0235)•	.3100(.0256)•	.3890(.0297)•	.4482(.0359)⊙	.4422(.0250)⊙	**.4583(.0339)**
			0.1	.7041(.0060)•	.6380(.0169)•	.5629(.0204)•	.5893(.0403)•	.6718(.0527)•	**.8231(.0049)**
			0.2	.6631(.0131)•	.5924(.0108)•	.5649(.0279)•	.5341(.0387)•	.6318(.0678)•	**.7862(.0230)**
			0.3	.6145(.0075)•	.5547(.0122)•	.5201(.0224)•	.5215(.0148)•	.6058(.0473)•	**.7763(.0144)**
			0.4	.5734(.0067)•	.5254(.0080)•	.4937(.0123)•	.5011(.0513)•	.5937(.0708)•	**.7655(.0101)**
HW	.7745	.7020	0.5	.5325(.0114)•	.4964(.0086)•	.4601(.0163)•	.4835(.0199)•	.5674(.0552)•	**.7613(.0186)**
			0.6	.5048(.0098)•	.4802(.0077)•	.4526(.0144)•	.4563(.0273)•	.5408(.0486)•	**.7441(.0150)**
			0.7	.4941(.0105)•	.4584(.0088)•	.4314(.0159)•	.4213(.0088)•	.5248(.0304)•	**.7351(.0165)**
			0.8	.4892(.0133)•	.4429(.0060)•	.4184(.0098)•	.4041(.0226)•	.5096(.0300)•	**.7267(.0099)**
			0.9	.4846(.0179)•	.4354(.0101)•	.4145(.0171)•	.3743(.0299)•	.4809(.0336)•	**.7272(.0271)**
			0.1	.7925(.0081)•	.8006(.0126)•	.7336(.0063)•	.2952(.3154)•	.7159(.0426)•	**.9701(.0030)**
			0.2	.7824(.0088)•	.7812(.0124)•	.7291(.0062)•	.2846(.3006)•	.6830(.0574)•	**.9678(.0051)**
			0.3	.7565(.0267)•	.7617(.0253)•	.7219(.0041)•	.3124(.3299)•	.6852(.0565)•	**.9615(.0074)**
			0.4	.7782(.0112)•	.7796(.0098)•	.7175(.0148)•	.3166(.3343)•	.6834(.0568)•	**.9574(.0097)**
WebKB	.8563	.8249	0.5	.7723(.0272)•	.7692(.0420)•	.6993(.0120)•	.3364(.3548)•	.6728(.0538)•	**.9006(.0302)**
			0.6	.7047(.0748)•	.7174(.0763)•	.6946(.0234)•	.3461(.3650)•	.6626(.0404)•	**.8680(.0260)**
			0.7	.5834(.0134)•	.5834(.0134)•	.6916(.0170)•	.3580(.3779)•	.6463(.0527)•	**.8418(.0231)**
			0.8	.5568(.0107)•	.5568(.0107)•	.6737(.0286)•	.3532(.3728)•	.6422(.0488)•	**.8092(.0313)**
			0.9	.5264(.0102)•	.5264(.0102)•	.6564(.0235)•	.3541(.3737)•	.6197(.0566)•	**.7857(.0250)**
win\tie\lose				54 \ 0 \ 0	54 \ 0 \ 0	51\ 3 \ 0	46 \ 8 \ 0	43 \ 11 \ 0	

the initial graphs and the consistency between views. And the learned graphs contain ideal clustering structures.

One may be also interested in the reason why our method has a considerable improvement when PER is high. When PER is high, for most of the subspace learning methods, it is hard to accurately estimate the common representation P_c simply from the little common complete data. IMG utilizes a general global structure to remedy this deviation. However, the global structure overlooks the specific intrinsic structure of each individual view. Our structures are more detailed and specific.

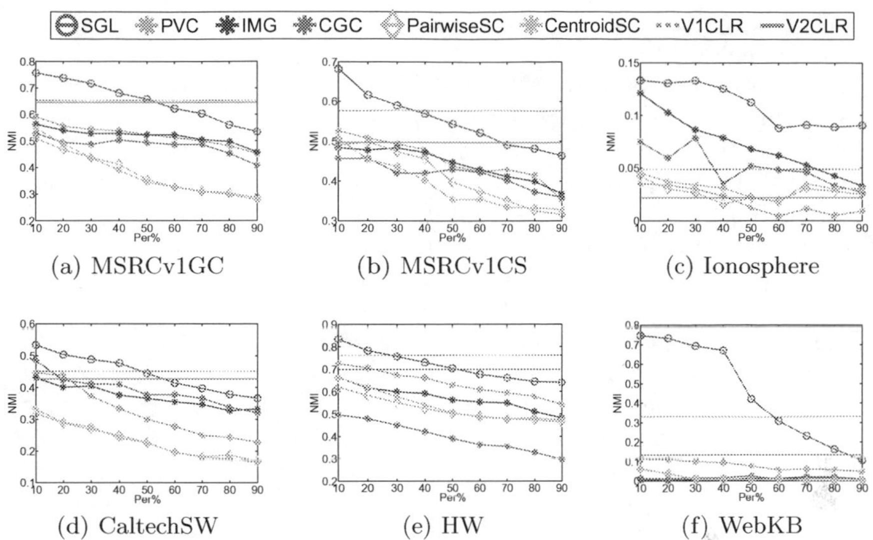

Fig. 3. The NMI (the higher the better) results for the six data sets. PER (partial example ratio) is the ratio of partial examples. Partial examples are evenly distributed to the two views.

5.4 Convergence Study

We experiment on data set MSRCv1 to show the convergence property. The convergence curves and corresponding NMI performances with $PER = 30\%$ and $PER = 70\%$ setting are plotted in Fig. 4. For $PER = 30\%$ setting, we set $\{\lambda1, \lambda2, \mu\}$ as $\{50, 50, 2.0\}$. For $PER = 70\%$ setting, we set $\{\lambda1, \lambda2, \mu\}$ as $\{50, 50, 9.0\}$. The objective function during each iteration is drawn in black. We can see that the value of objective function decreases rapidly with the increasing of iteration round. Inspiringly, it only takes around 12 rounds to converge. The NMI value during each iteration is drawn in red, from which we can see 12 round is enough to get good clustering performance.

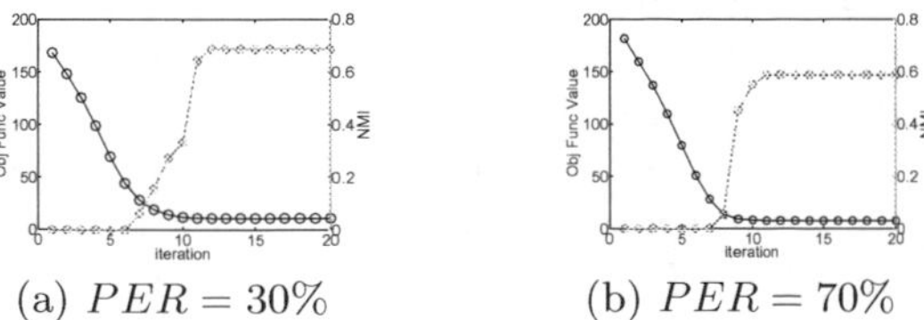

Fig. 4. Convergence curve of Objective function value and corresponding NMI performance curve *vs* number of iterations of our with $PER = 30\%$ and $PER = 70\%$ on MSRCv1GC data set. (Color figure online)

5.5 Parameter Study

We study parameters on four data sets: MSRCv1GC, MSRCv1SW CaltechSW and HW. There are three parameters to explore: λ_1, λ_2 and μ. Following [16], we determined both λ_1 and λ_2 in a heuristic way : in each iteration, we computed the numbers of zero eigenvalues of L_{S1} and L_{S2}, if one is larger (smaller) than k, we divide (multiply) it by two (respectively). Following [12], We tune μ for three different PER 30%, 50% and 70%. As above experiment, we randomly select a ratio of examples to be partial and repeat such process 10 times to record the average results. The effect of the parameter μ is showed in Fig. 5.

From Fig. 5, it is easy to see that on all data sets, our method achieves steadily good performance for NMI with a very large range of μ in all settings, which validates the robustness of our method. Our method usually has a relatively good performance when μ is in the range of $[2.0, 4.0]$ for the $PER = 30\%$ and $PER = 50\%$ settings, while the best range becomes $[7.0, 9.0]$ for the $PER = 70\%$ setting.

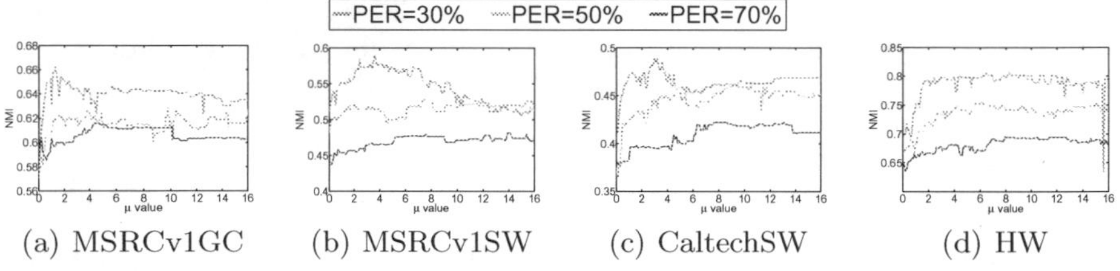

(a) MSRCv1GC (b) MSRCv1SW (c) CaltechSW (d) HW

Fig. 5. Effect of the parameter μ on four data set with three different PER.

6 Conclusion

In this paper, we propose a method to handle multi-view clustering problem in the case that all the views suffer from the missing of some data. Different from existing approaches, we simultaneously manipulate and cluster incomplete multi-view data. We excavate and maintain the intrinsic structure of each individual view, and establish interaction between the different views through the shared data. For each view, a graph with exactly c connected components can be learned so that the clustering results can be derived from graphs without any post-clustering. To optimize our proposed objective, we provide the solution which can simultaneously handle both the whole and partial regularization problem. Experimental results on six real-world multi-view data sets compared with several baselines validate the effectiveness of our method. In the future, we will study how to reduce the computational cost of our method.

References

1. Bickel, S., Scheffer, T.: Multi-view clustering. In: Proceedings of the 4th IEEE International Conference on Data Mining (ICDM), pp. 19–26 (2004)
2. Brand, M.: Incremental singular value decomposition of uncertain data with missing values. In: Computer Vision - ECCV 7th European Conference on Computer Vision, pp. 707–720 (2002)
3. Cheng, W., Zhang, X., Guo, Z., Wu, Y., Sullivan, P.F., Wang, W.: Flexible and robust co-regularized multi-domain graph clustering. In: Proceedings of the 19th ACM SIGKDD International Conference on Knowledge Discovery and Data Mining, pp. 320–328 (2013)
4. Chung, F.R.: Spectral Graph Theory, vol. 92. American Mathematical Society, New York (1997)
5. Fan, K.: On a theorem of Weyl concerning eigenvalues of linear transformations i. Proc. Natl. Acad. Sci. **35**(11), 652–655 (1949)
6. Greene, D., Cunningham, P.: A matrix factorization approach for integrating multiple data views. In: Proceedings of Machine Learning and Knowledge Discovery in Databases, European Conference, ECML PKDD 2009, pp. 423–438 (2009)
7. Guo, Y.: Convex subspace representation learning from multi-view data. In: Proceedings of the 27th AAAI Conference on Artificial Intelligence (2013)
8. Huang, J., Nie, F., Huang, H.: A new simplex sparse learning model to measure data similarity for clustering. In: Proceedings of the Twenty-Fourth International Joint Conference on Artificial Intelligence IJCAI, pp. 3569–3575 (2015)
9. Huang, J., Nie, F., Huang, H., Lei, Y., Ding, C.H.Q.: Social trust prediction using rank-k matrix recovery. In: Proceedings of the 23rd International Joint Conference on Artificial Intelligence IJCAI, pp. 2647–2653 (2013)
10. Kumar, A., Rai, P., Daume, H.: Co-regularized multi-view spectral clustering. In: Advances in Neural Information Processing Systems 24: 25th Annual Conference on Neural Information Processing Systems, pp. 1413–1421 (2011)
11. Lee, D.D., Seung, H.S.: Learning the parts of objects by non-negative matrix factorization. Nature **401**(6755), 788–791 (1999)
12. Li, S., Jiang, Y., Zhou, Z.: Partial multi-view clustering. In: Proceedings of the 28th AAAI Conference on Artificial Intelligence, pp. 1968–1974 (2014)
13. Lin, Z., Chen, M., Ma, Y.: The augmented lagrange multiplier method for exact recovery of corrupted low-rank matrices. arXiv preprint arXiv:1009.5055 (2010)
14. Liu, J., Wang, C., Gao, J., Han, J.: Multi-view clustering via joint nonnegative matrix factorization. In: Proceedings of the 2013 SIAM International Conference on Data Mining, pp. 252–260. SIAM (2013)
15. Mohar, B., Alavi, Y., Chartrand, G., Oellermann, O.: The laplacian spectrum of graphs. Graph theory, combinatorics, and applications **2**(871–898), 12 (1991)
16. Nie, F., Wang, X., Jordan, M.I., Huang, H.: The constrained laplacian rank algorithm for graph-based clustering. In: Proceedings of the 30th AAAI Conference on Artificial Intelligence, pp. 1969–1976 (2016)
17. Shao, W., He, L., Yu, P.S.: Multiple incomplete views clustering via weighted nonnegative matrix factorization with $L_{2,1}$ regularization. In: Appice, A., Rodrigues, P.P., Santos Costa, V., Soares, C., Gama, J., Jorge, A. (eds.) ECML PKDD 2015. LNCS (LNAI), vol. 9284, pp. 318–334. Springer, Cham (2015). https://doi.org/10.1007/978-3-319-23528-8_20
18. Shao, W., Shi, X., Philip, S.Y.: Clustering on multiple incomplete datasets via collective kernel learning. In: 2013 IEEE 13rd International Conference on Data Mining (ICDM), pp. 1181–1186. IEEE (2013)

19. Wang, Q., Si, L., Shen, B.: Learning to hash on partial multi-modal data. In: Proceedings of the 24th International Joint Conference on Artificial Intelligence, IJCAI, pp. 3904–3910 (2015)
20. Zhao, H., Liu, H., Fu, Y.: Incomplete multi-modal visual data grouping. In: Proceedings of the 25th International Joint Conference on Artificial Intelligence, IJCAI, pp. 2392–2398 (2016)

DeepRSD: A Deep Regression Method for Sequential Data

Xishun Wang[1(✉)], Minjie Zhang[2], and Fenghui Ren[2]

[1] Bitmain Technologies Inc., Beijing, China
xw357@uowmail.edu.au

[2] School of Computing and Information Technology, University of Wollongong, Wollongong, Australia
{minjie,fren}@uow.edu.au

Abstract. Regressions on Sequential Data (RSD) are widely used in different disciplines. This paper proposes DeepRSD, which utilizes several different neural networks to result in an effective end-to-end learning method for RSD problems. There have been several variants of deep Recurrent Neural Networks (RNNs) in classification problems. The main functional part of DeepRSD is the stacked bi-directional RNNs, which is the most suitable deep RNN model for sequential data. We explore several conditions to ensure a plausible training of DeepRSD. More importantly, we propose an alternative dropout to improve its generalization. We apply DeepRSD to two different real-world problems and achieve state-of-the-art performances. Through comparisons with state-of-the-art methods, we conclude that DeepRSD can be a competitive method for RSD problems.

Keywords: Sequential data · Deep recurrent neural network
Alternative dropout · Regression

1 Introduction

In many regression problems, the predictor variables come from sequential data. For instance, predicting the hourly energy demand given weather forecasting in each hour, or estimating the valence of a facial expression from a video (sequence of images). Similar problems are widely seen in different disciplines. In this paper, we name these problems as Regressions on Sequential Data (RSD). RSD can be formally defined as follows.

$$\mathbf{y} = f_\theta(\mathbf{X}), \tag{1}$$

where f_θ is a transformation parameterized by θ, $\mathbf{X} = [\mathbf{x}_1, \mathbf{x}_2, \cdots, \mathbf{x}_T]$ is a $T \times N$ matrix, representing T steps and N predictor variables (features) in each step, and $\mathbf{y}$ can be a scalar or a T-dimension vector (a simple structured output).

X. Wang—Work done in University of Wollongong. Now the author is in Bitmain Technologies Inc.

X. Geng and B.-H. Kang (Eds.): PRICAI 2018, LNAI 11012, pp. 113–125, 2018.
https://doi.org/10.1007/978-3-319-97304-3_9

The challenge of RSD is how to simultaneously model the (complex) features in each step and the temporal information. Gradient boosting [3] is an effective method to handle complex features, but it cannot naturally model temporal information. People have to make extra effort to encode temporal information when using gradient boosting. Continuous conditional random fields [16] can simultaneously model step features and temporal information, but it is relatively weak to deal with complex features. Feature engineering or other models are introduced [21] to compensate its weakness.

In this paper, we propose DeepRSD to solve the RSD problem. DeepRSD takes advantages of several variants of neural networks to construct an effective end-to-end learning method. In the family of neural networks, Recurrent Neural Networks (RNNs) [17] gain the capacity of modeling sequential data. There have been some variants of deep RNN [7,14] in discrete problems. We deeply study different deep RNNs and choose stacked bi-directional RNN (Bi-RNN) to represent the sequential data $\mathbf{X}$ efficiently. The stacked Bi-RNNs can learn not only the temporal transitions, but also the complex relations in the heterogeneous step feature $\mathbf{x}_i$ through its nonlinear representations. As a result, stacked Bi-RNNs outperforms other deep RNNs in RSD problems.

It is challenging to train DeepRSD for two reasons. (1) RNN itself is hard to train. (2) Comparing to classification problems, the input and output are both unbounded in regression. We explore several conditions for a plausible training, including data preprocessing, initializations and preventing gradient vanishing/exploding for RNN. More importantly, we deeply study the dropout for stacked Bi-RNNs. The previous dropout methods do not work in DeepRSD. Instead, we propose an alternative dropout to effectively improve the generalization of DeepRSD. We also provide an explanation of alternative dropout through visualizations.

To show the advantages of DeepRSD, we insist to construct a universal model with an end-to-end learning manner to solve actual problems. We demonstrate the performance of DeepRSD in AMS solar energy prediction contest on Kaggle[1]. To the best of our knowledge, DeepRSD gets the best result evaluated by Kaggle server. We further evaluate DeepRSD on a dataset of electricity demand prediction, from NPower Forecasting Challenge 2016[2]. It is found that DeepRSD is still competitive even though the dataset is small. We also make general comparisons of DeepRSD and other state-of-the-art methods to demonstrate the effectiveness of DeepRSD.

The contributions of this paper are in three aspects: (1) We propose DeepRSD using several variants of neural networks for RSD problems and explore several conditions to reliably train DeepRSD. (2) We propose alternative dropout to effectively improve the generalization of DeepRSD. (3) We apply DeepRSD to two real-world problems and achieve state-of-the-art performances.

---

1 https://www.kaggle.com/c/ams-2014-solar-energy-prediction-contest.

2 https://www.npowerjobs.com/graduates/forecasting-challenge. Data are publicly available. Competition results are also published on this webpage.

2 Designs of DeepRSD

In this section, the standard RNN is briefly reviewed at first, and then the architecture of DeepRSD is illustrated. In the following, we discuss how to choose a proper activation function for DeepRSD. We also describe alternative dropout in detail.

2.1 RNN Review

As RNN is the core module for DeepRSD, we have a brief review of standard RNN [17]. For the input sequence $\mathbf{x}_1, \mathbf{x}_2, \cdots, \mathbf{x}_T$, each in $\mathbb{R}^N$, RNN computes a sequence of hidden states $\mathbf{h}_1, \mathbf{h}_2, \cdots, \mathbf{h}_T$, each in $\mathbb{R}^M$, and a sequence of predictions $\hat{\mathbf{y}}_1, \hat{\mathbf{y}}_2, \cdots, \hat{\mathbf{y}}_T$, each in $\mathbb{R}^K$, by iterating the equations

$$\mathbf{h}_i = \varphi_h(\mathbf{W}_{hx}\mathbf{x}_i + \mathbf{W}_{hh}\mathbf{h}_{i-1} + b_h) \tag{2}$$

$$\hat{\mathbf{y}}_i = \varphi_y(\mathbf{W}_{yh}\mathbf{h}_i + b_y) \tag{3}$$

where $\mathbf{W}_{hx}, \mathbf{W}_{hh}, \mathbf{W}_{yh}$ are weight matrices, b_h, b_y are bias terms, and φ_h, φ_y are activation functions. Equation 2 defines the input-to-hidden layer and Eq. 3 defines the hidden-to-output layer.

2.2 The Overall Architecture

Figure 1(a) illustrates the overall architecture of DeepRSD. We describe the network layers and their functions from bottom to top. DeepRSD consists of three modules: input processing module, main functional module and output processing module.

Input processing module includes the input layer and the Network-In-Network (NIN) layer [10]. The input layer is at the bottom, where sequential features are fed into DeepRSD. On the top of the input layer is the NIN layer that reduces the dimension of features using a linear activation function. The NIN layer contributes to accelerating the training process; meanwhile, NIN layer does not affect the precision of final predictions.

Main functional module is a stack of Bi-RNN layers with different sizes. RNN is suitable to model sequential data because it introduces hidden layer to encode the temporal information. Bi-RNN [8] can effectively represent the correlations, and has been widely used to model sequential data. The structure of Bi-RNN is illustrated in Fig. 1(b). The stacked Bi-RNNs supply sufficient nonlinearities for the sequence and also for step feature $\mathbf{x}_i$. Even the features in $\mathbf{x}_i$ are heterogeneous and have complex functional relationships, the stacked Bi-RNNs can learn to represent them automatically.

Output processing module is a step-wise dense layer that outputs the predicted value at each step. In Fig. 1(a), we show the unrolled T dense layers, corresponding to the T predictions. The T predictions can also be added up for a scalar prediction if necessary. Therefore, the final output $\mathbf{y}$ can be a T-dimension vector or a simple scalar.

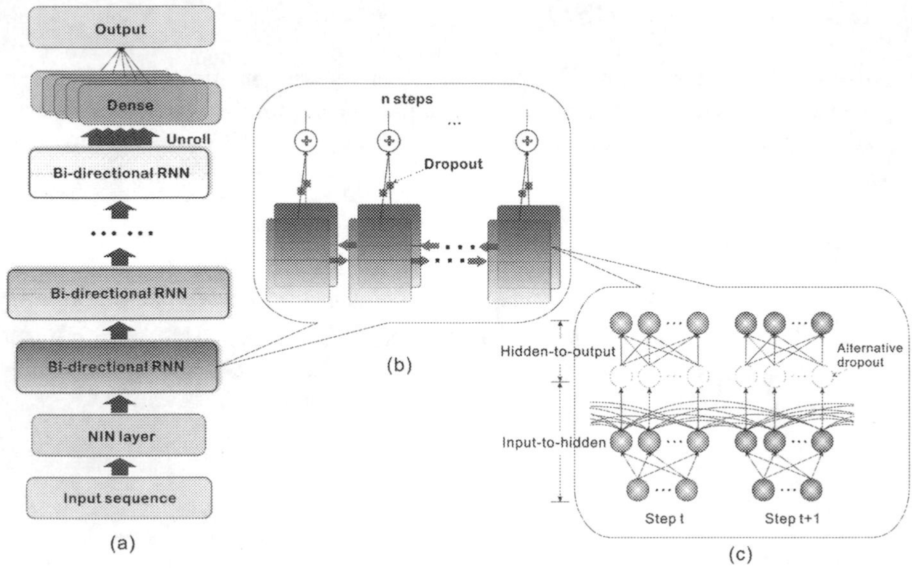

Fig. 1. The overall architecture of DeepRSD

Stacked Bi-RNNs, the main functional module in DeepRSD, is designed catering the characteristics of RSD problems. In discrete problems, Pascanu et al. [14] discussed how to construct deep RNN and proposed three variants of deep RNN, which are deep input-to-hidden, deep hidden-to-output and deep transition networks. Graves [6] used RNN with stacked hidden layers to generate sequences. Much effort in RNN is made to handle long dependency in sequences in discrete problems, while in RSD, we aim to model the sequential information as well as the functional relationships among step features. For many RSD problems in practice, the sequential data is not so long that a standard hidden layer is adequate to handle the dependencies, thus no necessary to introduce deep transitions. In the stacked Bi-RNNs, there are dense connections in input-to-hidden and hidden-to-output layers, which supply plenty of nonlinearities to encode the heterogeneous step features. We tried deep input-to-hidden and deep hidden-to-output networks, and neither of them worked as well as stacked Bi-RNNs in our experimented datasets. The advantages of stacked Bi-RNNs over other deep RNNs are further shown in experiments in Subsect. 4.1.

2.3 Activation Function

For the nonlinear activation function, we use leaky rectified linear unit (leaky ReLU) [1], shown in Eq. 4.

$$\varphi(x) = \begin{cases} x \quad if \quad x > 0 \\ \alpha x \; if \quad x \leq 0 \end{cases} \tag{4}$$

For RNN, traditional activations–sigmoid or hyperbolic tangent functions, which have saturated zones, may lead to the gradient vanishing problem [15]. ReLU [12] is advantageous since (1) it alleviates the vanishing gradient and (2) it offers a simple gradient computation. However, it often makes DeepRSD diverge. When using leaky ReLU, we can train DeepRSD more reliably. For the above reasons, we choose leaky ReLU as the activation function for DeepRSD.

2.4 Alternative Dropout

Dropout [19] has been a simple and effective way to improve the generalization of feed-forward neural networks. However, people struggle to develop effective dropout for RNN. Zaremba et al. [22] applied dropout to the input and hidden-to-output but not to the transition layer in RNN. Gal et al. [4] proposed a theoretically grounded dropout to the hidden layer in RNN and got improved performance. These methods work effectively for discrete problems. However, they do not work in DeepRSD.

Considering the structure of stacked Bi-RNNs, we propose a special dropout scheme. For the standard RNN shown in Fig. 1(c), we apply dropout between the input-to-hidden and hidden-to-output layers, while for the stacked second Bi-RNN, this dropout is applied alternatively. To be specific, dropout is applied only to the *forward* RNN for the first Bi-RNN. For the stacked second Bi-RNN, dropout is applied to the *backward* RNN. Dropout is applied alternatively in the forward and backward directional RNNs, so we name this dropout scheme as alternative dropout.

For the stacked Bi-RNNs, the alternative dropout between input-to-hidden and hidden-to-output layer is crucial to improve generalization. We supply a possible explanation for alternative dropout. We assume that the input-to-hidden layer of forward RNN outputs a vector in range $[a, b]$. The hidden-to-output layer is simplified as an identity map. If we do not apply any dropout, Bi-RNN sums the outputs of each direction and thus gives an output range of approximate $[2a, 2b]$ (the output range of two RNNs should be similar). For dropout with a keep rate γ ($\gamma < 1$), to keep the invariance of expectation, we re-scale the vector and lead to an inflated approximate range $[a/\gamma, b/\gamma]$ (Re-scaling is the default manner in dropout [19]). If dropout with a keep rate γ is applied to both directions, the output range of Bi-RNN will be $[2a/\gamma, 2b/\gamma]$. In contrast, for alternative dropout, the output range of Bi-RNN will be $[a/\gamma + a, b/\gamma + b]$. We can see that the dropout on both directions lead to a larger fluctuation range than alternative dropout. The large fluctuations may bring difficulty to optimization algorithms to find a good local minimum. We experiment and visualize alternative dropout in Subsect. 4.1 to support our explanation.

3 Training and Inference

We first set the cost function for DeepRSD. For regression problems, Mean Square Error (MSE) and Mean Absolute Error (MAE) are widely used. As MAE is more robust to very large or small values, we use MAE as the cost function for DeepRSD. If the output $\mathbf{y}$ is a T-dimension vector, the cost function can be written as:

$$C(\theta) = \frac{1}{ST} \sum_{i}^{S} \sum_{i}^{T} |y_i - \hat{y}_i|, \tag{5}$$

where S is the total number of sequence samples, and θ is parameters to be learned (see Eq. 1). If $\mathbf{y}$ is a scalar, the summation $\sum_i^T$ can be omitted.

DeepRSD is hard to train for several reasons. Comparing to classification problems, the inputs and outputs are both unbounded in regression problems, which may lead to divergence in the training of DeepRSD. Moreover, improper initializations will result in divergence or invalid learning in deep networks. Besides, there are gradient vanishing/exploding problems in (deep) RNN, which may hamper the training process. In our study, we find the conditions in Table 1 are necessary to ensure a plausible training.

Table 1. Conditions for DeepRSD training

Condition	Description
Data preprocessing	Normalize and trim data
Initializations	Introduce proper initializations for RNN
Gradient vanishing preventing	Use leaky ReLU activation
Gradient exploding preventing	Use gradient clipping

Data Preprocessing. Sutskever et al. [20] pointed out it is essential to normalize data (both inputs and outputs) to obtain a reliable training for RNN. We follow this rule and normalize the inputs and outputs for DeepRSD. We further trim the extreme values to result in a bounded region $[-a, a]$. If we set $a = 5$, the extreme values outside the 5σ region of Gaussian will be trimmed.

Initializations. Initializations are critical to ensure the convergence of RNN [20]. We use Gaussian and orthogonal initializations [5,18] for the stacked Bi-RNNs. A correct scale of Gaussian is essential for a plausible training. For normalized data, we find $\sigma = 0.01$ is a good scale to ensure convergence.

Gradient Vanishing Preventing. RNN is difficult to train because they suffer from gradient vanishing/exploding problems [15]. We use leaky ReLU activation to prevent vanishing gradients(see Subsect. 2.3).

Gradient Exploding Preventing. We simply use gradient clipping [15] to prevent gradient exploding for RNN.

Applying the above conditions, DeepRSD can be trained reliably. We resort to mini-batch Stochastic Gradient Decent (SGD) with Nesterov's momentum [13], with learning rate decay [20], to train DeepRSD. We also try other optimization algorithm, such as Adadelta [23] and Adam [9], but the results are not so good as SGD with Nesterov's momentum. Therefore, we recommend to use SGD with Nesterov's momentum to train DeepRSD.

Inference in DeepRSD can be quite efficient. As DeepRSD introduces dropout, we simply employ the inference process of dropout networks to predict $\mathbf{y}$ [19].

4 Experiment

DeepRSD is evaluated on two different real-world problems from data science competitions. We apply DeepRSD to the AMS solar energy prediction problem to predict a scalar value. We further evaluate DeepRSD on an electricity demand prediction problem, where the output is structured.

For both problems, we used DeepRSD to construct a universal end-to-end learning model. We used the same conditions in training for the two problems. In data preprocessing, the data were normalized to standard Gaussian. We set the bound for trimming, $a = 5$. To cope with the gradient vanishing problem, DeepRSD used leaky ReLU activation with a leakiness $\alpha = 0.15$, For gradient exploding, DeepRSD used gradient clipping to normalize the gradients if their norm exceeded 1.0 [15]. In initializations, for the transition matrix W_{hh} in the RNN layer, DeepRSD used orthogonal initialization [18] with a gain $(1+\alpha^2)^{\frac{1}{2}}$. For the input-to-hidden weight matrix W_{hx}, DeepRSD used Gaussian distribution with 0 mean and 0.01 standard variance to initialize it.

4.1 Evaluations on AMS Solar Energy Prediction Contest

The objective of the problem is to predict the daily incoming solar energy at 98 Oklahoma Mesonet sites [11]. Detail information can be found on Kaggle's website (see footnote 1).

Solutions Using DeepRSD. We use DeepRSD to construct one universal model for the 98 Mesonet sites. For each Mesonet site, we extract the weather data from its neighbouring four GEFS grids. We also supply the distances of the Mesonet site to its neighbouring four grids. Besides, we add the temporal and the Mesonet site specific information. All the above information is combined to be a step feature with 77 variables. The raw features are input to DeepRSD, without any feature engineering. DeepRSD uses alternative dropout to improve its generalization. DeepRSD not only learns the transitions in weather forecasting sequences, but also hiddenly learns to approximate the weather states at the Mesonet site from the heterogeneous features.

The hyperparameters were set using random search [2], followed by handcraft tuning. The input dimension was 77 for the input layer. The output dimension of NIN layer was 64, reducing the input dimension by 16.9%. DeepRSD introduced 4 stacked Bi-RNN and dense layers, with the size 128, 224, 128 and 16. The following dense layer had an output dimension of 1. The last layer was a mean-pooling layer to output the daily production. The dropout rate for both forward and backward RNN before the summation was 0.3, and the drop rate of alternative dropout was 0.5. Dropout was applied in the first 3 layers of the stacked Bi-RNNs.

Test Results. Table 2 shows DeepRSD's result measured by MAE and the top three results in the Kaggle competition. We can see that GBDT is the dominant method that holds the top three places in the past competition. The top three methods used complex feature engineering, post-processing or model combinations to improve the results [11]. In contrast, DeepRSD simply averaged 10 differently trained models and got an MAE of 2.10M.

Table 2. Ours and the top three results in the Kaggle contest

Solution	MAE (MW)	Method
1st Place	2.11	GBDT
2nd Place	2.13	GBDT
3rd Place	2.16	GBDT
Ours	*2.10*	*DeepRSD*

Comparing DeepRSD to Other Deep RNNs. In this experiment, we compare the performance of deep RNNs. Besides stacked Bi-RNNs, we also constructed deep input-to-hidden (DeepIH) network and deep hidden-to-output (DeepHO) network. We used DeepIH and DeepHO to replace stack Bi-RNNs in the architecture of DeepRSD. The other parts of DeepRSD stayed the same. Besides, we also use standard RNN and multi-layer dense neural networks (DNN) as the baseline.

The configurations of DeepRSD stayed the same as introduced in the second paragraph in Sect. 4. The configurations of DeepIH and DeepHO were optimized by random search [2]. DeepIH used two dense layers, with size 32 and 32, for each time step; and two RNN layers, with size 192 and 128. DeepHO used two RNN layers with size 128 and 128, followed by two dense layers with size 128 and 64. The DNN had 4 dense layers, with size 128, 256, 192 and 128. The standard RNN had a size of 128. The performances of the five different RNNs are shown in Fig. 2.

In Fig. 2, we use standard RNN and DNN as the baseline. RNN obtains an MAE of 2.20 MW, and DNN obtains an MAE of 2.21 MW. Though DNN is a deep network that has 4 layers, it does not utilize the temporal information, and therefore has a low performance. Comparing to the two baselines, DeepIH, DeepHO and DeepRSD make significant improvements on this problem.

We then analyze the three deep RNNs in detail. For DeepIH, it first uses dense networks to represent step features, and then input the representations into RNN. For DeepHO, it first represents features using two layers of RNNs, and then uses dense network to refine the output of RNN. In contrast, DeepRSD, which uses stacked Bi-RNNs, always combines the nonlinear representations of step features and temporal information. We can see that DeepRSD has advantages over DeepIH and DeepHO in Fig. 2. That is the reason we choose stacked Bi-RNNs for sequential data regression.

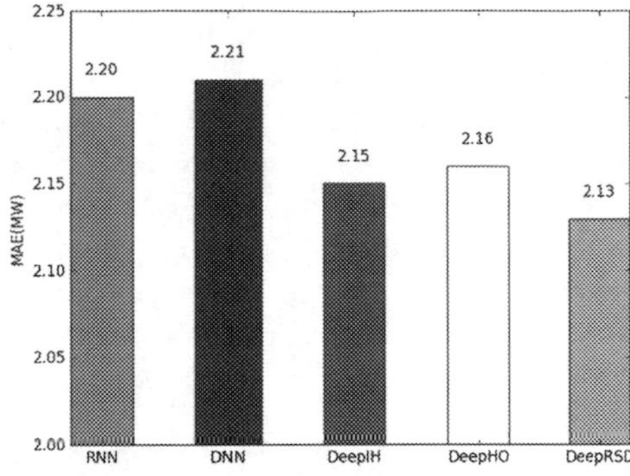

Fig. 2. The performance comparisons of different networks

Analysis of Alternative Dropout. In this experiment, we compare and analyze three dropout ways for DeepRSD. The first way is naive dropout, where dropout is only applied in the input projection and output projection [22]. The second way is variational dropout, where dropout is applied to the hidden layer besides the input and output projections [4]. The third way is the proposed alternative dropout. The three dropout methods are applied to DeepRSD with the same other configurations.

The MAEs and epochs to converge are shown in Table 3 for the three dropout methods. Without any dropout, DeepRSD achieves an MAE of 2.17 MW. Though different dropout rates have been tried, naive dropout and variational dropout do not improve the generalization of DeepRSD. Moreover, variational dropout converges very slow, up to 40 epochs. Alternative dropout effectively enhances the generalization of DeepRSD by near 2%. In discrete problems, networks with dropout will consume more training time. This is also seen in regression problems in Table 3. DeepRSD without dropout converges in 4 epochs, while DeepRSD with alternative dropout converges in 6 epochs.

Table 3. Comparisons of different dropout ways

Methods	MAE (MW)	Epoches to converge
No dropout	2.17	4
Naive dropout	2.17	6
Variational dropout	2.17	40
Alternative dropout	2.13	6

We intuitively explain the alternative dropout via data visualizations. When the network was near convergence in training, we collected the output of the first step of the third Bi-RNN. The output was sampled every 100 mini-batches from batch 30000 to 35000. In the same manner, we visualized the output using naive dropout. The visualization of alternative dropout and naive dropout are shown in Fig. 3a and b, respectively. We can see that the outputs are consistent for the alternative dropout in Fig. 3a, while the outputs fluctuate in the naive dropout in Fig. 3b. The inconsistency and fluctuations in traditional dropout bring difficulty for the optimization algorithms, resulting in a poor local minimum. Even though we decrease the dropout rate, naive dropout does not work well. In contrast, alternative dropout provides a mild dropout way for stacked Bi-RNNs.

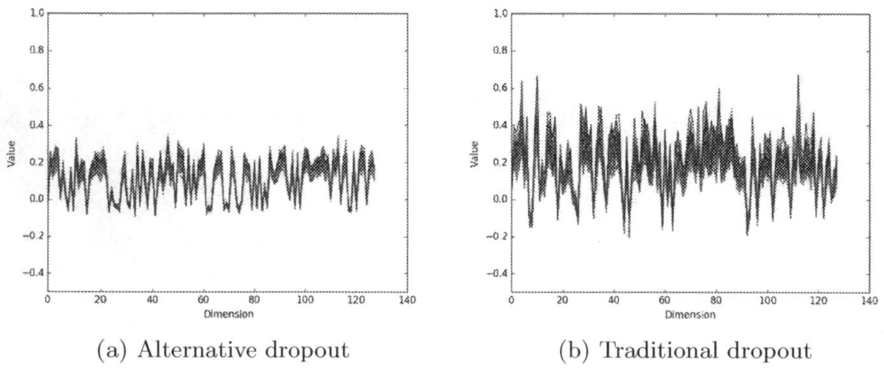

(a) Alternative dropout (b) Traditional dropout

Fig. 3. Data visualization of dropout

4.2 Evaluations on Electricity Demand Forecasting Competition

The task of this competition is to predict the future power demand in every half hour according to weather data. Detail information can be found on NPower Demand Forecasting Challenge website (see footnote 2).

Solutions Using DeepRSD. We use DeepRSD to model this sequential data prediction problem. The extracted raw features include weather feature, temporal feature, and calendar feature, 13 variables in total. We use a data sequence with length 48, which corresponds to electricity usages of half hour in a day. This competition used Mean Absolute Percentage Error (MAPE) for the final score, while we can still use MAE as the cost function to train DeepRSD.

In this problem, the hyperparameters for DeepRSD were set as follows. The input dimension was 13. DeepRSD introduced 2 stacked Bi-RNNs with the size 16 and 16. The following dense layer had an output dimension of 1. The final output was a 48-dimension vector. DeepRSD used alternative dropout with a drop rate of 0.2.

Results and Comparisons. We compare the performance of DeepRSD with the winning methods and several state-of-the-art methods in this competition. The results, measured by MAPE, are shown in Table 4.

Table 4. Evaluation results of the two rounds in NPower Forecasting Challenge 2016.

Model	MAPE in round 1	MAPE in round 2
1st Place	3.14%	7.13%
2nd Place	6.43%	4.89%
3rd Place	7.84%	7.48%
ARIMA	8.95%	8.77%
SGCRF	5.83%	6.64%
GBDT	5.40%	4.97%
DeepRSD	$(4.88 \pm 0.21)\%$	$(4.56 \pm 0.20)\%$

The evaluations are based on a rolling forecasting mode, same as the competition. The top three methods did not employ complex machine learning methods, but relied heavily on feature engineering[3]. ARIMA is employed as the baseline model, which is not as competitive as the top three methods.

The following methods are popular in recent. The overall performance of SGCRF is comparable to the second place in the competition. The results of GBDT are close to the first place. DeepRSD achieves the best performance, with an average MAPE of 4.72%, better than the first place. Besides, DeepRSD only uses the raw feature without any feature engineering. The results of DeepRSD fluctuates due to the instability of neural networks, but this can be compensated by model ensemble.

5 Conclusion

In this paper, we proposed DeepRSD for the regressions on sequential data. DeepRSD used stacked Bi-RNNs to represent the sequential data. We pointed out four conditions to ensure a plausible training. We also proposed an alternative dropout to effectively improve the generalization of DeepRSD. We applied DeepRSD to two real-world sequential data prediction problems and achieved state-of-the-art performances. According to the experimental results, DeepRSD showed two major advantages over other methods. (1) DeepRSD can simultaneously represent step features and temporal information. (2) DeepRSD has strong nonlinear presentation capacity to achieve a good performance without feature engineering. Therefore, we conclude that DeepRSD can be an effective solution for regressions on sequential data.

---

[3] http://blog.drhongtao.com/2016/12/winning-methods-from-npower-forecasting-challenge-2016.html.

References

1. Agostinelli, F., Hoffman, M., Sadowski, P., Baldi, P.: Learning activation functions to improve deep neural networks. arXiv preprint arXiv:1412.6830 (2014)
2. Bergstra, J., Bengio, Y.: Random search for hyper-parameter optimization. J. Mach. Learn. Res. **13**(Feb), 281–305 (2012)
3. Chen, T., Guestrin, C.: XGBoost: a scalable tree boosting system. arXiv preprint arXiv:1603.02754 (2016)
4. Gal, Y.: A theoretically grounded application of dropout in recurrent neural networks. arXiv preprint arXiv:1512.05287 (2015)
5. Glorot, X., Bengio, Y.: Understanding the difficulty of training deep feedforward neural networks. In: AISTATS, vol. 9, pp. 249–256 (2010)
6. Graves, A.: Generating sequences with recurrent neural networks. arXiv preprint arXiv:1308.0850 (2013)
7. Graves, A., Jaitly, N., Mohamed, A.-R.: Hybrid speech recognition with deep bidirectional LSTM. In: 2013 IEEE Workshop on Automatic Speech Recognition and Understanding (ASRU), pp. 273–278. IEEE (2013)
8. Graves, A., Schmidhuber, J.: Framewise phoneme classification with bidirectional LSTM and other neural network architectures. Neural Netw. **18**(5), 602–610 (2005)
9. Kingma, D., Ba, J.: Adam: a method for stochastic optimization. arXiv preprint arXiv:1412.6980 (2014)
10. Lin, M., Chen, Q., Yan, S.: Network in network. arXiv preprint arXiv:1312.4400 (2013)
11. McGovern, A., Gagne, D.J., Basara, J., Hamill, T.M., Margolin, D.: Solar energy prediction: an international contest to initiate interdisciplinary research on compelling meteorological problems. Bull. Am. Meteorol. Soc. **96**(8), 1388–1395 (2015)
12. Nair, V., Hinton, G.E.: Rectified linear units improve restricted Boltzmann machines. In: Proceedings of the 27th International Conference on Machine Learning (ICML 2010), pp. 807–814 (2010)
13. Nesterov, Y.: A method of solving a convex programming problem with convergence rate $\mathcal{O}(1/k^2)$. In: Soviet Mathematics Doklady, vol. 27, pp. 372–376 (1983)
14. Pascanu, R., Gulcehre, C., Cho, K., Bengio, Y.: How to construct deep recurrent neural networks. arXiv preprint arXiv:1312.6026 (2013)
15. Pascanu, R., Mikolov, T., Bengio, Y.: On the difficulty of training recurrent neural networks. In: ICML, vol. 28, no. 3, pp. 1310–1318 (2013)
16. Qin, T., Liu, T.-Y., Zhang, X.-D., Wang, D.-S., Li, H.: Global ranking using continuous conditional random fields. In: Advances in Neural Information Processing Systems, pp. 1281–1288 (2009)
17. Rumelhart, D.E., Hinton, G.E., Williams, R.J.: Learning representations by back-propagating errors. Cognit. Model. **5**(3), 1 (1988)
18. Saxe, A.M., McClelland, J.L., Ganguli, S.: Exact solutions to the nonlinear dynamics of learning in deep linear neural networks. arXiv preprint arXiv:1312.6120 (2013)
19. Srivastava, N., Hinton, G.E., Krizhevsky, A., Sutskever, I., Salakhutdinov, R.: Dropout: a simple way to prevent neural networks from overfitting. J. Mach. Learn. Res. **15**(1), 1929–1958 (2014)
20. Sutskever, I., Martens, J., Dahl, G.E., Hinton, G.E.: On the importance of initialization and momentum in deep learning. In: ICML, vol. 28, no. 3, pp. 1139–1147 (2013)

21. Wytock, M., Kolter, Z.: Sparse Gaussian conditional random fields: algorithms, theory, and application to energy forecasting. In: International Conference on Machine Learning, pp. 1265–1273 (2013)
22. Zaremba, W., Sutskever, I., Vinyals, O.: Recurrent neural network regularization. arXiv preprint arXiv:1409.2329 (2014)
23. Zeiler, M.D.: ADADELTA: an adaptive learning rate method. arXiv preprint arXiv:1212.5701 (2012)

Single Image Super-Resolution via Perceptual Loss Guided by Denoising Auto-Encoder

Zhong-Han Niu(✉), Lu-Fei Liu, Kai-Jun Zhang, Jian-Feng Dong, Yu-Bin Yang(✉), and Xiao-Jiao Mao

State Key Laboratory for Novel Software Technology, Nanjing University, Nanjing 210023, China
niuzh@smail.nju.edu.cn, yangyubin@nju.edu.cn

Abstract. Image restoration is a difficult task due to its non-uniqueness of solution. Owing to the power of Convolution Neural Networks (CNNs), we can generate images with high PSNR (Peak Signal to Noise Ratio) and SSIM (Structural SIMilarity index) by using a per-pixel loss between the outputs and the ground-truth images. Unfortunately, these images usually suffer from over-smoothing problem. The previous perceptual loss based on high-level features was then proposed to replace the traditional per-pixel loss. But the low-level information such as color, shape and texture will be lost. In order to alleviate this problem, we design a new perceptual loss extracted from a pre-trained denoising auto-encoder with symmetric skip connections (SDAE). The encoder in SDAE is extracted as a perceptual function. We carry out the experiments on single image super-resolution to validate the proposed method. The results show that the images generated by our method have both better visual quality and higher PSNR and SSIM than the state-of-the-art methods.

Keywords: Image restoration · Convolutional neural network
Perceptual loss · Denoising auto-encoder · Skip connection

1 Introduction

The task of image restoration is to recover the clean image from its corrupted version, which is a well-known ill-posed inverse problem. Taking advantage of increased depth and architecture development, CNNs have set new records on image restoration such as image denoising [1–3] and image super-resolution [1,4–7]. Existing CNN-based methods can be classified into two categories, which are focusing on the design of network architecture [8,9] and loss functions [10,11] respectively.

This work is funded by the Natural Science Foundation of China (No. 61673204), State Grid Corporation of Science and Technology Projects (Funded No. SGLNXT00DKJS1700166), and the Program for Distinguished Talents of Jiangsu Province, China (No. 2013-XXRJ-018).

X. Geng and B.-H. Kang (Eds.): PRICAI 2018, LNAI 11012, pp. 126–136, 2018.
https://doi.org/10.1007/978-3-319-97304-3_10

The CNN-based methods focused on the design of network architecture can greatly improve both PSNR and SSIM, the crucial measurements for evaluating image quality, but always result in generating over-smoothing images. The perceptual loss function was then proposed to measure the similarity between images according to the difference between image features. The perceptual loss function used to train the network should be based on high-level features extracted from pre-trained classification networks [10]. However, by doing so, image contents and the overall spatial layouts and structures can be kept, but the low-level information such as color, shape and texture will be lost. Moreover, it is very difficult to reconstruct the original images from extracted high-level features, thus the use of high-level features in classification tasks will result in a great discrepancy in image details. Which layer of features can be used to restore the original picture is Johnson's [10] criteria for selecting perceptual function [11].

To address the above issue, we expect to be able to find such a perceptual feature that can be used to classify and minimize the loss of image details at the same time. In this paper, we propose a new method to train deep neural network based on a new perceptual loss function. First, the new perceptual loss functions are based on muti-scale features. These muti-scale features are essential to restoring image details. Second, these perceptual features are extracted from pre-trained denoising auto-encoder (DAE) rather than a pre-trained classification network. Denoising auto-encoder [12,13] has shown the extremely good effectiveness on learning features for CNN pre-training on classification, detection tasks, either stand-alone or as initialization for non-parametric methods [14]. Third, we combine denoising auto-encoder with symmetrical skip connections [1] which is conducive to train DAE. Inspired by ResNet [15], skip connections can solve the problem of gradient vanishing. Meanwhile, it can also pass image details from bottom layers to top layers.

In the proposed method, auto-encoder is made up of two parts, encoder and decoder. We set encoder as the perceptual loss function.

2 Related Work

Extensive work has been done to improve the image restoration performance. A more promising category of methods for image restoration is the CNN-based methods. For the first category, Dong et al. [3] proposed to learn an end-to-end mapping between low/high-resolution images. For the second category, Johnson et al. [10] replaced a per-pixel loss with a perceptual loss. In their work, perceptual loss function is based on high-level features extracted from pre-trained VGG-16 network [7]. Based on their work, Ledig et al. [16] proposed a more abundant perceptual loss function consisting an adversarial loss [17] and a content loss. The adversarial network [18] was trained to differentiate between real images (high-resolution images) and fake images (low-resolution images), while the content loss function was provided by a pre-trained VGG-19 network.

It is worth mentioning that Mao et al. [1] proposed a new architecture using encoder-decoder networks with symmetric skip connections, which obtained very high PSNR and SSIM. Their network consists of multiple layers of convolution and de-convolution operator. The convolution behaves like feature extractor, while the deconvolution is used to restore clean images from the features extracted by convolution. Moreover, with the network going deeper, high pass of images will be lost. The skip connections can directly pass image details from bottom layers to top layers, which reduces the loss of information.

Not only the network structure, but also the design of loss function have been widely studied. In order to prevent the recovered images from over-smoothing, Johnson et al. [10] pointed out that the similarity between two images should not be measured by the difference between the corresponding pixels, but by encouraging them to have similar feature representations. Beyond that, Ledig et al. [16, 17] even expected that the generated images have almost the identical data distribution to the high-resolution images. Their methods yielded visually pleasure pictures with low PSNR and SSIM. For a classification network, as we restore the original image using high-level features, image contents and overall spatial structures are preserved, but color, texture and exact shape are not. It shows that it is hard to recover details from only high-level features. Unfortunately, low-level features have little spatial information which can be useful to generate smooth images.

3 The Proposed Method

3.1 Motivation

In this section, we propose a new perceptual loss functions based on muti-scale features. Using Denoise Auto-Encoder (DAE) instead of classification network to extract features. Features extracted from DAE contain sufficient information about the original image, which ensures the recovered image to be more similar to the original image. Moreover, unlike the traditional Denoising Auto-Encoder, our DAE is a deep convolution encoder-decoder network with symmetric skip connections. Firstly, with the benefit of skip connections, deconvolution achieve better recovering results. More image details are directly passed from bottom layers to top layers, which reduces the loss of information. Secondly, skip connections can tackle the problem of gradient vanishing elegantly.

3.2 The Architecture

Architecture of our method is composed of two parts: an image restoration network G, and a perceptual loss network. For network G, given a corrupted image $\hat{X} \in R^{w \times h \times 3}$, $G(\hat{X})$ will generate a corresponding clean version. For perceptual loss network, our DAE is a deep convolutional encoder-decoder network with symmetric skip connections. We use the encoder network as the perceptual loss function. The whole structure is shown in Fig. 1. For the first step of training the combined network, we start by training the auto-encoder, and then add the encoder network to the image restoration network G. Afterwards, the parameters in the encoder network are fixed to finally train network G.

3.3 Denoising Auto-Encoder

In this Section, we present the details of the DAE in our method. Let $Y_i \in R^{w \times h \times 3}$, Y_i denotes a clean image, $\hat{X}_i$ denote the corresponding noisy version of Y_i, $\hat{X}_i \in R^{w \times h \times 3}$, a denoising auto-encoder takes an input $\hat{X}_i$ and maps it (with an encoder network) to a hidden representation Z_i, $Z_i = encoder(\hat{X}_i)$. The latent representation Z_i is then mapped back (with a decoder network) into $\hat{Y}_i$, $\hat{Y}_i = decoder(encoder(\hat{X}_i))$. Both encoder and decoder are multilayer neural network, and the reconstruct loss are be measured with Euclidean distance.

$$L(Y, \hat{Y}) = \frac{1}{n} \sum_{i=1}^{n} ||Y_i - \hat{Y}_i||^2 \quad (1)$$

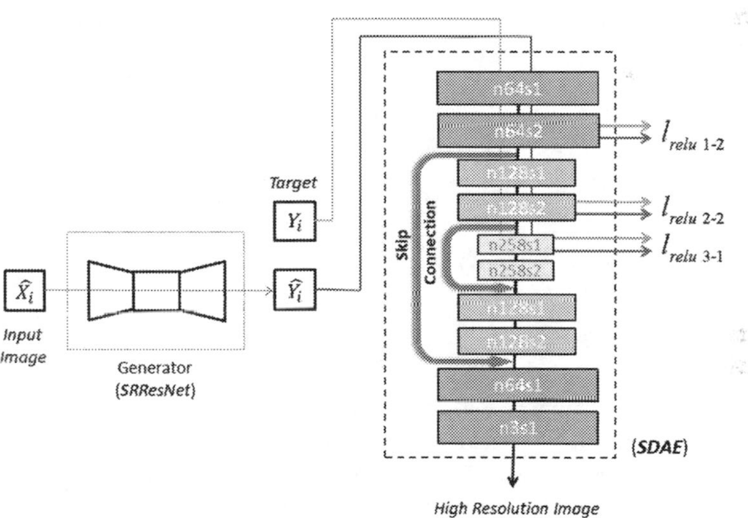

Fig. 1. The full network structure is composed of two parts: (1) Image generator (*left*) whose architecture is consistent with SRResNet proposed in [16]; (2) Denoising autoencoder with symmetric skip connections (*right*) with number of feature maps(n), stride(s) and consistent kernel size (3) All convolutional layers are followed by batch normalization (BN) and leaky ReLU nonlinearities except the last layer.

3.4 Perceptual Loss Function

For the integrity of article, here we briefly describe how to select features as the perceptual loss function from a classification network. For a middle layer i in the pre-trained network, the first i layers in the original network are extracted as a new convnet (encoder). Then we symmetrically add un-pooling and deconvolution layers as a deconvnet (decoder) behind the new convnet. The new network is also an auto-encoder, except that the parameters in the convnet are all fixed. In the denoising auto-encoder, the items contained in the loss is related to the output of encoder. As shown in Fig. 1, the output of encoder is composed of *relu*1_2, *relu*2_2 and *relu*3_1. Herewith, the perceptual loss function is then defined as:

$$\begin{aligned} loss_{\{SDAE\}}(Y,\hat{Y}) = \alpha||relu1\_2(Y) - relu1\_2(\hat{Y})||_2 \\ + \beta||relu2\_2(Y) - relu2\_2(\hat{Y})||_2 \\ + \gamma||relu3\_1(Y) - relu3\_1(\hat{Y})||_2 \end{aligned} \quad (2)$$

In order to make the generated images look like real ground truth, we follow the idea proposed in SRGAN [16] to learn a good generator so as to fool the learned discriminator, and make the discriminator good enough to distinguish the generated images from real ground truth. After the system achieves Nash Equilibrium, the generator can exactly generate image which is similar to real ground truth in vision. Thus, the whole loss function is then defined as:

$$loss = \lambda_a * l_{gan} + \lambda_b * loss_{\{SDAE\}} \quad (3)$$

For comparison, the effect of using DAE without skip connections on image restoration tasks is also tested. Similar to the above definition, the perceptual loss function in the DAE without skip connections is defined as:

$$loss_{\{DAE\}}(Y,\hat{Y}) = ||relu3\_1(Y) - relu3\_1(\hat{Y})||_2 \quad (4)$$

4 Experiments

We performed experiments on the widely used datasets **Set5**, **Set14** and **BSD100**, all reported PSNR(Peak Signal to Noise Ratio) and SSIM(Structural SIMilarity index) measures were calculated on the y-channel.

In all our experiments, we choose SRResNet [16] as the generator. To test the $loss_{\{SDAE\}}$(SRGAN-SDAE) defined in Sect. 3.4, we compare it with other two perceptual loss function. The one is the activations at *relu*5_4 layer of the pre-trained VGG-19 network(SRGAN), the other is $loss_{\{DAE\}}$(SRGAN-DAE). Experiment results show that using the proposed $loss_{\{SDAE\}}$ function can generate images with better super-resolution performance, higher PSNR and SSIM.

4.1 Training Details and Parameters

In our paper, since the code of original SRGAN was not released, so we adopted a tensorflow implementation of the impressive work SRGAN[1], the results of SRGAN that they reproduced are slightly lower than the original results. The reason for this phenomenon may be adopting different initialization methods and training with data of different scales. However, it has no negative impact on measuring the effectiveness of our proposed approach.

[1] https://github.com/brade31919/SRGAN-tensorflow.

Training Denoising Auto-Encoder. The denoising autoencoders with/without skip connections (SDAE/DAE) are shown in Fig. 1. In order to keep as much information as possible, we replaced the pooling operator with a 3×3 convolution kernel using a stride of 2 in the upsampling and downsampling layers. We used **mirflick25k**[2] as the training dataset, and for each mini-batch we randomly cropped 32 sub-images with the size of 64×64. We trained our SDAE and DAE on a Gaussian noise with zero mean and standard deviation $\sigma = 10$. These methods are implemented and trained in Tensorflow. Let $Y_i \in R^{64\times64\times3}$, $\hat{X}_i \in R^{64\times64\times3}$, $N_i \in R^{64\times64\times3}$ and $N_i(k, j) \sim normal(0, 10)$.

$$\hat{X}_i = Y_i + N_i \tag{5}$$

Y_i denotes the clean image, i.e., the expected output of DAE. N_i denotes the Gaussian noise, and $\hat{X}_i$ denotes the corrupted images, i.e., the input of DAE. The traditional loss function based on Euclidean distances between Y_i and $DAE(\hat{X}_i)$ is adopted in our experiments. For optimization we use Adam with $\beta_1 = 0.9$. We train with $1.5 * 10^5$ update iterations at a learning rate 10^{-4} and also $0.5 * 10^5$ update iterations at a lower learning rate of 10^{-5}.

Training SRResNet. We trained our SRResNet using **mirflick25k** datasets, then constructed the LR images by downsample the HR images with bicubic interpolation. All experiments were performed with a scale factor of $4\times$ between low- and high-resolution images. For training SRResNet, we cropped 16 random 96×96 HR sub-images for each mini-batch, the use Adam with $\beta_1 = 0.9$ to optimize it. We trained SRResNet with a learning rate of 10^{-4} and 10^6 update iterations.

Finetuning SRResNet with Perceptual Loss and GANs. After the training of SRResNet was complete, the trained SRResNet network was employed as initialization for the generator. Then we further trained three SRGANs (SRGAN-VGG, SRGAN-SDAE, SRGAN-DAE), In SRGAN-VGG and SRGAN-DAE, there are 2 hyper parameters λ_a and λ_b, we set them to 0.001 and 0.006, In SRGAN-SDAE, they are 5 hyper parameters: λ_a, λ_b, α, β and γ, we set them to 0.001, 0.005, 1, 1 and 4. All SRGAN variants were trained with 10^5 update iterations at a learning rate of 10^{-4} and another with 10^5 update iterations at a learning rate of 10^{-5}.

4.2 Results

We perform experiments on single-image super-resolution tasks to validate the proposed method. SRResNet, SRGAN-VGG and SRGAN-DAE are compared with our SRGAN-SDAE. Results for $4\times$ super-resolution in Fig. 2. Our method can recover visually more convincing HR images. Compare the performance of SRGAN-SDAE and SRGAN-DAE, we can observe that using skip connections

[2] http://press.liacs.nl/mirflickr/mirdownload.html.

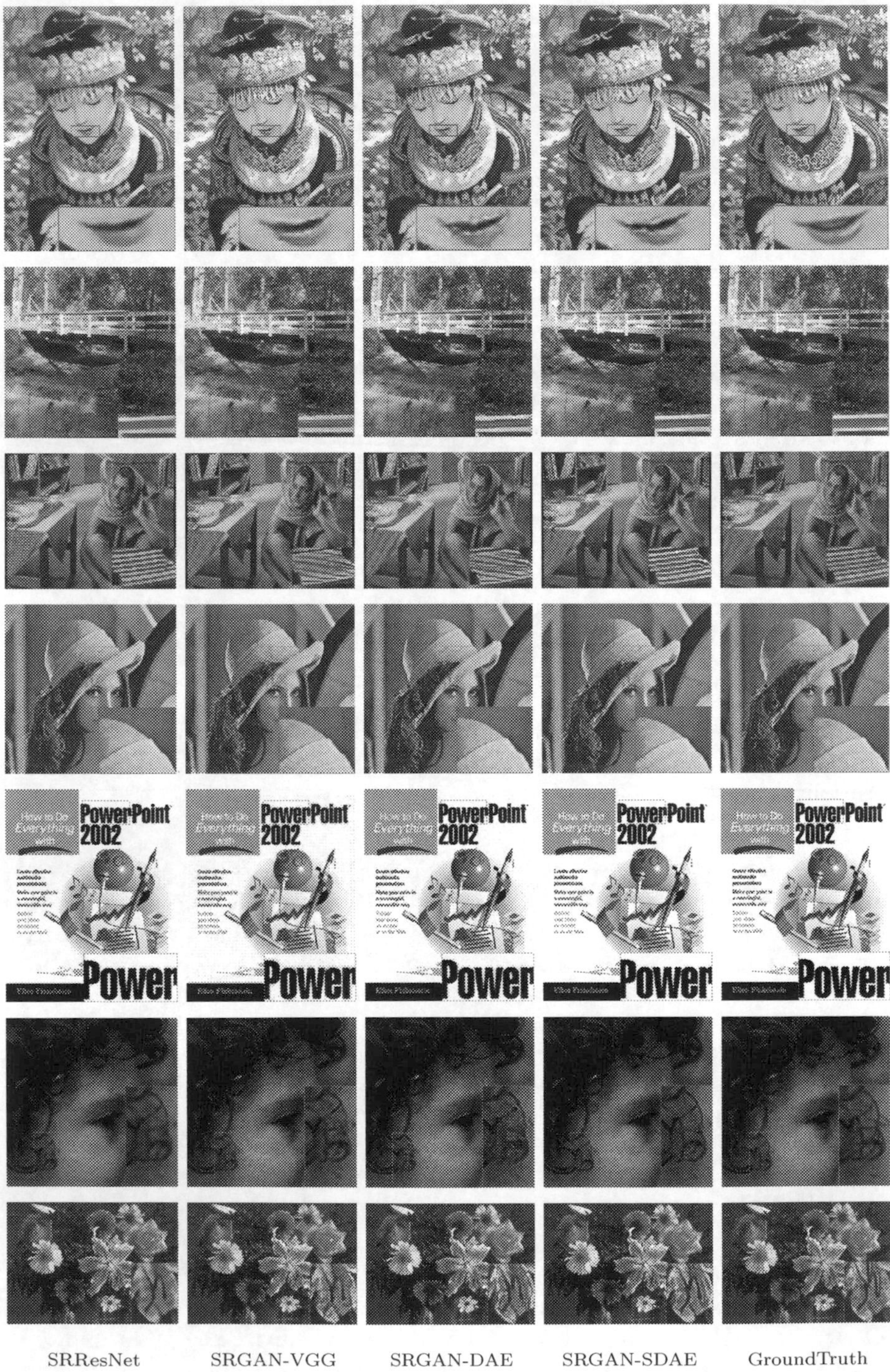

Fig. 2. Super resolution results on images (4×) from Set14

can retains more texture details, which is essential to alleviate over-smoothing. Along with much improved visual effects, the PSNR and SSIM of images produced by three different perceptual loss function are compared in Tables 1 and 2. For efficiency, we don't apply any image enhancement, we test each image for only once and then report PSNR and SSIM on **Set5**, **Set14** and **BSD100** respectively. Compared to other methods, the proposed SRGAN-SDAE actually does a good job at reconstructing high contrast image with higher values of PSNR and SSIM.

Table 1. Average PSNR on Set5, Set14 and BSD100 benchmark data

	Set5	Set14	BSD100
SRResNet	30.51	26.78	25.183
SRGAN-VGG	27.69	23.70	21.63
SRGAN-DAE	24.78	23.72	22.21
SRGAN-SDAE	**28.28**	**24.24**	**22.49**

Table 2. Average SSIM on Set5, Set14 and BSD100 benchmark data

	Set5	Set14	BSD100
SRResNet	0.8898	0.7781	0.7337
SRGAN-VGG	0.8274	0.6631	0.6041
SRGAN-DAE	0.8211	0.6659	0.6031
SRGAN-SDAE	**0.8471**	**0.6944**	**0.6316**

In our experiments, we also test both pretrained VGG and DAE on three different noises: (1) Gaussian noise, (2) Poisson noise and (3) Salt & Peppy noise. For the two inputs x and Generator(x'), a perceptual loss function $p(\cdot)$ should meet the following conditions:

$$\frac{|x - G(x')|}{|p(x) - p(G(x'))|} < C \tag{6}$$

where C is a constant. Under this condition, we can measure the performance of generator(G) by $|p(x) - p(G(x'))|$. However, suppose that there is now a series of perceptual functions to be selected, we should choose the most sensitive function for input x. Therefore we optimize the objective function $|p(x) - p(G(x'))|_2$ simultaneously to ensure $G(x')$ is the closest one to x. Sensitivity can be measured as fellow:

$$sensitivity = \frac{|p(x) - p(G(x'))|_2}{|p(x) + \epsilon|_2}, \epsilon > 0 \tag{7}$$

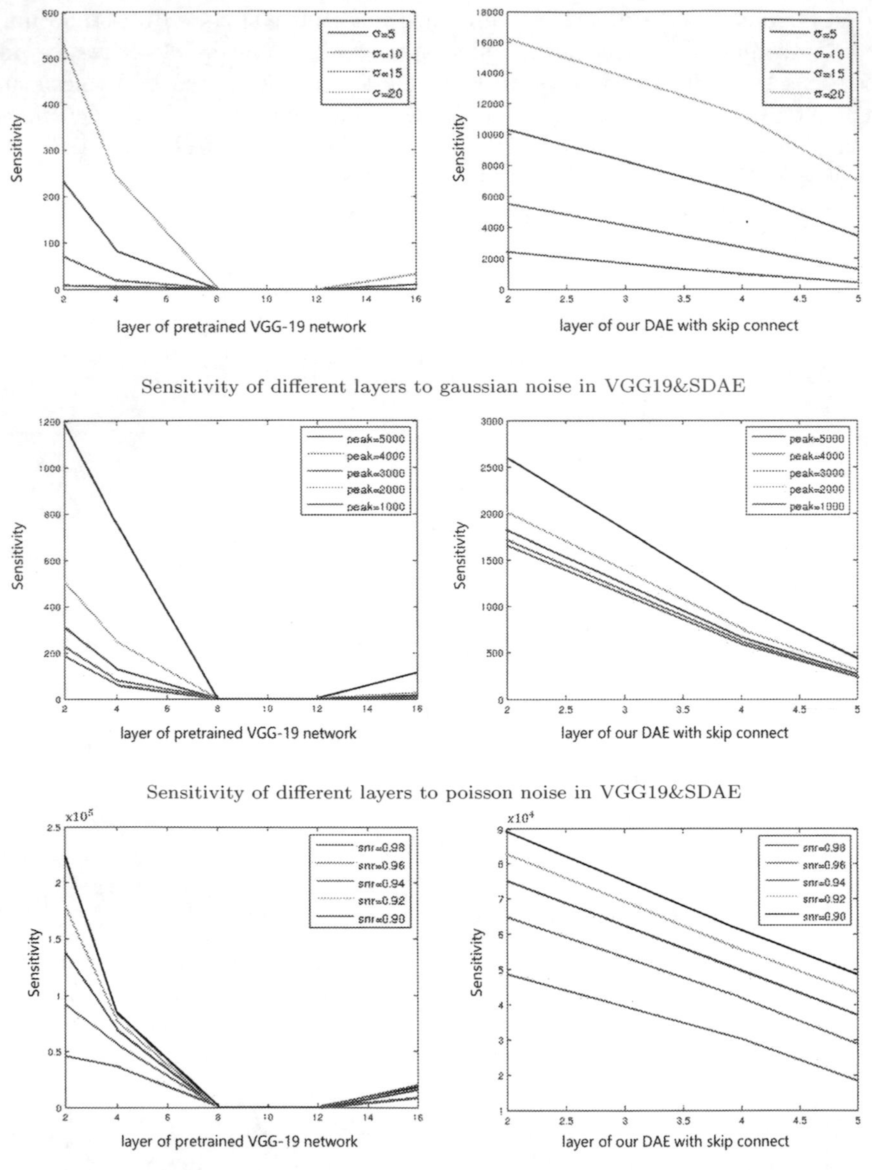

Sensitivity of different layers to gaussian noise in VGG19&SDAE

Sensitivity of different layers to poisson noise in VGG19&SDAE

Sensitivity of different layers to salt&peppy noise in VGG19&SDAE

Fig. 3. In the same layer of two networks, feature maps extracted from SDAE is more able to capture the difference of inputs than VGG19, which in return back-propagates a larger gradient.

Experimental results are shown in Fig. 3. The difference between noisy input and its clean version measured by VGG is far less than that by DAE, which leading to VGG be easy to receive the noisy input. It demonstrates that DAE is more suitable for extracting perceptual loss functions than VGG. VGG fails to handle input disturbances as good as DAE can do. This also explains the generated picture guided with DAE has higher PSNR value.

5 Conclusion

In this paper, we have presented a new perceptual loss function for single image super-resolution(SR), combined the benefits of Denoising Auto-Encoder and symmetry skip connections. The new perceptual loss functions are based on muti-scale features. Features extracted from pre-trained DAE are vital to prevent over-smoothing. Experimental results show that training with a new perceptual loss obtains better visual quality, higher PSNR and SSIM.

References

1. Mao, X., Shen, C., Yang, Y.-B.: Image restoration using very deep convolutional encoder-decoder networks with symmetric skip connections. Adv. Neural Inf. Process. Syst. **29**, 2802–2810 (2016)
2. Cui, Z., Chang, H., Shan, S., Zhong, B., Chen, X.: Deep network cascade for image super-resolution. In: Fleet, D., Pajdla, T., Schiele, B., Tuytelaars, T. (eds.) ECCV 2014. LNCS, vol. 8693, pp. 49–64. Springer, Cham (2014). https://doi.org/10.1007/978-3-319-10602-1_4
3. Dong, C., Loy, C.C., He, K., Tang, X.: Image super-resolution using deep convolutional networks. IEEE Trans. Pattern Anal. Mach. Intell. **38**(2), 295–307 (2016)
4. Gu, S., Zuo, W., Xie, Q., Meng, D., Feng, X., Zhang, L.: Convolutional sparse coding for image super-resolution. In: Proceedings of the IEEE International Conference on Computer Vision, pp. 1823–1831 (2015)
5. He, K., Zhang, X., Ren, S., Sun, J.: Deep residual learning for image recognition. In: Proceedings of the IEEE Conference on Computer Vision and Pattern Recognition, pp. 770–778 (2016)
6. Jain, V., Seung, S.: Natural image denoising with convolutional networks. In: Advances in Neural Information Processing Systems, pp. 769–776 (2009)
7. Simonyan, K., Zisserman, A.: Very deep convolutional networks for large-scale image recognition. In: Proceedings of International Conference on Learning Representations, pp. 1–14 (2015)
8. Wang, Z., Liu, D., Yang, J., Han, W., Huang, T.: Deep networks for image super-resolution with sparse prior. In: Proceedings of the IEEE International Conference on Computer Vision, pp. 370–378 (2015)
9. Xie, J., Xu, L., Chen, E.: Image denoising and inpainting with deep neural networks. In: Advances in Neural Information Processing Systems, pp. 341–349 (2012)
10. Johnson, J., Alahi, A., Fei-Fei, L.: Perceptual losses for real-time style transfer and super-resolution. In: Leibe, B., Matas, J., Sebe, N., Welling, M. (eds.) ECCV 2016. LNCS, vol. 9906, pp. 694–711. Springer, Cham (2016). https://doi.org/10.1007/978-3-319-46475-6_43
11. Zeiler, M.D., Fergus, R.: Visualizing and understanding convolutional networks. In: Fleet, D., Pajdla, T., Schiele, B., Tuytelaars, T. (eds.) ECCV 2014. LNCS, vol. 8689, pp. 818–833. Springer, Cham (2014). https://doi.org/10.1007/978-3-319-10590-1_53

12. Vincent, P., Larochelle, H., Lajoie, I., Bengio, Y., Manzagol, P.-A.: Stacked denoising autoencoders: learning useful representations in a deep network with a local denoising criterion. J. Mach. Learn. Res. **11**(Dec), 3371–3408 (2010)
13. Rifai, S., Vincent, P., Muller, X., Glorot, X., Bengio, Y.: Contractive auto-encoders: explicit invariance during feature extraction. In: Proceedings of the 28th International Conference on Machine Learning (ICML-2011), pp. 833–840 (2011)
14. Pathak, D., Krahenbuhl, P., Donahue, J., Darrell, T., Efros, A.A.: Context encoders: feature learning by inpainting. In: Computer Vision and Pattern Recognition, pp. 2536–2544 (2016)
15. He, K., Zhang, X., Ren, S., Sun, J.: Identity mappings in deep residual networks. In: Leibe, B., Matas, J., Sebe, N., Welling, M. (eds.) ECCV 2016. LNCS, vol. 9908, pp. 630–645. Springer, Cham (2016). https://doi.org/10.1007/978-3-319-46493-0_38
16. Ledig, C., et al.: Photo-realistic single image super-resolution using a generative adversarial network. In: The IEEE Conference on Computer Vision and Pattern Recognition (CVPR), July 2017
17. Goodfellow, I., et al.: Generative adversarial nets. In: Advances in Neural Information Processing Systems, pp. 2672–2680 (2014)
18. Makhzani, A., Shlens, J., Jaitly, N., Goodfellow, I., Frey, B.: Adversarial autoencoders. In: International Conference on Learning Representations (2016)

Context-Aware Phrase Representation for Statistical Machine Translation

Zhiwei Ruan[1], Jinsong Su[1,3], Deyi Xiong[2], and Rongrong Ji[1](✉)

[1] Xiamen University, Xiamen, China
zw_ruan@stu.xmu.edu.cn, {jssu,rrji}@xmu.edu.cn
[2] Soochow University, Suzhou, China
dyxiong@suda.edu.cn
[3] Fujian Provincial Key Laboratory of Information Processing and Intelligent Control, Minjiang University, Fuzhou, China

Abstract. Phrases are the basic translation units in the conventional (phrase-based) statistical machine translation (SMT), and learning compact vector representations for the basic phrasal translation units is the essential and fundamental work. However, most existing works focus on exploring internal relationship among words within phrases, which are lack of context information and not sufficient for phrase representation learning. To solve this problem, we propose a context-aware phrase representation learning framework, which extends the bilingually-constrained recursive autoencoder with context modeling component. By this way, we obtain context-aware phrase representation. Furthermore, for the word and topic form the base of the our model, we regard the word and topic as two different vertexes and construct a bipartite network. Thus, we naturally introduce the bipartite network embedding method to learn better word and topic embedding, which further improve the quality of the phrase representation. To evaluate the effectiveness of our method, we conduct experiments on Chinese-English translation. Experimental results show that the proposed method significantly improves the translation quality on NIST test sets.

Keywords: Context-aware phrase embedding
Bilingually-constrained recursive autoencoders
Statistical machine translation

1 Introduction

Statistical machine translation (SMT) has attracted a great interest and made great progress in the past decade. Phrase-based SMT systems have achieved state-of-the-art performance largely benefit from the fact that long phrases are used as translation units so that more useful context information can be obtained in selecting translations. Generally, translation models [1,2] are trained with bilingual data, in which longer phrases occur less often. Due to this, the sparsity

X. Geng and B.-H. Kang (Eds.): PRICAI 2018, LNAI 11012, pp. 137–149, 2018.
https://doi.org/10.1007/978-3-319-97304-3_11

issue hinders the model training. In the context of deep learning, it is conventional to convert the basic unit to a continuous feature vector. To this end, most prior works mainly focus on learning bilingual word embeddings to improve individual components of SMT systems [3–12]. However, phrase-level vector representation, intuitively, is a more sufficient way for deep neural network based SMT.

There has been a plethora of research on projecting a phrase into a continuous feature vector [13–17], which is named as phrase embeddings. With the success of those work, researchers extend the monolingual phrase embeddings to bilingual phrase embeddings, which learning phrase embeddings for the bilingual phrase pair simultaneously [18–23]. The motivation is intuitive, a phrase and its corresponding translation share the same semantics, so their representations should be close in the shared embedding space. However, existing works only take semantic compositions of internal words within phrases into consideration, which ignore the context information beyond phrases.

To address the aforementioned issue, we propose a context-aware phrase representation learning framework, which extends the bilingually-constrained recursive autoencoder (BRAE) [19] with context modeling component. From the observation that the semantics of phrases are often context-dependent, we represent the document-level context of each phrase with its document-topic distribution. Then, we combine the obtained contextual clues with recursive autoencoder (RAE) based phrase representation and produce the context-aware phrase representation. Furthermore, for the word and topic form the base of the our model, we regard the word and topic as two different vertexes and construct a bipartite network, which consists of words and topics. In this way, we introduce the bipartite network embedding method to learn better word and topic embedding, which results in better phrase representation. Comparing with existing work on bilingual phrase embedding, the proposed model not only considers the context information beyond phrases, but also improves phrases representation by introducing a word-topic bipartite network. For our model is an extension of BRAE and we use document-level topic distribution as context information, in the following, we name our model as Topically-informed Bilingually-constrained Recursive Auto-encoders (TBRAE). To summarize, we make the following contributions:

- By introducing the document-level topic distribution as context information, we augment the presentation capability of phrase representation.
- We construct a word-topic bipartite network for better word and topic vector representation, both of which are the basis of our model and directly affect the quality of the phrase representation. To the best of our knowledge, this has not been investigated yet.
- Based on the proposed model, we enhance a state-of-the-art SMT system with two phrase-level similarity features. Experimental results on Chinese-English translation task show the effectiveness of the proposed model.

2 Related Work

Recently, learning bilingual text embeddings has attracted great attention, especially for SMT. Li et al. proposed an RAE-based ITG reordering classifier [24]. Kalchbrenner and Blunsom introduced recurrent continuous translation models that comprise a class of purely continuous sentence-level translation models [4]. Lu et al. applied the deep autoencoder to automatically learn new features for the phrase-based translation model [20]. Gao et al. presented a continuous-space phrase translation model to project bilingual phrases into the continuous-valued vector representations [18]. Zhang et al. proposed the BRAE model [19], which is the basis of our model. Cho et al. proposed a novel Encoder-Decoder that consists of two RNNs for bilingual phrase embeddings [21]. Su et al. explored inner structures and semantic correspondence inside bilingual phrases for better phrase embeddings [22] . Hu et al. proposed a context-dependent convolutional matching model to capture the semantic similarities between context-sensitive phrase pairs [25]. Significantly different from these studies, our model introduces latent topics to improve bilingual phrase embeddings.

Specifically, we exploited latent topics in two ways in our model. Inspired by topic-based SMT [26–31], we introduce introduce the document-level topic distribution as context information for learning context-aware phrase representation. More importantly, we construct a word-topic bipartite network for better word and topic vector representation, both of which are the basis of our model and directly affect the quality of the phrase representation. In this aspect, recently, Liu et al., introduced the latent topic model to globally cluster words into different topics according to their contexts [32] . Furthermore, Liu et al. used a tensor layer to capture more interactions between words and topics under different contexts [33]. Different from the methods mentioned here, our model further exploits 2-step semantic correlations between words and topics for phrase embeddings, which, to the best of our knowledge, has never been investigated before.

3 The TBRAE Model

In this section, we first give an overview of our model, followed by the methods of modeling words, phrases and contexts, word-topic semantic constraints, respectively. Afterwards, we describe the model objective and the strategy for model training.

Figure 1 provides the architecture of the TBRAE model, which is an extension of the BRAE [19]. It consists of four components: (1) ***two recursive auto encoders*** that separately summarize the semantic meanings of the source and target phrases; (2) ***two context representation models*** which are respectively used to model the source-side and the target-side topical contexts; (3) ***bidirectional semantic constraints for topical phrase embeddings*** that minimize the bidirectional semantic distances between phrases and their translations in topical contexts; (4) ***two word-topic semantic constraints*** which exploit the word topic assignments to constrain word and topic embeddings in two languages, respectively.

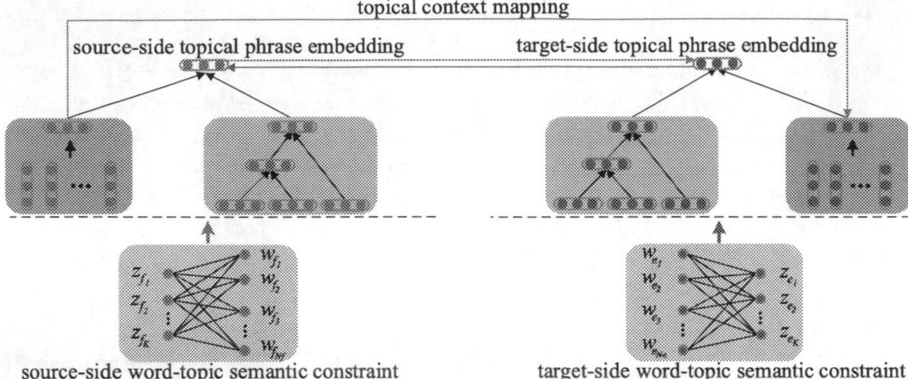

Fig. 1. The illustration of the TBRAE architecture. w_* and z_* represent the words and topics for two languages, respectively. Rectangles in mauve stand for the context representation models while canary yellow and light green rectangles represent the RAE-based phrase embeddings and the word-topic semantic constraints separately. (Color figure online)

In the last decade, topic models have drawn much attention and been applied successfully in various NLP tasks. Among these topic models, LDA is the most commonly used one at present, and therefore we use it to mine topics in our work. Before training the model, we employ LDA to obtain the topic distributions of documents and the word topic assignments. The former is available for the topical phrase embeddings, while the latter is used to constrain the learning of word and topic embeddings.

3.1 RAE-Based Phrase Modeling

In our model, each word in the vocabulary V corresponds to an n-dimensional real-valued vector, and all the vectors are stacked into a word embedding matrix $L_w \in \mathbb{R}^{n\times|V|}$. Regarding the phrase p as the meaningful composition of its internal words, we apply an RAE to learn its vector representation $\boldsymbol{p}$, as shown in the canary yellow part in Fig. 1. Assuming the vector representations (x_1, x_2, x_3) of the ordered words in the phrase serve as the input to the RAE. For two children vectors $\boldsymbol{x}_1$ and $\boldsymbol{x}_2$, the parent vector $\boldsymbol{y}_1$ is:

$$\boldsymbol{y}_1 = f(W^{(1)}[\boldsymbol{x}_1; \boldsymbol{x}_2] + b^{(1)}) \tag{1}$$

where $W^{(1)} \in \mathbb{R}^{n\times 2n}$ is a parameter matrix, $b^{(1)} \in \mathbb{R}^{n\times 1}$ is a bias term, and f is an element-wise activation function such as $tanh(\cdot)$, which is used in our experiments. In this way, $\boldsymbol{y}_1$ is also a n-dimensional vector. To evaluate how well $\boldsymbol{y}_1$ represents its children, we reconstruct the vector representations $\boldsymbol{x}'_1$ and $\boldsymbol{x}'_2$ of the original children nodes in the following way:

$$[\boldsymbol{x}'_1; \boldsymbol{x}'_2] = f(W^{(2)}\boldsymbol{y}_1 + b^{(2)}) \tag{2}$$

where $W^{(2)} \in \mathbb{R}^{2n \times n}$ and $b^{(2)} \in \mathbb{R}^{2n \times 1}$. Considering two children vectors $\boldsymbol{y}_1$ and $\boldsymbol{x}_3$, we then further apply Eq. (1) to compute the parent vector $\boldsymbol{y}_2$. This combination and reconstruction process of auto-encoder repeats at each node until the entire phrase vector is generated. To obtain the optimal binary tree and phrase representation for p, we employ a greedy algorithm [14] to minimize the sum of the *reconstruction error* at each node in the binary tree $T(p)$:

$$E_{rec}(p;\theta) = \sum_{y \in T(p)} \frac{1}{2} \parallel [\boldsymbol{c}_1; \boldsymbol{c}_2]_y - [\boldsymbol{c}_1'; \boldsymbol{c}_2']_y \parallel^2 \tag{3}$$

where y represents a non-leaf node in $T(p)$. It has two children vectors $\boldsymbol{c}_1$ and $\boldsymbol{c}_2$ which are reconstructed as the vectors $\boldsymbol{c}_1'$ and $\boldsymbol{c}_2'$.

3.2 Context Modeling

Based on the "bag-of-words" assumption, LDA views each document as a mixture of underlying topics, and generates each word according to the multinomial distribution conditioned on a topic. After training, LDA learns the document-topic distribution, which records the topic distribution of each document. Those parameters are often used to capture the document-level context in topic-based SMT [26 31]. Inspired by topic-based SMT, we use the document-topic distribution to represent the document-level context of phrases in each document. To make topical context computable, we regard each topic z in the topic set Z outputted by LDA as a pseudo word, of which semantic representation is also an n-dimensional real-valued vector. Thus, all topic embeddings can also be stacked to form a matrix $L_z \in \mathbb{R}^{n \times |Z|}$.

For the phrase p with the vector representation $\boldsymbol{p}$ in the document d, we define the semantic representation $\boldsymbol{dc}$ of its document-level context as the weighted sum of topic embeddings $\boldsymbol{z}$:

$$\boldsymbol{dc} = \sum_z p(z|d) \cdot \boldsymbol{z} \tag{4}$$

During training, we apply the above-mentioned approach to obtain the topical contexts of the phrase pair (f, e) in two languages, which are represented as $\boldsymbol{dc}_f$ and $\boldsymbol{dc}_e$, respectively. It has the advantage of exploiting extra monolingual corpora for better topic modeling. However, only source language documents are available during translation. To obtain the target-side topical context, we conduct topical context mapping in the source-to-target direction, and minimize the semantic distance $E_{tcm}(f|e;\theta)$ between the topical context embeddings in two languages as below:

$$E_{tcm}(f|e;\theta) = \frac{1}{2} ||\boldsymbol{dc}_e - f(W^{(3)}_{f2e} \cdot \boldsymbol{dc}_f + b^{(3)}_{f2e})||^2 \tag{5}$$

where $W^{(3)}_{f2e} \in \mathbb{R}^{n \times n}$ is the mapping matrix and $b^{(3)}_{f2e} \in \mathbb{R}^{n \times 1}$ is the corresponding bias term.

3.3 Bilingually-Constrained Topical Phrase Embeddings

Similar to the BRAE model, our TBRAE model exploits cross-lingual semantic equivalence to learn the topical phrase embeddings. The intuition behind TBRAE is that the source- and target-side parts of each phrase pair share the same semantic meanings under topical contexts. Thus, they can consider each other as the gold vector representation to learn the phrasal semantic representations under the topical contexts in two languages.

To model this intuition, we first introduce a standard neural network layer to produce the topical phrase embedding $\boldsymbol{p}_{dc}$

$$\boldsymbol{p}_{dc} = g(W^{(4)}[\boldsymbol{p}; \boldsymbol{dc}] + b^{(3)}) \tag{6}$$

where $W^{(4)} \in \mathbb{R}^{n \times 2n}$ and $b^{(4)} \in \mathbb{R}^{n \times 1}$.

Notice that all the embedding parameters for two languages are learned separately, and therefore the produced source- and target-side topical phrase embeddings $\boldsymbol{f}_{dc}$ and $\boldsymbol{e}_{dc}$ are located in different vector spaces. For this, we apply a semantic transformation matrix to map a topical phrase embedding to the semantic space in the other language, and then minimize the semantic distance between its transformed vector and the embedding vector of its translation. Formally, we calculate the semantic distance between $\boldsymbol{f}_{dc}$ and $\boldsymbol{e}_{dc}$ in the target-side embedding space as follows:

$$E_{sem}(f|e;\theta) = \frac{1}{2}||\boldsymbol{e}_{dc} - f(W^{(5)}_{f2e}\boldsymbol{f}_{dc} + b^{(5)}_{f2e})||^2 \tag{7}$$

where $W^{(5)}_{f2e} \in \mathbb{R}^{n \times n}$ is the semantic mapping matrix in the source-to-target direction, and $b^{(5)}_{f} \in \mathbb{R}^{n \times 1}$ is the corresponding bias term.

Then, we follow Zhang et al. to introduce a *max-semantic-margin error* $E^{*}_{sem}(f|e;\theta)$ to exploit the positive example (f, e) and the negative example (f, e') simultaneously [19]:

$$E^{*}_{sem}(f|e;\theta) = max\{0, E_{sem}(f|e;\theta) - E_{sem}(f|e',\theta) + 1\} \tag{8}$$

where e' is another candidate translation of f or a bad translation that replaces the words in e with randomly chosen target language words.

Note that the above-mentioned semantic transformation can also be performed in the target-to-source direction. Therefore, the semantic distance is bidirectional. Due to the limitation of space, we do not describe it.

3.4 Word-Topic Semantic Constraint Modeling

As stated previously, word and topic embeddings constitute the basis of the contextual phrase semantic representations in TBRAE. LDA learns the topic-word distribution that represents each topic as a distribution over words. Based on this distribution, LDA samples a topic to generate each word in a document. The word topic assignments reflect the semantic correlations between words and topics, which can be used as the semantic constraints when learning phrase embeddings. Inspired by Tang et al., who study heterogeneous text network embeddings [34] , we exploit the semantic correlation between words and topics for better topical phrase embeddings.

The basic idea of our approach is as follows. In LDA model training, one topic is sampled to generate each word in the document. Thus, the topic assignments of each word reflect its semantic information in the topic space. According to the principle of maximum likelihood estimation, we first define the empirical conditional probability $\hat{p}(z|w)$ of topic z given word w based on the topic assignments of words

$$\hat{p}(z|w) = \frac{count(w, z)}{\sum_{z'} count(w, z')} \tag{9}$$

where $count(w, z)$ denotes the number of times z sampled to generate w. Thus, the semantic correlation between words w and w' in the topic space can actually be determined by their conditional distributions $\hat{p}(z|w)$ and $\hat{p}(z|w')$. If they are semantically related, then w and w' should be represented closely in the embedding space.

To preserve the semantic correlations between words when learning topical phrase embeddings, we also define the conditional probability $p(z|w)$ based on the word and topic embeddings as follows:

$$p(z|w) = \frac{exp(\boldsymbol{w} \cdot \boldsymbol{z})}{\sum_{z'} exp(\boldsymbol{w} \cdot \boldsymbol{z}')} \tag{10}$$

where $\boldsymbol{w}$ denotes the embedding vector of word w. Then, we choose the Kullback-Leibler divergence $E_{wt}(w; \theta)$ to encourage $p(*|w)$ to be close to $\hat{p}(*|w)$:

$$E_{wt}(w; \theta) = \lambda_w \cdot d(p(*|w), \hat{p}(*|w)) \tag{11}$$

Here we introduce the weight λ_w that is defined as the frequency of w to distinguish the effects of different words. Omitting some constants, the objective function imposed on w becomes

$$E_{wt}(w; \theta) = \sum_{z} count(w, z) logp(z|w) \tag{12}$$

Similarly, the word-topic semantic constraints mentioned here can apply to the embedding learning in two languages.

3.5 The Model Objective

The above objective functions either act on each phrase pair or are used as global word-topic semantic constraints to learn the topical phrase embeddings.

For a phrase pair (f, e), there are three kinds of errors involved: (1) ***reconstruction error*** $E_{rec}(f, e; \theta)$: how well the learned vector representations $\boldsymbol{f}$

and $\boldsymbol{e}$ represent the phrases f and e respectively? (2) ***topical context mapping error*** $E_{tcm}(f|\ e;\theta)$: what is the semantic distance between the learned vector representations of topical contexts $\boldsymbol{dc}_f$ and $\boldsymbol{dc}_e$? (3) ***semantic error*** $E_{sem}(f,e;\theta)$: what is the semantic distance between the learned topical phrase embeddings $\boldsymbol{f}_{dc}$ and $\boldsymbol{e}_{dc}$? Formally, the joint error of (f,e) is defined as below:

$$E(f,e;\theta) = \alpha \cdot E_{rec}(f,e;\theta) + \beta \cdot E_{tcm}(f|e;\theta) + (1-\alpha-\beta) \cdot E_{sem}(f,e;\theta) \quad (13)$$

where the hyper-parameters α and β are used to weight different error functions, $E_{rec}(f,e;\theta)$ is the sum of $E_{rec}(f;\theta)$ and $E_{rec}(e;\theta)$, while $E_{sem}(f,e;\theta)$ equals $E^*_{sem}(f|e;\theta)$ plus $E^*_{sem}(e|f;\theta)$.

Besides, we impose the word-topic semantic constraint, mentioned in Sect. 3.4, on words in two languages. Thus, the final objective over the training set D becomes

$$\begin{aligned} J_{TBRAE} = & \frac{1}{N}\sum_{(f,e)\in D} E(f,e;\theta) + \gamma \cdot \Big(\frac{1}{|V_f|}\sum_{f\in V_f} E_{wt}(f;\theta) \\ & + \frac{1}{|V_e|}\sum_{e\in V_e} E_{wt}(e;\theta)\Big) + R(\theta) \end{aligned} \quad (14)$$

where γ is the hyper-parameter used to reflect the effect of the word-topic semantic constraints, $E_{wt}(*;\theta)$ denotes the error functions of the word-topic semantic constraints for two languages, and $R(\theta)$ is the regularization term involving the following parameter sets:[1] (1) θ_{L_w}: the word embedding matrices; (2) θ_{L_z}: the topic embedding matrices; (3) θ_{rec}: the RAE parameter matrices $W^{(1)}$, $W^{(2)}$ and bias terms $b^{(1)}$, $b^{(2)}$; (4) θ_{tcm}: the topical context mapping matrix $W^{(3)}_{f2e}$ and bias term $b^{(3)}_{f2e}$; (5) θ_{tp}: the topical phrase embedding parameter matrices $W^{(4)}$ and bias terms $b^{(4)}$; (6) θ_{sem}: the phrase semantic transformation matrices $W^{(5)}$ and bias terms $b^{(5)}$. Here we assign parameter sets different weights for regularization:

$$\begin{aligned} R(\theta) = & \frac{\lambda_{L_w}}{2}||\theta_{L_w}||^2 + \frac{\lambda_{L_z}}{2}||\theta_{L_z}||^2 + \frac{\lambda_{rec}}{2}||\theta_{rec}||^2 \\ & + \frac{\lambda_{tcm}}{2}||\theta_{tcm}||^2 + \frac{\lambda_{tp}}{2}||\theta_{tp}||^2 + \frac{\lambda_{sem}}{2}||\theta_{sem}||^2 \end{aligned} \quad (15)$$

We apply a similar co-training style algorithm as [19] to train the model parameters. Specifically, for each phrase pair, we fix its target-side contextual phrase representation to update its source-side parameters, and vice versa. In this process, we apply mini-batch to tune parameters based on gradients over the joint error. In each batch, we only use the forced decoding phrase pairs of a document for model training. Note that the word-topic semantic constraints are imposed on words rather than phrases. For this, we just consider the topic assignments of words occurring in the document and calculate their semantic

[1] Note that the source and target languages have different sets of parameters.

constraint errors. This procedure repeats until either the joint error (shown in Eq. (14)) reaches a local minimum or the number of iterations is larger than the pre-defined one (25 is used in experiments).

4 Experiments

To validate the effectiveness of our TBRAE model, we conducted experiments on NIST Chinese-English translation task. Given a bilingual phrase (f, e) used to translate the source document, we successively implemented RAE-based phrase embeddings, topical context modelings and mapping, topical phrase embeddings, and semantic transformations. Finally, we calculated the cosine similarities between f and e in two directions, which are used as two additional features in the log-linear framework of SMT system.

4.1 Setup

Following Zhang et al. we chose a phrase-based translation system with a maximum entropy based reordering model (MEBTG) [35,36] as our experiment system [19]. Our training data consists of the FBIS corpus and the Hansards part of LDC2004T07 corpus, with 1.0M parallel sentences (25.2M Chinese words and 29M English words). Following Zhang et al., we performed forced decoding with Leaving-One-Out [37] on the parallel sentences to collect 3.65M phrase pairs of high quality for the model training [19]. We trained a 5-gram language model on the Xinhua portion of Gigaword corpus using *SRILM* Toolkits.[2] Besides, we used NIST MT05 and MT06/MT08 data set as the development and test set, respectively. For translation results, we chose the case-insensitive BLEU-4 [38] as the evaluation metric, and performed paired bootstrap sampling [39] to calculate the statistical significance in BLEU score differences.

For the topic model, we used the GibbsLDA++[3] for estimation and inference. Following [27,40], we set the parameters as follows: the topic number $N_z = 30$, the hyper-parameters $\alpha_z = 50/N_z$ and $\beta_z = 0.1$, and the iteration number $N_{iter} = 1000$.

In the experiments, we set the vector dimension as 50 and the learning rate as 0.01, as implemented in [19]. To tune the hyper-parameters, we randomly selected 250,000 forced decoding bilingual phrases as training set, 5000 as development set, and another 5000 as test set. We first incrementally drew α from 0.05 to 0.3, β from 0.05 to 0.25 with step 0.05, γ from 0.01 to 0.1 with step 0.01, and λ_* exponentially from 10^{-5} to 10^{-2}, and then determined the optimal hyper-parameters according to the overall error of the proposed model on the test set. Noting that too many hyper-parameters will lead to difficulties in model training, we first learned word embeddings, RAE parameters, and some hyper-parameters such as λ_{L_w}, λ_{rec}, λ_{sem} using the BRAE model. Then, we fixed these

[2] http://www.speech.sri.com/projects/srilm/download.html.
[3] http://gibbslda.sourceforge.net/.

Table 1. Experiment results on the test sets when setting dimension $n = 50$. */**: significantly better than MEBTG ($p < 0.05/0.01$), +/++: significantly better than BRAE ($p < 0.05/0.01$)

Model	MEBTG	BRAE	TBRAE(cont)	TBRAE(ss)	TBRAE(ts)	TBRAE
MT06	29.66	30.27	30.35**	30.88**+	30.68**	31.16**++
MT08	21.52	22.53	22.77**	23.34**++	23.11**+	23.71**++

parameters, hyper-parameters and tuned the others during the TBARE model training. Finally, we set $\alpha = 0.1, \beta = 0.1, \gamma = 0.08, \lambda_{L_w} = 10^{-5}$, $\lambda_{L_t} = 10^{-5}$, $\lambda_{rec} = 10^{-2}$, $\lambda_{tcm} = 10^{-5}$, $\lambda_{tp} = 10^{-3}$ and $\lambda_{sem} = 10^{-5}$.

4.2 Overall Performance

First, we investigated the overall performance of the TBRAE model. Following Zhang et al., we set the dimensionality of the word and the topic embedding as 50 [19]. In addition to the conventional MEBTG system and the BRAE model, we also compared our model with its three variants: (1) TBRAE(cont) which explores only topical contexts while ignoring the word-topic semantic constraints; (2) TBRAE(ss) that uses only the cosine similarity feature in the source-side semantic space; (3) TBRAE(ts) that uses only the cosine similarity feature in the target-side semantic space.

Table 1 summarizes the comparison results of different models on the test sets. In all cases, TBRAE performs better than MEBTG, BRAE and TBRAE(cont), even if it use only one similarity feature. When using bidirectional similarity features together, TBRAE achieves the best performance, which is better than MEBTG, BRAE and TBRAE(cont) by 1.5/2.19, 0.89/1.18 and 0.81/0.94 BLEU points on the two sets, respectively. These experiments show that the exploitation of latent topics, especially word-topic constraints, contributes to outperforming MEBTG and BRAE both of which consider only internal semantic information of bilingual phrases.

5 Conclusions and Future Work

We have presented a topically-informed BRAE model which exploits latent topics to improve phrase embeddings for SMT. Topical contexts are introduced to enhance the determinativeness of phrase embeddings in different contexts. Word topic assignments are also used to constrain the learning of word and topic embeddings, both of which directly affect the learned contextual phrase embeddings. The experiment results on Chinese-English translation demonstrate the superiority of our model over a state-of-the-art baseline and BRAE [19].

There are some valuable research directions in future. First, it is interesting to follow Liu et al. to directly model the interaction between words and topics for bilingual phrase embeddings [33]. Second, our model holds the potential to be extended to other phrase-based and even syntax-based systems.

Acknowledgments. This work is supported by the National Key R&D Program (No. 2017YFC0113000, and No. 2016YFB1001503), Nature Science Foundation of China (No. U1705262, No. 61772443, and No. 61572410), Post Doctoral Innovative Talent Support Program under Grant BX201600094, China Post-Doctoral Science Foundation under Grant 2017M612134, Scientific Research Project of National Language Committee of China (Grant No. YB135-49), Nature Science Foundation of Fujian Province, China (No. 2017J01125 and No. 2018J01106), and the Open Fund Project of Fujian Provincial Key Laboratory of Information Processing and Intelligent Control (Minjiang University) under Grant MJUKF201742.

References

1. Koehn, P., Och, F.J., Marcu, D.: Statistical phrase-based translation. In: Proceedings of NAACL 2003, pp. 48–54 (2003)
2. Chiang, D.: Hierarchical phrase-based translation. Comput. Linguist. **33**, 201–228 (2007)
3. Auli, M., Galley, M., Quirk, C., Zweig, G.: Joint language and translation modeling with recurrent neural networks. In: Proceedings of EMNLP 2013, pp. 1044–1054 (2013)
4. Kalchbrenner, N., Blunsom, P.: Recurrent continuous translation models. In: Proceedings of EMNLP 2013, pp. 1700–1709 (2013)
5. Liu, L., Watanabe, T., Sumita, E., Zhao, T.: Additive neural networks for statistical machine translation. In: Proceedings of ACL 2013, pp. 791–801 (2013)
6. Vaswani, A., Zhao, Y., Fossum, V., Chiang, D.: Decoding with large-scale neural language models improves translation. In: Proceedings of EMNLP 2013, pp. 1387–1392 (2013)
7. Yang, N., Liu, S., Li, M., Zhou, M., Yu, N.: Word alignment modeling with context dependent deep neural network. In: Proceedings of ACL 2013, pp. 166–175 (2013)
8. Zou, W.Y., Socher, R., Cer, D., Manning, C.D.: Bilingual word embeddings for phrase-based machine translation. In: Proceedings of EMNLP 2013, pp. 1393–1398 (2013)
9. Devlin, J., Zbib, R., Huang, Z., Lamar, T., Schwartz, R., Makhoul, J.: Fast and robust neural network joint models for statistical machine translation. In: Proceedings of ACL 2014, pp. 1370–1380 (2014)
10. Garmash, E., Monz, C.: Dependency-based bilingual language models for reordering in statistical machine translation. In: Proceedings of EMNLP 2014, pp. 1689–1700 (2014)
11. Tran, K.M., Bisazza, A., Monz, C.: Word translation prediction for morphologically rich languages with bilingual neural networks. In: Proceedings of EMNLP 2014, pp. 1676–1688 (2014)
12. Wu, H., et al.: Improve statistical machine translation with context-sensitive bilingual semantic embedding model. In: Proceedings of EMNLP 2014, pp. 142–146 (2014)
13. Socher, R., Manning, C.D., Ng, A.Y.: Learning continuous phrase representations and syntactic parsing with recursive neural networks. In: Proceedings of the NIPS 2010 Workshop, pp. 1–9 (2010)
14. Socher, R., Pennington, J., Huang, E.H., Ng, A.Y., Manning, C.D.: Semi-supervised recursive autoencoders for predicting sentiment distributions. In: Proceedings of EMNLP 2011, pp. 151–161 (2011)

15. Socher, R., Huang, E.H., Pennington, J., Ng, A.Y., Manning, C.D.: Dynamic pooling and unfolding recursive autoencoders for paraphrase detection. In: Proceedings of NIPS 2011 (2011)
16. Collobert, R., Weston, J., Bottou, L., Karlen, M., Kavukcuoglu, K., Kuksa, P.: Natural language processing (almost) from scratch. J. Mach. Learn. Res. **16**, 2493–2537 (2011)
17. Mikolov, T., Sutskever, I., Chen, K., Corrado, G.S., Dean, J.: Distributed representations of words and phrases and their compositionality. In: Proceedings of NIPS 2013, pp. 3111–3119 (2013)
18. Gao, J., He, X., Yih, W.T., Deng, L.: Learning continuous phrase representations for translation modeling. In: Proceedings of ACL 2014, pp. 699–709 (2014)
19. Zhang, J., Liu, S., Li, M., Zhou, M., Zong, C.: Bilingually-constrained phrase embeddings for machine translation. In: Proceedings of ACL 2014, pp. 111–121 (2014)
20. Lu, S., Chen, Z., Xu, B.: Learning new semi-supervised deep auto-encoder features for statistical machine translation. In: Proceedings of ACL 2014, pp. 122–132 (2014)
21. Cho, K., et al.: Learning phrase representations using RNN encoder-decoder for statistical machine translation. In: Proceedings of EMNLP 2014, pp. 1724–1734 (2014)
22. Su, J., Xiong, D., Zhang, B., Liu, Y., Yao, J., Zhang, M.: Bilingual correspondence recursive autoencoder for statistical machine translation. In: Proceedings of EMNLP 2015, pp. 1248–1258 (2015)
23. Wang, X., Xiong, D., Zhang, M.: Learning semantic representations for nonterminals in hierarchical phrase-based translation. In: Proceedings of EMNLP 2015, pp. 1391–1400 (2015)
24. Li, P., Liu, Y., Sun, M.: Recursive autoencoders for ITG-based translation. In: Proceedings of EMNLP 2013, pp. 567–577 (2013)
25. Hu, B., Tu, Z., Lu, Z., Li, H., Chen, Q.: Context-dependent translation selection using convolutional neural network. In: Proceedings of ACL 2015 Short Paper, pp. 536–541 (2015)
26. Zhao, B., Xing, E.P.: Bitam: Bilingual topic admixture models for word alignment. In: Proceedings of ACL 2006, pp. 969–976 (2006)
27. Xiao, X., Xiong, D., Zhang, M., Liu, Q., Lin, S.: A topic similarity model for hierarchical phrase-based translation. In: Proceedings of ACL 2012, pp. 750–758 (2012)
28. Eidelman, V., Boyd-Graber, J., Resnik, P.: Topic models for dynamic translation model adaptation. In: Proceedings of ACL 2012, Short paper, pp. 115–119 (2012)
29. Xiong, D., Zhang, M.: A topic-based coherence model for statistical machine translation. In: Proceedings of AAAI 2013 (2013)
30. Hu, Y., Zhai, K., Eidelman, V., Boyd-Graber, J.: Polylingual tree-based topic models for translation domain adaptation. In: Proceedings of ACL 2014, pp. 1166–1176 (2014)
31. Hasler, E., Blunsom, P., Koehn, P., Haddow, B.: Dynamic topic adaptation for phrase-based MT. In: Proceedings of EACL 2014, pp. 328–337 (2014)
32. Liu, Y., Liu, Z., Chua, T.S., Sun, M.: Topical word embeddings. In: Proceedings of AAAI 2015, pp. 2418–2424 (2015)
33. Liu, P., Qiu, X., Huang, X.: Learning context-sensitive word embeddings with neural tensor skip-gram model. In: Proceedings of IJCAI 2015, pp. 1284–1290 (2015)
34. Tang, J., Qu, M., Mei, Q.: PTE: predictive text embedding through large-scale heterogeneous text networks. In: Proceedings of KDD 2015, pp. 1165–1174 (2015)

35. Wu, D.: Stochastic inversion transduction grammars and bilingual parsing of parallel corpora. Comput. Linguist. **23**(3), 377–403 (1997)
36. Xiong, D., Liu, Q., Lin, S.: Maximum entropy based phrase reordering model for statistical machine translation. In: Proceedings of ACL 2006, pp. 521–528 (2006)
37. Wuebker, J., Mauser, A., Ney, H.: Training phrase translation models with leaving-one-out. In: Proceedings of ACL 2010, pp. 475–484 (2010)
38. Papineni, K., Roukos, S., Ward, T., Zhu, W.: BLEU: a method for automatic evaluation of machine translation. In: Proceedings of ACL 2002, pp. 311–318 (2002)
39. Koehn, P.: Statistical significance tests for machine translation èvaluation. In: Proceedings of EMNLP 2004, pp. 388–395 (2004)
40. Griffiths, T.L., Steyvers, M.: Finding scientific topics. In: Proceedings of the National Academy of Sciences 2004 (2004)

Collaborating Aesthetic Change and Heterogeneous Information into Recommender Systems

Zongze Jin[1,2], Yun Zhang[1,2](✉), Weimin Mu[1,2], Weiping Wang[2,4], and Hai Jin[2,3]

[1] School of Cyber Security, University of Chinese Academy of Sciences, Beijing, China
[2] Institute of Information Engineering, Chinese Academy of Sciences, Beijing, China
{jinzongze,zhangyun,muweimin,wangweiping}@iie.ac.cn
[3] School of Computer Science and Technology, Huazhong University of Science and Technology, Wuhan, China
hjin@hust.edu.com
[4] National Engineering Research Center Information Security Common Technology, NERCIS, Beijing, China

Abstract. Recently, with the increasing of heterogeneous information, recommender system has gradually transferred from a single view of rating to multi-dimensional information integration. However, the existing approaches cannot fully exploit the users' information. In this paper, we propose a deep learning based framework, which uses heterogeneous information and also considers temporal changes in users' interests to extract the users' features. Experiments on several real world datasets demonstrate that our proposed model outperforms the state-of-the-art methods for recommendation task.

Keywords: Recommender system · Feature representation
Deep learning

1 Introduction

With the explosive growth of information, recommender systems have been an effective technique to discover what the users need [2,23]. Traditional recommender systems, such as collaborative filtering (CF) [16,22], mainly utilize the users' historical behavior or interests. While these approaches have shown good performance, they also have some limitations. Firstly, the CF techniques cannot solve the sparsity problem very well. In addition, the interpretability of the CF techniques is poor. With the development of recommender systems, some researches [6,28,29] have exploited users' information to improve recommendation in order to tackle these problems.

Zheng et al. [31] adopts reviews with convolutional neural network (CNN) to capture the users' feature, but ignores the user-changed interests. Song et al. [24]

X. Geng and B.-H. Kang (Eds.): PRICAI 2018, LNAI 11012, pp. 150–162, 2018.
https://doi.org/10.1007/978-3-319-97304-3_12

has considered the user-changed interests with long-short term memory (LSTM) to capture the temporal changes in users' interests, but the approach uses only reviews. However, as different types of information come into being, users' interests do not focus on a single view, but come from the mixture of multiple views (e.g., images, reviews or ratings) of the various data. In recommendation, numeric ratings reflect users' comprehensive evaluation through multiple views. For example, in movie recommendations, reviews represent users' opinions, posters reflect the direct visual feeling and the movie descriptions express the key information (e.g., directors or actors). Many researchers have demonstrated that heterogeneous information can improve the accuracy and make the users' profiles completely. Previous work [28,29] about users' representations using heterogeneous information mainly use deep learning techniques to represent the textual feature, the audio feature and the visual feature. However, these methods ignore the temporal changes in users' interests. Users not only change the aesthetic or understanding abilities, but also pay attention to some important information. For example, as time goes on, the users' aesthetic on movie posters will change with the needs and trends of the market. Besides, the reason why the user chose the movie is that it is the best picture Oscar or directed by Spielberg.

In this paper, we propose a novel framework, named Aesthetic-changed Heterogeneous Information Collaborative Representation Framework (AHICRF), which uses heterogeneous information and also considers temporal changes in users' interests to extract the users' features. The framework is illustrated in Fig. 1. In this framework, we regard each information source as a view and utilize deep learning techniques to capture the features from multiple views. For users' visual representations, we have fully taken the visual feelings (e.g., movie's posters or book covers) and the key information (e.g., directors or authors) into account. For users' visual representations, we use CNN to get the image features and leverage LSTM to capture temporal changes in users' interests. For review view, we regard this view as the subjective view and we use CNN to obtain the users' interests. And for the description, we regard this view as the objective view and also use CNN to gain what the users focus on. In addition, our contributions can be summarized as follows:

- We present an end-to-end model, AHICRF, which uses deep learning techniques to extract user features from heterogeneous information.
- To the best of our knowledge, AHICRF is the first model which considers the temporal changes in users' interests when fusing the heterogeneous information.
- We compare AHICRF with the state-of-the-art methods on three real world datasets to demonstrate its effectives.

The rest of the paper is organized as follows. In Sect. 2, we represent the related work about AHICRF. Besides, problem definitions about our model are presented in Sect. 3. Then we describe AHICRF in detail in Sect. 3. In Sect. 4, we present our experiments and analyze the experimental results. Finally, conclusions are presented in Sect. 5.

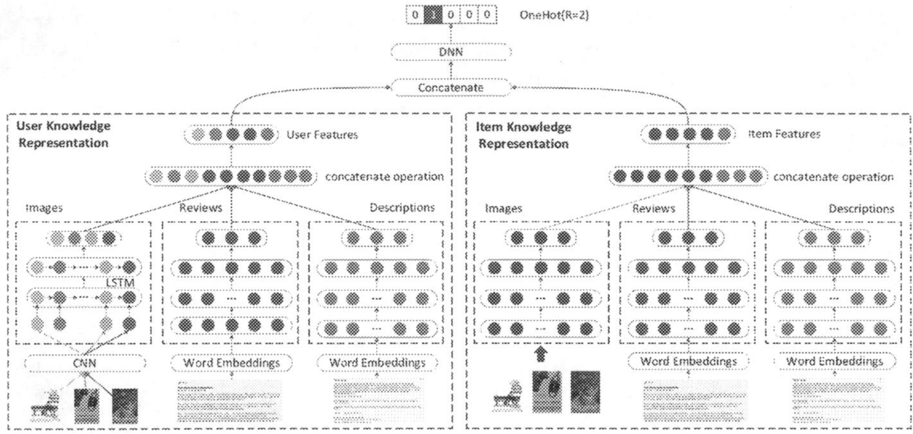

Fig. 1. The architecture of AHICRF.

2 Related Work

Recently, many researches [11,24,27–29] have demonstrated fully exploiting users' representations can improve recommendation performance. Most existing tasks focus on leveraging the single view to represent users' features. Aciar et al. [1] has developed and employed an ontology to translate opinions quality and content into a form the recommender process can use. The text-mining process automatically maps the review comments into the ontologys information structure. However, the manual selection of ontology construction limits the development of these methods. Many researches [3,17,18] have presented topic discovery from the text information to improve recommendations. Moveover, some approaches [9,26] which use probabilistic graphical models to mine the reviews have enhanced recommendations. In addition, many methods [4,30] have adopted sentiment analysis to capture the feature through reviews or descriptions. For example, Zhang et al. [30] has proposed the model which leverages phrase-level sentiment analysis to complete multi-matrix factorization for recommendations. Furthermore, Bauman et al. [4] has adopted item aspects to give users better choices using reviews. Recently, some approaches [24,25,31] which use word embeddings to capture the semantic information in text. Zheng et al. [31] adopts word2vec[1] to extract the features of reviews in preprocessing stage and uses CNN to capture the users' features using reviews, but ignoring the temporal changes in users' interests. Besides, Song et al. [24] has leveraged the deep semantic structured model (DSSM) [14] to capture the semantic features and introduces LSTM to obtain the temporal changes in users' interests.

In addition, some approaches [8,13,19,28] leverage the visual informations to improve recommendations. McAuley et al. [19] has proposed the co-purchase recommendations based on images and He et al. [13] has presented the top-

[1] https://code.google.com/archive/p/word2vec/.

N recommendation to capture the implicit feedbacks through Visual Bayesian Personalized Ranking (VBRP). Besides, Covington et al. [8] has utilized deep learning techniques to gain the video features to improve recommendations and Zhang et al. [28] has used convolutional neural networks (CNN) to capture the image features.

However, with the explosive growth of heterogeneous information, a single view can not fully express the users' interests, and more and more researches have integrated more views. In [27], Yu et al. applies matrix factorization techniques [16] on the diffused user interests to calculate latent representations for users and items accordingly through heterogeneous information. Grad-Gyenge et al. [11] has proposed the rating prediction leveraging knowledge base's network features. With the development of deep learning, existing approaches follow the research trend. Elkahky et al. [10] has proposed the deep learning approach extended from the DSSM [14] to map users and items to a shared semantic space and recommend items that have maximum similarity with users in the mapped space. Zhang et al. [28] has proposed the framework, named Collaborative Knowledge Base Embedding (CKE), to jointly learn the latent representations in collaborative filtering as well as items semantic representations from the knowledge base. In addition, Zhang et al. [29] has proposed a Joint Representation Learning (JRL) approach as a general framework for recommendation, which builds representation learning on top of pair-wise learning to rank for top-N recommendation.

3 Framework

In this section, we describe our framework, named Aesthetic-changed Heterogeneous Information Collaborative Representation Framework (AHICRF). Firstly, we present the problem definition. Secondly, we provide a simple overview of our framework in Sect. 3.2. Then we describe preprocessing part, user knowledge representation part, item knowledge representation part and output layers, respectively. After that, we propose the loss function of our framework in Sect. 3.6 and present how to train our framework in Sect. 3.7.

3.1 Problem Definition

Given a user U, we utilize $V = \{v_{t1}^1, v_{t2}^2, \cdots, v_{tn}^n\}$ to represent the images about what he has evaluated, in which tn represents the time of evaluating the image. And $R = \{R_1, R_2, \cdots, R_n\}$ and $D = \{D_1, D_2, \cdots, D_n\}$ separately represent the user's reviews and the descriptions on which he has focused. Thus, we adopt the triple tuples $H = \{(v_{t1}^1, R_1, D_1), (v_{t2}^2, R_2, D_2), \cdots, (v_{tn}^n, R_n, D_n)\}$ to express heterogeneous information of the user U. We aim to recommend items to each user through heterogeneous information H.

3.2 Overview

In our framework, we adopt the visual view V_v, the review view V_R and the description view V_D. By fully exploiting the features from different views, our model focus on the user-changed information. From Fig. 1, our framework mainly consists of four parts: (1) Preprocessing Part (2) User Knowledge Representation Part (3) Item Knowledge Representation Part and (4) Joint Learning Part. From Fig. 1, we can observe that the left part is the user knowledge representation part and the other is the item knowledge representation part. Then we utilize joint learning to get the predicted ratings.

3.3 Preprocessing Part

In this subsection, we first present the visual feature preprocessing, which is an important task before extracting the visual feature. Additionally, we adopt word embedding to deal with the textual information.

Visual Feature Preprocessing. Before we capture the aesthetic-changed visual features, we should get the visual features of images or videos as the input. We adopt CNN architectures to learn the representations in the visual views V_v. Same as [19], we use the same CNN architecture, which contains 5 convolutional layers followed by 3 fully-connected layers with pre-training on ImageNet (ILSVRC2010) images, to capture the visual features. We use the output of $FC8$, the last fully-connected layer, which results in a feature vector of length $F = 1000$. And the user-changed visual features is presented in User Knowledge Representation Part.

Word Embedding. Before we capture the textual features, we should prepropress the text for neural networks. The embedding layer maps each non-zero word feature into a dense vector representation. Recently, many natural language processing (NLP) tasks [5,7] demonstrate word embedding can enhance the performance on semantic analysis. In our framework, we pre-train the dictionary of words using word2vec[2]. Then we use V_R and V_D to represent the reviews and descriptions word embeddings matrices, respectively.

3.4 User Knowledge Representation Part

In this subsection, we present visual feature representation, review feature representation, description feature representation and integrated strategy. We adopt CNN and LSTM to capture the users' aesthetic change. In addition, we use reviews to represent the user' subjective habits and use descriptions to represent the impact of objective factors. Finally, we use integrated strategy to concatenate these features.

Visual Feature Representation. Users' visual feelings will change over time. There are many reasons for this phenomenon, such as the changed interests or

[2] https://code.google.com/archive/p/word2vec/.

the popular trend. To capture the user-changed visual features, we adopt long-short term memory (LSTM) to obtain the temporal trends. In Fig. 1, we show the architecture of this part and we show the input which is the visual feature $F^{U_n}_{v^n_{tn}}$ about the user U from the preprocessing as follows.

$$F^U_{v^n_{tn}} = (f^U_{v^1_{t1}}, f^U_{v^2_{t2}}, \cdots, f^U_{v^n_{tn}}) \tag{1}$$

where v^n_{tn} represents the images about what the user U has evaluated. We adopt LSTM in our model to capture the dynamic feature of the users. Each LSTM unit at time t consists of a memory cell c_t, an input gate i_t, a forget gate f_t and the output gate o_t. These gates are computed from previous hidden state h_{t-1} and the current input z_t. The memory cell c_t is updated by partially forgetting the existing memory and adding a new memory content l_t. The details are as follows.

$$[f_t, i_t, o_t] = \sigma[W_{lstm}[h_{t-1}, z_t] + b_{lstm}] \tag{2}$$

$$l_t = tahn[V[h_{t-1}, z_t] + d] \tag{3}$$

$$c_t = f_t * c_{t-1} + i_t * l_t \tag{4}$$

Once the memory content of the LSTM unit is updated, the hidden state at time step t is given by $h_t = o_t * tahn(c_t)$. The output features F^U_V of LSTM is expressed by

$$F^U_V = LSTM(h_t, F^U_{v^n_{tn}}) \tag{5}$$

Review Feature Representation. In order to highlight the features of user reviews, which reflect users' subjective language habits, interests and so on, we adopt the CNN to obtain the review features. In our model, we apply the word embedding matrix V^R_U and use C^U_R to denote the output of convolutional layers and some maxpooling layers. Then we use a fully connected layer with the weight W^c_R and the bias term b^c_R. After that, we use a maxpooling layer to get the review features. At last we use ReLUs (Rectified Linear Units) [20] to get the output features F^U_R:

$$F^U_R = ReLU(max(W^c_R * C^U_R + b^c_R)) \tag{6}$$

Description Feature Representation. Compared to Review Feature Representation, Description Feature Representation is more concerned with the objective information. The reason why the user watch the movie is that the actor is his/her favorite star. The network is the same as the Review Feature Representation. But in this way, we adopt the different word embedding matrix V^D_U and use C^U_D to denote the output of convolutional layers and some maxpooling layers. Then through a fully connected layer, a maxpooling layer and the non-linear mapping, we can get that the output features F^D_R:

$$F^U_D = ReLU(max(W^c_D * C^U_D + b^c_D)) \tag{7}$$

Integrated Strategy. When we obtain the features from the different views, we should integrate the above representations. In this way, we concatenate the above features as the input feature X_U:

$$X_U = W_V^U * F_V^U + W_R^U * F_R^U + W_D^U * F_D^U \tag{8}$$

where W_V^U, W_R^U and W_D^U are the weights of the fusion features of the Visual View, Review View and Description View. After that, we use Deep Neural Network (DNN) to obtain the final user output F_o^U:

$$F_o^U = DNN(X_U) \tag{9}$$

where $DNN(.)$ means that we use deep neural network to get our final output F_o^U.

3.5 Item Knowledge Representation Part

In this subsection, same as user knowledge representation, we also present visual feature representation, review feature representation, description feature representation and integrated strategy. We adopt CNN to capture the items' visual information. Besides, we use reviews to represent the impact of different users and use descriptions to represent the official properties. Finally, we use integrated strategy to concatenate these features.

Visual Feature Representation. Unlike users' visual representation, this part uses only CNN for feature extraction, the reason why we do not use LSTM is that the visual features of items do not change over time. In this part, we should pre-train the network and fine-tune our model. And we use F_V^I to represent the visual features of items as follows.

$$F_V^I = ReLU(max(W_I^V * C_V^I + b_I^V)) \tag{10}$$

Review Feature Representation. For items, the review is the users' view and the description is the official view. Same as the user part, we also leverage CNN to capture the features of reviews. But in this part, we apply the word embedding matrix V_I^R and use C_R^I to denote the output of convolutional layers and some maxpooling layers. Then we get the output F_R^I:

$$F_R^I = ReLU(max(W_I^R * C_R^I + b_I^R)) \tag{11}$$

Description Feature Representation. Compared to Review Feature Representation, Description Feature Representation focus on the offical information in item part. The network is the same as the Review Feature Representation. So we can get that the output features F_R^D:

$$F_D^I = ReLU(max(W_I^D * C_D^I + b_I^D)) \tag{12}$$

Integrated Strategy. Same as the user part, when we obtain the features from the different views, we should integrate the above representations. In this way, we adopt concatenate the features and use Deep Neural Network to get the final features X_I:

$$X_I = W_V^I * F_V^I + W_R^I * F_R^I + W_D^I * F_D^I \tag{13}$$

where W_V^I, W_R^I and W_D^I are the weights of the fusion features of the Visual View, Review View and Description View in item part. After that, we use Deep Neural Network (DNN) to obtain the final item output F_o^I:

$$F_o^I = DNN(X_I) \tag{14}$$

3.6 Output Layers

When we get the final user feature F_o^U and the final item features F_o^I, we use DNN to predict the ratings. Firstly, we concatenate the features and get X_O.

$$X_O = W_o^U * F_o^U + W_o^I * F_o^I \tag{15}$$

where W_o^U denotes the weight of F_o^U and W_o^I denotes the weight of F_o^I. And we use DNN to obtain the final output features F_o:

$$F_o = DNN(X_O) \tag{16}$$

In our framework, we utilize the One-Hot encoding method to obtain the supervised value $y = OneHot(R)$. We utilize softmax method to obtain the prediction y^*:

$$y^* = softmax(W_o * F_o + b_o) \tag{17}$$

where W_o denotes the weight of F_o and the b_o is the bias.

Last we adopt a cross-entropy method to capture the difference between the supervised value y and the predicted results y^*:

$$C = -\sum(y_i ln(y_i^*) + (1 - y_i) ln(1 - y_i^*)) \tag{18}$$

Then we predict the ratings R and y_k^* denotes the probability of getting the rating k.

$$R = arg \max_k(y_k^*)$$

3.7 Training

We take the derivative of the loss with respect to the whole set of parameters through back-propagation, and use stochastic gradient descent with mini-batch to update the parameters. Word vectors are learned with word2vec. We empirically set vector dimension d as 300. We use dropout to avoid the neural network being over-fitting.

4 Experiment

In this section, we firstly describe three real datasets and metrics in our experiments. Then in Sect. 4.2, we present the baselines and the experiments settings. Finally, we give the experimental results and analyze them.

4.1 Datasets and Metrics

We use the following benchmark real-world datasets for performance evaluation:

MovieLens-20M dataset[3]: It contains more than 100,000 movie ratings with the scales from 1 to 5 provided by 27,000 movies by 138,000 users.

Amazon-Book and Amazon-Clothing dataset[4]: This dataset is collected by McAuley [12,19]. It contains different types of data from Amazon. The dataset covers user interactions on items and contains the metadata spanning May 1996-July 2014. In our framework, we utilize the Amazon-Book and Amazon-Clothing information. This book part contains 123960 users and 50052 items with the scales from 1 to 5. The clothing part contains 39387 users and 23033 items with the scales from 1 to 5.

To check the performances of different methods, we use 2 popular metrics for evaluations: mean squared error (MSE) and mean absolute error (MAE). The lower values of them indicate better performance.

4.2 Baselines

In this section, we evaluate our model AHICRF by comparing with several state-of-the-art approaches using each single view (image, review and description):

BPR-MF [21]: This method utilizes numeric ratings to complete the top-N recommendation.

VBPR [13]: This method is the state-of-the-art approach based on visual images of the items.

MVDNN [10]: This method is a novel multi-view model that discovers a single mapping for user features in the latent space such that it is jointly optimized with features of items from all domains.

DeepCoNN [31]: It learns hidden latent features for users and items jointly using two coupled neural networks such that the rating prediction accuracy is maximized.

CKE [28]: It integrates collaborative filtering with items semantic representations from the knowledge base to learn different representations in a unified model jointly.

JRL [29]: It is a general framework for recommendation, which builds representation learning on top of pair-wise learning to rank for top-N recommendation.

We utilize stochastic gradient descent with batch size 128 and train each model for 50 epochs. For baselines, we adopt the recommended parameters. For our model, in the visual representations part, we use the output of $FC8$ in [19], the last fully-connected layer, which results in a feature vector of length $F = 1000$. In the review representations part and description representations part, we adopt the texual features which have been presented in [15].

---

[3] https://grouplens.org/datasets/movielens/.

[4] http://jmcauley.ucsd.edu/data/amazon/.

4.3 Results

In this subsection, we firstly present performance evaluation and analyze the results. Then we consider the impact the temporal changes in users' interests and the impact of embedding size.

Performance Evaluation. The performances of AHICRF and the baselines are listed in Table 1. From the results, we have the following observations: (1) The performance of BPR-MF is the worst, and VBPR is a little better than BPR-MF. The reason for this results is that traditional approaches cannot integrate multiple information. (2) We find MVDNN and DeepCoNN are better than BPR-MF and VBPR but worse than the others. Although MVDNN has considered the multiple views, but it has not integrated multiple information into its model. For DeepCoNN, it has only chosen the single view using reviews. (3) CKE, JRL and AHICRF, which integrate rich information from different views into their models are better than the above. The reason why CKE is worse than JRL and AHICRF is that CKE uses unsupervised approaches to integrate heterogeneous information and ignores users' impact. (4) AHICRF, which captures fully users' information through multiple views, achieves the best performances. In addition, by observing the experimental results in Table 1, we draw the following conclusions: (1) Our approach is better than the others, which demonstrates that fully exploiting the users' information is effective. (2) Under the same conditions, the experimental results that MSE value is larger than MAE value, which means the MSE metric is a better indicator of the performance of our model.

Table 1. MSE and MAE comparison with baselines

Method	MovieLens		Book		Clothing	
	MAE	MSE	MAE	MSE	MAE	MSE
BPR-MF	0.792	1.245	0.985	1.154	0.879	1.213
VBPR	0.765	1.134	0.749	1.112	0.792	1.112
MVDNN	0.659	1.025	0.688	0.978	0.695	0.997
DeepCoNN	0.649	1.013	0.642	0.973	0.672	0.985
CKE	0.621	1.007	0.612	0.966	0.632	0.967
JRL	0.602	0.975	0.594	0.953	0.621	0.942
AHICRF	**0.589**	**0.956**	**0.583**	**0.942**	**0.608**	**0.933**

Impact of Temporal Changes in User's Interests. Our model focus on the user feature representation, especially capturing aesthetic change. In order to measure the impact of users' aesthetic changes, we show the impact of temporal changes about user's interests in Fig. 2(a). We use M, B and C denotes Movielens, Amazon-Book and Amazon-Clothing, respectively. In this experiment, we use CNN and LSTM to extract the users' visual features, respectively. From

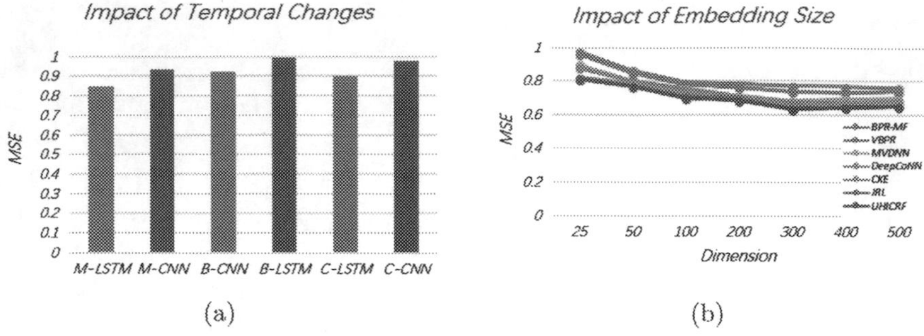

Fig. 2. The impact of temporal changes and word embedding size.

Fig. 2(a), we observe that the performance of using LSTM is better than CNN on three datasets. We can obtain the conclusion that using LSTM to capture the temporal changes in users' interests can improve recommendations.

Impact of Embedding Size. From Fig. 2(b), we show the impact of word embedding size. We fix the other factors and tune the embedding size from 25 to 500. In Fig. 2(b), we find that with the increasing of embedding size, the performance of our model tends to be stable. And we achieve the best performance when we set the embedding size to 300. Through experiments, we can also observe that other deep learning baselines can achieve the best performance when the size is from 200 to 300. So in our experiment, we use 300 as the embedding size.

5 Conclusions

In this paper, we propose a novel heterogeneous information recommendation framework, named Aesthetic-changed Heterogeneous Information Collaborative Representation Framework (AHICRF). The AHICRF model contains two key parts: User Knowledge Representation and Item Knowledge Representation. We utilize User Knowledge Representation which uses heterogeneous information and also considers temporal changes in users interests to extract the users' features. And we adopt the Item Knowledge Representation to obtain the item features. At last, we integrate these features to predict the ratings. The experimental results show that our proposed AHICRF model indeed can improve recommendation through heterogeneous information. Meanwhile, AHICRF outperforms the state-of-the-art approaches.

Acknowledgment. This work was supported by National Key Research and Development Plan (2016QY02D0402).

References

1. Aciar, S., Zhang, D., Simoff, S., Debenham, J.: Informed recommender: basing recommendations on consumer product reviews. IEEE Intell. Syst. **22**(3), 39–47 (2007)
2. Adomavicius, G., Tuzhilin, A.: Toward the next generation of recommender systems: a survey of the state-of-the-art and possible extensions. IEEE Trans. Knowl. Data Eng. **17**(6), 734–749 (2005)
3. Bao, Y., Fang, H., Zhang, J.: TopicMF: simultaneously exploiting ratings and reviews for recommendation. In: Twenty-Eighth AAAI Conference on Artificial Intelligence, pp. 2–8 (2014)
4. Bauman, K., Liu, B., Tuzhilin, A.: Aspect based recommendations: recommending items with the most valuable aspects based on user reviews. In: The ACM SIGKDD International Conference, pp. 717–725 (2017)
5. Blunsom, P., Grefenstette, E., Kalchbrenner, N.: A convolutional neural network for modelling sentences. In: Proceedings of the 52nd Annual Meeting of the Association for Computational Linguistics (2014)
6. Bobadilla, J., Ortega, F., Hernando, A.: Recommender systems survey. Knowl.-Based Syst. **46**(1), 109–132 (2013)
7. Collobert, R.: Natural language processing from scratch. J. Mach. Learn. Res. **12**, 2393–2537 (2011)
8. Covington, P., Adams, J., Sargin, E.: Deep neural networks for YouTube recommendations. In: ACM Conference on Recommender Systems, pp. 191–198 (2016)
9. Diao, Q., Qiu, M., Wu, C.Y., Smola, A.J., Jiang, J., Wang, C.: Jointly modeling aspects, ratings and sentiments for movie recommendation (JMARS). In: KDD, pp. 193–202 (2014)
10. Elkahky, A.M., Song, Y., He, X.: A multi-view deep learning approach for cross domain user modeling in recommendation systems. In: International Conference on World Wide Web, pp. 278–288 (2015)
11. Grad-Gyenge, L., Filzmoser, P., Werthner, H.: Recommendations on a knowledge graph. In: MLREC 2015 International Workshop on Machine Learning Methods for Recommender Systems (2015)
12. He, R., Mcauley, J.: Ups and downs: modeling the visual evolution of fashion trends with one-class collaborative filtering. In: International Conference on World Wide Web, pp. 507–517 (2016)
13. He, R., Mcauley, J.: VBPR: visual Bayesian personalized ranking from implicit feedback. In: Thirtieth AAAI Conference on Artificial Intelligence, pp. 144–150 (2016)
14. Huang, P.S., He, X., Gao, J., Deng, L., Acero, A., Heck, L.: Learning deep structured semantic models for web search using clickthrough data. In: ACM International Conference on Information and Knowledge Management, pp. 2333–2338 (2013)
15. Kim, Y.: Convolutional neural networks for sentence classification. In: Empirical Methods in Natural Language Processing, pp. 1746–1751 (2014)
16. Koren, Y., Bell, R., Volinsky, C.: Matrix factorization techniques for recommender systems. Computer **42**(8), 30–37 (2009)
17. Ling, G., Lyu, M.R., King, I.: Ratings meet reviews, a combined approach to recommend. In: Proceedings of the 8th ACM Conference on Recommender systems, pp. 105–112. ACM (2014)

18. Mcauley, J., Leskovec, J.: Hidden factors and hidden topics: understanding rating dimensions with review text. In: ACM Conference on Recommender Systems, pp. 165–172 (2013)
19. Mcauley, J., Targett, C., Shi, Q., Van Den Hengel, A.: Image-based recommendations on styles and substitutes. In: SIGIR, pp. 43–52 (2015)
20. Nair, V., Hinton, G.E.: Rectified linear units improve restricted Boltzmann machines. In: International Conference on International Conference on Machine Learning, pp. 807–814 (2010)
21. Rendle, S., Freudenthaler, C., Gantner, Z., SchmidtThieme, L.: BPR: Bayesian personalized ranking from implicit feedback. In: Proceedings of the Twenty-Fifth Conference on Uncertainty in Artificial Intelligence, pp. 452–461 (2012)
22. Sarwar, B., Karypis, G., Konstan, J., Riedl, J.: Item-based collaborative filtering recommendation algorithms. In: International Conference on World Wide Web, pp. 285–295 (2001)
23. Shen, H.W., Wang, D., Song, C., Barabsi, A.L.: Modeling and predicting popularity dynamics via reinforced poisson processes. In: Twenty-Eighth AAAI Conference on Artificial Intelligence, pp. 291–297 (2014)
24. Song, Y., Elkahky, A.M., He, X.: Multi-rate deep learning for temporal recommendation. In: International ACM SIGIR Conference on Research and Development in Information Retrieval, pp. 909–912 (2016)
25. Tang, D., Qin, B., Liu, T., Yang, Y.: User modeling with neural network for review rating prediction. In: International Conference on Artificial Intelligence, pp. 1340–1346 (2015)
26. Wu, Y., Ester, M.: Flame: a probabilistic model combining aspect based opinion mining and collaborative filtering. In: WSDM, pp. 199–208 (2015)
27. Yu, X., et al.: Personalized entity recommendation: a heterogeneous information network approach. In: Proceedings of the 7th ACM International Conference on Web Search and Data Mining, pp. 283–292 (2014)
28. Zhang, F., Yuan, N.J., Lian, D., Xie, X., Ma, W.Y.: Collaborative knowledge base embedding for recommender systems. In: ACM SIGKDD International Conference on Knowledge Discovery and Data Mining, pp. 353–362 (2016)
29. Zhang, Y., Ai, Q., Chen, X., Croft, W.B.: Joint representation learning for top-n recommendation with heterogenous information sources. In: The ACM International Conference on Information and Knowledge Management (2017)
30. Zhang, Y., Lai, G., Zhang, M., Zhang, Y., Liu, Y., Ma, S.: Explicit factor models for explainable recommendation based on phrase-level sentiment analysis. ACM (2014)
31. Zheng, L., Noroozi, V., Yu, P.S.: Joint deep modeling of users and items using reviews for recommendation. In: Tenth ACM International Conference on Web Search and Data Mining, pp. 425–434 (2017)

Latent Subspace Representation for Multiclass Classification

Jing Hu[1], Changqing Zhang[1](✉), Xiao Wang[2], Pengfei Zhu[1], Zheng Wang[3], and Qinghua Hu[1]

[1] School of Computer Science and Technology, Tianjin University, Tianjin, China
{jinghu,zhangchangqing,zhupengfei,huqinghua}@tju.edu.cn
[2] School of Computer Science, Beijing University of Posts and Telecommunications, Beijing, China
wangxiao_cv@tju.edu.cn
[3] School of Computer Software, Tianjin University, Tianjin, China
wzheng@tju.edu.cn

Abstract. Self-representation based subspace representation has shown its effectiveness in clustering tasks, in which the key assumption is that data are from multiple subspaces and can be reconstructed by the data themselves. Benefiting from the self-representation manner, ideally, subspace representation matrix will be block-diagonal. The block-diagonal structure indicates the true segmentation of data, which is beneficial to the multiclass classification task. In this paper, we propose a Latent Subspace Representation for Multiclass Classification (LSRMC). With the help of a projection, our method focuses on exploiting the subspace representation based on the low-dimensional latent subspace, which further ensures the quality of subspace representation. We learn the projection, subspace representation and classifier in a unified model, and solve the problem efficiently by using Augmented Lagrangian Multiplier with Alternating Direction Minimization. Experiments on benchmark datasets demonstrate that our approach outperforms the state-of-the-art multiclass classification methods.

Keywords: Subspace representation · Latent space
Multiclass classification

1 Introduction

Classification is a basic and important problem in machine learning and computer vision, which has a wide range of applications. Originally, people propose various methods to solve the binary classification problem. Then there are many approaches that extend the binary classification to multiclass case [1]. For example, according to the principle of Maximum A Posteriori (MAP) and the assumption of conditional independence, Naive Bayes [2] has been extended to a multiclass model with a satisfactory result. Decision tree is a powerful framework for classification tasks, especially well-known by its variants (e.g., ID3, C4.5) [3].

X. Geng and B.-H. Kang (Eds.): PRICAI 2018, LNAI 11012, pp. 163–176, 2018.
https://doi.org/10.1007/978-3-319-97304-3_13

Random Forest (RF) [4] considers to build an ensemble structure based on decision trees by introducing the bootstrap sampling. In addition, k-Nearest Neighbor (kNN) [5], a non-parametric classification, is regarded as a classical method for many tasks. Support vector machine (SVM) [6] model is generally acknowledged as one of the most successful machine learning methods. A large number of studies focus on how to innovate on the basis of SVM and apply it to numerous problems [7,8]. Initially, it is designed for the binary classification. For tackling a K-class problem, LIBSVM[1] utilizes the method of one-versus-one, which build a classifier for any two classes of samples and requires $\mathrm{K}(\mathrm{K}-1)/2$ binary classifiers in total. Recently, deep learning [9] has shown its promising performance on the image classification tasks. However, there are still some disadvantages such as the incompleteness of theory and the high complexity.

The high-dimensionality of the data not only increases time and space costs, but also makes the data difficult to be classified, commonly known as the "curse of dimensionality" [10]. A typical solution is to perform dimensionality reduction with Principal Component Analysis (PCA) [11] or Linear Discriminate Analysis (LDA) [12]. However, PCA is sensitive to outliers and LDA subjects to the sample size problem. Sparse representation can find the underlying low-dimensional structures and reduce the effect of noise from high-dimensional space simultaneously, which makes the data easily divisible. Feature selection is an effective way to remove irrelevant features from high-dimensional data. Regularization based feature selection [13] commonly adds a $\ell_{2,1}$-norm constraint to the selection matrix so as to achieve the sparseness. Sparse dictionary learning [14] also aims at seeking a sparse representation of the input data in the form of a linear combination of atoms, which compose a dictionary. For most high dimensional data, it holds the self-representation property of features, which makes the data itself a dictionary without learning. In some fundamental signal and image processing tasks, self-representation has a good performance and evolves rapidly.

Recently, self-representation-based subspace clustering models have been proposed. Generally, self-representation based subspace learning holds the assumption that the samples can be linearly represented mutually by data points which belong to the same subspace. For instance, trajectories of a rigidly moving object in a video, face images under various illumination conditions and hand-written digits with different rotations all lie in the low-dimensional underlying subspaces. For subspace learning, researchers have paid great attentions to subspace clustering, which has achieved promising performances. The representative approaches include Sparse Subspace Clustering (SSC) [15] and Low Rank Representation (LRR) [16]. Considering to promote dimensionality reduction, SSC is further improved by projecting the original features to a low-dimensional latent space, termed as Latent Space Spares Subspace Clustering (L3SC) [17]. Besides, low rank representation have shown strong advantages and been studied deeply in many works [18–20].

Motivated by the success of subspace representation in clustering tasks, we focus on learning subspace representation for multiclass classification. Ideally,

[1] https://www.csie.ntu.edu.tw/~cjlin/libsvm/.

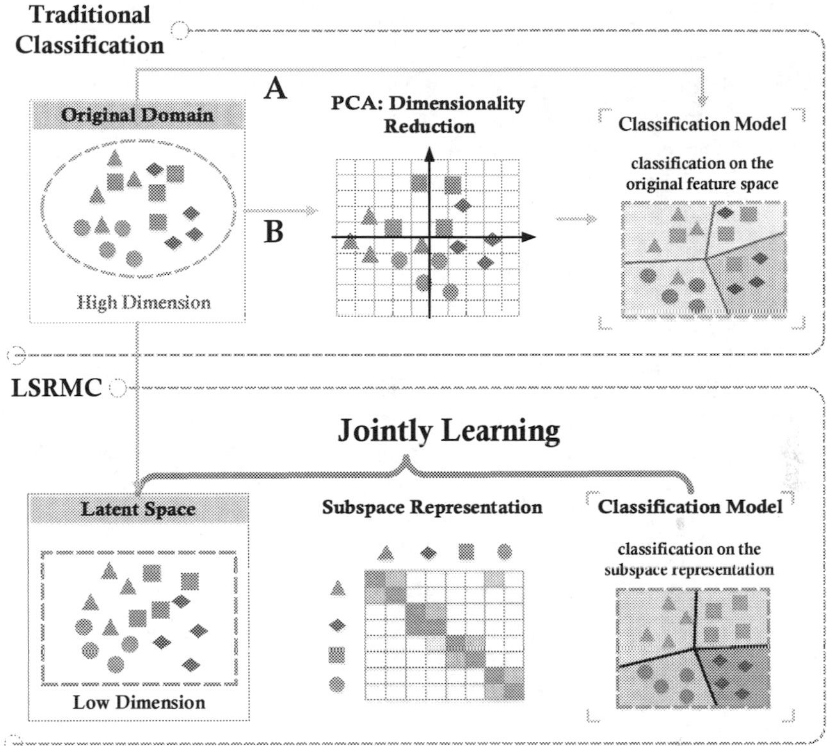

Fig. 1. Overview of the latent subspace representation for multiclass classification. Traditional methods usually train classifier on raw features (A) or on the preprocessed features by PCA in the off-line manner (B). LSRMC tries to find a new latent subspace representation to build a better classifier.

under the subspace assumption, the instances of the same class can be represented with each other, which makes the representation with high discriminative ability. Accordingly, the classification task will benefit from the subspace representation and promising classification performance could be expected. However, considering that the original features may be high-dimensional and noisy, it is risky to use the original features directly to learn the subspace representation. Therefore, we propose to seek a latent subspace representation and based on which the classification model is learned. The overview of our model is shown in Fig. 1. To summarize, the key contributions of our work are as follows:

- We extend the self-representation based subspace learning to multiclass learning, and propose a multiclass model by combining the linear classification model with subspace representation.
- The proposed model jointly learns the subspace representation, latent space projection and classifier in a unified framework, which achieves a promising classification result.

• Experimental results on benchmark datasets demonstrate the superiority of the proposed method compared with other multiclass classification approaches.

The remainder of this paper is organized as follows. In Sect. 2, we will give the details of our proposed method. Section 3 describes the optimization process and presents the convergence analysis. The experiments are shown in Sect. 4. Finally, there is a conclusion to summarize our work briefly in Sect. 5.

2 The Proposed Method

2.1 Motivation

When we handle the multiclass problem, the classes are considered to be disjoint, so as to separate each sample into only one class. It can be said to be linearly separable that datasets whose classes can be separated exactly by linear decision surfaces.

Multiclass extension of binary linear classification can be implemented by minimizing a sum-of-squares error function

$$L(\mathbf{W}) = ||\mathbf{W}\mathbf{X} - \mathbf{Y}||_F^2. \tag{1}$$

Here we use $\mathbf{X} = [\mathbf{x_1}, ..., \mathbf{x_n}] \in R^{d \times n}$ to denote a data matrix, where the i-th column represents the i-th data with d-dimensional features and n is the number of instances. $\mathbf{Y} = [\mathbf{y_1}, ..., \mathbf{y_n}] \in R^{c \times n}$ is a category matrix. Here c is the number of classes. If instance $\mathbf{x}_i$ belongs to the j-th class, $\mathbf{y}_i(j) = 1$, and the rest elements are zeros in the case of multiple classes. Our goal is to obtain a weight matrix $\mathbf{W} \in R^{c \times d}$ to predict the class of a new instance.

Inspired by subspace learning, in our work, we aim to train a multiclass classifier taking advantage of a new low-rank representation from latent subspace. Instead of using the original data to construct a linear classification model directly, we will map the data to a reduced-dimensional latent space and obtain a subspace coefficient representation matrix.

Self-representation expresses each sample as a linear combination of all other samples in the dataset. Its formulation can be described as

$$\mathbf{X} = \mathbf{X}\mathbf{Z}, \tag{2}$$

where $\mathbf{Z} = [\mathbf{z_1}, ..., \mathbf{z_n}] \in R^{n \times n}$ is the coefficient matrix, i.e., the representation. Based on the self-representation, subspace learning attempts to find the combination coefficients with block-diagonal property ideally, which means that the corresponding coefficients are zeros if the samples are from different subspaces.

2.2 Problem Formulation

In this paper, we develop a model integrating dimension reduction, low rank representation and classification into a unified framework. We assume the original data $\mathbf{X}$ are drawn from several fixed subspaces while noise may exist in the whole ambient space. For the purpose of dimension reduction, a linear transformation matrix $\mathbf{P} \in R^{t \times d}$ is applied to map the observations from the original space R^d to the t-dimensionality latent space. Based on this latent space, we can learn the low rank representation $\mathbf{Z}$ and obtain a classifier $\mathbf{W} \in R^{c \times n}$ with promising performance simultaneously. To avoid a trivial solution and due to its effectiveness, we adopt the low-rank constraint on $\mathbf{Z}$ and a regularization on $\mathbf{W}$. Our objective function is defined as follows:

$$[\mathbf{P}^*,\mathbf{Z}^*,\mathbf{W}^*] = \min_{\mathbf{P},\mathbf{Z},\mathbf{W}} Q(\mathbf{P},\mathbf{Z},\mathbf{W}) \quad s.t. \quad \mathbf{P}\mathbf{P}^\mathbf{T} = \mathbf{I}, \tag{3}$$

where $Q(\mathbf{P},\mathbf{Z},\mathbf{W}) =$

$$\underbrace{||\mathbf{WZ} - \mathbf{Y}||_F^2}_{Loss} + \underbrace{\lambda_1||\mathbf{PX} - \mathbf{PXZ}||_F^2}_{Reconstruction\ Error} + \underbrace{\lambda_2||\mathbf{Z}||_*}_{Rank\ Constraint} + \underbrace{\lambda_3||\mathbf{W}||_F^2}_{Model\ Regularization}. \tag{4}$$

Here $||\cdot||_*$ denotes the nuclear norm and $||\cdot||_F$ is the Frobenius norm. We define our classification loss function as in the first term. It is novel that we use the new representation instead of the raw features. The second term introduces a subspace representation $\mathbf{Z}$ in a latent space with the help of a projection $\mathbf{P}$. The third term of Q is a constraint which enforces the subspace representation to be low-rank. The last term is a model regularization preventing over-fitting problems. λ_1, λ_2 and λ_3 are non-negative constants that control reconstruction error, rank constraint and model regularization terms respectively. Furthermore, the rows of $\mathbf{P}$ are required to orthogonal and normalized to unit norm, which avoids a degenerated solution.

3 Optimization

3.1 Optimization for LSRMC

The proposed model learns the projection $\mathbf{P}$, the subspace representation $\mathbf{Z}$ and the classifier $\mathbf{W}$ at the same time. Our problem can be solved efficiently by Augmented Lagrangian Multiplier (ALM) with Alternating Direction Minimization (ADM) [21]. Firstly, we need to introduce one auxiliary variable $\mathbf{J}$ to replace $\mathbf{Z}$ in the nuclear norm term of our objective function. Consequently, the function in Eq. (3) converts to the equivalent problem

$$\begin{aligned}&\min_{\mathbf{P},\mathbf{Z},\mathbf{W},\mathbf{J}} ||\mathbf{WZ} - \mathbf{Y}||_F^2 + \lambda_1||\mathbf{PX} - \mathbf{PXZ}||_F^2 + \lambda_2||\mathbf{Z}||_* + \lambda_3||\mathbf{W}||_F^2\\ &s.t. \quad \mathbf{P}\mathbf{P}^T = \mathbf{I}, \mathbf{J} = \mathbf{Z}.\end{aligned} \tag{5}$$

We further rewrite the constraint $\mathbf{J} = \mathbf{Z}$ as a penalty term via ALM and have the following equivalent function

$$\begin{aligned}L(\mathbf{P},\mathbf{Z},\mathbf{W},\mathbf{J}) = {} & ||\mathbf{WZ} - \mathbf{Y}||_F^2 + \lambda_1||\mathbf{PX} - \mathbf{PXZ}||_F^2\\ & +\lambda_2||\mathbf{J}||_* + \lambda_3||\mathbf{W}||_F^2 + \langle \mathbf{H}, \mathbf{J} - \mathbf{Z}\rangle + \frac{\mu}{2}||\mathbf{J} - \mathbf{Z}||_F^2\\ s.t. \quad & \mathbf{P}\mathbf{P}^T = \mathbf{I}.\end{aligned} \tag{6}$$

Note that, $\langle \cdot, \cdot \rangle$ denotes the matrix inner product. Here $\mathbf{H}$ is known as the Lagrange multiplier and μ is an increasing positive parameter for enforcing the equality constraints. To optimize our loss function in Eq. (6) with the technique of ALM-ADM, we separate it into the following subproblems. We can optimize one variable by fixing the others and update it iteratively.

1. $\mathbf{Z}$-subproblem: Fixing $\mathbf{P}, \mathbf{W}, \mathbf{J}$, update $\mathbf{Z}$ by solving the following problem

$$\begin{aligned} \mathbf{Z}^* = argmin \quad & ||\mathbf{WZ} - \mathbf{Y}||_F^2 + \lambda_1 ||\mathbf{PX} - \mathbf{PXZ}||_F^2 \\ & + \langle \mathbf{H}, \mathbf{J} - \mathbf{Z} \rangle + \frac{\mu}{2} ||\mathbf{J} - \mathbf{Z}||_F^2. \end{aligned} \tag{7}$$

The above function is a smooth convex problem. Taking the derivative with respect to $\mathbf{Z}$ and setting it to zero, we obtain the solution

$$\mathbf{Z}^* = \mathbf{A}^{-1}\mathbf{B}, \tag{8}$$

where $\mathbf{A}^{-1} = (2\lambda_1 \mathbf{X}^T\mathbf{P}^T\mathbf{PX} + 2\mathbf{W}^T\mathbf{W} + \mu\mathbf{I})^{-1}$ and $\mathbf{B} = (2\lambda_1 \mathbf{X}^T\mathbf{P}^T\mathbf{PX} + 2\mathbf{W}^T\mathbf{Y} + \mathbf{H} + \mu\mathbf{J})$.

2. $\mathbf{P}$-subproblem: Fixing $\mathbf{Z}, \mathbf{W}, \mathbf{J}$, update $\mathbf{P}$ by solving the following problem

$$\mathbf{P}^* = argmin \quad \lambda_1 ||\mathbf{PX} - \mathbf{PXZ}||_F^2, \quad s.t. \quad \mathbf{PP}^T = \mathbf{I}. \tag{9}$$

This problem can be solved in the similar manner by referring to the work [17].

3. $\mathbf{W}$-subproblem: Fixing $\mathbf{P}, \mathbf{J}, \mathbf{Z}$, update $\mathbf{W}$ by solving the following problem

$$\mathbf{W}^* = argmin \quad ||\mathbf{WZ} - \mathbf{Y}||_F^2 + \lambda_3 ||\mathbf{W}||_F^2. \tag{10}$$

By setting the derivative of Eq. (10) with respect to W to zero, we get the closed form solution

$$\mathbf{W}^* = \mathbf{YZ}^T(\mathbf{ZZ}^T + \lambda_3 \mathbf{I})^{-1}. \tag{11}$$

4. $\mathbf{J}$-subproblem: Fixing $\mathbf{Z}, \mathbf{P}, \mathbf{W}$, update $\mathbf{J}$ by solving the following problem

$$\mathbf{J}^* = argmin \quad \lambda_2 ||\mathbf{J}||_* + \langle \mathbf{H}, \mathbf{J} - \mathbf{Z} \rangle + \frac{\mu}{2} ||\mathbf{J} - \mathbf{Z}||_F^2. \tag{12}$$

The subproblem with respect to $\mathbf{J}$ can be converted to

$$\mathbf{J}^* = argmin \quad \frac{\lambda_2}{\mu} ||\mathbf{J}||_* + \frac{1}{2} ||\mathbf{J} - (\mathbf{Z} - \frac{\mathbf{H}}{\mu})||_F^2. \tag{13}$$

We can employ the singular value thresholding operator [22] to solve the above problem efficiently. Finally, we update the Lagrange multiplier matrix $\mathbf{H}$ by the following formulas

$$\mathbf{H} = \mathbf{H} + \mu(\mathbf{J} - \mathbf{Z}). \tag{14}$$

Intuitively, the multiplier is updated to increase the weight of the penalty term in each iteration.

For testing data $\mathbf{X}_{test} \in R^{d \times m}$, we implement the same mechanism as the training data. Firstly, we need to find its latent subspace representation $\mathbf{Z}_{test} \in R^{n \times m}$ based on $\mathbf{X}$ by using the projection $\mathbf{P}$. It can be solved by minimizing the following function

$$\min_{\mathbf{Z}_{test}} \lambda_1 \left\|\mathbf{P}\mathbf{X}_{test} - \mathbf{P}\mathbf{X}\mathbf{Z}_{test}\right\|_F^2 + \lambda_2 \|\mathbf{Z}_{test}\|_*. \tag{15}$$

Similarly, the above problem can be solved by referring to the manner in [16]. Then we apply the classifier $\mathbf{W}$ to predict the class of each sample from testing set. The complete procedure of the proposed multiclass classification approach is displayed in Algorithm 1 clearly.

Algorithm 1. Multiclass Classification by LSRMC

Input: Train data $\mathbf{X}, \mathbf{Y}$, Test data $\mathbf{X}_{test}$, Parameters $\lambda_1, \lambda_2, \lambda_3$, Dimension of latent subspace t.

Initialization:
$\mathbf{P} = 0, \mathbf{W} = 0, \mathbf{J} = \mathbf{Z} = 0, \mathbf{H} = 0, \mathbf{Y}_{test} = 0, \mathbf{Z}_{test} = 0, \mu = 10^{-6}, \mu_{\max} = 10^6$, $\rho = 1.05, \epsilon = 10^{-4}$.

while *not converged* **do**

  Update variables $\mathbf{Z}, \mathbf{P}, \mathbf{W}, \mathbf{J}$ by solving their respective Eq. (7),(9),(10),(12);

  Update multiplier $\mathbf{H}$ according to Eq. (14) ;

  Update parameter by $\mu = \min(\mu_{\max}, \rho\mu)$;

  Check the convergence condition: $||\mathbf{J} - \mathbf{Z}||_\infty < \varepsilon$.

end

Map $\mathbf{X}_{test}$ to the latent space to obtain the low-rank representation $\mathbf{Z}_{test}$ by solving the problem in Eq. (15).

Obtain predicted class by $\mathbf{Y}_{test} = \mathbf{W}\mathbf{Z}_{test}$.

Find the maximum of $\mathbf{Y}_{test}$ and convert it to a binary label matrix $\tilde{\mathbf{Y}}_{test}$.

Output: $\mathbf{Z}, \mathbf{P}, \mathbf{W}, \tilde{\mathbf{Y}}_{test}$

3.2 Complexity and Convergence

As shown in Algorithm 1, the optimization of our objective function is split mainly into 4 subproblems. Note that d, t are the dimension of features and latent representation respectively. And c, n denote the numbers of classes and samples. For updating $\mathbf{Z}$, the complexity of this step is $O(dtn + dn^2 + cn^2 + n^3)$. Updating $\mathbf{P}$ includes the eigen decomposition operator, whose complexity is $O(dn^2 + n^3)$. When we compute $\mathbf{W}$, the main complexity is $O(n^3)$. Dealing with the J-subproblem, the nuclear norm proximal operator costs $O(n^3)$. Overall, the total complexity is $O(dtn + dn^2 + cn^2 + n^3)$ for each iteration. In reality, considering the situation $c \ll n$ and the condition $t \ll d$, the total complexity is $O(dn^2 + n^3)$. With alternating optimization, our model is guaranteed to converge. During the optimizations of $\mathbf{Z}, \mathbf{W}$, we can easily find a closed form solution with respect to a convex function. There is an optimal solution for updating $\mathbf{P}$ in [17]. Moreover, the subproblems of $\mathbf{J}$ have been guaranteed to converge in the work [22]. Therefore, our method has a stable convergence behavior.

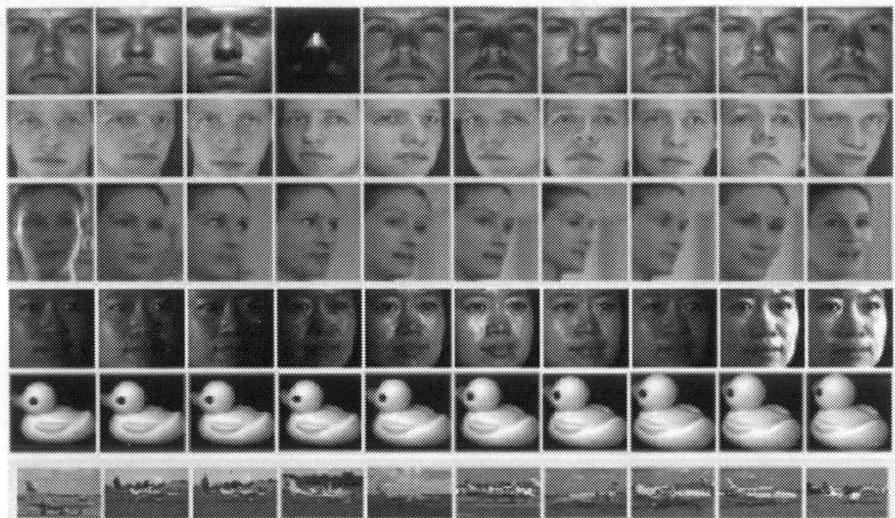

Fig. 2. Images from six datasets. The rows from top to bottom correspond to YaleB, ORL, NothingHill, PIE, COIL20 and MSRCv1, respectively.

4 Experiments

4.1 Experiment Setting

In the experiments, we employ six real-world datasets to evaluate the performances of our model. There are four face images datasets (YaleB[2], ORL[3], Notting Hill [23] and PIE [24]), and two object image datasets (COIL-20[4], MSRCv1[5]). There are 38 subjects in the Extended YaleB Database. Each class contains 64 frontal face images taken under different illuminations. We resize each image to 48×42 pixels and just use the first 10 subject classes as in the work [16]. ORL consists of 40 distinct individuals, 10 different images per person. The Notting Hill dataset is derived from the movie "Notting Hill", where five main cast members are used. For each person, we select 110 distinct face images. The PIE database contains over 40,000 images of 68 people, each one under different poses, illuminations, and with different expressions. We select 10 images of each person. COIL-20 is from Columbia Object Image Library, including 20 objects and 72 different images for each. MSRCv1 contains 240 images and 8 classes. 7 classes of them are used to our experiment as in [19]. The detailed statistics information and samples of these datasets are shown in Table 1 and Fig. 2.

2 http://vision.ucsd.edu/~leekc/ExtYaleDatabase/ExtYaleB.html
3 http://www.cl.cam.ac.uk/research/dtg/attarchive/facedatabase.html.
4 http://www.cs.columbia.edu/CAVE/software/softlib/coil-20.php.
5 https://www.microsoft.com/en-us/research/project/image-understanding/.

Table 1. Datasets description

Dataset	YaleB	ORL	NottingHill	PIE	COIL-20	MSRCv1
Domains	Face	Face	Face	Face	Object	Object
#Feature	2016	3304	6750	484	3304	1302
#Instance	640	400	550	680	1440	210
#Class	10	40	5	68	20	7

We compare our method with the following several baselines. PCA [11] and LDA [12] are proposed to reduce dimension efficiently. However the resulting linear combination of features by LDA can be used as a classifier to separate two or more classes of objects. Similar to [25], we utilize the hybrid classifier jointly using PCA and LDA as a comparison method. k-Nearest Neighbors (kNN) [5] is a relatively mature method in theory and one of the most popular machine learning algorithms. Random Forest (RF) [4] is a kind of the ensemble learning methods for classification. Support Vector Machine (SVM) [6] is defined to seek a linear classifier with the largest interval in feature space. We utilize the program from LIBSVM for the linear SVM method to handle multiclass classification problem. The Multiclass Capped ℓ_p-Norm SVM (SVMcapLp) [7] utilizes a new formulation to build SVM model. The multi-class Optimal margin Distribution Machine (mcODM) [8] can solve the margin distribution optimization problem efficiently. In addition, we add the same model regularization term $||\mathbf{W}||_F^2$ by referring to [26] as the Basic Linear Classification model (denoted by BLC) in Eq. (1), which is one of comparison methods.

For experiment settings, we randomly select 3/4 from each dataset as training set and the rest is testing set. In our experiment, we select the parameters referring to the average results of 10 times on validation set, which is drawn from 1/4 of training data randomly. We tune λ_1 from the set $\{0.01, 0.1, 0.5, 1, 1.5, 2\}$ with fixing λ_2, λ_3, both of which choose a value from $\{0.001, 0.01, 0.1, 1\}$ and the latent space dimension t is selected from $\{30, 60, 90, 120, 150, 180\}$. Owing to the randomness, we run 30 times for each dataset to compute the average results with standard deviation. For other algorithms, we try our best to tune the parameters to have the best experiment performance. We use four evaluation metrics to measure the performance, i.e. Accuracy, F-score, Precise and Recall [23]. The larger the values of these metrics are, the better the classifier performs.

4.2 Experimental Results

Table 2 shows the comparison results of different methods on the six benchmark datasets. Our approach almost outperforms all the algorithms in terms of four diverse metrics. Observing these results, several pieces of information can be obtained as follows: (1) Intuitively, the proposed method is effective on the multiclass classification tasks, which works very well on benchmark datasets. Classification accuracies of our model performed on four datasets all reach to

Table 2. Performance comparison results (mean ± std %) on six benchmark datasets.

Datasets	Methods	Accuracy	F-score	Precise	Recall
YaleB	PCA+LDA	95.38 ± 1.65	90.73 ± 3.55	90.43 ± 4.02	91.05 ± 3.16
	kNN	72.58 ± 3.50	55.57 ± 4.62	55.22 ± 4.87	55.95 ± 4.47
	RF	93.38 ± 2.15	87.28 ± 3.94	87.34 ± 4.12	87.24 ± 3.86
	SVM	94.17 ± 1.42	88.53 ± 2.86	88.26 ± 3.16	88.80 ± 2.72
	SVMcapLp	91.88 ± 3.60	84.76 ± 5.90	83.43 ± 6.28	86.17 ± 5.75
	mcODM	95.62 ± 1.98	91.38 ± 3.84	91.26 ± 4.00	91.50 ± 3.74
	BLC	96.25 ± 1.77	92.44 ± 3.62	92.23 ± 4.01	92.67 ± 3.30
	Ours	**98.33 ± 1.19**	**96.61 ± 2.45**	**96.46 ± 2.68**	**96.77 ± 2.25**
ORL	PCA+LDA	93.00 ± 2.91	86.62 ± 5.90	88.26 ± 5.92	85.10 ± 6.39
	kNN	88.20 ± 2.78	75.82 ± 4.61	74.51 ± 5.34	77.32 ± 4.92
	RF	78.10 ± 3.38	57.89 ± 7.48	57.89 ± 7.25	58.00 ± 8.26
	SVM	90.50 ± 3.63	82.40 ± 5.43	82.72 ± 5.84	82.17 ± 5.64
	SVMcapLp	93.90 ± 2.69	88.84 ± 6.28	89.19 ± 7.59	88.62 ± 5.89
	mcODM	96.60 ± 2.99	93.16 ± 5.80	93.71 ± 5.84	92.64 ± 5.89
	BLC	93.50 ± 3.54	87.82 ± 7.57	87.86 ± 6.99	87.82 ± 8.35
	Ours	**97.70 ± 1.77**	**95.59 ± 3.07**	**96.18 ± 2.86**	**95.03 ± 3.46**
NottingHill	PCA+LDA	98.57 ± 1.33	97.33 ± 2.34	97.14 ± 2.47	97.52 ± 2.31
	kNN	97.13 ± 1.71	95.24 ± 2.78	94.69 ± 3.17	95.81 ± 2.58
	RF	93.16 ± 2.36	87.90 ± 4.36	86.82 ± 5.01	89.05 ± 3.82
	SVM	98.21 ± 1.24	97.13 ± 2.10	97.30 ± 1.99	96.97 ± 2.38
	SVMcapLp	93.04 ± 1.57	87.25 ± 3.07	85.04 ± 3.82	89.60 ± 2.53
	mcODM	98.99 ± 1.09	98.11 ± 2.03	98.07 ± 2.06	98.15 ± 2.04
	BLC	97.22 ± 1.51	95.69 ± 2.46	95.55 ± 2.56	95.84 ± 2.55
	Ours	**99.25 ± 0.62**	**98.71 ± 1.13**	**98.68 ± 1.18**	**98.75 ± 1.12**
PIE	PCA+LDA	80.12 ± 3.64	59.62 ± 7.82	56.52 ± 9.58	63.44 ± 6.46
	kNN	59.00 ± 3.46	37.69 ± 4.96	35.18 ± 5.60	40.75 ± 4.53
	RF	74.94 ± 3.08	54.40 ± 3.92	52.55 ± 4.61	56.53 ± 4.09
	SVM	73.53 ± 3.34	52.92 ± 5.22	49.89 ± 6.23	56.59 ± 4.96
	SVMcapLp	84.76 ± 2.26	67.72 ± 6.32	66.00 ± 7.68	69.70 ± 5.43
	mcODM	83.88 ± 1.74	67.64 ± 4.57	66.33 ± 5.61	69.14 ± 4.45
	BLC	81.94 ± 2.62	66.02 ± 4.60	64.56 ± 4.64	67.64 ± 5.33
	Ours	**85.53 ± 2.73**	**70.08 ± 6.32**	**67.16 ± 7.28**	**73.40 ± 5.59**
COIL-20	PCA+LDA	97.81 ± 0.78	95.90 ± 1.46	95.86 ± 1.44	95.95 ± 1.55
	kNN	99.08 ± 0.72	98.17 ± 1.46	98.13 ± 1.50	98.22 ± 1.43
	RF	93.08 ± 1.22	87.92 ± 2.35	87.82 ± 2.19	88.02 ± 2.56
	SVM	98.56 ± 1.03	97.09 ± 2.12	96.96 ± 2.27	97.21 ± 1.97
	SVM_capLp	97.83 ± 0.98	95.78 ± 1.89	95.64 ± 1.91	95.92 ± 1.92
	mcODM	99.47 ± 0.42	98.96 ± 0.81	98.98 ± 0.80	98.94 ± 0.84
	BLC	97.44 ± 1.20	95.23 ± 2.28	95.12 ± 2.25	95.34 ± 2.36
	Ours	**99.61 ± 0.27**	**99.23 ± 0.50**	**99.2 ± 0.60**	**99.25 ± 0.42**
MSRCv1	PCA + LDA	83.77 ± 4.37	70.09 ± 7.99	70.58 ± 7.58	69.75 ± 8.94
	kNN	76.23 ± 8.11	60.80 ± 12.57	59.33 ± 13.15	62.43 ± 12.12
	RF	69.62 ± 5.73	50.23 ± 8.59	49.13 ± 8.66	51.47 ± 8.77
	SVM	84.72 ± 4.99	71.60 ± 8.79	**71.75 ± 9.09**	71.48 ± 8.58
	SVMcapLp	62.64 ± 8.43	45.25 ± 8.40	34.53 ± 8.77	68.64 ± 9.05
	mcODM	82.45 ± 4.54	68.20 ± 7.86	67.78 ± 8.05	68.69 ± 7.98
	BLC	84.15 ± 4.00	70.92 ± 6.90	70.34 ± 7.04	71.63 ± 7.35
	Ours	**85.28 ± 4.06**	**71.88 ± 6.76**	69.97 ± 7.48	**74.01 ± 6.49**

97% or more. (2) Comparing with the basic linear classification model (BLC), our method is better especially on ORL dataset. It proves that our learned latent subspace representation is superior to the original features. (3) The performances of all methods on MSRCv1 are not very promising, since the backgrounds are usually much more complex than other datasets, which increases the difficulty of the object classification task. Moreover, the size of images and on PIE is relatively small, even though LSRMC still achieves promising performance compared with other methods, i.e., about 85% in terms of accuracy.

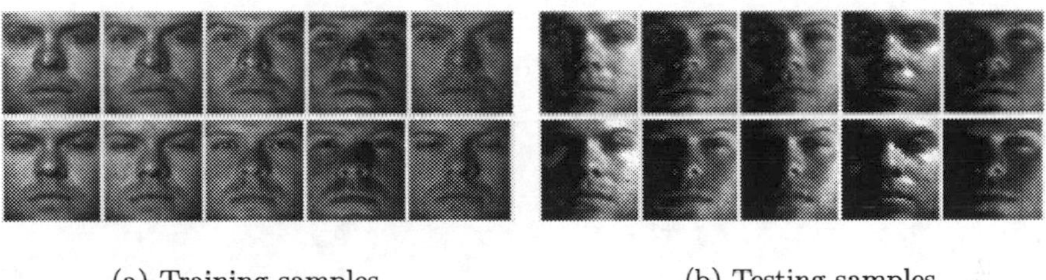

(a) Training samples. (b) Testing samples.

Fig. 3. The reconstructions of the YaleB samples. The first row is the reconstruction images ((a) ($\mathbf{P}^{\mathbf{T}}\mathbf{PXZ}$), (b) ($\mathbf{P}^{\mathbf{T}}\mathbf{PXZ}_{\mathbf{test}}$)). The second row represents original faces.

Figure 3 shows the reconstruction of the images on YaleB data. The reconstructed images are quite similar to the original ones, which demonstrates the learned latent subspace representation encodes the information of original data. The reconstructed results on test images are also of good quanlity, which verifies the rationality of both the latent subspace representation $\mathbf{Z}_{test}$ based on $\mathbf{X}$ and the learned projection $\mathbf{P}$.

4.3 Parameter Tuning and Convergence Experiment

Figure 4(a) shows the parameter λ_1, λ_2 tuning experiment with fixing $\lambda_3 = 1, t = 120$ on YaleB data. As λ_1 gets lager, the average accuracy of the classifier tends

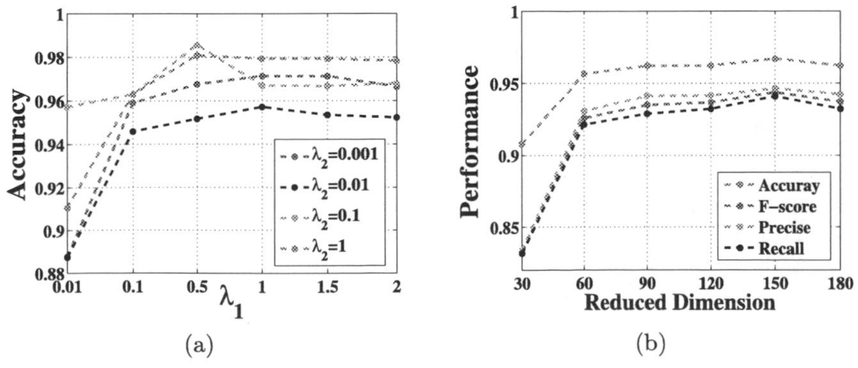

(a) (b)

Fig. 4. Parameters tuning on YaleB.

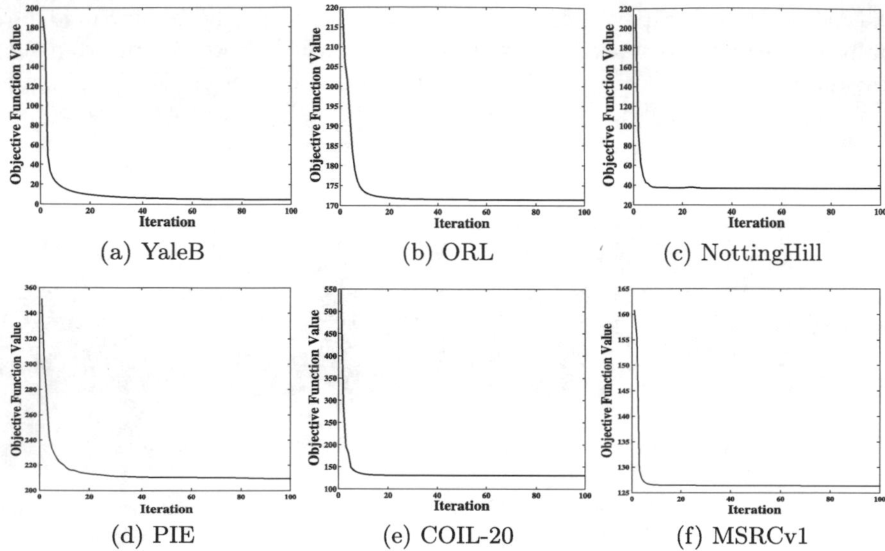

(a) YaleB (b) ORL (c) NottingHill

(d) PIE (e) COIL-20 (f) MSRCv1

Fig. 5. Convergence experimental results on diverse datasets.

to be stable at a high level. It is reasonable that the smaller reconstruction error, the better performance. It proves that the parameter λ_1 is effective in our model.

Figure 4(b) shows the performance with different dimensions of latent space. With the relatively low dimension such as 60, it is sufficient for LSRMC to achieve a stable and promising result on YaleB whose original feature dimension is 2016. In the meanwhile, when the reduced dimension is 30, the performance is not very satisfied. It demonstrates that a higher dimensional data may be needed to preserve more information from the original data, because the dimension of the latent space is too low to discard the important and useful information. Our model is expected to give the latent space a sufficient dimension.

Figure 5 gives the results from convergence experiments on six datasets. It is clearly that our model can converge fast within a small number of iterations. The convergence of our model is verified in accordance with experimental results.

5 Conclusions

In this paper, we propose a new latent subspace representation to explore the relationship of different classes. Specially, we regard it as a new feature for samples to perform classification tasks. It is the main novelty that we put forward a new low-dimensional but efficient subspace representation to build a classifier. Experiments on benchmark datasets verify the advantages of our method. In the future, large scale and nonlinearity data will be considered to be solved by our model. Furthermore, it will be extend to a semi-supervised version with less class information but a higher accuracy.

Acknowledgments. This work was supported in part by National Natural Science Foundation of China (Grand No: 61602337, 61732011, 61702358, 61702296, 61772360).

References

1. Aly, M.: Survey on multiclass classification methods. Neural Netw. **19**, 1–9 (2005)
2. Rish, I.: An empirical study of the naive Bayes classifier. In: IJCAI (2001)
3. Quinlan, J.R.: Induction of decision trees. Mach. Learn. **1**, 257–264 (1986)
4. Ho, T.K.: Random decision forests. In: ICDAR (1995)
5. Bay, S.D.: Combining nearest neighbor classifiers through multiple feature subsets. In: ICML (1998)
6. Cortes, C., Vapnik, V.: Support-vector networks. Mach. Learn. **20**, 273–297 (1995)
7. Nie, F., Wang, X., Huang, H.: Multiclass capped ℓ_p-norm SVM for robust classifications. In: AAAI (2017)
8. Zhang, T., Zhou, Z.: Multi-class optimal margin distribution machine. In: ICML (2017)
9. Lecun, Y., Bengio, Y., Hinton, G.: Deep learning. Nature **521**, 436–444 (2015)
10. Bellman, R.E.: Dynamic Programming. Princeton University Press, Princeton (1957)
11. Vidal, R., Ma, Y., Sastry, S.S.: Principal Component Analysis. IEEE Computer Society, Silver Spring (2005)
12. Riffenburgh, R.H., Clunies-Ross, C.W.: Linear discriminant analysis. Chicago (1960)
13. Nie, F., Huang, H., Cai, X., Ding, C.: Efficient and robust feature selection via joint $\ell_{2,1}$-norms minimization. In: NIPS (2010)
14. Kreutz-Delgado, K., Murray, J.F., Rao, B.D., Engan, K., Lee, T.W., Sejnowski, T.J.: Dictionary learning algorithms for sparse representation. Neural Comput. **15**, 349–396 (2014)
15. Elhamifar, E., Vidal, R.: Sparse subspace clustering. In: CVPR (2009)
16. Liu, G., Lin, Z., Yu, Y.: Robust subspace segmentation by low-rank representation. In: ICML (2010)
17. Patel, V.M., Van Nguyen, H., Vidal, R.: Latent space sparse subspace clustering. In: ICCV (2013)
18. Zhang, Z., Zhao, M., Li, F., Zhang, L., Yan, S.: Robust alternating low-rank representation by joint l_p- and $l_{2,p}$-norm minimization. Neural Netw. **96**, 55–70 (2017)
19. Zhang, C., Hu, Q., Fu, H., Zhu, P., Cao, X.: Latent multi-view subspace clustering. In: CVPR (2017)
20. Zhang, Z., Li, F., Zhao, M., Zhang, L., Yan, S.: Joint low-rank and sparse principal feature coding for enhanced robust representation and visual classification. IEEE Trans. Image Process. **25**, 2429–2443 (2016)
21. Lin, Z., Liu, R., Su, Z.: Linearized alternating direction method with adaptive penalty for low-rank representation. In: NIPS (2011)
22. Cai, J., Candès, E.J., Shen, Z.: A singular value thresholding algorithm for matrix completion. Soc. Ind. Appl. Math. **20**, 1956–1982 (2010)
23. Cao, X., Zhang, C., Fu, H., Liu, S., Zhang, H.: Diversity-induced multi-view subspace clustering. In: CVPR (2015)
24. Sim, T., Baker, S., Bsat, M.: The cmu pose, illumination, and expression (pie) database. In: Proceedings of the IEEE International Conference on Automatic Face and Gesture Recognition (2002)

25. Zhao, W., Chellappa, R., Krishnaswamy, A.: Discriminant analysis of principal components for face recognition. In: Wechsler, H., Phillips, P.J., Bruce, V., Souliè, F.F., Huang, T.S. (eds.) Face Recognition. NATO ASI Series (Series F: Computer and Systems Sciences), vol. 163, pp. 73–85. Springer, Heidelberg (1998). https://doi.org/10.1007/978-3-642-72201-1_4
26. Zhang, Y., Zhou, G., Jin, J., Zhao, Q., Wang, X., Cichocki, A.: Sparse Bayesian classification of EEG for brain-computer interface. IEEE Trans. Neural Netw. Learn. Syst. **27**(11), 2256–2267 (2016)

Low-Rank Graph Regularized Sparse Coding

Yupei Zhang[1(✉)], Shuhui Liu[1], Xuequn Shang[1(✉)], and Ming Xiang[2]

[1] School of Computer Science, Northwestern Polytechnical University, Xi'an, China
{ypzhaang, shang}@nwpu.edu.cn

[2] Department of Computer Science and Technology, Xi'an Jiaotong University, Xi'an, China

Abstract. In this paper, we propose a solution to the instability problem of sparse coding with the technique of low-rank representation (LRR) which is a promising method of discovering subspace structures of data. Graph regularized sparse coding has been extensively studied for keeping the locality of the high-dimensional observations. However, in practice, data is always corrupted by noises such that samples from the same class may not inhabit the nearest area. To this end, we present a novel method for robust sparse representation, dubbed low-rank graph regularized sparse coding (LogSC). LogSC uses LRR to capture the multiple subspace structures of the data and aims to preserve this structure into the resultant sparse codes. Different from the traditional methods, our method, jointly rather than separately, learns the sparse codes and the LRR; our method maintains the global structure of the data no longer the local structure. Thus, the yielding sparse codes can be not only robust to the corrupted samples thanks to the LRR, but also discriminative arising from the multiple subspaces preserving. The optimization problem of LogSC can be effectively tackled by the linearized alternating direction method with adaptive penalty. To evaluate our approach, we apply LogSC for image clustering and classification, and meanwhile probe it in noisy scenes. The inspiring experimental results on the public image data sets manifest the discrimination, the robustness and the usability of the proposed LogSC.

Keywords: Laplacian sparse coding · Multiple subspaces preserving
Low-rank representation · Image clustering and classification

1 Introduction

Sparse coding, as a promising technique for capturing the high-level semantic features and yielding a parsimonious representation of data [1], has attracted great interest in the past two decades and achieved numerous inspirational results in wide range domains, including image retrieval [2], dimensionality reduction [3], image clustering and classification [1, 4–6]. Traditional sparse coding (TSC) aims at learning a dictionary composed of numerous atoms from the given data and meanwhile reaping the sparse representation of each datum with respect to the learned dictionary [1, 6]. Wherein, the atoms are just the bases/features for spanning the space that encompasses all samples and the sparse representation is a linear combination that faithfully reconstructs each datum by selecting as few atoms as possible. Therefore, studies related to sparse coding

X. Geng and B.-H. Kang (Eds.): PRICAI 2018, LNAI 11012, pp. 177–190, 2018.
https://doi.org/10.1007/978-3-319-97304-3_14

can be mainly grouped into sparse decomposition, dictionary learning and sparse representation-based applications [6]. Reviewing them is outside the scope of this article and see the references therein. One crucial work of them is to enhance the smoothness of the resultant sparse codes, since the aim of sparse coding is actually learning a feature mapping. That is, if two data points is similarity in the original space, then their images should be near in the new space [7]. Nevertheless, this prior criterion is often violated in the traditional formulation of sparse coding, on account of the overcomplete dictionary and the independent coding process [4, 5].

To preserve the similarity among the data, an intuitional and widely used method is introducing the prior knowledge of similarity into sparse coding. Two solutions, smooth sparse coding [8] and graph regularized sparse coding (GSC) [4], have been presented. The former considers the similarity prior as weights on reconstruction term. It encourages the similar samples to have similar reconstruction errors and thus to yield similar sparse codes. The latter employs the graph Laplacian as a smooth operator, inspired by manifold learning [4, 5], to preserve the similarity information into the resulting sparse codes. Due to the explicitness of GSC, it has been extensively studied. In [5], Laplacian sparse coding uses histogram intersection-based metric instead of Euclidean distance; and hypergraph Laplacian sparse coding replaces the normal graph with the hypergraph which encodes the more complicated relationship of the data. In [9], the authors, adopting the ensemble manifold regularizer, present multiple graph sparse coding and multiple hypergraph sparse coding to avoid the hype-parameter selection. Recently, in [10], the multi-hypergraph incidence consistent sparse coding extra integrates a new regularization termed hypergraph incidence consistency.

Although many above studies of GSC have been developed, all of them still rest in the original noose by: constructing graph/hypergraph to capture the similarity prior and then doing sparse coding with graph regularization. The route of GSC has the following shortages. (1) The pre-specified distance metric is data-oblivious and fails to capture the hidden structure of the data. Moreover, distance metric is always sensitive to noises in data, leading to unreliable local prior graph. (2) The real-world data is always corrupted by noises such that samples from the same class may not be locally distributed. Hence, local structure often delivers an ineffective graph. (3) In GSC, the step of knitting graph is completely independent of the step of leaning sparse codes. Such two-stage scheme likely makes GSC be lost in local optimum, since no unified objective can be available. (4) The feature-sign search algorithm has a low convergence rate and gives rise to many small coefficients that ought to be zeroed out. To remedy the shortcomings, learning a discriminative graph from the given samples is crucial and of great concern, such as the low-rank representation (LRR) [11].

LRR aims at seeking the lowest rank representation of the entire data set on the given dictionary, under the assumption that the data approximately inhabits a mixture of several low-rank subspaces [11]. Because of the belief that the samples from the same class exist in a linear subspace while the samples of different classes exist in different linear subspace, the sample matrix can be used as dictionary to achieve the LRR of itself [1]. It is just the low-rank self-representation property [12, 13]. With the property, LRR can effectively recover the global structure of multiple linear subspaces, implicitly corresponding to the class structure of the data. Therefore, LRR can grasp the discriminative structure, even if no class tags are available [13]. More importantly,

LRR can "correct" the possible errors and then give correct subspace segmentation, by introducing a sparse noise matrix. Its related analysis in theory has been already provided under certain condition [11]. In addition, LRR can be solved cheaply by using the linearized alternating direction method with adaptive penalty (LADMAP) [14]. In summary, LRR is discriminative, robust and economic.

Inspired by the merits of LRR, in this paper, we aim to solve the instability issue of sparse coding with the nonnegative LRR method [13]. Following the workflow of GSC, we first construct the graph using the nonnegative low-rank coefficient matrix and then learn sparse codes regularized by the LRR graph. However, it is likely to be lost in local optimum. We here integrate the objective of LRR and the objective of GSC into a unified optimization problem. The problem is just our proposed method, dubbed **Lo**w-rank **g**raph regularized **S**parse **C**oding (LogSC). Our main contributions are as follows:

(1) We propose a new way of sparse coding, called LogSC, to learn dictionary, sparse code and LRR simultaneously. Such jointed strategy can encourage LogSC to fully exploit the low-rank structure and avoid the hyper-parameter selection.
(2) Our LogSC preserves the global structure of multiple linear subspaces, no longer the local structure, into sparse code. Benefiting from LRR, the resultant sparse features are not only discriminative but also robust to various noises [11–13].
(3) We extend the LADMAP optimization framework to tackle the objective problem of LogSC, where the accelerated proximal gradient [15] is utilized for graph regularized sparse decomposition.

The rest of this paper is organized as follows. In Sect. 2, we review the ingredients and present our objective problem of LogSC, followed by its optimization method in Sect. 3. Our experimental results and discussions are shown in Sect. 4. Finally, we conclude this paper in Sect. 5.

2 LogSC: Low-Rank Graph Regularized Sparse Coding

The goal of LogSC is to learn sparse code, Laplacian regularization, and low-rank representation together. Thus, we here review the three ingredients and then integrate them into our method for sparse coding.

2.1 Traditional Sparse Coding (TSC)

Given a matrix $\mathbf{Y} = [\mathbf{y}_1, \mathbf{y}_2, \cdots, \mathbf{y}_n] \in \mathbb{R}^{m \times n}$ with each $\mathbf{y}_i$ being an m-dimensional sample, let $\mathbf{D} = [\mathbf{d}_1, \mathbf{d}_2, \cdots, \mathbf{d}_d] \in \mathbb{R}^{m \times d}$ be the dictionary matrix where each $\mathbf{d}_l \in \mathbb{R}^m$ denotes a dictionary atom, and $\mathbf{X} = [\mathbf{x}_1, \mathbf{x}_2, \cdots, \mathbf{x}_n] \in \mathbb{R}^{d \times n}$ be the coefficient matrix where $\mathbf{x}_i \in \mathbb{R}^d$ is the sparse code corresponding to the sample $\mathbf{y}_i$. With these notations, usually, the problem of TSC can be formulated as [6]:

$$\min_{\mathbf{D},\mathbf{X}} \|\mathbf{Y} - \mathbf{D}\mathbf{X}\|_F^2 + \lambda_1 \sum_{i=1}^{n} \|\mathbf{x}_i\|_1 \ \text{ subject to } \ \|\mathbf{d}_l\|_2^2 = 1, \ l \in \mathcal{I}_n, \tag{1}$$

where the Frobenius norm is used for measuring the reconstruction error; the ℓ_1 norm is adopted for inducing sparsity; $\lambda_1 > 0$ is a free parameter for balancing the reconstruction error and the sparsity; and the imposed constraint is to remove the scaling problem. However, this route of TSC often suffers the instability problem, due to the overcomplete dictionary and the independent encoding process for each sample [4, 5].

2.2 Laplacian Regularization

To mitigate the instability of TSC, GSC and its most variations integrate the Laplacian regularization into problem (1), which can be described as [4, 12]:

$$\min_{\mathbf{X}} \frac{1}{2} \sum_{i=1}^{n} \sum_{j=1}^{n} w_{ij} \|\mathbf{x}_i - \mathbf{x}_j\|_2^2, \tag{2}$$

where w_{ij} indicates the similarity between $\mathbf{y}_i$ and $\mathbf{y}_j$, and is usually assigned by:

$$w_{ij} = \begin{cases} 1 & \text{if } \mathbf{y}_i \in \mathcal{N}_k(\mathbf{y}_j) \text{ or } \mathbf{y}_j \in \mathcal{N}_k(\mathbf{y}_i) \\ 0 & \text{otherwise} \end{cases}, \tag{3}$$

where $\mathcal{N}_k(\mathbf{y}_i)$ indicates the set of k nearest neighbors of $\mathbf{y}_i$. However, the neighborhood graph constructed from Eq. (3) is data-oblivious as well as sensitive to noise, and thereby cannot correctly depict the similarity structure of the noisy data. Besides, this scheme using two independent stages likely makes GSC be lost in local optima. Many improved methods have been presented, yet the predicament is still not broken [9, 10].

2.3 Low-Rank Representation (LRR)

Utilizing the LRR technique for the sample similarity discovery, i.e., the low-rank self-expression property [11, 13], is formulated as follows:

$$\min_{\mathbf{Z}} \|\mathbf{Z}\|_* + \lambda_4 \|\mathbf{E}\|_{2,1} \ \text{ subject to } \ \mathbf{Y} = \mathbf{YZ} + \mathbf{E}, \tag{4}$$

where $\mathbf{Z}$ is the representation matrix of $\mathbf{Y}$ using the dictionary matrix $\mathbf{Y}$, and its nuclear norm is adopted for approximately seeking the lowest rank solution; $\mathbf{E}$ denotes a sparse additive error matrix, and its $\ell_{2,1}$ norm is used for tackling the corruptions and noises in data samples; $\lambda_4 > 0$ is a tradeoff parameter.

In problem (4), $\mathbf{Z}$ matrix is enforced to be block-diagonal and thus recovers the structure of multiple linear subspaces existed in the noisy data, implicitly corresponding to the class structure [11]. That is, each elements $z_{i,j}$ of $\mathbf{Z}$ indicates the similarity relationship between $\mathbf{y}_i$ and $\mathbf{y}_j$. Moreover, this similarity from LRR is more robust and discriminative than the distance metric used in GSC [13]. As a result, it motivates us to employ this novel technique to tackle the instability problem of sparse coding. For obtaining an explicit explanation of similarity metric, we here exploit the non-negative LRR through adding the non-negativity constraint into (4).

2.4 Objective Problem of LogSC

Based on the above ingredients, we aim to preserve the low-rank subspace structure of the data into sparse codes, with the hope of alleviating the drawbacks of GSC. Rather than simply replacing with LRR graph, we combine the objective of LRR, the Laplacian regularization and the objective of sparse coding into the unified objective as follows:

$$\begin{aligned} &\min_{\mathbf{D},\mathbf{X},\mathbf{Z},\mathbf{E}} \|\mathbf{Y}-\mathbf{D}\mathbf{X}\|_F^2 + \lambda_1 \sum_{i=1}^{n} \|\mathbf{x}_i\|_1 + \tfrac{1}{2}\lambda_2 \sum_{i=1}^{n}\sum_{j=1}^{n} w_{ij}\left\|\mathbf{x}_i - \mathbf{x}_j\right\|_2^2 + \lambda_3\|\mathbf{Z}\|_* + \lambda_4\|\mathbf{E}\|_{2,1} \\ &\text{subject to } \mathbf{Y} = \mathbf{Y}\mathbf{Z} + \mathbf{E};\, \mathbf{W} = \mathbf{Z}^T + \mathbf{Z};\, \mathbf{W} \geq 0 \\ &\qquad\qquad \|\mathbf{d}_l\|_2^2 = 1,\ l \in \mathcal{I}_n \end{aligned}, \quad (5)$$

where $\lambda_2 > 0$ and $\lambda_3 > 0$ are both tradeoff parameters; letting $\mathbf{W} = \mathbf{Z}^T + \mathbf{Z}$ aims to build Laplacian regularization by low-rank self-expression; the constraint $\mathbf{W} > 0$ is imposed for giving an explicit similarity. Problem (5) is just our proposed method, referred to as the **Lo**w-rank **g**raph regularized **S**parse **C**oding (LogSC). As can be seen, LogSC avoids any hype-parameter, like the neighborhood size k in GSC.

3 Objective Optimization by LADMAP

The problem of LogSC is an optimization of multi-block variables, like the ones in [12, 16], and can be effectively solved by the framework of LADMAP. By introducing two Lagrange multipliers $\mathbf{M}_1$ and $\mathbf{M}_2$, the augmented Lagrangian function of (5) is:

$$\begin{aligned} &\mathcal{F}(\mathbf{D},\mathbf{X},\mathbf{Z},\mathbf{E},\mathbf{M}_1,\mathbf{M}_2) \\ &\quad = \|\mathbf{Y}-\mathbf{D}\mathbf{X}\|_F^2 + \lambda_1 \sum_{i=1}^{n} \|\mathbf{x}_i\|_1 + \tfrac{\lambda_2}{2} \sum_{i=1}^{n}\sum_{j=1}^{n} w_{ij}\left\|\mathbf{x}_i - \mathbf{x}_j\right\|_2^2 + \lambda_3\|\mathbf{Z}\|_* + \lambda_4\|\mathbf{E}\|_{2,1} \\ &\quad + \tfrac{\mu}{2}\left(\left\|\mathbf{W} - \mathbf{Z}^T - \mathbf{Z} + \tfrac{\mathbf{M}_1}{\mu}\right\|_F^2 + \left\|\mathbf{Y} - \mathbf{Y}\mathbf{Z} - \mathbf{E} + \tfrac{\mathbf{M}_2}{\mu}\right\|_F^2\right) \\ &\quad - \tfrac{1}{2\mu}\left(\|\mathbf{M}_1\|_F^2 + \|\mathbf{M}_2\|_F^2\right) \end{aligned}, \quad (6)$$

where $\mu > 0$ is a penalty parameter. The objective (6) is separable with respect to each block variable, by the spirit of LADMAP, and thus we can minimize it through updating each variable while holding the others constant, respectively.

3.1 Updating E

For updating $\mathbf{E}$, we should solve the following problem:

$$\min_{\mathbf{E}} \lambda_4\|\mathbf{E}\|_{2,1} + \frac{\mu}{2}\|\mathbf{E} - \mathbf{Q}_E\|_F^2, \quad (7)$$

where $\mathbf{Q}_E = \mathbf{Y} - \mathbf{YZ} + \mathbf{M}_2/\mu$. The optimal solution $\mathbf{E}^*$ can be given by [11]:

$$\mathbf{e}_i^* = \begin{cases} \frac{\|[\mathbf{q}_E]_i\|_2 - \lambda_4/\mu}{\|[\mathbf{q}_E]_i\|_2} & \text{if } \|[\mathbf{q}_E]_i\|_2 > \lambda_4/\mu \\ 0 & \text{otherwise} \end{cases} \tag{8}$$

where $[\mathbf{q}_E]_i$ and $\mathbf{e}_i^*$ are respectively the column of the matrix $\mathbf{Q}_E$ and $\mathbf{E}^*$.

3.2 Updating Z

Given **E**, **W**, **X** and **D**, the matrix **Z** can be updated by:

$$\min_{\mathbf{Z}} \frac{\lambda_3}{\mu} \|\mathbf{Z}\|_* + \mathcal{G}(\mathbf{Z}), \tag{9}$$

where $\mathcal{G}(\mathbf{Z}) = \frac{1}{2}\left(\left\|\mathbf{Z}^T + \mathbf{Z} - (\mathbf{W} + \mathbf{M}_1/\mu)\right\|_F^2 + \|\mathbf{YZ} - (\mathbf{Y} - \mathbf{E} + \mathbf{M}_2/\mu)\|_F^2\right)$.

Denote by $\mathbf{Z}^{(t)}$ the coefficient matrix obtained from the previous iteration or the initial value. Linearizing the smooth term $\mathcal{G}(\mathbf{Z})$ at $\mathbf{Z}^{(t)}$ and adding a proximal term, we arrive at the following approximation problem of (9) [14]:

$$\min_{\mathbf{Z}} \frac{1}{2}\left\|\mathbf{Z} - \left(\mathbf{Z}^{(t)} - \nabla_{\mathbf{Z}}\mathcal{G}\left(\mathbf{Z}^{(t)}\right)/\eta\right)\right\|_F^2 + \frac{\lambda_3}{\mu\eta}\|\mathbf{Z}\|_*, \tag{10}$$

where η is a balance parameter for proximal term. Its closed-form solution [17] is:

$$\mathbf{Z}^{(t+1)} = \Theta_\varepsilon\left(\mathbf{Z}^{(t)} - \nabla_{\mathbf{Z}}\mathcal{G}\left(\mathbf{Z}^{(t)}\right)/\eta\right), \tag{11}$$

where $\Theta_\varepsilon(\cdot)$ is the singular value thresholding operator (SVT) and $\varepsilon = \lambda_3/(\mu\eta)$.

3.3 Updating W

Fixing **E**, **Z**, **X** and **D**, we learn the weight matrix **W** (or Laplacian matrix) by:

$$\min_{\mathbf{W} \geq 0} \lambda_2 \mathrm{tr}\left(\mathbf{W}^T\mathbf{H}\right) + \mu \mathrm{tr}\left(\mathbf{W}^T\mathbf{W} - 2\mathbf{W}^T\mathbf{Q}_W + \mathbf{Q}_W^T\mathbf{Q}_W\right), \tag{12}$$

where $\mathbf{Q}_W = \mathbf{Z}^T + \mathbf{Z} - \mathbf{M}_1/\mu$, and $h_{ij} = \left\|\mathbf{x}_i - \mathbf{x}_j\right\|_2^2$. We set the derivative of the objective function of (12) with respect to **W** to zero, and then obtain its closed-form solution by:

$$\mathbf{W} = \max\left\{\frac{2\mu\mathbf{Q}_W - \lambda_2\mathbf{H}}{2\mu}, 0\right\}. \tag{13}$$

3.4 Updating X

Updating **X** with other variables fixed is to solve the following problem:

$$\min_{\mathbf{X}} \|\mathbf{Y} - \mathbf{D}\mathbf{X}\|_F^2 + \lambda_1 \sum_{i=1}^{n} \|\mathbf{x}_i\|_1 + \lambda_2 \sum_{i=1}^{n} \sum_{j=1}^{n} l_{ij} \mathbf{x}_i^T \mathbf{x}_j, \tag{14}$$

where **L** is actually the Laplacian matrix for **W** [4, 5]. Then we solve the following sub-problem for each vector $\mathbf{x}_i$ individually while holding all the others constant.

$$\min_{\mathbf{x}_i} \left\| \begin{bmatrix} \mathbf{y}_i \\ \sqrt{\lambda_2 l_{ii}} \mathbf{q}_i \end{bmatrix} - \begin{bmatrix} \mathbf{D} \\ -\sqrt{\lambda_2 l_{ii}} \mathbf{I} \end{bmatrix} \mathbf{x}_i \right\|_2^2 + \lambda_1 \|\mathbf{x}_i\|_1, \tag{15}$$

which can be solved by fast iterative shrinkage-thresholding algorithm (FISTA) [18].

3.5 Updating D

We update the dictionary matrix **D** with fixing the other variables by:

$$\min_{\mathbf{D}} \|\mathbf{Y} - \mathbf{D}\mathbf{X}\|_F^2 \text{ subject to } \|\mathbf{d}_l\|_2^2 = 1,\ l \in \mathcal{I}_n. \tag{16}$$

We here solve (16) by using a Lagrange dual that is clearly exhibited in [4]. In brief, by introducing the diagonal matrix of Lagrange multipliers $\mathbf{\Lambda}$, we arrive at the Lagrange dual problem of (16), shown as:

$$\min_{\mathbf{\Lambda} \geq 0} \operatorname{tr}\left(\mathbf{Y}\mathbf{X}^T \left(\mathbf{X}\mathbf{X}^T + \mathbf{\Lambda}\right)^{-1} \mathbf{X}\mathbf{Y}^T + \mathbf{\Lambda}\right), \tag{17}$$

which can be effectively optimized by Newton's method or conjugate gradient.

3.6 Updating $\mathbf{M}_1$ and $\mathbf{M}_2$

At the end of each iteration, the two Lagrange multipliers $\mathbf{M}_1$ and $\mathbf{M}_2$ are updated by:

$$\begin{cases} \mathbf{M}_1 = \mathbf{M}_1 + \mu(\mathbf{W} - \mathbf{Z}^T - \mathbf{Z}) \\ \mathbf{M}_2 = \mathbf{M}_2 + \mu(\mathbf{Y} - \mathbf{Y}\mathbf{Z} - \mathbf{E}) \end{cases}. \tag{18}$$

In summary, we outline the learning scheme for LogSC in Algorithm 1. For terminating the iteration, with the constants δ_1 and δ_2, we set the two following conditions:

$$\max\left\{\|\mathbf{Y} - \mathbf{D}\mathbf{X}\|_F / \|\mathbf{Y}\|_F, \|\mathbf{Y} - \mathbf{Y}\mathbf{Z} - \mathbf{E}\|_F / \|\mathbf{Y}\|_F\right\} \leq \delta_1, \tag{19}$$

$$\max\left\{\left\|\mathbf{D}^{(t)} - \mathbf{D}\right\|_F, \left\|\mathbf{Z}^{(t)} - \mathbf{Z}\right\|_F, \left\|\mathbf{E}^{(t)} - \mathbf{E}\right\|_F, \left\|\mathbf{W}^{(t)} - \mathbf{W}\right\|_F, \left\|\mathbf{X}^{(t)} - \mathbf{X}\right\|_F\right\} \leq \delta_2. \tag{20}$$

Algorithm 1. Low-rank Graph Regularized Sparse Coding Algorithm (LogSC)

Input: Data **Y**; dictionary size d; parameters: λ_1, λ_2, λ_3, λ_4.

Initialization: $\mathbf{E} = 0$, $\mathbf{Z} = 0$, $\mathbf{W} = 0$, $\mathbf{M}_1 = 0$, $\mathbf{M}_2 = 0$;

$\mu = 1e\text{-}6$, $\mu_{\max} = 1e{+}6$, $\rho = 1.9$, $\delta_1 = 1e\text{-}4$, $\delta_2 = 1e\text{-}3$.

While not converged **do**

1. Update error matrix **E** by (8);
2. Update low-rank matrix **Z** by (11);
3. Update weight matrix **W** by (13);
4. Update sparse codes **X** by solving (15) for each datum;
5. Update dictionary matrix **D** by solving (17);
6. Update Lagrange multipliers $\mathbf{M}_1$ and $\mathbf{M}_2$ by (18);
7. Update parameter μ by $\mu = \min(\rho\mu, \mu_{\max})$;
8. Check the convergence conditions by (19) and (20).

Output: Dictionary matrix **D**; Sparse codes **X**.

4 Experiments

In this section, we conduct experiment to evaluate the efficacy of LogSC using publicly available image datasets: Yale, AR, USPS and COIL20, shown in Fig. 1. By performing clustering and classification, we survey the discrimination and the robustness of sparse code yielded by our method. Since LogSC is to get more effective sparse representation, we mainly compare with TSC and GSC in experiments. Due to the limited space here, more experimental results can be found in http://www.escience.cn/people/yupeizhang, together with our experimental codes and the used data sets.

Fig. 1. Example images from Yale (1-left), AR (1-right), USPS (2-left) and COIL20 (2-right)

4.1 Image Clustering on Yale

Yale dataset contains 165 face images from 15 individuals. Each individual has 11 images and each image is caught with different facial expression (e.g., happy) or configuration (e.g., w/no glasses). We here adopt the cropped version, in which each image is resized to 32 × 32 gray pixels, displayed in Fig. 1. First, we perform PCA to reduce the data dimensionality via keeping 98% information in the sense of reconstruction error. Then, TSC/GSC/LogSC is applied to learn the sparse representation of the given data. On the resulting sparse codes, we adopt the K-means algorithm with cosine metric for clustering. To evaluate the clustering results, we employ two standard metrics: clustering accuracy (CA) and normalized mutual information (NMI) [12]. In experiments, the parameters are set as follows: $d = 128$; $\lambda_1 = 0.1$ for TSC; $\lambda_1 = 0.1$, $\lambda_2 = 0.01$ and $k = 3$ for GSC; $\lambda_1 = 0.1$, $\lambda_2 = 0.005$ and $\lambda_3 = \lambda_4 = 1$ for LogSC.

On the resulting sparse codes, we carry out the clustering experiments with the cluster number q ranging from 2 to 15. For each q except 15, 20 test runs are done using different randomly chosen q clusters and the final performance scores are computed by averaging over the 20 results. In each test, we repeat 50 times K-means with different initializations and record the best result in terms of the objective function of K-means. The results are listed in Table 1, where the average scores (Avg) corresponding to all methods are also computed for comparison. As can be seen, the proposed LogSC consistently outperforms the other compared approaches on Yale.

Table 1. Cluster results on the Yale face database. ORG is using the original image pixels.

q	Clustering accuracy (CA, %)				
	ORG	PCA	TSC	GSC	LogSC
2	66.59	72.04	84.12	85.68	**92.27**
4	48.29	51.25	64.66	64.32	**80.12**
6	48.54	46.06	52.58	54.17	**64.39**
8	44.03	46.70	51.65	49.38	**59.95**
10	44.22	44.09	47.55	51.86	**56.96**
12	43.25	43.37	45.12	51.74	**56.44**
14	41.03	42.40	42.92	51.18	**53.25**
15	40.06	41.29	42.27	51.55	**53.27**
Avg	47.00	48.40	53.86	57.49	**64.58**
q	Normalized mutual information (NMI, %)				
	ORG	PCA	TSC	GSC	LogSC
2	37.93	39.85	47.71	48.68	**65.96**
4	27.94	32.40	44.17	43.33	**61.55**
6	40.27	34.41	41.53	43.25	**53.57**
8	41.16	43.36	47.30	44.07	**55.57**
10	45.90	46.42	47.12	49.65	**55.29**
12	47.53	48.07	47.68	51.27	**56.54**
14	48.01	48.97	47.95	52.82	**56.06**
15	48.12	49.89	48.14	53.89	**56.37**
Avg	42.11	42.92	46.45	48.37	**57.61**

In order to probe the effects of the four tradeoff parameters $\{\lambda_1, \lambda_2, \lambda_3, \lambda_4\}$, we compare LogSC with the other approaches. Concretely, we vary one parameter in a specific range and fix the others. Briefly, only CA is measured using Yale, shown in

Fig. 2. In Fig. 2, all compared methods are shown with its best CA. From the results in Fig. 2, we can note that the choices of λ_1 and λ_2 are of importance, while the performance of LogSC is insensitive to the selection of λ_3 and λ_4. Besides, we can find that LogSC can achieve better clustering performance than TSC and GSC in a wide range of parameter values. Moreover, our method has no hyper-parameter any more. Thereby, LogSC has stronger practical usability. By the way, in experiments, λ_3 and λ_4 can be set to one simply.

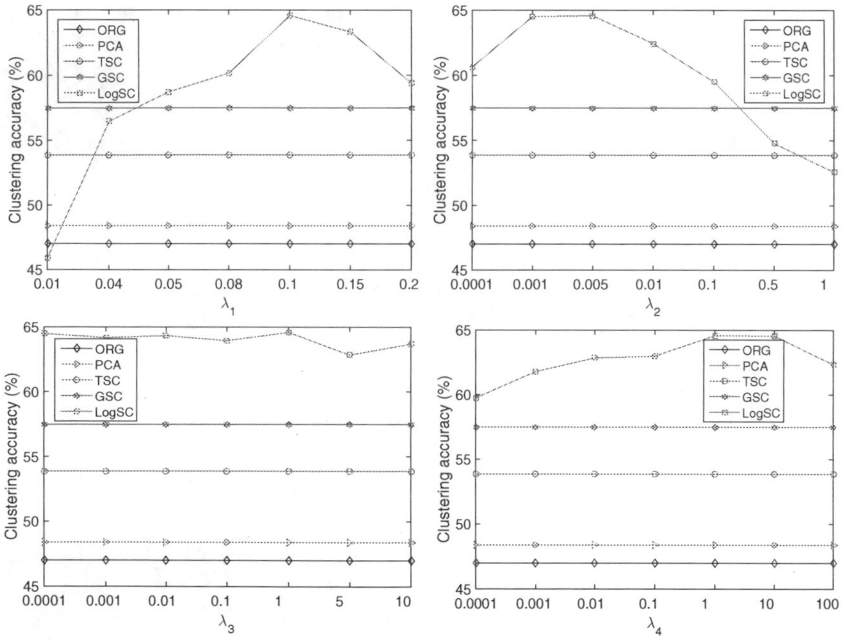

Fig. 2. The effects of parameters on the average clustering results using Yale.

4.2 Image Classification on AR

AR dataset is composed of over 4000 frontal face images in gray pixels from 126 people. We use the subset containing 2600 images from 50 men and 50 women; each person has 26 pictures taken under different facial expressions, illumination conditions and occlusions. Firstly, with keeping 95% information, we obtain the PCA subspace of AR, where TSC/GSC/LogSC learns the dictionary matrix **D** from training data. Then the sparse code of each sample from training/test set is achieved by the Lasso problem individually [6, 19]. Finally, we train SVM classifier with linear kernel [20] and 1-NN classifier with cosine metric using the sparse codes of training samples and calculate the classification accuracy on the sparse codes of test samples. Note that the classification scheme of LogSC is general without any special handling, while the generalization of GSC is realized by the strategy in [4]. Besides, we adopt 5-fold cross validation on training set for determining λ_1 and λ_2, meanwhile assigning $\lambda_3 = \lambda_4 = 1$.

We randomly extract $a \in \{5, 8, 11, 15, 20\}$ images per person from AR for training and take the rest for test. For each a, we yield 20 training/test splits. In each split, TSC/GSC/LogSC learns the dictionary of size 128 on the training samples. Then, on the test samples, classification accuracy is achieved using SVM and NN for each split. Finally, the average accuracy is computed over the 20 splits. The classification results are plotted in Fig. 3. In addition, the standard deviations of LogSC are shown together with its accuracies. As can be seen from Fig. 3, LogSC can arrive at the best classification performance, especially on small sample sizes and using 1-NN classifier.

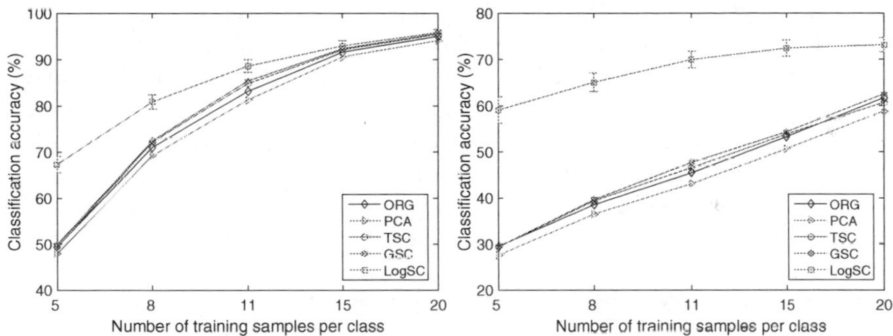

Fig. 3. Classification results of various sample sizes on AR by SVM (left) and NN (right).

To investigate the effect of dictionary size, we carry out the classification experiment with $d \in \{32, 64, 128, 256, 512\}$ on the training/test split of $a = 11$. For each d, we also obtain the average classicization accuracy over the 20 splits. Figure 4 exhibits the results and extra depicts the standard deviations of LogSC. From Fig. 4, we can find that our LogSC consistently outperforms the other methods in term of classification accuracy at any dictionary size. In addition, a small dictionary size is insufficient for partitioning the samples, while a big one lead to annoying instability issue.

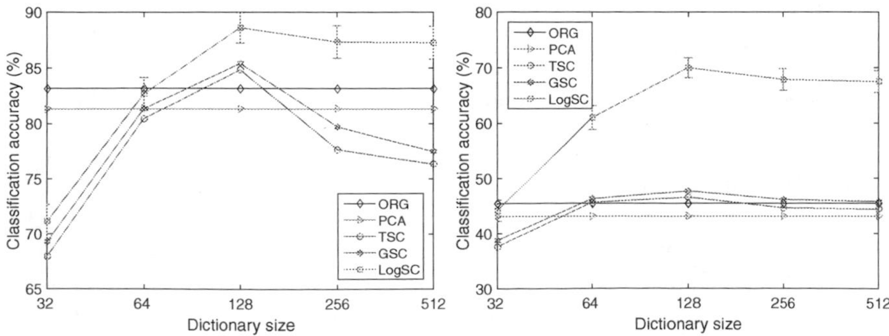

Fig. 4. Classification results of various dictionary sizes on AR by SVM (left) and NN (right).

4.3 Robust Image Classification on USPS and COIL20

USPS database contains normalized gray scale images of size 16 × 16. It totally has 9298 images and is originally partitioned into a training set of 7291 images and a test set of 2007 images. To raise the bar, we inject the "salt & pepper" noise with density 0.1 into half of the samples in both training set and test set, denoted as USPS_sp. We randomly extract $a = \{10, 30, 50, 100, 200, 500\}$ images per digit from the training set to learn the dictionary of size 128 and then compute accuracy with the test set. For each a, we randomly draw out 10 training subsets. Figure 5 (left) exhibits the average classification accuracy by SVM over the 10 test runs. Extra, the classification results on original training/test split of USPS_sp are also achieved. As can be seen from Fig. 5, our LogSC can result in the best performance among all methods.

COIL20 database is comprised of 1440 gray images from 20 objects. For each object, 72 images of size 32 × 32 are taken 5° apart during the process of rotating the turntable 360°. For testing the robustness, we randomly lose contiguous pixels of size 8 × 32 for the nearly half of the images of COIL20 (COIL20_co for short). We randomly draw out 36 images per class from COIL20_co as training set and take the rest images as test set. Then, we compute the classification accuracies varying dictionary size $d \in \{32, 64, 128, 256, 512\}$ on 10 training/test splits. Figure 5 (right) depicts the average classification results by 1-NN for each d over the 10 test runs. From the results, we can find that our LogSC gives rise to the significantly improved classification performance in comparison with the other approaches.

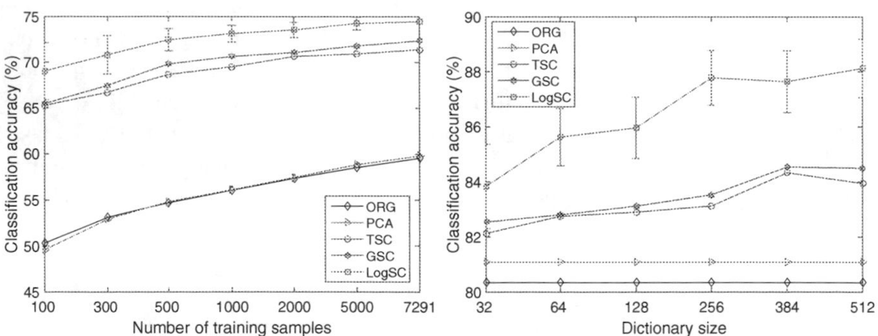

Fig. 5. Classification results on USPS_sp by SVM (left) and COIL20_co by 1-NN (right)

5 Conclusion

In this paper, we put forth a novel strategy for sparse coding, dubbed Low-rank graph regularized Sparse Coding (LogSC), towards removing the instability problem. LogSC integrates sparse coding, graph Laplacian regularization and low-rank representation into a uniform optimization problem, which is effectively tackled exploiting the framework of LADMAP. The encouraging experimental results of clustering and classification manifest that LogSC not only yields discriminative features, but also has preferred capability of generalization and robustness. It is worth mentioning that there only exist two free parameters needed attention in LogSC. However, more theoretical and experimental results are required in future work.

Acknowledgments. This research was funded by the Fundamental Research Funds for the Central Universities (Grant No. G2018KY0301) and the National Natural Science Foundation of China (Grants No. 61332014 and 61772426).

References

1. Elhamifar, E., Vidal, R.: Sparse subspace clustering: algorithm, theory, and applications. IEEE Trans. Pattern Anal. Mach. Intell. **35**(11), 2765–2781 (2013)
2. Zhang, Y., Xiang, M., Yang, B.: Graph regularized nonnegative sparse coding using incoherent dictionary for approximate nearest neighbor search. Pattern Recogn. **70**, 75–88 (2017)
3. Zhang, Y., Xiang, M., Yang, B.: Linear dimensionality reduction based on hybrid structure preserving projections. Neurocomputing **173**, 518–529 (2016)
4. Zheng, M., et al.: Graph regularized sparse coding for image representation. IEEE Trans. Image Process. **20**(5), 1327–1336 (2011)
5. Gao, S., Tsang, I.W.-H., Chia, L.-T.: Laplacian sparse coding, hypergraph laplacian sparse coding and applications. IEEE Trans. Pattern Anal. Mach. Intell. **35**(1), 92–104 (2013)
6. Zhang, Z., Xu, Y., Yang, J., Li, X., Zhang, D.: A survey of sparse representation: algorithms and applications. IEEE Access **3**, 490–530 (2015)
7. Bengio, Y., Courville, A., Vincent, P.: Representation learning: a review and new perspectives. IEEE Trans. Pattern Anal. Mach. Intell. **35**(8), 1798–1828 (2013)
8. Balasubramanian, K., Yu, K., Lebanon, G.: Smooth sparse coding via marginal regression for learning sparse representations. Artif. Intell. **238**, 83–95 (2016)
9. Jin, T., Yu, Z., Li, L., Li, C.: Multiple graph regularized sparse coding and multiple hypergraph regularized sparse coding for image representation. Neurocomputing **154**, 245–256 (2015)
10. Feng, X., Wu, S., Zhou, W., Tang, Z.: Multi-hypergraph incidence consistent sparse coding for image data clustering. In: Bailey, J., Khan, L., Washio, T., Dobbie, G., Huang, J.Z., Wang, R. (eds.) PAKDD 2016. LNCS (LNAI), vol. 9652, pp. 79–91. Springer, Cham (2016). https://doi.org/10.1007/978-3-319-31750-2_7
11. Liu, G., Lin, Z., Yan, S., Sun, J., Yu, Y., Ma, Y.: Robust recovery of subspace structures by low-rank representation. IEEE Trans. Pattern Anal. Mach. Intell. **35**(1), 171–184 (2013)
12. Yin, M., Gao, J., Lin, Z.: Laplacian regularized low-rank representation and its applications. IEEE Trans. Pattern Anal. Mach. Intell. **38**(3), 504–517 (2016)
13. Zhang, Y., Xiang, M., Yang, B.: Low-rank preserving embedding. Pattern Recogn. **70**, 112–125 (2017)
14. Lin, Z., Liu, R., Su, Z.: Linearized alternating direction method with adaptive penalty for low-rank representation. In: Proceedings of Advance in Neural information Processing System, pp. 612–620 (2011)
15. Parikh, N., Boyd, S.: Proximal algorithms. Found. Trends Optim. **1**(3), 127–239 (2014)
16. Xu, Y., Fang, X., Wu, J., Li, X., Zhang, D.: Discriminative transfer subspace learning via low-rank and sparse representation. IEEE Trans. Image Process. **25**(2), 850–863 (2016)
17. Cai, J.-F., Candès, E.J., Shen, Z.: A singular value thresholding algorithm for matrix completion. SIAM J. Optim. **20**(4), 1956–1982 (2010)

18. Beck, A., Teboulle, M.: A fast iterative shrinkage-thresholding algorithm for linear inverse problems. SIAM J. Imaging Sci. **2**(1), 183–202 (2009)
19. Zhang, Y., Xiang, M., Yang, B.: Hierarchical sparse coding from a Bayesian perspective. Neurocomputing **272**, 279–293 (2018)
20. Chang, C.-C., Lin, C.-J.: LIBSVM: a library for support vector machine. ACM Trans. Intell. Syst. Technol. **2**(3), Article no. 27 (2011)

Decentralized Multiagent Reinforcement Learning for Efficient Robotic Control by Coordination Graphs

Chao Yu(✉), Dongxu Wang, Jiankang Ren, Hongwei Ge, and Liang Sun

School of Computer Science and Technology,
Dalian University of Technology, Dalian 116024, Liaoning, China
{cy496,wdx,rjk,hwge,liangsun}@dlut.edu.cn

Abstract. Reinforcement learning is widely used to learn complex behaviors for robotics. However, due to the high-dimensional state/action spaces, reinforcement learning usually suffers from slow learning speed in robotic control applications. A feasible solution to this challenge is to utilize structural decomposition of the control problem and resort to decentralized learning methods to expedite the overall learning process. In this paper, a multiagent reinforcement learning approach is proposed to enable decentralized learning of component behaviors for a robot that is decomposed as a coordination graph. By using this approach, all the component behaviors are learned in parallel by some individual reinforcement learning agents and these agents coordinate their behaviors to solve the global control problem. The approach is validated and analyzed in two benchmark robotic control problems. The experimental validation provides evidence that the proposed approach enables better performance than approaches without decomposition.

Keywords: RL · Robotic control · Multiagent learning · CG

1 Introduction

Robot learning is going to be a key ingredient for the future of autonomous robots that are able to learn and react to uncertain and unforeseen changes in stochastic and dynamic environments. Among various forms of learning approaches, Reinforcement Learning (RL) [1] is commonly used to learn complex behaviors for a wide variety of robots, from multi-link robotic manipulators, mobile robots, aerial vehicles to humanoid robots [2]. However, many real-world robotic control applications feature high-dimensional state and action spaces, i.e. multiple actuators or effectors, through which the individual actions work together to make the robot perform a desired task. In such applications, RL suffers from the combinatorial explosion of complexity, which makes classical RL methods directly inapplicable. For example, value function based approaches usually face high variance in the policy due to a small change in the estimated value function,

X. Geng and B.-H. Kang (Eds.): PRICAI 2018, LNAI 11012, pp. 191–203, 2018.
https://doi.org/10.1007/978-3-319-97304-3_15

while policy search approaches often require carefully chosen task-specific pre-structured policy parameterizations before seeking out a proper solution [15]. Impressive progress has been recently achieved using end-to-end deep RL in various robotic control applications, relying on sophisticated network architectures and heavy hyper-parameter tuning. However, deep RL approaches usually require a large number of training episodes to find solutions. Moreover, it is still an unsolved issue to propose a general method that can perform well in a variety of tasks [12].

In contrast to direct learning approaches, another way of dealing with the complexity of RL in high-dimensional robotic control is to specify or discover hierarchically structured policies, by decomposing tasks into more manageable subtasks [8]. This decomposition has the additional advantage of reducing the total amount of information required to solve the problem, if subtasks are appropriately defined. There are two main structured RL approaches: Modular RL (MRL) [10] for executing concurrent subtasks and Hierarchical RL (HRL) [11] for executing a hierarchical structure of tasks. All these approaches, however, rely heavily on the designer's knowledge of the domain and ability to select appropriate subtasks. Although some approaches have been proposed to automatically discover and learn the hierarchical structure, extra computational complexity might be introduced in order to achieve a satisfactory learning performance.

In this paper, we still resort to the decomposition paradigm to solve a high-dimensional robotic control problem, due to its promise in scalability and efficiency. Unlike the traditional decomposition methods of MRL and HRL that require extra mechanisms such as module/action selection policy or hand-crafted task decomposition using domain knowledge, we directly decompose the control learning problem into several sub-problems in the multi-dimensional state and action spaces, with each sub-problem corresponding to controlling some particular components of the robot. In this decomposition, each sub-problem is controlled and solved individually by an agent, and all the agents work toward a common goal by properly coordinating their behaviors. In order to model the interplay of interrelated sub-problems, the Coordination Graph (CG) [7] is applied to realize the structural decomposition. It is then possible to use Multi-Agent RL (MARL) approaches [5] for decentralized learning of the sub-problems. The approach is validated and analyzed in two robotic control problems. The experimental validation provides evidence that the proposed approach shows better performance and faster learning speed than approaches without decomposition. Moreover, different ways of constructing CG can bring about various learning performance, and thus, trade-off between simplicity and effectiveness is required.

2 RL, MARL and CG

This section introduces single agent RL with its multiagent extension, and the concept of CG. These are the foundations of this paper.

2.1 MDP and RL

RL is a general class of algorithms in the field of machine learning that aims at allowing an agent to learn how to make sequential decisions in an environment, where the only feedback consists of a scalar reward signal [4]. An MDP is a commonly adopted framework for RL problems, which can be defined by a 4-tuple $M = (S, A, P, R)$, where S is a finite state space, A is a set of actions available to the agent, $P(s, a, s') : S \times A \times S \rightarrow [0, 1]$ is a Markovian transition function when the agent transits from state s to s' after taking action a, and $R : S \times A \rightarrow R$ is a reward function that returns immediate reward $R(s, a)$ to the agent after taking action a in state s. An agent's *policy* $\pi : S \times A \rightarrow [0, 1]$ is a probability distribution that maps a state $s \in S$ to an action $a \in A$. The goal in an MDP is to learn a policy π so as to maximize the expected discounted reward $V^{\pi}(s)$ for each state $s \in S$. The reward function is given by Eq. (1).

$$V^{\pi}(s) = E_{\pi}\left[\sum_{t=0}^{\infty} \gamma^t R(s_t, \pi(s_t))|s_0 = s\right], \tag{1}$$

where E_{π} is the expectation of policy π, s_t denotes the state at time t, and $\gamma \in [0, 1)$ is a discount factor. For any finite MDP, there is at least one *optimal policy* π^*, such that $V^{\pi^*}(s) \geq V^{\pi}(s)$ for every policy π and every state $s \in S$.

For small discrete domains, the optimal policy can be computed using some simple model-free RL methods, such as tabular Q-learning [9]. When the problem gets more complex, efficient techniques (e.g., batch learning and model-based learning), and representational techniques (e.g., function approximation and hierarchical decomposition) can be applied to enable feasible learning in solving the problem. More background knowledge of RL can be found in [4].

2.2 MARL and CG

MDP and its RL solutions deal with single agent's sequential decision making problems. When multiple agents coexist in the same environment and conduct learning simultaneously, it becomes the MARL problem. MARL has been successfully applied to a variety of virtual as well as real-life domains ranging from distributed control, multi-robot systems and resource management to automated trading [5]. The main problem in MARL is that the concurrent multiple learning processes can make the learning environment non-stationary for each individual learner. Learning to achieve coordinated behaviors in such a non-stationary environment is a challenging problem, especially when agents also need to deal with incomplete information caused either by their communication constraints or by their observability limits.

Computationally, the complexity in MARL grows exponentially with the number of agents. One way to alleviate this problem is to exploit certain level of independence among agents. CG [7] is one of such effective techniques, which enables the decomposition of the global payoff function $Q(\mathbf{s}, \mathbf{a})$ into a linear combination of local payoff functions. This decomposition can be depicted using an undirected graph $G = (V, E)$, in which each node $i \in V$ represents an agent and an edge $(i, j) \in E$ indicates the corresponding agents having to coordinate their actions. Allowing payoff functions defined over at most two agents, the global payoff function $Q(\mathbf{s}, \mathbf{a})$ can be given by:

$$Q(\mathbf{s}, \mathbf{a}) = \sum_{(i,j) \in E} Q_{ij}(\bar{s_{ij}}, a_i, a_j), \tag{2}$$

where $\mathbf{s} = \langle s_1, \ldots, s_n \rangle \in S$ and $\mathbf{a} = \langle a_1, \ldots, a_n \rangle \in A$ are the joint state and joint action of all agents, respectively, and $\bar{s_{ij}}$ represents the relevant state variables for agent i and j.

The main goal of CG is to find a coordination strategy of actions for the agents to maximize $Q(\mathbf{s}, \mathbf{a})$ at state $\mathbf{s}$. The Variable Elimination (VE) algorithm [7] can be applied to solve the coordination problem and find the optimal $\mathbf{a}$. In VE, an agent first collects all payoff functions related to its edges before it is eliminated. It then computes a conditional payoff function, which returns the maximal value that it is able to contribute to the system for every action combination of its neighbors, and a best-response function (or conditional strategy), which returns the action corresponding to the maximizing value. The conditional payoff function is communicated to its neighbors and the agent is eliminated from the graph. The agents are iteratively eliminated until one agent remains. This agent selects the action that maximizes the final conditional payoff function. A reverse order is then performed in which every agent computes its optimal action based on its conditional strategy and fixed actions of its neighbors. A more detailed description of the VE process can be found in [6].

After computing the optimal joint action in a group of agents, it is then possible to employ distributed MARL approaches for solving sequential decision making problems. For example, Guestrin *et al.* [7] proposed three forms of *coordinated RL* algorithm on CG. Kok and Vlassis [6] proposed the *Sparse Cooperative Q-Learning* that enables learning under local rewards on CG. The main concepts, techniques and algorithms of MARL can be found in detail in [5].

3 Decentralized MARL for Robotic Control

A large number of sophisticated RL approaches have been recently proposed to solve continuous control problems in robotics [12–14,17,18]. Relying on some training tricks such as in the neural network structure, or activation functions related to specific tasks, these approaches have achieved tremendous progress in solving relatively high-dimensional robotic control problems. However, as these approaches still search in the whole space of the problem, they inevitably undergo high computational complexity, causing slow or sometimes divergent learning performance. A direct solution to this problem is to decompose the whole control problem into several sub-problems that can be more easily solved. In this way, the high computation complexity can be greatly reduced. For example, a humanoid robot usually has 19 rigid links including the head, body, arms and legs, along with 28 actuated joints, resulting in 142-dimensional state including the joint angles, joint velocities, vector of contact forces, and the coordinates of the center of mass [12]. Directly learning in such a high-dimensional space is intractable. But if we can decompose the robot into several single components, e.g., the legs, the torso, and the head, and use efficient coordination mechanisms to coordinate these components, then the computation complexity for the whole robotic control problem can be greatly alleviated. The global learning problem is now transformed into a distributed multiagent coordination problem, with each agent representing a single component of the robot. In this section, we first give a specific example to illustrate how to decompose a robotic control problem based on CG, and then discuss how to handle the coordination of the decomposed components with continuous actions.

3.1 Robot Decomposition Using CG

We use a simple 2D humanoid robot to illustrate how the robot can be structurally decomposed. Walker2d (Fig. 1(a)) is one of the RL benchmarks provided by OpenAI gym. It consists of 17-dimensional state space and 6-dimensional action space. The state space contains positions and velocities of the thigh, knee, and ankle joints. The action space contains the movement range of these joints. A straightforward method to decompose the robot is to model each joint as an agent and build an edge to link two directly connected joints according to the physical structure. Figure 1(b) shows the structural decomposition and construction of CG in Walker2d, in which D_1, D_2, and D_3 represent the thigh, knee and ankle joints on the left leg, respectively, and the other three on the right leg.

We can see that this kind of decomposition is directly induced by the physical structure of a robot. Thus, it is simple and easy to implement. We should also emphasize that such a decomposition is not unique. In fact, we can conduct various decompositions in different levels of granularity by grouping different number of joints into a single agent. For example, the Walker2d can be simply decomposed to a CG with only two agents, each of which represents one leg of the robot. Moreover, the CG can be initialized in a way to incorporate some preliminary domain knowledge, such as which components of the robot are comparatively more critical, and which components require closer coordination, etc. By utilizing such knowledge, learning efficiency can be further increased.

3.2 Problem Formalization

For a robot agent D, a specific coordination graph G can be built according to the decomposition method described in the previous subsection. In G, there are n agents $d_1, d_2, \ldots, d_n$, and a set of m edges e_{ij} to connect two linked agents d_i and d_j. Let $\mathcal{S}, \mathcal{A}$ denote the robot's state space and action space, $\mathcal{S}_1, \mathcal{S}_2, \ldots, \mathcal{S}_n$ and $\mathcal{A}_1, \mathcal{A}_2, \ldots, \mathcal{A}_n$ denote the state spaces and action spaces of agent $d_1, d_2, \ldots, d_n$, respectively. Then, the global value function $Q(\mathbf{s}, \mathbf{a})$ ($\mathbf{s} \in \mathcal{S}, \mathbf{a} \in \mathcal{A}$) can be

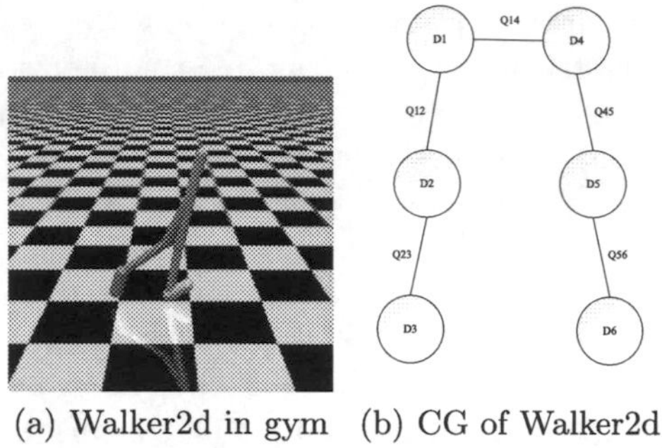

(a) Walker2d in gym (b) CG of Walker2d

Fig. 1. Structural decomposition of Walker2d in OpenAI gym

decomposed into a linear combination of local value functions $Q_{ij}(\mathbf{s}_{e_{ij}}, \mathbf{a}_{e_{ij}})$ ($\mathbf{s}_{e_{ij}} \in \mathcal{S}_i \times \mathcal{S}_j, \mathbf{a}_{e_{ij}} \in \mathcal{A}_i \times \mathcal{A}_j$) according to Eq. (2). Then the optimal joint action can be given as $\mathbf{a}^* = argmax_a Q(\mathbf{s}, \mathbf{a})$.

At each time step during learning, the robot performs the optimal joint action $\mathbf{a}^*$ and receives the next state $\mathbf{s}'$ and reward $\mathbf{r}$. Assuming the value function to be approximated by some parameters w_{ij} (e.g., weights in the neural networks), then each local value functions $Q_{ij}(\mathbf{s}_{e_{ij}}, \mathbf{a}_{e_{ij}})$ can be updated along the gradient of the mean square TD error, resulting the following update rule:

$$\Delta w_{ij} = \alpha[r + \gamma \max_{\mathbf{a}} Q(\mathbf{s}', \mathbf{a}) - Q(\mathbf{s}, \mathbf{a})] \nabla_{w_{ij}} Q_{ij}(\mathbf{s}_{e_{ij}}, \mathbf{a}_{e_{ij}}), \quad (3)$$

in which the optimal joint action $\mathbf{a}$ in the new state $\mathbf{s}'$ can be computed by applying the VE on the CG, and the previous joint Q-value $Q(\mathbf{s}, \mathbf{a})$ can be computed by fixing the optimal action of every agent to the one assigned in $\mathbf{a}$.

However, since the action space in robotic control problems is high-dimensional and continuous, directly applying VE on the CG to compute the optimal joint actions is infeasible. Next, we will propose an MARL method to enable coordinated learning with continuous actions on CG.

3.3 Computation of the Continuous Joint Optimal Actions

The proposed method is called Multi-Agent Normalized Advantage Functions (MA-NAF), which is a multiagent extension of continuous RL method of Normalized Advantage Functions (NAF) [19]. The idea behind NAF is to represent the Q-function $Q(\mathbf{s}, \mathbf{a})$ in such a way that its maximum, i.e., $argmax_{\mathbf{a}} Q(\mathbf{s}, \mathbf{a})$, can be determined easily and analytically during the Q-learning update. NAF separates the Q-value function to two terms: advantage term $A(\mathbf{s}, \mathbf{a})$ and state-value function term $V(\mathbf{s})$ as follows:

$$Q(\mathbf{s}, \mathbf{a}) = A(\mathbf{s}, \mathbf{a}) + V(\mathbf{s}), \quad (4)$$

in which $V(\mathbf{s})$ is independent of actions, while $A(\mathbf{s},\mathbf{a})$ is parameterized as a quadratic function of actions with nonlinear features of the states as follows [19]:

$$A(s,a) = -\frac{1}{2}(\mathbf{a}-\mu(\mathbf{s}))^T\mathbf{P}(\mathbf{s})(\mathbf{a}-\mu(\mathbf{s})), \quad (5)$$

in which $\mu(\mathbf{s})$ is a vector function dependent on state s, and $\mathbf{P}(\mathbf{s})$ is an action-independent positive-definite square matrix parameterized by $\mathbf{P}(\mathbf{s}) = \mathbf{L}(\mathbf{x})\mathbf{L}(\mathbf{x})^T$, where $\mathbf{L}(\mathbf{x})$ is a lower-triangular matrix whose entries are determined by the linear output layer of a neural network, with a diagonal terms exponentiated. It should be noted that, the values of $V(\mathbf{s})$, $\mathbf{L}(\mathbf{x})$ and $\mu(\mathbf{s})$ are all determined by the output of neural networks. Although neural networks are usually nonlinear, but these functions are still convex functions since they are independent of actions.

Since $A(s,a)$ is a quadratic function of actions, the optimal action in current state s can be easily computed as:

$$\frac{\partial Q}{\partial \mathbf{a}} = -\mathbf{P}(\mathbf{s})(\mathbf{a}-\mu(\mathbf{s})), \quad (6)$$

Since P is an invertible matrix, let $\frac{\partial Q}{\partial \mathbf{a}} = 0$, then we can get

$$\mathbf{a}^* = \mu(\mathbf{s}). \quad (7)$$

Therefore, when NAF needs to compute the optimal action, the only thing that needs to do is to obtain the value of $\mu(\mathbf{s})$.

The idea behind MA-NAF is to represent the overall Q-function $Q(\mathbf{s},\mathbf{a})$ as a linear combination of agents' local Q-function $Q_{ij}(\mathbf{s}_{e_{ij}},\mathbf{a}_{e_{ij}})$, and each Q_{ij} uses the form of NAF as follows:

$$Q_{ij}(\mathbf{s}_{e_{ij}},\mathbf{a}_{e_{ij}}) = A_{ij}(\mathbf{s}_{e_{ij}},\mathbf{a}_{e_{ij}}) + V_{ij}(\mathbf{s}_{e_{ij}}). \quad (8)$$

Each V_{ij} is also independent of actions, and each A_{ij} is also parameterized as a quadratic function of actions related to e_{ij}. The definitions of V and A are the same as NAF. The only difference is that each agent now has an independent V and A. The overall Q-function then can be given as follows:

$$Q(\mathbf{s},\mathbf{a}) = \sum_{i=1}^{m} A_{ij}(\mathbf{s}_{e_{ij}},\mathbf{a}_{e_{ij}}) + \sum_{i=1}^{m} V_{ij}(\mathbf{s}_{e_{ij}}) \quad (9)$$

It is clear that $Q(\mathbf{s},\mathbf{a})$ is also a quadratic function of actions. Therefore, the optimal actions can be easily computed by differentiating $Q(\mathbf{s},\mathbf{a})$ over actions:

$$\frac{\partial Q}{\partial \mathbf{a}} = \sum \frac{\partial A_{ij}}{\partial \mathbf{a}} = -\frac{1}{2}\sum \frac{\partial(\mathbf{a}-\mu(\mathbf{s}))^T\mathbf{P}(\mathbf{s})(\mathbf{a}-\mu(\mathbf{s}))}{\partial \mathbf{a}} = 0 \quad (10)$$

To simplify the calculation of this equation, we can first compute the gradient of each edge on the graph G, and then combine this gradient information into a matrix. Then, the overall action gradient can be computed by Eq. (11).

$$\frac{\partial Q}{\partial a} = \mathbf{U}\mathbf{a} - \mathbf{H}(\mathbf{s}), \quad (11)$$

in which $\mathbf{U}$ is the combining matrix of $\mathbf{P}$, and $\mathbf{H}(\mathbf{s})$ is the combining matrix of $\mathbf{P}\mu$. The overall joint optimal action can be computed by solving the following linear equation functions:

$$\mathbf{U}\mathbf{a} = \mathbf{H}(\mathbf{s}). \tag{12}$$

The order of this equations is equal to the size of the actions dimension. The Gaussian elimination method can be directly used in a relatively low dimension, while the conjugate gradient method can be used when the dimension is higher.

To clarify, we illustrate the above calculation using a simple example. Let $\langle d_1, d_2\rangle$ be the agents connected by edge e_{12}, and let $\langle d_1, d_3\rangle$ be the agents connected by edge e_{13}, then joint action gradients of $\langle d_1, d_2\rangle$ and $\langle d_1, d_3\rangle$ are:

$$\frac{\partial Q_{e12}}{\partial a_{e_{12}}} = \mathbf{P}(\mathbf{s}_{e_{12}})\mathbf{a}_{e_{12}} - \mathbf{P}(\mathbf{s}_{e_{12}})\mu(\mathbf{s}_{e_{12}}). \tag{13}$$

$$\frac{\partial Q_{e13}}{\partial a_{e_{13}}} = \mathbf{P}(\mathbf{s}_{e_{13}})\mathbf{a}_{e_{13}} - \mathbf{P}(\mathbf{s}_{e_{13}})\mu(\mathbf{s}_{e_{13}}). \tag{14}$$

Let $\mathbf{P}(\mathbf{s}_{e_{12}}) = \begin{pmatrix} \mathbf{p}_1^{12} \\ \mathbf{p}_2^{12} \end{pmatrix}$, $\mathbf{P}(\mathbf{s}_{e_{13}}) = \begin{pmatrix} \mathbf{p}_1^{13} \\ \mathbf{p}_3^{13} \end{pmatrix}$, $\mu(\mathbf{s}_{e_{12}}) = [\mu_1^{12}(s_1), \mu_2^{12}(s_2)]^T$ and $\mu(\mathbf{s}_{e_{13}}) = [\mu_1^{13}(s_1), \mu_3^{13}(s_3)]^T$, in which the subscript represents the agent and the superscript represents the edge. Then we can get:

$$\mathbf{U} = \begin{pmatrix} \mathbf{p}_1^{12} + \mathbf{p}_1^{13} \\ \mathbf{p}_2^{12} \\ \mathbf{p}_3^{13} \end{pmatrix}, \tag{15}$$

$$\mathbf{H}(\mathbf{s}) = \begin{pmatrix} \mathbf{p}_1^{12}\mu_1^{12}(s_1) + \mathbf{p}_2^{12}\mu_1^{13}(s_2) \\ \mathbf{p}_2^{12}\mu_2^{12}(s_2) \\ \mathbf{p}_3^{13}\mu_3^{13} \end{pmatrix} \tag{16}$$

Then combing Eqs. (15), (16) and (12), the optimal joint action can be computed using various methods.

4 Experiments

This section gives the experimental evaluation of our approach in two benchmark robotic control problems: Hopper and Walker2d [12]. We also investigate how different ways of building CG can impact the learning performance of our approach. We use a separate neural network with two layers of 200 rectified linear units (ReLU) to approximate each Q value function. To be consistent with previous approaches, a replay buffer with a length of 100,000 is adopted to stabilize the neural network and avoid divergence. We mainly compare our approach with the original NAF, in order to show the benefits of structural decomposition of our approach. As we also apply the NAF approach to model each agent on CG, a target network is also applied to stabilize the neural network. Other parameter settings are the same with previous work in [19].

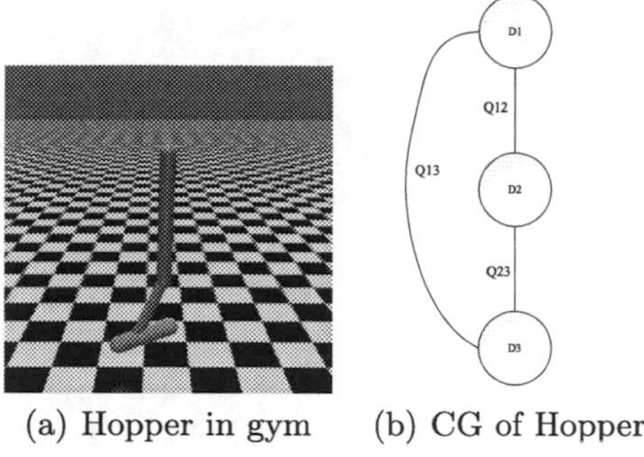

(a) Hopper in gym (b) CG of Hopper

Fig. 2. Illustration of structural decomposition of the Hopper

The Hopper is a one-footed humanoid robot, with 11-dimensional state space and 3-dimensional action space, as shown in Fig. 2(a). The state space contains positions and velocities of single thigh, knee, and humerus joints. The action space contains the movement range of these joints. We build a CG for the Hopper as in Fig. 2(b), which consists of three agents (D_1, D_2, D_3) representing the thigh, knee and ankle, respectively. The thigh and knee, and the knee and ankle are connected on the CG, to indicate direct coordination between these agents (i.e., Q_{12}, Q_{23} on the CG, respectively). An indirect coordination edge between the thigh and ankle (i.e., Q_{13}) is also built to further increase coordination. As shown in Sect. 3, the Walker2d can be seen as a more complex version of the Hopper as it has two legs. So Walker2d robot must learn to walk like real humans, which is an extremely challenging task for general RL approaches. In this experiment, we simply adopted the structure in Fig. 1(b) to represent the CG of Walker2d.

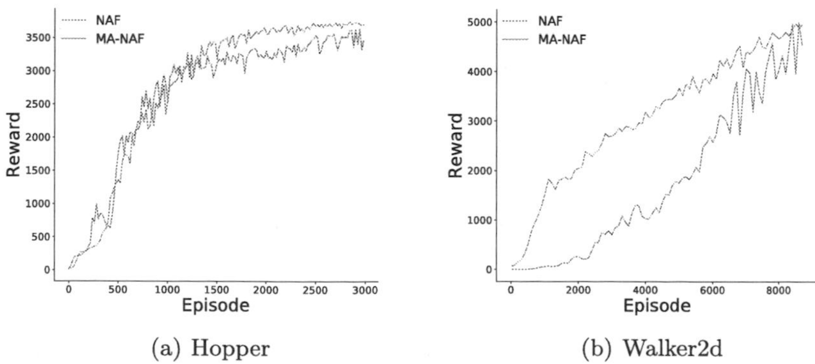

(a) Hopper (b) Walker2d

Fig. 3. The comparison of our approach MA-NAF and the approach NAF in two benchmark robotic control experiments: Hopper and Walker2d.

Figure 3(a) shows the performance of MA-NAF and NAF in Hopper. Our approach performs slightly better than the NAF in this experiment. However, our approach is more stable than NAF. Especially in the final stage, our approach achieved convergence at almost 1500 iterations, while NAF is still fluctuating violently. The reason why there is no significant difference between our approach and NAF is due to the relatively small problem size of Hopper. This can be verified by the result in Walker2d domain, as shown in Fig. 3. In this higher dimensional problem, the advantage of structural decomposition using our approach becomes more prominent. Especially in the early period, the performance of NAF has only improved slightly for the first 2000 iterations, while our approach can achieve a significant improvement. Also, in the later period after 6000 iterations, NAF is still fluctuating dramatically, while our approach is more stable. Therefore, we can conclude that the structural decomposition and distributed coordinated learning in our approach are indeed effective means in solving high-dimensional learning problems in robotic control.

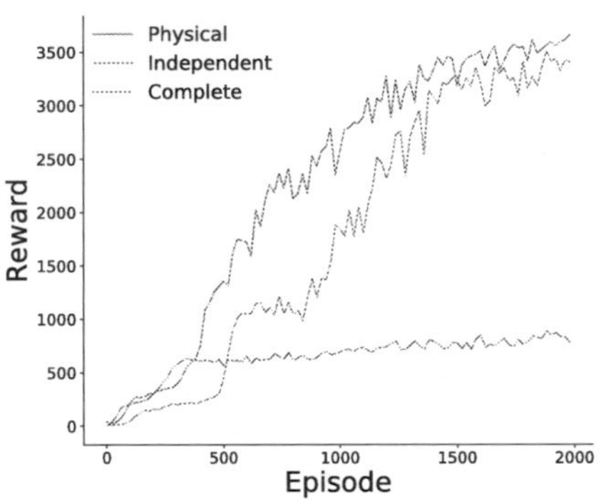

Fig. 4. Applying different structures of CG in our approach in the Hopper domain

As the way of constructing the CG is a key point in determining the overall coordination level and thus affecting the final learning performance, we further investigate how different structures of CG impact the performance of our approach. We propose three different ways of constructing CG. The first one is called *independent graph*, in which no edges exist on CG to indicate coordination among the agents. In other words, all the agents on CG make decisions independently. The second one is called *complete graph*, in which all the agents are linked to each other and the input of a Q value includes the information of all the agents. The last one is the *physical graph* as in Fig. 2(b) in which agents are linked by physical constraints of robots and the input of each Q value only includes the information of the connected agents. Figure 4 shows the learning performance of these three different graph structures in the Hopper domain. It is clear that the independent graph method performs the worst, due to lack of coordination among agents. The physical graph approach outperforms the complete graph approach throughout the learning process. The result provides some useful insights into constructing a CG for robotic applications.

(1) If the structure of CG is too simple to reflect the coordination dependencies among agents, the learning performance can be significantly impaired. This can be observed in the extreme case when using the independent graph approach in the Hopper domain (Fig. 4).
(2) On the contrary, a over complex structure of CG will lead to an increase in the number of nonlinear function approximators, which in turn may cause instability during learning. In addition, a too complex graph structure often embodies a large amount of redundant information, which may lead to inefficiency caused by mutual interference in training.
(3) Therefore, a careful trade-off between simplicity and effectiveness in constructing a CG is required. The basic principle is that the graph structure should be as simple as possible, while capturing the basic and most critical coordination relationship among different components of a robot. For example, we found that the coordination between the Hopper's thigh and ankle had an impact on the learning performance. So we increase the structure complexity a bit by adding an edge to connect the thigh with the ankle to promote the coordination.

5 Related Work

RL in robotic control is a topic of interest for decades [2]. There are broadly two directions for robotic control through RL in both research and applications. One direction is to apply traditional RL approaches, combined with some specific efficient or representational techniques. Among these approaches, the policy search approaches have attracted increasingly high attention due to its effectiveness compared to value-based approaches [15]. For example, Schulman *et al.* [13] proposed and analyzed trust region methods for optimizing stochastic control policies. Silver *et al.* [14] proposed deterministic policy gradient algorithms for RL with continuous actions. All these approaches still search in the whole problem space. Our work, however, focuses on structural decomposition of the global problem into some easier sub-problems. The other direction is to employ task decomposition methods to facilitate learning in robotic control [8]. Particularly, there is plenty work in Hierarchical RL (HRL) [11] for executing a hierarchical structure of tasks. However, HRL approaches rely heavily on the designer's knowledge of the domain and ability to select appropriate subtasks. Our work resorts to the structural decomposition, rather than the task decomposition as in HRL approaches. This significantly simplifies the problem formulation and also reduces the computational complexity.

Continuous control in robotics using RL has been extensively studied in recent years. For example, Google DeepMind [17] uses Deep Deterministic Policy Gradient (DDPG) to enable a robot to learn walking. Gu [18] utilized a deep RL algorithm based on off-policy training of deep Q-functions to scale to complex 3D manipulation tasks and to train on real physical robots. Duan *et al.* [12] compared some state-of-the-art continuous control RL approach in a variety of domains. Our work stands out of these studies by proposing a multiagent extension of continuous RL methods in robotic control.

Finally, MARL has gained a great deal of interest in the agent community [5]. Drawing on techniques and concepts from various areas such as artificial intelligence, game theory, psychology and sociology, MARL provides a promising paradigm to learn satisfactory agent behaviors in complex environments, ranging from distributed control, multi-robot systems and resource management to social networks [3,6,16,20]. However, most research in MARL still focuses on coordinated learning for multiple agents, whereas our work focuses on coordinating behaviors for a single agent. Moreover, most research is still in simple and discrete domains, while our work focuses on high-dimensional continuous domains in robotic control.

6 Conclusions

In this paper, we resort to structural decomposition to solve a high-dimensional robotic control problem. We showed illustratively how to decompose a robotic control problem into several sub-problems and how to build a CG to capture the interplay and dependencies among different sub-problems. We then proposed a distributed MARL approach, named MA-NAF, to enable coordinated learning of joint continuous actions on the constructed CG. The approach is validated and analyzed in two robotic control problems. The experimental validation proves that the proposed approach can achieve better performance and faster learning speed than the approaches that learn without decomposition. Moreover, we analyzed the impact of different ways of constructing a CG on the learning performance and draw a general principle of trading off between simplicity and effectiveness in constructing a CG for robotic control applications.

Our work motivates several directions for future research. First, some prior knowledge can be integrated into the construction of CG, so as to further improve the learning performance. For example, the Q values can be initialized in a way of reflecting the importance of components in the robot. Second, although our work has shown that the graph structure induced by the physical structure of the robot enables efficient learning performance, this physical decomposition becomes more implicit and harder when the structure of robots gets more and more complex. So, more sophisticated decomposition methods are needed to enable the application of our approach in higher dimensional complex domains. An extremely challenging yet interesting issue is: can we build an efficient CG autonomously from scratch? Last but not the least, all the component agents in our approach learn and explore at the same speed. This can be improved by drawing on various existing MARL principles or mechanisms to differentiate the learning behaviors of the agents.

Acknowledgments. This work is supported by the National Natural Science Foundation of China under Grant 61502072, 61572104 and 61403059, Hongkong Scholar Program under Grant XJ2017028, and Dalian High Level Talent Innovation Support Program under Grant 2017RQ008.

References

1. Sutton, R.S., Barto, A.G.: Reinforcement Learning: An Introduction. The MIT Press, Cambridge (1998)
2. Kober, J., Peters, J.: Reinforcement learning in robotics: a survey. Int. J. Robot. Res. **32**(11), 1238–1274 (2013)
3. Yu, C., Zhang, M., Ren, F., Tan, G.: Emotional multiagent reinforcement learning in spatial social dilemmas. IEEE Trans. Neural Netw. Learn. Syst. **26**(12), 3083–3096 (2015)
4. Wiering, M., Van Otterlo, M.: Reinforcement Learning. Adaptation, Learning, and Optimization. Springer, Berlin (2012). https://doi.org/10.1007/978-3-642-27645-3
5. Busoniu, L., Babuska, R., De Schutter, B.: A comprehensive survey of multiagent reinforcement learning. IEEE Trans. Syst. Man Cybern. Part C Appl. Rev. **38**(2), 156–172 (2008)
6. Kok, J.R., Vlassis, N.: Collaborative multiagent reinforcement learning by payoff propagation. J. Mach. Learn. Res. **7**, 1789–1828 (2006)
7. Guestrin, C., Lagoudakis, M., Parr, R.: Coordinated reinforcement learning. In: ICML 2002, pp. 227–234 (2002)
8. Grana, M., Fernandez-Gauna, B., Lopez-Guede, J.M.: Cooperative multi-agent reinforcement learning for multi-component robotic systems: guidelines for future research. Paladyn **2**(2), 71–81 (2011)
9. Watkins, C.J.C.H., Dayan, P.: Q-learning. Mach. Learn. **8**(3–4), 41 (1992)
10. Takahashi, Y., Edazawa, K., Asada, M.: Modular learning system and scheduling for behavior acquisition in multi-agent environment. In: Nardi, D., Riedmiller, M., Sammut, C., Santos-Victor, J. (eds.) RoboCup 2004. LNCS (LNAI), vol. 3276, pp. 548–555. Springer, Heidelberg (2005). https://doi.org/10.1007/978-3-540-32256-6_51
11. Barto, A.G., Mahadevan, S.: Recent advances in hierarchical reinforcement learning. Discret. Event Dyn. Syst. **13**(1–2), 41–77 (2003)
12. Duan, Y., Chen, X., Houthooft, R., Schulman, J., Abbeel, P.: Benchmarking deep reinforcement learning for continuous control, pp. 1329–1338 (2016)
13. Schulman, J., Levine, S., Moritz, P., Jordan, M.I., Abbeel, P.: Trust region policy optimization. Comput. Sci. **2**(2), 1889–1897 (2015)
14. Silver, D., Lever, G., Heess, N., Degris, T., Wierstra, D., Riedmiller, M.: Deterministic policy gradient algorithms. In: ICML 2014, pp. 387–395 (2014)
15. Deisenroth, M.P., Neumann, G., Peters, J.: A Survey on Policy Search for Robotics. Now Publishers Inc., Breda (2013)
16. Yu, C., Zhang, M., Ren, F.: Collective learning for the emergence of social norms in networked multiagent systems. IEEE Trans. Cybern. **44**(12), 2342–2355 (2014)
17. Lillicrap, T.P., et al.: Continuous control with deep reinforcement learning. Comput. Sci. **8**(6), A187 (2015)
18. Gu, S., Holly, E., Lillicrap, T., Levine, S.: Deep reinforcement learning for robotic manipulation with asynchronous off-policy updates. In: ICRA 2017, pp. 3389–3396 (2017)
19. Gu, S., Lillicrap, T., Sutskever, I., Levine, S.: Continuous deep q-learning with model-based acceleration. In: ICML 2016, pp. 2829–2838 (2016)
20. Yu, C., Zhang, M., Ren, F.: Multiagent learning of coordination in loosely coupled multiagent systems. IEEE Trans. Cybern. **45**(12), 2853–2867 (2015)

Construction of Microblog-Specific Chinese Sentiment Lexicon Based on Representation Learning

Li Kong[1,2], Chuanyi Li[1,2(✉)], Jidong Ge[1,2(✉)], Yufan Yang[1,2], Feifei Zhang[1,2], and Bin Luo[1,2]

[1] State Key Laboratory for Novel Software Technology, Nanjing University, Nanjing, China
kl_nju@126.com, yyfnju@163.com, 257561343@qq.com, luobin@nju.edu.cn

[2] Software Institute, Nanjing University, Nanjing, China
lcynju@126.com, gjdnju@163.com

Abstract. Sentiment analysis is a research hotspot in Nature Language Processing, and high-quality sentiment lexicon plays an important part in sentiment analysis. In this paper, we explore an approach to build a microblog-specific Chinese sentiment lexicon from massive microblog data. In feature learning, in order to enhance the quality of word embedding, we build a neural architecture to train a sentiment-aware word embedding by integrating three kinds of knowledge, including the context words and their composing characters, the polarity of sentences and the polarity of labeled words. Experiments conducted on several public datasets show that in both unsupervised and supervised microblog sentiment classification, the lexicon generated by our approach achieves the state-of-the-art performance compared to several existing Chinese sentiment lexicons and our feature learning method successfully catches both semantics and sentiment information.

Keywords: Sentiment lexicon · Representation learning · Microblog

1 Introduction

Sentiment analysis, also known as opinion mining, is a branch of Nature Language Processing (NLP). Its purpose is to help users acquire, organize and analyze relevant information, and analyze, process, induce and reason the subjective text [1]. Sentiment lexicon is an important component in sentiment analysis systems as it provides rich sentiment information. Sentiment lexicon consists of a list of subjective words or phrases, each of which is assigned with a sentiment polarity score. There have been some universal sentiment lexicons such as General Inquirer (GI), WordNet, HowNet, etc. However, compared to English sentiment lexicons, quality of existing Chinese sentiment lexicons is relatively low. That makes the automatic construction of domain-specific Chinese sentiment lexicon a meaningful and challenging task in the field of sentiment analysis.

Unlike English, texts of Chinese, Japanese and some other languages do not have obvious space between single words. Instead, a word of these languages consists of one

X. Geng and B.-H. Kang (Eds.): PRICAI 2018, LNAI 11012, pp. 204–216, 2018.
https://doi.org/10.1007/978-3-319-97304-3_16

or more characters and the semantics of each composing character is often related to the semantics of the word [2, 3]. For instance, '摇篮' (cradle) consists of '摇' (sway) and '篮' (basket). Considering the particularity of Chinese, researchers start from granularity finer than words and work on the level of characters, even structural parts to obtain better representation. Final representation for each word is the addition of word embedding and character embeddings, even structural part embeddings.

Microblog is a type of social media popular among young people where they can freely express emotional opinions and discuss various topics. Microblogs contain more free writing style which corresponds to people's expression custom, and richer emotions than traditional media. Various emoticons, such as and , are provided and widely used to directly convey positive or negative emotion, which can be seen as the indicator or label of the polarity of a microblog [4–6, 19]. With the help of microblog API, it is very easy to collect millions of posts.

In this paper, we utilize the Sina microblog (Weibo[1]) data as our corpus and attempt to learn a sentiment lexicon from massive collection of microblogs with emoticons indicating the polarity of sentences. We use the framework of [7] and make some modifications to realize a representation learning approach, as is shown in Fig. 1. Since a Chinese word is composed of one or more characters, it is helpful to take its composing characters into consideration when learning the semantic of the word. In addition, since we focus on sentiment polarity, known polarity of sentences and expanded seed words (labeled words) are used to optimize the feature learning of words. Based on these, we learn the continuous representation of Chinese words from three aspects: the context words and their composing characters, the polarity of sentences and the polarity of labeled words. The representation of each word in the corpus is then used as the features in a classifier to predict the sentiment polarity.

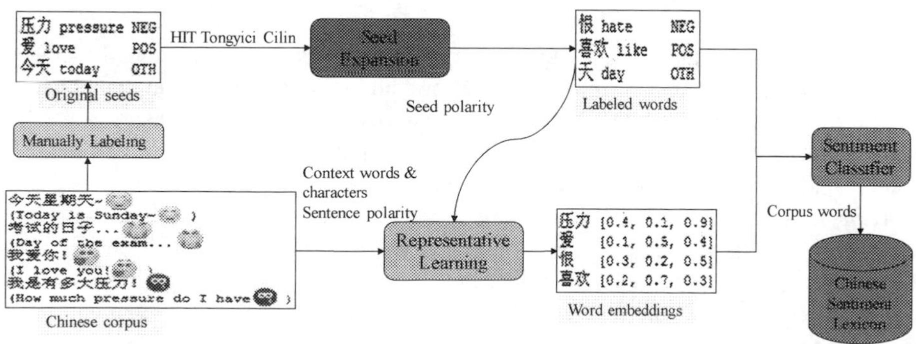

Fig. 1. The representation learning approach for building microblog-specific Chinese sentiment lexicon.

---

[1] https://weibo.com/.

The main contributions of our work are as follows:

- We combine context information and sentiment information to learn the embedding of both Chinese words and composing characters.
- We construct a microblog-specific Chinese sentiment lexicon using a sentiment classification framework.
- Our lexicon obtains the state-of-the-art performance compared to several existing sentiment lexicons, when used for microblog sentiment classification.

The rest of the paper is organized as follows. Section 2 introduces the related work on sentiment lexicon building. Our approach for microblog Chinese sentiment lexicon building is presented in Sect. 3. In Sect. 4 we provide the experimental results. Section 5 concludes the paper and presents future work.

2 Related Work

In this section, we will introduce two main approaches for sentiment lexicons construction: dictionary-based methods and corpus-based methods.

Dictionary-based methods rely on a seed sentiment dictionary which is usually small and a semantic knowledge base, such as WordNet[2] and Urban Dictionary[3], to explore the relationship between words, including synonymy, antonymy, upper and lower relationship etc. Hu and Liu accept a word as positive if it is a synonym of a positive seed word or an antonym of a negative seed word with the help of WordNet. The expansion of negative words is similar [8]. Heerschop et al. realize the emotion propagation of the seed word set utilizing the semantic relationship in WordNet [9]. A random walk-based algorithm is proposed in [10] to rank the word polarities in WordNet. They assume that the occurrence of the words in the glosses can express polarity properties.

Compared to semantic knowledge base, corpora are easier to get. Manually-labeled seed words and patterns in unlabeled corpora are used to induce domain-specific lexicons. Corpus-based methods can be further classified into two categories: conjunction methods and co-occurrence methods. Conjunction methods utilize conjunctions to judge the relationship of words around. For example, words around ‘and’ are probable to have the same polarity while words around ‘but’ may convey opposite polarities [11, 12]. A double propagation (DP) method is proposed in [13], which uses both sentiment and target relation and various connectives to extract sentiment words. Co-occurrence methods are based on the assumption that if two words often appear in the same sentence or document, they tend to have the same polarity or if a word often appear in positive (negative) sentences, it is more likely to express positive (negative) emotion. The degree of co-occurrence is usually measured by Point Mutual Information (PMI) [14]. Some researchers put forward several variants of PMI, such as positive PMI (PPMI) [15] and second order co-occurrence PMI (SOC-PMI) [16].

---

[2] https://wordnet.princeton.edu/.

[3] https://www.urbandictionary.com/.

The latest corpus-based approaches normally utilize the up-to-date machine learning models, such as neural networks, to learn a sentiment-aware distributed representation of words. In [17] sentiment attribute scores of each word are obtained through a neural network model based on tweets emoticons. Tang et al. modify the skip-gram model [18] and integrate the sentiment information of text into its hybrid loss function to learn sentiment-specific embedding. Then a softmax classifier is trained to predict the polarity according to a word embedding [7]. Wang et al. consider information on both word-level and document-level to learn word embedding and a logistic regression model is used later as the classifier [19].

Apart from techniques above, construction of Chinese sentiment lexicon also utilizes particularity of Chinese words and considers information of characters and structural parts to obtain better representation. Convolutional auto-encoder (convAE) is utilized in [20] to learn bitmap of characters to obtain semantics information. Since one character may have several meanings, Chen et al. learn one representation for each semantics [2]. Final representation for each word here is the addition of word embedding and character embeddings. It is worth noting that different characters make different contributions to the semantics of the word [21]. Considering from the finer granularity, radical is found to play an important part in the semantics of a character, e.g. '吃' (meal) has close connection with its radical '口' (mouth) [22]. Some researchers also make the assumption that characters with the same radicals have similar semantics and usage [23]. Yu et al. extend the work of [2] and jointly learn the embeddings of words, characters, and subcharacter components [3].

3 The Proposed Approach

In this section, we will introduce our approach for building a microblog-specific Chinese sentiment lexicon in detail. We follow [7] to form a classification framework. The major difference is the way we learn the representations of words. When modifying the skip-gram model to predict word embeddings according to the context, we also utilize information of characters of the context words. Besides considering sentiment polarity of each sentence in the corpus, we also utilize sentiment polarity of labeled words to guide the learning of word embeddings.

3.1 Microblog-Specific Word Embedding

Our feature learning method (*NJUWE*) is comprised of three parts: the context words and their composing characters, the polarity of sentences and the polarity of labeled words, as is shown in Fig. 2. Given a target word w_i, we will utilize its embedding x_i to predict its context words w_{i-1}, w_{i+1} and their composing characters c_{i-1}, c_{i+1}. Obviously the window size is 3 in this example and we can set it to 5 or others. As w_i is contained in the sentence s_j whose representation is se_j, x_i is also used to predict $spol_j$, the polarity of s_j. If w_i is a seed word, its polarity pol_i will also be predicted.

Context Information: We follow [2] to build a character-enhanced word embedding model as the first part of our feature learning method. We will realize this part based on

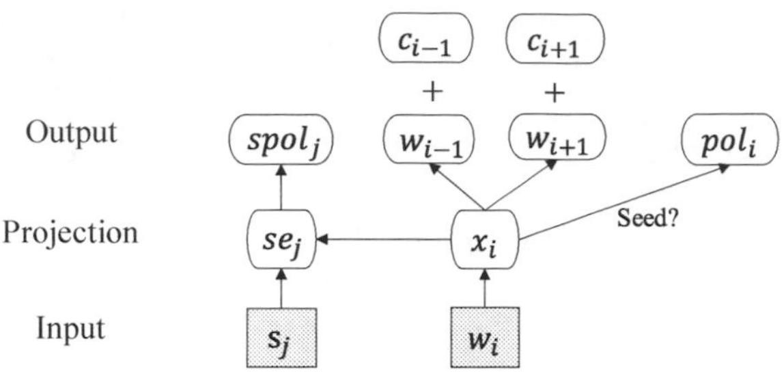

Fig. 2. Model of *NJUWE.*

skip-gram model to better integrate with the other parts. Skip-gram aims at predicting the context words given the target word. The optimization target is to maximize the average log probability below:

$$f_1 = \sum\nolimits_{w \in T} \log p(context(w)|w) \tag{1}$$

Where T is the occurrence of each word in the corpus, w is the target word and *context(w)* is the corresponding context words in the window. In order to accelerate the training procedure, we adopt Negative Sampling [24]. The objective is to distinguish the target word from the noise distribution using logistic regression. In the ideal situation, the probability of predicting the target word as w should be maximized and the probability of predicting the target word as other words should be minimized. We represent a context word x_j with both character embeddings and word embedding to get its embedding $\boldsymbol{x_j}$. The formula can be then written as:

$$\begin{aligned} f_1 = \sum_{w \in T} \sum_{w' \in context(w)} \sum_{u \in \{w\} \cup NEG\{w\}} & [L_{(u)}^{w'} * log(\sigma(\boldsymbol{x}_w^T * \theta^u)) \\ & + \left(1 - L_{(u)}^{w'}\right) * log\left(1 - \sigma\left(\boldsymbol{x}_w^T * \boldsymbol{\theta}^u\right)\right)] \end{aligned} \tag{2}$$

$$\boldsymbol{x_w} = \frac{1}{2} * \left(\boldsymbol{e_w} + \frac{1}{m}\sum\nolimits_{k=1}^{m} \boldsymbol{c_k}\right) \tag{3}$$

Where $\boldsymbol{e_w}$ is the word embedding of w, $\boldsymbol{c_k}$ is the embedding of the k-th character in w, m is the number of characters in w and $L_{(u)}^{w'}$ is an indicator function which equals 1 if the sample u is predicted as w', otherwise 0. $\boldsymbol{\theta}^u$ is the auxiliary vector of u.

Sentence Sentiment Information: In this part, each sentence s is represented as a vector $\boldsymbol{s}$ which is the average of addition of embeddings of words in it. Since we deal with microblog sentences with emoticons indicating their sentiment polarities, we can utilize a sentence representation to predict the sentence polarity, which is actually a golden standard. The objective of the second part is to maximize the log sentiment probability below:

$$f_2 = \sum\nolimits_{s \in S} logp(spol \mid s) \tag{4}$$

Where S is the occurrence of each sentence in the corpus and *spol* is the polarity of a sentence. An optimization borrowing Negative Sample is used here. We treat the predicted polarity that equals the golden standard as the positive sample and otherwise negative sample. Then the formula can be written as:

$$\begin{aligned} f_2 = \sum_{s \in S} \sum_{p\_s \in \{spol\} \cup NEG\{spol\}} & [L_{(p\_s)}^{spol} * log\left(\sigma\left(s^T * \theta^{p\_s}\right)\right) + \\ & \left(1 - L_{(p\_s)}^{spol}\right) * log\left(1 - \sigma\left(s^T * \theta^{p\_s}\right)\right)] \end{aligned} \tag{5}$$

$$s = \frac{1}{n} * \sum\nolimits_{w \in s} w \tag{6}$$

Where n is the number of words in a sentence and p_s is the predicted polarity of the sentence. Other parameters are similar to the description above.

Word Sentiment Information: Inspired by the discovery that sentence sentiment information greatly improves the quality of representation learning [7], we try to utilize sentiment information of labeled words to get better performance. We hope to predict the polarity of a word, which is actually known after seed expansion, with the corresponding word representation. Optimization similar to Negative Sampling is also used here. The objective of this part is to maximize the log sentiment probability:

$$\begin{aligned} f_3 = \sum_{w \in D} logp(pol \mid x_w) = \sum_{w \in D} \sum_{pol \in \{p\_w\} \cup NEG\{p\_w\}} & [L_{(p\_w)}^{pol} * \\ log\left(\sigma\left(x_w^T * \theta^{p\_w}\right)\right) + \left(1 - L_{(p\_w)}^{pol}\right) * log\left(1 - \sigma\left(x_w^T * \theta^{p\_w}\right)\right)] & \end{aligned} \tag{7}$$

Where D is the occurrence of each labeled word, *pol* is the polarity of the word, p_w is the golden standard and other parameters are similar to parameters in Eq. (5).

As a whole, we try to maximize the linear combination of the three parts:

$$f = \alpha_1 * f_1 + \alpha_2 * f_2 + \alpha_3 * f_3 \tag{8}$$

Where the parameters α_1, α_2 and α_3 weigh the different parts and the value is limited to 0 or 1. We train our neural model with stochastic gradient ascent. The window size is 5, the embedding length is 200 and the initial learning rate is 0.025 in our experiment.

3.2 Lexicon Construction

In this section, we follow the method introduced in [7] to build a machine learning based classifier to predict the sentiment polarity of a word in the corpus according to the word representation learned in Sect. 3.1. The feature vector of the word is the input of the classifier and word sentiment polarity is the output. Words of the same polarity are grouped together and a sentiment lexicon is formed.

Firstly, we collect and sort all the words in the Sina microblog corpus by Jieba[4] tokenizer. We select the most frequent 700 words and arrange 5 native speakers to annotate the sentiment polarity (positive, negative or others). Majority voting method is used when they have disagreement about the annotation. We get 135 positive words, 66 negative words and 299 most frequent other words as seeds.

Then we expand seed words in the same way as [7] utilizing HIT IR-Lab Tongyici Cilin[5]. After this step, we obtain 1175 positive words, 897 negative words and 1176 other words. These serve as labeled data.

A Random Forest (RF) classifier is trained in the next step. The input is the embeddings of each labeled word and the output is the sentiment score. The score of positive words, negative words and other words is 1, 2 and 3 respectively.

Finally, each of the words sorted in the first step except the labeled words, is mapped into a vector through *NJUWE* and the vector is fed to the RF classifier to predict the sentiment polarity. Positive and negative words obtained in this step are added to the sentiment lexicon together with labeled words.

4 Experimental Evaluation

We will evaluate the quality of our approach in this section. Since sentiment lexicon is built with the purpose of guiding sentiment classification, we will first evaluate the result of sentence-level classification utilizing lexicon information. The better the effect of the classification is, the higher the quality of the lexicon is. Next, we will evaluate the quality of our feature learning approach. Specifically, we will carry on word similarity computation and word-level sentiment classification which is based on word embeddings obtained from different feature learning approaches.

4.1 Corpus and Settings

We use Weibo corpus offered by [4] to train our model and collect our lexicon. This corpus contains about 5.88 million Chinese microblogs with emoticons from October 1, 2011 to July 31, 2012. We make the assumption that if a microblog only contains positive emoticon(s), it conveys positive emotion, so does a microblog with only negative emoticon(s). So we respectively pick one million sentences with only positive emoticons and another one million with only negative emoticons. Word segmentation using Jieba tokenizer and stop words removing are done in advance. Sentences with only stop words or emoticons or without Chinese words are ignored.

[4] https://www.python.org/pypi/jieba/.

[5] https://pypi.ltp-cloud.com.

4.2 Evaluation of Lexicon

We will evaluate the effect of sentiment lexicon when it is used to guide sentence-level sentiment classification, by both supervised and unsupervised methods. Accuracy and Macro-averaged F-measure (Macro-F1) are calculated to show the result of classification and measure the usability of sentiment lexicon in classification.

Unsupervised Sentiment Classification. For unsupervised sentiment classification, we calculate the sum of scores of all sentiment words in a sentence with the help of the sentiment lexicon. If the sum score is greater than 0, then the sentence will be judged as positive, otherwise negative.

Supervised Sentiment Classification. To evaluate the effect of the sentiment lexicon in supervised sentiment classification, besides counting the sum of scores of sentiment words, we also combine some pre-defined features. Considering characteristics of Sina microblogs, we follow [25] to extract some features as follows: (1) negative words; (2) degree words; (3) punctuation; (4) emoticon. Each sentence is represented as a feature vector made up of the extracted features. Details about the features are present in [25]. Then the feature vector is put into a traditional machine learning based classifier (here we use a RF model) to predict the sentiment polarity of the sentence.

Table 1. Statistic of sentence-level classification datasets.

Dataset	Training set		Test set	
	Positive	Negative	Positive	Negative
SC2012	407	1757	41	229
SC2013	4951	4991	1883	2660
SC2014	2078	1943	1037	892

Setups. For supervised classification, we utilize data offered by microblog sentence-level sentiment classification task in NLPCC2012–2014 (*SC2012–2014*) to train a RF classifier respectively. For simplicity, we group fine-grained sentiment labels (e.g., "happiness", "like", "disgust", "anger") into two classes: positive and negative. Since training data offered by the tasks is too little compared to the respective test data, we use test data in NLPCC tasks as our training data to train the RF model and check the classification performance on the given training data, which is our test data. We apply the RF model to predict our test data in which polarities are offered as the golden standard. For unsupervised classification, we use sentences in the original training data in *SC2012–2014*. The distribution of positive and negative sentences in the three data sets is present in Table 1. Notice that for each data set, the training set and test set have been exchanged here.

We compare the performance of our lexicon (*NJUSD*) with several existing Chinese sentiment lexicon[6], including *NTUSD* from National Taiwan University, the

[6] https://download.csdn.net/download/yunliangshen/9945179.

Table 2. Statistic of sentiment lexicons.

Lexicon	NJUSD	NTUSD	HowNet	THUD
Positive	4183	2812	836	5568
Negative	5087	8278	1254	4469

Chinese part of *HowNet* and Chinese Derogatory Dictionary from Tsinghua University (*THUD*). Statistics of these lexicons are shown in Table 2.

Results. Accuracy and Macro-F1 of classifying microblog sentences using different lexicons are present in Fig. 3. As we can see, both unsupervised and supervised classification tasks guided by *NJUSD* achieve the best performance. Only considering sentiment words, our lexicon yields 7.14% improvement on Accuracy and 1.02% improvement on Macro-F1 on average. By utilizing other features, our lexicon yields 7.69% improvement on Accuracy and 5.11% improvement on Macro-F1 on average.

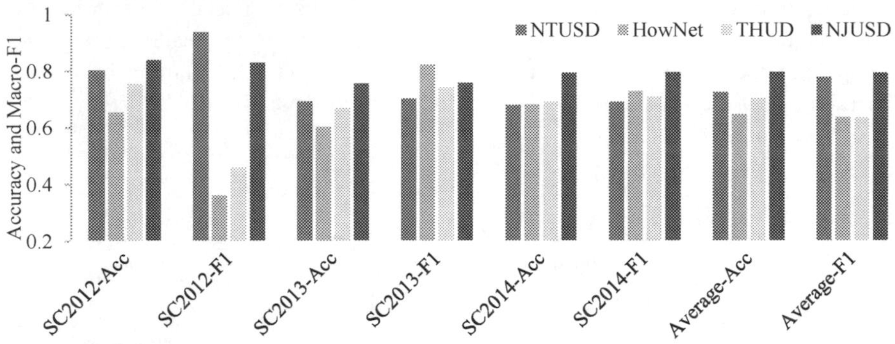

(a) Unsupervised method

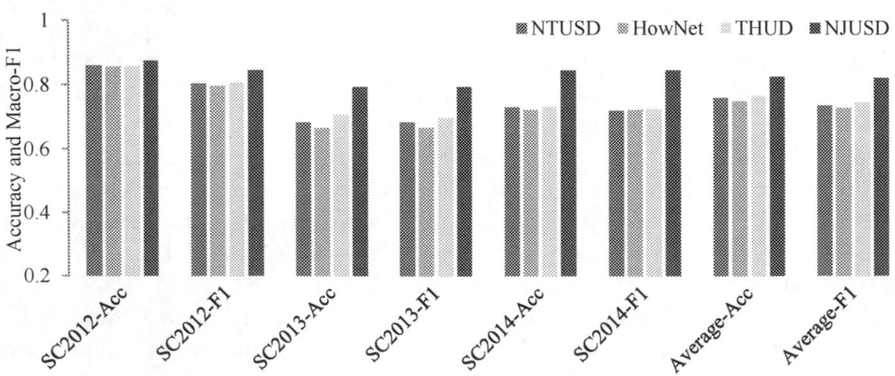

(b) Supervised method

Fig. 3. Accuracy and Macro-F1 on sentiment classification datasets using different lexicons.

That proves the availability and superiority of *NJUSD* in sentence-level sentiment classification. Performances of most lexicons are improved by adding pre-defined features, which agrees with the results in [7, 19].

4.3 Evaluation of Feature Learning

In order to demonstrate the effectiveness and advantage of our feature learning approach, we test the performances of our method and some existing methods when: (1) they are used in words semantic similarity computation; (2) they are used in word-level sentiment classification. In addition, we will see the influence of each composing part in Eq. (8), by ignoring one part at a time and testing the performance of the corresponding performance in word-level sentiment classification.

We use several state-of-the-art word embedding algorithms for comparison, including *CBOW*, *skip-gram* [18], *CWE* [2] and *JWE* [3]. For justice, we implement the last two algorithms based on skip-gram model and accelerate with Negative Sampling, the same as our approach.

Semantic Similarity. In this task, words are represented as vectors through a word embedding method. For a word pair with similar semantics, the similarity score, which is computed as the cosine similarity of word embeddings of the two words, should be high and vice versa. We compute the Spearman's rank correlation coefficient ρ_s [26] between the human-labeled scores and similarity scores computed by embeddings. If ρ_s is close to 1, it means there is a positive correlation the two compared data set. That is, the word embedding properly expresses the word's semantics.

The widely used data sets WordSim-240 and WordSim-297 are selected for word semantics similarity evaluation, which contain 240 and 297 Chinese word pairs respectively. A human-labeled similarity score, ranging from 1 to 10, is assigned to each pair. We remove a word pair if not both words are in the corpus or if the two words are the same. After that, we get 221 word pairs from WordSim-240 and 228 word pairs from WordSim-297.

ρ_s of each data set between given similarity scores and calculated scores are shown in Table 3. From the results, we can see that ρ_s between the human-labeled similarity score and the score got by computing the embeddings trained by *NJUWE* is the highest compared to the state-of-the-art methods. It yields 1.32% improvement on WordSim-240 and 2.33% improvement on WordSim-297. That means that our word embedding method can catch a word's semantics. Our Spearman correlation is smaller than that in [3] when the same word embedding method is applied with the same settings. It arises from our informal corpus and the different word segmentation tools. However, it is still passable.

Table 3. Results of word similarity evaluation.

Dataset	CBOW	Skip-gram	CWE	JWE	NJUWE
WordSim-240	0.4224	0.4443	0.4607	0.4276	**0.4739**
WordSim-297	0.3721	0.4194	0.4099	0.4015	**0.4427**

Sentiment Classification. In this task, words embeddings obtained from different feature learning methods are fed to a RF sentiment classifier to predict the polarity of the word. That requires the feature learning algorithm should not only catch the semantics, but also the sentiment information of a word.

We make the assumption that words appear in all three referential lexicons mentioned in Sect. 4.2 and have the same polarity are correctly labeled with sentiment polarity. We extract 900 such words, in which 450 are positive and 450 are negative. We randomly choose 300 positive and 300 negative words to serve as the training data. The rest of the words are the test data.

Since polarities of these words are known to us, accuracy and Macro-F1 can be calculated to present the performance, as is shown in Table 4. The results show that given a word, *NJUWE* can judge whether it is positive or negative more accurately than other methods. It yields 6.90% improvement on Accuracy and 7.71% improvement on Macro-F1 compared to *CWE*, which achieves the best performance among other methods. It is because our method considers not only the words' context, but also the sentiment of the sentences the words make up.

Table 4. Results of word sentiment classification.

Metric	CBOW	Skip-gram	CWE	JWE	NJUWE
Accuracy	0.5898	0.6289	0.6351	0.5959	**0.7041**
Macro-F1	0.5817	0.6263	0.6332	0.5619	**0.7043**

Influence of Composing Parts. In this part, we will see how the three composing parts in Eq. (8) influence the performance in word-level sentiment classification. Each time a composing part is ignored in training the word embeddings. Then the obtained embeddings are used as features to conduct word-level sentiment classification. Data set and setting are the same as above. Accuracy and Macro-F1 are present in Table 5. *NJUWE-*P_i means the i-th part is not considered in *NJUWE*. We can see that we get the best result if we consider all the three aspects, which proves the meaning of combination of different information in feature learning. However, our experiment shows that if we do not consider the context of words, the classification result will become much worse and if we do not consider the sentence polarity, the classification performance will not decrease that much, which is discordant with the conclusion in [7] that even if the context information is ignored, the performance is still remarkable only utilizing sentiment information. We think it may be because the language we deal with is different and Chinese character information greatly improves the positive influence of word context in feature learning.

Table 5. Results of word sentiment classification ignoring each part.

Metric	NJUWE	NJUWE-P_1	NJUWE-P_2	NJUWE-P_3
Accuracy	**0.7041**	0.5395	0.6562	0.6820
Macro-F1	**0.7043**	0.4978	0.6463	0.6785

5 Conclusion

In this paper, we propose the construction of a microblog-specific Chinese sentiment lexicon. We combine context information, sentence-level sentiment polarity and word-level sentiment polarity to learn features of words in the corpus and classify the words with a RF classifier. Experimental results demonstrate the worth of our sentiment lexicon in helping predict sentiment polarity and the benefits of our feature learning algorithm in learning semantic representations.

In the future, we will try more flexible weights to each of the three aspects in feature learning to optimize the result. We also plan to take more aspects, like user information, time information and domain information into consideration to build a more accurate and flexible sentiment lexicon. We hope to realize customized sentiment analysis in our work afterwards.

Acknowledgment. This work was supported by the National Key R&D Program of China (2016YFC0800803).

References

1. Liu, B.: Sentiment Analysis and Opinion Mining. University of Illinois at Chicago, Chicago (2012)
2. Chen, X., Xu, L., Liu, Z.: Joint learning of character and word embeddings. In: Proceedings of the Twenty-Fourth International Joint Conference on Artificial Intelligence, pp. 1236–1242 (2015)
3. Yu, J., Jian, X., Xin, H.: Joint embeddings of chinese words, characters, and fine-grained subcharacter components. In: Proceedings of the 2017 Conference on Empirical Methods in Natural Language Processing, pp. 286–291 (2017)
4. Feng, S., Song, K., Wang, D.: A word-emoticon mutual reinforcement ranking model for building sentiment lexicon from massive collection of microblogs. World Wide Web **18**, 949–967 (2015)
5. Wu, F., Huang, Y., Song, Y.: Towards building a high-quality microblog-specific Chinese sentiment lexicon. Decis. Support Syst. **87**, 39–49 (2016)
6. Tan, J., Xu, M., Shang, L., Jia, X.: Sentiment analysis for images on microblogging by integrating textual information with multiple kernel learning. In: Booth, R., Zhang, M.-L. (eds.) PRICAI 2016. LNCS, vol. 9810, pp. 496–506. Springer, Cham (2016). https://doi.org/10.1007/978-3-319-42911-3_41
7. Tang, D., Wei, F., Qin, B.: Building large-scale Twitter-specific sentiment lexicon: a representation learning approach. In: Proceedings of the 25th International Conference on Computational Linguistics: Technical Papers, pp. 172–182 (2014)
8. Hu, M., Liu, B.: Mining and summarizing customer reviews. In: Proceedings of the Tenth ACM SIGKDD International Conference on Knowledge Discovery and Data Mining, pp. 168–177 (2004)
9. Heerschop, B., Hogenboom, A., Frasincar, F.: Sentiment lexicon creation from lexical resources. In: Abramowicz, W. (ed.) BIS 2011. LNBIP, vol. 87, pp. 185–196. Springer, Heidelberg (2011). https://doi.org/10.1007/978-3-642-21863-7_16

10. Esuli, A., Sebastiani, F.: PageRanking WordNet synsets: an application to opinion mining. In: Proceedings of the 45th Annual Meeting of the Association for Computational Linguistics, ACL, pp. 424–431 (2010)
11. Hatzivassiloglou, V., McKeown, K.: Predicting the semantic orientation of adjectives. In: Proceedings of the Eighth Conference on European Chapter of the Association for Computational Linguistics, pp. 174–181 (1997)
12. Kanayama, H., Nasukawa, T.: Fully automatic lexicon expansion for domain-oriented sentiment analysis. In: Proceedings of the 2006 Conference on Empirical Methods in Natural Language Processing, pp. 355–363 (2006)
13. Qiu, G., Liu, B., Bu, J., Chen, C.: Opinion word expansion and target extraction through double propagation. Comput. Linguist. **37**(1), 9–27 (2011)
14. Turney, P.: Thumbs up or thumbs down?: Semantic orientation applied to unsupervised classification of reviews. In: Proceedings of the 40th Annual Meeting on Association for Computational Linguistics, pp. 417–424 (2002)
15. Hamilton, W., Clark, K., Leskovec, J.: Inducing domain-specific sentiment lexicons from unlabeled corpora. In: Proceedings of the 2016 Conference on Empirical Methods in Natural Language Processing, pp. 595–605 (2016)
16. Islam, M., Inkpen, D.: Second order co-occurrence PMI for determining the semantic similarity of words. In: Language Resources and Evaluation, pp. 1033–1038 (2006)
17. Vo, D., Zhang, Y.: Don't count, predict! An automatic approach to learning sentiment lexicons for short text. In: Proceedings of the 54th Annual Meeting of the Association for Computational Linguistics, pp. 219–224 (2016)
18. Mikolov, T., Chen, K., Corrado, G.: Efficient estimation of word representations in vector space. http://arxiv.org/abs/1309.4168 (2013)
19. Wang, L., Xia, R.: Sentiment lexicon construction with representation learning based on hierarchical sentiment supervision. In: Proceedings of the 2017 Conference on Empirical Methods in Natural Language Processing, pp. 513–521 (2017)
20. Su, T., Lee, H.: Learning Chinese word representations from glyphs of characters. In: Proceedings of the 2017 Conference on Empirical Methods in Natural Language Processing, pp. 264–273 (2017)
21. Xu, J., Liu, J., Zhang, L.: Improve Chinese word embeddings by exploiting internal structure. In: Proceedings of NAACL-HLT, pp. 1041–1050 (2016)
22. Yin, R., Wang, Q., Liu, R.: Multi-granularity Chinese word embedding. In: Proceedings of the 2016 Conference on Empirical Methods in Natural Language Processing, pp. 981–986 (2016)
23. Sun, Y., Lin, L., Yang, N., Ji, Z., Wang, X.: Radical-enhanced Chinese character embedding. In: Loo, C.K., Yap, K.S., Wong, K.W., Teoh, A., Huang, K. (eds.) ICONIP 2014. LNCS, vol. 8835, pp. 279–286. Springer, Cham (2014). https://doi.org/10.1007/978-3-319-12640-1_34
24. Mikolov, T., Sutskever, L., Chen, K.: Distributed representations of words and phrases and their compositionality. In: Advances in Neural Information Processing Systems, pp. 3111–3119 (2013)
25. Mohammad, S.: Building the state-of-the-art in sentiment analysis of tweets. In: Proceedings of the Seventh International Workshop on Semantic Evaluation Exercises, SemEval 2013, pp. 321–327 (2013)
26. Myers, J., Well, A., Lorch, R.: Research Design and Statistical Analysis, 2nd edn. Routledge, London (2010)

Phonologically Aware BiLSTM Model for Mongolian Phrase Break Prediction with Attention Mechanism

Rui Liu, FeiLong Bao(✉), Guanglai Gao, Hui Zhang, and Yonghe Wang

Inner Mongolia Key Laboratory of Mongolian Information Processing Technology, College of Computer Science, Inner Mongolia University, Hohhot 010021, China
liurui_imu@163.com, csfeilong@imu.edu.cn

Abstract. Phrase break prediction is the first and most important component in increasing naturalness and intelligibility of text-to-speech (TTS) systems. Most works rely on language specific resources, large annotated corpus and feature engineering to perform well. However, phrase break prediction from text for Mongolian speech synthesis is still a great challenge because the data sparse problem due to the scarcity of resources. In this paper, we introduce a Bidirectional Long Short-Term Memory (BiLSTM) model with attention mechanism which uses the position-based enhanced phonological representations, word embeddings and character embeddings to achieve state of the art performance. The position-based enhanced phonological representations, derived from a separately BiLSTM model, are comprised of phoneme and syllable embeddings which take along position information. By using an attention mechanism, the model is able to dynamically decide how much information to use from a word or phonological component. To handle Out-of-Vocabulary (OOV) problem, we incorporated word, phonological and character embeddings together as inputs to the model. Experimental results show the proposed method significantly outperforms the systems which only used the word embeddings by successfully leveraging position-based phonologically information and attention mechanism.

Keywords: Mongolian · Phrase break · Phonologically
Attention mechanism · Position

1 Introduction

Phrase break plays an important role in both naturalness and intelligibility of speech [1]. It breaks long utterances into meaningful units of information and

This research was supports by the China national natural science foundation (No. 61563040, No. 61773224), Inner Mongolian nature science foundation (No. 2016ZD06) and the Enhancing Comprehensive Strength Foundation of Inner Mongolia University (No. 10000-16010109-23).

X. Geng and B.-H. Kang (Eds.): PRICAI 2018, LNAI 11012, pp. 217–231, 2018.
https://doi.org/10.1007/978-3-319-97304-3_17

makes the speech more understandable. Therefore, identifying the break boundaries of prosodic phrases from the given text is crucial in speech synthesis. Many statistical methods have been investigated to model speech prosody, including classification and regression tree [2], hidden Markov model [3], maximum entropy model [4] and conditional random fields (CRF) with linguistic class features (such as part-of-speech (POS), length of word etc.) [5–13]. However, the linguistic class features are discrete linguistic representations of words, which don't take into account the distributional behavior of words. Recent developments in neural architecture and representation learning have opened the door to models that can discover useful features automatically from the unlabelled data. With this development, neural networks and word embeddings have been increasingly investigated in order to minimize the effort of feature engineering and achieved similar or even superior performance over conventional method in phrase break prediction tasks [14–21]. Vadapalli et al. [17] utilized deep neural networks (DNNs) and recurrent neural networks (RNNs) to model phrase break by using word embeddings. Zheng et al. [20] proposed a character-enhanced word embedding model and a multi-prototype character embedding model for Mandarin phrase break prediction. Klimkov et al. [21] investigated how various types of textual features can improve phrase break prediction and BiLSTM and word embeddings proved to be beneficial.

All these methods mentioned have made great contributions, while they heavily rely on the availability of hand-labeled training data. As a result, these methods can not be used for languages where the necessary linguistic resources are not readily available, and manual annotation of data is expensive and time-consuming. Thus it is hard to work with scripts of Mongolian languages, which are agglutinative in nature and lacks sufficient training corpus. A better solution may lie in dealing with sub-word units like stem and suffixes. Liu et al. [22] proposed a suffix segmentation method, they segmented the ending suffix followed by the Narrow No-Break Space (NNBSP) [23–25] in Mongolian nouns according to the characteristics of Mongolia word formation and then treated them as individual tokens to model Mongolian phrase break. However, the naturalness of synthetic speech is less than satisfactory, especially without a good rhythm.

In this work, we make full use of phonological information to model Mongolian phrase break. Our underlying assumption is that prosodic phrases are likely to be transliterated. Additionally, phenomena such as vowel harmony manifest explicitly in phoneme and syllable representation and can potentially be helpful for Mongolian phrase break.

We first identify the sequence of phonemes and syllables automatically and use Bidirectional Long Short-Term Memory (BiLSTM) networks to encode phoneme and syllable level information to a phonological representation, which captures the phonological information of the word. Then we combine word level representation and phonological level representation to a complex representation. In addition, we use character embeddings to handle the Out-of-Vocabulary (OOV) problem as in [26]. At last, the complex representation and character embeddings are comprised together to a joint embedding and we feed it in another separately BiLSTM to model context information of each Mongolian word and decode the corresponding right phrase break label. Second, we propose a position-based enhanced method for phonological embeddings. General phonological embeddings cannot distinguish between uses of the same phoneme and syllable in different contexts. We add a positional tag, e.g. the first/second/third/etc., for each phoneme and syllable in each word. We learn phoneme and syllable embeddings from each positionally tagged sequence of phonemes and syllables for each word. Third, we also propose an attention module which chooses the most informative component among available ones (in our case, word embeddings, phonological embeddings) to extract context form.

We experiment our approach with Mongolian languages, and the reported results show the proposed approach achieves the best performance. The phoneme and syllable representation provides richer phonological information for word representation and plays an important role in the neural network architecture. Finally, we incorporate the proposed phrase break model in a Mongolian Text-to-Speech (TTS) system and demonstrate its usefulness with listening tests.

Our contributions are the three-fold: (1) We propose a BiLSTM approach to predict Mongolian prosody phrase labels leverage phonologically information from Mongolian phoneme and syllable without any feature engineering. (2) The position-based enhanced phonological embedding method, which takes into account the positional information in different contexts of the same phoneme and syllable, are investigated. (3) We propose a general attention module that selectively chooses information sources to extract primary context form, maximizing information gain from each component: words, phonological information (comprised of phoneme and syllable embeddings).

2 Proposed Model

Figure 1 shows the overall architecture of the Mongolian phrase break prediction model. The set of input features for each token is basically formed by three distinct components: the word embedding (WE), phonologically embedding (PE) derived from phoneme (PhoE) and syllable embeddings (SylE), and character embeddings (CE). For each given token, we first obtain PhoE and SylE, then we concatenate these two embeddings to get a new embedding called PE. Attach the PE to WE to form a complex embedding with attention mechanism. At last, CE is used along with the complex embedding as a joint embedding. We fed the joint embedding into BiLSTM [27,28] phrase break prediction model to decode the corresponding right phrase break label. We formulate each component of the model in the following subsections.

2.1 Input Features

2.1.1 Word Embeddings

Word embedding map words into a space where semantically similar words have similar vector representations [29]. Based on this idea, more and more embedding

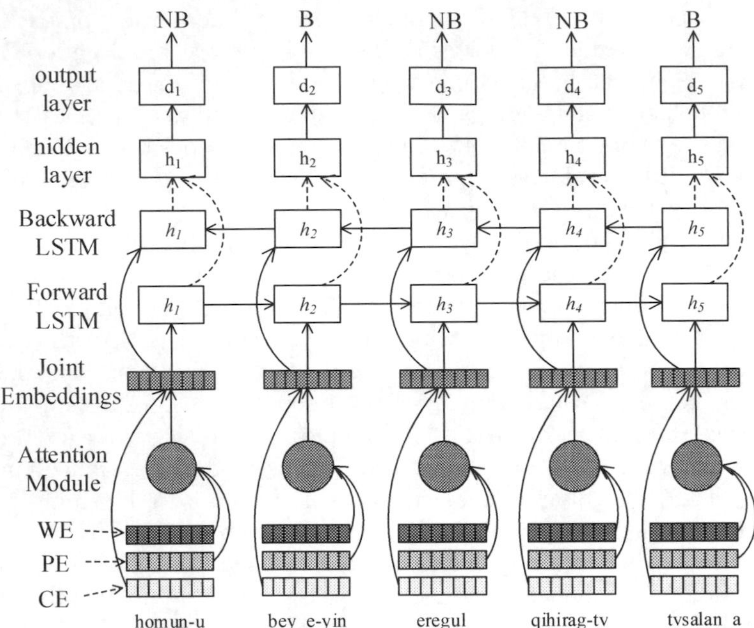

Fig. 1. Mongolian phrase break prediction model. The WE and PE (Fig. 2) are concatenated with attention mechanism, CE is used along with the concatenated embedding to form a joint embedding as input; a BiLSTM produces context-dependent representations; the information is passed through a hidden layer and the output layer. The outputs are either probability distributions for softmax. (WE: word embedding; PE: Phonological embedding; CE: Character embedding)

models have been developed, including continuous bag-of words model (CBOW), Skip-Gram model [30], and Global C&W (GloVe) [31]. We use Skip-Gram model to train the word embedding representation.

The training objective of the Skip-Gram model is to find word representations that are useful for predicting the surrounding words in a raw text. More formally, given a sequence of training words $w_1, w_2, w_3, \ldots, w_T$, the objective of the Skip-Gram model is to maximize the average log probability

$$\frac{1}{T}\sum_{t=1}^{T}\sum_{-c\leq j\leq c, j\neq 0} \log p(w_{t+j}|w_t) \tag{1}$$

where c is the size of the training context (which can be a function of the center word w_t). Larger c results in more training examples and thus can lead to a higher accuracy, at the expense of the training time. The basic Skip-Gram formulation defines $p(w_{t+j}|w_t)$ using the *softmax* function:

$$p(w_O|w_I) = \frac{\exp({v'_{wO}}^\top v_{wI})}{\sum_{w}^{W=1}\exp({v'_w}^\top v_{wI})} \tag{2}$$

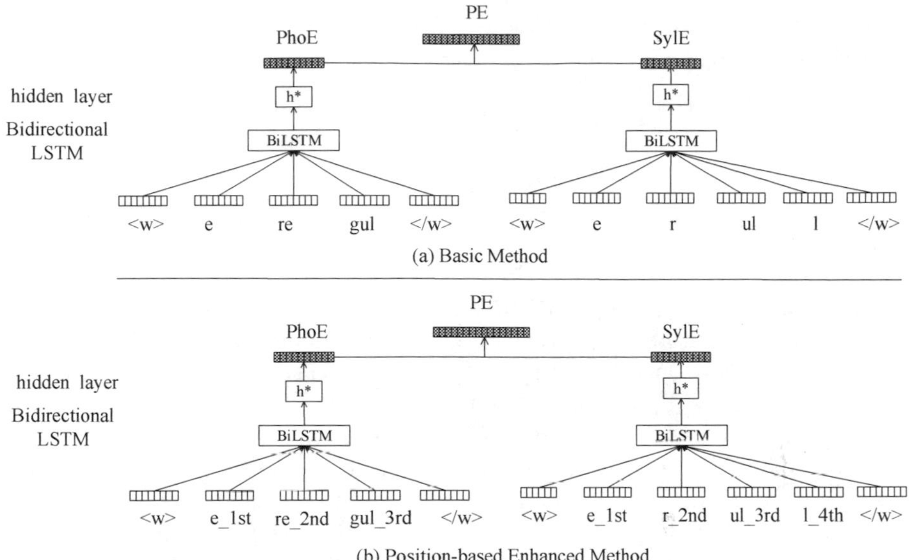

Fig. 2. (a) Basic method, (b) Position-based enhanced method for PE. Take a Mongolian word "eregul" for example, it contains three syllables: 'e', 're', 'gul' and four phonemes: 'e', 'r', 'ul', 'l'. (PhoE: phoneme embeddings; SylE: syllable embeddings)

where v_w and $v_w^{'}$ are the "input" and "output" vector representations of w, and W is the number of words in the vocabulary. This formulation is impractical because the cost of computing $\bigtriangledown \log p(w_O|w_I)$ is proportional to W, which is often large (10^5–10^7 terms).

2.1.2 Phonological Embeddings

PE are abstracted from these two vectors: PhoE and SylE. Figure 2 shows the process of obtaining the PE, through BiLSTM embedding network architecture, by using two methods in detail. We investigate two embedding methods for PE as shown in Fig. 2(a) and (b). We denote the two methods as "*Basic Method*" and "*Position-based Enhanced Method*".

Basic Method. In Fig. 2(a), each words in a Mongolian sentences is broken down into individual smaller phonological unit: phoneme and syllable, these are then mapped to a sequence of vectors $(v_1, \ldots, v_t)$, which are passed through a BiLSTM:

$$\overrightarrow{h_i^*} = LSTM(v_i, \overrightarrow{h_{i-1}^*}) \tag{3}$$

$$\overleftarrow{h_i^*} = LSTM(v_i, \overleftarrow{h_{i-1}^*}) \tag{4}$$

We then use the last hidden vectors from each of the LSTM components, concatenate them together, and pass the result through a separate non-linear layer.

$$h^* = [\overrightarrow{h^*_R}; \overleftarrow{h^*_l}] \qquad PhoE(SylE) = \tanh(W_m h^*) \tag{5}$$

where W_m is a weight matrix mapping the concatenated hidden vectors from both LSTMs into output representation *PhoE* or *SylE*. We then concatenate the PhoE and SylE to obtain PE.

Position-Based Enhanced Method. In the case of Mongolian phonemes and syllable, the same token holds different pronunciation information in different contexts. General *PhoE* and *SylE* in Fig. 2(a) cannot distinguish between uses of the same phoneme and syllable in different contexts. Motivated by [32], we add a positional tag for each phoneme and syllable in each word. Instead of keep three embeddings for each token corresponding to its three types of positions in a word, i.e., Begin, Middle and End. We add the novel positional tag, e.g. the **first/second/third/etc.** as shown in Fig. 2(b), according to the count of phonemes and syllables within a word, and then allow the model to learn more exquisite phonologically information for each specific word.

As demonstrated in Eqs. (3) and (4), we take a word (w_i) and its phonemes and syllables, $(p_1, \ldots, p_t)$ or $(s_1, \ldots, s_t)$, for example. We will take different embeddings of a phoneme and syllable according to its position within (w_i). That is, when building the embeddings (v_i), we will take the embeddings (v_first_i) for the beginning phoneme p_1 or syllable s_1 of the word w_i, take the embeddings (v_second_i) for the second phoneme p_2 or syllable s_2, and take the embeddings (v_third_i) for the third phoneme p_3 or syllable s_3. The rest is similar. Hence, Eqs. (3) and (4) can be rewritten as if we rename the new embeddings v_i as v_pos_i:

$$\overrightarrow{h^*_i} = LSTM(v\_pos_i, \overrightarrow{h^*_{i-1}}) \tag{6}$$

$$\overleftarrow{h^*_i} = LSTM(v\_pos_i, \overleftarrow{h^*_{i-1}}) \tag{7}$$

In the position-based enhanced phoneme and syllable embedding method, we learn new phoneme and syllable embeddings from positional tagged sequence of phonemes and syllables for each word. Various embeddings of each phoneme and syllable are differentiated by the position in the word, and the embedding assignment for a specific phoneme and syllable in a word can be automatically determined by the position. The position-based enhanced PE is obtained by concatenating the new PhoE and SylE.

2.1.3 Character Embeddings

CE are obtained using the same BiLSTM as described in Sect. 2.1.2. The BiLSTM takes as input a sequence of character of each Mongolian word and the last hidden states are used to create CE for the input word.

2.2 Attention Mechanism

We now have three alternative feature representation for each word - WE_t is an embedding learned on the word level as described in Sect. 2.1.1, PE_t is a representation dynamically built from the individual unit in the *t-th* word of the input Mongolian text, and CE_t is a representation learned from character unit as described in Sect. 2.1.3. Motivated by [33], instead of concatenating PE with the WE, the two vectors are added together using a weight sum, where the weights are predicted by a two-layer network:

$$w = \sigma(M_z^{(3)} \tanh(M_z^{(1)} \cdot WE + M_z^{(2)} \cdot PE)) \tag{8}$$

$$WE^* = w \cdot WE + (1 - w) \cdot PE \tag{9}$$

where $M_z^{(1)}$, $M_z^{(2)}$ and $M_z^{(3)}$ are weight metrics for calculating w, and $\sigma()$ is the logistic function with values in the range [0, 1]. The vector w has the same dimensions as WE or PE, acting as the weight between the two vectors. It allows the model to dynamically decide how much information to use from the phonologically component or the word embedding.

We concatenate the WE_t and PE_t into a complex vector (WE^*) using attention module, and then append the CE_t to WE^* to generate the joint embeddings (JE) as a new word-level representation for the phrase break prediction model: $JE = [WE^*; CE]$.

2.3 BiLSTM Phrase Break Model

As shown in Fig. 1. JE which concatenate word, phonological and character embeddings are given as input to two LSTM components moving in opposite directions through the text, creating context-specific representations. The respective forward- and backward-conditioned representations are concatenated for each word position, resulting in representations that are conditioned on the whole sequence:

$$\overrightarrow{h_t} = LSTM(JE_t, \overrightarrow{h_{t-1}}) \tag{10}$$

$$\overleftarrow{h_t} = LSTM(JE_t, \overleftarrow{h_{t-1}}) \tag{11}$$

$$h_t = [\overrightarrow{h_t}; \overleftarrow{h_t}] \tag{12}$$

We include an extra narrow hidden layer on top of the LSTM, which allows the model to detect higher-level feature combinations, while constraining it to be small forces it to focus on more generalisable patterns:

$$d_t = \tanh(W_d h_t) \tag{13}$$

where W_d is a weight matrix between the layers, and the size of d_t is intentionally kept small.

Finally, to produce phrase break label predictions, we use a softmax layer. An alternative approach for the output layer is using a CRF layer as in [34], but we find that softmax output layer yields better results in our experiments. The softmax calculates a normalised probability distribution over all the possible labels of each word:

$$P(y_t = k|d_t) = \frac{e^{W_{o,k}d_t}}{\sum_{\tilde{k}\epsilon K} e^{W_{o,\tilde{k}}d_t}} \tag{14}$$

where $P(y_t = k|d_t)$ is the probability of the label of the t-th word (y_t) being k, K is the set of all possible labels, and $W_{o,k}$ is the k-th row of output weight matrix W_o. To optimise this model, we minimise categorical cross entropy, which is equivalent to minimising the negative log-probability of the correct labels:

$$E = -\sum_{T}^{t=1} \log(P(y_t|d_t)) \tag{15}$$

This approach assumes that the word-level, phonological-level components learn somewhat disjoint information, and it is beneficial to give word embedding only as input to the Mongolian phrase break prediction system. It allows the model to take advantages of phonological information from the phoneme and syllable in Mongolian.

3 Experiments and Analysis

3.1 Datasets

In the experiments, each word in a sentence was assigned to one of the following two PB labels: "B" and "NB" means *"break after a word"* and *"non-break"* respectively. For evaluating the effectiveness of the proposed approach, we rely on a corpus corresponding to the TTS database recorded by a professional native Mongolian female speaker. The corpus contains 59k sentences, more than 409k words, 1065k syllables and 1885k phonemes. The whole corpus is partitioned into training and test set for all experiments according to 4:1.

The word embedding train data were crawled from mainstream websites in Mongolian. After cleaning web page tags and filtering longer sentences, its token size and vocabulary are about 200 million and 3 million respectively.

3.2 Setup

For data preprocessing, all digits were replaced with the character "0". Any words that occurred only once in the training data were replaced by the generic OOV token for word embeddings, but were still used in the phonological embedding components. All tokens are initialized with 200 dimensional pre-trained vectors as illustrated in Sect. 2.1.1 and updated during training. The embeddings for phoneme and syllable parts were set to length 100 respectively and initialised randomly.

The LSTM layer size was set to 200 in each direction for different level components. The hidden layer d has size 50. Parameters were optimised using *AdaDelta* with default learning rate 1.0 and sentences were grouped into batch of size 64. *Softmax* was used as the output layer for all the experiments. Performance on the training set was measured at every epoch and training was stopped if performance had not improved for 7 epoches; the best-performing model on training stage was then used for evaluation on the test set. Results are reported on the test set in terms of the Precision (P), Recall (R) and F-score (F) which is defined as the harmonic mean of the P and R.

3.3 Main Results

With this experiment, all Mongolian phrase break prediction systems are built at different input features. Table 1 report results from ablation tests experiments, with or without *Attention mechanism* (Att) or *Position-based enhanced method* (Pos), on various input features in Mongolian.

Our proposed method performs better than other benchmarks with the optimal configuration. Firstly, word embeddings alone perform rather poorly due to the challenges of reliably estimating them for a large vocabulary given a small dataset. Attach the PhoE or SylE to the word embeddings provide a significant performance boost. This indicates that phonological information benefits the Mongolian phrase break prediction from phoneme or syllable components. Using 'WE+PE' yields a further improvement in F score. Secondly, usage of attention mechanism seems to improve performance in all system in Table 1. This indicates that the attention mechanism is able to focus on the most effective information (word or phonological) adaptive to each token to maximize the information gain. Thirdly, results show the effectiveness of the position-based enhanced method for all model as well. In most cases, position-based phoneme and syllable embeddings can effectively distinguish different meanings of a word, which indicates, (1) modeling multiple senses of phonemes and syllables are important for phonological embeddings; (2) position information is adequate in addressing ambiguity. Among these, the proposed joint embedding ('WE+PE+CE') reaches the best performance for the usage of phonological information as well as the capability to fix the OOV problem.

3.4 Comparison of Phonological Embeddings Dimensions

In this experiment, we study the effect of varying the phonological embedding dimension on the performance of the model for Mongolian phrase break prediction. We use the best system ('WE+PE+CE' system with attention mechanism and position-based enhanced method) as described in Sect. 3.3 with all the parameters and hyperparameters unchanged, except for the dimension of PE (WE has the same dimensions as PE). We vary the PE dimension and compute the performance, in terms of F-Score. Figure 3 shows the results of this experiment.

Here we can see an indistinctive change in the performance on phrase break prediction when the PE dimension is varied. As it show in Fig. 3, the 200 dimension PE reach the best, while too much dimension will include other boring

Table 1. Ablation tests on different input features for Mongolian phrase break. (Att: Attention Mechanism; Pos: Position-based Enhanced Method)

Input features	Model	Att	Pos	P	R	F
WE	DNN [17]	No	No	86.92	82.20	82.95
	LSTM [17]	No	No	87.12	85.41	86.26
	BiLSTM	No	No	88.73	90.24	88.58
WE+PhoE	BiLSTM	No	No	91.13	90.58	89.94
		No	Yes	90.53	91.01	90.12
		Yes	No	90.24	90.96	90.04
		Yes	Yes	90.12	91.33	90.20
WE+SylE	BiLSTM	No	No	91.15	90.15	89.79
		No	Yes	91.09	90.17	90.03
		Yes	No	91.07	90.70	90.06
		Yes	Yes	90.18	91.27	90.13
WE+PE	BiLSTM	No	No	91.47	90.46	90.04
		No	Yes	90.32	91.03	90.23
		Yes	No	90.15	91.07	90.19
		Yes	Yes	90.83	91.43	90.40
WE+PE+CE	BiLSTM	No	No	91.04	91.21	90.27
		No	Yes	90.86	91.49	90.41
		Yes	No	90.85	91.38	90.39
		Yes	Yes	90.98	91.73	**90.82**

information that classifier cannot utilize, too small dimension can not learn the enough information. This is a somewhat surprising and counterintuitive result, as one would expect at least 1–2% increase in the performance corresponding to the increase in the PE dimensions.

3.5 Comparison of Position-Based Enhanced Method

In this experiment, we compare the performance of the position-based enhanced method by using two tagging schemes. A phoneme or syllable usually plays different roles when it is in different positions within a word. Here we utilize multiple-prototype phonological embeddings to address this issue. The idea is that, we keep multiple vectors for one phoneme and syllable, each corresponding to one of the meanings. We compare two tagging schemes in position-based enhanced method for multiple-prototype PE: (1) Tag location index for each token, e.g. the first/second/third/etc., according to the count of phonemes and syllables within a word; and (2) Keep three embeddings for each tokens corresponding to its three types of positions in a word, i.e., Begin, Middle and End. The first scheme, used in previous experiments, is named after 'Pos'. We denote

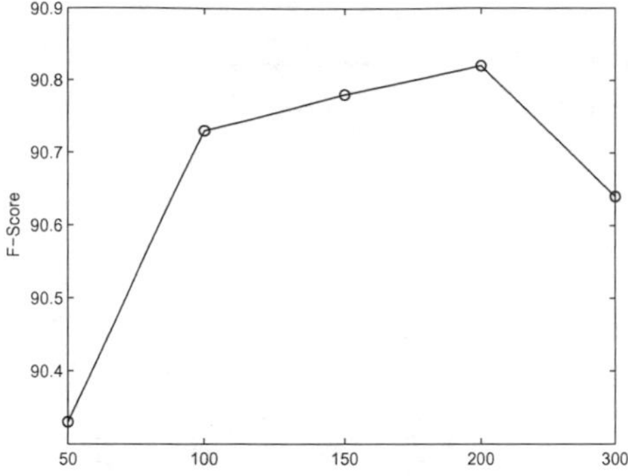

Fig. 3. Effect of varying the PE dimension on the performance (in terms of the F Score) of the 'WE+PE+CE' system on the Mongolian phrase break prediction.

Table 2. Effect of different position-based enhanced method on the performance of the 'WE+PE+CE' system for the Mongolian phrase break prediction.

Input features	Model	Att	Pos	Pos(BME)	P	R	F
WE+PE+CE	BiLSTM	No	No	Yes	90.49	90.92	90.29
		No	Yes	No	90.86	91.49	90.41
		Yes	No	Yes	90.74	91.51	90.75
		Yes	Yes	No	90.98	91.73	90.82

the second scheme as 'Pos(BME)'. Compared to the Basic Method (Sect. 2.1.2), with the two methods the count of (phoneme, syllable) can be increased from (61, 200) to (158, 378) and (546, 434) respectively.

We also use the 'WE+PE+CE' system as described in Sect. 3.3 with all the parameters and hyperparameters unchanged. Table 2 presents the results of this experiment. As examination of the results in Table 2 shows that 'Pos' method significantly outperform the 'Pos(BME)' method with or without attention mechanism. This proves that capturing more exquisite phonologically information using the scheme according to the count of phonemes and syllables within a word improves the performance, as compared to the 'Pos(BME)' method. Armed with 'Pos' method, the model can learn more rich phonologically information.

3.6 Comparison of Output Layer

In this experiment, we study the effect of different output layer on the performance for phrase break prediction. For sequence labeling task, it is effective to consider the correlation between taggers and jointly decode the best output for a given tokens. Following [34], we can also use a CRF as the output layer, which conditions each prediction on the previously predicted label. We denote the system using softmax or CRF output layer as 'BiLSTM-softmax' and 'BiLSTM-CRF'.

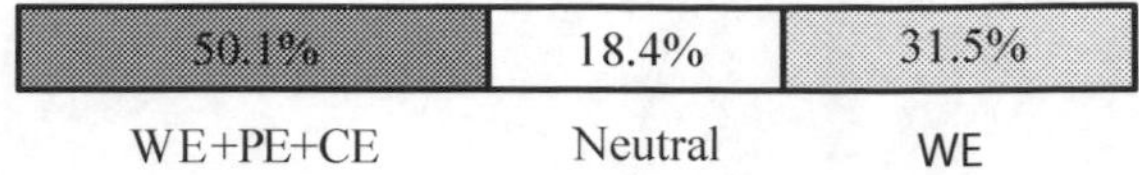

Fig. 4. The percentage preference of Subjective Evaluations.

Table 3 summarizes the experimental results for best system ('WE+PE+CE') by using BiLSTM-softmax or BiLSTM-CRF model. Surprisingly, we observe that BiLSTM-softmax model outperforms BiLSTM-CRF model in all metrics. This results conflicts with the empirical fact that CRF output layer is likely to work better than softmax output layer in other sequential labeling tasks, e.g., Part-of-Speech (POS) tagging [35] and Name Entity Recognition (NER) [36]. We believe that the abnormal phenomenon may owing to the nature of the specific tasks. For NER, which gives every word a entity label (e.g., time, location, organization, person, money, ...), the distribution of different labels in the corpus is approximately equal due to the grammar rules. It is important to consider the previous and future entity labels when decoding the current label. On the contrary, the distribution of output labels in phrase break prediction task is highly unequal, the proportion of 'NB' and 'B' is 85% versus 15% in our corpus. Thus the CRF layer may learn more knowledge about transiting from 'NB' to 'NB', and it will be more likely to predict the output label to be 'NB'. Modeling the output label dependencies, by the addition of a CRF layer on top of an BiLSTM, does not improve performance for Mongolian phrase break prediction model.

Table 3. Effect of BiLSTM model with different output layer on the performance of the WE+PE+CE system on the Mongolian phrase break prediction.

Input features	Model	P	R	F
WE+PE+CE	BiLSTM-softmax	90.98	91.73	90.82
	BiLSTM-CRF	89.67	89.08	89.69

3.7 Listening Tests

To compare the performance of the 'WE+PE+CE' system vs 'WE' one, a subjective preference listening test was conducted. A set of 20 sentence pairs of each session was randomly selected from the 100 pairs with different phrase break prediction results and speech was generated through a DNN-based Mongolian TTS system [37]. A group of 10 subjects were asked to choose which one was better in terms of the naturalness of synthesis speech, they could choose "Neutral" if they did not have any preference. The percentage preference is shown in Fig. 4. We can clearly see that the 'WE+PE+CE' system can achieve better naturalness of synthesized speech as compared with 'WE' system.

4 Conclusions

In this paper, we introduce a BiLSTM model with attention mechanism which uses the word embeddings, phonological representations and character embeddings to achieve state of the art performance. Our experiments show that including a phonological representation component in the BiLSTM model provides substantial performance improvements on all the benchmarks for Mongolian phrase break prediction. In addition, the attention mechanism and position-based enhanced method for phonological representations achieve the best results on all evaluations. Moreover, all of this is achieved without any extra feature engineering specific to the task or language. Our method can also be applied to various languages.

References

1. Chen, Z., Hu, G., Jiang, W.: Improving prosodic phrase prediction by unsupervised adaptation and syntactic features extraction. In: 11th Annual Conference of the International Speech Communication Association, Makuhari, Chiba, Japan, pp. 1421–1424 (2010)
2. Chu, M., Qian, Y.: Locating boundaries for prosodic constituents in unrestricted mandarin texts. Comput. Linguist. Chin. Lang. Process. **6**, 61–82 (2001)
3. Nie, X., Wang, Z.: Automatic phrase break prediction in Chinese sentences. J. Chin. Inf. Process. **17**(4), 39–44 (2003)
4. Li, J.F., Hu, G.P., Wang, R.: Chinese prosody phrase break prediction based on maximum entropy model. In: 8th Proceedings of INTERSPEECH, Jeju Island, Korea, pp. 729–732 (2004)
5. Qian, Y., Wu, Z., Ma, X., Soong, F.: Automatic prosody prediction and detection with conditional random field (CRF) models. In: 7th Proceedings of ISCSLP, Tainan, Taiwan, pp. 135–138 (2010)
6. Rosenberg, A., Fernandez, R., Ramabhadran, B.: Phrase boundary assignment from text in multiple domains. In: 13th Annual Conference of the International Speech Communication Association, Portland, Oregon, USA, pp. 2558–2561 (2012)
7. Vadapalli, A., Bhaskararao, P., Prahallad, K.: Significance of word-terminal syllables for prediction of phrase breaks in text-to-speech systems for Indian languages. In: 8th ISCA Tutorial and Research Workshop on Speech Synthesis (2013)
8. Ananthakrishnan, S., Narayanan, S.: An automatic prosody recognizer using a coupled multi-stream acoustic model and a syntactic-prosodic language model. In: 30th International Conference on Acoustics. Speech, and Signal Processing, pp. 269–272. IEEE Press, Philadelphia (2005)
9. Hasegawa-Johnson, M., et al.: Simultaneous recognition of words and prosody in the Boston University radio speech corpus. Speech Commun. **46**, 418–439 (2005)
10. Sridhar, V.K.R., Bangalore, S., Narayanan, S.S.: Exploiting acoustic and syntactic features for automatic prosody labeling in a maximum entropy framework. IEEE Trans. Audio Speech Lang. Process. **16**, 797–811 (2008)
11. Busser, B., Daelemans, W., van den Bosch, A.: Predicting phrase breaks with memory-based learning. In: 4th ISCA Tutorial and Research Workshop on Speech Synthesis, Perthshire Scotland (2001)

12. Fernandez, R., Ramabhadran, B.: Driscriminative training and unsupervised adaptation for labeling prosodic events with limited training data. In: 11th Conference of the International Speech Communication Association, Makuhari, Chiba, Japan, pp. 1429–1432 (2010)
13. Rosenberg, A., Fernandez, R., Ramabhadran, B.: Modeling phrasing and prominence using deep recurrent learning. In: 16th Conference of the International Speech Communication Association, Dresden, Germany, pp. 3066–3070 (2015)
14. Vadapalli, A., Prahallad, K.: Learning continuous-valued word representations for phrase break prediction. In: 15th Conference of the International Speech Communication Association, Singapore, pp. 41–45 (2014)
15. Watts, O., et al.: Neural net word representations for phrase-break prediction without a part of speech tagger. In: 34th IEEE International Conference on Acoustics, Speech, and Signal Processing (ICASSP), Florence, Italy, pp. 2599–2603 (2014)
16. Watts, O., Yamagishi, J., King, S.: Unsupervised continuous-valued word features for Phrase-break prediction without a part-of-speech tagger. In: 12th Conference of the International Speech Communication Association, Florence, Italy (2011)
17. Vadapalli, A., Gangashetty, S.V.: An investigation of recurrent neural network architectures using word embeddings for phrase break prediction. In: 17th Conference of the International Speech Communication Association, San Francisco, CA, USA, pp. 2308–2312 (2016)
18. Rendel, A., Fernandez, R., Hoory, R., Ramabhadran, B.: Using continuous lexical embeddings to improve symbolic-prosody prediction in a text-to-speech front-end. In: 36th IEEE International Conference on Acoustics, Speech, and Signal Processing (ICASSP), Shanghai, China, pp. 5655–5659 (2016)
19. Ding, C., Xie, L., Yan, J., Zhang, W., Liu, Y.: Automatic prosody prediction for Chinese speech synthesis using BLSTM-RNN and embedding features. In: IEEE Automatic Speech Recognition and Understanding Workshop, Scottsdale, Arizona, USA, pp. 98–102 (2015)
20. Zheng, Y., Li, Y., Wen, Z., Ding, X., Tao, J.: Improving prosodic boundaries prediction for mandarin speech synthesis by using enhanced embedding feature and model fusion approach. In: 17th Conference of the International Speech Communication Association, San Francisco, CA, USA, pp. 3201–3205 (2016)
21. Klimkov, V., et al.: Phrase break prediction for long-form reading TTS: exploiting text structure information. In: 18th Conference of the International Speech Communication Association, Stockholm, Sweden, pp. 1064–1068 (2017)
22. Liu, R., Bao, F., Gao, G., Wang, W.: Mongolian prosodic phrase prediction using suffix segmentation. In: International Conference on Asian Language Processing, pp. 250–253. IEEE (2017)
23. Gertai, Q.: Mongolian Syntax, pp. 77–133. Mongolia People Publishing House, Hohhot (1991)
24. Temusurvn and Otegen: Mongolian Orthography Dictionary, pp. 77–133. Inner Mongolia People Publishing House, Hohhot (1999)
25. Bao, F., Gao, G., Yan, X., Wang, W.: Segmentation-based Mongolian LVCSR approach. In: Proceedings of International Conference on Acoustics, Speech and Signal Processing, pp. 8136–8139 (2013)
26. Ling, W., et al.: Finding function in form: compositional character models for open vocabulary word representation. Computer Science, pp. 1899–1907 (2015)
27. Greff, K., Srivastava, R.K., Koutnik, J., Steunebrink, B.R., Schmidhuber, J.: LSTM: a search space odyssey. IEEE Trans. Neural Netw. Learn. Syst. **28**(10), 2222–2232 (2016)

28. Schuster, M., Paliwal, K.K.: Bidirectional recurrent neural networks. IEEE Trans. Signal Process. **45**(11), 2673–2681 (2002)
29. Mikolov, T., et al.: Efficient estimation of word representations in vector space. Computer Science (2013)
30. Mikolov, T., Sutskever, I., Chen, K., Corrado, G.S., Dean, J.: Distributed representations of words and phrases and their compositionality. In: Advances in Neural Information Processing Systems, pp. 3111–3119 (2013)
31. Pennington, J., Socher, R., Manning, C.: Glove: global vectors for word representation. In: Proceedings of the 2014 Conference on Empirical Methods in Natural Language Processing (EMNLP), pp. 1532–1543 (2014)
32. Chen, X., Xu, L., Liu, Z., Sun, M., Luan, H.B.: Joint learning of character and word embeddings. In: International Conference on Artificial Intelligence, pp. 1236–1242, AAAI Press (2015)
33. Bahdanau, D., Cho, K., Bengio, Y.: Neural machine translation by jointly learning to align and translate. Computer Science (2014)
34. Huang, Z., Xu, W., Yu, K.: Bidirectional LSTM-CRF models for sequence tagging. Computer Science (2015)
35. Liu, R., Bao, F., Gao, G., Wang, Y., et al.: Character-based joint segmentation and POS tagging for Chinese using bidirectional RNN-CRF. In: 8th International Joint Conference on Natural Language Processing (IJCNLP 2017), Taipei, Taiwan (2017)
36. Lample, G., Ballesteros, M., Subramanian, S., Kawakami, K., Dyer, C.: Neural architectures for named entity recognition. In: Proceedings of the 2016 Conference of the North American Chapter of the Association for Computational Linguistics: Human Language Technologies, San Diego, California, pp. 260–270 (2016)
37. Liu, R., Bao, F., Gao, G., Wang, Y.: Mongolian text-to-speech system based on deep neural network. In: Tao, J., Zheng, T.F., Bao, C., Wang, D., Li, Y. (eds.) NCMMSC 2017. CCIS, vol. 807, pp. 99–108. Springer, Singapore (2018). https://doi.org/10.1007/978-981-10-8111-8_10

Multi-label Crowdsourcing Learning with Incomplete Annotations

Shao-Yuan Li and Yuan Jiang(✉)

National Key Lab for Novel Software Technology, Nanjing University, Nanjing 210023, China
{lisy,jiangy}@lamda.nju.edu.cn

Abstract. In this paper we consider multi-label crowdsourcing (MLC) learning with labeling information from non-expert crowds. Previous crowdsourcing works typically care about single-label tasks, which ignore the label correlations. While the preliminary MLC studies concern themselves with the label correlations, they focus on *local* correlations whose estimation relies heavily on the annotations' quality and requires complete annotations for the labeled instances. However, annotations' quality in MLC is often various and incomplete annotations are common. For example, the crowds may just tag a few labels and leave the other labels untouched due to the heavy workload or labeling uncertainty. In this paper, we deal with the incomplete annotation issue. We propose a two stage approach considering the *global* low-rank structure correlation between the labels and crowds. Being able to learn with incomplete annotations, we also extend the proposed model to active annotation collection which significantly reduces the labeling cost. Experiments validate the effectiveness of our proposals.

Keywords: Multi-label · Crowdsourcing · Incomplete annotation
Low-rank structure · Tensor completion · Active query

1 Introduction

A rising challenge faced by machine learning algorithms is the scenario of multiple labels associated with data, e.g., one image may be tagged with labels *'urban'* and *'road'*, and one document may involve topics like *'economics'* and *'politics'*. To handle such tasks, multi-label learning (MLL) has received significant attention [30]. Typical MLL requires the groundtruth labels, which are rather expensive resources. Through distributing the task to multiple workers and estimating the true labels via some aggregation schemes, crowdsourcing [9] provides an economic alternative to collect labels.

Previous crowdsourcing works mainly care about single-label tasks [6,11,17,20,26,27,31], whereas using crowdsourcing for MLL is still in the preliminary stage. [1,7,22] extended the single-label methods by considering the *local*

Supported by NSF of China (61673201).

X. Geng and B.-H. Kang (Eds.): PRICAI 2018, LNAI 11012, pp. 232–245, 2018.
https://doi.org/10.1007/978-3-319-97304-3_18

label correlations estimated from the crowds' annotations, which rely heavily on the annotations' quality. Furthermore, they require complete annotations for the labeled instances, i.e., they assume the positive labels are tagged and the untagged labels are negative. In practice, the crowds may just tag a few labels and leave the others untouched due to the heavy workload of examining the whole label set or labeling uncertainty. Simply regarding the untagged labels as negative would deteriorate the label correlation estimation and subsequent learning.

In this paper, we consider the incomplete annotation issue. We propose a two-stage approach **CRIA** (CRowdsourcing with Incomplete Annotations) to first estimate the incomplete annotations and then estimate the groundtruth. Considering that the labels are correlated and determined by a few factors, we assume a low-rank structure between labels; besides, with the basic crowdsourcing assumption that most workers are willing to provide good annotations, the tagged labels are very likely to be correct. As the workers are labeling the same task, their annotations should be closely related. Regarding the annotations as a three-mode (instance, label, worker) tensor, we assume a *global* low-rank structure of the tensor and propose an optimization objective to estimate the missing annotations, and then infer the groundtruth labels using ensemble over crowds.

Besides, motivated by the low-rank structure which means the full annotations can be approximated by only a subset of them, we also propose strategies to actively select the few most helpful annotations to reduce the labeling burden and cost. Based on the groundtruth prediction of the proposed **CRIA** model, we define criteria to measure the uncertainty, informativeness and reliability of instances, labels and workers, and select the most informative labels of the most uncertain instances to collect annotations from the most reliable workers.

2 Related Work

Dealing with examples associated with multiple labels, multi-label learning has received significant attention. The simplest way is to deal with each label independently. To exploit the label correlations, various advanced approaches were proposed, see [30] and references therein. Typical multi-label algorithms require the groundtruth labels for learning, which are expensive.

With the advent of crowdsourcing platforms such as Amazon Mechanical Turk (AMT), crowdsourcing [9] provides an alternative to collect supervised information by distributing the task to multiple easy to access workers. As workers may make mistakes, the common wisdom is to estimate the higher quality labels via some aggregation schemes. Numbers of studies for single-label tasks have been proposed, mainly by using probabilistic models and estimating the workers' expertise from different perspectives, such as measures with explicit explanation like accuracy [11,27], confusion matrix [16,17,31], and more complex multidimensional vectors [26]. In the multi-label learning field, using crowdsourcing is in the preliminary stage. To estimate the groundtruth labels, methods extending the single-label methods by exploiting label correlations were explored.

[7] proposed three implementations P-DS, D-DS, ND-DS respectively extending DS [6] by incorporating dependency relationships among all label power set, label set of two labels, and conditional label dependency. [22] captured the co-occurrence dependencies between labels exploiting the notion of latent label clusters. But they assume that the workers annotate the positive labels and the rest are negative, i.e., the annotations are complete, which may not be true in practice.

We also note works constructing the taxonomy of labels using crowdsourcing [1,5,21]. Among them, [1,5] collected annotations for items, the similar setting as ours. [1] also implemented an approach considering the label co-occurrence to estimate the 'true' labels of items. Whereas the methodology assumes that all annotations are equally reliable, thus the same parameter value for all workers are used, whose inferiority is demonstrated in our experiments.

Our technique of low-rank tensor completion is related to the field of matrix, tensor completion [3,4,8,15,18,25]. The trace norm has been shown to be the tightest convex approximation for the rank of matrices, and efficient algorithms for matrix completion using trace norm were proposed [3,4,18]. As there is no direct way to determine the rank for tensors, heuristic models such as Tucker model based tensor factorization [25], parallel factor analysis model [8], and tensor trace norm definition using matrix trace norm [15] were proposed. Similar to [32] which exploited tensor for multi-class problem, considering that the well developed tools of matrix completion can be exploited, we build our approach based on the model of [15]. Different from [32] which inserted a groundtruth layer into the tensor, and relied on prior information of results of other crowdsourcing methods, we estimate the groundtruth through ensemble over the completed annotations, which is more efficient, robust and stable.

Other related work may contain partial label learning (PLL) and multi-label active learning (MLA). Our awareness that workers may not tag all labels shares the similar concern with PLL, which learns from a partial set of groundtruth labels [2,28]. Our active annotation collection idea is inspired by MLA, which reduces the labeling cost by collecting the most valuable labels, using measures like uncertainty and informativeness [10,14,19]. Our previous work [13] considered active multi-label crowdsourcing by incorporating the local neighborhoods' label correlations, which are solicited from the initial set of groundtruth labels.

3 Crowdsourcing with Incomplete Annotations

We use bold capital letters such as $\mathbf{X}$ to denote matrix, $\|\cdot\|_*$, $\|\cdot\|_F$ the trace and Frobenious norm of one matrix. Calligraphic letters, such as $\mathcal{X}$ denote tensors. For a 3-mode tensor $\mathcal{X}$, its (i,j,t)-th element is represented as $\mathcal{X}_{ijt}$. $\mathcal{X}_{(k)}$ denotes the output matrix of the *unfold* operation along the k-th dimension on $\mathcal{X}$. The opposite operation *fold* is the inverse of *unfold* and returns the tensor. The Frobenius norm of a 3-mode tensor is defined as $\|\mathcal{X}\|_F = (\sum_{i,j,t} |\mathcal{X}_{ijt}|^2)^{1/2}$.

We represent the annotations for a set of multi-label instances $\mathbf{X} \in \mathbb{R}^{N\times d}$ as a 3-mode tensor $\mathcal{T} \in \{+1,-1,0\}^{N\times L\times M}$, where N, L, M, d respectively denotes the number of instances, labels, workers and feature dimension. $\mathcal{T}_{ijt}$ denotes worker t's annotation result on label j for instance i. $\mathcal{T}_{ijt} = 1(-1)$ denotes worker t tags label j as positive (negative) for instance i, and $\mathcal{T}_{ijt} = 0$ denotes worker t doesn't tag label j. Note that the column $\mathcal{T}_{i:t} = 0^{L\times 1}$ means that worker t doesn't tag instance i. Our target is to estimate groundtruth labels from $\mathcal{T}$.

Previous MLC assumes that positive labels are tagged and the remaining are negative, i.e., each column $\mathcal{T}_{i:t}$ is either $\{+1,-1\}^{L\times 1}$ or $0^{L\times 1}$. This is not true in practice. To deal with this issue, we propose to first estimate the untagged annotations by exploiting the low rank structure between labels and annotations, and then estimate the groundtruth using ensemble.

3.1 Missing Annotation Estimation

Following typical crowdsourcing learning, we assume that most workers are acting with *good will*, i.e., they are willing to provide good annotations. Considering that the labels are correlated and determined by a few factors, and the annotation results of different workers should be closely related, the full annotation tensor is expected to be low rank. We adopt the tensor completion model in [15] to recover the untagged annotations. Formally, we wish to estimate an annotation tensor $\mathcal{X} \in \mathbb{R}^{N\times L\times M}$ whose entries in the observed positions should be close to the observed annotations, and at the same time, it should be low rank:

$$\min_{\mathcal{X}} \ \sum_{k=1}^{3} \alpha_k \|\mathcal{X}_{(k)}\|_* \quad s.t. \ \mathcal{X}_\Omega = \mathcal{T}_\Omega \tag{1}$$

Here $\Omega = \{(i,j,t)|\mathcal{T}_{ijt} \neq 0\}$ denotes the index set of observed annotations. $\mathcal{X}_{(1)}, \mathcal{X}_{(2)}, \mathcal{X}_{(3)}$ are respectively the unfolded annotation matrix along the instance, label and worker dimension. α_k are predefined scalars with $\sum_{k=1}^{3} \alpha_k = 1, \alpha_k \geq 0$. From Eq. 1, we can see that the tensor completion is essentially fulfilled by conducting low rank matrix completion on each of the unfolded annotation matrix along the instance, label and worker dimension. By using this model, we can easily exploit well developed techniques such as side information utilization and efficient optimization methods for low rank matrix completion.

Since the trace norms in Eq. 1 are not independent, to conduct optimization, matrices $\mathbf{M}_1, \mathbf{M}_2, \mathbf{M}_3$ are introduced and the optimization is converted as:

$$\min_{\mathcal{X},\mathbf{M}_k} \ \sum_{k=1}^{3} \alpha_k \|\mathbf{M}_k\|_* + \frac{\beta_k}{2}\|\mathcal{X}_{(k)} - \mathbf{M}_k\|_F^2 \quad s.t. \ \mathcal{X}_\Omega = \mathcal{T}_\Omega \tag{2}$$

To exploit the instance features as side information to augment the learning, we assume a linear relationship between the crowds' annotations and the instances' features, and the unfolded matrix $\mathcal{X}_{(1)}$ can be represented by $\mathcal{X}_{(1)} = \mathbf{XW}$, where $\mathbf{W}$ is the coefficients. Thus our learning objective becomes:

$$\min_{\mathcal{X},\mathbf{W},\mathbf{M}_2,\mathbf{M}_3} \alpha_1\|\mathbf{XW}\|_* + \frac{\beta_1}{2}\|\mathcal{X}_{(1)} - \mathbf{XW}\|_F^2 + \sum_{k=2}^{3} \alpha_k\|\mathbf{M}_k\|_* + \frac{\beta_k}{2}\|\mathcal{X}_{(k)} - \mathbf{M}_k\|_F^2$$
$$s.t. \ \mathcal{X}_\Omega = \mathcal{T}_\Omega \tag{3}$$

Algorithm 1. $\mathcal{X}$ Estimation

1: **Initialization:** $\mathcal{X} = \mathcal{T}, \Omega = \{(i,j,k)|\mathcal{T}_{ijk} \neq 0\}$, β_k, stopping criterion ϵ
2: **while** stopping criterion is not satisfied **do**
3: Calculate $\mathcal{X}$ by Eq. 5
4: Calculate $\mathbf{M}_2, \mathbf{M}_3$ by Eq. 6
5: Calculate $\mathbf{W}$ by Eq. 7 using APGD
6: **end while**

Incorporating the features into learning, we achieve two advantages: (1) it allows us to predict labels for novel unseen examples; (2) in cases where the feature dimension d is much smaller than the number of instances N, the matrix $\mathbf{W} \in \mathbb{R}^{d \times LM}$ mode would be much smaller than the matrix $\mathbf{M}_1 \in \mathbb{R}^{N \times LM}$, we reduce the number of parameters to learn and speed up the computation.

To estimate $\mathcal{X}, \mathbf{W}, \mathbf{M}_2, \mathbf{M}_3$, we employ block coordinate descent (BCD) [23] to estimate them iteratively which converges at rate $O(1/T)$.

Computing $\mathcal{X}$: With the other variables fixed, the optimization with respect to $\mathcal{X}$ is given by the following subproblem:

$$\min_{\mathcal{X}} \frac{\beta_1}{2}\|\mathcal{X}_{(1)} - \mathbf{XW}\|_F^2 + \sum_{k=2}^{3} \frac{\beta_k}{2}\|\mathcal{X}_{(k)} - \mathbf{M}_k\|_F^2 \quad s.t. \quad \mathcal{X}_\Omega = \mathcal{T}_\Omega \tag{4}$$

The closed form solution is induced:

$$\mathcal{X}_{ijt} = \begin{cases} \mathcal{T}_{ijt} & (i,j,t) \in \Omega \\ \left(\frac{\beta_1 fold_1(\mathbf{XW}) + \sum_{k=2}^{3} \beta_k fold_k(\mathbf{M}_k)}{\sum_{k=1}^{3} \beta_k}\right)_{ijt} & (i,j,t) \notin \Omega \end{cases} \tag{5}$$

Computing $\mathbf{M}_k$: With the other variables fixed, the optimization with respect to $\mathbf{M}_k$ is given by:

$$\min_{\mathbf{M}_k} \frac{1}{2}\|\mathcal{X}_{(k)} - \mathbf{M}_k\|_F^2 + \frac{\alpha_k}{\beta_k}\|\mathbf{M}_k\|_* \tag{6}$$

which has closed form solution by SVT [3].

Computing $\mathbf{W}$: With the other variables fixed, the optimization with respect to $\mathbf{W}$ is given by:

$$\min_{\mathbf{W}} \frac{\alpha_1}{\beta_1}\|\mathbf{XW}\|_* + \frac{1}{2}\|\mathcal{X}_{(1)} - \mathbf{XW}\|_F^2 \tag{7}$$

Following [28], we exploit Accelerated Proximal Gradient Descend (APGD) [24] to optimize Eq. 7 iteratively, which converges at rate $O(1/T^2)$.

3.2 Groundtruth Inference

After the tensor completion, we get one full annotation estimation tensor $\mathcal{X} \in \mathbb{R}^{N \times L \times M}$. To infer the groundtruth $\{\hat{\mathbf{z}}_{ij}\}$, we conduct ensemble over the recovered annotations. Compared to the observed discrete $\{1, -1\}$ labeling results, the recovered annotations are signed real valued. We test two voting strategies:

(1) **Signed Voting:** we use the sign $\{1, -1\}$ of the estimated annotations as the hard label annotation, and conduct voting over the workers:

$$\hat{\mathbf{z}}_{ij} = \sum_t sign(\mathcal{X}_{ijt})/M \tag{8}$$

This scheme is named as $\mathbf{CRIA}_S$ (CRowdsourcing with Incomplete Annotations).

(2) **Valued Voting:** we believe that the estimation values can represent some confidence level for the workers, for example, given the annotation estimation of two workers t, t' on label j of instance i $\mathcal{X}_{ijt} = 0.9$, $\mathcal{X}_{ijt'} = -0.1$, label j is more likely to be positive on instance i.

$$\hat{\mathbf{z}}_{ij} = \sum_t(\mathcal{X}_{ijt})/M \tag{9}$$

This scheme is named as $\mathbf{CRIA}_V$.

For a set of novel instances $\mathbf{X}_s$, to predict their groundtruth, we first estimate the crowds' annotations $\mathcal{X}_s = fold_1(\mathbf{X}_s\mathbf{W})$, and then conduct the above voting.

4 Active Annotation Collection

Considering that the labeling budget is often limited, whereas collecting annotations without control may lead to not only unnecessary information redundancy, but also possible out of control labeling errors (e.g., incomplete annotation in this paper), we propose to actively collect the most valuable annotations.

Instance Selection. To select the most informative instance, typical active methods defined some uncertainty measure for the instances considering the prediction uncertainty over labels. As the proposed **CRIA** model gives real valued prediction without hard label prediction, we define an uncertain measure for the instance, computed as the gap between its largest and smallest prediction of labels. The smaller the gap, it means the more difficult to split the positive and negative labels for the instance. The instance with the smallest gap is selected:

$$i^* = \arg\min_i U(\mathbf{x}_i) := \max_j \hat{\mathbf{z}}_{ij} - \min_j \hat{\mathbf{z}}_{ij} \tag{10}$$

Label Selection. Different from traditional active methods querying the most uncertain labels, we consider the *label sparsity* property of multi-label tasks, i.e., while the label size can be large, the number of positive labels is usually very small, whose information however is critical to learning. E.g., for the two image tasks concerning 6 and 16 labels in our experiment, the average number of positive labels are respectively 1.24 ± 0.45 and 1.80 ± 0.90. This *label sparsity* phenomenon is also observed on numerous multi-label benchmark data.[1] Driven by this, we propose to query the most possibly *positive* labels for annotation:

$$L_j^* = \{j^* \mid \hat{\mathbf{z}}_{i^*j} \text{ ranks top } l \text{ among label predictions}\} \tag{11}$$

[1] http://mulan.sourceforge.net/datasets-mlc.html.

Algorithm 2. Active Crowdsourcing Procedure

Input: instances $\mathbf{X}$, initial annotations $\mathcal{T}$

Repeat:
  Estimate the full annotations $\mathcal{X}$ and groundtruth for $\mathbf{X}$ respectively by Alg. 1 and Eq. 9
  Select instance, labels, worker $(\mathbf{x}_{i^*}, L_j^*, t^*)$ respectively by Eq. 10, 11, 12
  Query annotations for $(\mathbf{x}_{i^*}, L_j^*, t^*)$ and add into $\mathcal{T}$
Until The maximum number of queries is reached

The number l can be determined based on reality, e.g., if the cardinality of positive labels is large (small), we can set l large (small). We test l with varying values in the experiments.

Worker Selection. Given the selected instance and label (i^*, L_j^*) by Eqs. 10 and 11, we select the worker which most possibly gives the positive annotations:

$$t^* = \arg\max_t \sum_{j^* \in L_j^*} \mathcal{X}_{i^* j^* t} \tag{12}$$

After the instance, label, worker indices (i^*, L_j^*, t^*) are selected, the corresponding annotations are collected and added into $\mathcal{T}_{i^* j^* t^*}$ to update the full annotation tensor and groundtruth label estimation using the CRIA model. The overall process is summarized in Algorithm 2. We compare with a few baselines in the experiment, which shows significant annotation savings.

5 Running Time Analysis

For $\mathbf{CRIA}_S$ ($\mathbf{CRIA}_V$), the computation mainly comes from the SVT while computing $\mathbf{M}_k$ for Eq. 6 and $\mathbf{W}$ for Eq. 7, which can be implemented very efficiently using readily available high-quality packages, see [3] for details. As approximate solution is good enough, early stop can be employed for the iterative BCD and APGD, e.g., their maximum iteration number are set as 200, 100 in our experiment. Thus compared to the probabilistic crowdsourcing learning methods which rely on the EM procedure over all labels and workers, $\mathbf{CRIA}_S$ ($\mathbf{CRIA}_V$) is very efficient, especially in the case of not small number of workers and labels.

6 Experiment

6.1 Data Sets

We distributed two multi-label image annotation tasks with different instance and label size on AMT, and ask the workers to tag the positive label for the image they see, the same way as existing multi-label crowdsourcing works do. Thus the annotations are expected to be a fair comparison benchmark.

Scene. *Scene* contains 700 images concerning 6 labels. On average each image has 1.24 ± 0.45 labels. 18 workers annotating the most images (each no less than

70) are kept for experiment. On average each worker annotated 267 ± 201 images, each image was annotated by 6.9 ± 2.3 workers.

Image. *Image* contains 1495 images concerning 16 labels. On average each image has 1.80 ± 0.90 labels. 15 workers annotating the most images (each no less than 100) are kept. On average each worker annotated 397 ± 453 images, each image was annotated by 10.1 ± 1.41 workers.

The groundtruth labels are annotated by human volunteers, and a 1248 dimension fisher vector is extracted as the feature. We conduct some rough analysis to get some idea about the data quality. For each worker, we compute its MacroF1 score on its annotated instances. MacroF1 [30] is the macro average of the F1 score over all labels, with value in [0, 1], the larger, the better. Respectively 15 and 14 workers' macroF1 range in $[0.70, 0.85]$ for *Scene* and *Image*, indicating that annotations from most workers are reliable. In the following, we first conduct experiments concerning the incomplete annotation issue, then test the effect of active annotation collection strategies.

6.2 Crowdsourcing Learning

We test two settings for the incomplete annotation learning. In the *transductive* setting, we make annotations of the whole data uniformly random missing, and our target is to estimate the groundtruth labels for the data set. We vary the observed fraction of annotations p from 100% to 10%. In the *inductive* setting, we randomly split the data into 10% test data with no annotations and 90% training data with annotations, with the observation varies also from 100% to 10%. Results on the *test data* are reported. Each experiment is repeated for 10 times and the average and standard deviation results are recorded.

We compare with four multi-label baselines **D-DS**, **P-DS**, **ND-DS** [7], **MLNB** [1], and four state of the art single-label baselines **MV**, **DS** [6], **Yutc** [17], **MaxEn** [31]. The single-label baselines can deal with the incomplete annotation issue by learning on each label separately, but they ignore the label correlations thus are expected to work worse than ours. The multi-label baselines treat the untagged labels for the annotated instances as negative. For the proposed method, parameters are set as $\alpha_k = 1/3$, $\beta_k = 0.1$, $\epsilon = 10^{-2}$. The maximum iteration for BCD, APGD are set as 200, 100. The codes of the baselines are provided by their authors and the default parameter suggested there are used. Except for DS, the two coin model implemented by [16] is used. Besides, we also incorporate another baselines **LinEn**, which builds a linear classifier for each label on each worker using its corresponding instances, and the prediction is the ensembles of workers. To prevent overfitting, l2 regularization with trade-off parameter 1 is used. As our method uses linear classifier, and also considers the missing annotation issue and the label/worker correlations, we choose LinEn as a fair baseline to demonstrate the importance of the above two factors.

As our method currently learns no threshold to separate the positive and negative predictions, to evaluated the classification performance, we treat the top k ranked labels as positive and rest as negative. Here k is the number of true positive labels of each example. For comparison fairness, the best result among this strategy and the heuristic thresholding strategy (0.5 for crowdsourcing baselines and 0 for LinEns) for baselines are used. We report the macroF1 (macF.) results, performance on other measures such as hamming loss, microF1, average arecision and ranking loss are similar and we omit them due to space limitation.

Transductive Results. The results for the *transductive* setting are shown in Table 1. We can see that CRIA_V outperforms other methods significantly in most time, whereas the signed voting scheme CRIA_S is inferior. When $p = 100\%$ which is the same scenario of previous multi-label baselines, our approach also achieves significantly better performance. It's notable that when the annotations are small, e.g., 10% for *Scene* and 20% for *Image*, LinEn performs the best. This may be due to the information insufficiency for the crowdsourcing methods to learn reliable parameters. When the annotations increase, LinEn is not able to gain as much benefit as the crowdsourcing baselines. Among the multi-label baselines, MLNB ranks the worst. Two reasons may explain this, first, MLNB considering label co-occurrence is designed for learning the label hierarchy, but for problems lacking such hierarchies, label co-occurrence is not as common; more importantly, MLNB uses the same parameter for all workers, which ignores their expertise variance. Comparing D-DS, P-DS, and ND-DS which extend DS [6] by considering label relationship among all label powersets, label set of two labels, ND-DS performs most effectively by learning the conditional label dependency.

Comparing the single-label baselines, when the annotations are no less than 60%, MaxEn which models each worker's confusion on each example performs the best. Whereas when annotations are less, Yutc utilizing the instances' feature performs better. Besides, the multi-label baselines are not necessarily always better than the single-label ones, which is reasonable in crowdsourcing. Since their local label correlations are solicited solely from the collected annotations, whose quality would rely heavily on the annotations' quality and quantity.

Inductive Results. The results for the *inductive* setting are shown in Table 2. Except for Yutc and LinEn, the other baselines didn't consider the feature information and learned no classifier, thus no results are reported for them. The comparison is similar with the transductive setting, but with much lower performance, indicating that inductive crowdsourcing learning is more challenging.

6.3 Active Results

In the above, we have validated the superiority of the proposed **CRIA** model, in this section, we test the proposed active strategies. Using the real valued voting scheme $\mathbf{CRIA}_V$ as learning model, we test: (1) **Rand** which selects instance, labels, worker randomly; (2) **LabAct** which selects instance and worker randomly, selects labels using the proposed strategy; (3) **InstLabAct** which selects worker randomly, selects instance and labels using the proposed strategy; (4) $\mathbf{CRIA}_a$ which selects instance, labels, worker using the proposed strategy. Each time one instance is first selected, then l labels for this instance are selected, and the worker is selected. We also compare with one totally random strategy (5) **RandT** which selects l random entries of the tensor at each time.

Table 1. The *MacF1* results for the *transductive* setting. The randomly observed annotations p varies from 100% to 10%. CRIA$_S$ and CRIA$_V$ are the proposed approach with signed and real valued voting. mean ± std results over 10 times random repetitions are recorded. The best results on each row are bolded, with the comparable ones (pairwise single-tailed t-test at 95% confidence level) marked by •.

	p	100%	80%	60%	40%	20%	10%
Scene	D-DS	.869 ± .000	.854 ± .006	.812 ± .006	.744 ± .012	.598 ± .019	.419 ± .019
	P-DS	.421 ± .000	.411 ± .003	.394 ± .003	.357 ± .008	.271 ± .011	.181 ± .011
	ND-DS	.883 ± .000	.863 ± .008	.813 ± .007	.751 ± .009	.607 ± .014	.422 ± .020
	MLNB	.186 ± .000	.207 ± .014	.207 ± .013	.196 ± .008	.176 ± .011	.151 ± .006
	MV	.895 ± .000	.871 ± .006	.840 ± .005	.780 ± .008	.620 ± .015	.441 ± .018
	DS	.853 ± .003	.833 ± .010	.799 ± .010	.775 ± .014	.692 ± .014	.533 ± .019
	MaxEn	.893 ± .001	.884 ± .007	.863 ± .006	.828 ± .010	.716 ± .013	.537 ± .019
	YuTc	.854 ± .004	.847 ± .010	.833 ± .013	.835 ± .017	.764 ± .039	.571 ± .102
	LinEn	.809 ± .000	.798 ± .005	.788 ± .006	.777 ± .009	.754 ± .009	**.726 ± .009**
	CRIA$_S$	.907 ± .000	.900 ± .004	.882 ± .007	.847 ± .012	.743 ± .015	.617 ± .013
	CRIA$_V$	**.918 ± .000**	**.914 ± .005**	**.900 ± .009**	**.871 ± .010**	**.783 ± .013**	.647 ± .012
Image	D-DS	.794 ± .000	.757 ± .006	.703 ± .007	.623 ± .013	.462 ± .012	.293 ± .002
	P-DS	.161 ± .000	.156 ± .005	.148 ± .007	.129 ± .010	.086 ± .009	.049 ± .007
	ND-DS	.803 ± .000	.752 ± .002	.686 ± .001	.607 ± .000	.454 ± .014	.294 ± .001
	MLNB	.120 ± .000	.115 ± .007	.113 ± .005	.114 ± .009	.103 ± .005	.093 ± .004
	MV	.850 ± .000	.811 ± .005	.760 ± .004	.662 ± .005	.476 ± .008	.311 ± .006
	DS	.769 ± .004	.753 ± .010	.747 ± .011	.699 ± .009	.516 ± .010	.339 ± .008
	MaxEn	.845 ± .000	.827 ± .006	.796 ± .004	.717 ± .008	.522 ± .011	.337 ± .004
	YuTc	.813 ± .003	.797 ± .012	.781 ± .008	.738 ± .022	.568 ± .040	.366 ± .057
	LinEn	.707 ± .000	.693 ± .003	.675 ± .011	.652 ± .012	**.621 ± .020**	**.558 ± .040**
	CRIA$_S$	.877 ± .000•	.852 ± .003	.805 ± .006	.702 ± .007	.508 ± .005	.363 ± .009
	CRIA$_V$	**.877 ± .000**	**.864 ± .005**	**.832 ± .005**	**.760 ± .006**	.599 ± .007	.471 ± .006

Table 2. The *MacF1* results for the *inductive* setting. The randomly observed annotations p varies from 100% to 10%. CRIA$_S$ and CRIA$_V$ are the proposed approach with signed and real valued voting. mean ± std results over 10 times random repetitions are recorded. The best results on each row are bolded, with the comparable ones (pairwise single-tailed t-test at 95% confidence level) marked by •.

	p	100%	80%	60%	40%	20%	10%
Scene	YuTc	.286 ± .018	.291 ± .028	.270 ± .020	.246 ± .041	.060 ± .022	.114 ± .062
	LinEn	**.293 ± .000**	**.303 ± .021**	.286 ± .018	.287 ± .023	.270 ± .025	.241 ± .038
	CRIA$_S$	.279 ± .000	.286 ± .033	.286 ± .023	.283 ± .019	.293 ± .030	.286 ± .029
	CRIA$_V$	.286 ± .000	.301 ± .033•	**.290 ± .029**	**.291 ± .031**	**.303 ± .012**	**.300 ± .044**
Image	YuTc	.368 ± .000	.331 ± .000	.311 ± .000	.274 ± .000	.195 ± .000	.094 ± .000
	LinEn	.339 ± .000	.314 ± .014	.272 ± .022	.237 ± .019	.186 ± .022	.163 ± .019
	CRIA$_S$	.369 ± .000	.337 ± .008	.299 ± .018	.264 ± .019	.224 ± .019	.199 ± .021
	CRIA$_V$	**.399 ± .000**	**.374 ± .015**	**.348 ± .021**	**.324 ± .020**	**.278 ± .017**	**.235 ± .015**

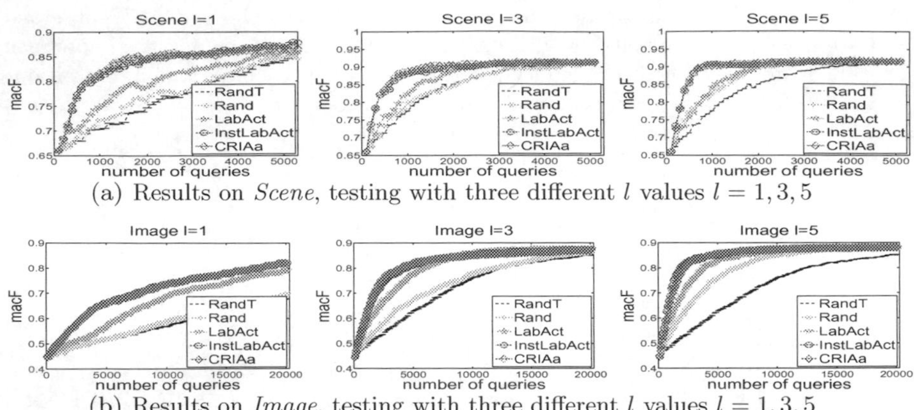

(a) Results on *Scene*, testing with three different l values $l = 1, 3, 5$

(b) Results on *Image*, testing with three different l values $l = 1, 3, 5$

Fig. 1. The MacF1 results of different annotation collection strategies.

Here we don't compare with active matrix/tensor completion method like adaptive column subset selection [12], because with the target of recovering the matrix, they require a whole column each time which corresponds to all the labels of an instance, whereas our concern is just that the worker may not annotate all labels. We do not compare with traditional multi-label active learning because they learn with groundtruth labels. We also do not compare with related but different work [29] for single-label crowdsourcing tasks and [13] which relies on groundtruth for label correlation exploitation.

For each data, we randomly select 10% of the annotations as the initial data, and iteratively select (instance, label, worker) to query annotations and update the groundtruth estimation. The average MacF1 results over 10 times repetition in the *transductive* setting are shown in Fig. 1, $l = 1, 3, 5$ are tested. It can be seen that both the instance and label active query strategies (InstLabAct vs LabAct; LabAct vs Rand) play significant role in finding the most helpful annotations. Besides, comparing Rand and RandT, we can see some subtle advantage of Rand at the early stage, indicating that focusing on querying labels of specific instances is more preferred. For worker selection, no much difference between the random and active strategy is observed. This may be explained by the overall uniform annotation quality of the workers. On the two experiment data, $l = 3$ is a moderate number for $\mathbf{CRIA}_a$, which converges much faster than $l = 1$ and no slower than $l = 5$. This is due to that, the average number of positive labels for *Scene* and *Image* are respectively 1.24 and 1.80, for which 3 is large enough.

6.4 Parameter Study

In the experiment, parameters α_k and β_k are fixed. α_k is conventionally set as 1/3 (3 is the mode number). β_k trade-off between the approximation to the observed annotations and the low-rank property of annotations. We study the effect of β_k to our multi-label learning. Let $\gamma = \alpha_k/\beta_k$, we vary γ in $[10^{-3}, \ldots, 10^{3}]$, and plot in Fig. 2 the results with observed annotation rate $10\%, 40\%, 70\%$ in the transductive setting. From Fig. 2 we can see that when γ is no less than 10, the learning performance is fairly stable, which is consistent with [15].

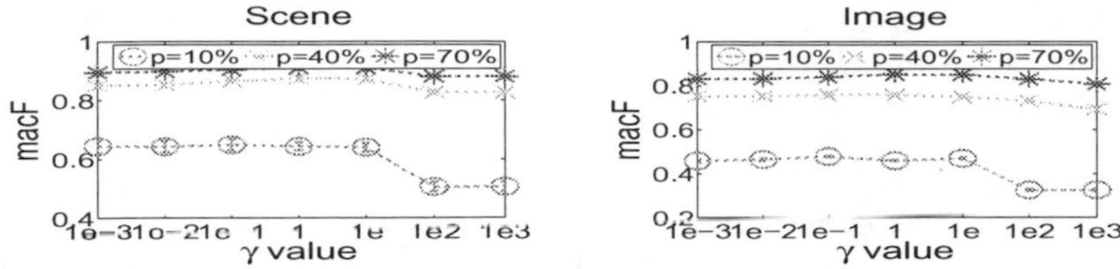

Fig. 2. The influence of β with three different observation rate

7 Conclusion

In this paper, we deal with multi-label crowdsourcing learning where annotations for the tagged instances are incomplete. We exploit the low-rank structure between labels and crowds to estimate the unobserved annotations and infer the groundtruth. Experiments show the superiority of the proposed approach, even in the complete annotation case. We also propose active annotation collection strategies to effectively reduce the labeling workload and cost. Currently, we do not pay special attention to spammer workers which would provide no beneficial annotations, for future work, we would like to deal with such problem.

References

1. Bragg, J., Mausam, Weld, D.: Crowdsourcing multi-label classification for taxonomy creation. In: First AAAI Conference on Human Computation and Crowdsourcing (2013)
2. Bucak, S.S., Jin, R., Jain, A.K.: Multi-label learning with incomplete class assignments. In: Proceedings of the IEEE Computer Society Conference on Computer Vision and Pattern Recognition, Colorado Springs, CO, pp. 2801–2808 (2011)
3. Cai, J.F., Candès, E.J., Shen, Z.: A singular value thresholding algorithm for matrix completion. SIAM J. Optim. **20**(4), 1956–1982 (2010)
4. Candes, E., Tao, T.: The power of convex relaxation: near-optimal matrix completion. IEEE Trans. Inform. Theory **56**(5), 2053–2080 (2009)
5. Chilton, L., Little, G., Edge, D., Weld, D., Landay, J.: Cascade: crowdsourcing taxonomy creation. In: Proceedings of the SIGCHI Conference on Human Factors in Computing Systems, pp. 1999–2008 (2013)
6. Dawid, A.P., Skene, A.M.: Maximum likeihood estimation of observer error-rates using the em algorithm. J. Roy. Stat. Soc. **28**(1), 20–28 (1979)
7. Duan, L., Oyama, S., Sato, H., Kurihara, M.: Separate or joint? Estimation of multiple labels from crowdsourced annotations. Expert Syst. Appl. **41**(13), 5723–5732 (2014)

8. Harshman, R.A.: Foundations of the PARAFAC procedure: models and conditions for an explanatory multi-modal factor analysis. In: UCLA Working Papers in Phonetics, vol. 16, pp. 1–84 (1970)
9. Horvitz, E.: Reflections on challenges and promises of mixed-initiative interaction. AI Mag. **28**(2), 13–22 (2007)
10. Huang, S.J., Zhou, Z.H.: Active query driven by uncertainty and diversity for incremental multi-label learning. In: Proceedings of the 13th IEEE International Conference on Data Mining, pp. 1079–1084 (2013)
11. Karger, D., Oh, S., Shah, D.: Iterative learning for reliable crowdsourcing systems. In: Shawe-Taylor, J., Zemel, R., Bartlett, P., Pereira, F., Weinberger, K. (eds.) Advances in Neural Information Processing Systems 24, pp. 1953–1961 (2011)
12. Krishnamurthy, A., Singh, A.: Low-rank matrix and tensor completion via adaptive sampling. In: Advances in Neural Information Processing Systems 26, Lake Tahoe, Nevada, pp. 836–844 (2013)
13. Li, S.Y., Jiang, Y., Zhou, Z.H.: Multi-label active learning from crowds. CoRR abs/1508.00722 (2015)
14. Li, X., Guo, Y.: Active learning with multi-label SVM classification. In: Proceedings of the 23rd International Joint Conference on Artificial Intelligence, pp. 1479–1485 (2013)
15. Liu, J., Musialski, P., Wonka, P., Ye, J.: Tensor completion for estimating missing values in visual data. IEEE Trans. Pattern Anal. Mach. Intell. **35**(1), 208–220 (2011)
16. Liu, Q., Peng, J., Ihler, A.: Variational inference for crowdsourcing. In: Bartlett, P., Pereira, F., Burges, C., Bottou, L., Weinberger, K. (eds.) Advances in Neural Information Processing Systems 25, pp. 692–700 (2012)
17. Raykar, V., Yu, S., Zhao, L., Valadez, G., Florin, C., Bogoni, L., Moy, L.: Learning from crowds. J. Mach. Learn. Res. **11**, 1297–1322 (2010)
18. Recht, B., Fazel, M., Parrilo, P.A.: Guaranteed minimum-rank solutions of linear matrix equations via nuclear norm minimization. SIAM Rev. **52**(3), 471–501 (2010)
19. Singh, M., Curran, E., Cunningham, P.: Active learning for multi-label image annotation. In: Proceedings of the 19th Irish Conference on Artificial Intelligence and Cognitive Science (2008)
20. Snow, R., O'Connor, B., Jurafsky, D., Ng, A.: Cheap and fast - but is it good? Evaluating non-expert annotations for natural language tasks. In: Proceedings of the Conference on Empirical Methods in Natural Language Processing, Honolulu, Hawaii, pp. 254–263 (2008)
21. Sun, Y., Singla, A., Fox, D., Krause, A.: Building hierarchies of concepts via crowdsourcing. In: Proceedings of the Twenty-Fourth International Joint Conference on Artificial Intelligence, pp. 844–853 (2015)
22. Tam, N.T., Viet, H.H., Hung, N.Q.V., Weidlich, M., Yin, H., Zhou, X.: Multi-label answer aggregation for crowdsourcing. Technique report (2016)
23. Tseng, P.: Convergence of a block coordinate descent method for nondifferentiable minimization. J. Optim. Theory Appl. **109**, 475–494 (2001)
24. Tseng, P.: On accelerated proximal gradient methods for convex-concave optimization. Technical report, University of Washington, Seattle (2008)
25. Tucker, L.R.: Some mathematical notes on three-mode factor analysis. Psychometrika **31**, 279–311 (1966)
26. Welinder, P., Branson, S., Belongie, S., Perona, P.: The multidimensional wisdom of crowds. In: Lafferty, J., Williams, C.I., Shawe-Taylor, J., Zemel, R., Culotta, A. (eds.) Advances in Neural Information Processing Systems 23, pp. 2024–2432 (2010)

27. Whitehill, J., Ruvolo, P., Wu, T., Bergsma, J., Movellan, J.: Whose vote should count more: optimal integration of labels from labelers of unknown expertise. In: Bengio, Y., Schuurmans, D., Lafferty, J., Williams, C., Culotta, A. (eds.) Advances in Neural Information Processing Systems 22, pp. 2035–2043 (2009)
28. Xu, M., Jin, R., Zhou, Z.H.: Speedup matrix completion with side information: application to multi-label learning. In: Burges, C., Bottou, L., Ghahramani, Z., Weinberger: K. (eds.) Advances in Neural Information Processing Systems 26, pp. 2301–2309 (2013)
29. Yan, Y., Rosales, R., Fung, G., Dy, J.: Active learning from crowds. In: Proceedings of the 28th International Conference on Machine Learning, pp. 1161–1168 (2011)
30. Zhang, M.L., Zhou, Z.H.: A review on multi-label learning algorithms. IEEE Trans. Knowl. Data Eng. **26**(8), 1819–1837 (2014)
31. Zhou, D., Basu, S., Mao, Y., Platt, J.: Learning from the wisdom of crowds by minimax entropy. In: Bartlett, P., Pereira, F., Burges, C., Bottou, L., Weinberger, K. (eds.) Advances in Neural Information Processing Systems 25, pp. 2195–2203 (2012)
32. Zhou, Y., He, J.: Crowdsourcing via tensor augmentation and completion. In: Proceedings of the Twenty-Fifth International Joint Conference on Artificial Intelligence, New York, NY, pp. 2435–2441 (2016)

Multiple Kernel Fusion with HSIC Lasso

Tinghua Wang(✉) and Fulai Liu

School of Mathematics and Computer Science, Gannan Normal University, Ganzhou 341000, People's Republic of China
wthgnnu@163.com

Abstract. Multiple kernel learning (MKL) is a principled way for kernel fusion for various learning tasks, such as classification, clustering and dimensionality reduction. In this paper, we develop a novel multiple kernel learning model based on the Hilbert-Schmidt independence criterion (HSIC) for classification (called HSIC-MKL). In the proposed HSIC-MKL model, we first propose a HSIC Lasso-based MKL formulation, which not only has a clear statistical interpretation that minimum redundant kernels with maximum dependence on output labels are found and combined, but also the global optimal solution can be computed efficiently by solving a Lasso optimization problem. After the optimal kernel is obtained, the support vector machine (SVM) is used to select the prediction hypothesis. It is evident that the proposed HSIC-MKL is a two-stage kernel learning approach. Extensive experiments on real-world data sets from UCI benchmark repository validate the superiority of the proposed model in terms of prediction accuracy.

Keywords: Kernel method · Kernel fusion · Multiple kernel learning (MKL) Support vector machine (SVM) · Hilbert-Schmidt independence criterion (HSIC) Lasso

1 Introduction

Kernel methods such as support vector machines (SVM) and kernel Fisher discriminant analysis (KFDA) have been successfully applied to a wide variety of machine learning problems [1]. These methods map data points from the input space to some feature space, i.e., higher dimensional reproducing kernel Hilbert space (RKHS), where even relatively simple algorithms such as linear methods can deliver very impressive performance. The mapping is determined implicitly by a kernel function (or simply a kernel), which computes the inner product of data points in the feature space. Despite the popularity of kernel methods, there is not yet a mechanism in place that can serve to guide the kernel leaning and selection. It is well known that selecting an appropriate kernel, thereby, an appropriate feature space is of great importance to the success of kernel methods [2]. To address this issue, recent years have witnessed the active research on learning effective kernels automatically from data. One popular technique for kernel learning and selection is multiple kernel learning (MKL) [3–5], which aims at learning a linear or nonlinear combination of a set of predefined kernels (base kernels) in order to identify a good target kernel for the applications. Compared with traditional kernel methods employing a fixed kernel, MKL exhibits its flexibility of

X. Geng and B.-H. Kang (Eds.): PRICAI 2018, LNAI 11012, pp. 246–255, 2018.
https://doi.org/10.1007/978-3-319-97304-3_19

automated kernel learning, and also reflects the fact that typical learning problems often involve multiple, heterogeneous data sources.

The idea of MKL can be generally applied to all kinds of kernel methods, such as the commonly used SVM and KFDA, leading to SVM-based MKL and discriminant MKL, respectively. Our work in this paper will only focus on the SVM-based MKL formulation. Specifically, we present a two-stage multiple kernel learning model based on the Hilbert-Schmidt independence criterion (HSIC), called HSIC-MKL. HSIC, which was initially introduced for measuring the statistical dependence between random variables or random processes [6], has been successfully applied in various machine learning problems [7], such as feature selection, clustering and subspace learning. The success is based on the fact that many existing learning tasks can be cast into problems of dependence maximization (or minimization). Motivated by this, in the first stage, we propose a HSIC-Lasso-based MKL formulation, which not only has a clear statistical interpretation that minimum redundant kernels with maximum dependence on output labels are found and combined, but also the global optimal solution can be computed efficiently by solving a Lasso optimization problem[1]. In the second stage, the SVM is used to select the prediction hypothesis, i.e., the SVM is trained to induce the final decision function to show classification results. It should be pointed out that the HSIC Lasso [8, 9] was originally proposed for high-dimensional feature selection, which needs to predefine the kernels (for example, Gaussian kernel for inputs and delta kernel for outputs) before feature selection, whereas our work employs the HSIC Lasso for MKL, aiming to learn an optimal composite kernel to train a kernel classifier.

2 Multiple Kernel Learning

In this section, we briefly review the MKL. Suppose we are given a set of labeled training samples $\{(\boldsymbol{x}_i, y_i)\}_{i=1}^n$ in a binary classification problem, where $\boldsymbol{x}_i \in \mathrm{X} \subset R^d$ is the input data and $y_i \in \{+1, -1\}$ is the corresponding class label. The goal of the SVM is to find an optimal hyperplane $\boldsymbol{w}^{\mathrm{T}}\phi(\boldsymbol{x}) + b = 0$ that separates the training points into two classes with the maximal margin, where $\boldsymbol{w}$ is the normal vector of the hyperplane, b is a bias, and ϕ is a feature map which maps $\boldsymbol{x}_i$ to a high-dimensional feature space. This hyperplane can be obtained by solving the following optimization problem

$$\begin{aligned} &\min \frac{1}{2}\|\boldsymbol{w}\|^2 + C\sum_{i=1}^{n} \xi_i \\ &\text{s.t.} \quad y_i(\boldsymbol{w}^{\mathrm{T}}\phi(\boldsymbol{x}_i) + b) \geq 1 - \xi_i \\ &\qquad \xi_i \geq 0, \quad i = 1, \cdots, n \end{aligned} \tag{1}$$

[1] In statistics and machine learning, Lasso (least absolute shrinkage and selection operator) (also LASSO) is a regression analysis method that performs both variable selection and regularization in order to enhance the prediction accuracy and interpretability of the statistical model it produces.

where $\boldsymbol{\xi} = (\xi_1, \cdots, \xi_n)^{\mathrm{T}}$ is the vector of slack variables and C is the regularization parameter used to impose a trade-off between the training error and generalization.

To solve the SVM optimization problem, suppose α_i be the Lagrange multiplier corresponding to the ith inequality in (1), the dual problem of (1) is shown to

$$\begin{aligned} \max & \sum_{i=1}^{n} \alpha_i - \frac{1}{2}\sum_{i=1}^{n}\sum_{j=1}^{n} y_i y_j \alpha_i \alpha_j k(\boldsymbol{x}_i, \boldsymbol{x}_j) \\ \text{s.t.} & \sum_{i=1}^{n} \alpha_i y_i = 0, \\ & 0 \le \alpha_i \le C, \quad i = 1, \cdots, n. \end{aligned} \tag{2}$$

where $k(\boldsymbol{x}_i, \boldsymbol{x}_j) = \phi(\boldsymbol{x}_i)^{\mathrm{T}} \phi(\boldsymbol{x}_j)$ is the kernel function which implicitly defines the feature map ϕ.

Instead of formulating an optimization criterion with a fixed kernel k, one can leave the kernel k as a combination of a set of predefined kernels, which results in the issue of MKL [3–5]. MKL maps each sample to a multiple-kernel-induced feature space and a linear classifier is learned in this space. The feature mapping used in MKL takes the form of $\phi(\cdot) = [\phi_1^{\mathrm{T}}(\cdot), \cdots, \phi_M^{\mathrm{T}}(\cdot)]^{\mathrm{T}}$, which is induced by M pre-defined base kernels $\{k_m(\cdot,\cdot)\}_{m=1}^{M}$ with different kernel forms or different kernel parameters. The linear combination of the base kernels is given by $k = \sum_{m-1}^{M} \mu_m k_m$, where μ_m is the corresponding combination coefficient. Let $\boldsymbol{\mu} = (\mu_1, \cdots, \mu_M)^{\mathrm{T}} \in \Delta$, where Δ is the domain of $\boldsymbol{\mu}$. With different constraints on $\boldsymbol{\mu}$, different MKL models can be obtained. For example, when $\boldsymbol{\mu} \in \Delta$ lies in a simplex, i.e.:

$$\Delta = \left\{ \boldsymbol{\mu} : \|\boldsymbol{\mu}\|_1 = \sum_{m=1}^{M} \mu_m = 1, \mu_m \ge 0 \right\} \tag{3}$$

we call it L_1-norm of kernel weights and the resulting model L_1-MKL [10]. Most MKL methods fall in this category. When

$$\Delta = \left\{ \boldsymbol{\mu} : \|\boldsymbol{\mu}\|_p \le 1, p > 1, \mu_m \ge 0 \right\} \tag{4}$$

we call it L_p-norm of kernel weights and the resulting model L_p-MKL [11].

Like SVM, the dual problem of MKL can be represented as

$$\begin{aligned} \max & \sum_{i=1}^{n} \alpha_i - \frac{1}{2}\sum_{i=1}^{n}\sum_{j=1}^{n} y_i y_j \alpha_i \alpha_j \sum_{m=1}^{M} \mu_m k_m(\boldsymbol{x}_i, \boldsymbol{x}_j) \\ \text{s.t.} & \sum_{i=1}^{n} \alpha_i y_i = 0, \ \boldsymbol{\mu} \in \Delta, \\ & 0 \le \alpha_i \le C, \quad i = 1, \cdots, n. \end{aligned} \tag{5}$$

The goal of training MKL is to learn μ_m, α_i and b with the given M base kernels, and the final decision function is given by

$$f(\boldsymbol{x}) = \mathrm{sgn}\left(\sum_{i=1}^{n} \alpha_i y_i \sum_{m=1}^{M} \mu_m k_m(\boldsymbol{x}_i, \boldsymbol{x}) + b\right) \tag{6}$$

where the samples $\boldsymbol{x}_i$ with $\alpha_i > 0$ are called support vectors.

3 MKL-HSIC

In this section, we detailedly discuss the two-stage MKL method (HSIC-MKL) for learning kernels in the form of linear combination of M base kernels $\{k_m(\cdot,\cdot)\}_{m=1}^{M}$ or kernel matrices $\{\mathbf{K}_m\}_{m=1}^{M}$. The corresponding combination coefficient μ_m is selected subject to the condition $\mu_m \geq 0$. In the first stage, the algorithm determines the combination coefficient μ_m, and in the second stage, an SVM is trained with the learned kernel.

We first introduce the notion of the HSIC. Let $\mathbf{e} = (1, \cdots, 1)^{\mathrm{T}} \in \mathrm{R}^n$ and $\mathbf{I} \in \mathrm{R}^{n \times n}$ be the identity matrix. Given the centering matrix $\mathbf{H} = \mathbf{I} - \mathbf{e}\mathbf{e}^{\mathrm{T}}/n \in \mathrm{R}^{n \times n}$, the centered kernel matrix associated with $\mathbf{K}$ is given by $\bar{\mathbf{K}} = \mathbf{HKH}$. Given two kernels k_1 and k_2, the HSIC between these two kernels is defined as

$$HSIC(\mathbf{K}_1, \mathbf{K}_2) = \frac{1}{n^2}\mathrm{tr}(\mathbf{K}_1\mathbf{H}\mathbf{K}_2\mathbf{H}) \tag{7}$$

Let $\bar{\mathbf{L}} = \mathbf{HLH}$ and $\bar{\mathbf{K}} = \mathbf{HKH}$, where $\mathbf{K}$ and $\mathbf{L}$ are the kernel matrix for input data an kernel matrix for output labels, respectively. We here propose using HSIC Lasso [8, 9] for estimating the combination coefficient $\boldsymbol{\mu}$:

$$\begin{aligned} \min\ & \frac{1}{2}\left\| \bar{\mathbf{L}} - \sum_{m=1}^{M} \mu_m \bar{\mathbf{K}}_m \right\|_{\mathrm{F}}^2 + \lambda \|\boldsymbol{\mu}\|_1 \\ \text{s.t.}\ & \mu_1, \cdots, \mu_M \geq 0 \end{aligned} \tag{8}$$

where $\|\cdot\|_{\mathrm{F}}$ is the Frobenius norm and $\lambda > 0$ is the regularization parameter. In (8), the first term means that we are aligning the centered output kernel matrix $\bar{\mathbf{L}}$ by a linear combination of the centered input base kernel matrices $\{\bar{\mathbf{K}}_m\}_{m=1}^{M}$, and the second term means that the combination coefficients for irrelevant base kernels become zero since the L_1-regularizer tends to produce a sparse solution. After estimating $\boldsymbol{\mu}$, we normalize each element of $\boldsymbol{\mu}$ as $\mu_m \rightarrow \mu_m / \sum_{m=1}^{M} \mu_m$.

Noting that $<\bar{\mathbf{K}}, \bar{\mathbf{L}}>_{\mathrm{F}} = <\bar{\mathbf{K}}, \mathbf{L}>_{\mathrm{F}} = <\mathbf{K}, \bar{\mathbf{L}}>_{\mathrm{F}} = \mathrm{tr}\mathbf{KHLH} = n^2 HSIC(\mathbf{K}, \mathbf{L})$, we can rewrite the first term of (8) as

$$
\begin{aligned}
&\frac{1}{2}\left\|\bar{\mathbf{L}} - \sum_{m=1}^{M} \mu_m \bar{\mathbf{K}}_m\right\|_{\mathrm{F}}^2 \\
&= \frac{1}{2}\left\langle \bar{\mathbf{L}} - \sum_{m=1}^{M} \mu_m \bar{\mathbf{K}}_m, \bar{\mathbf{L}} - \sum_{m=1}^{M} \mu_m \bar{\mathbf{K}}_m \right\rangle_{\mathrm{F}} \\
&= \frac{1}{2}\langle \bar{\mathbf{L}}, \bar{\mathbf{L}}\rangle_{\mathrm{F}} - \left\langle \bar{\mathbf{L}}, \sum_{m=1}^{M} \mu_m \bar{\mathbf{K}}_m \right\rangle_{\mathrm{F}} + \frac{1}{2}\left\langle \sum_{m=1}^{M} \mu_m \bar{\mathbf{K}}_m, \sum_{m=1}^{M} \mu_m \bar{\mathbf{K}}_m \right\rangle_{\mathrm{F}} \\
&= \frac{1}{2}\langle \bar{\mathbf{L}}, \bar{\mathbf{L}}\rangle_{\mathrm{F}} - \sum_{m=1}^{M} \mu_m \langle \bar{\mathbf{L}}, \bar{\mathbf{K}}_m\rangle_{\mathrm{F}} + \frac{1}{2}\sum_{m=1}^{M}\sum_{o=1}^{M} \mu_m \mu_o \langle \bar{\mathbf{K}}_m, \bar{\mathbf{K}}_o\rangle_{\mathrm{F}} \\
&= \frac{n^2}{2} HSIC(\mathbf{L}, \mathbf{L}) - n^2 \sum_{m=1}^{M} \mu_m HSIC(\mathbf{L}, \mathbf{K}_m) + \frac{n^2}{2}\sum_{m=1}^{M}\sum_{o=1}^{M} \mu_m \mu_o HSIC(\mathbf{K}_m, \mathbf{K}_o)
\end{aligned}
\tag{9}
$$

In (9), the n^2 and $HSIC(\mathbf{L}, \mathbf{L})$ are constant and can be ignored. We have a clear statistical interpretation of MKL using HSIC Lasso. First, if the m-th kernel matrix $\mathbf{K}_m$ has high dependence on the output matrix $\mathbf{L}$, $HSIC(\mathbf{L}, \mathbf{K}_m)$ takes a large value and thus μ_m should also be large so that (9) is minimized. On the other hand, if $\mathbf{K}_m$ and $\mathbf{L}$ are independent, $HSIC(\mathbf{L}, \mathbf{K}_m)$ is close to zero and thus μ_m tends to be removed by the L_1-regularizer. This means that relevant kernels that have strong dependence on output $\mathbf{L}$ tend to be selected by the HSIC Lasso. Second, if $\mathbf{K}_m$ and $\mathbf{K}_o$ are strongly dependent, which means one of them is redundant kernel, $HSIC(\mathbf{K}_m, \mathbf{K}_o)$ takes a large value and thus either μ_m or μ_o tends to be zero. This means that redundant kernels tend to be removed by the HSIC Lasso. In one word, HSIC Lasso tends to find non-redundant kernels with strong dependence on output $\mathbf{L}$, which is a preferable property in kernel learning.

To solve the HSIC Lasso problem in (9), many Lasso optimization techniques can be applied in practice, such as dual augmented Lagrangian (DAL) [12, 13], which has been successfully employed for high-dimensional feature selection [8, 9].

We sketch the overall procedure of the proposed HSIC-MKL in Algorithm 1, where the centered kernel matrix can be calculated by

$$
\bar{\mathbf{K}}_{ij} = \mathbf{K}_{ij} - \frac{1}{n}\sum_{i=1}^{n} \mathbf{K}_{ij} - \frac{1}{n}\sum_{j=1}^{n} \mathbf{K}_{ij} + \frac{1}{n^2}\sum_{i=1}^{n}\sum_{j=1}^{n} \mathbf{K}_{ij}
\tag{10}
$$

Algorithm 1. HSIC-MKL

Input: Labeled data $\{(x_i, y_i)\}_{i=1}^n$, base kernels $\{k_m(\cdot,\cdot)\}_{m=1}^M$ or kernel matrices $\{\mathbf{K}_m\}_{m=1}^M$, and regularization parameters C and λ.

Output: SVM classifier $f(x)$.

1: Initialize $\boldsymbol{\mu} = \boldsymbol{e}/M$.

2: Calculate the kernel matrix $\mathbf{L} = \boldsymbol{y}\boldsymbol{y}^{\mathrm{T}}$, where $\boldsymbol{y} = (y_1, \cdots, y_n)^{\mathrm{T}}$.

3: Calculate the centered kernel matrices $\bar{\mathbf{L}}$ and $\{\bar{\mathbf{K}}_m\}_{m=1}^M$.

4: Obtain $\boldsymbol{\mu}$ by solving (8).

5: Normalize each element of $\boldsymbol{\mu}$ as $\mu_m \to \mu_m / \sum_{m=1}^M \mu_m$.

6: Combine the kernel matrices using the weight $\boldsymbol{\mu}$ and train an SVM classifier.

We analyze the computational complexity of Algorithm 1 with the O notation. Firstly, the computational complexity of calculating centered kernel matrices in Step 3 is $O(Mn^2)$. Secondly, the complexity of the quadratic programming solver in Step 4 is $O(TM^3)$ with T being the number of iterations in solving (8). Finally, note that empirically the SVM training complexity is $O(n^{2.3})$ [14], the computational complexity of Step 6 is $O(M + n^{2.3})$. Thus, the total computational complexity of our proposed HSIC-MKL is

$$O(Mn^2) + O(M^3) + O(M + n^{2.3}) = O(Mn^2 + M^3 + n^{2.3}) \quad (11)$$

It should be noted that we here suppose that multiple base kernels (kernel matrices) can be precomputed and loaded into memory before the HSIC-MKL training. Then, the computational cost of calculating the base kernels is ignored.

4 Experimental Evaluation

In this section, we perform extensive experiments on binary classification problems to evaluate the efficacy of the proposed HSIC-MKL approach. We compare HSIC-MKL with the following state-of-the-art kernel learning algorithms:

- AvgMKL: The average combination of multiple base kernels. It was reported that AvgMKL is competitive with many algorithms [3, 4].
- SimpleMKL [10]: An algorithm reformulates the mixed-norm regularization of MKL problem as the weighted 2-norm regularization, and L_1-norm is imposed on kernel weights.
- LpMKL [11]: An algorithm generalizes the regular L_1-norm MKL to arbitrary L_p-norm ($p > 1$) MKL. We adopt the cutting plane algorithm with second order Taylor approximation of L_p.

- CKA-MKL [15]: The two-stage MKL with centered kernel alignment. The two-stage MKL first learns the optimal kernel weights according some criteria, and then applies the learned optimal kernel to train a kernel classifier.

For parameter settings, the regularization parameters C and λ are determined by 5-fold cross-validation on the training set. Specifically, we perform grid-search in one dimension (i.e., a line-search) to choose the regularization parameters C from the set $\{10^{-2}, 10^{-1}, \cdots, 10^{2}\}$ for all the compared methods. For our proposed HSIC-MKL approach, we perform grid-search over two dimensions, i.e., $C = \{10^{-2}, 10^{0}, \cdots, 10^{2}\}$ and $\lambda = \{10^{-2}, 10^{-1}, \cdots, 10^{2}\}$. In addition, for LpMKL, we examine $p = 2, 3, 4$ and report the best results. In the aspect of implementation, all the methods are implemented using MATLAB in the framework of SVM-KM toolbox[2]. Note that SimpleMKL has been implemented in the SimpleMKL software package[3], which needs the SVM-KM toolbox.

We select eight popular binary classification data sets, i.e., *Australian Credit Approval*, *Breast Cancer Wisconsin (Original)*, *Pima Indians Diabetes*, *German Credit Data*, *Heart*, *Ionosphere*, *Liver Disorders*, and *Sonar*, from the UCI machine learning repository [16]. For *Breast Cancer Wisconsin (Original)*, we directly eliminated the samples that contain missing attribute values. Table 1 provides the statistics of these data sets. It presents, for each data set, the short name of data set, the number of samples, the number of features, and the original name of data set.

Table 1. Statistics of the selected eight data sets from UCI

Data set	#Samples	#Features	Original data set
Australian	690	14	Australian credit approval
Breast	683	9	Breast cancer wisconsin (original)
Diabetes	768	8	Pima indians diabetes
German	1000	20	German credit data
Heart	270	13	Heart
Ionosphere	351	34	Ionosphere
Liver	345	7	Liver disorders
Sonar	208	60	Sonar

For each data set, we partition it into a training set and a test set by stratified sampling (by which the object generation follows the class prior probabilities): 50% of the data set serves as training set and the left 50% as test set. The training samples are normalized to be of zero mean and unit variance, and the test samples are also normalized using the same mean and variance of the training data. Following the settings of previous For each data set, we partition it into a training set and a test set by stratified sampling (by which the object generation follows the class prior probabilities): 50% of the data set serves as

[2] http://asi.insa-rouen.fr/enseignants/~arakoto/toolbox/.

[3] http://asi.insa-rouen.fr/enseignants/~arakoto/code/mklindex.html.

training set and the left 50% as test set. The training samples are normalized to be of zero mean and unit variance, and the test samples are also normalized using the same mean and variance of the training data. Following the settings of previous MKL studies [10], we use the Gaussian kernel $k(\boldsymbol{x}_i, \boldsymbol{x}_j) = \exp(-\|\boldsymbol{x}_i - \boldsymbol{x}_j\|^2 / 2\sigma^2)$ and polynomial kernel $k(\boldsymbol{x}_i, \boldsymbol{x}_j) = (\boldsymbol{x}_i \cdot \boldsymbol{x}_j + 1)^d$ as the base kernels:

- Gaussian kernels with ten different widths $\sigma \in \{2^{-3}, 2^{-2}, \cdots, 2^6\}$ for each individual dimension as well as all dimensions.
- Polynomial kernels with three different degrees $d \in \{1, 2, 3\}$ for each individual feature as well as all features.

All kernel matrices are normalized to unit trace and precomputed prior to running the algorithms.

Table 2. Classification accuracy comparison among different MKL algorithms on UCI data sets

Data set	Classification accuracy (%)				
	AvgMKL	SimpleMKL	LpMKL	CKA-MKL	HSIC-MKL
Australian	66.8 ± 4.5	85.1 ± 1.3	84.6 ± 1.7	**87.2 ± 0.4**	86.7 ± 1.3
Breast	95.4 ± 0.9	**96.6 ± 0.7**	96.1 ± 0.6	96.4 ± 0.9	96.6 ± 1.0
Diabetes	65.3 ± 1.8	75.9 ± 2.3	72.7 ± 2.4	75.3 ± 3.5	**77.1 ± 2.2**
German	69.6 ± 1.4	71.5 ± 2.6	**74.4 ± 1.5**	72.0 ± 1.2	72.4 ± 0.9
Heart	75.5 ± 5.3	83.1 ± 2.8	80.6 ± 3.6	82.1 ± 1.8	**83.3 ± 2.6**
Ionosphere	91.2 ± 1.8	93.5 ± 1.2	94.8 ± 2.1	93.7 ± 1.0	**95.5 ± 0.8**
Liver	57.4 ± 2.1	62.4 ± 4.3	69.3 ± 2.8	68.8 ± 1.6	**70.0 ± 2.9**
Sonar	59.0 ± 8.7	78.2 ± 3.5	**84.7 ± 3.3**	81.3 ± 2.8	81.8 ± 3.2

To get stable results, we independently repeat splitting each data set, and then run each algorithm on it for 20 times. The average classification accuracy and the standard deviations of each algorithm are reported in Table 2. The bold numbers denote the best performance of MKL methods on each data set. To conduct a rigorous comparison, the paired t-test [17] is performed. The paired t-test is used to analyze if the difference between two compared algorithms on one data set is significant or not. The p-value of the paired t-test represents the probability that two sets of compared results come from the distributions with an equal mean. A p-value of 0.05 is considered statistically significant. The win-tie-loss (W-T-L) summarizations based on the paired t-test are listed in Table 3, where HSIC-MKL and SimpleMKL, HSIC-MKL and LpMKL, and HSIC-MKL and CKA-MKL are compared, respectively. For two compared algorithms, assuming Algorithm 1 vs. Algorithm 2, a win or a loss means that Algorithm 1 is better or worse than Algorithm 2 on a data set. A tie means that both algorithms have the same performance.

From Tables 2 and 3, we find that the proposed HSIC-MKL consistently achieves the overall best classification performance. Among the evaluated 8 data sets, SimpleMKL, LpMKL and CKA-MKL report 1, 2 and 1 best results, respectively, while our

Table 3. Significance test of classification results on UCI data sets

Data set	Win-tie-loss (W-T-L)		
	HSIC-MKL vs. SimpleMKL	HSIC-MKL vs. LpMKL	HSIC-MKL vs. CKA-MKL
Australian	W	W	T
Breast	T	T	T
Diabetes	W	W	W
German	W	L	T
Heart	T	W	W
Ionosphere	W	W	W
Liver	W	W	W
Sonar	W	L	T

HSIC-MKL reports 4 best results. From the viewpoint of significance test, we have the following observations. For HSIC-MKL, although it is outperformed by LpMKL on the *German* and *Sonar* data sets, it produces significantly better classification performance than LpMKL on the *Australian*, *Diabetes*, *Heart*, *Ionosphere* and *Liver* data sets. Compared with SimpleMKL, HSIC-MKL significantly outperforms SimpleMKL on the *Australian*, *Diabetes*, *German*, *Ionosphere*, *Liver*, *Sonar* data sets, and yields the same performance on the rest of the data sets. Compared with CKA-MKL, HSIC-MKL significantly outperforms CKA-MKL on the *Diabetes*, *Heart*, *Ionosphere* and *Liver* data sets, and yields the same performance on the rest of the data sets. Overall, HSIC-MKL is better than SimpleMKl, LpMKL and CKA-MKL.

5 Conclusion

We have presented an effective two-stage MKL algorithm based on the notion of HSIC. By discussing the connection between MKL and HSIC Lasso, we find that the proposed algorithm not only has a clear statistical interpretation that minimum redundant kernels with maximum dependence on output labels are found and combined, but also the global optimal solution can be computed efficiently by solving a Lasso optimization problem. Comprehensive experiments on a number of benchmark data sets demonstrate the promising results of our proposed algorithm. Future investigation will focus on the further validation of the use of the proposed algorithm on more real-world applications, such as computer vision, speech and signal processing, and natural language processing. Moreover, expending the proposed model to extreme learning machine and domain transfer learning, as well as investigating theoretical properties of the proposed algorithm are important issues to be investigated.

Acknowledgements. This work is supported in part by the National Natural Science Foundation of China (No. 61562003).

References

1. Shawe-Taylor, J., Cristianini, N.: Kernel Methods for Pattern Analysis. Cambridge University Press, New York (2004)
2. Wang, T., Zhao, D., Tian, S.: An overview of kernel alignment and its applications. Artif. Intell. Rev. **43**(2), 179–192 (2015)
3. Gönen, M., Alpayın, E.: Multiple kernel learning algorithms. J. Mach. Learn. Res. **12**, 2211–2268 (2011)
4. Bucak, S.S., Jin, R., Jain, A.K.: Multiple kernel learning for visual object recognition: a review. IEEE Trans. Pattern Anal. Mach. Intell. **36**(7), 1354–1369 (2014)
5. Gu, Y., Chanussot, J., Jia, X., Benediktsson, J.A.: Multiple kernel learning for hyperspectral image classification: a review. IEEE Trans. Geosci. Remote Sens. **55**(11), 6547–6565 (2017)
6. Gretton, A., Bousquet, O., Smola, A., Schölkopf, B.: Measuring statistical dependence with Hilbert-Schmidt norms. In: Jain, S., Simon, H.U., Tomita, E. (eds.) ALT 2005. LNCS (LNAI), vol. 3734, pp. 63–77. Springer, Heidelberg (2005). https://doi.org/10.1007/11564089_7
7. Wang, T., Li, W.: Kernel learning and optimization with Hilbert-Schmidt independence criterion. Int. J. Mach. Learn. Cybern. 1–11 (2017). https://doi.org/10.1007/s13042-017-0675-7
8. Yamada, M., Kimura, A., Naya, F., Sawada, H.: Change-point detection with feature selection in high-dimensional time-series data. In Proceedings of the 23rd International Joint Conference on Artificial Intelligence, Beijing, China, pp. 1827–1833 (2013)
9. Yamada, M., Jitkrittum, W., Sigal, L., Xing, E.P., Sugiyama, M.: High-dimensional feature selection by feature-wise kernelized Lasso. Neural Comput. **26**(1), 185–207 (2014)
10. Rakotomamonjy, A., Bach, F.R., Canu, S., Grandvalet, Y.: SimpleMKL. J. Mach. Learn. Res. **9**, 2491–2521 (2008)
11. Kloft, M., Brefeld, U., Sonnenburg, S., Zien, A.: l_p-norm multiple kernel learning. J. Mach. Learn. Res. **12**, 953–997 (2011)
12. Tomioka, R., Sugiyama, M.: Dual-augmented Lagrangian method for efficient sparse reconstruction. IEEE Sig. Process. Lett. **16**(12), 1067–1070 (2009)
13. Tomioka, R., Sugiyama, M.: Super-linear convergence of dual augmented Lagrangian algorithm for sparsity regularized estimation. J. Mach. Learn. Res. **12**, 1537–1586 (2011)
14. Platt, J.C.: Fast training of support vector machines using sequential minimal optimization. In: Advances in Kernel Methods: Support Vector Learning, pp. 185–208 (1999)
15. Cortes, C., Mohri, M., Rostamizadeh, A.: Algorithms for learning kernels based on centered alignment. J. Mach. Learn. Res. **13**, 795–828 (2012)
16. Lichman, M.: UCI machine learning repository. University of California, School of Information and Computer Science, Irvine (2013). http://archive.ics.uci.edu/ml/
17. Demšar, J.: Statistical comparisons of classifiers over multiple data sets. J. Mach. Learn. Res. **7**, 1–30 (2006)

Visualizing and Understanding Policy Networks of Computer Go

Yuanfeng Pang(✉) and Takeshi Ito

The University of Electro-Communications, Tokyo, Japan
yuanfengpang@gmail.com, uecitotake@gmail.com

Abstract. In May 2017, the application of deep learning to the game "Go" enjoyed a tremendous victory when the AlphaGo computer program beat one of the top professional players. However, there is no clear understanding of why deep learning elicits such strong performance. In this paper, we introduce visualization techniques used in image recognition to investigate the functions of the intermediate layers and operations of the Go policy network. Used as a diagnostic tool, these visualization techniques allow us to understand what happens during the training of policy networks. We also introduce a visualization technique that performs a sensitivity analysis of the classifier output by occluding portions of the input Go board, revealing which parts of the board are important for predicting the next move.

Keywords: Deep learning · Computer Go · Visualization

1 Introduction

Since their introduction by Clark and Storkey [1], convolutional networks have demonstrated excellent performance as the basis for computer learning of the strategy board game "Go". Several studies have shown that convolutional networks can perform as well as regular Monte Carlo tree search (MCTS)-based approaches. This idea was extended in developing Darkforest [2], which is a Deep Convolutional Neural Network (DCNN) designed for long-term predictions. Darkforest substantially improves the win rate for pattern matching approaches against MCTS-based approaches, even with looser search budgets. This paved the way for AlphaGo [3], which combines MCTS with policy and value networks. Since 2016, AlphaGo has defeated three human Go champions, becoming the first computer program to defeat human professional players in a full-sized game of Go.

Despite the encouraging fact that deep neural networks are better at recognizing shapes than MCTS-based approaches, there is still little insight into the internal operation and behavior of these complex networks, or how they achieve such good performance. Without a clear understanding of how and why they work, we cannot fully utilize DCNN-based computer Go and continue its encouraging progress. In this paper, we introduce visualization techniques used in image recognition that provide an insight into the functional intermediate layers of DCNNs and apply them to visualize the operation of the Go policy network. Used as a diagnostic tool, these visualizations allow us to understand what happens during the training process. We also introduce a

X. Geng and B.-H. Kang (Eds.): PRICAI 2018, LNAI 11012, pp. 256–267, 2018.
https://doi.org/10.1007/978-3-319-97304-3_20

visualization technique that performs a sensitivity analysis of the classifier output by occluding portions of the input Go board, revealing which parts of the board are important for predicting the next move.

2 Related Work

Policy Network of Computer Go: Currently, the most successful Go programs are based on MCTS with a policy and a value network. The strongest programs, such as AlphaGo and Darkforest, apply convolutional networks to construct a move selection policy, which is used to bias the exploration when training the value network. A supervised learning strategy enabled AlphaGo to achieve 57% move prediction accuracy using a database of human professional games [4]. Moreover, the probability that the expert's move is within the top-5 predictions of the network exceeded 87%. Recently, using a combined policy and value network architecture and assigning a low weight to the value component, it became possible to avoid overfitting to the values. After 72 h, the move prediction accuracy exceeded that of the state-of-the-art method, reaching 60.4% on the KGS test set [5].

Visualization: Recent work on image recognition has demonstrated the considerable advantages of deep convolutional networks over alternative architectures. Moreover, our understanding of how these models work has progressed significantly. One relatively simple method is to use visualizing filters, but these are generally limited to the first layer, where projections to pixel space are possible. Because we take a direct inner product between the weights of the convolution layer and the pixels in the original image, we can get some sense of what these filters are looking for by visualizing the learned weights of these filters. Clark and Storkey [1] visualized the weights of some randomly selected channels from the randomly selected convolution filters of a five-layer convolutional neural network trained on the Games of Go on Disk (GoGoD) dataset. They found that some filters learned to acquire a symmetric property; however, as they are not connected directly to the input image, the visualized filters of intermediate layers are less interpretable, and alternate methods must be used in higher layers. One method involves visualizing the activation maps of intermediate layers. In convolution networks, filters are applied in a way that respects the underlying geometry of the input. Visualizing activation maps is a simple way to gain intuition about what types of things in the input are each of those features in that layer looking for. In 2015, Zeiler and Fergus [6] introduced a novel visualization technique that provides an insight into the function of the intermediate feature layers and the operation of the classifier. Their approach provides a non-parametric view of invariance, showing which patterns from the training set activate the feature map. They conducted occlusion experiments using an image dataset, masking part of the image before feeding it to the CNN, then constructed a probability heatmap at each masked location [6]. When parts of the original input image corresponding to the pattern were occluded, Zeiler and Fergus observed a distinct drop in activity within the feature map. Used in a diagnostic role, these visualizations allowed them to find model architectures that outperform older ones. The generality of this visualization technique suggests its applicability to other "visual" domains, such as computer Go. That is, it should be possible to gain intuition about the policy network by examining the inputs.

3 Network

Recent progress has involved the application of DCNNs rather than shallow networks to predict the next move based on simple patterns extracted from previous games. In this study, we train a DCNN that predicts the next move given the current board situation as an input. We treat the 19×19 board as a 19×19 image with five channels. Each channel encodes information from a different aspect of the board, (e.g., the player's stones or the opponent's stones).

3.1 Data

The dataset used in this study was taken from GoGoD [7], which consists of sequences of board positions for complete games played between humans of professional rank. The data are saved in the SGF computer file format. A move is encoded as an indicator (1 of 361) for each position on the 19×19 board. The board state information includes the positions of all stones on the board, and the sequence allows the order of individual moves to be determined. We collected 17.6 million board-state next-move pairs (corresponding to 86329 games) and used 100000 of these pairs as the test dataset.

Table 1. Features used as inputs to the CNN

Feature	# of planes	Description
Stone colour	3	Player's stone/opponent's stone/empty
Last move	2	Last move of player and opponent

The features that we use come directly from the raw representation of the game rules. The feature planes are listed in Table 1. There are three differences between our features and those used in the policy network of AlphaGo. First, considering the future visualization work, we added the empty position plane to the stone color features; thus, the first three feature planes represent the board. Moreover, three planes can be easily visualized using the RGB color model. Second, to accelerate the training, we reduced the last move information to two feature planes (only the last two moves are considered). Third, we encoded the stone color features by specifying whether each stone belongs to the player or the opponent (rather than as black and white stones) and omitted the feature that records whether it as black's turn or white's turn.

3.2 Network Architecture

Compared to previous works, we use a simpler feature set and shallower CNN to accelerate the training process. Each convolution layer is followed by batch normalization. All layers use the same width, w = 64, with no pooling. This is because pooling reduces the amount of input information that is retained and negatively affects the performance. Instead, we use only one softmax layer to predict the next move. Figure 1 shows the architecture of the network for our model. The differences between our Lite Policy network and the AlphaGo-Zero network are listed in Table 2. The neural network parameters are optimized by stochastic gradient descent with momentum and learning rate annealing. After feeding the current position into the network, the softmax output with the maximum probability will be selected.

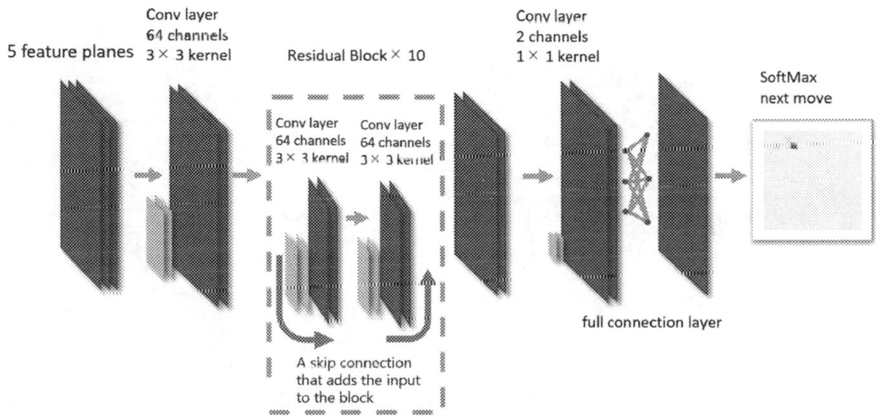

Fig. 1. Our network structure (d = CNN * 2 and Residual Block * 10, w = 64). The input is the current board situation, the output is the predicted next move.

Table 2. Differences between the two networks

Description	Lite policy net	AlphaGo-Zero net
Input planes	5	17
Residual block	10	40
Width	64	256
Network head	Policy head	Policy head/value head
Output	Next move	Board value/next move
Batch size	128	32 × 19
Dataset	86329 professional games (GoGoD)	4.9 million games of self-play
Policy iteration	No	Yes

3.3 Training Results

To understand the performance of our network, we measured the prediction accuracy and the loss on the training set and test set during training (10 epochs). Though the accuracy on the test dataset was less than 50%, we found that the top-n performance of the DCNN was quite strong. As shown in Fig. 2, the network can predict the correct next move 80% of the time when n = 9. We consider the accuracy of our network to be good enough to make it worthwhile conducting occlusion sensitivity experiments.

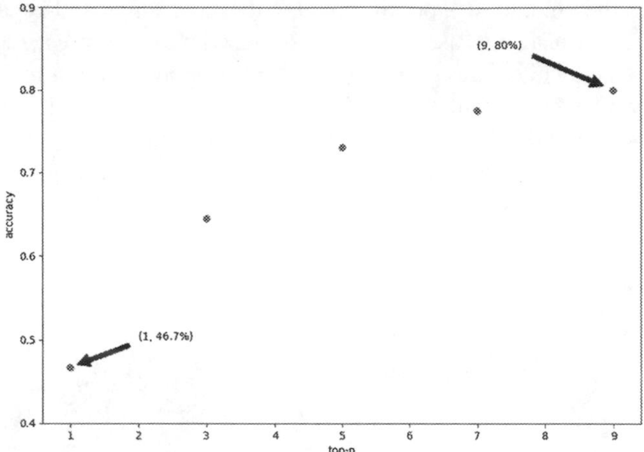

Fig. 2. Probability that the right next move is within the top-n predictions of the network.

4 Visualization

To understand our policy network, we applied four visualization techniques used in image recognition. These methods focus on understanding how the model changes during the process of training.

4.1 Visualize the Weight of Filters

Visualization of the Weight: The method of visualizing the weight of filters is shown in Fig. 3. This visualization allows us to see how the model evolves over time.

4.2 Visualize the Activation

The second visualization method involves plotting the activation values for the neurons in each layer of a convolution network in response to a specific board. In convolutional networks, filters are applied in a way that respects the underlying geometry of the input in lower layers, and each channel is also arranged spatially. Figures 4 and 5 show examples of this type of visualization. Except for the last convolution layer, which has a size of $2 \times 19 \times 19$ depicted as two separate 19×19 grayscale images, all convolution layers have a size of $64 \times 19 \times 19$ depicted as 64 separate 19×19 grayscale images. Each of the 64 small images contains activations in the same (1–19)–(A–T) spatial layout as the input board data. Figure 5 shows 64 images tiled into an 8×8 grid in row-major order.

Activation Visualization of Successive Moves: Figure 4 shows the visualization of the activation map in our trained model after feeding successive moves into the policy network.

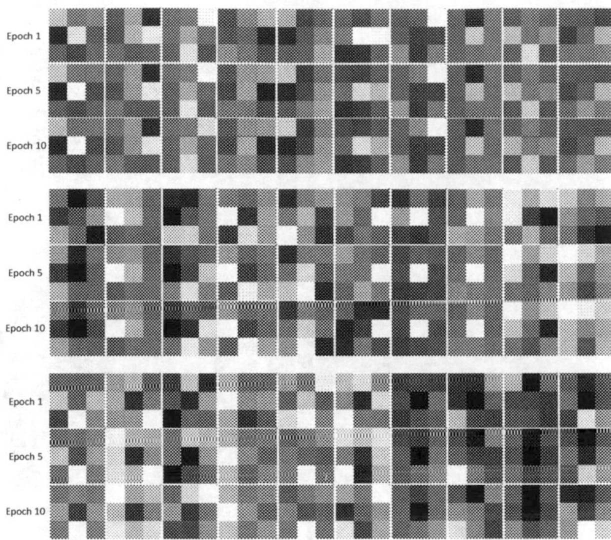

Fig. 3. Evolution of the first ten filter weights of the first layer during training. Filters for the first three feature planes (stone colour), the fourth feature plane (last move of player), and the fifth feature (last move of opponent) are displayed in different blocks. Within each block, we show the visualized weights at epochs 1, 5, and 10. We use the RGB color model to visualize the filters of first three features and grayscale to visualize the filters of the fourth and fifth feature planes. Note: (i) Because of the smaller filter size (3×3), the symmetric property acquired by previous, larger filters is not observed (e.g., 7×7, Clark and Storkey [7]); (ii) The first three feature planes represent the player's stone, opponent's stone, and empty squares by separate one-hot encoding. This means that the same position cannot have values of 1 or 0 simultaneously. The red, green, and blue visualized weights detect the player's stone, opponent's stone, or empty position. The visualization shows that only a few weights have a clear assignment, whereas most of the filters did not learn to acquire a clear recognition of the Go board like a human player; (iii) throughout the training process, weights from the filters of stone colour features changed less significantly than weights from the filters of last move features. After five epochs, unlike the filters of stone colour features, the filters of last move features are still trying to converge to the optimal solution, e.g., filters in block 2, row 3, column 6 and block 3, row 3, column 10. (Color figure online)

Activation Visualization of Different Layers: Figure 5 shows the visualization of the activation map in different layers.

4.3 Visualization with a Transposed Convolution Network

Visualization with a transposed convolution network (also known as deconvnet) can interpret the feature activity in intermediate layers. This method maps these activities back to the input pixel space, showing what input pattern originally caused a given activation in the feature. The transposed convolution network [7] can be thought of as a convolution network model that uses the same components, but in reverse. Like Zeiler and Fergus [7], we used rectification and flipped filters (flip each filter vertically and horizontally) to reconstruct the activity in the layer beneath, which gave rise to the

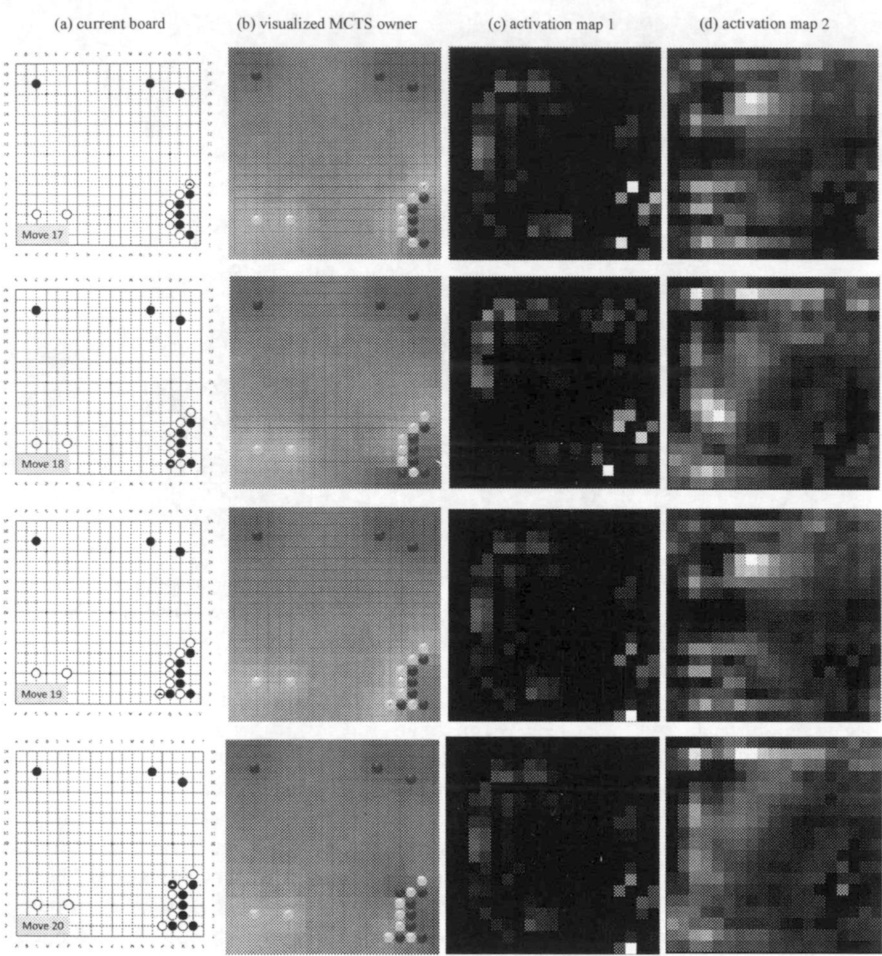

Fig. 4. Visualization of the activation map in our trained model. We analyze four successive moves (moves 17–20) from a game in which AlphaGo Zero (white) beat Ke Jie (black). These visualizations are not samples from the model, but are grayscale maps of given features with a specific input move. In column (b), we visualize the all board owner calculated by MCTS. In columns (c) and (d), we visualize the convolution network activations of the last-layer features. Although much of the lower computation is robust to small changes, the last layer is more sensitive. As we encode the stone colour features as the player's stone and opponent's stone, the input from neighbouring moves is nearly opposite, whereas the input from separated moves is similar. On activation map 1, although the inputs (e.g., move 17 and move 18, move 18 and move 19) fed to the network are nearly opposite, the map remains similar except in the lower right, where the furikawari (exchange) happened. Moreover, on activation map 2, the input from separated moves (move 17 and move 19, move 19 and move 20) is similar. It seems that activation map 1 is more interpretable than activation map 2, and has a closer connection with the original board.

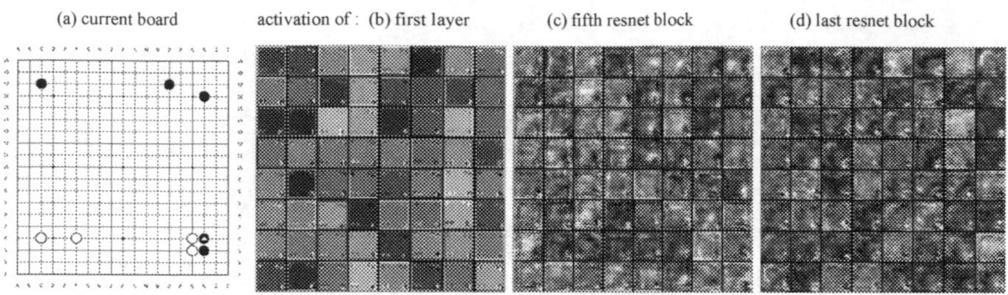

Fig. 5. Visualization of the activation map from different layers in our trained model. We analyze one move (move 10) in a game played by AlphaGo Zero (white) and Ke Jie (black). Seeing the activation of first layer (a), it is apparent that much of the lower layers are encoding information about the original board and partially recognizing the board edge (though the board edge is not one of the input features). As they are not connected directly to the input image, the activation of intermediate layers are less interpretable, such as the activation of a layer from the fifth resnet block (c) and one from the last (tenth) resnet block (d). However, (c) still exhibits some properties different from (d). Comparing each feature map from activation map (c) with those from the deeper activation map (d), there is more pure space in the middle area of the board in (c), which corresponds with the blank area on the original board.

chosen activation. Moreover, we used an upresidual layer to invert the residual layer. This reconstruction is repeated until the input space is reached.

Upresidual: Unlike the image convolution network used by Zeiler and Fergus, we did not use a pooling layer in our policy network, so there is no uppooling layer in our deconvnet. However, we used an upresidual layer to invert the residual layer. By recording the gradients added to the layer output, we obtain a set of variables. The upresidual operation in the deconvnet deletes these variables from the gradients.

Unlike the input (RGB model) to the image convolution network, the input to the Go policy network has more than three channels. Thus, it is impossible to present all reconstructed input at once. In Figs. 6 and 7, we only visualize reconstructed input of the first three channels, which belong to stone color features (representing the board information).

In Fig. 6, the first convolution layers have a size of $64 \times 19 \times 19$, and we depict them as 64 separate 19×19 RGB images. These 64 images are tiled into an 8×8 grid in row-major order. In Figs. 6 and 7, the last convolution layers are RGB images of size $2 \times 19 \times 19$, and we depict them as two separate 19×19 grayscale images. Each of the small images contains reconstructed inputs in the same (1–19)–(A–T) spatial layout as the input board data.

Reconstructed Input Visualization: Figure 6 shows feature visualizations from our model when predicting the same next move.

Reconstructed Input Evolution During Training: Figure 7 shows the visualization of reconstructed input from different training step.

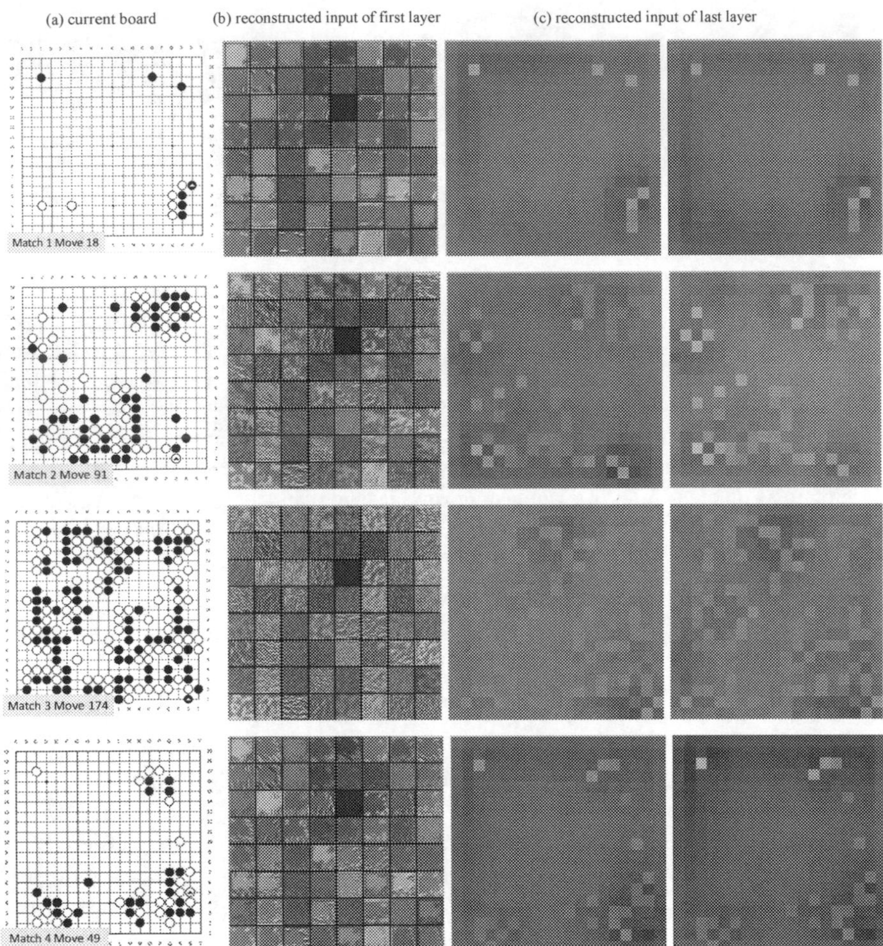

Fig. 6. Visualization of the reconstructed input in our trained model. We analyze four moves (move 18 of match 1, move 91 of match 2, move 174 of match 3, move 49 of match 4) in the games played by AlphaGo Zero. Column (b) visualizes the reconstructed input starting from the first layer. Each of the first layer reconstructed inputs correspond to the original board, and each has a different direction, which is similar to the texture of the convolution network image. Columns (c) and (d) visualize the reconstructed input starting from the last layer. Though these boards from four games are different, when fed into the policy network, we get the same output (predicted next move is position R-2). Some parts of the reconstructed input are very discriminative (e.g., lower right of the image in rows 1 and 3, lower part of the image in row 1). It is obvious that though the features do not have a strong grouping, there is clear invariance to input deformations.

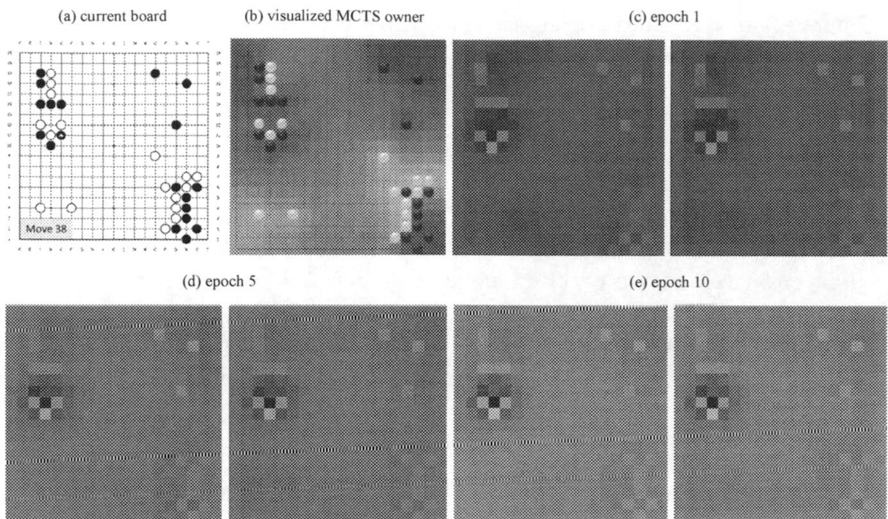

Fig. 7. Visualization of the reconstructed input in our trained model at epochs 1, 5, and 10. From images (b) (c) (d), we can see that color contrast around the next move position (D-12) is enhanced during traning.

4.4 Occlusion Experiment

With DCNNs, it is unclear whether the model can truly identify certain areas on the board like an image classifier, or simply focuses on the surrounding area. We attempted to answer this question by occluding different portions of the input board in a systematic manner with an empty square, recalculating the features of the occluded board as a new input of the network, then monitoring the rank of the correct move in the top-n confident predictions. As shown in Fig. 8, we visualize the rank of the correct move in the top-n confident predictions using gradations of color.

Go board are sensitive to small changes, but we found that removing one stone generally has little effect on the rank of the correct move in the top-n confident predictions. We believe there are two main reasons for this. First, removing one stone could alter this area to a certain death situation, which makes the network give up the capturing race (Semeai in Japanese, where both players have groups striving to capture each other) and ignore the changed area. Second, removing one stone could change a regular group of stones into a strange group. A lack of training means the features of the group barely activate the deeper layer of our network, and the changed area is ignored.

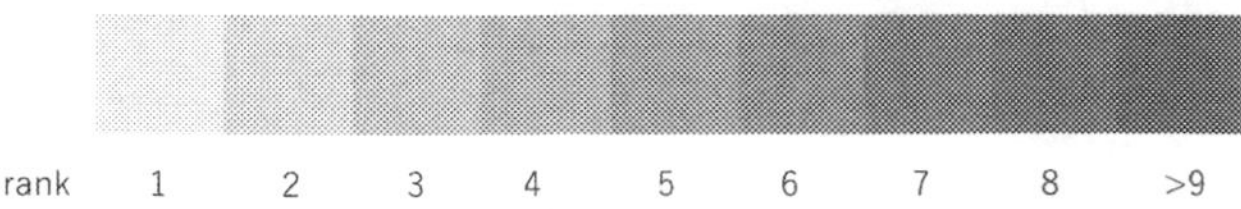

Fig. 8. Gradations representing the rank of the correct move in the top-n confident predictions.

Figure 9(a) shows an example board in which we systematically covered different portions of the board with an empty square and recorded the changes in the network's predictions. Figure 9(b) shows the rank of the correct move in the top-n predictions as a function of removing one stone from its position (occlusion area size 1 × 1). When a specific area (e.g., white stone – P11, black stone – N9, Q5) of the board is obscured, the rank for the correct next move "N11" drops significantly. We evaluated the sensitivity to the occlusion area; the results are given in Fig. 9(c), (d). These results suggest that specific stones (e.g., white stone – P11, P9, black stone – N9, R9) or specific areas have a strong effect on move prediction. When more than one of these stones or areas is occluded, our DCNN will be unable to output the correct next move. The example clearly shows that the model is localizing the pattern within the board, as when the center-right of the board is obscured, the rank for the correct next move "N11" drops.

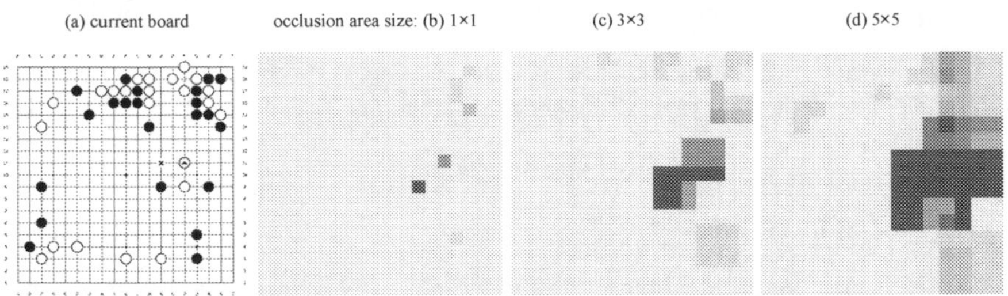

Fig. 9. Maps showing the rank of the correct move in the top-n confident predictions as a function of removing stones from occlusion area with different size.

In Fig. 10, with a 3 × 3 occlusion area, we analyze two moves in a game played by AlphaGo (white) and Sedol (black), which was won by AlphaGo. The ability to be activated by a specific area allows the DCNN to implicitly understand many sophisticated concepts of Go. In the left part of Fig. 10, after pushing once on the left, AlphaGo capped Black on the lower side and stopped two stones (H6 and H4) from running out to the center. The white stone at M4 makes it difficult for black to make a

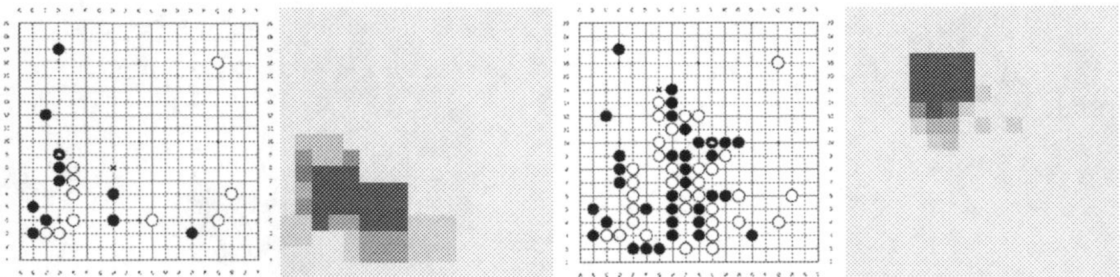

Fig. 10. Maps showing the rank of the correct move in the top-n predictions as a function of removing stones from the position. Left: current board (last move 21 (D9), next move 22 (H8)). Right: current board (last move 69 (L10), next move 70 (G14))

connection between H4 and O3. The figure shows that the left area and stones H6, H4, M4 have a strong influence on the next move prediction. In the right part of Fig. 10, the move L10 was ugly but necessary, giving white the Sente (a move that overwhelmingly compels a player into a follow-up move) to return to the left side. We set the most recent move as one of the input features, but once get the Sente, the network can turn to now area whenever necessary.

5 Conclusion and Future Work

This paper has reported the results of visualization experiments that demonstrate the learning ability of a DCNN model for playing Go. When trained to predict the next move, the DCNN is highly sensitive to local patterns on the board, rather than simply using broad information. During training, attention is focused on some special areas. In future work, with a partial understanding of how and why DCNNs work, we hope to target the development of better models. We plan to use the visualization methods as diagnostic tools for identifying problems that occur during training and improving the performance of the policy network. Additionally, we believe that identifying the critical area will allow Go beginners to understand the board visually, which should remove some aspects of confusion.

References

1. Clark, C., Storkey, A.: Training deep convolutional neural networks to play go. In: Proceedings of the 32nd International Conference on Machine Learning (ICML 2015), pp. 1766–1774 (2015)
2. Tian, Y., Zhu, Y.: Better computer go player with neural network and long-term prediction. arXiv preprint arXiv:1511.06410 (2015)
3. Silver, D., Huang, A., Maddison, C.J., Guez, A., Sifre, L., et al.: Mastering the game of go with deep neural networks and tree search. Nature **529**(7587), 484–489 (2016)
4. Maddison, C.J., et al.: Move evaluation in go using deep convolutional neural networks. arXiv preprint arXiv:1412.6564 (2014)
5. Silver, D., Schrittwieser, J., Simonyan, K., Antonoglou, I., et al.: Mastering the game of Go without human knowledge. Nature **550**(7676), 354–359 (2017)
6. Zeiler, M.D., Fergus, R.: Visualizing and understanding convolutional networks. In: Fleet, D., Pajdla, T., Schiele, B., Tuytelaars, T. (eds.) ECCV 2014. LNCS, vol. 8689, pp. 818–833. Springer, Cham (2014). https://doi.org/10.1007/978-3-319-10590-1_53
7. GoGoD. https://gogodonline.co.uk

A Multi-objective Optimization Model for Determining the Optimal Standard Feasible Neighborhood of Intelligent Vehicles

Lei Huang[1], Ying Xu[1(✉)], and Hailiang Zhao[2]

[1] College of Computer Science and Electronic Engineering, Hunan University, Changsha, China
{hnu_hl, hnxy}@hnu.edu.cn

[2] School of Mathematics, Southwest Jiaotong University, Chengdu, China
hailiang@home.swjtu.edu.cn

Abstract. Due to the complex conditions on the roads, intelligent vehicles need to face infinite environments. Based on the neighborhood control theory, the infinite world can be reduced to a limited and irregular feasible area. By constructing a finite number of feasible neighborhoods within the feasible region, an optimal standard feasible neighborhood can be determined for intelligent vehicle. This paper proposes a standard feasible neighborhood for the intelligent vehicle based on the ladder-sector. Then a new multi-objective optimization model for determining the optimal standard feasible neighborhood has been proposed. A partition method has been designed by transforming the problem from the infinite feasible domain into a series of feasible neighborhoods. Finally, simulations have been carried out on some representative road conditions. Simulation results demonstrate the effectiveness of the proposed multi-objective optimization model.

Keywords: Intelligent vehicle · Robot planning · Multi-objective optimization

1 Introduction

With the rapid development of computer technology and artificial intelligence, the robotic has been greatly improved in function and technical level. Intelligent mobile robots are an important branch in the robotics. For intelligent mobile robots, they are required to move and complete the task in any environment and without intervention. An overview of research on ICT-based support and assistance services for the safety of future connected vehicles is presented in [1]. To realize the independent movement of intelligent wheeled robots such as smart cars, it is the most feasible way to imitate the decision process of intelligent creatures. In the face of complex dynamic environment, a quick or a relatively stable environment is usually selected as the next action for decision-making. The range of decision-making is called the feasible neighborhood, a series of feasible neighborhoods constitute the neighborhood system. A dynamic decision-making model based on the neighborhood system is proposed in [2] to describe such a decision process. The model decomposes the dynamic decision-making process in a complex macro environment into a series of simple decision-making

X. Geng and B.-H. Kang (Eds.): PRICAI 2018, LNAI 11012, pp. 268–281, 2018.
https://doi.org/10.1007/978-3-319-97304-3_21

processes within the neighborhood, so that it is faced with a finite simple environments rather than an infinite complex world.

During the decision-making process, the determination of feasible neighborhoods and the selection of a satisfactory feasible neighborhood are critical. Normally, for a feasible neighborhood, two conditions need to be satisfied, one is that no obstacles in the neighborhood, the second is that the controlled object can move in its traveling direction. The shape of this feasible neighborhood is usually complex and hard to calculate. But for intelligent vehicles and other independent wheeled mobile robots, the mathematical model of determining feasible neighborhood should be easy to build and fast to solve.

Multi-objective optimization is a hot research topic in the field of intelligent computation. Generally, a multi-objective optimization problem with m optimization objectives and r constraints can be formally defined as follows:

$$Optimise\ \ F(x) = (f_1(x), f_2(x), \ldots, f_m(x)) \tag{1}$$

$$s.t.\ e(x) = (e_1(x),\ e_2(x), \ldots,\ e_r(x)) \geq 0 \tag{2}$$

where $x = (x_1,\ x_2, \ldots,\ x_r)$ is a decision variable, X denotes a decision (variable) space containing all feasible solution spaces, $F(x)$ contains the objective vector determined by m sub-objectives function $f_i(x),\ i \in \{1, \ldots, m\}$ and r constraints $e(x) \geq 0$ limits the range of feasible solutions. For a multi-objective optimization problem with minimization objectives, u and v are two decision variables, if $f_i(u) \leq f_i(v)$ for all $j \in [1, .., m]$, and there exist at least one $j \in [1, .., m]$ which satisfies $f_i(u) < f_i(v)$, then u dominates v denoted by $u \prec v$. If there is no solution which dominates x^* in X, then x^* is the Pareto optimal solution. The set of all Pareto optimal solutions in X is called the Pareto-optimal Set (PS). The objective vectors of solutions in Pareto-optimal Set form the Pareto Front (PF) in objective space. The purpose of multi-objective optimization algorithm is to search a set of non-dominated Pareto solutions so that these solutions are scattered and uniformly distributed to reach the real Pareto Front as much as possible [3]. Various multi-objective optimization algorithms have been proposed in the literature to solve different types of optimization problems in the literature [4–7].

In this work, we investigate the problem of determining the standard feasible neighborhood for intelligent vehicles in the feasible area. According to the relative relationship between the actual controlled object and the feasible region, the standard feasible neighborhood of the ladder sector is selected in this work. A novel multi-objective optimization model has been defined for the first time to determine the optimal standard feasible neighborhood, where three optimization objectives have been considered including maximizing the radius length, the width of neighborhood and the speed of vehicle. Based on our proposed multi-objective optimization model, a partition method has been proposed to transform the infinite feasible domain of the problem into a finite feasible domain. Different types of simulated roads have been generated by using MATLAB. Simulation results demonstrate the effectiveness of our proposed model.

2 Related Works

Based on the neighborhood control theory, the environment faced by intelligent vehicles is infinite on complex roads. The infinite world can be reduced to a limited and irregular feasible area by constructing a finite number of feasible neighborhoods in the feasible area. Finally, we can choose an optimal standard feasible neighborhood in this limited standard feasible neighborhood for decision-making.

Here, some basic concepts are given for determining feasible neighborhoods for the intelligent vehicles as follows:

Definition 1 (the feasible area [2]): The area in which the vehicle can travel normally in its moving direction is called a feasible area.

Definition 2 (the standard feasible neighborhood [2]): A region of the shape and size of the feasible region is called the standard feasible neighborhood.

According to the actual control of the object and the feasibility of different areas, we can get different shapes of standard feasible neighborhood. The characteristics of the controlled object should be taken into consideration when selecting the shape of a standard neighborhood. The selected shape should be convenient for mathematical description. To simplify the model of the standard feasible neighborhood, we only consider the two-dimensional standard feasible neighborhood which is more simple and convenient for the simulation of vehicle driving. The commonly used shapes of feasible neighborhood are circle, sector and rectangle. The shape of the circular and sector neighborhood is rather special, which is more suitable for the controlled objects with relatively small feasible area, such as the aircraft, small robots and so on. However, for smart cars with special contours and larger dimensions, circular or sector neighborhoods are not easy to describe their relative positions in their feasible areas. The rectangular neighborhood is the same as the shape of the vehicle, which ensures the safety of the vehicle, but it is difficult to provide the direction information for the next decision.

Combined with the characteristics of rectangular and sector neighborhood, the mathematical definition $L(r, l_1, l_2, l_3)$ of the ladder-sector standard feasible neighborhood is as follows:

$$L(r, l_1, l_2, l_3) = \left\{ (x, y) \middle| \begin{array}{c} y > 0 \\ l_1 : A_1x + B_1y + C_1 > 0 \\ l_2 : A_2x + B_2y + C_3 > 0 \\ l_3 : A_3x + B_3y + C_3 > 0 \end{array} \right\} \tag{3}$$

Where r is the radius of the neighborhood, l_1, l_2 is the side of the ladder-sector neighborhood, the length of l_1 and l_2 are equal to r. l_3 is the front boundary of the neighborhood as shown in Fig. 1(a). (x, y) represents a point in the ladder-sector neighborhood. The direction of l_1, l_2 and l_3 depends on the corresponding parameters A, B and C. It can be seen that when $B_1 = 0$, $B_2 = 0$, $A_3 = 0$, the ladder-sector standard neighborhood becomes the rectangular neighborhood.

To ensure the safety, an intelligent vehicle should be completely inside the ladder-sector feasible neighborhood as shown in Fig. 1(b). The neighborhood can be adjusted by changing the angle between l_1 and l_2. If the direction of the line that connects point O and the middle of l_3 represents the turning direction of the road, which provides the direction information for the vehicle choose the neighborhood. Therefore, it is safe and practical to construct the standard feasible neighborhood of intelligent vehicle with the ladder-sector feasible neighborhood.

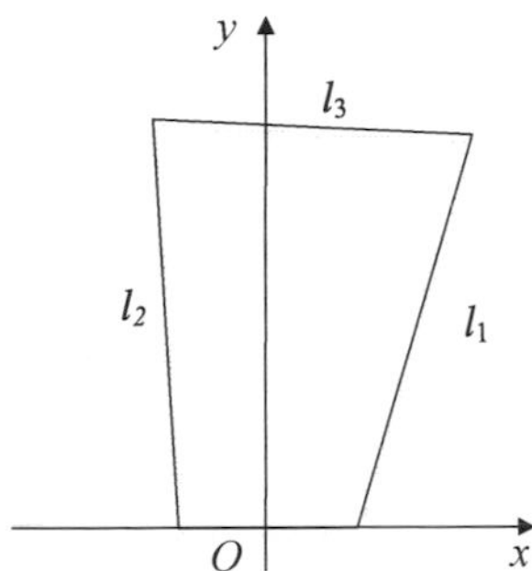

(a) The shape of the ladder-sector

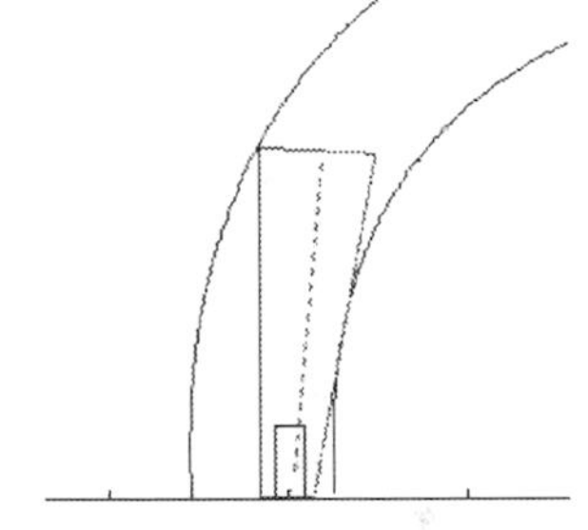

(b) The ladder-sector standard feasible neighborhood with one vehicle

Fig. 1. The ladder-sector standard feasible neighborhood

A lot of works have been carried out to solve the real-time positioning and map creation of robots [8–10]. The main methods of mobile robot map construction include Kalman filter based method [8], global optimization method based on EM (Expectation Maximization) algorithm [9], particle filter based method [10] and so on. Most of these methods are mature and have been applied for some applications. However, the actual environment is often dynamic, such as the movement of pedestrian, vehicles and so on. Existing static environment map building methods are not directly applicable to map building in dynamic environments [11–13]. The construction of maps in unstructured, dynamic or large-scale environments remains a challenging problem to be studied and solved. The fundamental problem of goal-directed path planning in an uncertain environment is addressed in [14]. A feasible region extraction method based on self-growth network is proposed in [15]. Based on the neighborhood system theory, the concept of sector neighborhood and rectangular neighborhood for intelligent vehicle has been proposed, and a road model has been given [16–20]. A circular neighborhood suitable for vehicle reversing is proposed in [19], but this only applies when the vehicle is reversing and the speed is slow.

3 The Multi-objective Optimization Model for the Standard Feasible Neighborhood

3.1 The Definition of the Multi-objective Optimization Model

When establishing the standard feasible neighborhoods, the safety and the speed are two key issues for an intelligent vehicle, which are affected by the length of the neighborhood radius, the width of the neighborhood, and the speed of the vehicles. As shown in Fig. 2, the angle between l_1 and the positive direction of x-axis is β_1, and the angle between the negative direction of x-axis is β_2. $d_{rear} = d_c + d_l + d_r$ is the width of the rear of the neighborhood, where d_c is the length of vehicle, d_l is the length to the left and d_r is the length to the right. The car length is s_c. The width of the front boundary of the neighborhood d_{front} is calculated as follows:

$$d_{front} = \sqrt{(r\cos\beta_1 + r\cos\beta_2 + d_{rear})^2 + (r\sin\beta_1 - r\sin\beta_2)^2} \tag{4}$$

Based on the above definition, in the multi-objective optimization model, we consider the following three objectives:

(1) Maximize the Length of neighborhood radius r.
(2) Maximize the width of the front of the neighborhood to meet the vehicle turning, speed adjusting and other behavior decisions.
(3) Maximize the speed v while the safety is ensured.

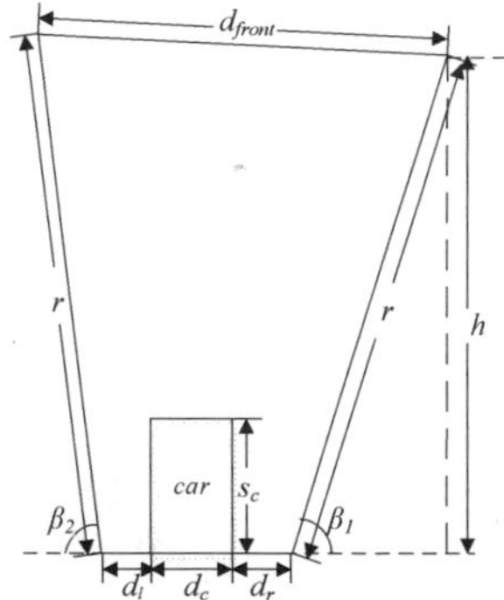

Fig. 2. The ladder-sector standard feasible neighborhood model

In addition, we consider the following constraints:

(1) The Radius Length Constraint

If the length of the radius r of the ladder-sector is too short, it affects the behavior decision of the vehicle in the neighborhood; and if the radius r is too long, the ladder-sector internal width may be too narrow to the traffic safety. Therefore, the radius should be within the range of the maximum and minimum length of the ladder-sector.

$$r_{min} \leq r \leq r_{max} \tag{5}$$

(2) The Angle Constraint

In order to facilitate the decision-making of vehicles in the neighborhood, the angles β_i (for i = 1, 2) cannot be too large to change the direction of the neighborhood, or too small to make the front of the neighborhood narrower, which make the vehicle cannot run normally. We define the length of the neighborhood $h = min\{r * sin(\beta_i)\}$. Obviously, the car length should satisfy $s_c < h$, i.e. $s_c < r * sin(\beta_i)$. So we can get $\beta_i > arcsin(s_c/r)$. If the width of the front of the neighborhood is too narrow which makes the vehicle cannot pass, it means $\beta_i \leq \pi/2$. So we can get:

$$arcsin\,(s_c/r) < \beta_i \leq \pi/2\;(\text{for}\; i = 1, 2) \tag{6}$$

(3) The Width Constraint

The ladder-sector has two widths d_{front} and d_{rear} (see Fig. 2), which affect the vehicle's direction turning and speed changing. It is easy to know that $d_{front} \geq d_{rear}$ (if and only if $\beta_1 = \beta_2 = \pi/2$). Here, we set the minimum and maximum values of d_l and d_r as follows:

$$\begin{aligned} d_{min} \leq d_r \leq d_{max} \\ d_{min} \leq d_l \leq d_{max} \end{aligned} \tag{7}$$

(4) The Speed Constraint

The braking process of a vehicle can be divided into two parts: the brake preparation time t_0, and the brake time t_1. Assuming the vehicle speed is v, the average deceleration is a, then the safe distance can be calculated as:

$$S = t_0 v + \frac{v^2}{2a} \tag{8}$$

Since the neighborhood length $h = min\{r * sin(\beta_i)\}$ (for i = 1, 2), let $S = h$, so we can get the maximum speed of the vehicle in the neighborhood is:

$$v_{max} = \sqrt{a^2 + t_0^2 + 2ah} - at_0 \tag{9}$$

So the speed limit for the speed v_t at time t is set as:

$$v_t \leq v_{max} \tag{10}$$

Based on the above definitions, given a standard feasible neighborhood u, we can define the multi-objective optimization model for the standard feasible neighborhood of intelligent vehicles as follows:

(1) $f_1(u)$: Maximize the neighborhood radius length

$$f_1(u) = \text{Max}(r) \tag{11}$$

(2) $f_2(u)$: Maximize the width of the front of the neighborhood

$$f_2(u) = \text{Max}(d_{front}) \tag{12}$$

(3) $f_3(u)$: Maximize the speed

$$f_3(u) = \text{Max}(v) \tag{13}$$

$$s.t. \quad \begin{array}{l} r_{min} < r < r_{max} \\ v < v_{max} \\ d_{min} < d_l < d_{max} \\ d_{min} < d_r < d_{max} \\ d_{rear} = d_r + d_l + d_c \\ arcsin(s_c/r) < \beta_i \leq \frac{\pi}{2} \ (i = 1,\ 2) \end{array} \tag{14}$$

3.2 The Proposed Algorithm for the Multi-objective Optimization Model

An ideal standard feasible neighborhood requires that the vehicle drives fast while the safety is maintained. In this paper, the problem on the infinite feasible domain is transformed into a finite feasible domain. A weight vector is used to determine the final standard feasible neighborhood, here we set the weight vector $[w_1, w_2, w_3]$ ($\sum w_i = 1$) to each objective. So we transform the multi-objective optimization problem into a weighted sum function as follows:

$$max\, f = \sum_{i=1}^{3} w_i f_i(u) \tag{15}$$

Finally, the standard feasible neighborhood with the largest f-value is the final standard feasible neighborhood.

Since the three objectives are required to achieve the maximum, we use the λ-method [21] to determine the weight coefficient:

$$\lambda_i = 1/f_i^* \tag{16}$$

Where $f_i^* = max\, f_i(u)$. The weight coefficient w_i is set as the normalized λ_i:

$$w_i = \frac{\lambda_i}{\sum \lambda_j} \tag{17}$$

Table 1. The division of r (m)

Parameter	Values of the division							
r	5	6	8	10	12	15	20	30
	40	60	80	100	120	150	180	200

Table 2. The actual division of d_l, and d_r (m)

Parameter	Values of the division							
d_l	0.2	0.4	0.6	0.8	1	1.5	2	2.5
d_r	0.2	0.4	0.6	0.8	1	1.5	2	2.5

Table 3. The division of β

Parameter	Values of the division			
β	π/9	π/6	2π/9	5π/18
	π/3	7π/18	4π/9	π/2

The multi-objective programing model is thus solved as follows [19]:

(1) In order to simplify the solution process and to find a satisfactory standard feasible neighborhood, we divide the radius r, the width d_{rear} and the angle β of the neighborhood to find the standard feasible neighborhood. An example division is as follows:

(a) The division of r

According to the speed limits and the corresponding safety distances of all kinds of road conditions in China, the division of r is shown in Table 1.

(b) The division of d_{rear}

From Fig. 2, we can see that the width of the rear of the neighborhood $d_{rear} = d_c + d_l + d_r$. So the division of d_{rear} is equal to the division of d_l and d_r. Considering the general situation, the division of d_l and d_r is shown in Table 2.

(c) The division of angle β

Since the minimum value of β is related to the radius, and the maximum value is π/2 (see Formula (6)). Therefore, the minimum value of β needs to be calculated and the suitable division is selected in Table 3.

(2) Find the corresponding standard feasible neighborhood based on the partition in (1). Based on the width d_{rear} and the angle β, a finite feasible neighborhood base is thus defined as $U = Q_1 \cup Q_2 \cup \ldots \cup Q_m$, where Q_i consists of a set of neighborhoods of the same width d_{rear} and angle β.

(3) Then the optimal standard feasible neighborhood u_i in Q_i $(i = 1, 2, \ldots, m)$ is determined. A set of discrete optimal solution sets $U = \{u_i\}$ are formed by all optimal standard feasible neighborhoods.

(4) By setting the weight w_i to each objective, the weighted sums of objective function values of each optimal standard feasible neighborhood u_i in U are calculated according to Eq. (15). The standard feasible neighborhood with the largest value is selected as the final standard feasible neighborhood.

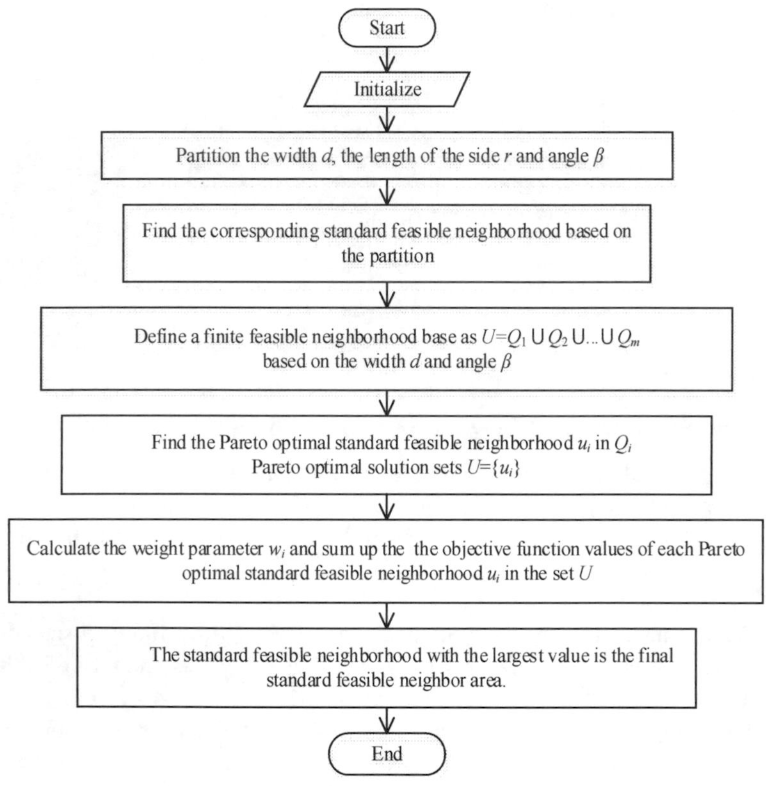

Fig. 3. The flow chart of the proposed algorithm

3.3 An Illustrative Example of the Partition Method

As shown in Fig. 1(b), the vehicle can find the standard feasible neighborhood according to the partition method described in Sect. 3.2. The standard feasible neighborhoods are classified according to their widths and angles. Some of the objective values are shown in Table 4. The optimal solutions obtained by the algorithm are shown in Fig. 3.

After a finite division of the neighborhood, we construct a set of finite feasible neighborhoods. We calculate the weight vector as $[w_1 = 0.1435,\ w_2 = 0.5704,\ w_3 = 0.2861]$ based on Eq. (17). Then we calculate the weighted sum by using Eq. (15) to select the optimal standard feasible neighborhood as shown in Fig. 4, the objective values are $f_1(u) = 20$, $f_2(u) = 8.87$, $f_3(u) = 29.79$.

Table 4. Objective values of the optimal solutions

Objective function	The objective values						
$f_1(u)$	6	8	12	12	15	20	20
$f_2(u)$	9.66	9.77	9.36	8.56	5.60	5.40	8.87
$f_3(u)$	12.01	16.20	21.38	21.17	25.01	30.08	29.79

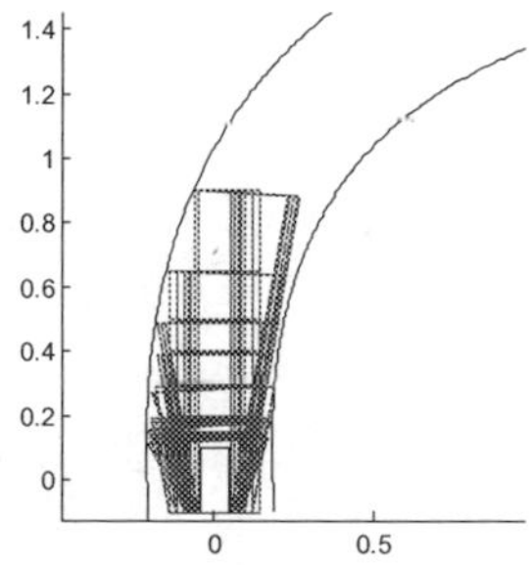

(a) The set of finite feasible neighborhoods

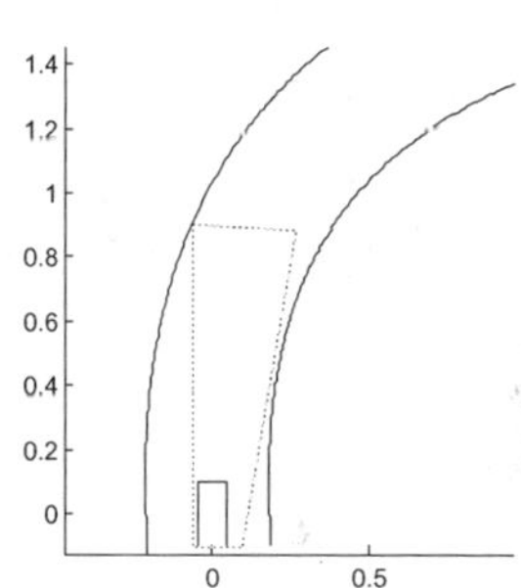

(b) The optimal solution u

Fig. 4. An example of the partition method

4 Performance Evaluation

To evaluation the performance of our proposed algorithm, a number of simulations have been carried out. The parameters used in the simulation are shown in Table 5.

Table 5. Parameter setting

Parameter	Value	Parameter	Value
r_{min}	0.25	r_{mas}	6
d_{min}	0.025	d_{max}	0.15
s_c	0.2	d_c	0.09
w (road width)	0.6		

4.1 Comparison on Different Road Conditions

According to the division method in Sect. 3.2, a series of standard feasible neighborhoods meeting the road conditions can be obtained. Matlab is used to carry on the simulation experiments, we set the starting point $P_0(x_0, y_0)$ of the vehicle and the starting angle θ_0 in the road model. Using the weight vector calculation method defined in Eq. (17), an optimal feasible neighborhood can be obtained. A number of simulations on different road conditions have been shown in Figs. 5, 6, 7 and 8. It can be seen that our proposed algorithm based on the multi-objective optimization model can always find satisfactory results.

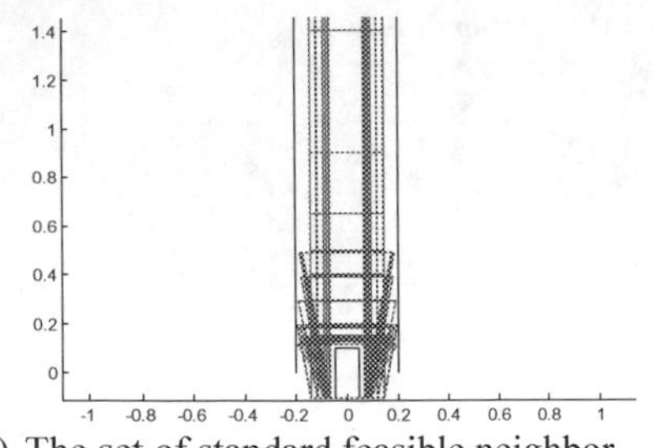

(a) The set of standard feasible neighborhoods

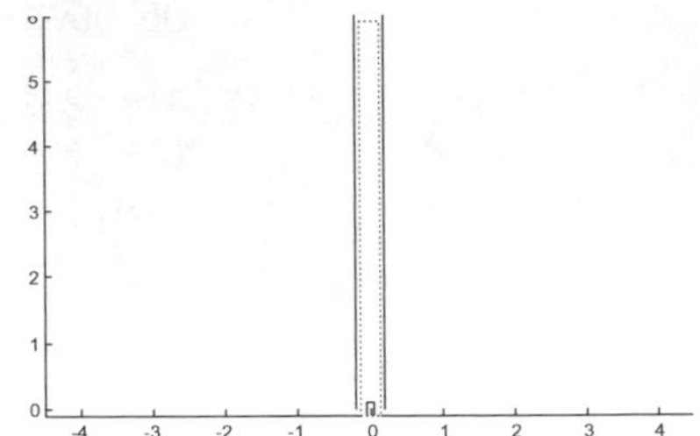

(b) The optimal standard feasible neighborhood

Fig. 5. The simulation on a straight road

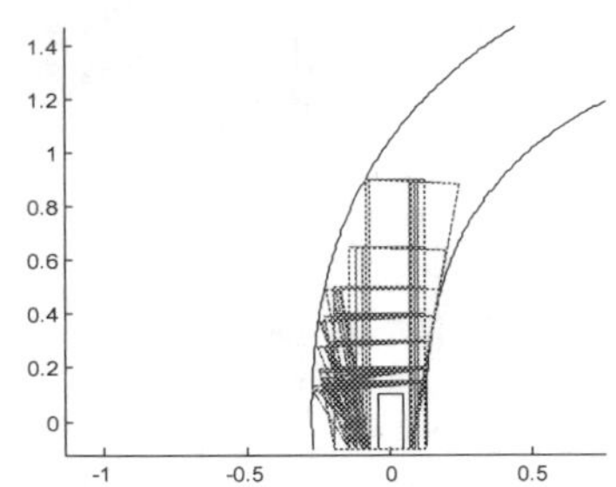

(a) The set of standard feasible neighborhoods

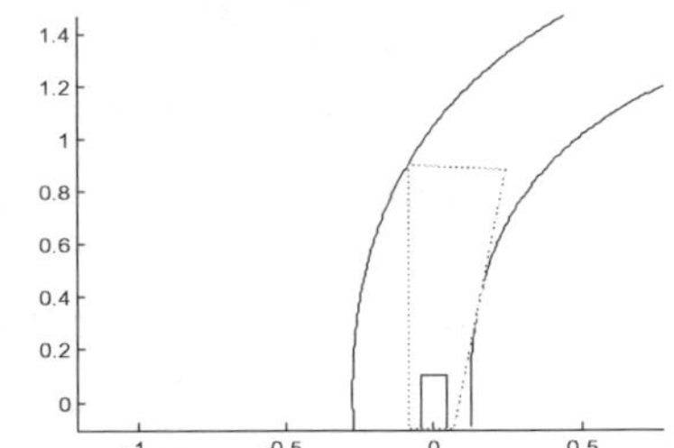

(b) The optimal standard feasible neighborhood

Fig. 6. The simulation on the curve road

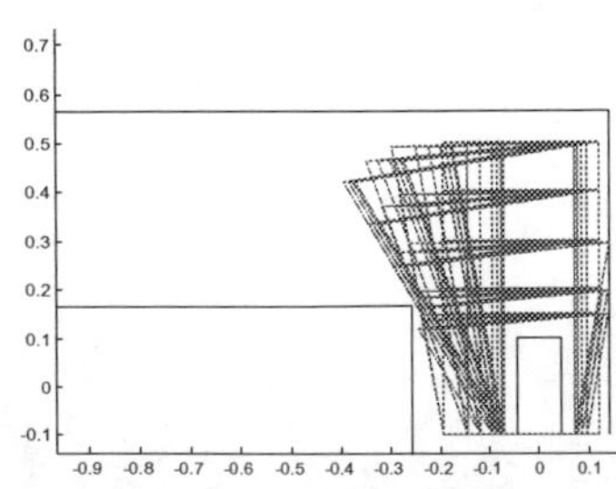

(a) The set of standard feasible neighborhoods

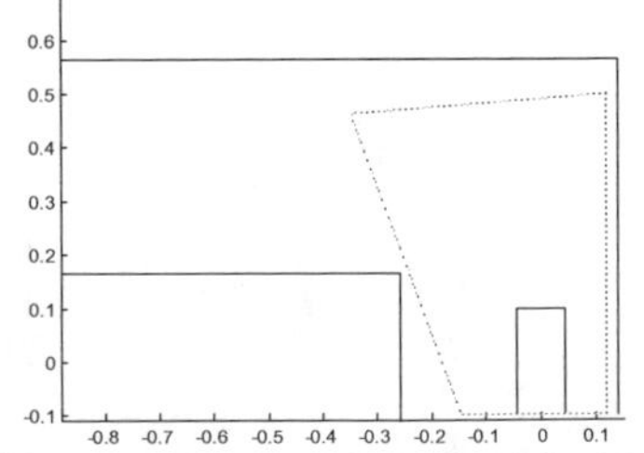

(b)The optimal standard feasible neighborhood

Fig. 7. Simulation on the road with a left turn

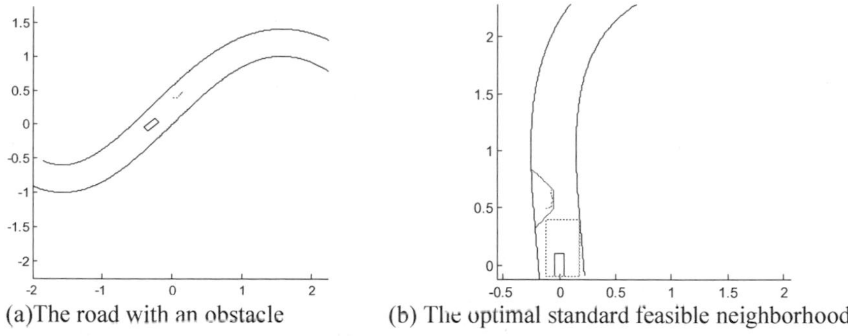

(a)The road with an obstacle (b) The optimal standard feasible neighborhood

Fig. 8. Simulation on the road with obstacles

4.2 Comparison of Different Neighborhood Models

We compare the simulation results of our proposed algorithm with the results in [17], using the same simulation data.

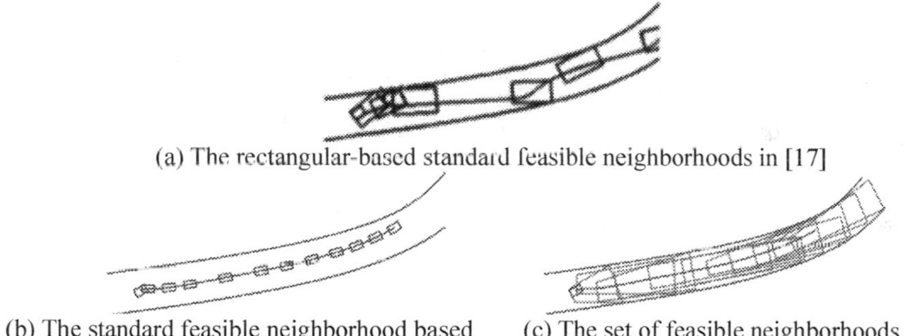

(a) The rectangular-based standard feasible neighborhoods in [17]

(b) The standard feasible neighborhood based on our work (the route) (c) The set of feasible neighborhoods based on our work (the neighborhoods)

Fig. 9. The comparison of simulation results

Figure 9(a) is the simulation result of the rectangular-based standard feasible neighborhood [17]. The small rectangular block represents a vehicle, the large rectangular block is a rectangular neighborhood. Figure 9(b) and (c) are the simulation results of the ladder-Sector feasible neighborhoods. The simulation of the vehicle moving route is given in Fig. 9(b), and (c) shows the ladder-Sector neighborhoods of the vehicle during the decision making process. It can be seen in Fig. 9(b) that the traveling route of the vehicle is basically consistent with that of the road which shows the good performance of the ladder-sector-based standard feasible neighborhood proposed in the this work.

We also compare two metrics (1) the average distance d_{ave} between the driving route of the vehicle and the center line of the road; (2) the average angle deviation θ_{ave} between the driving angle of the vehicle and the angle of the road. As shown in

Table 6, the average distance of the ladder-sector neighborhood model between the vehicular route and the road center line is only 0.0395, and the average deviation angle is only 0.0512, which are superior to the rectangular neighborhood model. Experimental results demonstrate again that the proposed ladder-sector neighborhood model is better than the rectangular neighborhood model (Fig. 10).

Table 6. Simulation results of d_{ave} and θ_{ave}

Rectangular neighborhood		Ladder-sector neighborhood	
d_{ave}	0.0974	d_{ave}	0.0395
θ_{ave}	0.1216	θ_{ave}	0.0512

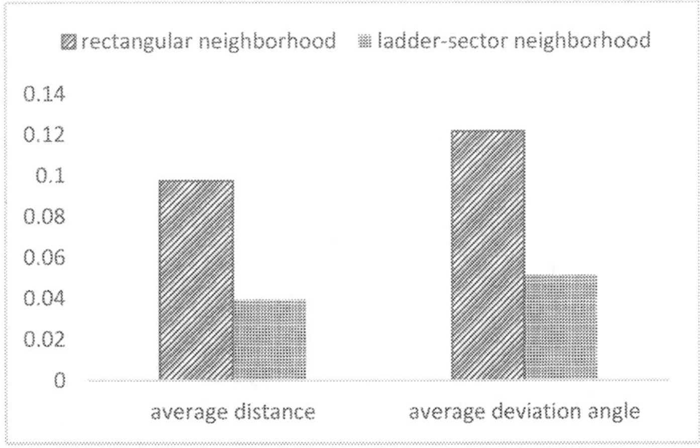

Fig. 10. Comparison of the ladder-sector neighborhood model with the rectangular neighborhood model

5 Conclusion

Based on the multi-objective optimization and neighborhood system theory, a new ladder-sector neighborhood model has been proposed for the intelligent vehicle. We use the ladder-sector to build the standard feasible neighborhood. Then a novel multi-objective optimization model for determining the feasible neighborhood of the optimal standard is given. A partition method has been designed by transforming the problem from the infinite feasible domain into a finite partition. A number of simulation results demonstrate the effectiveness of the proposed ladder-sector-based multi-objective optimization model for determining feasible neighborhood.

References

1. Bila, C., Sivrikaya, F., Khan, M.A., Albayrak, S.: Vehicles of the future: a survey of research on safety issues. IEEE Trans. Intell. Transp. Syst. **18**(5), 1046–1065 (2017)
2. Zhao, H.: A dynamic optimization decision and control model based on neighborhood systems. In: International Congress on Image and Signal Processing, pp. 1329–1334. IEEE (2014)
3. Eckart, Z., Thiele, L.: Multi-objective Optimization Using Evolutionary Algorithms. Wiley, Hoboken (2001)
4. Deb, K., AgRWAal, S., Pratap, A., Meyarivan, T.: A fast and elitist multi-objective genetic algorithm: NSGA II. IEEE Trans. Evol. Comput. **6**(2), 182–197 (2002)
5. Zhang, Q., Li, H.: MOEA/D: a multiobjective evolutionary algorithm based on decomposition. IEEE Trans. Evol. Comput. **11**(6), 712–731 (2007)
6. Xu, Y., Qu, R.: Solving multi-objective multicast routing problems by evolutionary multi-objective simulated annealing algorithms with variable neighbourhoods. J. Oper. Res. Soc. **62**(2), 313–325 (2011)
7. Qu, R., Xu, Y., Castro, J., Landa-Silva, D.: Particle swarm optimization for the Steiner tree in graph and delay-constrained multicast routing problems. J. Heuristics **19**(2), 317–342 (2013)
8. Bailey, T., Nieto, J., Guivant, J., Stevens, M.: Consistency of the EKF-SLAM algorithm. In: IEEE/RSJ International Conference on Intelligent Robots and Systems, pp. 3562–3568. IEEE (2006)
9. Corff, S.L., Fort, G., Moulines, E.: Online Expectation Maximization algorithm to solve the SLAM problem. In: Statistical Signal Processing Workshop, pp. 225–228. IEEE (2011)
10. Lee, H.C., Park, S.K., Choi, J.S., Lee, B.H.: PSO-FastSLAM: an improved FastSLAM framework using particle swarm optimization. In: IEEE International Conference on Systems, Man and Cybernetics, pp. 2763–2768. IEEE Press (2009)
11. Biswas, R., Limketkai, B., Sanner, S., Thrun, S.: Towards object mapping in non-stationary environments with mobile robots. In: IEEE/RSJ International Conference on Intelligent Robots and Systems, pp. 1014–1019 (2002)
12. Wolf, D.F., Sukhatme, G.S.: Towards mapping dynamic environments. In: Proceedings of the International Conference on Advanced Robotics, pp. 594–600 (2003)
13. Wang, C.C., Thorpe, C.: Simultaneous localization and mapping with detection and tracking of moving objects. In: Proceedings of the IEEE International Conference on Robotics and Automation, pp. 2918–2924. IEEE (2002)
14. Bhattacharya, S., Ghrist, R., Kumar, V.: Persistent homology for path planning in uncertain environments. IEEE Trans. Robot. **31**(3), 578–590 (2017)
15. Zhong, C., Liu, S., Yang, F.: Topological map building based on GNG network dynamic environment. J. East China Univ. Sci. Technol. (Nat. Sci. Ed.) **38**(1), 63–68 (2012)
16. Sun, L., Shi, Q.: Neighborhood based decision making model for microscopic pedestrians simulation. Highw. Eng. **04**, 68–72 (2009)
17. Xiong, S., Zhao, H.: Simulations on the movement of intelligent vehicle based on rectangular safe neighborhood. Appl. Res. Comput. **30**(12), 3593–3596 + 3621 (2013)
18. Zhao, H.: Motion planning for intelligent cars following roads based on feasible neighborhood. In: IEEE International Conference on Control Science and Systems Engineering, pp. 27–31. IEEE (2015)
19. Fu, H., Zhao, H., Jiang, Y.: A control method for intelligent car parking based on neighborhood system. Fuzzy Syst. Math. (02), 103–115 (2016)
20. Jiang, Y., Zhao, H., Fu, H.: A control method to avoid obstacle for an intelligent car based on rough sets and neighborhood systems. In: 10th International Conference on Intelligent Systems and Knowledge Engineering, pp. 66–70. IEEE (2016)
21. Qian, S., et al.: Operational Research, 3rd edn. Tsinghua University Press, Beijing (2005)

Efficient Detection of Critical Links to Maintain Performance of Network with Uncertain Connectivity

Kazumi Saito[1,2], Kouzou Ohara[3(✉)], Masahiro Kimura[4], and Hiroshi Motoda[5,6]

[1] Faculty of Science, Kanagawa University, Hiratsuka, Japan
k-saito@kanagawa-u.ac.jp
[2] Center for Advanced Intelligence Project, RIKEN, Tokyo, Japan
kazumi.saito@riken.jp
[3] Department of Integrated Information Technology, Aoyama Gakuin University, Sagamihara, Japan
ohara@it.aoyama.ac.jp
[4] Department of Electronics and Informatics, Ryukoku University, Kyoto, Japan
kimura@rins.ryukoku.ac.jp
[5] Institute of Scientific and Industrial Research, Osaka University, Suita, Japan
motoda@ar.sanken.osaka-u.ac.jp
[6] School of Computing and Information Systems, University of Tasmania, Hobart, Australia

Abstract. We address the problem of efficiently detecting critical links in a large network in order to maintain network performance, e.g., in case of disaster evacuation, for which a probabilistic link disconnection model plays an essential role. Here, critical links are such links that their disconnection exerts substantial effects on the network performance such as the average node reachability. We tackle this problem by proposing a new method consisting of two new acceleration techniques: reachability condition skipping (RCS) and distance constraints skipping (DCS). We tested the effectiveness of the proposed method by using three real-world spatial networks. In particular, we show that the proposed method achieves the efficiency gain of around 10^4 compared with a naive method in which every single link is blindly tested as a critical link candidate.

1 Introduction

Developing new methods/tools that enable us to quantify the importance of each individual node and link is crucially important in exploring essential properties of the structure and functions of large networks that are studied in many different fields of science and engineering. The most fundamental approach is using traditional centrality metrics based on network topology such as degree centrality and betweenness centrality. Another approach based on more realistic settings is to assess nodes or links using a certain network performance metric [6–8,12–14], that is to answer "Which links/nodes are most critical in maintaining

X. Geng and B.-H. Kang (Eds.): PRICAI 2018, LNAI 11012, pp. 282–295, 2018.
https://doi.org/10.1007/978-3-319-97304-3_22

a desired network performance?". To maintain the performance we need to find nodes and links that degrade the performance substantially if not functioning, and have to provide adequate maintenance so that they don't fail to function. For example, if the desired performance is to maximize evacuation or minimize isolation, the problem is to detect critical links that maximally reduce the overall performance if these links do not function. This problem is mathematically formulated as an optimization problem when a network structure is given and a performance measure is defined.

In this paper, similarly to the studies of Saito *et al.* [12,13], we take the second approach to identify critical links in a general setting that could be extended to take into account detailed features specific to an actual network such as road capacities. On the other hand, unlike their studies, we introduce a probabilistic link disconnection model which corresponds to a probabilistic road blockage model in case of disaster evacuation over spatial networks. We also employ the performance defined by the average node reachability with respect to a link deletion, *i.e.*, the contribution value defined as the difference of expected number of nodes that are reachable from a given set of nodes such as evacuation facilities in a road network, when a particular link is deleted/blocked. The problem is to rank the links in accordance with the contribution values and identify the most critical link(s).

Below we summarize our contributions in this paper. (1) We presented a unified problem framework of detecting critical links based on a probabilistic link disconnection model with disaster evacuation and others in mind. (2) We proposed an efficient method to compute the contribution values for every individual link by devising two new techniques of avoiding unnecessary computations, which is referred to as reachability condition skipping (RCS) and distance constraints skipping (DCS), (3) We experimentally demonstrated the effectiveness of our proposed method for the real-world spatial networks in case of disaster evacuation, showing the efficiency gain of around 10^4 over a naive method, and revealed the characteristics of detected links with high contribution values for the settings we used of the probabilistic link disconnection model.

The paper is organized as follows. Section 2 briefly explains some studies related to this paper. Section 3 formulates our critical link detection problem based on probabilistic link disconnection models. Section 4 presents the proposed method consisting of two techniques for skipping unnecessary computations. Section 5 reports three datasets used and the experimental results: computational efficiency and characterization of detected links. Section 6 summarizes the main achievements and future plans.

2 Related Work

The structure and functions of spatial networks have been studied by many researchers [2,4,9], for the sake of understanding and improving the usage of these networks embedded in the real space. From structural viewpoints, centrality measures have been widely used to analyze spatial networks [4,6,7,9], especially by extending the conventional notions of centrality measures on simple networks to those of weighted networks based on road usage frequency of urban streets [9] and to those of spatial networks based on geodesic distance [6,7]. From functional viewpoints, traffic usage patterns in urban streets have been investigated [2]. Shen *et al.* considered the total pairwise connectivity in undirected weighted graphs as the network performance metric to be optimized [14]. Oliveira *et al.* investigated several network performance metrics that had been proposed for road networks from two different viewpoints, congestion and vulnerability [8]. Those metrics are commonly based on traveling time for a link or a path in a road network. Our work is different from these existing studies. We rather focus on critical link detection problem in a situation where links are probabilistically blocked.

The critical link detection problem is closely related to the contamination minimization addressed in [5] where an effective method that minimizes the spread of contamination through a network was explored by blocking a small number of links. We borrow the same idea in [5] that samples graphs from a given network by probabilistically determining connectivity of each link to estimate the expected number of nodes that are reachable from a set of target nodes under the situation where each link is probabilistically disconnected. However, as this method [5] requires a quite large number of simulation samples for each link as it has to compute the expected value both when it is connected and disconnected, it has a limitation when the disconnection probability is small. In this paper, we overcome this limitation by explicitly dealing with the differences of reachability sizes for both connected and disconnected cases.

The problem of inserting k new links into a network for improving network performance has been studied by many researchers [10,11]. For instance, Papagelis [10] addressed a problem of finding new k shortcut links in a network such that adding them to the network could minimize the average shortest path distance over all pairs of nodes. The problem of maximizing the gain of closeness centrality of a specific node u by adding k new links was tackled in [11]. We focus on the reachability size, unlike these studies, in a situation that certain links are probabilistically disconnected.

The reachable size computation becomes harder as the network size increases, since it needs to take the global network structure into account. To overcome this problem, for instance, in the context of influence maximization, Borgs *et al.* [1] proposed an algorithm based on reverse reachability search, and proved that it runs in near linear time and provides theoretical guarantees on the approximation quality. Cohen *et al.* [3] presented a bottom-k sketch-based method of the greedy algorithm, which is called the greedy Sketch-based Influence Maximization (SKIM). Here in this paper, unlike the above approximation approaches, we focus on exactly computing the contribution value for each link from a set of simulation samples whereby there is no need to worry about the error introduced by approximation.

3 Problem Formulation

Let $G = (\mathcal{V}, \mathcal{E})$ be a given simple undirected (or bidirectional) network without self-loops, where $\mathcal{V} = \{u, v, w, \cdots\}$ and $\mathcal{E} = \{e, \cdots\}$ are sets of nodes and undirected links, respectively. We also express each link e as a pair of nodes, *i.e.*, $e = (u, v)$, and assume $(u, v) = (v, u)$. For each link $e = (u, v) \in \mathcal{E}$, we define its distance over network G by $d(u, v; G) = r(u, v)$, where $r(u, v)$ is supposed to be assigned some value such as physical distance between two positions u and v on a spatial network, among others. For each pair of nodes that does not have the direct connection, *i.e.*, $(u, w) \notin \mathcal{E}$, we define the distance $d(u, w; G)$ as the geodesic distance over the network G, as usual. For each node $v \in \mathcal{V}$, we assume that v has some weight denoted by $\rho(v)$ which is intended to represent a population around node v in a road network.

In our problem setting, we assume a fixed group of nodes $\mathcal{U} \subset \mathcal{V}$ such as evacuation facilities on a spatial network. Let $\mathcal{R}(u; G)$ be the set of reachable nodes by following links from a node u over G, where note that $u \in \mathcal{R}(u; G)$. Then, we can define a set $\mathcal{R}(\mathcal{U}; G)$ of reachable nodes by following links from every node $u \in \mathcal{U}$ over G, *i.e.*,

$$\mathcal{R}(\mathcal{U}; G) = \bigcup_{u \in \mathcal{U}} \mathcal{R}(u; G).$$

Also, let $\mathcal{R}_1(v; G)$ be the set of nodes adjacent to v, *i.e.*, $\mathcal{R}_1(v; G) = \{w \mid (v, w) \in \mathcal{E}\}$, and for a set of nodes $\mathcal{T} \subset \mathcal{V}$, let $\mathcal{R}_1(\mathcal{T}; G)$ be the set of nodes adjacent to every node $v \in \mathcal{T}$, *i.e.*, $\mathcal{R}_1(\mathcal{T}; G) = \bigcup_{v \in \mathcal{T}} \mathcal{R}_1(v; G)$. We also assume a model prescribed by a set of link disconnection probabilities denoted by $\mathcal{P}$, where $\mathcal{P} = \{p_{(v,w)} \mid (v, w) \in \mathcal{E}\}$. Note that in terms of disaster evacuation over a spatial network, those probabilities are assigned according to some road blockage model based on geographical properties, and then the expected reachable size from $\mathcal{U}$ can be interpreted as the expected number of persons who can successfully move to one of these evacuation facilities.

Let $\mathcal{H}$ be a set of integers defined by $\mathcal{H} = \{1, \cdots, H\}$. Now, we repeat simulations H times based on the probabilistic model prescribed by $\mathcal{P}$, and sample a set $\mathcal{G}_H$ of H graphs constructed by excluding the disconnected links determined by a Bernoulli trial based on $p_{(v,w)}$ for each link $(u, v) \in \mathcal{E}$. *i.e.*, $\mathcal{G}_H = \{G_h = (\mathcal{V}, \mathcal{E}_h) \mid h \in \mathcal{H}\}$, where $\mathcal{E}_h \subset \mathcal{E}$ is the set of non-disconnected links at the h-th simulation. The first step of Fig. 1 illustrates this H graphs generation. Some links are removed from a given network G in each graph G_h. Note that the black nodes denote ones in $\mathcal{U}$, while the white nodes denote the nodes not in $\mathcal{U}$ in this figure. For each graph G_h, let $G_h^+(e)$ and $G_h^-(e)$ be graphs constructed by adding and removing a link e, respectively, *i.e.*, $G_h^+(e) = (\mathcal{V}, \mathcal{E}_h \cup \{e\})$ and $G_h^-(e) = (\mathcal{V}, \mathcal{E}_h \setminus \{e\})$. The second step in Fig. 1 illustrates the construction of graphs $G_h^+(e)$ and $G_h^-(e)$ for a certain link e in $\mathcal{E}$ of G. Since the link e is not included in G_1, G_1 is different from $G_1^+(e)$ that has an added link e denoted by a red broken line, but is identical to $G_1^-(e)$. On the other hand, G_H that has the link e is identical to $G_H^+(e)$, but is different from $G_H^-(e)$ from which e

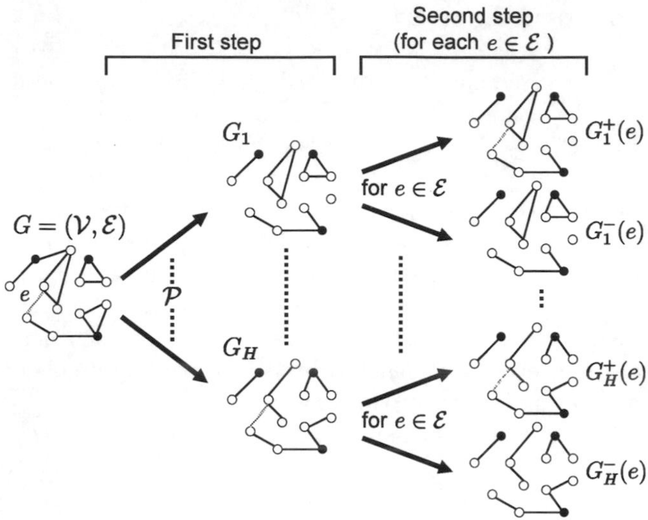

Fig. 1. Generation of H graphs $G_1, \ldots, G_H$ from a given network $G = (\mathcal{V}, \mathcal{E})$ based on the link disconnection probabilities $\mathcal{P}$ (first step) and generation of $G_h^+(e)$ and $G_h^-(e)$ by adding and removing each link $e \in \mathcal{E}$ to and from each graph G_h (second step). (Color figure online)

is removed. Note that the isolated node in G_1 is not reachable from any black node, and thus it is not included in $\mathcal{R}(\mathcal{U}; G_1)$. Adding the link e to G_1 does not contribute to improving its reachability. Thus, it is not included in $\mathcal{R}(\mathcal{U}; G_1^+(e))$, either. The three nodes composing a single component having no black node in G_1 are not included in $\mathcal{R}(\mathcal{U}; G_1)$, but are included in $\mathcal{R}(\mathcal{U}; G_1^+(e))$ because they are reachable from the black node at the bottom right of $G_1^+(e)$.

Based on $G_h^+(e)$ and $G_h^-(e)$, we define the following reachability contribution value of a link $e \in \mathcal{E}$ over G_h.

$$\phi_h(e) = \phi_h^+(e) - \phi_h^-(e), \tag{1}$$

where

$$\phi_h^+(e) = \sum_{v \in \mathcal{R}(\mathcal{U}; G_h^+(e))} \rho(v), \quad \phi_h^-(e) = \sum_{v \in \mathcal{R}(\mathcal{U}; G_h^-(e))} \rho(v),$$

Then, we can define the reachability contribution value $F(e; \mathcal{G}_H)$ of a link $e \in \mathcal{E}$ for $\mathcal{G}_H$ as follows:

$$F(e; \mathcal{G}_H) = \frac{1}{H} \sum_{h \in \mathcal{H}} \phi_h(e). \tag{2}$$

Here note that for a given probabilistic model prescribed by $\mathcal{P}$, when H is a sufficiently large number, $F(e; \mathcal{G}_H)$ can be a close approximation to the expected reachability contribution value. Here we emphasize that unlike the approach based on a certain approximation strategy such as the bottom-k sketch-based

Table 1. Notation

$\mathcal{G}_H = \{G_h = (\mathcal{V}, \mathcal{E}_h) \mid h \in \mathcal{H}\}$	Set of H graphs generated according to probabilistic model $\mathcal{P}$
$G_h^+(e) = (\mathcal{V}, \mathcal{E}_h \cup \{e\})$	Graph constructed by adding a link e to G_h
$G_h^-(e) = (\mathcal{V}, \mathcal{E}_h \setminus \{e\})$	Graph constructed by removing a link e from G_h
$\phi_h(e) = \phi_h^+(e) - \phi_h^-(e)$	Reachability contribution value of a link e for G_h
$F(e; \mathcal{G}_H) = H^{-1} \sum_{h \in \mathcal{H}} \phi_h(e)$	Reachability contribution value of a link e for $\mathcal{G}_H$

method [3] mentioned in previous section, we are computing the contribution value $F(e; \mathcal{G}_H)$ exactly for each link $e \in \mathcal{E}$ from given simulation samples $\mathcal{G}_H$. Thus, there is no error introduced in here. Hereafter, we refer to this unified framework as a probabilistic model-based critical link detection problem. In this paper, we focus on the task of accurately and efficiently calculating $F(e; \mathcal{G}_H)$ for every $e \in \mathcal{E}$. Of course, network performance measure is not unique. It varies from problem to problem, but computing $\phi_h(e)$ for every node $e \in \mathcal{E}$ can be a fundamental task. Note that our proposed method and techniques can directly contribute to this task.

For ease of reference, we summarize the frequently used symbols in Table 1.

4 Proposed Method

A naive method would be to straightforwardly compute the reachability size. Here, note that $G_h^+(e) = G_h$ if $e \in \mathcal{E}_h$; $G_h^-(e) = G_h$ otherwise. Thus, for each $h \in \mathcal{H}$, by computing $\mathcal{R}(\mathcal{U}; G_h)$ by following links from $\mathcal{U}$ over G_h and $\phi_h = \sum_{v \in \mathcal{R}(\mathcal{U}; G_h)} \rho(v)$ in advance, for each $e \in \mathcal{E}$, we can obtain $\phi_h(e)$ as $\phi_h - \phi_h^-(e)$ by computing $\phi_h^-(e)$ if $e \in \mathcal{E}_h$; $\phi_h^+(e) - \phi_h$ by computing $\phi_h^+(e)$ otherwise. Below we summarize the naive method (NM for short) that computes $F(e; \mathcal{G}_H)$ for every link $e \in \mathcal{E}$ from a given set $\mathcal{G}_H$ of networks produced from an original network G and a given subset of nodes $\mathcal{U}$.

1: Perform the following step **2:** for every $h \in \mathcal{H}$.
2: Compute ϕ_h, and then compute $\phi_h(e)$ for every $e \in \mathcal{E}$.
3: Output $F(e; \mathcal{G}_H)$ defined in Eq. (2) for every $e \in \mathcal{E}$ and terminate.

For $\mathcal{G}_H$, let $E(\mathcal{G}_H)$ be the average number of links followings from $\mathcal{U}$ over each G_h,

$$E(\mathcal{G}_H) = \frac{1}{H} \sum_{h \in \mathcal{H}} |\{(v, w) \in \mathcal{E}_h \mid (\{v, w\} \cap \mathcal{R}(\mathcal{U}; G_h)) \neq \emptyset\}|.$$

Then, the computational complexity of NM is approximately $O(H \times |\mathcal{E}| \times E(\mathcal{G}_H))$ under the situation that $\mathcal{R}(\mathcal{U}; G_h^+(e)) \approx \mathcal{R}(\mathcal{U}; G_h^-(e))$ for most links $e \in \mathcal{E}$. Thus it generally requires a large amount of computation for large-scale networks. In fact, in case that most probabilities $p_e \in \mathcal{P}$ are quite small, *i.e.*, it is assumed that $E(\mathcal{G}_H) \approx |\mathcal{E}|$, we obtain $H \times |\mathcal{E}|^2 \in [3.6 \times 10^{13}, 1.6 \times 10^{15}]$ for our networks used in our experiment, where H is set to $100,000$ ($= 10^5$) as performed in our experiments. In order to overcome this problem, we present our methods by proposing new techniques of skipping unnecessary computations.

4.1 RCS: Reachability Condition Skipping

For each $h \in \mathcal{H}$, we consider obtaining $\phi_h(e)$ by only following links within a relatively small portion of network. To this end, for each link $e = (v, w) \in \mathcal{E}$, we introduce a function $\psi_h(e)$ defined by $\psi_h(e) = |\{v, w\} \cap \mathcal{R}(\mathcal{U}; G_h)| \in \{0, 1, 2\}$, which returns the number of nodes included in $\mathcal{R}(\mathcal{U}; G_h)$ for the node pair $\{v, w\}$. Now, in case of $\psi_h(e) = 0$, we obtain $\phi_h(e) \leftarrow 0$ because $\mathcal{R}(\mathcal{U}; G_h^+(e)) = \mathcal{R}(\mathcal{U}; G_h^-(e))$. In case of $\psi_h(e) = 1$, it must hold that $e \notin \mathcal{E}_h$, and thus we obtain

$$\phi_h(e) \leftarrow \begin{cases} \sum_{x \in \mathcal{R}(w; G_h)} \rho(x) & \text{if} \quad v \in \mathcal{R}(\mathcal{U}; G_h), \\ \sum_{x \in \mathcal{R}(v; G_h)} \rho(x) & \text{if} \quad w \in \mathcal{R}(\mathcal{U}; G_h). \end{cases}$$

In case of $\psi_h(e) = 2$, we further classify it into two patterns whether e is included in $\mathcal{E}_h$ or not, *i.e.*, $e \in \mathcal{E}_h$ and $e \notin \mathcal{E}_h$. In the former pattern we obtain

$$\phi_h(e) \leftarrow \begin{cases} \sum_{x \in \mathcal{R}(v; G_h^-(e))} \rho(x) & \text{if} \quad \mathcal{R}(v; G_h^-(e)) \cap \mathcal{U} = \emptyset, \\ \sum_{x \in \mathcal{R}(w; G_h^-(e))} \rho(x) & \text{if} \quad \mathcal{R}(w; G_h^-(e)) \cap \mathcal{U} = \emptyset, \\ 0 & \text{otherwise.} \end{cases}$$

In the latter pattern we also obtain $\phi_h(e) \leftarrow 0$ because $\mathcal{R}(\mathcal{U}; G_h^+(e)) = \mathcal{R}(\mathcal{U}; G_h^-(e))$.

Based on the above considerations, we can revise the step 2 of NM as follows:

2: Compute $\mathcal{R}(\mathcal{U}; G_h)$, and after computing $\psi_h(e)$, perform the following steps for every $e = (v, w) \in \mathcal{E}$:
2-1: If $\psi_h(e) = 1$, set $\phi_h(e) \leftarrow \sum_{x \in \mathcal{R}(w; G_h)} \rho(x)$ if $v \in \mathcal{R}(\mathcal{U}; G_h)$, and $\phi_h(e) \leftarrow \sum_{x \in \mathcal{R}(v; G_h)} \rho(x)$ if $w \in \mathcal{R}(\mathcal{U}; G_h)$.
2-2: If $\psi_h(e) = 2$ and $e \in \mathcal{E}_h$, set $\phi_h(e) \leftarrow \sum_{x \in \mathcal{R}(v; G_h^-(e))} \rho(x)$ if $\mathcal{R}(v; G_h^-(e)) \cap \mathcal{U} = \emptyset$, $\phi_h(e) \leftarrow \sum_{x \in \mathcal{R}(w; G_h^-(e))} \rho(x)$ if $\mathcal{R}(w; G_h^-(e)) \cap \mathcal{U} = \emptyset$, and $\phi_h(e) \leftarrow 0$ otherwise.

Hereafter, we refer to this technique as RCS (reachability condition skipping), and the detection method employing this technique as the RCS method (RM for short).

4.2 DCS: Distance Constraints Skipping

We consider further reducing the computational load for the step 2-2 of RM by applying distance constraints. For each $x \in \mathcal{R}(\mathcal{U}; G_h)$, let $\delta_h(x)$ be the minimum distance from $\mathcal{U}$ to x over G_h, *i.e.*, $\delta_h(x) = \min\{d(u, x; G_h) \mid u \in \mathcal{U}\}$. Here, note that we can efficiently compute $\delta_h(x)$ as follows: for each $h \in \mathcal{H}$, after the initialization of $\delta_h(x) \leftarrow 0$ if $x \in \mathcal{U}$ and $\delta_h(x) \leftarrow \infty$ otherwise, we can compute $\delta_h(x)$ for every $x \in \mathcal{R}(\mathcal{U}; G_h) \setminus \mathcal{U}$ by performing best first search with respect to $\delta_h(x)$. Then, for each $e = (v, w) \in \mathcal{E}_h$ such that $\psi_h(e) = 2$, we can immediately know that $\mathcal{R}(v; G_h^-(e)) \cap \mathcal{U} \neq \emptyset$ if $\delta_h(v) \leq \delta_h(w)$ and $\mathcal{R}(w; G_h^-(e)) \cap \mathcal{U} \neq \emptyset$ if $\delta_h(w) \leq \delta_h(v)$. Hereafter, we assume $\delta_h(v) \leq \delta_h(w)$ without loss of generality. Now, we can easily see that if the condition $\mathcal{R}(w; G_h^-(e)) \cap \mathcal{U} = \emptyset$ holds, it must satisfy that $\delta_h(w) + d(w, x; G_h^-(e)) = \delta_h(x)$ for arbitrary node $x \in \mathcal{R}(w; G_h^-(e))$. Thus, from its contraposition, if there exists some node $x \in \mathcal{R}(w; G_h^-(e))$ such that $\delta_h(w) + d(w, x; G_h^-(e)) > \delta_h(x)$, we can immediately conclude that $\mathcal{R}(w; G_h^-(e)) \cap \mathcal{U} \neq \emptyset$.

Based on the above considerations, we can revise the step 2 of RM as follows:

2: Compute $\mathcal{R}(\mathcal{U}; G_h)$ together with $\delta_h(v)$ by performing best-first search with respect to $\delta_h(v)$, and after computing $\psi_h(e)$, perform the following steps for every $e = (v, w) \in \mathcal{E}$:
2-1: If $\psi_h(e) = 1$, set $\phi_h(e) \leftarrow \sum_{x \in \mathcal{R}(w; G_h)} \rho(x)$ if $v \in \mathcal{R}(\mathcal{U}; G_h)$, and $\phi_h(e) \leftarrow \sum_{x \in \mathcal{R}(v; G_h)} \rho(x)$ if $w \in \mathcal{R}(\mathcal{U}; G_h)$.
2-2: If $\psi_h(e) = 2$ and $e \in \mathcal{E}_h$, after initializing a subset of nodes as $\mathcal{T} \leftarrow \{w\}$, set $x \leftarrow \arg\min_{y \in \mathcal{R}_1(\mathcal{T}; G_h^-(e))} d(w, y; G_h^-(e))$ and $\mathcal{T} \leftarrow \mathcal{T} \cup \{x\}$ unless $\mathcal{T} = \mathcal{R}_1(\mathcal{T}; G_h^-(e))$ or $\delta_h(w) + d(w, x; G_h^-(e)) > \delta_h(x)$, and then set $\phi_h(e) \leftarrow \sum_{x \in \mathcal{T}} \rho(x)$ if $\mathcal{T} = \mathcal{R}_1(\mathcal{T}; G_h^-(e))$, and $\phi_h(e) \leftarrow 0$ otherwise.

Hereafter, we refer to this technique as DCS (distance constraints skipping), and the detection method employing both RCS and DCS as the proposed method (PM for short).

5 Experiments

We focused on three cities referred to as Hamamatsu, Shizuoka and Numazu in our experiments because these medium-sized regional cities in Japan face the Pacific Ocean and are relatively close to Mt. Fuji, namely, detecting critical links in these networks is an extremely important task against the tsunami in a large-scale earthquake and a volcanic eruption. We used spatial road networks extracted from the OSM[1] data of each city, as performed in Ohara *et al.*'s previous studies [6,7]. In our experiments, for the sake of evaluating the fundamental performance of our proposed method, we set $d(v, w; G) = 1$ and $p_{v,w} = p$ for every $(v, w) \in \mathcal{E}$, where p is the only parameter for controlling the degree of road blockage (disconnection probability). Moreover, we set $\rho(v) = 1$ for simplicity and H is set to $100,000$ $(= 10^5)$ as mentioned earlier.

[1] https://openstreetmap.jp/.

Table 2. Basic statistics as network.

Name	$\|\mathcal{V}\|$	$\|\mathcal{E}\|$	$\|\mathcal{U}\|$	*deg*	*avg*	*s.d.*	*max*
Hamamatsu	104,813	127,648	432	2.43	16.62	9.29	74
Shizuoka	53,903	66,444	363	2.47	15.69	11.98	59
Numazu	15,483	19,053	232	2.46	12.88	10.00	122

Table 2 shows the basic statistics of the Hamamatsu, Shizuoka and Numazu networks, where $|\mathcal{V}|$, $|\mathcal{E}|$ and $|\mathcal{U}|$ are the numbers of nodes, links and evacuation facilities, *deg* means the average degree of nodes calculated by $deg = 2|\mathcal{E}|/|\mathcal{V}|$, *avg* and *s.d.* stand for the average and standard deviation of distance $\delta(v) = \min\{d(u, v; G) \mid u \in \mathcal{U}\}$ for every $v \in \mathcal{V}$, respectively, and *max* shows the maximum distance of $\delta(v)$. From this table, we can see that although the numbers of nodes and links, $|\mathcal{V}|$ and $|\mathcal{E}|$, are substantially different, the average degrees (*deg*) are quite similar as a common characteristic of spatial networks, and the average distances (*avg*) and their standard deviations (*s.d.*) are similar too. These are considered to be common requirements to evacuation facilities.

5.1 Evaluation of Computational Efficiency

In order to investigate how efficiently the proposed method (PM) works, we compared its computation time with those of the RCS method (RM) and the naive method (NM), by setting the disconnection probability p to $p = 2^{-k}$, where $k = 1, \cdots, 9$, *i.e.*, $0.0019 < p \leq 0.5$. We show our experimental results in Fig. 2, where Figs. 2(a), (b) and (c) are those for Hamamatsu, Shizuoka and Numazu networks, respectively. Here, our programs implemented in C were executed on a computer system equipped with two Xeon X5690 3.47 GHz CPUs and a 192 GB main memory with a single thread within the memory capacity. From Fig. 2, for all the networks, we can see that for most of the disconnection probability settings, NM and RM required substantial amount of computation time, about 10^4 and 10^2 times larger than those of PM, respectively, except at $p = 2^{-1}$ for which they were almost compatible. These experimental results indicate that our proposed method (PM) successfully achieved a significant amount of computational reduction.

Below we examine our experimental results more closely. From Fig. 2, we can see that, as naturally expected, larger networks required more computation time, which is in the order of Hamamatsu (Fig. 2(a)), Shizuoka (Fig. 2(b)) and Numazu (Fig. 2(c)) networks, as shown in Table 2. On the other hand, we can observe a quite similar tendency of curves with respect to the disconnection probability p regardless of the network size for all the three methods, *i.e.*, they were almost horizontally flat when $p \leq 2^{-3}$, and the minimum values were achieved when $p = 2^{-1}$. This can be naturally explained by the fact that the size of the largest connected component for G_h when $p \leq 2^{-3}$ is almost equal to that of the original network G, while the size for G_h when $p = 2^{-1}$ becomes

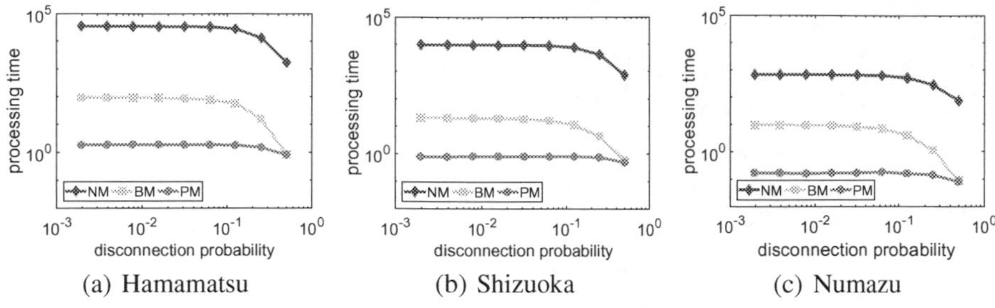

(a) Hamamatsu (b) Shizuoka (c) Numazu

Fig. 2. Evaluation of computational efficiency.

extremely small, *i.e.*, in the latter case, the number of links to be followed from each node generally becomes quite small. This fact is experimentally confirmed in the next subsection. Another notable characteristic is that the computation time difference of PM when $p \leq 2^{-3}$ and $p = 2^{-1}$ was much smaller than those of NM and RM. This result suggests that our proposed DCS technique worked quite effectively.

5.2 Evaluation of Contribution Values

We investigated how much the network performance potentially degrades for each link $e \in \mathcal{E}$ by varying the disconnection probability $p = 2^{-k}$, where $k = 1, \cdots, 7$. We show our experimental results in Fig. 3, where the horizontal and the vertical axes stand for the rank for e in terms of the contribution value and its actual value $F(e; \mathcal{G}_H)$, respectively, and Figs. 3(a), (b), and (c) are those of the Hamamatsu, Shizuoka and Numazu networks, respectively. From Fig. 3, for all the networks, we can see that for some disconnection probability settings, there exist some links which bring about substantially large contribution values, *i.e.*, there exist a significant number of isolated persons who cannot move to any evacuation facility. Here we should emphasize that it is extremely important to minimize isolation in case of disaster evacuation.

Below we examine our experimental results more closely. From Fig. 3, we can see that, as also expected, larger networks produced much larger contribution values, in the order of Hamamatsu (Fig. 3(a)), Shizuoka (Fig. 3(b)) and Numazu (Fig. 3(c)) networks. On the other hand, regardless of the network size, we can see that the contribution values were relatively large when $p = 2^{-2}$, in comparison to those of $p = 2^{-1}$ or $p = 2^{-3}$. This can also be naturally explained by the fact that the size of the largest connected component for G_h when $p \leq 2^{-3}$ is almost equal to that of the original network G while the size for G_h when $p = 2^{-1}$ becomes extremely small. Thus, the best value is in the middle.

We performed further experiments to confirm our conjectures above. We show the experimental results in Fig. 4 for the three cities, abbreviated as H for Hamamatsu, S for Shizuoka and N for Numazu networks. Here the disconnection probability p were also varied as $p = 2^{-k}$ where $k = 1, \cdots, 9$, Fig. 4(a) shows

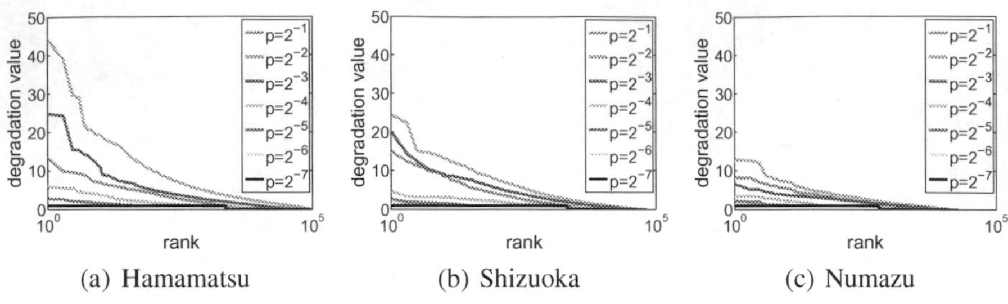

(a) Hamamatsu (b) Shizuoka (c) Numazu

Fig. 3. Evaluation of degradation value.

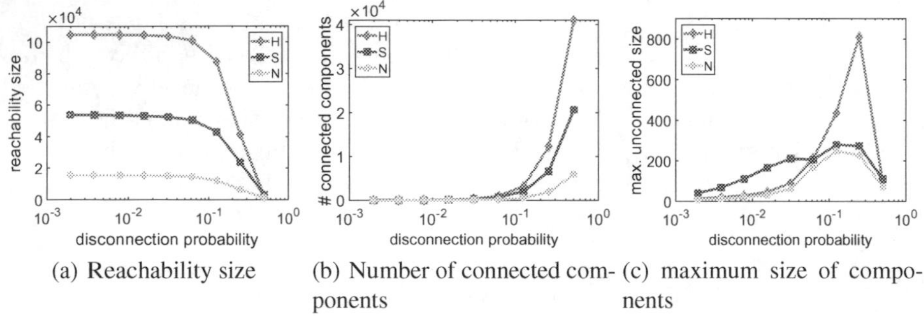

(a) Reachability size (b) Number of connected components (c) maximum size of components

Fig. 4. Analysis of experimental results.

the average reachability size from $\mathcal{U}$, *i.e.*, $\sum_{h \in \mathcal{H}} |\mathcal{R}(\mathcal{U}; G_h)|/H$. We can confirm that all the sizes were extremely small when $p = 2^{-1}$, while they are almost equal to the original ones when $p \leq 2^{-3}$. Here we note that the original sizes of the Hamamatsu, Shizuoka and Numazu networks are 104,813, 53,903 and 15,483, respectively, as shown in Table 2. Figure 4(b) shows the average number of connected components among nodes unreachable from $\mathcal{U}$ for G_h, *i.e.*, among $\mathcal{V} \setminus \mathcal{R}(\mathcal{U}; G_h)$, from which we can confirm that there exist quite large numbers of components when $p = 2^{-1}$, while they become much smaller when $p \leq 2^{-3}$. Figure 4(c) shows the average size of the maximum connected components among nodes unreachable from $\mathcal{U}$. We can confirm that they are largest when $p = 2^{-2}$ and/or $p = 2^{-3}$ for all the three networks, which reasonably coincides with our experimental results shown in Fig. 3. Thus, we consider that these experimental results reasonably support our conjectures.

5.3 Visualization of Detected Link Locations

We investigated how differently the detected links in each network are distributed on each map. We show our visualization results in Fig. 5. More specifically, we plotted each node $v \in \mathcal{V}$ by a green dot according to the position described by a pair of latitude and longitude, and then depicted each link $e = (v, w) \in \mathcal{E}$ by a cyan line which directly connects between nodes v and w. After that, we plotted

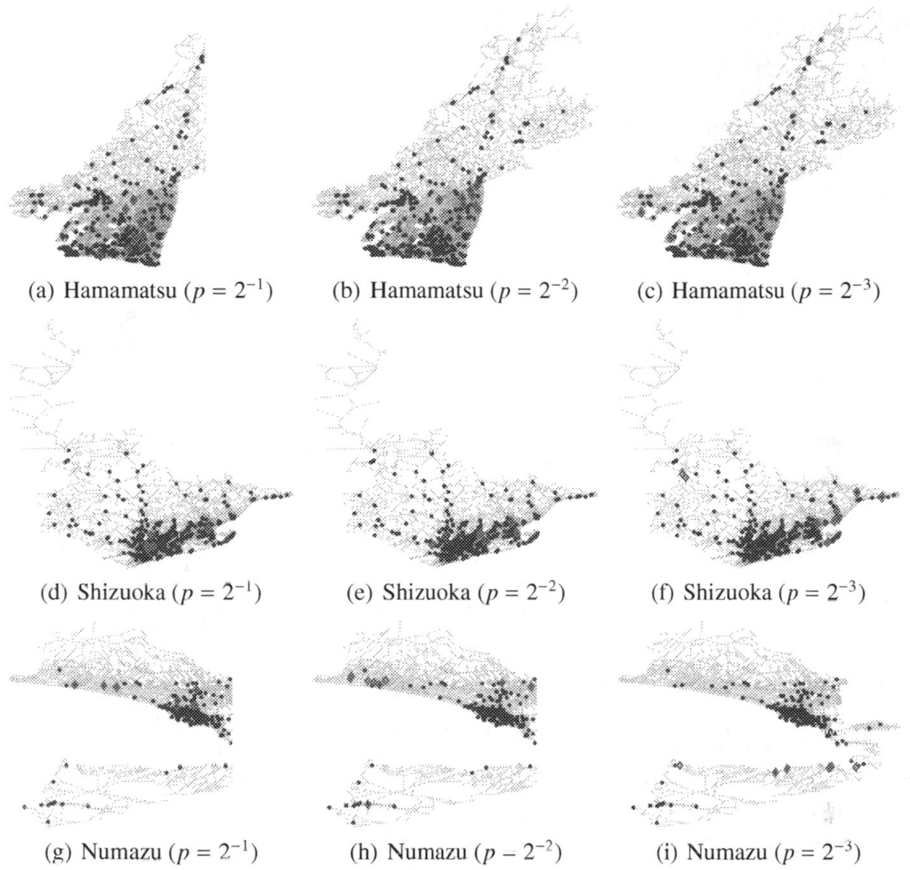

(a) Hamamatsu ($p = 2^{-1}$) (b) Hamamatsu ($p = 2^{-2}$) (c) Hamamatsu ($p = 2^{-3}$)

(d) Shizuoka ($p = 2^{-1}$) (e) Shizuoka ($p = 2^{-2}$) (f) Shizuoka ($p = 2^{-3}$)

(g) Numazu ($p = 2^{-1}$) (h) Numazu ($p = 2^{-2}$) (i) Numazu ($p = 2^{-3}$)

Fig. 5. Visualization results. (Color figure online)

each node $u \in \mathcal{U}$ corresponding to the position of an evacuation facility by a small blue circle, and then depicted the middle position of each link $e = (v, w)$ which is ranked within the top-10 score according to the contribution value by a slightly larger red diamond. We show the results for each of the Hamamatsu, Shizuoka and Numazu networks with three values of the disconnection probability, i.e., $p = 2^{-1}$, $p = 2^{-2}$ and $p = 2^{-3}$. The corresponding results are given in Figs. 5(a), (d), and (g) for $p = 2^{-1}$, in Figs. 5(b), (e), and (h) for $p = 2^{-2}$, and in Figs. 5(c), (f), and (i) for $p = 2^{-3}$, respectively.

First of all, we can see that the entire configurations of these networks are substantially different to each other. However, it should be emphasized that we obtained similar experimental results to these three networks in terms of the computational efficiency and the contribution values as shown in Figs. 2 and 3, respectively. This would suggest the generality of our probabilistic model-based critical link detection problem. From the visualization results in Fig. 5, we can see that the critical links with high contribution values may change substantially depending on the disconnection probability when $p \geq 2^{-3}$, but the visualization results for the probability $p < 2^{-3}$ were sufficiently close to those with $p = 2^{-3}$ for all the network.

Below we examine our experimental results more closely. We notice from Fig. 5 that in case of $p = 2^{-1}$ the top-10 scored links appeared around the city center area as shown in Figs. 5(a), (d), and (g), in case of $p = 2^{-2}$ they somewhat moved to the suburb area as shown in Figs. 5(b), (e), and (h) and in case of $p = 2^{-3}$ they further moved out to the surrounding area as shown in Figs. 5(c), (f), and (i) for all the networks, but their locations differ depending on the network and the disconnection probability. Here, it should be noted that we can observe a few number of detected links which commonly appear in at least two cases. For example, the link denoted by the top red diamond in Fig. 5(a) appears in Fig. 5(b), too. We can conjecture that these commonly appeared links are particularly important, but we need further investigations to confirm our conjecture.

6 Conclusion

We have proposed a unified problem framework of critical link detection and its novel solution method for a large network under a given probabilistic model of link disconnectivity. Namely, we formalized this detection problem as the problem of computing the contribution value of each link, that is, the amount of the network performance degradation in terms of reachability, and presented two new techniques for avoiding unnecessary computations: reachability condition skipping (RCS) and distance constraints skipping (DCS). In our experiments using three real-world spatial networks, we showed that the method achieved the efficiency gain of around 10^4 compared with a naive method in which every single link is blindly tested as a critical link candidate. Our immediate future plan is to apply our method to a real world application and show that it can solve a difficult problem efficiently, e.g., identifying important critical spots in transportation network or evacuation network.

Acknowledgments. This material is based upon work supported by JSPS Grant-in-Aid for Scientific Research (C) (No. 17K00314).

References

1. Borgs, C., Brautbar, M., Chayes, J., Lucier, B.: Maximizing social influence in nearly optimal time. In: Proceedings of the 25th Annual ACM-SIAM Symposium on Discrete Algorithms (SODA 2014), pp. 946–957 (2014)
2. Burckhart, K., Martin, O.J.: An interpretation of the recent evolution of the city of Barcelona through the traffic maps. J. Geograph. Inf. Syst. **4**(4), 298–311 (2012)
3. Cohen, E., Delling, D., Pajor, T., Werneck, R.F.: Sketch-based influence maximization and computation: scaling up with guarantees. In: Proceedings of the 23rd ACM International Conference on Conference on Information and Knowledge Management, pp. 629–638 (2014)

4. Crucitti, P., Latora, V., Porta, S.: Centrality measures in spatial networks of urban streets. Phys. Rev. E **73**(3), 036125 (2006)
5. Kimura, M., Saito, K., Motoda, H.: Blocking links to minimize contamination spread in a social network. ACM Trans. Knowl. Discov. Data **3**, 9:1–9:23 (2009)
6. Ohara, K., Saito, K., Kimura, M., Motoda, H.: Accelerating computation of distance based centrality measures for spatial networks. In: Calders, T., Ceci, M., Malerba, D. (eds.) DS 2016. LNCS (LNAI), vol. 9956, pp. 376–391. Springer, Cham (2016). https://doi.org/10.1007/978-3-319-46307-0_24
7. Ohara, K., Saito, K., Kimura, M., Motoda, H.: Maximizing network performance based on group centrality by creating most effective k-links. In: Proceedings of the 4th IEEE International Conference on Data Science and Advanced Analytics (DSAA 2017), pp. 561–570 (2017)
8. Oliveira, E.L., Portugal, L.S., Junior, W.P.: Determining critical links in a road network: vulnerability and congestion indicators. Procedia - Soc. Behav. Sci. **162**, 158–167 (2014)
9. Opsahl, T., Agneessens, F., Skvoretz, J.: Node centrality in weighted networks: generalizing degree and shortest paths. Soc. Netw. **32**(3), 245–251 (2010)
10. Papagelis, M.: Refining social graph connectivity via shortcut edge addition. ACM Trans. Knowl. Discov. Data (TKDD) **10**(2), 12 (2015)
11. Parotsidis, N., Pitoura, E., Tsaparas, P.: Centrality-aware link recommendations. In: Proceedings of of the Ninth ACM International Conference on Web Search and Data Mining (WSDM 2016), pp. 503–512 (2016)
12. Saito, K., Kimura, M., Ohara, K., Motoda, H.: Detecting critical links in complex network to maintain information flow/reachability. In: Booth, R., Zhang, M.-L. (eds.) PRICAI 2016. LNCS (LNAI), vol. 9810, pp. 419–432. Springer, Cham (2016). https://doi.org/10.1007/978-3-319-42911-3_35
13. Saito, K., Ohara, K., Kimura, M., Motoda, H.: An accurate and efficient method to detect critical links to maintain information flow in network. In: Kryszkiewicz, M., Appice, A., Ślęzak, D., Rybinski, H., Skowron, A., Raś, Z.W. (eds.) ISMIS 2017. LNCS (LNAI), vol. 10352, pp. 116–126. Springer, Cham (2017). https://doi.org/10.1007/978-3-319-60438-1_12
14. Shen, Y., Nguyen, N.P., Xuan, Y., Thai, M.T.: On the discovery of critical links and nodes for assessing network vulnerability. IEEE/ACM Trans. Netw. **21**(3), 963–973 (2013)

Mixed Neighbourhood Local Search for Customer Order Scheduling Problem

Vahid Riahi(✉), M. M. A. Polash, M. A. Hakim Newton, and Abdul Sattar

Institute for Integrated and Intelligent Systems (IIIS),
Griffith University, Brisbane, Australia
{vahid.riahi,mdmasbaulalam.polash}@griffithuni.edu.au,
{mahakim.newton,a.sattar}@griffith.edu.au

Abstract. Customer Order Scheduling Problem (COSP) is an NP-Hard problem that has important practical applications e.g., in the paper industry and the pharmaceutical industry. The existing algorithms to solve COSP still either find low quality solutions or scramble with large-sized problems. In this paper, we propose a new constructive heuristic called *repair-based mechanism (RBM)* that outperforms the best-known heuristics in the literature. We also propose a mixed neighbourhood local search (MNLS) algorithm. MNLS embeds a number of move operators to diversify the local exploitation making different areas around the current solution accessible. Moreover, we also propose a greedy diversification method to keep the search focussed even when it is in a plateau. Our experimental results on 960 well-known problem instances indicate statistically significant improvement obtained by the proposed MNLS over existing state-of-the-art algorithms. MNLS has found new best solutions for 721 out of the 960 problem instances.

Keywords: Scheduling · Customer order · Local search

1 Introduction

A customer order scheduling problem (COSP) has n customer orders and m parallel machines. Each customer order j contains m items. Each item i can be processed by a particular machine i. Machines can execute different items of a customer order j simultaneously. Each item i of a customer order j needs a non-negative period of processing time $p_{ij} \geq 0$ at machine i. The completion time of a customer order j is the time point when processing of all corresponding items is finished. The aim is to find a sequence of the customer orders such that the summation of the completion times of the customer orders is minimised.

The COSP problem was first introduced by [2]. It has several real-life applications, e.g., car repair shops [10], pharmaceutical industry [5], manufacturing of semi finished lenses [1], and paper industry [6]. Consider a car repair shop that possesses several particular mechanics. Each entering car contains multiple broken parts. Each broken part needs a particular mechanic to fix it. The

X. Geng and B.-H. Kang (Eds.): PRICAI 2018, LNAI 11012, pp. 296–309, 2018.
https://doi.org/10.1007/978-3-319-97304-3_23

mechanics are able to work on a single car at the same time. A car leaves the shop only when all broken parts are repaired. This car repair shop model can also be adapted to aircraft maintenance and ship repair [10].

The COSP is an NP-Hard problem [6], meaning that it is difficult to be optimally solved especially when the size of the problem is large. Therefore, researchers recently put much more attention on heuristic and metaheuristic algorithms to solve COSP. The very first heuristic proposed for COSP is *Shortest Total Processing Time (STPT)*[8]. Recently, two other heuristics are proposed based on the idea of STPT: *Earliest Completion Time (ECT)* [6] and FP [3] (named after the authors' names). As metaheuristics, a Tabu Search (TS) [6] and a Greedy Search Algorithm (GSA) [3] are proposed.

In this paper, we study possible drawbacks of existing methods (explained in Sect. 3) and then propose efficient approaches, which outperform the state-of-the-art methods. First, we propose a constructive heuristic called *repair-based mechanism (RBM)*. RBM is an improved version of STPT heuristic. STPT starts with an empty sequence. It then iteratively appends the unscheduled customer order with the smallest total processing time at the end of the partial sequence. However, based on the repair mechanism, RBM seeks better positions for unscheduled customer orders by inserting them to earlier positions of the partial sequence as well instead of only at the end.

As the metaheuristics, we propose a Mixed Neighbourhood Local Search (MNLS) algorithm. MNLS is made up of two main steps: intensification and diversification. In the intensification phase, we use a number of neighbourhood operators instead of only one. The idea behind this is that different neighbourhoods will generate different local optima and different landscapes [9]. Therefore, different neighbourhoods will help our algorithm search different regions around the current solution. In the diversification phase, we use the idea of a multi-start procedure that produces different initial solutions from where local search can start. In the classical multi-start procedure, the initial solutions are completely randomly generated; which typically cause exploration of inferior solutions in terms of the objective value [9]. We use a greedy procedure to generate initial solutions by keeping a part of the current local optima and changing another part of it. The intuition is that the proposed greedy approach will create a solution that shares the properties of both new and good areas of the search space in terms of the objective function.

The proposed RBM and MNLS algorithms are tested on 960 well-known large instances generated by [3]. First, our results showed the superiority of the proposed RBM against STPT as well as FP heuristic (the best-preforming heuristic in the literature) with a substantial margin. Experimental results showed that the proposed MNLS algorithm with RBM and even with FP as initialisation significantly outperform GSA, the best existing metaheuristic in the literature. Finally, for 721 out of the 960, a new upper bound is found by the proposed MNLS.

In the rest of the paper, Sect. 2 outlines the formulation of COSP, Sect. 3 describes the literature, Sect. 4 introduces the constructive heuristic and MNLS algorithm, Sect. 5 presents the experimental results, and Sect. 6 concludes the paper.

2 Preliminaries

The COSP with n customer orders and m machines has $n!$ possible permutations on each machine and a total of $(n!)^m$ possible permutations. However, [4] has proved that the optimal case happens when the permutation of the customer orders is the same for all machines.

Suppose π be a permutation of the given n customer orders and π_k denotes the customer order in the kth position of π. Also, let C_{i,π_k} be the completion time of the customer order at position k on machine i. To calculate the total completion time TCT(π) of solution π, first, the completion time of each customer j order on each machine i is calculated as $C_{i,\pi_k} = C_{i,\pi_{k-1}} + p_{i\pi_k}$ where $k = 1, 2, \ldots, n$, $i = 1, 2, \ldots, m$, and for convenience of the computation, $C_{i,[0]} = 0$. Then, the completion time of customer order occupied in position k is computed $C_{\pi_k} = max\{C_{i,\pi_k}\}$. Finally, $TCT(\pi) = \sum_{k=1}^{n} C_{\pi_k}$ computes the total completion time of solution π.

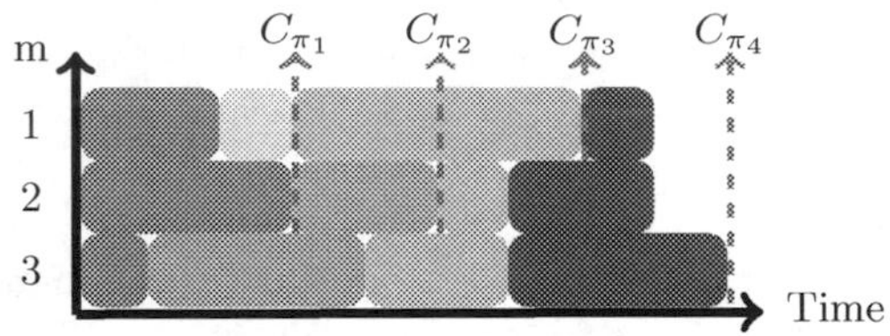

Fig. 1. A COSP with three machines and four orders. (Color figure online)

In Fig. 1, a COSP with three machines and four customer orders is depicted to help understand the problem. The total completion times are computed by summing up the four completion times shown in red arrows.

3 Related Works

To solve COSP, a heuristic named *Shortest Total Processing Time (STPT)* is proposed in [8]. STPT starts with an empty sequence and constructs a schedule by appending the unscheduled customer order with the smallest total processing time at the end of the partial sequence. This heuristic is very fast. However, the performance significantly decreases especially when the problem size increases since it only focuses on the end of the partial solution. Another existing heuristic is *Earliest Completion Time (ECT)* [6]. In ECT, all unscheduled customer orders are appended one by one at the end of the partial sequence, and the permutation with lowest objective value is picked. This process continues until all customer orders are scheduled. Another heuristic called FP [3] is also proposed. FP starts with an initial sequence obtained by another heuristic called SPT-B. The SPT-B first obtains m permutations by sorting the customer orders in a non-decreasing order of the processing times on each machine. After calculating the objective value of each m sequences, the best one is selected as the initial sequence of FP. Next, similar to ECT, customer orders are tested on the end of the partial sequence. However, FP always considers a complete sequence considering those unscheduled customer orders based on the STP-B ordering as the trailing customer orders of the sequence. Focusing only again on the end of partial sequence leads to performance degradation for both FP and ECT especially when problem size increases.

As metaheuristics, a Tabu Search (TS) [6] and a Greedy Search Algorithm (GSA) [3] are proposed. TS uses ECT to generate an initial solution and then uses the swap operator in local search. GSA employs FP for the initial solution. Then, it goes through the main loop which contains three steps. At the first step, one customer order is randomly selected and inserted at the end of the solution. At the second step, GSA finds the best neighbour for the customer order newly placed at the end, and finally applies an exhaustive swap operator on the solution obtained from the second step. It is continued until the stopping criterion is met. The results show the efficiency of GSA over TS algorithm. Both algorithms exhaustively uses all possible swap moves; which increases the required CPU times as well as the risk of getting stuck in the local optima.

4 Our Approach

In order to solve COSP, we propose a heuristic called *repair-based mechanism (RBM)* and a metaheuristic algorithm named Mixed Neighbourhood Local Search (MNLS). The proposed algorithms are explained in the following sections.

4.1 The Proposed RBM Heuristic

RBM is an improved version of *STPT* heuristic [8]. *STPT* starts with an empty sequence π, calculates the total processing time $\sigma[j] = \sum_{i=1}^{m} P_{ij}$ of each order j over all machines, sorts them in a list L in a non-decreasing order of $\sigma[j]$. At each iteration $1 \leq k \leq n$, it appends the kth customer order from the list L at the end of the sequence π.

One possible criticism of *STPT*, *ECT* and *FP* is that they are position-oriented method as their focus is to find the best customer order just for the end of the current partial sequence, and the positions of previously scheduled customer orders are not changed any more as the construction phase progresses.

We propose a heuristic to modify the above-mentioned drawback and improve the performance. *RBM* is an order-oriented method seeking the 'best' position for each customer order. To do this, the current unscheduled customer order is inserted not only at the end of the current partial solution, but also inserted at the beginning and all other positions of the partial sequence. In addition, when a customer order is at its best position, a new partial sequence would be created. The already scheduled customer orders may then find better positions in the new partial sequence. Thus, reinserting those already scheduled customer orders may be useful as well.

In the proposed RBM shown in Algorithm 1, in each iteration k, the current unscheduled customer order $L[k]$ is inserted at the last position $k' = k$ of the partial sequence π, and all other possible positions $1 \leq k' < k$ of the partial sequence. Then, the position with the lowest total order completion time is selected as the position $\bar{k}$ of the customer order currently being placed. After finding the best position for the current customer order $L[k]$ in the partial sequence π, we again repair the π focusing on the neighbours of the newly placed customer order. Two customer orders around position $\bar{k}$, $h = \bar{k} \pm 1$ ($h \geq 1$ or $h \leq n$), are also inserted in all positions of the partial sequence π. Note that we select two orders around position $\bar{k}$ for the repair process since they were adjacent before inserting the current order $L[k]$ at position $\bar{k}$, so they are highly likely to be affected than others. It is also worth mentioning that although our proposed heuristic requires slightly more CPU times, it obtains remarkably better results.

Algorithm 1. RBM Heuristic

$\sigma[j] = \sum_{i=1}^{m} P_{ij}$ for each customer order j ($j = 1, 2, \ldots, n$)
Sort the customer orders in the list L in a non-decreasing order of $\sigma[j]$.
Let π be a partial sequence with only one customer order, $\pi_1 \leftarrow L[1]$.
for $k = 2$ *to* n **do**
  $\pi[k] \leftarrow L[k]$ *// The STPT heuristic*
  // The proposed repair-based mechanism
  $\bar{k} \leftarrow k$, $BestObj \leftarrow TCT(\pi)$, $\pi' \leftarrow \pi$
  for $k' = k - 1$ *to* 1 **do**
    $\pi'' \leftarrow$ Insert customer order π'_k in the position k' in π'.
    if $TCT(\pi'') < BestObj$ **then**
      $\bar{k} \leftarrow k'$, $BestObj \leftarrow TCT(\pi'')$, $\pi \leftarrow \pi''$
  $\pi \leftarrow$ Sequence with lowest $TCT(\pi)$ by inserting customer order π_h in all possible positions of π, where $h = \bar{k} \pm 1$ ($h \geq 1$ or $h \leq k$)
return π

4.2 Search Algorithm

There exist some algorithms to solve the COSP, however those algorithms either find low quality solutions or struggle with large-sized problems. One reason is that they get stuck in the local optima because of an exhaustive use of a move operator or a weak diversification method. In order to deal with these issues, we propose an efficient local search-based algorithm, called MNLS that embeds a number of neighbourhood operators in a mixed fashion as intensification process and also a greedy diversification method as the diversification approach. The use of mixed neighbourhood operator creates different local optima and allows our algorithm to explore more search areas and diversify the intensification process. Besides, in the diversification phase, we replace the typical random method with a greedy approach that produces a new solution by keeping a part of the local optima and changing the remaining part of it, i.e., intensify the diversification process. The greedy diversification, allows our algorithm to share the information of both good and new areas in the search space at the time of generating new solution for the intensification procedure.

The proposed search algorithm given in Algorithm 2 starts with an initial solution obtained by RBM heuristic. The initial solution is then improved by the proposed mixed neighbourhood search. Then, the algorithm goes through the loop in which the search restarts with a greedy method followed by mixed neighbourhood search. To escape from strong local optima, an acceptance criterion is also used to decide whether to accept or reject the solution obtained by the intensification phase.

Algorithm 2. Proposed Search algorithm

$\pi \leftarrow$ Generate an initial solution using the RBM heuristic
$\pi \leftarrow$ Use the intensification method on π
$iter \leftarrow 1$, $\pi_{best} \leftarrow \pi$
while $++iter \leq MaxIter$ **do**
    $\pi' \leftarrow$ Use the diversification method on π
    $\pi'' \leftarrow$ Use the intensification method on π'
    if $TCT(\pi'') < TCT(\pi)$ **then**
        $\pi \leftarrow \pi''$
        if $TCT(\pi'') < TCT(\pi_{best})$ **then**
            $\pi_{best} \leftarrow \pi''$
    else if $random() < P$ **then**
        $\pi \leftarrow \pi''$
return π_{best}

Intensification Method. In this paper, we propose a Mixed Neighbourhood Local Search (MNLS) method that contains four move operators $N_k(k = 1, \ldots, 4)$. In MNLS, instead of a single neighbourhood, we explore a number of given neighbourhoods to obtain a better solution with respect to the objective value. The intuition is that different neighbourhoods create different landscapes and consequently different local optima. The use of mixed neighbourhoods thus enables our algorithm to navigate through the search area, to explore more regions around the current solution, and also to escape from local optima.

The selection of neighbourhood operators is important and is considerably affects the performance of MNLS. Among several types of operator, we select Insert, Swap, Insert-Pair, and Swap-Pair since these moves are widely used when solutions are permutations. These operators are as follows:

1. Insert (N_1): A random customer order π_j is removed from its position j and then reinserted at a random position k ($k \neq j$) (Fig. 2a).
2. Swap (N_2): Two random customer orders, π_j and π_k ($k \neq j$), are selected and their positions are exchanged (Fig. 2b).
3. Insert-Pair (N_3): Two consecutive random customer orders, π_j and π_{j+1} are removed from their positions, j and $j+1$ ($j = 1, 2, \ldots, n-1$), and reinserted into random positions k and $k+1$ ($k = 1, 2, \ldots, n-1$ and $k > j+1$ or $k+1 < j$) (Fig. 2c).
4. Swap-Pair (N_4): Two consecutive random customer orders, π_j and π_{j+1} ($j = 1, 2, \ldots, n-1$) are selected and their positions are exchanged with two different consecutive random customer orders, π_k and π_{k+1} ($k = 1, 2, \ldots, n-1$ and $k > j+1$ or $k+1 < j$) (Fig. 2d).

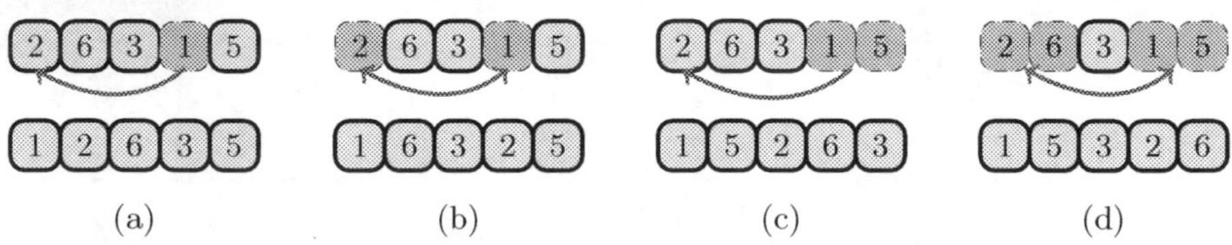

Fig. 2. Example of operators (a) Insert (b) Swap (c) Insert-Pair (d) Swap-Pair

Recall that one possible drawback of existing metaheuristic algorithms is the exhaustive use of a single operator. Evaluating all neighbouring solutions would be hugely time-consuming particularly for the large instances. For example, an exhaustive use of only Swap operator generates a total of $n(n-1)/2$ candidate solutions. To tackle this drawback, in this paper we employ two approaches: an *acceleration method* (a fast neighbourhood evaluation strategy) and a random-based operator selection.

The *acceleration method* is based on the one proposed by [7]. The idea is to compute only the completion time of the changed part of the permutation after employing each move, and reuse the computation of the unchanged part of the permutation. With this *acceleration method*, we can speed up the calculation of the total customer orders completion time to 50% that is notable. Based on the second approach, the random-based operator selection, MNLS selects an operator at each iteration randomly. This procedure gives our four operators the same chance to be applied on the current solution. This procedure, compared to exhaustive operators, keeps open the search space but saves the computation time remarkably.

In the proposed intensification method given in Algorithm 3, at each iteration, one of the operators is randomly selected and applied to the current solution. If a better solution in terms of total completion time is obtained, the current solution is updated and the iteration counter is reset to 1; otherwise the iteration counter is increased. This process is continued until the iteration counter is less than $20 \times n$ (it is set through experimentation).

Algorithm 3. Proposed MNLS

Let π is input solution, and $iter \leftarrow 1$.
Set N_1: Insert, N_2: Swap, N_3: Insert-Pair, and N_4: Swap-Pair.
while $++iter \leq 20n$ **do**
  k = random(1,4) *// Generate a random number between 1 and 4.*
  $\pi' \leftarrow N_k(\pi)$ *//Apply operator N_k on the current solution π.*
  if $TCT(\pi') < TCT(\pi)$ **then**
    $\pi \leftarrow \pi'$, $iter \leftarrow 1$
return π

Diversification Method. To avoid getting stuck and convergence towards local optima, we propose a multi-start MNLS for COSP. In the classical multi-start procedure, a solution at each iteration is randomly generated and most likely unrelated to the previously visited local optima. The randomly generated solution is then improved by the local search. However, [9] pointed out that 'the quality of the local optima obtained by a local search method depends on the initial solution' and a random solution in most cases is a low quality solution. In this paper, we propose a greedy diversification method that creates a new solution at each iteration relying on the preliminary idea of our RBM heuristic. The proposed greedy method holds a part of the current local optima and shuffles the remaining parts. The intuition is that we do not fully erase the information of the properties of the local optima and use a part of it for the next initial solution as good solutions often cluster around (e.g., in a range of mountains).

In the proposed diversification method, at each iteration, a set of customer orders, $ExtractedOrder = 2$ (it is fixed with a preliminary test), are randomly extracted and removed from the current solution π and saved into a list ω as the unscheduled customer orders. After that, the extracted customer orders, one by one, leaves the list ω and goes back to the end of the partial sequence π. Unlike the RBM heuristic, this newly placed customer order is then swapped with all other customer orders in the partial sequence π and its best position $\bar{k}$ is selected based on the objective. Then, its new neighbours (the customer orders at positions $p = \bar{k} \pm 1$ ($p \geq 1$ or $p \leq n$)) are inserted in all positions of the current partial sequence. The best solution with respect to the objective value would be considered as the partial sequence for the next unscheduled customer order.

Note that, using only one move in the diversification procedure may increase the risk of returning to a previously visited solutions at the time of using the intensification phase. Therefore, we use swap as well as insert operator to decrease this probability. Additionally, the proposed diversification method keeps some parts of the solution and destroys another part of the solution with the hope of obtaining a better search area. Consequently, although a new initial solution for intensification is created, it is not far away from the previously found local optima, and has some of their properties as well. This is why we propose a greedy diversification method for MNLS instead of a fully randomly generated solution. The proposed greedy diversification method is presented in Algorithm 4.

Algorithm 4. Proposed greedy diversification method

Input: π: Solution, *ExtractedOrder*: number of customer orders removed.
Set $\omega = \emptyset$.
for $k = 1$ *to ExtractedOrder* **do**
  Remove a random customer order (without repetition) from π and save in ω
for $k = 1$ *to ExtractedOrder* **do**
  $\bar{k} \leftarrow LastPos \leftarrow n - ExtractedOrder + k$
  $\pi[LastPos] \leftarrow \omega[k]$
  $BestObj \leftarrow TCT(\pi)$, $\pi' \leftarrow \pi$
  for $k' = LastPos - 1$ *down to* 1 **do**
    $\pi'' \leftarrow$ Swap the customer orders at positions $\pi'_{LastPos}$ and $\pi'_{k'}$
    if $TCT(\pi'') < BestObj$ **then**
      $\bar{k} \leftarrow k'$, $\pi \leftarrow \pi''$, $BestObj \leftarrow TCT(\pi'')$
  $\pi \leftarrow$ Schedule with lowest $TCT(\pi)$ by inserting customer orders π_p in all possible positions of π where $p = \bar{k} \pm 1$ ($p \geq 1$ or $p \leq LastPos$)
return π

Acceptance Criterion. After the intensification phase, it should be decided whether to accept or reject the new solution obtained by the intensification phase as the current solution for the next iteration. Thus, we propose a simple acceptance criterion that accepts worse solutions with the probability of $P = 0.5$ (it is fixed through experimentation). This acceptance criterion helps the algorithm keep a balance between intensification and diversification. In terms of intensification, only improving solutions are acceptable (strong selection), however, based on the diversification, any solution with any quality with respect to the objective function is acceptable (weak selection).

5 Experimental Results

Experiments are carried out using Framinan's benchmark [3]. This benchmark is made up of 1680 instances: 720 small and 960 large instances. In this paper, we have used the 960 large instances. This instance set is divided into two testbeds (480 instances each): Test-1 and Test-2. In the former, each customer order requests m items with $p_{ij} > 0$, while in the latter, $p_{ij} \geq 0$ i.e., the processing times of some items are zero. Both these testbeds are categorized in 16 sets with 30 instances. The sets include different combinations of the numbers of customer orders $n \in \{20, 50, 100, 200\}$ and machines $m \in \{2, 5, 10, 20\}$.

FP and GSA [3] are respectively the best existing heuristic and metaheuristic in the literature. Thus, the proposed methods are compared with these algorithms. The programs are implemented in the programming language C and tested on the same computer. To evaluate the results, the deviation of total completion time of method A from the total completion time of the best-known solutions for each instance is calculated, $TCT(A^i)$ - $TCT(\pi^i)$. The smaller the deviation, the better the methods' performance. Note that we evaluate the idea of using mixed neighbourhood operators instead of a single one as well as a greedy diversification instead of a random one. The results confirm the efficiency of the proposed idea of mixed neighbourhood operators and greedy diversification. However we do not show related results in detail due to space restriction.

Table 1 gives a comparison of RBM, FP and STPT heuristics. STPT is also included in this experiment since RBM is a modification of this heuristic. Table 1 shows that RBM significantly improves the performance of STPT heuristic in all instance groups. In addition, the proposed heuristic outperforms FP heuristic in 27 out of 32 instance sets. We also use a student *t-test* with level of significance $\alpha = 0.05$ between heuristics. On both Test-1 and Test-2 p-value were 0.000 ($<\alpha$) that confirm a statistically significant difference among FP and RBM heuristic.

Table 1. Deviation from best-known solutions for the heuristics.

Instances	TEST-1				TEST-2			
$n \times m$	Best	STPT	FP	RBM	Best	STPT	FP	RBM
20 × 2	8952	432	48	**24**	6298	462	65	**12**
20 × 5	10461	654	101	**78**	5385	716	86	**53**
20 × 10	11491	976	145	**138**	5805	862	109	**107**
20 × 20	12320	972	**138**	181	6231	821	105	**92**
50 × 2	51965	1968	223	**91**	35373	2594	269	**82**
50 × 5	58741	4105	643	**523**	30577	4008	601	**527**
50 × 10	63779	5638	**951**	986	30479	5048	703	**621**
50 × 20	66752	5842	**993**	1195	31916	5181	794	**733**
100 × 2	202005	6896	809	**379**	134113	8449	943	**243**
100 × 5	228602	15162	2519	**1910**	111054	12519	2568	**1381**
100 × 10	241551	18259	3395	**3302**	109886	15904	2778	**2286**
100 × 20	253401	20878	**3519**	4557	109940	16428	2654	**2596**
200 × 2	783719	21729	2718	**1330**	518665	20336	2888	**638**
200 × 5	884242	44777	10470	**5689**	433946	45810	11215	**4833**
200 × 10	935949	52661	10813	**9150**	403657	48816	10087	**7674**
200 × 20	979527	60983	**11521**	14127	407541	51613	8984	**8781**
Average	-	16371	3063	**2729**	-	14973	2803	**1916**

We assess the efficiency of the proposed MNLS algorithm against GSA. GSA algorithm used FP heuristic as initialisation. To have a better view about the performance of the proposed mixed neighbourhood operators and the greedy diversification, we also use the FP heuristic as our initial solution (MNLS-FP for short). As the stopping criterion, a maximum number of iteration, *MaxIter = 100* is considered for all algorithms. However, two other values 10 and 50 are also considered for *MaxIter*to show the performance of the algorithms from short to long duration. The results are given in Table 2. To display that the differences

Table 2. Deviation from best-known solutions for the search algorithms.

TEST-1	Best	GSA	GSA	GSA	MNLS-FP	MNLS-FP	MNLS-FP	MNLS	MNLS	MNLS
n × m		10	50	100	10	50	100	10	50	100
20 × 2	8952	5	1	**0**	1	**0**	**0**	1	**0**	**0**
20 × 5	10461	15	6	4	5	1	**0**	5	1	**0**
20 × 10	11491	29	11	9	15	3	**0**	13	2	**0**
20 × 20	12320	30	12	9	22	3	1	19	3	**1**
50 × 2	51965	38	21	17	8	1	**0**	8	2	**0**
50 × 5	58741	153	86	59	69	20	8	44	13	**2**
50 × 10	63779	229	98	77	179	49	21	109	32	**7**
50 × 20	66752	273	126	93	244	56	11	147	40	**7**
100 × 2	202005	137	94	86	25	7	**2**	35	8	**2**
100 × 5	228602	449	246	229	267	89	28	169	42	**9**
100 × 10	241551	592	346	288	734	239	87	289	90	**11**
100 × 20	253401	751	296	197	1386	440	130	509	155	**17**
200 × 2	783719	299	241	227	94	23	7	90	20	**2**
200 × 5	884242	1563	872	746	884	287	110	371	98	**11**
200 × 10	935949	2548	907	664	3248	1088	552	597	136	**15**
200 × 20	979527	3651	715	290	6702	2887	1630	1467	347	**67**
Average	299591	673	255	187	868	324	162	242	62	**9**
TEST-2	Best	GSA	GSA	GSA	MNLS-FP	MNLS-FP	MNLS-FP	MNLS	MNLS	MNLS
n × m		10	50	100	10	50	100	10	50	100
20 × 2	6298	4	2	1	**0**	**0**	**0**	**0**	**0**	**0**
20 × 5	5385	13	2	1	3	**0**	**0**	2	**0**	**0**
20 × 10	5805	13	2	1	9	1	**0**	5	1	**0**
20 × 20	6231	18	3	3	7	1	**0**	6	1	**0**
50 × 2	35373	37	18	13	6	1	**0**	6	1	**0**
50 × 5	30577	132	73	59	69	28	**18**	57	25	**18**
50 × 10	30479	185	96	77	120	45	30	97	40	**30**
50 × 20	31916	218	94	74	158	62	39	108	51	**33**
100 × 2	134113	127	72	66	23	9	**7**	30	10	**7**
100 × 5	111054	385	260	251	286	137	98	193	108	**77**
100 × 10	109886	519	326	294	539	241	172	337	173	**134**
100 × 20	109940	537	312	281	702	305	190	461	251	**174**
200 × 2	518665	254	220	198	63	30	22	82	33	**21**
200 × 5	433946	968	703	661	779	367	265	521	284	**214**
200 × 10	403657	1365	839	746	2067	891	578	928	546	**389**
200 × 20	407541	1523	759	545	3093	1366	791	1424	717	**465**
Average	148804	394	236	204	495	218	138	266	140	**98**

between algorithms are statistically significant, the 95% confidence interval plot of them are also shown in Fig. 3. No overlapping of intervals for a pair denotes a significant difference between the two methods compared.

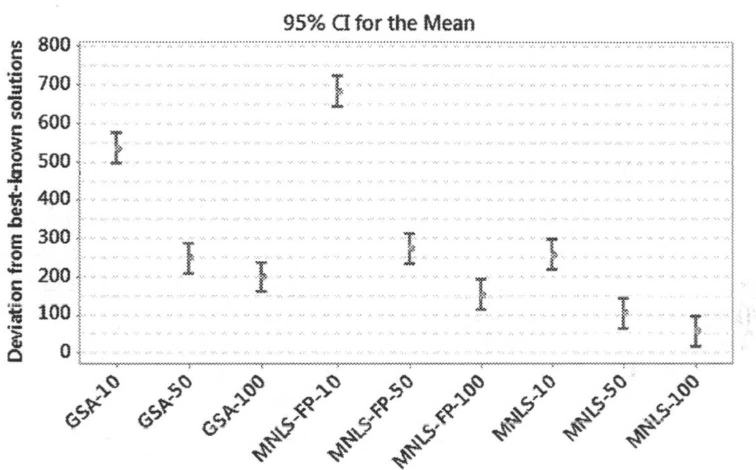

Fig. 3. 95% confidence interval plot of compared algorithms.

From Table 2 and Fig. 3, MNLS with $MaxIter = 100$ (MNLS-100 for short) has the best performance in both of the testbeds on average, and statistically outperforms other algorithms. Additionally, not only MNLS-100, but MNLS-50 (MNLS with 50 iterations) is also statistically superior to GSA-100. Interestingly, MNLS-10 (with only 10 iterations) is statistically equivalent to GSA-100. Comparison of MNLS-FP and GSA also reveals some points that are worth to be mentioned. GSA-10 and GSA-50 have better performance compared to MNLS-FP-10 and MNLS-FP-50 respectively. However, MNLS-FP-100 has smaller average deviations than GSA-100 in 30 out of 32 instance groups. To have a better view, we present the convergence graphs of the algorithms for two instances: TEST-1-318 ($n = 200$ and $m = 10$) and TEST-2-179 ($n = 50$ and $m = 5$) in various iterations in Fig. 4. It can be seen that GSA can find better solutions in the earlier stage of the search. However, when the algorithms proceed for more iterations, MNLS outperforms GSA. In fact, the proposed algorithm is able to jump out of the local optima later in the search. We do not show the convergence of other instances as they are similar.

In each iteration of the search, what MNLS does is not the same as what GSA does, e.g., MNLS uses repeatedly one of the given neighbourhood operator while GSA uses an exhaustive swap. Therefore, The CPU execution times of the algorithms must be compared instead of considering the number of iterations. The CPU times used by the algorithms based on the number of orders and machines, respectively, are shown in Fig. 5. This figure shows that MNLS is much faster than GSA but still obtains better results. Finally, it is worth noting that for TEST-1 and TEST-2, 379 and 349 new best-known solutions are obtained by MNLS respectively out of the 480 each.

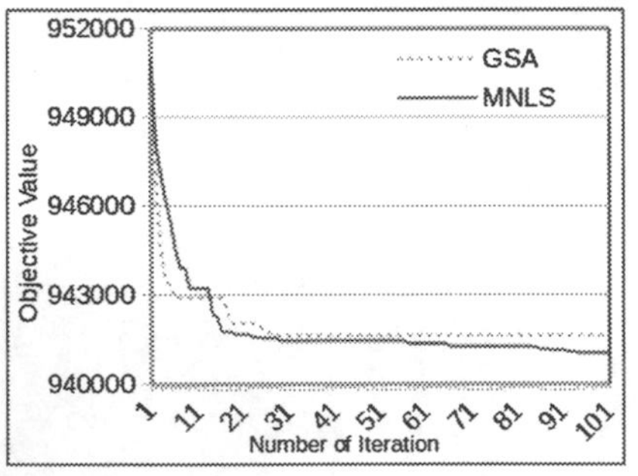

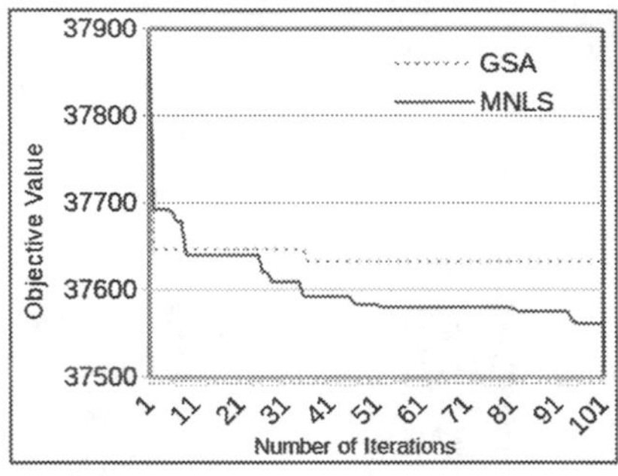

Fig. 4. Convergence of GSA and MNLS for TEST-1-318 (left), TEST-2-179 (right).

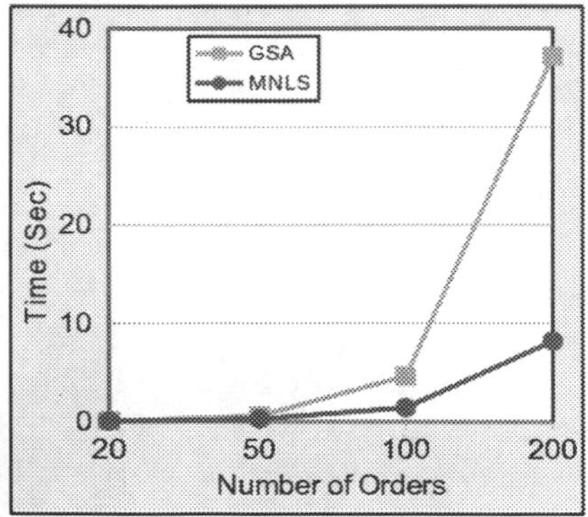

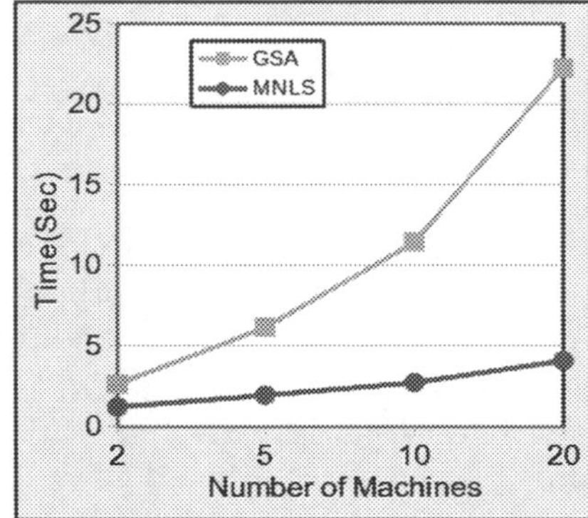

Fig. 5. Interaction between CPU times of algorithms and number of orders/machines.

6 Conclusion

In this paper, we consider a Customer Order Scheduling Problem (COSP) that has realistic applications such as the paper industry and the pharmaceutical industries. The COSP is known to be NP-hard. To solve this problem, an effective local search algorithm is proposed that comprises a new constructive heuristic to generate the initial solution, a mixed neighbourhood for intensification, and also a greedy approach for diversification to keep the search focussed even when it is in a plateau. The results show that the proposed algorithm significantly outperforms the state-of-the-art algorithms. Moreover, the proposed algorithm has also found new upper bounds for 721 out of 960 problem instances.

References

1. Ahmadi, R., Bagchi, U., Roemer, T.A.: Coordinated scheduling of customer orders for quick response. Naval Res. Logist. (NRL) **52**(6), 493–512 (2005)
2. Ahmadi, R., Bagchi, U.: Scheduling of Multi-job Customer Orders in Multi-machine Environments. ORSA/TIMS, Philadelphia (1990)
3. Framinan, J.M., Perez-Gonzalez, P.: New approximate algorithms for the customer order scheduling problem with total completion time objective. Comput. Oper. Res. **78**, 181–192 (2017)
4. Lee, I.S.: Minimizing total tardiness for the order scheduling problem. Int. J. Prod. Econ. **144**(1), 128–134 (2013)
5. Leung, J.Y.T., Li, H., Pinedo, M.: Order scheduling models: an overview. In: Kendall, G., Burke, E.K., Petrovic, S., Gendreau, M. (eds.) Multidisciplinary Scheduling: Theory and Applications. Springer, Boston (2005). https://doi.org/10.1007/0-387-27744-7_3
6. Leung, J.Y.T., Li, H., Pinedo, M.: Order scheduling in an environment with dedicated resources in parallel. J. Sched. **8**(5), 355–386 (2005)
7. Li, X., Wang, Q., Wu, C.: Efficient composite heuristics for total flowtime minimization in permutation flow shops. Omega **37**(1), 155–164 (2009)
8. Sung, C.S., Yoon, S.H.: Minimizing total weighted completion time at a pre-assembly stage composed of two feeding machines. Int. J. Prod. Econ. **54**(3), 247–255 (1998)
9. Talbi, E.G.: Metaheuristics: From Design to Implementation, vol. 74. Wiley, Hoboken (2009)
10. Yang, J.: Scheduling with batch objectives. Ph.D. thesis, The Ohio State University (1998)

Graph Based Family Relationship Recognition from a Single Image

Chao Xia[1], Siyu Xia[2(✉)], Yuan Zhou[2], Le Zhang[3], and Ming Shao[4]

[1] School of Biomedical Engineering, Shanghai Jiao Tong University, Shanghai, China
[2] School of Automation, Southeast University, Nanjing, China
xia081@gmail.com
[3] School of Aerospace, Xi'an Jiao Tong University, Xi'an, China
[4] Department of Computer and Information Science, University of Massachusetts Dartmouth, Dartmouth, USA

Abstract. Kinship recognition from facial images is an important task of social network analysis. However, previous studies mainly focus on kinship verification between two people. Very few attempts have been conducted on analyzing kinship relations of whole family. In this paper, we present a graph based method to recognize kinship relations of the whole family members from a single family photo. After pre-processing and feature extraction, we recognize kinship relations of all pairs of people in the family and then select a group of pair-wise kinship relations to construct connected subgraph of all family members. After that, we use kinship rules to infer and check all potential relationships on the graph and choose the best relationship graph as output. The key idea is to use connected subgraph model and kinship relation rules to select the best subset of the pairwise kinship, which can help us recover from the incorrect pairwise kinship classification results. Extensive experimental results demonstrate the effectiveness of the proposed method.

Keywords: Family relationship recognition · Graph model Social network

1 Introduction

With the development of digital camera and network techniques, people tend to share photos on social media websites such as Facebook, YouTube and Flickr. There are enormous number of images on these platforms, and most of them are group images. Compared with single person images, group images contain two or more people and usually have more complex events. So, it makes sense for us to understand image of group people.

Facial image contains many important features, such as eye shape, skin color, nose position and so on. In recent years, extensive researches have been conducted using computer vision and pattern recognition technologies to find significant information from facial images, such as person identification [1,2], age

X. Geng and B.-H. Kang (Eds.): PRICAI 2018, LNAI 11012, pp. 310–320, 2018.
https://doi.org/10.1007/978-3-319-97304-3_24

prediction [3]. For group people image, facial cues are also informative for understanding the relationship of people in the image. Typically, the relationship of people in groups can be classified into kinship among family members and social relationship between friends and colleagues.

In this paper, we investigate the problem of kinship recognition in a family photo. As an universal kind of social relationship, kinship recognition has many potential applications, such as finding missing children, analyzing family photo and assisting criminal investigations [4]. However, to the best of our knowledge, few researchers have tackled this problem, possibly due to lacking of publicly available family photo databases and great challenges of this problem.

Kinship verification was first mentioned at 2010 [5]. After that, several attempts have been done in this area [5–10]. They aimed to identify whether a given pairs of people have kinship or not. Usually, this verification was conducted on a certain relationship type, such as we know all the test image pairs are father and son, just to identify whether they have kinship or not. These works ignored the exact kinds of kinship, besides, in practice, people often upload family photos containing more than two people. Guo et al. [11] mentioned a full connected graph based method to recognize kinship in a family, however, the maximum number of people they can deal with is four due to the computational limitation.

Motivated by the aforementioned problems of prior works, in this paper, we introduce a graph based method to organize kinship between all family members. Instead of using a full-connected graph, we only use connected subgraph to organize all family members. For a big family with several family members, it is not necessary to recognize the relationship between all pairs of people. Further more, the relationship between some pairs maybe complex, such as a child and his aunt, which is even hard for people to recognize. Compared with full connected graph, the total number of edges needed in connected subgraph decrease significantly with the increase of node number. The general framework of our method is illustrated in Fig. 1.

There are two main contributions in our work. Firstly, graph based method can shares information between pairwise classifiers, so we can infer potential kinship relations based on the existing information on the graph and kinship knowledge. Secondly, compared with full connected network, the key advantage of our connected subgraph is that it can choose the most reliable group from all the pairwise kinship. Through this way, we have chance to choose the best pairwise relationship combination and avoid some incorrect pairs.

In the rest of the paper, we will discuss some related works in Sect. 2. Section 3 is the method. Experimental results are provided in Sect. 4. Section 5 is conclusions and future plan.

2 Related Work

Fang et al. [5]. is the first attempt to tackle kinship verification problem using facial images. In the subsequent works, researchers proposed different methods

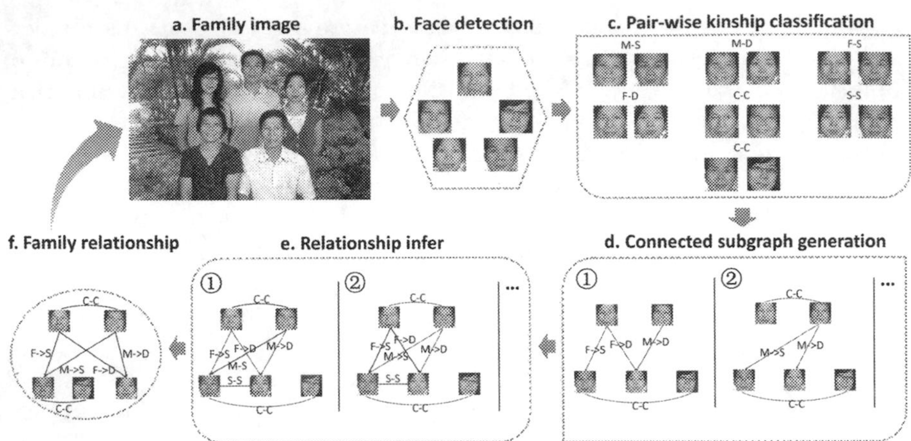

Fig. 1. Overview of the family relationship recognition system. The relationships in the graph contain father → son(F → S), father → daughter(F → D), mother → son(M → S), mother → daughter(M → D), couple ↔ couple(C ↔ C), sibling ↔ sibling(S ↔ S). (f) The final relationship network of the family in (a)

to solve this problem, such as metric learning [7,8], deep convolution neural network [9], transfer learning [6,18], subspace clustering [10] and so on. The most representative method is Neighborhood Repulsed Metric Learning (NRML) mentioned by Lu [8]. They tried to learn a distance metric that aims to pull kinship samples get close and repel non-kinship samples as far as possible. Nevertheless, all these methods focused on bi-subjects kinship verification, they ignored to recognize the specific kinship types between tested pairs, besides, they only focused on the relation of two people.

In contrast to the aforementioned methods, Zhang et al. [12] aimed at recognizing whether a group photo is a family photo or a collective photo taken with friends and colleagues. This method used three dedicated local features under Multiple Instance Learning framework to recognize kinship in group photos.

Overall, the above methods focused on binary classification problem, they intended to find whether two or a group of people have kinship or not, but they ignored specific kind of kinship in the image. Guo et al. [11] mentioned a full-connected graph-based approach to recognize kinship in a family. Different from them, we use a connected subgraph based method to organize family members and infer their potential relationship, which can help us to choose the best combination of pairwise kinship and avoid the incorrect ones. Besides, through extracting deep face features, we can predict age more exactly, which is a significant information for pairwise kinship recognition.

3 Proposed Method

In this paper, we propose a graph based method to construct family relationship network using a group of pairwise kinship classification result. Instead of using a full-connected graph, we only use connected subgraph to organize all family members and infer the potential relationships in the graph. For family relationship recognition, we assuming that each people in the image has at least one kinship with the others. The main procedure of our method is listed in Algorithm 1.

Algorithm 1. Main procedure of our family network recognition method

Input: An image of family people.
Output: Family relationship network
1: Detect and crop face from input image I and get face image $I_1, I_2, \ldots I_n$, n is people number;
2: Extract face feature X_{face} of each image using VGGFace;
3: Recognize age X_{age}, gender X_{gender} of each face image I_i;
4: Kinship classification of image pair (I_i, I_j);
5: Select part of pairwise kinship and generate all feasible connected subgraph set $V = \{G_1, G_2, \ldots, G_m\}$, where G_i is the ith connected subgraph;
6: **repeat**
7:    Inference all potential relationship in each graph G_i
8: **until** There is no more potential relationship in the graph
9: Judge and exclude infeasible candidates graph;
10: Choose the most reliable graph G as relationship graph;

3.1 Face Feature Extraction

There are many kinds of descriptors to express facial appearance, such as local binary pattern (LBP) features [2], histogram of gradient (HOG) features [13] and so on. Besides these handcraft features, VGGFace [14], a face recognition model, uses a Convolutional Neural Network (CNN) to extract face features from origin images. In our method, we use pre-trained VGGFace model to extract face feature of family people. We get a 4096 dimension vector $X_{face}(I_i)$ of an input face image I_i.

For a family image with several people, we first use a public available face detector to detect and crop facial region from the image. From this, we can get the number of family members. Then, we align face images based on the detected key points and resize face images to 224 * 224 pixels, which are fitted to the input of the VGGFace model.

After that, we use the method in [3] to predict age from face image. Through fine tuning VGGFace model on several age datasets, we get a deep model for age prediction. This model returns a 90 dimensional vector representing the distribution of age from 1 to 90 (assuming the age range is 1 to 90). The predicted age A^* of the extracted distribution vector t^* is given by:

$$A^* = \sum_{n=1}^{N} A_n K(t^*, t_n) \quad (1)$$

where N is the number of images in the training set, t_n is the age distribution vector of the nth training image, A_n is the age of the nth image, K (*,*) is distance measurement, defined as:

$$K\left(t^{*}, t_n\right) = \exp(-\alpha \times ||t^{*} - t_n||_2^2) \tag{2}$$

where α is the parameter selected by 10-fold cross validation. Through this, we get age feature $X_{age}\left(I_i\right)$ of the input image I_i.

For gender, we build a binary support vector machine (SVM) classifier and use VGGFace feature $X_{face}\left(I_i\right)$ as input, then we get a binary result $X_{gender}\left(I_i\right) \in \{0, 1\}$ as gender feature of input image I_i.

Apart from single image feature, we verify kinship between any pair of people in the family using method in [8]. Instead of using a binary result (a pair of people have or not have kinship), we compute the degree of kinship between test pairs. For a pair of input image I_i and I_j, we get kinship feature $X_{kinship}\left(I_i, I_j\right)$. Besides, in order to improve classification accuracy, we first ignore which one is older or younger and compute age difference $X_{age}\left(I_i, I_j\right)$ between a pair of people i, j as follows:

$$X_{age}\left(I_i, I_j\right) = \left|X_{age}\left(I_i\right) - X_{age}\left(I_j\right)\right| \tag{3}$$

3.2 Pairwise Kinship Classification

In order to get particular type of kinship between pairs of family people. We define 8 types of basic directional kinship relations and 2 types of undirected kinship relations, that is father $\rightarrow$ son, father $\rightarrow$ daughter, mother $\rightarrow$ son, mother $\rightarrow$ daughter, son $\rightarrow$ father, daughter $\rightarrow$ father, son $\rightarrow$ mother, daughter $\rightarrow$ mother, couple $\leftrightarrow$ couple, sibling $\leftrightarrow$ sibling, because sibling relation and couple relation are mutual. Complex relationship, such as grandfather $\rightarrow$ grandson can be generated by the combination of basic kinship relations.

We complete this classification work in two stages to improve accuracy and reduce calculations. In the first stage, we classify all types of kinship relation into four undirected relationships, which is parent-child, couple-couple, sibling-sibling and others. In the second stage, we use age and gender feature dividing parent-child relationship into 8 types of directional relationship defined before.

For the first stage classification, we concatenate the extracted features of the image pair (I_i, I_j) to obtain the final feature vector X_{ij}:

$$X_{ij} = \left[X_{face}\left(I_i\right), X_{face}\left(I_j\right), X_{kinship}\left(I_i, I_j\right), X_{age}\left(I_i, I_j\right)\right]$$

We build a multi-class support vector machine (SVM) classifier for this classification. From this, we can get specific types of kinship between a pair of people. Apart from the final classification result of a pair of people, we calculate conditional probability of each class and use this probability as the score of the branch belongs to corresponding classes.

3.3 Family Relationship Network Construction

In this step, we construct relationship network of all the family members using pairwise kinship relations recognized before. Network construction process have three steps. For a relationship graph $G = (V, E)$, we first choose part of pairwise kinship to generate all feasible connected subgraph containing all vertices in G, which means connecting all family people as a whole. Then we use kinship generation rules listed in Table 1 to get potential relationship in each connected subgraph. After that, we check all the relations on the graph and remove the candidates which violate the constraint rules (Table 2). Since the number of branches in each graph may be different, we choose the kinship graph which have the highest average branches score as final result.

Generate Connected Subgraph. For a graph with n nodes, the maximum number of brunches is C_n^2, which is full connected graph. To construct a connected subgraph, the minimum number of brunches needed is $n-1$, which means we can choose $n-1$ pairwise kinship from all the C_n^2 pairwise kinship. This gives us opportunities to avoid incorrect classification result. Figure 2 is some sketch map of full connected graph and connected subgraph, the node number in this example is defined as 4.

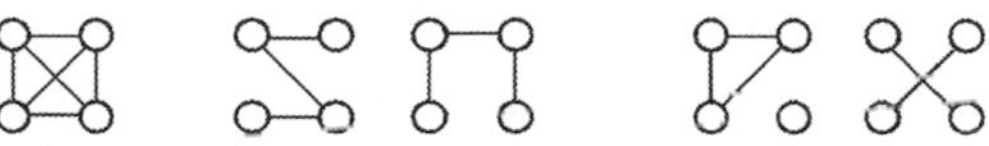

Fig. 2. An example of the generated networks with 4 nodes. The first graph on the left is full connected network, the next two are connected subgraph, the last two are disconnected subgraph

Inference Potential Relationship. Considering that graph based method can share information between branches, we use existing relationship on the graph and kinship generation rules listed in Table 1 to generate potential relationship. For example, we know A $\rightarrow$ B is father $\rightarrow$ son, B $\leftrightarrow$ C is sibling $\leftrightarrow$ sibling, we can infer A $\rightarrow$ C is father $\rightarrow$ son (suppose C is male). In this step, we only consider the basic relationships defined before and ignore the complex relations. With the increasing of people number, complex relation will be a large part of pairwise relationships and these relationships is hard to distinguish even for people. In each graph, we only use the information directly or indirectly offered by $n-1$ pairwise kinship classification results and ignore the others, which can help us avoid the incorrect classification result as much as possible. After analyzing all connected subgraph, we can make full use of the pairwise classification results and get the best candidates. Figure 3 is an example of kinship inference.

Table 1. Kinship generation rules

Definition	Instance
• Father and mother are couples	[(A → B: Son/Daughter → Father) ∧ (A → C: Son/Daughter → Mother)] ⇒ (C-B: Couple-Couple)
• Siblings have the same parents	[(A-B: Sibling-Sibling) ∧ (A → C: Son/Daughter → Mother/Father)] ⇒ (B → C: Son/Daughter → Mother/Father)
• Couples have the same child	[(A-B: Couple-Couple) ∧ (A → C: Mother/Father → Son/Daughter)] ⇒ (B → C: Father/Mother → Son/Daughter)
• Children of the same parents are siblings	[(A → B: Son/Daughter → Mother/Father) ∧ (C → B: Son/Daughter → Mother/Father)] ⇒ (A-C: Sibling-Sibling)
• Siblings have the same siblings	[(A-B: Sibling-Sibling) ∧ (C-B: Sibling-Sibling)] ⇒ (A-C: Sibling-Sibling)

Exclude Infeasible Results. So far, we have obtained all possible kinship on the graph. It may not be a fully connected graph because there may be some kinship that we do not care. Then we use kinship constraint rules listed in Table 2 to check all the relations and remove the graph which violates the rules.

Table 2. Kinship constraint rules

Definition	Instance
• Child have only one father/mother	[(A → B: Son/Daughter → Father/Mother)] ⇒ ¬ (A → C: Son/Daughter → Father/Mother)
• Couples have different gender	[(A-B: Couple-Couple)] ⇒ ¬ (A, B have the same gender)
• There should not be kinship between couples	[(A-B: Couple-Couple)] ⇒ ¬ (A, B have kinship)
• Child should be younger than parents	[(A → B: Son/Daughter → Father/Mother)] ⇒ ¬ (A is older than B)

Finally, for each feasible graph, we use the conditional probability calculated in pairwise kinship classification part representing the score of the branch belong to corresponding classes. Then we calculate average score of all the branches on the graph and use this score to measure the reliability of a graph. We choose the most reliable graph as final result.

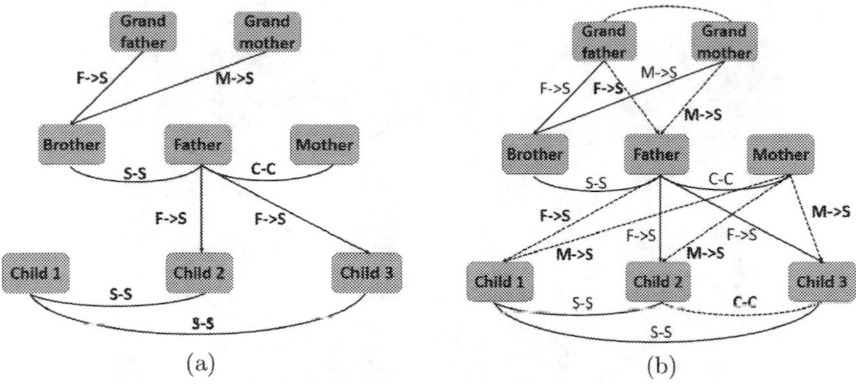

Fig. 3. An example of kinship inference, where (b) is family relationship network inferred from (a) and kinship generation rules. The dotted branches on the graph shows the relationship generated by kinship generation rules.

4 Experiment

4.1 Databases

Existing databases related to family relationship includes: Family101 [15], FIW [4], TSKinFace [16] and The images of groups databases [17]. The first two databases have multiple image of a people taken in different years, besides, there is no family photo in the databases. TSKinFace [16] only contains three types of family, that is: father-mother-son, father-mother-daughter, father-mother-daughter-son. People number and relationships in these family are very limited. Images of groups databases [17] contains family photos of different number of people. In our experiments, we choose part of family photo from Images of groups databases and collect the rest from the Internet. The total number of images in our databases is 115, including 550 people, each image represents a different family and the family size ranges from 3 to 8 people. Some samples in our database are shown in Fig. 4.

4.2 Result

We set a 5-fold cross validation experiments on our databases. Family member distribution and the average classification accuracy of all folds are reported in Fig. 5. Our method gets the best performs at the image of 4–5 people, with the accuracy of 76.38% and 72.13% respectively. The results become worse with the family photo of 7 or more people. This may be the kinship relations between people are too hard to identification in a big family. For a big family, we may need some branch photos to provide extra information for relationship network construction.

Moreover, we compare our graph based method with our pairwise kinship classification method on TSKinFace [16] databases. That is to verify the

Fig. 4. Some family images in our database.

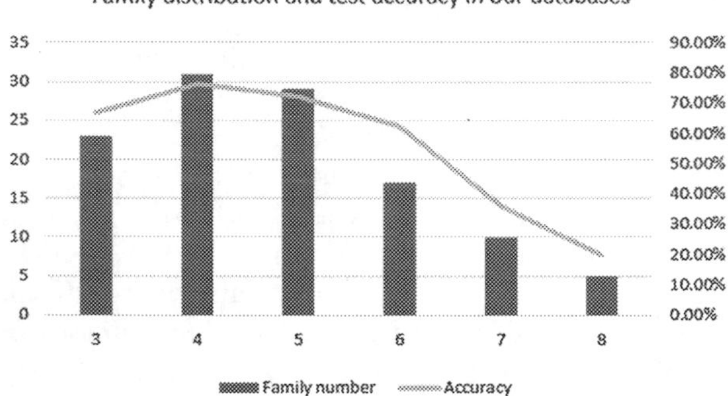

Fig. 5. Family member distribution and tests accuracy.

selecting and correcting ability of graph based model. We select 228 father-mother-daughter-son family for experiments. There are Father-Son pair, Father-Daughter pair, Mother-Son pair, Mother-Daughter pair, Sibling-Sibling pair, Couple-Couple pair in this kind of family. Test results are listed in Table 3. From the result, we can know that the mistakes are mainly due to the Sibling-Sibling pair and Couple-Couple pair, which may be the error of kinship verification. Besides, in a family, the recognized age of the mother is usually younger than that of the father, which may mistake their relationship as Father-Daughter. Compared with pairwise classification results, the accuracy of our graph based method improved significantly. These results also demonstrate the effects of our graph based method.

Table 3. Test results on TSKinFace databases

Relationship	Pairwise (%)	Graph based (%)
Father-Son	79.39	92.54
Father-Daughter	76.32	92.11
Mother-Son	75.44	90.79
Mother-Daughter	78.51	92.98
Sibling-Sibling	68.42	88.60
Mother-Daughter	59.21	87.28
Average	72.88	90.72
Whole family		82.89

5 Conclusions

In this paper, we proposed a graph based method to recognize family relationship network from a family photo. Compared with pairwise kinship classification results, extensive experiments demonstrated the effects of graph based method in selecting the best combination of pairwise kinship classification results, and the mechanism of sharing information between different pairs. In the future, we aim to improve the accuracy of pairwise kinship classification, which is the foundation of the network construction. Besides, we plan to find more efficient method for network construction to deal with family with more people.

Acknowledgment. This work is supported by the National Natural Science Foundation of China under Grant 61671151 and 61728103.

References

1. Schroff, F., Kalenichenko, D., Philbin, J.: FaceNet: a unified embedding for face recognition and clustering, pp. 815–823 (2015)
2. Ahonen, T., Hadid, A., Pietikainen, M.: Face description with local binary patterns: application to face recognition. IEEE Trans. Pattern Anal. Mach. Intell. **28**(12), 2037–2041 (2006)
3. Yang, X., Gao, B.B., Xing, C., Huo, Z.W.: Deep label distribution learning for apparent age estimation. In: IEEE International Conference on Computer Vision Workshop, pp. 344–350 (2015)
4. Robinson, J.P., Shao, M., Wu, Y., Fu, Y.: Families in the wild (FIW): large-scale kinship image database and benchmarks. In: ACM on Multimedia Conference, pp. 242–246 (2016)
5. Fang, R., Tang, K.D., Snavely, N., Chen, T.: Towards computational models of kinship verification. In: IEEE International Conference on Image Processing, pp. 1577–1580 (2010)
6. Xia, S., Shao, M., Fu, Y.: Kinship verification through transfer learning. In: International Joint Conference on Artificial Intelligence, pp. 2539–2544 (2011)

7. Hu, J., Lu, J., Tan, Y.P.: Discriminative deep metric learning for face verification in the wild. In: Computer Vision and Pattern Recognition, pp. 1875–1882 (2014)
8. Lu, J., Zhou, X., Tan, Y.P., Shang, Y., Zhou, J.: Neighborhood repulsed metric learning for kinship verification. IEEE Trans. Pattern Anal. Mach. Intell. **36**(2), 331–45 (2014)
9. Zhang, K., Huang, Y., Song, C., Wu, H., Wang, L.: Kinship verification with deep convolutional neural networks. In: British Machine Vision Conference, pp. 148.1–148.12 (2015)
10. Zhao, H., Ding, Z., Fu, Y.: Block-wise constrained sparse graph for face image representation. In: IEEE International Conference and Workshops on Automatic Face and Gesture Recognition, pp. 1–6 (2015)
11. Guo, Y., Dibeklioglu, H., Van Der Maaten, L.: Graph-based kinship recognition. In: International Conference on Pattern Recognition, pp. 4287–4292 (2014)
12. Zhang, J., Xia, S., Shao, M., Fu, Y.: Family photo recognition via multiple instance learning. In: ACM on International Conference on Multimedia Retrieval, pp. 424–428 (2017)
13. Dalal, N., Triggs, B.: Histograms of oriented gradients for human detection. In: IEEE Computer Society Conference on Computer Vision and Pattern Recognition, pp. 886–893 (2005)
14. Parkhi, O.M., Vedaldi, A., Zisserman, A.: Deep face recognition. In: British Machine Vision Conference, pp. 41.1–41.12 (2015)
15. Fang, R., Gallagher, A.C., Chen, T., Loui, A.: Kinship classification by modeling facial feature heredity. In: IEEE International Conference on Image Processing, pp. 2983–2987 (2014)
16. Qin, X., Tan, X., Chen, S.: Tri-subjects kinship verification: understanding the core of a family. In: IAPR International Conference on Machine Vision Applications, pp. 580–583 (2015)
17. Gallagher, A.C., Chen, T.: Understanding images of groups of people. In: IEEE Conference on Computer Vision and Pattern Recognition, CVPR 2009, pp. 256–263 (2009)
18. Xia, S., Shao, M., Luo, J., Yun, F.: Understanding kin relationships in a photo. IEEE Trans. Multimedia **14**(4), 1046–1056 (2012)

ACGAIL: Imitation Learning About Multiple Intentions with Auxiliary Classifier GANs

Jiahao Lin and Zongzhang Zhang(✉)

School of Computer Science and Technology,
Soochow University, Suzhou, People's Republic of China
zzzhang@suda.edu.cn

Abstract. As an important solution to decision-making problems, imitation learning learns expert behavior from example demonstrations provided by experts, without the necessity of a predefined reward function as in reinforcement learning. Traditionally, imitation learning assumes that demonstrations are generated from single latent expert intention. One promising method in this line is generative adversarial imitation learning (GAIL), designed to work in large environments. It can be thought as a model-free imitation learning built on top of generative adversarial networks (GANs). However, GAIL fails to learn well when handling expert demonstrations under multiple intentions, which can be labeled by latent intentions. In this paper, we propose to add an auxiliary classifier model to GAIL, from which we derive a novel variant of GAIL, named ACGAIL, allowing label conditioning in imitation learning about multiple intentions. Experimental results on several MuJoCo tasks indicate that ACGAIL can achieve significant performance improvements over existing methods, e.g., GAIL and InfoGAIL, when dealing with label-conditional imitation learning about multiple intentions.

Keywords: Imitation learning · Generative adversarial networks
Multiple intentions · Auxiliary classifier

1 Introduction

To deal with sequential decision-making problems modeled as Markov decision processes (MDPs), reinforcement learning (RL) requires the access to a well-defined reward function or reinforcement signal to find an optimal behavior [19]. Deep RL has achieved remarkable successes in many complex and high-dimensional tasks recently. However, in many complex situations, an appropriate reward function is difficult to be predefined [8]. As a potential alternative solution, imitation learning has no requirement about the access to any knowledge of reward signals and learns to behave by imitating expert demonstrations.

This work was in part supported by National Natural Science Foundation of China (61502323) and High School Natural Foundation of Jiangsu (16KJB520041).

X. Geng and B.-H. Kang (Eds.): PRICAI 2018, LNAI 11012, pp. 321–334, 2018.
https://doi.org/10.1007/978-3-319-97304-3_25

Most of imitation learning algorithms traditionally assume that the demonstrations come from an expert under single latent intention. Among them, generative adversarial imitation learning (GAIL) [12] is state of the art. It is sample efficient in terms of expert data and can scale well to relatively high dimensional environments. Its key idea is to use generative adversarial networks (GANs) [9] to match distributions of states and actions defining expert behavior.

However, in real-world scenarios, we often need to deal with imitation tasks with multiple expert intentions, where single-intention imitation learning algorithms such as GAIL are no longer suitable for learning. They are obsessed with matching the state-action distributions demonstrated by experts blindly, while ignoring latent multiple intentions that lead to difference in performance.

This paper aims to develop an algorithm for imitation learning about multiple intentions in complicated and high-dimensional learning tasks. To our knowledge, the most similar existing work is InfoGAIL [14], which can not only imitate complex behaviors, but also learn interpretable and meaningful representations of complex behavioral data without supervision. This paper takes a different way. We are not willing to apply imitation learning about multiple intentions in an unsupervised way, which can lead to an interpretation beyond understanding easily. We prefer that a single agent can simultaneously employ accurate label-conditional imitation learning about multiple intentions. As a motivating example, imagine that parents as a couple are teaching their kid to drive, the mom demonstrates in a slow fashion with the intention to be careful, while the dad demonstrates in a fast way with the intention to be efficient. Provided the different actions in particular situations, e.g. the dad chooses second gear to accelerate while the mom slows down elegantly to give way to pedestrians, the kid is required to learn from the mixture of demonstrations and imitate parents to cohere with their different intentions simultaneously.

To achieve this goal, we propose a new algorithm, called auxiliary classifier GAIL (ACGAIL), by combining ideas from GAIL and auxiliary classifier GAN [16] (in Sect. 3). ACGAIL uses an auxiliary classifier in GAIL, along with a novel adversarial game, to learn from multiple intentions. The auxiliary classifier plays a role of assisting the adversary which is known as adversarial networks to reconstruct the side information about the multiple latent intentions. This is followed by a closer look at the relationship between ACGAIL and InfoGAIL [14]. Experimental results on several MuJoCo tasks (in Sect. 4) show that ACGAIL can reconstruct the side information and perform label-conditional imitation learning provided by the labeled demonstrations under multiple intentions. ACGAIL can also appear better performance than existing methods, e.g., GAIL and InfoGAIL, in these label-conditional imitation learning scenarios.

2 Background

This section briefly introduces the notations and basic definitions in MDPs, and single-intention/multiple-intention imitation learning methods.

2.1 MDPs

An MDP can be defined by a tuple $(\mathcal{S}, \mathcal{A}, P, r, \rho_0, \gamma)$. In it $\mathcal{S}$ is the state space; $\mathcal{A}$ is the action space; $P : \mathcal{S} \times \mathcal{A} \times \mathcal{S} \rightarrow [0, 1]$ is the state transition probability distribution, where $P(s' \mid s, a)$ means the probability over state s' after the agent takes action a in state s; $r : \mathcal{S} \times \mathcal{A} \rightarrow \mathbb{R}$ is the reward function, where $r(s, a)$ means the reward obtained after taking action a in state s; $\rho_0 : \mathcal{S} \rightarrow [0, 1]$ is the distribution of the initial state s_0; $\gamma \in (0, 1)$ is the discount factor which balances the immediate and delayed rewards. This paper focuses on dealing with the tasks that have continuous state and action spaces. We define $\pi : \mathcal{S} \times \mathcal{A} \rightarrow [0, 1]$ as a stochastic policy and η as the expected cumulative discounted reward of π:

$$\eta(\pi) = \mathbb{E}_{s_0, a_0, \ldots}\left[\sum\nolimits_{t=0}^{\infty} \gamma^t r(s_t, a_t)\right] \tag{1}$$

where $s_0 \sim \rho_0(s_0)$, $a_t \sim \pi(a_t \mid s_t)$, and $s_{t+1} \sim P(s_{t+1} \mid s_t, a_t)$. Let ρ_π be the discount visitation frequencies, i.e., $\rho_\pi(s) = P(s_0 = s \mid \pi) + \gamma P(s_1 = s \mid \pi) + \gamma^2 P(s_2 = s \mid \pi) + \ldots$, where $s_0 \sim \rho_0$ and the actions are taken by π. We can rewrite Eq. 1 in a sum over states rather than time steps: $\eta(\pi) = \sum_{t=0}^{\infty} \int_{s \in \mathcal{S}} P(s_t = s \mid \pi) \int_{a \in \mathcal{A}} \pi(a \mid s) \gamma^t r(s, a) = \int_{s \in \mathcal{S}} \rho_\pi(s) \int_{a \in \mathcal{A}} \pi(a \mid s) r(s, a)$.

2.2 Single-Intention Imitation Learning

Single-intention imitation learning addresses the task of learning a policy from the behavior of an expert driven by one intention, without any access to an explicit reinforcement signal. It mainly includes the following three categories:

Behavioral Cloning [17] learns a policy over state-action pairs in a supervised learning way. One recent work is an end-to-end system that uses a convolutional neural network (CNN) to represent a policy and learns it by behavioral cloning with raw images as inputs [4]. Due to compounding error caused by covariate shift, behavioral cloning suffers from poor generalization.

Inverse Reinforcement Learning (IRL) [1,15] considers that the expert policy is learned under an unknown reward function. Thus, compounding error, a challenging problem for methods that fit single time-step decisions, is no longer a problem for IRL. It learns a policy by iteratively executing the following two steps: it recovers the unknown reward function using expert demonstrations; and it (approximately) solves the RL problem with the learned reward function. However, IRL has the so-called degeneracy issue, i.e., there exist many reward functions making the observed policy optimal. The issue can be eliminated by introducing a casual entropy regularization to the optimization objective, which encourages the algorithm to find a reward function to maximize the casual entropy of the policy [21,22]. Due to the high computational complexity of solving the inner RL problem inside one learning loop, IRL methods are usually inefficient in addressing relatively high-dimensional learning problems.

Generative Adversarial Imitation Learning [9] is a recent imitation learning method inspired by GANs which have achieved prominent successes in the field of image processing. GANs introduce a two-player minmax game, where a generator captures a data distribution and a discriminator estimates the probabilities whether samples came from the example data. In the training process, the generator tries to confuse the discriminator and the discriminator tries to achieve an accurate estimation. As the discriminator guides the generator to recover the distributions of example data, the discriminator is unable to differentiate between the two distributions eventually. To avoid the inner RL process in IRL, GAIL directly extracts a policy from expert demonstrations based on GANs.

In GAIL, the policy plays a generator role which makes discriminator confusing the state-action pair samples from either the generator or the expert, while the reward function serves as the discriminator trying to distinguish the samples accurately. By training, the reward function guides the policy to match the generated state-action distribution with the expert distribution. The formal GAIL minmax game is denoted as $\min_\theta \max_\omega V(\theta, \omega)$, where $V(\theta, \omega)$ is:

$$\mathbb{E}_{(s,a)\sim\pi_\theta}\left[\log(D_\omega(s,a)\right] + \mathbb{E}_{(s,a)\sim\pi_E}\left[\log(1 - D_\omega(s,a)\right] - \lambda_H H(\pi_\theta) \quad (2)$$

Here, the policy π_θ serves as the generator and the reward function D_ω serves as the discriminator. Both of them are represented as deep neural networks, with parameters θ and ω respectively. The causal entropy of the policy π, denoted as $H(\pi)$, is used as a regularization term together with hyper-parameter λ_H. The policy π_θ can be trained by policy gradient methods such as trust region policy optimization (TRPO) [18], while the discriminator can be optimized using ADAM [13]. By taking advantage of deep neural networks and avoiding the weakness of IRL, GAIL can perform well in relatively high-dimensional problems.

2.3 Multiple-Intention Imitation Learning

There are some existing works that closely relate to imitation learning about multiple intentions. Babes et al. [3] proposed to cluster unlabeled demonstrations by the expectation maximization method. Dimitrakakis and Rothkopf [7] proposed a multi-task learning approach, generalizing the Bayesian approach to IRL. Choi and Kim [6] presented a nonparametric Bayesian approach to IRL by integrating the Dirichlet process mixture model into Bayesian IRL. The algorithms introduced above are based on IRL. However, these IRL-based algorithms require high computational cost of solving RL problems inside the learning loops. Focusing on solving high-dimensional problems, there are some works that extend the GAIL framework, such as InfoGAIL [14] and multi-modal imitation learning [11]. These two extensions learn a single policy that can imitate skills from unlabeled and unstructured demonstrations by maximizing the mutual information between the latent variables and the observed state-action pairs. As shown detailedly in the next section, this paper focuses on learning from labeled demonstrations with multiple intentions instead of unlabeled demonstrations. The most similar work to ours is ACGAN [16], which employs label conditioning that results in image samples exhibiting global coherence by a novel variant of GANs.

3 ACGAIL: Imitation Learning with Auxiliary Classifier

In this section, we first describe the ACGAIL algorithm and its detailed implementation. Then, we take a closer look at its relation to InfoGAIL.

3.1 ACGAIL

In many real-world situations, due to differences of individuals or various purposes, the experts can behave with multiple intentions. So, the example demonstrations provided by experts are mixed with multiple expert intentions. As is often the case, each demonstration can be labeled by a particular intention. Therefore, we can get a mixed set of demonstrations that are labeled by multiple expert intentions. In this paper, we propose that the agent learns from multiple expert intentions simultaneously using one policy. Formally, in this case, we assume that there exists a finite set of K intentions. It can be represented as follows: $\boldsymbol{c_K} = \{c_1, \ldots, c_K\}$. Let us define the prior distribution of intentions as $c \sim p(c)$. For convenience, we simplify the expert policy that includes multiple intentions as π_E, i.e., $\pi_E = \{\pi_{E_{c_1}}, \ldots, \pi_{E_{c_K}}\}$. Instead of learning a policy solely based on the state, the policy can be extended to include a dependence on the intention c as $\pi(a|s, c)$, where c is sampled from the prior $p(c)$.

To reconstruct the side information and perform imitation learning about multiple intentions, we add more structure to the latent space in GAIL along with a specialized optimization objective following the theory of ACGAN. Specifically, we add an auxiliary classifier to adversary which is now composed of two models: an auxiliary classifier defined as C_ψ with parameters ψ and a discriminator defined as D_ω with parameters ω. Furthermore, the policy playing the role of a generator is defined as π_θ with parameters θ. They are all represented by deep neural networks. Working similarly to the discriminator in GAIL, the discriminator in ACGAIL outputs probabilities whether the samples of state-action pairs come from the expert or not. The auxiliary classifier model we added can classify the latent intention labels of state action pairs and output the softmax cross entropy between the latent label variables and logits of classification. In other words, the output of the auxiliary classifier can be interpreted as the probability error of classification. Moreover, the latent intention label variables can be represented as one-hot vectors. The auxiliary classifier assists the adversary reconstructing the side information over latent intention labels. Therefore, we call this new method as auxiliary classifier GAIL. In it, the games for the discriminator and the classifier are given respectively as follows:

$$\min_{\pi_\theta} \max_{D_\omega} \mathbb{E}_{\pi_\theta}[\log(D_\omega(s, a))] + \mathbb{E}_{\pi_E}[\log(1 - D_\omega(s, a))] - \lambda_H H(\pi_\theta) \tag{3}$$

$$\max_{\pi_\theta, C_\psi} \mathbb{E}_{\pi_\theta}[\log(C_\psi(c|s, a))] + \mathbb{E}_{\pi_E}[C_\psi(c|s, a))] \tag{4}$$

where we simplify the $\mathbb{E}_{c\sim p(c),(s,a)\sim\pi(a|s,c)}[\cdot]$ as $\mathbb{E}_{\pi}[\cdot]$. As a result, we can acquire the corresponding objectives for the discriminator and the classifier:

$$L_D = \max_{D_\omega} \mathbb{E}_{\pi_\theta}[\log(D_\omega(s,a))] + \mathbb{E}_{\pi_E}[\log(1 - D_\omega(s,a))] \tag{5}$$

$$L_C = \max_{C_\psi} \mathbb{E}_{\pi_\theta}[\log(C_\psi(c|s,a))] + \mathbb{E}_{\pi_E}[\log(C_\psi(c|s,a))] \tag{6}$$

In our method, the objective of adversary is now composed of the functions from both the discriminator and the classifier:

$$L_{adversary} = L_D + L_C \tag{7}$$

The adversary is trained to maximize the novel optimization objective $L_{adversary}$. It can be considered that the adversary tries to make both the differentiation of the discriminator over sample sources and the classification of the classifier over intention label variables to be more accurate.

By combining the Eqs. 3 and 4 with respect to generator π_θ, we can obtain the optimization objective for the generator π_θ as follows:

$$L_{\pi_\theta} = \min_{\pi_\theta} \mathbb{E}_{\pi_\theta}[\log(D_\omega(s,a))] - \lambda_C \mathbb{E}_{\pi_\theta}[\log(C_\psi(c|s,a))] - \lambda_H H(\pi_\theta) \tag{8}$$

where hyper-parameter λ_C is used to trade off the influence of the discriminator and the classifier to the generator. The discriminator and the classifier can be jointly interpreted as a reward function providing learning signals to the policy. The detailed reward function provided by the adversary can be represented as $-\log(D_\omega(s,a)) + \lambda_C \log(C_\psi(c|s,a))$. It can be thought that the discriminator tries to make the distribution of samples generated by the generator close to the expert distribution. Meanwhile, the auxiliary classifier encourages the policy generated from the generator to match the latent intention label. In such a combination, the adversary guides the policy to confuse the discriminator as well as to reduce the classification error of the classifier, resulting in a policy employing label-conditional imitation learning about multiple intentions.

To sum up, the total minmax game between the adversary and the generator in ACGAIL can be summarized as Eq. 9:

$$\begin{aligned} \min_{\pi_\theta, C_\psi} \max_{D_\omega} \; & \mathbb{E}_{\pi_\theta}[\log(D_\omega(s,a))] + \mathbb{E}_{\pi_E}[\log(1 - D_\omega(s,a))] \\ & - \mathbb{E}_{\pi_\theta}[C_\psi(c|s,a))] - \lambda_C \mathbb{E}_{\pi_E}[C_\psi(c|s,a))] - \lambda_H H(\pi_\theta) \end{aligned} \tag{9}$$

3.2 Algorithm Implementation

ACGAIL needs to update four networks basically: the discriminator network D_ω, the classifier network C_ψ, the policy network π_θ and a value function working as a baseline. We use TRPO to update π_θ to ensure a monotonic improvement of policy optimization and generalized advantage estimation to reduce the variance of policy gradient estimates. We use ADAM to update both D_ω and

Algorithm 1. ACGAIL

Input: Expert demonstrations with multiple intentions $T_E \sim \pi_E$; initial policy, discriminator, classifier parameters $\theta_0, \omega_0, \psi_0$; initial batch size B; initial the number of steps to apply to adversary M, the number of step to apply to the generator N.
Output: Learned policy π_θ.

for $i = 0, 1, 2, \ldots$ **do**
  Sample a random intention label $c_i \sim p(c)$;
  for M steps **do**
    Sample trajectories from policy π_θ: $\tau_i \sim \pi_{\theta_i}(c_i)$;
    Roll out samples $\mathcal{X}_i \sim \tau_i$ and $\mathcal{X}_E \sim T_E$ with same batch size B;
    Update the discriminator parameters from ω_i to ω_{i+1} with gradient:

$$\Delta_\omega = \mathbb{E}_{\mathcal{X}_i}[\nabla_\omega \log(D_\omega(s,a))] + \mathbb{E}_{\mathcal{X}_E}[\nabla_\omega \log(1 - D_\omega(s,a))]$$

    Update the classifier parameters from ψ_i to ψ_{i+1} with gradient:

$$\Delta_\psi = \mathbb{E}_{\mathcal{X}_i}[\nabla_\psi \log(C_\psi(c|s,a))] + \mathbb{E}_{\mathcal{X}_E}[\nabla_\psi \log(C_\psi(c|s,a))]$$

  end for
  for N steps **do**
    Sample trajectories from policy π_θ: $\tau_i \sim \pi_{\theta_i}(c_i)$ and roll out samples $\mathcal{X}_i \sim \tau_i$;
    Take a policy step from θ_i to θ_{i+1}, using the TRPO update rule with the following objective:

$$-\mathbb{E}_{\mathcal{X}_i}[\log(D_{\omega_{i+1}}(s,a))] + \lambda_C \mathbb{E}_{\mathcal{X}_i}[\log(C_{\psi_{i+1}}(c|s,a))] - \lambda_H H(\pi_\theta)$$

  end for
end for

C_ψ. Since the classifier and the discriminator form jointly as the adversary and work closely, we introduce a structure that the classifier and the discriminator share their parameters and update jointly according to the optimization objective of the adversary, which is similar to the optimization of the dueling network architecture [20]. Moreover, we consider the training improvements of the discriminator and the classifier to be the same since they are equally important to update. As a result, it is not proper to use the hyper-parameter λ_C to trade off the training step sizes in updating the discriminator and the classifier. However, the influences of the discriminator and the classifier towards the generator should not be the same. Therefore, we use the hyper-parameter λ_C in the reward function to balance the influences properly. The training procedure of ACGAIL is presented in Algorithm 1. In it, the finite-horizon trajectory samples include the label information of intention c_i as $\tau_{c_i} = (s_0, a_0, \ldots, s_h, a_h \mid c_i)$, where h represents the length of trajectory. As a result, the set of expert demonstrations $T_E = \{\tau_1, \ldots, \tau_n\}$ is extended to a mixture of state-action pairs labeled by different intentions as $T_E = \{s_0, a_0, c_0, s_1, a_1, c_1, \ldots\}$. So, the input of Algorithm 1 can be considered as a batch of tuples (s_i, a_i, c_i) selected from T_E randomly.

In the iteration of training, we set the numbers of inner loop steps for both the adversary and the generator, denoted as M and N, to balance the training step sizes of the adversary and the generator. Our setting follows the trick of training GANs, which suggests the adversary to maintain proper accuracy to prevent the generator from vanishing gradient. To speed up training, we suggest to use the behavioral cloning method to initialize policy in some tasks. Note that there are some works to improve the training, such as Wasserstein GAN [2] and improved WGAN [10]. However, due to we are dealing with an adversary constructed by two models, here we follow the training trick of vanilla GAN.

3.3 Relation to InfoGAIL and Mutual Information

Both ACGAIL and InfoGAIL focus on the learning problem about multiple intentions. InfoGAIL tends to interpret the latent intentions by maximizing the mutual information between the latent intention variables and the state-action pairs generated from the generator, where the maximization of the mutual information can be understood that the samples generated by a policy exhibit higher relevance to the corresponding intention labels. However, due to lack of the access to posterior, InfoGAIL can not maximize the mutual information directly. It tries to optimize the surrogate minmax game as follows:

$$\begin{aligned} \min_{\pi_\theta, Q_\psi} \max_{D_\omega} \; & \mathbb{E}_{\pi_\theta}[\log(D_\omega(s,a))] + \mathbb{E}_{\pi_E}[\log(1 - D_\omega(s,a))] \\ & - \lambda_Q \mathbb{E}_{\pi_\theta}[Q_\psi(c|s,a))] - \lambda_H H(\pi_\theta) \end{aligned} \tag{10}$$

The corresponding objectives of the discriminator D_ω, the posterior Q_ψ, and the generator π_θ are:

$$L_{D_\omega} = \max_{D_\omega} \mathbb{E}_{\pi_\theta}[\log(D_\omega(s,a))] + \mathbb{E}_{\pi_E}[\log(1 - D_\omega(s,a))] \tag{11}$$

$$L_{Q_\psi} = \max_{Q_\psi} \mathbb{E}_{\pi_\theta}[\log(Q_\psi(c|s,a))] \tag{12}$$

$$L_{\pi_\theta} = \min_{\pi_\theta} \mathbb{E}_{\pi_\theta}[\log(D_\omega(s,a))] - \lambda_Q \mathbb{E}_{\pi_\theta}[\log(Q_\psi(c|s,a))] - \lambda_H H(\pi_\theta) \tag{13}$$

Here, Eq. 11 is similar to Eq. 5 in guiding the generator to imitate the expert behavior. Equation 13, similar to Eq. 8, is the objective for π_θ. By comparing them, we find that ACGAIL can also be interpreted as trying to maximize the mutual information between the latent label variables and the state-action pairs.

The difference arises from Eq. 12 compared to Eq. 6. Following the GAN fashion, the training of the auxiliary classifier in ACGAIL is actually fed either labeled expert samples or generated samples. Leveraging the training through labeled expert samples, the auxiliary classifier can acquire the access to a relatively accurate posterior of the state-action pairs. Thus, ACGAIL maximizes the mutual information directly rather than the surrogate objective. Thus, the auxiliary classifier introduced in ACGAIL is able to reconstruct the side information about latent intention labels, which results in the policy employing label-conditional imitation learning in coherence with corresponding expert intentions. Meanwhile, dealing with unlabeled demonstrations, InfoGAIL finds a set of most significant latent representations as intentions and learns from it in an unsupervised way. Notice that ACGAIL is training with labeled demonstrations while

Table 1. Parameters of tasks and expert's average performance

Task	State space	Action space	Expert label 0	Expert label 1
Hopper-v1	11	3	3589.09	672.55
Walker2d-v1	17	6	3550.94	725.99
HalfCheetah-v1	17	6	3889.23	1487.27
Humanoid-v1	376	117	2267.36	488.31

InfoGAIL is training with unlabeled demonstrations. The difference of preconditions about demonstrations leads to the prominent difference in performance. Compared to InfoGAIL which can result in an interpretation beyond understanding easily, the advantage of ACGAIL is that the auxiliary classifier assists the algorithm to achieve accurate label-conditional imitation learning about multiple intentions provided with labeled demonstrations.

4 Experiments

This section aims to answer the following questions: (1) Can ACGAIL use only one policy to employ label-conditional imitation learning about multiple expert intentions? (2) Can ACGAIL scale well to high-dimensional tasks?

4.1 Environmental Setup

We evaluate Algorithm 1 against two baselines, GAIL and InfoGAIL, in a series of challenging high-dimensional simulated robotic tasks in MuJoCo. Each task comes with a true reward function, defined in the OpenAI Gym [5]. The expert policies with multiple intentions are generated by running TRPO in different numbers of iterations with these true reward functions. Then, we would like to use the expert policies to sample 1,500 trajectories and label the trajectories with the corresponding latent intention variables. The labeled trajectories sampled from expert policies are shuffled as labeled state-action pairs. For conciseness, we generate two latent expert intentions for each task. Table 1 shows the information of tasks and the expert's average performance under each intention. Columns 2–3 list the dimensions of the state space and the action space for each task, and Columns 4–5 list the expert's average performance under latent intentions label variables 0 and 1. Each expert's performance is averaged over the cumulative discounted rewards (a.k.a. returns) of 1,500 expert trajectories.

4.2 Imitation Learning About Multiple Intentions

In our algorithm, we get four neural networks to update: discriminator, auxiliary classifier, policy and value function. The setting of neural networks is the same as in GAIL: 2 hidden layers of 100 units each, with tanh nonlinearities between

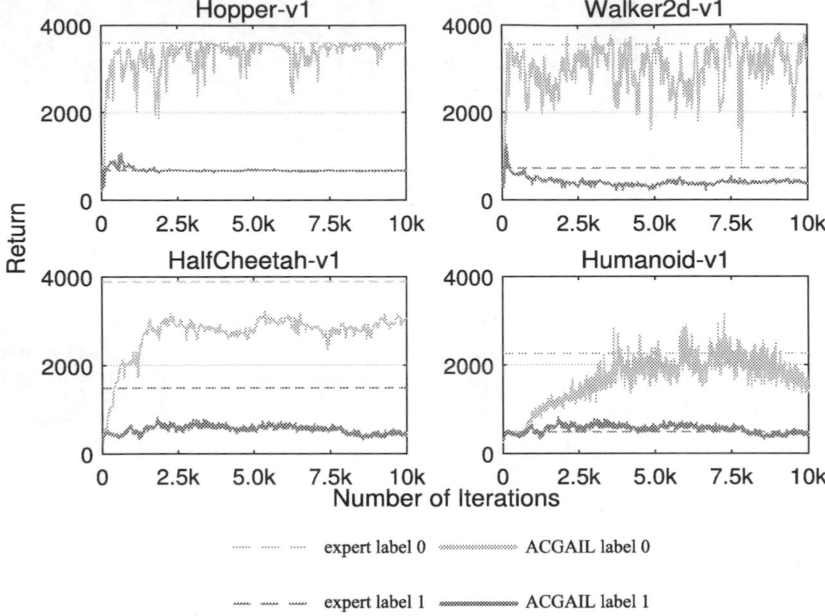

Fig. 1. ACGAIL's results on four tasks. The dashed lines represent the average return of trajectories performed by expert; the bold lines represent the return of one trajectory generated by ACGAIL. The red and blue lines, respectively, represent the results under intention label variables 0 and 1. The horizontal axis shows the number of training iterations, and the vertical axis shows the return averaged over last 40 trajectories representing the performance of learned policy. (Color figure online)

them. The same networks are also used in the two baseline algorithms. As we share the parameters in ACGAIL, the discriminator and the auxiliary classifier are also structured by 2 hidden layers of 100 units each, while the hidden layers are shared and the output layers work differently. We use TRPO and ADAM to train the policy and the value function respectively, and also use ADAM to train the adversary. We set the learning rate of ADAM for the adversary to 5×10^{-5}, a relatively small value, according to the training trick of GANs. We choose to set $\lambda_H = 0$ since we find that the empirical performance of ACGAIL is insensitive to this parameter, and set $\lambda_C = 0.5$.

In Fig. 1, we present the results of running ACGAIL on four different tasks by showing 10,000 training iterations. The results show that, at the beginning of training, the policies under two different intentions are roughly similar; when the training process goes on, the policies under different intentions exhibit discriminating performance, each of which performs closely to the expert behavior under the corresponding intention. On Hopper-v1 and Walker2d-v1, our algorithm begins to employ label-conditional imitation learning after about 200 training iterations, while on HalfCheetah-v1 and Humanoid-v1, the differences begin after around 1,000 training iterations. Furthermore, on Hopper-v1, each of the

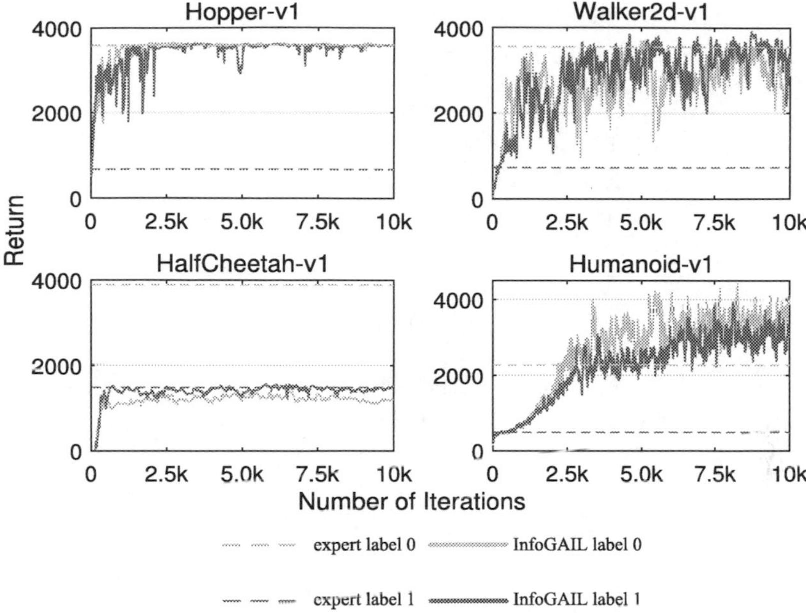

Fig. 2. InfoGAIL's results on four tasks. The dashed lines represent the average return of trajectories performed by expert; the bold lines represent the return of one trajectory generated by generator. The red and blue lines, respectively, represent the results under intention label variables 0 and 1. The horizontal axis shows the number of training iterations, and the vertical axis shows the return averaged over last 40 trajectories representing the performance of learned policy. (Color figure online)

policies conditioned under two different intention labels perfectly converges to the corresponding expert returns. On Walker2d-v1, the return of the policy under intention label 0 exhibits more fluctuation. It can be interpreted that the returns of expert demonstrations exhibit volatility since the dimensions or cardinalities of both state and action spaces become larger. On HalfCheetah-v1, the returns of policies vary and converge to the returns under the corresponding expert intentions. On Humanoid-v1, due to the issue of high dimensionality, the training is quite slow and quite difficult to achieve a perfect convergence. Above all, the results of all tasks show that ACGAIL can exhibit different returns close to the expert's returns under the corresponding latent intentions and scale well to high-dimensional tasks.

In Fig. 2, we demonstrate the results of InfoGAIL on the four MuJoCo tasks. The results of GAIL are listed in Table 2. The setting for InfoGAIL is the same as in ACGAIL. From the results of the four tasks in Figs. 1 and 2, we can see that ACGAIL is able to exhibit different behaviors/performance under different latent intention label variables. Furthermore, ACGAIL is able to generate label-conditional behavior samples that precisely approximate to expert performance under corresponding latent intention labels. While InfoGAIL struggles to

Table 2. Performance errors over all latent intentions

Task	ACGAIL	InfoGAIL	GAIL
Hopper-v1	**0.0097**	2.1340	2.1678
Walker2d-v1	**0.2796**	1.6167	1.7951
HalfCheetah-v1	**0.2921**	0.3642	0.5546
Humanoid-v1	**0.1256**	2.7784	3.0664

interpret the latent intentions ignoring the side information over labeled demonstrations.

We suggest to use the sum of the differences in average returns over all intentions as a quantitative criterion of the similarity between generated state-action samples and expert samples over multiple intentions:

$$X = \sum_{c_i \in \boldsymbol{c_K}} p(c_i) \frac{\left| \bar{R}_{\pi_\theta, c_i} - \bar{R}_{\pi_E, c_i} \right|}{\bar{R}_{\pi_E, c_i}} \tag{14}$$

where $\bar{R}_{\pi_\theta}$ or $\bar{R}_{\pi_E}$ represents the average return of sampled trajectories given a policy π_θ or π_E, and $p(c_i)$ represents the prior probability of intention label variable c_i. Specifically, $p(c_i)$ should be 0.5 since we sample the two intention label variables randomly in our algorithm. The criterion represents performance errors over all latent intentions. It uses absolute values to accept both positive and negative deviations to the expert's performance, and take the expert's performance as the denominator. Its output X can be interpreted as the degree of the performance variance between the expert and the generator over all intentions. It is obvious that a smaller value of X is preferred. For quantifying the differences over all intentions for the algorithms, we use the trajectory samples with training iterations from $8,000$ to $9,000$ for each algorithm. The outputs of the criterion are reported in Table 2.

Table 2 shows that ACGAIL has lower variance over latent intentions than InfoGAIL as it employs label-conditional imitation learning about multiple intentions. Because InfoGAIL tries to interpret the latent intentions, it exhibits lower variance than GAIL which only works properly under single intention.

5 Conclusion and Future Work

In this paper, we introduce auxiliary classifier as an additional model to vanilla GAIL, which is able to use single policy to employ label-conditional imitation learning about multiple intentions. Furthermore, the experimental results show that ACGAIL can better deal with the situations where the demonstrations are labeled by multiple latent expert intentions.

We noticed that there are some drawbacks in the current ACGAIL implementation. Its performance appears worse as the number of latent expert intentions increases. In addition, it is tricky to search proper hyper-parameters of time steps to improve training for particular tasks. In the future, we will explore ways of eliminating the tricky issue of searching time steps of training. As a matter of fact, we are digging into the possibility of extending the remarkable work of Wasserstein GAN to ACGAIL. Moreover, we are trying to find a more stable structure to achieve imitation learning about multiple intentions, and then use it to learn from several latent intentions.

References

1. Abbeel, P., Ng, A.Y.: Apprenticeship learning via inverse reinforcement learning. In: ICML, pp. 1–8 (2004)
2. Arjovsky, M., Chintala, S., Bottou, L.: Wasserstein generative adversarial networks. In: ICML, pp. 214–223 (2017)
3. Babes, M., Marivate, V., Subramanian, K., Littman, M.L.: Apprenticeship learning about multiple intentions. In: ICML, pp. 897–904 (2011)
4. Bojarski, M., et al.: End to end learning for self-driving cars. arXiv preprint arXiv:1604.07316 (2016)
5. Brockman, G., et al.: OpenAI Gym. arXiv preprint arXiv:1606.01540 (2016)
6. Choi, J., Kim, K.E.: Nonparametric Bayesian inverse reinforcement learning for multiple reward functions. In: NIPS, pp. 305–313 (2012)
7. Dimitrakakis, C., Rothkopf, C.A.: Bayesian multitask inverse reinforcement learning. In: Sanner, S., Hutter, M. (eds.) EWRL 2011. LNCS (LNAI), vol. 7188, pp. 273–284. Springer, Heidelberg (2012). https://doi.org/10.1007/978-3-642-29946-9_27
8. Finn, C., Levine, S., Abbeel, P.: Guided cost learning: deep inverse optimal control via policy optimization. In: ICML, pp. 49–58 (2016)
9. Goodfellow, I., et al.: Generative adversarial nets. In: NIPS, pp. 2672–2680 (2014)
10. Gulrajani, I., Ahmed, F., Arjovsky, M., Dumoulin, V., Courville, A.C.: Improved training of Wasserstein GANs. In: NIPS, pp. 5769–5779 (2017)
11. Hausman, K., Chebotar, Y., Schaal, S., Sukhatme, G., Lim, J.J.: Multi-modal imitation learning from unstructured demonstrations using generative adversarial nets. In: NIPS, pp. 1235–1245 (2017)
12. Ho, J., Ermon, S.: Generative adversarial imitation learning. In: NIPS, pp. 4565–4573 (2016)
13. Kingma, D.P., Ba, J.: ADAM: a method for stochastic optimization. ICLR (2015)
14. Li, Y., Song, J., Ermon, S.: InfoGAIL: interpretable imitation learning from visual demonstrations. In: NIPS, pp. 3815–3825 (2017)
15. Ng, A.Y., Russell, S.J.: Algorithms for inverse reinforcement learning. In: ICML, pp. 663–670 (2000)
16. Odena, A., Olah, C., Shlens, J.: Conditional image synthesis with auxiliary classifier GANs. In: ICML, pp. 2642–2651 (2017)
17. Pomerleau, D.A.: Efficient training of artificial neural networks for autonomous navigation. Neural Comput. **3**(1), 88–97 (1991)
18. Schulman, J., Levine, S., Abbeel, P., Jordan, M., Moritz, P.: Trust region policy optimization. In: ICML, pp. 1889–1897 (2015)
19. Sutton, R.S., Barto, A.G.: Reinforcement Learning: An Introduction. MIT Press, Cambridge (1998)

20. Wang, Z., Schaul, T., Hessel, M., Hasselt, H., Lanctot, M., Freitas, N.: Dueling network architectures for deep reinforcement learning. In: ICML, pp. 1995–2003 (2016)
21. Ziebart, B.D., Bagnell, J.A., Dey, A.K.: Maximum causal entropy correlated equilibria for Markov games. In: AAMAS, pp. 207–214 (2011)
22. Ziebart, B.D., Maas, A.L., Bagnell, J.A., Dey, A.K.: Maximum entropy inverse reinforcement learning. In: AAAI, pp. 1433–1438 (2008)

Matching Attention Network for Domain Adaptation Optimized by Joint GANs and KL-MMD

Yuan-Zhu Gan[1(✉)], Hai-Qing Wang[2], Lu-Fei Liu[1], and Yu-Bin Yang[1(✉)]

[1] State Key Laboratory for Novel Software Technology, Nanjing University, Nanjing 210023, China
ganyz@smail.nju.edu.cn, yangyubin@nju.edu.cn

[2] The 28th Research Institute of China Electronics Technology Group Corporation, Nanjing 210007, China

Abstract. Although deep neural networks have brought impressive advances in a variety of machine learning tasks, it is more difficult to train a top-performing model in the absence of the labeled data. To alleviate this issue, domain adaptation has been extensively researched, which aims to reduce the difference between the distributions of the source and target domain by imposing restrictions on features. Adversarial learning method is the most promising approach to generate data that obeys a complex distribution. However, generator model often sinks into partial or full collapse. In this paper, we transform the complex data into a simple distribution, then calculate KL divergence (KL-MMD). We combine the Matching Gate with Attention Mechanism and put forward Matching Attention to learn feature vectors. Extensive experiments and analysis are conducted on three different digits datasets: MNIST, USPS, SVHN. To our knowledge, our method achieves state-of-the-art digit recognition performance on three unsupervised adaptation results.

Keywords: Domain adaptation · Generative adversarial network Matching gate · Attention mechanism · KL divergence

1 Introduction

Convolutional Neural Networks (CNNs) have made new records on a variety of visual tasks with the rapid development of deep learning. But most of them are trained on large-scale datasets and can be not generalized well to new datasets or tasks. Data bias and domain shift greatly impedes the reusability of the

This work is funded by the Natural Science Foundation of China (No. 61673204), State Grid Corporation of Science and Technology Projects (Funded No. SGLNXT00DKJS1700166), and the Program for Distinguished Talents of Jiangsu Province, China (No. 2013-XXRJ-018).

X. Geng and B.-H. Kang (Eds.): PRICAI 2018, LNAI 11012, pp. 335–347, 2018.
https://doi.org/10.1007/978-3-319-97304-3_26

model trained on a specified dataset. Studies have indicated that the supervised approaches always behave not well on the testing set if the testing and training inputs have different distributions. In the field of deep learning, the typical and feasible solution is to fine-tune the pre-trained model on the other datasets. However it is often prohibitively expensive and time-consuming to gather enough labeled data to fine-tune the neural network well.

Domain adaptation attempts to alleviate the influence of data bias in the target domain where labels are sparse or non-existent. More specifically, it learns a deep neural network that maps both domains into a common feature space. Some methods have been proposed to solve such a problem. Tzeng et al. [17] and Long et al. [10] achieved this by optimizing the network to minimize the discrepancy metric: Maximum Mean Discrepancy (MMD). Sun et al. [12,13] used correlation distance to measure the domain shift. The most popular method recently is the adversarial domain adaptation which is based on Generative Adversarial Networks (GANs) [5]. ADDA [16] used a discriminator network to distinguish the distributions of two domain examples.

In this paper, we improve the existing approaches in two ways. First, a new CNN architecture is proposed to learn more expressive features. To be specific, we add a Matching Attention (MA) layer between the SourceCNN and TargetCNN shown in Fig. 1 based on the Attention Mechanism [21] and the Matching Gate [18]. The SourceCNN and TargetCNN are respectively feature extractors on the source and target domains and MA layer aims to pay more emphasis on informative features and suppress useless ones, which has a tendency to learn the representations with lower correlations. Second, we use the idea of perceptual similarity [8] to measure whether two distributions are similar. And the new loss function extremely improves the classification accuracy for domain adaptation.

2 Related Work

2.1 Domain Transfer Learning

Extensive works have been done on domain transfer learning and its task is to transfer the network representations from a labeled source domain to a target domain and simultaneously minimize the testing error on target datasets where no labels are available at the training time. Owing to the power of Convolution Neural Networks (CNNs), a lot of CNN-based approaches have been put forward.

The main strategy is to minimize the difference between the source and target feature distributions. Several typical methods based on this strategy are listed as follows: (1) Measuring the difference between two domain feature distributions with Maximum Mean Discrepancy (MMD) [17] loss. Tzeng [17] proposed a new CNN architecture with a newly added adaptation layer which is based on MMD to learn representations jointly to optimize for classification and domain invariance. (2) Using an adversarial loss to minimize the domain shift. The principle of this way is to ensure that the distributions of the source and target domain examples can not be distinguished by the discriminator network. Ganin [3] learns a discriminative feature within a domain and simultaneously invariant with data bias between the domains. Tzeng [16] combines Generative Adversarial Nets with the domain adaptation and proposes a unified framework called Adversarial Discriminative Domain Adaptation (ADDA).

Another category pays more attention to the feature similarity between the various categories of source and target domains instead of directly optimizing the difference between the source and target feature distribution. Haeusser [6] proposed a novel association loss as an alternative discrepancy measure. This category is more fine-grained compared with the first one due to the lack of annotation information in the target datasets. Actually it is more challenging when it comes to effectiveness.

2.2 Attention Mechanism

Since [21] is proposed to apply visual attention in neural image caption generation, extensive attention models have been shown effective in various tasks such as image captioning and classification.

Attention mechanism can be divided into two categories: spatial attention and channel attention. For the first category, the size of feature maps is $W \times H \times C$. It can be considered as a $W \times H$ image and the representation of every pixel is C dimensional. The attention model will learn to re-weigh every pixel. Xu [21] applied this kind of model to refine the spatial attention. Residual attention model [19] add this to the residual network and achieves 0.6% top-1 accuracy improvement compared to *ResNet*-200. The second category pays more attention to each channel of a feature map which is viewed as a process of selecting semantic attributes. The most famous application of it is SEnet [7] which is the foundation of the ILSVRC 2017 top classification submission. SCA-CNN [2] combined spatial attention with channel attention and performs the state-of-the-art image captioning method. From the view of optimization, there are soft attention and hard attention and the biggest difference between them is that soft attention can be optimized by the standard back-propagation while hard attention is optimized by REINFORCE algorithms [20].

The original spark of attention mechanism is that people only focus on selective parts when they process the whole image. The analysis is always based on experiment results that it gives the relevant parts of the image bigger weight or it can learn richer descriptions.

3 The Proposed Method

In this section, we first describe baseline Adversarial Discriminative Domain Adaptation (ADDA) architecture, then introduce the Matching Attention mechanism to solve the limitation of complete separation of two feature extraction networks in ADDA model. Then we describe how to use a classification function to transform complex feature distributions to a simple multinomial distribution.

3.1 Model Architecture

Baseline ADDA Architecture. The fundamental ADDA [16] architecture is composed of four components: SourceCNN(S), TargetCNN(T), Classifier(C) and Discriminator(D). The first two components are convolutional feature extractors of the source datasets and target datasets separately. The classifier trained on the source datasets can be shared by the target datasets during the testing phase. The fourth component is trained to differentiate the distribution of the outputs of two different CNNs.

Matching Attention Mechanism. Inspired by the recent researches in deep neural networks, attention mechanism can bring more discriminative feature representations and also can be incorporated with deep network structures in an end-to-end training fashion. Simply stated, for each location i of hidden layer h_j, the attention mechanism gives a positive weight a_i which is computed by a function f_{att} whose input can be the output of any hidden layer before j. Thus the output of Attention Module H is:

$$\begin{aligned} e_{ji} &= f_{att}(h_{j-1}) \\ a_{ji} &= \frac{exp(e_{ji})}{\sum_{k=1}^{c} exp(e_{jk})} \\ h_{ji} &= h_{ji} * a_{ji} \end{aligned} \tag{1}$$

where c is the number of channels for h_j. Following the previous attention mechanism idea in Residual Attention Network [19], we choose soft attention with residual learning. Thus the output H of attention residual learning is:

$$h_{ji} = h_{ji} * (1 + a_{ji}) \tag{2}$$

On the one hand, soft attention model can be used directly as a branch of the main network, which is easier to implement than hard attention. On the other hand, residual learning can enhance the representation ability of model and simultaneously make the training process more stable. The matching gate mechanism has achieved excellent results in the field of human re-identification. The paper [18] puts forward a new opinion that the comparison between two images should not always be done at the final level and finer local pattern can be extracted by comparing the mid-level features across the pair of images. On their basis, we extend the above attention mechanism to our Matching Attention (MA). The output of our MA is:

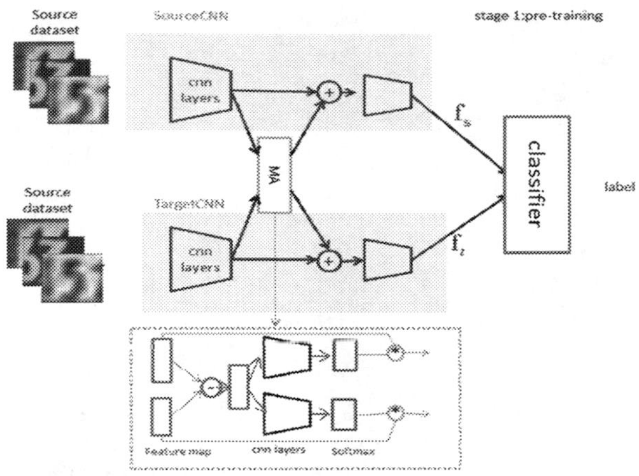

Fig. 1. In the first step, we pre-train SourceCNN, TargetCNN, MA and Classifier using labeled source image examples. Using the pairs (SourceDataset, SourceDataset) to train the above network can get a good initialization weights for adaptation learning.

$$
\begin{aligned}
g_{j-1} &= h^s_{j-1} - h^t_{j-1} \\
e^s_{ji} &= f^s_{att}(g_{j-1}) \\
e^t_{ji} &= f^t_{att}(g_{j-1}) \\
a^s_{ji} &= \frac{exp(e^s_{ji})}{\sum_{k=1}^{c} exp(e^s_{jk})} \\
a^t_{ji} &= \frac{exp(e^t_{ji})}{\sum_{k=1}^{c} exp(e^t_{jk})} \\
h^s_{ji} &= h^s_{ji} * (1 + a^s_{ji}) \\
h^t_{ji} &= h^t_{ji} * (1 + a^t_{ji})
\end{aligned}
\tag{3}
$$

where h^s_j and h^t_j represent the output of hidden layer j of SourceCNN and TargetCNN respectively, g_{j-1} is the feature similarity computation proposed in [18], which is alterable.

The KL Divergence. While a theoretical basis for the GAN criterion has been proved by Goodfellow et al. [5], the convergence of GAN is based on the hypothesis that the game between the generator and discriminator achieves Nash Equilibrium, which is not easy to be satisfied in practice. It is a common observation that generator model often sinks into partial or full collapse. Thus, it is insufficient to judge whether two distributions are similar by using only the discriminator.

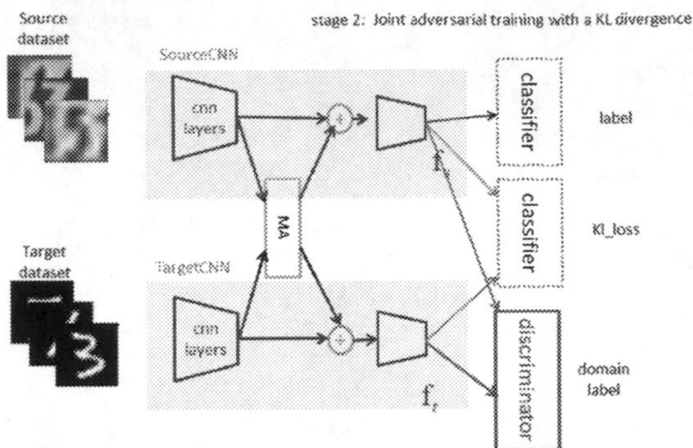

Fig. 2. In the second step, after pre-training, we fix the Classifier and then perform adversarial adaptation by finetuning the remainings such that a discriminator that sees encoded source and target examples cannot reliably predict their (f_s, f_t) domain label.

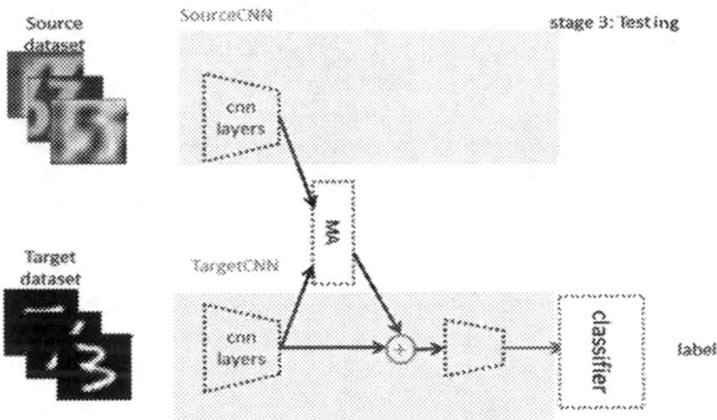

Fig. 3. During testing, for each testing image $x_t \in X_T$, we randomly select a source image $x_s \in X_S$, then combine x_t and x_s to form a new input pair(x_s, x_t), the classification result of x_t is classifier(f_t) as shown above.

One way is to combine the discriminator and MMD (Maximum Mean Discrepancy) to measure the distance between two distributions. MMD is computed as followed:

$$MMD(X_S, X_T) = \left\| \frac{1}{|X_S|} \sum_{x_s \in X_S} \phi(x_s) - \frac{1}{|X_T|} \sum_{x_t \in X_T} \phi(x_t) \right\| \tag{4}$$

In this case, $\phi(\cdot)$ is a representation which operates on source data points, $x_s \in X_S$, and target data points $x_t \in X_T$. $\phi(\cdot)$ is data-independent, such as Gaussian Kernels [11]. Johnson et al. [8] has shown the use of perceptual function based on high-level features extracted from pretrained network can capture perceptual differences between two inputs. In this paper we combine the original MMD and perceptual function. We define $\phi(\cdot)$ as a classifier, then $\frac{1}{|F_S|}\sum_{f_s \in F_S} classifier(f_s)$ and $\frac{1}{|F_T|}\sum_{f_t \in F_t} classifier(f_t)$ are simple multinomial distributions. $f_s \in F_S$ and $f_t \in F_T$ are features extracted from source dataset(X_S) and target dataset(X_T). Concretely, let $\frac{1}{|F_S|}\sum_{f_s\in F_S} classifier(f_s)$ approximately equal to $[q_1, q_2, \ldots, q_c]^c$, c is the output dimension of the classifier and $\sum_{i=1}^{c} q_i = 1$. For the data sampled from the target dataset, we assume that $\frac{1}{|F_T|}\sum_{f_t\in F_t} classifier(f_t)$ represents $[p_1, p_2, \ldots, p_c]^c$, $\sum_{i=1}^{c} p_i = 1$. Thus we define $\mathcal{L}_{kl}$ as:

$$\mathcal{L}_{kl} = \sum_{i=1}^{c} p_i * log\frac{p_i}{q_i} + Constant \tag{5}$$

when the $\mathcal{L}_{kl}$ is minimized, $p_i = q_i$. The simple KL loss can greatly improve the classification results of target datasets.

Our Architecture. The final architecture including training and testing process is shown in Figs. 1, 2 and 3, which can be divided into three parts: Feature Extractor(SourceCNN & TargetCNN & MA), Classifier(C), Discriminator(D). Let X_S, X_T represent the source dataset and the target dataset, Y_S represents the labels corresponding to X_S. F_S, F_T are features extracted from X_S, X_T. Thus the whole formulation for our proposed method is below:

$$\begin{aligned}
\mathcal{L}_{cls}(x_s, x_t, y_s) &= -\sum_{k=1}^{K} \mathbb{1}_{[y_s=k]} logC(f_s) \\
\mathcal{L}_{adv_D}(x_s, x_t) &= -(logD(f_s) + log(1 - D(f_t))) \\
\mathcal{L}_{adv_G}(x_s, x_t) &= -logD(f_t) \\
\min_{D} \sum_{(x_s,x_t)\in(X_S,X_T)} &\frac{1}{|X_S||X_T|}\mathcal{L}_{adv_D}(X_s, X_t) \\
\min_{FE,C} \sum_{(x_s,y_s,x_t)\in(X_S,Y_S,X_T)} &\frac{1}{|X_S||X_T|}(\alpha * \mathcal{L}_{cls} + \beta * \mathcal{L}_{adv_G} + \gamma * \mathcal{L}_{kl})
\end{aligned} \tag{6}$$

where K is the number of categories in the source dataset.

3.2 Training and Testing

The final architecture can be trained from the scratch in an end-to-end manner, for the stability of the discriminator in the training process. But we decide to divide the whole training process into two steps. The first step only uses the source dataset to train Feature Extractor and Classifier. To be specific, we choose to optimize the following loss function:

$$\begin{aligned}
\mathcal{L}_{cls}(x_s, x_s') &= \mathbb{1}_{[y_s=k]} logC(f_s) + \mathbb{1}_{[y_s'=k]} logC(f_t) \\
&\min_{FE,C} - \sum_{(x_s,x_s')\in(X_S,X_S)} \mathcal{L}_{cls}(x_s, x_s')
\end{aligned} \tag{7}$$

Table 1. Average classification accuracy on unsupervised adaptation among MNIST, SVHN, USPS and backbone network is the same as that in ADDA

Method	Domains(source → target)		
	MNIST → USPS	USPS → MNIST	SVHN → MNIST
Source only	0.752	0.571	0.601
Gradient reversal [4]	0.771	0.730	0.739
Domain confusion [15]	0.791	0.665	0.681
CoGAN [9]	**0.912**	0.891	-
ADDA(ADDA-R) [16]	0.910	0.902	0.766
ADDA-S(Ours)	0.899	-	0.794
ADDA-S-MA(Ours)	0.910	0.918	0.827
ADDA-S-MA-KL(Ours)	0.907	**0.924**	**0.878**

Table 2. Average classification accuracy on unsupervised adaptation among MNIST and backbone network is the same as that in Associate Domain Adaption

Method	Domains(source → target)
	SVHN → MNIST
DANN [4]	0.426
DSN w/DANN [1]	0.583
DSN w/MMD [1]	0.323
DA_{assoc} [6]	0.937
Larger-ADDA-S-MA-KL(Ours)	**0.944**

After the completion of the training, we train D and simultaneously fine tune Feature Extractor and fix the Classifier. In particular, we set $\alpha = 10, \beta = 0.4, \gamma = 0.1$ in Eq. 6, then using Adam with 0.0002 to optimize the whole architecture. During testing, because Feature Extractor has two inputs, each target image has to be paired with arbitrary source image and then pass to Feature Extractor together. Because the generative adversarial networks' training is extremely unstable, we repeatedly train the whole architecture six times and report the average classification accuracy of target datasets.

4 Expriments

In order to validate the proposed method, we perform experiments for unsupervised classification adaptation across three different domain shifts. We take three different digits datasets: **MNIST**[1], **USPS**[2], **SVHN**[3]. Consistent

[1] http://yann.lecun.com/exdb/mnist/.
[2] https://www.otexts.org/1577.
[3] http://ufldl.stanford.edu/housenumbers/.

Table 3. Three different networks: the leftmost is the basic network, the middle is deeper network, the rightmost is the basic network with attention mechanism

ConvNet configuration		
Base model	Deeper model	Attention model
conv5-20		
maxpool		
conv5-50		
maxpool		
flatten		
FC-500	FC-500	FC-500
	FC-500	Residual attention model
FC-10		
softmax		

with ADDA, we demonstrate adaptation in three directions: MNIST $\rightarrow$ USPS, USPS $\rightarrow$ MNIST, and SVHN $\rightarrow$ MNIST. The results show that our method achieves comparable performance to the state-of-the-art.

4.1 Setup and Results

For three adaptation, we use the full training sets of the source and target datasets. Following ADDA [16], the size and format of the source dataset and the target dataset pictures are unified. The SourceCNN (TargetCNN), Classifier and Discriminator are provided by ADDA and the different things are that we use the Sigmoid activation function instead of the Relu activation function at the last layer of the SourceCNN and the TargetCNN. The advantage of doing this is to increase the expressive ability of features and simultaneously reduce the information loss. We use ADDA-R, ADDA-S, ADDA-S-MA and ADDA-S-MA-KL represent the initial ADDA provided by [16], the ADDA with sigmoid activation function, the ADDA-S with the proposed Matching Attention mechanism and ADDA-S-MA with the proposed KL loss respectively. Additionally, in order to explore the influence of different network structures, following the Associate Domain Adaption (ADA) [6], we use their classification network as SourceCNN (TargetCNN) to perform the same experiment as above, which is represented as Larger-ADDA-S-MA-KL. All results are shown in Tables 1 and 2. The good results validate the advantages of the KL loss and attention model.

4.2 Analysis

In this section, we mainly analyze the roles of the $\mathcal{L}_{kl}$ and attention model. We compare $\mathcal{L}_{kl}$ values of the four models (ADDA-R, ADDA-S, ADDA-S-MA and ADDA-S-MA-KL) which are taken in Fig. 4. Figure 4 shows that the value

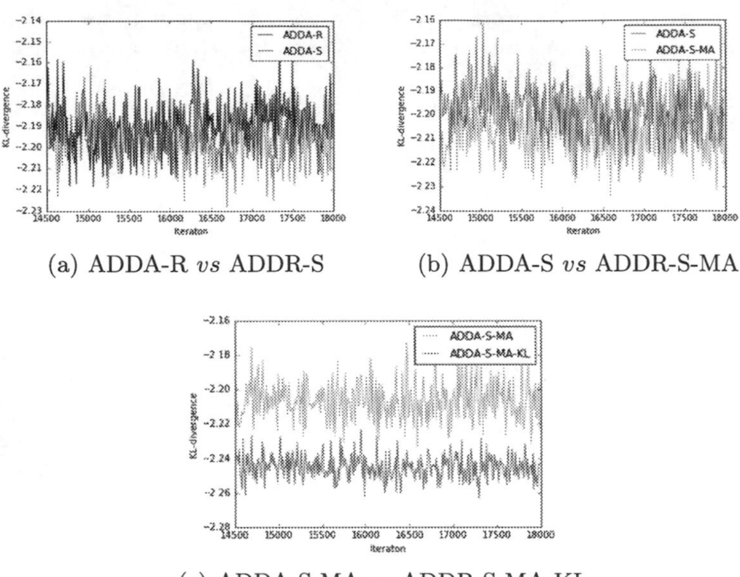

(a) ADDA-R *vs* ADDR-S (b) ADDA-S *vs* ADDR-S-MA

(c) ADDA-S-MA *vs* ADDR-S-MA-KL

Fig. 4. The $\mathcal{L}_{kl}$ values of four models, which can measure the distance between two generated feature distributions (F_S and F_T). It can be seen from figures that ADDA-R is the worst model, ADDA-S-MA-KL is the best model. (a) ADDA-R *vs* ADDR-S. (b) ADDA-S *vs* ADDR-S-MA. (c) ADDA-S-MA *vs* ADDR-S-MA-KL.

of $\mathcal{L}_{kl}$ does correspond to the performance of the trained model. This explains why we choose to propose such a loss function. For attention model, we have an intuition that the reason why attention model can improve the effect is not only that it makes the model notice several pixels of the input, but also it can extract a feature vector with better expressive abilities. The expressive ability of vectors is equivalent to their correlations. How to evaluate the vector correlations is mentioned in paper SVDNet [14]. Given a matrix W : $[\boldsymbol{\omega}_1\, \boldsymbol{\omega}_2\, \ldots\, \boldsymbol{\omega}_k]$, the gamma matrix of W is defined as:

$$
\begin{aligned}
G = W^T W &= \begin{bmatrix} \boldsymbol{\omega}_1^T \boldsymbol{\omega}_1\; \boldsymbol{\omega}_1^T \boldsymbol{\omega}_2 \ldots \boldsymbol{\omega}_1^T \boldsymbol{\omega}_k \\ \boldsymbol{\omega}_2^T \boldsymbol{\omega}_1\; \boldsymbol{\omega}_2^T \boldsymbol{\omega}_2 \ldots \boldsymbol{\omega}_2^T \boldsymbol{\omega}_k \\ \\ \boldsymbol{\omega}_k^T \boldsymbol{\omega}_1\; \boldsymbol{\omega}_k^T \boldsymbol{\omega}_2 \ldots \boldsymbol{\omega}_k^T \boldsymbol{\omega}_k \end{bmatrix} \\
&= \begin{bmatrix} g_{11}\; g_{12} \cdots g_{1k} \\ g_{21}\; g_{22} \cdots g_{2k} \\ \\ g_{k1}\; g_{k2} \cdots g_{kk} \end{bmatrix}
\end{aligned} \tag{8}
$$

where k is the number of vectors in W, g_{ij} are the entries in G, and $\boldsymbol{\omega}_i$ are the weight vectors in W. Thus we can define $S(.)$ as a metric to measure correlation between all the column($\boldsymbol{\omega}_i$) of W:

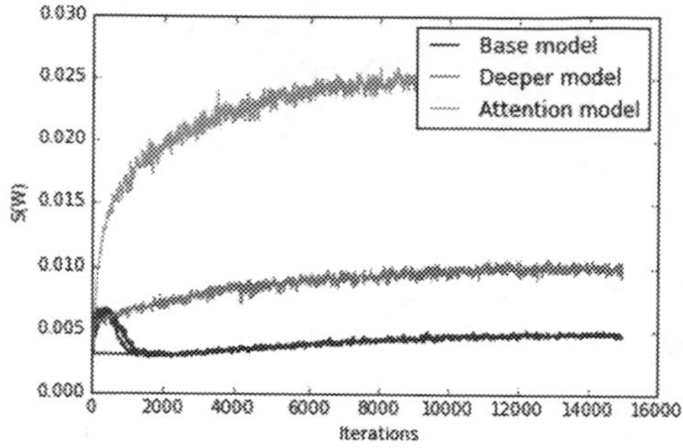

Fig. 5. The S(W) values of the features of the last layer before the softmax layers in three different networks. Network architectures are listed in Table 3 and all three models are trained on SVHN. It can be seen from the line chart that the S(W) values of the feature vector extracted from attention model is larger than other two, which means the feature vector has lower correlations.

$$S(W) = \frac{\sum_{i=1}^{k} g_{ij}}{\sum_{i=1}^{k} \sum_{j=1}^{k} g_{ij}} \tag{9}$$

where S(W) is inversely proportional to correlations.

In our analytical experiments whose architectures are shown in Table 3, we only calculate the S(W) values of the feature vectors of the last layer before the softmax layer in three different networks, the results in Fig. 5 demonstrate that the correlation of features is positively related to the model depth and usage of attention mechanism. Through the comparison, we can find the model with attention mechanism can learn more expressive features than the deep model with the same number of parameters. The discovery also gives birth to a new idea that we can improve shallow model through reducing the correlation of features in different layers.

5 Conclusion

In this paper, we have improved two aspects of the ADDA model. First, we combine the matching gate with attention mechanism and put forward matching attention to learn a feature vector with better expressive ability. Simultaneously, we analyse the attention mechanism and get a conclusion that the model with attention is helpful to generate feature vectors with lower correlation compared with deeper model. Second, we adopt a deterministic function (classification function) to transform a complex and indescribable distribution to a simple and discrete distribution, which makes us be able to use simple KL divergence to measure the difference between two indescribable distributions. Extensive experiments demonstrate that our proposed network achieves state-of-the-art digit recognition performance on three unsupervised adaptation results.

References

1. Bousmalis, K., Silberman, N., Dohan, D., Erhan, D., Krishnan, D.: Unsupervised pixel-level domain adaptation with generative adversarial networks. In: The IEEE Conference on Computer Vision and Pattern Recognition (CVPR), vol. 1, p. 7 (2017)
2. Chen, L., et al.: SCA-CNN: spatial and channel-wise attention in convolutional networks for image captioning. In: IEEE Conference on Computer Vision and Pattern Recognition, pp. 6298–6306 (2017)
3. Ganin, Y.: Unsupervised domain adaptation by backpropagation. In: International Conference on International Conference on Machine Learning, pp. 1180–1189 (2015)
4. Ganin, Y., et al.: Domain-adversarial training of neural networks. J. Mach. Learn. Res. **17**(59), 1–35 (2016)
5. Goodfellow, I.J., et al.: Generative adversarial networks. Adv. Neural Inf. Process. Syst. **3**, 2672–2680 (2014)
6. Haeusser, P., Frerix, T., Mordvintsev, A., Cremers, D.: Associative domain adaptation. In: IEEE International Conference on Computer Vision, pp. 2784–2792 (2017)
7. Hu, J., Shen, L., Sun, G.: Squeeze-and-excitation networks. arXiv preprint arXiv:1709.01507 (2017)
8. Johnson, J., Alahi, A., Fei-Fei, L.: Perceptual losses for real-time style transfer and super-resolution. In: Leibe, B., Matas, J., Sebe, N., Welling, M. (eds.) ECCV 2016. LNCS, vol. 9906, pp. 694–711. Springer, Cham (2016). https://doi.org/10.1007/978-3-319-46475-6_43
9. Liu, M.Y., Tuzel, O.: Coupled generative adversarial networks. In: Advances in Neural Information Processing Systems, pp. 469–477 (2016)
10. Long, M., Cao, Y., Wang, J., Jordan, M.I.: Learning transferable features with deep adaptation networks. In: International Conference on Machine Learning, pp. 97–105 (2015)
11. Long, M., Zhu, H., Wang, J., Jordan, M.I.: Deep transfer learning with joint adaptation networks. arXiv preprint arXiv:1605.06636 (2016)
12. Sun, B., Feng, J., Saenko, K.: Return of frustratingly easy domain adaptation. In: National Conference on Artificial Intelligence, pp. 2058–2065 (2016)
13. Sun, B., Saenko, K.: Deep CORAL: correlation alignment for deep domain adaptation. In: Hua, G., Jégou, H. (eds.) ECCV 2016. LNCS, vol. 9915, pp. 443–450. Springer, Cham (2016). https://doi.org/10.1007/978-3-319-49409-8_35
14. Sun, Y., Zheng, L., Deng, W., Wang, S.: SVDNet for pedestrian retrieval. In: IEEE International Conference on Computer Vision, pp. 3820–3828 (2017)
15. Tzeng, E., Hoffman, J., Darrell, T., Saenko, K.: Simultaneous deep transfer across domains and tasks. In: 2015 IEEE International Conference on Computer Vision (ICCV), pp. 4068–4076. IEEE (2015)
16. Tzeng, E., Hoffman, J., Saenko, K., Darrell, T.: Adversarial discriminative domain adaptation. In: IEEE Conference on Computer Vision and Pattern Recognition, pp. 2962–2971 (2017)
17. Tzeng, E., Hoffman, J., Zhang, N., Saenko, K., Darrell, T.: Deep domain confusion: maximizing for domain invariance. In: Computer Vision and Pattern Recognition, arXiv (2014)

18. Varior, R.R., Haloi, M., Wang, G.: Gated Siamese convolutional neural network architecture for human re-identification. In: Leibe, B., Matas, J., Sebe, N., Welling, M. (eds.) ECCV 2016. LNCS, vol. 9912, pp. 791–808. Springer, Cham (2016). https://doi.org/10.1007/978-3-319-46484-8_48
19. Wang, F., et al.: Residual attention network for image classification. In: Computer Vision and Pattern Recognition, pp. 6450–6458 (2017)
20. Williams, R.J.: Simple statistical gradient-following algorithms for connectionist reinforcement learning. Mach. Learn. **8**(3–4), 229–256 (1992). https://doi.org/10.1007/BF00992696
21. Xu, K., et al.: Show, attend and tell: neural image caption generation with visual attention. In: Computer Science, pp. 2048–2057 (2015)

Attention Based Meta Path Fusion for Heterogeneous Information Network Embedding

Houye Ji, Chuan Shi(✉), and Bai Wang

Beijing University of Posts and Telecommunications, Beijing, China
{jhy1993,shichuan,wangbai}@bupt.edu.cn

Abstract. Recently, there is a surge of network embedding algorithms, which embed information network into a low dimensional space. However, contemporary network embedding algorithms focus on homogeneous networks, while we know that many real-world systems can be constructed with heterogeneous information networks (HINs). Compare to homogeneous networks, HINs contain heterogeneity types of nodes and edges, which leads to new challenges for traditional network embedding: handing mixed heterogeneous nodes and fusing rich semantic information. Although several HIN embedding algorithms have been proposed, these challenges have not been well dressed. How to explore the rich semantic information and integrate these information still remain to be solved. In this paper, we propose a novel attention based meta path fusion model for HIN embedding (called AMPE). In order to handle node heterogeneity and extract rich information, AMPE first extracts multiple homogeneous networks from HIN with meta paths, and then employs adopted AutoEncoders to embed these homogeneous networks. After that, AMPE fuses these embeddings learned from homogeneous networks with attention mechanism. Experimental results on two real-world datasets demonstrate the effectiveness of the proposed model.

1 Introduction

Recent years, network representation learning [1–3] (e.g. network embedding) has attracted a great deal of attention. The goal of network representation learning is to embed a network into a low dimensional latent space, in which each node is represented as a latent vector. Such representations can preserve the proximities between the nodes, which can be treated as feature vectors and applied in subsequent data mining tasks, such as node classification, community detection and link prediction.

However, most network embedding algorithms focus on homogeneous network containing the same types of node or edge. In the real world, networks usually contain multiple types of nodes or edges, named heterogeneous information networks (HINs). Since HINs can model much more complex relationships and structures than homogeneous information networks, it has been widely used

X. Geng and B.-H. Kang (Eds.): PRICAI 2018, LNAI 11012, pp. 348–360, 2018.
https://doi.org/10.1007/978-3-319-97304-3_27

in graph mining [4,5]. Meanwhile, meta path [4], a relation composition connecting two types of nodes, has been widely used to capture rich semantic information contained in HIN. Taking Fig. 1(b) as an example, a meta path between two businesses can be Business-City-Business, which means these businesses located in the same city. Due to the complexity of HIN, traditional homogeneous network embedding methods cannot be directly applied to HIN because of the following two reasons:

(1) Heterogeneous information networks have various types of nodes and edges. How to preserve the heterogeneous neighbors of each node is an urgent problem that need to be solved. (2) Heterogeneous information networks contain rich and complex semantic information. How to extract and fuse these information is an open problem. A novel fusion model that can select some useful information and combine them will be desired.

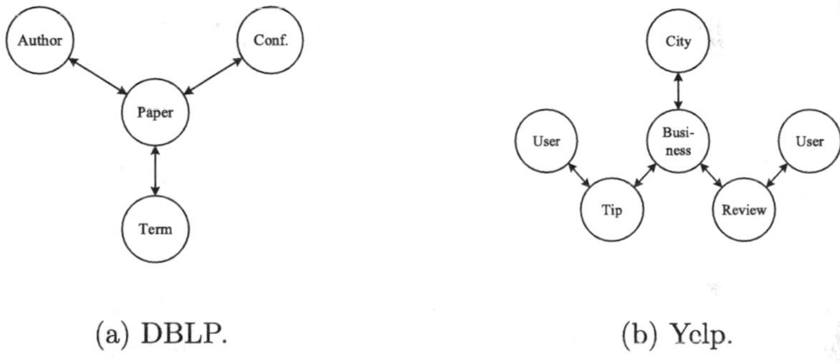

(a) DBLP. (b) Yelp.

Fig. 1. Two examples of heterogeneous information network in experiments.

Some HIN embedding algorithms have been proposed to overcome above challenges. Dong et al. [6] introduce meta path based random walk to embed heterogeneous network, which only utilizes single meta path to extract semantic information. HIN2Vec [7] is designed to capture the semantic embedded by exploiting different meta paths among nodes. Esim [8] tries to capture semantic information from multiple meta paths. However, it relies heavily on user-specified meta path and adopts grid search to obtain the weights of meta paths. The network embedding algorithms aforementioned usually embed the semantic information via random walk model, which maybe unable to fully capture the deep semantic information. What's more, since HINs contain rich semantic information, instead of utilizing a single meta path, the combination of multiple meta paths can give a more comprehensive description of HINs.

To better solve challenges faced by HIN embedding, we propose a novel **A**ttention based **M**eta **P**ath fusion heterogeneous network **E**mbedding model, named AMPE, which can embed various kinds of semantic information extracted from multiple meta paths and fuses them for specific tasks. In AMPE, we first transform the original heterogeneous network into several homogeneous networks based on corresponding meta paths. Then AMPE extends AutoEncoder to the heterogeneous scenario that can extensively embed these semantics information simultaneously. Significantly different from current weight learning for meta paths, we propose an attention based deep fusion module, which can weight the importance of each meta path and fuses them for specific tasks.

The remainder of this paper is organized as follows. We first review the related work in Sects. 2 and 3 gives the preliminary concepts in heterogeneous information network. In Sect. 4, we introduce the proposed model in details. Datasets and experiments are presented in Sect. 5. Finally, some conclusions and future works are showed in Sect. 6.

2 Related Work

Originally, network embedding algorithms were proposed to embed network into a low dimensional latent space, in which each node is represented as a latent vector. The motivation behind those algorithms is to preserve the structural information of nodes, so the learned embeddings can be applied to further data mining tasks.

Recently, some network embedding algorithms based on random walk and deep learning have been proposed. Inspired by word embedding [9], DeepWalk [10] embeds network structures by truncated random walk. Along with DeepWalk, node2vec [11] designs a biased random walk to sample the neighbors. Meanwhile, LINE [12] is an efficient network embedding method that can deal with large-scale networks. Wang et al. [13] introduce deep learning to perform network embedding. However, all of these algorithms cannot be applied to HINs directly because they didn't consider the heterogeneity of HINs.

There are also some heterogeneous network embedding algorithms. Esim [8] proposes a meta path guided embedding method to perform similarity search for HINs. Metapath2vec [6] designs a meta path based random walk and apply skip-gram to learn network representations. HIN2Vec [7] captures the rich semantics information in HINs by exploiting different types of relationships among nodes. However, most of existing methods can't learn the importance of meta paths and combine them for specific tasks.

3 Preliminaries

A heterogeneous information network is a special kind of information network, denoted as $\mathcal{G} = (\mathcal{V}, \mathcal{E})$, which consists of an object set $\mathcal{V}$ and a link set $\mathcal{E}$. A HIN is also associated with a node type mapping function $\phi : \mathcal{V} \rightarrow \mathcal{A}$ and a link type mapping function $\psi : \mathcal{E} \rightarrow \mathcal{R}$. $\mathcal{A}$ and $\mathcal{R}$ denote the sets of predefined object types and link types, where $|\mathcal{A}| + |\mathcal{R}| > 2$.

The complexity of heterogeneous information network drives us to provide the meta level (i.e., schema-level) description for understanding the object types and link types better in the network. Given the typed essence, a HIN can be abstracted as a network schema, denoted as $\mathcal{S} = (\mathcal{A}, \mathcal{R})$ [5,14], which is a meta template define over object types. Figure 1 gives network schemas on both DBLP and Yelp.

A meta path Φ [4] is a path defined on a schema $\mathcal{S} = (\mathcal{A}, \mathcal{R})$, and denoted in the form of $A_1 \xrightarrow{R_1} A_2 \xrightarrow{R_2} \ldots \xrightarrow{R_l} A_{l+1}$. Given a meta path Φ, we can translate the original HIN G into a homogeneous network G_Φ which can capture the semantic information of meta path. The adjacency matrix of G_Φ can be represented as $M_\Phi \in \mathbb{R}^{n \cdot n}$, where $M_\Phi(i,j) = 1$ iff node i connects to node j via meta path Φ.

4 The Proposed Method

In this section, we propose a novel deep model to embed nodes in HIN into low-dimensional vectors, called AMPE. AMPE is composed of three major components. First, we transform the original HIN into several homogeneous networks. After that, AMPE embeds these homogeneous network simultaneously by an adopted AutoEncoders. Finally, AMPE can learn the weight of each meta path based embedding and fuses them via attention mechanism. Figure 2 presents the framework of AMPE.

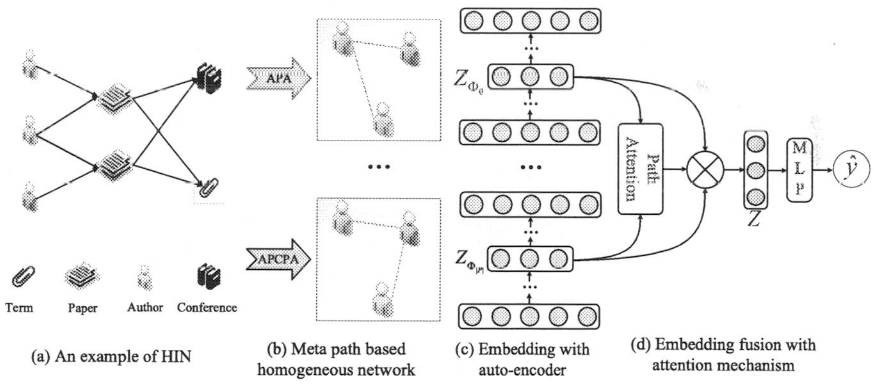

Fig. 2. The framework illustration of the proposed AMPE approach.

4.1 Meta Path Based Homogeneous Network

Heterogeneous information networks usually have various kinds of complex semantic information. Here we utilize a set of meta paths (e.g., $\Phi_0, \Phi_1, \ldots, \Phi_{|P|}$) to extract semantic information and transform the original HIN G into several homogeneous networks (e.g., $G_{\Phi_0}, G_{\Phi_1}, \ldots, G_{\Phi_{|P|}}$). Each homogeneous network G_Φ contains one type of semantic information which means every node is connected to its neighbors through meta path Φ. Here we give the adjacency matrix of each homogeneous network G_Φ, denoted as M_Φ. In homogeneous network G_Φ, if node i is connected to node j through meta path Φ, then $M_\Phi(i,j) = 1$.

4.2 Homogeneous Network Embedding via AutoEncoder

After obtaining several meta path based homogeneous networks, we extend traditional AutoEncoder to embed these homogeneous networks simultaneously.

Here we give a brief review of AutoEncoder. AutoEncoder [15] is an unsupervised deep learning model that can copy its input to its output. It usually involves two parts: encoder, which encodes the original feature representations into a latent space; decoder, which try to reconstruct the original representations from latent space. Formally, let x_i denotes the original feature representation of node i, and $\{y_i^1, y_i^2, \ldots, y_i^k\}$ denote the hidden representation of each encoder layer. The relationships between these representations can be shown as follows:

$$y_i^1 = \sigma(W^1 x_i + b^1), \tag{1}$$

$$y_i^k = \sigma(W^k y^{k-1} + b^k), k = 2, \ldots, K, \tag{2}$$

$$z_i = \sigma(W^{K+1} y_i^k + b^{K+1}). \tag{3}$$

Here z_i means the learned representation and σ is sigmoid function. After obtaining z_i, we try to reconstruct the original representation, denoted as $\hat{x}_i$. In decoder, the latent representations of hidden layers can be denoted as $\{\hat{y}_i^k, \hat{y}_i^{k-1}, \ldots, \hat{y}_i^1\}$ and the relationships between them can be shown as follows:

$$\hat{y}^K = \sigma(\hat{W}^{K+1} z_i + \hat{b}^{K+1}), \tag{4}$$

$$\hat{y}_i^{k-1} = \sigma(\hat{W}^k \hat{y}^k + \hat{b}^k), k = 2, \ldots, K, \tag{5}$$

$$\hat{x}_i = \sigma(\hat{W}^1 \hat{y}_i^1 + \hat{b}^1). \tag{6}$$

The learning process of AutoEncoder is to minimize the distance between the original feature representation x_i and the reconstructed representation $\hat{x}_i$, denoted as follows:

$$L = \sum_{i=1}^{n} ||x_i - \hat{x}_i||_2^2. \tag{7}$$

Unfortunately, such an AutoEncoder cannot directly be applied to network embedding due to the sparsity problem, which means the number of zero elements in adjacency matrix is far more than non-zero elements. In order to solve this problem, we impose more penalty on non-zero elements. Then AutoEncoder will pay more attention to these non-zero elements and gives priority to reconstructing them. The modified loss function can be shown as follows:

$$L = \sum_{i=1}^{n} ||(x_i - \hat{x}_i) \odot b_i||_2^2 = ||(\hat{X} - X) \odot B||_F^2. \tag{8}$$

where $\odot$ means Hadamard product, b_i is a weight vector and $b_{i,j} = x_{i,j} * (\beta - 1) + 1$. Here β is penalty coefficient.

By fitting these AutoEncoders adjacency matrix of each homogeneous network simultaneously, we can obtain a group of node embeddings. The overall loss function for these AutoEncoders can be summarized as below:

$$L_{ae} = \sum_{i=1}^{|P|} ||(\widehat{X_{\Phi_i}} - X_{\Phi_i}) \odot B_{\Phi_i}||_F^2. \tag{9}$$

After training these AutoEncoders, we can obtain $|P|$ groups of node embeddings, denoted as $\{Z_{\Phi_0}, Z_{\Phi_1}, \ldots, Z_{\Phi_{|P|}}\}$.

4.3 Fusing Embeddings via Attention Mechanism

After obtaining $|P|$ groups of node embeddings, the proposed AMPE can automatically fuse these embeddings and learn their importances via attention mechanism for the specific task. The fusion process F can be shown as follows:

$$Z = F(Z_{\Phi_0}, Z_{\Phi_1}, \ldots, Z_{\Phi_{|P|}}). \tag{10}$$

Inspired by the attention mechanism in neural machine translation [16], we define the attention value as follows:

$$att'_{\Phi_i} = h^T \cdot Tanh(W \cdot Z_{\Phi_i} + b), \tag{11}$$

$$att_{\Phi_i} = \frac{exp(att'_{\Phi_i})}{\sum_{i=1}^{|P|} exp(att'_{\Phi_i})}, \tag{12}$$

where W is a weight matrix, b is a bias vector, h is weight vector, att_{Φ_i} is the weight of meta path Φ_i. Obviously, the higher att_{Φ_i}, the more important meta path Φ_i is. With the learned weights as coefficients, we can weight combine these embeddings to obtain the final embedding. The final embedding Z is shown as follows:

$$Z = \sum_{i=1}^{|P|} att_{\Phi_i} \cdot Z_{\Phi_i}. \tag{13}$$

Then we can apply the final embedding to specific tasks and learn the attention value via the back propagation algorithm. For example, in node classification, we try to minimize the *Cross Entropy* between the ground-truth and the predictions:

$$L_{att} = -\sum y_i \log(wz_i), \tag{14}$$

where w is the parameter of the classifier, y_i is the label of z_i. With the guide of labeled data, we can optimize the proposed model and learn the weights of meta paths. Here we only need a few labeled data to fine-tune the pre-trained AutoEncoders.

Table 1. Statistics of the datasets

Dataset	Relations (A-B)	Number of A	Number of B	Number of A-B	Avg. degree of A	Avg. degree of B
DBLP	Paper-Author	14328	4057	19645	1.3	4.8
	Paper-Conf	14328	20	14328	1.0	716.4
	Paper-Term	14327	8789	88420	6.2	10.1
Yelp	Business-City	4352	253	4352	1.0	17.2
	Business-Tip	4352	41359	52262	12.0	1.3
	Tip-User	41359	25608	42262	1.0	1.7
	User-Review	125684	176860	176860	1.4	1.0
	Review-Business	176860	4352	176860	1.0	40.6

5 Experiments

5.1 Datesets

To verify the effectiveness of the proposed AMPE, we conduct some experiments on two real-world datasets. The detailed descriptions of these datasets are shown in Table 1, and their schemas are shown in Fig. 1.

- **DBLP**[1]. We extracted a subset of DBLP which contains papers (P), authors (A), conferences (C), terms (T). We obtain the ground truth from the dataset $dblp - 4area$ [4], which labels each author according to their research area. Here we employ the meta path set {APA, APCPA, APTPA} to extract homogeneous networks.
- **Yelp**[2]. We extracted businesses located in North Carolina (NC), Wisconsin (WI), Pennsylvania (PA) and Edinburgh (EDH). Then we constructed a HIN that comprises businesses (B), users (U), cities (C), reviews (R) and tips (T). We employ the meta path set {BCB, BRURB, BTUTB} to extract homogeneous networks. Here we use the state information provided in the dataset as the ground truth.

5.2 Baselines

We compare with the following network embedding methods:

- DeepWalk [10]: A random walk based network embedding method for homogeneous network. Here we run DeepWalk on whole HIN and ignore the heterogeneity of nodes.
- AE [15]: A deep AutoEncoder (AE) that can embed networks via a series of non-linear mappings. Here we only report the best result of single meta path.

[1] https://dblp.uni-trier.de.

[2] https://www.yelp.com/dataset/download.

- AE_{concat}: A variant of the AutoEncoder model. We first apply AutoEncoders to learn node representations for each meta path, and concatenate them as the final representation.
- Metapath2vec [6]: A heterogeneous network embedding method which can embed the semantic information extract from a single meta path. Here we only report the best result of single meta path.
- ESim [8]: A heterogeneous network embedding method which can capture semantics information from multiple meta paths. Since it is difficult to search the weights of a set of meta paths, we assign the weights learned from AMPE to ESim.
- $AMPE_{avg}$: A variant of the proposed AMPE. We treat all meta paths equally and average the learned embeddings.
- AMPE: Our proposed approach for heterogeneous network embedding, which can fuse multiple meta paths according to their importances.

5.3 Parameter Settings

For DBLP, the architecture of AutoEncoder is 4057-1000-100-1000-4057 and β is set to 30. We use RMSprop to optimize AMPE and the learning rate is 0.001. Here we select 400 labeled data to fine-tune the AutoEncoder and learn the weights of meta paths. For Yelp, the architecture of AutoEncoder is 4352-100-4352. Here we utilize 200 balanced labeled data to fine-tune the model. Since such an AutoEncoder already work well, we don't need a deeper model.

For DeepWalk and metapath2vec, we set window size as 5, walk length as 20, walks per node as 40, num of negative samples as 5. For a fair comparison, we set embedding dimension as 100 for all above algorithms.

Table 2. Quantitative results on the node classification task

Datasets	Algorithms	30%		50%		70%	
		Macro-F1	Micro-F1	Macro-F1	Micor-F1	Macro-F1	Micro-F1
DBLP	DeepWalk	0.7456	0.7488	0.7785	0.7785	0.7930	0.7947
	AE	0.8928	0.8931	0.8978	0.8979	0.8894	0.8998
	AE_{concat}	0.8889	0.9055	0.9068	0.9068	0.9086	0.9086
	metapath2vec	0.8894	0.8889	0.8910	0.8905	0.8991	0.8998
	ESim	0.9135	0.9144	0.9125	0.9134	0.9172	0.9177
	$AMPE_{avg}$	0.9042	0.9041	0.9087	0.9085	0.9136	0.9138
	AMPE	**0.9237**	**0.9239**	**0.9239**	**0.9239**	**0.9248**	**0.9248**
Yelp	DeepWalk	0.8970	0.8970	0.9189	0.9233	0.9333	0.9378
	AE	0.9218	0.9272	0.9500	0.9522	0.9606	0.9642
	AE_{concat}	0.9491	0.9639	0.9808	0.9844	0.9846	0.9879
	metapath2vec	0.9728	0.9690	0.9760	0.9718	0.9742	0.9688
	Esim	0.9818	0.9793	0.9882	0.9890	0.9890	0.9890
	$AMPE_{avg}$	0.9510	0.9673	0.9682	0.9771	0.9746	0.9824
	AMPE	**0.9855**	**0.9866**	**0.9926**	**0.9927**	**0.9968**	**0.9965**

5.4 Classification

We start by conducting a task of multi-label classification to evaluate the effectiveness of the proposed model. First, we randomly divide the dataset into training set and test set. Then, we utilize KNN classifier with $k = 5$ to predict the labels of the test samples. We repeat the process for 10 times and report the average Macro-F1 and Micro-F1. The results are presented in Table 2.

The results show that, by distinguishing the importances of meta paths, AMPE achieves the best performance. Compare to HIN embedding methods, homogeneous network embedding methods including DeepWalk and AutoEncoder fail to perform well. For HIN embedding, through integrating multiple meta paths to perform HIN embedding, ESim and AMPE perform much better than other methods. Taking one step further, with weight learning for meta paths, AMPE performs much better than AMPE$_{avg}$. Overall, by utilizing deep model to embed and fusing semantics information extracted from HIN, AMPE achieves the best results in node classification task.

Table 3. Quantitative results on the node clustering task

Algorithms	DBLP	Yelp
DeepWalk	0.6656	0.6460
AE	0.6647	0.6631
AE$_{concat}$	0.6874	0.6386
metapath2vec	0.7195	0.8563
ESim	0.6205	0.6292
AMPE$_{avg}$	0.5225	0.6578
AMPE	**0.7474**	**0.9681**

5.5 Clustering

We also conduct clustering task to evaluate the embeddings learned from above algorithms. Here we introduce the K-Means to perform node clustering and use NMI to evaluate the performances. Since the performance of K-Means is affected by initial centroids, we repeat the process for 10 times and report the average results. The results are shown in Table 3.

It's obviously that AMPE performs better than all baselines. Similar to the node classification, homogeneous network embedding methods fail to perform well. It's interesting that AMPE$_{avg}$ has the worst performance in DBLP. We will explain this phenomenon by analysing the attention value in next section. Besides, by concatenating the embeddings learned from different meta paths, the AE$_{concat}$ also performs well. Generally speaking, AMPE can give a comprehensive description of HIN.

5.6 Analysis of Attention Mechanism

An interesting characteristic of AMPE is that it can learn the importances of meta paths via attention mechanism. In Fig. 3, we record the performances based on single meta path and corresponding attention value. For DBLP, AMPE gives APCPA the highest weight, which means AMPE considers the APCPA to be the most important meta path in identifying the author's research area. This is reasonable because we labeled the authors according to the conferences they submit. Meanwhile, APA cannot identify the author's research area. If we treat these meta paths equally (e.g., AMPE_{avg}), the performance will drop significantly. For Yelp, the results show that AMPE gives the largest weight to BRURB. One possible explanation is that users usually visit and review the businesses which is located near to their home for convenience. Obviously, there is a positive correlation between performance of single meta path and its attention value. It proves that the proposed AMPE can reveal the difference among these meta paths and weights them properly.

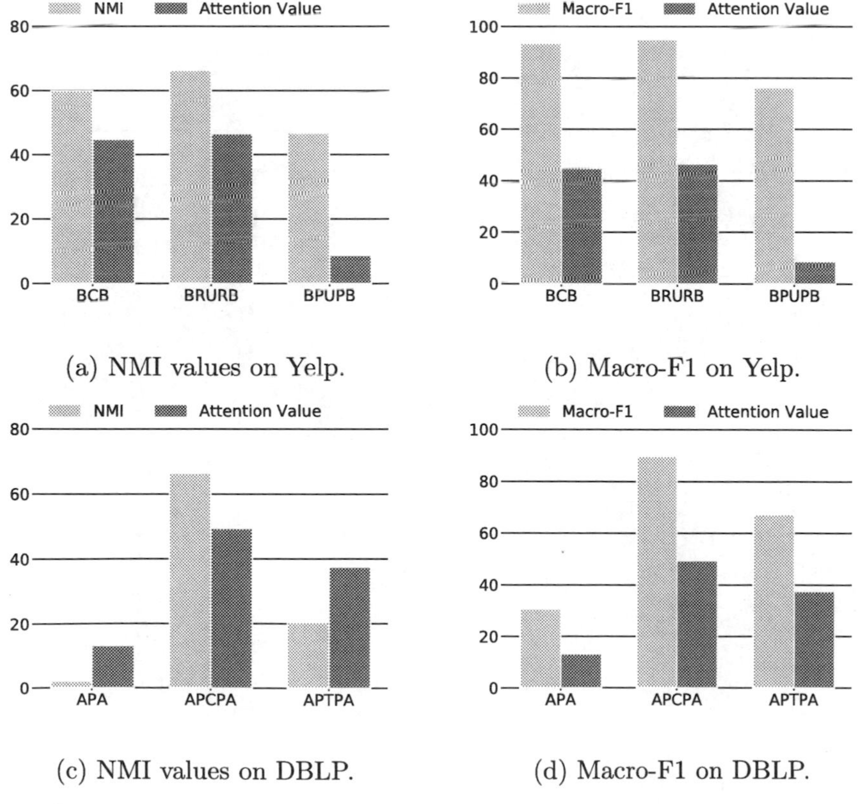

Fig. 3. Performance of single meta path and corresponding attention value.

5.7 Visualization

For a more intuitive comparison, we visualize the learned embeddings on a 2-dimensional space. Here we utilize t-SNE to visualize the author embedding in DBLP. The results are shown in Fig. 4.

It's obvious that single AutoEncoder barely separates the authors from different groups (represented by the same color), but the distribution of blue points are scattered. Deepwalk can basically separate the authors without sharp boundaries. Metapath2vec performs much better than above methods, but the boundary is still blurry. Finally, AMPE achieves the best performance among these methods, since it can separate the authors in different research area clearly with obvious borders among these clusters.

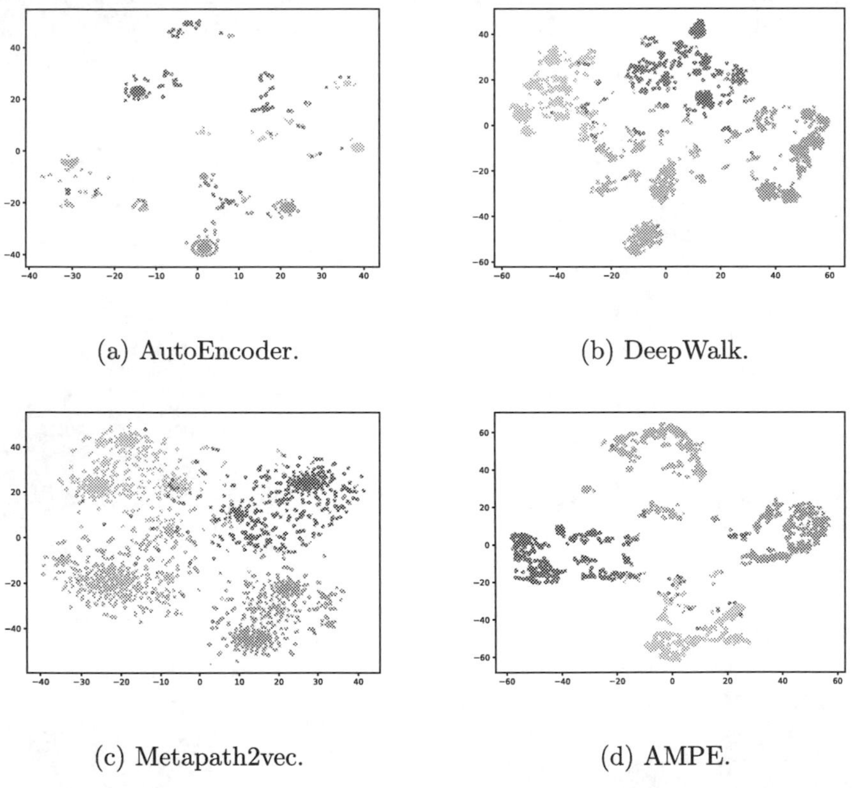

(a) AutoEncoder. (b) DeepWalk.

(c) Metapath2vec. (d) AMPE.

Fig. 4. Visualization results on DBLP. (Color figure online)

5.8 Parameters Experiments

Here we investigate the sensitivity of different parameters in our model, including embedding dimension and non-zero element penalty β. We first compare the performances of AMPE on DBLP with various numbers of embedding dimensions.

The results are shown in Fig. 5. We can see that with the growth of embedding dimension, the performance raises first and then remains stable. The reason is that AMPE needs a suitable dimension to encode these semantics information and larger dimension may introduce some redundancies. Then we show how the β affects the performances. Large β means that the model will pay more attention to non-zero elements. From the Fig. 5, We can see that AMPE achieves the best performance with a balanced β.

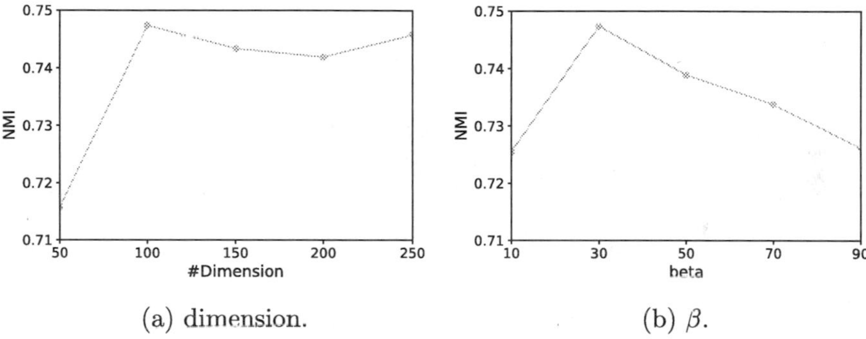

(a) dimension. (b) β.

Fig. 5. Parameter study on the number of embedding dimensions and the value of non-zeros element penalty β.

6 Conclusion

In this paper, we study the problem of heterogeneous information network embedding, which aims to embed heterogeneous information network into a low-dimensional space. And we propose a novel heterogeneous information network embedding model, named AMPE, which can capture rich semantics information in HIN and fuses them for specific tasks. By extending the AutoEncoder to the heterogeneous scenario, AMPE can embed the semantics information extracted by meta paths simultaneously. In addition, the proposed AMPE can combine these information via attention mechanism. Experiment results including node classification and node clustering demonstrate the effectiveness of AMPE.

Acknowledgments. This work is supported by the National Natural Science Foundation of China (No. 61772082, 61375058), the National Key Research and Development Pro- gram of China (2017YFB0803304), and the Beijing Municipal Natural Science Foundation (4182043).

References

1. Cui, P., Wang, X., Pei, J., Zhu, W.: A survey on network embedding. arXiv preprint arXiv:1711.08752 (2017)
2. Goyal, P., Ferrara, E.: Graph embedding techniques, applications, and performance: a survey. arXiv preprint arXiv:1705.02801 (2017)
3. Zhang, D., Yin, J., Zhu, X., Zhang, C.: Network representation learning: a survey. arXiv preprint arXiv:1801.05852 (2017)
4. Sun, Y., Han, J., Yan, X., Yu, P.S., Wu, T.: PathSim: meta path-based top-k similarity search in heterogeneous information networks. Proc. VLDB Endow. **4**(11), 992–1003 (2011)
5. Sun, Y., Han, J.: Mining heterogeneous information networks: a structural analysis approach. ACM SIGKDD Explor. Newsl. **14**(2), 20–28 (2013)
6. Dong, Y., Chawla, N.V., Swami, A.: metapath2vec: Scalable representation learning for heterogeneous networks. In: Proceedings of the 23rd ACM SIGKDD International Conference on Knowledge Discovery and Data Mining, pp. 135–144. ACM (2017)
7. Fu, T.Y., Lee, W.C., Lei, Z.: Hin2vec: explore meta-paths in heterogeneous information networks for representation learning. In: Proceedings of the 2017 ACM on Conference on Information and Knowledge Management, pp. 1797–1806. ACM (2017)
8. Shang, J., Qu, M., Liu, J., Kaplan, L.M., Han, J., Peng, J.: Meta-path guided embedding for similarity search in large-scale heterogeneous information networks. CoRR abs/1610.09769 (2016)
9. Mikolov, T., Sutskever, I., Chen, K., Corrado, G.S., Dean, J.: Distributed representations of words and phrases and their compositionality. In: Advances in Neural Information Processing Systems, pp. 3111–3119 (2013)
10. Perozzi, B., Al-Rfou, R., Skiena, S.: DeepWalk: online learning of social representations. In: Proceedings of the 20th ACM SIGKDD International Conference on Knowledge Discovery and Data Mining, pp. 701–710. ACM (2014)
11. Grover, A., Leskovec, J.: node2vec: Scalable feature learning for networks. In: Proceedings of the 22nd ACM SIGKDD International Conference on Knowledge Discovery and Data Mining, pp. 855–864. ACM (2016)
12. Tang, J., Qu, M., Wang, M., Zhang, M., Yan, J., Mei, Q.: Line: large-scale information network embedding. In: Proceedings of the 24th International Conference on World Wide Web, International World Wide Web Conferences Steering Committee, pp. 1067–1077 (2015)
13. Wang, D., Cui, P., Zhu, W.: Structural deep network embedding. In: Proceedings of the 22nd ACM SIGKDD International Conference on Knowledge Discovery and Data Mining, pp. 1225–1234. ACM (2016)
14. Sun, Y., Yu, Y., Han, J.: Ranking-based clustering of heterogeneous information networks with star network schema. In: Proceedings of the 15th ACM SIGKDD International Conference on Knowledge Discovery and Data Mining, pp. 797–806. ACM (2009)
15. Bengio, Y., Lamblin, P., Popovici, D., Larochelle, H.: Greedy layer-wise training of deep networks. In: Advances in Neural Information Processing Systems, pp. 153–160 (2007)
16. Bahdanau, D., Cho, K., Bengio, Y.: Neural machine translation by jointly learning to align and translate. arXiv preprint arXiv:1409.0473 (2014)

An Efficient Auction with Variable Reserve Prices for Ridesourcing

Chaoli Zhang[1], Fan Wu[1(✉)], and Xiaohui Bei[2]

[1] Shanghai Jiao Tong University, Shanghai, China
{chaoli_zhang,fwu}@sjtu.edu.cn
[2] Nanyang Technological University, Singapore, Singapore
xhbei@ntu.edu.sg

Abstract. Ridesourcing refers to the service that matches passengers who need a car to personal drivers. In this work, we study an auction model for ridesourcing that sells multiple items to unit-demand single-parameter agents with variable reserve price constraints. In this model, there is an externally imposed reserve price set for every item, and the price is both item- and bidder-dependent. Such auctions can also find applications in a number of other traditional and online markets, such as ad auction or online laboring market.

Our main result is a truthful, individually rational, and computationally efficient mechanism that respects the reserve price constraints and always achieves at least half of the optimal social benefit (*i.e.*, the sum of the valuations of the winning agents). Furthermore, we show such efficiency approximation is tight by proving that even without any computational constraints, no truthful and individually rational mechanism can achieve better than 2-approximation for social benefit maximization. Finally, we evaluate the performance of our mechanism based on real taxi-trace data. The empirical results show that our mechanism outperforms other benchmark mechanisms in terms of both social benefit and revenue.

Keywords: Ridesourcing · Reserve Prices Auction

1 Introduction

Ridesourcing provides a wealth of efficiency and flexibility to urban transportation and has been injected new vigor in recent years due to the popularization of smartphones[1]. More specifically, an online transportation network company

This work was supported in part by the State Key Development Program for Basic Research of China (973 project 2014CB340303), in part by China NSF grant 61672348, 61672353, and 61472252, and in part by Shanghai Science and Technology fund 15220721300. The opinions, findings, conclusions, and recommendations expressed in this paper are those of the authors and do not necessarily reflect the views of the funding agencies or the government.

[1] Example companies in this domain include Lyft, Uber, Didi, etc.

X. Geng and B.-H. Kang (Eds.): PRICAI 2018, LNAI 11012, pp. 361–374, 2018.
https://doi.org/10.1007/978-3-319-97304-3_28

takes ride requests from passengers, and dispatches the available cars in the nearby location to serve the passengers. There are two fundamental functions of such platforms: ride-matching (*i.e.*, assigning the drivers to the passengers) and pricing [7].

The above ridesourcing scenario can be modeled as a single-parameter auction design problem: each passenger has a single-parameter valuation for getting a ride. As one of the classical mechanism design problems, auctions have been widely studied as a powerful instrument for resource allocation due to their perceived fairness and allocation efficiency. In addition, each potential ride has a *reserve price*, usually set by the government as a regulation, so as to guarantee the minimum profit from each ride and to prevent destructive competition, which is determined mainly by the driver's cost (*i.e.*, fuel consumption and labor time, etc.) or some other factors of the driver (*i.e.*, different drivers may have different critical values for a ride picking). Hence these reserve prices would depend on not only the trip length, but the locations of the driver and the passenger, as the driver needs to pick up the passenger before continuing their ride. It is reasonable and necessary to set different reserve prices for different passengers when they are to be allocated to different drivers.

Reserve price has been a salient feature in many single-parameter auctions and many practical scenarios, such as online auction markets like eBay [3], either to boost the revenue [16], or to favor a particular group of agents [15]. However, in most previous works, the reserve price is set by the auctioneer and only simple and symmetric price rules are considered. That is, either the auctioned item has a common reserve price for all agents, or in certain cases, though the price can be set differently for different agents, different units of the same item always have the same reserve price.

In this paper, we study a simple auction model that captures the most salient aspect of the ridesourcing problem above. Our goal is to design mechanisms that is truthful and individually rational, with the objective of maximizing the *social benefit* of the allocation, defined as the sum of valuations of all agents who win an item individually.

1.1 Our Results

Our results in this paper are listed as follows.

- We propose a truthful, individually rational, and 2-approximation mechanism in terms of social benefit for the auctions with variable reserve prices.
- We also exploit limitations of auctions with variable reserve prices, and show that when restricted to truthful and individually rational mechanisms, the 2-approximation social benefit guarantee of our mechanism is optimal.
- Finally, we demonstrate the performance of our mechanism in a case study that considers taxi matching using real taxi-trace data. Experiment results show that our mechanism outperforms other benchmark mechanisms by a clear margin in terms of both social benefit and revenue.

The rest of the paper is organized as follows. In Sect. 2, we review related works. In Sect. 3, we show the preliminaries for our work. In Sect. 4, we give our truthful approximation mechanism and show that the 2-approximation achieved by our mechanism is actually tight. In Sect. 5, we report the evaluation results. We make a conclusion in Sect. 6.

2 Related Work

Many works have been done for ridesourcing (sometimes also called ridesharing) in recent years [1,5,6,9–13,17,20,21]. Due to the complexity of the ridesourcing problem, they focused on many different issues, scheduling, pricing, market analysis and so on.

Some of them which are based on market-based mechanisms design are most related with our work. [13] modified the VCG payment scheme proposed in [17] to adapt it to the dynamic requirements of the open-world ridesourcing problem. [21] showed that the deficit generated by the VCG mechanism can be arbitrarily large and proposed less efficient alternatives based on fixed prices and two-sided reserve prices that have deficit control. [6] proposed a coalition game for ridesourcing problem. [9] focused on sharing the resulting cost among passengers which is also different from the pricing problem in ridesourcing.

A majority of the literature on auction design have restricted their study to the single-parameter framework. Such a framework includes many practical scenarios, such as single-item auctions [4], digital goods auctions [8], multicast auctions [19], to name a few.

In many single-parameter auctions, reserve price are set to boost the revenue [16], or to favor a particular group of agents [15]. Although the reserve price constraints are widely used and play an important role to achieve certain design goal, they also bring challenges to the mechanism design field, as the reserve price constraints restrict the space of the possible allocations. Different from many existing works, variable reserve prices are considered in this paper.

We combine the classical greedy weighted maximum matching design technique [18] with the Myerson's Lemma [2,16] in a creative way to design the novel truthful and individually rational mechanism for social benefit maximization with the variable reserve prices constraints and the approximation ratio achieved by the mechanism we design is actually tight in theory.

3 Preliminary

We present the ridesharing problem model in a general auction framework. Consider a multi-unit auction with m items and n unit-demand, single-parameter agents. Each agent i has a private value v_i for getting an item. The auction collects agent bids $(b_1, \ldots, b_n)$, and outputs an allocation A of the items to the agents as well as payment p_i for each agent i. We assume agents have *quasi-linear* utilities defined as $u_i = v_i - p_i$ if i wins an item, and $u_i = 0$ otherwise. Further, there is an externally imposed reserve price $\bar{p}_{ij}$ for agent i to buy item j. That is, when item j is assigned to agent i, the payment p_i of agent i should not be less than $\bar{p}_{ij}$. We assume that reserve prices $\bar{p}_{ij}$ are public information, but the valuation v_i is private information to agent i.

We aim to design auctions with the following properties.

- *Truthfulness* (also known as *incentive compatibility* or *strategy-proofness*): for every agent i and fixed bids of other agents b_{-i}, agent i can always maximize her utility by reporting $b_i = v_i$.
- *Individual Rationality*: for each agent i whose value is v_i, assume that she is charged p_i ($p_i = 0$ if she loses the auction) when bidding v_i, then $v_i - p_i$ must be non-negative.
- *Computational Efficiency*: the allocation and payments can be computed in polynomial time.

Objectives. We study the following objectives in this paper. Let $\mathbb{W}(A)$ be the set of agents who are individually assigned to an item in allocation A.

- The *social benefit* of an allocation A is defined as the sum of valuations of all winning agents $SB(A) = \sum_{i \in \mathbb{W}(A)} v_i$.
- The *revenue* of the mechanism is defined as $REV(A) = \sum_{i \in \mathbb{W}(A)} p_i$. In this paper we focus mainly on the social benefit objective.

Due to the reserve price constraints, the notion of "optimal social benefit" needs to be defined carefully. Because an allocation that simply maximizes the social benefit may assign a certain item to an agent whose valuation is smaller than its corresponding reserve price. Such an allocation is unfavored because it does not admit any pricing scheme that satisfies both reserve price constraints and individual rationality. Thus, in this paper we define the optimal social benefit as

$$SB_{\mathrm{OPT}} = \max\{SB(A) \mid v_i(j) \geq \bar{p}_{ij} \text{ if } A \text{ assigns item } j \text{ to } i\}.$$

A mechanism is said to have c-approximation if it always outputs an allocation with social benefit no less than $\frac{SB_{\mathrm{OPT}}}{c}$.

3.1 Discussion on VCG-type Mechanisms

The Vickrey-Clarke-Groves (VCG) mechanism is a cornerstone method in mechanism design when it comes to the optimization of global objective. It is a truthful mechanism that achieves optimal global objective and can be applied to a variety of domains. However, it does not take reserve prices into consideration, hence the resulting payments might violate these constraints.

One might also be tempted to consider variants of the VCG mechanism. One possibility is to restrict the domain of feasible allocations to the ones in which every winning agent has valuation not less than the corresponding reserve price. The reserve price constraints can then be satisfied. Such change, however, might break the truthfulness of the mechanism.

Example 1. Consider two agents $\{1, 2\}$ and two items $\{a, b\}$, with variable reserve prices $\bar{p}_{1a} = \bar{p}_{2a} = 1$, $\bar{p}_{1b} = \infty$, $\bar{p}_{2b} = 2$ and $v_1 = 1$, $v_2 = 2$. When reporting truthfully, the VCG-type mechanism will assign item a to agent 1 and item b to agent 2, and charge them 1 and 2 respectively. However, agent 2 can get item a with price 1 if she misreports her valuation as 1.5.

Another variant is to view the reserve price as the "cost" of allocating an item to an agent, and use the allocation that maximizes the total valuation minus the allocation costs as the resulting allocation. Such mechanism could preserve truthfulness. However, it no longer provides any social benefit guarantee.

Example 2. Consider two agents $\{1, 2\}$ and one item a, which reserve prices $\bar{p}_{1a} = 0, \bar{p}_{2a} = 1$ and valuations $v_1 = \epsilon, v_2 = 1$. The mechanism that maximizes the sum of valuation minus the reserve prices would allocate the item to agent 1 because $\epsilon - 0 > 1 - 1$. While the optimal social benefit, when defined as only the sum of valuations, is obviously 1.

3.2 Interpretation in Ridesourcing

The above model describes a general framework that can be applied to many applications. Below we demonstrate its interpretation in the ridesourcing scenario.

In the basic online ridesourcing problem [7], passengers requiring rides are the agents and available drivers offering rides can be considered as the items. Passenger i reports her request $\theta_i = \{l_i^o, l_i^d, b_i\}$ to the platform where l_i^o and l_i^d are the origin and destination of her required ride respectively, b_i is agent i's valuation for the ride.

The platform collects the location information l_j of each driver j through GPS, and calculates the cost of assigning driver j to passenger i as the reserve price $\bar{p}_{ij}$. For instance, one way to define $\bar{p}_{ij}$ is to let $\bar{p}_{ij} = p_u * (dis(l_j, l_i^o) + dis(l_i^o, l_i^d))$, where $dis(m, n)$ denotes the distance between two points m and n, and p_u denotes the specific fuel consumption of the car. Then the platform needs to produce an assignment of the drivers to the passengers and the corresponding payment that each passenger pays to her driver.

The goal of the platform is to design a mechanism that motivates passengers to report their true valuations, and ensures that the payment of each passenger always covers the corresponding reserve price, and simultaneously maximizing the social benefit or revenue of the allocation.

4 A Truthful Approximation Mechanism

In this section, we present and analyze a truthful, individually rational and 2-approximation mechanism for social benefit maximization in the variable reserve price setting.

In the following, we consider a weighted bipartite graph $G = (V_A, V_I, E)$, where V_A is a subset of the agents, V_I is a subset of the items. Every edge

$(i, j) \in E$ is associated with the corresponding reserve price $\bar{p}_{ij}$. We will add or remove vertices and edges of G during the process of the mechanism.

We define a left-perfect matching in G as follows.

Definition 1. A matching M with size $|V_A|$ in G is called a *left-perfect matching* in G.

Clearly, a left-perfect matching is also a maximum matching in G.

The intuition behind our mechanism is that, at any moment, we only consider the agents with bids higher than $\bar{p}$ and edges with reserve prices below or equal $\bar{p}$, for some threshold value $\bar{p}$. We continuously decrease the value of $\bar{p}$. Such process will add agents to the graph while removing edges. We will maintain the following invariants throughout the mechanism.

Invariants:

---

1. Graph G always has a left-perfect matching.
2. There exists a threshold value $\bar{p}$, such that every agent in G has valuation not less than $\bar{p}$, and every edge in G has reserve price below or equal $\bar{p}$.

Each agent added to the graph will pay the smallest threshold value of $\bar{p}$ with which the graph still has a left-perfect matching.

The details of the mechanism are shown below.

Lemma 1. *The invariants hold throughout the run of the mechanism.*

Theorem 1. EROS *is a truthful, individually rational, and computationally efficient mechanism with 2-approximation for social benefit maximization.*

We prove each part of Theorem 1 separately in the following subsections.

4.1 Truthfulness

Our mechanism design problem belongs to the single-parameter domain (*i.e.*, the private information of every agent is a single value). By the well known characterization of truthful mechanisms in single-parameter domains [16], it suffices to show that our mechanism satisfies the following two properties.

- *Allocation Monotonicity.* For every agent i and fixed bids b_{-i} by other agents, i can win an item when bidding b_i, then she can still win if she bids any value $b'_i > b_i$.
- *Critical Payment Rule.* The payment charged to each winning agent equals to the minimal bid for this agent to win. This value is also called the *critical bid* of this agent.

Mechanism 1. EROS: a truthful, individually rational, 2-approximation mechanism.

```
Input: reported bids (b_1, ..., b_n);
1  Let C be the union set of all agents and edges, the value v(e) for element e in C
   is defined as its bid if e is an agent, and its reserve price if e is an edge.
2  Remove all edges (i, j) with b_i < p̄_ij in C.
3  Let V_A = ∅, V_I be the set of all items.
4  Let bipartite graph G = (V_A, V_I, E = ∅).
5  for each element e in C in decreasing order of v(e) do
6      if e is an edge (i, j) in G and i ∈ V_A then
7          Remove (i, j) from G.
8          if G no longer has a left-perfect matching then
9              Assign item j to agent i, let i pay p̄_ij.
10             Remove i and j from G.
11     if e is an agent i then
12         if G ∪ {i} has a left-perfect matching then
13             Add vertex i and its incident edges to G.
14         else
15             for each agent i' in G do
16                 Let M be a left-perfect matching in G
17                 if G \ {i'} ∪ {i} has a left-perfect matching then
18                     Assign agent i' her matched item j in M, let i' pay b_i.
19                     Remove i' and j from G.
20                     i remains unallocated.
```

Allocation Monotonicity

Lemma 2. *The allocation rule in* EROS *is monotone.*

Proof. First, it is easy to see from the mechanism that, every agent that is added to graph G in line 11 of the mechanism will end up being assigned an item in the output allocation. Thus the allocation monotonicity rule is equivalent of saying that, if agent i can be added to G with bid b_i, i will still be added to G if she bids any value $b_i' > b_i$, assuming all other bids remain the same.

We focus on the agent adding process in EROS. Without loss of generality, assume that $k(k')$ agents, denoted as $A_k(A_{k'})$, have been added to G before agent i bidding $b_i(b_i')$ is considered at moment $t_i(t_i')$. Note that $A_k(A_{k'})$ does not only contain agents in G at $t_i(t_i')$, but also the ones that have been matched and removed from G before $t_i(t_i')$.

When processing elements (*i.e.*, agents and edges) in the union set C in decreasing order of their values, agent i will be processed earlier when bidding b_i' than bidding b_i. Thus we have $t_i' \leq t_i$. With all the other information remaining unchanged, it is easy to see that $A_{k'} \subseteq A_k$. Furthermore, if graph $(A_k \cup \{i\}, I, E)$

has a left-perfect matching, graph $(A_{k'} \cup \{i\}, I, E)$ will have a left-perfect matching as well. Therefore when bidding b'_i, agent i will still be added to graph G, and thus be assigned an item in the final mechanism outcome.

Critical-bid Payment. Next we show the payment specified by our mechanism coincides with the critical bid of the monotone allocation rule.

Lemma 3. *The payment of a winning agent i is her critical bid in* EROS.

Proof. Here we show that the payment of each assigned agent is the minimum bid that she needs to report to be added in G. That is, the agent will lose the item if she bids anything less than that payment.

There are two places in the mechanism where items are assigned to agents. We consider them separately.

1. When the element e being processed is an edge (i, j) (line 8, 9). Here agent i is assigned item j and pays $\bar{p}_{ij}$. Let G be the bipartite graph at this moment. Based on line 7 condition, we know that $G \backslash \{(i, j)\}$ does not have a left-perfect matching.
   Now assume that agent i bids $b'_i = \bar{p}_{ij} - \varepsilon$ for some small $\varepsilon > 0$. Note that in this case, edge (i, j) will be removed from C at line 2 of the mechanism. Therefore when agent i is being processed, adding it will give us exactly the graph $G \backslash \{(i, j)\}$. Because it does not have a left-perfect matching, we know in this case agent i will not be added to G and hence will be left unassigned.
2. When the element e being processed is an agent i (line 15, 16).
   Here agent i' is assigned her matched item in matching M and pays b_i, where i is the agent failing to be added to G.
   Assume i' bids $b_i - \varepsilon$. According to the mechanism, the following events will happen.
   (a) Agent i will be picked in C before agent i'.
   (b) When processing agent i, she will be added to the graph since $G \backslash \{i'\} \cup \{i\}$ has a left-perfect matching.
   (c) After i is added, agent i' will not be able to added to G any more when processed. Because otherwise it would violate the condition that agent i is not added to G with the original bidding.

   We conclude that in this case, agent i' will also not be assigned if she bids below the payment.

Lemmas 2 and 3 together imply the truthfulness of EROS.

4.2 Individual Rationality and Reserve Price Constraints

Individual rationality and reserve price constraints can be easily proved by the invariant properties of the mechanism.

Lemma 4. EROS *respects the reserve price constraints and is individually rational.*

Proof. Note that at each iteration of the mechanism, the value of element e in C is exactly the threshold value mentioned in Invariant 2. Furthermore, whenever we assign an item j to an agent i in the iteration (at line 9 or line 18), the payment charged to the agent is exactly this threshold value. Hence we always have $v_i \geq p_i \geq \bar{p}_{ij}$. This proves both reserve price constraints and individual rationality of the mechanism.

4.3 Approximation Ratio

To show the social benefit approximation of EROS, we relate the winning set of agents to the outcome of the following simple greedy allocation algorithm.

Greedy Algorithm

Consider each agent i in decreasing order of v_i, if there is an unassigned item j with $v_i \geq \bar{p}_{ij}$, assign item j to agent i (if there are more than one such items, pick an arbitrary one).

This is a variant of the greedy matching algorithm, which is known to achieve 2-approximation for social benefit maximization. The proof is omitted due to space constraints.

Lemma 5. *The Greedy Algorithm is a 2-approximation to the optimal social benefit solution.*

Next we will show that the allocation produced by EROS coincides with a particular run of this greedy algorithm.

Lemma 6. EROS *always achieves at least half of the optimal social benefit.*

Proof. Let M be the matching output by our mechanism. We assume that this matching is produced by the following process:

For each agent i in decreasing order of v_i, if $i \in M$, assign agent i her matched item in M. Otherwise discard this agent. To prove this allocation is 2-approximation, it suffices to show that the above process is also a valid running process of the greedy algorithm. That is, we want to show that for each agent $i \notin M$, when i is considered in the greedy algorithm, there is no unassigned item j left with $v_i \geq \bar{p}_{ij}$.

Assume by contradiction that we can find an unassigned item j with $v_i \geq \bar{p}_{ij}$ when processing agent i. This means that when processing agent i in line 11 of EROS, the graph $G \cup \{i\}$ will have a left-perfect matching $M \cup (i, j)$. Hence according to the mechanism, agent i will be added to graph G at this step. However, we also observe that every agent added to the graph G in the mechanism will all end up being assigned to an item. This contradicts the assumption that $i \notin M$ and proves the lemma.

4.4 Lower Bounds

In this subsection we focus on the lower bounds for the approximation ratio of any truthful and individually rational mechanism. We show that the 2-approximation achieved by our mechanism is actually tight in this model.

Theorem 2. *There is no truthful and individually rational mechanism that can achieve an approximate ratio better than 2 for social benefit maximization, even with only two items.*

Proof. We prove this theorem through a concrete counter example. Assume otherwise that such a mechanism exists. We focus on the following 2 scenarios.

First, consider two agents $\{1,2\}$ and two items $\{a,b\}$, with variable reserve prices $\bar{p}_{1a} = \bar{p}_{2a} = 1$, $\bar{p}_{1b} = \infty$, $\bar{p}_{2b} = 1+\varepsilon$ and $v_1 = 1$, $v_2 = 1+\varepsilon/2$ where $\varepsilon > 0$. Since neither agent can afford item b, and agent 2 has a higher value than agent 1, the truthful mechanism must assign item a to agent 2 with price $p_2 \in [1, 1+\varepsilon/2]$ and leave item b unassigned.

Next, consider a similar case where from the above example we change the value v_2 from $1+\varepsilon/2$ to $1+\varepsilon$. Note that although agent 2 can now afford to have item b, a truthful mechanism must still assign item a to agent 2 with price $p_2 \in [1, 1+\varepsilon/2]$ when they are bidding truthfully. This is because agent 2 can always get this allocation by reporting $b_2 = 1+\varepsilon/2$, and this is always a better result for agent 2 than assigning item b to her.

Note that in the later instance, the optimal social benefit is $2+\varepsilon$ from assigning item a to agent 1 and item b to agent 2. Hence any truthful and individually rational mechanism cannot have approximation ratio better than $\frac{2+\varepsilon}{1+\varepsilon}$, whose limit is 2 when $\varepsilon \to 0$.

5 Evaluation

We conduct experiments in a ridesourcing scenario on a real taxi-trace dataset to evaluate the performance of our mechanism. Please refer to Sect. 3 "Example in ridesourcing" paragraph for the model details.

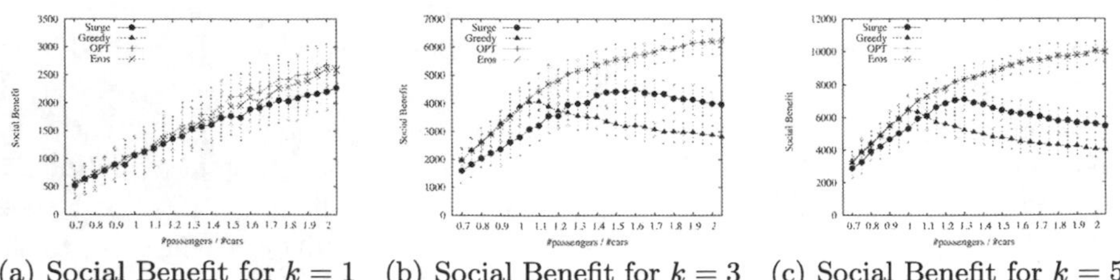

(a) Social Benefit for $k = 1$ (b) Social Benefit for $k = 3$ (c) Social Benefit for $k = 5$

Fig. 1. Social benefit comparison

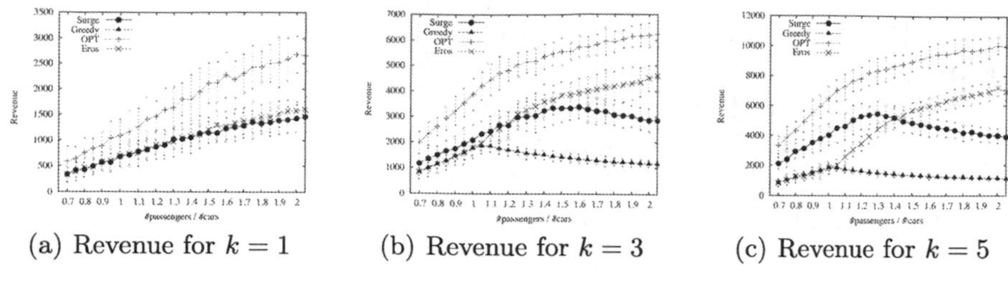

(a) Revenue for $k = 1$ (b) Revenue for $k = 3$ (c) Revenue for $k = 5$

Fig. 2. Revenue comparison

5.1 Simulation Setup

Our experimental evaluation is based on a taxi-trace dataset of city Shanghai in 2015. The data contains the locations of about 100 taxis in that city at a particular time.

We then randomly sample the information of passengers [14]. For each passenger i, her origin l_i^o and destination l_i^d are randomly sampled from a uniform distribution over the main city area. Recall that the reserve price of assigning taxi j to passenger i is $\bar{p}_{ij} = p_u * (dis(l_j, l_i^o) + dis(l_i^o, l_i^d))$, where l_j is the location of taxi j, and p_u is the specific fuel consumption of a car in that city. Note the actual value of p_u is not important since it is a common factor in all costs and passenger valuations.

The individual valuation v_i of each passenger i is sampled from a Gaussian distribution over the interval $2\mu \geq v_i \geq 0$ with mean $\mu = k * p_u * dis(l_i^o, l_i^d)$ and variance $\delta = 20$. The idea is to let μ represent the standard taxi fare for the trip, and use Gaussian distribution to model that with high probability a passenger would be willing to pay a price close to that taxi fare. The taxi price is on average 5 times the gas or oil cost of the trip in the targeted city. In order to examine the effects of different valuation distributions on the mechanism performance, we run the entire set of experiments with three different values $k = 1, 3, 5$.

To investigate the influence of different levels of supply and demand on the performance of each mechanism, we run all the aforementioned mechanisms with different passenger quantities $\mathcal{P}$, ranging from 70 to 200. For every value of $\mathcal{P}$, we simulate the mechanisms on 50 sets of passenger samples and take the average result. Each data point is also plotted together with the 95% confidence interval.

5.2 Benchmark Mechanisms

To evaluate the performance of Eros, we compared Eros with several other mechanisms.

- Greedy. We use this mechanism to model the simplest strategy of assigning each passenger to its nearest car in a greedy fashion. The mechanism runs as follows: Repeatedly pick passenger i and car j with the smallest distance $dis(l_j, l_i^o)$, offer this car to this passenger at price $p_i = \bar{p}_{ij}$. If passenger i

accepts this offer (*i.e.*, her bid is not less than this price), make the match and remove this pair from the system. Otherwise mark passenger i as unassigned and remove her from the system (because under individual budget balance condition this passenger cannot be assigned to any car). Clearly this mechanism is truthful and individually rational.

- Surge. Surge pricing is a dynamic pricing strategy used by many online ridesourcing companies. It is an effective way to extract more revenue from the discrepancy between demand and supply. Here we consider a very simple version of this pricing strategy. Let $\alpha \geq 1$ be the surge factor. We simply employ the Greedy mechanism described above, but replace the offered price $\bar{p}_{ij}$ by $\alpha \cdot \bar{p}_{ij}$. We vary the value of α from 1 to 5 and pick the allocation with the largest revenue as our final allocation. Note that this is *not* a truthful mechanism.

Finally, we use OPT to denote the optimal social benefit in each problem instance. Note that as shown in Sect. 4.4, no truthful and individually rational mechanism can always achieve optimal social benefit. Thus it only serves as an upper bound of all mechanisms' performances. Also note that when considering revenue as the performance metric, the optimal social benefit still serves as a (perhaps loose) upper bound on the possible revenue that any mechanism can achieve.

5.3 Results

Figure 1(a)–(c) show the social benefit achieved by different mechanisms with $k = 1, 3, 5$ respectively[2]. We can see from the results that our mechanism outperforms all other mechanisms by a clear margin. In particular, when the ratio between the number of passengers and the number of taxis is large, *i.e.*, the market is in high demand, our mechanism achieves near optimal social benefit most of the time, while the performances of Greedy and Surge start to drop down.

Figure 2(a)–(c) show the revenue comparisons between each mechanism. Note that in this work we did not provide any theoretical analysis on the revenue aspect of our mechanism. Yet empirical results show that our mechanism is able to generate competitive revenue performance. In particular, when the demand is high compared with the supply, our mechanism again outperforms Surge, which is a non-truthful mechanism designed specifically for the purpose of revenue extraction.

5.4 Discussion

From the experiments we can also form the following observations and discussions.

[2] In Fig. 1(a) Surge mechanism achieves optimal performance with surge factor $\alpha = 1$, *i.e.*, it coincides with the Greedy mechanism. Thus its plot is not displayed in the figure. The same is true also for Fig. 2(a).

Low Demand vs. High Demand. The discrepancy between supply and demand plays an important role in different mechanisms. Note that as the number of passengers increases, OPT also increases. However, such correlation is not reflected in Greedy and Surge. The reason is that these two mechanisms assign cars to passengers based on the distances between them, hence they do not take advantage of the increasing number of high-valuation passengers. On the other hand, our mechanism is able to exploit such discrepancy and picks passengers selectively based on their valuations. This partially explains why our mechanism always gives good performance in the cases with high demand.

Theory vs. Practice. In Sect. 4.4 we established a lower bound of 2 on the social benefit approximation ratio for any truthful mechanisms in this model. However, as the empirical results suggest, in practice one can usually go beyond this lower bound and achieve much better social benefit. This is because practical data usually have special structures and properties. How to formally analyze these properties from a theoretical point of view, and obtain better lower/upper bounds for auctions in specific application domains is an interesting open question in this area.

6 Conclusion and Future Work

In this paper, we study an mechanism design model for ridesourcing that allocates cars to unit-demand single-parameter agents with variable reserve price constraints. We give a truthful, individually rational, and computationally efficient mechanism that respects the reserve price constraints and achieves 2-approximation for social benefit maximization. We further evaluate the performance of our mechanism based on real taxi-trace data, and empirical results show that our mechanism outperforms other benchmark mechanisms in terms of both social benefit and revenue.

There are a number of future working directions that worth pursuing. First, given the online nature of the ridesourcing application, an important challenge is to design a dynamic online mechanism. Second, given the simplicity of our mechanism, it would be interesting to know how it can be generalized to be applied in other related domains. Third, appropriate design of the formulation of the social benefit can make our mechanism be adapted to practical applications with more interesting social objectives.

References

1. Agatz, N., Erera, A., Savelsbergh, M., Wang, X.: Optimization for dynamic ride-sharing: a review. Eur. J. Oper. Res. **223**(2), 295–303 (2012)
2. Archer, A., Papadimitriou, C., Talwar, K., Tardos, É.: An approximate truthful mechanism for combinatorial auctions with single parameter agents. Internet Math. **1**(2), 129–150 (2004)
3. Bajari, P., Hortacsu, A.: The winner's curse, reserve prices, and endogenous entry: empirical insights from ebay auctions. RAND J. Econ. **34**, 329–355 (2003)

4. Baker, J., Song, J.: A review of single-item internet auction literature and a model for future research. J. Electron. Commer. Org. **5**(1) (2007)
5. Banerjee, S., Johari, R., Riquelme, C.: Pricing in ride-sharing platforms: a queueing-theoretic approach. In: Proceedings of the Sixteenth ACM Conference on Economics and Computation, EC 2015, p. 639. ACM (2015)
6. Bistaffa, F., Farinelli, A., Ramchurn, S.D.: Sharing rides with friends: a coalition formation algorithm for ridesharing. In: Proceedings of the 2015 AAAI Conference on Artificial Intelligence, AAAI 2015. AAAI (2015)
7. Furuhata, M., Dessouky, M., Ordóñez, F., Brunet, M.E., Wang, X., Koenig, S.: Ridesharing: the state-of-the-art and future directions. Transp. Res. Part B: Methodol. **57**, 28–46 (2013)
8. Goldberg, A.V., Hartline, J.D., Wright, A.: Competitive auctions and digital goods. In: Proceedings of the Twelfth Annual ACM-SIAM Symposium on Discrete Algorithms, SODA 2001, pp. 735–744. Society for Industrial and Applied Mathematics (2001)
9. Gopalakrishnan, R., Mukherjee, K., Tulabandhula, T.: The costs and benefits of ridesharing: sequential individual rationality and sequential fairness. In: Proceedings of the 8th ACM Conference on Electronic Commerce, EC 2016. ACM (2016)
10. Herbawi, W., Weber, M.: The ridematching problem with time windows in dynamic ridesharing: a model and a genetic algorithm. In: 2012 IEEE Congress on Evolutionary Computation (CEC), pp. 1–8. IEEE (2012)
11. Herbawi, W.M., Weber, M.: A genetic and insertion heuristic algorithm for solving the dynamic ridematching problem with time windows. In: Proceedings of the 14th Annual Conference on Genetic and Evolutionary Computation, pp. 385–392. ACM (2012)
12. Jacob, J., Roet-Green, R.: Ride solo or pool: the impact of sharing on optimal pricing of ride-sharing services (2017)
13. Kamar, E., Horvitz, E.: Collaboration and shared plans in the open world: studies of ridesharing. In: International Joint Conference on Artificial Intelligence, IJCAI 2009, vol. 9, p. 187 (2009)
14. Kleiner, A., Nebel, B., Ziparo, V.: A mechanism for dynamic ride sharing based on parallel auctions. In: International Joint Conference on Artificial Intelligence, IJCAI 2011, pp. 266–272 (2011)
15. Kotowski, M.H.: On asymmetric reserve prices. Technical report, Mimeo (2015)
16. Myerson, R.B.: Optimal auction design. Math. Oper. Res. **6**(1), 58–73 (1981)
17. Parkes, D.C., Kalagnanam, J.R., Eso, M.: Achieving budget-balance with Vickrey-based payment schemes in exchanges. In: International Joint Conference on Artificial Intelligence, IJCAI 2001, pp. 1161–1168 (2001)
18. Preis, R.: Linear time 1/2-approximation algorithm for maximum weighted matching in general graphs. In: Meinel, C., Tison, S. (eds.) STACS 1999. LNCS, vol. 1563, pp. 259–269. Springer, Heidelberg (1999). https://doi.org/10.1007/3-540-49116-3_24
19. Varshney, U.: Multicast over wireless networks. Commun. ACM **45**(12), 31–37 (2002)
20. Zhang, D., Li, Y., Zhang, F., Lu, M., Liu, Y., He, T.: coRide: carpool service with a win-win fare model for large-scale taxicab networks. In: Proceedings of the 11th ACM Conference on Embedded Networked Sensor Systems, p. 9. ACM (2013)
21. Zhao, D., Zhang, D., Gerding, E.H., Sakurai, Y., Yokoo, M.: Incentives in ridesharing with deficit control. In: Proceedings of the 2014 International Conference on Autonomous Agents and Multi-agent Systems, AAMAS 2014, pp. 1021–1028. International Foundation for Autonomous Agents and Multiagent Systems (2014)

Matrix Entropy Driven Maximum Margin Feature Learning

Dong Zhang, Jinhui Tang(✉), and Zechao Li

School of Computer Science and Engineering,
Nanjing University of Science and Technology, Nanjing 210094, China
{dongzhang,jinhuitang,zechao.li}@njust.edu.cn

Abstract. This paper proposes an efficient supervised Matrix Entropy Driven Maximum Margin Feature Learning method (M3FL) to optimize all the discriminative features simultaneously. Specifically, we first present an in-depth investigation to the heteroscedastic problem in the maximum margin criterion, and then propose a new Maximum Margin Framework (MMF) based on the analysis to improve the traditional maximum margin criterion. The proposed MMF is robust to the initialization by exploring the ℓ_1-norm property. We further analyze the proposed MMF and find that it is necessary to learn the projection matrix from the perspective of matrix entropy. Consequently, the M3FL method is proposed to make the matrix entropy of the projection matrix as small as possible, and the corresponding optimization algorithm is developed. In addition, we discuss the relationship between the proposed optimization algorithm w.r.t. M3FL and the optimization algorithm w.r.t. MMF. Experiments are conducted on six widely-used data sets and experimental results demonstrate that the proposed method outperforms the state-of-the-art methods.

Keywords: Feature learning · Maximum margin · Matrix entropy

1 Introduction

Feature learning is one of the most important issues in machine learning community [30,35]. In the past, many effective approaches have been proposed to generate meaningful features, such as Principal Component Analysis [18], Marginal Fisher Analysis [28], and Fisher Linear Discriminant (FLD) [12]. Thanks to the excellent performance of the supervised methods, in particular, FLD has attracted a lot of attention, which extracts the meaningful features by maximizing the trace ratio value between the between-class scatter matrix S_b and the within-class scatter matrix S_w.

However, FLD suffers from issues of singularity and small sample size (SSS) [24,25]. In order to address these shortcomings, many corrective methods of FLD have been proposed, such as Local FLD [5], Tensor FLD [23], 2D-FLD [9] and Maximum Margin Criterion (MMC) [8]. As an excellent one, MMC extracts features by maximizing the difference between S_b and S_w. From [8], we know that

X. Geng and B.-H. Kang (Eds.): PRICAI 2018, LNAI 11012, pp. 375–387, 2018.
https://doi.org/10.1007/978-3-319-97304-3_29

MMC can extract more discriminative features than FLD. Except for the classical MMC, a modified MMC is proposed in [13], in which $\mathbf{S}_b$ and $\mathbf{S}_w$ are firstly preprocessed by eigenvectors of the total scatter matrix $\mathbf{S}_t$ corresponding to the zero eigenvalues. However, the ℓ_2-norm in $\mathbf{S}_b$ and $\mathbf{S}_w$ causes the heteroscedastic problem, in which the variance of some classes or other will be excessively wide [31,36]. Moreover, the ℓ_2-norm-driven learning approaches mentioned above are not robust to the noisy data and outliers [31,32]. It is well-known that the ℓ_1-norm is introduced as an alternative to the ℓ_2-norm in resisting the noisy data and outliers [3,11,14]. However, there are two limitations of the ℓ_1-norm methods. The first one is that the optimal results are easy to get stuck in local solutions when they are solved by iterative algorithms [4,34]. The other one is that results to the ℓ_1-norm approaches are sensitive to initializations, such that different initializations may lead to different local solutions. Based on the two points, we can obtain a flawed performance.

In this paper, we propose an efficient supervised Matrix entropy driven Maximum Margin Feature Learning method (M3FL), in which all discriminative features are generated simultaneously. Specifically, we first give an in-depth investigation to the heteroscedastic problem in MMC. Then, we propose a new Maximum Margin Framework (MMF), in which the ℓ_1-norm is used to regularize the difference between S_b and S_w. We further give an analyze to the proposed MMF and find that it is necessary to learn the projection matrix from the perspective of matrix entropy, and M3FL is proposed to make the matrix entropy of the projection matrix as small as possible and the corresponding optimization algorithm is developed. In addition, we discuss the relationship between proposed optimization algorithms to M3FL and MMF. Experiments are conducted on six widely-used data sets and results demonstrate that the proposed method outperforms state-of-the-art methods.

2 Related Work

The training set $\mathbf{X} \in \mathbb{R}^{m \times n}$ is supplied as n samples $\{\mathbf{x}_1, \mathbf{x}_2, \ldots, \mathbf{x}_n\}$ belonging to c different classes and takes values in a m-dimensional space, n_i is number of samples in class i, $\mathbf{x}_{i,j}$ is the j-th training sample in class i, where $j = 1, 2, \ldots, n_i$ and $i = 1, 2, \ldots, c$. The mean vector of class i is $\boldsymbol{\mu}_i = \frac{1}{n_i}\sum_{j=1}^{n_i} \mathbf{x}_{i,j}$, and the mean vector of whole samples is $\boldsymbol{\mu} = \frac{1}{n}\sum_{i=1}^{n} \mathbf{x}_i$. For feature classification, a good feature learning approach should maximize the difference between the S_b and S_w. For this purpose, Maximum Margin Criterion (MMC) [8] is written as

$$\begin{aligned} &\max_{\mathbf{w}_d} \mathbf{w}_d^T (\mathbf{S}_b - \mathbf{S}_w) \mathbf{w}_d \\ &s.t. \;\; \mathbf{w}_d^T \mathbf{w}_d - 1 = 0, \end{aligned} \tag{1}$$

where $\mathbf{w}_d \in \mathbb{R}^{m \times 1}$ is the projection vector, the projection matrix $\mathbf{W} = (\mathbf{w}_1, \mathbf{w}_2, \ldots, \mathbf{w}_d) \in \mathbb{R}^{m \times d}$. $\mathbf{S}_b$ is the between-class scatter matrix:

$$\mathbf{S}_b = \frac{1}{n} \sum_{i=1}^{c} n_i (\boldsymbol{\mu}_i - \boldsymbol{\mu})(\boldsymbol{\mu}_i - \boldsymbol{\mu})^T = \mathbf{H}_b \mathbf{H}_b^T \tag{2}$$

and $\mathbf{S}_w$ is the within-class scatter matrix:

$$\mathbf{S}_w = \frac{1}{n}\sum_{i=1}^{c}\sum_{j=1}^{n_i}(\mathbf{x}_{i,j} - \boldsymbol{\mu}_i)(\mathbf{x}_{i,j} - \boldsymbol{\mu}_i)^T = \mathbf{H}_w\mathbf{H}_w^T, \tag{3}$$

where

$$\mathbf{H}_b = \frac{1}{\sqrt{n}}[\sqrt{n_1}(\boldsymbol{\mu}_1 - \boldsymbol{\mu}), \ldots, \sqrt{n_c}(\boldsymbol{\mu}_c - \boldsymbol{\mu})], \tag{4}$$

$$\mathbf{H}_w = \frac{1}{\sqrt{n}}[\mathbf{x}_{1,1} - \boldsymbol{\mu}_1, \ldots, \mathbf{x}_{n_1,1} - \boldsymbol{\mu}_1, \ldots, \mathbf{x}_{n_c,c} - \boldsymbol{\mu}_c]. \tag{5}$$

To obtain the projection vector $\mathbf{w}_d$, the Lagrangian is introduced with a multiplier α_d, which leads to

$$(\mathbf{S}_b - \mathbf{S}_w)\mathbf{w}_d = \alpha_d\mathbf{w}_d. \tag{6}$$

In Eq. (6), α_d is the eigenvalue of $\mathbf{S}_b - \mathbf{S}_w$, and $\mathbf{w}_d$ is the corresponding eigenvector. Therefore, the objective value will be maximized if the projection direction $\mathbf{W}$ is composed of the first d largest eigenvectors of $\mathbf{S}_b - \mathbf{S}_w$. To improve the robustness, MMC with the ℓ_1-norm (MMC-ℓ_1) is proposed in [19], which aims to maximize the following formulation:

$$\begin{aligned} &\max_{\mathbf{w}_d} \sum_{i=1}^{c} n_i\|\mathbf{w}_d^T(\boldsymbol{\mu}_i - \boldsymbol{\mu})\|_1 - \nu\sum_{i=1}^{c}\sum_{j=1}^{n_i}\|\mathbf{w}_d^T(\mathbf{x}_{i,j} - \boldsymbol{\mu}_i)\|_1 \\ &s.t.\ \ \mathbf{w}_d^T\mathbf{w}_d - 1 = 0, \end{aligned} \tag{7}$$

where $\|\cdot\|_1$ denotes the ℓ_1-norm, and ν is a nonnegative weight parameter of one vector. We can use the gradient ascent strategy to solve this problem. The detailed process to solve MMC-ℓ_1 can be found in [15].

3 Robust Maximum Margin Framework

In this section, we first give an investigation to the heteroscedastic problem in MMC, and show the rationality of the ℓ_1-norm. Then a novel and efficient Maximum Margin Framework (MMF) is proposed.

3.1 Rationality of the ℓ_1-norm

Recall that the objective function in Eq. (1) is based on the difference between $\mathbf{S}_b$ and $\mathbf{S}_w$, then we can rewrite the objective function of Eq. (1) as

$$\max_{\mathbf{w}_d} \sum_{i=1}^{c} \mathbf{w}_d^T(\mathbf{S}_{b,i} - \mathbf{S}_{w,i})\mathbf{w}_d, \tag{8}$$

where $\mathbf{S}_{b,i}$ is the between-class scatter matrix of the i-th class with others,

$$\mathbf{S}_{b,i} = \frac{1}{n_i}\sum_{i\in C}(\boldsymbol{\mu}_i - \boldsymbol{\mu})(\boldsymbol{\mu}_i - \boldsymbol{\mu})^T \tag{9}$$

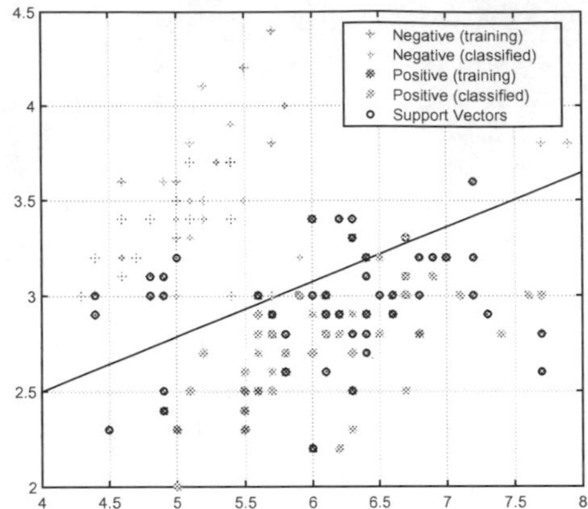

Fig. 1. A brief description to the heteroscedastic problem.

and $\mathbf{S}_{w,i}$ is the within-class scatter matrix of the i-th class.

$$\mathbf{S}_{w,i} = \frac{1}{n_i} \sum_{i \in C} \sum_{j=1}^{n_i} (\mathbf{x}_{i,j} - \boldsymbol{\mu}_i)(\mathbf{x}_{i,j} - \boldsymbol{\mu}_i)^T. \tag{10}$$

From the perspective of statistics, $\mathbf{S}_{b,i}$ and $\mathbf{S}_{w,i}$ are both "plug-in" estimates [37], which implying that if the scatter of training samples are heteroscedastic in essence, for instance, the distance between the l-th training sample and the v-th training sample in the same class is excessively large, then the "plug-in" estimates would be inappropriate [16,21]. Figure 1 gives a show to the heteroscedastic problem. We can see from Fig. 1 that the distribution of negative samples is wider than that of positive samples, which may result in a larger proportion of negative samples in the wrong points and result in the optimal classification plane being closer to the sample points of the positive class. Let us consider a special case, if all the training samples in the same class are widely uniformly distributed across the domain of values, then the difference between $\mathbf{S}_b$ and $\mathbf{S}_w$ will be relatively small. According to Eqs. (2)–(3) and Eq. (8), the ℓ_2-norm based formulations can enlarge the effect of values for $\mathbf{S}_{b,i}$ and $\mathbf{S}_{w,i}$, such that differences among $\mathbf{S}_{b,i}$ or $\mathbf{S}_{w,i}$ will be amplified [7,22]. Compared with the ℓ_2-norm, the ℓ_1-norm can repress the heteroscedastic problem since the ℓ_1-norm consists of the absolute values. Therefore, in MMC, the utilizations of the ℓ_1-norm are more appropriate than the ℓ_2-norm in S_w and S_b. Besides, from [4,14,33], we know that the ℓ_1-norm is more robust than the ℓ_2-norm. Especially, when facing with outliers, the ℓ_1-norm can achieve robust performance than the ℓ_2-norm.

3.2 Maximum Margin Framework

Before the proposed method is described in detail, we show some basal principles behind MMF. We first make a LU decomposition to $\mathbf{S}_b - \mathbf{S}_w$ as follows [10]

Algorithm 1. A traditional algorithm to solve MMF

Input: Training samples $\mathbf{X} = \{x_1, x_2, ..., x_n\}$, d.
Initialize $\mathbf{W} = \{\mathbf{w}_1, \mathbf{w}_2, ..., \mathbf{w}_d\} \in \mathbb{R}^{m\times d}$, each $\mathbf{w}_d^T\mathbf{w}_d = 1$.
Process:
for $k = 1$ **to** d
  Let $t = 1$, $w_d^t = w_d$.
  Compute μ, μ_i, $\mathbf{S}_d$ and $\mathbf{H}_{di}(i = 1, 2, ..., c)$.
  While not converge **do**
    Compute $\beta_i = sign[\mathbf{w}_d^T\mathbf{H}_{di}]$, and $\mathbf{Y} = \sum_{i=1}^{c}\beta_i\mathbf{H}_{di}$;
    Find $\mathbf{w}_d^{t+1} = \mathbf{Y}/||\mathbf{Y}||_2$;
    Let $t = t + 1$;
  end while.
  Update the samples$\mathbf{X} = \mathbf{X} - (\mathbf{w}_d^t(\mathbf{w}_d^t)^T)\mathbf{X}$, and $\mathbf{w}_d = \mathbf{w}_d^t$.
end
Output: The optimal projection matrix:$\mathbf{W} \in \mathbb{R}^{m\times d}$.

$$\begin{aligned}\mathbf{S}_b - \mathbf{S}_w &= \mathbf{H}_b\mathbf{H}_b^T - \mathbf{H}_w\mathbf{H}_w^T \\ &= \mathbf{H}_d\mathbf{I}\mathbf{I}_d^T.\end{aligned} \tag{11}$$

Based on Eqs. (8)–(11), the objective function of (1) can be written as

$$\max_{\mathbf{w}} \mathbf{w}_d^T(\mathbf{H}_d\mathbf{H}_d^T)\mathbf{w}_d = \max_{\mathbf{w}} \parallel \mathbf{w}_d^T\mathbf{H}_d \parallel_2^2, \tag{12}$$

where $\| \cdot \|_2^2$ denotes the ℓ_2-norm. Note that the ℓ_1-norm can suppress the heteroscedastic problem. Therefore, a more rational formulation can be expressed as

$$\begin{aligned}&\max_{\mathbf{w}} ||\mathbf{w}_d^T\mathbf{H}_d||_1 \\ &s.t.\ \ \mathbf{w}_d^T\mathbf{w}_d - 1 = 0,\end{aligned} \tag{13}$$

which is based on the ℓ_1-norm, where $||\mathbf{w}_d^T\mathbf{H}_d||_1 = |\mathbf{w}_d^T\mathbf{H}_d|_1$. For a more convenient solution to the problem, we can rewrite the problem (13) as

$$\begin{aligned}&\max_{\mathbf{w}} \beta_i\mathbf{w}_d^T\mathbf{H}_{di} \\ &s.t.\ \ \mathbf{w}_d^T\mathbf{w}_d - 1 = 0,\end{aligned} \tag{14}$$

where $\beta_i = sign(\mathbf{w}_d^T\mathbf{H}_{di})$ and $\sum_{i=1}^{n}\mathbf{H}_{di} = \mathbf{H}_d$. We suppose that if $(\mathbf{w}_d^T\mathbf{H}_{di}) < 0$, then $\beta_i = -1$; if $(\mathbf{w}_d^T\mathbf{H}_{di}) > 0$, then $\beta_i = 1$; if $(\mathbf{w}_d^T\mathbf{H}_{di}) = 0$, then $\beta_i = 0$. Based on β_i, we define a new matrix $\mathbf{Y} = \sum_{i=1}^{c}\beta_i\mathbf{H}_{di}$, the problem (14) can be exprcssed as

$$\begin{aligned}&\max_{\mathbf{w}} \mathbf{w}_d^T\mathbf{Y} \\ &s.t.\ \ \mathbf{w}_d^T\mathbf{w}_d - 1 = 0.\end{aligned} \tag{15}$$

The formulation (15) is the proposed feature learning method in this work and can be solved by an iterative algorithm. Since the problem (15) has the similar formulation as PCA with ℓ_1-norm, which has been discussed in [4], then we know that the optimal solution of Eq. (15) is $\mathbf{w}_{d+1} = \mathbf{Y}/ \parallel \mathbf{Y} \parallel_2$ As shown in Algorithm 1, the projection vectors can be generated one by one via the iterative process.

4 Matrix Entropy Driven Maximum Margin Feature Learning

In this section, we further present an analyze to the proposed MMF method. Then, we propose an efficient supervised Matrix entropy driven Maximum Margin Feature Learning method (M3FL).

4.1 Theoretical Analysis

As shown in [6,26,27], solutions to the ℓ_1-norm based problems are sensitive to the initial experiment setting. Figure 2 gives a brief sketch to this problem. For a convenient expression, we only enumerate three local optimal solutions. As we can see from Fig. 2, if the initial vector $\mathbf{w}_0$ is placed on the position of the initialization 1, then the solution is likely to fall into the local optimal solution 1. If the initial vector $\mathbf{w}_0$ is placed on the position of the initialization 3, then the solution is likely to fall into the local optimal solution 1 or the local optimal solution 3, which depends on the selection of the learning rate. If the initial vector $\mathbf{w}_0$ is placed on the position of the initialization 2, then the solution is likely to fall into any one of the local optimal solutions or none of the local solutions. In such case, the optimization algorithm will be non-convergence. Suppose there are s different local solutions for the training samples ($s \geq 1$), then the projection matrix $\mathbf{M}$ will at most have $s!$ different statuses as $\mathbf{M}_1, \mathbf{M}_2, \ldots, \mathbf{M}_{s!}$. Suppose $P(\mathbf{M}_i)$ is the probability of $\mathbf{M}_i$ where ($i = 1, 2, \ldots, s!$), then the matrix entropy of this matrix can be expressed as

$$H(\mathbf{M}) = -\sum_{i=1}^{s!} P(\mathbf{M}_i) \cdot log_2(P(\mathbf{M}_i)), \tag{16}$$

$$P(\mathbf{M}_i) = T(\mathbf{M}_i)/s!, \tag{17}$$

where $T(\mathbf{M}_i)$ is the frequency for the status of $\mathbf{M}_i$ from $s!$ different statuses of $\mathbf{M}$, $0 \leq T(\mathbf{M}_i) \leq s!$, $0 \leq P(\mathbf{M}_i) \leq 1$, $\sum_{i=1}^{s!} P(\mathbf{M}_i) = 1$, and we assume that $0log_2(0) = 0$ when $P(\mathbf{M}_i) = 0$. Suppose that for every $\mathbf{M}_i$ of $\mathbf{M}$ we have $P(\mathbf{M}_1) = P(\mathbf{M}_2) = \ldots = P(\mathbf{M}_{s!})$, implying that $P(\mathbf{M}_i) = 1/s!$, then the matrix entropy for $\mathbf{M}$ will be a monotone increasing function. The matrix entropy $H(\mathbf{M})$ has its maximal value as $H(\mathbf{M})_{max} = log_2 s!$, and $0 \leq H(\mathbf{M}) \leq H(\mathbf{M})_{max}$. One can use $H(\mathbf{M}) - H(\mathbf{M})_{max}$ or $\frac{H(\mathbf{M}}{H(\mathbf{M})_{max}}$ as any status of $\mathbf{M}$ to measure its uncertainty degree. When $H(\mathbf{M})_{max} - H(\mathbf{M}) = 0$ or $\frac{H(\mathbf{M}}{H(\mathbf{M})_{max}} = 1$, then the status of $\mathbf{M}$ has the biggest uncertainty degree. Based on the above analysis, we find that the projection matrix calculated by the gradient strategy will have a large matrix entropy value yet uncertain performance.

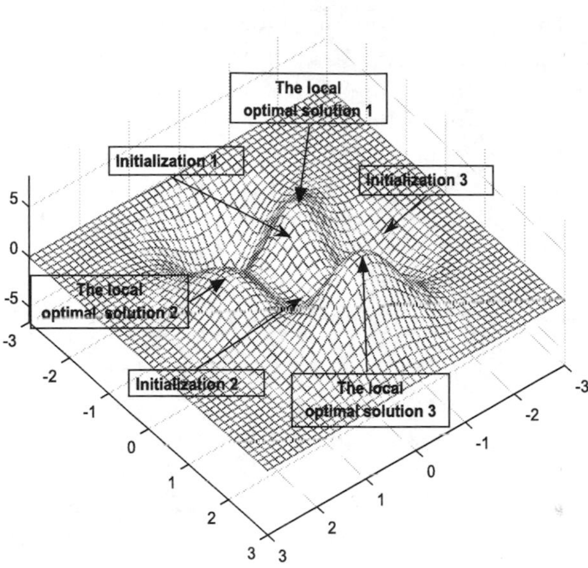

Fig. 2. Illustration of the uncertain state to solutions of the ℓ_1-norm approaches.

4.2 M3FL Approach

To obtain much certain performance, the matrix entropy of the feature matrix should as small as possible while preserving wealthy information. One attractive way to achieve this goal is to extract features as few times as possible. Therefore, the formulation of M3FL is defined as

$$\begin{array}{l} \max_{\mathbf{W}} ||\mathbf{W}^T\mathbf{H}_d||_1 \\ s.t.\ \ \min H(\mathbf{W}), \mathbf{W}^T\mathbf{W} = \mathbf{I}, \end{array} \tag{18}$$

where $\mathbf{I}$ is an identity matrix. Based on the analyses of Eqs. (11)–(15), we know that the pivotal step is to solve the following problem

$$\max_{\mathbf{W}} tr(\mathbf{W}^T\mathbf{Y}). \tag{19}$$

The constraint $\min H(\mathbf{W})$ can met when all the projection vectors are generated with one-time, then $H(\mathbf{W}) = 0$. We adopt the optimization algorithm as the one in [4] to solve the remainders of Eq. (18). The principle can be explained by the following theory. Suppose the SVD decompose of $\mathbf{Y}$ is $\mathbf{Y} = \mathbf{U}\Lambda\mathbf{V}^T$, in which $\mathbf{U} \in \mathbb{R}^{m\times m}$, $\Lambda \in \mathbb{R}^{m\times d}$ and $\mathbf{V} \in \mathbb{R}^{d\times d}$. Then Eq. (19) is expressed as

$$\begin{array}{l} tr(\mathbf{W}^T\mathbf{Y}) \\ = tr(\mathbf{W}^T\mathbf{U}\Lambda\mathbf{V}^T) \\ = tr(\Lambda\mathbf{V}^T\mathbf{W}^T\mathbf{U}) \\ = tr(\Lambda\mathbf{Z}), \end{array} \tag{20}$$

Algorithm 2. An efficient algorithm for M3FL

Input: Training samples $\mathbf{X} = \{x_1, x_2, ..., x_n\}$, d.
Initialize $t = 1$ and $\mathbf{W}_t \in \mathbb{R}^{m \times d}$, each $\mathbf{w}_d^T \mathbf{w}_d = 1$.
  Compute μ, μ_i, $\mathbf{S}_d$ and $\mathbf{H}_{di} (i = 1, 2, ..., c)$.
  While not converge **do**
    $\beta_i = sign[\mathbf{W}_t^T \mathbf{H}_{di}]$, and $\mathbf{Y} = \sum_{i=1}^{c} \beta_i \mathbf{H}_{di}$;
    Compute the SVD decompose of $\mathbf{Y}$, and$\mathbf{Y} = \mathbf{U}\Lambda\mathbf{V}^T$;
    Let $\mathbf{W}_{t+1} = \mathbf{U}[\mathbf{I}; \mathbf{0}]\mathbf{V}^T$, and $t = t + 1$;
  end while.
Output: The optimal projection matrix:$\mathbf{W} \in \mathbb{R}^{m \times d}$.

where $\mathbf{Z} = \mathbf{V}^T \mathbf{W}^T \mathbf{U} \in \mathbb{R}^{d \times m}$, $\mathbf{Z}\mathbf{Z}^T = \mathbf{I}$ and $\mathbf{I}$ is an d by d identity matrix, so $\mathbf{Z}_{i,i} \leq 1$, where $\mathbf{Z}_{i,i}$ is the (i, i)-th element of $\mathbf{Z}$. Combined with the condition that $\mathbf{Y} = \sum_{i=1}^{c} \beta_i \mathbf{H}_{di}$ then $tr(\Lambda\mathbf{Z}) \geq 0$, we further have the (i, i)-th element Λ_{ii} in matrix $\mathbf{\Lambda}$ that meets $\Lambda_{ii} \geq 0$. Hence, we have $tr(\mathbf{W}^T\mathbf{Y}) \leq \sum_i \Lambda_{ii}$. Especially, if and only if $Z_{ii} = 1$, the equality holds. Therefore, the objective function achieves the maximum value when $\mathbf{Z} = [\mathbf{I}; \mathbf{0}]$. That means the maximum solution to the problem (18) is

$$\mathbf{W}^T = \mathbf{U}\mathbf{Z}^T\mathbf{V}^T = \mathbf{U}[\mathbf{I}; \mathbf{0}]\mathbf{V}^T. \tag{21}$$

Based on above analysis, we continue describing an efficient algorithm to solve the M3FL approach in Algorithm 2. From Algorithm 2, all meaningful features can be obtained simultaneously.

5 Discussion

In this section, we give a discussion between the solutions of Algorithms 1 and 2. We consider an arbitrary p-order projection matrix as $\mathbf{M} = \{m_1, m_2, \ldots, m_p\}$, and $m_l (l = 1, 2, \ldots, p)$ is the optimal column vector. Suppose that the difference among all the projection vectors is very small. Then if we continue using Algorithm 1 to generate projection vectors, the projection matrix can easily fall into a disorder condition. Based on this rational assumption, $\mathbf{M}$ will at most have $p!$ different statuses as $\mathbf{M}_1, \mathbf{M}_2, \ldots, \mathbf{M}_{(p!)}$, and the probability of each status is almost the same. Therefore, the matrix entropy of the solution Algorithm 1 at most is

$$\begin{aligned} H(\mathbf{M}^g) &= (-1/(p!) \cdot log_2(1/(p!))) + (-1/(p!) \cdot log_2(1/(p!))) + \ldots \\ &+ (-1/(p!) \cdot log_2(1/(p!)))(\text{p! times}) \\ &= -(p!)/(p!) \cdot log_2(1/(p!)) \\ &= -log_2(1/(p!)) \\ &= log_2(p!) \gg 0, \end{aligned}$$

where $\mathbf{M}^g$ is the projection matrix generated by Algorithm 1. However, if all the projection vectors can be generated simultaneously, then the projection matrix will have only one status. The probability of this status is 1, and the matrix entropy of the projection matrix will be

$$H(\mathbf{M}^n) = 1 \cdot log_2(1) = 0, \tag{22}$$

where $\mathbf{M}^n$ is the projection matrix generated by Algorithm 2. Then we have

$$H(\mathbf{M}^n) \ll H(\mathbf{M}^g). \tag{23}$$

Therefore, the matrix entropy value of Algorithm 2 has a smaller value than the matrix entropy value of Algorithm 1, which means that the Algorithm 2 can generate a more certain solution. Only when all the vectors in $\mathbf{M}$ have a distinctly difference, such as $m_1 > m_2 > \ldots > m_p$, then the projection matrix generated by the two algorithms may have a small difference, such that $H(\mathbf{M}^n) \approx H(\mathbf{M}^g)$.

Table 1. Statistical analysis of the experimental data sets.

NO.	Name	Class	Samples	Dimensionality
1	ALLAML	2	72	7129
2	LUNG	5	203	12600
3	Carcinomas	11	174	9182
4	Prostate-GE	2	102	5966
5	ORL face database	40	400	4096
6	extended Yale Face Database B	15	165	4096

Table 2. Classification accuracies with STD on the gene expression data ($T = 5$).

Data Set	Method				
	FLD	MMC	MMC-L1	MMF	**M3FL**
ALLAML	78.67 ± 3.17	68.6 ± 4.12	79.7 ± 3.05	80.2 ± 2.71	$\mathbf{83.4 \pm 2.25}$
LUNG	83.9 ± 5.75	81.1 ± 4.56	84.5 ± 5.32	88.7 ± 5.24	$\mathbf{90.5 \pm 4.56}$
Carcinomas	81.5 ± 5.25	82.7 ± 5.64	86.0 ± 4.58	88.5 ± 4.19	$\mathbf{90.1 \pm 3.27}$
Prostate-GE	76.5 ± 5.52	72.7 ± 4.93	74.6 ± 5.37	80.2 ± 4.38	$\mathbf{84.3 \pm 4.15}$

6 Experiments

In this section, we conduct the experiments on six benchmark data sets, which are four gene expression data sets including ALLAML [2], LUNG [1], Carcinomas [29] and Prostate-GE [20] and two image data sets including the ORL face database [25] and the extended Yale Face Database B database [14]. Table 1 shows the statistical analysis of data sets used in this work, including the class and dimensionality.

To demonstrate the efficiency of M3FL, we compare it with four different methods, including FLD [12], MMC [13], MMC-ℓ_1 [19] and MMF. All the used data sets are firstly standardized to be the optimal zero-mean via the technology proposed in [17]. To reduce the computation complexity in the training process, the training data are firstly handled with PCA [18]. We set $d = 25$ for the gene expression data, $d = 50$ for the ORL face database and $d = 35$ for the extended Yale Face Database B database. The parameter ν is set to 0.8 for MMC-ℓ_1. The nearest neighbour classifier is selected. For each experiment, the training set is randomly chosen in each data set and the experiment is carried out 10 times. We adopt the average value of the accuracies over these 10 repetitions.

6.1 Results on Gene Expression Data

In this experiment, we set the training number $T = 5$ and remainders are for testing. Table 2 shows the classification results with the corresponding standard deviation (STD). Compared with other methods, M3FL can achieve a higher classification accuracy in most cases and M3FL is around 5%–13% better than other methods, which indicates that M3FL has a higher and more certain performance than other methods.

6.2 Results on Image Data

We set the training number $T = (5, 6, 7, 8)$ for the ORL database and $T = (20, 30, 40, 50)$ for the extended Yale Face Database B, remainders are for testing. The results are shown in Figs. 3 and 4. Compared with other methods, we can draw the same conclusion as the one in last experiment. To test the robustness, the ORL database and the extended Yale B database are contaminated by the 10% and 20% of the Gaussian noise, respectively. Then we chose the same experimental settings as the ones in the last experiment. As we can see in Figs. 5 and 6, the performance of robustness is verified from the high classification accuracy of M3FL.

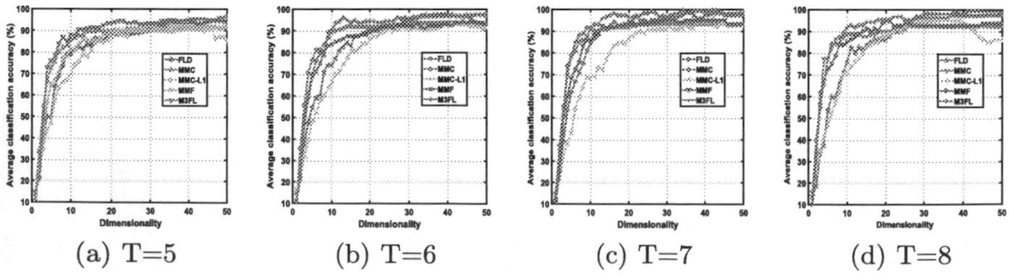

Fig. 3. Average classification accuracies for different number of training samples on ORL data set.

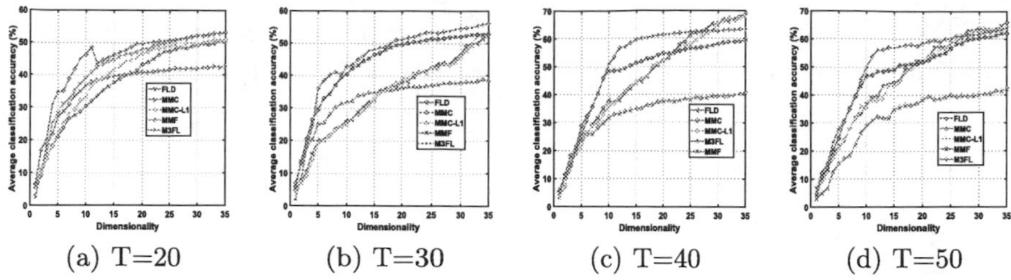

(a) T=20 (b) T=30 (c) T=40 (d) T=50

Fig. 4. Average classification accuracies for different number of the training samples on extended Yale Face Database B.

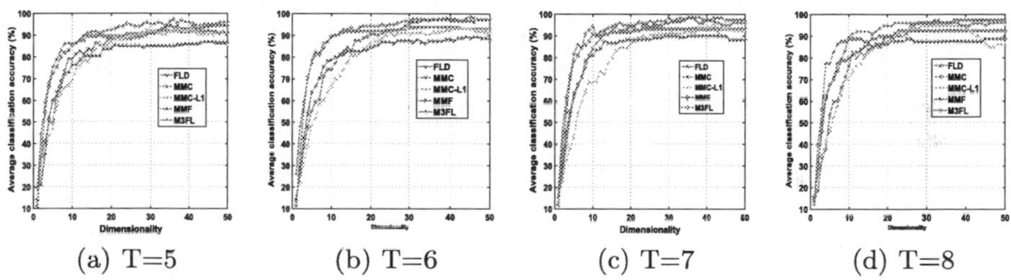

(a) T=5 (b) T=6 (c) T=7 (d) T=8

Fig. 5. Average classification accuracies for different number of the training samples on the contaminated ORL data set.

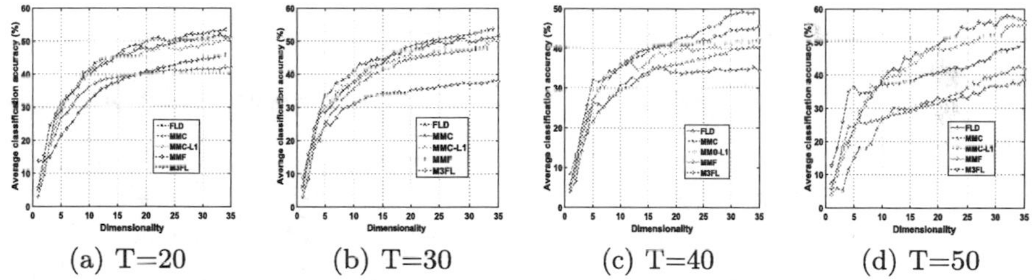

(a) T=20 (b) T=30 (c) T=40 (d) T=50

Fig. 6. Average classification accuracies for different number of training samples on the contaminated extended Yale Face Database B.

7 Conclusions and Future Work

In this paper, we propose a M3FL method, in which all the discriminative features can be generated simultaneously. From the perspective of matrix entropy, we analyze the proposed MMF and find that the performance can be improved by making the matrix entropy of the projection matrix as small as possible, and the corresponding optimization algorithm is developed. In addition, we discuss the relationship between the proposed optimization algorithm w.r.t. M3FL and the optimization algorithm w.r.t. MMF. Experimental results on six benchmark data sets demonstrate the superiority of M3FL. Further more, we will improve M3FL with graph embedding for the semi-supervised feature learning in the future. We also look forward to combine M3FL with other models, such as convolutional neural network, recurrent neural network, and so on.

References

1. Bhattacharjee, A., et al.: Classification of human lung carcinomas by mRNA expression profiling reveals distinct adenocarcinoma subclasses. Proc. Nat. Acad. Sci. USA **98**(24), 13790–13795 (2001)
2. Fodor, S.P.A.: DNA sequencing: massively parallel genomics. Science **277**(5324), 393–395 (1997)
3. Hou, C., Jiao, Y., Nie, F., Luo, T., Zhou, Z.: 2D feature selection by sparse matrix regression. IEEE Trans. Image Process. **26**(9), 4255–4268 (2017)
4. Li, B.N., Yu, Q., Wang, R., Xiang, K., Wang, M., Li, X.: Block principal component analysis with nongreedy l1-norm maximization. IEEE Trans. Cybern. **46**(11), 2543–2547 (2016)
5. Li, B., Zheng, C.H., Huang, D.S.: Locally linear discriminant embedding: an efficient method for face recognition. Pattern Recogn. **41**(12), 3813–3821 (2008)
6. Li, C., Liu, Q., Dong, W., Wei, F., Zhang, X., Yang, L.: Max-margin-based discriminative feature learning. IEEE Trans. Neural Netw. **27**(12), 2768–2775 (2016)
7. Li, C., Shao, Y., Deng, N.Y.: Robust l1-norm two-dimensional linear discriminant analysis. Neural Netw. **65**(C), 92–104 (2015)
8. Li, H., Jiang, T., Zhang, K.: Efficient and robust feature extraction by maximum margin criterion. IEEE Trans. Neural Netw. **17**(1), 157–165 (2006)
9. Li, M., Yuan, B.: 2D-LDA: a statistical linear discriminant analysis for image matrix. Pattern Recogn. Lett. **26**(5), 527–532 (2005)
10. Li, Z., Tang, J.: Unsupervised feature selection via nonnegative spectral analysis and redundancy control. IEEE Trans. Image Process. **24**(12), 5343–5355 (2015)
11. Li, Z., Tang, J., He, X.: Robust structured nonnegative matrix factorization for image representation. IEEE Trans. Neural Netw. **29**, 1947–1960 (2018)
12. Liu, C., Wechsler, H.: Gabor feature based classification using the enhanced fisher linear discriminant model for face recognition. IEEE Trans. Image Process. **11**(4), 467–476 (2002)
13. Liu, J., Chen, S., Tan, X., Zhang, D.: Comments on efficient and robust feature extraction by maximum margin criterion. IEEE Trans. Neural Netw. **18**(6), 1862–1864 (2007)
14. Liu, Y., Gao, Q., Miao, S., Gao, X., Nie, F., Li, Y.: A non-greedy algorithm for l1-norm LDA. IEEE Trans. Image Process. **26**(2), 684–695 (2016)
15. Lu, G.F., Tang, G., Zou, J.: Spare l1-norm-based maximum margin criterion. J. Vis. Commun. Image Represent. **38**(C), 11–17 (2016)
16. Muller, H., Stadtmuller, U.: Estimation of heteroscedasticity in regression analysis. Ann. Stat. **15**(2), 610–625 (1987)
17. Nie, F., Yuan, J., Huang, H.: Optimal mean robust principal component analysis. In: International Conference on Machine Learning, pp. 1062–1070 (2014)
18. Price, A.L., Patterson, N.J., Plenge, R.M., Weinblatt, M.E., Shadick, N.A., Reich, D.: Principal components analysis corrects for stratification in genome-wide association studies. Nat. Genet. **38**(8), 904–907 (2006)
19. Si, C., Dao, C., Bin, L.: L1-norm-based maximum margin criterion. Chin. J. Electron. **44**(6), 1383–1388 (2016)

20. Singh, D., et al.: Gene expression correlates of clinical prostate cancer behavior. Cancer Cell **1**(2), 203–209 (2002)
21. Tang, J., Li, Z., Wang, M., Zhao, R.: Neighborhood discriminant hashing for large-scale image retrieval. IEEE Trans. Image Process. **24**(9), 2827–2840 (2015)
22. Tang, J., et al.: Tri-clustered tensor completion for social-aware image tag refinement. IEEE Trans. Pattern Anal. Mach. Intell. **39**(8), 1662–1674 (2017)
23. Tao, D., Li, X., Wu, X., Maybank, S.J.: General tensor discriminant analysis and gabor features for gait recognition. IEEE Trans. Pattern Anal. Mach. Intell. **29**(10), 1700–1715 (2007)
24. Wan, M., Lai, Z.: Multi-manifold locality graph embedding based on the maximum margin criterion (MLGE/MMC) for face recognition. IEEE Access **5**, 9823–9830 (2017)
25. Wang, H., Lu, X., Hu, Z., Zheng, W.: Fisher discriminant analysis with l1-norm. IEEE Trans. Cybern. **44**(6), 828–842 (2013)
26. Wang, Q., Gao, Q.: Two-dimensional PCA with f-norm minimization. In: Proceedings of the Thirty-First AAAI Conference on Artificial Intelligence, pp. 2718–2724 (2017)
27. Xie, J., Jian, Y., Qian, J., Ying, T., Zhang, H.: Robust nuclear norm-based matrix regression with applications to robust face recognition. IEEE Trans. Image Process. **5**(99), 2286–2295 (2017)
28. Xu, D., Yan, S., Tao, D., Lin, S., Zhang, H.: Marginal fisher analysis and its variants for human gait recognition and content-based image retrieval. IEEE Trans. Image Process. **16**(11), 2811–2821 (2007)
29. Yang, K.J., Cai, Z., Li, J., Lin, G.: A stable gene selection in microarray data analysis. BMC Bioinform. **7**(1), 228–244 (2006)
30. Ye, Q., Yang, J., Liu, F., Zhao, C., Ye, N., Yin, T.: L1-norm distance linear discriminant analysis based on an effective iterative algorithm. IEEE Trans. Circuits Syst. Video Technol. **28**(1), 114–129 (2018)
31. Ye, Q., Yang, J., Yin, T., Zhang, Z.: Can the virtual labels obtained by traditional LP approaches be well encoded in WLR. IEEE Trans. Neural Netw. **27**(7), 1591–1598 (2016)
32. Ye, Q., Yin, T., Gao, S., Jing, J., Zhang, Y., Sun, C.: Recursive dimension reduction for semisupervised learning. Neurocomputing **171**, 1629–1636 (2016)
33. Zhang, D., Zhang, L., Ye, Q., Ruan, H.: Robust learning-based prediction for timber-volume of living trees. Comput. Electron. Agric. **136**, 97–110 (2017)
34. Zhang, Z., Chow, T.W.S.: Robust linearly optimized discriminant analysis. Neurocomputing **79**, 140–157 (2012)
35. Zhang, Z., Chow, W.S.: Tensor locally linear discriminative analysis. IEEE Sig. Process. Lett. **18**(11), 643–646 (2011)
36. Zhang, Z., Yan, S., Zhao, M.: Pairwise sparsity preserving embedding for unsupervised subspace learning and classification. IEEE Trans. Image Process. **22**(12), 4640–4651 (2013)
37. Zheng, W., Lai, J., Li, S.Z.: 1D-LDA vs. 2D-LDA: when is vector-based linear discriminant analysis better than matrix-based? Pattern Recogn. **41**(7), 2156–2172 (2008)

Spectral Image Visualization Using Generative Adversarial Networks

Siyu Chen(✉), Danping Liao, and Yuntao Qian

College of Computer Science, Zhejiang University, HangZhou, China
{sychen,liaodanping,ytqian}@zju.edu.cn

Abstract. Spectral images captured by satellites and radio-telescopes are analyzed to obtain information about geological compositions distributions, distant asters as well as undersea terrain. Spectral images usually contain tens to hundreds of continuous narrow spectral bands, so the visualization based on information fusion and dimensional reduction is required for proper display on a trichromatic monitor which is important for spectral image processing and analysis system. The visualizations of spectral images should preserve as much information as possible from the original signal and facilitate image interpretation. However, most of the existing visualization methods display spectral images in false colors, which contradicts with human's expectation and experience. In this paper, we present a novel visualization method based on generative adversarial network (GAN) to display spectral images in natural colors, in which a structure loss and an adversarial loss are combined to form a new loss function. The adversarial loss fits the visualized image to the natural image distribution using a discriminator network that is trained to distinguish false-color images from natural-color images. At the same time, we use an improved cycle loss as the structure constraint to guarantee structure consistency. Experimental results show that our method is able to generate structure-preserved and natural-looking visualizations.

Keywords: Image visualization · Spectral image
Generative adversarial nets

1 Introduction

The rapid development of imaging technology brings about the ability to capture images with high spectral resolution. Hyperspectral imaging sensors, for example, routinely capture more than 100 channels of spectral data. Ultimately, it is often human observers who interpret these images for analysis and diagnosis. However, human's eyes are merely capable of sensing a very narrow range of the electromagnetic wavelength. It is thus crucial to reduce the dimensionality of spectral images so that the images can be displayed on an visual output device. Although the requirements of visualization are task dependent, there are some common goals such as consistent rendering, information preservation and natural palette [11]. Many methods are developed following some, or all, of these requirements.

X. Geng and B.-H. Kang (Eds.): PRICAI 2018, LNAI 11012, pp. 388–401, 2018.
https://doi.org/10.1007/978-3-319-97304-3_30

The most straightforward visualization method is to select three representative bands from the original image to display. Band selection methods such as linear prediction (LP) was applied to select the most informative bands [24]. One disadvantage of band selection methods is that, except for the selected bands, all the information contained in other channels is ignored.

To preserve the information across the whole range of wavelength, dimension reduction methods such as principle component analysis [25] and independent component analysis [29] were proposed. To better preserve the nonlinear and local structures, manifold learning methods were applied to spectral image visualization tasks [2]. In [13], in order to preserve the edge information, bilateral filtering is applied to calculate the band weights at each pixel for band image fusion. These local structure-based approaches perform well in preserving the intrinsic information of spectral images.

To achieve balanced trade-off between multiple information preservation requirements, optimization-based approaches [14,19,20] are also used for spectral image visualization. These methods try to meet specific visualization criteria by defining corresponding cost functions. In [20], for instance, by combining a global and a local stochastic search using the Metropolis criterion, a nonlinear bicriteria optimization is proposed to obtain three representative bands. The primary challenge of optimization-based methods is determining the optimal cost function for complex criteria, requirement of pixel-wise labeling, and inference-time complexity.

While most existing visualization methods try to preserve as much information as possible from the original data, most of them display spectral images in false colors. The false-color visualizations brings interpretation difficulties because the colors of objects are very different from what is expected by humans. Moreover, most data-adaptive methods suffer from "inconsistent rendering" problem, i.e., very different colors might be assigned to the same objects/materials in different images, which also hinders the interpretation of spectral images. Therefore, "natural palette" and "consistent rendering" gradually become two important criteria for visualization quality evaluation.

To produce consistent natural-looking images, Jacobson *et al.* [11] proposed a stretched color matching function (CMF) for visualization, which stretches the CIE 1964 tristimulus color matching functions from the visible range to the invisible range. However, the stretched CMF is fixed for each type of hyperspectral imaging sensor, which limits its capability in preserving the specific information in different spectral images.

Connah *et al.* [3] used a constrained contrast mapping paradigm in the gradient domain to generate a visualization that shares similar colors with a corresponding natural-looking RGB image. This method requires pixel-wise matching between the spectral image and the corresponding RGB image, which limits its applications in general scenarios where pixel-wise matching is hard to obtain.

Liao *et al.* utilized manifold alignment to transfer colors from natural RGB images to hyperspectral images [15–17]. The approach is capable of visualizing the hyperspectral image in natural colors as well as preserving local similarity

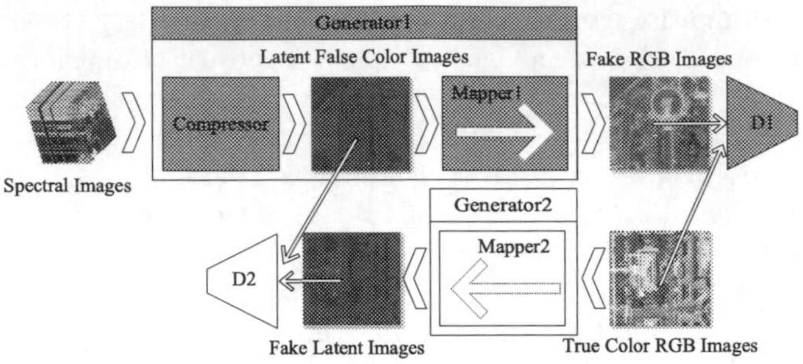

Fig. 1. The model structure of VGAN. (Color figure online)

between hyperspectral pixels. However, manifold alignment also requires a set of matching pixels between the hyperspectral image and the referencing RGB image. As a result, the corresponding RGB image should be captured at exactly the same site as the hyperspectral image and should not have large geometric distortion in order to obtain precise image registration.

Recently, Generative Adversarial Network (GAN) based techniques have demonstrated remarkable effectiveness in colorization and style transfer [10,22, 28]. Unlike traditional style transfer methods that specifically and explicitly design objectives for the model, GAN utilizes a discriminator network to guide the generator. Such an adversarial learning technique makes it possible to train a strong generative model in an unsupervised way without pixel labeling or paired samples. These advantages make GAN a promising visualization technique.

In this work we propose an end-to-end visualization generative adversarial network (VGAN), in which a deep residual structure (ResNet) is used. Our goal is to generate natural and structure-preserved visualizations for spectral images. Different from previous methods that require image-pairing and pixel-wise matching between natural images and the spectral images to "transfer" colors, our model is totally unsupervised and can automatically learn the correspondence between different data distributions. To achieve our goal, we propose a loss function which consists of an adversarial loss and a cycle-consistency loss. The adversarial loss pushes our solution to the natural image manifold using a discriminator network that is trained to distinguish false-color images from natural-color images. The cycle-consistency loss guarantees the structure preservation of the spectral image during color mapping. The model structure of the VGAN is shown in Fig. 1. Based on Cycle-GAN [28], VGAN comprises two generators and two discriminators. Generator_1 contains: 1. a *compressor* network that fuses input spectral images to a 3-band image; 2. a *mapper* that translates the output of the compressor to a natural-looing image. Discriminator_1 encourages Generator_1 to produce visualizations indistinguishable from natural color images. We also use a second generator, a mapper from natural-looking images to the latent output space of the compressor, to guarantee structure consistency by minimizing the cycle loss. Both compressor and mapper networks use very small convolution kernels which allows the feature maps to be more structural consistent. Application of small kernels makes the model faster and easier to train, as pointed out by recent model compression researches [8,9].

In this paper we make the following contributions. First, we propose a new method in which GAN is utilized to visualize spectral image. To our knowledge, this is the first time that GAN is used for spectral image visualization. Introducing GAN into this task also makes the visualization natural in a data-driven way with unsupervised-training. Second, we propose a novel cycle loss based on [28], to preserve the spatial structure as well as information. Finally, we present a new network architecture which is light-weight yet effective for high quality spectral image visualizations.

This paper is organized in the following order: Sect. 2 explains GAN and its adversarial learning techniques; Sect. 3 introduces the proposed GAN for spectral image visualization; Sect. 4 shows the experimental results and comparisons. The conclusions are presented in Sect. 5.

2 Generative Adversarial Nets

GAN was firstly introduced by Goodfellow [5], in which, noise z sampled from uniform distribution is passed to an up-sampling network G to generate image $G(z)$ from some latent distribution. The goal of network G is to generate images that are highly similar to real images and thus difficult to classify by a differentiable discriminator D. This is achieved by maximizing the targets L_D and L_G alternately.

$$L_D = \mathop{\mathbb{E}}_{\substack{x \sim p_{data} \\ z \sim p_{noise}}} \log(D(x)) + \log\left(1 - D(G(z))\right), \tag{1}$$

$$L_G = \mathop{\mathbb{E}}_{z \sim p_{noise}} \log(D(G(z))), \tag{2}$$

in which, $\mathbb{E}$ is the mathematical expectation notation. p_{data} stands for the distribution of true data (real images, for example) while p_{noise} is the random noise distribution.

D takes in real image $x \sim p_{data}$ and fake image $G(z)$ and gives discriminative confidence $y \in [0, 1]$. Higher confidence indicates more likely of being a real image.

This adversarial process has an optimal solution where nash equilibrium is achieved. The following equations hold when the optimal solution is reached.

$$\mathop{\mathbb{E}}_{\substack{x \sim p_{data} \\ z \sim p_{noise}}} \log(D^*(G^*(z))) - \log(D^*(x)) = 0, \tag{3}$$

$$\mathop{\mathbb{E}}_{z \sim p_{noise}} D^*(G^*(z)) = 0.5, \tag{4}$$

$$\mathop{\mathbb{E}}_{x \sim p_{data}} D^*(x) = 0.5. \tag{5}$$

3 Proposed Method

The goal of VGAN is to estimate a structure-preserved and natural-looking visualization for an input spectral image.

In our model, a spectral image from domain A is transformed to domain B by a *compressor* network. The compressor compresses the number of image channels down to 3, and outputs a false-color image.

Then the false-color image is mapped to domain C where images have natural color distributions. This mapping is performed by a *Mapper* network, whose input and output are of the same size but different in color style.

The compressor and mapper network together form our desired generator network that can change both the channel number and the color style. In order to generate structure-consistent visualizations, we impose a cycle loss by using a second heterogeneous generator that maps images from domain C to domain B when training the model.

VGAN is constructed with heterogeneous generator network architectures. The generator $G_{A \to C}$ contains two parts: compressor Cpr and mapper M_1. The generator $G_{C \to B}$ contains only one mapper M_2. The M_1, M_2 and Cpr correspond with *Mapper 1*, *Mapper 2* and *Compressor* in Fig. 1.

3.1 Formulation

The objective of VGAN is to learn a mapping function from spectral image domain A to natural RGB domain C via a latent false-color domain B as a bridge, given training samples $\{x_i\}_{i=1}^{N}$ where $x_i \in A$, and $\{y_j\}_{i=1}^{M}$ where $y_i \in C$. There are three mapping functions to be learned.

One of the mapping functions maps the image from domain A to B, one from B to C and another one maps the image from C back to B. We denote the data distribution as $x \sim \mathbb{P}_A$, $y \sim \mathbb{P}_C$ and $z \sim \mathbb{P}_B$ where z is translated from domain A. Formally, the three mappings are $Cpr : A \to B$, $M_1 : B \to C$ and $M_2 : C \to B$, which compose two generative mappings $G_{A \to C}(x) = M_1(Cpr(x))$ and $G_{C \to B}(y) = M_2(y)$.

In addition, we use two adversarial discriminators D_C and D_B, where D_C aims to distinguish between images $\{y\}$ and visualized images $G_{A \to C}(x)$; in the same way, D_B aims to discriminate between $\{z\}$ and $G_{C \to B}(y)$.

Our objective contains two types of terms: *adversarial losses* to constrain the output of mapping functions to be as similar as possible to the target domain; and *cycle consistency losses* to preserve the structure.

Adversarial Loss. Adversarial losses are applied to both of the generators. For the generator $G_{A \to C}$ its discriminator D_C, the objective is formulated as follows:

$$\begin{aligned} \mathcal{L}_{GAN}(G_{A \to C}, D_C, A, C) = & \mathop{\mathbb{E}}_{y \sim \mathbb{P}_C} \log(D_C(y)) \\ & + \mathop{\mathbb{E}}_{x \sim \mathbb{P}_A} \log(1 - D_C(G_{A \to C}(x))), \end{aligned} \tag{6}$$

where $G_{A \to C}$ takes in images from domain A and generate images similar to images from domain C, while D_C aims to distinguish fake images generated by $G_{A \to C}$ from images in domain C. A similar adversarial loss is introduced for the generator $G_{C \to B}$ and its discriminator D_B as well:

$$\min_{G_{C \to B}} \max_{D_B} \mathcal{L}_{GAN}(G_{C \to B}, D_B, C, B), \tag{7}$$

where the samples of domain B is generated by $Cpr(x), x \sim \mathbb{P}_A$.

Cycle Consistency Loss. Because of the implications of adversarial loss that, given a mapping function M, any mappings obtained by permutating the images in the target domain gives similar loss value. Thus, with only adversarial loss, it cannot be guaranteed that the learned function can map input x_i to a desired y_i. Cycle consistency loss can help to prevent the function from mapping all the x_i to a single highly realistic y_i, as has been reported in [23]. If the mapping functions are cycle-consistent, for each image x from domain A, the mapping cycle should bring x back to a specified stage, i.e. $x \to Cpr(x) \to G_{A \to C}(x) \to G_{C \to B}(G_{A \to C}(x)) \approx Cpr(x)$. This means, to recover $Cpr(x)$ from $G_{C \to B}(x)$, the information contained in $Cpr(x)$ such as structure/texture should be preserved by $G_{A \to C}$. The cycle consistency loss is formulated as:

$$\begin{aligned} \mathcal{L}_{cyc}(M_1, M_2) = & \mathop{\mathbb{E}}_{x \sim \mathbb{P}_A} [\|M_2(M_1(Cpr(x))) - Cpr(x)\|] \\ & + \mathop{\mathbb{E}}_{y \sim \mathbb{P}_C} [\|M_1(M_2(y)) - y\|]. \end{aligned} \tag{8}$$

Full Objective. Our overall objective is:

$$\begin{aligned} \mathcal{L}(G_{A \to C}, G_{C \to B}, D_C, D_B) = & \mathcal{L}_{GAN}(G_{A \to C}, D_C, A, C) \\ & + \mathcal{L}_{GAN}(G_{C \to B}, D_B, C, B) \\ & + \lambda \mathcal{L}_{cyc}(M_1, M_2). \end{aligned} \tag{9}$$

Earth-Mover distance from WGAN [1] is used to formulate objectives for optimization. In WGAN, discriminators are constrained to be 1-Lipschitz functions and their losses are constructed using the Kantorovich-Rubinstein duality.

There are works show that the original WGAN tends to have extreme-valued or extremely distributed weights because of the weight clipping scheme [6]. To alleviate this phenomenon, we optimize the expectation using sigmoid cross-entropy metric. The removal of the commonly-used softmax activation in discriminator prevents the weights from growing too large. We argue that together with sigmoid cross-entropy metric, softmax activation removal, batch normalization and data augmentation which averts large weights caused by over-fitting, the discriminators can be efficient approximations to k-Lipschitz functions.

The adversarial loss of discriminator that distinguishes real samples in domain C from fake samples generated by mapping functions $G_{A \to C}$ is:

$$\begin{aligned} & \mathcal{L}_D(C, G_{A \to C}) \\ & = \mathop{\mathbb{E}}_{y \sim \mathbb{P}_C} CE(S(D_C(y)), \mathbf{1}) + \mathop{\mathbb{E}}_{x \sim \mathbb{P}_A} CE(S(D_C(G_{A \to C}(x))), \mathbf{0}) \end{aligned} \tag{10}$$

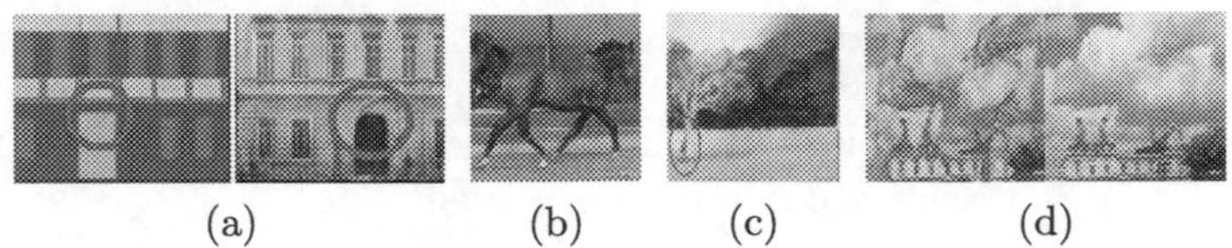

Fig. 2. Common problems in GANs. (a) Inconsistent structure in pix2pix. (b) Fabricated patterns in Progressive-GAN. (c) Incorrect coloring in Cycle-GAN. (d) Inconsistent coloring in Cycle-GAN. (Color figure online)

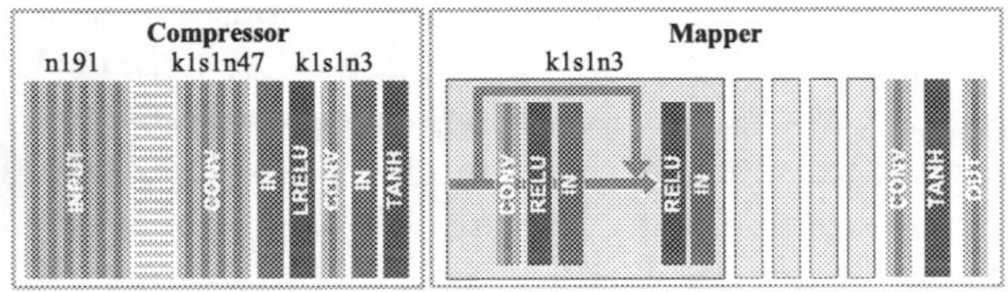

Fig. 3. Network architecture of the generator (ours).

where CE stands for cross-entropy function and S is softmax function.

The adversarial loss of generator that takes input from domain A and generate samples in domain C is:

$$\mathcal{L}_G(A, C) = \mathop{\mathbb{E}}_{x \sim \mathbb{P}_A} CE\left(S(D_C(G_{A \rightarrow C}(x))), \mathbf{1}\right). \tag{11}$$

We learn the discriminative models via performing the minimization:

$$J^{D^*} = \min_{\theta_D} \mathcal{L}_D(C, G_{A \rightarrow C}) + \mathcal{L}_D(B, G_{C \rightarrow B}). \tag{12}$$

The generators are learned by the following optimization:

$$J^{G^*} = \min_{\theta_G} \mathcal{L}_G(A, C) + \mathcal{L}_G(C, B) + \lambda \mathcal{L}_{cyc}(M_1, M_2). \tag{13}$$

3.2 Architecture

Prevailing architectures of generators like in most of cGANs [21] are based on encoder-decoder structure for color stylization and transfer [10,28]. However, the auto-encoder architecture is prone to generating fabricated textures with inconsistent shapes and coloring as shown in Fig. 2, making it not suitable for visualization tasks which require precision and preciseness. Some attempts have been made to use U-net to preserve the image structure [10,27] but the improvement is not significant.

The architecture of VGAN differs from previous GANs in two primary aspects. First, the images is not down-sampled or up-sampled spatially. This ensures that the original details are not destroyed by down-sampling and no extra texture is created by up-sampling. Second, the kernel size of all the convolutions are set to 1 to prevent the network from generating blurred texture.

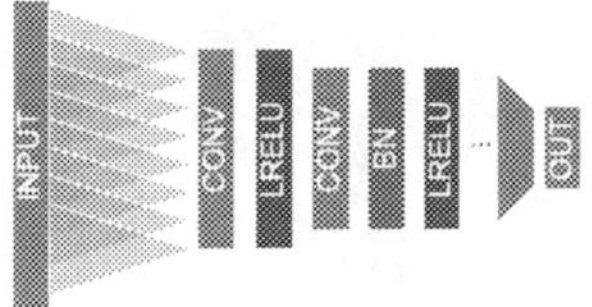

(a) General structure.

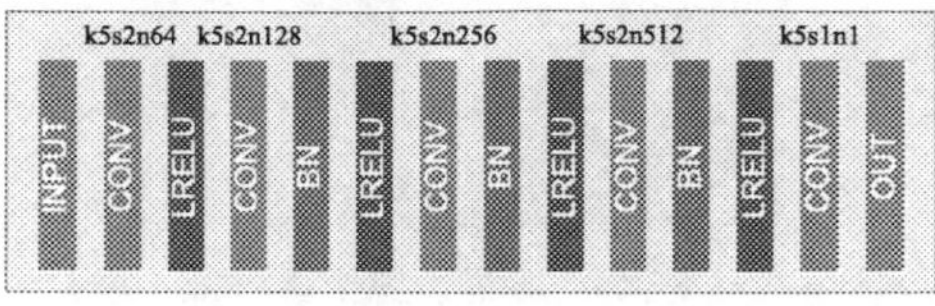

(b) Details about the structure used.

Fig. 4. Architecture of the discriminator.

The architecture of generator $G_{A \to C}$ is shown in Fig. 3, in which k stands for kernel size, s is the stride size of the convolutional layer and n is the depth/filters of the layer. The network architecture of the mapper in generator $G_{C \to B}$ is identical to the mapper in $G_{A \to C}$. The compressor network contains two stride-1 convolutions. The output of compressor is activated by $tanh$ so that the output is in the same range with the output of generator $G_{C \to B}$. The mapper network in generator $G_{A \to C}$ contains 5 residual blocks and one convolution layer with stride set to 1. We leverage the residual blocks in our architecture based on [7]. Instance normalization is used in generator networks to diminish the influence of instance-specific contrast information in each input image [26].

The architecture of the discriminator is shown in Fig. 4. It consists of 4 convolutional layers with batch-normalization and Leaky-ReLU activation. The leak ratio is set to 0.2. Each convolutional layer reduce both the height and width of an image by a factor of 2. At the end of the network, the values given by the last convolution operation are reshaped to a vector as the output. For better gradient behaviour, the final output is not passed to fully-connected layers [18].

In our model, the kernel size is set to 1. It is highly unlikely to generate excessive fabricated artifacts and textures by such an pixel-wise computation. On the contrary, pixel-wise operations are inclined to cause topology simplification and feature merging. With the explicit cycle-consistency constraint reinforcing the information preservation and the implicit constraint reducing unwanted excessive creations, the networks is optimized to be structure consistent and nature in color style.

We also tried a GAN model without the cycle architecture. The colors and spatial structure in those visualization results were incorrect. Several losses were explored to improve the performance but no significant improvement is observed.

4 Experiments

We compare our method with several well-known/recent methods that have been introduced in Sect. 1, including Stretched CMF [11], LP Band Selection [24], Bicriteria Optimization [20], Bilateral Filtering [13] and Manifold Alignment [16]. The data, detailed experiment settings and results will be introduced in the following subsections.

Fig. 5. The 50th band of the HSI

Fig. 6. One of the RGB images taken from Google Maps. (New York city) (Color figure online)

4.1 Datasets

In our experiment, we used a remote sensing hyperspectral image and a set of RGB images obtained from Google Earth for training. It is worth mentioning that, since a well-accepted distribution of *natural color* is hard to depict, and this paper is not aimed at defining one, here we treat the RGB images from Google Earth as an approximation to real natural color images in the true nature image distribution. Because VGAN is a data-driven approach that can map the spectral images into any target domain specified by the training set, when provided with actual natural color images, VGAN will perform the mapping from spectral images to true natural color images.

The hyperspectral image is taken over Washington D.C. mall by the Hyperspectral Digital Imagery Collection Experiment sensor. There are 191 bands in the image after noisy bands are removed. The size of each band image is 1208×307. Its 50th band image is shown in Fig. 5. We collected 12 RGB images including scenes of New York (see Fig. 6), Orlando, and Washington. These images are of roughly the same size (about 1600×800) and have different spatial resolution. The spectral images and RGB images are sliced into 6000 overlapped patches with the size of 128×128 for training. We augmented the data set by applying flipping and rotation on the patches. For testing, the spectral image of D.C. mall is cut into non-overlapping patches. The visualization result is obtained by stitching the non-overlapping patches together.

4.2 Implementation Details

We used ADAM [12] for optimization and set the learning rate of the generator and the discriminator to 0.0001 and 0.00001, respectively. The weight of cycle-loss λ is set to 50. In order for the generator to produce more diverse outputs,

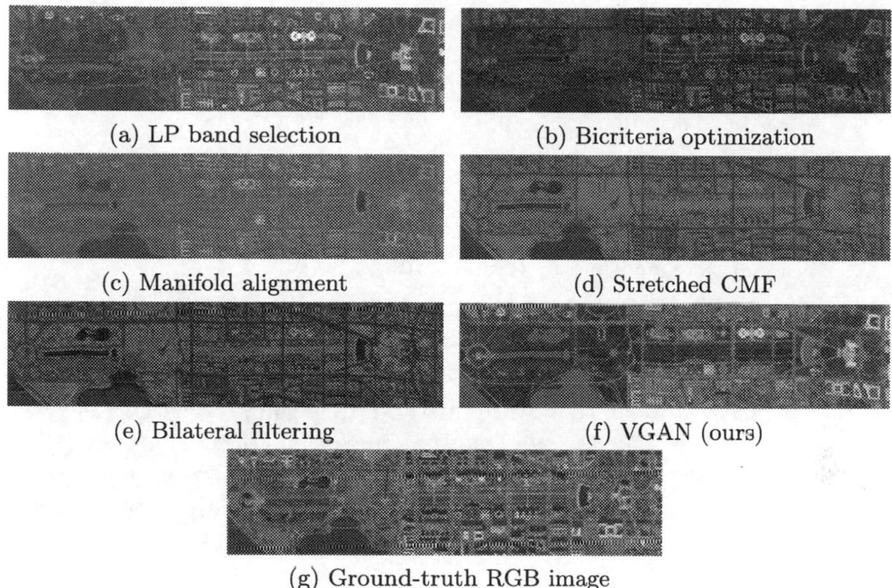

Fig. 7. Comparison of different approaches on the Washington DC Mall data set. The D.C. Mall spectral image was taken in Aug, 1995, and the RGB image from Google Earth was taken in 2017 winter. (Color figure online)

we follow the mini-batch technique proposed in [23], i.e., the discriminators are equipped with cached queues that store the most recent 50 fake images and 50 real images. The epoch size is set to 6000 and the model is trained for 2 epochs using A and B training data with a batch size of 1.

4.3 Visual and Quantitative Comparisons

Figure 7 shows the visual comparison of different visualization approaches on the Washington D.C. mall data.

It can be seen that the result of VGAN not only has a very natural tone but also preserves fine details.

Since there is no universally accepted standard for the quantitative assessment of spectral image visualization, we adopt 4 metrics including entropy [13], root-mean-square error(RMSE) [29], separability of features [4] and correlation coefficients between the RGB components (CORR) [29].

Entropy: Higher entropy indicates richer information in an image. The entropy of a 1-channel image is defined by $t = -\sum_i p(i) \ln p(i)$, in which $p(i)$ is the probability density of the intensity level i. The entropy of an RGB image is the average of all channels' entropy.

Table 1. Performance comparisons.

Method	Entropy	RMSE	CORR	Separabilit
LP band selection	6.59	68.35	0.92	55.68
Stretched CMF	3.89	92.46	0.36	30.08
Bilateral filtering	3.31	102.43	0.73	47.54
Bicriteria optimization	5.75	98.47	0.63	52.43
Manifold alignment	**10.32**	**33.23**	0.89	34.64
Ours	8.25	49.99	**0.98**	**64.89**

RMSE: RMSE is a straight-forward method to evaluate whether the visualization has natural colors [29]. Let $I(x)$ and $I'(x)$ denote the RGB vector of pixel x in the visualized image and the true color image, respectively. The RMSE between I and I' over the whole image is given by: $rmse = \sqrt{\frac{1}{N}\sum_x (I(x) - I'(x))}$.

CORR: Since natural images have a high degree of correlation between the RGB components [29], the correlation between the RGB components of the visualizations indicates the similarity of the visualizations to natural images. The two-dimensional normalized correlation function for images is defined as $CORR_{X,Y} = \frac{\sum_{m,n}(X_{mn}-\bar{X})(Y_{mn}-\bar{Y})}{\sum_{m,n}(X_{mn}-\bar{X})^2 \sum_{m,n}(Y_{mn}-\bar{Y})^2}$, where X, Y are two grey-scale images; and $\bar{X}$, $\bar{Y}$ are the means of X and Y, respectively. The overall CORR is obtained as the mean value of $C_{R,G}$, $C_{R,B}$ and $C_{B,G}$.

Separability of Features: Separability of features shows how well different pixels are mapped to distinct colors. The idea behind is that, in the color space, the average distance between two pixels should be as large as possible [4]. Separability of features is given by $\gamma = \frac{1}{(N-1)^2}\sum_{x \neq y} g(x,y)$, in which, $g(x,y)$ is the Euclidean distance between RGB pixels x and y. N denotes the number of all pixels. γ represents the average pairwise Euclidean distance in terms of all pixel pairs. Larger γ yields better separability.

The quantitative comparison results are shown in Table 1. Comparisons on entropy and RMSE shows that the performance of manifold alignment method stands out by solving the tradeoff between information preservation and natural rendering. Without supervision provided by paired labeling, our method still performs well under entropy and RMSE metrics. The results indicate that VGAN can visualize images with rich information and similar color to the unseen ground-truth. Compared to manifold alignment, which requires matching pixels for color transfer, our method achieves better CORR, which indicates the strong capability of VGAN in producing visualizations with natural color distribution. Also, the separability of our approach ranks the first place. This means our approach can render the image in natural color and also preserve the pixel separability in a way that doesn't need extra explicit constraints or supervision.

Notably, from the results shown in Fig. 7f we can see that even when the RGB training samples and the spectral image were taken in different seasons, VGAN is able to learn the most likely appearance of trees in summer instead of the sallow color directly transferred by manifold alignment. Our previous exploratory experiments show that this is not coincidental. By inspecting spectral pixel values, we found that the spectral character of plants is distinguishable from that of the ground. When mapped to vegetational-covered color distribution in a pixel-wise way, either the most representative colors are correctly assigned to ground and trees, or the mapping is done completely in the opposite way. It seems that the discriminator always awards the more natural mapping, which leads to all the pixels of lush plants being colored correctly.

In our experiments we found that, the network without cycle-loss performs much worse in terms of separability. This meets our expectation since cycle-loss requires the separability be preserved so that the details can be best recovered.

5 Conclusion

In this paper we present an unsupervised end-to-end approach VGAN for displaying spectral images in natural colors. By minimizing the adversarial loss of the discriminator which is trained to differentiate between false-color images and natural-color images, VGAN is able to generate natural-looking visualizations. In addition, we use a cycle-loss to overcome the ambiguity and structure inconsistent problem of classic GANs. Visualization results show that VGAN is capable of producing visualizations with rich information and very natural color distributions. Pixels in the spectral images are also well separated in the RGB space.

Acknowledgement. This work was supported by the National Natural Science Foundation of China 61571393, and the National Key Research and Development Program of China 2018YFB0505000.

References

1. Arjovsky, M., Chintala, S., Bottou, L.: Wasserstein GAN. ArXiv e-prints, January 2017
2. Bachmann, C.M., Ainsworth, T.L., Fusina, R.A.: Exploiting manifold geometry in hyperspectral imagery. IEEE Trans. Geosci. Remote Sens. **43**(3), 441–454 (2005)
3. Connah, D., Drew, M.S., Finlayson, G.D.: Spectral edge image fusion: theory and applications. In: Fleet, D., Pajdla, T., Schiele, B., Tuytelaars, T. (eds.) ECCV 2014 Part V. LNCS, vol. 8693, pp. 65–80. Springer, Cham (2014). https://doi.org/10.1007/978-3-319-10602-1_5
4. Cui, M., Razdan, A., Hu, J., Wonka, P.: Interactive hyperspectral image visualization using convex optimization. IEEE Trans. Geosci. Remote Sens. **47**(6), 1673–1684 (2009)
5. Goodfellow, I.J., et al.: Generative adversarial networks. arXiv:Machine Learning (2014)

6. Gulrajani, I., Ahmed, F., Arjovsky, M., Dumoulin, V., Courville, A.: Improved training of Wasserstein GANs. ArXiv e-prints, March 2017
7. He, K., Zhang, X., Ren, S., Sun, J.: Deep residual learning for image recognition. ArXiv e-prints, December 2015
8. Howard, A.G., et al.: MobileNets: efficient convolutional neural networks for mobile vision applications. ArXiv e-prints, April 2017
9. Iandola, F.N., Han, S., Moskewicz, M.W., Ashraf, K., Dally, W.J., Keutzer, K.: Squeezenet: Alexnet-level accuracy with 50x fewer parameters and <0.5MB model size. arXiv:1602.07360 (2016)
10. Isola, P., Zhu, J., Zhou, T., Efros, A.A.: Image-to-image translation with conditional adversarial networks. In: Computer Vision and Pattern Recognition, pp. 1125–1134 (2016)
11. Jacobson, N.P., Gupta, M.R.: Design goals and solutions for display of hyperspectral images. IEEE Trans. Geosci. Remote Sens. **43**(11), 2684–2692 (2005)
12. Kingma, D.P., Ba, J.: Adam: a method for stochastic optimization. arXiv preprint arXiv:1412.6980 (2014)
13. Kotwal, K., Chaudhuri, S.: Visualization of hyperspectral images using bilateral filtering. IEEE Trans. Geosci. Remote Sens. **48**(5), 2308–2316 (2010)
14. Kotwal, K., Chaudhuri, S.: An optimization-based approach to fusion of hyperspectral images. IEEE J. Sel. Topics Appl. Earth Obs. Rem. Sens. **5**(2), 501–509 (2012)
15. Liao, D., Qian, Y., Zhou, J.: Visualization of hyperspectral imaging data based on manifold alignment. In: 2014 22nd International Conference on Pattern Recognition (ICPR), pp. 70–75. IEEE (2014)
16. Liao, D., Qian, Y., Zhou, J., Tang, Y.Y.: A manifold alignment approach for hyperspectral image visualization with natural color. IEEE Trans. Geosci. Remote Sens. **54**(6), 3151–3162 (2016)
17. Liao, D., Ye, M., Jia, S., Qian, Y.: Visualization of hyperspectral imagery based on manifold learning. In: 2013 IEEE International Geoscience and Remote Sensing Symposium (IGARSS), pp. 1979–1982. IEEE (2013)
18. Lin, M., Chen, Q., Yan, S.: Network in network. arXiv preprint arXiv:1312.4400 (2013)
19. Mignotte, M.: A multiresolution Markovian fusion model for the color visualization of hyperspectral images. IEEE Trans. Geosci. Remote Sens. **48**(12), 4236–4247 (2010)
20. Mignotte, M.: A bicriteria-optimization-approach-based dimensionality-reduction model for the color display of hyperspectral images. IEEE Trans. Geosci. Remote Sens. **50**(2), 501–513 (2012)
21. Mirza, M., Osindero, S.: Conditional generative adversarial nets. ArXiv e-prints, November 2014
22. Radford, A., Metz, L., Chintala, S.: Unsupervised representation learning with deep convolutional generative adversarial networks. In: International Conference on Learning Representations (2016)
23. Salimans, T., Goodfellow, I., Zaremba, W., Cheung, V., Radford, A., Chen, X.: Improved techniques for training GANs. ArXiv e-prints, June 2016
24. Su, H., Du, Q., Du, P.: Hyperspectral image visualization using band selection. IEEE J. Select. Topics Appl. Earth Observ. Remote Sens. **7**(6), 2647–2658 (2014)
25. Tyo, J.S., Konsolakis, A., Diersen, D.I., Olsen, R.C.: Principal-components-based display strategy for spectral imagery. IEEE Trans. Geosci. Remote Sens. **41**(3), 708–718 (2003)

26. Ulyanov, D., Vedaldi, A., Lempitsky, V.: Instance normalization: the missing ingredient for fast stylization. ArXiv e-prints, July 2016
27. Yi, Z., Zhang, H., Tan, P., Gong, M.: DualGAN: unsupervised dual learning for image-to-image translation. ArXiv e-prints, April 2017
28. Zhu, J.Y., Park, T., Isola, P., Efros, A.A.: Unpaired image-to-image translation using cycle-consistent adversarial networks. arXiv preprint arXiv:1703.10593 (2017)
29. Zhu, Y., Varshney, P.K., Chen, H.: Evaluation of ICA based fusion of hyperspectral images for color display, pp. 1–7 (2007)

Fusing Semantic Prior Based Deep Hashing Method for Fuzzy Image Retrieval

Xiaolong Gong, Linpeng Huang(✉), and Fuwei Wang

Department of Computer Science, Shanghai Jiao Tong University, Shanghai, China
{gxl21438,lphuang,wfwzy2012}@sjtu.edu.cn

Abstract. Fuzzy image retrieval is a novel visual application about designing a multi-modal retrieval system that supports querying across image modalities, e.g., a fuzzy type image searches for some similar images. However, most existing deep hashing methods are not suitable for obtaining a robust image hash code on multi-modal retrieval task. In this paper, we propose *Fusing Semantic Prior based Deep Hashing* (FSPDH) method, which is the first attempt to integrate unsupervised semantic prior into end-to-end deep architecture for fuzzy image retrieval task. The major contribution in this work is extracting the prior information from images and incorporating it effectively into hash learning process. In addition, our strategy can be usefully used in single-modal retrieval task. Extensive experiments show that our FSPDH approach yields state-of-the-art results in both multi-modal and single-modal image retrieval tasks on our image datasets.

Keywords: Fuzzy image retrieval · Deep hashing · Multi-modal

1 Introduction

In the past decades, information retrieval techniques have attracted increasing attention in the presence of massive web datasets. Especially in multimedia cross-modal retrieval application, many previous works [7,9,11,12] attempt to approximate nearest neighbors search across different media modalities by using hashing method that brings both computation efficiency and search quality, e.g. search for relevant images through text queries. However, thousands of images are uploaded to the Internet every day, which increases the difficulty to retrieve correct images through complicated semantic text. Some search engines of app like Taobao[1] and Amazon[2] have product search function by uploading an image and taking the picture to search similarity products. However, many uploaded images from mobile devices are not clear due to lots of external reasons, such as camera pixel is too low, the surrounding light is not appropriate. All of the

[1] https://www.taobao.com/.
[2] https://www.amazon.com/.

X. Geng and B.-H. Kang (Eds.): PRICAI 2018, LNAI 11012, pp. 402–415, 2018.
https://doi.org/10.1007/978-3-319-97304-3_31

fuzzy images contribute to the bad search quality and poor user experience, which motivates us to focus on multi-modal fuzzy image retrieval task. In this work, we list four possible scenarios as our fuzzy image: pixel dropouts, noisy, high exposure, blurry.

To address the above problem, an advantageous solution is hashing method with shallow architectures. The goal of hashing is to learn binary code representation for data point while preserving the similarity in the original feature space. Some recent works [4,13] learn hash codes across modalities based on *Matrix Factorization (MF)* framework, demonstrating some promising results. Other methods [16,20,26] take advantage of the intra-modal similarity, trying to alleviate the semantic gap between multi-modal. However, without learning deep representation, existing methods based on shallow architectures cannot effectively work well in weaken semantic gap between high-level semantics and cannot exploit inherent correlation structure from different modalities. Recently, several deep models for hashing methods [3,18,21] have been proposed to capture heterogeneous correlation more effectively than shallow learning methods. They have integrated both feature learning and hashing encoding by using adaptive deep neural networks. Meanwhile, the latest deep hashing methods [12,15,23] have presented efficient performance on image-text retrieval task, but also their algorithms are limited to single-modal retrieval.

To date, most of effective deep hashing methods remain a challenge due to the semantic gap between the native features of modalities and the learned semantic representation, especially in our task. The key point in our work is how to extract intrinsic semantic characteristics behind images from different modalities. In this paper, we propose a novel multi-modal approach in fuzzy image retrieval application, called *Fusing Semantic Prior based Deep Hashing* (FSPDH) which has a great performance in both single-modal and multi-modal retrieval tasks. In addition, we create two multi-modal image datasets based on *Cifar-10* and *NUS-WIDE*, which can be used to simulate the fuzzy image retrieval process. FSPDH chooses *Auto-encoder* as an unsupervised semantic prior extractor, preserving similarity between unsupervised native features and the supervised semantic representation. The main contributions of FSPDH can be summarized as follows:

- We firstly construct two fuzzy image retrieval datasets and consider four common types of fuzzy image modality, including blurry images, noisy images, pixel dropouts and high exposure.
- The proposed FSPDH exploits unsupervised semantic representation as the prior distribution for multiple modalities. We utilize compressed code in auto-encoder as an inherent semantic information of images. Such prior information will be considered to avoid inherent semantic loss in the learning process of deep structure network.
- Extensive experiments on two datasets demonstrate the outstanding performance of our proposed FSPDH compared to other deep hashing methods in multi-modal retrieval task. And FSPDH also achieves great performance in single-modal retrieval task.

Table 1. Summary of the notations

Notation	Definition
n	The number of data points
K	The length of hash code
H_i^x, H_j^y	Hash code for two modalities
U_i^x, U_j^y	Unsupervised semantic prior representation
A	The semantic similarity matrix
l_i	The label of i_{th} data point
λ, γ, η	All hyper-parameters

2 Related Works

Cross-modal retrieval [1,14,22] has been a hot topic in the field of information retrieval. Most of researchers [12,19] applied their algorithm into image-text retrieval cross-modal task, while others focused on the modality like video [10,24] and music [5,6]. In particular, [3] created a multi-modal dataset that contains five common modalities. Recently, a deep hashing method has been proposed by Liu et al. [12], using Convolutional Neutral Network to learn the hash code for the image data in the single-modality retrieval task. Lin [11] learned the hash code in a point-wised manner which can improve CNN learning performance in some large-scale datasets. Castrejon [3] proposed a strategy that all weight parameters of last few layers in one CNN is the initialization of the other CNN. Zhao [25] considered the condition of multiple labels of one image in retrieval task rather than one label information. Wang [17] proposed an algorithm that can preserve both discriminability and similarity for hash codes, and thus enhance retrieval accuracy compared with those who only consider the similarity.

Above related works, they still have several limitations in multi-modal image retrieval. None of these methods explore the unsupervised semantic prior before they optimize the objection function. In the following section, we will introduce our innovative algorithm in details and show that these improvements how to affect the final retrieval performance.

3 Approach

3.1 Problem Statement

Some notations that we will use in this paper are shown in Table 1. We use uppercase letters to denote matrices, which represent the training data. Subscript is used to represent one sample from dataset and superscript is used to represent each modality. For example, H represents the hash matrix, H_i is a hash vector of the i-th sample, H_{ij} is an element in matrix H and H^x denotes a hash matrix

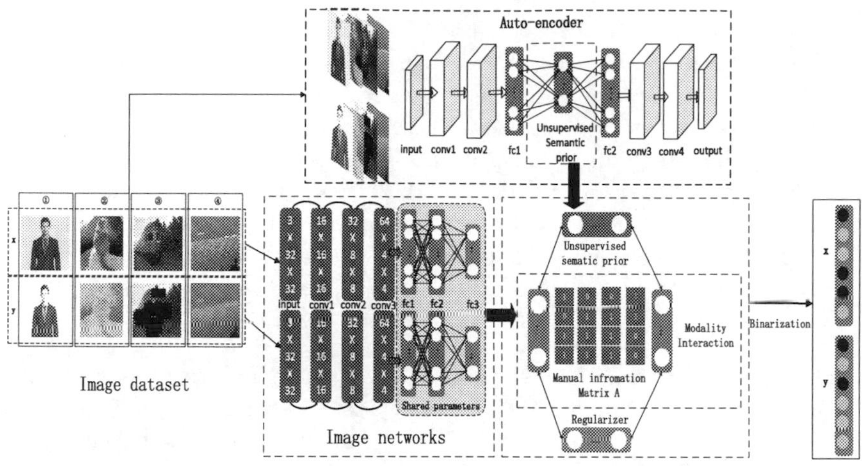

Fig. 1. Whole framework of FSPDH

for modality x. $\mathrm{tr}(\cdot)$ and $\|\cdot\|_F$ denote the trace and the Frobenius norm of a matrix, respectively. $Sign(\cdot) \in \{-1, 1\}$ is a mapping function.

Suppose that we have n training data points[3], each data point includes two modalities, represented by an image-image pair. Let $\{x_i\}_{i=1}^n$ and $\{y_j\}_{j=1}^n$ represent two modalities, respectively. $x_i \in \mathbb{R}^{D_x}$ denotes the D_x-dimensional feature vectors of the original image modality, and $y_j \in \mathbb{R}^{D_y}$ denotes the D_y-dimensional feature vectors of the damage image modality. $A = \{A_{ij}\} \in \mathbb{R}^{n \times n}$ is a manual similarity matrix of the training data, where element $A_{ij} = l_i^T \cdot l_j \in \{0, 1\}$ can be constructed from the semantic labels of data points and represents the similarity between sample i and sample j. l_i is a manual label vector of sample i. All modalities in the same data point share the same label information. The goal of multimodal search is to learn two desired hash functions $f_x(\mathbf{x}) : \mathbb{R}^{D_x} \longmapsto \{-1, 1\}^K$ and $f_y(\mathbf{y}) : \mathbb{R}^{D_y} \longmapsto \{-1, 1\}^K$ which can be used for quick retrieve in search engine. The learned hash functions can be utilized to generate K-bit hash codes for query and retrieval database in all modalities.

3.2 Deep Architecture

The hybrid deep architecture for learning multi-modal hash codes are shown in Fig. 1. Our deep architecture is composed of two parts. The first part is the unsupervised semantic information extractor, which is *Auto-encoder*. In detail, convolutional layers *conv1, conv4* have size $16 \times 16 \times 16$, *conv2, conv3* have size $32 \times 8 \times 8$ and *fc1, fc2* have size 1×256 (width, length). Our semantic prior layer has size $1 \times K$. The second part is called hash code generator, it is made up of *Convolutional Neural Networks (CNN)*. It is used for generating the

[3] In this paper, "data point" represents an image-image pair and "sample" represents an image for one modality.

final hash code from different modalities. Each CNN has same structure: three convolutional layers (*conv1–conv3*) and three fully connected layers (*fc1–fc3*). Five layers (*conv2–fc2*) utilize ReLU [8] as activation function and *fc3* is followed by Softmax function. In our approach, the corresponding fully connected layers share their parameters, i.e. each $fc1$ in CNN has the same parameters (see Fig. 1). Specifically, *conv1* layer has size $16 \times 16 \times 16$ (channel, width, length), *conv2* layer has size $32 \times 8 \times 8$ and *conv3* has size $64 \times 4 \times 4$. *fc1* has size 1×1024 (width, length), *fc2* has size 1×256 and the size of *fc3* is $1 \times K$.

3.3 FSPDH Framework

Modality Interaction. We should preserve the similarity between given pairs in manual similarity matrix A. For a pair of samples x_i and y_j, we use euclidean distance as the metric to quantify their similarity between H_i^x and H_j^y: $D(H_i^x, H_j^y) = \|H_i^x - H_j^y\|_2^2$. The maximum a posteriori estimation of H_i^x and H_j^y is defined as

$$P(H_i^x, H_j^y|A) \propto P(A|H_i^x, H_j^y) \cdot P(H_i^x) \cdot P(H_j^y) \tag{1}$$

If H_i^x and H_j^y are generated by input data points that come from the same category, our likelihood function should be close to 1, and vice versa. The likelihood function can be written as:

$$P(A_{ij}|H_i^x, H_j^y) = \begin{cases} \phi(D(H_i^x, H_j^y)) & A_{ij} = 1 \\ 1 - \phi(D(H_i^x, H_j^y)) & A_{ij} = 0 \end{cases} \tag{2}$$

where $\phi(z) = 1/(1 + e^{-\gamma z})$ is sigmoid function with hyper-parameter γ. While γ is too large, the gradient of sigmoid function is close to zero, which is an obstacle for an effective optimization. So we use a parameter γ to keep the function stay in an active area. The value of γ should be smaller than 1, which is more effective in back-propagation optimization than $\gamma = 1$. Hence, the inter-modal logarithm likelihood is formulated as:

$$\begin{aligned} \mathcal{L}_1^{xy} &= -\log P(A|H_i^x, H_j^y) = -\sum_{A_{i,j} \in A} \log P(A_{ij}|H_i^x, H_j^y) \\ &= \sum_{A_{i,j} \in A} \log(1 + e^{\gamma D(H_i^x, H_j^y)}) - \gamma A_{i,j} D(H_i^x, H_j^y) + C_1 \end{aligned} \tag{3}$$

where C_1 represents a constant term. In FSPDH, the hash codes not only preserve the semantic similarity across different modalities, but have good discriminative abilities to capture semantic correlation in their own modality. Thus, we also consider about the intra-modal pairwise loss in our framework and the formulation can be written as:

$$\begin{aligned} \mathcal{L}_1^{x+y} &= \sum_{t \in x,y} -\log P(A|H_i^t, H_j^t) \\ &= \sum_{t \in x,y} \sum_{A_{i,j} \in A} \log(1 + e^{\gamma D(H_i^t, H_j^t)}) - \gamma A_{i,j} D(H_i^t, H_j^t) \end{aligned} \tag{4}$$

Unsupervised Semantic Loss. In order to generate accurate binary codes from the input training set, we need to strength the relationship between the learned codes and the semantic representation. Above loss functions try to utilize the manual semantic prior information to quantify the consistency in terms of correlation between different hash matrices. However, they ignore the semantic prior information inside samples, which we call **unsupervised semantic prior**.

Generally, maximum a posterior performs better than maximum likelihood estimation if the prior distribution is chosen appropriately. Intuitively, we should enhance our learning architecture by importing a reasonable prior information. In our work, we decide to use auto-encoder to get unsupervised semantic prior information for our architecture. Those compressed representation codes indicate that the natural underlying semantic information of data points and exclude information from supervised labels, which can be regarded as a mean value parameters in our prior distribution. Thus, we put a novel Gaussian distribution on $P(H_i^t)$ as our prior estimation,

$$P(H_i^t) = \mathcal{N}(H_i^t | U_i^t, \sigma^2 I) \tag{5}$$

where $t \in \{x, y\}$, $\mathcal{N}(\cdot)$ denotes the Gaussian distribution, I is an identity matrix, σ represents variance of the Gaussian distribution and $U_i^t \in \mathbb{R}^{1\times K}$ is an unsupervised semantic vector generated by auto-encoder. It is clear that our unsupervised semantic loss function can be defined as,

$$\begin{aligned} \mathcal{L}_2^{x+y} &= -\sum_{t\in x,y} \log P(H_i^t) = \sum_{t\in x,y} \frac{1}{2\sigma^2} D(H_i^t, U_i^t) + C_2 \\ &= \eta[D(H_i^x, U_i^x) + D(H_i^y, U_i^y)] + C_2 \end{aligned} \tag{6}$$

where C_2 is a constant term. For convenience, we let $\eta = \frac{1}{2\sigma^2}$.

Discrepant Regularization Loss. However, directly optimizing on H is infeasible because the binary constraints on H^y and H^y will lead to an intractable training in CNN network. So we relax the discrete constraint of $H \in \{-1, 1\}^{n\times K}$ to be a real valued matrix $H \in \mathbb{R}^{n\times K}$. In our work, we replace the Hamming distance by Euclidean distance, which is a normal relaxation trick for optimization. Therefore, we should impose an discrepant regularizer to resolve the problem of binary constraints and approach the desired discrete values $\{-1, 1\}$. We need to minimize the discrepancy between our continuous codes and a vector of all ones $\mathbf{1}$. Then, our discrepant regularization loss can be defined as,

$$\mathcal{R} = \sum_{i=1}^{N} \| |H_i^x| - \mathbf{1} \|_2^2 + \sum_{j=1}^{N} \| |H_j^y| - \mathbf{1} \|_2^2 \tag{7}$$

where $\| \cdot \|_2$ is the l_2-norm of vector, $| \cdot |$ is the element-wise absolute value operation.

Algorithm 1. FSPDH algorithm

Input: Original set $\{x_i\}$, fuzzy set $\{y_j\}$, manual similarity matrix A, parameters λ, η, K;
Output: Parameters (θ_x, θ_y) of two CNN networks, hash codes matrix of training set H;
Initialize H and θ_x, θ_y by using random matrices;
Extract prior U^x and U^y by using auto-encoder;
Set mini-batch size as 100, and max iteration number $\tau = 100$;
repeat
  for l *from 1 to* τ **do**
    for i *from 1 to* $\lfloor n/100 \rfloor$ **do**
      Update θ_x, θ_y using BP algorithm;
      Update H according to Eq.15:
    end
  end
until *the preset maximum iteration is reached*;

Objective Function. Our goal is to maximize logarithm posterior which can be rewritten as,

$$\log(P(H_i^x, H_j^x | A_{ij})) \propto \log(P(A_{ij} | H_i^x, H_j^x)) + \log(P(H_i^x)) + \log(P(H_j^x)) \tag{8}$$

We let θ_x, θ_y represent our two CNN networks' parameters, the above overall loss function is defined as,

$$\min_{\theta, H_i^x, H_j^y} \mathcal{L} = \Big(\sum_{i,j}^{n} \mathcal{L}_1^{xy} + \mathcal{L}_1^{x+y} + \mathcal{L}_2^{x+y}\Big) + \lambda \mathcal{R} \tag{9}$$

where λ is a weighting parameter that controls the strength of the regularizer.

3.4 Optimization

We jointly train our deep network with mini-batch *stochastic gradient descent (SGD)*. The FSPDH algorithm is summarized in Algorithm 1. We derive the learning algorithms for the FSPDH model in Eq. 9 w.r.t H_i^x, it can be separated into four components, we will take derivatives for them separately. It should be noted that updating H_j^y is the same as updating H_i^x.

$$\frac{\partial \mathcal{L}_1^{xy}}{\partial H_i^x} = 2\gamma\phi(D(H_i^x, H_j^y))(H_i^x - H_j^y) - 2\gamma A_{i,j}(H_i^x - H_j^y) \tag{10}$$

we use $\|H_i^x - H_j^y\|_2^2 = \mathrm{tr}((H_i^x - H_j^y)^T (H_i^x - H_j^y))$ in derivation. Similarly, the intra-modal pairwise loss w.r.t H_i^x can be calculated by

$$\frac{\partial \mathcal{L}_1^{x+y}}{\partial H_i^x} = 2\gamma(\phi(D(H_i^x, H_j^x)) - A_{i,j})(H_i^x - H_j^x) \tag{11}$$

And gradient of unsupervised semantic loss w.r.t H_i^x can be written as:

$$\frac{\partial \mathcal{L}_2^{x+y}}{\partial H_i^x} = \eta \frac{\partial \text{tr}((H_i^x - U_i^x)^T (H_i^x - U_i^x))}{\partial H_i^x} = 2\eta(H_i^x - U_i^x) \tag{12}$$

The last gradient of discrepant regularization can be written as:

$$\frac{\partial \mathcal{R}}{\partial H_i^x} = [\frac{\partial \mathcal{R}}{\partial H_{i,1}^x}, \cdots, \frac{\partial \mathcal{R}}{\partial H_{i,K}^x}], \qquad \frac{\partial \mathcal{R}}{\partial H_{i,*}^x} = 2(|H_{i,*}^x| - 1)\Delta(H_{i,*}^x) \tag{13}$$

where

$$\Delta(H_{i,*}^x) = \begin{cases} 1, & -1 \leq H_{i,*}^x \leq 0 \quad or \quad H_{i,*}^x \geq 1 \\ -1, & otherwise \end{cases} \tag{14}$$

Eventually, the overall loss function w.r.t H_i^x is represented as follow:

$$\begin{aligned} \frac{\partial \mathcal{L}}{\partial H_i^x} &= (\sum_j^n 2\gamma(\phi(D(H_i^x, H_j^y)) - A_{i,j})(H_i^x - H_j^y) \\ &+ 2\gamma(\phi(D(H_i^x, H_j^x)) - A_{i,j})(H_i^x - H_j^x) + 2\eta(H_i^x - U_i^x)) \\ &+ \lambda[2(|H_{i,o}^x| - 1)\Delta(H_{i,o}^x)]_{o=1}^K \end{aligned} \tag{15}$$

Discussion. This architecture can be easily applied to single-modal retrieval task with tiny changes in objective function which can be denoted as:

$$\begin{aligned} \mathcal{L}(H, U) = &\sum_{i,j}^n \sum_{A_{i,j} \in A} \log(1 + e^{\gamma D(H_i, H_j)}) - \gamma A_{i,j} D(H_i, H_j) \\ &+ \eta D(H_i, U_i) + \lambda \sum_{i=1}^N \||H_i| - \mathbf{1}\|_2^2 + C \end{aligned} \tag{16}$$

where C is a constant term. We show its promising performance in experiment. For a new point that is not in the training set, its binary code can be generated by an element-wise sign function which can be written as,

$$b_k^t = sign(f_t(t_k; \theta_t)) \quad t \in \{x, y\} \tag{17}$$

where $f(\cdot)$ represent our learning function.

4 Experiment

4.1 Dataset

Cifar-10+: *Cifar-10*[4] dataset, which is widely accepted and utilized in single-modal algorithm. It originally consists of 60,000 32 × 32 images belonging to 10

[4] http://www.cs.toronto.edu/~kriz/cifar.html.

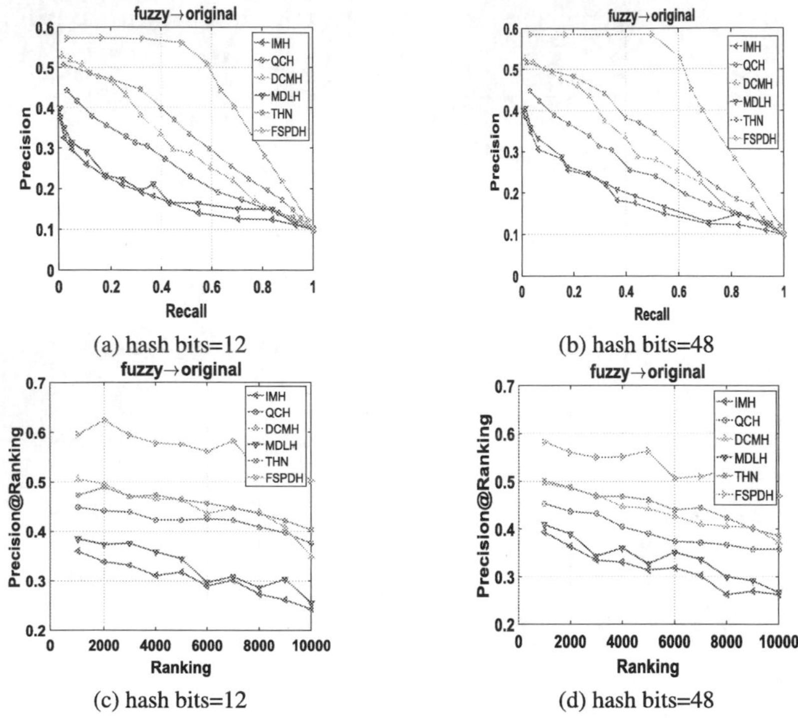

Fig. 2. Multi-modal retrieval on **Cifar-10+**. Precision-recall curve (a), (b) and Precision@Ranking curve (c), (d).

mutually independent classes (6,000 images per category). We randomly select 50,000 images as our training set and 10,000 images as our query set. After our processing, each data point in **Cifar-10+** has an original image and its associated fuzzy state. Considering the real scene in applications, we randomize four types of fuzzy state: blurry image, noisy image, pixel dropouts and high exposure. **NUS-WIDE+**: *NUS-WIDE*[5] is a public web image dataset containing 269,648 images collected from *Flickr*. There are 81 concepts manually annotated as final ground truth. We extract 100,000 images which belong to the 20 most frequent concepts in our experiment. These images are resized to 64×64 as an input for CNN. Similarly, we select 80,000 images as our training set and the rest part is query set.

4.2 Experimental Results

We compare the proposed FSPDH with five multi-modal hashing algorithms. **MDLH** [15], **IMH** [16] and **THN** [2] are unsupervised method and apply matrix factorization strategy, **DCMH** [7] and **QCH** [21] are supervised multi-modal

[5] http://lms.comp.nus.edu.sg/research/NUS-WIDE.htm.

Table 2. MAP (fuzzy→ original) comparison with baselines on two multi-modal datasets. The best accuracy is shown in boldface, while second best results are underlined.

Method	Cifar-10+				NUS-WIDE+			
	bits = 12	bits = 24	bits = 36	bits = 48	bits = 12	bits = 24	bits = 36	bits = 48
IMH	0.3289	0.3716	0.3805	0.3875	0.3312	0.3798	0.3729	0.3751
QCH	0.4150	0.4512	0.4687	0.4685	0.5381	0.5492	0.5517	0.5607
DCMH	0.4991	0.4876	0.4754	0.4955	0.6006	0.5983	0.5901	0.6017
MDLH	0.3373	0.3810	0.3893	0.3974	0.3877	0.4110	0.4293	0.4374
THN	<u>0.5005</u>	<u>0.5077</u>	<u>0.5100</u>	<u>0.5104</u>	<u>0.6213</u>	<u>0.6291</u>	<u>0.6309</u>	<u>0.6300</u>
FSPDH	**0.5546**	**0.5360**	**0.5261**	**0.5484**	**0.6782**	**0.6701**	**0.6619**	**0.6733**

Table 3. MAP (original→ original) comparison with baselines on **Cifar-10**.

Method	bits = 12	bits = 24	bits = 36	bits = 48
CNNH	0.5425	0.5604	0.5640	0.5574
DLBHC	0.5503	0.5803	0.5778	0.5885
DNNH	0.5708	0.5875	0.5899	0.5904
DSH	<u>0.6175</u>	<u>0.6512</u>	<u>0.6607</u>	<u>0.6755</u>
FSPDH	**0.7685**	**0.7450**	**0.7495**	**0.7426**

deep hashing methods. In single-modal retrieval task, we select four state-of-the-art approaches based on CNN network: **CNNH** [23], **DLBHC** [11], **DNNH** [9] and **DSH** [12]. Above all methods are implemented by using their source codes. Some methods put more emphasis on retrieval task between text and image, which are not directly suitable for our method. The part of text or some modality different from image is changed to be suitable for image input, and the following structure is also changed to be same as the image layers to keep symmetric. To be more fair, we change their network to our structure and all parameters are set according to the suggestions of authors. We utilize cross-validation strategy to choose our five hyper-parameters: γ, λ, η, K and *mini-batch size*. According to the results in the validation set, we set $\gamma = 0.5$ empirically, and we find that the best performance can be achieved with $\lambda = 0.25$, $\eta = 0.15$. We explore the influence of λ, η and *mini-batch size* in the following part. To evaluate the retrieval performance based on three widely accepted metrics: *Mean Average Precision (MAP)*, *Precision-recall* curves and *Precision@Ranking*.

In multi-modal retrieval task: broken image query on retrieval database, we compare our proposed FSPDH with five baseline methods on the two datasets **Cifar-10+** and **NUS-WIDE+** in terms of *MAP*, *Precision-recall* curve and *Precision@Ranking* curve. We evaluate all methods with different lengths of hash codes, i.e., 12, 24, 36 and 48 bits. All *MAP* results are reported in Table 2.

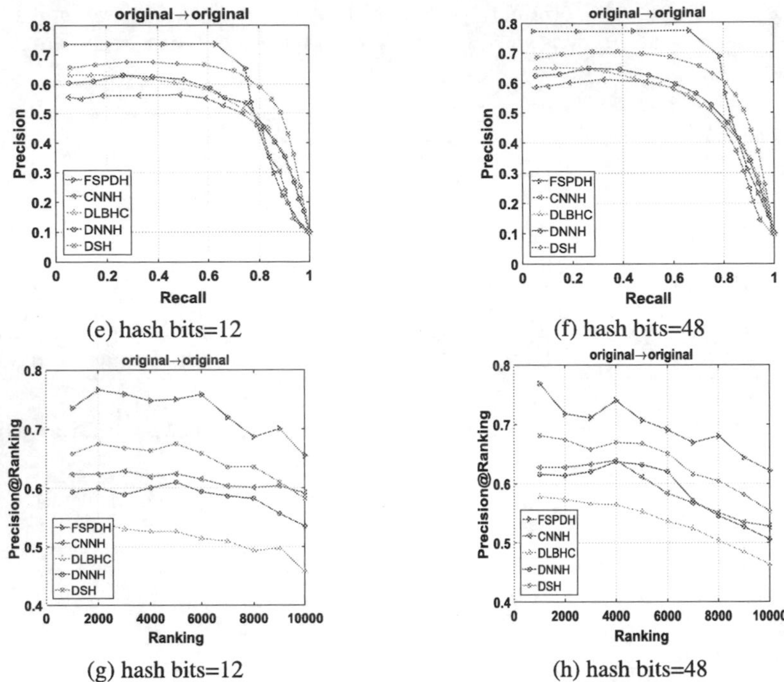

Fig. 3. Single-modal retrieval on **Cifar-10**. Precision-recall curve (e), (f) and Precision@Ranking curve (g), (h).

We take $K = 12$ and $K = 48$ as an example and exhibit promising result on **Cifar-10+** in Fig. 2. Specifically, methods based on deep architecture are much better than those shallow methods, which means the deep learning framework can capture better feature representation and improve the performance. Among all the CNN models, FSPDH has the highest performance. There are two reasons: (1) the unsupervised semantic prior is important for improve fuzzy image retrieval performance. This makes complete sense, FSPDH is a better framework that can flexible hold the supervised manual semantic information and unsupervised prior information together. (2) Another reason is that the share of parameters in full connected layers of CNN. Different modalities may have different representations, we should strength correlation between two modalities for our multi-modal task. Intuitively, sharing parameters of full connected layers can project latent feature information to the similar space in order to fulfill information gap between two modalities. Meanwhile, we apply our method to traditional single-modal retrieval task, MAP results on **Cifar** are shown in Table 3 and we demonstrate *Precision-recall/Precision@Ranking* curve in Fig. 3, which shows that FSPDH also has great performance in single-modal retrieval task.

4.3 Parameter Sensitivity

In terms of mini-batch size, we put emphasis on speed of convergence. As shown in Fig. 4, FSPDH has a faster convergence speed if mini-batch size equals 50, but result of loss shows instability. Considering the trade-off between stability and speed, we choose 100 as our mini-batch size. And η is a hyper-parameter that controls the contribution of the unsupervised semantic prior information. In fact, value of η represents the variance of the prior distribution. We compare our MAP results with different values of η (see Fig. 5) in two retrieval tasks. The results demonstrate that our unsupervised semantic prior information has a significant impact on retrieval performance. Similarly, λ that controls the element of the learned hash code can be close to -1 or 1. We should note that λ is much smoother in variance than η. The regularizer serves as an auxiliary loss to help constrain the output of hash code.

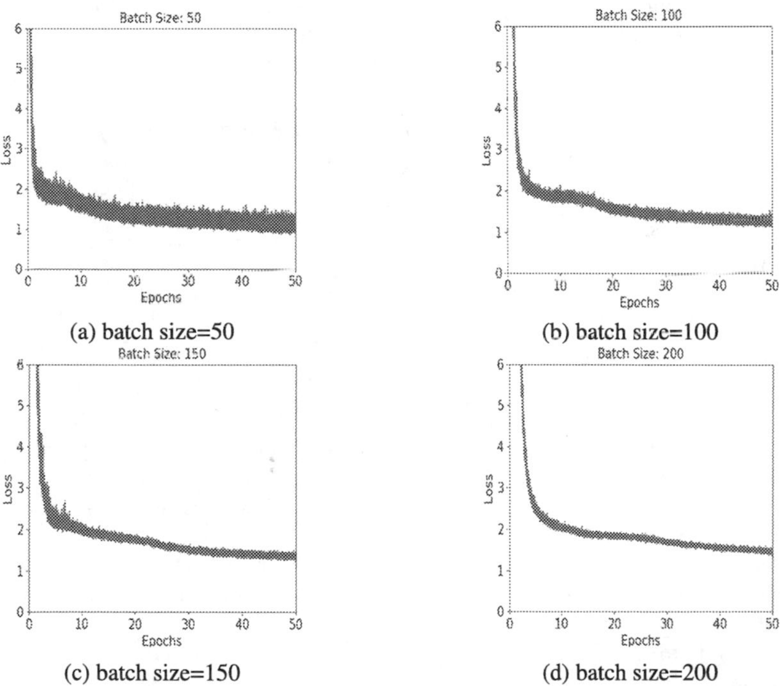

(a) batch size=50 (b) batch size=100 (c) batch size=150 (d) batch size=200

Fig. 4. Convergence curve with different mini-batch sizes.

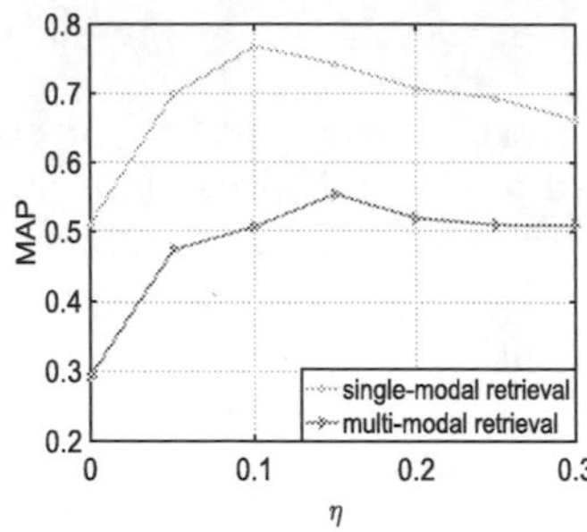

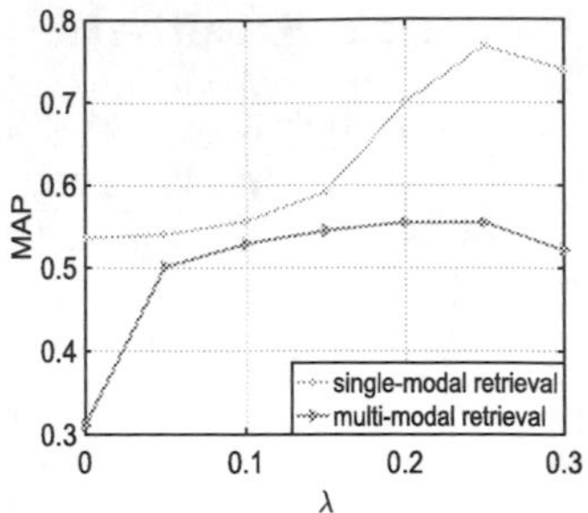

Fig. 5. MAP in terms of various λ and η on two tasks.

5 Conclusion

In this paper, we presented a new (FSPDH) deep hashing method to enable efficient multi-modal retrieval of images in response to fuzzy images. Specifically, we select auto-encoder as the unsupervised semantic prior extractor, which plays an important role in improving retrieval performance. In addition, FSPDH can be completely applied to single-modal retrieval and any other applications such as classification, detection and so on. Extensive experiments on datasets validate that FSPDH can yield great improvement over state-of-the-art hashing methods.

Acknowledgments. This work was partially supported by Shanghai Municipal Commission of Economy and Informatization (No. 201701052). We thank Zhongyi Zhou from Shanghai Jiao Tong University for his useful discussions and feedback.

References

1. Bu, S., Wang, L., Han, P., Liu, Z., Li, K.: 3D shape recognition and retrieval based on multi-modality deep learning. Neurocomputing **259**, 183–193 (2017)
2. Cao, Z., Long, M., Wang, J., Yang, Q.: Transitive hashing network for heterogeneous multimedia retrieval, pp. 81–87 (2017)
3. Castrejon, L., Aytar, Y., Vondrick, C., Pirsiavash, H., Torralba, A.: Learning aligned cross-modal representations from weakly aligned data, pp. 2940–2949 (2016)
4. Ding, G., Guo, Y., Zhou, J., Gao, Y.: Large-scale cross-modality search via collective matrix factorization hashing. IEEE Trans. Image Process. **25**(11), 5427–5440 (2016)
5. Dorfer, M., Schlüter, J., Vall, A., Korzeniowski, F., Widmer, G.: End-to-end cross-modality retrieval with CCA projections and pairwise ranking loss. arXiv preprint arXiv:1705.06979 (2017)
6. Drai-Zerbib, V., Baccino, T.: The effect of expertise in music reading: cross-modal competence. J. Eye Mov. Res. **6**(5) (2014)
7. Jiang, Q.Y., Li, W.J.: Deep cross-modal hashing. arXiv preprint arXiv:1602.02255 (2016)
8. Krizhevsky, A., Sutskever, I., Hinton, G.E.: Imagenet classification with deep convolutional neural networks, pp. 1097–1105 (2012)

9. Lai, H., Pan, Y., Liu, Y., Yan, S.: Simultaneous feature learning and hash coding with deep neural networks, pp. 3270–3278 (2015)
10. Li, Y., Wang, R., Huang, Z., Shan, S., Chen, X.: Face video retrieval with image query via hashing across euclidean space and riemannian manifold, pp. 4758–4767 (2015)
11. Lin, K., Yang, H.F., Hsiao, J.H., Chen, C.S.: Deep learning of binary hash codes for fast image retrieval, pp. 27–35 (2015)
12. Liu, H., Wang, R., Shan, S., Chen, X.: Deep supervised hashing for fast image retrieval, pp. 2064–2072 (2016)
13. Liu, H., Ji, R., Wu, Y., Hua, G.: Supervised matrix factorization for cross-modality hashing (2016)
14. Masci, J., Bronstein, M.M., Bronstein, A.M., Schmidhuber, J.: Multimodal similarity-preserving hashing. IEEE Trans. Pattern Anal. Mach. Intell. **36**(4), 824–830 (2014)
15. Qu, W., Wang, D., Feng, S., Zhang, Y., Yu, G.: A novel cross-modal hashing algorithm based on multimodal deep learning. Sci. China Inf. Sci. **60**(9), 092104 (2017)
16. Song, J., Yang, Y., Yang, Y., Huang, Z., Shen, H.T.: Inter-media hashing for large-scale retrieval from heterogeneous data sources, pp. 785–796 (2013)
17. Wang, D., Gao, X., Wang, X., He, L., Yuan, B.: Multimodal discriminative binary embedding for large-scale cross-modal retrieval. IEEE Trans. Image Process. **25**(10), 4540–4554 (2016)
18. Wang, W., Ooi, B.C., Yang, X., Zhang, D., Zhuang, Y.: Effective multi-modal retrieval based on stacked auto-encoders. Proc. VLDB Endow. **7**(8), 649–660 (2014)
19. Wang, W., Yang, X., Ooi, B.C., Zhang, D., Zhuang, Y.: Effective deep learning-based multi-modal retrieval. VLDB J. **25**(1), 79–101 (2016)
20. Weiss, Y., Torralba, A., Fergus, R.: Spectral hashing, pp. 1753–1760 (2009)
21. Wu, B., Yang, Q., Zheng, W.S., Wang, Y., Wang, J.: Quantized correlation hashing for fast cross-modal search, pp. 3946–3952 (2015)
22. Wu, P., Hoi, S.C., Zhao, P., Miao, C., Liu, Z.Y.: Online multi-modal distance metric learning with application to image retrieval. IEEE Trans. Knowl. Data Eng. **28**(2), 454–467 (2016)
23. Xia, R., Pan, Y., Lai, H., Liu, C., Yan, S.: Supervised hashing for image retrieval via image representation learning, vol. 1, pp. 2156–2162 (2014)
24. Xia, S., Li, T., Ge, S., Dong, Z.: Efficient web video classification via cross-modality knowledge transferring, pp. 211–216 (2016)
25. Zhao, F., Huang, Y., Wang, L., Tan, T.: Deep semantic ranking based hashing for multi-label image retrieval, pp. 1556–1564 (2015)
26. Zhu, X., Huang, Z., Shen, H.T., Zhao, X.: Linear cross-modal hashing for efficient multimedia search, pp. 143–152 (2013)

Topic-Guided Automatical Human-Simulated Tweeting System

Zongyue Liu, Fuhai Chen, Jinsong Su, Chen Shen, and Rongrong Ji(✉)

Xiamen University, Xiamen, Fujian, China
rrji@xmu.edu.cn

Abstract. Social network grows increasingly popular in our life nowadays. It's an interesting intelligent behaviour to automatically post tweets in social network, which has not yet been explored. However, the associated researches are trapped in the problem of "multivalued mapping" where the agent should generate various appropriate tweets given a certain topic. In this paper, a human-simulated tweeting system is first designed to generate the multiple and appropriate tweets for given topics. In this system, a novel topic-image-tweet scheme is proposed with a Keyword-Based Retrieval Module (KBR-Module) and a Topic-Guided Image Captioning Module (TGIC-Module), where multiple topic-related images are searched in KBR-Module and encoded to generate the accurate tweets in TGIC-Module. The effectiveness of the proposed system and the superiority of our specific image captioning model are evaluated by sufficient quantitative comparisons and qualitative analysis in a real-world Twitter dataset.

Keywords: Human-simulated · Automatically tweeting Topic-guided · Social media · Twitter · Image captioning

1 Introduction

In recent years, it has been witnessed the great popularity of social networks such as Twitter and Sina Weibo. Take Twitter for example, Twitter hits a remarkable amount of 328 million monthly active users by the time of July 2017. More and more users record their life and express their opinions for a variety of hot topics, *e.g.*, food and clothes, on social networks. An interesting inspiration comes from the question, *i.e.*, how does machine post the generated tweets automatically? Automatically tweeting is actually useful under many circumstances, *e.g.*, during travel, during which people tend to have no time to post the tweets but still want to keep plenty of fans.

However, automatically tweeting is not an easy task at all. The challenges lie in two aspects: on the one hand, it is an uncertain problem (similar to "multi-valued mapping") to generate the multiple various tweets given a certain topic, which puts forward the requirement on the multiple-choice mechanism for intelligent system. On the other hand, the tweets should be generated appropriately,

X. Geng and B.-H. Kang (Eds.): PRICAI 2018, LNAI 11012, pp. 416–428, 2018.
https://doi.org/10.1007/978-3-319-97304-3_32

i.e., the generated contents need to be not only relevant to the topics but also correct in the textual expression.

In this paper, we design a topic-guided human-simulated tweeting system, which provides a novel topic-image-tweet scheme for the challenges of the multiple-choice and appropriate tweet generation. Specifically, on the one hand, we design a Keyword-Based Retrieval Module (termed KBR-Module) to search the images (with the corresponding captions) queried by the keywords of the topics, where the multiple topic-related images can be obtained in this topic-image scheme. On the other hand, we propose a Topic-Guided Image Captioning Module (termed TGIC-Module), where the obtained images are encoded into a Topic-Guided Context Sequence Memory Network (T-CSMN) to generate the topic-related and well-expressed tweets. It's noted that the Context Sequence Memory Network (CSMN) is first proposed in [1] for tweet image captioning, where the memory sequentially stores the contexts of images and tweeting styles at each step of word generation. However, it ignores the guide of the topic, where the contexts of images and tweeting styles are both highly relevant with tweet topics, *i.e.*, different topic leads to different focuses on images and different tweeting mood. To this end, we advance the CSMN model by embedding the topic to attend the contexts of sequential generation. By carrying out sufficient quantitative comparisons and qualitative analysis in the real-word Twitter dataset, we have shown the effectiveness of the designed topic-guided human-simulated tweeting system and the superiority of the proposed T-CSMN method for automatically tweeting.

The contributions of our work lie in three folds as below:

- We design a human-simulated tweeting system, serving as the first of its kind;
- We propose a novel topic-image-tweet scheme for the challenges of the multiple-choice and appropriate tweet generation;
- We advance the Context Sequence Memory Network (CSMN) model with the guide of topic, *i.e.*, T-CSMN, for the real application of the tweet image captioning.

The rest of the paper is organized as: Related work are first reviewed in Sect. 2. We then introduce our human-simulated tweeting system integrally in Sect. 3. The proposed Topic-Guided Image Captioning Module with T-CSMN model is emphatically described in Sect. 4. The evaluation experiments are conducted in Sect. 5. Finally, we make the conclusion in Sect. 6.

2 Related Work

2.1 Analysis Systems on Tweet Data

As far as our knowledge, existing analysis systems on tweet data refer to the sentiment analysis, the information push, and the user analysis. For examples, Wang *et al.* [2] proposed a system for real-time analysis of public sentiment towards presidential candidates in the 2012 U.S. election. As for the information push, Uchida *et al.* [3] have achieved a real-time information sharing system in the aftermath of a disaster which can post information on Twitter. For the user analysis, owing to the users in Twitter may not be all real people, Chu *et al.* [4] designed a classification system to determine whether an unknown user is a human, bot or cyborg. However, there was not a automatically tweeting system yet, which also left unexplored so far in research.

2.2 Image Caption

Image captioning is a task to generate the descriptions of the images. There have been a lot of works published on this task [5–14]. Most of the existing image captioning methods are inspired by Machine Translation's encoder-decoder framework. From this perspective, image captioning is similar to image text translation. Vinyals *et al.* [15] and Karpathy *et al.* [16] proposed a CNN-RNN architecture, where CNN encodes the feature of the image and RNN decodes the image feature to generate words sequence. Mao *et al.* [17] proposed to generate caption by using the multimodal recurrent neural networks (m-rnn). Donahue *et al.* [18] used long short-term memory (LSTM), a advanced RNN model, to boost the performance of the image captioning. Recently, Xu *et al.* [19] and You *et al.* [20] proposed the attention based models to generate more accurate descriptions of images automatically. However, for the tweeting system, the contexts of images and tweeting styles would be weakly kept at each step of the word generation in the CNN-RNN based image captioning model. To this end, a memory based architecture is needed.

3 Human-Simulated Tweeting System

The overall structure of the system we proposed is illustrated in Fig. 1. The system, based on Twitter, consists of two major modules. One major module is the Topic-Guided Image Captioning module and the other is the Keyword-Based Retrieval module.

3.1 Keyword-Based Retrieval Module

There is a big database that stores a large number of twitter in the KBR-Module. The contents of the data stored in the database include the information required by the system, such as texts, images, topics and keywords. The input of the module is topic and keywords and what we want to output is some texts related to the topic. A number of images, together with the text and keywords, will be obtained by retrieving in the dataset through the specific topic and target images will be produced in these candidate images. Because the images are diverse on the same topic and the descriptions of the same topic is varied, it still needs the keywords to further reduce the range of the image retrieval results and gets the images which is more related to the topic. These images are used to generate text that we will post on Twitter in the Topic-Guided Image Captioning module.

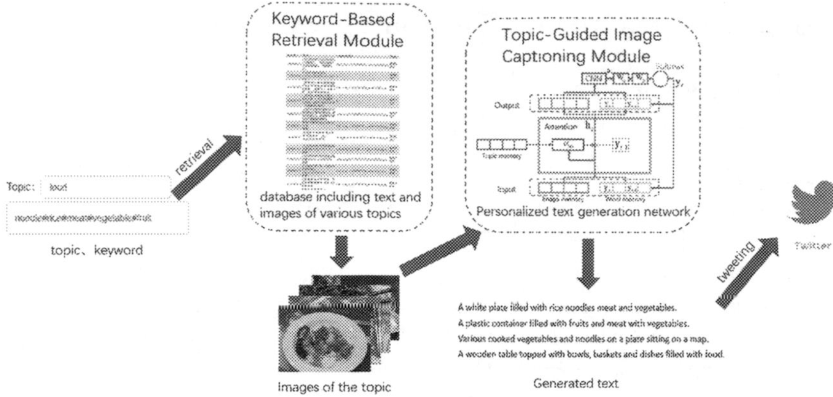

Fig. 1. The framework of the proposed human-simulated tweeting system. The system contains a Keyword-Based Retrieval Module (KBR-Module) and a Topic-Guided Image Captioning Module (TGIC-Module). The input of our system is a specific topic and we will show the result of image retrieval and the text generated.

3.2 Topic-Guided Image Captioning Module

In the GFIC-Module, we take the image as the input. We save the feature of the image and the embedding of the topic and the generated words in the memory. Then, we apply CNN to fuse multiple heterogeneous cells with different filters and after softmax, the probability is computed. We select the most precise word by the probability. We will give a more detailed description of this module in the Sect. 4.

3.3 System Mechanism

As the goal of our system is to post human-simulated text on Twitter, it is crucial for our system to be able to log in to Twitter and post text successfully. In order to log in like a real person, our system prefer to use the request module of Python. We all know the communication between the client and the server is achieved through sending packages. We first send a request of "GET" to get the package from the server, which includes "pubkey", "servertime" and other useful information. Next, we post a request with username encrypted with Base64, password encrypted with RSA and other necessary information. What we get from the server shows whether we log in successfully. Certainly, there is much more operation in this communication, the request of "GET" and "POST" is the most important part. While finishing logging in, we design to save the cookies and set the valid time for the cookies to facilitate the next access. As for posting the text, it is much simpler after completing the login step. What we need to do is pack the text, image and client information into the package that will be sent to the server. It is worth nothing that in order to avoid the response timeout, we need to set up a waiting time to make sure that our system is able to run normally.

4 Topic-Guided Image Captioning Module

4.1 Memory Component

Figure 2 illustrates the structure of this module and the module's output is a sequence of predicted words: $\{y_t\} = y_1, \ldots, y_T$ which is equivalent to the generated sentence while the input of the module is the images retrieved from the previous module together with the context information of topic. All the inputs are added in to the memory and are divided into two parts to save: the image memory and the topic memory. The third part of the memory, the word memory, is used to store all the words predicted by the model. These three parts make up the memory of our algorithm.

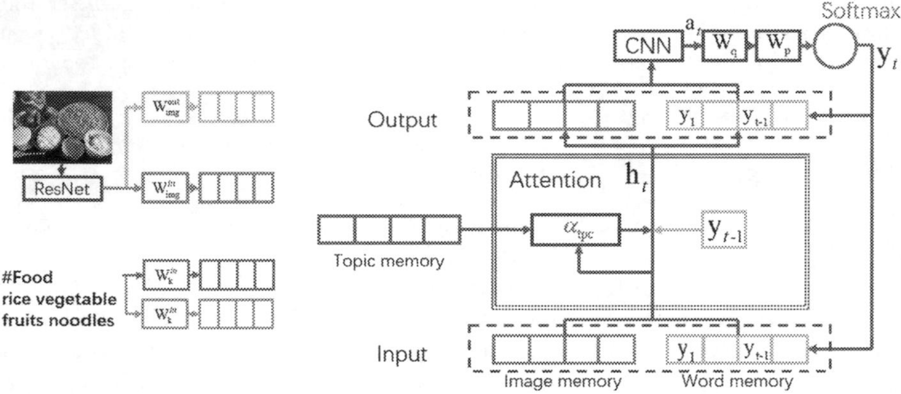

Fig. 2. The structure of the Topic-Guided Image Captioning Module. The feature vector extracted from the image and the embedding vector are used as the input of the module. After computing the weight factor α_{tpc}, the attention $\mathbf{h}_t$ is obtained by considering the word of the last step and will be used to update the memory. Through CNN and Softmax, a new predicted word will be obtained.

According to [21], the input of each part of the memory is embedded into two kinds of vector: the input representation and the output representation. We represent both the input and output formulas as a single representation without indices *in* and *out*. Meanwhile, we select the most frequent D words from the dataset to produce a dictionary $\mathcal{D}$. The predicted words are selected from this dictionary through the probability computed by the CNN.

Image Memory. This part of memory is the vector representation of image features. We extract the feature vector of the image by using the model of ResNet101 which is pre-trained on the ImageNet dataset. In order to test the effect of image features on the result of text generation, we experiment with two different features of the image: the feature maps of res5c layer $\mathbf{I}^{5c} \in \mathbb{R}^{2,048 \times 7 \times 7}$ and the output vector of pool5 layer $\mathbf{I}^{p5} \in \mathbb{R}^{2,048}$. The former focus more on the spatial attention and the latter represents the whole image. Compared with the pool5, the res5c feature map takes up more memory for 49 cells. In the experiments, the two feature representation will be compared.

The vector (take res5c feature as an example) representing the res5c feature which is stored in image memory is computed separately for 49 dimensions by

$$\mathbf{v}_{img} = ReLU(\mathbf{W}_{img}\mathbf{I}^{5c} + \mathbf{b}_{img}), \tag{1}$$

where $\mathbf{W}_{img} \in \mathbb{R}^{1,024\times 2,048}$ and $\mathbf{b}_{img} \in \mathbb{R}^{1,024}$ are the parameters that the model needs to be learned and ReLU represents the activation of Rectified Linear United.

Topic Memory. In the TGIC-Module, the input query image is related to the particular topic, so we select $\mathcal{N}$ topics in the dataset to form the vocabulary list $\{k_i\}_{i=1}^{\mathcal{N}}$. To enhance the performance of the follow-up CNN, we arrange $\{k_i\}_{i=1}^{\mathcal{N}}$ in fixed order and put it into the topic memory. The topic memory pays more attention on the specific topic, thus improving the performance of TGIC-Module. We choose the $\mathcal{N}$ topics by statistics of all the data in the database and the memory contains all the topics we selected. Our vector of the topic memory becomes

$$\mathbf{v}_{tpc,i} = ReLU(\mathbf{W}_w[\mathbf{W}_k\mathbf{k}_i] + \mathbf{b}_w); \qquad i \in 1,\ldots,\mathcal{N}, \tag{2}$$

where k_i is the representation of i-th topic. The parameters that needs to be learned are $\mathbf{W}_w \in \mathbb{R}^{1,024\times 512}$, $\mathbf{W}_k \in \mathbb{R}^{512\times \mathcal{D}}$ and $\mathbf{b}_w \in \mathbb{R}^{1,024}$.

Word Memory. All the words $y_1,\ldots,y_{t-1}$ generated previously are stored in the word memory presented as

$$\mathbf{v}_{word,i} = ReLU(\mathbf{W}_w[\mathbf{W}_k y_i] + \mathbf{b}_w); \qquad i \in 1,\ldots,t-1, \tag{3}$$

where y_i represents the one-hot representation for the i-th word generated before. The parameters $\mathbf{W}_w$, $\mathbf{b}_w$ and embedding matrices $\mathbf{W}_k$ are the same as we used in the Eq. (2). After each iteration we will recalculate $\mathbf{v}_{word,i}$ and update it to the memory when a new generated word is output by the module.

Finally, we splice the input and output representations of the image and word parts of the memory separately: $\mathbf{V}_t = [\mathbf{v}_{img,1} \oplus \cdots \oplus \mathbf{v}_{img,49} \oplus \mathbf{v}_{word,1} \oplus \cdots \oplus \mathbf{v}_{word,t-1}]$. (Take res5c feature as an example and the image memory occupies 49 cells. If we use pool5 feature, the vector is 1,024-dimensional and only takes one cell.) We define $m = m_{img} + m_{word}$ as the overall size of the whole memory.

4.2 Text Generation

The algorithm we use stores all the previously generated words into memory and the model can generate the next word by using the previous information of image feature, topics list and the word generated before. We also introduce the attention model in our algorithm to make the text generated by the network more related to the topic we gave.

Attention Information. Generating a new word y_t needs to use all the information in the memory. We first use y_{t-1}, the one-hot vector of the previous word, to generate an input vector $\mathbf{s}_t$ at time t of the memory network by:

$$\mathbf{s}_t = ReLU(\mathbf{W}_s(\mathbf{W}_e y_{t-1}) + \mathbf{b}_s), \tag{4}$$

where trained to learn $\mathbf{W}_s \in \mathbb{R}^{1,024\times 512}$ and $\mathbf{W}_e \in \mathbb{R}^{512\times D}$. The topic memory will take the input vector $\mathbf{s}_t$ to compute "attention", the matching scores between the input vector $\mathbf{s}_t$ and every cell of the input memory $\mathbf{V}_t^{in}$. Besides, in order to emphasize the influence of the topic on the generated text and predict the text related to the particular topic, we define α_{tpc} as a weight factor to guide the generation of text by the specific topic:

$$\mathbf{M} = \mathbf{V}_{tpc}\mathbf{U}_{tpc}\mathbf{V}_t^{in}, \tag{5}$$

$$\alpha_{tpc} \propto exp\left(\sum_j^m \mathbf{M}_{i=i_0,j}\right), \tag{6}$$

$$\mathbf{h}_t = softmax(\alpha_{tpc}\mathbf{V}_t^{in}\mathbf{s}_t), \tag{7}$$

where $\mathbf{U}_{tpc} \in \mathbb{R}^{1,024\times 1,024}$ is a matrix, i_0 is the specific topic, and α_{tpc} is the parameter describing the relevance between the topic and the predicted words. $\mathbf{V}_t^{in}$ is the memory representation of the image and the predicted words. $\mathbf{h}_t$ tells the correlation between the input vector $\mathbf{s}_t$ and the input memory, and we use the topic to guide which part the next word needs to pay more attention to. Then we change the dimensions of the representation of the output memory $\mathbf{V}_t^{out} \in \mathbb{R}^{m\times 1,024}$ by element-wise multiplication (represented by the symbol $\odot$) of each column with $\mathbf{h}_t \in \mathbb{R}^m$:

$$\mathbf{V}_t^{attention}(*, i) = \mathbf{h}_t \odot \mathbf{V}_t^{out}(*, i), \tag{8}$$

where the rescaled representation of the output memory $\mathbf{V}_t^{attention}$ into two parts, image and word, as $\mathbf{V}_t^{attention} = [\mathbf{v}_{img,1:49}^{attention} \oplus \mathbf{v}_{word,1:t-1}^{attention}]$.

Word Prediction. We design to apply CNN to the output representation $\mathbf{V}_t^{attention}$ mainly due to that by fusing information of different cells with different filters, CNN can output a more precise sequence of representations. Three filters with different window sizes whose depth is 300 is applied to the model and the window sizes we set is $d = [3, 4, 5]$. For each memory type, we use a single convolutional layer and max-pooling layer as:

$$\mathbf{a}_{img,t}^d = maxpool(ReLU(\mathbf{W}_{img}^d \otimes \mathbf{v}_{img,1:49}^{attention} + \mathbf{b}_{img}^d)); \qquad d = [3, 4, 5], \tag{9}$$

where the convolutional operation is signed with the symbol of $\otimes$. $\mathbf{b}_{img}^d \in \mathbb{R}^{49\times 300}$ are the biases and $\mathbf{W}_{img}^d$ are the filters. $\mathbf{a}_{img,t}^d$ whose size is $(300 \times [47, 46, 45])$ is reduced to $(300 \times [1, 1, 1])$ and we get $\mathbf{a}_{img,t}$ by concatenating $\mathbf{a}_{img,t}^d$ from $d = 3$ to 5. The other type of memory take the same operation of

Eq. (9). Thus, we achieve $\mathbf{a}_t$ by connecting two types memory whose dimension is $1,800 = 2 \times 3 \times 300$.

$$\mathbf{a}_t = [\mathbf{a}_{img,t} \oplus \mathbf{a}_{word,t}]. \tag{10}$$

Next we obtain the probability of the predicted word $\mathbf{p}_t \in \mathbb{R}^D$ by a softmax layer over the dictionary $\mathcal{D}$:

$$\mathbf{p}_t = softmax(\mathbf{W}_p(ReLU(\mathbf{W}_q\mathbf{a}_t + \mathbf{b}_q))), \tag{11}$$

where $\mathbf{W}_q \in \mathbb{R}^{1,800\times 1,800}$ and $\mathbf{b}_q \in \mathbb{R}^{1,800}$ are the weight matrix and the bias of a hidden state, respectively.

To predict the most precise result, we choose the word whose probability is the highest in the dictionary $\mathcal{D}$: $y_t = argmax(\mathbf{p}_t)$. If the word y_t is not the symbol indicating the end, the next word y_{t+1} will be generated by inputting y_t into the Eqs. (3) and (4). The sentence generated by this approach is the best because the model is greedy for it selects the best word at each step sequentially.

5 Experiments

5.1 Dataset and Experimental Setting

Dataset. We prefer to use the dataset proposed in [1] and make some improvements on it. First we get a list of basic topics (*e.g.* sports, movie, food) by sorting the frequency of the various words appearing in the tags of the images except for stopwords like "*a*", "*the*". Next, we filter all the topic according to the category of the word. For example, we combine the topic "holiday" and the topic "vacation" because they have the same content. Moreover, "sandwiches" belong to the topic "food", so we integrate the topic "sandwiches" into the topic "food" and label a keyword "sandwiches" to the images that was previously a "sandwich" topic. Then we preprocess these data by labelling the image and text by the topics and keywords which are extracted from the content and save the data into the database.

Experimental Setting. We use the image retrievaled from the retrieval module as the query input and the original text of the image as the groundtruth (GT). In order to evaluate the text generated by the model, we measure the similarity between the generated sentences and GTs by using BLEU [22], CIDEr [23], METEOR [24], and ROUGE-r [25] scores. The higher the score, the better the performance. For the system, we will evaluate the performance of the whole system including time of logging in, time of image retrieval, time of text generation and time of tweeting text.

We take 90% of the dataset as the training data, 5K data as the test data and others for validation. Because our system is topic-based, we split the dataset by topics in order to separate the training and test data. If the data of a topic appears in both training and testing, text generated by the model will be close to the text in the training set and will affect the evaluation results.

We take *Attend2u* as our baseline, proposed by Park *e.g.* 2017 [1] which designed a model that can generate personalized sentences and hashtags of a query image. And we also compare the various kinds of deformation produced by our algorithm in order to verify the effect of each part of the algorithm.

5.2 Quantitative Comparison

The quantitative results of the text generation is shown in Table 1. It shows our algorithms have better performance than the baseline according to all the metrics we have listed.

Table 1. Evaluation of text generation between different methods. We use language similarity metrics (BLEU, CIDEr, METEOR, ROUGE-L). The methods with [*] generate text unrelated to the topic.

Methods	B-1	B-2	B-3	B-4	CIDEr	METEOR	ROUGE-L
(Attend2U)	0.093	0.035	0.012	0.006	0.103	0.043	0.108
(seq2seq)	0.050	0.012	0.003	0.000	0.034	0.024	0.065
(OURS-5c)	0.091	0.031	0.011	0.004	0.112	0.036	0.126
(OURS-p5)	**0.114**	**0.043**	**0.016**	**0.006**	**0.146**	**0.045**	**0.127**
(OURS-noTPC)*	0.098	0.039	0.014	0.006	0.105	0.037	0.120
(OURS-noWORD)	0.088	0.033	0.002	0	0.055	0.026	0.117
(OURS-noCNN)	0.092	0.038	0.002	0	0.060	0.029	0.144

We first find that the pool5 feature vector of the query image which takes only one cell of the memory outperforms the res5c feature vector. In our opinion, it is because computing attention is too hard for a large image feature and people describe the image by the whole content of the image instead of the detail. Thus, the feature of the whole image is more useful for the generation of the text.

We experiment our algorithms from two aspects whether the text is related to the topic or not. The latter contains the baseline and (OURS-noTPC), while the former contains the others. (OURS-noTPC) shows a little bit better than others in generating the text unrelated to topic, while (OURS-p5) gives the best results. We also find that if we remove one of the three kinds of memory, our approach turns to show worse performance. For example, if we remove the structure of CNN, the sentences generated become incoherence.

5.3 Qualitative Analysis

We show some examples of the text generated by our algorithm in Fig. 3. Every example contains the query image, predicted text and the GTs. Because the GT sentences are private and diverse from different users, it is really difficult to

Fig. 3. Six examples of the text prediction with query images, groundtruths (GT), and the text generated by our algorithm (OURS). Most of the generated texts are related to the images and meaningful.

predict the same sentence as the GT. However, a large number of sentences predicted by our model are the description of query images related to the particular topic and some of them even contains different emojis. For example, in Fig. 3, the second image contains just some texts and a cup of coffee, however, our model can predict that this image means to hope for a good day. It means that our model can not only describe the content of the image, but also understand the deep meaning of the image.

Figure 4 shows the generated text of different images under the same topic. We choose the topic of "food" and change the images to predict sentences. The text generated by our model can describe the images of the topic successful.

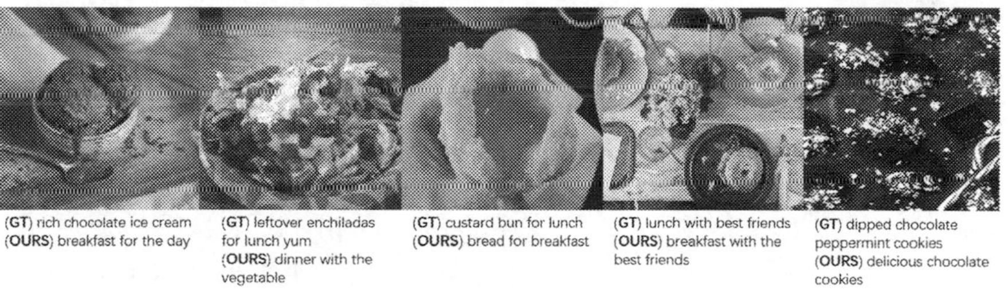

(GT) rich chocolate ice cream
(OURS) breakfast for the day
(GT) leftover enchiladas for lunch yum
(OURS) dinner with the vegetable
(GT) custard bun for lunch
(OURS) bread for breakfast
(GT) lunch with best friends
(OURS) breakfast with the best friends
(GT) dipped chocolate peppermint cookies
(OURS) delicious chocolate cookies

Fig. 4. Five examples of the text prediction for the topic "food" with query images, groundtruths (GT), and the text generated by our algorithm (OURS).

5.4 System Performance

Our system is shown in Fig. 5 and our system can post the generated text successfully to Twitter and it performance is the same as a real person. On the left, we get the input topic and list the retrieved images below. The text post by which account is displayed on the right. Other users can comment the text we post while they even don't know it is not tweeting by a tweeting system.

We also analyze the performance of our system in Table 2, including retrieval time, generation time, login time and posting time. The time of generating a text is very fast while the retrieval time is long due to the large dataset. As for

Fig. 5. The human-simulated tweeting system. We show the input and the retrieved images on the left and on the right we show the generated text.

login and posting, it needs to communicate with the server for three times. As a result, our system has a very good performance, and it is of great significance in practical applications.

Table 2. The performance of our system. We calculate the retrieval time and generation time of our model and count the login time and posting time of our system.

Retrieval time	Generation time	Login time	Posting time
1741 ms	17 ms	671 ms	347 ms

6 Conclusions

In this paper, we design a topic-guided human-simulated tweeting system, which provides a novel topic-image-tweet scheme, *i.e.*, the pipeline of the our Keyword-Based Retrieval Module (KBR-Module) and our Topic-Guided Image Captioning Module (TGIC-Module). The problem of the multiple-choice and appropriate tweet generation is well dealt with in this scheme. Additionally, we propose the Topic-Guided Context Sequence Memory Network (T-CSMN) to encode the obtained images and generate the topic-related and well-expressed tweets. Sufficient quantitative comparisons and qualitative analysis have been carried out to evaluate the effectiveness of the designed system and the superiority of the proposed T-CSMN model in a real-world Twitter dataset.

Our future work will focus on the design of the automatically tweeting system with emotion-oriented information. Additionally, we will consider the transformation of our tweeting system to more other social network platforms.

Acknowledgments. This work is supported by the National Key R&D Program (No. 2017YFC0113000, and No. 2016YFB1001503), Nature Science Foundation of China (No. U1705262, No. 61772443, and No. 61572410), Post Doctoral Innovative Talent

Support Program under Grant BX201600094, China Post-Doctoral Science Foundation under Grant 2017M612134, Scientific Research Project of National Language Committee of China (Grant No. YB135-49), and Nature Science Foundation of Fujian Province, China (No. 2017J01125 and No. 2018J01106).

References

1. Park, C.C., Kim, B., Kim, G.: Attend to you: personalized image captioning with context sequence memory networks (2017)
2. Wang, H., Can, D., Kazemzadeh, A., Bar, F., Narayanan, S.: A system for real-time Twitter sentiment analysis of 2012 us presidential election cycle. In: Proceedings of the ACL 2012 System Demonstrations, Association for Computational Linguistics, pp. 115–120 (2012)
3. Uchida, O., et al.: A real-time information sharing system to support self-, mutual-, and public-help in the aftermath of a disaster utilizing Twitter. IEICE Trans. Fundam. Electron. Commun. Comput. Sci. **99**(8), 1551–1554 (2016)
4. Chu, Z., Gianvecchio, S., Wang, H., Jajodia, S.: Who is tweeting on Twitter: human, bot, or cyborg? In: Proceedings of the 26th Annual Computer Security Applications Conference, pp. 21–30. ACM (2010)
5. Ordonez, V., Kulkarni, G., Berg, T.L.: Im2Text: describing images using 1 million captioned photographs. In: Advances in Neural Information Processing Systems, pp. 1143–1151 (2011)
6. Kuznetsova, P., Ordonez, V., Berg, A.C., Berg, T.L., Choi, Y.: Collective generation of natural image descriptions. In: Proceedings of the 50th Annual Meeting of the Association for Computational Linguistics: Long Papers, vol. 1, pp. 359–368. Association for Computational Linguistics (2012)
7. Kuznetsova, P., Ordonez, V., Berg, A., Berg, T., Choi, Y.: Generalizing image captions for image-text parallel corpus. In: Proceedings of the 51st Annual Meeting of the Association for Computational Linguistics: Short Papers, vol. 2, pp. 790–796 (2013)
8. Kuznetsova, P., Ordonez, V., Berg, T., Choi, Y.: TREETALK: composition and compression of trees for image descriptions. Trans. Assoc. Comput. Linguist. **2**(1), 351–362 (2014)
9. Mason, R., Charniak, E.: Nonparametric method for data-driven image captioning. In: Proceedings of the 52nd Annual Meeting of the Association for Computational Linguistics: Short Papers, vol. 2, pp. 592–598 (2014)
10. Kiros, R., Salakhutdinov, R., Zemel, R.: Multimodal neural language models. In: International Conference on Machine Learning, pp. 595–603 (2014)
11. Sutskever, I., Vinyals, O., Le, Q.V.: Sequence to sequence learning with neural networks. In: Advances in Neural Information Processing Systems, pp. 3104–3112 (2014)
12. Fang, H., et al.: From captions to visual concepts and back (2015)
13. Park, C.C., Kim, G.: Expressing an image stream with a sequence of natural sentences. In: Advances in Neural Information Processing Systems, pp. 73–81 (2015)
14. Vinyals, O., Toshev, A., Bengio, S., Erhan, D.: Show and tell: lessons learned from the 2015 mscoco image captioning challenge. IEEE Trans. Pattern Anal. Mach. Intell. **39**(4), 652–663 (2017)
15. Vinyals, O., Toshev, A., Bengio, S., Erhan, D.: Show and tell: a neural image caption generator. In: 2015 IEEE Conference on Computer Vision and Pattern Recognition (CVPR), pp. 3156–3164. IEEE (2015)

16. Karpathy, A., Fei-Fei, L.: Deep visual-semantic alignments for generating image descriptions. In: Proceedings of the IEEE Conference on Computer Vision and Pattern Recognition, pp. 3128–3137 (2015)
17. Mao, J., Xu, W., Yang, Y., Wang, J., Huang, Z., Yuille, A.: Deep captioning with multimodal recurrent neural networks (m-RNN). arXiv preprint arXiv:1412.6632 (2014)
18. Donahue, J., et al.: Long-term recurrent convolutional networks for visual recognition and description. In: Proceedings of the IEEE Conference on Computer Vision and Pattern Recognition, pp. 2625–2634 (2015)
19. Xu, K., et al.: Show, attend and tell: neural image caption generation with visual attention. In: International Conference on Machine Learning, pp. 2048–2057 (2015)
20. You, Q., Jin, H., Wang, Z., Fang, C., Luo, J.: Image captioning with semantic attention. In: IEEE Conference on Computer Vision and Pattern Recognition, pp. 4651–4659 (2016)
21. Weston, J., Chopra, S., Bordes, A.: Memory networks. In: 2015 International Conference on Learning Representations, ICLR 2015 (2015)
22. Papineni, K., Roukos, S., Ward, T., Zhu, W.J.: BLEU: a method for automatic evaluation of machine translation. In: Proceedings of the 40th Annual Meeting on Association for Computational Linguistics, pp. 311–318. Association for Computational Linguistics (2002)
23. Vedantam, R., Lawrence Zitnick, C., Parikh, D.: CIDEr: consensus-based image description evaluation. In: Proceedings of the IEEE Conference on Computer Vision and Pattern Recognition, pp. 4566–4575 (2015)
24. Banerjee, S., Lavie, A.: METEOR: an automatic metric for MT evaluation with improved correlation with human judgments. In: Proceedings of the ACL Workshop on Intrinsic and Extrinsic Evaluation Measures for Machine Translation and/or Summarization, pp. 65–72 (2005)
25. Lin, C.Y.: ROUGE: a package for automatic evaluation of summaries. In: Text Summarization Branches Out (2004)

Network Embedding Based on a Quasi-Local Similarity Measure

Xin Liu[1(✉)], Natthawut Kertkeidkachorn[1], Tsuyoshi Murata[2], Kyoung-Sook Kim[1], Julien Leblay[1], and Steven Lynden[1]

[1] Artificial Intelligence Research Center, National Institute of Advanced Industrial Science and Technology, AIST Waterfront ANNEX, 2-4-7 Aomi, Koto-ku, Tokyo 135-0064, Japan
{xin.liu,n.kertkeidkachorn,ks.kim,julien.leblay,steven.lynden}@aist.go.jp

[2] Department of Computer Science, Tokyo Institute of Technology, 2-12-1 Ookayama, Meguro-ku, Tokyo 152-8552, Japan
murata@c.titech.ac.jp

Abstract. Network embedding based on the random walk and skip-gram model such as the DeepWalk and Node2Vec algorithms have received wide attention. We identify that these algorithms essentially estimate the node similarities by random walk simulation, which is unreliable, inefficient, and inflexible. We propose to explicitly use node similarity measures instead of random walk simulation. Based on this strategy and a new proposed similarity measure, we present a fast and scalable algorithm AA$^+$Emb. Experiments show that AA$^+$Emb outperforms state-of-the-art network embedding algorithms on several commonly used benchmark networks.

1 Introduction

In the era of big data, the study of networks has received an enormous amount of attention. Of recent interest is network embedding—learning representations of network nodes in a low dimensional vector space, such that the proximity structure between nodes are maximally preserved [2,4,6]. The learned embeddings can be used as feature inputs for downstream machine learning algorithms, and this technology is beneficial for many network analysis tasks, such as community detection [19,22], label classification [16,17], link prediction [5], recommendation [21], and visualization [14].

One of the important algorithms for tackling the network embedding problem is based on random walk and skip-gram model [9,10]. DeepWalk [12] and Node2Vec [5] are representatives of this research direction. Their main idea is to use random walks to transform a network to an ordered sequence of nodes, which are then taken as input to the skip-gram model to learn the embeddings. The key point is that the sequence of nodes encodes the node proximity information, and this ensures the success of the algorithms. Therefore, DeepWalk and Node2Vec essentially estimate the node similarities by random walk simulation,

X. Geng and B.-H. Kang (Eds.): PRICAI 2018, LNAI 11012, pp. 429–440, 2018.
https://doi.org/10.1007/978-3-319-97304-3_33

or by counting the frequency of two nodes appearing together as the visited node and the corresponding context node in the walks. However, this method cannot efficiently and reliably estimate the node similarities when the size of the network becomes large. To overcome this weak point, we propose a fast network embedding algorithm AA$^+$Emb that explicitly uses a quasi-local node similarity instead of random walk simulation. We demonstrate that AA$^+$Emb outperforms DeepWalk, Node2Vec and several state-of-the-art network embedding algorithms on six benchmark networks based on standard tests of multilabel classification and link prediction.

Our main contributions are as follows.

- We identify that the success of DeepWalk and Node2Vec lies in estimating the node similarities by random walk simulation, which, however, has several weak points.
- We propose an objective function that integrates node similarities instead of random walk simulation. The new objective function has the merits of high reliability, efficiency, and flexibility over the one used by DeepWalk and Node2Vec.
- We introduce a novel similarity measure. This measure does not require global topological information but makes use of more information than local measures. Thus, it is a quasi-local measure and can reach a good tradeoff between accuracy and computational complexity.
- Based on the new objective function and similarity measure, we propose the AA$^+$Emb algorithm. AA$^+$Emb is superior to state-of-the-art algorithms in terms of generating high quality embeddings. Moreover, it is fast and scalable to large networks with near linear time complexity.

The rest of the paper is organized as follows. Section 2 reviews DeepWalk and Node2Vec. Section 3 introduces the new objective function, as an improvement of the one used in DeepWalk and Node2Vec. Section 4 proposes the new similarity measure. Section 5 presents the AA$^+$Emb algorithm, including the complexity analysis and the parameter selection discussion. Section 6 reports the experiment results. Section 7 surveys related work. Finally, Sect. 8 gives our conclusion.

2 DeepWalk and Node2Vec

We begin with the symbols and definitions that will be used. For clarity, we consider a simple network $\mathcal{G} = (\mathcal{V}, \mathcal{E})$, where $\mathcal{V} = \{v_i \mid i = 1, \cdots, n\}$ is the node set, and $\mathcal{E} \subseteq \mathcal{V} \times \mathcal{V}$ is the edge set. $n = |\mathbf{V}|$ and $m = |\mathbf{E}|$ are the number of nodes and edges, respectively. $\mathbf{A}$ denotes the adjacency matrix, with the element $A_{ij} = A_{ji} \in \{0, 1\}$ indicating whether $(v_i, v_j) \in \mathcal{E}$.

The aim of network embedding is to map each node v_i to a vector or *embedding* $\boldsymbol{e}_i \in \mathbb{R}^d$ for $\forall i = 1, \ldots, n$. $d \ll n$ is the embedding dimension. The sense of a good mapping is that the embeddings preserve the proximity structure between nodes. In other words, the (dis)similarity of embeddings in the $\mathbb{R}^d$ space should, to some extent, approximate the (dis)similarity of nodes in the original network.

Next, let us review DeepWalk and Node2Vec, which are representatives of the algorithms based on random walk and skip-gram model [9,10]. The two algorithms basically follow two steps. First, we sample a series of random walks, and create a corpus $\mathcal{C}$ comprised of pairs of visited nodes and the corresponding context nodes in the walks[1]. Then, we learn the embeddings by feeding $\mathcal{C}$ to the skip-gram model. The objective function of the skip-gram model with negative sampling can be expressed as[2]

$$O = \sum_{(v_i,v_j)\in\mathcal{C}} \left[\left(\log \sigma(\boldsymbol{e}_i^\top \boldsymbol{e}_j) \right) + \beta \cdot \mathbb{E}_{v_t \sim P_t} \left(\log \sigma(-\boldsymbol{e}_i^\top \boldsymbol{e}_t) \right) \right], \tag{1}$$

where $\sigma(x) = 1/(1+\exp(-x))$; β is a hyperparameter representing the number of negative samples for each $(v_i, v_j) \in \mathcal{C}$; P_t is the probability for selecting a negative sample v_t; Usually, the unigram distribution raised to the 3/4rd power are used for P. That is

$$P_t = \frac{(n_t^{\mathcal{C}})^{\frac{3}{4}}}{\sum_t (n_t^{\mathcal{C}})^{\frac{3}{4}}}, \tag{2}$$

where $n_t^{\mathcal{C}} = \#(v_t, \cdot)$ denotes the number of times that v_t appears as the first element of the pairs in $\mathcal{C}$.

By maximizing (1) we get a relative high value of $\boldsymbol{e}_i^\top \boldsymbol{e}_j$ for a positive example $(v_i, v_j) \in \mathcal{C}$ and a relative low value of $\boldsymbol{e}_i^\top \boldsymbol{e}_t$ for a negative example (v_i, v_t) where v_t is randomly sampled according to P_t. Note that the dot product $\boldsymbol{e}_i^\top \boldsymbol{e}_j$ expresses the similarity between the embeddings $\boldsymbol{e}_i$ and $\boldsymbol{e}_t$. Therefore, the positive examples that repeatedly emerge in $\mathcal{C}$, or the node pairs that frequently appear together as visited nodes and context nodes in random walks will have similar embeddings; the other node pairs have dissimilar embeddings.

3 New Objective Function

Recall that the requirement of network embedding is that similar nodes should have similar embeddings and dissimilar nodes have dissimilar embeddings. Therefore, DeepWalk and Node2Vec essentially estimate the node similarities by random walk simulation, *i.e.*, counting the frequency of two nodes appearing together as the visited node and the corresponding context node. However, this method cannot efficiently and reliably estimate the node similarities when the size of the network is large enough.

Our idea is to replace random walk simulation by explicitly using node similarities. Suppose $\boldsymbol{S}$: $(v_i, v_j) \rightarrow \mathbb{R}^+$ is a similarity measure for a pair of nodes

[1] A difference between DeepWalk and node2vec is that the former uses a pure random sampling strategy, while the latter introduces two hyper-parameters to use 2nd-order random walks in order to bias the walks towards a particular search strategy.

[2] DeepWalk originally uses hierarchical softmax [9] with an objective similar to this.

(we will see the definition of the measure in the next section). The greater S_{ij} is, the more similar v_i and v_j are. Our objective function is defined as

$$O = \sum_{v_i} \Big[\sum_{v_j \in \mathcal{C}_i^+} (S_{ij} \log \sigma(\boldsymbol{e}_i^\top \boldsymbol{e}_j)) + \beta \cdot (\sum_{v_j \in \mathcal{C}_i^+} S_{ij}) \cdot \mathbb{E}_{v_t \sim P_t^i} \big(\log \sigma(-\boldsymbol{e}_i^\top \boldsymbol{e}_t) \big) \Big], \quad (3)$$

where

$$\mathcal{C}_i^+ = \begin{cases} \{v_j \mid S_{ij} > \rho_i^+\} & \text{if } |\{v_j \mid S_{ij} > \rho_i^+\}| \leq \tau; \\ \{v_j \mid v_j \text{ is among the } \tau \text{ most similar nodes to } v_i\} & \text{otherwise.} \end{cases} \quad (4)$$

is the set of nodes that are similar to v_i. ρ_i^+ and τ are hyperparameters for controlling the size of $\mathcal{C}_i^+$. Each node $v_j \in \mathcal{C}_i^+$ is paired with v_i to compose a positive example. Each positive example (v_i, v_j) is weighted by S_{ij} in the objective function. $\mathcal{C}_i^- = \{v_j \mid S_{ij} < \rho_i^-\}$ is the set of nodes that are dissimilar to v_i. Again, ρ_i^- is a hyperparameter for controlling the size of $\mathcal{C}_i^-$. The distribution for selecting a negative sample for v_i is defined as

$$P_t^i = \begin{cases} \frac{1}{|\mathcal{C}_i^-|} & \text{if } v_t \in \mathcal{C}_i^-; \\ 0 & \text{otherwise.} \end{cases} \quad (5)$$

$\beta \cdot (\sum_{v_j \in \mathcal{C}_i^+} S_{ij})$ is the number of samples that are paired with v_i to form negative examples. So, on average, we still generate β negative examples for a positive example.

Our new objective function have the following advantages over the one used by DeepWalk and Node2Vec.

- **Reliable.** Estimation based on random walks introduces random factors, resulting in unstable results in different runs of the algorithm. On the other hand, researchers have proposed a bunch of measures for stably estimating node similarities in networks [7,8]. Integrating the similarity measures into our new objective function leads to more reliable results. Moreover, based on the distribution (2) it is possible to sample a false negative sample (*i.e.* a node that is similar to v_i), leading to less accurate results. Our negative sampling distribution (5) avoids such a situation.
- **Efficient.** Estimating the node similarities directly based on the network information is much more efficient than estimation based on counting the frequency of visited and context node pairs from random walks. This is because the latter requires an enormous number of samples.
- **Flexible.** The similarity measure can be based on any definitions, providing the flexibility for accommodating different types of networks. For example, many networks contain some "metadata" such as the age or gender of individuals in a social network. We can easily use both network topology and such metadata for defining node similarities. However, random walk based similarity estimation cannot use metadata to estimate node similarities.

4 Similarity Measure

In this section, we propose a new similarity measure called AA$^+$, as an extension of Adamic-Adar (AA) similarity [1]. AA similarity is defined as

$$S_{ij}^{\text{aa}} = \sum_{v_t \in \Gamma_i \cap \Gamma_j} \frac{1}{\log k_t}, \tag{6}$$

where $\Gamma_i = \{v_j \mid A_{ij} > 0\}$ indicates the set of neighbors of v_i and $k_i = \sum_{j=1}^{n} A_{ij}$ denotes the degree of v_i. It is apparent that AA similarity is a local measure, because v_i and v_j's similarity S_{ij}^{aa} is just related to information on their common neighbors, or length-2 paths. Our idea is to use more information on paths with longer lengths.

The specific definition of AA$^+$ similarity follows. Suppose $p_{ij}^l = (v_{i_0}, v_{i_1}, \ldots, v_{i_l})$ where $i_0 = i, i_l = j$ is a length-l path between v_i and v_j. First, we assume the contribution of p_{ij}^l to v_i and v_j's similarity is equal to the reciprocal of the product of the logarithms of the degrees of the intermediate nodes of the path. That is,

$$c(p_{ij}^l) = \frac{k_{i_0} k_{i_l}}{k_{i_0} (\log k_{i_1} \log k_{i_2} \cdots \log k_{i_{l-1}}) k_{i_l}}, \tag{7}$$

where we set $\log 1 = 0.1$. Secondly, we suppose the contribution decays with the path length by a factor of α^l, where α is a parameter for decay rate. Finally, the similarity is defined as the contributions over all $l \leq \eta$ paths

$$S_{ij}^{\text{aa}^+} = \sum_{l=1}^{\eta} \alpha^l \sum_{p_{ij}^l} c(p_{ij}^l), \tag{8}$$

where η is a hyperparameter.

We can derive that AA$^+$ degrades to AA similarity if we only consider the path length $l = 2$, as

$$S_{ij}^{\text{aa}^+} \mid_{l=2} = \sum_{p_{ij}^{l=2}} c(p_{ij}^{l=2}) = \sum_{v_t \in \Gamma_i \cap \Gamma_j} \frac{1}{\log k_t} = S_{ij}^{\text{aa}}, \tag{9}$$

where we have omitted the overall multiplicative factor α^2.

Note that local measure has the advantage of ease of computing. However, local measures are based on information of common neighbors. Consequently, many node pairs have the similarity score of 0, which is insufficient for our objective function. Global measures, on the other hand, consider all of the paths and require high computational complexity. AA$^+$ similarity does not need global topological information but make use of more information than local measures (length $l \leq \eta$ *vs.* $l = 2$ paths), thus it is a quasi-local measure and can reach a good tradeoff between accuracy and computational complexity.

Algorithm 1 AA$^+$Emb

Input: network: $\mathcal{G} = (\mathcal{V}, \mathcal{E})$
embedding dimension: d
similarity threshold: ρ_i^+, ρ_i^- $(i = 1, \cdots, n)$
maximum size of the similar node set: τ
maximum path length: η
decay rate: α
average number of negative examples per positive example: β
batch size: ι

Output: node embeddings: $\boldsymbol{e_i}$ for $i = 1, \ldots, n$

begin
  Initiate $\boldsymbol{e_i}$ for $i = 1, \ldots, n$ randomly
  `// Preparation procedure`
  for $i \leftarrow 1$ **to** n **do**
    Calculate and store the node similarities S_{ij} for $j = 1, \ldots, n$
    Create and store the similar and dissimilar node sets $\mathcal{C}_i^+$ and $\mathcal{C}_i^-$
  end
  `// Learning procedure`
  repeat
    for a batch of nodes $\{v_{i_1} \cdots v_{i_\iota}\}$ **do**
      for $i \leftarrow i_1$ **to** i_ι **do**
        Sample negative samples from $\mathcal{C}_i^-$
      end
      Update related $\boldsymbol{e_i}$ by batch gradient decent of Eq. (3)
    end
  until *convergence*
end

5 The Algorithm

With the new objective function and similarity measure, we propose the AA$^+$Emb algorithm for network embedding, which is shown in Algorithm 1. Next, we discuss the computational complexity. For calculating the node similarities, for each node v_i we successively traverse v_i's neighbors, the neighbors' neighbors, and so on until the neighbors of η-hops away. Thus, the preparation procedure requires a complexity of $\mathrm{O}(\bar{k}^{\eta} \cdot n)$, where $\bar{k}$ is the average degree of nodes. The update operation based on batch gradient decent is linear with the multiplication of the embedding dimension and the number of embeddings to be updated. For convenience, we suppose a batch of a single node. The number of the positive and negative examples in the worst case is $\mathrm{O}(\tau \cdot \beta)$, *i.e.*, the update operation for this batch requires a complexity of $\mathrm{O}(\tau \cdot \beta \cdot d)$. Thus, the complexity of the learning procedure is $\mathrm{O}(\kappa \cdot \tau \cdot \beta \cdot d \cdot n)$, where κ is the number of epochs for training. Finally, the overall complexity of AA$^+$Emb is $\mathrm{O}(\bar{k}^{\eta} \cdot n + \kappa \cdot \tau \cdot \beta \cdot d \cdot n)$. For huge networks, it requires much memory to store S_{ij} $(j = 1, \ldots, n)$, $\mathcal{C}_i^+$, and $\mathcal{C}_i^-$ for each v_i. To avoid it, we can even calculate S_{ij}, $\mathcal{C}_i^+$, and $\mathcal{C}_i^-$ in an online fashion. That is, we calculate them in the learning procedure, resulting a total algorithm complexity of $\mathrm{O}((\bar{k}^{\eta} + \tau \cdot \beta \cdot d) \cdot \kappa \cdot n)$. Because the parameters $\bar{k}, \kappa, \tau, \beta, d$ are bounded by some constants, both of the complexities can be roughly viewed as near linear to the size of the network.

AA$^+$Emb involves a number of parameters. We provide some suggestions on how to select their values. We set the decay rate $\alpha = 0.9/\lambda_1^{\mathrm{AD}^{-1}}$, where $\mathbf{D} = \mathrm{diag}(\log k_1, \log k_2, \cdots, \log k_n)$ and $\lambda_1^{\mathrm{AD}^{-1}}$ denotes the spectral radius of $\mathbf{AD}^{-1}$. We select η from $[5, 10]$ and τ from $[\bar{k}^2, \bar{k}^4]$, depending on the size of the network. We choose ρ_i^+ and ρ_i^- based on the values that correspond to 75–95 cumulative percent of v_i's similarities (in descending order). Moreover, we suggest to divide the nodes into n/ι batches, such that the nodes in a batch have balanced values on $\sum_{v_j \in C_i^+} S_{ij}$, or we can simply set $\iota = 1$. Finally, we set $\beta = 5$ for the average number of negative examples per positive example.

6 Experiments

We evaluate AA$^+$Emb based on two applications: multilabel classification [12] and link prediction [5]. We compare AA$^+$Emb with DeepWalk, Node2Vec, and the following three state-of-the-art algorithms for network embedding.

- GraRep [3] defines a loss function by integrating the transition probabilities. Minimizing this loss function is equivalent to factorizing a matrix that is related to the s-step transition probability matrix. For each k the factorization produces a sub-embedding. Then GraRep concatenates sub-embeddings on different s as the final embedding solution. Note that calculating the transition probability matrix requires a high time and space complexity, so this algorithm is not scalable to large networks.
- HOPE [11] obtains embeddings by factorizing the Katz similarity matrix using a generalized singular value decomposition algorithm.
- LINE [15] learns two different embeddings, one is for preserving the 1st-order proximity and the other for preserving the 2nd-order proximity. Finally, the two embeddings are concatenated together.

We uniformly set the embedding dimension as 120 for all algorithms. The parameter settings are as follows. For DeepWalk and Node2Vec, we set the window size to 10, the walk length to 80, the number of walks per node to 10. For GraRep, we set the maximum matrix transition step to 6. For HOPE, we set the decay rate to $0.95/\lambda_1^{\mathrm{A}}$. For LINE, we set the number of negative samples to 5. Lastly, for Node2Vec, we learn the best in-out and return hyperparameters with a grid search over $\{0.25, 0.50, 1, 2, 4\}$.

We use eight real-world network datasets, which come from various domains and are commonly used by other researchers. A brief description of these networks follows.

- EuropeAir [13] and USAir [13]: The air-traffic networks of Europe and the USA, respectively. The nodes indicate airports and the edges denote the existence of commercial flights. The labels represent the capacity levels of the airports.
- Cora [20] and DBLP [14]: Paper citation networks. The labels represent the topics of the papers.

- BlogCatalog [16]: A network of social relationships of the bloggers listed on the BlogCatalog website. The labels represent topic categories provided by the bloggers.
- Flickr [16]: A network for the contacts between users in Flickr. The labels represent the interest groups of the users.

We remove self-loop edges and transform bi-directional edges to undirected edges for each network. The statistics of the networks after pre-processing are summarized in Table 1.

Table 1. Statistics of the networks

Dataset	$\|\mathcal{V}\|$	$\|\mathcal{E}\|$	$\|\mathcal{L}\|$
EuropeAir	399	5,993	4
USAir	1,190	13,599	4
Cora	2,708	5,278	7
DBLP	13,184	47,937	5
BlogCatalog	10,312	333,983	39
Flickr	80,513	5,899,882	195

6.1 Multilabel Classification

In the multilabel classification settings, every node is associated with one or more labels from a set $\mathcal{L}$. The task is executed according to the following procedure [12]. First, we randomly sample a portion of the labeled nodes for training, with the rest for testing. Then, we use the learned embeddings and the corresponding labels of the training nodes to train a one-vs-all logistic regression (LR) classifier. Finally, feeding the embeddings of the testing nodes to the classifier we predict their labels, which will be compared to the true labels for evaluation. We repeat this procedure 10 times and evaluate the performance in terms of *Macro-F1*[3].

The results are displayed in Fig. 1. It is evident to see that AA$^+$Emb has the best performance in all of the networks. In particular, it outperforms DeepWalk and Node2Vec by a large margin in the air-traffic networks. For example, it achieves a performance gain of 25.9% over DeepWalk and 18.7% over Node2Vec in the USAir network when the prediction is made based on 60% labeled nodes. This attributes to the superiority of AA$^+$ measure over random walk simulation for estimating node similarities. AA$^+$Emb also has considerable advantages over the other three state-of-the-art algorithms. For example, it achieves an improvement over GraRep of 36.4%, HOPE of 10.7%, and LINE of 21.9% in the BlogCatalog network when the prediction is made based on 90% labeled nodes.

[3] We omitted evaluation in terms of Micro-F1 because the trends are basically similar to Macro-F1.

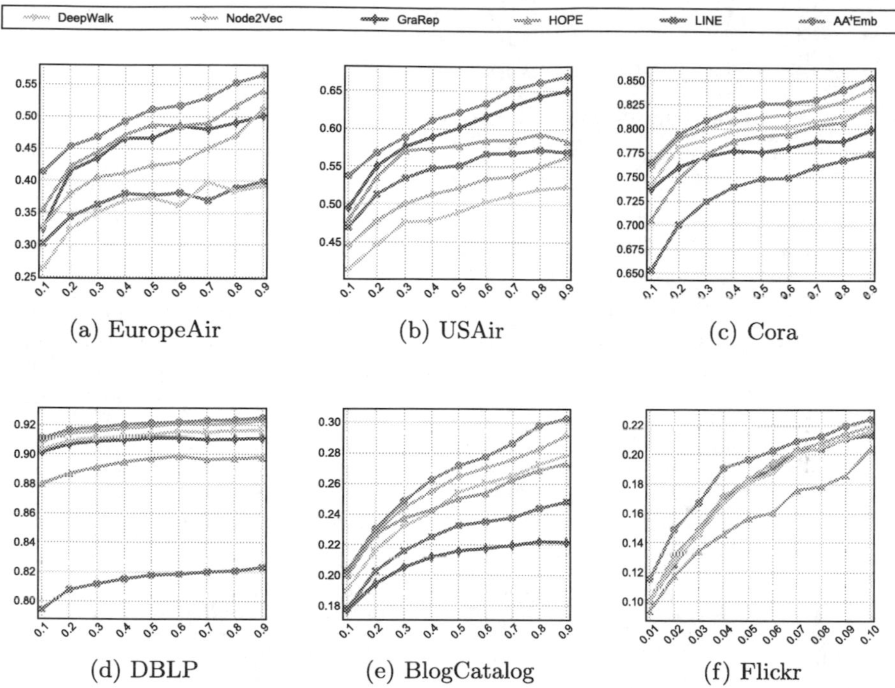

Fig. 1. Macro-F1 scores for the multilabel classification task. The x-axis represents the ratio of nodes with known labels. The y-axis represents the Macro-F1 scores. (a) EuropeAir (b) USAir (c) Cora (d) DBLP (e) BlogCatalog (f) Flickr

6.2 Link Prediction

In the link prediction task, we are given a network $\mathcal{G}'$ with 50% of edges removed from the original network $\mathcal{G}$. We predict the missing edges (*i.e.* the 50% removed edges) according to the procedures in [5]. First, based on the node embeddings learned from $\mathcal{G}'$, we generate edge embeddings for pairs of nodes using the element-wise operators listed below. We label an edge embedding as positive if the corresponding edge exists in $\mathcal{G}'$ and negative otherwise. Then, we train a binary LR classifier using all of the edge embeddings that have positive labels and the same amount of randomly sampled edge embeddings that have negative labels. After that, feeding an edge embedding to the LR classifier we can calculate the existence probability of the corresponding edge. Finally, we evaluate the performance based on the probabilities of the missing edges and non-existent edges (*i.e.* the edges that do not exist in $\mathcal{G}$) in terms of the *Area Under the Curve (AUC)*.

The element-wise operators for generating edge embeddings are:

- Average: $[\boldsymbol{e}_{ij}]_t = \big([\boldsymbol{e}_i]_t + [\boldsymbol{e}_j]_t\big)/2$,
- Hadamard: $[\boldsymbol{e}_{ij}]_t = [\boldsymbol{e}_i]_t \cdot [\boldsymbol{e}_j]_t$,

– Weighted L1: $[e_{ij}]_t = |[e_i]_t - [e_j]_t|$,
– Weighted L2: $[e_{ij}]_t = |[e_i]_t - [e_j]_t|^2$,

where $t \in 1, \cdots, d$ denotes the subscript of the t-th element of an embedding.

Table 2 shows the results. We can find that AA$^+$Emb consistently outperforms the baselines in all of the networks. Remarkably, it outperforms both DeepWalk and Node2Vec with gain up to 10.5% and 8.4% in the EuropeAir network. Comparatively speaking, HOPE performs the second best, but it has less success in the paper citation networks. Note that HOPE is based on factorizing the Katz similarity matrix, while AA$^+$Emb is based on sampling positive and negative examples using AA$^+$ similarity. On the one hand, this implies that preserving higher order proximity by directly using similarity measures is conducive to link prediction. On the other hand, this also demonstrates that AA$^+$ similarity is superior to Katz similarity.

Table 2. AUC scores for the link prediction task (based on the best results of choosing different operators for edge embedding)

Dataset	DeepWalk	Node2Vec	Grarep	HOPE	LINE	AA$^+$Emb
EuropeAir	0.8226	0.8383	0.9083	0.8992	0.7236	**0.9090**
USAir	0.8650	0.8934	0.9434	0.9501	0.8372	**0.9529**
Cora	0.7324	0.7381	0.6947	0.7018	0.6780	**0.7407**
DBLP	0.9224	0.9231	0.9216	0.9078	0.8812	**0.9302**
BlogCatalog	0.8774	0.8878	0.9307	0.9387	0.8788	**0.9445**
Flickr	0.9184	0.9201	–	0.9286	0.8996	**0.9342**

7 Related Work

While finalizing this manuscript, we have been made aware of a related approach developed independently by Tsitsulin et al. [18]. They propose a network embedding algorithm that learns the distribution of a similarity measure. There are several differences between the two contemporary works. First, we identify that DeepWalk and Node2Vec essentially estimate node similarities by random walk simulation, while they do not. Secondly, we integrate the node similarities into the objective function, while they incorporate the similarity distribution into the objective function. Thirdly, we propose the new AA$^+$ similarity, while they use the existent PageRank similarity.

8 Conclusion

We have proposed AA$^+$Emb algorithm for network embedding. It is based on the idea of explicitly using AA$^+$ similarity instead of random walk simulation in formulating the objective function. AA^+Emb is superior to state-of-the-art algorithms in terms of generating high quality embeddings. Moreover, it is fast and scalable to large networks with near linear time complexity.

This work only deals with unweighted and undirected networks. However, the similarity in the proposed objective function (3) can be based on any user-defined measures. This implies that our work is not limited to simple networks but can be extended to different types of networks. For example, if we give a proper definition of the similarity, (3) also applies to multiplex networks that contain multiple types of nodes and edges. Embedding of different types of networks is left for our future work.

Acknowledgment. This paper is based on results obtained from a project commissioned by the New Energy and Industrial Technology Development Organization (NEDO).

References

1. Adamic, L.A., Adar, E.: Friends and neighbors on the web. Soc. Netw. **25**(3), 211–230 (2003)
2. Cai, H., Zheng, V.W., Chang, K.C.C.: A comprehensive survey of graph embedding: problems, techniques and applications. arXiv preprint arXiv:1709.07604 (2017)
3. Cao, S., Lu, W., Xu, Q.: GraRep: learning graph representations with global structural information. In: Proceedings of CIKM, pp. 891–900 (2015)
4. Goyal, P., Ferrara, E.: Graph embedding techniques, applications, and performance: a survey. arXiv preprint arXiv:1705.02801 (2017)
5. Grover, A., Leskovec, J.: node2vec: scalable feature learning for networks. In: Proceedings of KDD, pp. 855–864 (2016)
6. Hamilton, W.L., Ying, R., Leskovec, J.: Representation learning on graphs: methods and applications. arXiv preprint arXiv:1709.05584 (2017)
7. Lü, L., Medo, M., Yeung, C.H., Zhang, Y., Zhang, Z., Zhou, T.: Recommender systems. Phys. Rep. **519**, 1–49 (2012)
8. Lü, L., Zhou, T.: Link prediction in complex networks: a survey. Physica A **390**, 1150–1170 (2011)
9. Mikolov, T., Chen, K., Corrado, G., Dean, J.: Efficient estimation of word representations in vector space. arXiv preprint arXiv:1301.3781 (2013)
10. Mikolov, T., Sutskever, I., Chen, K., Corrado, G., Dean, J.: Distributed representations of words and phrases and their compositionality. In: Proceedings of NIPS, pp. 3111–3119 (2013)
11. Ou, M., Cui, P., Pei, J., Zhang, Z., Zhu, W.: Asymmetric transitivity preserving graph embedding. In: Proceedings of KDD, pp. 1105–1114 (2016)
12. Perozzi, B., Al-Rfou, R., Skiena, S.: DeepWalk: online learning of social representations. In: Proceedings of KDD, pp. 701–710 (2014)
13. Ribeiro, L.F.R., Saverese, P.H.P., Figueiredo, D.R.: struc2vec: learning node representations from structural identity. In: Proceedings of KDD, pp. 385–394 (2017)
14. Tang, J., Qu, M., Mei, Q.: PTE: predictive text embedding through large-scale heterogeneous text networks. In: Proceedings of KDD, pp. 1165–1174 (2015)
15. Tang, J., et al.: Line: large-scale information network embedding. In: Proceedings of WWW, pp. 1067–1077 (2015)

16. Tang, L., Liu, H.: Relational learning via latent social dimensions. In: Proceedings of KDD, pp. 817–826 (2009)
17. Tang, L., Liu, H.: Scalable learning of collective behavior based on sparse social dimensions. In: Proceedings of CIKM, pp. 1107–1116 (2009)
18. Tsitsulin, A., Mottin, D., Karras, P., Müller, E.: Verse: versatile graph embeddings from similarity measures. In: Proceedings of WWW, pp. 539–548 (2018)
19. Wang, X., et al.: Community preserving network embedding. In: Proceedings of AAAI, pp. 203–209 (2017)
20. Yang, C., Sun, M., Liu, Z., Tu, C.: Fast network embedding enhancement via high order proximity approximation. In: Proceedings of IJCAI, pp. 3894–3900 (2017)
21. Yu, X., et al.: Personalized entity recommendation: a heterogeneous information network approach. In: Proceedings of WSDM, pp. 283–292 (2014)
22. Zhang, Y., Lyu, T., Zhang, Y.: Cosine: community-preserving social network embedding from information diffusion cascades. In: Proceedings of AAAI, pp. 2620–2627 (2018)

Reinforcement Learning for Mobile Robot Obstacle Avoidance Under Dynamic Environments

Liwei Huang, Hong Qu[(✉)], Mingsheng Fu, and Wu Deng

School of Computer Science and Engineering,
University of Electronic Science and Technology of China, Chengdu 611731, China
hlw_legend@163.com, hongqu@uestc.edu.cn

Abstract. Collision avoidance under dynamic environments is a challenging problem for mobile robots. Navigating the robot safely to the target is extremely significant especially in the dynamic environments. In this paper, a new approach based on reinforcement learning is proposed to navigate the robot from the start location to the target location without collisions with static and dynamic obstacles. In the proposed method, we improve the original Q-learning algorithm in environment modeling, reward function, and the adapted policy to make the robot stay away from obstacles, reduce the probability of collisions, and reach the target as fast as possible. Finally, simulations of some test scenarios and the comparisons between the original Q-learning and improved Q-learning are respectively conducted to validate that the proposed approach has high efficiency and adaptability in solving dynamic obstacle avoidance problem.

Keywords: Obstacle avoidance · Reinforcement learning
Dynamic environments · Mobile robot

1 Introduction

The path planning problem is considered an indispensable part in mobile robots navigation, which requires the robot to reach the target from a start location without collision with the obstacles in a specified environment. According to the obstacles' movement situation, the path planning problem has been classified into two categories: static path planning and dynamic path planning. Many researches have been done on mobile robot path planning problem for several decades under static environments [4,6,7,10–14]. In traditional dynamic path planning methods, the movements of dynamic obstacles should be predicted in advance to avoid collisions, which makes it time-consuming in building and updating of the dynamic environment map. Also, the accuracy of the prediction cannot be guaranteed.

Planning has long been studied in artificial intelligence, but research in reinforcement learning has brought a number of powerful innovation [9]. Reinforcement learning has been widely applied in robotics [8]. A multi Q-learning

X. Geng and B.-H. Kang (Eds.): PRICAI 2018, LNAI 11012, pp. 441–453, 2018.
https://doi.org/10.1007/978-3-319-97304-3_34

algorithm is presented to synchronously re-plan the paths for multi-agents [15]. Duguleana proposed a new reinforcement learning approach to solve the problem of obstacle avoidance in [1], which had a good average speed and a satisfying target reaching success rate. The authors addressed a new approach for combination of supervised learning and reinforcement learning [3] in robot navigation by taking advantages of the two methods. A solution was developed in [2] using Q-learning and a neural network planner to solve path planning problems under dynamic environments. In [5], a new approach was presented for solving the problem of mobile robot path planning in an unknown dynamic environment based on Q-learning, and the authors redefined the states space to solve the curse of dimensionality problem.

Reinforcement learning has inherent advantage dealing with dynamic environments, of which the learning process is executed by interacting with the environment. Through off-line learning under varieties of environments, the trained reinforcement learning based methods can directly get the collision free path in the simulated situations.

Therefore, we build our work on basis of reinforcement learning, and propose an improved Q-learning algorithm to deal with robot navigation problem under dynamic environment. The contributions of this paper mainly include: (1) we take account of the obstacle's moving direction in the states redefinition phase to get rid of confusions in the updates of Q-values; (2) a hybrid selection strategy combining ε-greedy and closer to target is utilized to choose the robot's next action, thus increasing the diversities of optional solutions; (3) we redefine the reward functions to make it more reasonable and more applicable; (4) some complicated environments with static and dynamic obstacles are tested to validate the merits of our method.

This paper is organized as follows. Sect. 2 is devoted to the problem statement and the states redefinition. The detailed presentation of path planning obtained by improved Q-learning is illustrated in Sect. 3. Several simulations and comparisons are conducted in Sect. 4. Conclusions and outlooks are drawn in the last section.

2 The Environment Model

In this paper, we consider the same environment model as [5], and make some improvements on it. In the environment, there are obstacles and target, which can be either static or dynamic. The robot's goal is to find a collision free path from its start position to the target position through applying Q-learning algorithm.

2.1 The State Space

In the states and actions definition, we care about only the approximate distance and relative directions between the robot and the target, and between the robot and the closest obstacle. At each time instant, the robot is considered as the center, and the environment around it is divided into four regions: $R1$, $R2$, $R3$ and $R4$. To avoid the situation that the obstacle and the target may locate at the same region which will confuse the robot, the angle between d_{r-t} (the line from robot to target) and d_{r-o} (the line from robot to obstacle) is considered, as shown in Fig. 1(a). The range of θ is $[0, 2\pi]$, as we only need to know the range of the angle, thus, we divide the interval into eight angular regions, which is shown in Fig. 1(b).

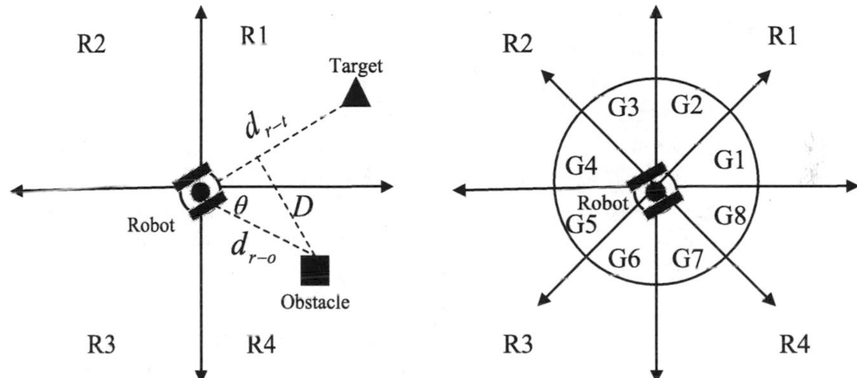

(a) The initial environment model. (b) The environment model containing angle θ.

Fig. 1. The mobile robot environment containing one target and one closest obstacle.

Assume that at time instant t, the robot's position is $P_r = [P_x \ P_y]^t$, the target position is $P_t = [P_{t-x} \ P_{t-y}]^t$, and the closest obstacle location is $P_o = [P_{o-x} \ P_{o-y}]^t$. Then we have

$$\theta = \arcsin \frac{D}{d_{r-o}}, \tag{1}$$

where

$$D = \frac{|(P_{t-y} - P_y)P_{o-x} + (P_x - P_{t-x})P_{o-y} + P_{t-x}P_y - P_xP_{t-y}|}{\sqrt{(P_{t-x} - P_x)^2 + (P_{t-y} - P_y)^2}}, \tag{2}$$

and

$$d_{r-o} = \sqrt{(P_{o-x} - P_x)^2 + (P_{o-y} - P_y)^2}. \tag{3}$$

The current angular region G containing θ is depicted as follows:

$$G = \begin{cases} G1, \theta \in [0, \pi/4) \\ G2, \theta \in [\pi/4, \pi/2) \\ G3, \theta \in [\pi/2, 3\pi/4) \\ G4, \theta \in [3\pi/4, \pi) \\ G5, \theta \in [\pi, 5\pi/4) \\ G6, \theta \in [5\pi/4, 3\pi/2) \\ G7, \theta \in [3\pi/2, 7\pi/4) \\ G8, \theta \in [7\pi/4, 2\pi). \end{cases} \tag{4}$$

If we just use the target region R_g, the closest obstacle region R_o, and the current angular region G_n to determine the state, the update confusion problem of Q-values may happen. For example, in the training phase, as in Fig. 2(a), the robot and obstacle move in the same direction at time instant t, and the robot is in the safe state $S_t = (R_1, R_1, G_1)$, then it moves forward to get closer to target, and reaches the dotted rectangle position, which is also a safe state. Then, the robot will get a positive reward, and the Q-value at t is updated according to the reward function and Q-value update equation in Section 3. Nevertheless, under the situation shown in Fig. 2(b), the robot and obstacle move in the opposite direction. The robot is in the safe state $S_t = (R_1, R_1, G_1)$, then if the robot still move forward and reach the dotted rectangle location, it will go into the failure state, and collide with the obstacle. Thus, the robot will receive a negative reward as punishment, and the update of Q-value will be different from that of the situation illustrated in Fig. 2(a).

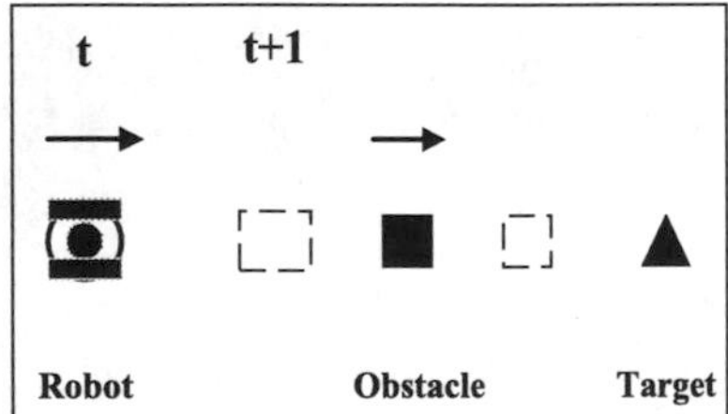

(a) The robot and obstacle move in the same direction.

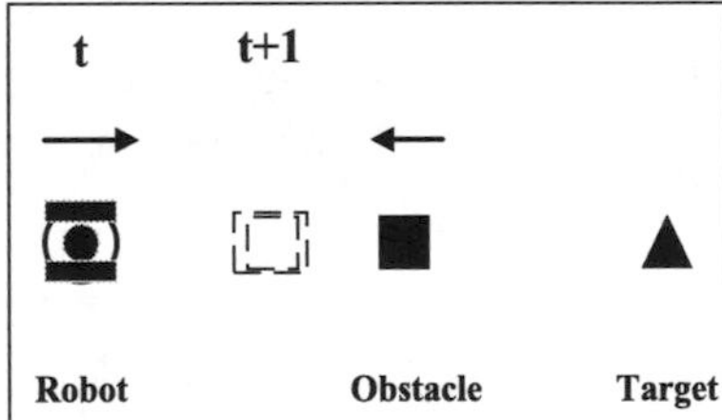

(b) The robot and obstacle move in the opposite direction.

Fig. 2. Confusions created by taking no consideration of obstacle's moving direction

Therefore, to overcome the update confusion problem of Q-values, we add the additional obstacle's direction to the state definition, which is:

$$S_t = (R_g, R_o, G_n, D_o), n \in [1, 8], \tag{5}$$

where D_o is the obstacle's moving direction.

2.2 The Action Space

The action space should be defined after the states space is determined. In this paper, we consider three actions for the robot: move forward, turn left, and turn right. For the robot, moving forward is to move to the target in a straight line. Turning left and right actions are applied when the robot meets obstacles, and the turning degree depends on the situations and the required degree of avoidance.

3 Collision Avoidance Using Improved Q-Learning

In this section, we make some adjustments to the reward function, and the selection strategy to improve Q-learning, and to make it more superior in solving the robot path planning problem under dynamic environments.

3.1 The Reward Function

The reward function indicates wether the performed action at a specific situation is good or not. Before the definition of the reward function, we firstly classify the states into 4 types: Safe States (SS), which means the robot has a low or no possibility colliding with the obstacles; Non-safe States (NS), which means the robot has a high possibility colliding with the obstacles, Winning States (WS), which means the robot reaches the goal, Failure States (FS), which the robot collides with the obstacles.

The states sets are clustered according to a series of distances, which are d_{win}, d_{min}, d_{col}, d_{r-o}, and d_{r-t}, where d_{win} is the radius of the winning region around the target, d_{min} is the radius of the non-safe region around the obstacle, d_{col} is the radius of collision region around the obstacle, d_{r-o} is the distance between the robot and the closest obstacle, and d_{r-t} is the distance between the robot and the target. These distances are shown in Fig. 3, and the current transition state of the robot is determined by

$$S = \begin{cases} WS, d_{r-t} \leq d_{win} \\ SS, \;\; d_{r-o} \geq d_{min} \\ NS, \; d_{col} < d_{r-o} \leq d_{min} \\ FS, \;\; d_{r-o} \leq d_{col}. \end{cases} \tag{6}$$

Based on the transition states, we define the reward function as:

$$r = \begin{cases} 1, & S \subset NS \rightarrow SS \\ -1, & S \subset NS \rightarrow NS, d_{r-t}(n+1) \leq d_{r-t}(n) \\ 0, & S \subset NS \rightarrow NS, d_{r-o}(n+1) > d_{r-o}(n) \\ -2, & S \subset NS \rightarrow FS \\ -0.1, & S \subset NS. \end{cases} \tag{7}$$

Specially, for $S \subset NS$, we give it a -0.1 reward to make the robot arrive at the target as fast as possible.

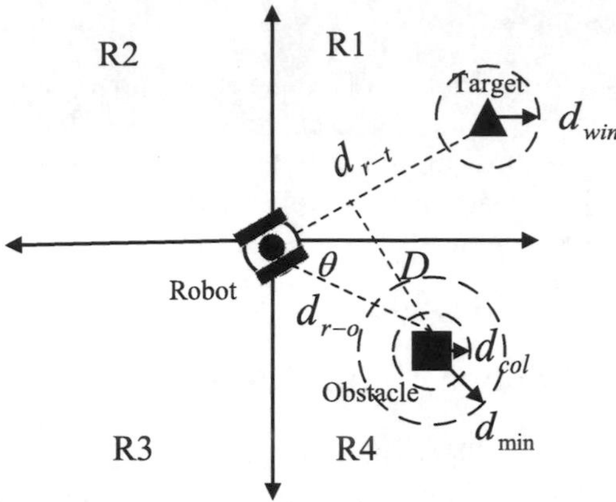

Fig. 3. The main distances contributing to the robot states classification

3.2 The Q-Values

In the Q-learning algorithm, the Q-values are stored in a matrix called Q table, in which the rows stand for the different states and the columns represent the actions performed by the robot. The Q table will be filled and updated by Q-values in the training phase, and the value usually has relations to the immediate reward and the maximum reward in the new state for all actions, which is:

$$Q(S_t, a_t) = r(S_t, a_t) + \gamma \max(Q, S_{t+1}), \tag{8}$$

where S_t is the state at time instant t, a_t is the action taken by the robot at that time, $r(S_t, a_t)$ is the immediate reward which can be calculated by Eq. (7), $\max(Q, S_{t+1})$ is the maximum Q-value among all the possible actions in the new state S_{t+1}, and γ is the discount factor.

3.3 The Selection Policy

The selection policy determines which action the robot will take, and helps updating the Q-table in the training stage, then in the testing phase, the learned policy guides the robot to the target without collisions and generates the terminal path.

In [5], the authors prescribed that when in the SS state, the robot changed its orientation toward the target, and moved one step forward; while in the NS state, the robot compared the turning right or left actions, and chose the one that would lead to a closer location to the target in the training phase, which we call the "closer to target" strategy in this paper.

After training the robot in different dynamic environments, the resulting policy can be used for future navigation. Therefore, in the testing phase, the robot just move toward the target until the current transition state is Non-safe. Then, the robot makes decisions of turning right or left according to the Q-table, and chooses the action with a higher Q-value. If the two actions have the same Q-value, the robot chooses one direction randomly.

In order to increase the diversity of solutions, we add the classical ε-greedy strategy to the“closer to target” strategy in the training phase to explore more about the environment, and to improve the chances of recognizing the optimal action. In ε-greedy exploration, parameter ε represents exploration probability which is introduced to balance the ratio between random action selection and greedy action selection. In this paper, we take advantages of the two selection strategies, and combine them to make the robot arrive at the targets as fast as possible, as well as to find more optimal solutions. The hybrid ε-greedy-closer to target strategy is displayed as follows.

Algorithm 1. The hybrid ε-greedy-closer to target strategy

```
Randomly generate p, p ∈ (0,1)
If p < ε
   a = rand(A)
Else
   a = closer to target(A)
End if.
```

Then, the flowchart of Q-learning algorithm for training the robot using the new hybrid selection strategy is shown in Fig. 4.

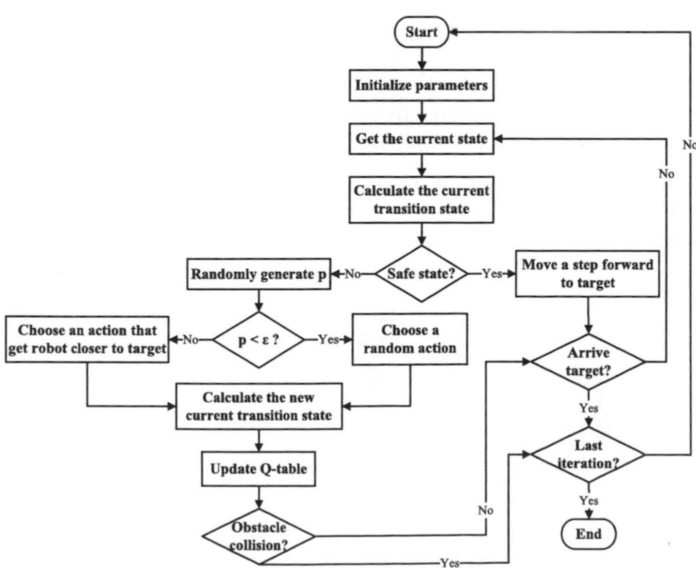

Fig. 4. The robot training process using the new selection strategy.

After training, the robot can be tested in future environment using the learned policy, and the corresponding flowchart is shown in Fig. 5.

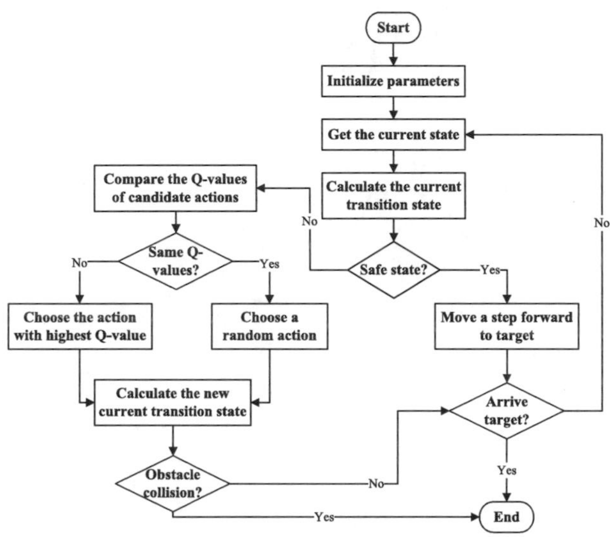

Fig. 5. The robot navigation process using the learned policy.

4 Simulation and Analysis

In order to demonstrate the feasibility and effectiveness of the Improved Q-learning (IQL) method dealing with obstacle avoidance problems under dynamic environments, a series of simulations were conducted. These simulations were all implemented in Anaconda software with version 2.74 programming environment on an Intel Core 4 PC running windows 10. In these simulations, the path planning region (150×50 units) is made up of targets and obstacles generated randomly with either regular or random motions.

Aside the prerequisites described above, based on the physical constraints from the real environment, the dynamic obstacles are defined as squares with a width/length of 1, d_{min} is set to 4, and the collision radius d_{col} is set to 2. The target is defined as a pentagram which occupies one grid, and the wining region radius d_{win} is set to 2. The mobile robot has a radius of 0.5 and the turning angle (left/right) is set to 45° throughout all scenarios.

4.1 Some Test Simulations

In this subsection, we tested some simple scenarios, as well as some complex situations with dynamic obstacles. The initial points of the robot were (0, 25) in all test scenarios. Firstly, we give two simple test scenarios to show the performance of our algorithm.

In the first simple scenario, we set the obstacle and the target both dynamic. The obstacle moved vertically from the initial location (19, 42.29) to the X axis, and then bounced back, as shown in Fig. 6(a). The target started its movement from location (75, 50), moving in the southeast direction.

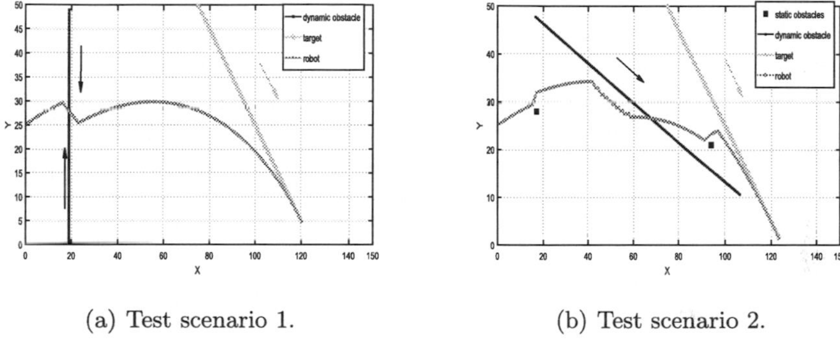

(a) Test scenario 1.

(b) Test scenario 2.

Fig. 6. Simple test scenarios.

As shown in Fig. 6(a), the robot successfully catched the goal. At the beginning, the robot was in SS state, and moved in northeast direction, directly moving to the target until iteration 17. The robot met the upcoming obstacle, and it chose to turn right to avoid collision until iteration 25 it was in SS again. Finally, the robot gradually adjusted its direction to the goal and arrived at the target.

On basis of scenario 1, we added two static obstacles in the environment, changed the moving direction of the dynamic obstacle, which can be seen in Fig. 6(b). The locations of the two static obstacles are (17, 28), and (94, 21), respectively. The start locations the dynamic obstacle and target are (16.65, 47.73), and (75, 50), respectively.

In Fig. 6(b), the robot still catched up with the target without collisions. What's more notable was that there was an oscillation path between X-axis 40 and 60, which revealed that the robot adjusted its direction to the target in real time while avoiding collisions with the moving obstacle. At iteration 64, the robot was in SS state again, and just chased the target before meeting the static obstacle. After evading the static obstacle, the robot catched up with the target safely.

Then, we tested some complicated situations with more dynamic obstacles. In the third scenario, we set three static obstacles with corresponding locations (25, 18), (44, 22), and (83, 32). Also, four dynamic obstacles with regular movements were added, and their moving directions were shown in Fig. 7. The starting points of the dynamic obstacles (from left to right) are (19, 36.99), (33, 48.29), (72.65, 22.61), and (114.29, 3.5), respectively. The initial points of the moving target are (120, 25).

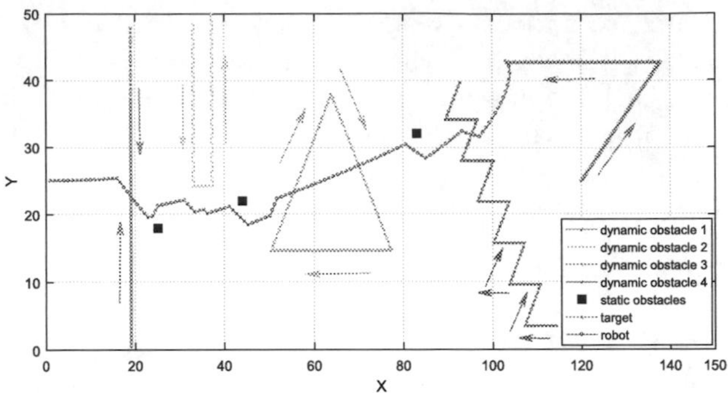

Fig. 7. Test scenario 3.

Figure 7 shows the final path planned by the improved reinforcement learning method. From this figure, we can see that the robot moved towards the target on the whole while avoiding collisions with all the obstacles.

In the fourth test scenario, we set four static obstacles with locations (7.05, 23.17), (60.66, 25.55), (84.34, 24.53), and (101.67, 29.45), respectively. The dynamic obstacles under this situation all moved randomly and their initial points (from left to right) were (25, 25), (50, 25), (75, 25), (100, 25), and (125, 25), respectively. The target with initial location (150, 25) also had random movements, as shown in Fig. 8.

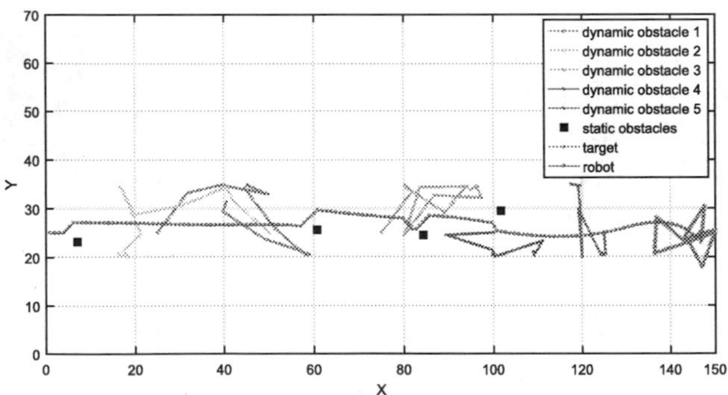

Fig. 8. Test scenario 4.

From Fig. 8, we can see that even under situations with obstacles and target in random movements, the robot still found a safe path. What's more, this also reveals that our algorithm has high adaptability and effectiveness dealing with random situations.

4.2 Comparison Results

In order to see the performance of the improved Q-learning (IQL) algorithm, we compared it with the Q-learning (QL) algorithm in [5]. Hit is defined as the total number of test scenarios the robot reaches its goal successfully among all test scenarios. Correspondingly, hit rate is the ratio of the hits to the number of all test scenarios.

In the following comparisons, we studied the effect of the two algorithms on number of obstacles. We started by 1 dynamic obstacle in the simulated environment, and then increased the number of obstacles by adding 1 dynamic obstacle and 1 static obstacle each time. In each situation, we applied 500 randomly generated test scenarios, and counted the number of hits. The comparison results on hits are shown in Fig. 9(a). To clearly see the percentage of hits among all test situations, we also give the relationship between the number of obstacles and the hit rates, as plotted in Fig. 9(b).

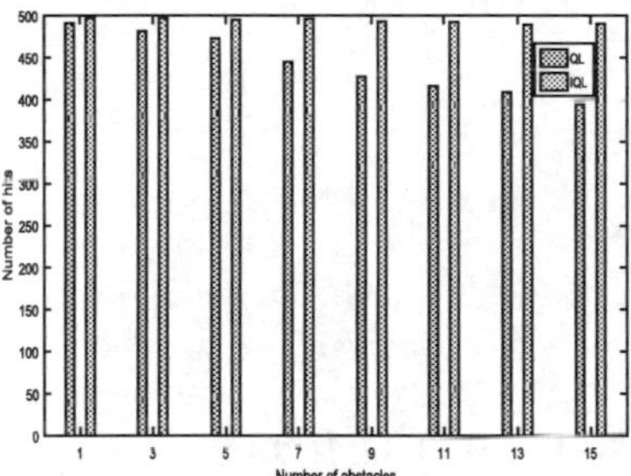

(a) Comparison results of the hits.

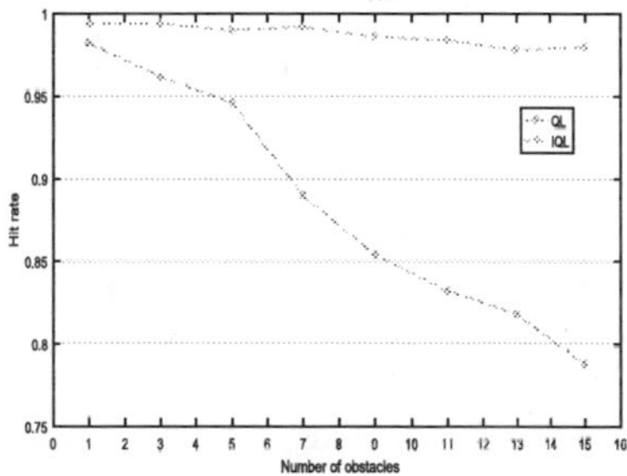

(b) Comparisons results of hit rates.

Fig. 9. Comparison results. (Color figure online)

In Fig. 9(a), the blue bar represents data obtained by QL, while the red one stands for the data obtained by IQL. We can see from the figure that the number of hits descends rapidly with increasing number of obstacles for QL. However, our algorithm holds a stable results with averagely 494 hits (out of 500). Besides, when the number of obstacles turns to 15, the successful hits of robots is 394 for QL, and for IQL, the successful hits is as high as 490.

More intuitively, we can see from Fig. 9(b) that the hit rate stays approximately constant for IQL (the red dotted line). However, for QL (the blue dotted line), the hit rate decreases rapidly from the original 98.2% to 78.8% with increasing number of obstacles. Therefore, our algorithm is more stable and more effective in dealing with dynamic obstacle avoidance problems.

5 Conclusions and Future Work

In this paper, we proposed an improved reinforcement learning method to deal with the mobile robot navigation problem under dynamic environments. In the improved method, the state space is redefined by adding the moving direction of the closest obstacle to overcome the update confusion problem of Q-values. In the reward function, we give a punishment for the non-safe states to make the robot arrive at the target as fast as possible. Besides, a hybrid selection policy which combines "closer to target" and traditional ε-greedy is presented to increase the diversity of solutions. Finally, simulations about some simple and complex test scenarios, and comparisons between Q-learning and the improved Q-learning are conducted to validate the feasibility and effectiveness of the presented algorithm.

However, the definition of reward function has a great influence on the results, thus, we will try different reward functions and compare our algorithm with some newly presented algorithms to see its performance. What's more, our algorithm has limitations in dealing with continuous control problem for the robot teams. Therein, we will also focus on multi-agent control problems using deep reinforcement learning for future research.

Acknowledgement. This research is supported by the National Natural Science Foundation of China under Grant 61573081.

References

1. Duguleana, M., Barbuceanu, F.G., Teirelbar, A., Mogan, G.: Obstacle avoidance of redundant manipulators using neural networks based reinforcement learning. Robot. Comput. Integr. Manufact. **28**(2), 132–146 (2012)
2. Duguleana, M., Mogan, G.: Neural networks based reinforcement learning for mobile robots obstacle avoidance. Expert Syst. Appl. **62**, 104–115 (2016)
3. Fathinezhad, F., Derhami, V., Rezaeian, M.: Supervised fuzzy reinforcement learning for robot navigation. Appl. Soft Comput. **40**(C), 33–41 (2016)
4. Huang, R., Zaruba, G.V.: Static path planning for mobile beacons to localize sensor networks. In: IEEE International Conference on Pervasive Computing and Communications Workshops, pp. 323–330 (2007)
5. Jaradat, M.A.K., Al-Rousan, M., Quadan, L.: Reinforcement based mobile robot navigation in dynamic environment. Robot. Comput. Integr. Manufact. **27**(1), 135–149 (2011)
6. Kala, R., Shukla, A., Tiwari, R.: Robotic path planning in static environment using hierarchical multi-neuron heuristic search and probability based fitness. Neurocomputing **74**(14), 2314–2335 (2011)
7. Kamil, F., Hong, T.S., Khaksar, W., Moghrabiah, M.Y., Zulkifli, N., Ahmad, S.A.: New robot navigation algorithm for arbitrary unknown dynamic environments based on future prediction and priority behavior. Expert Syst. Appl. **86**, 274–291 (2017)
8. Jens Kober, J., Bagnell, A., Peters, J.: Reinforcement learning in robotics: a survey. Int. J. Robot. Res. **32**(11), 1238–1274 (2013)
9. Littman, M.L.: Reinforcement learning improves behaviour from evaluative feedback. Nature **521**(7553), 445–451 (2015)
10. Montiel, O., Orozco-Rosas, U., Seplveda, R.: Path planning for mobile robots using bacterial potential field for avoiding static and dynamic obstacles. Expert Syst. Appl. **42**(12), 5177–5191 (2015)

11. Gmez Ortega, J., Camacho, E.F.: Mobile robot navigation in a partially structured static environment, using neural predictive control. Control Eng. Pract. **4**(12), 1669–1679 (1996)
12. Hong, Q., Xing, K., Alexander, T.: An improved genetic algorithm with co-evolutionary strategy for global path planning of multiple mobile robots. Neurocomputing **120**(10), 509–517 (2013)
13. Hong, Q., Yang, S.X., Willms, A.R., Yi, Z.: Real-time robot path planning based on a modified pulse-coupled neural network model. IEEE Trans. Neural Netw. **20**(11), 1724 (2009)
14. Hong, Q., Yang, S.X., Yi, Z., Wang, X.: A novel neural network method for shortest path tree computation. Appl. Soft Comput. **12**(10), 3246–3259 (2012)
15. Su, X., Zhao, M., Zhao, L., Zhang, Y.: A novel multi stage cooperative path re-planning method for multi UAV. In: Booth, R., Zhang, M.-L. (eds.) PRICAI 2016. LNCS (LNAI), vol. 9810, pp. 482–495. Springer, Cham (2016). https://doi.org/10.1007/978-3-319-42911-3_40

Subclass Maximum Margin Tree Error Correcting Output Codes

Fa Zheng[1,2] and Hui Xue[1,2](✉)

[1] School of Computer Science and Engineering, Southeast University, Nanjing 210096, People's Republic of China
{faaronzheng,hxue}@seu.edu.cn

[2] Key Laboratory of Computer Network and Information Integration, Southeast University, Ministry of Education, Nanjing, People's Republic of China

Abstract. Error Correcting Output Codes (ECOC) is an effective method to handle multi-class classification problems, whose performance is heavily affected by encoding strategies. However, traditional encoding strategies are usually data-independent which more likely leads to a less representation coding matrix. Therefore, recent researches emphasize more on the data-dependent construction of coding matrix. However, these methods usually can not guarantee that the binary problems in coding matrix are linearly separable. When the problems are linearly non-separable, the difficulty of designing base classifiers will increase. Even the non-linear base classifiers can not ensure that they can handle each binary problem well, which will decrease the performance of ECOC. In this paper, we propose subclass maximum margin tree error correcting output codes (SM^{2}ECOC) which aims to make each binary problem simple and linearly separable. Concretely, SM^{2}ECOC firstly uses hierarchical clustering techniques to split original classes into a series of linearly separable subclasses. Then it takes the margin as a criterion to evaluate the separability among subclasses and guide the construction of coding matrix. As a result, the binary problems in coding matrix more likely tend to be linearly separable which can reduce the difficulty in base classifiers effectively. Experimental results show the superiority of SM^{2}ECOC.

Keywords: Error correcting output codes · Maximum margin tree Subclass

1 Introduction

Error Correcting Output Codes (ECOC) is applied widely in multi-class classification problems [5], which usually involves encoding and decoding steps. The encoding step addresses the multi-class problem into a series of binary problems by generating a coding matrix. Each row and column of the coding matrix represent a class and binary problem respectively. The coding matrix is first coded by +1 and −1 as Table 1(a) shown, where +1 and −1 show that the corresponding

X. Geng and B.-H. Kang (Eds.): PRICAI 2018, LNAI 11012, pp. 454–462, 2018.
https://doi.org/10.1007/978-3-319-97304-3_35

base classifier regards this class as positive and negative respectively. Allwein et al. [1] further presented a ternary coding matrix which introduces symbol zero into the coding matrix as Table 1(b) shown. The symbol zero means that the corresponding classification does not include the relevant class. The decoding step makes a prediction for unseen data. Firstly, the predictions of all base classifiers will be combined as an output code word. The class which has the most similar code word with output code word will be selected as the class of the unseen data.

The researches of ECOC can generally be divided into three fields: encoding strategy, decoding strategy and other strategy.

Encoding strategy focuses on building a representative coding matrix. One-Versus-All(OVA) [13] obtains a binary coding matrix by considering one class as positive while the rest as negative. One-Versus-One (OVO) [8] generates a ternary coding matrix, each column of coding matrix only regards two classes as positive and negative respectively. Dense random and sparse random [1] generate the coding matrix randomly, where the dense one randomly obtains a binary coding matrix and the sparse one randomly generates a ternary one. Hadamard ECOC [2] uses Hadamard matrix to build coding matrix. Hadamard ECOC can ensure enough separability between the row and column of the coding matrix.

All aforementioned encoding strategies are data-independent which leads to a longer code words or worse performance. Therefore, more and more attention has been paid to construct the code matrix by a data-driven way. Discriminant ECOC (DECOC) [15] utilizes sequential forward floating search and mutual information to generate the tree by a top-down strategy. Based on the partition of tree, a coding matrix is constructed. Hierarchical ECOC (HECOC) [11] and Maximum Margin Tree ECOC (M^2ECOC) [17] use different criteria: support vector domain description and maximum margin to estimate inter-class separability and further generate the partition of tree. Subclass problem-dependent ECOC (Subclass ECOC) [7] splits the linearly non-separable problem into linearly separable ones on the basis of DECOC.

Decoding strategy emphasizes on enhance the error-correcting capability. Traditional decoding strategies are based on the distance between code word and output code word, such as Hamming distance (HD) [13] and Euclidean distance [8]. Allwein et al. [1] shown the advantage of using a loss-based function to decode. Loss-weighted [6] decoding applies the performance of base classifiers to adjust the classification decision.

Other strategy aims to improving the performance of ECOC beyond the encoding and decoding. ECOC-optimizing node embedding [14] algorithm iteratively adds a new classifier to classify the most confusing binary problems. Through selecting the most representative base classifiers from a group of similar base classifiers, Anderson and Siome [16] avoided the efficiency problem of ECOC. Liu et al. [12] mined the relationships among the base classifiers and proposed using a unified objective function to represent the relationships and boost the learning performances.

In this paper, we focus on encoding strategy and propose Subclass Maximum Margin Tree Error Correcting Output Codes (SM^2ECOC) which emphasizes on

Table 1. Coding matrix for a four-class problem

(a) Binary

	h_1	h_2	h_3	h_4
C_1	+1	-1	-1	-1
C_2	-1	+1	-1	-1
C_3	-1	-1	+1	-1
C_4	-1	-1	-1	+1

(b) Ternary

	h_1	h_2	h_3	h_4	h_5	h_6
C_1	+1	+1	+1	0	0	0
C_2	-1	0	0	+1	+1	0
C_3	0	-1	0	-1	0	+1
C_4	0	0	-1	0	-1	-1

making each binary problem in coding matrix tend to be linearly separable. SM^{2}ECOC firstly adopts the hierarchical clustering algorithm to split the original classes into a series of simple and linearly separable subclasses. Then it uses the margin to estimate the separability among the classes and further guide the construction of coding matrix. Consequently, the binary problems in coding matrix are more likely reorganized to be linearly separable ones which further makes the selection of base classifiers more flexible.

The paper is organized as follows. Section 2 introduces the related encoding algorithms Subclass ECOC. Section 3 introduces SM^{2}ECOC approach in detail. Section 4 shows the compared experiments. Finally, Sect. 5 concludes the paper.

2 Related Encoding Algorithms

Subclass ECOC [7] considers the linearly non-separable problems in coding matrix. On the basis of DECOC, when the partition is linearly non-separable, Subclass ECOC uses k-means to split the linearly non-separable partition into simpler and smaller sub-partitions. As Fig. 1 shown, when $\{C_1, C_3\}$ is linearly non-separable, different from DECOC, Subclass ECOC splits $\{C_1, C_3\}$ into two linearly separable partition $\{C_1, C_{3\_1}\}$ and $\{C_1, C_{3\_2}\}$. Therefore, through several times of decompositions, Subclass ECOC can transform a linearly non-separable binary problem into linearly separable ones. However, Subclass ECOC usually leads to an unstable splitting result because it uses the unstable k-means clustering algorithm hierarchically.

3 Subclass Maximum Margin Tree ECOC (SM^{2}ECOC)

The complexity of the binary problems in coding matrix has an important impact on the performance of ECOC. When the binary problems are linearly non-separable, even the non-linear base classifiers can not guarantee that they can handle each binary problem well. Subclass ECOC solves linearly non-separable problem by using k-means hierarchically in encoding step. Different from Subclass ECOC, SM^{2}ECOC splits subclasses before encoding and uses a more stable

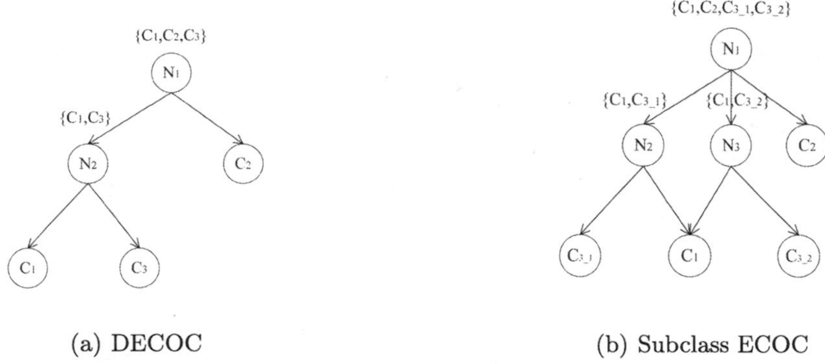

(a) DECOC (b) Subclass ECOC

Fig. 1. Illustration of building the tree in DECOC and Subclass ECOC

clustering method. As a result, SM^{2}ECOC tries to recombine classes in order to make each binary problem tend to be linearly separable. SM^{2}ECOC involves two steps: splitting subclasses and building coding matrix. The splitting subclasses step splits original classes into a series of simple and linearly separable subclasses. The building coding matrix step uses M^{2}ECOC to explore data-dependent information from subclasses and obtain the coding matrix.

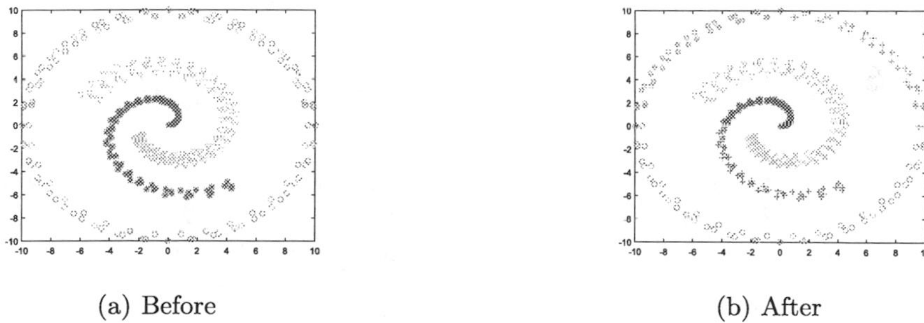

(a) Before (b) After

Fig. 2. Effect of DIANA algorithm DIANA

Splitting Subclasses: We use Divisive Analysis (DIANA) [9] to split original classes, which is a divisive hierarchical clustering algorithm. Different with k-means, DIANA can get a stable clustering result without specifying the number of clusters. Concretely, DIANA firstly splits data into two clusters with the biggest differences, and then for each cluster, repeats the process until the termination condition is satisfied. A threshold *termination* controls the partition granularity of each cluster. The number of the samples in each cluster becomes larger when the value of the *termination* gets bigger. The effect of DIANA is shown in Fig. 2. The original three classes are divided into eight linearly separable subclasses. Therefore, each binary problem in coding matrix is much more easier to be linearly separable.

Since that DIANA is an unsupervised algorithm, one cluster sometimes involves different classes. If the proportion of the data in one cluster compared to the whole data of this class is less than a threshold *drop*, we will consider these data as noises and drop them from the cluster, which can avoid generating redundant subclasses. Furthermore, if the data in one class are split into different subclasses, we will give them new labels which should contain the original class label information in order to backtrack the true label in prediction.

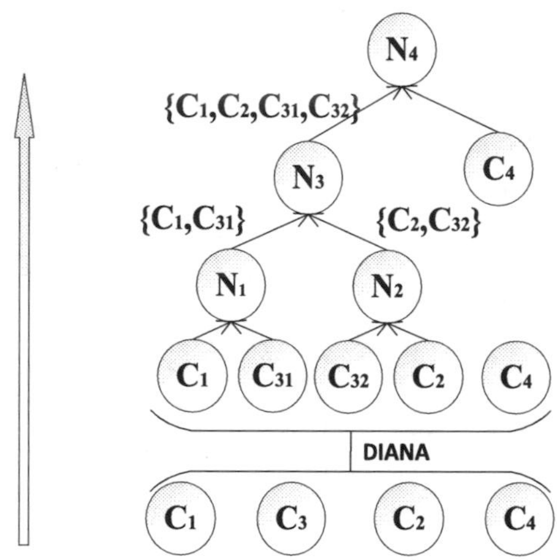

Fig. 3. Procedure of building a bottom-up maximum margin

Building Coding Matrix: After the splitting step, we obtain a series of linearly separable subclasses. In order to obtain the coding matrix, we use the margin as the separability measure standard to guide the construction of coding matrix. Margin is one of the basic concepts in Support Vector Machine (SVM) [4], which is defined as follow:

$$margin = \frac{2}{||\boldsymbol{w}||} \tag{1}$$

where $\boldsymbol{w}$ is the normal vector of hyperplane. The maximum margin can be computed between subclasses according to (1), and then a maximum margin matrix can be obtained through all maximum margins:

$$\begin{bmatrix} 0 & m_{12} & \dots & m_{1(k-1)} & m_{1k} \\ m_{21} & 0 & \dots & m_{2(k-1)} & m_{2k} \\ \dots & \dots & \dots & \dots & \dots \\ m_{(k-1)1} & m_{(k-1)2} & \dots & 0 & m_{(k-1)k} \\ m_{k1} & m_{k2} & \dots & m_{k(k-1)} & 0 \end{bmatrix}$$

where m_{ij} is the maximum margin between the ith and jth subclasses.

According to the maximum margin matrix, a bottom-up strategy is utilized to build the maximum margin tree. Concretely, for subclasses with the maximal

Algorithm 1. The Produce of SM^{2}ECOC

```
Input: The data set S has N samples
Threshold t for clustering method
Threshold d for dropping step
Output: The final subclasses subclasses

//Finding subclasses
cluster=Clustering(S, t);
//Ignoring the noise
subclasses=drop(cluster,d);
Relabeling the samples
while num(subclasses)>0 do
    // Computing maximum margin among subclasses according to (1)
    maximum_margin_matrix=compute_maximum_margin(subclasses)
    max_margin=max(maximum_margin_matrix)
    //Merging the subclasses corresponding to the maximal maximum margin
    new_subclass={row(max_margin),column(max_margin)}
    //Recording the left subclasses
    left_classes=subclasses − new_subclass
    //Creating a partition of the tree
    partlength(part+1)=new_subclass
    subclasses={new_subclass, left_classes}
end while
Obtaining a coding matrix according to (2)
```

maximum margin, we merge them into one until there is only one subclass left. As Fig. 3) shown, the original four classes are divided into five subclasses after splitting. $\{C_1\}$, $\{C_{31}\}$ and $\{C_{32}\}$, $\{C_2\}$ are merged as a new subclass orderly. Repeating the above process, we take $\{C_1, C_{31}\}$ and $\{C_2, C_{32}\}$ as another new subclass. Finally, all subclasses will be integrated as a new subclass.

We can obtain a coding matrix M according to the maximum margin tree as follows:

$$M(r,l) = \begin{cases} 1 & C_r \in P_l^{left} \\ 0 & C_r \notin P_l \\ -1 & C_r \in P_l^{right} \end{cases} \tag{2}$$

where $M(r,l)$ indicates the element lying in row r, column l of coding matrix. C_r stand for the class r, P_l^{left} is the left and P_l^{right} is the right partition of the lth partition.

Finally, we can obtain a coding matrix in which the binary problems are more likely to be linearly separable. The Produce of SM^{2}ECOC is as Algorithm 1 shown.

4 Experiments and Analyses

In this section, SM^{2}ECOC is compared with DECOC [15], HECOC [11], M^{2}ECOC [17] and Subclass ECOC [7] to validate its superiority.

In the experiments, ten multi-class UCI data sets [3] are used. Each data set is randomly split into two non-overlapping training and testing sets ten times. Seventy percent of the samples constitutes the training set and the rest constitutes the testing set. Moreover, the parameter set $\Theta = \{\Theta_{size}, \Theta_{perf}, \Theta_{impr}\}$ in Subclass ECOC is fixed to $\Theta_{size} = \frac{|J|}{50}$, $\Theta_{perf} = 0$ and $\Theta_{impr} = 0.95$ according to [7]. In SM^{2}ECOC, the threshold *termination* is selected according to the accuracy of classification from the interval $\{N, \lfloor N/2 \rfloor, \lfloor N/3 \rfloor ... \lfloor N/10 \rfloor\}$, where N is the size of data. The threshold *drop* is selected from the interval $\{0.05, 0.1\}$ also according to the accuracy of classification.

Linear base classifier Nearest Mean Classifier (NMC) and non-linear base classifier SVM are applied as the base classifier. In the radial basis function kernel, the regularization parameter C is set to 1 [7] and the width σ is selected from the interval $\{2^{-6}, 2^{-5}, ..., 2^5, 2^6\}$. Hamming distance (HD) [13] is used to as decoding strategy.

Table 2. Classification results (mean ± std) of NMC and HD on ten datasets (•/◦ indicates that our algorithm is significantly better or worse than other algorithms based on the t-test at 5% significance level)

Data set	DECOC	Subclass ECOC	HECOC	M^{2}ECOC	SM^{2}ECOC
Balance	80.32 ± 3.72	81.60 ± 5.27	81.60 ± 3.16	83.42 ± 3.24•	**84.01 ± 2.72**
Cmc	46.29 ± 1.19•	46.31 ± 1.18•	45.48 ± 2.38•	46.97 ± 1.60•	**50.88 ± 0.90**
Ecoli	74.20 ± 8.27•	77.90 ± 4.07•	71.90 ± 13.40•	83.80 ± 2.67•	**86.00 ± 2.71**
Glass	42.15 ± 11.40•	49.08 ± 6.97•	42.31 ± 10.00•	49.23 ± 4.53•	**62.15 ± 5.04**
Iris	79.78 ± 8.35•	85.11 ± 3.93•	86.22 ± 5.52•	86.00 ± 5.55•	**92.00 ± 4.34**
Lenses	78.75 ± 8.44•	78.75 ± 8.44•	71.25 ± 11.90•	80.00 ± 8.74•	**92.50 ± 8.74**
Tea	53.26 ± 5.64•	55.87 ± 5.80•	54.13 ± 6.44•	56.09 ± 5.21•	**61.52 ± 5.33**
Thyriod	92.97 ± 3.40•	93.44 ± 3.59•	94.06 ± 2.42•	94.53 ± 2.68•	**97.34 ± 1.29**
Vehicle	40.04 ± 3.37•	43.94 ± 5.22•	40.67 ± 3.40•	49.25 ± 4.86•	**66.22 ± 3.26**
Wine	**97.36 ± 3.11**	**97.36 ± 3.11**	95.09 ± 3.47	93.40 ± 3.59	94.72 ± 3.42
Average	68.51 ± 5.69	70.94 ± 4.76	68.27 ± 6.21	72.36 ± 4.27	**78.73 ± 3.78**
Win/tie/loss	8/2/0	8/2/0	8/2/0	9/1/0	/

From the Tables 2 and 3, it can be seen that SM^{2}ECOC can reach better or comparable performance, especially with linear base classifier. Meanwhile, the standard deviations and average accuracies are listed in the bottom of the tables. The pairwise t-tests [10] at 5% significance level are also shown. The win/loss with marker •/◦ indicates that SM^{2}ECOC can achieves significantly better/worse performance than the compared algorithms respectively. Otherwise, a tie with no marker. As the tables shown, SM^{2}ECOC achieves statistically better or comparable performance which just validates the effectiveness of SM^{2}ECOC and accords with our conclusions.

Table 3. Classification results(mean ± std) of SVM and HD on ten datasets (•/∘ indicates that our algorithm is significantly better or worse than other algorithms based on the t-test at 5% significance level)

Data set	DECOC	Subclass ECOC	HECOC	M^2ECOC	SM^2ECOC
Balance	76.84 ± 1.99•	77.17 ± 2.03•	89.79 ± 1.02	90.16 ± 0.92	**90.27 ± 0.94**
Cmc	51.97 ± 1.46•	52.83 ± 1.35	**54.52 ± 1.19**	53.21 ± 1.27	53.51 ± 1.45
Ecoli	80.30 ± 15.10	83.10 ± 6.59•	70.30 ± 15.50•	86.90 ± 2.59	**87.80 ± 1.87**
Glass	62.31 ± 9.84	64.15 ± 9.97	61.85 ± 5.88•	62.15 ± 3.78•	**68.00 ± 2.49**
Iris	72.89 ± 4.42•	74.67 ± 2.81•	**95.11 ± 3.60**	94.89 ± 1.83	94.89 ± 1.83
Lenses	56.25 ± 8.84•	58.75 ± 6.04•	62.50 ± 0.00•	75.00 ± 10.20	**82.50 ± 8.74**
Tea	44.35 ± 5.99•	47.83 ± 5.02•	51.30 ± 3.58•	55.43 ± 4.94•	**61.52 ± 5.98**
Thyriod	94.37 ± 1.32•	94.37 ± 1.32•	95.78 ± 1.06•	96.09 ± 1.11	**97.03 ± 1.37**
Vehicle	72.76 ± 2.37•	72.76 ± 2.37•	74.53 ± 1.93	75.08 ± 1.76	**75.35 ± 1.51**
Wine	96.23 ± 1.99•	97.36 ± 1.82•	98.30 ± 1.65	98.30 ± 1.97	**99.25 ± 0.97**
Average	70.83 ± 5.33	72.30 ± 3.93	75.40 ± 3.54	78.72 ± 3.04	**81.01 ± 2.72**
Win/tie/loss	8/2/0	8/2/0	5/5/0	2/8/0	/

5 Conclusion

In this paper, we present an encoding algorithm SM^2ECOC which focuses on making each binary problem linearly separable in coding matrix. SM^2ECOC includes two steps: splitting subclasses and building coding matrix. The splitting subclasses step splits original classes into a series of linearly separable subclasses by DIANA algorithm. Then, the building coding matrix step uses the maximum margin between subclasses to guide the construction of coding matrix. Experimental results show the superior performance of SM^2ECOC compared with some related algorithms.

Acknowledgments. This work is supported by the National Key R&D Program of China (No. 2017YFB1002801), the National Natural Science Foundations of China (Grant Nos. 61375057, 61300165 and 61403193), the Natural Science Foundation of Jiangsu Province of China (Grant No. BK20131298) and Fundamental Research Funds for the Central Universities (SJLX_160053) and Research Innovation Program for College Graduates of Jiangsu Province of China (SJLX_160053). It is also supported by Collaborative Innovation Center of Wireless Communications Technology.

References

1. Allwein, E.L., Schapire, R.E., Singer, Y.: Reducing multiclass to binary: a unifying approach for margin classifiers. J. Mach. Learn. Res. **1**(Dec), 113–141 (2000). https://doi.org/10.1162/15324430152733133
2. An-rong, Y., Xiang, X., Jing-ming, K.: Application of hadamard ECOC in multiclass problems based on SVM. Chin. J. Electron. **36**(1), 122–126 (2008). https://doi.org/10.3321/j.issn:0372-2112.2008.01.022

3. Asuncion, A., Newman, D.: UCI machine learning repository (2007)
4. Cortes, C., Vapnik, V.: Support-vector networks. Mach. Learn. **20**(3), 273–297 (1995). https://doi.org/10.1007/BF00994018
5. Dietterich, T.G., Bakiri, G.: Solving multiclass learning problems via error-correcting output codes. J. Artif. Intell. Res. **2**, 263–286 (1995). https://doi.org/10.1613/jair.105
6. Escalera, S., Pujol, O., Radeva, P.: Loss-weighted decoding for error-correcting output coding. In: VISAPP, no. 2, pp. 117–122 (2008)
7. Escalera, S., Tax, D.M., Pujol, O., Radeva, P., Duin, R.P.: Subclass problem-dependent design for error-correcting output codes. IEEE Trans. Pattern Anal. Mach. Intell. **30**(6), 1041–1054 (2008). https://doi.org/10.1109/TPAMI.2008.38
8. Hastie, T., Tibshirani, R., et al.: Classification by pairwise coupling. Ann. Stat. **26**(2), 451–471 (1998). https://doi.org/10.1214/aos/1028144844
9. Kaufman, L., Rousseeuw, P.J.: Finding Groups in Data: An Introduction to Cluster Analysis, vol. 344. Wiley, Hoboken (2009)
10. Kuncheva, L.I.: Combining Pattern Classifiers: Methods and Algorithms. Wiley, Hoboken (2004)
11. Lei, L., Xiao-Dan, W., Xi, L., Ya-Fei, S.: Hierarchical error-correcting output codes based on SVDD. Pattern Anal. Appl. **19**(1), 163–171 (2016)
12. Liu, M., Zhang, D., Chen, S., Xue, H.: Joint binary classifier learning for ECOC-based multi-class classification. IEEE Trans. Pattern Anal. Mach. Intell. **38**, 2335–2341 (2016). https://doi.org/10.1109/TPAMI.2015.2430325
13. Nilsson, N.J.: Learning Machines: Foundations of Trainable Pattern-Classifying Systems. McGraw-Hill, New York (1965)
14. Pujol, O., Escalera, S., Radeva, P.: An incremental node embedding technique for error correcting output codes. Pattern Recogn. **41**(2), 713–725 (2008). https://doi.org/10.1016/j.patcog.2007.04.008
15. Pujol, O., Radeva, P., Vitria, J.: Discriminant ECOC: a heuristic method for application dependent design of error correcting output codes. IEEE Trans. Pattern Anal. Mach. Intell. **28**(6), 1007–1012 (2006). https://doi.org/10.1109/TPAMI.2006.116
16. Rocha, A., Goldenstein, S.K.: Multiclass from binary: expanding one-versus-all, one-versus-one and ECOC-based approaches. IEEE Trans. Neural Netw. Learn. Syst. **25**(2), 289–302 (2014). https://doi.org/10.1109/TNNLS.2013.2274735
17. Zheng, F., Xue, H., Chen, X., Wang, Y.: Maximum margin tree error correcting output codes. In: Booth, R., Zhang, M.-L. (eds.) PRICAI 2016. LNCS (LNAI), vol. 9810, pp. 681–691. Springer, Cham (2016). https://doi.org/10.1007/978-3-319-42911-3_57

A Multi-latent Semantics Representation Model for Mining Tourist Trajectory

Yanpeng Sun[1,2], Tianlong Gu[1], Chenzhong Bin[1(✉)], Liang Chang[1], Haili Kuang[1], Zhaowei Huang[1], and Lei Sun[1]

[1] Guangxi Key Lab of Trusted Software, Guilin University of Electronic Technology, Guilin 541004, China
{yanpeng_sun, sunlei92}@yeah.net, {cctlgu, changl}@guet.edu.cn, binchenzhong@163.com, 18624379808@163.com, 316413286@qq.com
[2] School of Mechanical and Electrical Engineering, Guilin University of Electronic Technology, Guilin 541004, China

Abstract. With the development of location- based social network, there are a variety of ways provided to record user tourist trajectories. Although the tourist trajectory is of great value for many applications, mining tourist trajectories is still challenging due to the fact that a series of hidden complex characteristics affecting the user's travel behavior. In this paper, according to the impact of different factors on user travel trajectory, we present a multiple latent semantics representation model (*MLS2vec*) that represents latent semantic information of travel trajectories in a flexible manner. Various latent semantic information include user-level, temporal-level, and attraction-level latent semantics, which represents different feature in the same dimensional space. Using negative sampling to train parameters, we apply the *MLS2vec* model to challenging attractions recommendation tasks. Extensive experiments are conducted in the real crawled data set, and the experimental results show the validity and accuracy of our proposed model over several mainstream methods.

Keywords: Tourist trajectory · Latent semantics · Multi-latent semantics Attractions recommendation

1 Introduction

With the popularity of mobile devices and the rapid growth of social networks, people can use different forms to record travel activities, such as tweets, pictures and videos, which make social network a mirror of human behavior patterns. It provides a deep understanding of people's personalized behavioral preferences over a particular time and space, meanwhile, it offers opportunities for personalized travel recommendations.

Since trajectory data reflects human mobility, it can naturally be used in location-based applications, including location prediction [1] and user mobility modeling [2]. In addition, the previous work shows that public temporal and spatial data, such as the user's check-in data, strongly indicate that the trajectory information contains a variety of latent semantic information such as geographical information of the location and

X. Geng and B.-H. Kang (Eds.): PRICAI 2018, LNAI 11012, pp. 463–476, 2018.
https://doi.org/10.1007/978-3-319-97304-3_36

user's mobile behavior, which can be used to obtain personalized preferences of users. Although it is of great practical value to analyze trajectory data, it is still a challenge to study and mine tourist trajectory data owing to users' complex travel behavior. Hence, we need a flexible way to mine the semantic meaning of the tourist trajectory data.

In this paper, we propose a Multi-Latent Semantics Tourist Trajectory Representation Model (*MLS2vec*). Inspired by neural networks and deep learning research [3], we propose to use distributed representations to model tourist trajectory data and use multiple contexts in a flexible way to represent multiple latent information in tourist trajectory data. Our model ensure each latent semantic a unique distributed vector.

The main contributions of this paper are as follows:

(1) Based on the distributed representation model, a multi-latent semantics tourist trajectory representation model is proposed. The model can effectively learn multiple semantic of tourist trajectory.
(2) In the model training, we use the negative sampling method to further improve the model training speed, which can make the model adapt to massive trajectory data mining scenarios.
(3) By using different latent semantic embedding, we design a personalized recommendation method of attractions, which can achieve high-precision and high-quality recommendation effects.
(4) Experimental results of test evaluation conducted on the actual tourist trajectory dataset obtained in Guilin has proved the validity and accuracy of the model.

2 Related Works

2.1 Spatio-Temporal Trajectory Mining

The main target of mining Spatio-Temporal trajectory is to find latent semantic in trajectory model from visiting sequences and sports lasting time of users. Traditional trajectory mining methods mostly rely on Discriminative model, including Markov model [4], Mining Frequent Patterns [5] and improved Markov model [6] and so on. The main idea of these methods is mapping location of the trajectory into a series of discrete states, and then describing easy sports pattern of people in different conditions with probabilistic method, which hence ignoring latent complex semantic in trajectory data. These methods mainly focus on depict the observed Spatio-Temporal trajectory itself, instead of the latent user mobile pattern.

In recent years, there are some researches exploring the Spatio-Temporal trajectory by the topic model, such as utilizing LDA [7] model and ATM other topic model to mine implicit information in trajectory [8]. For the reason that it's hard to get the prior distribution for these models, the similar recommendation results of models using topic models directly is ineffective. Recent years, neural network and deep learning model are applied in mining the Spatio-Temporal trajectory in some research, for example, tensor model [9] can capture user potential preference with tensor, while establishing fine-grained awareness framework and generating model depend on distributional hypothesis of user habit to decide feature space. Methods mentioned above introduce composite tuples to varying degrees to represent high-dimensional information of user trajectory, which brings higher complexity and computation.

2.2 Travel Attraction Recommendation

The aim of travel recommendation is to recommend attraction that users may visit according to their historical tourism behavior. The existing methods usually utilize contextual information, social network, geographical influence and temporal effect to obtain users' interview preference. It is showed by geographical influence and social network that people prefer to visit somewhere friends have already travelled [10]. Many researches take geographical and social information into consideration, including methods based CF (collaborating filtering) [11, 16] and methods based matrix decomposition [10]. Yin [1] uses location category labels to search personal interest and location preference; adding labels and user annotation in clustering LDA and MF model [12] shows nice performance. Whereas, introducing composite tuples to represent high-dimensional information of user trajectory makes complexity and computation increasing enormously, which means it's not suitable for mining mass trajectory data. Previous work has extended CF based user, combining temporal effect and geographical information by linear combination [13]. While the temporal effect and geographical information contained by location itself is not considered for mining more latent semantic information. Therefore, based on the distributed representation model [14, 15], we propose a framework to mining tourist trajectory with multi-latent semantics.

3 A Multi-latent Semantics Tourist Trajectory Representation Model

Before introducing the model, we present some basic definition.

Definition 1 (Visit Location Record). When the user u visits the attraction l at time t, the visit location record l_s has three elements $<u, t, l>$.

Here is a visit location record example <*Tom, 2017-8-18, Rival Li*>, indicating the user id is *Tom*, who visited *Rival Li* on *Aug 18th, 2017.*

Definition 2 (Visit Trajectory). Associating every visit location record of user u by spatial attribution to generate visit trajectory, the form of visit trajectory t is: $<u, t_1, l_1>, \ldots, <u, t_i, l_i>, \ldots, <u, t_N, l_N>$. N signifies the length of series and $s_i < s_{i+1}$ for $i \leq N-1$.

Table 1 show all illustration of symbols used in the paper.

Table 1. Notations and descriptions

Symbols	Descriptions
u, m, l	Index users, month, attractions variables
N_t	Number of attractions in the tourist trajectory
U	Consisting of a set of all users
D	Consisting of a set of all attractions
T	Collection of all time intervals
v_u, v_m, v_l	User-level, time-level, and attraction-level latent semantic feature vectors
t	Timestamps
v_f	Latent eigenvectors containing context f
$Window$	The size of the training window
K	The length of the recommended list
P	The number of attractions that the user has played

3.1 Framework of the Model

The latent semantics of the travel trajectory represent the factors that affect the generation of travel trajectory, such as different travel preferences of the user, user's travel preferences at different time intervals, geographic location of the attraction, etc. Therefore, finding the latent semantics of tourism routes has become a way to understand user travel behavior.

The user's travel trajectory includes user preferences, spending habits, seasonality of attraction tours, attraction types, and other latent semantics. Now we focus on how to model latent semantics in different travel routes through different contextual information. We find that each visit location record in the travel route consists of three elements. Therefore, there are at least three different latent semantic features contained in tour route, namely the user-level latent semantic features that reflect the user's travel preferences, the temporal-level latent semantic features that show travel preference under the specific time interval and the attractions-level latent semantic features with sight geographical information. Therefore, we will adopt a three-level structure and obtain corresponding latent semantic features through different contextual information. We can understand the user's travel behavior more comprehensively by three aspects above, and provide useful help for personalized recommendations and urban planning (Fig. 1).

3.1.1 User-Level Latent Semantics

We need to learn each user's travel reference from their own tourist trajectory.

Obviously, user's travel reference directly influence user's option of location in tourist trajectory, which indicating user's personal behavior pattern, travel appetite and travel custom. For example, a user u enjoys visiting scenic of landscapes or humanity and riding to visit locations, then it's more possible that user u choose riding for location visiting and locations are more likely to be landscapes or humanity. In consequence, user's history of travel trajectory hides the travel preference. We can represent the latent semantic feature of user travel preference in tourist trajectory by Z-dimension feature vector v_u.

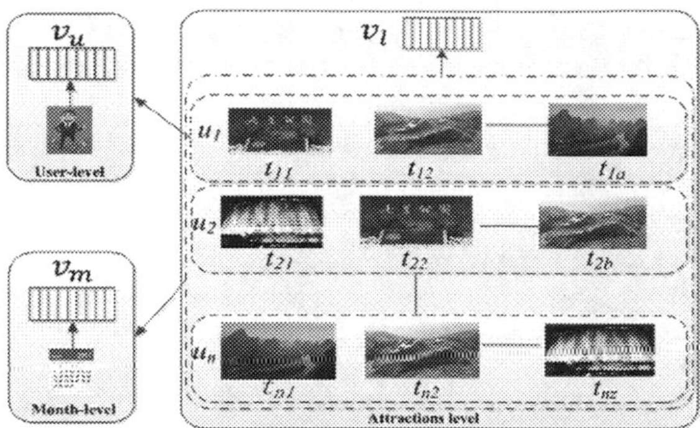

Fig. 1. Framework of the model

3.1.2 Temporal-Level Latent Semantics

For the seasonality of location, it has huge impact on user's travel temporal option. So we can learn user's travel preference conveyed by all their tourist trajectories in a certain time section, reflecting their travel reference, behavior pattern and POI.

The semantics of temporal also directly impact user's option of tourist trajectory, with such a reason that seasonality feature greatly influences the ornamental value of attractions. For instance, the seasonality semantic of the Longsheng Hot Spring is strong, which means when it's December or November, the best time for visiting here, the probability for people to visit here is much higher. But the probability becomes low when it's February. Because of the great diversity of travel option in different months, we select month as our temporal interval. We represent the latent semantic feature of user travel preference in the present month by *Z*-dimension feature vector v_m.

3.1.3 Attractions-Level Latent Semantics

Finally, we learn the latent semantic features of each attraction through the collection of surrounding attractions.

It is quite clear that people get used to the next attraction close to the present one, hence, we can tell that the present attraction is influenced by surrounding attractions. We regard that the former attractions *C* and the later attractions *C* have impact on the existing of the present one, so the two sets of *C* is ought to be a window in the training process. Inspired by the word embedding model *Word2Vec* [14], it considers that one word's semantic information is affected by the surrounding words. We let $l_{i-C} : l_{i+C}$ be the attractions list: $l_{i-C}, \ldots l_{i-1}, l_{i+1} \ldots, l_{i+C}$ in the window of attraction l_i. We set window to show that each attraction is only related to the surrounding *2C* attractions. For example, when *C* equals 2, using Skip-gram model, we can predict the information of its surrounding 4 attractions according to the present one, thus making the present one contains latent semantics of the surrounding 4 attractions.

3.2 Modeling

Given the travel trajectory t $= <(\mathrm{u}, t_1, l_1), (\mathrm{u}, t_2, l_2), \ldots\ldots, (\mathrm{u}, t_n, l_n)>$ of user *u* over *m* months, based on conditional probability formula, let probability p{(u, t_1, l_1), (u, t_2, l_2) ,……, (u, t_n, l_n)} be the occurrence rate of this trajectory, we formulate the probability as follows:

$$\mathrm{P}\{(\mathrm{u},t_1,l_1),\ (\mathrm{u},t_2,l_2),\ \ldots\ldots,\ (\mathrm{u},t_n,l_n)\} = \mathrm{P}\{(\mathrm{u},t_1,l_1)\} \times \mathrm{P}\{(\mathrm{u},t_2,l_2)|(\mathrm{u},t_1,l_1)\} \times \ldots \times \mathrm{P}\{(\mathrm{u},t_n,l_n)|(\mathrm{u},t_1,l_1),(\mathrm{u},t_2,l_2),\ \ldots\ldots,\ (\mathrm{u},t_{n-1},l_{n-1})\} \tag{1}$$

With instantiating multi-latent semantics feature vector, we get the goal function in the model as follows:

$$\sum\nolimits_{u\in U}\sum\nolimits_{t\in T}\sum\nolimits_{i=1}^{N_t}\log P\left(l_i\middle|\underbrace{u}_{user-level},\underbrace{m}_{temporal-level},\underbrace{l_{i-C}:l_{i+C}}_{attractions-level}\right) \tag{2}$$

where U, T is the set of users and months respectively and N_t is the length of trajectory. Semantic features in each level are associated with feature vectors in the corresponding space. In addition, the target attractions are generated by aggregating multiple semantic representation vectors, so that vectors of the target attractions contain multi-level context information.

3.3 Parameter Estimation and Optimization

Now we show the detailed process and evaluation methods of the model solution. The key to training the multi-latent semantic tourist trajectory representation model is to maximize the objective function of the model. In machine learning, the conditional probability is generally constructed using the softmax function, but in the training model of this paper, the standard softmax function is computationally expensive, so we apply Negative sampling techniques to training and update parameters.

Given a trajectory list $t = <(u,\ t_1,\ l_1),\ (u,\ t_2,\ l_2),\ \ldots\ldots,\ (u,\ t_n,\ l_n)>$, the overall target function is maximize the probability of each attraction on the basis of given context information:

$$\sum\nolimits_{i=1}^{N_t}\log P\left(l_i|f^{(i)}\right) \tag{3}$$

where N_t denotes the length of trajectory, and l_i is the context information containing all the latent semantic.

Knowing the context $f^{(i)}$ of the current attraction l_i, we need to predict l_i. Therefore, for a given $f^{(i)}$, the attraction l_i is a positive sample, and attractions beyond the context of this one are negative samples. For a given positive sample $\left(f^{(i)}, l_i\right)$, we maximize the following probability:

$$g(l_i) = \prod\nolimits_{\alpha\in\{l_i\}\cup NEG(l_i)} P\left(\alpha|f^{(i)}\right) \tag{4}$$

where $NEG(l_i)$ denotes the non-empty negative sample subset $NEG(l_i)$ about l_i and:

$$P\left(\alpha|f^{(i)}\right) = \begin{cases} \sigma\left(X_{f(i)}^T \theta^\alpha\right), & L^{l_i}(\alpha) = 1 \\ 1 - \sigma\left(X_{f(i)}^T \theta^\alpha\right), & L^{l_i}(\alpha) = 0 \end{cases} \tag{5}$$

Where $X_{f(i)}$ devotes the sum of vectors under each context $f^{(i)}$, $\theta^\alpha \in R^m$ indicates the auxiliary vector of attraction l_i, waiting to be trained. The purpose of training is to increase the probability of a positive sample while reducing the probability of a negative sample, so the final objective function is:

$$\mathcal{L} = \log \prod\nolimits_{l_i \epsilon t} g(l_i) = \sum\nolimits_{l_i \epsilon t} \left\{ \log\left[\sigma\left(X_{f(i)}^T \theta^\alpha\right)\right] + \sum\nolimits_{\alpha \in NEG(l_i)} \log\left[\sigma\left(-X_{f(i)}^T \theta^\alpha\right)\right] \right\} \tag{6}$$

To simplify the following update process, we mark the contents of the brackets in the above formula as $\mathcal{L}(l_i, \alpha)$. We apply Random Gradient Rising Method to optimizing the objective function, and the gradient formula of $\mathcal{L}(l_i, \alpha)$ about θ^α is as following:

$$\frac{\partial \mathcal{L}(l_i, \alpha)}{\partial \theta^\alpha} = \left[L^{l_i}(\alpha) - \sigma\left(X_{f(i)}^T \theta^\alpha\right)\right] X_{f(i)} \tag{7}$$

So the updating formula of θ^α can be given as:

$$\theta^\alpha := \theta^\alpha + \eta\left[L^{l_i}(\alpha) - \sigma\left(X_{f(i)}^T \theta^\alpha\right)\right] X_{f(i)} \tag{8}$$

Where η devotes the learning rate. Note that variable $X_{f(i)}$ and θ^α are symmetrical, we can get gradient calculation of $\mathcal{L}(l_i, \alpha)$ about $X_{f(i)}$:

$$\frac{\partial \mathcal{L}(l_i, \alpha)}{\partial X_{f(i)}} = \left[L^{l_i}(\alpha) - \sigma\left(X_{f(i)}^T \theta^\alpha\right)\right] \theta^\alpha \tag{9}$$

Then we update all the embedding vectors, the renovate can be computed as follows:

$$v_f := v_f + \eta \sum\nolimits_{\alpha \in \{l_i\} \cup NEG(l_i)} \frac{\partial \mathcal{L}(l_i, \alpha)}{\partial X_{f(i)}}, f \epsilon \; Context(l_i) \tag{10}$$

The solution method of the model has been determined. The model is trained by using the sequence of attractions in trajectories. Given the input of the sample, the parameters of the model are trained using the random gradient method, and then updated to the current position of the training.

3.4 Model Application

We will apply the trained model to the real attraction recommendation task. In the real attraction recommendation task, the user is generally not likely to select the previously visited sight. Therefore, we generate a TOP-K recommendation list according to the recommendation formula $S_1(u,\ l)$ based on the user's demand at the time point m, the set l_p which consists of P attractions that the user has previously visited, and the candidate list of other attraction l.

$$S_1(u,\ l) \propto \left(v_u + v_m + v_{lp}\right)^T \cdot v_l \tag{11}$$

Where v_u represents a user-level latent semantic feature vector of user u, v_m represents a temporal-level latent semantic feature vector, v_l devotes an attraction-level latent semantic feature vector of all the attractions, and v_{l_p} represents the sum of latent semantic feature vector of all the sights in the dataset that the tourist has visited.

We find that the *MLS2vec* model can effectively solve the cold start problem in attraction recommendation. When a new user comes in the recommendation system, a recommended list of TOP-k is generated using the recommendation formula $S_2(u,\ l)$ based on the user travel time point m and the candidate list composed of attraction l.

$$S_2(u,l) \propto v_m^T \cdot v_l \tag{12}$$

3.5 Datasets

Crawled travel notes information of 193,470 users from CTRIP, Mafengwo and other travel portals, extracted information on each scenery point from each user's travel information and arranged in chronological order, a complete travel spatial-temporal trajectory can be formed. The data set used by the experiment is created not only by removing the data and geographical location information, such as districts and counties in the travel records, that is repeatedly shared by a single user on different websites, but also by removing the trajectory data of a single attraction from the user's travel trajectory. The processed data has a total of 135,027 users' travel trajectory data. The total number of tourist attractions is 245 and the time span is between January and December.

4 Experiment

4.1 Parameter Training

Parameter training is an important step in machine learning. In the actual application process, model algorithm, datasets and result feedback are collaborated to optimize the training parameters. Table 2 shows the correspondence between the main parameters in Algorithm 1 and the *MLS2vec* model and their default values. Model training and experiments are performed on the DELL PRECISION T1700 workstation.

Table 2. Main parameters

Parameter	Descriptions	Corresponding parameter	Defaults
Size	Vector dimension	Z	200
Window	The window size	$2C$	3
Negative	Negative sample number	-	5
Alpha	Initial learning rate	-	0.05
Iter	Number of iterations	-	5
Threads	Number of program threads	-	8

4.2 Latent Semantic Analysis of Model

The seasonal latent semantics implied by attractions is that the attraction is of most ornamental value in a particular season, so the number of visitors in this place during this season will be higher than other seasons. Taking Longsheng Hot Spring as an example, the best visit time is from November to mid-December, so the place is of strong seasonal latent semantics. By simply counting the number of people who visited Longsheng Hot Spring in each month, the results are shown in Fig. 2a. It shows the proportion of tourists visiting Longsheng Hot Spring in each month. During November and December, the number of visitors accounts for more than 40% of the total number of visitors.

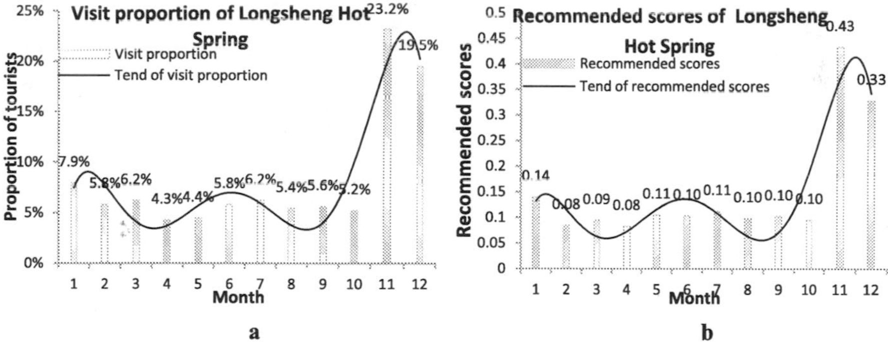

Fig. 2. Seasonal latent semantics analysis of model.

Using formula (11) to calculate the recommended scores for Longsheng Hot Spring under different months, we can conclude the model has completely preserved the seasonal latent semantics of the spot by the comparison of the statistical results showed in Fig. 2b.

The results of the experiment are shown in Fig. 2. In November and December, the recommending scores for Longsheng Hot Spring are the highest, and the trend of visiting proportions is the same as the trend of model recommendation. Therefore, the model preserves the seasonal latent semantics of the spot more accurately. It shows that the *MLS2vec* model can relatively preserve the latent seasonal latent semantics in the attraction.

4.3 Evaluation Criterion

Selecting 20% of the data in the database randomly as a test set, using the user-level latent semantic feature vector, the temporal-level latent semantic feature vector, and the attraction-level latent semantic feature vector to generate a sorting list of attractions calculated by the scoring formula (11), we select top-K attractions by sorting scores as a list of recommendations. Define $hit\_r@k$ for a single test user, the recall rate for this user is:

$$hit\_r@k = \frac{k}{TP_u} \tag{13}$$

Where k is the number of attraction which user has already visited in the top-k recommendations, and TP_u is the total number of attractions which user has already visited. For the recall rate of all test visitors, $Recall@k$ is the probability of successful prediction for all test sets:

$$Recall@k = \frac{\sum hit\_r@k}{\#all\_test\_user} \tag{14}$$

Randomly selecting 20% of user's trajectory data as a test set, selecting P attractions in each user's tourist trajectory as known tourist attractions, predicting the next attraction the user will go to by the model, and we can use the scoring formula (12) generating a list of top-K recommendations. Defining $hit\_a@k$ for a single test user, if the next attraction actually visited by the user is included in the top-K list, let $hit\_a@k = 1$, or $hit\_a@k = 0$. The total accuracy rate is the possibility of users who get the correct recommendation:

$$Accuracy@k = \frac{\sum hit\_a@k}{\#all\_test\_user} \tag{15}$$

4.4 Comparison Experiment

We conduct comparative experiments with two methods as follows: (1) doc2vec [15], for every tourists u, we can not only learn his embedded vector $x^{(u)}$ through the tourist trajectory, but also learn vector representation of every attractions. We can generate candidate list of attractions by calculating similarity distance between users and attractions. (2) LCA-LDA [1], we take into account with the individual interests and local preferences of each city by utilizing location access mode. According to formula (14) and formula (15), the model's recall rate and accuracy rate are obtained.

Figure 3a and b separately denotes change of recall ratio and accuracy ration of the model with the influence of K when P equals 3. It can clearly be seen through the graph that with the increase of the recommended list's length K, the recall rate and accuracy rate show an increasing trend. Because the list of model recommendations increases as the value of K increases, the probability of recommending accurate attractions to users will increase. Therefore, the recall rate and accuracy rate show an increasing trend. Our experimental results indicate that the latent semantics information contained in the *MLS2vec* model is more abundant and complete.

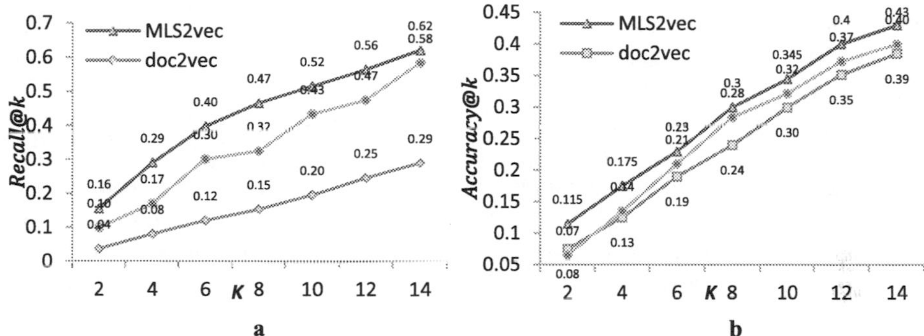

Fig. 3. Performance comparison on attractions recommendation

The setting of the window in the model training may affect the recall rate. Selecting $K = 10$, we train the model with $2C$ as the size of the window to calculate the recall rate. Because of errors in the process of training, we take average of the sum of recalls. The results shown in Fig. 4a show that with the increase of the recall rate of windows, there will be subtle fluctuations. When C changes, the recall rate of *MLS2vec* model appears to increase and then decrease. When C is 3, the model recall rate reaches the peak. The experimental results show that the latent semantics information stored in the *MLS2vec* model is the most complete and the semantics contained in the model is saturated when C is 3, so the X of the *MLS2vec* model is set to 3.

When the P attractions visited by the user are known, we need to judge the accuracy rate of *MLS2vec*. Fixing K be 10, the experimental results is shown in Fig. 4b, from which we can tell that the accuracy increases as P increases, indicating that the more gained attractions that tourists have visited, the more accuracy in recommendation attractions. The accuracy of the recommended results demonstrates that the latent

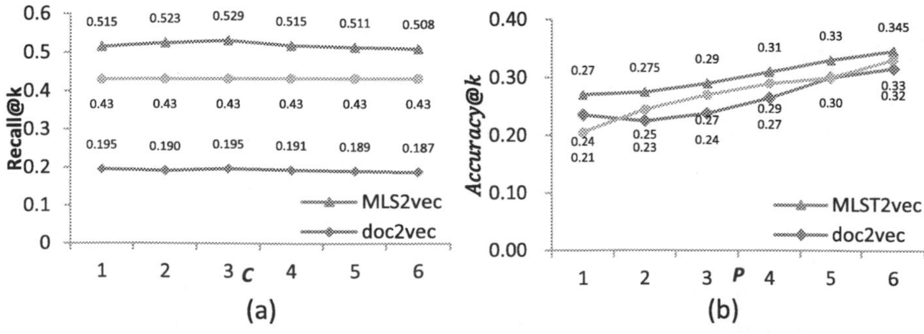

Fig. 4. Effect of parameter changes on model performance

semantics information contained in the *MLS2vec* model is more complete and richer for accurately predict the user's amusement attractions.

For the cold start problem, we compared the experiments of the hot recommends to verify the effectiveness of the *MLS2vec* model on this problem. For new user issues, hot recommends method provide the new user with Top-K attractions according to the visiting ratio from high to low. *MLS2vec* model calculates the TOP-K recommendation list according to the formula (12). Finally calculates the recall rate of the two models according to the formula (14).

The results shown in Fig. 5 show that the *MLS2vec* model performs better than the hot recommendation on the cold start problem for the attraction recommendation. With the increase of the number of recommended attractions, the recall rate of the model shows an increasing trend, and the recall rate of the *MLS2vec* is about 2 percentage points higher. With the above statements, it has proved the validity and accuracy of the *MLS2vec* model on the cold start problem of attractions recommendation.

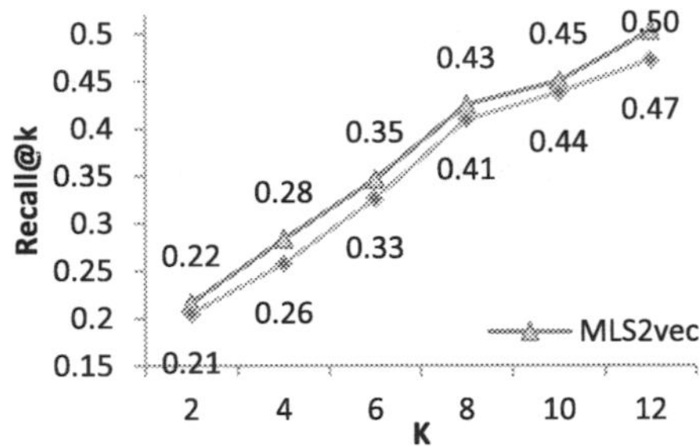

Fig. 5. Performance comparison on attractions recommendation in cold start

Based on the above experimental results, it can be concluded that the *MLS2vec* model can learn multiple latent semantics in user travel behavior and each level latent semantics is stored in a more complete manner. In real life, the user's tourist trajectory information is relatively sparse, and the *MLS2vec* model can completely discover user's latent travel preferences in the user's visiting trajectory, so that high-quality, high-accuracy recommendation results can be achieved.

5 Conclusion

This paper proposes a multi-latent semantic tourist trajectory representation model *MLS2vec*, which can efficiently learn multiple latent semantics in the tourist trajectory. It obtains the vector corresponding to multiple latent semantics through training to achieve high-quality attractions recommendation. Considering the position information, the visiting sequence and the play time of the spots in the track is of great significance for understanding the user's visiting mode. User-level latent semantics are trained through all the attractions in the trajectory, temporal-level latent semantic is trained by play trajectories of users in different months, and the attraction-level latent semantics are trained according to the context information of the user's trajectory, then the final model is obtained. Finally, using tourists' trajectory data set in Guilin, a comparative test between our model and doc2vec [15] model of recall rate and accuracy rate is conducted. The test results prove that the model is efficient and accurate.

Acknowledgments. This work was partially supported by the National Natural Science Foundation of China (Nos. U1501252, 61572146, U1711263), the Natural Science Foundation of Guangxi Province (No. 2016GXNSFDA380006), then Guangxi Innovation-Driven Development Project (No. AA17202024), and the Innovation Project of GUET Graduate Education (Nos. 2018YJCX12, YCSW2018139).

References

1. Yin, H., Sun, Y., Cui, B., et al.: LCARS: a location-content-aware recommender system. In: ACM SIGKDD International Conference on Knowledge Discovery and Data Mining, pp. 221–229. ACM (2013)
2. Yuan, Q., Cong, G., Ma, Z., et al.: Who, where, when and what: discover spatio-temporal topics for twitter users. In: ACM SIGKDD International Conference on Knowledge Discovery and Data Mining, pp. 605–613. ACM (2013)
3. Mikolov, T., Chen, K., Corrado, G., et al.: Efficient estimation of word representations in vector space. Comput. Sci. (2013)
4. Chen, M., Liu, Y., Yu, X.: NLPMM: a next location predictor with markov modeling. In: Tseng, V.S., Ho, T.B., Zhou, Z.-H., Chen, A.L.P., Kao, H.Y. (eds.) PAKDD 2014. LNCS (LNAI), vol. 8444, pp. 186–197. Springer, Cham (2014). https://doi.org/10.1007/978-3-319-06605_9_16
5. Monreale, A., Pinelli, F., Trasarti R, et al.: WhereNext: a location predictor on trajectory pattern mining. Proceedings of the KDD 2009, pp. 637–646 (2009)
6. He, J., Li, X., Liao, L., et al.: Inferring a personalized next point-of-interest recommendation model with latent behavior patterns. In: Thirtieth AAAI Conference on Artificial Intelligence, pp. 137–143. AAAI Press (2016)
7. Long, X., Jin, L., Joshi, J.: Exploring trajectory-driven local geographic topics in foursquare. In: International Workshop on Location-Based Social Networks, pp. 927–934 (2012)
8. Wang, X.: Action recognition using topic models. In: Moeslund, T., Hilton, A., Krüger, V., Sigal, L. (eds.) Visual Analysis of Humans, pp. 311–332. Springer, London (2011). https://doi.org/10.1007/978-0-85729-997-0_16
9. Yang, D., Zhang, D., Yu, Z., et al.: Fine-grained preference-aware location search leveraging crowdsourced digital footprints from LBSNs. In: ACM International Joint Conference on Pervasive and Ubiquitous Computing, pp. 479–488. ACM (2013)
10. Cheng, C., Yang, H., King, I., et al.: Fused matrix factorization with geographical and social influence in location-based social networks. In: AAAI Conference on Artificial Intelligence (2012)
11. Ye, M., Yin, P., Lee, W.C., et al.: Exploiting geographical influence for collaborative point-of-interest recommendation. In: SIGIR 2011 Proceedings of the 34th International ACM SIGIR Conference on Research and Development in Information Retrieval, pp. 325–334. ACM (2011)
12. Gao, H., Tang, J., Hu, X., et al.: Content-aware point of interest recommendation on location-based social networks. In: Twenty-Ninth AAAI Conference on Artificial Intelligence, pp. 1721–1727. AAAI Press (2015)

13. Yuan, Q., Cong, G., Ma, Z., et al.: Time-aware point-of-interest recommendation. In: International ACM SIGIR Conference on Research and Development in Information Retrieval, pp. 363–372. ACM (2013)
14. Mikolov, T., Sutskever, I., Chen, K., et al.: Distributed representations of words and phrases and their compositionality. In: Advances in Neural Information Processing Systems, pp. 3111–3119 (2013)
15. Le, Q.V., Mikolov, T.: Distributed Representations of Sentences and Documents. **4**, pp. II–1188 (2014)
16. He, X., Liao, L., Zhang, H., et al.: Neural collaborative filtering. In: Proceedings of the 26th International Conference on World Wide Web, pp. 173–182. International World Wide Web Conferences Steering Committee (2017)

Two-Stage Unsupervised Deep Hashing for Image Retrieval

Yuan-Zhu Gan(✉), Hao Hu(✉), and Yu-Bin Yang(✉)

State Key Laboratory for Novel Software Technology,
Nanjing University, Nanjing 210023, China
ganyz@smail.nju.edu.cn, {myou,yangyubin}@nju.edu.cn

Abstract. In this paper, we propose a two-stage unsupervised deep hashing method to map the high-dimensional images to compact binary codes for large-scale image retrieval. We employ a neural network to look for the non-linear complex transformations to learn the binary representations in an unsupervised way which is suitable for the unlabeled data. Our method consists of two stages. The first stage trains a stacked convolutional autoencoder with the binary relaxation criterion. Then the second stage adopts the encoder part of the first-stage autoencoder and iteratively updates the parameters with back-propagation algorithm under the following criterions: (1) preserving original information, (2) producing balanced codes, (3) keeping bits independent and (4) the above binary relaxation criterion. For the new-coming image, we can easily obtain its compact binary codes by propagating it through the trained network and quantizing the network's output. We evaluate our proposed method on two widely-used datasets and achieve very competitive result compared to the state-of-the-arts.

Keywords: Deep hashing · Unsupervised · Image retrieval

1 Introduction

With the large-scale image data, the content-based image retrieval [9] has attracted much attention in recent years. When giving a query image, the task of image retrieval is to find the closest or the most similar images from the dataset by means of ranking their distances to the query image. Considering the high dimension and huge quantity of images, the cost of computation can be expensive and the query speed can't meet today's requirements. In order to deal with the inefficiency, the approximate nearest neighbor search methods [1] have been proposed to save time and memory.

This work is funded by the Natural Science Foundation of China (No. 61673204), State Grid Corporation of Science and Technology Projects (Funded No. SGLNXT00DKJS1700166), and the Program for Distinguished Talents of Jiangsu Province, China (No. 2013-XXRJ-018).

X. Geng and B.-H. Kang (Eds.): PRICAI 2018, LNAI 11012, pp. 477–489, 2018.
https://doi.org/10.1007/978-3-319-97304-3_37

The hashing techniques transfer the original image space to the Hamming space, i.e., mapping the original images to compact binary codes with hashing functions. The generated hash codes can preserve the similarity of the original semantics so the similar images can be encoded to the similar binary hash codes. With the binary codes, the data dimension decreases so it can gain significant reduction in storage and distance computation cost.

Traditional hashing-based methods [2,18,22] usually first present the images to hand-crafted visual features [16] and then implement the projection stage and quantization stage to generate compact binary codes. But the well-designed hand-crafted features can't capture the images' richer semantic presentations and these separate steps may produce suboptimal results. In recent years the development of the neural networks and the deep architecture [8,17] have achieved great success in a lot of fields [19,20]. Many deep learning approaches have shown powerful learning ability in different applications. Deep convolutional neural networks (CNNs) [8] have non-linear architectures and can extract robust and powerful features. Autoencoder [7] is an unsupervised learning method which aims to learn a low dimension representation of the data from itself without any labels. With the numerous benefits of the neural networks and the deep architecture, several deep hashing methods have been proposed [10,24] and these methods usually perform better results compared to the traditional ones.

In this paper, we propose a deep unsupervised two-stage hashing method. Our method has no need to image labels and additional image data or pre-trained model. The first stage trains an autoencoder using the unlabeled images which adds a binary-like criterion. The second stage iteratively updates the encoder of the autoencoder and introduce more criterions to keep the codes independent, balanced and preserving the original image information. We conduct experiments on two widely-used datasets and the experimental results show very competitive performance compared to the state-of-the-arts.

2 Related Work

2.1 Hashing Techniques

In recent years, the hashing-based methods have become more popular in large scale image retrieval. The existing hashing methods can be divided into two categories: data-dependent and data-independent. The data-independent methods adopt random projections or manually to construct hash functions. The representative data-independent method is locality sensitive hashing (LSH) [2]. The data-dependent methods learn hash functions from the training data and can be categorized into three classes: supervised, semi-supervised, and unsupervised. The supervised methods will be given some supervised information, such as class labels, pairwise labels or triplet labels to learn hash functions. For example, kernel-based supervised hashing (KSH) [13] proposes a kernel-based hashing model with pairwise information and can deal with the linearly inseparable problems. The semi-supervised methods make use of labeled and unlabeled images. Semi-supervised hashing [21] adopts the empirical fitness on labeled data and set an information theoretic regularizer on both labeled and unlabeled samples. The unsupervised methods have no requirement for label information. PCA-based hashing (PCAH) [22] uses the principal component analysis (PCA) method to learn hash functions. PCA-ITQ [3] is the extension of ITQ with unsupervised data after PCA projections. K-means hashing (KMH) [4] proposes an Affinity-Preserving K-means algorithm to decrease the distance between the clustering and quantized cells. Spectral hashing [23] shows that spectral relaxation can lead to an eigenvector solution and balanced binary codes can be created by spectral graph partitioning. Spherical hashing [5] proposes a hypersphere-based hashing technique to minimize the spherical Hamming distance.

2.2 Deep Learning

Deep learning becomes a hot topic all over the world attributed to its significant feature learning and presentation power. In various vision tasks such as image classification [8], object detection [19], researchers adopt the convolutional neural networks (CNNs), autoencoder [7] and other deep learning methods to achieve great success. Similarly, deep learning can be applied to the large scale image retrieval. Xia et al. [24] first learns the approximate hash codes then learns hash functions and image representations by a convolutional neural network. Lin et al. [11] proposes an easy but effective deep supervised architecture to create binary codes which only adds a latent layer in the classification model. Liu et al. [12] adopts a binary-like and discriminative loss to decrease the discrepancy between Hamming space and real-valued space. Lu et al. [14] proposes a deep framework to learn hash codes which adopts the multiple dense non-linear transformations instead of the popular deep convolutional networks. Most of these methods are supervised and supervised hashing methods can take full advantage of the label information so that it can usually achieve better performance.

3 The Proposed Approach

In this section, we will introduce our proposed two-stage hashing method in detail. Figure 2 presents the training framework of our approach. As we can see, the approach consists of two training stages. The first stage contains a convolution autoencoder whose middle layer has K nodes and K denotes the length of binary codes. We train the autoencoder with the reconstructed content loss and the binary relaxation constraint. Then we initialize the second-stage's network with the parameters of the first-stage autoencoder's encoder and adopt more criterions and iteratively update parameters with back-propagation algorithm to make codes more balanced, independent and binary-like. In the following part we first introduce our notation, then explain the criterions of different stages, finally state the training process (Fig. 1).

The training data set has n images $\{x_1, x_2, \ldots, x_n\}$, $x_i \in \mathbb{R}^d$ where d is the dimension of the input images. For the first stage, the parameters denote $\mathcal{W}_1$ and the middle layer's output is $\{a_1, a_2, \cdots, a_n\}$, $a_i \in \mathbb{R}^K$. For the second stage, the parameters denote $\mathcal{W}_2$ and the network's output denotes $v_i = \psi(x_i; \mathcal{W}_2)$ where $v_i \in \mathbb{R}^K$ and the mapping function $\psi(\cdot)$ is the combination of a series of non-linear functions which can be expressed as:

$$\psi(x; \mathcal{W}_2) = f_k(\cdots f_2(f_1(x; w_1); w_2) \cdots ; w_k) \tag{1}$$

The function f_i means the i-th layer's non-linear operation which takes parameters w_i and data as inputs and its output will be token to the next layer function f_{i+1} as data input. k denotes the maximum number of the layers. $\mathcal{W}_2 = (w_1, w_2, \ldots, w_k)$ denotes the collections of the parameters. Then we can binarize the v_i by the function $sgn(\cdot)$ to get binary codes $b_i \in \{-1, +1\}^K$ where $sgn(v) = 1$ if $v > 0$ and -1 otherwise. It can be summarized as:

$$b_i = sgn(v_i) = sgn(\psi(x_i; \mathcal{W}_2)) \tag{2}$$

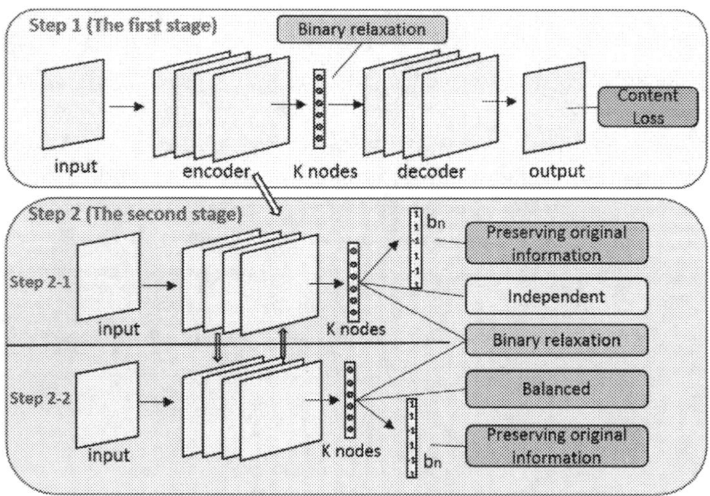

Fig. 1. The illustration of our method's training process.

3.1 The First-Stage Training

The main idea of the first-stage training is to train an autoencoder with our unlabeled images to serve for the second-stage training. Autoencoder is a good unsupervised method to learn the data's hidden information representations in low dimensions from data itself. Our first-stage training can be regarded as the pre-training of the second-stage training and this pre-training process doesn't involve additional image data and pre-trained models. We make some variations on the architecture and append a binary-like criterion to decrease the discrepancy when quantizing the middle layer's output nodes to binary codes.

The autoencoder consists of the encoder and the decoder. The middle hidden layer has K nodes which is the same as the length of hash codes. The encoder contains four convolution layers and the decoder contains four deconvolution layers symmetrically. Following [17], we set the kernel size of convolution and deconvolution layers 3×3 and the number of their feature maps is all 64. We don't use pooling and unpooling layers in the network because we think pooling and unpooling operations will lose some useful and detailed semantic information which can be used for better feature representations. All layers are followed by the rectified linear unit (relu) [15] except the middle hidden layer and the last deconvolution layer.

The training loss function is made up of two parts. The content loss computes the difference between the input image and the reconstruction image. We adopt the mean square error of the two images to express the loss. We assume the reconstruction image is x_i^R for the input image x_i. n denotes the number of total images. The content loss is expressed as follows:

$$\ell_{11} = \frac{1}{n} \sum_{i=1}^{n} \|x_i - x_i^R\|_2^2 \tag{3}$$

We adopt a binary relaxation criterion to force the output of the middle layer close to the discrete values. Usually, we transform the real-valued space to the Hamming space with the function $sgn(\cdot)$. In the process, we should consider two kinds of errors. The first error directly computes the difference before and after quantization which can be expressed as $||a_i - sgn(a_i)||_2^2$. But the function $sgn(\cdot)$ is a non-differentiable operation and it is intractable when we train our network using the back propagation algorithm. The second error considers the difference when we replace the real-valued distance of two vectors with the Hamming distance of two binary codes. To reduce the gap of the two space and make training available through the back-propagation technique, motivated by [12], we employ the binary relaxation constraint on the real-valued vectors.

$$\ell_{12} = \frac{1}{n} \sum_{i=1}^{n} \| \, |a_i| - \mathbf{1} \|_1 \tag{4}$$

$\mathbf{1}$ denotes the vector filled with ones. With the binary relaxation criterion, the network's output is closer to the desirable values $(+1/-1)$, then we can easily binarize the real-valued vectors to binary codes by the function $sgn(\cdot)$. The following second stage also adopts this binary relaxation criterion.

In summary, the first stage aims to minimize the following total loss to train the autoencoder where the λ_1 is the weighting parameter to balance the content loss and the binary relaxation criterion.

$$\min_{\mathcal{W}_1} \mathcal{L}_1 = \ell_{11} + \lambda_1 \ell_{12} \tag{5}$$

3.2 The Second-Stage Training

In this stage, we try to produce more balanced and independent binary codes under the condition of maintaining the original input's semantic information.

Preserving Original Information. We will iteratively update the network in the second stage and in every iteration, we will keep the output maintain the original image's discriminative information. We minimize the loss between the network's output and the binary output from the last iteration:

$$\ell_{21} = \frac{1}{N}\sum_{i=1}^{N}\|b_i - v_i\|_2^2 = \frac{1}{N}\sum_{i=1}^{N}\|b_i - \psi(x_i; \mathcal{W}_2)\|_2^2 \tag{6}$$

N denotes the number of each mini-batch for the training set. We fix the parameter W_2 and obtain b_i using Eq. (2). The created b_i have preserved latent semantic information of the input data in the last iteration though it may be suboptimal and the binary form is helpful to diminish the above two kinds of errors. The image's original semantic information is inherited from the first iteration so in order to preserve the original information in every iteration, we just need to maintain the information from the last iteration by minimizing ℓ_{21}. At the same time we add other criterions to make the outputs more robust.

Keeping Independent. We desire our produced binary codes are highly informative and the bit is independent and uncorrelated to each other. It's good for avoiding coding redundancy. In [23], the author sets the correlation matrix to be close to the identity matrix to ensure the pairwise uncorrelated. We make some variations and more relaxed constrains due to the nondifferentiable $sgn(\cdot)$ function and the stochastic gradient descent technique with mini-batches to train our network. We assume the number of each mini-batch is N, and the code length is K. $V \in \mathbb{R}^{N\times K}$ denotes the collections of N outputs $v_i \in \mathbb{R}^K$ of the neural network in a mini-batch. I denotes the identity matrix. The loss function can be written as follows:

$$\ell_{22} = \left\|\frac{1}{N}V^TV - I\right\|_F^2 \tag{7}$$

By attaching the relaxed orthogonality criterion, the different bits can be pairwise uncorrelated which is contribute to creating more efficient and independent binary codes.

Keeping Balanced. We also desire our generated binary codes are balanced which means the codes are evenly distributed and every bit could be 1 or -1 with the 50% probability. It's helpful for maximizing the entropy of probability distribution and the information capacity of codes can be enlarged. We average all the values on each bit and make it close to 0 which indicates the numbers of 1 and -1 are equal. We add the loss on each bit to form the loss function. We assume that v_{ik} means the k-th bit value of the network's output v_i for input x_i and the loss function can be written as follows:

$$\ell_{23} = \sum_{k=1}^{K}\left(\frac{1}{N}\sum_{i=1}^{N}v_{ik}\right)^2 \tag{8}$$

Algorithm 1. Our two-stage hashing method

Input: Training set $X = \{x_1, x_2, \ldots, x_n\} \in \mathbb{R}^{n \times d}$, max iterative number R, R_1, R_2, parameters λ_1, λ_2, λ_3 and λ_4
Output: The two stages' parameters $\mathcal{W}_1$ and $\mathcal{W}_2$
Step 1 (The first-stage training):
Train the convolution autoencoder with the training set X according to Eq. (5) then initialize $\mathcal{W}_2$ with the well-trained first-stage parameters.
Step 2 (The second-stage training):
for $r = 1, 2, \cdots, R$ **do**
  Step 2-1:
  update b_n fixing $\mathcal{W}_2$ according to Eq. (2).
  for $r_1 = 1, 2, \cdots, R_1$ **do**
    update $\mathcal{W}_2$ fixing b_n according to Eq. (10).
  end
  Step 2-2:
  update b_n fixing $\mathcal{W}_2$ according to Eq. (2).
  for $r_2 = 1, 2, \cdots, R_2$ **do**
    update $\mathcal{W}_2$ fixing b_n according to Eq. (11).
  end
end

The loss function is a relaxed version for a mini-batch. This criterion try to keep the balance property by equaling the probability of being 1 or -1 to make our produced binary codes contain richer information.

Keeping Binary-Like. This criterion is the same as the binary relaxation constrain employed in the first stage. We only need to replace the middle output in Eq. (4) with the output of the second-stage's network:

$$\ell_{24} = \frac{1}{N} \sum_{i=1}^{N} \| \, |\psi(x_i; \mathcal{W}_2)| - \mathbf{1} \|_1 \tag{9}$$

Our training process is represented in the Algorithm 1.

The first-stage training is important because we need the autoencoder to assist us to find the low-dimension representations which can still keep the original rich semantic information. The relaxed binary criterion makes the output inherit discriminative information after quantization but it achieves a suboptimal result. Inspired by [3], in the second-stage training, we iteratively update the parameters to seek a more balanced and independent result. In each iteration, we first get b_n by taking the input images going through the network. Then we respectively add the independent and balanced criterions to update the network's parameters on the basis of remaining the original information extracted in the last iteration. We minimize the following loss to improve the independent property.

$$\min_{\mathcal{W}_2} \mathcal{L}_{21} = \ell_{21} + \lambda_2 \ell_{22} + \lambda_4 \ell_{24} \tag{10}$$

To improve the balanced property we minimize the loss:

$$\min_{\mathcal{W}_2} \mathcal{L}_{22} = \ell_{21} + \lambda_3 \ell_{23} + \lambda_4 \ell_{24} \tag{11}$$

We hold the binary relaxation criterion in both training stages. It can decrease the two errors which come from transforming the real-valued vectors to binary codes.

4 Experiments

In this section, we conduct experiments on two widely-used benchmark datasets, MNIST and CIFAR-10 datasets. We first state our experiment's settings including the introductions of datasets, the evaluation metric and the details of the implementation. Then we present the experiment results compared to the state-of-the-arts.

4.1 Datasets

The MNIST dataset is a handwritten digit database, which contains 10 classes (labeled from 0 to 9), and consists of 70000 28×28 grayscale images. Following [14], we randomly select 100 per class and totally 1000 images as our query data, and keep the remaining images as the gallery set.

The CIFAR-10 dataset contrains 10 classes and consists of 60000 32×32 color images. We also randomly sample 1000 images (100 per class) as the query data, and use the rest as the gallery set.

4.2 Evaluation Metric

We propose two evaluation metrics to measure the different methods' performance. (1) Mean Average Precision (mAP): It's an overall measurement to the performance of hashing methods. For every query, we rank all the gallery set according to their Hamming ranking to the query and compute the average precision (AP) which is the average of top-k results' precision values. Then we compute the average value of all the queries' average precision (AP) as the mean average precision (mAP). (2) Precision@r: The value computes the average precision of the retrieved images within the Hamming radius r and we set $r = 2$ in this paper. Following [14], we evaluate the first metric on 16, 32 and 64 bits and the second metric on 16 and 32 bits.

4.3 Compared Methods

We compare our method with state-of-the-art hashing methods. They are all unsupervised methods including DH [14], LSH [2], PCA-ITQ [3], KMH [4], Spherical [5], SH [23] and PCAH [22]. Among them, DH [14] is the deep hashing method and the others are non-deep hashing methods. The denotation First-Stage in the table means the evaluations of the created hashing codes after the first-stage training and the denotation TwoStages means the results after two stages' training, i.e., our final results. The denotation OneStage means the model implemented by adding all the criterions (preserving original information, keeping independent, keeping balanced and keeping binary-like) on the latent vector in the first stage.

4.4 Implementation Details

We implement our method with Keras platform. In the first-stage training, we adopt the stochastic optimization algorithm Adam [6] with the learning rate 10^{-3} and the parameter λ_1 sets 10^{-4}. In the second-stage training, we adopt the stochastic gradient descent method with the learning rate 10^{-3} and set the parameters λ_2, λ_3, λ_4 0.01, 0.01 and 0.1 respectively. The size of the mini-batch is 128.

Table 1. Results on the MNIST dataset

Method	Hamming ranking (mAP,%)			Precision(%)@r=2	
	16	32	64	16	32
PCA-ITQ [3]	41.18	43.82	45.37	65.73	73.14
KMH [4]	32.12	33.29	35.78	61.88	68.85
Spherical [5]	25.81	30.77	34.75	51.71	64.26
SH [23]	26.64	25.72	24.10	57.52	65.31
PCAH [22]	27.33	24.85	21.47	36.36	65.54
LSH [2]	20.88	25.83	31.71	25.10	55.61
DH [14]	43.14	44.97	46.74	66.10	73.29
FirstStage	35.43	35.72	36.81	57.61	56.68
TwoStages	**44.23**	**45.87**	**47.12**	**67.01**	**74.23**
OneStage	37.88	39.58	41.74	62.18	69.32

4.5 Results

Results on the MNIST Dataset. The MNIST dataset is a widely-used public handwritten digit images dataset. Following the setting of [14], each image is represented as a 784-D gray-scale feature vector by using its intensity and DH [14] adopts the settings in their paper. Table 1 shows the evaluation results of different hashing methods. As shown in Table 1, our method outperforms the other hashing methods on the two metrics and we contribute it to that the encoder in the first-stage training can extract more informative features on the MNIST dataset and then with more criterions and iterative trainings the performance is improved much especially when increasing code length. Figure 2 shows

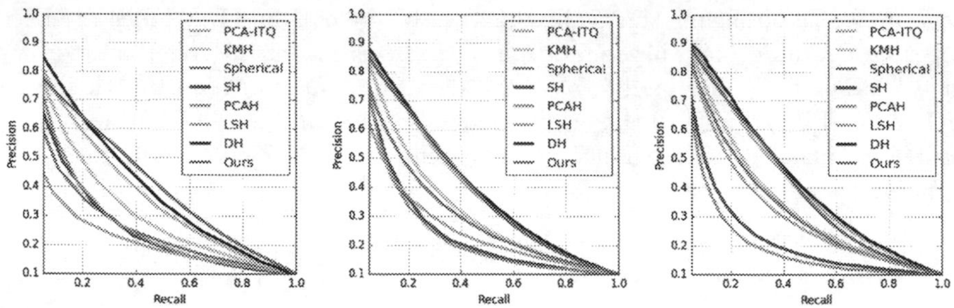

Fig. 2. Precision/Recall curves on the MNIST dataset for different unsupervised hashing methods with respect to 16, 32 and 64 bits (from left to right).

Table 2. Results on the CIFAR-10 dataset

Method	Hamming ranking (mAP,%)			Precision(%)@r=2	
	16	32	64	16	32
PCA-ITQ [3]	15.67	16.20	16.64	22.60	14.99
KMH [4]	13.59	13.93	14.46	22.08	5.72
Spherical [5]	13.98	14.58	15.38	20.96	12.50
SH [23]	12.55	12.42	12.56	18.52	20.60
PCAH [22]	12.91	12.60	12.10	21.29	2.68
LSH [2]	12.55	13.76	15.07	16.73	7.07
DH [14]	16.17	16.62	16.96	**23.33**	15.77
FirstStage	16.09	16.84	18.69	13.86	18.18
TwoStages	**18.65**	**19.79**	**20.72**	18.56	**28.59**
OneStage	16.82	17.23	18.95	15.78	19.55

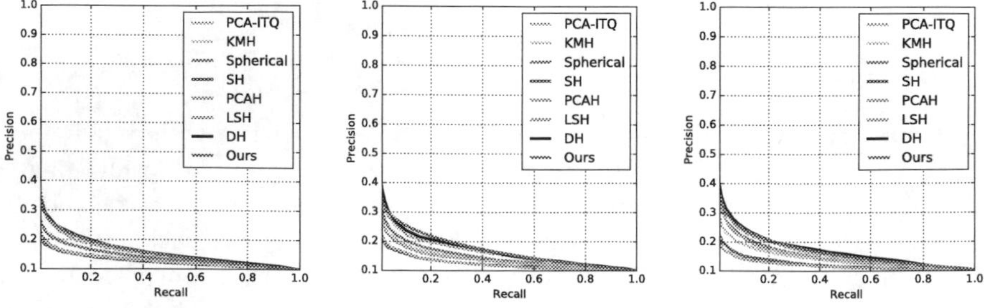

Fig. 3. Precision/Recall curves on the CIFAR-10 dataset for different unsupervised hashing methods with respect to 16, 32 and 64 bits (from left to right).

the precision-recall curves of different methods. We observe that our method outperforms the LSH, KMH, Spherical, SH, PCA-ITQ and PCAH, and is competitive with DH.

Results on the CIFAR-10 Dataset. The CIFAR-10 color images contain more complicated visual information. Each image is represented as a 512-D GIST feature vector in traditional hashing methods and DH [14] follows the same settings in the MNIST dataset. Table 2 reports our experiment results compared with the state-of-the-arts. As we can see, the CIFAR 10 dataset is more challenging so the performance is much lower than that on the MNIST dataset. Our method outperforms the other hashing methods except the evaluation metric precision@r=2 on 16 bits where we think the first-stage training in low encoding length on the CIFAR-10 dataset doesn't produce that compact codes but the second-stage training improves it a lot and the mAP evaluation performs well. With the increasing of code length, the overall evaluations outperform the other methods. Figure 3 shows the precision-recall curves of different methods on the CIFAR-10 dataset and our method performs better than LSH, KMH, Spherical, SH, PCA-ITQ and PCAH, and has very competitive performance with DH.

Results on Comparing with the OneStage Model. The OneStage model adds all the criterions on the latent vector in the first stage and it outperforms the FirstStage because these criterions are useful for better coding. But the first stage's task is the images' reconstruction and this task will constrain the latent vector to fit for the robust hashing codes. So we only employ the first stage to learn the hidden representations preparing for the second stage and just one criterion is adopted because less criterions in the first stage mean low degree of fitting which is more suitable for the following iterative training. The second stage is free from the reconstruction task and more criterions can better contribute to the iterative training. Experiments results show that TwoStages' performance is much better than the OneStage's.

5 Conclusion

In this paper, we have presented a deep unsupervised two-stage hashing method which has no requirement for image labels. The approach consists of two training stages. The first stage trains an autoencoder with the reconstructed content loss and the binary relaxation constraint. The second-stage training inherits the first-stage's parameters, adopts more criterions and iteratively updates parameters with back-propagation algorithm to make produced codes more balanced, independent and binary-like. We conduct experiments on two widely-used datasets and the experimental results show very competitive performance compared to the state-of-the-arts.

References

1. Andoni, A., Indyk, P.: Near-optimal hashing algorithms for approximate nearest neighbor in high dimensions. In: 47th Annual IEEE Symposium on Foundations of Computer Science, FOCS 2006, pp. 459–468. IEEE (2006)
2. Gionis, A., Indyk, P., Motwani, R., et al.: Similarity search in high dimensions via hashing. In: VLDB 1999, pp. 518–529 (1999)
3. Gong, Y., Lazebnik, S., Gordo, A., Perronnin, F.: Iterative quantization: a procrustean approach to learning binary codes for large-scale image retrieval. IEEE Trans. Patt. Anal. Mach. Intell. **35**(12), 2916–2929 (2013)
4. He, K., Wen, F., Sun, J.: K-means hashing: an affinity-preserving quantization method for learning binary compact codes. In: Proceedings of the IEEE Conference on Computer Vision and Pattern Recognition, pp. 2938–2945 (2013)
5. Heo, J.P., Lee, Y., He, J., Chang, S.F., Yoon, S.E.: Spherical hashing. In: 2012 IEEE Conference on Computer Vision and Pattern Recognition (CVPR), pp. 2957–2964. IEEE (2012)
6. Kingma, D., Ba, J.: Adam: a method for stochastic optimization. arXiv preprint arXiv:1412.6980 (2014)
7. Krizhevsky, A., Hinton, G.E.: Using very deep auto encoders for content-based image retrieval. In: ESANN (2011)
8. Krizhevsky, A., Sutskever, I., Hinton, G.E.: Imagenet classification with deep convolutional neural networks. In: Advances in Neural Information Processing Systems, pp. 1097–1105 (2012)
9. Lew, M.S., Sebe, N., Djeraba, C., Jain, R.: Content-based multimedia information retrieval: state of the art and challenges. ACM Trans. Multimed. Comput. Commun. Appl. (TOMM) **2**(1), 1–19 (2006)
10. Li, W., Wang, S., Kang, W.: Feature learning based deep supervised hashing with pairwise labels. In: Proceedings of the Twenty-Fifth International Joint Conference on Artificial Intelligence, IJCAI 2016, New York, NY, USA, 9–15 July 2016, pp. 1711–1717 (2016)
11. Lin, K., Yang, H.F., Hsiao, J.H., Chen, C.S.: Deep learning of binary hash codes for fast image retrieval. In: Proceedings of the IEEE Conference on Computer Vision and Pattern Recognition Workshops, pp. 27–35 (2015)
12. Liu, H., Wang, R., Shan, S., Chen, X.: Deep supervised hashing for fast image retrieval. In: Proceedings of the IEEE Conference on Computer Vision and Pattern Recognition, pp. 2064–2072 (2016)
13. Liu, W., Wang, J., Ji, R., Jiang, Y.G., Chang, S.F.: Supervised hashing with kernels. In: 2012 IEEE Conference on Computer Vision and Pattern Recognition (CVPR), pp. 2074–2081. IEEE (2012)
14. Lu, J., Liong, V.E., Zhou, J.: Deep hashing for scalable image search. IEEE Trans. Image Process. **26**(5), 2352–2367 (2017)
15. Nair, V., Hinton, G.E.: Rectified linear units improve restricted boltzmann machines. In: Proceedings of the 27th International Conference on Machine Learning (ICML-10), pp. 807–814 (2010)
16. Oliva, A., Torralba, A.: Modeling the shape of the scene: a holistic representation of the spatial envelope. Int. J. Comput. Vis. **42**(3), 145–175 (2001)
17. Simonyan, K., Zisserman, A.: Very deep convolutional networks for large-scale image recognition. arXiv preprint arXiv:1409.1556 (2014)
18. Strecha, C., Bronstein, A., Bronstein, M., Fua, P.: Ldahash: improved matching with smaller descriptors. IEEE Trans. Pattern Anal. Mach. Intell. **34**(1), 66–78 (2012)

19. Szegedy, C., Toshev, A., Erhan, D.: Deep neural networks for object detection. In: Advances in Neural Information Processing Systems, pp. 2553–2561 (2013)
20. Taigman, Y., Yang, M., Ranzato, M., Wolf, L.: Deepface: closing the gap to human-level performance in face verification. In: Proceedings of the IEEE Conference on Computer Vision and Pattern Recognition, pp. 1701–1708 (2014)
21. Wang, J., Kumar, S., Chang, S.F.: Semi-supervised hashing for scalable image retrieval. In: 2010 IEEE Conference on Computer Vision and Pattern Recognition (CVPR), pp. 3424–3431. IEEE (2010)
22. Wang, J., Kumar, S., Chang, S.F.: Semi-supervised hashing for large-scale search. IEEE Trans. Pattern Anal. Mach. Intell. **34**(12), 2393–2406 (2012)
23. Weiss, Y., Torralba, A., Fergus, R.: Spectral hashing. In: Advances in Neural Information Processing Systems, pp. 1753–1760 (2009)
24. Xia, R., Pan, Y., Lai, H., Liu, C., Yan, S.: Supervised hashing for image retrieval via image representation learning. In: AAAI, vol. 1, pp. 2156–2162 (2014)

A Fast Heuristic Path Computation Algorithm for the Batch Bandwidth Constrained Routing Problem in SDN

Dongjun Qian[1], Peng Yang[2(✉)], and Ke Tang[2]

[1] School of Computer Science and Technology, University of Science and Technology of China, Hefei 230027, China
horizon@mail.ustc.edu.cn

[2] Shenzhen Key Laboratory of Computational Intelligence, Department of Computer Science and Engineering, Southern University of Science and Technology, Shenzhen 518055, China
{yangp,tangk3}@sustc.edu.cn

Abstract. This paper presents a new path computation algorithm for the batch bandwidth constrained routing problem, aiming to reduce the end-to-end running time of a routing algorithm while maintaining the quality of the solution set. The batch bandwidth constrained routing problem arises along with the emergence of the Software Defined Networking (SDN) framework. A network is a bidirectional graph and most bandwidth constrained routing algorithms use Constrained Shortest Path First (CSPF) algorithm to compute a path meeting a certain bandwidth demand. However, available CSPF algorithms' time complexities have a super-linear relation with the graph size. In fact, we think the entire graph is unnecessary for bandwidth constrained routing algorithms in that a comparatively small subgraph can be enough to cover a feasible path. Based on this thought, we present an algorithm to figure out different subgraphs for different requests of a batch with the help of a graph partitioning process in advance. We achieve an end-to-end time saving of up to a proportion of 69% in our experiments.

Keywords: Path computation · Bandwidth constrained routing · SDN

1 Introduction

With the rapid development of Internet, using network terminal devices has become a part of people's everyday life. However, the traditional network infrastructures are becoming outdated. In a traditional network, forwarding decisions are made on different switches, so it is hard to control and manage the network. Switches from different manufacturers or of different models may have different standards, in which case the developers need to study many different standards to develop a new application. Besides, developers need to configure all the devices for testing. All these increase the complexity and cost of innovations.

X. Geng and B.-H. Kang (Eds.): PRICAI 2018, LNAI 11012, pp. 490–502, 2018.
https://doi.org/10.1007/978-3-319-97304-3_38

Software Defined Networking (SDN [8]) is an emerging architecture that can alleviate the above difficulties. It decouples the control plane and the data plane. Developers only need to deploy their applications on the control plane. SDN is a more centralized system compared to a traditional one and thus Traffic Engineering (TE) could be performed more efficiently. The bandwidth constrained routing problem, requesting a feasible non-bifurcation path from a source node to a target node, is a fundamental problem since the emergence of network. A truth for any communication networking is that all links have a bandwidth limit thus congestions may occur. In SDN, the controllers of the control plane process all the routing requests. As the network becomes large, there will be a great number of requests for every short interval. Computing a feasible path in a large scale network needs much more computation than in a small one. And because a link has limited total amount of bandwidth, the routing requests cannot be simply processed in a parallel way as it may lead to congestion. Thus the problem solving speed has been restricted if we want to keep congestion at a low seriousness level. With the network growing larger, the average processing time of a single request gets longer. Besides, more requests come within a certain long interval. Therefore, the requests may continue getting piled up if the processing speed is slower than the request arising frequency. So the capability of quickly processing the bandwidth constrained routing requests is a bottleneck limiting the size of a SDN system to be practical.

Possible ways to enhance the request processing capability of SDN are improving the hardware performance, enhancing the scalability of SDN or developing path computation algorithms that are more efficient. Improving the hardware performance is out of the scope of this article. For enhancing the scalability of SDN, many controller platforms such as Onix [7], HyperFlow [15], Kandoo [5], Floodlight [13], Opendaylight [11], Ryu [12] and ONOS [2] supporting distributed controller architectures have been developed. But with the increase of node number in a network, the number of controllers should increase at least proportionally to maintain the balance between the request arising frequency and processing speed. As a result, the cost of synchronizing information across controllers will increase sharply. Developing a more efficient path computation algorithm can improve every single controller's request processing capability therefore fewer controllers will be needed in a large scale SDN system or an even larger network can be satisfied with current controllers. CSPF is a class of algorithms most widely used to compute a feasible path satisfying the bandwidth constraint. Based on an unconstrained shortest path algorithm like Dijkstra's algorithm or Bellman-Ford algorithm, CSPF works by filtering out unfeasible links in advance or by ignoring unfeasible links during searching. The time complexity of a specific CSPF algorithm is just the same as the underlying unconstrained shortest path algorithm. Most popularly used shortest path first algorithm in CSPF is Dijkstra's algorithm, its time complexity can be $\mathcal{O}(|V|^2)$ or $\mathcal{O}(|E| + |V| \log |V|)$ where $|V|$ represents the node number of a network and $|E|$ the link number for $|E| = \mathcal{O}(|V|^2)$. For the batch bandwidth constrained routing problem in SDN, the time complexity of Dijkstra's algorithm based CSPF is $\mathcal{O}(K \times |V|^2)$ or $\mathcal{O}(K \times (E + |V| \log |V|))$ where K represents the request number. It rises sharply along with $|V|$ not only because the order of $|V|$ in the time complexity is high but also because the number of requests will rise proportionally when the network gets larger for any given interval.

Although the number of nodes of an optimal path differs from request to request, it is usually the case that most paths obtained by CSPF involve only a small fraction of the nodes of the whole graph. Therefore, it will definitely be more efficient if we can figure out an exact subgraph that a request really needs in a very short time.

Inspired by this thought, we define a domain as a subgraph that enjoys relatively good connectivity inside it. Then we can build a quotient graph each of whose nodes denotes a different domain. Then map the requests onto the quotient graph and compute paths with a specially designed routing algorithm. Each of the paths corresponds to a subset of nodes of the original graph and thus a subgraph. In this way, we can figure out a certain subgraph for each request. A graph of a communication network is not always a flat graph and there may exist domains recognized or not. A subset of the entire node set of a graph, along with all the edges starting and ending inside it, can denote a specific subgraph exclusively. Noticing that graph partitioning techniques minimize the total weights of edges crossing subgraphs denoted by node subsets, in other words maximize the total weights of edges within subgraphs, we think the connectivity inside subgraphs can be maximized correlatively if we set the edge bandwidths as edge weights, thus these subgraphs can be viewed as domains. From our experiment results, the path computation time can get reduced proportionally up to 69%, while maintaining the quality of the solutions.

2 Problems Definition and Related Works

2.1 The Bandwidth Constrained Routing

The batch bandwidth constrained routing problem is defined as following:

Network $G = (V, E)$ is a bidirectional graph, V represents the node set and E represents the edge set. $\delta : E \to \mathbb{R}_{>0}$ defines the bandwidth of each edge. K is a request set, $\forall k \in K, k = (s, t, d)$, in which s represents the source node, t represents the target node and d represents the demanded bandwidth. The requested output is a solution set R corresponding to the request set K. Each element of R is either a list of nodes implying a feasible path or a rejection. R cannot break the bandwidth limit of any edge.

Routing algorithms for this problem try to get a near-optimal solution set R on some metrics like throughput, reject ratio, average path length and load balance, meanwhile they minimize the computation time. And the routing algorithms for this problem basically can be classified into two categories:

1. Sequentially process all the requests, first setting the cost of each edge and then using CSPF to find a feasible path minimizing the total cost. Such algorithms include Minimum Hops (MH), Widest Shortest Path (WSP [1]), Shortest-dist Path (SP [9]), MIRA [6] and DORA [3].
2. Other algorithms process all the requests simultaneously, like LPF-RR [16].

The first kind of routing algorithms use CSPF to compute the path. Difference among these algorithms is the cost function of edges. In MH, all edges have a constant cost value 1. In WSP, all edges still have a constant cost value 1 while an edge with higher available bandwidth will be preferred during the search. In SP, the cost of an edge is the reciprocal value of its available bandwidth. MIRA determines the edges' cost by computing the max-flow min-cut between all the possible source node target node pairs. The time complexity of this algorithm is $\mathcal{O}(|V|^5)$, which is unacceptable in a large scale network. DORA computes all the disjoint paths between all the pairs of source nodes and target nodes to get a vector named PPV (Path potential value) for each edge in advance. For each request on processing, the costs of edges are determined according to their available bandwidths and PPV vectors. The length of a PPV vector is the number of possible pairs of source nodes and target nodes. Thus in a large scale network, DORA will need huge amount of space to save very long PPV vectors for every edge which makes DORA unpractical. Whether the cost of an edge is a constant value or a function, CSPF is applicable. The advantage of this kind of routing algorithms is that the total processing time basically increases linearly with the number of requests, which is comparatively efficient and makes these algorithms most popular.

The second kind of routing algorithms do not set a cost value for each edge. They solve all the requests simultaneously by optimizing one or more network performance metrics. A typical example is LPF-RR, which formulates the batch bandwidth constrained routing problem as an integer programming problem to optimize the load balance of a network. This kind of algorithms have time complexities increase super-linearly with the number of requests and thus are not widely used.

This paper will focus on improving the CSPF computation process in the first kind of routing algorithms. As mentioned in the first section, CSPF is based on the unconstrained path computation algorithms, among which most frequently used ones are Dijkstra's algorithm, Bellman-Ford algorithm and Floyd-Warshall algorithm. Although Dijkstra's algorithm and Bellman-Ford algorithm both computes a shortest path from a single source node to all other nodes, Bellman-Ford algorithm is slower than Dijkstra's algorithm. On the other hand, Dijkstra's algorithm cannot handle graphs with negative edge costs while Bellman-Ford algorithm is capable of. Floyd-Warshall algorithm computes shortest paths between all pair of nodes with a time complexity of $\mathcal{O}(|V|^3)$. Because different requests have different bandwidth demands and the edges' available bandwidths change over time, Floyd-Warshall algorithm is less time efficient than Dijkstra's algorithm and Bellman-Ford algorithm. Besides, as the cost of an edge is always positive in a reasonable routing algorithm, Dijkstra's algorithm is usually the prime choice.

2.2 The Graph Partitioning

The graph partitioning is a classical NP-hard problem that requests a partition $V_1, V_2, \ldots, V_q$ of node set V from graph $G = (V, E, c, w)$, where $c : V \to \mathbb{R}_{\geq 0}$

defines the weights of nodes and $w : E \to \mathbb{R}_{>0}$ defines the weights of edges. And for convenience of notation, the definitions of c and w can be generalized to $\forall V' \subseteq V, c(V') = \sum_{v \in V'} c(v)$ and $\forall E' \subseteq E, w(E') = \sum_{e \in E'} w(e)$. Then the graph partitioning problem can be formulated as following:

$$\min \sum\nolimits_{i<j} w(E_{ij}), E_{ij} = \{(u,v)|(u,v) \in E, u \in V_i, v \in V_j\} \tag{1}$$

$$\text{subject to} \quad \bigcup\nolimits_{i=1}^{q} V_i = V \tag{2}$$

$$\forall i,j \in \{1,2,\ldots,q\} \text{ and } i \neq j, V_i \cap V_j = \emptyset \tag{3}$$

$$c(V_i) \leq \frac{(1+\epsilon)c(V)}{q} + \max\nolimits_{v \in V} c(v) \tag{4}$$

Where ϵ is a hyper parameter representing the balance of weights of nodes among node subsets. Equation (1) is the objective function. It minimizes the total weights of edges whose source and target belonging to different subsets of V. Equation (2) means the partition $\{V_1, V_2, \ldots, V_q\}$ should cover all nodes in G, (3) means they should not have a common node. Equation (4) means each subset of nodes should have a near total weight of nodes.

There has been a lot of works on the graph partitioning problem including exact algorithms like spectral partitioning and graph growing, heuristic algorithms like Kernighan-Lin algorithm, and multilevel methods like KaFFPa [14]. The proposed method uses KaFFPa to partition the graph. KaFFPa first contracts the edges to get a coarsened graph, then conducts the initial partitioning, at last uncoarsens the graph and applys local search at the same time. More details of these algorithms can be referred to Buluç et al. [4]. Among these algorithms, the multilevel partitioning method based ones perform best on large graphs.

3 A Fast Path Computation Algorithm

In this section, we present our heuristic fast path computation algorithm. Let $G = (V, E)$ represent a bidirectional graph, K represent a request set on G. q represents the number of node subsets of V obtained by the graph partitioning algorithm. There are 4 procedures in our algorithm:

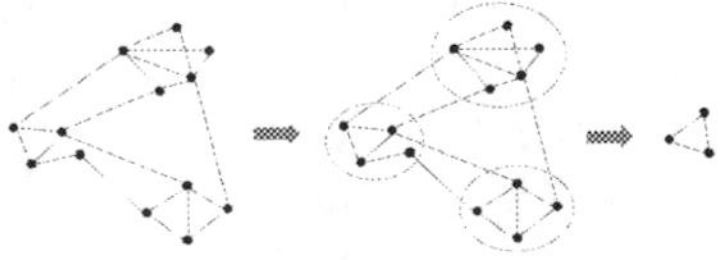

Fig. 1. Partition $G = (V, E)$ and build quotient graph $Q = (VQ, EQ)$

1. First set the weights of edges equal to the bandwidths of edges. Set the weights of nodes all identical to 1. Set q, the number of subsets of nodes, to $\lceil 0.25\sqrt{|V|}\rceil$. Then use KaFFPa to partition G to get a partition $\{V_1, V_2, \ldots, V_q\}$.

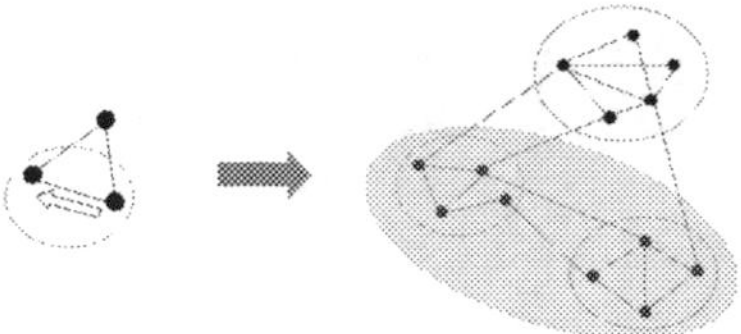

Fig. 2. Map a path on Q to a subgraph of G

2. Build quotient graph $Q = (VQ, EQ)$. Each node of Q corresponds to a node subset of G and $VQ = \{V_1, V_2, \ldots, V_q\}$, where $V_i, i = 1, 2, \ldots, q$ represents a node subset of G and a node of Q at the same time for convenience. Each edge of Q denotes a edge subset of G and $\forall (V_i, V_j) \in EQ, bandwidth((V_i, V_j)) = \sum_{u \subset V_i, v \in V_j, (u,v) \in E} bandwidth((u, v))$.
3. For each request $k = (s, t, d) \in K$, map it onto Q to get $k' = (V_i, V_j, d), s \in V_i, t \in V_j$. Route all the requests on Q with our specially designed routing algorithm and the solution set on Q is called R'.
4. Map R' onto graph G. Then we can get certain subgraphs of G for requests not rejected on Q. Then route these requests within their corresponding subgraphs. For the requests that have a feasible path on Q but failed to find a feasible path on the corresponding subgraph, reroute them on the entire graph G and then we get the final solution set R.

The procedures of the graph partitioning and the construction of the quotient graph are illustrated in Fig. 1 and the procedures of getting a subgraph corresponding to a path on the quotient graph is illustrated in Fig. 2. With the node weights all identical to 1, the node subsets $V_1, V_2, \ldots, V_q$ obtained by the graph partitioning have approximately the same amount of nodes. With the edge bandwidths as edge weights, the least bandwidth is cut by the partitioning operation thus most bandwidth is within the subgraphs denoted by $V_1, V_2, \ldots, V_q$.

3.1 Routing Algorithm on Quotient Graph

A bandwidth constrained routing algorithm is specially designed for routing requests on the quotient graph Q obtained above. Its edge cost function is defined as following:

$$\text{cost}(e) = \begin{cases} \ln\left(\frac{1+\beta}{1-\frac{d}{\text{available\_bandwidth}(e)}+\beta}\right) + \alpha, & \text{if available\_bandwidth}(e) \geq d \\ +\infty, & \text{otherwise} \end{cases}$$

where $\alpha, \beta > 0$ are two hyper-parameters, d is the bandwidth demanded by the request on processing and available_bandwidth(e) is the unallocated bandwidth of edge $e \in EQ$. cost(e) increases with the demanded bandwidth d and decreases with the available bandwidth of edge e.

Let $\hat{\rho}(e) = 1 - \frac{d}{b}, b = \text{available\_bandwidth}(e)$. $\hat{\rho}(e)$ is our estimate of $\rho(e)$ which represents the possibility that there exists an edge having available bandwidth more than d in the edge subset of G denoted by edge e. $\lim_{b \to \infty} \hat{\rho}(e) = 1, \lim_{b \to d} \hat{\rho}(e) = 0$ and $\hat{\rho}(e)$ increases monotonically with b. When $\alpha \to 0, \beta \to 0$, $\text{cost}(e) = \ln(\frac{1}{\hat{\rho}(e)})$. Let $path \subseteq EQ$ denote a path on Q for the request. Then the total edge cost of the path is $\text{cost}(path) = \sum_{e \in path} \text{cost}(e) = \ln\left(\frac{1}{\prod_{e \in path} \hat{\rho}(e)}\right)$. Then to minimize the cost($path$) is to maximize the possibility that there exists a feasible path within the subgraph of G denoted by $path$ on Q. When $\alpha, \beta >> 1$, with $\ln\left(\frac{1+\beta}{1-\frac{d}{\text{available\_bandwidth}(e)}+\beta}\right)/\alpha \approx 0$, and $\text{cost}(e) \approx \alpha$, we have $\text{cost}(path) \approx \alpha \times \sum_{e \in path} 1$. Then to minimize cost($path$) is to minimize the number of nodes of $path$, thereby minimize the node number of the subgraph of G denoted by $path$ because as mentioned above all the node subsets have approximately the same amount of nodes. And minimizing the size of the subgraph for a request correlates to the minimizing of the path computation time.

To summarize, a smaller α and β lead to a larger $\hat{\rho}$, a larger α and β lead to a smaller subgraph, and vice versa. In other words, by tuning α and β we can make a trade-off between the path computation time on the subgraph and the possibility that a feasible path exists in the subgraph. Then we can use CSPF to compute paths for requests on the quotient graph with this cost function.

3.2 The Path Computation Time

Assume the time complexity of CSPF is $\mathcal{O}(N^p), p > 1$ where N represents the node number of the graph being operated on. Let g represent the node number of the graph $G = (V, E)$. Let q represent the number of nodes of the corresponding quotient graph $Q = (VQ, EQ)$. Let m represent the number of nodes each node subset approximately holds. We can get $g \approx qm$. H is a CSPF based bandwidth constrained routing algorithm. H's time complexity is the same as CSPF. If we use H alone to solve the problem, then $T_0 = \mathcal{O}(g^p) \approx \mathcal{O}(q^p m^p)$ is the running rime. For the proposed algorithm, $T_1 = \mathcal{O}(q^p)$ is the running time on Q. With l denoting the number of nodes of a path on Q, the node number of the subgraph denoted by the path is approximately $h = lm$. Then we apply H on the subgraph for the request and the running time on the subgraph is $T_2 = \mathcal{O}(h^p) \approx \mathcal{O}(l^p m^p)$. Because $q = 0.25\sqrt{g} = \mathcal{O}(\sqrt{g}), m \approx 4\sqrt{g} = \mathcal{O}(\sqrt{g})$ in our algorithm, we have

$$\frac{T_1 + T_2}{T_0} = \frac{\mathcal{O}(q^p + l^p m^p)}{\mathcal{O}(g^p)} = \frac{\mathcal{O}(g^{0.5p} + l^p g^{0.5p})}{\mathcal{O}(g^p)} = \frac{\mathcal{O}(1 + l^p)}{\mathcal{O}(g^{0.5p})} = \frac{\mathcal{O}(1 + l^p)}{\mathcal{O}(q^p)}$$

Since $l \leq q$ and most commonly $l << q$ for l is the node number of a path in Q which has q nodes, $T_1 + T_2 << T_0$. It means the path computation time for a single request of our algorithm is basically less than the original algorithm H. The larger the size of the request set is, the more time can be saved. If the size of the request set is large enough, the extra running time mainly caused by the graph partitioning operation can be offset and the end-to-end running time can get reduced.

4 Performance Evaluation

In this section, we evaluate the performance of our algorithm on the accelerating of two different routing algorithms, MH and SP, both using Dijkstra's algorithm based CSPF to compute feasible paths. The proposed algorithm used them as the routing algorithms applied on the subgraphs.

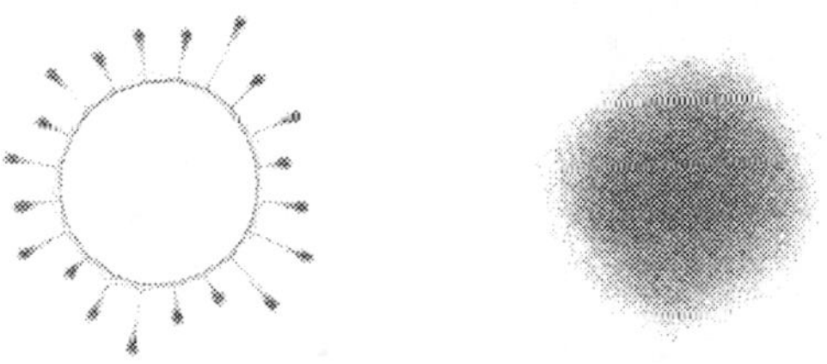

Fig. 3. Visualization of the generated graphs. Left: the ring graph. Right: the flat graph

4.1 Graphs and Request Sets

Two different graphs are used in our experiment, namely the ring graph and the flat graph, both of which are generated with a computer program.

The generation of the ring graph and the request set on it are described as following:

1. Generate 20 undirected flat graphs using Brite [10] with a Waxman model [17]. Each graph has 500 nodes and 1000 edges.
2. Take 10 nodes from each of the 20 graphs to form a ring by connecting each node from graph_i to all 10 nodes from $\text{graph}_{(i+1)\%20}$, $i = 1, 2, \ldots, 20$.
3. Replace each undirected edge with two directed edges of opposite directions and set random bandwidth within $[1000, 5000]$ following uniform distribution pattern and we get graph $G = (V, E)$.
4. Randomly choose two different nodes $s, t \in V$, find a shortest path from s to t namely *path*. Generate a random number $d \sim U[1000, 5000]$ and add $0.01d$ to the bandwidths of all edges in *path*. Repeat this procedure 1,000,000 times to make the bandwidth setting of G more reasonable.
5. Randomly choose two different nodes $s, t \in V$ and generate a random number $d \sim U[1000, 5000]$, then we get a random request (s, t, d). Repeat this procedure 100,000 times to get the request set K.

The generation of the flat graph and the request set on it are described as following:

1. Generate an undirected flat graph using Brite with a Waxman model. The generated graph has 2000 nodes and 16000 edges.

2. Replace each undirected edge with two directed edges of opposite directions and set random bandwidth within $[1000, 5000]$ following uniform distribution pattern and we get graph $G = (V, E)$.
3. Randomly choose two different nodes $s, t \in V$, find a shortest path from s to t namely *path*. Generate a random number $d \sim U[1000, 5000]$ and add $0.01d$ to all edges in *path*. Repeat this procedure 1,000,000 times to make the bandwidth setting of G more reasonable.
4. Randomly choose two different nodes $s, t \in V$ and generate a random number $d \sim U[1000, 5000]$, then we get a random request (s, t, d). Repeat this procedure 100,000 times to get the request set K.

The visualization of the ring graph and the flat graph is illustrated in Fig. 3.

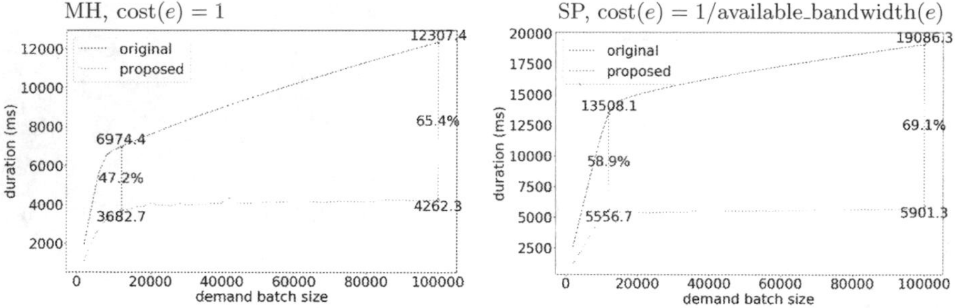

Fig. 4. Running time on the ring graph

4.2 Results

We run all the experiments 10 times and present the mean value of the results. We use the original MH or SP algorithm to solve all 100,000 requests on the ring graph and the flat graph, and record results of other request batch sizes at an interval of 2000 during each run. Since the proposed algorithm processes a request set in a batch manner, we use it to solve request sets of different batch size with independent runs. Thus there are in total $10 \times 2 \times 50 \times 2 = 2000$ independent trials of the proposed algorithm tested on $2 \times 50 \times 2 = 200$ different circumstances.

The running times are illustrated in Figs. 4 and 5. When the request batch size is smaller than 12000, both of the two running times of the original algorithm and the proposed algorithm grow linearly with the batch size. Besides, the proposed algorithm consumes less running time than the original one does, and the advantage rises steadily with the increase of the batch size. When the request batch size is larger than 12000, both of the two running time slows down, because the bandwidths of the edges of graph G is seriously consumed so that only a few edges are feasible to a request in terms of bandwidth. Thus only very few amount of edges get relaxed and Dijkstra's algorithm terminates early for no more nodes reachable. The proposed algorithm's running time grows much

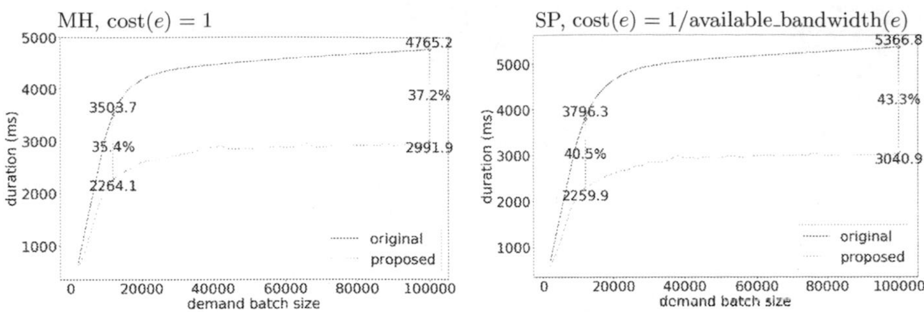

Fig. 5. Running time on the flat graph

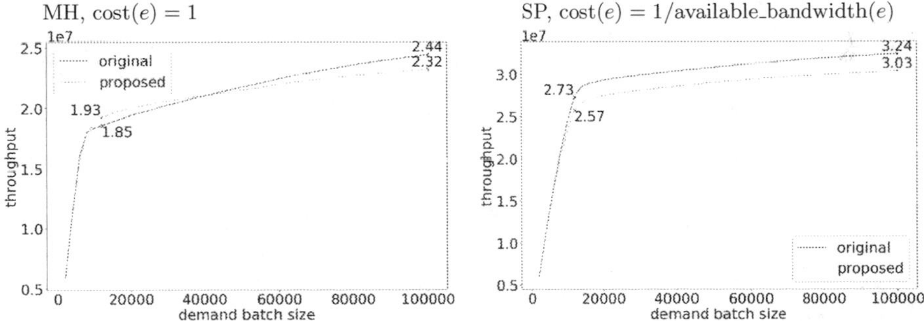

Fig. 6. Throughput on the ring graph

slower than the original one's because in this situation the quotient graph Q's bandwidth is consumed seriously too, and thus if a request does not have a feasible path on Q, then the request is rejected immediately. Processing the largest request set composed of 100,000 requests, the proposed algorithm saves 65.4% on the ring graph by accelerating MH, 69.1% on the ring graph by accelerating SP (see Fig. 4), 37.2% on the flat graph by accelerating MH and 43.3% by accelerating SP (see Fig. 5), in terms of end-to-end running time.

The corresponding throughput and reject ratio are illustrated in Figs. 6, 7, 8 and 9. On the ring graph, when the request batch size is smaller than 12000, the proposed algorithm's throughputs and reject ratios are no worse than the original one's, when the batch size is larger than 12000 the proposed algorithm's throughputs are slightly lower than the original one's while the reject ratios are almost the same. On the flat graph, when the request batch size is smaller than 10000, the proposed algorithm's throughput curve overlaps the original one's and the reject ratios are small but larger than the original one's, when the request batch size is larger than 10000 the proposed algorithm's throughputs are a bit smaller than the original one's and the reject ratios are a bit larger than the original one's, but both of the two gaps reach a maximum with the batch size of around 20000 and keeps not enlarged along with the increasing of the request batch size after that point. The proposed algorithm finds a shortest feasible

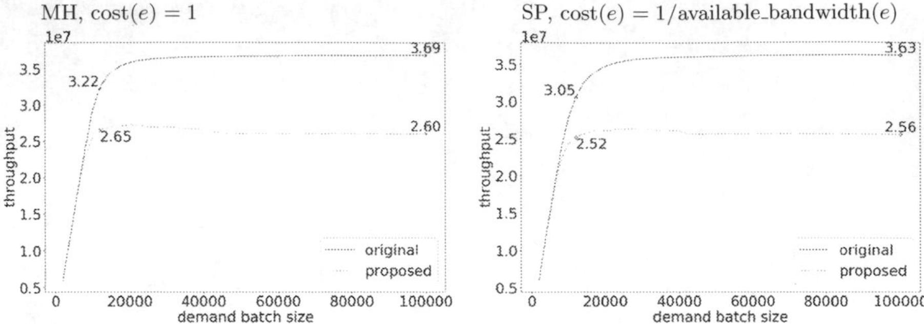

Fig. 7. Throughput on the flat graph

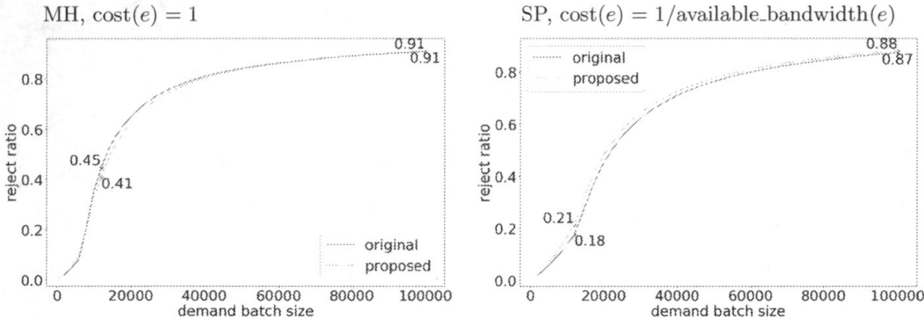

Fig. 8. Reject ratio on the ring graph

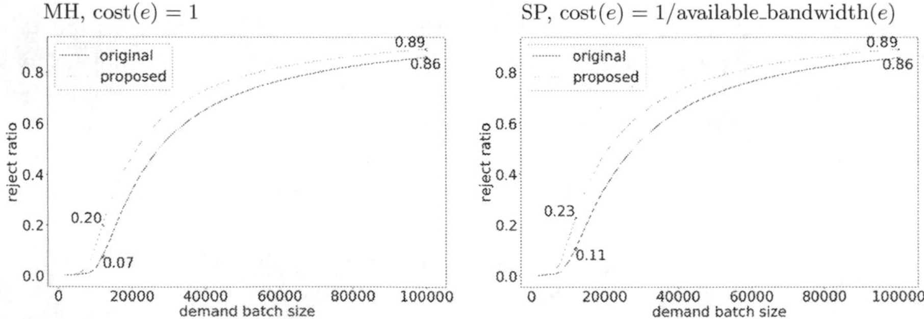

Fig. 9. Reject ratio on the flat graph

path in a small subgraph. But the path found is not always the global shortest feasible path. When the size of the request set is small, the bandwidth resource is sufficient whether the paths are optimal or not, so the quality of the solution sets are near on these two quality metrics. When the request set size is very large, the solution set consisting of suboptimal paths suffers. The proposed algorithm has a better performance on the ring graph because natural domains exist in the ring graph while not in the flat graph. Because the proposed algorithm assumes the subsets of nodes obtained by the graph partitioning algorithm making up domains. Although the proposed algorithm's solution qualities are slightly worse than the original ones in some circumstances in the figures, the original ones cannot get solution sets in time with a practical time limit while the proposed algorithm can.

5 Conclusion

We proposed an heuristic algorithm to figure out the subgraphs that requests really need to accelerate the bandwidth constrained routing algorithms. First we partition the graph. Then we build a quotient graph and map the request set onto it. After that we solve the request set on the quotient graph. Then we map the solution set to subgraphs of the original graph and solve the requests. At last we reroute those requests, which were accepted on the quotient graph but rejected on their corresponding subgraphs, on the entire original graph to get the final solution set.

For the batch bandwidth constrained routing problem with a large scale graph and a large request set, previous algorithms may fail to complete processing request sets in time, which leads to the unceasingly piling up of requests. Our algorithm enormously reduced the end-to-end running time to make the problem solving quick enough, saving proportionally up to 69% end-to-end running time in our experiments, while keeping a fine solution quality.

6 Further Discussion

Since we have figured out different subgraphs for different requests, it is possible that some subgraphs have no overlap with each other thus the corresponding requests can be solved on parallel without any risk of breaking links' bandwidth limits to save even more time.

Acknowledgments. This work was supported by the Ministry of Science and Technology of China (2017YFC0804003), Shenzhen Peacock Plan (Grant No. KQTD2016112514355531), the Natural Science Foundation of China (61672478), the Science and Technology Innovation Committee Foundation of Shenzhen (ZDSYS201703031748284), and the Royal Society Newton Advanced Fellowship (NA150123).

References

1. Apostolopoulos, G., Kama, S., Williams, D., Guerin, R., Orda, A., Przygienda, T.: QoS routing mechanisms and OSPF extensions. RFC 2676, RFC Editor, August 1999
2. Berde, P., et al.: ONOS: towards an open, distributed SDN OS. In: Proceedings of the Third Workshop on Hot Topics in Software Defined Networking, pp. 1–6. ACM (2014)

3. Boutaba, R., Szeto, W., Iraqi, Y.: DORA: efficient routing for MPLS traffic engineering. J. Netw. Syst. Manag. **10**(3), 309–325 (2002)
4. Buluç, A., Meyerhenke, H., Safro, I., Sanders, P., Schulz, C.: Recent advances in graph partitioning. In: Kliemann, L., Sanders, P. (eds.) Algorithm Engineering. LNCS, vol. 9220, pp. 117–158. Springer, Cham (2016). https://doi.org/10.1007/978-3-319-49487-6_4
5. Hassas Yeganeh, S., Ganjali, Y.: Kandoo: a framework for efficient and scalable offloading of control applications. In: Proceedings of the First Workshop on Hot Topics in Software Defined Networks, pp. 19–24. ACM (2012)
6. Kar, K., Kodialam, M., Lakshman, T.V.: Minimum interference routing of bandwidth guaranteed tunnels with mpls traffic engineering applications. IEEE J. Sel. Areas Commun. **18**(12), 2566–2579 (2000)
7. Koponen, T., et al.: Onix: a distributed control platform for large-scale production networks. In: OSDI, vol. 10, pp. 1–6 (2010)
8. Kreutz, D., Ramos, F.M., Verissimo, P.E., Rothenberg, C.E., Azodolmolky, S., Uhlig, S.: Software-defined networking: a comprehensive survey. Proc. IEEE **103**(1), 14–76 (2015)
9. Ma, Q., Steenkiste, P., Zhang, H.: Routing high-bandwidth traffic in max-min fair share networks. In: ACM SIGCOMM Computer Communication Review, vol. 26, pp. 206–217. ACM (1996)
10. Medina, A., Lakhina, A., Matta, I., Byers, J.: BRITE: an approach to universal topology generation. In: Proceedings of the Ninth International Symposium on Modeling, Analysis and Simulation of Computer and Telecommunication Systems, pp. 346–353. IEEE (2001)
11. Medved, J., Varga, R., Tkacik, A., Gray, K.: OpenDaylight: towards a model-driven SDN controller architecture. In: 2014 IEEE 15th International Symposium on a World of Wireless, Mobile and Multimedia Networks (WoWMoM), pp. 1–6. IEEE (2014)
12. Nippon Telegraph and Telephone Corporation: RYU Network Operating System (2012). http://osrg.github.com/ryu/. Accessed 11 Apr 2018
13. Project Floodlight: Floodlight (2012). http://www.projectfloodlight.org/floodlight/. Accessed 11 Apr 2018
14. Sanders, P., Schulz, C.: Think locally, act globally: highly balanced graph partitioning. In: Bonifaci, V., Demetrescu, C., Marchetti-Spaccamela, A. (eds.) SEA 2013. LNCS, vol. 7933, pp. 164–175. Springer, Heidelberg (2013). https://doi.org/10.1007/978-3-642-38527-8_16
15. Tootoonchian, A., Ganjali, Y.: HyperFlow: a distributed control plane for OpenFlow. In: Proceedings of the 2010 Internet Network Management Conference on Research on Enterprise Networking, p. 3 (2010)
16. Wang, Y., Wang, Z.: Explicit routing algorithms for internet traffic engineering. In: International Conference on Computer Communications and Networks, pp. 582–588. IEEE (1999)
17. Waxman, B.M.: Routing of multipoint connections. IEEE J. Sel. Areas Commun. **6**(9), 1617–1622 (1988)

3SP-Net: Semantic Segmentation Network with Stereo Image Pairs for Urban Scene Parsing

Lingli Zhou and Haofeng Zhang(✉)

School of Computer Science and Engineering, Nanjing University of Science and Technology, Nanjing, China
zhanghf@njust.edu.cn

Abstract. Image semantic segmentation has a wide range of applications, especially scene parsing. During the past several years, Convolutional Neural Networks (CNNs) have been shown to have a great potential in image semantic segmentation of scenes. However, due to the existence of invariance in CNN, images will lose structural details which are important to elaborate semantic segmentation results during the feature extraction stage. We are not committed to seeking methods to restore these hard-to-restore structural information, instead, we propose a novel method namely Semantic Segmentation Network with Stereo Image Pairs (3SP-Net), which utilise pairwised stereo images to generate segmentation results, and add an Adversarial Network (GAN) to make the generated maps more similar to the real ones. 3SP-Net computes a pair of left and right stereo features which provides additional information about the 3D structure of the physical environment to compensate for the loss of structural information in 2D images, to improve the performance of semantic segmentation. Furthermore, we adopt adversarial training to enhance the high-order consistency between results generated by the image semantic segmentation network and ground-truth segmentation maps. Experiments on Cityscapes show that the performances with the assistance of depth features can be improved greatly to the widely-used architectures such as Fully Convolutional Network (FCN) and DeepLab.

1 Introduction

Image classification, object detection and image semantic segmentation are three core research issues in computer vision. Among them, image semantic segmentation is most challenging, its task is to classify each pixel of images into several categories, so as to facilitate subsequent image analysis and visual understanding. Image semantic segmentation fuses two tasks of traditional image segmentation and target recognition, and the substantive goal of which is to classify and locate each pixel in images.

With the rapid development of deep learning, the field of computer vision also ushered in a wave of development. The deep neural network [29,30] has

X. Geng and B.-H. Kang (Eds.): PRICAI 2018, LNAI 11012, pp. 503–517, 2018.
https://doi.org/10.1007/978-3-319-97304-3_39

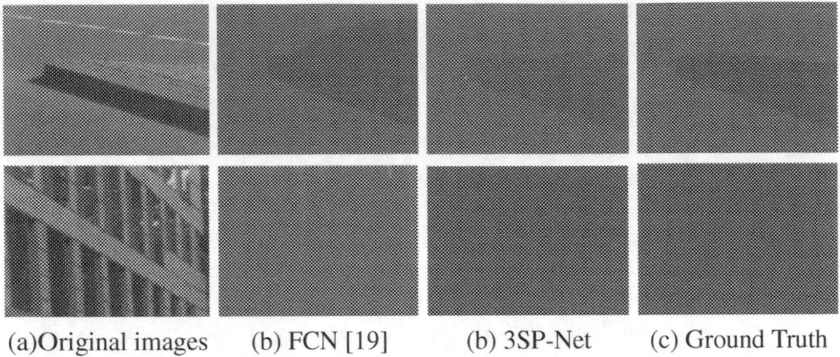

Fig. 1. Two kinds of typical errors produced by FCN-VGG on Cityscapes Dataset [7].

been proved to be an effective means in the field of computer vision. Convolutional Neural Network (CNN) is a kind of useful visual models, which can obtain the hierarchical structure of image features. By taking the best of location information from underlying structure and semantic information from high-rise structure, the researchers can not only improve the classification performance of the entire image, but also make progress in the localization task with structural output for image semantic segmentation. One of main problems in image semantic segmentation using CNN is the existence of down-sampling in image feature extraction. These operations, such as pooling, reduce the resolution of images, resulting in the loss of location information of images, as a result, the segmentations become less accurate. But pooling layers are necessary as they enlarge the receptive field of the upper convolution kernel and satisfy the invariance required in image classification. In order to make a precise adjustment to the score maps, some models have been proposed to save and restore lost structural information during the down-sampling process. Researchers have proposed two different forms of network architectures to solve this problem, one is the encoder-decoder structure [2,18,26], and the other is called dilated convolution or atrous convolution [3,33]. Although improved results has been obtained, these methods still have difficulties in segmenting details. From the segmentation results in conventional method such as Fully Convolutional Network (FCN) [19] based on VGGNet [29] in the first row of Fig. 1, we can find that the results at the boundary of two objects are inaccurate.

No matter how large the receptive field is, each pixel is predicted independently in the above methods. It is inevitable that it will bring some noises in the results as shown in the second row of Fig. 1. Moreover, due to the lack of constraints of CNN on space and edge information, the segmentation results can be relatively rough. To deal with this problem, some works exploited post-processing methods like fully-connected Conditional Random Fields (CRFs) [15] to recover object boundaries and enforce spatial-contiguity of output maps. Even though these methods can further optimize the segmentation results, a mount of parameters need to be learned, which lead to the increasing of computational complexity heavily.

Recent works [8,12,28] try to learn features from RGB-D images using CNNs. These features including more spatial characteristics contribute to semantic segmentation, but most of them attach the off-the-shelf depth data as the forth channel directly. Although depth is helpful to the segmentation, the previously designed feature extraction networks have to be changed with the direct usage of depth information.

In order to continue to maintain the original network architectures, as well as gain the benefit from depth to segmentation, we proposed a Semantic Segmentation Network with Stereo Image Pairs (3SP-Net), which attempts to improve the performance of semantic segmentation with the help of depth information. Stereo image pairs can construct 3D structural information about the physical structure of images, which is helpful to provide more structural information. Although our method need the usage of depth information, we do not destroy original representation learning networks for RGB images, and the depth information is calculated from RGB images easily, and plays the same role as depth images.

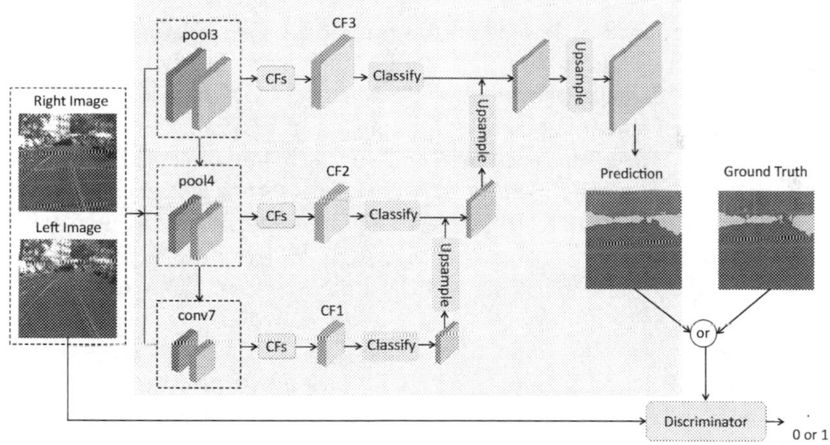

Fig. 2. The framework of our 3SP-Net based on FCN

Besides, inspired by the recent popular and effective Generative Adversarial Network (GAN) [11], we add an adversarial structure [11] follows the semantic segmentation generative network, which is then encouraged to generate finer segmentation maps. We applied the concept of depth guided training and GAN to several popular methods of semantic segmentation such as FCN and DeepLab, and the experimental results show that the modified network can outperform greatly the original ones. The framework of our 3SP-Net based on FCN is illustrated in Fig. 2. It is worthwhile to list the contributions of our work,

(1) We propose a novel Semantic Segmentation Network with Stereo Image Pairs (3SP-Net) as input for urban scene parsing, which utilise the depth feature to compensate for the short of structural information in traditional methods;
(2) In order to generate more accurate segmentation map, we adopt the concept of adversarial network to improve the performance of our method;
(3) The experiments on the popular city scene dataset shows that our method can significantly improve the performance of conventional methods, especially on some classes with small areas, such as pole or pedestrian.

The rest of this paper is organized as follows. In Sect. 2, we give a brief review of recent methods of Semantic Segmentation and Adversarial Learning. The details of our method is described in Sect. 3. Section 4 reports the experimental results of our method combined with several conventional methods, and analyses the performance by the influence of adversarial learning. Finally, we conclude this paper in Sect. 5.

2 Related Work

Semantic Segmentation. In this part, we review recent advances of CNNs in the image semantic segmentation task and some works involving depth. Since Long et al. first published the paper [19] in 2014, FCN has been adopted in almost all recent systems of semantic segmentation [4,10,14,34]. The proposed structure of FCN makes the segmentation input to an image of any size, as well as improves the processing speed compared with the classification methods [10,14] based on image block. In order to enlarge the receptive field without reducing the resolution of the image, the paper [33] proposed the concept of dilated convolution for the first time, and DeepLab [3–5] of Chen et al. also used dilated convolution. DeepLab proved that dilated convolution is very effective in image semantic segmentation. Apart from DeepLab, PSPNet [34] is also based on dilated convolution. Its most important contribution is exploiting the capability of the pyramid pooling module to aggregate local and global context information based on different regions. Contextual content of different ranges together makes the final prediction more reliable. Our baseline networks are FCN, DeepLab Network and PSPNet [4,19,34].

In addition to the above considerations, many other structures can ameliorate semantic segmentation results from the point of localization ability of scene parsing. One line is to deal with the existence of multi-scale objects, including using multi-scale images [6,24] or convolutional features at multiply scales [4,19]. Another direction is to seek mathematical means to improve the performance of the final result [3,15]. The most representative of them is fully-connected Conditional Random Fields [3]. However, these post-processing method is completely separated from the CNN, they just use the result of CNNs as unitary potential function. Another is to put CRF and FCN together to form a model of end-to-end training [30]. Although the models can further enhance the performance of segmentation, there are still many details need to be improved.

Depth information helps to understand geometric information of the scene images. RGB images combined with location information provided by depth can achieve complementary effect, and some progress has been made in tasks of scene labeling, object recognition [35], and stereo estimation. With more and more data sets providing depth for images, there is an increasing number in applying depth to the image semantic segmentation task these years [12,13]. Recently, some methods [8,13] learned the features of the 3D scene from RGB-D images for segmentation using deep learning. Lin et al. [17] think other works did not make the best of useful information from the depth channel, therefore they presented a better method of learning features with RGB-D images. But the relationship between RGB information and depth is difficult to capture, moreover, RGB information plays a more important role in semantic segmentation task than depth information. In our scenario, we just adopt depth as condition to play a guiding role in the network structure.

Adversarial Learning. The GAN is a generative model [11] proposed by Goodfellow. The core idea of GAN comes from the Nash equilibrium of game theory. The theory sets the participants to be a generator and a discriminator. The former captures the potential distribution of real data samples and generates new data samples; the latter discriminates whether the input is the real data or the generated sample. In order to win the game, these two game participants need to constantly improve their generative ability and discriminative ability respectively. This optimization process is to find a Nash equilibrium between the two players. Early GAN models [22,25,27] are mainly used in unsupervised learning tasks, which is to generate data with the same distribution as the real data samples. The work [32] of Tarlow and Zemel suggested to learn with higher-order loss terms which are not included in the generative model. Higher-order loss terms can correct CNN-induced errors by reducing the CNN performance. Inspired by [23,31,32], the paper [20] applied adversarial training to semantic segmentation firstly. It optimized an objective function in the respect of the high-order consistency between generated label maps and ground truth label maps. By enforcing long-range spatial label contiguity of generated label maps, segmentation model will produce results closer to ground-truth that cannot be distinguished by a binary classification model. We also design a discriminative network to predict the possibility of the input label to be ground truth. Its field-of-view is the entire input image, so the discriminative loss can penalty the mismatch considered from the perspective of high-order consistency. For the loss of the segmentation model, we will add an adversarial loss term which degrades the performance of the discriminative network but improve its own performance.

3 Methodology

We elaborate our general framework for 3SP-Net in Sects. 3.1 and 3.2. First, we combine RGB features with depth features calculated from the former and send the hybrid information to the classifier. Then preliminary results will be further optimized through adversarial training. We explain how to conduct adversarial training in Sect. 3.3. We describe three architectures used in our experiments in Sect. 3.4.

3.1 Combine RGB Features and Depth Features

We hold that in the image segmentation task, the dominant role should be RGB information, and depth information only plays a guiding role. For example, when two pixels in the boundary of the objects have similar features and their 2D positions are adjacent, their depth can help to distinguish and make a correct judgment. Therefore 3SP-Net just adds depth information before the final score layer, rather than uses the depth information from the beginning of the network. At this point, the features of the RGB images have been extracted, we refer to the method of calculating disparity using the left and right RGB features in the paper [21] and concatenating the depth information with the RGB features to get final results.

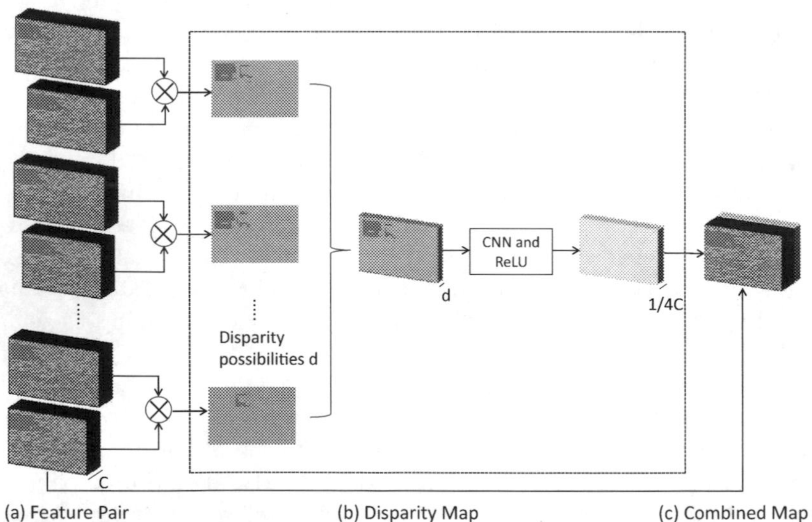

Fig. 3. The details of Combination of RGB Features and Depth Features (CFs) block. The right feature map need to be appropriately larger in order to calculate disparity of each pixel in the left image.

3SP-Net converts an existing semantic segmentation network into an siamese network, whose two branches share the parameters. Each branch processes the left and right image respectively to get their corresponding representation, and then the disparity of each pixel in the left feature map can obtained. According to [21], we treat the problem of calculating disparity map as multi-class classification, where the classes are all possible disparities. Given a pair of left and right features, we calculate its disparity with d possibilities by calculating respectively its inner products with d pixels which have location from (x, y) to $(x - d, y)$ in the right feature map for a pixel which has location (x, y) in the left feature map. The resulting matching scores for all pixels in the left feature maps make up a 3-dimensional cost volume, namely a disparity map. We refer the reader to Fig. 3 for more details. In the actual experiment, the corresponding right image need to be appropriately larger in order to calculate disparity of each pixel in the left image.

Next, we fuse the two types of features. As mentioned before, depth information only plays a guiding role, while at the same time, we can't let the RGB information dominate the depth information excessively. So before combination of the two maps, we convert the number of the latter channels through convolution operations to a certain proportion β of the number of the RGB feature map channels. In this illustration, we choose the proportion β as 1/4 for an example. Then the disparity map after convolution is cascaded with the RGB feature map. Specially, it is preferred to normalize each individual feature before cascading, which makes training more stable and improves the segmentation performance. Finally, we use the combined feature map to learn the classifier.

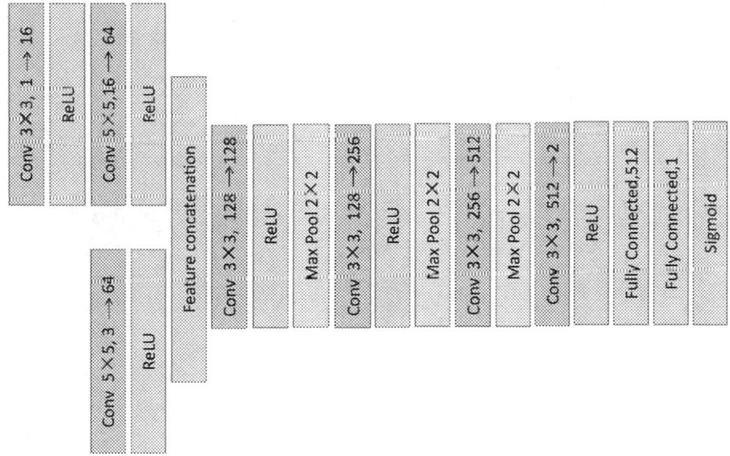

Fig. 4. Summary of the architecture used for the discriminative network. The up and down branches process respectively the label map and the RGB image.

3.2 Discriminative Network

In order to conduct adversarial training, we need to design a discriminative network, which discriminates whether the input is a generated label map or a ground-truth label map. It has two inputs for the discriminative network. One is a label map to be judged; the other is the corresponding RGB image, which provides a matching reference. In [20], the label maps to input are multi-channel, but this kind of inputs potentially gives discriminative network information that can help to distinguish between generated label maps (consist of zeros and ones) and ground-truth label maps (values between zero and one), even authors provided methods to deal with the problem. So we feed the label maps with one channel representing classification of each pixel to avoid this potential identification information to the discriminative network. As shown in Fig. 4, the up and down branch processes respectively the label map and the RGB image. Both inputs need to do some convolutional operations before concatenation, so as that they have equal status with 64 channels. Then the fused signals are passed into stack of convolutional layers and fully connected layers, after which we can get the binary class probability of the label map by a sigmoid activation. Since the discriminative network has a field-of-view of the entire image, the loss of it can punish mismatches from the point of higher-order consistency.

3.3 Adversarial Training

We alternately train two networks, where we minimize the loss with regard to the parameters θ_g of the segmentation network while maximizing it w.r.t the parameters θ_d of the discriminative network. We utilise the back-propagation (BP) algorithm to minimize losses of the two networks. Given N training images, we define the loss functions for the two networks respectively. In the following formulas, $g(x_n)$ denotes the generated result of image x_n and y_n denotes the corresponding ground-truth annotation.

Training the Discriminative Model. We use $d(x, y) \in [0, 1]$ to denote the scalar probability with which the discriminative network predicts that y is the ground-truth label map of x. The loss of the discriminative network is defined as

$$\mathcal{L}(\theta_d) = \sum_{i=0}^{N} \mathcal{L}_b(d(x_n, y_n), 1) + \mathcal{L}_b(d(x_n, g(x_n)), 0), \tag{1}$$

where $\mathcal{L}_b(z, \hat{z}) = -[zlog\hat{z} + (1 - z)log(1 - \hat{z})]$ denotes the binary cross-entropy loss. In the experiment, we add a minimum value to each value before making log calculation for this value, so as to avoid data overflow like $log0$. We describe the discriminative network's architecture in Sect. 3.2 above.

Training the Segmentative Model. Given the discriminative network, apart from the multi-class cross-entropy loss $\mathcal{L}_m(g(x_n), y_n)$ for the prediction of each pixel, we need to adjust the loss function by adding another loss term for the generative model. This second loss term encourages the segmentation network to generate results that confused by the discriminative network, namely to degrade the performance of the discriminative model. The objective function for adversarial training in the segmentation network is

$$\mathcal{L}(\theta_g) = \sum_{i=0}^{N} \mathcal{L}_m(g(x_n), y_n) + \alpha\mathcal{L}_b(d(x_n, g(x_n)), 1). \tag{2}$$

We replace the term $-\alpha\mathcal{L}_b(d(x_n, g(x_n)), 0)$ with $+\alpha\mathcal{L}_b(d(x_n, g(x_n)), 1)$ following [20], with which we minimize the probability of $g(x_n)$ to be synthetic label map for x_n in the segmentation network. The smaller second loss term means it is more difficult to distinguish the generated label maps from the ground-truth ones for the discriminative network, thus, the resulting segmentation label maps are optimized for higher-order consistency.

3.4 Network Architectures

We now detail the architecture of 3SP-Net based on FCN [19] as an example. Besides, we can also apply our method to other semantic segmentation networks such as DeepLab and PSPNet [4,34].

3SP-Net Based on FCN. FCN replaced all fully connected layers with convolutional layers so as to accept an arbitrary-size image as input and achieve end-to-end learning. Authors of FCN picked the VGG 16-layer net for the experiment, whose feature layers encode images in a nonlinear local-global pyramid form. To balance classification and location, a skip structure is designed, which takes advantage of the feature spectrum to combine deep and rough semantic information with subtle and superficial appearance information.

Figure 2 explains how we apply our method to FCN. We experiment directly with the final version FCN-8s. We follow its skip structure while adding our depth information. For conv7, pool3, pool4 layers of left images, we calculate their disparity maps and cascade them with the left feature maps to get CF1, CF2, CF3 respectively (see Fig. 3). After getting three combined features, we add three 1×1 convolutional layers on them to produce corresponding class predictions. Until now, we get three score layers under the guidance of depth information which have 8, 16, 32 pixel stride respectively. Then we fuse these outputs by using skip connection. We fuse the predictions of the CF1 with the predictions computed from CF2 by adding a $2\times$ deconvolution layer on the former to unite the dimension of two predictions. Again, the stride 16 predictions are upsampled to fuse with the output of CF3. At this point our fusion has stride 8, so we upsample it back to the size of the left image. After further optimizing the results through adversarial training, our method improves the performance on Cityscapes testing set by 2.18 to 94.75 and 0.9 to 63.69 in terms of pixel accuracy and mIOU. More experimental results are presented in Sect. 5.

3SP-Net Based on DeepLab. We carry out experiments on DeepLab of Chen et al. [4] based on ResNet50 [18]. The paper used atrous convolution, which has the ability to enlarge the receptive field without increasing the number of parameters, while controlling the resolution of features. We add depth information to the network by combing the last left features with disparity features calculated from Res-3 layers. ResNet has very deep layers but the error will increase as the network deepening. We choose the left and right features of Res-3 layer to calculate disparity, because, on the one hand, it has a relatively small error; on the other hand, it has the same resolution as the last feature map so we need not to upsample it before cascading them. We finally upsample the predictions to the original image size.

3SP-Net Based on PSPNet. PSPNet [34] is another network that is widely used for semantic segmentation. Its greatest contribution is exploiting global and local context information to enhance the contextual awareness of each pixel. We use PSPNet based on ResNet50 [4] as our baseline. The disparity map is also calculated from the features of Res-3 layer and we cascade the depth information with the last RGB features of the left image to carry out the next classification.

4 Experiments

Dataset and Evaluate Metrics. Cityscapes Dataset [7] is a dataset tailored for autonomous driving in an urban environment. It is comprised of a large, diverse set of images annotated for pixel-level labeling and these images are recorded in streets from 50 different cities in different seasons. 5000 of these images have high quality pixel-level annotations; 20000 additional images have coarse annotations. In our experiments, we only use 5000 finely annotated images for experimental comparison. Among the 5000 finely annotated images, there are 3475 for training, 500 for validation and 1525 for testing. Specially, Cityscapes provides the right images corresponding to all the left images which are vital to our method. There are 34 visual classes for annotation, which are grouped into eight categories, but only 19 classes are included in the assessment. Cityscapes also includes a benchmark suite, its two main indicators are the PASCAL VOC intersection-over-union metric IOU [9] and the instance-level intersection-over-union metric iIoU [7]. In addition to the two indicators of IOU and iIOU, we add pixel accuracy as a standard for the evaluation of the experiments jointly.

Implementation Details. Our implementation is based on the public deep learning system TensorFlow [1]. We use "exponential decay" learning rate policy to control speed of parameter update where current learning rate equals to $l_{rate} * d_{rate}^{(g_{step}/d_{step})}$. Among them, l_{rate} is base learning rate, d_{rate} is attenuation coeffcient and d_{step} is attenuation velocity. The poly can let us approach the better solution in the early stage of training while ensuring that the solution will not fluctuate much later in the training, so that the ultimate result is closer to the local optimal solution. We set l_{rate}, d_{rate}, d_{step} to 0.01, 0.96 and 5000 respectively. We choose the Adam optimizer and carry on multiple iterations for improving performance. A random crop is sampled from an original image randomly, with the per-pixel mean subtracted for training. According to [34], the "cropsize" should be as large as possible. Due to limited physical memory of GPU, we set "batchsize" to 4 during training. Dropout is included in each network to resist overfitting. For networks based on Resnet [18], we normalize both features before the combination of them. We train the base classification nets from scratch and restore part of parameters to 3SP-Net. Then we fine-tune all layers of these networks by back propagation through the whole net. In order to get corresponding disparity for each pixel in left images during the testing phase and considering the limited GPU memory, we refer to the test method in [16]. We extract five large patches (the center patch and the four corner patches) to make predictions for each image in the testing set.

4.1 Results of 3SP-Net Based on FCN

Ablation Study for Combing Features. To evaluate the effectiveness of our method, we conduct contrast experiments based on FCN [19] with several settings firstly. The trade-off weight β has a very important influence on the results of the segmentation. If this value is too large, depth information will interference the effect of RGB information on classification. But too small of it will make depth information unable to play its guiding role. We experiment with setting the weight β 1/3, 3/10, 1/4 and 1/5 and we show the results in Table 1. Comparing the results in the table, $\beta = 1/4$ works better than other settings, and the best setting yields results 93.67/62.87/43.48 in terms of Pixel Acc.(%), mIOU(%) and iIOU(%) on Cityscapes validation set. We believe suitable value of β will benefit performance. Our method of using depth to guide segmentation outperforms the baseline FCN [19] of 92.95/61.29/42.38 by 0.75/1.58/1.1 in terms of absolute improvement.

Table 1. Setting an appropriate trade-off weight β during combing two types of features is important. Empirically, $\beta = 1/4$ yields the best performance. The results are tested on Cityscapes validation set based on FCN.

Method	Pixel Acc.(%)	mIoU(%)	iIoU(%)
FCN	92.95	61.29	42.38
FCN + Depth ($\beta = 1/3$)	92.67	55.22	40.02
FCN + Depth ($\beta = 3/10$)	93.54	62.50	**43.49**
FCN + Depth ($\beta = 1/4$)	**93.67**	**62.87**	43.48
FCN + Depth ($\beta = 1/5$)	92.87	60.96	42.50

Ablation Study for Adversarial Training. We set trade-off weight $\alpha = 0.2$ for the loss of the segmentative model. In order to ensure that the discriminative loss is meaningful, we pre-train the discriminative network about 30k before using the adversarial loss to fine-tune the segmentation network. Then we alternately train the generative network and the discriminative network after every 500 iterations of each. Statistics in Table 2 show the comparisons of our 3SP-Net based on FCN with or without adversarial training on Cityscapes testing set. Only using depth information, our result exceeds FCN by 1.08/0.48/0.35 and reaches 93.65/63.27/44.06 in terms of Pixel Acc.(%), mIOU(%) and iIOU(%). Using the adversarial training can further improve performance by 1.1/0.42 and reaches 94.75/63.69 in terms of Pixel Acc. and mIOU. Detailed per-class results

Table 2. Comparison results on Cityscapes testing set with baseline FCN.

Method	Pixel Acc.(%)	mIoU(%)	iIoU(%)
FCN	92.57	62.79	43.71
3SP-Net w/o AT	93.65	63.27	**44.06**
3SP-Net w/ AT	**94.75**	**63.69**	43.81

Table 3. Per-class results on Cityscapes testing set of contrast experiments with baseline FCN

Model	Road(%)	Swalk(%)	Build.(%)	Wall(%)	Fence(%)	Pole(%)	Tlight(%)	Sign(%)	Veg.(%)
FCN	96.01	72.42	85.12	32.74	40.44	45.87	51.97	61.41	87.88
3SP-Net w/o AT	96.05	72.51	85.52	**34.16**	41.81	47.24	51.79	62.52	87.80
3SP-Net w/ AT	**96.36**	**73.44**	**85.97**	33.79	**42.15**	**48.18**	**52.20**	**63.17**	**88.01**
Terrain(%)	Sky(%)	Person(%)	Rider(%)	Car(%)	Truck(%)	Bus(%)	Train(%)	Mbike(%)	Bike(%)
56.80	91.46	72.85	43.91	**90.69**	50.04	51.66	50.76	41.80	69.14
55.92	91.39	74.56	44.82	90.08	50.69	52.48	**51.97**	41.12	69.76
56.84	**91.88**	**74.97**	**45.92**	90.41	**51.00**	**53.04**	51.12	**41.88**	**70.83**

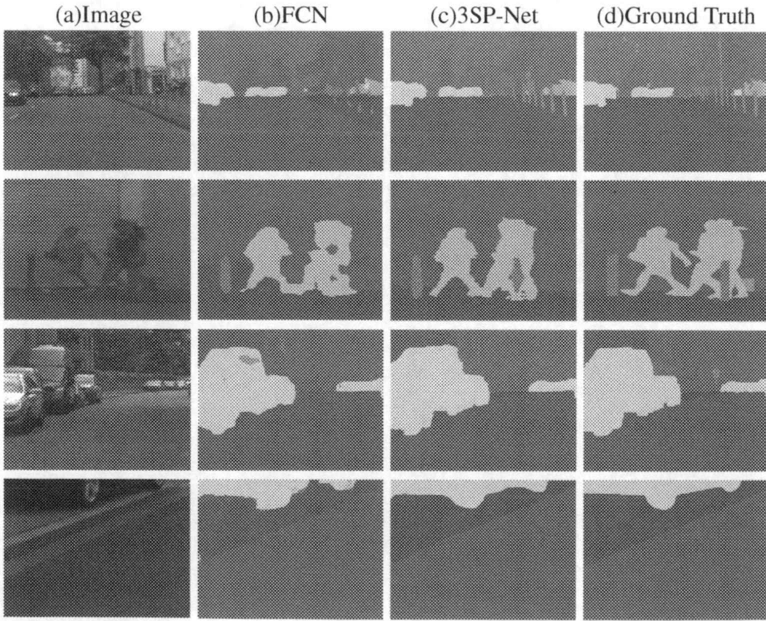

Fig. 5. Visual improvements on Cityscapes validation set. For every row we list input image (a), the baseline FCN (b), 3SP-Net (c), and Ground Truth (d)

of IOU are shown in Table 3, 18 of 19 classes get promoted in terms of IOU compared with FCN.

Visual Performance Analysis. Figure 5 shows few qualitative comparisons on the validation set. We can see that pieces have been significantly improved including poles, pedestrians owing to depth information providing more guiding role and the noises in the scenes are effectively removed in the last two rows of Fig. 5. The qualitative results indicate that our method can refine boundary segmentation results as well as smooth parts of noises in FCN, so 3SP-Net produces more detailed and accurate segmentation results.

4.2 Results of 3SP-Net Based on Other Networks

Our method also works satisfyingly on DeepLab and PSPNet [4,34]. Table 4 shows 3SP-Net with adversarial training can outperform the baseline DeepLab50 with approving advantage on Cityscapes testing set. For the baseline, we obtain 84.14/37.54/30.69 in terms of Pixel Acc.(%), mIOU(%) and iIOU(%), while for 3SP-Net with adversarial training we obtain 86.35/39.61/32.07 respectively. Results of 3SP-Net based on PSPNet50 are shown in Table 5, which confirm that our proposed method is also applicable to PSPNet.

Table 4. Comparison results on Cityscapes testing set with baseline DeepLab50.

Model	Pixel Acc.(%)	mIOU(%)	iIOU(%)
DeepLab50	84.14	37.54	30.69
3SP-Net w/o AT	85.70	38.84	31.72
3SP-Net w/ AT	**86.35**	**39.61**	**32.07**

Table 5. Comparison results on Cityscapes testing set with baseline PSPNet50.

Model	Pixel Acc.(%)	mIOU(%)	iIOU(%)
PSPNet50	85.45	43.83	35.02
3SP-Net w/o AT	88.61	44.80	**36.93**
3SP-Net w/ AT	**89.00**	**45.18**	35.09

5 Conclusions

We have proposed an effective architecture 3SP-Net to improve performances of semantic segmentation networks. We do not use depth images directly to avoid hand-crafted operations so that we can achieve end-to-end training. Our method for calculating disparity maps is simple and effective, which provide more structural information to guide the segmentation. Preliminary results for the segmentation can be further optimized through adversarial training by increasing high-order consistency. Our experimental results show that our method can significantly advance the widely-used semantic segmentation networks, including FCN, DeepLab and PSPNet.

Acknowledgement. This work was supported in part by the Key Research and Development Plan of Jiangsu Province (BE2015162) and the Major Special Project of Core Electronic Devices, Highend Generic Chips and Basic Software (2015ZX01041101). We are thankful to Haofeng Zhang for proofreading the paper and his helpful comments.

References

1. Abadi, M., et al.: TensorFlow: a system for large-scale machine learning (2016)
2. Badrinarayanan, V., Kendall, A., Cipolla, R.: SegNet: a deep convolutional encoder-decoder architecture for image segmentation. PAMI **39**(12), 2481–2495 (2017)
3. Chen, L.C., Papandreou, G., Kokkinos, I., Murphy, K., Yuille, A.L.: Semantic image segmentation with deep convolutional nets and fully connected CRFs. Comput. Sci. **4**, 357–361 (2014)
4. Chen, L.C., Papandreou, G., Kokkinos, I., Murphy, K., Yuille, A.L.: Deeplab: Semantic image segmentation with deep convolutional nets, atrous convolution, and fully connected CRFs. PAMI **PP**(99), 1 (2018)
5. Chen, L.C., Papandreou, G., Schroff, F., Adam, H.: Rethinking atrous convolution for semantic image segmentation. arXiv preprint arXiv:1706.05587 (2017)
6. Chen, L.C., Yang, Y., Wang, J., Xu, W., Yuille, A.L.: Attention to scale: Scale-aware semantic image segmentation. In: CVPR, pp. 3640–3649 (2016)
7. Cordts, M., et al.: The cityscapes dataset for semantic urban scene understanding. In: CVPR, pp. 3213–3223 (2016)
8. Couprie, C., Farabet, C., Najman, L., LeCun, Y.: Indoor semantic segmentation using depth information. arXiv preprint arXiv:1301.3572 (2013)
9. Everingham, M., Eslami, S.M.A., Gool, L.V., Williams, C.K.I., Winn, J., Zisserman, A.: The pascal visual object classes challenge: a retrospective. Int. J. Comput. Vis. **111**(1), 98–136 (2015)
10. Girshick, R., Donahue, J., Darrell, T., Malik, J.: Rich feature hierarchies for accurate object detection and semantic segmentation. In: CVPR, pp. 580–587 (2014)
11. Goodfellow, I.J., et al.: Generative adversarial nets. In: ICONIP, pp. 2672–2680 (2014)
12. Gupta, S., Arbelaez, P., Malik, J.: Perceptual organization and recognition of indoor scenes from RGB-d images. In: CVPR, pp. 564–571. IEEE (2013)
13. Gupta, S., Girshick, R., Arbeláez, P., Malik, J.: Learning rich features from RGB-D images for object detection and segmentation. In: Fleet, D., Pajdla, T., Schiele, B., Tuytelaars, T. (eds.) ECCV 2014. LNCS, vol. 8695, pp. 345–360. Springer, Cham (2014). https://doi.org/10.1007/978-3-319-10584-0_23
14. Hariharan, B., Arbeláez, P., Girshick, R., Malik, J.: Simultaneous detection and segmentation. In: Fleet, D., Pajdla, T., Schiele, B., Tuytelaars, T. (eds.) ECCV 2014. LNCS, vol. 8695, pp. 297–312. Springer, Cham (2014). https://doi.org/10.1007/978-3-319-10584-0_20

15. Krähenbühl, P., Koltun, V.: Efficient inference in fully connected CRFs with gaussian edge potentials. In: Advances in Neural Information Processing Systems, pp. 109–117 (2011)
16. Krizhevsky, A., Sutskever, I., Hinton, G.E.: Imagenet classification with deep convolutional neural networks. In: ICONIP, pp. 1097–1105 (2012)
17. Lin, D., Chen, G., Cohen-Or, D., Heng, P.A., Huang, H.: Cascaded feature network for semantic segmentation of RGB-d images. In: ICCV, pp. 1320–1328 (2017)
18. Lin, G., Milan, A., Shen, C., Reid, I.: Refinenet: multi-path refinement networks for high-resolution semantic segmentation (2016)
19. Long, J., Shelhamer, E., Darrell, T.: Fully convolutional networks for semantic segmentation. In: CVPR, pp. 3431–3440 (2015)
20. Luc, P., Couprie, C., Chintala, S., Verbeek, J.: Semantic segmentation using adversarial networks (2016)
21. Luo, W., Schwing, A.G., Urtasun, R.: Efficient deep learning for stereo matching. In: CVPR, pp. 5695–5703 (2016)
22. Mirza, M., Osindero, S.: Conditional generative adversarial nets. arXiv preprint arXiv:1411.1784 (2014)
23. Nguyen, A., Yosinski, J., Clune, J.: Deep neural networks are easily fooled: high confidence predictions for unrecognizable images, pp. 427–436 (2014)
24. Papandreou, G., Kokkinos, I., Savalle, P.A.: Modeling local and global deformations in deep learning: epitomic convolution, multiple instance learning, and sliding window detection. In: CVPR, pp. 390–399. IEEE (2015)
25. Radford, A., Metz, L., Chintala, S.: Unsupervised representation learning with deep convolutional generative adversarial networks. arXiv preprint arXiv:1511.06434 (2015)
26. Ronneberger, O., Fischer, P., Brox, T.: U-Net: convolutional networks for biomedical image segmentation. In: Navab, N., Hornegger, J., Wells, W.M., Frangi, A.F. (eds.) MICCAI 2015. LNCS, vol. 9351, pp. 234–241. Springer, Cham (2015). https://doi.org/10.1007/978-3-319-24574-4_28
27. Salimans, T., Goodfellow, I., Zaremba, W., Cheung, V., Radford, A., Chen, X.: Improved techniques for training gans. In: Advances in Neural Information Processing Systems, pp. 2234–2242 (2016)
28. Schwarz, M., Schulz, H., Behnke, S.: RGB-D object recognition and pose estimation based on pre-trained convolutional neural network features. In: ICRA, pp. 1329–1335. IEEE (2015)
29. Simonyan, K., Zisserman, A.: Very deep convolutional networks for large-scale image recognition. arXiv preprint arXiv:1409.1556 (2014)
30. Szegedy, C., et al.: Going deeper with convolutions. In: CVPR, pp. 1–9 (2015)
31. Szegedy, C., et al.: Intriguing properties of neural networks. arXiv preprint arXiv:1312.6199 (2013)
32. Tarlow, D., Zemel, R.: Structured output learning with high order loss functions. In: Artificial Intelligence and Statistics, pp. 1212–1220 (2012)
33. Yu, F., Koltun, V.: Multi-scale context aggregation by dilated convolutions. arXiv preprint arXiv:1511.07122 (2015)
34. Zhao, H., Shi, J., Qi, X., Wang, X., Jia, J.: Pyramid scene parsing network. In: CVPR, pp. 2881–2890 (2017)
35. Zia, S., Yüksel, B., Yüret, D., Yemez, Y.: RGB-D object recognition using deep convolutional neural networks. In: CVPR, pp. 896–903 (2017)

An Interactivity-Based Personalized Mutual Reinforcement Model for Microblog Topic Summarization

Lu Zhang[1,2], Liangjun Zang[1(✉)], Longtao Huang[1], Jizhong Han[1], and Songlin Hu[1,2]

[1] Institute of Information Engineering, Chinese Academy of Sciences, Beijing 100093, China
{zhanglu, zangliangjun, huanglongtao, hanjizhong, husonglin}@iie.ac.cn

[2] School of Cyber Security, University of Chinese Academy of Sciences, Beijing 100049, China

Abstract. Microblog topic summarization aims to provide readers with a concise and representative set of high-quality messages for efficient digestion. Unlike previous traditional text summarization, microblog posts are companied by user interactive behaviors such as thumbs-ups, comments and retweets. Intuitively, messages with more social influence are more important and should have higher probability to be included in the summary. We proposed a two-stage approach to solve microblog topic summarization problem, named Interactivity based Personalized Mutual Reinforcement Model (IPMR Model). Firstly, we extract keywords from all posts of a given topic and then collect relevant sentences which contain keywords as candidates. Secondly, we rank candidate sentences using a mutual reinforcement model based on interactivity statistics with keywords. We conducted a series of experiments on a corpus of microblog posts from five topics, and used Rouge-N as evaluation metric. Experimental results show that our model achieves the best overall performance consistently when compared with several state-of-the-art models.

Keywords: Microblog topic summarization · Social interactivity
Keywords extraction · Mutual reinforcement model

1 Introduction

Microblogging is one of the most popular social entertainment applications in recent years. The most representative examples may be *Twitter* (English) and *Sina Weibo* (Chinese). Taking *Sina Weibo* for example, according to accounting data of December 2017, it had 392 million active users per month.[1] People use microblog platform to interact with their favorite stars, share happiness of their lives and so on. *Microblog Topic* is the most popular item among various services, where users express and share

[1] See http://tech.sina.com.cn/i/2018-02-13/doc-ifyrmfmc2341675.shtml.

X. Geng and B.-H. Kang (Eds.): PRICAI 2018, LNAI 11012, pp. 518–530, 2018.
https://doi.org/10.1007/978-3-319-97304-3_40

their views on a topic by adding the corresponding hashtag to posts. Each topic has a separate page clustering posts with the same hashtag.

However, as there are many blog users and posting is convenient, the number of posts under hot topics is usually huge and posts quality is low. Thus a nice summary is needed to provide readers with representative messages for efficient digestion. To solve this problem, Chinese *Sina Weibo* has set up the '*elite posts*' page under each topic managed by human hosts. However the selection and maintenance of '*elite posts*' is a time-consuming job and may be subjective, which motivate researchers to study various methods to rank and select salient and diversified messages as a summary of each topic.

Recently researchers began to study on microblog topic summarization in Chinese. But it has many difficulties which are different from tweets, such as lack of public available large-scale datasets and so on. A notable work is CMiner [1] proposed in 2016, which aims at topic opinion targets extraction and summarization for Chinese microblog topics. However, it does not consider the '*interactivity*' characteristic of microblog messages, indicated by thumbs-ups, comments, and retweets. These attributes are also influential factors in determining whether a post or a sentence should be included in a summary.

We argue that a good summary should contain important sentences that satisfy the following conditions. Firstly, important sentences should be representative and central, i.e. being similar in content to many other sentences from the same topic. Secondly, important sentences should have more social influence, i.e. having more thumbs-ups, comments and retweets.

Our model is based on the Mutual Reinforcement Model [1, 2] by developing it with personalized 'interactivity' attribute of each microblog message, so we call it *I*nteractivity-based *P*ersonalized *M*utual *R*einforcement (IPMR) Model. Summaries are generated in two steps. Firstly, keywords are extracted from posts under a certain topic, and all sentences which contain at least one keyword are selected as candidates. Secondly, all candidate sentences and keywords are ranked simultaneously according to the IPMR model, where we assign the initial weight and jump probability of each sentence based on its interactivity. Finally, we choose top sentences to form a summary. We evaluate automatically generated summaries by Rouge-N metric against the 'elite posts' selected by human hosts of each topic. Compared with four other state-of-the–art models, experimental results show that our model performs best.

Our contributions are listed as follows:

(1) To the best of our knowledge, there is rare work about integrating 'interactivity' information into the task of microblog topic summarization.
(2) We propose an Interactivity-based Personalized Mutual Reinforcement model for Chinese microblog topic summarization, which does not require any manually labeled data.
(3) We show experimentally that the interactivity information of messages improves the quality of summaries greatly.

2 Related Work

2.1 Traditional Text Summarization

Researches of automatic text summarization have developed over fifty years with a mature system. These methods are divided into three types, extractive summarization, compressed summarization and abstractive summarization. Extractive summarization focuses on extracting salient sentences from original documents to form a summary. Abstractive summarization tends to generate each word automatically after training process. Compressed summarization is a compromise between the above two.

Early summarization generation methods are almost extractive, therefore extractive summarization system is the most complete one and its experimental results are also the best. Early algorithms select sentences based on some certain features by using unsupervised and supervised methods, called as feature-based methods. These features contain content word frequency [3], sentence position, named entities and so on. The task of selecting important sentences can also be seen as a classification problem, therefore many machine learning methods are utilized subsequently. For example, Markov models [4], conditional random fields [5] and so on.

Afterwards, some graph-based methods were proposed. The underlying assumption is that central sentences are more important as they carrying much information. Researchers defined central sentences as those which are more similar to other sentences. Typical ones are the LexRank algorithm [6] and the TextRank algorithm [7]. During this period, many other graph-based methods had been investigated. Zha [8] used mutual reinforcement principle to extract keyphrase and generate summaries simultaneously. Its theory is similar to the HITS algorithm [9] with a transition matrix between sentences and words. Wan et al. [2] developed [8] by adding the matrix between sentences and the other matrix between words in the same task. Its theory seems like the combination of PageRank [10] and HITS algorithm.

With the rapid growth of neural networks, there are more and more researches on abstractive summarization. In addition, abstractive summarization is more similar to the way that people writing summaries. Rush et al. [11] applied Convolutional Neural Network to the task of sentence-level summarization with a Neural Attention Model. Nallapati et al. [12] used sequence-to-sequence Recurrent Neural Networks model to address critical problems in summarization. However, it should be noted that abstractive summarization mainly focuses on headline generation of short texts. As the task is more difficult and neural network has just developed for a short time, there is still much room for improvement, such as readability, time complexity and so on. There is a survey of recent advances in document summarization from 2012 to 2017 by Yao et al. [13], besides latest approaches, it also forecasts the possible directions of future development.

2.2 Microblog Summarization

In recent years, the field of text summarization has changed dramatically. With the advent of the WEB 2.0 era, the need for summaries has gradually shifted to cyberspace texts. For example, summarization for products reviews on some websites [14], summarization for the Weibo blog posts and so on. When solving these new problems, extractive summarization methods are widely used.

Weng et al. [15] integrated posts and responses into the training model. It is a two-step scheme, classifying posts with responses into five classes, then applying different strategies to generate summaries for different classes, such as opinion analysis, response relevancy and so on. Bora [16] proposed a sentiment classification system for tweets. He built a Naïve Bayes Classifier to identify positive or negative emotions in posts, then generate public opinions summarization. Sharifi et al. [17] proposed the phrase reinforcement algorithm to generate summaries automatically. It aims at finding the most commonly used phrase as the summary. It usually begins with a trending topic as the root node, and adjacent of it are chains of common sequences of words collected from input posts. Zhao et al. [18] applied event detection to generate microblogs summarization by HITS algorithm. TREC 2017 has a relevant task called Real-Time Summarization Track [19], it aims at providing social media users with 'interest posts' timely. This task involves 'interest profiles' problem.

There is little work on the Chinese microblog summarization. Zhou et al. [1] presents a system *CMiner* that extracts opinion targets and opinion sentences as summaries simultaneously. They use a co-ranking algorithm in the model which is based on mutual reinforcement theory. Our task is different from it, since we devote to utilize posts specific 'interactivity' attribute to select sentences and our main task is generating summaries. Duan and Chen [20] designed a model of ranking tweets using social influence and content quality also in a mutually reinforcing manner. However they use user information such as authority to rank posts, in contrast, we pay more attention to the nature of posts. And these information is hard to acquire completely from Weibo, therefore we use only interactive statistics of posts like thumb-ups.

3 Our Model

In this section, we give a synthetic explanation for our IPMR Model. At first, we formulate the problem of microblog topic summarization as follows: given a topic t of *Sin-a Weibo*, we collect blogs of the topic. The collection can be regarded as a document, and we extract important sentences to form a summary. As microblog texts have specific attributes, the requirements for good summaries are different from traditional texts. We define 'important sentences' from the following two aspects:

a. Content. It means that important sentences should have high centrality in content. This feature is widely used in traditional extractive text summarization.

b. Interactivity. Microblog text has a specific property, interactivity. It is helpful for us to construct a summary containing hot opinions that interest people. Blog's interactivity can be measured by its retweets numbers, comments numbers and thumbs-up numbers.

There are two simple observations: (1) *elite posts* usually contain topical keywords; (2) *elite posts* usually have high interactivity such as large retweets. Therefore, we extend the mutual reinforcement model [1] which performed well on blogs summarization with two new factors: topical keywords and interactivity statistics.

Our model can be divided into two parts. In the first step, we extract keywords from blogs collection. Then we collect sentences that containing at least one keyword as candidates. In the second step, we applies the personalized mutual reinforcement model combining the keywords set and the candidate sentences set. The underlying principle of this model is Personalized PageRank algorithm by using interactivity to personalize sentences and HITS algorithm. In next sections, we will demonstrate these two main steps in detail. Figure 1 presents the structure of our model.

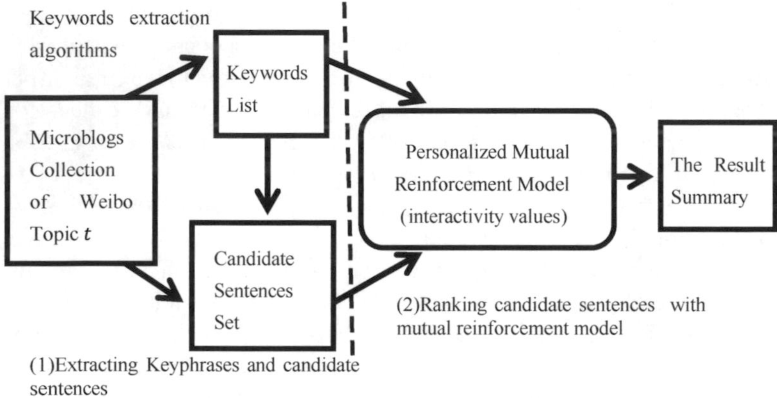

Fig. 1. Experimental method structure diagram

3.1 Extracting Keywords and Candidate Sentences

Based on the observation that elite posts usually contain topic central words which are similar to the definition of keywords, we integrated keywords into reinforcement model. As ideal summaries should have high coverage rate, we suppose that the number of keywords is the same as the number of clusters of blogs opinion targets. Zhou [1] proposed the method of obtaining the clusters number C based on *affinity propagation*. We compared typical keywords extraction methods by integrating them into our model, such as TF-IDF [21] and TextRank [22]. According to the experimental result, TextRank is more suitable for our model. After getting the keywords list, we collect relevant sentences that containing at least one keyword forming the candidate sentences set.

3.2 Ranking Candidate Sentences Based on Personalized Mutual Reinforcement Model

Keywords and candidate sentences sets are inputs of personalized mutual reinforcement model, and its output is the sorting results of these two datasets. Afterwards, top-C (the size of keywords list, in Sect. 3.1) sentences are selected to form the result summary. To ensure that popular sentences are selected, we developed the general reinforcement model by personalizing it with interactivity values. The other underlying assumption is the co-occurrence of salient sentences and keywords, the similarities of keywords and the similarities of salient sentences.

Interactivity. Before introducing the second model, we should give a clear explanation for posts 'interactivity'. Interactivity is the most prominent attribute of microblog texts. On Sina Weibo platform, users can retweet, comment and thumb up others' posts and these three operations reflect their attitudes. Retweeting represents users tend to share the post with others, commenting means users are interested in the blog, and thumbs-up stands for a feeling of approval. Therefore, the number of these three operations is closely related to the interactivity of microblogs text. In order to generate the ideal Weibo topic summarization, we should take these three values as measures of interactivity into consideration.

We assumed that all sentences in a blog share the same interactivity of this blog. We formulated the interactivity as a sum of linear addition of above three values, and calculated it as follows:

$$Score_{interactivity} = a \cdot x + b \cdot y + c \cdot z \tag{1}$$

Where a, b, c stand for three normalized coefficients. Their initial values are set according to their correlation coefficients to '*elite posts*' (see more information in Sect. 5.1). And x, y, z are set to the log value of the number of retweets, comments and thumbs-up respectively.

Personalized Mutual Reinforcement Model. Our model based on interactivity aims at increasing the probability of hot sentences been selected. In our mutual reinforcement model, there is a mutually reinforcing relationship between keywords and candidate sentences. On one hand, a sentence (word) which is similar to more other sentences is assumed to be more representative. On the other hand, a sentence (word) which is linked to more salient words (sentences) is also assumed to be more important. Following the PageRank and the HITS paradigm, we formulate above two types of relationship as four random walks, one among words, one among candidate sentences, one from keywords to sentences and one from sentences to keywords. It should be noted that initial weights and jump probabilities of sentences are assigned based on interactivity. The intuitive interpretation is that sentences with high interactivity are more important (personalizing initial weights) and have more influence on others (personalizing jump probabilities).

For keywords set A, we define the transition matrix $K \in \mathrm{R}^{|A|*|A|}$. Value K_{ij} represents similarity between word A_i and A_j, we calculate it based on Jaccard Index:

$$K_{ij} = \frac{|Character(A_i) \cap Character(A_j)|}{|Character(A_i) \cup Character(A_j)|} (1 \leq \mathrm{i}, \mathrm{j} \leq |A|) \tag{2}$$

The function $Character(A_x)$ is the Chinese character set of the x th word in set A, and $|A|$ is the total number of words in set A. Then we normalize the matrix and make the sum of each row is 1.

$$K_{ij} = \frac{K_{ij}}{\sum_{k=1}^{|A|} K_{ik}} \tag{3}$$

In the rand walk among words which are regarded as vertexes, there are two kinds of jump in each step, one is jumping to connected words and the other is jumping randomly to any words in the graph with probability p. This update iteration process can be formulated as:

$$K_{t+1} = (1-p)K_t + p \cdot M_k \tag{4}$$

Where $M_k \in \mathrm{R}^{|A|*|A|}$ is a matrix with all the values equal to 1.

For candidate sentences set B, we define the transition matrix S accordingly:

$$S_{ij} = \frac{CosineSimliarity(B_i,\ B_j)}{\sum_{k=1}^{|s|} CosineSimliarity(B_i,\ B_k)} \ (1 \le \mathrm{i},\ \mathrm{j} \le |B|) \tag{5}$$

Where $CosineSimliarity(B_i,\ B_j)$ refers to calculating the similarity of sentence vectors of B_i and B_j, $|B|$ is the total number of sentences in set B.

The random walk model among sentences is similar to the one among words, and the result matrix of each iteration is formulated as:

$$S_{t+1} = (1-p)S_t + p \cdot M_s \tag{6}$$

It should be noted that the matrix $M_s \in \mathrm{R}^{|B|*|B|}$ is different from $M_k \in \mathrm{R}^{|A|*|A|}$. Its values are assigned by sentences interactivity scores as follows:

$$\mathrm{M_{s\ ij}} = \frac{\mathrm{inter}(\mathrm{B_j})}{\sum_{\mathrm{j}=1}^{|\mathrm{B}|} \mathrm{inter}(\mathrm{B_j})} (1 \le \mathrm{i,j} \le |\mathrm{B}|) \tag{7}$$

Where $inter(B_i)$ stands for the interactivity value of i th sentence.

To formulate the third and fourth random walks between keywords and candidate sentences, we define two matrices $KS \in \mathrm{R}^{|A|*|B|}$ and $SK \in \mathrm{R}^{|B|*|A|}$. KS is the transition matrix from keywords to candidate sentences, SK is the transition matrix from candidate sentences to keywords. The value of these two matrices represents whether a word is included in a sentence, assigned as follows:

$$KS_{ij} = \frac{a_{ij}}{\sum_{k=1}^{|B|} a_{ik}} \ (a_{ij} = 1 \ if \ K_i \, in \, S_j, else \, a_{ij} = 0) \tag{8}$$

$$SK_{ij} = \frac{b_{ij}}{\sum_{k=1}^{|A|} b_{ik}} \ (b_{ij} = 1 \ if \ K_j \, in \, S_i, else \, b_{ij} = 0) \tag{9}$$

The mutual reinforcement model is a combination of these above four rand walks. As for a sentence (word), it can choose to jump to a sentence (word) of the graph at the probability of α (it is usually assigned as 0.85), or choose to jump to a word (sentence) at the probability of $(1-\alpha)$. The initial weight of each word is assigned equally as $1/|K|$. As for candidate sentences, they are initialized according to its own interactivity. We defined two vectors for keywords and sentences separately:

$$\vec{k} = \left(\frac{1}{|A|}, \frac{1}{|A|}, \ldots, \frac{1}{|A|}\right) \left(k \in R^{1*|A|}\right) \tag{10}$$

$$\vec{s} = \left(\frac{inter(B_1)}{\sum_{i=1}^{|B|} inter(B_i)}, \frac{inter(B_2)}{\sum_{i=1}^{|B|} inter(B_i)}, \ldots, \frac{inter\left(B_{|B|}\right)}{\sum_{i=1}^{|B|} inter(B_i)}\right) \left(s \in R^{1*|B|}\right) \tag{11}$$

Where $\vec{k}$ stands for keywords vector, $\vec{s}$ stands for sentences vector.

In each step, they are updated as follows:

$$k_{t+1} = \alpha \cdot k_t \cdot K + (1-\alpha) \cdot k_t \cdot KS \tag{12}$$

$$s_{t+1} = \alpha \cdot s_t \cdot S + (1-\alpha) \cdot s_t \cdot SK \tag{13}$$

After a period of iterations, the result converges gradually. In the last step, we chose top-C (the size of keywords list, in Sect. 3.1) sentences (deleting same sentences) according to the final values in the vector s as the result summary.

4 Experimental Settings

4.1 Datasets

We filtered tendentious topics related to stars and entertainment variety shows and compiled five datasets under five latest topics from December 2017 to February 2018, No. 1 'Jiang Ge trial' (#江歌案庭审#), No. 2 'Couples Joint Debt' (#夫妻共同债务#), No. 3 'the traveling frog game is brushing screen' (#旅行青蛙刷屏#), No. 4 'the second verdict of the admonishing smoking causes the sudden death in an elevator trail' (#电梯劝烟猝死案二审宣判#), No. 5 'hot search list and other items is temporarily closed for rectification' (#热搜榜等版块暂时下线整改#). These topics involved different fields, and having different sizes. Therefore, they help us test the robustness of our model.

For each topic, we collected all posts it contained, collected contents and interactivity values (number of retweets, number of comments, and number of thumbs-up). After that, we did sentences segmentation for each blog as pre-processing. The assumption is that sentences in a microblog share the same interactivity of this blog. Posts in the '*elite posts*' page under each topic are collected as standard datasets. Table 1 shows the detail information of each dataset.

Table 1. Dataset description (# denotes 'number of')

Topic number	#microblogs	#sentences	#'elite posts'	Fields
1	108	**411**	**43**	International cases
2	39	**111**	**9**	Law
3	148	**259**	**42**	Game
4	37	**132**	**15**	Domestic cases
5	202	**292**	**10**	Regulations

4.2 Evaluation Metric

We use Rouge-N method to analyze results. It is the most popular evaluation method in texts summarization, and is based on computing n-gram recall rate. In experiments, we evaluate results based on N = 1, 2, 3, 4, 5, 6.

4.3 Baselines

We use four state-of-the-art methods as baselines. They are Cminer, extended-CMiner (adding interactivity), LexRank and Submodular.

CMiner: It was proposed in 2016, it aims to extract opinion targets and generate opinion summarization at the same time. It is applied to Weibo topic summarization and has good performance.

Extended-CMiner (adding interactivity): Based on the CMiner system, we developed it by adding the interactivity attribute as a new one. By comparing it with the original one, we can learn the influence of the interactivity attribute. Besides, by comparing our method with this model, we can analyze the influence of keywords on summarization.

LexRank and Submodular: LexRank is a graph-based model and Submodular performs well in deleting redundant information. Both of them are typical algorithms of extractive summarization. Therefore, we choose them as baselines to make experiments results more compelling.

5 Experimental Results

We designed a series of experiments, their evaluation results and analysis are shown in following sections.

5.1 Testing the Relevance Between Interactivity and 'Elite Posts'

We conducted a correlation test on the Weibo topic # Jiang Ge trial #. There were 133 blogs and 516 sentences in this topic. After deleting the long reportable posts and irrelevant posts, there were altogether 108 microblogs with a total of 411 sentences. Collecting four attributes of posts: number of retweets, number of comments, number of thumbs-up, and whether it was an elite post. We performed logarithm operation on the first three attributes values. And if the post was an elite post, the fourth attribute

Table 2. T-tests and linear regression analysis results of three attributes

Operations	|t|	p	Corr-coef	Statistical conclusion
Retweet	2.222	0.028	0.191	significant ($\alpha = 0.05$)
Comment	2.086	0.039	0.180	significant ($\alpha = 0.05$)
Thumb up	3.127	0.002	0.227	extremely significant. ($\alpha = 0.01$)

would be set to 1 or 0 otherwise. We performed t-tests and linear regression analysis on the first three interactivity values with the fourth 'is' attribute respectively. The results are shown in Table 2.

According to Table 2, we can find that the correlation between posts' interactivity and the judgement of '*elite posts*'. Among these three values, the number of thumbs-up has the greatest influence on the judgement of '*elite posts*'. Therefore, these three values as interactivity attribute can help us to pick out '*elite posts*' which means that it is also useful for us to find salient sentences and generate a nice summary. And also we can get three correlation coefficients a, b, c for three operations correspondingly in the fourth column, which are used in the first equation (in Sect. 3.2).

5.2 Comparison with Baselines

We compare our IPMR Model with four baselines. We evaluate results by Rouge-N (N = 1, 2, 3, 4, 5, 6) and compute the average of five datasets as final results. According to the data showed in Fig. 2, our model performs best and exceeds the second one a lot.

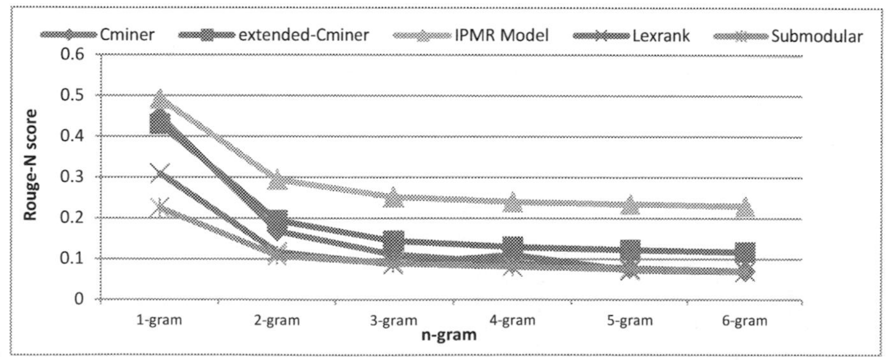

Fig. 2. Rouge-N experimental results

Firstly, We can see from Fig. 2 that two traditional baselines LexRank and Submodular have the lowest scores, and other three models are much better than them especially in 1-gram and 2-gram.

Then we compare CMiner and extended-CMiner, and the only difference between them is whether using 'interactivity' statistics. We can find that extended-CMiner performs better than CMiner, hence the 'interactivity' factor is helpful to improve experimental results.

Finally, we compare our model with extended-CMiner to learn the influence of topical keywords. Their only difference is the first step, extended-CMiner extracts nominal phrase while our model extracts keywords. According to results in Fig. 2, we find that our model performs much better than extended-CMiner under any evaluation metric. Therefore, it is reasonable to conclude that generating summaries by using keywords can improve results significantly.

In conclusion, our model has the best overall performance.

5.3 Parameter Sensitivity Analysis

In this section, we study the sensitivity of the parameter p in the second part of our model, the personalized mutual reinforcement model. It determines the jump probability in the first two random-walks (among words, among sentences), referring to Eqs. (4) and (6). To test its sensitivity, we select 0.2, 0.4, 0.6, and 0.8 for four values. The experimental Rouge-2 results are shown in Fig. 3. Based on the result, we conclude that the influence of the parameter p is slightly and our model is robust. According to the graph, parameter $p = 0.2$ has the best recall rate, we set it as 0.2 in experiments.

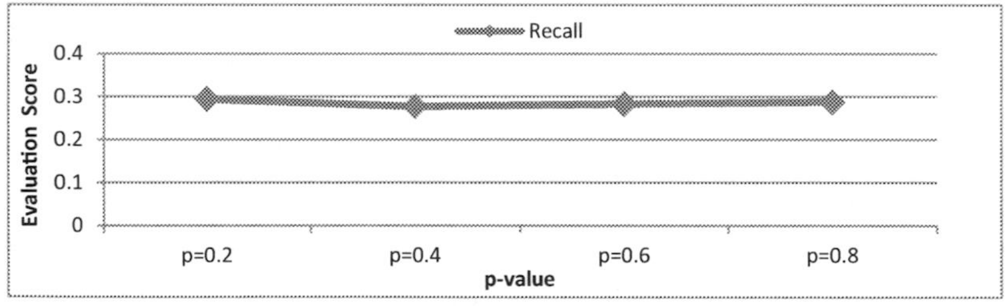

Fig. 3. Parameter p sensitivity analysis results

6 Conclusion and Future Work

In this paper we propose IMPR Model for automatic selection of important posts sentences as *Weibo* topics summaries, which consider interactive property of messages and topical keywords simultaneously. We show that the judgement of '*elite posts*' is highly relevant to interactive property of messages. Specifically, we verify the importance of interactivity and show that using keywords in personalized mutual reinforcement model can greatly improve the quality of summary compared with nominal phrases. We compare our model with four other state-of–the-art methods using Rouge-N evaluation metric, and the result show that our model has the best overall performance.

In the future, we consider incorporating user information into the model, based on the assumption that posts of high-level users or users with a large number fans are usually in high quality. In this way, their posts are more conducive to guiding the public and creating a friendly cyberspace environment.

Acknowledgments. This work is supported in part by the National Key Research and Development Program of China (No. 2017YFB1010000) and the National Natural Science Foundation of China (No. 61702500).

References

1. Zhou, X., Wan, X., Xiao, J., et al.: CMiner: opinion extraction and summarization for Chinese microblogs. IEEE Trans. Knowl. Data Eng. **28**(7), 1650–1663 (2016)
2. Wan, X., Yang, J., Xiao, J., et al.: Towards an iterative reinforcement approach for simultaneous document summarization and keyword extraction. In: Proceedings of the 45th ACL, pp. 552–559 (2007)
3. Vanderwende, L., Suzuki, H., Brockett, C., et al.: Beyond SumBasic: task-focused summarization with sentence simplification and lexical expansion. Inf. Process. Manage. **43** (6), 1606–1618 (2007)
4. Conroy, J.M., Oleary, D.P.: Text summarization via hidden Markov models. In: Proceedings of International ACM SIGIR Conference on Research and Development in Information Retrieval, pp. 406–407 (2001)
5. Shen, D., Sun, J.T., Li, H., et al.: Document summarization using conditional random fields. In: International Joint Conference on Artificial Intelligence, pp. 2862–2867 (2007)
6. Erkan, G., Radev, D.R.: LexRank: graph-based lexical centrality as salience in text summarization. J. Artif. Intell. Res. **22**(1), 457–479 (2004)
7. Mihalcea, R., Tarau, P.: TextRank: Bringing order into texts. In: Lin, D., Wu, D. (eds.) Proceedings of EMNLP 2004, Association for Computational Linguistics, pp. 404–411, Barcelona, Spain (2004)
8. Zha, H.: Generic summarization and key phrase extraction using mutual reinforcement principle and sentence clustering. In: Proceedings of the 25th ACM SIGIR, pp. 113–120 (2002)
9. Kleinberg, J.M.: Authoritative sources in a hyperlinked environment. J. ACM **46**(5), 604–632 (1999)
10. Page, L., Brin, S., Motwani, R., et al.: The PageRank citation ranking: bringing order to the web. Technical report. Stanford University, Stanford, CA (1999)
11. Rush, A.M., Chopra, S., Weston, J., et al.: A neural attention model for abstractive sentence summarization. In: Empirical Methods in Natural Language Processing, pp. 379–389 (2015)
12. Nallapati, R., Zhou, B., Santos, C.N., et al.: Abstractive text summarization using sequence-to-sequence RNNs and beyond. In: Conference on Computational Natural Language Learning, pp. 280–290 (2016)
13. Yao, J., Wan, X., Xiao, J.: Recent advances in document summarization. Knowl. Inf. Syst. **53**, 297–336 (2017). https://doi.org/10.1007/s10115-017-1042-4
14. Kim, S., Hovy, E.H.: Automatic identification of pro and con reasons in online reviews. In: Proceedings of the ACL, pp. 483–490, Barcelona, Spain (2006)
15. Weng, J., Yang, C., Chen, B., et al.: IMASS: an intelligent microblog analysis and summarization system. In: Proceedings of ACL, pp. 133–138, Barcelona, Spain (2011)

16. Bora, N.N.: Summarizing public opinions in tweets. Int. J. Comput. Linguist. Appl. **3**(1), 41–55 (2012)
17. Sharifi, B., Hutton, M., Kalita, J.K., et al.: Summarizing microblogs automatically. In: Proceedings of North American Chapter of the Association for Computational Linguistics, pp. 685–688 (2010)
18. Zhao, J., Liu, S., Liu, Y.: Towards event detection and summarization on microblogging platforms. Adv. Sci. Technol. Lett. **123**, 206–210 (2016)
19. TREC Real-Time Summarization Track Homepage. http://trecrts.github.io/. Accessed 29 Mar 2018
20. Duan, Y., Chen, Z., Wei, F., et al.: Twitter topic summarization by ranking tweets using social influence and content quality. In: Proceedings of the International Conference on Computational Linguistics, pp. 763–780 (2012)
21. Mihalcea, R.: Graph-based ranking algorithms for sentence extraction, applied to text summarization. In: Proceedings of 42nd ACL, Barcelona, Spain (2004)
22. Zhou, D., Orshanskiy, S.A., Zha, H., et al.: Co-ranking authors and documents in a heterogeneous network. In: Proceedings of International Conference on Data Mining, pp. 739–744 (2007)

Multiple Visual Fields Cascaded Convolutional Neural Network for Breast Cancer Detection

Haomiao Ni[1], Hong Liu[1(✉)], Zichao Guo[1], Xiangdong Wang[1], Taijiao Jiang[2,3], Kuansong Wang[4,5], and Yueliang Qian[1]

[1] Beijing Key Laboratory of Mobile Computing and Pervasive Device, Institute of Computing Technology, Chinese Academy of Sciences, Beijing 100190, China
hliu@ict.ac.cn

[2] Research Center for Big Data of Biomedical Sciences, Institute of Basic Medical Sciences, Chinese Academy of Medical Sciences and Peking Union Medical College, Beijing 100005, China

[3] Suzhou Institute of Systems Medicine, Suzhou 215123, China

[4] Department of Pathology, Xiangya Hospital, Central South University, Changsha, Hunan, China

[5] Department of Pathology, School of Basic Medical Sciences, Central South University, Changsha, Hunan, China

Abstract. This paper proposes a novel multiple visual fields cascaded convolutional neural network MVF-CasCNN to detect breast cancer metastases in the gigapixel whole slide image WSI. Here *visual field* is the total area of what the classifier can perceive from a particular input. Firstly, we perform patch-level classification using a large visual field CNN to coarsely locate possible lesion regions in a WSI. Then, a small visual field CNN is adopted to finely identify these tumor candidate areas and generate the final lesion probability heatmap for the WSI. Compared with single visual field based models, MVF-CasCNN achieves much higher performance in both slide classification and lesion localization. We also present a *tight* definition of tumor patch and an efficient *relatively hard* example mining method to enhance our network. Experimental results show that our method can surpass pathologist's level and achieve the state-of-the-art performance on public dataset Camelyon16.

Keywords: Breast cancer detection · Visual field · CNN · WSI

1 Introduction

Breast cancer is a common killing disease for women. But the examination of breast cancer requires pathologists to detect tumor regions from a huge histopathologic whole slide image, which can be extremely time-consuming and error-prone [1]. To assist in this diagnosis, more and more researchers focus on automated detection of cancer metastases in the whole slide image (WSI).

X. Geng and B.-H. Kang (Eds.): PRICAI 2018, LNAI 11012, pp. 531–544, 2018.
https://doi.org/10.1007/978-3-319-97304-3_41

However, computer-aided metastases detection in WSIs is not an easy task. First, WSI is typically stored in a multi-resolution pyramid structure (Fig. 1) and the number of pixels in level 0 can exceed 10 billion. Second, WSIs can have large color variation caused by stain difference (Fig. 2). Third, some normal areas can be very similar to diseased cells in the high resolution, e.g., 40× (Fig. 2).

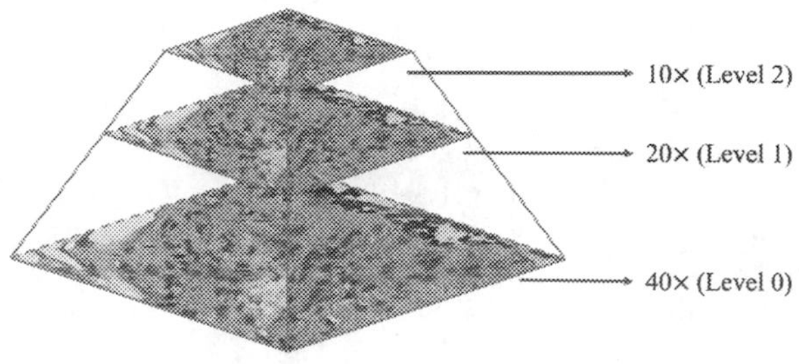

Fig. 1. The multi-resolution pyramid structure of whole slide image (Note that we only draw three layers here, but in fact slide image can have 8 layers).

More recently, with the Camelyon 2016 Challenge [1] held, many effective strategies are proposed to overcome the aforementioned difficulties. For detecting metastases in a huge WSI, researchers [3,7,12] generally divided the slide into millions of patches, and predicted the tumor probability of each patch. Then, they aggregated these patch-level predictions to generate the lesion likelihood heatmap for each WSI. Convolutional neural network (CNN) is commonly used to design the patch classifier because of its powerful ability to describe images [6] and the availability of numerous training patches. To handle the color difference between images, researchers have tried two useful ways. The first method [3] is to apply stain normalization [2] before feeding patches into network, and the second approach [7] is to adopt data augmentation [6] to train a color-insensitive model. To differentiate diseased cells from hard negative mimics, researchers also employed hard example mining (HEM) [12] to strengthen the deep network.

However, to capture finest cell-relevant information, existing methods [3,7,12] focus on detecting lesions using small patches of 40× magnification. But Fig. 2 shows that it is actually easier to distinguish tumors from some negative areas in a larger *visual field* (e.g., 10×) than a smaller one (e.g., 40×). Here, *visual field* is the total area of what the classifier can perceive from a particular input. Small visual field can better represent cell-level information, while large visual field can extract tissue-level features and thus help small visual field based model to discriminate lesions from hard mimics. Therefore, to combine small and large visual field, we propose a multiple visual fields cascaded CNN, MVF-CasCNN. Figure 3 shows the overview of MVF-CasCNN. When testing a WSI, we first preprocess the slide and divide it into those patches with large visual field, and then feed them into a large visual field CNN. Their predictions are later aggregated to create a coarse tumor likelihood heatmap, which is used to find those patches probably including lesions. Subsequently, new patches with small visual field are extracted from these candidate patches and fed into a small visual field CNN for finer classification. Finally, we aggregate their predictions to generate a finer heatmap. Section 4 will demonstrate these details.

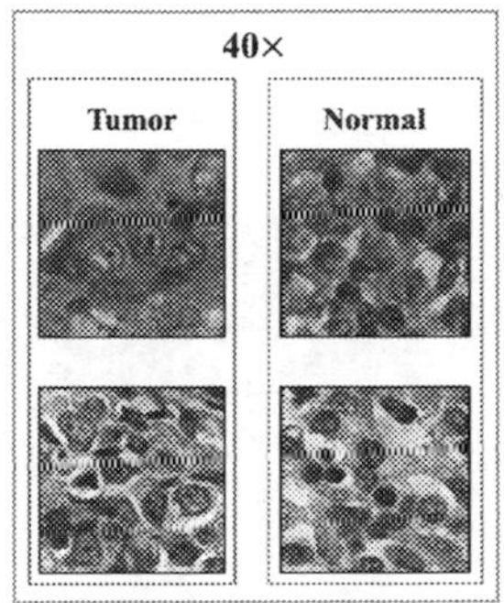

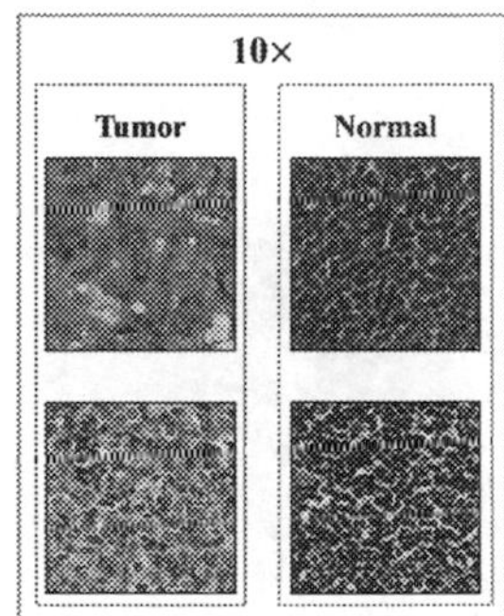

Fig. 2. Some examples of tumor and normal regions in different resolutions. (Color figure online)

To apply patch-level classification, researchers should define labels of their training patches sampled from the slide dataset. It is obvious to label a patch as normal only when all of its pixels are normal. But the question is how to define a patch as tumor. Liu et al. [7] defined a patch with the size of 299×299 as tumor if at least one pixel in its central region (128×128) is tumor. However, the area 128×128 is only about 18.33% of 299×299. This may include some tumor patches that very similar to normal cells and thus lead to the decrease of inter-class difference. On the contrary to this *loose* tumor patch definition, we propose a *tight* definition for our small visual field network: a patch is tumor only when all of its pixels are tumor, which can advance the model's performance. Section 2.2 will show these details.

To better distinguish between tumor and normal patches, Wang et al. [12] adopted hard example mining (HEM) [9] to add false positives to the original large training patch dataset (including about 0.3 million patches) and it generated a new dataset which was 1.2 times the size of the initial one for fine-tuning the initial trained model. This kind of HEM can make the training process much more time-costing and computational resources-demanding, especially for a large dataset. Another common HEM [5] is to keep all the positive samples while replacing all the initial normal samples by new reselected hard negatives. But remaining all positive samples is still inefficient since some tumor patches have already become *easy* for the original trained model. Therefore, to perform HEM much more efficiently, we apply data mining to both tumor and negative patches and just keep these new reselected examples in our final dataset. But unlike those HEM ways that just considering false examples, we also contain true samples that are not too easy for the trained model. Thus, we name our method *relatively hard* example mining (RHEM). We finally fine-tune the initial

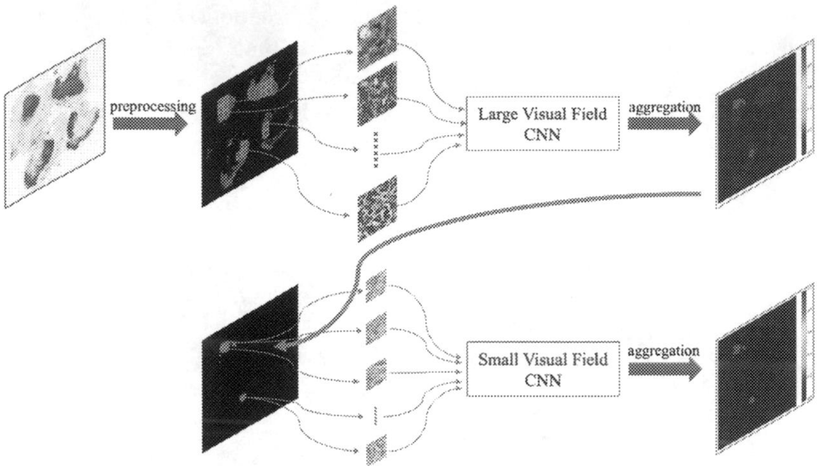

Fig. 3. The overview of our multiple visual fields cascaded CNN.

model on the small training dataset created by RHEM. The size of this dataset is only about 26% of the original one. Section 2.3 will illustrate these details.

The contribution of this paper can be summarized as follows: 1. We present a multiple visual fields cascaded CNN, MVF-CasCNN. This framework enables us to outstrip human expert and obtain state-of-the-art results on Camelyon16 dataset [1]. 2. We also propose a tight tumor patch definition that labels a patch as tumor only when all of its pixels are tumor, which can enhance the small visual field model's representation ability. 3. For more efficiently applying hard example mining to large training patch dataset, we propose a relatively hard example mining (RHEM) to build a new smaller patch dataset. Fine-tuning on this smaller dataset shows considerable improvement on metastases localization.

2 Small Visual Field CNN

When running inference on a WSI, our multiple visual fields cascaded CNN (MVF-CasCNN) firstly employs large visual field network and then utilizes small visual field model. But opposite to this testing process, during training, we firstly train a small visual field model and subsequently leverage it to train a large visual field network. So we first introduce our small visual field CNN, SVF-CNN. For facilitating the understanding, the definition of *visual field* is given as follows.

Visual field is the total area of what the classifier can perceive from a particular input. It depends on two factors: the size $m \times m$ of input patch and the magnification i where the patch is extracted. Figure 1 illustrates that patches with different sides m and magnifications i can have the same visual field. As Eq. (1) shows, for patches with the same side m, the higher magnification i they are from, the smaller visual field they have. And for patches from the same magnification i, the smaller side m they have, the smaller visual field they possess.

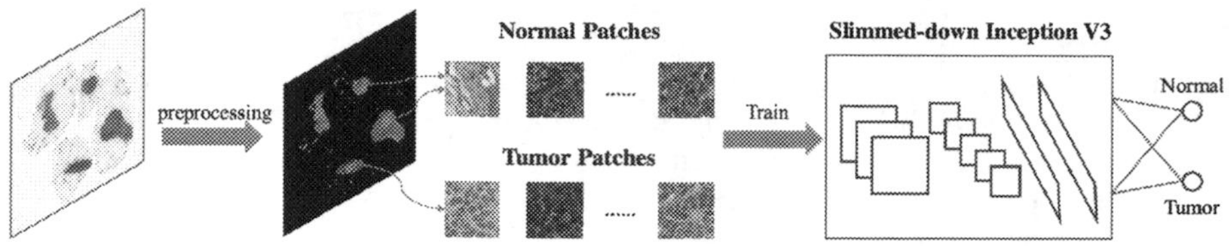

Fig. 4. The illustration of the training of our single visual field CNN (both small visual field model and large visual field network follow this framework).

To simplify the writing, if a patch sampled from the magnification i have the size of $m \times m$, we call the visual field of this patch is $i \otimes m$.

$$visual\ field \propto \left(\frac{m}{i}\right)^2 \tag{1}$$

Figure 4 shows the training of our SVF-CNN. Firstly, we preprocess slides to exclude the background. Then, we sample millions of normal patches and *tight* tumor samples for training our deep network, slimmed-down Inception V3 [7]. It has the same architecture as the original Inception V3 [11] but the number of filters per layer is only 10% of the initial one. Some typical data augmentation techniques [6], including color jittering, rotation and flip, are adopted to help the model learn color-invariant and orientation-insensitive features. Finally, we further enhance SVF-CNN with our relatively hard example mining (RHEM).

2.1 Slide Preprocessing

On average, about 82% of a whole slide image (WSI) is non-tissue area in Camelyon16 dataset [12]. So it is necessary to remove them for training or testing. Assuming that the WSI in the magnification i is I_i, and its corresponding groundtruth mask in the magnification i is G_i ($G_i = \emptyset$ if I_i is normal), we first apply OSTU algorithm [8] to the S channel of I_i in HSV color space. This results in a mask of regions of interest R_i. Then $G_i \cap R_i$ generates the tumor mask T_i, and $\neg G_i \cap R_i$ creates the normal mask N_i. Note that magnification i should be low (e.g., 0.625×) for fast preprocessing. Besides, in Camelyon16 dataset [1], G_i may incorrectly include some fat regions because of the difficulty of pixel-accurate annotation. Hence, our tumor mask T_i is not G_i but $G_i \cap R_i$.

2.2 Patch Sampling

To train a SVF-CNN, we extract patches with the size of 299×299 (the default size of Inception V3) from training slides in 40× using the masks mentioned in Sect. 2.1. So the visual field of these patches is $40 \otimes 299$. The Algorithm 1 shows the details of our patch sampling for constructing training patch dataset. Note that magnification j should be 40 and mask M_i can be either tumor or normal, depending on which class of patches is needed. Besides, to cover regions of interest, the sampling stride k_j should be less than the patch side m.

Algorithm 1. Patch sampling

Input: The whole slide image in the magnification j: I_j
The mask with certain label in the magnification i: M_i
The sampling stride of magnification j: k_j; The size of patch: $m \times m$
Output: Training patches in the magnification j: TP_j
Set (x, y) to be the coordinate of the first pixel in M_i
for x within the width of M_i **do**
  for y within the height of M_i **do**
    Extract patch P_j with the side m from I_j, where P_j is centered on $(\frac{j}{i}x, \frac{j}{i}y)$
    if P_j is the target label **then**
      $TP_j = TP_j \cup P_j$
    end if
    $y \leftarrow y + \frac{i}{j}k_j$
  end for
  $x \leftarrow x + \frac{i}{j}k_j$
end for
return TP_j

More importantly, we adopt our proposed *tight* definition for tumor patch, i.e., only when all pixels of the patch are tumor can it be defined as tumor. Using this definition is because of the following considerations. When we run inference in small visual field, most patches containing both of two classes will locate at the edge of lesion regions. Thus, their prediction results can only affect those values on the contour of the heatmap, which has little adverse effects on slide classification and tumor detection. However, tight definition will ignore those patches including isolated tiny diseased cells. But in Camelyon16 challenge [1], these isolated tumor cells (ITCs) are not used for evaluation. Furthermore, because of excluding those "tumor patches"that containing normal pixels, we increase the inter-class difference. And this will better help the model develop representation power. Our experiments will illustrate the effectiveness of this tight definition.

2.3 Relatively Hard Example Mining

Traditional hard example mining (HEM) [9,12] adds a considerable number of false positives to the original training dataset and retrains the initial model for improvement. This will obviously increase the size of initial dataset and make it harder to train a deep model when time and computational resources are limited, especially for a large dataset. Thus, to efficiently perform HEM, we propose a relatively hard example mining (RHEM) by constructing a small dataset H to fine-tune the initial trained model $\mathbb{M}$. Firstly, for running inference on training slides, we build a testing patch dataset of training slides D. Then we utilize $\mathbb{M}$ to predict the tumor probability p of each patch d in D. Dataset H will include false positives but exclude false negatives. This is because in Camelyon16 challenge [1], false negatives can be actually normal but falsely labeled as tumors due to the difficulty of detailed annotation. Since a complete dataset should contain both positive and negative samples, we also add those *relatively hard* true positives to

H. And because normal cells can be quite morphologically diverse, we also add *relatively hard* true negatives to H. Here *relatively hard* true samples are those patches that can be correctly recognized by $\mathbb{M}$ but the difference between their predictions p and 0.5 is less than a threshold T, i.e., $|p - 0.5| < T$. Finally, to increase the diversity of extracted samples, we randomly jitter each patch d in different directions for K times. This results in our final dataset H.

3 Large Visual Field CNN

As Sect. 2 mentions, visual field is the total area of what the classifier can perceive from a certain patch. Thus there are two types of patches with large visual field: 1. The patches have small size but are sampled from lower magnification (e.g., $10 \otimes 299$). 2. The patches are from high magnification but have larger size (e.g., $40 \otimes 1196$). So we build two types of training patch dataset for large visual field CNN, LVF-CNN. The training is similar to SVF-CNN, as Fig. 4 shows.

We first preprocess slides to remove their background. Then we build training patch datasets by utilizing the Algorithm 1 to sample patches. However, different from the tight definition used in SVF-CNN, here we use loose definition, which defines a patch as tumor if at least one pixel in its central region is tumor. This is because large visual field will cover much more tissues. So if we still employ tight definition, the number of tumor patches will decrease dramatically. It can lead to the extreme imbalance between two classes and the model may prefer to predict an unknown patch as normal. Besides, in Camelyon16 challenge, only those tumor regions with the longest diameter less than 1132 in $40\times$ can be ignored. But tight definition under some large visual fields (like $40 \otimes 1196$) will neglect those patches containing isolated tumor regions (e.g. a lesion area whose longest diameter is 1160). Thus, we choose loose definition and the side of central region is set to be $\frac{128}{299}$ of the patch side. These extracted patches will be later used to train a slimmed-down Inception V3 network. To accelerate training, we initialize most parameters of Inception V3 by the trained SVF-CNN. But due to the possible size change of input, we randomly initialize those parameters of fully-connected layers and some convolutional layers with size-related kernels.

4 Multiple Visual Fields Cascaded CNN

To effectively combine large visual field model LVF-CNN and small visual field network SVF-CNN, we present a multiple visual fields cascaded CNN, MVF-CasCNN. The main idea of MVF-CasCNN is from the actual diagnosis procedure of pathologists: they usually first locate regions of interest in a low magnification, that is, a large visual field, and then identify metastases in a high magnification, that is, a small visual field. As Fig. 3 shows, we firstly apply OSTU [8] to preprocess slide in the lowest magnification $0.3125\times$ (level 7) to faster get rid of background and generate the mask of regions of interest $R_{0.3125}$. Secondly, we sample patches of large visual field $j \otimes n$ by the Algorithm 1. Notice that the input mask $M_{0.3125}$ should be $R_{0.3125}$. Assuming that large visual field $j \otimes n$ is N times as large as our small visual field $40 \otimes 299$, using Eq. (1), we obtain:

$$N = \frac{(n/j)^2}{(299/40)^2} = \left(\frac{40n}{299j}\right)^2 \tag{2}$$

This means that in 40×, the sampling stride k^l_{40} of large visual field can be $\sqrt{N}$ times the length of the sampling stride k^s_{40} of small visual field $40 \otimes 299$. So given k^s_{40} , the stride k^l_j of large visual field model $j \otimes n$ is:

$$k^l_j = \frac{j}{40} k^l_{40} = \frac{j}{40} \sqrt{N} k^s_{40} = \frac{n k^s_{40}}{299} \tag{3}$$

Then we perform patch-level classification by LVF-CNN to produce a coarse tumor possibility heatmap $h^l(\cdot)$. We further continue to utilize Algorithm 1 to sample patches of small visual field $40 \otimes 299$ with stride k^s_{40}. But we only remain those patches whose central coordinates in 40× belong to set $\mathbb{S}$. Equation (4) shows how to get $\mathbb{S}$ by $h^l(\cdot)$. Note that P is a threshold of being tumor candidates. Then these patches are fed into SVF-CNN to create a finer heatmap.

$$\mathbb{S} = \left\{ (x, y) \;\middle|\; h^l\left(\left\lfloor \frac{x}{k^l_{40}} \right\rfloor, \left\lfloor \frac{y}{k^l_{40}} \right\rfloor \right) > P \right\}, \text{where } k^l_{40} = \sqrt{N} k^s_{40} \tag{4}$$

5 Experimental Evaluation

We evaluate our methods on Camelyon16 dataset [1]. It comprises 400 WSIs from lymph nodes. The training dataset consists of 270 slides, including 160 normal slides and 110 tumor slides, while the test dataset contains 130 WSIs, including 50 tumor slides and 80 normal slides. We separate 57 slides from the training dataset as validation dataset (34 normal and 23 tumor WSIs). This validation dataset will be later used for tuning parameters and finding the optimal models.

Two metrics will be used to assess the performance of algorithms. The first metric is to evaluate the performance of distinguishing between tumor and normal slides using the area under the receiver operating curve, i.e., AUC score. In this paper, we simply take the maximum value of the final heatmap as the probability of containing metastases for each WSI. The second evaluation measures the performance of lesion localization by FROC score, which is defined as the average sensitivity at 6 predefined false positive rate: 0.25, 0.5, 1, 2, 4, and 8 false positives per WSI. Similar to [4], we adopt non-maxima suppression to produce the coordinates of lesions. This approach iterates the following 2 steps until no pixels in the heatmap exceeds the threshold t: (1) output the maximum and its coordinate; (2) set all pixels within a radius r of the maximum to be 0. Here we set $r = 5$ and $t = 0.01$ to preserve a high sensitivity.

We design comprehensive experiments to measure our approaches: 1. For evaluating the influence of tumor patch definition, we compare the model using our tight definition with the network employing loose definition in [7]. 2. To

Table 1. Evaluation results of datasets with different tumor patch definitions.

Training patch dataset	AUC (%)	FROC (%)
Loose-Set (40 $\otimes$ 299)	94.58	70.52
Tight-Set (40 $\otimes$ 299)	**95.83**	**71.78**

measure our hard exampling mining, we compare online hard example mining OHEM [10] with our relatively hard example mining RHEM. 3. To show the superiority of proposed multiple visual fields cascaded CNN, MVF-CasCNN, we examine its performance and also compare it with other state-of-the-art methods.

5.1 Evaluation of Different Tumor Patch Definitions

To explore the effect of tumor patch definition, we define two kinds of tumor patch: the first one adopts tight definition, i.e., a patch is tumor only when all of its pixels are tumor, and the second one uses loose definition, i.e., a patch is tumor if at least one pixel in its central area is tumor. With these two definitions, two training datasets are built. We call them Tight-Set and Loose-Set respectively.

Implementation Details. To preprocess WSI quickly, we apply OSTU [8] to slides in the 0.625× (level 6, about 1000 by 1000 pixels). For building training patch dataset, we apply Algorithm 1 to sample patches with small visual field 40 $\otimes$ 299. Here the sampling stride $k_{40} = 64$ for tumor patch sampling and $k_{40} = 128$ for normal patches because the number of lesion regions are much less than that of normal areas. Using our tight tumor patch definition, we obtain a Tight-Set consisting of 3.6 million tumor samples and 21.5 million normal patches (about 25 million in total). But with the loose definition, Loose-Set includes 4.4 million tumor patches, which is a little more than Tight-Set.

Then, we train a small visual field network on these two patch datasets using a GeForce GTX 1080 Ti GPU. Our batch size is 256 and the initial learning rate is 0.05, with a decay of 0.5 every 2 million patches. Due to the large dataset size and the limitation of computational resource, we only iterate the training for at most 5 epochs and find the optimal models using validation dataset.

Experimental Results. As Table 1 shows, Tight-Set has 1.25% and 1.26% improvement in AUC and FROC than Loose-Set. The reason may be that our tight definition can remove those "tumor patches" that containing normal pixels, which helps to increase the inter-class difference. And this increase can further enhance model's description ability.

5.2 Evaluation of Hard Example Mining

For efficiently performing hard example mining (HEM) on large training dataset, we compare our proposed relatively hard example mining (RHEM) with online

Table 2. Evaluation results of different hard example mining on Camelyon16.

Method	AUC (%)	FROC (%)
Tight-Set ($40 \otimes 299$)	**95.83**	71.78
Tight-Set ($40 \otimes 299$ with OHEM [10])	94.77	72.88
Tight-Set ($40 \otimes 299$ with our RHEM)	95.52	**73.78**

hard example mining (OHEM) [10], which can automatically find hard examples in every training step and directly utilize them to update the gradients during the back-propagating. So OHEM doesn't increase the size of dataset and thus it is also a suitable training strategy for large patch dataset.

Implementation Details. We apply different HEM to the small visual field network trained on Tight-Set. For fine-tuning the trained model, we set a low initial learning rate: 4×10^{-6}. And training epochs of these algorithms are less than 3 due to the limitation of computational resources. For OHEM [10], we set it to find the top 64 hard examples in every training step. For our RHEM in Sect. 2.3, we randomly jitter extracted patches in different directions for 24 times, and the threshold $T = 0.4$, that is, we select those relatively hard true patches with predictions p satisfying $|p - 0.5| < 0.4$. So those true positives with p less than 0.9 and true negatives with p more than 0.1 are kept. Plus extracted false positives, this produces a small dataset including 5.8 million normal patches and 0.7 million tumor samples, which is only 26% of the Tight-Set.

Experimental Results. As Table 2 shows, our proposed RHEM can improve the original model in FROC by 2% while remaining the similar AUC. This shows the effectiveness of our RHEM. By contrast, though OHEM can bring 1.1% improvement in FROC, it reduces the AUC score by 1.06%. The reason may be that OHEM actually takes both false positives and false negatives into consideration while our RHEM only considers false positives. However, some false negative patches are in fact normal but mistakenly labeled as tumor due to the difficulty of detailed annotation. Thus, these false negative patches will constantly re-enter the training and confuse the deep network, which makes it more difficult for distinguishing slides. In addition, we employ randomly position jitter in our RHEM, which can introduce some new samples that the original Tight-Set doesn't have. These new samples may also help RHEM to take effect.

5.3 Evaluation of Multiple Visual Fields Cascaded CNN

As is mentioned in Sect. 4, we proposed a multiple visual fields cascaded CNN, MVF-CasCNN to effectively combine our large visual field model LVF-CNN and small visual field network SVF-CNN.

Implementation Details. MVF-CasCNN contains two networks, SVF-CNN and LVF-CNN. For SVF-CNN, we train the network using patches with small visual field $40 \otimes 299$ on Tight-Set and then enhance it by our RHEM. To train LVF-CNN, as Fig. 4 shows, we first apply OSTU [8] to preprocess slides in the 0.625× (level 6). Then, we adopt Algorithm 1 to sample patches with large visual field. After trying different types of large visual field, we finally choose $40 \otimes 1196$. The sampling stride $k_{40} = 256$ for tumor patch sampling and $k_{40} = 512$ for normal patches since the number of normal regions are generally far more than that of tumor areas in a WSI. This generates a dataset including 0.3 million tumor patches and 1.3 million normal samples. Because we leverage the trained SVF-CNN to train our LVF-CNN, the initial learning rate is set to be 0.002.

When testing, we first preprocess slide in the lowest magnification 0.3125× (level 7) to faster exclude background. Second, we sample patches of large visual field $40 \otimes 1196$ by Algorithm 1. Here we set the sampling stride of large visual field $k^l_{40} = 512$. Then we perform patch classification by LVF-CNN to create a coarse heatmap $h^l(\cdot)$. To obtain coordinate set $\mathbb{S}$ for SVF-CNN, we set threshold P to be 0.3 in Eq. (4) according to our experiments on the validation set. Subsequently, we extract patches of small visual field $40 \otimes 299$ using Algorithm 1 but just keep those patches satisfying set $\mathbb{S}$. Here using Eq. (3), the sampling stride of small visual field $k^s_{40} = (299 \times 512) \div 1196 = 128$. These patches are later fed into SVF-CNN to output a finer heatmap for computing AUC and FROC.

Comparison of Different Visual Field Models. We compare our proposed networks in Table 3. As Table 3 shows, compared with the best single visual field model, SVF-CNN, our MVF-CasCNN improves AUC and FROC by 1.33% and 6.81% respectively. It shows that the combination of multiple visual fields is useful to improve performance. Also, we compare our MVF-CasCNN with a simple fusion that takes average of heatmaps created separately by LVF-CNN and SVF-CNN. The results illustrate that this simple strategy MVF-Fusion can also enhance the performance. This in turn shows that the introduction of large visual field can be beneficial to small visual field network. But compared with MVF-Fusion, though our MVF-CasCNN perform 0.49% lower slightly in AUC, it achieves 2.07% higher FROC on lesion detection. The reason may be that our cascaded architecture can better mimic the pathologist's examination than this fusion scheme, since this fusion actually processes the information of different visual fields in parallel rather than in series.

Comparison of Different Multiple Visual Fields Models. To find better combination of small visual field network SVF-CNN and large visual field model LVF-CNN, we have tried different types of large visual field: $40 \otimes 1196$, $10 \otimes 299$, $40 \otimes 598$, and $20 \otimes 299$. According to Eq. (1), the visual field of $40 \otimes 1196$ is the same as that of $10 \otimes 299$, and $40 \otimes 598$ have the same visual field as $20 \otimes 299$. These four LVF-CNNs finally form four kinds of MVF-CasCNNs by combining with the same SVF-CNN ($40 \otimes 299$). Table 4 demonstrates results of these four MVF-CasCNNs. As Table 4 shows, MVF-CasCNN with $40 \otimes 1196$ achieves the

Table 3. Evaluation results of different visual field models on Camelyon16.

Method	AUC (%)	FROC (%)
LVF-CNN ($40 \otimes 1196$)	94.09	52.89
SVF-CNN ($40 \otimes 299$)	95.52	73.78
MVF-Fusion ($40 \otimes 1196$+$40 \otimes 299$)	**97.34**	78.52
MVF-CasCNN ($40 \otimes 1196$+$40 \otimes 299$)	96.85	**80.59**

best performance. However, tough $10 \otimes 299$ possesses the same visual field as $40 \otimes 1196$, it performs the worst. This may due to the low magnification. Although doctors can locate lesions exactly in the $10\times$, our large visual field CNN is still hard to distinguish between lesion and normal areas in such a coarse scale. So if we increase scale of large visual field from $10\times$ to $20\times$ but still keep the side to be 299, MVF-CasCNN using $20 \otimes 299$ will improve AUC and FROC by 0.94% and 11.48% respectively. This also shows that MVF-CasCNN using $10 \otimes 299$ suffers from the low magnification. We can also see that the network adopting $40 \otimes 1196$ can be better than the model with $40 \otimes 598$, especially in the tumor detection, which shows 4.44% gain. The reason may be that patches of $40 \otimes 1196$ enjoy larger visual field and thus can be easier to capture tissue-relevant information.

Table 4. Evaluation results of different MVF-CasCNNs on Camelyon16.

Method	AUC (%)	FROC (%)
MVF-CasCNN ($20 \otimes 299$ + $40 \otimes 299$)	94.90	73.48
MVF-CasCNN ($40 \otimes 598$ + $40 \otimes 299$)	96.48	76.15
MVF-CasCNN ($10 \otimes 299$ + $40 \otimes 299$)	93.96	62.00
MVF-CasCNN ($40 \otimes 1196$ + $40 \otimes 299$)	**96.85**	**80.59**

Comparison of Our Methods and State-of-the-Art Ways. As Table 5 shows, compared with top 2 methods [3], our MVF-CasCNN achieves comparable AUC and FROC in both slide classification and lesion detection. Following those top methods [3], we also take average of our MVF-CasCNN and another MVF-CasCNN trained in different step. We name this final model *Ensemble* MVF-CasCNN. Compared with the method [3] ranking 2nd, Ensemble MVF-CasCNN achieves 0.25% and 4.88% higher both in AUC and FROC. Compared with the top 1 approach [3], Ensemble MVF-CasCNN has 0.14% slight improvement on FROC but still performs 1.47% worse in AUC. However, the top 1 approach set the sampling stride to be 4 so the size of their heatmaps is $\frac{1}{16}$ of original slides in $40\times$. By contrast, our heatmaps are only the $\frac{1}{16384}$ of original slides in $40\times$ since our final stride is 128. But if we also set the stride to be 4, the number of testing patches will be 1024 times that of our current patches, which will be rather time-consuming. Though our heatmaps suffer the loss of resolution due to large stride, our model can still achieve state-of-the-art results with much less processing time. Compared with pathologists, who require about 14 min per WSI [3], the average running time of our MVF-CasCNN for a WSI is less than 8 min when using just one GTX 1080 Ti GPU: LVF-CNN takes 394 s to create a coarse heatmap, and the subsequent SVF-CNN spends 34 s in generating a finer result. But either MVF-CasCNN or Ensemble MVF-CasCNN outperforms human experts in both slide classification and lesion localization.

Table 5. Evaluation results of different approaches on Camelyon16.

Method	AUC (%)	FROC (%)
Pathologist [3]	96.60	72.40
HMS and MIT II [3] (Rank 1st)	**99.35**	80.74
HMS and MGH III [3] (Rank 2nd)	97.63	76.00
MVF-CasCNN ($40 \otimes 1196 + 40 \otimes 299$)	96.85	80.59
Ensemble MVF-CasCNN ($40 \otimes 1196 + 40 \otimes 299$)	97.88	**80.88**

6 Conclusion

This paper proposes a novel multiple visual fields cascaded CNN, MVF-CasCNN, to detect breast cancer metastases in WSIs. Using this framework, we achieve higher performance on both slide classification and lesion localization than either singe visual field based model. We also propose a tight tumor patch definition to advance the model's description ability. To further improve the metastases detection, we present a relatively hard example mining RHEM. Our final MVF-CasCNN and Ensemble MVF-CasCNN achieve state-of-the-art results on public dataset Camelyon16. In the future, we will evaluate our methods on more WSIs and explore more possible definitions of tumor patches.

Acknowledgement. This work is supported in part by Beijing Natural Science Foundation (4172058) and Central Public-interest Scientific Institution Basal Research Fund (2016ZX310195, 2017PT31026).

References

1. Camelyon (2016). https://camelyon16.grand-challenge.org/
2. Bejnordi, B.E., et al.: Stain specific standardization of whole-slide histopathological images. IEEE Trans. Med. Imaging **35**(2), 404–415 (2016)
3. Bejnordi, B.E., et al.: Diagnostic assessment of deep learning algorithms for detection of lymph node metastases in women with breast cancer. JAMA **318**(22), 2199–2210 (2017)
4. Cireşan, D.C., Giusti, A., Gambardella, L.M., Schmidhuber, J.: Mitosis detection in breast cancer histology images with deep neural networks. In: Mori, K., Sakuma, I., Sato, Y., Barillot, C., Navab, N. (eds.) MICCAI 2013. LNCS, vol. 8150, pp. 411–418. Springer, Heidelberg (2013). https://doi.org/10.1007/978-3-642-40763-5_51

5. Felzenszwalb, P.F., Girshick, R.B., McAllester, D., Ramanan, D.: Object detection with discriminatively trained part-based models. IEEE Trans. Pattern Anal. Mach. Intell. **32**(9), 1627–1645 (2010)
6. Krizhevsky, A., Sutskever, I., Hinton, G.E.: Imagenet classification with deep convolutional neural networks. In: Advances in Neural Information Processing Systems, pp. 1097–1105 (2012)
7. Liu, Y., et al.: Detecting cancer metastases on gigapixel pathology images. arXiv preprint arXiv:1703.02442 (2017)
8. Otsu, N.: A threshold selection method from gray-level histograms. IEEE Trans. Syst. Man Cybern. **9**(1), 62–66 (1979)
9. Rowley, H.A., Baluja, S., Kanade, T.: Neural network-based face detection. IEEE Trans. Pattern Anal. Mach. Intell. **20**(1), 23–38 (1998)
10. Shrivastava, A., Gupta, A., Girshick, R.: Training region-based object detectors with online hard example mining. In: Proceedings of the IEEE Conference on Computer Vision and Pattern Recognition, pp. 761–769 (2016)
11. Szegedy, C., Vanhoucke, V., Ioffe, S., Shlens, J., Wojna, Z.: Rethinking the inception architecture for computer vision. In: Proceedings of the IEEE Conference on Computer Vision and Pattern Recognition, pp. 2818–2826 (2016)
12. Wang, D., Khosla, A., Gargeya, R., Irshad, H., Beck, A.H.: Deep learning for identifying metastatic breast cancer. arXiv preprint arXiv:1606.05718 (2016)

Multi-view Learning and Deep Learning for Microscopic Neuroblastoma Pathology Image Diagnosis

Yuhan Liu[1], Minzhi Yin[2], and Shiliang Sun[1(✉)]

[1] Department of Computer Science and Technology, East China Normal University, Shanghai, China
slsun@cs.ecnu.edu.cn

[2] Department of Pathology, Shanghai Children's Medical Center, Shanghai Jiao Tong University School of Medicine, Shanghai, China

Abstract. Automated pathology image diagnosis is one of the most crucial research in the computer-aided medical field, and many studies on the recognition of various cancers are currently actively conducted. However, neuroblastoma, the most common extracranial solid tumor of childhood, has not got enough attention in the computer-aided diagnosis research. Accurate diagnosis of this cancer requires professional pathologists with sufficient experience, which makes lack of experts lead to misdiagnosis. In this paper, we apply multi-view and single-view maximum entropy discrimination, with traditional image representations and deep neural network representations respectively. The diagnosis is performed in three neuroblastoma subtypes, undifferentiated subtype (UD), poorly differentiated subtype (PD), differentiating subtype (D), and the normal type un-neoplasm tissues (UN). The best classification performance (94.25%), which far exceeds the diagnosis accuracy (56.5%) of a senior resident in the corresponding field, demonstrates the potential of neural network representations in analyzing microscopic pathology images of neuroblastoma tumors.

Keywords: Computer-aided diagnosis · Pathology image
Multi-view learning · Deep learning · Maximum entropy discrimination

1 Introduction

Peripheral neuroblastic tumors (pNTs) are a group of embryonal tumors arising from primitive sympathetic ganglia and containing variably differentiated neural elements and variable amounts of Schwannian stromal cells. They commonly affect children and are the most frequently extracranial solid tumors in childhood. There is one case in every 7000 live children, accounting for 8–10% of all childhood cancers [23]. The treatment and management of pNTs depend on the pathological diagnosis as well as the disease stage and some molecular information. The accurate pathological diagnosis plays the most important

X. Geng and B.-H. Kang (Eds.): PRICAI 2018, LNAI 11012, pp. 545–558, 2018.
https://doi.org/10.1007/978-3-319-97304-3_42

role in the whole treatment plan of patients. At this stage, the international neuroblastoma pathology classification (INPC) is recommended by the World Health Organization (WHO) for pNTs morphological categorization [18]. Based on morphologic criteria, mainly the differentiation of the neural elements and the variable amounts of Schwannian stromal cells, pNTs are classified into four basic morphological categories (shown in Fig. 1): (1) neuroblastoma (NB); (2) ganglioneuroblastoma, intermixed (GNBi); (3) ganglioneuroma (GN); and (4) ganglioneuroblastoma, nodular (GNBn).

The tumor usually varies from one microscopic field to another in the same tumor or from one tumor to another. Due to lack of pathologists especially pediatric pathologists, and the rise of patients in China, pathologists nowadays have to go over a large number of slides every day. Thus, it is not surprising that even the same pathologist would give different diagnoses for the same case, just because the slides were too much to examine. For each slide, the pathologists pick up several fields to observe, making the final decision about the entire slide based on these sampled regions. It was reported that there is a 20% discrepancy between central and institutional reviewers [24] because of experience, subjectivity and so on. Hence, it is necessary to find some ways to help the pathologist alleviate this time-consuming, experience-needed and non-objective work.

In all the cancer categories in pNTs, NB is the most common tumor type, composed of neoplastic neuroblasts in various differentiations with no or limited Schwannian stromal cells. By definition, the proportion of tumor tissues with Schwannian stromal cells should not exceed 50%. According to the INPC, NB can be further classified into three subtypes: undifferentiated (UD), poorly differentiated (PD), and differentiating (D). In this paper, we focus on the above three subtypes of the NB category as well as the un-neoplasm type (UN) which indicates the areas with no tumor cells, such as fibrous adipose tissue, blood vessels.

Different from regular natural images, microscopic tissue images have many unique characteristics. In this research, finding targeted kinds of image representations for microscopic pathology classification is one of the essential problems that we need to explore. Many traditional features have their distinctive superiorities and strong robustness, e.g., LBP [15] has been proved to be an efficient texture operator, aimed at describing the textural characteristics of target images. Pathology images, in a sense, show texture-like structures and are intuitively more suitable for texture representations, whereas other possible proper representations should also be considered to avoid the excessive deficiency of contributive information. Thus, different traditional features are supposed to be taken into consideration.

The uncertainty of proper representation and the limitation of information that one kind of feature contains both obstruct the further improvement of pathology image diagnosis. If several aspects of information can be utilized to diagnose at the same time and complement each other, which is called multi-view learning, then the above problems can be naturally solved. Multi-view learning, in recent years, is a rapidly developing research direction, having great theoretical

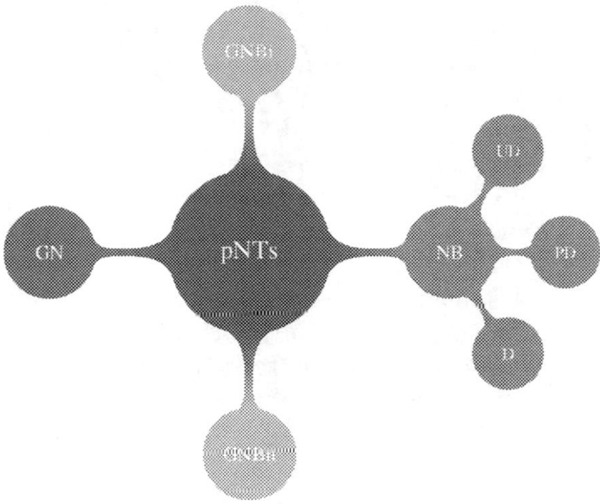

Fig. 1. The morphological categorization of pNTs

basis and enormous practical success [20,26,30]. We consider performing multi-view maximum entropy discrimination (MVMED) [21] to combine the contributive information of different representations, which can be various features of the same pathology image. Consequently, we can utilize a kind of typical feature that only emphasizes texture information to adapt the characteristics of tissue images and combine the texture feature with other types of features to make up for the limitation of information that it can contribute.

Despite traditional representations, deep neural network representations are also worthy of experimenting with. In recent years, many kinds of CNN networks, e.g., AlexNet [11], OverFeat [17], achieve excellent accuracy in natural image classification tasks, with large-scale datasets published in the ImageNet Large Scale Visual Recognition Challenge (ILSVRC) Competition. These trained networks can well extract semantic level features of natural images and show outstanding performance in many other kinds of natural image classification tasks [11,19,22]. Although the pattern of pathology images is far different from natural ones, the basic edge and figure information, which the deep networks have already been trained to gain, can still be reused. Also, the complexity and flexibility of CNN could provide the semantic information extraction of microscopic pathology image. Until now, there is no work about the application of deep learning in pNTs, and it was recently illustrated that it could be a future direction for research [4].

We highlight the main contributions as follows. (1) We are the first to successfully apply multi-view learning and deep learning technology on the microscopic neuroblastoma image diagnosis task, fully proving the effectiveness of the multi-view learning and deep learning algorithm. (2) We observe that deep neural network representations exceed traditional image representations, which illustrates the excellent potential of the application of deep neural network in computer-aided pNTs diagnosis. (3) From the experimental results, we achieve much better diagnosis performance comparing with a human senior resident, with both higher efficiency and accuracy.

2 Related Work

Pathological diagnosis is usually achieved by a professional human pathologist through observing a stained specimen on the slide glass with a microscope. Recently, thanks to the rapid progress in digitization technology of information, digital pathological images, which are called whole slide image (WSI) [16], can be accumulated by utilizing a scanner to capture the entire slide of the specimen. However, the tremendous amount of information that one WSI contained (more than a billion pixels) and the high morphology variability of one same disease both make it difficult to remember and diagnose with the human brain. Digital image analysis based on machine learning algorithms can assist pathologists to diagnose with lower misjudgment, regarding the detection efficiency and accuracy.

In Aug. 2016, research from Stanford University School of Medicine illustrated that computers could be trained to assess lung cancer pathological specimens with higher accuracy compared with pathologists [28]. In 2017, scientists from Google, Google Brain and Verily developed an artificial intelligence technique that can be used to diagnose breast cancer [12]. They segmented a single WSI into tens of thousands of 128×128-pixel patches for training. Ultimately, this algorithm learned to identify pixels within a single small patch that is labeled as a "tumor", effectively distinguishing tumor tissues from healthy tissues. Then in comparison with human pathologists, based on the sensitivity (how many correct tumors were found) and the false positive (how many normal tissues were diagnosed as tumors), the accuracy rate for human pathologists was 73.3% and the algorithm is 88.5%. In addition, artificial intelligence has been successfully applied in intestinal polyposis, prostate cancer, and lymph node metastasis [8,10,25]. There are also some papers predicting that artificial intelligence will be embedded in routine pathological workflows in the future, helping with repetitive tasks that require quantitative evaluation and counting, and reducing the time spent by pathologists for diagnosis. In this case, humans can undertake higher-level diagnosis and consultation tasks, e.g., integrating information on molecular changes, pathological diagnosis, and clinical manifestations, assisting clinical treatment planning and providing individualized health management for patients [5]. Relevant work has been carried out mainly in the diagnosis of adult cancer, such as the diagnosis of breast cancer, cervical cancer screening. However, no reports have been reported on children's tumors, and it is urgent to carry out relative researches.

3 Traditional Representations and Deep Representations

As mentioned above, the pattern of histopathology image is visually closer to texture rather than objects, and thus we consider choosing a classical kind of efficient texture operator: local binary pattern (LBP) [15]. LBP labels the pixels of an image by thresholding the neighborhood of each pixel and considers the result as a binary number, first proposed by Ojala et al. [14]. It describes the local texture construction of an image, having many remarkable strengths such as rotational and gray-scale invariance. A visualization example is shown in Fig. 2.

In spite of texture features, we also consider other traditional features. In this paper, we choose dense scale-invariant feature transform (DSIFT) [27] descriptor, which is often utilized in image matching or retrieval tasks. Average-DSIFT extracts SIFT [13] features densely, with a specific step size, from each image on a specified grid. Figure 2 displays the visualization result. SIFT features are detected through a staged filtering approach, which guarantees scale invariance of the algorithm. It recognizes stable extreme points in the scaled space and then extracts invariant values of position, rotation, and scale. Because image classification tasks require unified and fixed feature structures, DSIFT features are applied to get the normalized input of models. Since the dimension of the extracted feature is unnecessarily large, we pool it with the pooling size of 19×19. Two different mainstream ways are applied: one way is max-pooling, that is, keeping only the largest value (or the smallest) of the pool, and discarding the others; the other way is average-pooling, that is, averaging all the values in the pool. Max-pooling, in general, retains more texture information, while average-pooling retains more background information [2].

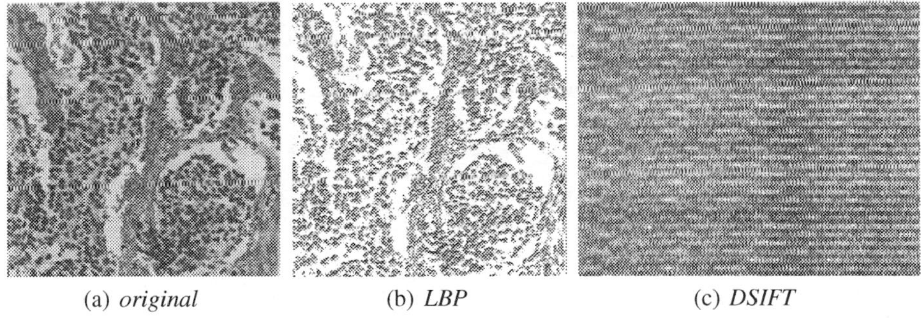

(a) *original* (b) *LBP* (c) *DSIFT*

Fig. 2. An example for LBP and DSIFT visualization (a) *original* (b) *LBP* (c) *DSIFT*

For deep neural network presentation, we choose the AlexNet architecture [11], which has won the ILSVRC12. This architecture consists of 5 convolutional layers, some of which are followed by the max-pooling layers, and three fully-connected layers. Each convolution layer contains 96 to 384 convolution kernels, each with a size range of 3×3 to 11×11. It was trained on the subset of the ImageNet dataset and achieved the best accuracy. Inside the architecture, the original images are center cropped and resized to 256×256. After these simple image preprocessing operations, they are treated as input data for network training. Data augmentation and dropout [6] are also utilized during the training process to avoid overfitting phenomenon. At the same time, in order to further improve the classification accuracy, local response normalization (LRN) [9] is also applied. We extract the representation output of the 7th layer in the network, which is the topmost feature extraction layer beneath the final classification layer inside the model and obtain features of 4096 dimensions. Also, we discard the ReLU part of the 7th layer to avoid the data sparsity caused by it. Since there is only one deep representation for MVMED, the classifier will be the degraded version MED instead.

4 Multi-view Learning with Maximum Entropy Discrimination

Multi-view learning focuses on machine learning problems that can be characterized by a variety of individual feature sets. Instead of using a single representation or simply concatenating multiple representations into one representation, multi-view learning explicitly uses different representations of the data and models the relationships between them or subsequent operations that they induce. The canonical correlation analysis (CCA) [7] and the co-training algorithm [1] are two representative work for the early study of multi-view learning. This type of learning mechanism comes from the fact that real-world objects can often be represented by many different views or features in various scenarios. For example, when understanding multimedia content, multimedia clips can be described with both image and audio. In the task of pathological diagnosis of cell or tissue images, the possible influence factors on the classification result are various, e.g., texture information may be an important basis, but at the same time, the color information that the doctor diagnoses as a part of the foundation cannot be ignored. The information contained in one set of features is often targeted and not comprehensive enough. In this problem, we need to obtain better accuracy by combining the advantages of different features and multi-view learning provides a natural solution for this purpose.

We consider using the MVMED algorithm [21] to combine multiple sets of features extracted from the original image and the main architecture of the model is shown in Fig. 3. In this algorithm, we have a multi-view dataset $\mathcal{D} = \{x_t^1, x_t^2, y_t\}_{t=1}^N$ with N examples, each of which has two views x_t^1 and x_t^2. For simpler expression, we let $v \in \{1, 2\}$ denote the index of views. For one pair $\{x_t^v, y_t\}$, x_t^v represents the tth input from view v, and $y_t \in \{1, -1\}$ denotes the corresponding label. Each view corresponds to a discriminant function $L_v(x^v|\boldsymbol{\Theta}_v)$ parameterized by a set of parameters $\boldsymbol{\Theta}_v$, satisfying $y_t L_v(x_t^v|\boldsymbol{\Theta}_v) \geq \gamma_t^v$, $t \in [N]$, $v \in [V]$. The discriminant functions from different views are regularized so that they classify the training samples with the same confidence. Margin consistency theory [20] is applied in this model, i.e., classification margins from different views are forced to be the same, namely, $\gamma_t \doteq \gamma_t^1 = \ldots = \gamma_t^V$, $t \in [N]$. Considering the case that specified margins may be not reasonable for some examples, the margins $\boldsymbol{\Theta} = \{\boldsymbol{\Theta}_v\}_{v\in[V]}$ are as random variables, assigned with prior $p_0(\boldsymbol{\gamma})$ as in the MED framework. The following optimization is solved for the posterior $p(\boldsymbol{\Theta}, \boldsymbol{\gamma})$.

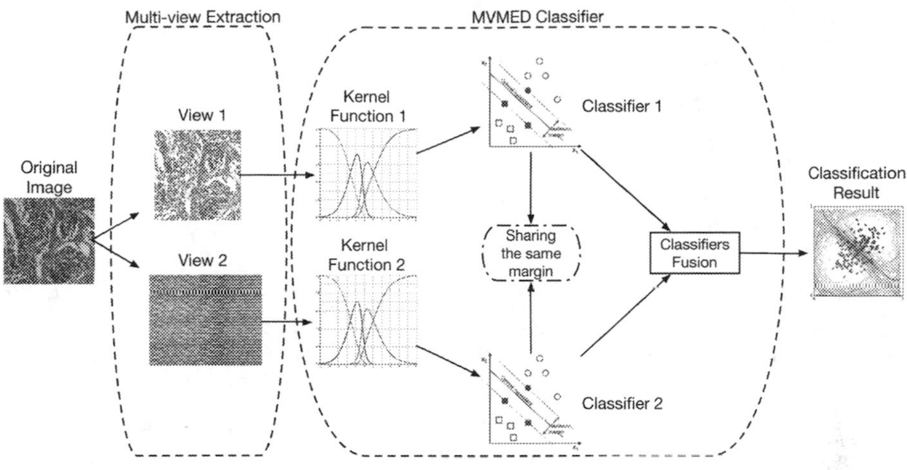

Fig. 3. The main architecture of MVMED

$$\begin{aligned} &\min_{p(\boldsymbol{\Theta},\boldsymbol{\gamma})} \mathrm{KL}(p(\boldsymbol{\Theta},\boldsymbol{\gamma}) \,||\, p_0(\boldsymbol{\Theta},\boldsymbol{\gamma})) \\ &\text{s.t.} \begin{cases} \int p(\boldsymbol{\Theta},\boldsymbol{\gamma})[y_t L_v(x_t^v|\boldsymbol{\Theta}_v) - \gamma_t] d\boldsymbol{\Theta}_v d\boldsymbol{\gamma} \geq 0, \\ t \in [N], v \in [V]. \end{cases} \end{aligned} \tag{1}$$

Afterwards, $p(\boldsymbol{\Theta}) = \int p(\boldsymbol{\Theta},\boldsymbol{\gamma}) d\boldsymbol{\gamma}$ can be recovered, and the following formula can be treated as decision rules

$$\hat{y} = \mathrm{sign}\left(\frac{1}{V}\sum_{v=1}^{V} \int p(\boldsymbol{\Theta})\, L_v(x^v|\boldsymbol{\Theta}_v)\, d\boldsymbol{\Theta}\right).$$

Also, the idea of sequential minimum optimization (SMO) [29] is adapted to the dual problem for efficient training, which is inspired by the original SMO for the standard SVM dual problem. This coordinate ascent algorithm decomposes the original quadratic programming problem for solving N parameters into amounts of sub-quadratic programming problems, each of which requires only two parameters to be addressed, saving time cost and memory requirements. It is guaranteed to converge to the global maximum because the optimization problem Eq. (1) is strictly convex and smooth. Especially, if there is only one view, MVMED will degenerate to MED.

5 Experiments

In this section, we will first introduce the detailed information about our pathology dataset and the specific partition configuration for training, validation, and testing. Then, we observe and compare the experimental results of deep neural representations and traditional representations through performing binary classification tasks, getting the characteristics of two kinds of features respectively.

Finally, we use the one-vs-rest method to get the multi-class classification results and compare the results with human doctor diagnosis.

5.1 Dataset Description

Between Jan. 1st, 2014 and Dec. 31st, 2015, 163 slides with a diagnosis of Peripheral neuroblastic tumors from 72 patients were seen at a third-level grade-A children's hospital, included ganglioneuroma (34 slides); ganglioneuroblastoma, intermixed (35 slides); and neuroblastoma (94 slides). Among the slides in the neuroblastoma category, there were 11 UD subtypes, 52 PD subtypes, and 31 D subtypes. These specimens were prepared according to the standard histopathologic protocol and subsequently digitized using ScanScope T2 digitizer (Aperio, Leica, Germany) at 40× magnification. The whole slide images are quite large, varying from 1 to 4.5 GB. To make the image analysis more tractable, we snapshot each histology slide image into multiple non-overlapping image tiles of the size 768 × 768 in pixels. All the snapshot images were reviewed histologically by a senior pediatric pathologist following the histological criteria according to INPC and classified into UD, PD, D, and UN. We name this dataset after neuroblastoma tumors (NBT) (Fig. 4).

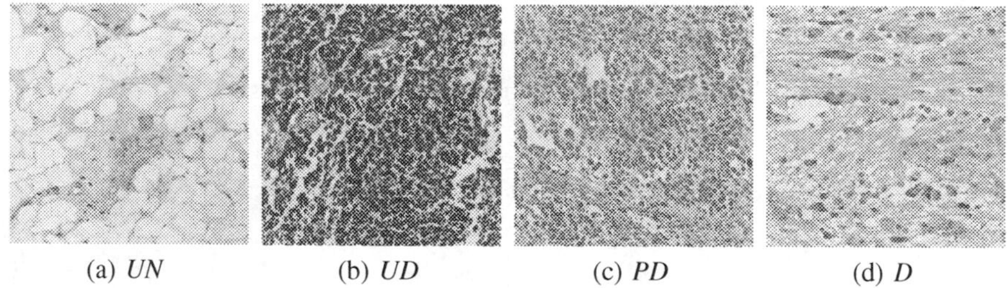

(a) *UN* (b) *UD* (c) *PD* (d) *D*

Fig. 4. Example for UN and three subtypes of NB.

As briefly mentioned in Sect. 2, one WSI contains enormous amounts of information and could consist of as many as tens of billions of pixels, which usually make it hard to analyze. Thus, sampling local mini patches is a useful method so that feature extraction and classification can be performed in each local patch. In this experiment, we choose to sample smaller patches from WSIs with size 768 × 768, since images of this size can contain just enough information for doctors to judge it and also comfortable for human vision.

Furthermore, since the real patient cases that can be collected are limited, and labeling requires a lot of labor, available training data that we can get are insufficient. In the four classes, there are only 100 patches in the class UN and around 300 patches in the other three classes, which are far not enough for general digital image analysis tasks. Therefore, data augmentation is necessary for us to perform. To achieve the data balance between four classes, we sample patches with size 740 × 740 from original patches to generate new samples to make the data amount of every class be 300 patches, and these samples can be considered independent ones. Afterwards, for both traditional and deep representations, we resize all the images to size 128 × 128, which is big enough for our model to see the details of one patch. Then, we rotate each patch by 90° for four times, flip the original patch horizontally and rotate again. This makes the image number in all classes increase from 300 to 2400. Also, we utilize the one-vs-rest method in the experiment, the training data of the class with the smaller number are copied by three times to avoid the unbalanced problem. The ratio of the partition in our dataset is $Training : Validation : Testing = 4 : 1 : 1$, i.e., the patch number of training data is 1600, and either of the other two is 400 for each class. To compare with the human doctor, 50 patches are sampled from the test sets of four classes, composing 200 test patches in total. All the labels of the human test patches are hidden and utilized to be compared with the diagnosis results of the human doctor.

5.2 Binary Classification

To analyze the classification difficulty of each class pair, we list the random combinations of two classes and treat each of them as one binary classification task respectively. Since we have four classes (UN, UD, PD, and D) in our dataset, there are $6 = 4 \times 3/div2$ binary pairs, which are UN-UD, UN-PD, UN-D, UD-PD, UD-D, and PD-D. As mentioned in Sect. 3, we utilize LBP, average-DSIFT and max-DSIFT representations as the traditional feature sets and AlexNet representation as the deep neural network feature. In the experiment, we obtain four results of each binary classification pair for traditional representations, which are gained from single LBP, single max-DSIFT or average-DSIFT, the concatenation of the two feature sets, and the combination of them with MVMED method separately. The experiment results are shown in Table 1.

Table 1. Results (%) of MVMED with traditional representations on NBT dataset.

Dataset	aver-DSIFT LBP	aver-DSIFT	LBP	aver-DSIFT LBP concat.	max-DSIFT LBP	max-DSIFT	max-DSIFT LBP concat.
UN - UD	97.15 ± 0.45	86.84 ± 0.95	96.74 ± 0.49	88.28 ± 0.80	**97.35 ± 0.53**	84.99 ± 0.54	84.48 ± 0.89
UN - PD	**97.03 ± 0.67**	84.13 ± 0.98	96.52 ± 0.57	89.26 ± 0.97	96.81 ± 0.78	84.15 ± 1.30	87.27 ± 1.29
UN - D	**93.62 ± 0.80**	84.58 ± 1.16	89.75 ± 1.25	86.27 ± 0.58	93.52 ± 0.62	84.06 ± 0.90	86.04 ± 1.09
UD - PD	74.00 ± 1.17	60.61 ± 1.46	**76.71 ± 0.94**	68.21 ± 1.16	75.03 ± 0.98	60.80 ± 1.04	64.99 ± 1.40
UD - D	90.36 ± 0.96	61.15 ± 1.91	**93.94 ± 0.77**	74.45 ± 1.06	90.66 ± 1.10	59.76 ± 1.75	67.75 ± 1.57
PD - D	83.36 ± 1.19	60.90 ± 1.06	**87.90 ± 1.16**	69.68 ± 1.13	83.54 ± 1.81	59.48 ± 1.45	62.04 ± 1.46

From Table 1, where aver-DSIFT means average-DSIFT and concat. means concatenation for simplicity, we can clearly see that utilizing LBP feature achieves much better performance than DSIFT features for every binary classification pair, which may potentially confirm that pathology images tend to contain the texture-like structures. Furthermore, it is not necessarily the case that one of max-DSIFT or average-DSIFT is better than the other, which means there is no apparent difference between the feature extraction effectiveness of the two. Also, if the two views can both well capture meaningful information of the image and achieve nice accuracy, the combination of them will perform better than either of them; if not so, the performance of the multi-view will be relatively unstable. In addition, the performance of the naive concatenation of two views cannot exceed either of them and is always between the two. At the same time, no matter the single representation is LBP, average-DSIFT or max-DSIFT, when it comes to the classification of UD-PD, the accuracy declines considerably. Thus, it can be illustrated that the classification between UD and PD is tougher than any other tasks, which also confirms the real diagnosis situations (the boundary between the two differentiating types is relatively blurred and usually influenced by the subjectivity of individual pathologists).

Table 2. Results (%) of MVMED with deep neural network representations on NBT dataset.

View	UN - UD	UN - PD	UN - D	UD - PD	UD - D	PD - D
AlexNet	99.80 ± 0.15	99.80 ± 0.15	98.93 ± 0.29	92.43 ± 0.74	99.81 ± 0.14	97.76 ± 0.35

Table 2 shows the classification accuracy of the deep representation in binary classification tasks. High accuracies in all case prove this neural network representation can efficiently extract useful features from pathology images. Although in the UD-PD classification case, the accuracy is still inferior a little comparing with other cases, it remains above 90%.

5.3 Multi-class Classification

Binary classification results can only convey us the concept the difficulty between random pairs from the four classes and our final goal is to classify one pathology patch into UN, UD, PD or D. We choose a typical multi-class classification method one-versus-rest (OvR) [3] to make the prediction. An OvR strategy requires the training of a single classifier for each category, samples of which are treated positive and all other samples are negative. This strategy requires the underlying classifier to generate real-valued confidence values for its decisions, not just class labels. Since when multiple classes are predicted to be a single sample, individual discrete class labels can cause ambiguities. The corresponding classifier is namely: $\hat{y} = \underset{k \in \{1 \ldots K\}}{\operatorname{argmax}} f_k(x)$, where $\hat{y} \in \{1, \ldots, K\}$ is the predicted label for the sample x and f_k is the confidence value of label k.

Table 3 shows the intermediate result of the classifier of each class. The deep representation is still superior to traditional ones and achieves brilliant performance. For traditional representations, the most cases illustrate that the multi-view learning helps the intermediate classification accuracy increase, which may further improve the final multi-class classification result when comparing with single views. Furthermore, the lowest accuracy of class PD in most cases demonstrates that this type of NB tumor is harder to recognize from other types. In contrast, the type UN is the easiest one to recognize, whose reason might be that healthy tissue is easy to distinguish from tumor tissue regarding morphology. Through the above OvR classifier, we obtain the final multi-view classification results afterwards, and the accuracies are shown in Table 4.

Table 3. Intermediate results (%) for one-vs-rest method on NBT dataset.

View	UN - UD PD D	UD - UN PD D	PD - UN UD D	D - UN UD PD
average-DSIFT LBP	**96.40 ± 0.40**	82.59 ± 0.55	79.50 ± 0.81	82.52 ± 0.70
average-DSIFT	90.54 ± 0.54	76.34 ± 0.20	69.86 ± 0.64	71.53 ± 0.90
LBP	93.68 ± 0.44	**85.64 ± 0.75**	80.33 ± 0.66	81.40 ± 1.08
average-DSIFT LBP concat	92.17 ± 0.41	78.65 ± 0.46	77.06 ± 0.91	76.36 ± 0.57
max-DSIFT LBP	96.24 ± 0.40	82.43 ± 0.81	**80.49 ± 0.77**	**82.77 ± 0.53**
max-DSIFT	90.89 ± 0.77	75.69 ± 0.25	70.29 ± 0.85	81.29 ± 1.07
max-DSIFT LBP concat	92.09 ± 0.50	77.10 ± 0.39	74.04 ± 0.62	73.35 ± 0.99
AlexNet	**99.70 ± 0.25**	**96.13 ± 0.41**	**93.88 ± 0.56**	**98.41 ± 0.35**

Table 4. Results (%) of multi-class classification via one-vs-rest method

View	Accuracy
AlexNet	**94.25 ± 0.75**
average-DSIFT LBP	72.59 ± 1.02
average-DSIFT	50.73 ± 0.91
LBP	72.52 ± 1.27
average-DSIFT LBP concat	60.97 ± 1.14
max-DSIFT LBP	**72.83 ± 1.37**
max-DSIFT	49.81 ± 0.85
max-DSIFT LBP concat	55.92 ± 0.55

From the final accuracies in Table 4, deep feature AlexNet achieves the best performance overall, exceeding the best result in traditional features by up to around 22%. We invite a doctor, who is a senior resident with eight years of experience from a general hospital, to try to diagnose the human test dataset. After four months reviewing all 163 slides with his supervisor via multi-microscope, he had been familiar with INPC and finished the image diagnosis himself. Four and a half hours were spent in total on human diagnosing and the time spent by the algorithm can almost be ignored, which confirms the efficiency of the model. The accuracy of AlexNet feature is far higher than the diagnosis results (56.5%) of the doctor (96.5% for the UN-UD, PD, D case). Since deep features show more excellent performance and robustness than traditional ones in this experiment, it is reasonable to believe that they have more potentials worthy of exploring. Also, they may be able to achieve higher accuracy when combined with other kinds deep features or traditional features through the end-to-end training, which will be a future work for us to do. For traditional representations, the multi-view learning combination of LBP and max-DSIFT features make the accuracy higher than either of the two of them, which demonstrates the effectiveness of MVMED in terms of utilizing the complementary information of different views.

6 Conclusion

Our work yields state-of-the-art sensitivity on the challenging task of diagnosing neuroblastoma tumors through digitally classifying pathology images with the multi-view learning method. We make explorations in the multi-view learning and single-view learning with traditional representations and deep representations on the NBT dataset. The binary classification results with both kinds of features help us analyze the task difficulty of random two classes and some primary characteristics of MVMED. Then, the intermediate and final results of OvR multi-class classification method demonstrates the excellence of multi-view learning and deep learning, especially when compared with the professional human diagnosis.

The number of the authoritative professional pathologists is nowadays far below the social requirement, whereas machine learning methods can "learn" the abundant medical human experience through the sample data labeled by these exports, achieving far higher accuracy than human doctors. This kinds of computer-aided diagnosis methods can possibly assist young pathologists who lack years of work experience. The potential shown by deep neural network representations provides our future work more possibilities, e.g., the end-to-end multi-view deep learning may the direction that we will focus on. Also, we will also attempt to apply pre-training through other hand-annotated tumor datasets with similar image conditions and further extend the size of our pathology dataset.

Acknowledgements. This work is supported by the National Natural Science Foundation of China under Project 61673179. The corresponding author is Prof. Shiliang Sun.

References

1. Blum, A., Mitchell, T.: Combining labeled and unlabeled data with co-training. In: Proceedings of the Eleventh Annual Conference on Computational Learning Theory, pp. 92–100. ACM (1998)
2. Boureau, Y.L., Bach, F., LeCun, Y., Ponce, J.: Learning mid-level features for recognition. In: Proceedings of Computer Vision and Pattern Recognition Conference, pp. 2559–2566. IEEE (2010)
3. Christopher, M.B.: Pattern Recognition and Machine Learning. Springer, New York (2016)
4. Gheisari, S., Charlton, A., Catchpoole, D.R., Kennedy, P.J.: Computers can classify neuroblastic tumours from histopathological images using machine learning. Pathology **49**, S72–S73 (2017)
5. Granter, S.R., Beck, A.H., Papke Jr., D.J.: Alphago, deep learning, and the future of the human microscopist. Pathol. Lab. Med. **141**(5), 619–621 (2017)
6. Hinton, G.E., Srivastava, N., Krizhevsky, A., Sutskever, I., Salakhutdinov, R.R.: Improving neural networks by preventing co-adaptation of feature detectors. arXiv preprint arXiv:1207.0580 (2012)
7. Hotelling, H.: Relations between two sets of variates. Biometrika **28**(3/4), 321–377 (1936)
8. Hou, L., Samaras, D., Kurc, T.M., Gao, Y., Davis, J.E., Saltz, J.H.: Patch-based convolutional neural network for whole slide tissue image classification. In: Proceedings of the Conference on Computer Vision and Pattern Recognition, pp. 2424–2433. IEEE (2016)
9. Jarrett, K., Kavukcuoglu, K., LeCun, Y., et al.: What is the best multi-stage architecture for object recognition? In: Proceedings of the 12th International Computer Vision Conference, pp. 2146–2153. IEEE (2009)
10. Korbar, B., et al.: Deep learning for classification of colorectal polyps on whole-slide images. J. Pathol. Inform. **8**, 1–9 (2017)
11. Krizhevsky, A., Sutskever, I., Hinton, G.E.: ImageNet classification with deep convolutional neural networks. In: Proceedings of Advances in Neural Information Processing Systems, pp. 1097–1105 (2012)
12. Liu, Y., et al.: Detecting cancer metastases on gigapixel pathology images. arXiv preprint arXiv:1703.02442 (2017)
13. Lowe, D.G.: Object recognition from local scale-invariant features. In: Proceedings of the Computer Vision International Conference, vol. 2, pp. 1150–1157. IEEE (1999)
14. Ojala, T., Pietikainen, M., Harwood, D.: Performance evaluation of texture measures with classification based on kullback discrimination of distributions. In: Proceedings of the 12th International Association for Pattern Recognition Conference, vol. 1, pp. 582–585. IEEE (1994)
15. Ojala, T., Pietikäinen, M., Harwood, D.: A comparative study of texture measures with classification based on featured distributions. Pattern Recogn. **29**(1), 51–59 (1996)
16. Pantanowitz, L.: Digital images and the future of digital pathology. J. Pathol. Inform. **1**, (2010)
17. Sermanet, P., Eigen, D., Zhang, X., Mathieu, M., Fergus, R., LeCun, Y.: Overfeat: integrated recognition, localization and detection using convolutional networks. arXiv preprint arXiv:1312.6229 (2013)

18. Shimada, H., et al.: The international neuroblastoma pathology classification (the Shimada system). Cancer **86**(2), 364–372 (1999)
19. Simonyan, K., Zisserman, A.: Very deep convolutional networks for large-scale image recognition. arXiv preprint arXiv:1409.1556 (2014)
20. Sun, S.: A survey of multi-view machine learning. Neural Comput. Appl. **23**(7–8), 2031–2038 (2013)
21. Sun, S., Chao, G.: Multi-view maximum entropy discrimination. In: Proceedings of International Joint Conferences on Artificial Intelligence, pp. 1706–1712 (2013)
22. Szegedy, C., et al.: Going deeper with convolutions. In: Proceedings of the Conference on Computer Vision and Pattern Recognition (2015)
23. Tang, J., Li, Z., Chen, J., et al.: Children's cancer diagnosis and treatment (2011)
24. Teot, L.A., Sposto, R., Khayat, A., Qualman, S., Reaman, G., Parham, D.: The problems and promise of central pathology review: development of a standardized procedure for the children's oncology group. Pediatr. Dev. Pathol. **10**(3), 199–207 (2007)
25. Wang, D., Khosla, A., Gargeya, R., Irshad, H., Beck, A.H.: Deep learning for identifying metastatic breast cancer. arXiv preprint arXiv:1606.05718 (2016)
26. Xu, C., Tao, D., Xu, C.: A survey on multi-view learning. arXiv preprint arXiv:1304.5634 (2013)
27. Yang, J., Yu, K., Gong, Y., Huang, T.: Linear spatial pyramid matching using sparse coding for image classification. In: Proceedings of the Conference on Computer Vision and Pattern Recognition, pp. 1794–1801. IEEE (2009)
28. Yu, K.H., et al.: Predicting non-small cell lung cancer prognosis by fully automated microscopic pathology image features. Nat. Commun. **7**, 12474 (2016)
29. Zeng, Z.Q., Yu, H.B., Xu, H.R., Xie, Y.Q., Gao, J.: Fast training support vector machines using parallel sequential minimal optimization. In: Proceedings of Intelligent System and Knowledge Engineering International Conference, vol. 1, pp. 997–1001. IEEE (2008)
30. Zhao, J., Xie, X., Xu, X., Sun, S.: Multi-view learning overview: recent progress and new challenges. Inf. Fusion **38**, 43–54 (2017)

Low-Rank Matrix Recovery via Continuation-Based Approximate Low-Rank Minimization

Xiang Zhang[1,4], Yongqiang Gao[2,4(✉)], Long Lan[1,4], Xiaowei Guo[1,4], Xuhui Huang[3,4], and Zhigang Luo[2,4(✉)]

[1] State Key Laboratory of High Performance Computing, NUDT, Changsha, China
zhangxiang08
[2] Science and Technology on Parallel and Distributed Laboratory, NUDT, Changsha, China
[3] Department of Computer Science and Technology, College of Computer, NUDT, Changsha, China
[4] College of Computer, NUDT, Changsha 410073, China
{gaoyongqiang16,zgluo}@nudt.edu.cn

Abstract. Low-rank matrix recovery (LRMR) is to recover the underlying low-rank structure from the degraded observations, and has myriad formulations, for example robust principal component analysis (RPCA). As a core component of LRMR, the low-rank approximation model attempts to capture the low-rank structure by approximating the ℓ_0-norm of all the singular values of a low-rank matrix, i.e., the number of the non-zero singular values. Towards this purpose, this paper develops a low-rank approximation model by jointly combining a parameterized hyperbolic tangent (tanh) function with the continuation process. Specificially, the continuation process is exploited to impose the parameterized tanh function to approximate the ℓ_0 norm. We then apply the proposed low-rank model to RPCA and refer to it as tanh-RPCA. Convergence analysis on optimization, and experiments of background subtraction on seven challenging real-world videos show the efficacy of the proposed low-rank model through comparing tanh-RPCA with several state-of-the-art methods.

Keywords: LRMR · RPCA · The continuation process
Background subtraction

1 Introduction

Low-rank matrix recovery (LRMR) attempts to recover the underlying low-rank structure from its corrupted observations, and has a wide range of applications in

X. Zhang and Y. Gao—Contributed equally to this work and this work was supported by the National Key Research and Development Program of China [2016YFB0200401], the National Natural Science Foundation of China [U1435222] and the National High-tech R&D Program [2015AA020108].

X. Geng and B.-H. Kang (Eds.): PRICAI 2018, LNAI 11012, pp. 559–573, 2018.
https://doi.org/10.1007/978-3-319-97304-3_43

computer vision, such as background subtraction [9,23], saliency detection [27, 39], face recognition [5,38], and image denosing [9,21] as well as machine learning, like principal component analysis (RPCA) [2,25,37], dictionary learning [22] and subspace clustering [14,24,36]. Thus, LRMR problems vary in different scenarios and can be formulated as RPCA, sparse and low-rank matrix decomposition or rank-sparsity incoherence. In this paper, we consider the LRMR problem [5,27] as RPCA, i.e.,

$$\min_{A,E} rank(A) + \lambda \|E\|_0, \quad s.t.\ D = A + E \tag{1}$$

where D is the data matrix, and A and E are the so-called low-rank and sparse components, respectively. λ is a parameter to balance the low-rank and sparse components, and $\|\cdot\|_0$ indicates ℓ_0-norm. Since solving the matrix rank and ℓ_0-norm of (1) are the NP-hard problem, [2] rewrites (1) as the convex relaxed objective function by replacing the rank and the ℓ_0-norm with the nuclear norm and the ℓ_1-norm, respectively. Although their model is convex, solving such the relaxed model might shrink all the singular values equally. This implies that large singular values are penalized more severely than small counterparts.

To address this issue, the non-convex versions of the nuclear norm such as weighted nuclear norm [9] and truncated nuclear norm [11] have been developed. Since the rank function and the nuclear norm are essentially the ℓ_0-norm and the ℓ_1-norm of the singular values, respectively, myriad non-convex approximations to them have been devised on the basis of the advances of ℓ_0-norm and ℓ_1-norm, such as minimax concave penalty [34], capped-ℓ_1 regularization [8], truncated ℓ_1-norm [31], etc. In light of these insights above, this paper also exploits a non-convex function to achieve this goal.

Inspired by [4,7,13] and the activation function of deep learning [16], this paper proposes a non-covex low-rank approximation model to solve LRMR problems, where a parameter is introduced into the hyperbolic tangent (tanh) function for the purpose of gradually approaching to the ℓ_0-norm via the continuation process. The convergent analysis on its optimization for tanh-RPCA is non-trivial due to the difficulty of the continuation process. To verify the efficacy of the proposed model, we apply it for RPCA on both synthetic data and several real-world videos. Experimental results show that it outperforms several state-of-the-art methods in terms of both quantitative and qualitative results.

The contributions of this paper embrace two aspects. A new non-convex low-rank approximation model is proposed by jointly combining the hyperbolic tangent (tanh) function with the continuation process to gradually approach to the ℓ_0-norm. To the best of our knowledge, it is the first attempt to adopt the activation function of deep learning and the continuation strategy to solve the rank approximation problem. In addition, we theoretically prove the convergence of the proposed model in the frame of augmented Lagrange multiplier (ALM).

The rest of paper is organized as follows. Section 2 reviews the related works briefly and Sect. 3 introduces our proposed model. The convergence analysis of the proposed optimization algorithm is given in Sect. 4. Experiments are performed in Sect. 5. Finally, we conduct the conclusion in Sect. 6.

2 Related Works

As is well-known in computer vision and machine learning, low-rank approximation has been studied thoroughly. Most existing efforts exploit the functions or schatten norms to approximate the rank function to solve LRMR problems and could be roughly divided into either convex or non-convex low-rank approximation.

In the convex methods, the nuclear norm is a frequently used convex approximation to the rank function. Candès *et al.* [3] claimed that the low-rank matrix can be recovered via the nuclear norm under the incoherence assumptions. Later, Recht *et al.* [26] also proved this claim. Due to the convex property of the nuclear norm, several sophisticated optimization techniques are developed concurrently. These optimization algorithms can efficiently yield a global optimal solution with theoretical guarantees, such as FISTA [1], APG [19], ADM [33] and ALM [20]. However, all the singular values are equally minimized so that large singular values are penalized more heavily than small ones.

The non-convex low-rank approximation method can be used to address the imbalanced penalization issue about singular values. It attempts to induce the large singular values to be larger as well as shrinks the small ones to be smaller. Since large singular values play a dominant role in determining the properties of a matrix, it is reasonable to emphasize the large singular values to maintain the major information. Numerious studies on the non-convex low-rank approximation have been widely developed, such as Capped ℓ_1-norm [35], Logarithm Determinant (logdet) [24] and the others [11,21]. Among them, the truncated nuclear norm [11] is a representative non-convex approximation method which refers to the nuclear norm subtracted by the summation of the largest few singular values. This is because the truncated nuclear norm can explicitly emphasize large singular values as well as penalize small singular values. Recent works show that the non-convex models might be more effective than convex counterparts for the LRMR problem. In this paper, our proposed low-rank approximation model also belongs to this category, but the difference from existing counterparts lies in where we approximate the ℓ_0-norm with a parameterized tanh function together with the continuation process. More importantly, the continuation process is very different from existing continuation processes used in LRMR. Thus, theoretical analysis on the convergence is very different from them as well.

3 The Proposed Model

This section elaborates our novel non-convex low-rank approximation model and then develops an optimization algorithm to solve it in the frame of ALM. In the end, we further analyze the convergence of the proposed optimization algorithm.

3.1 Problem Formulation

As stated above, LRMR focuses on recovering the low-rank structure within the dataset. Without loss of generality, we take RPCA as our basic model framework to evaluate our low-rank approximation model. RPCA can be formulated as the summation of both low-rank and sparse components. Given the data observations $D \in R^{m \times n}$, where m and n denote the number of dimensionalities and samples, respectively. According to [2], RPCA has the following formulation:

$$\min_{A,E} \|A\|_* + \lambda \|E\|_1, \quad s.t. D = A + E \tag{2}$$

where $\|A\|_*$ signifies the nuclear norm of A, which is defined as the summation of all of its singular values, and $\|E\|_1 = \sum_{ij} |E_{ij}|$. Based on the aforementioned approximation, the low-rank matrix can be effectively recovered under the incoherence assumption [2]. However, the nuclear norm in (2) is not tighter for the low-rank matrix approximation. In many studies, this point has been mentioned and is solved through the non-convex low-rank approximation [9,21]. Similarly, we propose a new low-rank approximation model for this problem as well. Then, we define our low-rank matrix approximation model as follows:

$$\|A\|_{\text{tanh},\beta} = \sum_i \tanh(\beta\sigma_i(A)) = \sum_i \left[\frac{2}{1 + \mathrm{e}^{-2\beta\sigma_i(A)}} - 1\right], \tag{3}$$

where $\sigma_i(A)$ signifies the i-th singular value of the matrix A, and $\beta > 0$ is a non-negative continuation parameter. Since our model is based on a parameterized tanh function, we abbreviate it as the "tanh-norm" for ease. Similar to [15], tanh-norm can be observed that $\lim_{\beta \to \infty} \|A\|_{\text{tanh},\beta} = \text{rank}(A)$. As shown in Fig. 1, the tanh-norm value approaches to the true rank as β increases, i.e. $\beta_c < \beta_b < \beta_g$. Thus, the tanh-norm is a proper candidate for the low-rank matrix approximation as well.

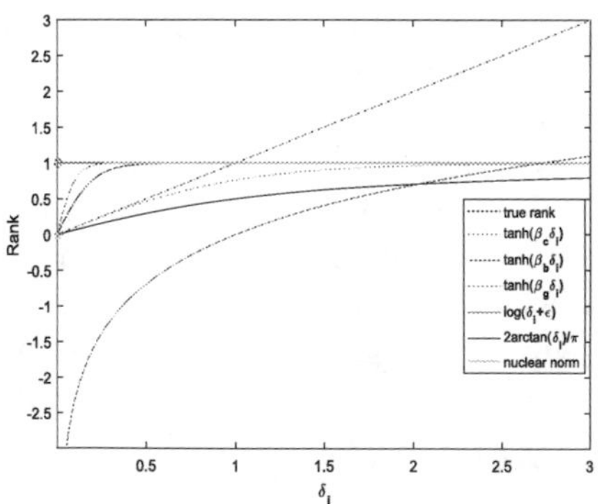

Fig. 1. The low-rank approximation functions versus the values of the i-th singular value δ_i.

By replacing the nuclear norm of (2) with (3), we define the tanh-RPCA model based on the tanh-norm as follows:

$$\min_{A,E} \|A\|_{\text{tanh},\beta} + \lambda \|E\|_1, s.t. D = A + E, \beta \to +\infty. \tag{4}$$

In light of (2) and (4), there are two highlighted aspects: 1) the tanh-norm for the low-rank matrix approximation is tighter than the nuclear norm, and 2) the objective (4) involves the continuation process where the continuation parameter β gradually increases to the positive infinity. Without loss of generality, in our experiments, we increase it with $\beta \leftarrow \beta + C$, where C is a predefined positive constant or integer. The second aspect greatly differs from existing studies [3,13,21,24] including the nuclear norm, log*det*, etc. In (4), the continuation process not only handles the non-convex optimization problem but also provides a dynamic way to reduce the gap between the tanh-norm and the rank function. Although [6,12] closely related with our work also introduce the continuation process into the optimization algorithm, it is designed for parameter selection rather than low-rank matrix approximation. Their involved continuation parameters gradually reduce to specific smaller value, contrary to our continuation process. More importantly, the continuation process makes the convergence proof to be non-trivial. Recently, the continuation process effectively used in [4] is similar to ours, but they follow different convergent behaviors in the objective function during the continuation process. Besides, the proof in [12,13] requires the objective value of approximation function to be unchanged when the continuation process is performed. Obviously, this condition is usually very strict in practical applications. Beyond this condition, our convergent analysis is more generalized than them.

3.2 Optimization

To optimize (4), we develop an optimization algorithm in the frame of the ALM. By introducing a Lagrange multiplier Y and a quadratic penalty term, the objective function of (4) can be rewritten as below:

$$\mathscr{L}(A,E,Y,\mu,\beta) = \sum_i \tanh(\beta\sigma_i(A)) + \lambda\|E\|_1 + \langle Y, A+E-D\rangle + \tfrac{\mu}{2}\|A+E-D\|_F^2, \tag{5}$$

where $\langle\cdot,\cdot\rangle$ denotes the matrix inner product, namely, $\langle P,Q\rangle = tr(P^TQ)$, and μ denotes a positive parameter. To solve (5), we need to make the objective function to be separable over all the variables. The detailed procedure can be shown as below:

Update A with the Other Variables Fixed. At the $(t+1)$-th step, we solve A^{t+1} with E^t, Y^t and μ^t fixed by optimizing the following sub-problem:

$$A^{t+1} = \arg\min_A \sum_i \tanh(\beta^t\sigma_i(A)) + \frac{\mu^t}{2}\left\|D - E^t - \frac{Y^t}{\mu^t} - A\right\|_F^2. \tag{6}$$

Solving this sub-problem (6) is similar to [14]. For concise, we omit here.

Update E with the Other Variables Fixed. At the $(t+1)$-th step, we optimize E^{t+1} with A^{t+1}, Y^t and μ^t fixed. The subproblem becomes:

$$E^{t+1} = \arg\min_E \lambda\|E\|_1 + \frac{\mu^t}{2}\left\|D - A^{t+1} - E - \frac{Y^t}{\mu^t}\right\|_F^2. \tag{7}$$

According to [1], (7) has the following closed-form solution:

$$E_{ij}^{t+1} = \max\left(\left|D - A^{t+1} - \frac{Y^t}{\mu^t}\right| - \frac{\lambda}{\mu^t}, 0\right)_{ij} sign\left(D - A^{t+1} - \frac{Y^t}{\mu^t}\right)_{ij}. \quad (8)$$

Update Y, μ and β with the Other Variables Fixed. The Lagrange multipliers Y^{t+1}, μ^{t+1} and β^{t+1} can be updated as below:

$$Y^{t+1}=Y^t + \mu^t(A^{t+1} + E^{t+1} - D), \quad (9)$$

$$\mu^{t+1} = \rho\mu^t, \quad (10)$$

and

$$\beta^{t+1} = \beta^t + C, \quad (11)$$

where $\rho > 1$. We can summarize the overall optimization procedure into Algorithm 1 (ALM for tanh-RPCA).

Algorithm 1. ALM for tanh-RPCA

Input: The data matrix $D \in R^{m\text{x}n}$.

1: Initialize: $\beta^0 > 1$, $\lambda > 1$, $\mu^0 > 0$, $\rho > 1$, $t = 0$, $A^0 = 0$, $E^0 = 0$ and $Y^0 = 0$
2: While not converged do
3: Update A^{t+1} by solving the subproblem (6);
4: Update E^{t+1} via (8);
5: Update Y^{t+1}, μ^{t+1} and β^{t+1} by (9), (10) and (11), respectively;
6: $t = t + 1$;
7: end While

Output: $A = A^{t+1}$ and $E = E^{t+1}$.

4 Convergence Analysis

This section mainly proves that our optimization algorithm converges to a stationary point. We first prepare several lemmas to verify the bound property of $\{Y^t\}$, $\{A^t\}$ and $\{E^t\}$, respectively. By these, we conclude that there exists a subsequence which converges to a local solution.

For convergence analysis, let $F(A)=\sum_i tanh(\beta\sigma_i(A))$, Eq. (5) is rewritten as:

$$\mathscr{L}(A,E,\beta,Y,\mu) =F(A)+\lambda\|E\|_1 + \langle Y, A + E - D\rangle + \frac{\mu}{2}\|A + E - D\|_F^2. \quad (12)$$

Lemma 1. *[30] The sequence $\{Y^t\}$ is bounded.*

Lemma 2. *Assume $\sum_{t=1}^{\infty} \frac{\mu^t+\mu^{t-1}}{2(\mu^{t-1})^2} < \infty$, $\{A^t\}$ and $\{E^t\}$ are bounded.*

Proof. We have the below equality by some algebra

$$\begin{aligned}
&\mathcal{L}(A^t,E^t,\beta^t,Y^t,\mu^t)\\
&= F_{\beta^t}(A^t) + \lambda\|E^t\|_1 + \langle Y^t, A^t + E^t - D\rangle + \tfrac{\mu^t}{2}\|A^t + E^t - D\|_F^2\\
&= F_{\beta^{t-1}}(A^t) + \lambda\|E^t\|_1 + \left\langle Y^{t-1}, A^t + E^t - D\right\rangle +\\
&\tfrac{\mu^{t-1}}{2}\|A^t + E^t - D\|_F^2 + F_{\beta^t}(A^t) - F_{\beta^{t-1}}(A^t) +\\
&\left\langle Y^t - Y^{t-1}, A^t + E^t - D\right\rangle + \tfrac{\mu^t - \mu^{t-1}}{2}\|A^t + E^t - D\|_F^2\\
&= \mathcal{L}(A^t,E^t,\beta^{t-1},Y^{t-1},\mu^{t-1}) + F_{\beta^t}(A^t) - F_{\beta^{t-1}}(A^t) + \tfrac{\mu^t+\mu^{t-1}}{2(\mu^{t-1})^2}\left\|Y^t - Y^{t-1}\right\|_F^2.
\end{aligned} \tag{13}$$

Then,

$$\begin{aligned}
&\mathcal{L}(A^{t+1},E^{t+1},\beta^t,Y^t,\mu^t) \le \mathcal{L}(A^{t+1},E^t,\beta^t,Y^t,\mu^t) \le \mathcal{L}(A^t,E^t,\beta^t,Y^t,\mu^t)\\
&\le \mathcal{L}(A^t,E^t,\beta^{t-1},Y^{t-1},\mu^{t-1}) + F_{\beta^t}(A^t) - F_{\beta^{t-1}}(A^t) + \tfrac{\mu^t+\mu^{t-1}}{2(\mu^{t-1})^2}\left\|Y^t - Y^{t-1}\right\|_F^2.
\end{aligned} \tag{14}$$

The inequality (14) can be recast as follows:

$$\begin{aligned}
&\mathcal{L}(A^{t+1},E^{t+1},\beta^t,Y^t,\mu^t)\\
&\le \mathcal{L}(A^1,E^1,\beta^0,Y^0,\mu^0) + \sum_{j=1}^{t}\left[F_{\beta^j}(A^j) - F_{\beta^{j-1}}(A^j)\right] + \sum_{j=1}^{t}\left[\tfrac{\mu^j-\mu^{j-1}}{2(\mu^{j-1})^2}\left\|Y^j - Y^{j-1}\right\|_F^2\right].
\end{aligned} \tag{15}$$

Since the tanh-norm starts with a small β and then gradually achieves the higher value to approach the rank function during the continuation process, this results in a series of sub-problems approaching to the original optimization problem. Suppose σ_i^j denotes the i-th singular value of A at the t-th iteration, there holds the following inequality:

$$\begin{aligned}
\sum_{j=1}^{t}\left[F_{\beta^j}(A^j) - F_{\beta^{j-1}}(A^j)\right] &= 2\sum_{i=1}^{l}\sum_{j=1}^{t}\frac{e^{-2\beta^{j-1}\sigma_i^j} - e^{-2\beta^j\sigma_i^j}}{(1+e^{-2\beta^j\sigma_i^j})(1+e^{-2\beta^{j-1}\sigma_i^j})}\\
&\le 2\sum_{i=1}^{l}\sum_{j=1}^{t}\frac{e^{-2\beta^{j-1}\sigma_i^j}}{(1+e^{-2\beta^{j-1}\sigma_i^j})}\\
&\le 2\sum_{i=1}^{l}\sum_{j=1}^{t}e^{-2\beta^{j-1}\sigma_i^j}.
\end{aligned} \tag{16}$$

where $l = \min\{m, n\}$, wherein m and n are the number of rows and columns of A, respectively. Let $n = \beta^{j-1} \in (0, +\infty)$. When $t \to +\infty$,

$$\begin{aligned}
\sum_{i=1}^{l}\sum_{j=1}^{+\infty}\mathrm{e}^{-2\beta^{j-1}\sigma_i^j} &= \sum_{i=1}^{l}\sum_{n=1}^{+\infty}(\mathrm{e}^{-2\sigma_i^j})^n = \sum_{i=1}^{l}\sum_{n=1}^{+\infty}\frac{(e^{-2\widetilde{\sigma}})^n}{(e^{-2\widetilde{\sigma}})^n}(e^{-2\sigma_i^j})^n\\
&= \sum_{i=1}^{l}\sum_{n=1}^{+\infty}(e^{-2\widetilde{\sigma}})^n(e^{-2(\sigma_i^j-\widetilde{\sigma})})^n.
\end{aligned} \tag{17}$$

If the singular value $\sigma_i^j \to +\infty$, $e^{-2\sigma_i^j} \to 0$. In this case, (16) is bounded due to the fact that the last inequality converges, when $n \to +\infty$. If this singular value is bounded, there exists a $\widetilde{\sigma}$ that meets $\sigma_i^j > \widetilde{\sigma}$. According to Theorem 1, (17) is convergent because the condition meets that $\sigma_i^j > \widetilde{\sigma} > 0$. Besides, if $\sigma_i^j = 0$, the second term of (15) is obviously bounded.

In light of the given condition $\sum_{t=1}^{\infty} \frac{\mu^t + \mu^{t-1}}{2(\mu^{t-1})^2} < \infty$, the inequality (15) is bounded.

Thus, under our continuation process, (16) always holds without any constrained condition.

As in Lemma 1, $\left\|Y^t - Y^{t-1}\right\|_F^2$ is bounded, and thus all the terms on the right side of (13) are bounded. This establishes the conclusion that $\mathscr{L}(A^{t+1},E^{t+1},\beta^t,Y^t,\mu^t)$ has the upper bound.

The formulation (12) can be rewritten as follows:

$$\begin{aligned} &\mathscr{L}(A^{t+1},E^{t+1},\beta^t,Y^t,\mu^t) + \tfrac{1}{2(\mu^t)^2}\left\|Y^t\right\|_F^2 \\ &= \mathrm{F}(A^{t+1}) + \lambda\left\|E^{t+1}\right\|_1 + \tfrac{\mu^t}{2}\left\|A^{t+1} + E^{t+1} - D - \tfrac{Y^t}{\mu^t}\right\|_F^2. \end{aligned} \tag{18}$$

As (18) is bounded, E^{t+1} is bounded. Likewise, A^t is bounded. ■

According to Lemma 2, the sequences $\{E^t, A^t\}$ induced by Algorithm 1 are bounded, when the continuation process continues to conduct $\beta \leftarrow \beta + C$. Besides, the other alternative increasing ways meet that $\beta \to +\infty$, and then Lemma 2 still holds.

Theorem 1. *Suppose the power series* $\sum_{n=0}^{\infty} a_n x_0^n$ *converges for some* $x_0 \in R$ *with* $x_0 \neq 0$. *So* $\sum_{n=0}^{\infty} a_n x^n$ *is absolutely convergent for every* $x \in R$ *with* $|x| < |x_0|$.

Proof. Since $\sum_{n=0}^{\infty} a_n x_0^n$ is convergent, so its terms are bounded and there exists $M \geq 0$ such that $a_n x_0^n \leq M$ *for* $n = 0, \cdots, +\infty$. Since $|x| < |x_0|$, there holds

$$|a_n x^n| = |a_n x_0^n| \left|\frac{x}{x_0}\right| \leq M r^n, \quad r = \left|\frac{x}{x_0}\right| < 1. \tag{19}$$

Comparing the power series with the convergent geometric series $\sum_{n=0}^{\infty} M r^n$, we conclude that $\sum_{n=0}^{\infty} a_n x^n$ is absolutely convergent. ■

Lemma 3. *Suppose* $\{A^t,E^t,Y^t\}$ *be the sequence generated from Algorithm 1 and* $\{A^*, E^*, Y^*\}$ *be an accumulation point. Then,* $\{A^*, E^*\}$ *is a stationary point of (5) if* $\sum_{t=1}^{\infty} \frac{\mu^t + \mu^{t-1}}{2(\mu^{t-1})^2} < \infty$.

Proof. Lemmas 1 and 2 show that Algorithm 1 generates the bounded sequence $\{A^t,E^t,Y^t\}$. According to the Bolzano-Weierstrass theorem, without loss of generality, the sequence $\{A^t,E^t,Y^t\}$ has a stationary point at least, e.g., $\{A^*,E^*,Y^*\}$.

Since $A^t + E^t - D = \frac{Y^t - Y^{t-1}}{\mu^{t-1}}$, we have $\lim_{t\to\infty} A^t + E^t = D$. Thus, this meets the primal feasibility condition. By the first-order optimality condition for A^{t+1}, we have

$$\begin{aligned} &\partial_A \mathscr{L}(A,E,Y,\mu)\,|_{A^{t+1}} \\ &= \partial_A F(A)|_{A^{t+1}} + Y^t + \mu^t(A^{t+1} + E^t - D) \\ &= \partial_A F(A)|_{A^{t+1}} + Y^{t+1} - \mu^t(E^{t+1} - E^t) \\ &= 0. \end{aligned} \tag{20}$$

If the singular value decomposition form of A is $Udiag(\delta_i)V^T$, according to the Theorem 6.10 of [17], we have $\partial_A F(A)|_{A^{t+1}} = Udiag(\theta)V^T$, where $\theta_i = (1 - \tanh^2(\sigma_i))\beta$. Since θ_i is finite, $\partial_A F(A)|_{A^{t+1}}$ is bounded.

As $\{Y^t\}$ is bounded, $\lim_{t\to\infty} \mu^t(E^{t+1} - E^t)$ is bounded. Under the assumption that $\lim_{t\to\infty} \mu^t(E^{t+1} - E^t) = 0$, we have $\partial_A F(A^*) + Y^* = 0$. Thus, $\{A^*,E^*,Y^*\}$ meets the KKT conditions of $\mathscr{L}(A,E,Y)$ and $\{A^*,E^*\}$ is a stationary of (4). ■

5 Experiments

In this section, we evaluate our tanh-RPCA by experiments of the low-rank matrix recovery on the synthetic data and experiments of background subtraction on seven real-world videos. The source code of our tanh-RPCA will be available later.

5.1 Synthetic Data

To evaluate the performance of the proposed tanh-RPCA model, we generate synthetic low-rank data matrix and then perform low-rank matrix recovery, according to [10]. The ground-truth low-rank data matrix $A = UV^T$, where $A \in R^{m\times n}$, $U \in R^{m\times r}$ and $V \in R^{n\times r}$. The $r = \rho_r \times m$ constrains the upper bound of $rank(A)$. In the simulations, each entry of U and V is randomly generated from the normal distribution. Then, we corrupt the ground-truth matrix with the sparse noise matrix which includes the $\rho_e \times m^2$ non-zero entries. These non-zero entries occur in random positions and follows the uniform distribution over $[-10, 10]$.

Two metrics serve as the performance evaluation: (1) relative reconstruction error (RRE): $RRE = \frac{\|A^* - A\|_F}{\|A\|_F}$, where A is the ground-truth low-rank matrix, and A^* is the reconstructed low-rank matrix, and (2) runtime ($TIME$): the execution CPU seconds.

Table 1. The *RRE* and *TIME* on synthetic data with ρ_e fixed 0.1 and ρ_r varying from 0.1 to 0.35 with step length 0.05.

Method	40	60	80	100	120	140
$RPCA_{RRE}$	0.1439	0.118	0.1025	0.0914	0.0832	0.0774
$RPCA_{TIME}$	10.7946	11.7768	10.4837	10.9941	10.0164	10.0323
$WNNM\text{-}RPCA_{RRE}$	6.37e-07	7.85e-07	9.43e-07	1.15e-06	1.39e-06	0.0036
$WNNM\text{-}RPCA_{TIME}$	9.878	12.9513	16.3728	18.2733	10.0336	10.418
$tanh\text{-}RPCA_{RRE}$	**5.46e-07**	**6.55e-07**	**8.54e-07**	**1.05e-06**	**1.32e-06**	**1.74e-06**
$tanh\text{-}RPCA_{TIME}$	**4.1822**	**4.6186**	**4.5554**	**4.6986**	**4.8355**	**5.7903**

Table 2. The *RRE* and *TIME* on synthetic data with ρ_e fixed 0.2 and ρ_r varying from 0.1 to 0.35 with step length 0.05.

Method	40	60	80	100	120	140
$RPCA_{RRE}$	0.2044	0.167	0.1441	0.1295	0.1177	0.1091
$RPCA_{TIME}$	11.1146	10.4599	10.6732	11.4856	11.329	11.2032
$WNNM\text{-}RPCA_{RRE}$	7.38e-07	9.46e-07	**1.20e-06**	**1.74e-06**	2.57e-02	5.94e-02
$WNNM\text{-}RPCA_{TIME}$	15.6525	15.1782	15.1762	19.2273	15.0298	15.2517
$tanh\text{-}RPCA_{RRE}$	**6.38e-07**	**8.66e-07**	1.21e-06	1.82e-06	**1.68e-02**	**5.08e-02**
$tanh\text{-}RPCA_{TIME}$	**5.4029**	**5.228**	**5.3386**	**6.1373**	**11.9624**	**11.7816**

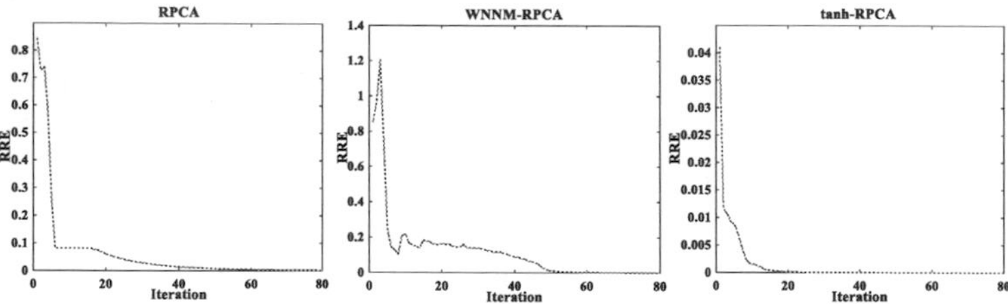

Fig. 2. The convergence curves of RPCA, WNNM-RPCA and tanh-PCA, respectively

In our experiments, we set $m = n = 400$, the values of both ρ_r and ρ_e from [0.1, 0.5]. λ is set to $1/\sqrt{m}$, following the suggested setting of [2] for RPCA and our tanh-RPCA, while, in WNNM-RPCA, λ is set as $\sqrt{mn}$ suggested by [9]. ρ of ADMM for all the methods is set to 1.03. For each parameter, we repeatly generate the synthetic low-rank matrix 10 times and the average performance over 10 runs is reported in term of *RRE* and *TIME*, as in Tables 1 and 2. WNNM-RPCA and tanh-RPCA are able to accurately recover the groundtruth matrix when either the rank of matrix or the number of corrupted entries is small. Nevertheless, the larger the rank of matrix or the number of corrupted entries, the bigger the estimation error of WNNN-RPCA. Unlike it, tanh-RPCA always induces the smaller square errors than WNNM-RPCA in most cases as above. Moreover, *TIME* of tanh-RPCA are the least in the compared methods. Besides, Fig. 2 shows the convergence curves of three above models at $\rho_e = 0.1$ and $\rho_r = 0.2$. In Fig. 2, tanh-RPCA quickly converges within the 20–30 round iterations, while RPCA and WNNM-RPCA converges in the 50–70 round iterations. In summary, experiments show that tanh-RPCA has a nice convergence behavior and low-rank recovery ability in case the matrices are largely corrupted by random noises.

5.2 Real-World Data

As a key step in video analysis, background subtraction has been extensively studied for many years. In background subtraction, the surveillance video captured by a camera is generally taken under a static scenario together with relatively static background and with relatively small moving objects over a period, where the low-rank matrix naturally corresponds to the background, and the sparse one captures the foreground. Thus, LRMR has inspired various effective techniques for background modeling [9,23,30,32].

We compare tanh-RPCA with several representative low-rank matrix recovery models, including WNNM-RPCA [9], RPCA [20], NoncvxRPCA [13] and PRMF [29] on seven challenging video sequences. Three video sequences provided by [18] are utilized in our experiments, including *WaterSurface*, *Hall* and *Airport*. In each sequence, 20 frames of ground truth foreground are utilized for quantitative comparison. Another four video sequences including *Bootstrap*, *Camouflage*, *TimeOfDay* and *WavingTrees*, and the corresponding ground truth foreground provided by [28] are exploited here as well. The background subtraction is treated as a binary classification problem. Since ground truth frames are available for the compared frames, we can calculate the F-measure[1] to evaluate the compared methods on seven videos.

Figure 3 shows the original, the groundtruth foreground, and recovered background on seven videos including *WaterSurface*, *Hall*, *Airport*, *Bootstrap*, *Camouflage*, *TimeOfDay* and *WavingTrees*. The background of the representative frame recovered by the WNNM-RPCA, RPCA, NoncvxRPCA and PRMF, respectively, contain some shadows.

Table 3 shows the F-measure of the compared methods, highlighted in bold for the best results. Both tanh-RPCA and WNNM-RPCA rank higher on seven video sequences. On the whole, tahn-RPCA achieves higher performance than the compared models. Experiments on real-world videos show the effectiveness of tanh-RPCA for background subtraction. This implies that our low-rank approximation model has great promising potential in low-rank matrix recovery.

[1] F-measure is the harmonic average of the precision and recall, with the best value at 1 (perfect precision and recall) and the worst at 0.

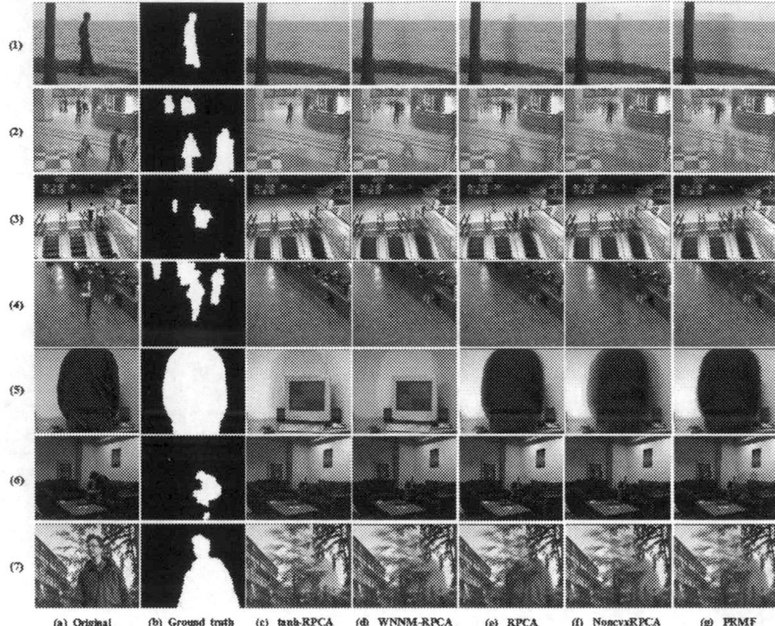

Fig. 3. (a) The original frame, (b) the groundtruth foreground, and the corresponding background respectively recovered by (c) tanh-RPCA (Ours), (d) WNNM-RPCA, (e) RPCA, (f) NoncvxRPCA and (g) PRMF on seven video sequences including (1) *WaterSurface*, (2) *Hall*, (3) *Airport*, (4) *Bootstrap*, (5) *Camouflage*, (6) *TimeOfDay* and (7) *WavingTrees*.

Table 3. The F-measure of the compared methods on seven video sequences, respectively.

Method	*WaterSurface*	*Hall*	*Airport*	*Bootstrap*	*Camouflage*	*TimeOfDay*	*WavingTrees*
tanh-RPCA	**0.8667**	**0.8042**	**0.6276**	**0.7859**	**0.6977**	0.6450	**0.6199**
WNNM-RPCA	0.8652	0.7861	0.6041	0.6446	0.5779	0.6736	0.5472
RPCA	0.6161	0.6847	0.4705	0.5637	0.1591	0.5912	0.2822
NoncvxRPCA	0.8598	0.5869	0.6080	0.5982	0.3993	**0.7082**	0.5482
PRMF	0.8602	0.5688	0.5752	0.5762	0.2166	0.4860	0.5092

6 Conclusion

This paper has developed a novel method of recovering the underlying low-rank matrix, termed as tanh-RPCA. It provides a new low-rank approximation function via the continuation process, in which the rise in a parameter imposes the hyperbolic tanh function to gradually approach to the rank function. The convergent proof of the corresponding optimization algorithm for tanh-RPCA is non-trivial due to the hardness of the continuation process. Experimental results verify the efficacy of tanh-RPCA compared with the baseline methods in both quantity and quality. This also implies the effectiveness of our low-rank approximation model.

References

1. Beck, A., Teboulle, M.: A fast iterative shrinkage-thresholding algorithm for linear inverse problems. SIAM J. Imaging Sci. **2**(1), 183–202 (2009)
2. Candès, E.J., Li, X., Ma, Y., Wright, J.: Robust principal component analysis? J. ACM **58**(3), 11 (2011)
3. Candès, E.J., Recht, B.: Exact matrix completion via convex optimization. Found. Comput. Math. **9**(6), 717 (2009)
4. Cao, Z., Long, M., Wang, J., Yu, P.S.: HashNet: deep learning to hash by continuation. In: IEEE International Conference on Computer Vision, pp. 5609–5618 (2017)
5. Chen, C.F., Wei, C.P., Wang, Y.C.F.: Low-rank matrix recovery with structural incoherence for robust face recognition. In: IEEE Conference on Computer Vision and Pattern Recognition, pp. 2618–2625 (2012)
6. Fan, Q., Jiao, Y., Lu, X.: A primal dual active set algorithm with continuation for compressed sensing. IEEE Trans. Sig. Process. **62**(23), 6276–6285 (2014)
7. Gao, Y., Cai, H., Zhang, X., Lan, L., Luo, Z.: Background subtraction via 3D convolutional neural networks. In: International Conference on Pattern Recognition. IEEE (2018)
8. Gong, P., Ye, J., Zhang, C.: Multi-stage multi-task feature learning. J. Mach. Learn. Res. **14**(1), 2979–3010 (2013)
9. Gu, S., Xie, Q., Meng, D., Zuo, W., Feng, X., Zhang, L.: Weighted nuclear norm minimization and its applications to low level vision. Int. J. Comput. Vis. **121**(2), 183–208 (2017)
10. Guo, X., Lin, Z., Center, C.M.I.: Route: robust outlier estimation for low rank matrix recovery. In: International Joint Conference on Artificial Intelligence, pp. 1746–1752 (2017)
11. Hu, Y., Zhang, D., Ye, J., Li, X., He, X.: Fast and accurate matrix completion via truncated nuclear norm regularization. IEEE Trans. Pattern Anal. Mach. Intell. **35**(9), 2117–2130 (2013)
12. Jin, Z.F., Wan, Z., Jiao, Y., Lu, X.: An alternating direction method with continuation for nonconvex low rank minimization. J. Sci. Comput. **66**(2), 849–869 (2016)
13. Kang, Z., Peng, C., Cheng, Q.: Robust PCA via nonconvex rank approximation. In: IEEE International Conference on Data Mining, pp. 211–220 (2015)
14. Kang, Z., Peng, C., Cheng, Q.: Robust subspace clustering via smoothed rank approximation. IEEE Sig. Process. Lett. **22**(11), 2088–2092 (2015)
15. Kang, Z., Peng, C., Cheng, Q.: Robust subspace clustering via tighter rank approximation. In: ACM International on Conference on Information and Knowledge Management, pp. 393–401 (2015)
16. LeCun, Y., Bengio, Y., Hinton, G.: Deep learning. Nature **521**(7553), 436 (2015)
17. Lewis, A.S., Sendov, H.S.: Nonsmooth analysis of singular values. Part i: theory. Set-Valued Anal. **13**(3), 213–241 (2005)
18. Li, L., Huang, W., Gu, I.Y.H., Tian, Q.: Statistical modeling of complex backgrounds for foreground object detection. IEEE Trans. Image Process. **13**(11), 1459–1472 (2004)

19. Lin, Z., Ganesh, A., Wright, J., Wu, L., Chen, M., Ma, Y.: Fast convex optimization algorithms for exact recovery of a corrupted low-rank matrix. J. Marine Biol. Assoc. UK **56**(3), 707–722 (2009)
20. Lin, Z., Liu, R., Su, Z.: Linearized alternating direction method with adaptive penalty for low-rank representation. In: Advances in Neural Information Processing Systems, pp. 612–620 (2011)
21. Lu, C., Tang, J., Yan, S., Lin, Z.: Generalized nonconvex nonsmooth low-rank minimization. In: IEEE Conference on Computer Vision and Pattern Recognition, pp. 4130–4137 (2014)
22. Mairal, J., Bach, F., Ponce, J., Sapiro, G.: Online learning for matrix factorization and sparse coding. J. Mach. Learn. Res. **11**(1), 19–60 (2010)
23. Mu, Y., Dong, J., Yuan, X., Yan, S.: Accelerated low-rank visual recovery by random projection. In: IEEE Conference on Computer Vision and Pattern Recognition, pp. 2609–2616 (2011)
24. Peng, C., Kang, Z., Li, H., Cheng, Q.: Subspace clustering using log-determinant rank approximation. In: ACM SIGKDD International Conference on Knowledge Discovery and Data Mining, pp. 925–934 (2015)
25. Peng, C., Kang, Z., Yang, M., Cheng, Q.: RAP: scalable RPCA for low-rank matrix recovery. In: Proceedings of the 25th ACM International on Conference on Information and Knowledge Management, pp. 2113–2118 (2016)
26. Recht, B., Fazel, M., Parrilo, P.A.: Guaranteed minimum-rank solutions of linear matrix equations via nuclear norm minimization. SIAM Rev. **52**(3), 471–501 (2010)
27. Shen, X., Wu, Y.: A unified approach to salient object detection via low rank matrix recovery. In: IEEE Conference on Computer Vision and Pattern Recognition, pp. 853–860 (2012)
28. Toyama, K., Krumm, J., Brumitt, B., Meyers, B.: Wallflower: principles and practice of background maintenance. In: IEEE International Conference on Computer Vision, pp. 255–261 (1999)
29. Wang, N., Yao, T., Wang, J., Yeung, D.-Y.: A probabilistic approach to robust matrix factorization. In: Fitzgibbon, A., Lazebnik, S., Perona, P., Sato, Y., Schmid, C. (eds.) ECCV 2012. LNCS, vol. 7578, pp. 126–139. Springer, Heidelberg (2012). https://doi.org/10.1007/978-3-642-33786-4_10
30. Wright, J., Ganesh, A., Rao, S., Peng, Y., Ma, Y.: Robust principal component analysis: exact recovery of corrupted low-rank matrices via convex optimization. In: Advances in Neural Information Processing Systems, pp. 2080–2088 (2009)
31. Xiang, S., Tong, X., Ye, J.: Efficient sparse group feature selection via nonconvex optimization. In: International Conference on Machine Learning, pp. 284–292 (2013)
32. Xin, B., Tian, Y., Wang, Y., Gao, W.: Background subtraction via generalized fused lasso foreground modeling. In: IEEE Conference on Computer Vision and Pattern Recognition, pp. 4676–4684 (2015)
33. Yuan, X., Yang, J.: Sparse and low rank matrix decomposition via alternating direction method. Pac. J. Optim. **9**(1) (2009)
34. Zhang, C.H., et al.: Nearly unbiased variable selection under minimax concave penalty. Ann. Stat. **38**(2), 894–942 (2010)
35. Zhang, T.: Analysis of multi-stage convex relaxation for sparse regularization. J. Mach. Learn. Res. **11**(3), 1081–1107 (2010)
36. Zhang, Z., Yan, S., Zhao, M.: Similarity preserving low-rank representation for enhanced data representation and effective subspace learning. Neural Netw. **53**, 81–94 (2014)

37. Zhang, Z., Zhao, M., Li, F., Zhang, L., Yan, S.: Robust alternating low-rank representation by joint lp-and l2, p-norm minimization. Neural Netw. **96**, 55–70 (2017)
38. Zheng, Y., Liu, G., Sugimoto, S., Yan, S., Okutomi, M.: Practical low-rank matrix approximation under robust ℓ_1-norm. In: IEEE Conference on Computer Vision and Pattern Recognition, pp. 1410–1417 (2012)
39. Zou, W., Kpalma, K., Liu, Z., Ronsin, J.: Segmentation driven low-rank matrix recovery for saliency detection. In: British Machine Vision Conference, pp. 1–13 (2013)

Inertial Constrained Hierarchical Belief Propagation for Optical Flow

Zixing Zhang and Ying Wen(✉)

Shanghai Key Laboratory of Multidimensional Information Processing,
Department of Computer Science and Technology,
East China Normal University, Shanghai, China
ywen@cs.ecnu.edu.cn

Abstract. In computer vision, optical flow estimation has attracted the researchers' interests for decades. Loopy belief propagation (LBP) is widely used for obtaining accurate optical flow in recent years. But its time-consumption and unfitness for large displacement scenes remains a challenging problem. In order to improve the performance of belief propagation in optical flow estimation, we propose an Inertial Constrained Hierarchical Belief Propagation (IHBPFlow) to estimate accurate optical flow. We treat input images as Markov random fields (MRF) and use possible displacements as labels and perform BP on hierarchical MRFs, i.e. superpixel MRF and pixel MRF. First we perform BP on the superpixel MRF, where the step of candidate displacements is enlarged so that the label space can be reduced. Then the basic displacements obtained from the superpixel MRF are used as initial values of the pixel MRF, which effectively compresses the space of labels, thus the process on the pixel MRF can be accelerated. Furthermore, we integrate multi-frame images and previous displacements as inertial constrained information into the proposed hierarchical BP model to enhance its ability to get reliable displacements in scenes where not enough texture information can be provided. Our method performs well on accuracy and speed and obtains competitive results on MPI Sintel dataset.

Keywords: Optical flow · Loopy belief propagation
Inertial constraint · Large displacement

1 Introduction

Optical flow estimation is a basic research field in computer vision which is extensively used for object segmentation, tracking, scene classification and many other applications. Since the work of Horn and Schunck [10], research on this

This work was supported by National Nature Science Foundation of China (No. 61773166), Natural Science Foundation of Shanghai (No. 17ZR1408200) and the Science and Technology Commission of Shanghai Municipality under research grant (No. 14DZ2260800).

X. Geng and B.-H. Kang (Eds.): PRICAI 2018, LNAI 11012, pp. 574–587, 2018.
https://doi.org/10.1007/978-3-319-97304-3_44

area has lasted for decades. Classical methods [5,17] minimize an energy function using a variational framework. These methods perform well in scenes with small displacements, but usually fail when large displacements and severe occlusions occur. Although conventional frameworks use coarse-to-fine strategy to convert large displacements into small ones on coarse level, they still have poor performance when the relative motion of a small-scale structure is larger than its own scale.

In order to overcome the drawback of variational framework, descriptor matching was introduced to improve the performance on large displacement optical flow estimation. Brox [4,6] integrates descriptor matching into the coarse-to-fine variational framework by penalizing the difference between the variational flow and the flow obtained by matches. Since then, more efforts have been spent on finding accurate correspondences to guide the solution to the variational framework. DeepFlow [19] retrieves quasi-dense correspondences by non-rigid matching. PatchMatch [3] based methods [2,11] advance the efficiency of computing correspondences by random search and propagation between neighbors. Most of these matching algorithms usually get sparse correspondences after removing mismatching points. Since sparse correspondences restrict the effect of matching algorithms, Jerome Revaud [16] proposed edge-preserving interpolation method to get dense correspondence field using an initial sparse set of matches. But its effect relies on the accuracy of matching algorithm.

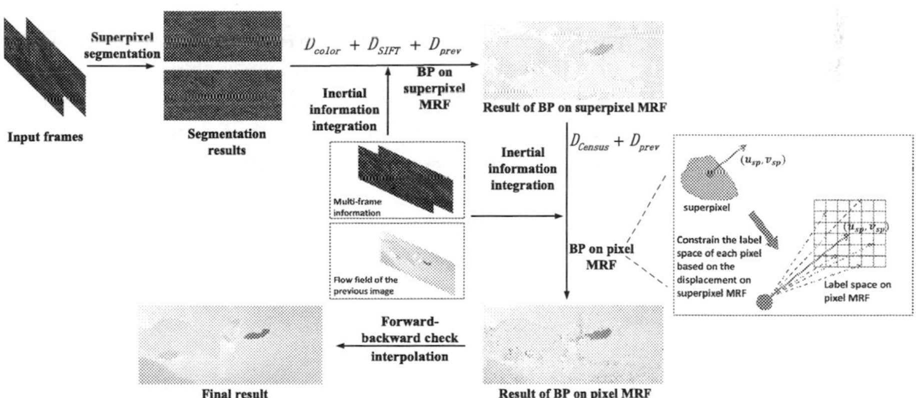

Fig. 1. The main procedure of our method. The input images are two adjacent frames. We segment the images into superpixels. BP is first performed on superpixel MRF and then BP is performed on pixel MRF based on the superpixel flow fields. Inertial information is used during BP to improve robustness of the model. After forward-backward consistency check and interpolation, we obtain the final result.

Markov random field (MRF) is another widely used framework for optical flow estimation. Inference algorithms for MRF like belief propagation (BP) provide good results in practice. However, these methods usually need a long running time. Felzenszwalb [9] introduced an efficient loopy belief propagation algorithm to make it possible to achieve a good result within a small fixed number of message passing iterations. SIFTFlow [14] uses a dual-layer loopy belief propagation to find correspondences between SIFT features. FullFlow [8] presents a global optimization algorithm using message passing and reduces the computational complexity of message update loop from quadratic to linear. SPM-BP [13] integrates message passing with PatchMatch-based particle generation algorithm. The key to applying BP to optical flow estimation is keeping a balance between the label space size and the accuracy of displacement field. Big label space means capability to éstimate large displacements accurately, but this usually leads to unacceptable cost in time and memory.

In this paper, we propose an inertial constrained hierarchical BP method for accurate optical flow estimation, named IHBPFlow. The main procedure is shown in Fig. 1. We construct two MRFs based on the input images: superpixel MRF and pixel MRF. First, we perform BP on the superpixel MRF to get a basic displacement field which is used as a reference for selection of candidate displacements on the pixel MRF. Then BP is performed on the pixel MRF based on the superpixel BP result. In this way, we obtain an accurate result by performing BP on the pixel MRF in a constrained label space. What's more, we incorporate multi-frame image and displacement information as inertial constraint into the proposed BP model to improve robustness of our method, especially in scenes where not enough image information can be provided in two-frame model to get reliable results.

Our work makes the following contributions: **(1)** We propose a novel hierarchical BP model to accurately obtain large displacement optical flow with two compressed label spaces that accelerate the process of BP. **(2)** We take inertial information into BP model to improve the robustness of the new model. When descriptors cannot provide enough information for finding correspondences, inertial information term becomes important to help obtain correct flow fields, especially in textureless and occluded areas.

2 Method

2.1 General Framework of BP

The general framework of belief propagation usually treats each pixel on the image as a node in MRF and connects the neighboring pixels with edges. Every possible quantity is a label for each node. For optical flow estimation, labels are candidate flow vectors. The object function is usually defined as

$$E(f) = \sum_{p \in \mathcal{P}} D_p(f_p) + \sum_{(p,q) \in N} V(f_p, f_q), \tag{1}$$

where $\mathcal{P}$ is set of nodes. f_p is the label assigned to node p, in optical flow estimation, each label represents a candidate displacement. N are the edges in the four-connected image grid graph. $D_p(f_p)$ is referred to as data cost and

$V(f_p, f_q)$ is the smoothness term to measure the difference of labels assigned to two neighboring nodes p and q.

This framework becomes intractable when facing high-resolution images with large displacements as the number of nodes and size of label space become too large. The method we use to accelerate BP is mainly inspired by the study of Felzenszwalb [9] and Li [13]. Felzenszwalb's method reduces the time of message update by computing the lower envelope of labels and the number of iteration by using multi-scale BP. Li uses PatchMatch-based particle generation method to get candidate movements efficiently and reduces the size of label space.

2.2 Inertial Constrained Hierarchical BP Model

We propose an inertial constrained hierarchical BP method for optical flow. Let I_1, I_2 be two input images. I_1 is treated as a MRF. Let $\mathcal{L}$ denotes a set of labels and each label is a candidate displacement vector. Our goal is to assign an appropriate displacement vector to every node.

Let $f_p \in \mathcal{L}$ be the discrete label to be assigned to node p, $f_p = (u_p, v_p)$ is the movement label that maps the node $p(x, y)$ in I_1 to $p'(x + u_p, y + v_p)$ in I_2. The proposed energy function is defined as

$$E(f) = \sum_{(p,q)\in N} V(f_p, f_q) + \sum_{p\in\mathcal{P}} (\alpha D_{color}(f_p) + \beta D_{desc}(f_p) + \gamma D_{prev}(f_p)) \tag{2}$$

where p is a node in I_1 and (p, q) is two neighboring nodes. The D_{color}, D_{desc} and D_{prev} are color difference, descriptor difference and multi-frame displacement consistency penalty between I_1 and I_2 respectively. $V(f_p, f_q)$ is the smoothness term to penalize the displacement difference between two neighboring nodes p and q. We define the data term as

$$D_p(f_p) = \alpha D_{color}(f_p) + \beta D_{desc}(f_p) + \gamma D_{prev}(f_p) \tag{3}$$

As Felzenszwalb's work shows, BP for minimizing Eq. (2) can be performed by message passing. The problem is converted to computing belief vector for each node. We compute belief vector for each node as follows

$$b_p(f_p) = D_p(f_p) + \sum_{(q\in N_p)} m_{qp}(f_p) \tag{4}$$

where $m_{qp}(f_p)$ means message sent from node q to node p. And the message update rule is defined as

$$m^t_{pq}(f_q) = \min_{f_p}(V(f_p, f_q) + D_p(f_p) + \sum_{s\in N_p\backslash q} m^{t-1}_{sp}(f_p)) \tag{5}$$

where $m^{t-1}_{sp}(f_p)$ denotes the message sent from node s to p at iteration $t-1$. s is neighboring node of p except q. After some iterations, the best label can be selected to minimize Eq. (4) at each node.

Hierarchical Scheme. Intuitively, each pixel can be treated as a node in MRF and BP can be used to assign labels to nodes. However, as $\mathcal{L}$ contains every possible displacement vector, $\mathcal{L}$ could have tens of thousands of labels when estimating a large displacement field. Considering the large label space and huge number of nodes, applying BP directly to each pixel is time-consuming, thus we introduce our hierarchical scheme to speed up the process.

We perform loopy BP on two MRFs: superpixel MRF and pixel MRF. Our method is based on the assumption that the displacements of pixels in local area on an object are usually consistent except for discontinuities on object boundaries, thus each of these small regions can be treated as a node in MRF. If we can obtain the approximate displacements of these small regions, the label space for pixels in these regions can be reduced greatly when performing BP on pixel MRF. In order to get these small regions in the input images, we segment the images into superpixels using efficient Simple Linear Iterative Clustering (SLIC) algorithm [1]. Compared to regular segmentation, superpixel can better adhere to boundaries of objects and preserve the motion details at edges. We first perform BP on the superpixel MRF and then perform it on the pixel MRF. On the superpixel MRF, the step of candidate displacements can be enlarged so that the label space can be reduced. Basic displacements obtained from the superpixel BP are used as initial values of the pixel MRF, which compresses the space of labels and accelerates the process on pixel MRF. Since we have two MRFs, node p denotes a superpixel and a pixel on the superpixel MRF and the pixel MRF respectively. On the superpixel MRF, the step of candidate displacements is constrained to ε (i.e. $f_p \in R^2$, $R = \{0, -\varepsilon, \varepsilon, -2\varepsilon, 2\varepsilon, ...\}$). We use Euclidean distance to compute $V(f_p, f_q)$ on superpixel MRF. We use two dimensional distance transform to update message iteratively [9]. In order to find the corresponding superpixel under candidate displacement, let x be the center point of superpixel p, we move x along f_p to pixel x' in I_2 and get corresponding superpixel p' in I_2 which $x' \in p'$.

After loopy belief propagation on the superpixel MRF, we obtain a basic displacement field. Using this underlying result as a guidance for computing the pixel MRF, we can limit the label space of each pixel to a small range when performing BP on the pixel MRF. Let (u_p, v_p) be candidate displacements at pixel p and (u_{sp}, v_{sp}) be the displacement obtained on the superpixel MRF, then $u_p = du + u_{sp}$ and $v_p = dv + v_{sp}$, $du \in [-\delta, \delta]$, $dv \in [-\delta, \delta]$. δ is a small shift on (u_{sp}, v_{sp}). As is shown on the right part of Fig. 1, the BP on the pixel MRF is a fine-tunning based on superpixel flow fields. The size of label space is constrained to $(2\delta + 1)^2$ on the pixel MRF. We use the min-convolution method in Full Flow [8] to perform message update on the pixel MRF. Since neighboring nodes belonging to different superpixels may have different underlying displacements, we modify the method to fix this problem. The message update procedure is decomposed into two sets of one-dimensional min-convolutions:

$$m_{pq}(u_q, v_q) = \min_{v_p} m_{pq|v_p}(u_q) + \rho(v_q - v_p) \tag{6}$$

$$m_{pq|v_p}(u_q) = \min_{u_p} \phi_{pq}(u_p, v_p) + \rho(u_q - u_p) \tag{7}$$

where $\rho(\cdot)$ is penalty function, and we use L_1 norm here. $f_p = (u_p, v_p)$ and $f_q = (u_q, v_q)$ are displacements of neighboring nodes p and q. $\phi_{pq}(u_p, v_p) = D_p(f_p) + \sum_{s \in N_p \backslash q} m_{sp}^{t-1}(f_p)$. We first compute Eq. (7) using one-dimensional min-convolution for every v_p. $\phi_{pq}(u_p, v_p)$ can be computed for only one time. Then Eq. (6) is computed for every u_q using one-dimensional min-convolution on v_q. When p and q have different basic displacements, we first assume that node p and q have the same basic displacements, the computation in Eqs. (6) and (7) can be seen as computing the lower envelope of the function. Then we will extend the lower envelope of the function to be outside the range if p and q have relative offsets. An explanation of computing Eq. (7) is shown in Fig. 2. In this example, we first compute the lower envelope of the function. If u_q have a 2-pixel offset relative to u_p, we then extend the lower envelope aside by 2 pixels. The same method can be applied to the computation of Eq. (6).

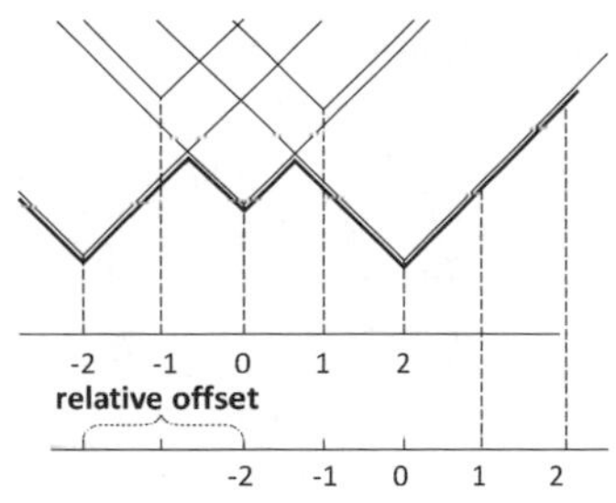

Fig. 2. The procedure of min-convolution in our method. The black line is the lower envelope of the function. We extend the lower envelope aside due to the relative offset.

Data Term Definition. For the sake of clarity, we rewrite Eq. (3) as

$$D_p(f_p) = D_{data}(f_p) + \gamma D_{prev}(f_p) \tag{8}$$

where $D_{data}(f_p) = \alpha D_{color}(f_p) + \beta D_{desc}(f_p)$. D_{data} and D_{prev} denote image information and displacements constraint at node p respectively.

The D_{data} consists of color information and descriptor information. We compute color errors in CIELab color space. On the superpixel MRF, the color of superpixel p is computed as mean of each channel of all pixels belonging to p. We use SIFT descriptor [15] to compute D_{desc} because SIFT is a widely used descriptor to extract local features. We compute dense sift [14] feature first. And then the feature of superpixel p is denoted by mean value of feature vectors of all pixels belonging to p. On the pixel MRF, instead of using SIFT, we use census transform [21] because it is resistant to illumination changes and its computation is more time-saving. D_{desc} is computed in L_2 distance on the superpixel MRF and is computed in hamming distance on the pixel MRF.

Inertial Constrained Information. Occlusions and textureless areas often cause failure in optical flow estimation. Kennedy [12] applied multi-frame images into data term $D_{data}(f_p)$ to improve the accuracy. In this paper, we not only consider multi-frame image information but also consider the displacement information of the previous frame.

Assuming there are four input frames I_{t-1}, I_t, I_{t+1} and I_{t+2}. We want to estimate the optical flow between I_t and I_{t+1}. For image information, we redefine D_{data} as

$$D_{data}(f_p) = \min\left\{D_{data}^{t+1}(f_p), D_{data}^{t-1}(-f_p) + \theta, D_{data}^{t+2}(2f_p) + \theta\right\} \tag{9}$$

$D_{data}^{t+1}(f_p)$ is the cost function of the standard two-frame model, $D_{data}^{t-1}(-f_p)$ is the cost when moving node p along $-f_p$ onto I_{t-1} and $D_{data}^{t+2}(2f_p)$ is the cost when moving node p along $2f_p$ onto I_{t+2}. θ is a constant to bias $D_{data}(f_p)$ towards $D_{data}^{t+1}(f_p)$.

In some scenes with great shadows or textureless areas, the data term $D_{data}(f_p)$ may not be able to provide enough information even if we take the previous and post images into account. Thus we introduce the displacement term D_{prev} to make the displacement field of the previous frame as a reference when images cannot provide enough information. D_{prev} is defined as follows

$$D_{prev}(f_p) = \sqrt{(u_{prev} - u)^2 + (v_{prev} - v)^2} \tag{10}$$

where $f_p = (u, v)$ is a candidate displacement of node p on I_t, and (u_{prev}, v_{prev}) is displacement of node $p - f_p$ (moving node p along $-f_p$) on I_{t-1}. An explanation is shown in Fig. 3. In this example, p_t is a node to be processed, and we want to compute the flow of p_t between I_t and I_{t+1}. p_{t-1}, p_{t+1} and p_{t+2} are the corresponding points when moving p_t along $(-u, -v)$ onto I_{t-1}, moving p_t along (u, v) onto I_{t+1} and moving p_t along $(2u, 2v)$ onto I_{t+2} respectively. We incorporate the image information of p_{t-1}, p_{t+1} and p_{t+2} according to Eq. (9) and displacement information of p_{t-1} according to Eq. (10) in our model. The D_{prev} is based on the assumption that movements of adjacent frames is usually inertial. Thus we prefer to keep flow fields consistent with the previous displacement field if not enough information can be used to obtain correct flow.

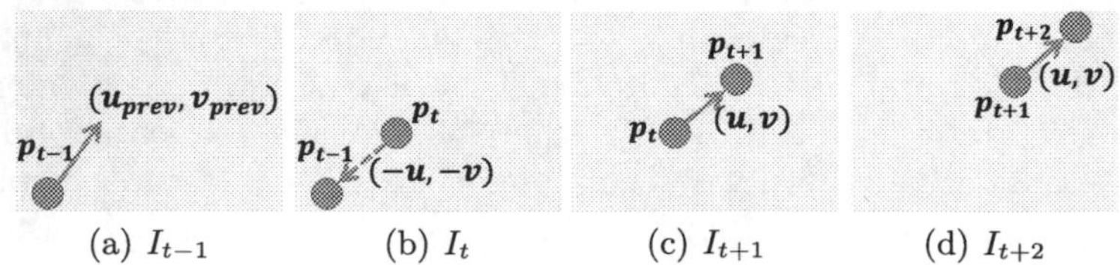

(a) I_{t-1} (b) I_t (c) I_{t+1} (d) I_{t+2}

Fig. 3. An explanation of the inertial information.

2.3 Postprocessing

After hierarchical BP, we get a pixel-accuracy displacement field. Forward-backward consistency check [8] is used for each pixel to remove inconsistent correspondences.

We get semi-dense displacement field after the procedure above. We use EpicFlow [16] interpolation method to obtain the final sub-pixel-accuracy optical flow as it is commonly used as postprocessing procedure to fill in blank areas by consistent matching points.

3 Experiments

We examine our method on the challenging MPI-Sintel optical flow dataset [7]. The MPI-Sintel dataset provides naturalistic video sequences including scenes with large displacements, motion blur and occlusions. It contains 23 training sequences with ground truths and 12 testing sequences without ground truths. Each of these sequences has two passes: clean pass and final pass. We evaluate our method on final pass as it contains more challenging effect of motion blur and atmospheric flow. Our experiments are performed on a PC with a 4-core Intel i5-4590 3.30 GHz CPU and 8 GB of RAM. In our experiments, the flow error is measured by endpoint error (EPE).

3.1 Parameter Analysis

We evaluate the impact of some parameters in our model in this section. We perform the evaluation using 10% of final training set on MPI Sintel dataset. In Eq. (3), the coefficients α, β and γ control the effect of color, descriptor and previous flow term respectively. ε mentioned in Sect. 2.2 controls the label space of BP on the superpixel MRF and δ controls the size of label space of BP on the pixel MRF. As the effect of color and SIFT descriptor in optical flow estimation has been validated by many researchers, we mainly focus on the effect of the candidate displacement step ε, the pixel displacement scope δ and the weight of previous displacement constraint γ. We set $\alpha = 1$, $\beta = 250$, $\theta = 40$ on the superpixel MRF and $\alpha = 0$, $\beta = 3$, $\theta = 40$ on the pixel MRF.

Figure 4 shows the experimental results of different parameters in our model. Figure 4(a) shows the effect of different ε when performing BP on the superpixel MRF. As we can see, high-accuracy candidate displacement is not necessary on superpixel BP. $\varepsilon = 4$ and $\varepsilon = 5$ both get satisfying results in our experiments. Since the larger ε is, the smaller label space size will be, and this will accelerate the computation effectively, thus we set $\varepsilon = 5$ in our experiments. Figure 4(b) shows the effect of δ. With δ increasing, the error decreases rapidly. A small δ is enough to get a satisfying result. We set $\delta = 10$ in our experiments. The curve indicates that our hierarchical model can effectively constrain the size of label space on the pixel MRF. Figure 4(c) and (d) show the impact of γ on the superpixel MRF and pixel MRF respectively. γ represents the weight of previous flow field constraint. We can see that on both two MRFs, with the increase of γ, the error drops effectively, but when γ becomes too large, the end point error rises again. This is because that too large γ limit the effect of image information in measuring the similarity between two nodes. We set $\gamma = 0.5$ on both two MRFs.

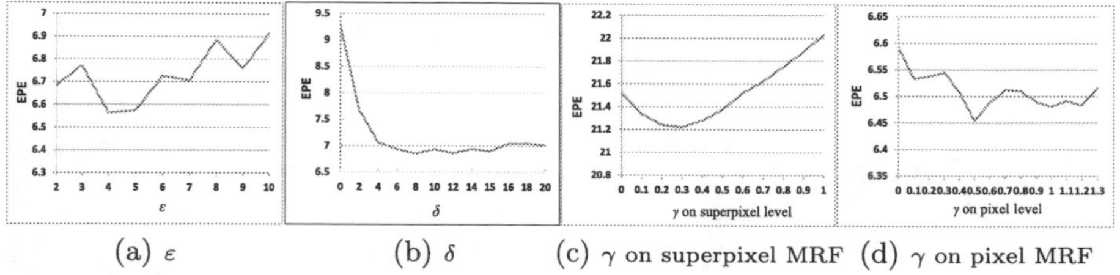

(a) ε (b) δ (c) γ on superpixel MRF (d) γ on pixel MRF

Fig. 4. Experimental results of different parameters.

3.2 Inertial Information Analysis

We incorporate multi-frame image and displacement information into our model to improve performance in scenes with severe occlusions and textureless areas. In this section, we analyse the effectiveness of inertial information in the proposed method by comparing the results of three models: IHBPFlow, IHBPFlow without previous displacement information (w/o prev) and IHBPFlow without previous displacement information and multi-frame image information (w/o multi+prev). Figure 5 compares some visual results. First two rows of Fig. 5 show the effect of our inertial constrained model. Figure 5(a) to (d) are four input images, Fig. 5(e) is the ground truth between Fig. 5(b) and (c). Figure 5(f) is an optical flow between Fig. 5(a) and (b). Now we want to estimate the flow between Fig. 5(b) and (c). Figure 5(g) is the result of IHBPFlow w/o multi+prev and Fig. 5(h) is the result of IHBPFlow. As is shown in areas marked by red rectangles, inertial constraint can better help capture the movement of arm. Another example is shown in the third and forth rows in Fig. 5. This case shows the effect of previous displacement information. Figure 5(i) to (l) are four adjacent images. The camera is moving forward, and the ground is moving backward relatively. The areas marked out by red rectangles have great shadows that not enough information can be extracted to help obtain correct flow. Figure 5(m) is an optical flow between Fig. 5(i) and (j). We want to estimate flow between Fig. 5(j) and (k). Figure 5(n) is the result obtained by IHBPFlow w/o multi+prev, Fig. 5(o) is the result of IHBPFlow w/o prev and Fig. 5(p) is obtained by IHBPFlow. Areas marked by red rectangles in Fig. 5(n) and (o) both have severe errors due to the shadow (lack of image information). After applying the displacement constraint, our method tends to keep the movements consistent between adjacent frames when little information can be extracted. Figure 5(p) shows a quite satisfying result.

We evaluate the effect of the inertial constraint numerically on MPI-Sintel final training set and results are shown in Table 1. In Table 1, 'total' means results

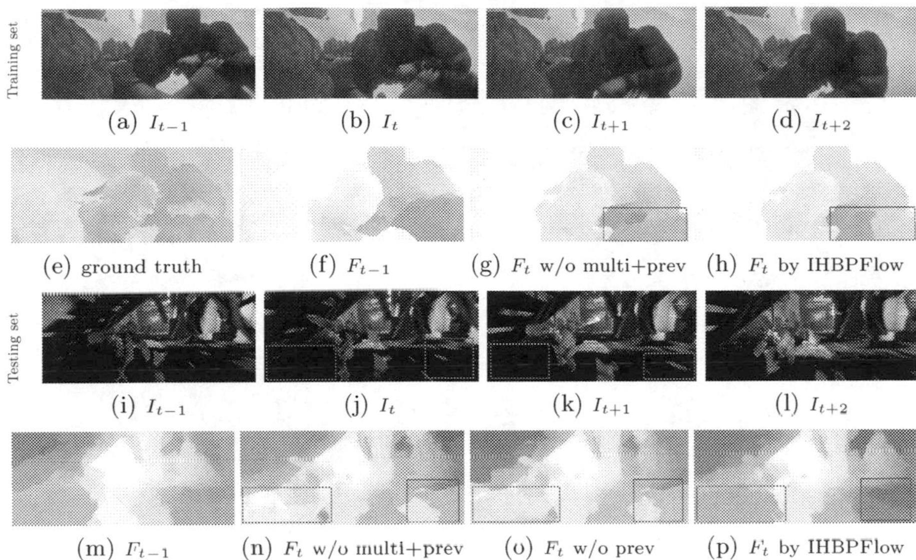

Fig. 5. Effects of inertial constraint on MPI Sintel dataset. (Color figure online)

Table 1. Experiments of IHBPFlow with/without inertial constraint on MPI-Sintel final training set. The performance is measured by endpoint error.

Sequence	IHBPFlow	w/o prev	w/o multi+prev
total	3.6980	3.7604	3.8162
ambush_2	29.9515	30.7528	30.6319
ambush_5	6.5926	6.8561	7.0650
cave_2	6.9905	7.4917	7.4432
market_5	11.4892	11.8180	11.7878
market_6	3.6121	3.7777	3.8065
temple_3	6.1957	6.3394	6.7218

obtained from the whole training set and the rest are results obtained from the sequences which have textureless areas and occlusions. The table presents that results of IHBPFlow are improved from 3.8162 to 3.6980 in total. It is noted that the proposed inertial constraint does improve the performance remarkably when facing images with little information.

3.3 Experiments on MPI-Sintel

On MPI Sintel dataset, we set $\alpha = 1$, $\beta = 250$, $\gamma = 0.5$, $\theta = 30$ when performing BP on the superpixel MRF and $\alpha = 0$, $\beta = 3$, $\gamma = 0.5$, $\theta = 40$, $\delta = 10$ when performing BP on the pixel MRF. The hierarchical BP is performed on 1/2-

Table 2. Comparison between IHBPFlow and some related methods on test set (final).

Methods	EPE All	Runtime(s)	Platform
FullFlow [8]	5.895	240	Intel I7(3.6 GHz) 64 GB
IHBPFlow	6.100	47	Intel I5(3.30 GHz) 8 GB
SPM-BP [13]	7.325	42	Intel I7(3.4 GHz) 8 GB
HCOF+multi [12]	8.799	1500	Intel Xeon(2 GHz) 4 GB

Table 3. Comparison between IHBPFlow and state-of-the-art methods on MPI Sintel test set (final).

Methods	EPE All	EPE Noc	EPE Occ
DCFlow [20]	5.119	2.283	28.228
FullFlow [8]	5.895	2.838	30.793
IHBPFlow	6.100	2.891	32.242
EpicFlow [16]	6.285	3.060	32.564
DeepFlow [19]	7.212	3.336	38.781
SPM-BP [13]	7.325	3.493	38.561
Classic+NLP [18]	8.291	4.287	40.925
HCOF+multi [12]	8.799	4.980	39.941
LDOF [6]	9.116	5.037	42.344
Classic+NL [17]	9.153	4.814	44.509

resolution images. We perform 2 iterations of BP on the superpixel MRF and 3 iterations on the pixel MRF. Tables 2 and 3 show the results of our method on MPI Sintel dataset compared with other methods. In these tables, 'EPE All', 'EPE Noc' and 'EPE Occ' denote endpoint error over the whole image, over regions that are visible in adjacent frames and over regions that are visible only in one of two adjacent frames respectively. Table 2 presents our method and some related works with corresponding platforms. These methods also use MRFs. It takes about 47 s for our method to process a frame with a low configuration. FullFlow slightly outperforms our method, but it requires much more memory and processing time than we do. The accuracy and processing time of the rest methods are lower and longer than ours. On the whole, the proposed method acquires a satisfying performance in view of accuracy and processing time.

Table 3 presents some results of state-of-the-art methods. As we can see in Table 3, the proposed model gets competitive results on this dataset. Among them, DCFlow outperforms all other methods as it uses deep learning to extract features that are more powerful than traditional descriptors. All results are available on MPI-Sintel dataset website[1].

[1] http://sintel.is.tue.mpg.de/results.

Some example results of the proposed model and some related methods on MPI Sintel dataset are shown in Fig. 6. The images on the first, second, third, forth and fifth row are input frames, the ground truths, EpicFlow results, SPM-BP results and our results respectively. In the first example, our model accurately captures the displacement of the leg and the stick on the top of the image. On the second and third column, the detail of the feet captured by our model is better. On the last column, our model reduces the displacement error effectively on the upper right part of the image. In short, the proposed IHBPFlow is a competitive and effective method.

Fig. 6. Some example results on MPI-Sintel dataset. Each column shows from top to bottom: mean of two input frames, ground truth, EpicFlow results, SPM-BP results and IHBPFlow results.

4 Conclusion

We present an inertial constrained hierarchical belief propagation framework to estimate accurate large displacement optical flow efficiently. In the proposed method, there are two issues solved. To obtain accurate optical flow, we integrate multi-frame images and previous displacements as inertial constrained information into the proposed hierarchical BP model to improve performance in scenes with occlusions and textureless areas. To overcome the time-consumption of belief propagation when faced with large displacements, we perform BP on superpixel MRF to obtain basic displacements and use it to guide the BP on the pixel MRF. Competitive results on datasets show that the proposed model is a powerful tool in optical flow estimation and more efforts can be made to promote the application of BP to obtaining accurate optical flow.

References

1. Achanta, R., Shaji, A., Smith, K., Lucchi, A., Fua, P., Süsstrunk, S.: SLIC superpixels compared to state-of-the-art superpixel methods. IEEE Trans. Pattern Anal. Mach. Intell. **34**(11), 2274–2282 (2012)
2. Bao, L., Yang, Q., Jin, H.: Fast edge-preserving patchmatch for large displacement optical flow. In: Proceedings of the IEEE Conference on Computer Vision and Pattern Recognition, pp. 3534–3541 (2014)
3. Barnes, C., Shechtman, E., Goldman, D.B., Finkelstein, A.: The generalized patchmatch correspondence algorithm. In: Daniilidis, K., Maragos, P., Paragios, N. (eds.) ECCV 2010. LNCS, vol. 6313, pp. 29–43. Springer, Heidelberg (2010). https://doi.org/10.1007/978-3-642-15558-1_3
4. Brox, T., Bregler, C., Malik, J.: Large displacement optical flow. In: Computer Vision and Pattern Recognition, pp. 41–48. IEEE (2009)
5. Brox, T., Bruhn, A., Papenberg, N., Weickert, J.: High accuracy optical flow estimation based on a theory for warping. In: Pajdla, T., Matas, J. (eds.) ECCV 2004. LNCS, vol. 3024, pp. 25–36. Springer, Heidelberg (2004). https://doi.org/10.1007/978-3-540-24673-2_3
6. Brox, T., Malik, J.: Large displacement optical flow: descriptor matching in variational motion estimation. IEEE Trans. Pattern Anal. Mach. Intell. **33**(3), 500–513 (2011)
7. Butler, D.J., Wulff, J., Stanley, G.B., Black, M.J.: A naturalistic open source movie for optical flow evaluation. In: Fitzgibbon, A., Lazebnik, S., Perona, P., Sato, Y., Schmid, C. (eds.) ECCV 2012. LNCS, vol. 7577, pp. 611–625. Springer, Heidelberg (2012). https://doi.org/10.1007/978-3-642-33783-3_44
8. Chen, Q., Koltun, V.: Full flow: optical flow estimation by global optimization over regular grids. In: IEEE Conference on Computer Vision and Pattern Recognition (2016)
9. Felzenszwalb, P.F., Huttenlocher, D.P.: Efficient belief propagation for early vision. Int. J. Comput. Vis. **70**(1), 41–54 (2006)
10. Horn, B.K., Schunck, B.G.: Determining optical flow. Artif. Intell. **17**(1–3), 185–203 (1981)
11. Hu, Y., Song, R., Li, Y.: Efficient coarse-to-fine patchmatch for large displacement optical flow. In: Proceedings of the IEEE Conference on Computer Vision and Pattern Recognition, pp. 5704–5712 (2016)
12. Kennedy, R., Taylor, C.J.: Hierarchically-constrained optical flow. In: IEEE Conference on Computer Vision and Pattern Recognition (2015)
13. Li, Y., Min, D., Brown, M.S., Do, M.N., Lu, J.: SPM-BP: Sped-up patchmatch belief propagation for continuous MRFS. In: IEEE International Conference on Computer Vision (2015)
14. Liu, C., Yuen, J., Torralba, A.: SIFT flow: dense correspondence across scenes and its applications. IEEE Trans. Pattern Anal. Mach. Intell. **33**(5), 978–994 (2011)
15. Lowe, D.G.: Object recognition from local scale-invariant features. In: International Conference on Computer Vision, vol. 2, pp. 1150–1157 (1999)
16. Revaud, J., Weinzaepfel, P., Harchaoui, Z., Schmid, C.: EpicFlow: edge-preserving interpolation of correspondences for optical flow. In: IEEE Conference on Computer Vision and Pattern Recognition (2015)
17. Sun, D., Roth, S., Black, M.J.: Secrets of optical flow estimation and their principles. In: Computer Vision and Pattern Recognition, pp. 2432–2439 (2010)

18. Sun, D., Roth, S., Black, M.J.: A quantitative analysis of current practices in optical flow estimation and the principles behind them. Int. J. Comput. Vis. **106**(2), 115–137 (2014)
19. Weinzaepfel, P., Revaud, J., Harchaoui, Z., Schmid, C.: Deepflow: large displacement optical flow with deep matching. In: Proceedings of the IEEE International Conference on Computer Vision, pp. 1385–1392 (2013)
20. Xu, J., Ranftl, R., Koltun, V.: Accurate optical flow via direct cost volume processing. In: IEEE Conference on Computer Vision and Pattern Recognition (CVPR) (2017)
21. Zabih, R., Woodfill, J.: Non-parametric local transforms for computing visual correspondence. In: Eklundh, J.-O. (ed.) ECCV 1994. LNCS, vol. 801, pp. 151–158. Springer, Heidelberg (1994). https://doi.org/10.1007/BFb0028345

ParallelNet: A Depth-Guided Parallel Convolutional Network for Scene Segmentation

Shiyu Liu and Haofeng Zhang(✉)

School of Computer Science and Engineering,
Nanjing University of Science and Technology, Nanjing, China
zhanghf@njust.edu.cn

Abstract. In the past few years, deep convolutional neural networks (CNN) have shown great superiority and also been the first choice in semantic segmentation. However, the pooling layers in the CNN cause the increasing loss (mainly positioning structure details) which is not favourable for segmentation. Moreover, the vast majority of previous studies only utilize the color or textural information of the image, without considering the depth information which is helpful for segmentation. In this paper, we propose a novel and effective end-to-end network for semantic segmentation namely Depth-guided Parallel Convolutional Network (ParallelNet). Compared to previous work, the contribution of our ParallelNet is that we have taken advantages of the mutual benefit and strong correlations between depth information and semantic information, which are combined to guide scene semantic segmentation. Besides, we utilise a new method to obtain the depth information of the image by calculating the correlation distance with $\mathcal{L}_1$-norm between left and right feature maps, thus, we just need to input the RGB images instead of RGB images and encoded 3D images in some conventional methods. Furthermore, we apply the concept of our ParallelNet to the current popular networks by exploiting the guidance of the depth information and transfer their learned representations with fine-tuning. The extensive experiments on the popular dataset Cityscape exhibit that our ParallelNet outperforms the original methods.

1 Introduction

Recently, semantic pixel-wise segmentation has been one of active research topics, since it has a very wide range of applications, including autonomous driving, three-dimensional reconstruction etc. Image semantic segmentation can be regarded as the cornerstone of image understanding technology, which plays a significant role in autonomous systems. Early approaches [24,28] which mostly dependent on low-level vision cues of image pixels have quickly been substituted by popular machine learning algorithms [21,23,26]. Especially, when deep convolution neural networks (CNN) were applied to object classification [15,25,27] with a great success, more and more researchers start to exploit CNN features to

X. Geng and B.-H. Kang (Eds.): PRICAI 2018, LNAI 11012, pp. 588–603, 2018.
https://doi.org/10.1007/978-3-319-97304-3_45

solve other structured prediction problems [10, 14]. To the end, a series of CNN based semantic segmentation methods have been proposed, and the accuracy of image semantic segmentation is repeatedly refreshed.

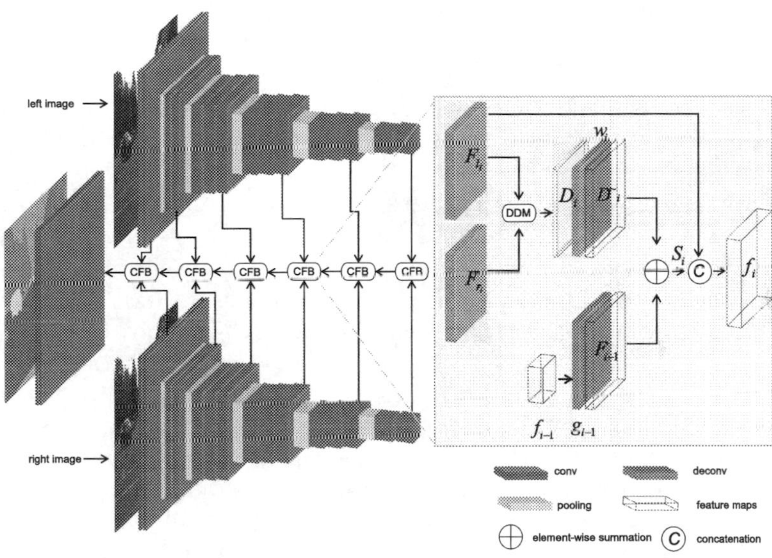

Fig. 1. An illustration of the framework of our proposed network, which contains two-parallel VGG branches to extract RGB features. The block namely CFB is exploited to calculate depth information, which is then combined with the RGB features to obtain the final results.

Most semantic segmentation methods based on CNN come from a common ancestor: Fully Convolutional Networks (FCN) [19]. FCN extended the well-known classification networks to dense pixel-wise labelling through convolutionalization. Its results, though very inspiring, is rough. This is mainly because the pooling layers reduce the spatial resolution of the feature maps, which results in the loss of positioning structure detail information. The increasingly lossy image feature representation is unfavourable for segmentation in which structural information is vital. In order to solve this limitation, various approaches have been proposed. One [1, 22] is the encoder-decoder architecture, another [3, 5, 6] exploits dilated convolution. In addition, some studies [2, 4, 31] apply conditional random fields as post-processing to obtain detailed prediction.

These above methods are all committed to capturing and storing boundary information. And these networks do have superior performance in delineating boundaries. However, the effect is less than satisfactory when the networks distinguish the certain indeterminate areas or the categories with geometric distinction. This is primarily because most of the current semantic networks only extract color or textual features of images, which only contains 2D information, while some 3D geometric information may be lost in RGB-only features and there will still be uncertainty for recognizing objects. Therefore, incorporating 3D scene information into 2D information is helpful for scene semantic segmentation as the 3D scene information can provides additional structural information to compensate the lossy structural representation in 2D images.

Depth as a type of 3D scene information is important in realistic scenarios. Depth information and semantic information have strong correlations and mutually beneficial: objects or pixels nearby with same depth have great opportunity to have the same semantic meanings. Besides, the Depth information provides rich and relatively accurate position information, which plays as an auxiliary guiding role in semantic segmentation.

Recently, some approaches have exploited multi-model feature fusion for semantic segmentation [9,12,29], most of these methods use RGB-D images as inputs, and apply two CNN branches to extract RGB and Depth features respectively, and then simply fuse the features from two branches. However, the learned feature representations using raw depth images with CNN is not rich. In order to effectively exploit the pre-trained network with fine-tuning to learn stronger features, the depthmap is encoded with three channels: horizontal disparity, height above ground, and angle with gravity (HHA [11]), which are computed from the original disparity map, and the disparity map should be calculated in advance, while the stereo images pairs are relatively more accessible.

Besides, inspired by Binocular Stereo Vision [13,17,20], which is based on the parallax principle that exploits two images obtained from different views and obtains the three-dimensional geometric information of the object by calculating the positional deviation between corresponding points of the image, we present a novel method to obtain the depth features of the image by calculating the correlation distance with $\mathcal{L}_1$-norm between image feature pairs, thus, we just need to input the RGB images instead of RGB images and HHA in those conventional methods.

In order to continue to exploit the learned rich representations of CNN pre-trained on RGB images with fine-tuning directly, as well as take the benefit from depth to segmentation, we design a Depth-guided Parallel Convolutional Network (ParallelNet) to incorporate depth features calculated from the RGB image pairs in the network into RGB features to improve segmentation accuracy. The framework of our ParallelNet is illustrated in Fig. 1. We utilize the Depth information of the image, which is combined with semantic information to guide scene semantic segmentation. Our network contains two-parallel VGG branches for extracting RGB features of the left and right image respectively. These two VGG branches share weights. Then several cascaded depth and RGB features fusion blocks (CFB) are exploited to obtain the final results. The CFB is crucial to our network. It consists of three vital blocks: the depth determination module (DDM), element-wise summation and concatenation. The DDM is essential for calculating the depth feature information. This block is inspired by the Binocular Stereo Vision with two inputs. The inputs are RGB features of the left and right image of a certain level. Then, perform the element-wise summation on the output of the DDM and the previously refined feature computed from the last

CFB, followed by concatenation which connects the summed results with the current level of the RGB feature. The CFB adaptively trains the RGB features of the image pair to effectively fuse the complementary features in depth and RGB modalities, while combing the high-level and low-level feature to finer the results. In this architecture, discriminative RGB and depth features in different level can be availably trained and fused, while retaining the advantage of skip architecture. Since the depth information is calculated inside the network, we can train the network end-to-end. It should be noted that, although we input image pairs, the left network branch is the main branch and the right branch is just an auxiliary branch to help obtain the depth information, the segmentation ground-truth is the left image in the supervised training process. We apply the concept of our ParallelNet to the current popular networks, and the extensive experiments on the popular dataset Cityscape [7] show that our parallel network can improve the performance over the original methods.

To sum up, the contribution of this paper mainly has the following three points:

(1) We propose a novel ParallelNet with RGB image pairs as input that exploits the advantage of the mutual benefit and strong correlations between depth and semantic information, which are combined to guide scene semantic segmentation.
(2) Inspired by Binocular Stereo Vision, we present an innovative module namely DDM which enables efficiently obtaining the depth information from the RGB images inputs instead of RGB images and HHA inputs in some previous methods.
(3) The experiments on the popular dataset Cityscape show that our method can improve the performance over the convolutional methods especially on these categories such as fences, Pole which have clear depth distinction.

2 Related Work

Since a great success in object classification employing deep CNN [15,25,27], a majority of studies on semantic segmentation have exploited deep CNN. Fully Convolutional Networks (FCN) [19] is the common ancestor of most current semantic segmentation methods. The advantage of FCN is that it employs the existing CNN as powerful visual models to learn hierarchies of features. FCN extended the well-known classification networks (AlexNet [15], GoogleNet [27], and the VGG [25]) into fully convolutional networks by replacing the last fully connected layers with convolutional layers, and produced feature maps instead of classification scores.

Although the results achieved by FCN is very encouraging, there are still some drawbacks. The first limitation is the low resolution of the feature maps due to the max pooling and sub-sampling, which leads to the results coarse. In order to solve this limitation, some approaches have been proposed. One [1,22] is an encoder-decoder architecture. Another [3,5,6] exploits astrous convolution, also named dilated convolution, which enlarges the receptive field in a exponential expansion way with no loss of resolution. Moreover, some researches [2,4,31] combine conditional random fields (CRF) into deep CNNs as post-processing to improve the segmentation accuracy.

Another limitation is the ensemble of multi-scale feature. FCN [19] exploited a skip architecture to combine what and where to obtain the finer prediction. To fully utilize global and local image-level features, Liu et al. [18] certified that global average pooling with FCN is efficient. Lin et al. [16] presented RefineNet that modified higher-level features by exploiting lower-level features via residual connections and achieved great increase. PSPNet [30] utilized the ability of global context information by integrating the contexts of different regions to generate good quality segmentation results.

Recently, some approaches utilizing depth information for segmentation have been studied. They extended the RGB based Convolutional networks to RGB-D situation. Early fusion method [8] was just concatenating depth into RGB channels as four-channel input. Later fusion method [19] added the two predictions computed by the two modalities. The architecture proposed by Wang et al. [29] is a network for deconvolution of multiple modalities. However, its training process included two stages, it can't be a end-to-end network. Moreover, in order to exploit the pre-trained network with fine-tuning to extract richer features, the depthmap should be encoded to a 3D image called HHA. In contrast, our proposed end-to-end architecture exploits the learned rich representations of CNN pre-trained on RGB images with fine-tuning directly and, as well as takes the benefit from depth to segmentation with the RGB images input.

3 Methodology

Our ParrelleNet benefits from the strong correlation and complementarity of depth and semantic information. We apply the concept of ParrelleNet to current popular networks FCN [19], Deeplab [5], PSPNet [30]. We mainly take FCN as basic network as an example to introduce our ParallelNet in detail. The other two variants are also introduced.

Our proposed ParallelNet's framework based on FCN is showed in Fig. 1. Our network contains two-parallel VGG branches to extract RGB features of different levels from bottom to up on the left and the right image respectively. The two VGG branches share weights. Following that, we employ several cascaded depth and RGB features fusion blocks (CFB) to get the final prediction with the skip architecture. CFB is the key to our network. The details of these modules will be elaborated in this section.

3.1 The Depth Determination Module (DDM)

An illustration of the depth determination module (DDM) is shown in Fig. 2. Given RGB features of the left and right images at certain level from the CNN, first we fix the left RGB feature maps, then we use a novel $right - shift - n$, $s.t. 0 < n < m$ operation to represent that the right feature maps are moved parallel n pixels to the right to match the corresponding points in the left feature maps. m is the depth level we set in advance. Then do the Correlation Distance Calculation (CDC) by $\mathcal{L}_1$-norm between the left and the new right feature maps obtained after $right - shift - n$, which generates a depth feature map. It is worth noting that the process of obtaining the first depth feature map don't perform the $right - shift - n$, but perform the CDC directly on the left and right RGB feature maps. Repeat the above processes for m times to finally receive m depth feature maps. Last, concatenate all the depth feature maps to get the depth information.

Specifically, let $h \times w \times g$ represents the spatial size of the given RGB feature maps and let $\mathcal{F}_l$, $\mathcal{F}_r$ denote the left and right RGB feature maps respectively. $\mathcal{F}_l$, $\mathcal{F}_r$ are both $h \times w$ matrix, $\boldsymbol{l}_{(x,y)}$ is a g-dimensional vector of the (x, y) position of the left RGB feature maps. Every element in the $\boldsymbol{l}_{(x,y)}$ is the feature value $l_{(x,y)_i}$ of the ith $s.t. 1 \leq i \leq g$ RGB feature map at (x, y) position. So does $\boldsymbol{r}_{(x,y)}$. In this case,

$$\boldsymbol{l}_{(x,y)} = [l_{(x,y)_1}, l_{(x,y)_2}, \ldots, l_{(x,y)_i}, \ldots, l_{(x,y)_g}] \tag{1}$$

$$\mathcal{F}_l = \begin{pmatrix} \boldsymbol{l}_{(1,1)} & \cdots & \boldsymbol{l}_{(1,w-n)} & \boldsymbol{l}_{(1,w-n+1)} & \cdots & \boldsymbol{l}_{(1,w)} \\ \vdots & \boldsymbol{l}_{(x,y)} & \vdots & \vdots & \vdots & \vdots \\ \boldsymbol{l}_{(h,1)} & \cdots & \boldsymbol{l}_{(h,w-n)} & \boldsymbol{l}_{(h,w-n+1)} & \cdots & \boldsymbol{l}_{(h,w)} \end{pmatrix} \tag{2}$$

Next, we utilize the above formulas to introduce two important parts of our DDM:

(1) $right - shift - n$: We do this $right - shift - n$ on the right RGB feature maps, keeping the left RGB feature maps unchanged. Connect the last n columns of the original matrix $\mathcal{F}_r$ to the left of the remainder. We let $\mathcal{F}^{\sim}{}_{r_n}$ denote the new right RGB feature maps after $right - shift - n$.

$$\mathcal{F}^{\sim}{}_{r_n} = \begin{pmatrix} \boldsymbol{r}_{(1,w-n+1)} & \cdots & \boldsymbol{r}_{(1,w)} & \boldsymbol{r}_{(1,1)} & \cdots & \boldsymbol{r}_{(1,w-n)} \\ \vdots & \vdots & \vdots & \vdots & \boldsymbol{r}_{(x,y)} & \vdots \\ \boldsymbol{r}_{(h,w-n+1)} & \cdots & \boldsymbol{r}_{(h,w)} & \boldsymbol{r}_{(h,1)} & \cdots & \boldsymbol{r}_{(h,w-n)} \end{pmatrix} \tag{3}$$

(2) Correlation Distance Calculation (CDC): We do the CDC on the $\mathcal{F}_l$ and $\mathcal{F}^{\sim}{}_{r_n}$ by $\mathcal{L}_1$-norm. Assuming that the $\boldsymbol{l}_{(x_1,y_1)}$ and the $\boldsymbol{r}_{(x_1,y_1)}$ are the vectors of the two feature maps in (x_1, y_1) position, their correlation distance can be calculated as follows:

$$d_{(x_1,y_1)} = \|\boldsymbol{l}_{(x_1,y_1)} - \boldsymbol{r}_{(x_1,y_1)}\|_1 = \sum_{i=1}^{g} |l_{(x_1,y_1)_i} - r_{(x_1,y_1)_i}| \tag{4}$$

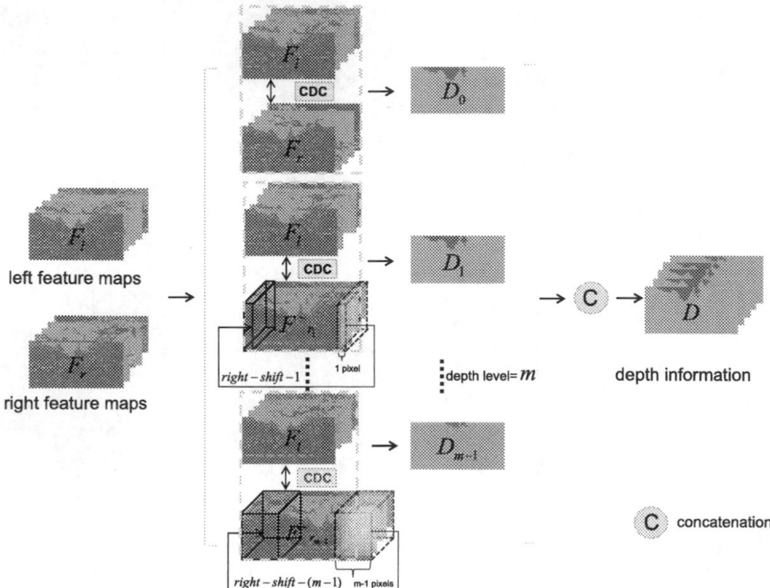

Fig. 2. A detailed illustration of the depth determination module. For the left and right feature maps extracted from the CNN, do the $right - shift - n$ operation, followed by the Correlation Distance Calculation (CDC) to obtain one feature map. Repeat the two operations for m times. Finally concatenate all the feature maps to get the depth features.

Based on this, do $\mathcal{L}_1$-norm on every corresponding position vector between $\mathcal{F}_l$ and $\mathcal{F}^{\sim}{}_{r_n}$, we can get the nth depth feature map D_n as follows:

$$D_n = \begin{pmatrix} \|\boldsymbol{l}_{(1,1)} - \boldsymbol{r}_{(1,w-n+1)}\|_1 & \cdots & \|\boldsymbol{l}_{(1,w)} - \boldsymbol{r}_{(1,w-n)}\|_1 \\ \vdots & \vdots & \vdots \\ \|\boldsymbol{l}_{(h,1)} - \boldsymbol{r}_{(h,w-n+1)}\|_1 & \cdots & \|\boldsymbol{l}_{(h,w)} - \boldsymbol{r}_{(h,w-n)}\|_1 \end{pmatrix} \tag{5}$$

3.2 Cascaded Depth and RGB Features Fusion Block (CFB)

Our proposed efficient cascaded depth and RGB features fusion block (CFB) is able to fuse the two complementary modalities features and combine coarse higher-level features with fine lower-level to generate higher-resolution semantic feature maps with skip architecture.

As shown in Fig. 1, the ith CFB has three inputs (except the first one): the refined feature maps f_{i-1} obtained from the previous CFB, the left and right RGB feature maps $\mathcal{F}_{l_i}$, $\mathcal{F}_{r_i}$. $\mathcal{F}_{l_i}$ and $\mathcal{F}_{r_i}$ are fed into the DDM to get the primary depth feature maps $\mathcal{D}_i$, then the $\mathcal{D}_i$ is passed through a 3×3 convolution layer

ω_i with the number of channels equals to the channels of $\mathcal{F}_{l_i}$ (Assuming equal to c), therefore, we obtain the new depth feature maps $\mathcal{D}^{\sim}{}_i$ with c channels. For the remaining input f_{i-1}, we get feature maps $\mathcal{F}_{i-1}$ of the same resolution as $\mathcal{D}^{\sim}{}_i$ by feeding the f_{i-1} into a deconvolution layer of stride 2 with c channels. Following that we perform element-wise summation on $\mathcal{F}_{i-1}$ and $\mathcal{D}^{\sim}{}_i$, the results are denoted as S_i. Later we concatenate $\mathcal{F}_{l_i}$ into S_i as f_i. The output of CFB block is f_i. The entire process can be expressed as follows:

$$f_i = T\{\mathcal{F}_{l_i}, \omega_i * D(\mathcal{F}_{l_i}, \mathcal{F}_{r_i}) + g_{i-1} * f_{i-1}\} \tag{6}$$

where the first $*$ represents convolution, the second $*$ denotes deconvolution. The $+$ represents element-wise summation. And $D(\cdot,\cdot)$ indicates the DDM operation, $T(\cdot,\cdot)$ indicates concatenation.

Last, the f_i are passed through two consecutive convolution layers, followed by a 1×1 convolutional layer with channel dimension 19 to predict the scores for each class at each location of the final high-resolution feature map.

In CFB, $\mathcal{D}_i$ obtained from DDM firstly passed through one 3×3 convolutional layer, which non-linearly transform the primary depth feature $\mathcal{D}_i$ to obtain rich and effective depth features. The output of previous CFB f_{i-1} provides the high-level information which includes both depth information and semantic information. For the purpose of getting finer prediction f_i, the left RGB features $\mathcal{F}_{l_i}$, the right RGB features $\mathcal{F}_{r_i}$, and the previous features f_{i-1} are embedded with ω_i, $D(\cdot)$ and g_{i-1}. We can also think that the $\mathcal{F}_{l_i}$ and $\mathcal{F}_{r_i}$ are used to provide residual low-level information including depth and RGB information between f_{i-1} and f_i. It is worth noting that f_i is the key value of CFB. The specific reasons are as follows: First, f_i not only fuses depth and RGB features at current layer, but also combines with the features at the previous layer. Second, the f_{i-1} provides coarse high-level feature maps from the deeper layers. Last, the supervision training on f_i can enable the network to continuously utilize the complementarity and mutual benefit of the two modalities to learn to transform and fuse the depth and RGB features by learning the parameters ω_i, g_{i-1} to achieve better performance than before.

3.3 Other Network Variants

ParallelNet-Deeplab Network is shown in Fig. 3. As we know, the conv1, conv2, conv3 in Deeplab have reduced resolution of image. So we feed the output of the last block of conv1, conv2 and ASPP to CFB with skip architecture to get final prediction. PSPNet and Deeplab are the same architecture except the combination method of the Pyramid Pooling Module output. Deeplab is sum-fusion, while PSPNet is concatenate-fusion. Based on this, the structure of ParallelNet-PSPNet is the same as ParallelNet-Deeplab.

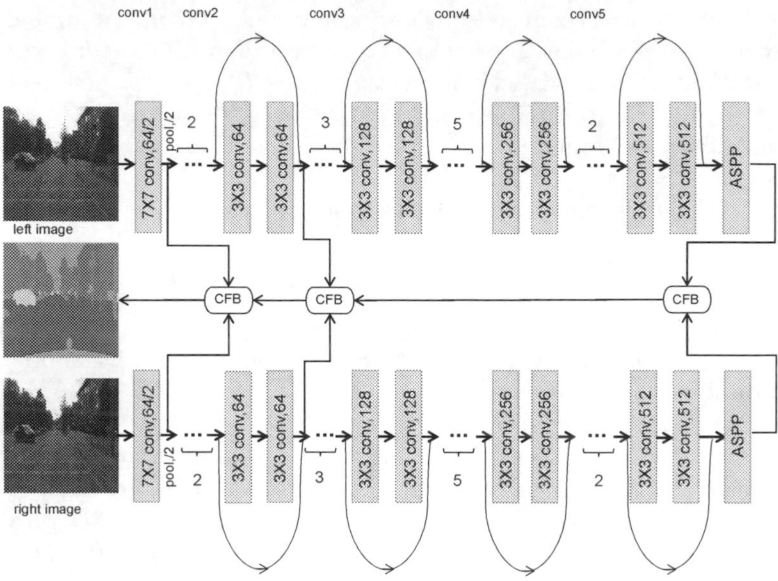

Fig. 3. The illustration of ParallelNet-Deeplab. We feed the output of the last module of the conv1, conv2 and ASPP to three CFBs with skip architecture to get the final results.

4 Experiments

Dataset. In this section, we evaluate our approach through a series of experiments on Cityscape Dataset for semantic segmentation. Cityscape Dataset is a large-scale dataset for autopilot-related aspects, focusing on pixels-wise scene semantic segmentation and instance annotation. The data scene includes different scenes from 50 different cities (mainly in Germany), with high quality pixel-level annotations of 5000 frames in addition to a larger set of 20000 weakly annotated frames. What's more, the dataset provides corresponding right images, which meets the requirements of the input image pairs required by our network. We use the left and right 8-bit images with 5000 frames (pixel-level) for our experiments. The image data is divided into 34 categories which contain both stuff and objects. And the 5000-frame fine-labelled (pixel-level) data are partitioned training, verification and test set. There are 2975 images for training, 500 images for verification and 1525 images for testing. It is noted that there are only 19 classes included in our experiments assessment.

Evaluation Metrics. We mainly employed three widely used metrics to evaluate our experimental results: the pixel-wise accuracy (Pixel Acc), the mean of class-wise intersection over union (Mean IoU) and the instance-level intersection-over-union (iIoU).

Implementation Details. Our experiments are implemented on the public platform Tensorflow. We apply the concept of ParallelNet to FCN, Deepalb and

PSPNet. We exploit the "exponential decay" learning rate method so that a better solution can be quickly obtained and the model can be more stable later in the training process. We set the $learning-rate$, $decay-steps$, $decay-rate$ to 0.1, 1000, 0.96 respectively. We train our network by Adam optimizer. Specially, for the three networks, the weights in the bottom-up RGB feature extraction (convolutional network) are initialized by employing the pre-trained net, while the weights in CFB are initialized with Xavier initialization, and zero-initializes the bias. Then we fine-tune all layers with back-propagation. Moreover, dropout is performed on each network to prevent overfitting. The input image pairs are randomly cropped during the training. And we set $batchsize$ to 4 due to our limited memory of GPU. During the testing, we cropped five patches (the four corner and the center patches) followed by averaging the predictions to make the final results.

4.1 Comprehensive Experiments

We compare our ParallelNet applied on FCN, Deeplab, PSPNet namely ParallelNet-FCN, ParallelNet-Deeplab, ParallelNet-PSPNet with the original networks. The results are shown in Table 1. It can be clearly seen that our ParallelNet outperforms the corresponding original network. For our ParallelNet-FCN, the results of Pixel acc, mIoU and iIoU are 93.63%, 63.68% and 43.82% respectively with our settings (depth level is 128, Num of CFBs is 5), and it improves the accuracy of FCN by 0.68%, 1.77% and 0.67% for Pixel acc, mIoU and iIoU respectively. For our ParallelNet-Deeplab, it increases the results of Deeplab by 0.79%, 1.16% and 0.55%. And for our ParallelNet-PSPNet, it enhance the accuracy of PSPNet by 0.82%, 1.22%, 0.56%. The results indicates combining depth with RGB features can help achieve better semantic segmentation.

Table 1. Comparison of our ParallelNet with original network. Ours outperforms the original network.

Method	Pixel Acc. (%)	mIoU (%)	iIoU (%)
FCN	92.95	61.91	43.15
PaallelNet-FCN	93.63	63.68	43.82
Deeplab	86.03	39.16	32.37
ParallelNet-Deeplab	86.82	40.32	32.92
PSPNet	88.65	44.74	35.11
ParallelNet-PSPNet	89.47	45.96	35.67

Class-wise accuracies of ParallelNet compared with the corresponding original networks are illustrated in Tables 2, 3 and 4. As it can be seen, the results of our ParallelNet have been improved in most categories by incorporating the

Table 2. Comparison of Class-wise semantic segmentation accuracy between FCN and ParallelNet-FCN (the bold fonts in the tables indicate the superiority of our results).

Method	Road(%)	swalk(%)	build(%)	wall(%)	fence(%)	pole(%)	tlight(%)
FCN	95.5	75.11	86.89	31.10	42.55	49.45	56.20
PallelNet-FCN	**96.36**	75.44	**89.46**	**34.79**	**47.64**	**55.17**	56.39
Method	sign(%)	Veg.(%)	terrain(%)	sky(%)	person(%)	rider(%)	car(%)
FCN	65.47	88.71	56.20	89.09	72.81	44.22	89.88
PallelNet-FCN	**67.37**	**90.5**	55.83	88.97	**76.96**	**47.92**	**90.4**
Method	trunk(%)	bus(%)	train(%)	mbike(%)	bike(%)	mIoU(%)	iIoU(%)
FCN	31.86	48.96	43.83	38.19	70.19	61.91	43.15
PallelNet-FCN	32.39	49.23	**44.52**	**39.83**	**70.83**	**63.68**	**43.82**

depth into RGB features especially in those categories with clear depth and geometric distinction, for example, wall, pole, fences, person, while in some classes which have little geometric distinction such as sky, terrain, our methods have shown no superiority.

Table 3. Comparison of Class-wise semantic segmentation accuracy (IoU) between Deeplab and ParallelNet-Deeplab (the bold fonts in the tables indicate the superiority of our results).

Method	Road(%)	swalk(%)	build(%)	wall(%)	fence(%)	pole(%)	tlight(%)
Deeplab	90.69	64.65	68.43	17.11	19.52	30.20	1.15
ParallelNet-Deeplab	**91.62**	65.21	**70.49**	**20.13**	**23.46**	**33.98**	1.36
Method	sign(%)	Veg.(%)	terrain(%)	sky(%)	person(%)	rider(%)	car(%)
DEeplab	32.35	82.42	45.40	44.39	51.56	7.72	80.64
ParallelNetDeeplab	**33.70**	**83.55**	45.60	44.17	**53.67**	**8.78**	**81.34**
Method	trunk(%)	bus(%)	train(%)	mbike(%)	bike(%)	mIoU(%)	iIoU(%)
Deeplab	5.27	24.33	17.05	12.45	48.61	39.16	32.37
ParallelNet-DEeplab	**6.09**	**25.03**	17.07	12.96	47.78	**40.32**	**32.93**

4.2 Ablation Studies

We conduct ablative experiments for ParallelNet-FCN by setting different depth levels and cascade numbers of CFB. The results are shown in Tables 5 and 6 respectively.

Table 5 shows the effect of different depth levels on the semantic segmentation. It is noted that we set the number of CFB to 5. We find that the pixel accuracy and the mIoU first increase and then decrease as the depth levels increase. We think that when the set depth level is relatively small, that is to say, for a certain pixel on the left image, the corresponding target pixel on the right image may not be matched. With the set depth level increases, the most pixels in the left can be matched correctly with the corresponding target pixels on the right images. In this case, the extracted depth information can play a positive role in guiding semantic segmentation. However, when the depth level increases continually, there may be additional pixels which matches the certain pixel in the

Table 4. Comparison of Class-wise semantic segmentation accuracy(IoU) between PSPNet and ParallelNet-PSPNet (the bold fonts in the tables indicate the superiority of our results).

Method	Road(%)	swalk(%)	build(%)	wall(%)	fence(%)	pole(%)	tlight(%)
PSPNet	92.56	67.84	77.22	21.32	25.02	38.47	3.00
PallelNet-PSPNet	**93.89**	**68.19**	**78.11**	**24.09**	**28.95**	**43.10**	2.90
Method	sign(%)	Veg.(%)	terrain(%)	sky(%)	person(%)	rider(%)	car(%)
PSPNet	27.16	85.30	50.09	75.43	58.30	11.62	83.40
PallelNet-PSPNet	**29.87**	**86.46**	48.55	75.71	**60.40**	**12.10**	84.00
Method	trunk(%)	bus(%)	train(%)	mbike(%)	bike(%)	mIoU(%)	iIoU(%)
PSPNet	22.45	38.35	7.48	15.20	49.92	44.74	35.11
PallelNet-PSPNet	22.55	37.69	**8.25**	**16.35**	**50.99**	**45.96**	**35.66**

left. So the number of disturbing pixels in the right image may increase and the errors correspondingly increase. At this time, the depth information will have a negative effect on semantic segmentation due to the existence of the errors, which causes both pixel accuracy and mIoU to decrease. We find that the depth level is set to 128 for the best performance.

Table 5. The results of different depth levels on semantic segmentation. And setting the depth level to 128 will achieve the best performance

Method	Pixel Acc. (%)	mIoU (%)	iIoU (%)
32	91.35	56.67	41.19
64	92.64	59.43	41.81
128	93.63	63.68	43.82
192	92.47	61.08	42.07

Table 6 shows the effect of diverse numbers of CFB on semantic segmentation. We have set the depth level to 128. From the bottom to the top of the network, we record the CFB at the top of the network as the first CFB and the CFB at the bottom of the network as the sixth CFB. From Table 6, we find that multiple CFBs which utilize the skip structure has improved performance, the pixel accuracy and the mIoU grow fast as the number of CFB increases from 2 to 5. The network using 5 CFBs achieve 63.97% mean IU and 93.63% pixel accuracy. And our cascaded improvements have met diminishing returns both with respect to the IU metric and also in terms of pixel-wise accuracy when the number of CFB increases from 5 to 6.

4.3 Qualitative Results

We show some qualitative results of ours proposed method compared with FCN network which only employ the RGB information on semantic segmentation in

Table 6. Refining ParallelNet by cascading different numbers of CFB improves semantic segmentation.

Num of CFB	Pixel Acc. (%)	mIoU (%)	iIoU (%)
6	93.79	63.59	43.88
5	93.63	63.68	43.82
4	92.34	60.57	42.07
3	91.87	58.41	42.38
2	91.3	55.88	40.69

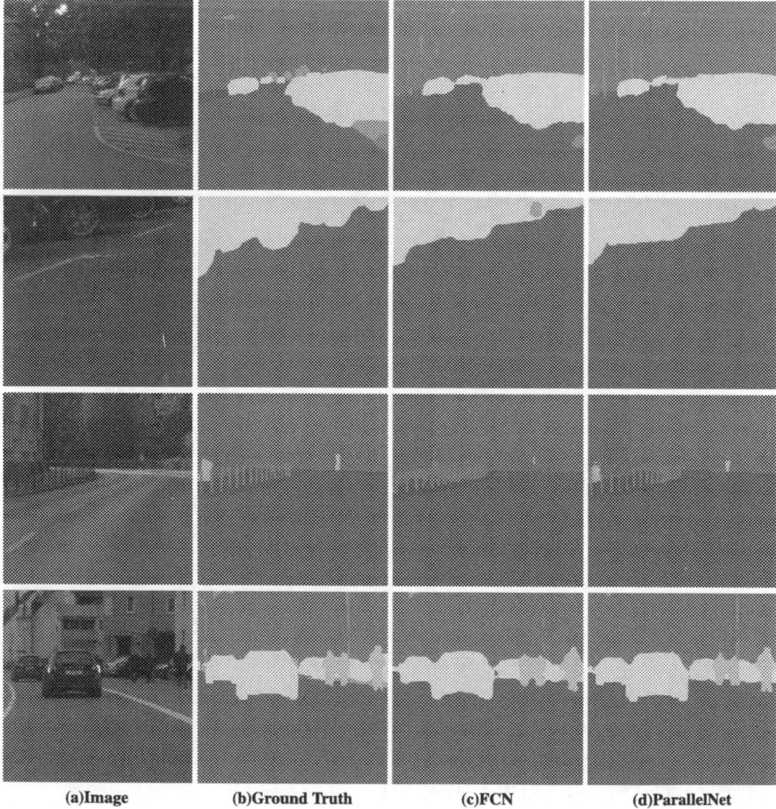

Fig. 4. Qualitative results of our ParallelNet-FCN compared with FCN. From the left to right for each example:image, Ground truth, the resluts of FCN and our ParallelNet. Note that our network shows significant improvement in these categories which have clear depth distinction, e.g., (a) the Pole which has clear depth distinction. (b) eliminating noise points with the help of depth to segmentation, (c) the fence which has geometric distinction, (d) the pedestrian which has obvious depth characteristic. Best viewed in color.

Fig. 3. We obtain the semantic segmentation results of FCN by running the available source code. We compare the results with our ParallelNet which employs image pairs as inputs and combines the depth information with the RGB information for segmentation (Fig. 4). We can see that our network shows significant improvement in fences, Pole, pedestrians categories which have clear depth distinction that may be lost in RGB-only features and our network helps eliminating noise points.

5 Conclusion

We present a novel ParallelNet for effectively segmenting images by taking benefit of the relevance and complementarity between depth and RGB modalities on the RGB images inputs. Our effective CFB with skip architecture can availably fuse the discriminative RGB and depth features in different level and combine the higher-level and lower-level features to get finer prediction. Our experiments demonstrate that our proposed ParallelNet outperforms the original network which only utilize the RGB features. In the future we plan to extend our proposed method to object detection and classification tasks to obtain more competitive results.

Acknowledgements. This work was supported in part by the Key Research and Development Plan of Jiangsu Province (BE2015162) and the Major Special Project of Core Electronic Devices, High-end Generic Chips and Basic Software (2015ZX01041101).

References

1. Badrinarayanan, V., Kendall, A., Cipolla, R.: SegNet: a deep convolutional encoder-decoder architecture for scene segmentation. PAMI **PP**(99), 2481–2495 (2017)
2. Chandra, S., Kokkinos, I.: Fast, exact and multi-scale inference for semantic image segmentation with deep Gaussian CRFs. In: Leibe, B., Matas, J., Sebe, N., Welling, M. (eds.) ECCV 2016. LNCS, vol. 9911. Springer, Cham (2016). https://doi.org/10.1007/978-3-319-46478-7
3. Chen, L.C., Papandreou, G., Kokkinos, I., Murphy, K., Yuille, A.L.: Semantic image segmentation with deep convolutional nets and fully connected crfs (2014). arXiv preprint arXiv:1412.7062
4. Chen, L.C., Papandreou, G., Kokkinos, I., Murphy, K., Yuille, A.L.: Semantic image segmentation with deep convolutional nets and fully connected CRFs. Comput. Sci. **4**, 357–361 (2014)
5. Chen, L.C., Papandreou, G., Kokkinos, I., Murphy, K., Yuille, A.L.: Deeplab: Semantic image segmentation with deep convolutional nets, atrous convolution, and fully connected crfs (2016). arXiv preprint arXiv:1606.00915
6. Chen, L.C., Papandreou, G., Schroff, F., Adam, H.: Rethinking atrous convolution for semantic image segmentation. arXiv preprint arXiv:1706.05587 (2017)
7. Cordts, M., et al.: The cityscapes dataset for semantic urban scene understanding (2016)

8. Couprie, C., Farabet, C., Najman, L., Lecun, Y.: Indoor semantic segmentation using depth information. Eprint Arxiv (2013)
9. Deng, Z., Todorovic, S., Jan Latecki, L.: Semantic segmentation of RGBD images with mutex constraints. In: ICPR, pp. 1733–1741 (2015)
10. Farabet, C., Couprie, C., Najman, L., LeCun, Y.: Learning hierarchical features for scene labeling. IEEE T-PAMI **35**(8), 1915–1929 (2013)
11. Gupta, S., Girshick, R., Arbeláez, P., Malik, J.: Learning rich features from RGB-D images for object detection and segmentation. In: Fleet, D., Pajdla, T., Schiele, B., Tuytelaars, T. (eds.) ECCV 2014. LNCS, vol. 8695, pp. 345–360. Springer, Cham (2014). https://doi.org/10.1007/978-3-319-10584-0_23
12. Hazirbas, C., Ma, L., Domokos, C., Cremers, D.: FuseNet: incorporating depth into semantic segmentation via fusion-based CNN architecture. In: Lai, S.-H., Lepetit, V., Nishino, K., Sato, Y. (eds.) ACCV 2016. LNCS, vol. 10111, pp. 213–228. Springer, Cham (2017). https://doi.org/10.1007/978-3-319-54181-5_14
13. Hirschmuller, H.: Accurate and efficient stereo processing by semi-global matching and mutual information. In: CVPR, vol. 2, pp. 807–814. IEEE (2005)
14. Khan, S.H., Bennamoun, M., Sohel, F., Togneri, R.: Geometry driven semantic labeling of indoor scenes. In: Fleet, D., Pajdla, T., Schiele, B., Tuytelaars, T. (eds.) ECCV 2014. LNCS, vol. 8689, pp. 679–694. Springer, Cham (2014). https://doi.org/10.1007/978-3-319-10590-1_44
15. Krizhevsky, A., Sutskever, I., Hinton, G.E.: Imagenet classification with deep convolutional neural networks. In: Advances in Neural Information Processing Systems, pp. 1097–1105 (2012)
16. Lin, G., Milan, A., Shen, C., Reid, I.: Refinenet: multi-path refinement networks for high-resolution semantic segmentation. In: CVPR (2017)
17. Liu, S., Zhao, L., Li, J.: The Applications and Summary of Three Dimensional Reconstruction Based on Stereo Vision (2012)
18. Liu, W., Rabinovich, A., Berg, A.C.: Parsenet: looking wider to see better. In: ICLR Workshop (2016)
19. Long, J., Shelhamer, E., Darrell, T.: Fully convolutional networks for semantic segmentation. In: CVPR, pp. 3431–3440 (2015)
20. Luo, W., Schwing, A.G., Urtasun, R.: Efficient deep learning for stereo matching. In: CVPR, pp. 5695–5703 (2016)
21. Muja, M., Lowe, D.G.: Scalable nearest neighbor algorithms for high dimensional data. PAMI **36**(11), 2227–2240 (2014)
22. Ronneberger, O., Fischer, P., Brox, T.: U-Net: convolutional networks for biomedical image segmentation. In: Navab, N., Hornegger, J., Wells, W.M., Frangi, A.F. (eds.) MICCAI 2015. LNCS, vol. 9351, pp. 234–241. Springer, Cham (2015). https://doi.org/10.1007/978-3-319-24574-4_28
23. Sánchez, A.V.D.: Advanced support vector machines and kernel methods. Neurocomputing **55**(1–2), 5–20 (2003)
24. Shi, J., Malik, J.: Normalized cuts and image segmentation. PAMI **22**(8), 888–905 (2000)
25. Simonyan, K., Zisserman, A.: Very deep convolutional networks for large-scale image recognition (2014). arXiv preprint arXiv:1409.1556
26. Smola, A.J., Schölkopf, B.: A tutorial on support vector regression. Stat. Comput. **14**(3), 199–222 (2004)
27. Szegedy, C., et al.: Going deeper with convolutions. In: CVPR, pp. 1–9 (2015)
28. Tang, M., Gorelick, L., Veksler, O., Boykov, Y.: Grabcut in one cut. In: ICCV, pp. 1769–1776. IEEE (2013)

29. Wang, J., Wang, Z., Tao, D., See, S., Wang, G.: Learning common and specific features for RGB-D semantic segmentation with deconvolutional networks. In: Leibe, B., Matas, J., Sebe, N., Welling, M. (eds.) ECCV 2016. LNCS, vol. 9909, pp. 664–679. Springer, Cham (2016). https://doi.org/10.1007/978-3-319-46454-1_40
30. Zhao, H., Shi, J., Qi, X., Wang, X., Jia, J.: Pyramid scene parsing network. In: CVPR, pp. 2881–2890 (2017)
31. Zheng, S., et al.: Conditional random fields as recurrent neural networks, pp. 1529–1537 (2015)

Aircraft Detection in Remote Sensing Images Based on Background Filtering and Scale Prediction

Jing Gao(✉), Haichang Li(✉), Zhongxing Han, Siyu Wang, and Xiaohui Hu

Institute of Software Chinese Academy of Sciences (ISCAS), Beijing, China
gaojing161@mails.ucas.cn, haichang@iscas.ac.cn

Abstract. Object detection is one of the most important tasks in remote sensing image analysis. A hot topic is aircraft detection. One challenge of aircraft detection is that the aircraft is relative small compared with the image, i.e., there are about fifteen million pixels per image in our aircraft data set, while the aircraft only accounts for about three thousand pixels. The large size difference between the image and the object makes it impossible to use a general object detection method to detect the aircraft in the remote sensing image. Another challenge of aircraft detection is that the sizes of aircrafts are various, i.e., the scale span of the aircraft is large due to the shooting distance and the scale of the aircraft itself. In order to solve these two problems, in this paper, we propose a new scheme containing two special networks. The first network is a background filtering network designed to crop partial areas where aircrafts may exist. The second network is a scale prediction network mounted on Faster R-CNN to recognize the scales of aircrafts contained in the areas that cropped by the first network. The scale problem is well solved, though the two networks are relatively simple in structure. Experiments on the aircraft data set show that our background filtering network can crop the areas containing the aircrafts from remote sensing images and our scale prediction network has improvement on the precision rate, recall rate and mean average precision (mAP).

Keywords: Convolutional Neural Networks (CNNs)
Aircraft detection · Remote sensing image · Multi-scale

1 Introduction

Object detection is one of the widely used computer vision applications in remote sensing image analysis. In recent years, many people have conducted a lot of researches to solve the problems faced by object detection of remote sensing images.

This work is supported in part by the Natural Science Foundation of China under Grants U1435220 and 61503365, Youth Innovation Foundation of the 4th China High Resolution Earth Observation Conference under Grant GFZX04061502, and STS project of Fujian Province and Chinese Academy of Sciences under Grant 2018T3009.

X. Geng and B.-H. Kang (Eds.): PRICAI 2018, LNAI 11012, pp. 604–616, 2018.
https://doi.org/10.1007/978-3-319-97304-3_46

The size of the remote sensing image in our data set is about (3000 × 5000), but the aircraft's size is about (50 × 60). According to our statistics, as shown in Table 1, the ratio of aircraft size to image size is less than 0.05 in all remote sensing images in our aircraft data set. The remote sensing image is large and the aircraft is relatively small, one example is shown in the first picture of Fig. 1. We can not use a simple scaling method to process the image into a fixed size and extract the features of objects very well. Han et al. [1] used an additional R-CNN, named region locating network, to select the regions where aircrafts locate with high probabilities, and then send these regions into Faster R-CNN [2] to detect aircrafts. However, the final detection accuracy of region locating network in [1] is not high due to the clustering algorithms and subsequent processing methods. As shown in Fig. 1, we used a simple structure network named Background-Filtering-Network to predict areas that may contain aircrafts, then we combined areas and adjusted the ratio and size of the predicted areas to obtain the final suitable cropping ares. Because of the relative concentration of aircraft in remote sensing images, our method is very effective. An example of using Background-Filtering-Network to crop the picture can be seen in Fig. 2.

Table 1. The proportion of aircraft size and remote sensing image size: *ratio* = $Area(box)/Area(image)$, *number* indicates the number of aircraft in this ratio range.

ratio	$(0, 0.01)$	$[0.01, 0.02)$	$[0.02, 0.03)$	$[0.03, 0.04)$	$[0.04, 0.05)$	$[0.05, 1]$
number	21970	0	2	2	0	0

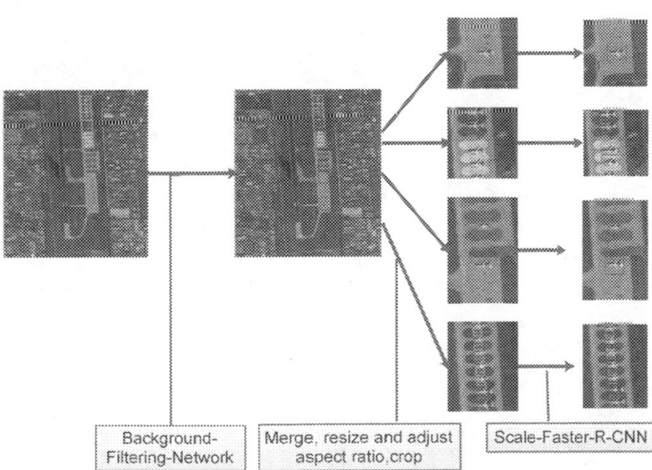

Fig. 1. The overall experimental procedure: we use Background-Filtering-Network identify areas that may contain aircrafts in large remote sensing images, then we combine these areas, resize, adjust the aspect ratio and crop the area containing aircrafts, finally using the Scale-Faster-R-CNN to detect the aircrafts.

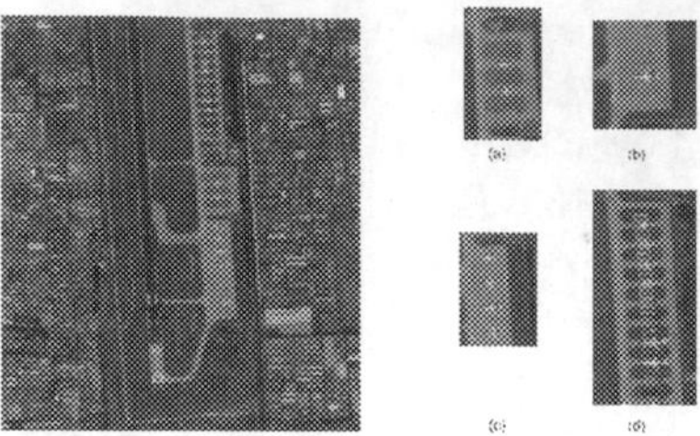

Fig. 2. The left is the original image, and the right is the cropped parts containing the aircrafts based on the Background-Filtering-Network prediction after adjusting size and aspect ratio. The size of original image is (2048×2353). The size of the cropped parts are $(300 \times 383), (300 \times 312), (300 \times 325), (300 \times 611)$, respectively

On our cropped aircraft data set, the aircraft's scale distribution is shown in Fig. 3, and the aircraft's scale is mainly between 16 and 640, however, the scale of anchors that produced by Faster R-CNN [2] is $(128, 256, 512)$. The scale of proposals produced by Faster R-CNN [2] do not match that of aircrafts. Using Faster R-CNN [2] directly in our cropped aircraft data set can not achieve high accuracy, especially when detecting relatively small aircraft. Regarding to the problem of relatively large spans in the scale of objects, Hao et al. [3] used a Scale-Proposal-Network to predict the scales of faces in a picture and then zoom the picture based on the scales for detecting faces. Since their method needs to scale the picture and calculate the feature map for each predicted scale of the picture, the amount of calculation is relatively large. And the scale Hao et al. [3] used is exponential of two and not precise enough. Therefore it does not work well in our remote sensing image aircraft detection. Both Faster R-CNN [2] and Scale-Proposal-Network Hao et al. [3] cannot be used directly to perfectly solve the problem of large spans in the scale of aircrafts, but they provide us with good inspiration. As shown in Fig. 1, we use Faster R-CNN [2] with a scale-prediction network named Scale-Faster-R-CNN to detect aircrafts on cropped aircraft data set. The scale-prediction network predicts the scales of aircrafts in the picture and use the predicted scales to produce anchors. By using the scale prediction network, we raise the mAP for Faster-R-CNN [2] on our cropped aircraft data set.

To sum up, our contributions in this paper are as follows: (1) Background-Filtering-Network to crop images: we scheme using Background-Filtering-Network to find the areas where the aircrafts may exist. And then we combine these areas, resize, adjust the aspect ratio and crop the areas. The first step makes common object detection methods can be used to detect aircrafts in remote sensing images. (2) Scale-Faster-R-CNN: we use a scale prediction network in the Faster-R-CNN [2], using the predicted scales to produce proposals. By using the scale prediction network, we raise precision rate, recall rate and mAP for Faster-R-CNN [2].

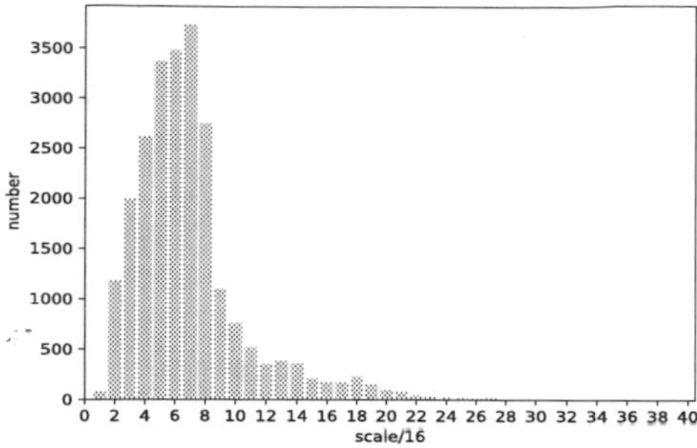

Fig. 3. Aircraft scale statistics on our cropped aircraft data set. The plane size is defined as $scale = \sqrt{w \times h}$, where w, h is the width and height of the box, respectively. The horizontal axis represents the scale of the aircraft divided by 16 and the vertical axis represents the number of aircraft at that scale.

2 Related Work

Now popular object detection methods can be mainly divided into two categories, the first is two-step method, like R-CNN [4], Fast R-CNN [5] and Faster R-CNN [2], the second is one-step method, such as YOLO [6], SSD [7]. From the experimental results, two-stage method is more accurate than the one-stage method. These methods are all based on convolution neural network (CNN). For CNN-based aircraft detectors, the variance in appearance can be handled by the large capacity of convolution neural network. The variance in scale, however, is not carefully considered and there is room for improvement.

Object detection in remote sensing images has been widely developed in recent years. Long et al. [8] proposed an accurate object localization framework for remote sensing images. Long et al. [8] used a two-stage object accurate localization method: non-maximum suppression and unsupervised score based bounding box regression. Pan et al. [9] proposed a cascade convolutional neural network framework based on transfer-learning and geometric feature constraints for aircraft detection. A saliency algorithm is used to preprocess the image to reduce the number of region proposals and improve the efficiency and accuracy of subsequent feature extraction and classification in [10]. Han et al. [11] combined weakly supervised learning with high-dimensional feature learning to detect objects in remote sensing images. Chen et al. [12] used a orientation classifier network to adjust the orientation of the boxes for the orientation problem existing in remote sensing image building detection. Han et al. [1] used a region locating network to select the regions where aircrafts locate with high probabilities. These methods all improve the target detection of remote sensing images, but they do not deal with scale issues in remote sensing images, so they are not suitable for our data sets and tasks.

The scale problem in object detection has been studied in recent years. There are mainly two ways to solve the scale problem, the first is the image pyramid and the second is RPN [2]. For image pyramid method, Li et al. [13] used three convolutional neural networks of roughly the same structure, the difference between the three networks is that the picture resolution and the complexity of the network are gradually increased. Sermanet et al. [14] resized the image to the corresponding scale for a given image to be processed, then performed an intensive sampling algorithm on each scale, and finally, combined the results at all scales to get the final result. Hao et al. [3] used a Scale-Proposal-Network to predict the scales of faces in a picture and then zoom the picture based on the scales for detecting faces. By using the image pyramid method, the detector only handle features in a certain range of scale and the variance is taken over by the image pyramid, which could reduce the fitting difficulty for detector but potentially increase the computational cost. For RPN [2] method, the size of the input image is fixed, and proposals of all scales are produced on the last convolution layer. Ren et al. [2] produced three scales $(128, 256, 512)$ and three aspect ratios $(0.5, 1, 2)$ proposals. The RPN [2] method are usually faster than image pyramid method [3,13,14] since it calculates feature map for image only once. However the scales used by RPN [2] are fixed, which are not fit all the pictures.

Our method has some differences with the methods mentioned above [1–3]. Although Faster R-CNN [2] uses multiple scales of proposals, the scales are fixed. We use an adaptive scale prediction based on the picture context information. Our method can choose the scales of the proposals in a wider range (from 16 to 640). Our method avails to detect small targets and the object of large scale span. Faster R-CNN [2] produces 9 anchors (3 scales, 3 ratios) at each sliding center, and we produce only 6 anchors (2 scales, 3 ratios). Compared with the method in [3] predicting exponent scales of faces, our scale-prediction is more elaborate and alternative. And our scales predicted are used to generate proposals, which do not have to generate feature map for each predicted scale picture. Compared with Region Locating Network [1], the data used by our Background-Filtering-Network is generated by a novel clustering methods, and then we use the subsequent processing methods. So our method have a better recall rate, and the pictures cropped by our method have the appropriate size and aspect ratio.

3 Our Method

In this section, we'll detail every step of the method we use. We first describe how to use Background-Filtering-Network to crop areas of the picture that may contain aircrafts. Then we introduce how to use Scale-Faster-R-CNN to detect the aircrafts in the pictures that are produced in the previous step.

3.1 Background-Filtering-Network to Crop Images

The Background-Filtering-Network that we use to crop pictures is based on RPN in ResNet [15]. As shown in Fig. 4, the Background-Filtering-Network calculates the feature map of the image and predicts proposals. The aircrafts are too small compared to the size of the remote sensing images. Therefore we can not directly use the aircraft annotation data to train the Background-Filtering-Network. We use clustering method to generate new annotation data for cropping images. The purpose of clustering is to divide the adjacent aircrafts into the same area, hence the boxes in clustered annotation data will be relatively large. The method of merging boxes is to merge two boxes with the smallest distance each time until only one box is left or the minimum distance is greater than the threshold. The distance between two boxes is defined as follows:

$$distance = Area^{increase} + \lambda distance^{center} \tag{1}$$

in which,

$$Area^{increase} = Area(b) - [Area(b1) + Area(b2) - Area(bb)] \tag{2}$$

where $b1, b2$ are the two boxes that need to be merged, b is the merged box of $b1$ and $b2$, bb is a block composed of overlapping parts of $b1$ and $b2$. The distance between the two boxes is weighted by the area newly added after the merging and the distance between two box center points. The λ is set to 100 for producing better annotation data for the Background-Filtering-Network.

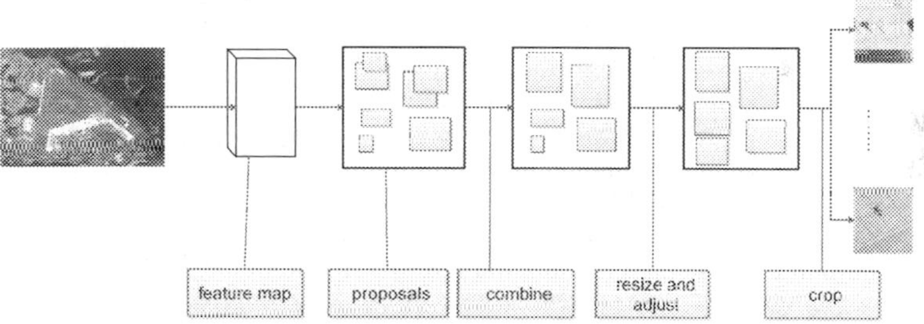

Fig. 4. The process of Background-Filtering-Network: the Background-Filtering-Network predicts proposals based on the image's feature maps. Then we combine the adjacent proposals and adjust the boxes' size and aspect ratio.

The new marked boxes generated by the clustering method can not be directly used to train the network. Because there are some boxes whose size or aspect ratio is not appropriate. It is not conducive for detecting object that a cropped picture is too large compared to object, so we stop merging the boxes once the area of the box is larger than the threshold. A cropped image that is too small may result in distorting the target when the image is scaled to a fixed size (600×1000). Too large aspect ratio is not conducive for Faster R-CNN [2] to detecting aircrafts. Therefore when we make a new annotation, we extend the boxes with an aspect ratio greater than five. One example of the result of clustering is shown in Fig. 5.

Fig. 5. New annotation data is generated based on the original annotation data. The blue box represents the original tag data, the red box represents the new tag data obtained after clustering, resizing and ratio adjustment.

As shown in Fig. 4, based on the Background-Filtering-Network prediction to crop images we also combine adjacent proposals and adjust the size and aspect ratio of the images so that cropped images' size is located between (300×300) to (1000×1000), aspect ratio is less than 3. One example of the results of cropping the picture is shown in Fig. 2. Since our method uses a novel clustering method and subsequent adjustments to the predicted region, the region cropped by our method can reach a better recall rate on Faster R-CNN [2] than the method in [1].

3.2 Scale-Faster-R-CNN

We use a scale-prediction network to predict the possible scales of aircrafts in the input pictures. The structure of the scale-prediction network is based on VGG16 [16]. This scale-prediction network shares convolutional layers with RPN and Fast R-CNN. As shown in Fig. 6, scale-prediction network inputs the feature maps from the shared convolutional layer into a 40 channel convolution layer to obtain 40 feature maps, and then generates a 40 dimension vector representing the probability through global max pooling layer.

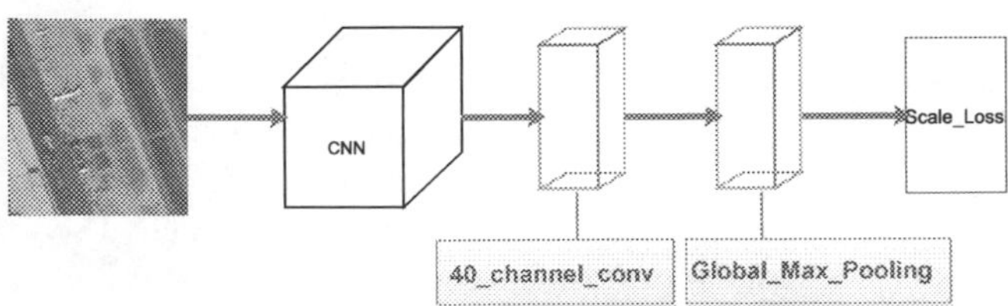

Fig. 6. The construction of scale-prediction network: the scale-prediction network and RPN share convolutional layers, only adding one convolutional layer and one pooling layer. The loss function of the scale prediction network is a cross-entropy loss function.

The scale used in our scale prediction network is an integer multiple of 16, for example, we predict that the scale is 3, in fact, the resulting anchor has a scale of $16 * 3$.

We define the size x of the aircraft based on the plane box b, x is defined as follows:

$$x = \sqrt{w \times h} \tag{3}$$

where w, h is the width and height of the box b, respectively.

We define a scale set from an aircraft size x. Scale set is $S = \{p_0, p_1, p_2, \ldots, p_{39}\}$, the index i in S is defined as follows:

$$i = round(x/16) - 1 \tag{4}$$

where $round()$ is a rounding function.

Following Hao et al. [3], the ground truth label setting method is as follows: for an occurring scale $i*$ set $p_{i*} = 1$, the scale of the neighbor in the occurring scale is defined by the mixed Gaussian model as follows:

$$p_i = \frac{1}{r} * Gaussian(i, \mu, \sigma), i \in N(i*) \tag{5}$$

where r is the number of scales existing in $N(i)$. The size of $N(i*)$ is 20. μ is $i*$. σ is $1/\sqrt{2\pi}$.

The loss function of scale-prediction network is defined as follows:

$$\hat{p_n} = sigmoid(x_n) = \frac{1}{1 + e^{-x_n}} \tag{6}$$

$$loss = -\frac{1}{N} \sum_{n=1}^{N} [p_n \log \hat{p_n} + (1 - p_n) \log(1 - \hat{p_n})] \tag{7}$$

where x is the output vector of the global max pooling layer, $\hat{p}$ is the predicted scale distribution vector and p is the ground truth scale distribution vector.

Since our pictures are cropped from the original remote sensing images, the number of scales contained in each picture is relatively small, usually two or three and we found out that choosing two scales for each picture would be sufficient after experiments. So we need to find the two most likely to appear in the picture using the output of the scale prediction network. As shown in Fig. 7, the scale prediction network outputs a vector representing the probability of occurrence at each scale. We need to find two scales with the highest probability of appearance in the picture based on the scale vector. Subtracting the mean from each point makes the probability distribution smoother. Then we use one-dimension non-maximum suppression (1D NMS) to find the two scales with the highest probability. Finally, RPN [2] uses the two predicted scales as the size of anchor to generate proposals, and Fast R-CNN [2] classifies and locates these proposals.

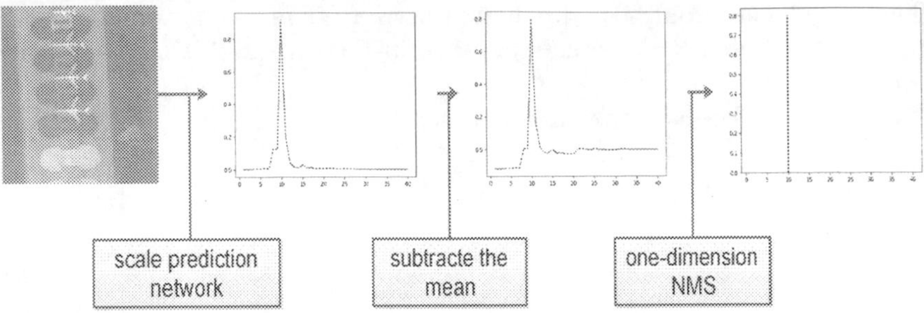

Fig. 7. The image is processed by the scale prediction network to output a histogram of probability distributions. This histogram contains a lot of noise. So some noise can be smoothed out by moving average. Then we use 1D NMS to find the prediction scales.

4 Experiments

There are 831 remote sensing images in our aircraft data set, with an average size of (3975×5535) pixels. There are 6783 pictures in our cropped aircraft data set. In the entire data set, a total of 21974 aircrafts were marked. 80% of the pictures are used as a training set, 10% of pictures are used as a validation set, and 10% of pictures are used as a test set.

For each picture, as shown in Fig. 1, we first input the picture to the Background-Filtering-Network to predict the areas that may contain aircrafts. Then we merge regions with confidence greater than 0.8 based on intersection-over-union (IOU). Next, we expand the areas with the aspect ratio greater than 3 by the short side into a square and resize the area between (300×300) and (1000×1000). Finally, the cropped areas are considered as the input of Scale-Faster-R-CNN. The recall rate on our aircraft test data set is 88.2%, and the recall rate on all aircraft data set is 91.9%. This higher recall rate guarantees that we miss less aircrafts after our cropping. Han et al. [1] used Faster R-CNN [2] to detect aircrafts after using the region locating network, and the accuracy and recall rate are 53.64%, 65.71%, respectively. After our Background-Filtering-Network crops the images, the accuracy and recall rate of detection using Faster R-CNN [2] are 65.82%, 92.24%, respectively. The improvement in recall and accuracy compared to [1] verifies that our cropping image method is better. As shown in Fig. 8, we compare the detection result of Faster R-CNN [2] on pictures that are cropped by our Background-Filtering-Network with that of pictures averagely cropped. When the image is averagely cropped into 16 pictures for detecting aircrafts, the aircraft is still small relative to the size of the picture, which is not conducive to Faster R-CNN [2] extracting features of aircrafts. And many of the 16 pictures contain no aircraft. Our method of cropping pictures makes the position and size of the aircraft more appropriate relative to the cropped pictures. Therefore, the pictures cropped by our method can be used to better detect the aircrafts even relatively small aircrafts.

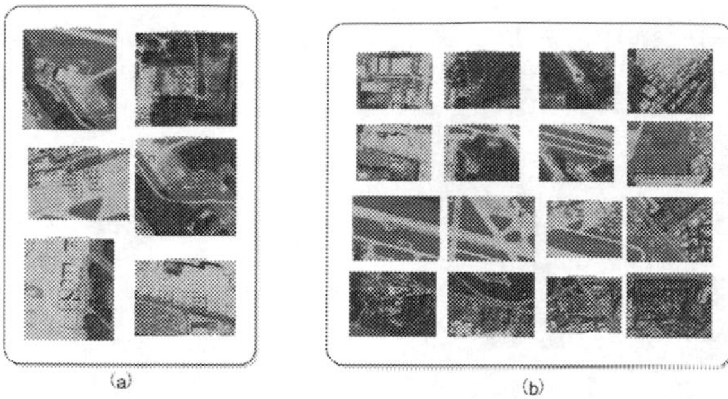

Fig. 8. Comparison between our cropping method and averagely cropping method. The pictures in (a) and (b) are cropped from the same large remote sensing image using the Background-Filtering-Network and averagely cropping method, respectively. (a) is a detection example of Faster R-CNN [2] on our cropped pictures, (b) is a detection example of Faster R-CNN [2] on averagely cropped pictures.

The procedure for using Scale-Faster-R-CNN to detect aircrafts is as follows: the scale prediction part predicts the scale vector, and based on the scale vector, the two most probable scales are found by using the method aforementioned. The RPN then uses these two scales as the scales of anchors to produce proposals and then inputs proposals to Fast R-CNN to generate the location and label of aircrafts. We test our method on the cropped aircraft data set. And we compare the results of Faster R-CNN [2] with that of our method. There are two definitions of scale in our method. One definition of scale is an integer in the range 1 to 40 as mentioned in the previous section, called our method-IS (integer scale). Another definition of scale is the exponent of two as defined in [3], called our method-ES (exponent scale). As shown by Table 2, our method is better than Faster R-CNN [2] and the mAP of integer scale in our method is slightly better than that of exponent scale. Compared to Faster R-CNN [2] on the cropped aircraft data set, our method-IS increases mAP by 0.81%, recall by 1.2%, and accuracy by 6.39%. We compare the predicted scales with the ground truth scales on the test data set. We define a method hitting an aircraft scale that: there exists at least one candidate scale given by this method that has a less than 3 difference with the ground true scale. Our Scale-Faster-R-CNN can hit the scale of the 95.2% aircrafts. And Faster R-CNN [2] can only hit the scale of the 61.3% aircrafts. These results verify that the proposal scales predicted by the scale prediction network are closer to the ground truth aircraft scales than the default proposal scales in Faster R-CNN [2]. The anchor number produced at each center point of sliding window by our method is less than that of Faster R-CNN [2], but it does not reduce the accuracy of the detection. This further shows that our method produces better proposals. As shown in Fig. 9, the P-R curve of our method is above of that of Faster R-CNN [2] on cropped aircraft data set. Because our method uses scale prediction, our method can adjust the size of the proposals according to the size of the aircrafts in the picture and we can produces proposals whose size is less than 128. Therefore, as shown in Fig. 10, our method is better than Faster R-CNN [2] to detect smaller aircraft in the picture.

Table 2. Result comparison on cropped aircraft data set: our method-IS represents our method using the integer scale, our method-ES represents our method using the exponent scale. In the aircraft data set, the mAP, recall and precision of our method is higher than that of Faster R-CNN [2].

	mAP(%)	Recall(%)	Precision(%)
Our method-IS	89.41	93.44	72.21
Our method-ES	89.23	93.87	73.29
Faster R-CNN	88.60	92.24	65.82

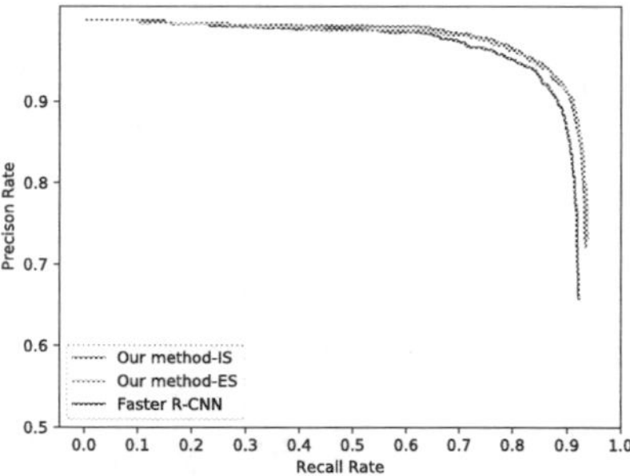

Fig. 9. The P-R curves of two methods: on the aircraft data set, our precision-recall curves (including using integer scale and exponent scale) can cover that of the Faster R-CNN [2].

Fig. 10. Comparison between our method and Faster R-CNN [2]. (a) is an example from Faster R-CNN [2], (b) is an example from our method. Our method performs better than the Faster R-CNN [2] when detecting smaller aircraft.

5 Conclusion

In this paper, we propose a two-stage aircraft detection pipeline. First, we use a Background-Filtering-Network to crop appropriately sized areas that may contain airplanes in remote sensing images. Since we used novel clustering methods and subsequent processing of regions predicted by the network, the recall rate of our method is relatively high and the sizes and aspect ratio of pictures cropped are appropriate. Cropping the image makes it possible to detect aircraft in remote sensing images using general object detection methods such as the Faster R-CNN [2]. Second, we use Scale-Faster-R-CNN which adds a scale forecast network based on Faster R-CNN [2] to better detect the aircrafts. The structure of scale prediction network is simple and the scale prediction network shares calculations with Faster R-CNN [2]. The scale prediction network can finely predict the scale within a relatively large range. Compared to Faster-R-CNN, our method has improved the precision rate, recall rate and mAP. The method we proposed can also be used to detect other objects in remote sensing images, such as ships and tanks.

References

1. Han, Z., Zhang, H., Zhang, J., Hu, X.: Fast aircraft detection based on region locating network in large-scale remote sensing images. In: 2017 IEEE International Conference on Image Processing (ICIP) (2017)
2. Ren, S., He, K., Girshick, R., Sun, J.: Faster R-CNN: towards real-time object detection with region proposal networks. In: Advances in Neural Information Processing Systems, pp. 91–99 (2015)
3. Hao, Z., Liu, Y., Qin, H., Yan, J., Li, X., Hu, X.: Scale-aware face detection. In: The IEEE Conference on Computer Vision and Pattern Recognition (CVPR), vol. 3 (2017)
4. Girshick, R., Donahue, J., Darrell, T., Malik, J.: Rich feature hierarchies for accurate object detection and semantic segmentation. In: Proceedings of the IEEE Conference on Computer Vision and Pattern Recognition, pp. 580–587 (2014)
5. Girshick, R.: Fast R-CNN. In: Proceedings of the IEEE International Conference on Computer Vision, pp. 1440–1448 (2015)
6. Redmon, J., Divvala, S., Girshick, R., Farhadi, A.: You only look once: unified, real-time object detection. In: Proceedings of the IEEE Conference on Computer Vision and Pattern Recognition, pp. 779–788 (2016)
7. Liu, W., et al.: SSD: single shot multibox detector. In: Leibe, B., Matas, J., Sebe, N., Welling, M. (eds.) ECCV 2016 Part I. LNCS, vol. 9905, pp. 21–37. Springer, Cham (2016). https://doi.org/10.1007/978-3-319-46448-0_2
8. Long, Y., Gong, Y., Xiao, Z., Liu, Q.: Accurate object localization in remote sensing images based on convolutional neural networks. IEEE Trans. Geosci. Remote Sens. **55**(5), 2486–2498 (2017)
9. Pan, B., Tai, J., Zheng, Q., Zhao, S.: Cascade convolutional neural network based on transfer-learning for aircraft detection on high-resolution remote sensing images. J. Sensors **2017** (2017)
10. Hu, G., Yang, Z., Han, J., Huang, L., Gong, J., Xiong, N.: Aircraft detection in remote sensing images based on saliency and convolution neural network. EURASIP J. Wirel. Commun. Netw. **2018**(1), 26 (2018)

11. Han, J., Zhang, D., Cheng, G., Guo, L., Ren, J.: Object detection in optical remote sensing images based on weakly supervised learning and high-level feature learning. IEEE Trans. Geosci. Remote Sens. **53**(6), 3325–3337 (2015)
12. Chen, C., Gong, W., Hu, Y., Chen, Y., Ding, Y.: Learning oriented region-based convolutional neural networks for building detection in satellite remote sensing images. Int. Arch. Photogramm. Remote Sens. Spat. Inf. Sci. **42**, 461 (2017)
13. Li, H., Lin, Z., Shen, X., Brandt, J., Hua, G.: A convolutional neural network cascade for face detection. In: Proceedings of the IEEE Conference on Computer Vision and Pattern Recognition, pp. 5325–5334 (2015)
14. Sermanet, P., Eigen, D., Zhang, X., Mathieu, M., Fergus, R., LeCun, Y.: OverFeat: integrated recognition, localization and detection using convolutional networks. arXiv preprint arXiv:1312.6229 (2013)
15. He, K., Zhang, X., Ren, S., Sun, J.: Deep residual learning for image recognition. In: Proceedings of the IEEE Conference on Computer Vision and Pattern Recognition, pp. 770–778 (2016)
16. Simonyan, K., Zisserman, A.: Very deep convolutional networks for large-scale image recognition. arXiv preprint arXiv:1409.1556 (2014)

Residual Convolutional Neural Networks with Global and Local Pathways for Classification of Focal Liver Lesions

Dong Liang[1], Lanfen Lin[1(✉)], Hongjie Hu[2], Qiaowei Zhang[2], Qingqing Chen[2], Yutaro Iwamoto[3], Xianhua Han[3], and Yen-Wei Chen[1,3(✉)]

[1] Department of Computer Science and Technology, Zhejiang University, Hangzhou, China
llf@zju.edu.cn, chen@is.ritsumei.ac.jp
[2] Department of Radiology, Sir Run Run Shaw Hospital, Hangzhou, China
[3] College of Information Science and Engineering, Ritsumeikan University, Shiga, Japan

Abstract. Computer-aided diagnosis (CAD) systems are useful in assisting radiologists with clinical diagnoses by classifying focal liver lesions based on computed tomography (CT) images. Extracting discriminative features from CT images is a crucial step in CAD systems. Although deep neural networks have demonstrated immense success in the computer vision community, there still remain two challenges in this field of medical image analysis. First, there are only limited dataset. Second, the local and global information of lesions both are necessary for this task. In this study, inspired by the importance of global and local information, we propose a novel model for distinguishing diverse types of focal liver lesions, called residual CNN with global and local pathways (ResNet-GL) model. The model uses both patches of lesion region (local information) and a whole-lesion region (global information) as inputs. Since the proposed ResNet-GL is a pixel-wise classification method (it assigns a label to each pixel of the lesion), we used the normalized label map produced by the ResNet-GL as an input of support vector machines (SVM) for classification of lesions. The effectiveness of our model is confirmed by the accuracy of our testing dataset, which is over 87%. Our results show that the proposed ResNet-GL model can not only achieves superior performance than state-of-the-art approaches, which are based on mid-level learning-based features, but also can achieve results better than other CNN-based approaches.

Keywords: Deep learning · Liver lesions classification · Local information Global information · Computer-aid diagnosis (CAD)

1 Introduction

Worldwide, liver cancer is the second most common cause of cancer-related deaths among men and the sixth among women. Hepatocellular carcinoma (HCC) is the most common type of the primary liver cancers [1]. In addition to HCCs, other types of

X. Geng and B.-H. Kang (Eds.): PRICAI 2018, LNAI 11012, pp. 617–628, 2018.
https://doi.org/10.1007/978-3-319-97304-3_47

masses, such as focal nodular hyperplasia (FNH), hemangiomas (HEM) and cysts are also very common. Radiological examinations, such as computed tomography (CT) images and magnetic resonance images (MRI) are primary methods of liver tumors diagnosis. However, assessments of tumor imagery humanly are generally subjective and are easily affected by radiologists' experience. Thus, computer-aided diagnosis (CAD) systems will play an important role in the early and accurate detection and classification of focal liver lesions (FLLs). A CAD system typically consists of two steps: (1) liver segmentation and lesion detection (segmentation) and (2) representation (feature extraction) of the detected lesions followed by classification (differential diagnosis). In this study, we focus on the second step (classification of FLLs).

Currently, contrast-enhanced CT images are widely used to detect, locate and diagnose focal liver lesions. Contrast-enhanced CT scans generally are divided into four phases. The non-contrast (NC) phase is scanned before contrast injection. The arterial (ART) phase is scanned 30–40 s after the contrast injection. The portal venous (PV) phase is scanned 70–80 s after the contrast injection. The delay (DL) phase is scanned 3–5 min after the contrast injection. From the non-contrast phase to the delay phase, vascularity and the contrast agent enhancement pattern of the liver masses can be assessed. There are several works that utilized single-phase (usually PV-phase) or multi-phase CT images to perform classification and retrieval of liver lesions. They often calculated the characteristics of the single-phase or different phases and then concatenated the features to represent the liver lesions. In this paper, we first introduce the approach based on a single phase that captures the PV phase from CT images. Then, we demonstrate how to extend our approach to multi-phase.

Most of existing approaches for classification of focal liver lesions used hand-crafted features (e.g. texture, density) or learning-based features (e.g. bag of visual words (BoVW) and its variants), which are known as mid-level features, to represent FLLs. Doron et al. [2] compared the effects of different texture combinations on the classification of focal liver lesions (i.e., Cyst, HEM, METS and healthy tissues) and found the combinations of three features (i.e., local binary patterns (LBP), grey-level co-occurrence matrix (GLCM) and intensities) achieved the best performance. Due to the limitation of the hand-crafted features, some learning-based methods had proposed to tackle the problem. Yang et al. [3] first applied the BoVW algorithm to the field of medical images analysis. Diamant et al. [4] improved the original BoVW algorithm. Compared with a single dictionary of original BoVW algorithm, they proposed a dual visual dictionary. One is an interior dictionary constructed from an interior region of focus. The other is a boundary dictionary constructed from a boundary region of focus, inspirited by the importance of the boundary region. Each dictionary can build a histogram. Thus, they stitched two histograms to represent the focus. Their result showed the effectiveness of a dual dictionary, which is better than a single dictionary. Furthermore, they utilized the mutual information to selected the most effective visual words from original dictionary [5]. Xu et al. [6] mentioned the bag-of-temporal co-occurrence words (BoTCoW) model, which extracts enhancement information from multi-phase CT images, to solve the retrieval of focal liver lesions problem. Xu et al. [7] also proposed a texture-specific BoVW variant. They used a rotation-invariant uniform (LBP) method to split the pixels of region-of-interest (ROI) into nine texture categories. They generated nine vocabularies for each, and the BoVW-based features were generated for them. Their model outperformed other BoVW-based methods in discriminating different lesions. To accurately approximate any local descriptor in coding produce, Wang et al. [8] used a sparse coding method, instead of K-means, for the dictionary learning.

In recent years, the high-level feature representation of deep convolutional neural networks (DCNN) has proven to be superior to hand-crafted low-level features and mid-level features [9]. Deep learning techniques have also been applied to medical image analysis and computer-aided detection and diagnosis. However, there have been very few studies on the classification of focal liver lesions. Yasaka et al. [10] proposed a convolutional neural network with three channels corresponding to three phases (NC, ART and DL) for the classification of liver tumors in dynamic contrast-enhanced CT images. The method can extract high-level temporal and spatial features, resulting in a higher classification accuracy compared with the state-of-the-art methods. Since they used a whole 2D sliced image as an input, it may lack local spatial information. Frid-Arar et al. [11] proposed a multi-scale patch-based classification framework to detect focal liver lesions. Since it is a pixel-wise classification method as well as other patch-based deep learning methods, how to combine the pixel-wise classification results for classification of lesions is a challenge task. The another limitation is that it only uses local information.

To solve the above problems, we proposed a novel model, called the "residual convolutional neural network with global and local pathways" (ResNet-GL) model. There are two main contributions. The first one is that our model provides two pathways. One is a local pathway, whose input is patches. The other is a global pathway, whose input is whole-lesion regions (ROIs: region of interests). Intuitively, patches represent the local information, whereas ROIs represent the global information. The second contribution is that the pixel-wise classification result by ResNet-GL, which is

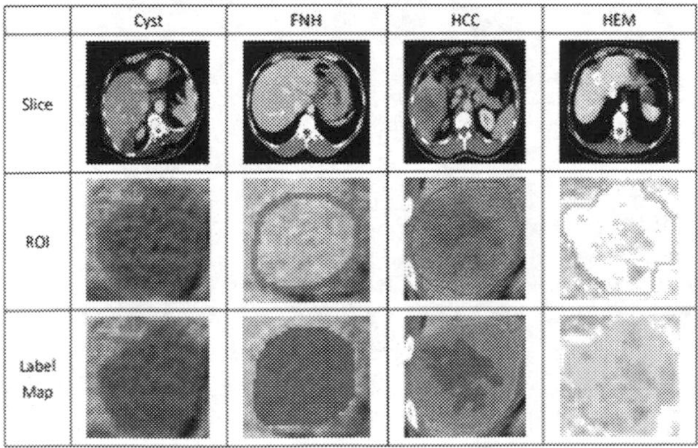

Fig. 1. First row shows the significant slice of different focal liver lesions. The red outline represents the result of segmentation. The second row shows the ROI of different types of focal liver lesions. The third row shows the label maps of different focal liver lesions. Green represents a cyst, blue represents a FNH, yellow represents a HCC and cyan represents a HEM. (Color figure online)

called as a label map, is used as an input of SVM for final lesion classification. Examples of different lesions and their label maps obtained by ResNet-GL are shown in Fig. 1.

2 Proposed Method

The flowchart of ResNet-GL model is shown in Fig. 2. Intuitively extracting global and local information will be described in detail in Sects. 2.1 and 2.2 respectively. The information will be combined before the last full connection layer. The softmax layer immediately behind the last full connection layer produces output that is the result of patch-based classification. We will introduce the loss function of our model in Sect. 2.3. In Sect. 2.4, we describe the method that extracts features from a label map and accomplishes the lesion-based classification. In Sect. 2.5, we explain how to extend our model to multi-phase CT images.

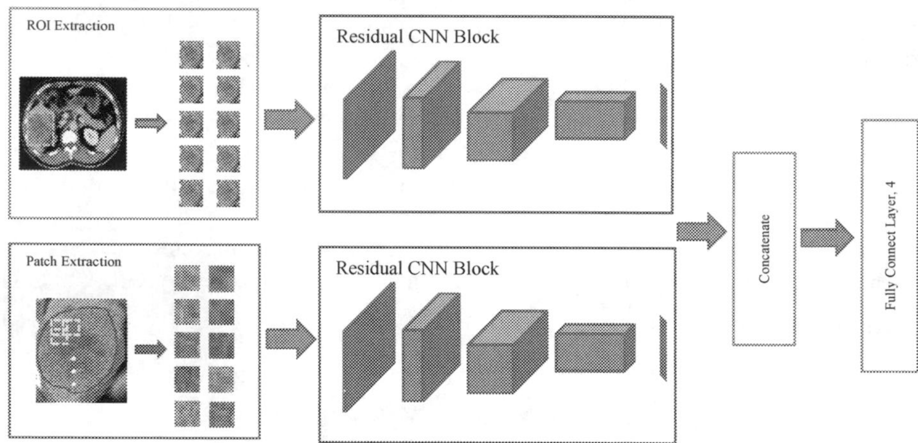

Fig. 2. The flowchart of the ResNet-GL model

2.1 Global Pathway

In this sub-section, we describe the global pathway, which uses the whole-lesion image ROI as an input. We first applied a random walk-based interactive segmentation algorithm [12] to segment healthy tissue and focal liver lesion in the significant layer. The segmented results were checked by two experienced radiologists. Each segmented lesion image (i.e., 2D slice image) was resized to 128 $\times$ 128. The resized images were then used as input for global pathway training and testing. Figure 1 displays the ROIs of the different types of lesions.

In ResNet block, we used 18 convolutional layers, one pooling layer (avg-pooling), and two fully connected layers. Each convolution layer was followed by a rectified linear unit (ReLU) activation function and a batch normalization layer. The number of

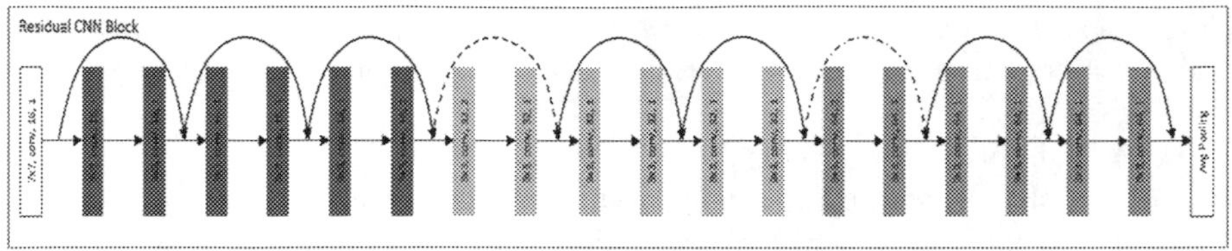

Fig. 3. Architecture of residual CNN block

parameters in this block is about 24K. The architecture of the ResNet block is shown in Fig. 3. Each convolution layer has three parameters: kernel size, depth, and stride, shown in the box. The merger of arrows represents addition. The dotted lines represent a shortcut [13] that decreases the size by setting the stride to 2.

2.2 Local Pathway

As described in this subsection, what our goal was to make use of local information. First, patches were extracted from ROIs. Each patch has a label, $c \in \{c_0, c_1, c_2, c_3\}$ where c_0 represents a cyst, c_1 represents a FNH, c_2 represents a HCC and c_3 represents HEM. Second, as in Sect. 2.1, before we used the ResNet block to extract local information, we resized the patches to 64 × 64. Although the ResNet block of the local pathway has the same architecture as the ResNet block of the global pathway, they do not share weights with each other.

Owing to the different lesions varying greatly in size, this causes an extreme imbalance among the patch categories. To solve this problem, we dynamically adjusted the pace that used to extract patches from the training dataset and validation dataset. The pace value is derived in Eq. (1):

$$pace_i = \begin{cases} floor\left(\sqrt{\frac{w_i * h_i}{\alpha}}\right), w_i * h_i > \alpha \\ 1, w_i * h_i \leq \alpha \end{cases} \quad (1)$$

where i represents the i-th ROI; $pace_i$ is the pace of i-th ROI to extract the patches, w_i and h_i represent the width and height of i-th ROI, α represents the threshold that can limit the number of patches, and the floor function represents rounding-down. By this piece-wise functionality, we can balance the number of patches extracted from different types of lesions as much as possible, and ensure that the patch is simultaneously obtained from as many different patients as possible. This means that the piecewise function not only ensures the balance between different categories, but also guarantees the diversity of patches. For the testing dataset, we still set the pace to 1.

2.3 Joint Loss Function

The vanishing gradient is the main concern during deep-CNN training, making the loss of back-propagation ineffective in early layers. Additionally, to fully utilize our data, we prefer our classification method for patches and ROI. Thus, we exploit the additional supervision injected into the local pathway and global pathway. Finally, the gradients were derived from both branches and the last output layer of mainstream network.

Let N be the batch size, ω^t be the weights in the t-th (t = 1, 2, …T) layer, we use the $W = [W_{local}, W_{local}, W_{FC}]$ be the weights of the mainstream network., where W_{local} and W_{global} represent the weights of the local and global convolutional layers, respectively and W_{FC} represents the weights of fully connected layers. $p(c|x_i; W)$ represents the probability of i-th patch belonging to the c-th class. Similarly we obtained the definition of $p(c|x_i; W_{global}, W_{FC\_G})$ and $p(c|x_i; W_{local}, W_{FC\_L})$, where W_{FC_G} and W_{FC_L} represent the weights of local and global fully connected layers. The cross-entropy loss of the mainstream network and these branches are as follows:

$$\mathcal{L} = \frac{1}{N}\sum\nolimits_{i=1}^{N}\sum\nolimits_{c=1}^{K} -p(c|x_i; W) * \log(p(c|x_i; W)) \tag{2}$$

$$\mathcal{L}_{local} = \frac{1}{N}\sum\nolimits_{i=1}^{N}\sum\nolimits_{c=1}^{K} -p(c|x_i; W_{local}, W_{FC\_L}) * \log(p(c|x_i; W_{local}, W_{FC\_L})) \tag{3}$$

$$\mathcal{L}_{global} = \frac{1}{N}\sum\nolimits_{i=1}^{N}\sum\nolimits_{c=1}^{K} -p(c|x_i; W_{global}, W_{FC\_G}) * \log\left(p(c|x_i; W_{global}, W_{FC\_G})\right) \tag{4}$$

Finally, we employed the back-propagation to learn the weights W, W_{local}, and W_{global}, by minimizing the following joint loss function:

$$\mathcal{L}_{joint} = \frac{1}{2} * \mathcal{L} + \frac{1}{4} * \mathcal{L}_{local} + \frac{1}{4} * \mathcal{L}_{global} \tag{5}$$

It should be noted that though W_{FC_L} and W_{FC_G} are also learned in the training phase, only the weights $W = \left[W_{local}, W_{global}, W_{FC}\right]$ for main stream are used in the test phase.

2.4 Post-processing of Label Map and Classification of Lesions by SVM

Since the proposed ResNet-GL assigned a label to each pixel of the lesion as shown in Fig. 1, we called is as a label map. In order to make a final classification of lesions, we use the normalized label map obtained by ResNet-GL as an input of SVM. The SVM, which demand relatively little training dataset, is used as a second classifier for lesion classifications. The normalized label map (input of SVM) is defined as:

$$F_i = \{\beta_{i0}, \beta_{i1}, \beta_{i2}, \beta_{i3}\} \tag{6}$$

where F_i represents the feature vector of the i-th label map. β_{ic} represents the proportion of pixels belonging to the c-th category in the i-th label map, which is defined in Eq. (7):

$$\beta_{ic} = \frac{\text{the number of pixels belong to } c - \text{th class}}{\text{total number of pixel in } i - \text{th lable map}} \tag{7}$$

As well as ResNet-GL, we use training dataset for SVM training and validation dataset for hyper parameter optimization.

2.5 Extension to Multi-phase CT Images

Although we presented our model only as a single phase, it is easy to extend to multi-phase CT images. Inspired by [7], we first employed a non-rigid registration technique based on the B-spline to align three phase images [14]. Then we used the different phases' CT images as a different channel. If we use three-phase CT images (NC, ART and PV phases), we used three channels in each pathway just like a color RGB image.

3 Experiments and Results

3.1 Setup

Data and Implementation. A total of 480 CT liver slice images were used, containing four types of lesions confirmed by pathologists, (i.e., Cyst, HEM, FNH, and HCC). The distribution of our dataset is shown in Table 1. The CT slices extracted from whole CT scan of 208 different patients. The slices were in close proximity to the significant layer that is marked by the pathologists. Additional, we guarantee that the different slices from same patient will not appear in training set and testing set at the same time. The CT images in our dataset are abdominal CT scans taken from 2015 through 2017. The CT scans were acquired with a slice collimation of 5–7 mm, a matrix of 512 × 512 pixels, and an in-plane resolution of 0.57–0.89. In our experiment, we randomly split our dataset into a training dataset, a validation dataset, and a testing dataset. In order to eliminate the effect of randomness, we conduct the partition operation twice, and form two groups of dataset. Each distribution is listed in Table 1.

Table 1. The distribution of dataset.

Type	Cyst		FNH		HCC		HEM		Total	
	Set1	Set2	Set1	Set2	Set1	Set2	Set1	Set2	Set1	Set2
Training	61	69	71	60	75	69	62	79	269	277
Validation	23	17	25	23	31	36	36	17	115	93
Testing	26	24	18	31	26	27	26	28	96	110
Total	110		114		132		124		480	

Our ResNet-GL model was implemented with Tensorflow library. We initialized the parameters of ResNet-GL block via. Gaussian distribution. We used a momentum optimizer to update our parameters by setting the learning rate initialized as 0.01 and the momentum coefficient to 0.9. We set the batch size to 100. We set the size of the patch as 7, α is 140. The reason will be explained in Sect. 3.2. The hardware environment as described as follow: Inter Core i7(3.7 GHz) with 32 GB RAM, NVIDIA 12 GB TITAN X GPU with CuDNN(v6.0) library for GPU acceleration.

Evaluation Measure. We evaluated the performance of our model by the mean and the standard deviation of the two testing set accuracies. Accuracy is defined as follows:

$$\text{Accuracy} = \frac{TP}{\mathrm{T}} \tag{8}$$

where the TP is the number of right classification samples and T is the number of all samples in the corresponding dataset.

3.2 Results

Optimization of Hyper Parameters. Patch size and α have an effect on the classification result. Thus, in our experiments, we varied them to achieve better performance. First, we determined the value of the patch size by using the metrics in the validation dataset, where the α is 140. The performance with different patch sizes is shown in Fig. 4(**a**). Note that a 7×7 patch size generates better classification performance than others. Then, we determined the value of α by using the metrics in the validation dataset. Performance is shown in Fig. 4(**b**). Note that when we set α to 140, it generates better performance than others.

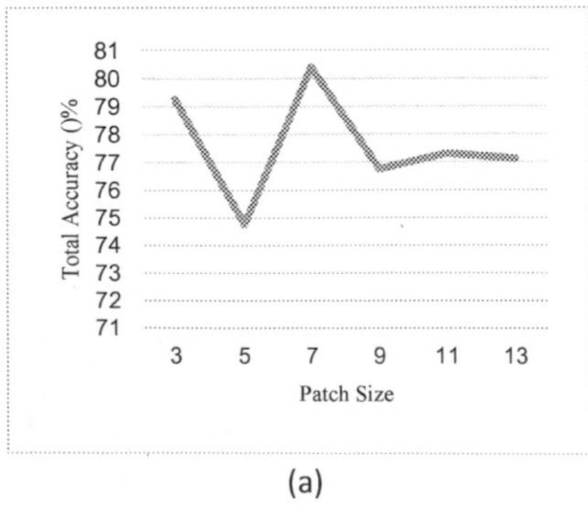

(a)

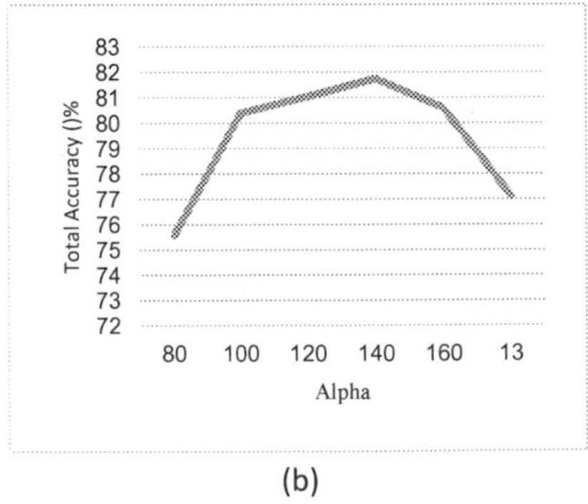

(b)

Fig. 4. Classification performance with various patch size and alpha

Effectiveness of Joint Loss. As we mentioned above, we propose the joint loss to avoid vanishing gradient and accelerate convergence. We compare the convergence of $\mathcal{L}_{\text{joint}}$ (Eq. (5)) and $\mathcal{L}$ (Eq. (2)) to demonstrate the effectiveness of the joint loss. We use

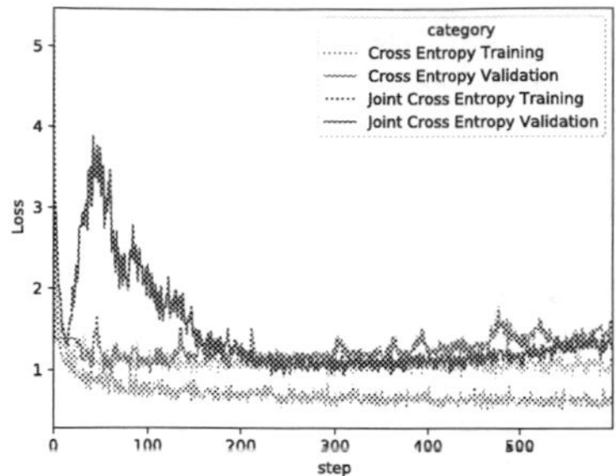

Fig. 5. The loss value of different loss function

$\mathcal{L}_{\text{joint}}$ and $\mathcal{L}$ to train the model, respectively. And the corresponding loss value of each step are given in Fig. 5. We can see that the joint loss $\mathcal{L}_{\text{joint}}$ can achieve faster convergence than the $\mathcal{L}$ loss.

Performance of Our Proposed Method. The effectiveness of the proposed ResNet GL model was verified on the testing dataset. The confusion matrix and accuracy are shown in Tables 2 and 3. It can be seen that the mean accuracies are 93.75%, 84.05%, 85.11% and 85.16% for Cyst, FNH, HCC and HEM, respectively.

Table 2. Confusion matrix for testing data1.

Type\Auto.	Cyst	FNH	HCC	HEM	Accuracy
Cyst	26	0	0	0	100.0%
FNH	0	14	0	4	77.77%
HCC	0	0	25	1	96.15%
HEM	1	0	3	22	84.61%

Table 3. Confusion matrix for testing data2.

Type\Auto.	Cyst	FNH	HCC	HEM	Accuracy
Cyst	21	2	0	1	87.50%
FNH	0	28	0	3	90.32%
HCC	3	4	20	0	74.07%
HEM	0	0	4	24	85.71%

Comparison to the Non-deep Learning Methods. We compared our model to typical methods representing state-of-the-art approaches using mid-level learning-based features [3, 4, 6–8], which are described in Sect. 1. For original BoVW algorithm [3], we set the size of dictionary is 128. For the dual dictionary BoVW [4], we set the size of the interior dictionary to 128, and the size of the boundary dictionary to 32. For the texture-specific BoVW method [7], we set the size of each vocabulary to 128. For the BoTCoW [6] model, we set the size of vocabulary of co-occurrence to 256. We attempted to find the parameters to achieve better performance in these experiments. The comparison results are shown in Table 4. Our model achieves better performance than the others.

Table 4. Comparison to the non-deep learning methods (classification accuracy (%) is represented as mean and standard deviation)

Method	Cyst	FNH	HCC	HEM	Total accuracy
Yang et al. [3]	88.30 ± 10.6	74.64 ± 28.1	75.50 ± 2.0	81.32 ± 6.2	78.81 ± 3.4
Wang et al. [8]	85.90 ± 3.6	65.14 ± 32.8	83.12 ± 7.5	67.99 ± 20.0	74.06 ± 5.7
Xu et al. [7]	68.75 ± 2.9	73.53 ± 4.1	87.25 ± 1.3	76.92 ± 10.8	77.04 ± 3.1
Diamant, et al. [4].	82.21 ± 7.4	70.00 ± 18.8	85.04 ± 10.2	76.90 ± 20.3	77.82 ± 1.2
Xu et al. [6]	92.15 ± 5.21	69.08 ± 20.1	85.04 ± 10.2	84.31 ± 0.4	82.11 ± 7.4
Our Method	93.75 ± 8.8	84.05 ± 8.8	85.11 ± 15.6	85.16 ± 0.7	87.58 ± 4.8

Comparison to the other Deep Learning Methods. Frid-Adar et al. [11] proposed a novel network for liver lesion detection that used different patch size. They showed that the performance of their model was better than a state-of-the-art fully convolutional network. Thus, we compared our proposed method (ResNet-GL+SVM) with Frid-Adar method (CNN with multi-scale local patch) + SVM. To make it fair, we also use the segmentation result by the pathologists as the input. Additionally, to verify the effectiveness of incorporating global information, we performed a comparative experiment using only the local pathway. What's more, due to the limitation of dataset, the model does not converge when we directly used ROI as input. Therefore, we cannot compare it with our method. The comparison results are listed in Table 5. Our proposed method, which extracts both local and global information, is better than networks that only extract local information. It is even better than multi-scale local information [11].

Table 5. Comparison to other deep learning methods (classification accuracy (%) is represented as mean and standard deviation)

Method	Cyst	FNH	HCC	HEM	Total Accuracy
Frid-Adar [11] + SVM (CNN with local)	100.0 ± 0.0	78.20 ± 0.5	84.37 ± 16.6	40.67 ± 16.2	76.16 ± 0.6
Our method(only local pathway)	100.0 ± 0.0	71.27 ± 6.5	80.89 ± 11.18	85.41 ± 8.8	84.12 ± 6.1
Our method	93.75 ± 8.8	84.05 ± 8.8	85.11 ± 15.6	85.16 ± 0.7	87.58 ± 4.8

4 Conclusion

We have proposed ResNet-GL, applying the CNN framework to the focal liver lesion classification for the first time. Our dataset comprises 480 lesions belonging to four categories. Our model was evaluated by total accuracy and confusion matrix on the testing dataset. Our model used the patches and ROIs as input for the ResNet-GL block, which integrated the local information and global information. The results of experiments show that by aggregating the label map, we can apply the CNNs to the small liver dataset; the performance of our model can achieve better performance than the methods based on hand-crafted features or learning-based features representing state-of-the-art method; and compared with other CNN models, our model is better at integrating the local and global information, and achieving better results. In future, we are going to develop a 3D ResNet-GL for treating 3D images to improve the classification accuracy. In addition, building a large scale liver lesions dataset remains a challenging task.

Acknowledgements. This work was supported in part by the National Key R&D Program of China under the Grant No. 2017YFB0309800, in part by the Key Science and Technology Innovation Support Program of Hangzhou under the Grant No. 20172011A038, and in part by the Grant-in Aid for Scientific Research from the Japanese Ministry for Education, Science, Culture and Sports (MEXT) under the Grant No. 18H03267 and No. 17H00754.

References

1. Ryerson, A.B., et al: Annual report to the nation on the status of cancer 1975–2012 featuring the increasing incidence of liver cancer. Cancer **122**(9), 1312–1337 (2016)
2. Doron, Y., et al.: Texture feature based liver lesion classification. In: Medical Imaging 2014: Computer-Aided Diagnosis. **9035**. International Society for Optics and Photonics (2014)
3. Yang, W.: Content-based retrieval of focal liver lesions using bag-of-visual-words representations of single-and multiphase contrast-enhanced CT images. J. Digit. Imaging **25**(6), 708–719 (2012)
4. Diamant, I.: Improved patch-based automated liver lesion classification by separate analysis of the interior and boundary regions. IEEE J. Biomed. Health Inform. **20**(6), 1585–1594 (2016)
5. Diamant, I., et al.: Multi-phase liver lesions classification using relevant visual words based on mutual information.In: IEEE 12th International Symposium on IEEE, pp. 407–410 (2015)
6. Xu, Y., et al.: Bag of temporal co-occurrence words for retrieval of focal liver lesions using 3D multiphase contrast-enhanced CT images. In: Proceedings of 23rd International Conference on Pattern Recognition (ICPR2016), pp. 2283–2288 (2016)
7. Xu, Y., et al.: Texture-specific bag of visual words model and spatial cone matching-based method for the retrieval of focal liver lesions using multiphase contrast-enhanced CT images. Int. J. Comput. Assist. Radiol. Surg. **13**(1), 151–164 (2018)
8. Wang, J., et al.: Sparse codebook model of local structures for retrieval of focal liver lesions using multiphase medical images. Int. J. Biomed. Imaging **2017**, 13 (2017)
9. Setio, A.: Pulmonary nodule detection in CT images: false positive reduction using multi-view convolutional networks. IEEE Trans. Med. Imaging **35**(5), 1160–1169 (2016)

10. Yasaka, K.: Deep learning with convolutional neural network for differentiation of liver masses at dynamic contrast-enhanced CT: a preliminary study. Radiology **286**(3), 887–896 (2017)
11. Frid-Adar, M., Diamant, I., Klang, E., Amitai, M., Goldberger, J., Greenspan, H.: Modeling the intra-class variability for liver lesion detection using a multi-class patch-based CNN. In: Wu, G., et al. (eds.) Patch-MI 2017. LNCS, vol. 10530, pp. 129–137. Springer, Cham (2017). https://doi.org/10.1007/978-3-319-67434-6_15
12. Dong, C., et al.: Simultaneous segmentation of multiple organs using random walks. J. Inf. Process. **24**(2), 320–329 (2016)
13. He, K., et al.: Deep residual learning for image recognition. In: Proceedings of the IEEE conference on computer vision and pattern recognition (2016)
14. Dong, C.: Non-rigid image registration with anatomical structure constraint for assessing locoregional therapy of hepatocellular carcinoma. Comput. Med. Imaging Graph. **45**, 75–83 (2015)

Intent Detection for Spoken Language Understanding Using a Deep Ensemble Model

Mauajama Firdaus(✉), Shobhit Bhatnagar, Asif Ekbal, and Pushpak Bhattacharyya

Indian Institue of Technology Patna, Patna, India
mauzama.03@gmail.com, shobhit.bhat@gmail.com, asif.ekbal@gmail.com, pushpakbh@gmail.com

Abstract. One of the significant task in spoken language understanding (SLU) is intent detection. In this paper, we propose a deep learning based ensemble model for intent detection. The outputs of different deep learning architectures such as convolutional neural network (CNN) and variants of recurrent neural networks (RNN) like long short term memory (LSTM) and gated recurrent units (GRU) are combined together using a multi-layer perceptron (MLP). The classifiers are trained using a combined word embedding representation obtained from both Word2Vec and Glove. Our experiments on the benchmark ATIS dataset show state-of-the-art performance for intent detection.

Keywords: Ensemble · Deep learning
Spoken language understanding

1 Introduction

Spoken Language Understanding (SLU) is one of the primary task of a dialog system, aiming to identify the semantic components in a user utterance expressed in natural language and take necessary steps to satisfy their requests. Natural language understanding (NLU) is still considered a very complex task and many practical task-oriented conversational systems have been developed for task-dependent domains. These systems aim to automatically detect the user's intention as expressed in natural language. The appropriate action to be taken by the system is decided according to the intent identified. The applications of SLU are becoming increasingly significant in our everyday lives. Numerous devices like smartphones have personal assistants that are constructed with SLU technologies.

Historically, intent detection has gained importance from the call classification system [4]. While this task has been broadly studied, it is still not possible to state that intent detection is a solved task. The task becomes challenging when the system has to deal with more natural and realistic sentences spoken by a group of people for the tasks more complicated than simple flight information

X. Geng and B.-H. Kang (Eds.): PRICAI 2018, LNAI 11012, pp. 629–642, 2018.
https://doi.org/10.1007/978-3-319-97304-3_48

requests. Irrespective of the approach employed for the task, the main problem is the "naturalness" of the user's input. The objective of SLU is to interpret user's intentions from their speech utterances [8].

In this paper, we focus on understanding the intentions of the user as stated in natural language. It basically deals with the extraction of the intended meaning i.e. the intent of an user utterance detected by the SLU module. The action to be taken is then decided by the dialog manager on the results of intent detection. Intents are global properties of an utterance, and these signify the main goal of a user. A robust intent detection system plays a crucial role in building an effective dialog system. For example, the user asking, *What is today's date?* should be classified as date enquiry so that the system can route the utterance to the correct natural language understanding system. The intent of the speaker is detected using a natural language understanding component. While it is a standard utterance classification task and clearly less complex than other tasks of semantic analysis, the errors made by a classifier for intent detection are more visible - as they often lead to wrong system responses. The focus of this work is to improve the accuracy of intent detection by employing the proposed deep learning based ensemble approach.

At first, we build several deep learning models based on CNN [34] and the variations of RNN such as LSTM [12], GRU [1]. Predictions obtained from all these models are finally combined together using a MLP model. Ensemble learning has been applied to various NLP tasks such as Part-of-Speech tagging [32], chunking [25], word sense disambiguation [20] and named entity recognition [3]. Several approaches, both classical and deep learning based, have been used for intent detection. However, to the best of our knowledge, none of the published works focus on deep learning based ensemble model for dialogue intent detection. Our empirical results show that an ensemble of different classifiers can indeed improve the efficiency of the classifier. Each deep neural network based model is trained with various representations obtained from Word2Vec and Glove. Experiments show that a combined representation of both Word2Vec and Glove are more effective in terms of efficiency.

The remainder of this paper is organized as follows: In Sect. 2, the related works and the motivation for taking up the task have been briefly described. We describe the proposed approach in detail in Sect. 3. Experimental setup and the datasets are discussed in Sect. 4. Results and it's analysis are discussed in Sect. 5. Finally, the concluding remarks and directions for future work are discussed in Sect. 6.

2 Related Works

Spoken Language understanding (SLU) in human/machine dialog systems aim to identify the intent of the user as expressed in natural language. It aims to classify a given user utterance x into one of the N pre-defined set of intent classes, y_i, based on the contents of the sentence:

$$y_i = \underset{\mathbf{i} \in \mathbf{N}}{\operatorname{argmax}} P(y_i/x) \quad (1)$$

Machine learning based approaches such as Support Vector Machines (SVMs) [6] and Adaboost [27,30,31] have been explored in the past. The authors in [7] detected the intents by using heterogeneous features extracted from semantic and syntactic graphs of the user utterances. For detecting the intents, the authors in [15] enriched word embeddings to improve the performance of the intent detection task. For efficient learning under low-resource SLU tasks, the authors in [19] have proposed a multi-scale RNN structure for identifying the intents. In [13], the authors proposed a triangular Conditional Random Field (CRF), that used an additional random variable on top of a standard CRF [29] for intent detection.

Deep learning is a promising direction, which integrates both classification and feature design into the learning procedure. Comparing to basic NBoW (neural bag of words) methods, the deep learning architectures can capture the structural patterns in the sequence of words. A number of deep learning techniques have been successively utilized for intent detection such as CNN [2,10]. In particular, [10] used CNN to extract query vector representations as features for intent detection. In [26], intent detection (call routing) was shown to benefit substantially from the use of a multi-layer neural network (NN) architecture. A comparative study of different neural network architectures considering only lexical information of the utterance as feature has been investigated in [23]. RNN and LSTM have also been previously explored for intent detection [24] along with word hashing to take care of the out-of-vocabulary words present in the corpus. In recent years, intent detection has been jointly done with slot filling using deep learning techniques. A CNN based triangular CRF model for joint intent detection and slot filling was proposed [35] in which the features were extracted through CNN layers, and was shared by both the tasks. A joint model has been proposed in [5] that made use of hierarchical representations of the input text which was learned using a recursive neural network (RecNN). RNN has also been employed for both intent detection and slot filling [9,18,36]. Recently, attention based bi-directional RNN was proposed for jointly addressing the task of intent detection and slot filling [17].

In our current work, we propose a novel ensemble based approach by combining the outputs of different deep learning models. The motivation for employing ensemble based approach is that, however, deep learning architectures such as LSTM, GRU and CNN have been used in the earlier works, they have been used in isolation, often on different datasets. There has not been any systematic attempt to build a model that could exploit the benefits of all these architectures for intent detection. Each of these models has different characteristics, and can achieve better performance on any target task if they are combined together in an efficient way.

3 Methodology

We propose an ensemble based approach for intent detection. The ensemble is constructed with various deep learning models, namely CNN, LSTM and GRU. Overall architecture of all the ensemble models is depicted in Fig. 1.

3.1 Word Embedding Representation

Word embeddings are very effective in capturing hidden semantic structures. This represents words as real-valued vectors as the input to the neural network based models as opposed to other traditional representations such as one-hot representation. Bag-of-words or one-hot word vectors, if fed into the model, generate feature vectors of extremely large dimension. As an alternative, word embeddings project the large sparse word vectors into a low dimensional, dense vector representation. Word embeddings are usually trained in an unsupervised manner on a huge dataset and then the embeddings are fine-tuned by the supervised training process. For word embeddings, we use two pre-trained embedding models: GloVe[1] [21] and Word2Vec[2]. We use these embeddings separately as input to the different deep learning models. To yield better performance on the task, we concatenate both the embeddings to serve as input to the different models. We observe that the combined word embedding performs better as they capture the meaning from both the embeddings, i.e. Glove and Word2Vec.

3.2 Baseline Models

In order to make a comparative study of different deep learning architectures we construct various baselines using CNN and the variations of RNN, namely LSTM and GRU.

Convolutional Neural Network: CNN [34] consists of an input and an output layer, along with numerous hidden layers. The hidden layers of CNN basically comprise of convolutional layers, pooling layers and the fully connected layers. The convolutional layers apply a convolution operation to the input. The output of the convolutional layer is fed to the pooling layers. In our model, we have used max pooling. The max pooling layer performs downsampling along the spatial dimensionality of the given input thereby reducing the number of parameters. Every neuron in one layer is connected to every neuron in another layer in the fully connected layer of the CNN. It is, in principle, similar to the traditional multi-layer perceptron neural network. The CNN model that we employ for our work uses three convolution layers followed by a max pooling layer, one dense layer and an output layer. Size of convolution filters dictates the hidden features to be extracted.

Recurrent Neural Network: RNN [14] is considered as an extension of feed-forward neural network, that handles the sequences of variable length by using a recurrent hidden state that captures the information of the previous states as well. Generally, given a sequence $x = (x_1, x_2, \ldots, x_T)$, the recurrent hidden state can be calculated by

$$h_t = \tanh(Wx_t + Uh_{t-1}) \tag{2}$$

[1] http://nlp.stanford.edu/projects/glove/.

[2] https://code.google.com/archive/p/word2vec/.

where the hidden state is denoted by h_t for a given time t. The transformation matrices for the input and the previous hidden states are represented by W and U, respectively. To capture long-distance dependencies, it is difficult to train RNN because of the vanishing or exploding gradient problem suffered by an RNN. In order to handle the problems of vanishing or exploding gradients, a few sophisticated activation functions with gating units were designed. Two improvements of RNN are the LSTM and the recently proposed GRU. Here we use both these variations, i.e. LSTM and GRU.

Long Short Term Memory: LSTM [12] is a special kind of RNN, which can efficiently learn long-term dependencies. LSTM uses three gating units such as input, forget and output to regulate the amount of the current, previous and output representations that should be incorporated in the current timestamp. Mathematically, it is represented by the following equations:

$$i_t = \sigma(W_i x_t + U_i h_{t-1}) \tag{3}$$

$$f_t = \sigma(W_f x_t + U_f h_{t-1}) \tag{4}$$

$$o_t = \sigma(W_o x_t + U_o h_{t-1}) \tag{5}$$

$$c_t = i_t \odot \tanh(W_c x_t + U_c h_{t-1}) + f_t \odot c_{t-1} \tag{6}$$

where x_t is the input at time t, the input, output and forget gates are denoted by i_t, o_t and f_t respectively and c_t denotes the memory unit. σ is the sigmoid function and $\odot$ denotes the element-wise product of two vectors. W and U are the transformation matrices. The hidden state h_t of LSTM at time t is calculated by:

$$h_t = o_t \odot \tanh(c_t) \tag{7}$$

For simplicity, the above equations are abbreviated with $h_t = \text{LSTM}(x_t, h_{t-1})$

Gated Recurrent Unit: GRU [1] is also a special kind of RNN, which overcomes the shortcomings of RNN. Unlike LSTM, GRU uses two gates - reset and update. The update gate takes care of the amount of past information that needs to be passed to the future whereas the reset gate decides the amount of past information to forget. Mathematically, the gates can be represented as:

$$r_t = \sigma(W_r x_t + U_r h_{t-1}) \tag{8}$$

$$c_t = \tanh(W x_t + r_t \odot (U h_{t-1})) \tag{9}$$

$$z_t = \sigma(W_z x_t + U_z h_{t-1}) \tag{10}$$

where the input at time t is given by x_t. The reset and update gates are r_t and z_t respectively and c_t is the current memory unit. W and U are the transformation matrices. The sigmoid function is denoted by σ and $\odot$ denotes the element-wise product of two vectors. The hidden state h_t of GRU at time t is calculated by:

$$h_t = (1 - z_t) \odot h_{t-1} + z_t \odot c_t \tag{11}$$

For simplicity, the above equations are abbreviated with $h_t = \text{GRU}(x_t, h_{t-1})$

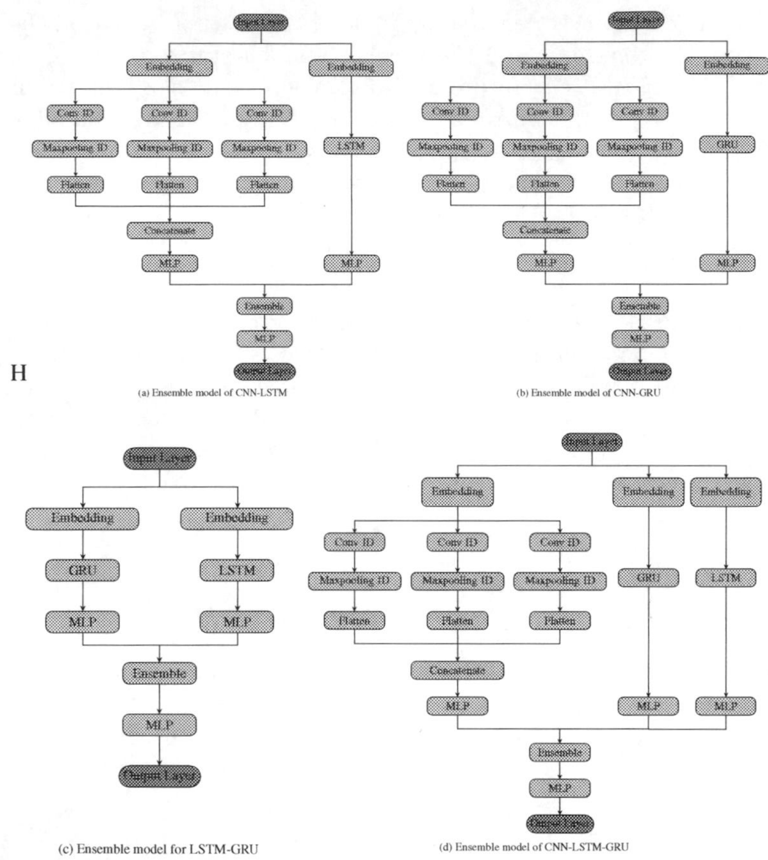

(a) Ensemble model of CNN-LSTM

(b) Ensemble model of CNN-GRU

(c) Ensemble model for LSTM-GRU

(d) Ensemble model of CNN-LSTM-GRU

Fig. 1. Block diagram of the Ensemble models for intent detection

3.3 Proposed Approach

In this paper, we propose an ensemble based deep learning approach for intent detection. We build several ensemble models as shown in Fig. 1. To capture the functionalities of different deep learning models we have ensembled them into one model for identifying the intents.

Model 1: The first ensemble model is shown in Fig. 1(a). Here, the outputs of CNN and LSTM is combined to capture the functionalities of both the architectures. The input of the ensemble layer in this case, can be computed as:

$$\overrightarrow{h}_n = [CNN(x_n, k), \overrightarrow{LSTM}(x_n, h_{n-1})] \tag{12}$$

where for CNN, x_n is the input and k is the filter size.

Model 2: In the model shown in Fig. 1(b), we combine the outputs of the CNN and GRU models. The input to the ensemble layer in this model is computed as:

$$\overrightarrow{h}_n = [CNN(x_n, k), \overrightarrow{GRU}(x_n, h_{n-1})] \tag{13}$$

Model 3: This model was implemented to capture the outputs of the LSTM and GRU as shown in Fig. 1(c). Though the architecture of both these models is similar, they still perform differently. LSTM is known to perform better for longer length utterances while GRU performs better with utterances of shorter length. We have combined them in one model to get the benefits of both the architectures for the task of intent detection. The input of the ensemble layer of this model can be calculated as:

$$\overrightarrow{h}_n = [\overrightarrow{LSTM}(x_n, h_{n-1}), \overrightarrow{GRU}(x_n, h_{n-1})] \tag{14}$$

Model 4: Finally, the last model integrates the outputs of the CNN, LSTM and GRU to capture the performance of all these techniques together as shown in Fig. 1(d). The input of the ensemble layer of this model, can be computed as:

$$\overrightarrow{h}_n = [CNN(x_n, k), \overrightarrow{LSTM}(x_n, h_{n-1}), \overrightarrow{GRU}(x_n, h_{n-1})] \tag{15}$$

The last layer of the ensemble models is the output layer with softmax activation function. The softmax activation function is applied to the representations to give the probability distribution with linear transformation at the output layer of all the ensemble models to predict the intent labels y_i for a given utterance. Formally,

$$y_i = softmax(W_i \overrightarrow{h}_n + b_i) \tag{16}$$

4 Dataset and Experiments

4.1 Dataset

A significant by-product of DARPA (Defence Advanced Research Program Agency) project was the ATIS (Airline Travel information System) corpus. The ATIS corpus [22] is one of the most extensively used datasets for the SLU task. There are a few variants of the ATIS corpus but in this paper, we follow the ATIS corpus used in [11]. The ATIS corpus comprises of utterances of people making flight reservations. There are 4,978 utterances in the training set of the corpus. The test set comprises of 893 utterances. There are 17 distinct intent classes in the corpus, such as Flight, Aircraft or Service, etc. Flight represents about 70% of the dataset hence making the corpus highly skewed (Fig. 2).

4.2 Experimental Setup

We use python based neural network package, Keras[3] for the implementation. The CNN model that we employ has 100 filters while sliding over 3, 4 and 5 words at a time. In our work, we use two layers of LSTM followed by a dense layer and an output layer. Each LSTM layer has 200 neurons. Similarly, for our GRU implementation we use two layers of GRU followed by one dense layer and

[3] www.keras.io.

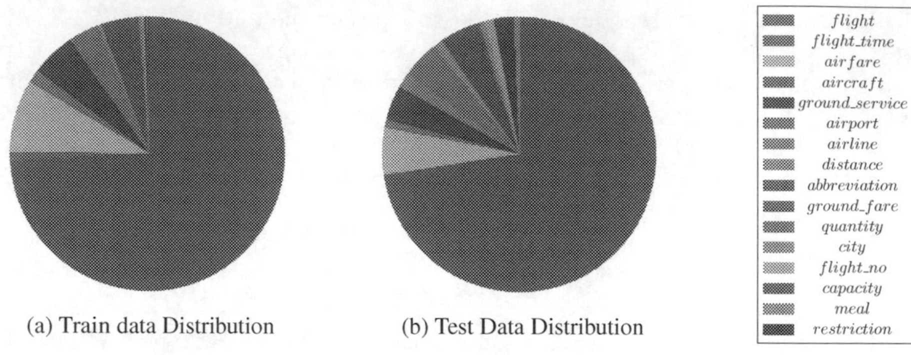

Fig. 2. Intent distribution of ATIS corpus.

an output layer. We fix the number of neurons in each GRU layer to be 200 to make a fair comparison between both the variants of RNN. The outputs of the CNN, LSTM and GRU models are fed to our ensemble model, which comprises of three dense layers. The models use a 300-dimensional word embedding for each Glove and Word2Vec models respectively. In case of combined word embedding, 600-dimensional embedding vectors are fed to the models as input.

We use ReLU activations for the intermediate layers of our model and softmax activation for the output layer. Dropout [28] is a very efficient regularization technique to avoid over-fitting of the network. During forward propagation, by randomly turning off the neurons it restricts convergence of weights to identical positions. We use 15% dropout and Adam [16] optimizer for regularization and optimization respectively. Model parameters are updated using the categorical cross-entropy.

5 Results and Discussions

In this section, we report the experiments conducted along with necessary analysis. We report accuracy and F-score as performance measures for intent detection.

5.1 Results

We demonstrate the evaluation results in Table 1. From the evaluation results, it is evident that our proposed ensemble based deep learning approach for intent detection performs better than the baseline models such as CNN, LSTM and GRU. The LSTM and GRU based models exhibit the best performance. This may be due to the fact that LSTM and GRU are designed to capture the long-term dependencies. The setup, where combined representation of both Glove and word2vec embeddings, are used perform better in all the cases. This may be due to the reason that neural network while trained using combined word embedding has more information (reduces the out-of-vocabulary word problem)

Table 1. Accuracy table

		Comparative Approaches						
		CNN	LSTM	GRU	Ensemble Methods			
					CNN-LSTM	CNN-GRU	LSTM-GRU	CNN-LSTM-GRU
Word Embedding	Glove	95.21	97.18	97.21	97.81	97.91	98.11	**98.35**
	Word2Vec	95.18	97.02	97.05	97.76	97.87	98.02	**98.17**
	Combined	95.70	97.43	97.56	98.12	98.15	98.41	**98.56**

Table 2. Comparison with previous state-of-the-art approaches on ATIS corpus

Model	Intent
Boosting (Tur et al. 2010)	96.46
Bi-LSTM [15]	97.31
Sentence simplification [31]	96.98
RecNN + Viterbi [5]	95.40
Our proposed ensemble model	**98.56**

rather when it is trained using just one of the word embedding representation. We also compare our results with the previous state-of-the-art approaches as shown in Table 2. Our proposed ensemble model outperforms the state-of-the-art approaches for the SLU task of intent detection.

5.2 Analysis

For more detailed analysis, we show the class-specific precision, recall and F1 score for our best performing ensemble model using combined word embeddings in Table 3. This shows that for most of the cases, the performances are quite high, even 100% recall, precision and F1-score are observed for a few classes (e.g. Abbreviation, Quantity, Distance, etc.). However, for some of the classes (e.g. Restriction, Day_name, etc.) the model demonstrates relatively low score. One of the reasons for such a low score may be the insufficient number of instances of these classes in the dataset.

In order to get an idea where our system fails we perform detailed error analysis of our best performing ensemble model. The quantitative analysis is shown in Table 4 in terms of a confusion matrix. As we can see, one of the major problems is that the *non-Flight* utterances are erroneously classified as *Flight*. This may be attributed to the fact that the corpus has unbalanced class distribution. Our detailed analysis further reveals that the errors are due to the embedding of prepositional phrases inside the noun phrase. For example, the phrase *Airfare of the flight from Texas to Chicago*, where the prepositional phrase

Table 3. ClassWise Precision, Recall and F1 Score

Intent	Precision	Recall	F1 Score
Flight	0.99	0.99	0.99
Flight_time	1	0.83	0.9
Airfare	0.97	0.97	0.97
Aircraft	0.66	0.66	0.66
Ground_service	1	1	1
Airport	1	0.94	0.96
Airline	1	0.97	0.98
Distance	1	1	1
Abbreviation	1	1	1
Ground_fare	0.94	1	0.96
Quantity	1	1	1
City	1	0.66	0.78
Flight_no	1	1	1
Capacity	1	0.66	0.79
Meal	1	1	1
Restriction	0.25	0.12	0.16
Day_name	0.37	0.54	0.44

suggests the utterance to be *flight* whereas the intent class is mainly determined by the head word of the noun phrase (*airfare* in this case). A number of errors were also encountered due to the incorrect annotation. Certain utterances in the dataset are ambiguous and also ill-formulated, such as *What's the airfare for a taxi to the Chicago airport?* In this case, the word *airfare* implies the intent class to be *Airfare*, whereas the actual intent class should be *Ground Service*. The absolute improvement in our results may not be very high, because the ATIS corpus have been studied for more than a decade and the score of the state-of-the-art approaches is already very high. Our proposed model has still been able to outperform the previous state-of-the-art approaches.

5.3 Statistical Test

A statistical hypothesis test named Welch's t-test [33] is conducted at the 5% (0.05) significance level to verify whether the improvement in our model is significant or not. This is done to show that the best accuracy obtained by our proposed method is statistically significant and has not occurred by chance. For statistical test on the ATIS corpus we execute the experiment 20 times. Table 5 reports p-values produced by Welch's t-test. All the p-values reported in the Table 5 are less than 0.05 (5% significance level).

Table 4. The confusion matrix for intent detection

Correct-estimated	a	b	c	d	e	f	g	h	i	j	k	l	m	n	o	p	q
a. Flight	624		1	1													
b. Flight_time	1																
c. Airfare	1		64														
d. Aircraft	1			8													
e. Ground_service					36												
f. Airport	1					16									1		
g. Airline	1						38										
h. Distance								10									
i. Abbreviation									32								
j. Ground_fare			1		1					6							
k. Quantity											8						
l. City	1											4					
m. Flight_no													8				
n. Capacity	1													20			
o. Meal															5		
p. Restriction									1								
q. Day_name	1																

Table 5. Statistical significance table

		CNN	LSTM	GRU	Ensemble Methods		
					CNN-LSTM	CNN-GRU	GRU-LSTM
Word Embedding	Glove	5.81E-061	1.8E-044	4.76E-044	2.9E-032	3.85E-029	1.93E-020
	Word2Vec	1.06E-059	3.44E-044	9.15E-044	4.41E-028	1.5E-023	1.35E-014
	Combined	5.67E-059	6.59E-044	5.97E-042	3.85E-029	4.41E-028	1.35E-014

6 Conclusion and Future Work

To understand the intent of an user's utterance, we have proposed a deep learning based ensemble approach for the SLU task of intent detection. The major contribution of our work is that by employing ensemble based deep learning approach, we are able to classify the intents well by using word embedding representations obtained from more than one source. As baseline models, we use CNN, LSTM and GRU, and outputs from these individual models are combined together using an MLP network. We performed experiments on the benchmark ATIS corpus. The proposed ensemble method outperforms the individual model in the task. We have observed that due to the natural advantage of working well on sequential data, LSTM and GRU perform better than CNN. We observe that concatenation of two word embeddings works better and improves the performance in all our settings. Evaluation results shows that the performance obtained by LSTM and GRU are better compared to the existing state-of-the-art models.

In the future, we would like to explore more complex deep learning models such as stacked bidirectional LSTM, hierarchical convnet and LSTM with memory networks for classifying intents. Also, we are in a process of using these models on a much larger corpora to examine whether the proposed approach behaves in a similar fashion. Furthermore, we would like to extend and apply our approach to a related SLU task, such as slot filling, which is a sequence labeling task. In the future we would also look at unsupervised adaptation of intent detection models due to the unavailability of labeled data for the task.

Acknowledgment. The research reported in this paper is partially supported by Accenture IIT AI Lab, IIT Patna.

References

1. Cho, K., et al.: Learning phrase representations using RNN encoder-decoder for statistical machine translation. arXiv preprint arXiv:1406.1078 (2014)
2. Collobert, R., Weston, J.: A unified architecture for natural language processing: deep neural networks with multitask learning. In: Proceedings of the 25th International Conference on Machine Learning, pp. 160–167. ACM (2008)
3. Ekbal, A., Saha, S.: Weighted vote-based classifier ensemble for named entity recognition: a genetic algorithm-based approach. ACM Trans. Asian Lang. Inf. Process. **10**(2), 9:1–9:37 (2011)
4. Gorin, A.L., Riccardi, G., Wright, J.H.: How may I help you? Speech Commun. **23**(1–2), 113–127 (1997)
5. Guo, D., Tur, G., Yih, W.t., Zweig, G.: Joint semantic utterance classification and slot filling with recursive neural networks. In: 2014 IEEE Spoken Language Technology Workshop (SLT), pp. 554–559. IEEE (2014)
6. Haffner, P., Tur, G., Wright, J.H.: Optimizing SVMs for complex call classification. In: 2003 IEEE International Conference on Acoustics, Speech, and Signal Processing, Proceedings (ICASSP 2003), vol. 1, p. I. IEEE (2003)
7. Hakkani-Tür, D., Tur, G., Chotimongkol, A.: Using syntactic and semantic graphs for call classification. In: Proceedings of the ACL Workshop on Feature Engineering for Machine Learning in Natural Language Processing (2005)
8. Hakkani-Tür, D., Riccardi, G., Tur, G.: An active approach to spoken language processing. ACM Trans. Speech Lang. Process. (TSLP) **3**(3), 1–31 (2006)
9. Hakkani-Tür, D., et al.: Multi-domain joint semantic frame parsing using bi-directional RNN-LSTM. In: INTERSPEECH, pp. 715–719 (2016)
10. Hashemi, H.B., Asiaee, A., Kraft, R.: Query intent detection using convolutional neural networks. In: International Conference on Web Search and Data Mining, Workshop on Query Understanding (2016)
11. He, Y., Young, S.: A data-driven spoken language understanding system. In: 2003 IEEE Workshop on Automatic Speech Recognition and Understanding, ASRU 2003, pp. 583–588. IEEE (2003)

12. Hochreiter, S., Schmidhuber, J.: Long short-term memory. Neural Comput. **9**(8), 1735–1780 (1997)
13. Jeong, M., Lee, G.G.: Triangular-chain conditional random fields. IEEE Trans. Audio Speech Lang. Process. **16**(7), 1287–1302 (2008)
14. Karpathy, A., Johnson, J., Fei-Fei, L.: Visualizing and understanding recurrent networks. arXiv preprint arXiv:1506.02078 (2015)
15. Kim, J.K., Tur, G., Celikyilmaz, A., Cao, B., Wang, Y.Y.: Intent detection using semantically enriched word embeddings. In: 2016 IEEE Spoken Language Technology Workshop (SLT), pp. 414–419. IEEE (2016)
16. Kingma, D., Ba, J.: Adam: a method for stochastic optimization. arXiv preprint arXiv:1412.6980 (2014)
17. Liu, B., Lane, I.: Attention-based recurrent neural network models for joint intent detection and slot filling. arXiv preprint arXiv:1609.01454 (2016)
18. Liu, B., Lane, I.: Joint online spoken language understanding and language modeling with recurrent neural networks. arXiv preprint arXiv:1609.01462 (2016)
19. Luan, Y., Watanabe, S., Harsham, B.: Efficient learning for spoken language understanding tasks with word embedding based pre-training. In: Sixteenth Annual Conference of the International Speech Communication Association (2015)
20. Pedersen, T.: A simple approach to building ensembles of naive Bayesian classifiers for word sense disambiguation. In: Proceedings of the 1st North American chapter of the Association for Computational Linguistics Conference, pp. 63–69. Association for Computational Linguistics (2000)
21. Pennington, J., Socher, R., Manning, C.: Glove: global vectors for word representation. In: Proceedings of the 2014 Conference on Empirical Methods in Natural Language Processing (EMNLP), pp. 1532–1543 (2014)
22. Price, P.J.: Evaluation of spoken language systems: the ATIS domain. In: Speech and Natural Language: Proceedings of a Workshop Held at Hidden Valley, Pennsylvania, 24 27 June 1990 (1990)
23. Ravuri, S., Stoicke, A.: A comparative study of neural network models for lexical intent classification. In: 2015 IEEE Workshop on Automatic Speech Recognition and Understanding (ASRU), pp. 368–374. IEEE (2015)
24. Ravuri, S.V., Stolcke, A.: Recurrent neural network and LSTM models for lexical utterance classification. In: INTERSPEECH, pp. 135–139 (2015)
25. Sang, E.F.: Noun phrase recognition by system combination. In: Proceedings of the 1st North American Chapter of the Association for Computational Linguistics Conference, pp. 50–55. Association for Computational Linguistics (2000)
26. Sarikaya, R., Hinton, G.E., Ramabhadran, B.: Deep belief nets for natural language call-routing. In: 2011 IEEE International Conference on Acoustics, Speech and Signal Processing (ICASSP), pp. 5680–5683. IEEE (2011)
27. Schapire, R.E., Singer, Y.: Boostexter: a boosting-based system for text categorization. Mach. Learn. **39**(2–3), 135–168 (2000)
28. Srivastava, N., Hinton, G.E., Krizhevsky, A., Sutskever, I., Salakhutdinov, R.: Dropout: a simple way to prevent neural networks from overfitting. J. Mach. Learn. Res. **15**(1), 1929–1958 (2014)
29. Sutton, C., McCallum, A., et al.: An introduction to conditional random fields. Found. Trends® Mach. Learn. **4**(4), 267–373 (2012)
30. Tur, G.: Model adaptation for spoken language understanding. In: Proceedings of the IEEE International Conference on Acoustics, Speech, and Signal Processing (ICASSP 2005), vol. 1, p. I-41. IEEE (2005)

31. Tur, G., Hakkani-Tür, D., Heck, L., Parthasarathy, S.: Sentence simplification for spoken language understanding. In: 2011 IEEE International Conference on Acoustics, Speech and Signal Processing (ICASSP), pp. 5628–5631. IEEE (2011)
32. Van Halteren, H., Zavrel, J., Daelemans, W.: Improving data driven wordclass tagging by system combination. In: Proceedings of the 36th Annual Meeting of the Association for Computational Linguistics and 17th International Conference on Computational Linguistics, vol. 1, pp. 491–497. Association for Computational Linguistics (1998)
33. Welch, B.L.: The generalization of 'student's' problem when several different population variances are involved. Biometrika **34**(1/2), 28–35 (1947)
34. Wu, J.: Introduction to convolutional neural networks. National Key Lab for Novel Software Technology, Nanjing University, China (2017)
35. Xu, P., Sarikaya, R.: Convolutional neural network based triangular CRF for joint intent detection and slot filling. In: 2013 IEEE Workshop on Automatic Speech Recognition and Understanding (ASRU), pp. 78–83. IEEE (2013)
36. Zhang, X., Wang, H.: A joint model of intent determination and slot filling for spoken language understanding. In: IJCAI, pp. 2993–2999 (2016)

Accurately Detecting Community with Large Attribute in Partial Networks

Wei Han[1,3], Guopeng Li[2], and Xinyu Zhang[1(✉)]

[1] Tsinghua University, Beijing 100084, China
han-wl3@mails.tsinghua.edu.cn,
xyzhang@tsinghua.edu.cn

[2] National University of Defense Technology, Xi'an 710106, China
wangqu_li@126.com

[3] Institute of Microelectronics of Chinese Academy of Sciences, Beijing 100029, China

Abstract. A community structure is the most significant feature of social networks. Fusing the relation information and the attribute information to is necessary to detect community in the attributed social network. However, both relation and attribute information will have non-uniform quality because of the meaningless or erroneous noise in a social network. Moreover, the nodes that lose relation or attribute information will make the network into a partial network. In those cases, it is unrealistic to split users into different communities correctly without considering the noise and incompleteness in combination processing. To solve this problem, we propose a non-negative matrix factorization (NMF)-based community detection framework. In this framework, common and correct community structures can be identified effectively and disagreements can be reconciled by introducing two regularizations in combination processing. The experimental results confirm the superior performance of the method and demonstrate its effectiveness for a partial network.

Keywords: Community detection · NMF · Partial networks
Multi-view clustering

1 Introduction

Numerous real-world networks have the structure of a community (module), which can be defined as a group of users who interact with each other more frequently than with those outside the group [1, 2]. A community provides an insight into the structure and function of the network [3, 4]. In the past few decades, numerous community detection algorithms were proposed [5]. However, accurately detecting a community and splitting the members into them is still a problem [6]. In a social network, combining relations and attributes is an efficient idea to improve the accuracy of community detection [7]. However, the predominantly sparse relations between users can often lead to them belonging to the same community, even when no relation exists between them. User attributes such as content are often of high dimensions. Many existing works [8] demonstrate that methods do not work perfectly when only relation or

X. Geng and B.-H. Kang (Eds.): PRICAI 2018, LNAI 11012, pp. 643–657, 2018.
https://doi.org/10.1007/978-3-319-97304-3_49

attribute information [9] is used. Methods fusing relation and attribute information tend to not only achieve a better accuracy but also provide useful semantic information for the communities [10, 11]. In general, relation and attribute data are essentially different types of data in social networks, so integrating them is a challenge for community identification. In recent years, some new approaches [12] have been proposed to deal with this problem.

However, these methods might not yield a higher clustering performance because all of them contain a lot of non-essential information. As mentioned earlier [13], it is no secret that better results can be obtained if the data sets are integrated with more relations and attributes. It is proven that the combination processing framework is also a key problem for accurate community detection, especially when some users have lost their relation information with others or have no attribute information in a network (we describe this network as a partial network). In a partial network, users with missing, meaningless, or erroneous information vary the quality of relation and attribute view to a great degree. The poor quality negatively affects the combination processing and results in the failure to capture common community structures of different views. Furthermore, incorporating excessive information regarding views can lead to worse results. Moreover, most methods [9, 14–16] based on NMF assume that both relation and attribute information appears for all users. However, owing to the nature of the data or the cost of data collection, some users might lose relation information. The missing information results in the methods failing to reconcile the disagreements, among different views, in combination processing. To summarize, integrating different views in such a manner that common and correct community structures can be effectively identified and disagreements could be reconciled remains a continuing problem.

In this paper, a novel NMF-based method was proposed to identify network communities using attributes and relations in the partial network. To split users into communities perfectly and actually, two useful regularizations are introduced in combination processing. Unlike previous studies that regularized the user cluster matrix toward a common consensus matrix, considering the attribute and relation to be different types of views, a pairwise constraint is added to the user cluster matrix from different views to complement each other. The pairwise constraint integrates the common structures from different views more effectively. To reconcile the disagreements, orthonormal constraint regularization between different user cluster matrices is proposed during the factorization process.

To deal with the users who lost relations in partial networks, based on the fact that users with similar local structures are closely related to the same community structures [17, 18], the nearest neighbor information of nodes is utilized to fill in the missing information during combination processing. For example, if the i-th node loses its relation information in partial networks, it can found that its nearest neighbor node j from the attribute view, so, in combination processing, the relation information from the j-th node can be used as the supplement information of the i-th node. In the same manner, when the i-th node loses its attribute information, the information of node j which is the nearest neighbor of the i-th node can be used as the supplement in combination processing.

Overall, the contribution of this paper can be summarized as follows:

(1) to obtain a more accurate community structure, a pairwise constraint is designed to integrate the common structures and an orthonormal constraint is used to reconcile the disagreements in combination processing.
(2) to deal with the missing information in each view, a method is proposed that can finds the nearest neighbor node information as supplement during combination processing.
(3) to evaluate the performances, experiments are analyzed in two kinds of real datasets. These are WebKB datasets, in which the quality of attribute view is better than the relation view and the Twitter datasets, in which the quality of relation view is better than the attribute view.

2 Related Works

The methods for community detection can be categorized into four types: relation-only methods, attribute-only methods [19], methods that combine multiple relation networks and methods that combine relations and attributes. As reviewed earlier [20], many methods have been developed to explore network relations, including NMF [21, 22], Random Walks Method [23], and spectral clustering [24].

NMF [25–27] is proved to be useful in many research areas. It enforces the constraint that the elements of the factor matrices must be nonnegative. Some studies show that when the Frobenius norm is used as a divergence, NMF is equivalent to a relaxed form of K-means clustering method [18]. One matrix contains cluster centroids, and the other is a cluster membership indicator matrix; hence, NMF is a useful method for data clustering. In particular, Ref. [21] improves a symmetric NMF (SNMF) for community detection. As the NMF-based clustering framework can integrate a wide range of social information seamlessly and flexibly, many methods based on NMF have been proposed for community detection.

To perfectly split users into communities, Pei et al. [9] integrate relations and contents as a NMTF (nonnegative matrix tri-factorization) problem that factorizes user words, tweet words and user-to-user matrices into lower rank representations of users and tweets with similarity regularization. Based on this study, Ozer et al. [28] show that user content and endorsement filtered connectivity information are complementary to each other in clustering politically motivated users into pure political communities. They model NMF frameworks to detect political communities on Twitter. However, these methods focus on utilizing more additional content information to detect communities and their framework lacks integration of partial data in relation and content. Jin et al. [29] adopted a random-graph null model-based NMF to faithfully capture community structures by preserving the expected node degrees in the model. The method is effective in discovering intrinsic and subtle community structures of numerous real-world networks. In Ref [12], a Bayesian probabilistic model for community detection was proposed for capturing both structural and attribute aspects of a graph. Wang et al. in [30] proposed a novel NMF model with two sets of parameters, the community membership matrix and community attribute matrix, and present efficient updating rules to evaluate the parameters with a convergence guarantee. The use of node attributes improves upon community detection and provides a semantic interpretation to the resultant network communities.

However, in reality, relations and attributes are two different types of data. A common consensus matrix cannot be correctly learned in networks with either missing, meaningless, or erroneous information in both relations and attributes. Appropriate methods need to be used to deal with the erroneous noise and missing information.

3 Model

In this section, the NMF model-based clustering framework with different types of regularization for community detection is presented.

3.1 Modeling Network Relations and Attributes

Let $G = (\boldsymbol{V}, \boldsymbol{E}, \boldsymbol{W})$ to denote the structure of a social network, where $\boldsymbol{V}$ is the set of all users and $\boldsymbol{E}$ is a $\boldsymbol{N} \times \boldsymbol{N}$ matrix, with each element $e_{u,v} = w_{u,v}$ indicating whether user v has a link to user u with weight $w_{u,v}$. $|V| = N$ denotes the number of users. According to [21], communities can be learned from the adjacency matrix $\boldsymbol{G} \in \mathbb{R}^{n \times n}$, which gives rise to the following function in the NMF matrix formulation:

$$\min_{U \geq 0, S \geq 0} \|\boldsymbol{G} - \boldsymbol{USU}^{\mathrm{T}}\|_F^2 \tag{1}$$

where $\boldsymbol{U} \in \mathbb{R}^{n \times k}$ is the user cluster matrix, k is the number of communities, $\boldsymbol{U}_{ij}(i = 1 \ldots n; j = 1 \ldots k)$ indicates the propensity of node i belonging to community j. $\boldsymbol{S} \in \mathbb{R}^{k \times k}$ is the associated matrix. Let $\hat{\boldsymbol{S}} = \boldsymbol{S} + \boldsymbol{S}^{\mathrm{T}}$ and $\hat{\boldsymbol{G}} = \boldsymbol{G} + \boldsymbol{G}^{\mathrm{T}}$, because $\boldsymbol{G}^{\mathrm{T}} = \boldsymbol{US}^{\mathrm{T}}\boldsymbol{U}^{\mathrm{T}}$. So for undirected and directed network, the following function can be obtained:

$$\min_{I \geq U \geq 0, S \geq 0} \|\hat{\boldsymbol{G}} - \boldsymbol{U}\hat{\boldsymbol{S}}\boldsymbol{U}^{\boldsymbol{T}}\|_F^2 \tag{2}$$

Suppose, $\boldsymbol{X} \in \mathbb{R}^{n \times m}$ is the m-dimensional nonnegative attribute of the users in the networks, and $\boldsymbol{H} \in \mathbb{R}^{n \times k}$ is the user cluster matrix. The NMF function formulation will be:

$$\min_{\boldsymbol{I} \geq \boldsymbol{H} \geq 0, \boldsymbol{V} \geq 0} L = \|\boldsymbol{X} - \boldsymbol{HV}\|_F^2 \tag{3}$$

where the values of $\boldsymbol{U}$ and $\boldsymbol{H}$ are between 0 and 1.

3.2 The Model with Regularization Constraints

Unlike previous studies that used a common cluster matrix in combination processing, we relax the constraint as follows:

$$\|\boldsymbol{H}-\boldsymbol{U}\|_F^2 \tag{4}$$

If there are some users who have no relation with other users, some studies [18, 31, 32] show that the neighborhood plays a critical role in community detection. When the node loses its relations, the relation information from its nearest neighbor can be used to act as a supplement, so it is a natural method to use the attributes view information to reconstruct the node's neighborhood relation structure. Hence, it can be done to build the nearest neighbor indicator matrix $\boldsymbol{M}_{\mathrm{C}} \in \mathbb{R}^{n\times n}$ for attributes view and $\boldsymbol{M}_{\mathrm{L}} \in \mathbb{R}^{n\times n}$ for relations view. For example, to build $\boldsymbol{M}_{\mathrm{C}}$, the missing indicator matrix $\boldsymbol{M}_{\mathrm{M\_C}} \in \mathbb{R}^{n\times n}$ can be built as follows:

$$\boldsymbol{M}_{\mathrm{M\_C}}(i,i) = \begin{cases} 1; & \boldsymbol{H}(i,:) \neq 0 \\ 0; & \boldsymbol{H}(i,:) = 0 \end{cases}$$

where $H(i,:)$ shows the i th node of the lost attribute information. Also, according to the nearest neighbor graph from the relations network, $\boldsymbol{M}_{\mathrm{C}}$ can be built as:

$$\boldsymbol{M}_{\mathrm{C}}(i,j) = \begin{cases} 1; & \text{if } j \text{ is the nearest neighbor of } i \text{ in } \boldsymbol{G} \\ \boldsymbol{M}_{\mathrm{M\_C}}(i,j); & \text{otherwise} \end{cases}$$

$\boldsymbol{M}_{\mathrm{L}}$ is built as the same way, and the nearest neighbor graph can be approximated using various methods [18, 33]. the node with the biggest weight is chosen in the weight matrix by Heat kernel weighting as the nearest neighbor.

To implement combination processing with missing information, a regularization constraint is designed to impose similarity constraints between different views:

$$\|\boldsymbol{M}_{\mathrm{C}}\boldsymbol{H}-\boldsymbol{M}_{\mathrm{L}}\boldsymbol{U}\|_F^2 \tag{5}$$

Through this regularization, it will make the user cluster matrix, approximated from two views, to complement each other to find common and correct community structures during the factorization process. Both relation and content have a lot of information in the form of noise. So in order to remove the influence of the noise and reconcile disagreements, orthonormal constraints can be imposed, such as:

$$\|\boldsymbol{M}_{\mathrm{C}}\boldsymbol{H}-\boldsymbol{M}_{\mathrm{L}}\boldsymbol{U}\|_F^2 + \left\|(\boldsymbol{M}_{\mathrm{C}}\boldsymbol{H})^{\mathrm{T}}(\boldsymbol{M}_{\mathrm{L}}\boldsymbol{U}) - \boldsymbol{I}\right\|_F^2 \tag{6}$$

where $\boldsymbol{I}$ is a $k \times k$ identity matrix.

To combine the objective functions of modeling the network relations and attributes, the following overall function is:

$$\begin{aligned} \min_{\boldsymbol{H}\geq 0,\boldsymbol{V}\geq 0,\boldsymbol{U}\geq 0,\boldsymbol{S}\geq 0} o = \theta\Big(\|\boldsymbol{X}-\boldsymbol{H}\boldsymbol{V}\|_F^2 + \left\|\boldsymbol{G}-\boldsymbol{U}\boldsymbol{S}\boldsymbol{U}^{\mathrm{T}}\right\|_F^2\Big) \\ \alpha\|\boldsymbol{M}_{\mathrm{C}}\boldsymbol{H}-\boldsymbol{M}_{\mathrm{L}}\boldsymbol{U}\|_F^2 + \beta\left\|(\boldsymbol{M}_{\mathrm{C}}\boldsymbol{H})^{\mathrm{T}}(\boldsymbol{M}_{\mathrm{L}}\boldsymbol{U}) - \boldsymbol{I}\right\|_F^2 \end{aligned} \tag{7}$$

4 Optimization

As the objective function in Eq. (7) is not convex, it is impractical to obtain the optimal solution. The local minima of Eq. (7) can be achieved using the method in [25]. The specific formulas are represented as the following four subproblems.

H-subproblem: when updating $\boldsymbol{H}$ with $\boldsymbol{U}$ and $\boldsymbol{V}$ fixed, we need to solve the following equation:

$$\min_{\boldsymbol{H}\geq 0} L(\boldsymbol{H}) = \theta\|\boldsymbol{X}-\boldsymbol{HV}\|_F^2 + \alpha\|\boldsymbol{M}_{\mathrm{C}}\boldsymbol{H}-\boldsymbol{M}_{\mathrm{L}}\boldsymbol{U}\|_F^2 \\ + \beta\left\|(\boldsymbol{M}_{\mathrm{C}}\boldsymbol{H})^{\mathrm{T}}(\boldsymbol{M}_{\mathrm{L}}\boldsymbol{U}) - \boldsymbol{I}\right\|_F^2 \tag{8}$$

To this end, a Lagrange multiplier matrix $\boldsymbol{\Theta} = (\boldsymbol{\Theta}_{ij})$ is introduced for the nonnegative constraints on $\boldsymbol{H}$, which results in the following equivalent objective function:

$$\begin{aligned} L(\boldsymbol{H}) &= \theta tr\left(\boldsymbol{XX}^{\mathrm{T}} - \boldsymbol{XV}^{\mathrm{T}}\boldsymbol{H}^{\mathrm{T}} - \boldsymbol{HVX}^{\mathrm{T}} + \boldsymbol{HVV}^{\mathrm{T}}\boldsymbol{H}^{\mathrm{T}}\right) \\ &+ \alpha tr\left(\boldsymbol{M}_{\mathrm{C}}\boldsymbol{HH}^{\mathrm{T}}\boldsymbol{M}_{\mathrm{C}}^{\mathrm{T}} - \boldsymbol{M}_{\mathrm{C}}\boldsymbol{HU}^{\mathrm{T}}\boldsymbol{M}_{\mathrm{L}}^{\mathrm{T}} - \boldsymbol{M}_{\mathrm{L}}\boldsymbol{UH}^{\mathrm{T}}\boldsymbol{M}_{\mathrm{C}}^{\mathrm{T}} + \boldsymbol{M}_{\mathrm{L}}\boldsymbol{UU}^{\mathrm{T}}\boldsymbol{M}_{\mathrm{L}}^{\mathrm{T}}\right) \\ &+ \beta tr\left(\boldsymbol{H}^{\mathrm{T}}\boldsymbol{M}_{\mathrm{C}}^{\mathrm{T}}\boldsymbol{M}_{\mathrm{L}}\boldsymbol{UU}^{T}\boldsymbol{M}_{\mathrm{L}}^{\mathrm{T}}\boldsymbol{M}_{\mathrm{C}}\boldsymbol{H} - \boldsymbol{H}^{\mathrm{T}}\boldsymbol{M}_{\mathrm{C}}^{\mathrm{T}}\boldsymbol{M}_{\mathrm{L}}\boldsymbol{U} - \boldsymbol{U}^{\mathrm{T}}\boldsymbol{M}_{\mathrm{L}}^{\mathrm{T}}\boldsymbol{M}_{\mathrm{C}}\boldsymbol{H} + I\right) \\ &+ tr\left(\Theta_1\boldsymbol{H}^{\mathrm{T}}\right) \end{aligned} \tag{9}$$

Using the Karush–Kuhn–Tucker conditions, given an initial value of $\boldsymbol{U}$ and $\boldsymbol{V}$, the successive update of $\boldsymbol{H}$ is:

$$\boldsymbol{H}_{ij} \leftarrow \boldsymbol{H}_{ij}\left(\frac{\theta\boldsymbol{XV}^{\mathrm{T}} + (\alpha+\beta)\boldsymbol{M}_{\mathrm{C}}^{\mathrm{T}}\boldsymbol{M}_{\mathrm{L}}\boldsymbol{U}}{\theta\boldsymbol{HVV}^{\mathrm{T}} + F(\boldsymbol{H})}\right)_{ij} \tag{10}$$

where $F(\boldsymbol{H}) = \alpha\boldsymbol{M}_{\mathrm{C}}^{\mathrm{T}}\boldsymbol{M}_{\mathrm{C}}\boldsymbol{H} + \beta\boldsymbol{M}_{\mathrm{C}}^{\mathrm{T}}\boldsymbol{M}_{\mathrm{L}}\boldsymbol{UU}^{T}\boldsymbol{M}_{\mathrm{L}}^{\mathrm{T}}\boldsymbol{M}_{\mathrm{C}}\boldsymbol{H}$. The update rule converges in accordance with the theorem in [25, 34].

V-subproblem: when updating $\boldsymbol{V}$ with $\boldsymbol{H}$, the following equation is:

$$\min_{\boldsymbol{V}\geq 0} L(\boldsymbol{V}) = \theta\|\boldsymbol{X}-\boldsymbol{HV}\|_F^2 + tr\left(\boldsymbol{\Theta}_2\boldsymbol{V}^{\mathrm{T}}\right) \tag{11}$$

Similarly, the successive update of $\boldsymbol{V}$ is:

$$\boldsymbol{V}_{ij} \leftarrow \boldsymbol{V}_{ij}\left(\frac{\boldsymbol{H}^{\mathrm{T}}\boldsymbol{X}}{\boldsymbol{H}^{\mathrm{T}}\boldsymbol{HV}}\right)_{ij} \tag{12}$$

U-subproblem: when updating $\boldsymbol{U}$ with $\boldsymbol{H}$, $\boldsymbol{S}$ fixed, the following equation is:

$$\min_{\boldsymbol{U}\geq 0} L(\boldsymbol{U}) = \theta\left\|\boldsymbol{G}-\boldsymbol{USU}^{\mathrm{T}}\right\|_F^2 + \alpha\|\boldsymbol{M}_{\mathrm{C}}\boldsymbol{H}-\boldsymbol{M}_{\mathrm{L}}\boldsymbol{U}\|_F^2 \\ + \beta\left\|(\boldsymbol{M}_{\mathrm{C}}H)^{\mathrm{T}}(\boldsymbol{M}_{\mathrm{L}}\boldsymbol{U}) - \boldsymbol{I}\right\|_F^2 + tr\left(\boldsymbol{\Theta}_3\boldsymbol{U}^{\mathrm{T}}\right) \tag{13}$$

Then use the auxiliary function approach [21] to find that the convergence of formula and the successive update of $\boldsymbol{U}$ is:

$$\boldsymbol{U}_{ij} \leftarrow \boldsymbol{U}_{ij}\left(\frac{\theta \boldsymbol{GUS}^{\mathrm{T}} + \theta \boldsymbol{G}^{\mathrm{T}}\boldsymbol{US} + (\alpha+\beta)\boldsymbol{M}_{\mathrm{L}}^{\mathrm{T}}\boldsymbol{M}_{\mathrm{C}}\boldsymbol{H}}{\theta \boldsymbol{USU}^{\mathrm{T}}\boldsymbol{US}^{\mathrm{T}} + \theta \boldsymbol{US}^{\mathrm{T}}\boldsymbol{U}^{\mathrm{T}}\boldsymbol{US} + F(\boldsymbol{U})}\right)_{ij}^{0.25} \tag{14}$$

where $F(\boldsymbol{U}) = \alpha \boldsymbol{M}_{\mathrm{L}}^{\mathrm{T}}\boldsymbol{M}_{\mathrm{L}}\boldsymbol{U} + \beta \boldsymbol{M}_{\mathrm{L}}^{\mathrm{T}}\boldsymbol{M}_{\mathrm{C}}\boldsymbol{HH}^{\mathrm{T}}\boldsymbol{M}_{\mathrm{C}}^{\mathrm{T}}\boldsymbol{M}_{\mathrm{L}}\boldsymbol{U}$.

$\boldsymbol{S}$-subproblem: when updating $\boldsymbol{S}$ with $\boldsymbol{U}$ fixed, the following equation is:

$$\min_{\boldsymbol{S} \geq 0} L(\boldsymbol{S}) = \theta \left\| \boldsymbol{G} - \boldsymbol{USU}^{\mathrm{T}} \right\|_F^2 + tr\left(\boldsymbol{\Theta}_4 \boldsymbol{S}^{\mathrm{T}}\right) \tag{15}$$

the successive update of $\boldsymbol{S}$ is:

$$\boldsymbol{S}_{ij} \leftarrow \boldsymbol{S}_{ij}\left(\frac{\boldsymbol{U}^{\mathrm{T}}\boldsymbol{GU}}{\boldsymbol{U}^{\mathrm{T}}\boldsymbol{USU}^{\mathrm{T}}\boldsymbol{U}}\right)_{ij} \tag{16}$$

To normalize the $\boldsymbol{H}$ and $\boldsymbol{U}$ to prevent scaling, normalization can be represented as: let $\boldsymbol{Q}_{jj}^{\mathrm{H}} = \sqrt{\sum_i (\boldsymbol{H}_{ij})^2}$, $\boldsymbol{Q}_{jj}^{\mathrm{U}} = \sqrt{\sum_i (\boldsymbol{U}_{ij})^2}$:

$$\boldsymbol{H} \leftarrow \boldsymbol{H}\left(\boldsymbol{Q}^{\mathrm{H}}\right)^{-1}, \boldsymbol{V} \leftarrow \boldsymbol{Q}^{\mathrm{H}}\boldsymbol{V}, \boldsymbol{U} \leftarrow \boldsymbol{U}\left(\boldsymbol{Q}^{\mathrm{U}}\right)^{-1}, \boldsymbol{S} \leftarrow \boldsymbol{Q}^{\mathrm{U}}\boldsymbol{U}\boldsymbol{Q}^{\mathrm{U}} \tag{17}$$

Summarizing the analysis, the algorithm framework is concluded as Algorithm 1.

Alg. 1.

Input: relations matrix $\boldsymbol{G}$, attributes matrix $\boldsymbol{X}$, number of communities k, parameters: α, β, θ

Output: user cluster matrix $\boldsymbol{U}$ and $\boldsymbol{H}$

1: initialize $\boldsymbol{H}$, $\boldsymbol{V}$, $\boldsymbol{U}$, $\boldsymbol{S}$,
2: **while** not converge **do**
3: normalize $\boldsymbol{H}$, $\boldsymbol{V}$, $\boldsymbol{U}$, $\boldsymbol{S}$ in Eq. (17)
4: update $\boldsymbol{H}$ in Eq. (10)
5: update $\boldsymbol{V}$ in Eq. (12)
6: update $\boldsymbol{U}$ in Eq. (14)
7: update $\boldsymbol{S}$ in Eq. (16)
8: **end while**

5 Experiments

5.1 Datasets

In the experiments, two real datasets is used: Twitter[1] and WebKB[2]. Twitter contains four sub datasets: football, olympics, politics-ie, politics-uk. They are described as follows:

(1) Football, it comprises 248 football players and clubs active on Twitter. The disjointed ground truth communities correspond to the 20 clubs.
(2) Olympics, it comprises 464 users, covering athletes and organizations that were involved in the London 2012 olympics. The ground truth communities correspond to 28 different sports.
(3) Politics-ie, it comprises 348 Irish politicians and political organizations, assigned to seven disjointed ground truth groups.
(4) Politics-uk, it comprises 419 Members of Parliament in the UK. The ground truth comprises five groups.

WebKB datasets also contains four sub datasets, which collected webpages from four universities, as: Cornell, Texas, Washington, and Wisconsin. In each dataset, The webpages are distributed over five classes: student, project, course, staff, and faculty, they are described by two views: the content view and the citation view. Each webpage is described by 1703 words in the content view and the number of citation links between other pages in the citation view. The statistics of the datasets are summarized in Table 1.

Table 1. Details of the datasets

Dataset	Nodes	Communities	Attributes	Relations
Cornell	195	5	1703	569
Texas	187	5	1703	578
Washington	230	5	1703	783
Wisconsin	265	5	1703	938
football	248	20	3601	3819
olympics	464	28	3097	10642
politics-ie	348	7	1051	16856
politics-uk	419	5	2879	27340

5.2 Baseline and Evaluation Metrics

To evaluate the community detection performance, several algorithms and our method Algorithm 1 are test on eight datasets. The algorithms which are evaluated are:

[1] http://mlg.ucd.ie/aggregation/.

[2] http://www.cs.umd.edu/projects/linqs/projects/lbc/.

(1) SNMF, The relation based community detection method developed by Wang et al. [21].
(2) Spectral, Spectral clustering is acceptable for both relation and attribute-based community detection; the best result from several results is chose as the final output.
(3) CAN, The attribute-based community detection developed by Nie et al. [33].
(4) RMSC, The multi-view spectral clustering method developed by Xia et al. [35].
(5) SCI, The methods that combine network relations and node attributes developed by Wang et al. [30].

Two metrics are sued to evaluate the community detection performances. The result is evaluated by comparing the cluster label of each node with the label provided by the dataset. First is accuracy (AC), which is used to measure the percentage of correct labels obtained. The second is the normalized mutual information (NMI), to measure how similar two sets of clusters are and takes a value between 0 and 1.

5.3 Results

Experiment is taken in these eight real networks which have node attributes and ground-truth community labels. In the experiment, like the SCI, θ is set as 0.01 in Algorithm 1; for α, β in Algorithm 1, it preforms the search within [0.1, 0.3, 0.5, 0.7, 1, 3, 5, 7, 10], then the highest AC value and its NMI as the final result to output. Algorithm 1 and SCI were repeated 10 times with different random initial matrices, and then averaged to obtain the final result.

Table 2 summarizes the AC and NMI results for community detection. Algorithm 1 outperforms the other methods on six networks completely. In WebKB datasets, as compared to the others, Algorithm 1 achieves 7% improvement in AC and 10% improvement in normalized mutual information. In the olympics dataset, although the AC value of Algorithm 1 is not as good as the value in SCI, it achieves almost 2% improvement in NMI. In the politics-ie and politics-uk datasets, Algorithm 1 achieves better improvement in AC and NMI than SCI.

Table 2. Performance comparison of communities.

Performance	Methods	Cornell	Texas	Washington	Wisconsin	Football	Olympics	Politics-ie	Politics-uk
AC	NMF	0.3672	0.4898	0.4035	0.3664	0.7923	0.7317	0.6848	0.6905
	Spectral	0.4795	0.6037	0.6000	0.4982	0.7629	0.6910	0.6483	0.5568
	CAN	0.4154	0.4706	0.4609	0.4000	0.8226	0.7414	0.6695	0.5990
	RMSC	0.4267	0.5513	0.5952	0.4970	0.8137	0.7325	0.5764	0.5876
	SCI	0.4718	0.6257	0.5087	0.5283	**0.8427**	**0.8082**	**0.8908**	0.8878
	Algorithm 1	**0.6328**	**0.6733**	**0.6509**	**0.5834**	0.8141	0.7821	**0.9052**	**0.9542**
NMI	NMF	0.0622	0.0690	0.0322	0.0500	0.8526	0.8366	0.7351	0.6697
	Spectral	0.1725	0.1951	0.2188	0.1722	0.8185	0.8261	0.6256	0.6215
	CAN	0.0681	0.0443	0.0575	0.0822	0.8124	0.8386	0.6414	0.6754
	RMSC	0.1320	0.1698	0.2204	0.1286	**0.8618**	0.8314	0.6100	0.6402
	SCI	0.1357	0.1687	0.1067	0.1933	**0.8611**	0.8387	0.8239	0.8639
	Algorithm 1	**0.3375**	**0.2896**	**0.3195**	**0.2604**	0.8508	**0.8552**	**0.8494**	**0.8899**

Missing Relations Information Study. However, in real tasks, it is often noticed that some nodes suffer from no relations or attributes information. To simulate this situation, a fraction of nodes are selected randomly to be incomplete examples, which are described only by the attributes or relations view. In the experiment, 5% to 50% of the nodes are selected randomly and their relationship with others is set as 0 in the relation network.

Now, Algorithm 1 is used to integrate relation network and attribute information to detect communities. This process is repeated 10 times and the average results are recorded.

Figures 1 and 2 show the results for the relations network suffering from missing information, on all the datasets. When partial example ratio (PER) is 0%, the dataset actually comes to the traditional multi-view data. Algorithm 1 performs better than single view. As the partial example ratio varies from 5% to 50%, both AC and NMI performances clearly decrease. On the contrary, in WebKB datasets, useful information provided by attributes view can be integrated to help discover the actual underlying structures in networks, so better performance can still be obtained by Algorithm 1.

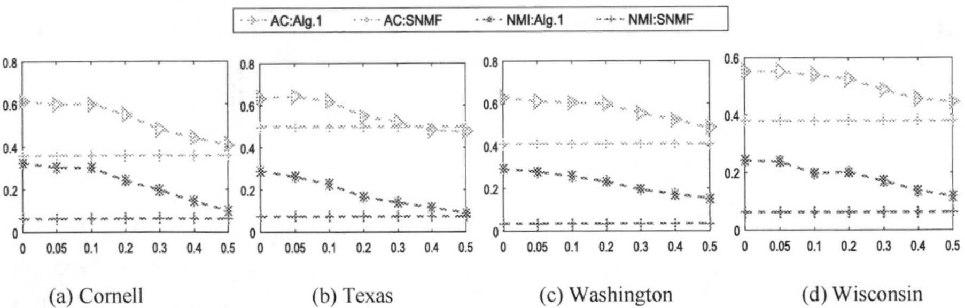

Fig. 1. The results for the WebKB data sets when the relations view misses information (X-axis shows the PER).

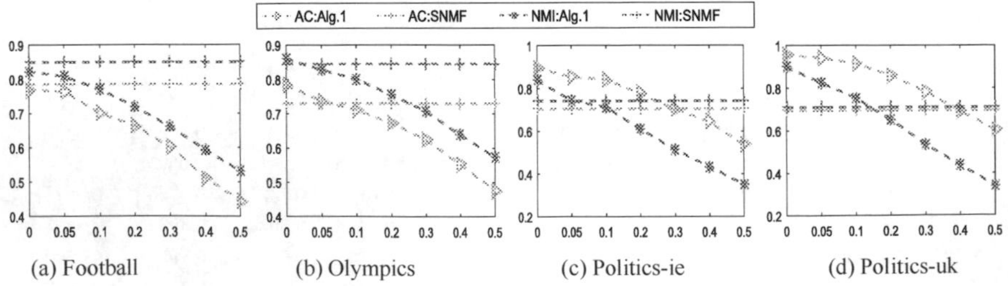

Fig. 2. The results for the Twitter data sets when the relations view misses information (X-axis shows the PER).

In Twitter datasets, when PER is small (such as in politics-ie, PER < 20%, in olympics, PER < 5%), it can still obtain better performance by integrating relations and attributes information. When PER is large, the performances become worse, because missing information of the relation network is more than the useful supplement information from the attributes matrix.

As the same way, in the experiment, 5% to 50% of the nodes are selected randomly and their attributes are set as 0. Figures 3 and 4 show the results of the Algorithm 1. In all datasets, both AC and NMI have better values in the relations view and the performance decreases with PER change. This is because the attributes view provides useful supplement information in Algorithm 1 to detect communities; The more is the information provided, the better is the performance.

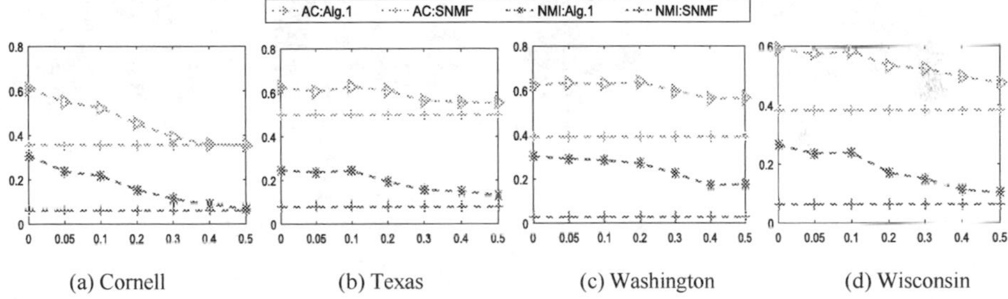

Fig. 3. The results for the WebKB data sets when the attributes view misses information (X-axis shows the PER).

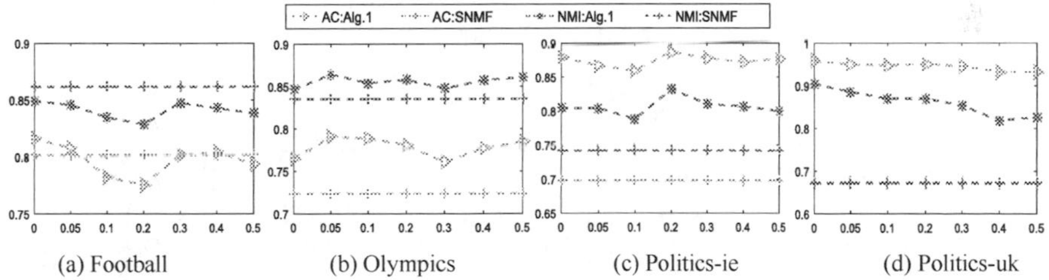

Fig. 4. The results for the Twitter data sets when the attributes view misses information (X-axis shows the PER).

Parameters Study. The effect of parameters α and β on real networks is tested as follow. it varied each parameter within [0.1, 0.3, 0.5, 0.7, 1, 3, 5, 7, 10] when $\theta = 0.01$, as shown in Figs. 5 and 6. β represents the weight of orthonormal constraints between two user cluster matrices. α represents the weight of the pairwise constraint. In WebKB datasets, the performances of Algorithm 1 decreases with varying parameter β. When $0.1 \leq \beta \leq 1$, the performances are relatively stable. When $\beta \geq 1$, the performances clearly decline. In football and olympics datasets, the performances of Algorithm 1 also decreases with β, while in politics-ie and politics-uk datasets, the performances of Algorithm 1 increases with β.

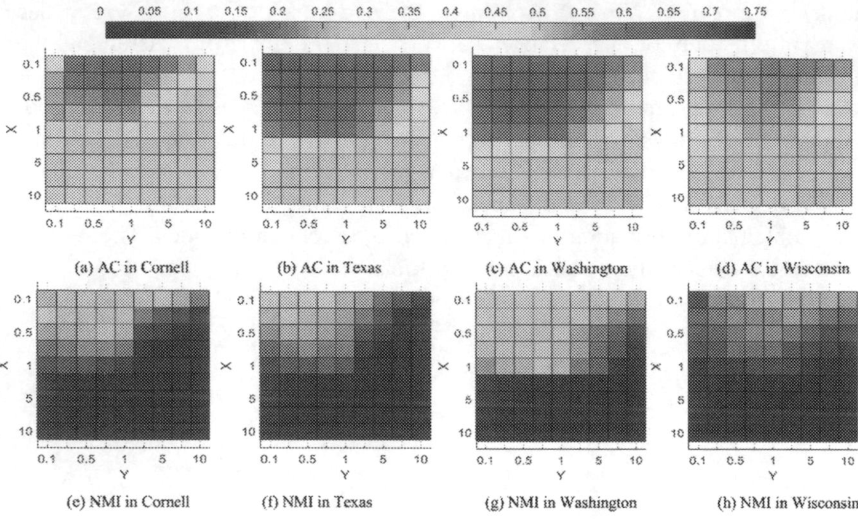

Fig. 5. Evaluating performance of Algorithm 1 with parameters in WebKB (X axis show the β, Y axis show the α)

For parameter α, the performances of Algorithm 1 keep stable roughly when $\alpha \leq 1$. When $\alpha \geq 1$, in politics-ie and politics-uk datasets, the performances increase first and then decrease. In other datasets, the performances decrease with α. As Algorithm 1 is significantly affected by parameters α and β, it suggests that parameters can be set between 0.1 and 10 to achieve a high performance.

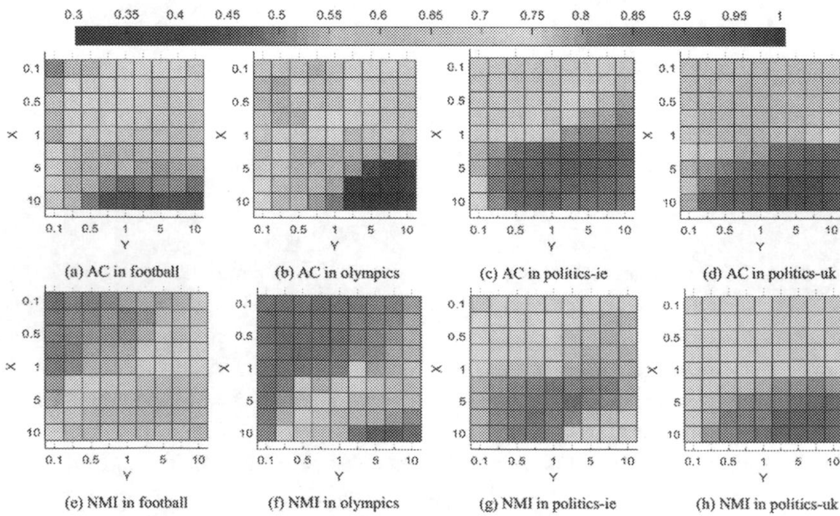

Fig. 6. Evaluating performance of Algorithm 1 with parameters in Twitter (X axis show the β, Y axis show the α)

6 Conclusions

A novel community identification method is proposed to split members into communities correctly by integrating relation and attribute information. The key idea is to adequately integrate two different types of views with the pairwise constraint and orthonormal constraint regularizations between different user cluster matrices. The salient property of the algorithm is its ability to make the user cluster matrices complement each other even with the presence of erroneous noise and missing relationships in a network. The experimental results from real networks demonstrated the superior performance of the algorithm in accurately detecting community structures. For future work, it is important to design a strong initialization method to improve the effectiveness, and to extend this method to integrate different types of information to networks with more relation and attribute information views.

Acknowledgements. This work was supported by the National High Technology Research and Development Program of 2016YFB0100903 and the Beijing Municipal Science and Technology Commission Special Major (D171100005017002, D171100005117002) and the National Natural Science Foundation of China (U1664263).

References

1. Yang, L., Jin, D., He, D., Fu, H., Cao, X., Fogelman-Soulie, F.: Improving the efficiency and effectiveness of community detection via prior-induced equivalent super-network. Sci. Rep. **7**, 634 (2017)
2. Porter, M.A., Onnela, J.P., Mucha, P.J.: Communities in networks. Not. AMS **56**, 4294–4303 (2009)
3. Tang, J., Chang, S., Aggarwal, C., Liu, H.: Negative link prediction in social media, pp. 87–96 (2014)
4. Tang, J., Aggarwal, C., Liu, H.: Recommendations in signed social networks. In: the 25th International World Wide Web Conference, pp. 31–40 (2016)
5. Cecile, B., David, C.J., Matteo, M., Barbora, M.: Clustering attributed graphs: models, measures and methods. Netw. Sci. **3**, 408–444 (2015)
6. Liu, X., Wang, W., He, D., Jiao, P., Jin, D., Cannistraci, C.V.: Semi-supervised community detection based on non-negative matrix factorization with node popularity. Inf. Sci. **381**, 304–321 (2017)
7. Greene, D.: Producing a unified graph representation from multiple social network views. In: the 5th Annual ACM Web Science Conference, pp. 118–121. ACM (2013)
8. Fang, Y., Cheng, R., Luo, S., Hu, J.: Effective community search for large attributed graphs. Proc. VLDB Endow. **9**, 1233–1244 (2016)
9. Pei, Y., Chakraborty, N., Sycara, K.: Nonnegative matrix tri-factorization with graph regularization for community detection in social networks. In: International Conference on Artificial Intelligence, pp. 2083–2089 (2015)
10. Yang, J., Mcauley, J., Leskovec, J.: Community detection in networks with node attributes, pp. 1151–1156 (2014)
11. Huang, X., Cheng, H., Yu, J.X.: Dense community detection in multi-valued attributed networks. Inf. Sci. **314**, 77–99 (2015)

12. Xu, Z., Ke, Y., Wang, Y., Cheng, H., Cheng, J.: A model-based approach to attributed graph clustering. In: The 2012 ACM SIGMOD International Conference on Management of Data, pp. 505–516. ACM (2012)
13. Palchykov, V., Gemmetto, V., Boyarsky, A., Garlaschelli, D.: Ground truth? Concept-based communities versus the external classification of physics manuscripts. EPJ Data Sci. **5**, 28 (2016)
14. Peng, C., Kang, Z., Cheng, Q.: Integrating feature and graph learning with low-rank representation. Neurocomputing **249**, 106–116 (2017)
15. Li, S.Y., Jiang, Y., Zhou, Z.H.: Partial multi-view clustering. In: AAAI Conference on Artificial Intelligence (AAAI 2014) (2014)
16. Shao, W., He, L., Yu, P.S.: Multiple incomplete views clustering via weighted nonnegative matrix factorization with $L_{2,1}$ regularization. In: Appice, A., Rodrigues, P.P., Santos Costa, V., Soares, C., Gama, J., Jorge, A. (eds.) ECML PKDD 2015. LNCS (LNAI), vol. 9284, pp. 318–334. Springer, Cham (2015). https://doi.org/10.1007/978-3-319-23528-8_20
17. Xiang, J., et al.: Enhancing community detection by local structural information. **2016**, 33–45 (2016)
18. Cai, D., He, X., Han, J., Huang, T.S.: Graph regularized nonnegative matrix factorization for data representation. IEEE Trans. Pattern Anal. Mach. Intell. **33**, 1548–1560 (2011)
19. Lee, K., Caverlee, J., Cheng, Z., Sui, D.Z.: Campaign extraction from social media. ACM Trans. Intell. Syst. Technol. **5**, 1–28 (2014)
20. Xie, J., Kelley, S., Szymanski, B.K.: Overlapping community detection in networks: The state-of-the-art and comparative study. ACM Comput. Surv. **45**, 1–35 (2011)
21. Wang, F., Li, T., Wang, X., Zhu, S., Ding, C.: Community discovery using nonnegative matrix factorization. Data Min. Knowl. Disc. **22**, 493–521 (2011)
22. Wu, W., Kwong, S., Zhou, Y., Jia, Y., Gao, W.: Nonnegative matrix factorization with mixed hypergraph regularization for community detection. Inf. Sci. **435**, 263–281 (2018)
23. Masuda, N., Porter, M.A., Lambiotte, R.: Random walks and diffusion on networks. Physics reports (2017)
24. Qin, X., Dai, W., Jiao, P., Wang, W., Ning, Y.: A multi-similarity spectral clustering method for community detection in dynamic networks. Sci. Rep. **6**, 31–54 (2016)
25. Lee, D.D., Seung, H.S.: Algorithms for non-negative matrix factorization. In: Advances in Neural Information Processing Systems 13, NIPS, pp. 556–562 (2000)
26. Liu, X., Wei, Y.M., Wang, J., Wang, W.J., He, D.X., Song, Z.J.: Community detection enhancement using non-negative matrix factorization with graph regularization. Int. J. Mod. Phys. B **30**, 130 (2016)
27. Ma, X., Sun, P., Qin, G.: Nonnegative matrix factorization algorithms for link prediction in temporal networks using graph communicability (2017)
28. Ozer, M., Kim, N., Davulcu, H.: Community detection in political Twitter networks using Nonnegative Matrix Factorization methods. In: IEEE/ACM International Conference on Advances in Social Networks Analysis and Mining, pp. 81–88 (2016)
29. Jin, D., Chen, Z., He, D., Zhang, W.: Modeling with node degree preservation can accurately find communities. New Media Soc. **18**, 1293–1309 (2016)
30. Wang, X., Jin, D., Cao, X., Yang, L., Zhang, W.: Semantic community identification in large attribute networks. In: Thirtieth AAAI Conference on Artificial Intelligence, pp. 265–271 (2016)
31. Whang, J.J., Gleich, D.F., Dhillon, I.S.: Overlapping community detection using neighborhood-inflated seed expansion. **28**, 1272–1284 (2015)
32. Bai, L., Cheng, X., Liang, J., Guo, Y.: Fast graph clustering with a new description model for community detection. Inf. Sci. **388**, 37–47 (2017)

33. Nie, F., Wang, X., Huang, H.: Clustering and projected clustering with adaptive neighbors. In: The 20th ACM SIGKDD International Conference on Knowledge Discovery and Data Mining, pp. 977–986. ACM (2014)
34. Chen, Y., Rege, M., Dong, M., Hua, J.: Non-negative matrix factorization for semi-supervised data clustering. Knowl. Inf. Syst. **17**, 355–379 (2008)
35. Xia, R., Pan, Y., Du, L., Yin, J.: Robust multi-view spectral clustering via low-rank and sparse decomposition. In: The 28th AAAI Conference on Artificial Intelligence, pp. 2149–2155 (2014)

Two-Step Multi-factor Attention Neural Network for Answer Selection

Pengqing Zhang, Yuexian Hou(✉), Zhan Su, and Yi Su

School of Computer Science and Techonology, Tianjin University, Tianjin, China
{zhangpq,yxhou,suzhan,suyi2016}@tju.edu.cn

Abstract. Attention-based neural network models recently proposed have achieved great success in question answering task. They focus on introducing the interaction information in sentence modeling rather than representing the question and the answer individually. However, there are some limitations of the previous work. First, in the interaction layer, most attention mechanisms do not make full use of the diverse semantic information of the question. Second, they have limited capability to construct interaction from multiple aspects. In this paper, to address these two limitations, we propose a two-step multi-factor attention neural network model. The two-step strategy encodes the question into different representations according to separate words in the answer, and these representations are employed to build dynamic-question-aware attention. Additionally, a multi-factor mechanism is introduced to extract various interaction information, which aims at aggregating meaningful facts distributed in different matching results. The experimental results on three traditional QA datasets show that our model outperforms various state-of-the-art systems.

Keywords: Answer selection · Neural network · Two-step attention
Multi-factor attention

1 Introduction

Answer selection (AS) is a crucial sub-task of the open domain question answering (QA) problem. Given a question, it aims to select the correct answers from a set of candidate sentences [1]. Each of the sentences is mapped to a representation, and a model is designed to predict the relationship between the question and the answer. Traditional models use lexical features such as Bag-of-Word (BOW) to model sentences. Hand-craft features design and selection are time-consuming and high dimension features may suffer from sparsity. Recently, neural network based approaches have been proposed and shown advantages in QA task [2,3]. The meaning of a sentence is represented in a vector space through a neural encoder such as convolutional neural network (CNN) [4–6] or long short-term memory (LSTM) [7]. A disadvantage of such models is that there is no explicit interaction between the question and answer during the encoding process, which may ignore some important information.

X. Geng and B.-H. Kang (Eds.): PRICAI 2018, LNAI 11012, pp. 658–670, 2018.
https://doi.org/10.1007/978-3-319-97304-3_50

To deal with this problem some work introduced attention mechanisms into sentence modeling. This strategy enables the information from the two input sentences (question and answer) can directly influence the computation of each other's representations [2,8]. For examples, Rocktaschel et al. [8] and Wang and Liu [2] constructed sentence level attention, in which each time-step hidden representation of a sentence is weighted by the attention caused by the other sentence. To grasp the fine-grained information, He and Lin [9] proposed word by word matching approaches which employ words representations to compute a matching matrix and adopt multiple convolution or recurrent layers to integrate the matching results. Aforementioned approaches built interaction in a single granular (word by word or sentence by sentence). Wang and Hamza [10] proposed a multi-perspective matching model to leverage multi-granular attention.

However, most attention approaches did not put more emphasis on utilizing flexible question representations to build question-aware attention. For examples, Wang and Liu [2] converted the question into a single vector regardless different answer words. Shen et al. [11] used each hidden state of the question to calculate the matching scores of the answer. These simple strategies ignore the fact that a question should be represented differently according to the different focuses of various answer words. Taking follow sentence as an example:

Question: How much is 1 tablespoon of the water?
Answer: The tablespoon has a capacity of about 15 ml.

We can see that the question has two key points: *how much* and *tablespoon*. Different answer words focus on different parts of the question, such as the phrase *tablespoon* in the answer is associated with the *tablespoon* in the question, *capacity* and *15ml* are related with *how much*. Thus, we should generate different semantic representations of the question and using these representations to calculate the attention weights of the words in the answer. Moreover, few attention based models extract interaction between sentence pairs from multiple aspects. We argue that building the attention from a single perspective is not easy to express the entire matching information between the sentence pairs.

In this paper, to tackle these problems, we propose a two-step multi-factor attention based neural network model. Two-step attention mechanism builds dynamic-question-aware attention by combining the bi-directional influence between question and answer to account for the attention, which consists of two components: the answer-towards-question attention and question-towards-answer attention. The former induces a series of flexible question representations and utilizing these representations to help the latter build dynamic-question-towards-answer attention. In order to obtain attention from multiple aspects, we exploit tensor-based transformation to integrate different aspects of matching results which are caused by different factors. This strategy merges the meaningful facts in a question-answer pair and helps the two-step attention strategy to represent answer precisely.

In general, the key contributions of this paper are:

- We propose a two-step attention strategy to construct dynamic-question-aware attention. The flexible question representations are learned in the first

step attention process and using these representations to establish the second step attention.
- We propose a multi-factor attention strategy to retain rich matching information for a question-answer pair.
- Experimental results on three QA datasets: WikiQA, TrecQA and YahooCQA evaluate the effectiveness of our two-step multi-factor attention neural network.

2 Two-Step Multi-factor Attention Model

In this section, we introduce the two-step multi-factor attention model. First, we use a bi-directional recurrent network [12] to build contextual representations of the words in the question and the answer (Sect. 2.1). Then, we propose the two-step multi-factor attention method, which takes these hidden representations as the input to get a semantic vector of the sentence (Sect. 2.2). At last, the semantic vectors of the question and the answer are used to compute a similarity score to determine their relationship (Sect. 2.3).

2.1 Question and Answer Encoder Layer

Consider a question Q and a candidate answer A, we convert the words to their respective word-level embeddings $e^q = (e^q_1, ..., e^q_n)$ and $e^a = (e^a_1, ..., e^a_m)$ where e^q_t is the embedding of the i-th word in the sentence Q, n and m denotes the length of Q and A respectively. To encode contextual embeddings, we use a bi-directional recurrent neural network (RNN) to build hidden representations of the words in the question and answer:

$$\overrightarrow{h}^q_t = \overrightarrow{\mathrm{RNN}}(h^q_{t-1}, e^q_t) \qquad t = 1, ..., n \tag{1}$$

$$\overleftarrow{h}^q_t = \overleftarrow{\mathrm{RNN}}(h^q_{t+1}, e^q_t) \qquad t = n, ..., 1 \tag{2}$$

$$\overrightarrow{h}^a_t = \overrightarrow{\mathrm{RNN}}(h^a_{t-1}, e^a_t) \qquad t = 1, ..., m \tag{3}$$

$$\overleftarrow{h}^a_t = \overleftarrow{\mathrm{RNN}}(h^a_{t+1}, e^a_t) \qquad t = m, ..., 1 \tag{4}$$

The forward and backward hidden states of each word are concatenated into a vector $h^q_t = [\overrightarrow{h}^q_t; \overleftarrow{h}^q_t], h^a_t = [\overrightarrow{h}^a_t, \overleftarrow{h}^a_t]$, where $h^a_t, h^q_t \in \mathbb{R}^{2d}$. Gated Recurrent Unit (GRU) [13] is adopted as recurrent unit implementation in our experiments since it performs similarly to LSTM [14] but is computationally cheaper.

2.2 Attention Layer

One-Step Attention. The attention-based models introduce the attention information into the representation of the sentence. Traditional approaches take

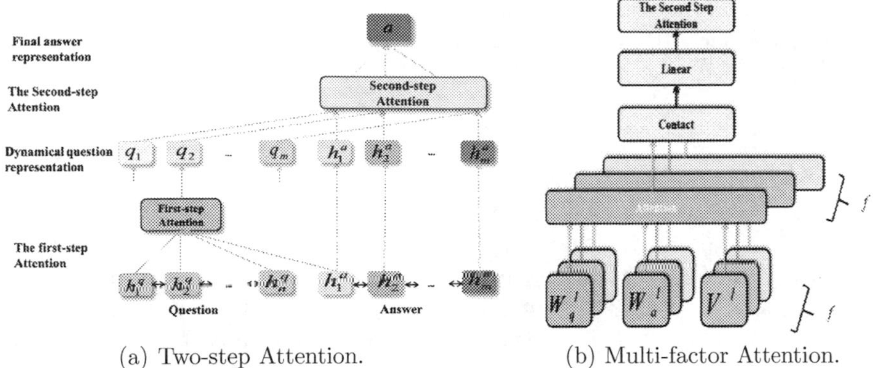

(a) Two-step Attention. (b) Multi-factor Attention.

Fig. 1. A two-step multi-factor attention model. (a) Consists of two parts: the first-step attention and the second-step attention, where q_i denotes the dynamic question representations, a denotes the final semantic vector of the answer. In (b) f denotes the number of factors in multi-attention layer.

a fixed question vector as the input of interaction layer and apply an unidirectional attention (question-towards-answer) to influence the representation of the answer. We denote it as one-step attention.

$$s_i^o = V^{o\top} \tanh(W_q^o \overline{q} + W_a^o h_i^a) \tag{5}$$

$$\tilde{s}_i^o = \frac{\exp(s_i^o)}{\sum_{k=1}^{m} \exp(s_k^o)} \tag{6}$$

where $\tilde{s}_i^o$ denotes the attention weight of the i-th word in the answer. $\overline{q}$ is an average over all hidden states, $\overline{q} = \frac{1}{n}\sum_{i=1}^{n} h_i^q$. $V \in \mathbb{R}^{2d}$, $W_q^o, W_a^o \in \mathbb{R}^{2d\times 2d}$ are trainable parameters. Obviously, for different answer words, one-step attention method employs a unitary representation $\overline{q}$ of the question to establish question-aware attention. These attention weights are employed to calculate a semantic vector to represent the answer:

$$a = \sum_{i=1}^{m} \tilde{s}_i^o h_i^a \tag{7}$$

Two-Step Attention. Different from traditional attention models, we use diverse semantic representations of the question to calculate the attention weights of the words in the answer. Concretely, the two-step attention model consists of two parts: (the first-step attention) each word in the answer focuses on different words in the question and resulting in a series of dynamic question representations. (The second-step attention) The flexible representations are employed to calculate the weights for the corresponding words in the answer. Figure 1(a) gives an overview of the two-step attention model.

First, when we read each word in an answer, we will reread the question to find out which part of the question should be more focused. We measure the importance score for different words in question by computing the similarity between each question word representation h_i^q and answer word representation h_j^a.

$$m_{ij} = \tanh(h_i^{a\top} U h_j^q) \tag{8}$$

$$\tilde{m}_{ij} = \frac{\exp(m_{ij})}{\sum_{k=1}^{n} \exp(m_{ik})} \tag{9}$$

where $\tilde{m}_{ij}$ denotes the weight from the i-th word in the answer to the j-th word in the question. $U \in \mathbb{R}^{2d \times 2d}$ is randomly initialized and updated during training. According to a specific word in the answer, we employ the attention weights to calculate a weighted sum of hidden states $\{h_i^q\}_{i=1}^n$, producing one representation of the question.

$$q_i = \sum_{k=1}^{n} \tilde{m}_{ik} h_k^q \tag{10}$$

A series of dynamic representations $q_1, ..., q_m$ can be generated according to different words $h_1^a, ..., h_m^a$ in the answer.

Second, we introduce diverse representations of the question to construct dynamic-question-towards-answer attention. The weight of each word in the answer is calculated based on its corresponding question representation.

$$s_i = V^\top \tanh(W_q \mathbf{q_i} + W_a \mathbf{h_i^a}) \tag{11}$$

$$\tilde{s}_i = \frac{\exp(s_i)}{\sum_{k=1}^{m} \exp(s_k)} \tag{12}$$

here q_i is the dynamic representation produced according to the answer word h_i^a. $\tilde{s}_i$ denotes the attention weight of q_i towards h_i^a, indicating which words in the answer should be more focused. $W_q, W_a \in \mathbb{R}^{2d \times 2d}$ and $V \in \mathbb{R}^{2d \times 1}$ are all randomly initialized and updated during training.

We first handle the attention from the answer to the question and resulting in different question representations, then taking these representations as the input of the second step attention layer which processes attention in the verse order. Bi-directional attention is both used for computing the importance of each word in the answer. At last these scores are employed to calculate the answer vector.

$$a = \sum_{i=1}^{m} \tilde{s}_i h_i^a \tag{13}$$

Multi-Factor Attention. We adopt tensor-based transformation function [15, 16] to build multi-factor attention which integrates rich matching results caused by different factors and helps the two-step attention to represent the answer precisely. Figure 1(b) gives an overview of the multi-factor model.

Let $\{q_i\}_{i=1}^m$ denotes the dynamic question representations generated by the first-step attention layer. Tensor-based transformation for multi-factor attention is used to calculate the answer's attention weights in the second-step attention layer.

$$s_i^f = V^{[1:f]\top} \tanh(W_q^{[1:f]} q_i + W_a^{[1:f]} h_i^a) \tag{14}$$

Here f is the number of factors, $W_q^{[1:f]}, W_a^{[1:f]} \in \mathbb{R}^{f \times 2d \times 2d}$, $V^{[1:f]} \in \mathbb{R}^{f \times 2d \times 1}$, $V^{[1:f]\top} \in \mathbb{R}^{f \times 1 \times 2d}$. Where the output attention weight $s_i^f \in \mathbb{R}^f$ is a vector with the dimension of f where each element $s_{i,l}^f$ is calculated according to the corresponding parameter matrix $W_q^{[l]}, W_a^{[l]} \in \mathbb{R}^{2d \times 2d}$, $V^{[l]} \in \mathbb{R}^{2d}$.

$$s_{i,l}^f = V^{[l]\top} \tanh(W_q^{[l]} q_i + W_a^{[l]} h_i^a) \tag{15}$$

We perform a weighted sum of all elements to obtain the resulting attention weight.

$$s_i = w^\top s_i^f \tag{16}$$

$$\tilde{s}_i = \frac{\exp(s_i)}{\sum_{k=1}^{m} \exp(s_k)} \tag{17}$$

here $\tilde{s}_i$ represents the final attention of the i-th word in the answer. $w \in \mathbb{R}^f$ is a trainable vector. The answer representation is computed as follow:

$$a = \sum_{i=1}^{m} \tilde{s}_i h_k^a \tag{18}$$

2.3 Loss Function

We use cosine similarity to measure the score between the representation of the question and the answer. And we adopt max-margin hinge loss as the objective function:

$$L = max\{0, M - cosine(\overline{q}, a_+) + cosine(\overline{q}, a_-)\} \tag{19}$$

where $\overline{q}$ is calculated by averagely pooling all the bi-GRU hidden states. a_+ denotes the positive candidate answer, a_- denotes the negative one, the scalar M is the predefined margin.

3 Experiments

In this section we evaluate our model on three QA datasets. The statics of datasets summarizes in Table 1.

3.1 Datasets

WikiQA [17] is a recently released open-domain questioning answer dataset in which all answers are collected from Wikipedia. We follow recent work [2,5,11] to remove all questions with no correct candidate answers.

Table 1. Statistics of datasets

	TrecQA			WikiQA			YahooCQA		
	TRAIN	DEV	TEST	TRAIN	DEV	TEST	TRAIN	DEV	TEST
Question	1227	82	100	873	126	243	56432	7082	7092
Pairs	53417	1148	1517	8672	1130	2351	287015	35880	35880
Correct	12.0%	19.3%	18.7%	12.0%	12.4%	12.5%	20%	20%	20%

TrecQA [18] was created by Wang et al. based on Text REtrieval Conference (TREC) QA track (8–13) data. The dataset contains two training sets: TRAIN and TRAIN-ALL. To verify the robustness of our model, we use TRAIN-ALL dataset which is larger and contains more noise. We remove the questions with only positive or negative answers.

YahooCQA is a benchmark dataset for community-based question answering. There are 142627 questions and answers in YahooCQA in which the answers are generally longer than those in TrecQA and WikiQA. We select the sentence pairs containing questions and the best answers of length 5–50 tokens after removing non-alphanumeric characters. For each question, we construct negative examples by randomly sampling 4 answers from the set of answer sentences.

3.2 Model Comparison

To check the effectiveness of our proposed attention approaches, we build four variations of the model: (1) one-step one-factor attention model; (2) two-step one-factor attention model; (3) one-step multi-factor attention model; (4) two-step multi-factor attention model. The other deep learning baseline models for comparison are as follows:

WikiQA:

- Attentive pooling CNN model (AP-CNN) by Santos et al. [5]. APCNN builds a sentence level attention based on hidden representations.
- Inner attention based RNN model (IARNN) by Wang and Liu [2]. The attention information is added before hidden states.
- A pairwise word interaction model (PWIM) by He and Lin [9] which captures fine-grained alignment.
- A bilateral multi-perspective matching model (BiMPM) by Wang and Hamza [10]. Multiple granular matching results are leveraged in BiMPM.
- An inter-weighted alignment model (IWAN) by Shen and Yang [11] which utilizes an inter-weighted layer to measure the importance for each word.

TrecQA: The baselines of TrecQA is similar to WikiQA. Additionally, we compare our model with the attention over attention model (AoA) (2016) [19] which introduces attended attention into representation procedure.

Table 2. Experimental results on the WikiQA

Models	MAP	MRR
AP-CNN (2016) [5]	0.688	0.695
INRNN (2016)	0.734	0.741
PWIM (2016) [9]	0.709	0.724
BiMPM (2017) [10]	0.718	0.731
IWAN (2017) [11]	0.733	0.750
One-step one-factor attention	0.713	0.723
Two-step one-factor attention	0.736	0.747
One-step multi-factor attention	**0.745**	**0.758**
Two-step multi-factor attention	<u>0.739</u>	<u>0.751</u>

YahooCQA: Three more baseline models are adopted on YahooCQA: IARNN-WORD (2016) [2] and AoA [19] and Holographic (HD-LSTM) (2017) [3] which builds the relationship between two sentences with holographic composition. We implemented IARNN-WORD model and AoA model on YahooCQA dataset.

3.3 Experimental Settings

We initialize word embeddings with 300-dimensional GloVe word vectors pre-trained from the 840B Common Crawl corpus [20]. For out of vocabulary (OOV) words, their embeddings are initialized randomly. During training, we do not update the pre-trained words embeddings. The GRU hidden size is set to 100 over WikiQA and TrecQA, and on YohooQA dataset the hidden variable's length is set to 150. AdamOptimizer is used for updating parameters with a learning rate of 0.005. The minibatch size is always 64. We add L2 penalty to train the model. The L2 regularization strength varies among $\{e^{-6}, e^{-5}\}$. Max-margin hinge loss is adopted as the training objective function. In all experiments, margin M is set to 0.05. We report the results in terms of mean average precision (MAP) and mean reciprocal rank (MRR) in WikiQA and TrecQA. Following Tay et al. [3] to use Precision@1 (P@1) and MRR as evaluation metrics in YahooCQA. Bi-GRU is adopted as recurrent unit implementation in all models and we share the GRU parameters between question and answer.

3.4 Experimental Results and Analysis

In this section, we present our empirical results and analysis on all datasets. For all reported results, the best result is in boldface and the second best is underlined. The model marked with $*$ indicates we implemented the model ourselves.

Experiments on WikiQA Dataset. The factor number of two-step multi-factor and one-step multi-factor attention model are set to 2 and 3 respectively.

Table 3. Experimental results on the TrecQA.

Models	MAP	MRR
IARNN (2016) [2]	0.709	0.775
AoA (2016)* [19]	0.739	0.840
PWIM (2016) [9]	0.738	0.827
BiMPM (2017) [10]	0.802	0.875
IWAN (2017) [11]	**0.822**	**0.889**
One-step one-factor attention	0.732	0.833
Two-step one-factor attention	0.792	<u>0.881</u>
One-step multi-factor attention	<u>0.805</u>	0.876
Two-step multi-factor attention	0.781	0.867

Table 2 reports the experimental results. First, we can see that two-step attention models outperforms one-step models by 2% on MAP and MRR. For one-step attention models, the multi-factor model outperforms one-factor model by 3%. It indicates the effectiveness of the two-step and multi-factor attention approaches.

Then, compared with recent deep learning models our multi-factor attention models achieve the best performance and arrive in the state-of-the-art result. Previous sentence level attention models built attention over hidden representations, such as AP-CNN. To avoid attention bias problem, INRNN model [2] added attention before hidden states and work significantly better than AP-CNN. PWIM (2016) [9] constructed 19-layer CNN to capture fine-grained interaction. IWAN (2017) [11] utilized much fewer parameters to build word level attention. As shown in Table 2 fine-grained attention model works better than coarse-grained attention model. Wang and Hamza propose BiMPM (2017) [10] to integrate multiple granular (word level and sentence level) matching results and achieve the state-of-the-art performance on many tasks. Our two-step attention models benefit from leveraging diverse semantic representations of the sentence and getting a better performance comparing with these deep learning models. Furthermore, due to integrating various aspects of attention, the multi-factor attention model achieves the best performance.

Experiments on TrecQA Dataset. The factors number of all multi-factor models are set to 3. Table 3 shows the experimental results on TrecQA. First, we can see that the two-step attention models and multi-factor models work better than the one-step models and one-factor models respectively. Then, compared to several state-of-the-art models, we obtain a clear performance gain of 0.05-0.07 in terms of MRR/MAP against models such as PWIM (2016) [9]. Attention over Attention (AoA) (2016) [19] model builds attended attention to produce final sentence representation. However, it neglects dynamic interaction between sentences pair. Our two-step attention models solve this problem and outperform it in all metrics. The BiMPM (2017) [10] and IWAN (2017) [11] achieve the state-of-the-art performances on many tasks. The manifestation from our model is on par with the two models. Therefore, our model is effective on TrecQA dataset.

Table 4. Experimental results on the YahooCQA.

Models	P@1	MRR
IARNN-WORD (2016)* [2]	0.604	0.762
AoA (2016)* [19]	0.601	0.761
HD-LSTM (2017) [3]	0.557	0.735
One-step one-factor attention	0.609	0.763
Two-step one-factor attention	**0.622**	**0.774**
Two-step multi-factor attention	<u>0.621</u>	**0.774**

Experiments on YahooCQA Dataset. We set the factor number of all multi-factor model to 3. As shown in Table 4, the two-step attention models outperform one-step one-factor attention model almost 2% on P@1 and 1% on MRR. Our model achieves the best performance comparing to other baseline models. Concretely, the two-step attention models significantly outperform the CNN or RNN-based sentence models which apply inflexible interaction information. The experimental results on YahooCQA further demonstrate the effectiveness of our two-step multi-factor attention model.

4 Model Properties

To demonstrate the properties of our model we conduct further experiments on WikiQA dataset.

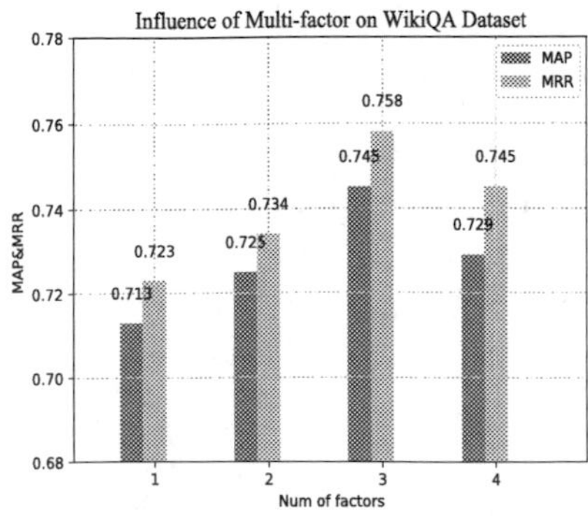

Fig. 2. Influence of multi-factor

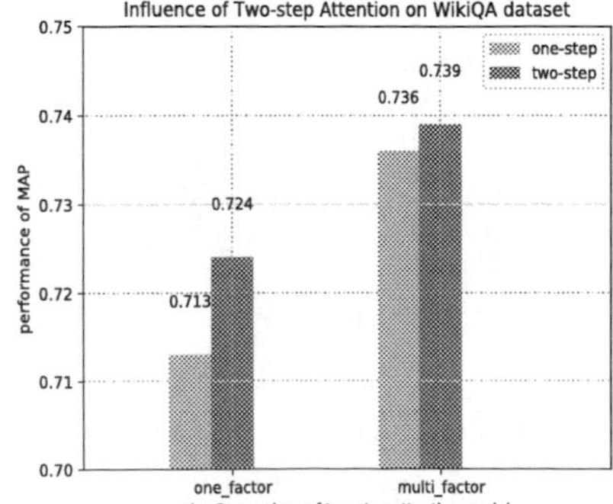

Fig. 3. Influence of two-step attention

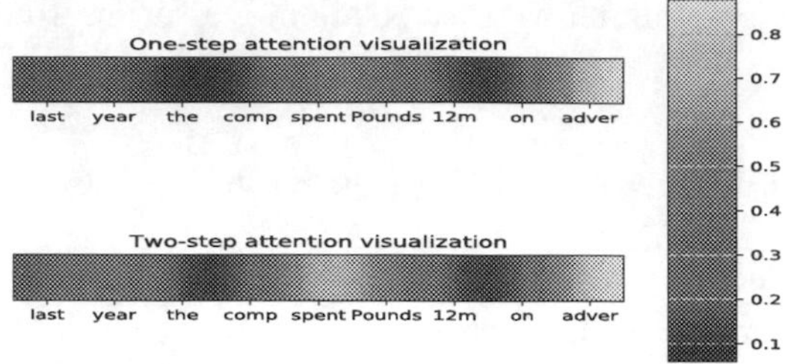

Fig. 4. Attention comparison between two-step and one-step. In the right of the figure, the number corresponding to different colors indicates the attention weights.

First, we study the influence of multi-factor attention strategy. In Fig. 2, we show the results of one-step attention model with different number of factors which varies among $\{1, 2, 3, 4\}$. We observe that when f is in $\{1, 2, 3\}$ increasing the number of factors leads to better performances. It verifies the advantages of leveraging rich information. However, the model with four-factor does not work better than the three-factor one. The four-factor models may extract some redundant information and result in over-fitting, while its performance is still significantly improved compared with the one-factor and two-factor models. Therefore, the number of factors plays a crucial role in the performance of the model. In practice, applying the proper factors often leads to better performance.

Second, we study the influence of two-step attention strategy. As shown in Fig. 3 the two-step attention model outperforms the one-step attention model with the same number of factors. When the number of factors is set to 1, two-step attention model improves the performance about 1% in MAP over one-step one. The models with multiple factors work better than one-factor models, where the two-step attention model achieve the best performance.

At last, we show attention visualization comparison between two-step and one-step strategies in Fig. 4. Given a question *How much did Mercury spend on advertising in 1993?*, we select a correct answer *last year the company spent Pounds 12 m on advertising.* Attention layer extracts the matching information and computes a score for each word in the answer. The scores of the words that matched with the question should be high. As shown in Fig. 4, one-step and two-step attention models both identify the phrase *advertising* which is the matching word in the question and the answer. Meanwhile, the two-step attention realizes the correlation between *pounds* and *how much* and gives a high weight to *pounds.* It indicates that the two-step attention strategy extracts matching information more effectively than one-step attention model.

5 Related Work

Many neural ranking models have been applied to QA tasks. There are two key ingredients to these models: an effective neural encoder and an attention layer. CNN and RNN are both widely used for sentence model. CNN extracts and combines important local contextual informations meanwhile builds sentences in a hierarchical way [4,5,16]. RNN models a sentence sequentially by updating the hidden state, which is more capable of exploiting the long-distance dependency [2,3,7]. Severyn and Moschitti [4] utilizes a multi-layered perception (MLP) to combine sentence representations of the question and answer.

The key difference among neural ranking models depends on the interaction layer. Hermann et al. [21] first applied attention mechanism into QA under an RNN architecture. Attentive pooling network leveraged the pooling layer to capture the interaction over hidden states and applying in both CNN and RNN [5]. Qiu et al. proposed a tensor network architecture to build attention with a tensor layer [16]. To solve the attention bias problem, inner attention mechanism fed the word embeddings into the attention layer to adjust the representation of each word [2]. We also employ an attention layer to influence the representation of the sentence. Different from previous work using a fixed representation of the sentence we exploit flexible representations to build dynamic-question aware attention. Meanwhile, different factors are utilized to build multi-interaction of sentence pairs in our model.

6 Conclusion

In this work, we focus on how to effectively formulate the interaction information between the sentence pairs. First, we consider the impact of the diverse representations of the question and propose a two-step attention model. Specifically, we feed the flexible question representations to the interaction layer and build dynamic-question-aware attention. Second, we explore the effect of various interaction information. The multi-factor attention strategy is introduced to compute attention from different aspects, which is helpful for catching meaningful matching information between the question and the answer. Experimental results on three answer selection datasets show that our model achieves the better performance compared to several state-of-art models.

Acknowledgements. This work is funded in part by the National Key R&D Program of China (2017YFE0111900), the Key Project of Tianjin Natural Science Foundation (15JCZDJC31100), the National Natural Science Foundation of China (Key Program, U1636203), the National Natural Science Foundation of China (U1736103) and MSCA-ITN-ETN - European Training Networks Project (QUARTZ).

References

1. Yao, X., Van Durme, B., Callison-Burch, C., Clark, P.: Answer extraction as sequence tagging with tree edit distance. In: HLT-NAACL, pp. 858–867 (2013)
2. Wang, B., Liu, K., Zhao, J.: Inner attention based recurrent neural networks for answer selection. In: ACL, vol. 1 (2016)
3. Tay, Y., Phan, M.C., Tuan, L.A., Hui, S.C.: Learning to rank question answer pairs with holographic dual LSTM architecture. arXiv preprint arXiv:1707.06372 (2017)

4. Severyn, A., Moschitti, A.: Learning to rank short text pairs with convolutional deep neural networks. In: Proceedings of the 38th International ACM SIGIR Conference on Research and Development in Information Retrieval, pp. 373–382. ACM (2015)
5. dos Santos, C.N., Tan, M., Xiang, B., Zhou, B.: Attentive pooling networks. CoRR, abs/1602.03609, vol. 2, no. 3, p. 4 (2016)
6. Yang, L., Ai, Q., Guo, J., Croft, W.B.: aNMM: ranking short answer texts with attention-based neural matching model. In: Proceedings of the 25th ACM International on Conference on Information and Knowledge Management, pp. 287–296. ACM (2016)
7. Tan, M., Santos, C., Xiang, B., Zhou, B.: LSTM-based deep learning models for non-factoid answer selection. arXiv preprint arXiv:1511.04108 (2015)
8. Rocktäschel, T., Grefenstette, E., Hermann, K.M., Kočiskỳ, T., Blunsom, P.: Reasoning about entailment with neural attention. arXiv preprint arXiv:1509.06664 (2015)
9. He, H., Lin, J.: Pairwise word interaction modeling with deep neural networks for semantic similarity measurement. In: Proceedings of the 2016 Conference of the North American Chapter of the Association for Computational Linguistics: Human Language Technologies, pp. 937–948 (2016)
10. Wang, Z., Hamza, W., Florian, R.: Bilateral multi-perspective matching for natural language sentences. arXiv preprint arXiv:1702.03814 (2017)
11. Shen, G., Yang, Y., Deng, Z.H.: Inter-weighted alignment network for sentence pair modeling. In: Proceedings of the 2017 Conference on Empirical Methods in Natural Language Processing, pp. 1190–1200 (2017)
12. Mikolov, T., Karafiát, M., Burget, L., Černockỳ, J., Khudanpur, S.: Recurrent neural network based language model. In: Eleventh Annual Conference of the International Speech Communication Association (2010)
13. Cho, K., et al.: Learning phrase representations using RNN encoder-decoder for statistical machine translation. arXiv preprint arXiv:1406.1078 (2014)
14. Hochreiter, S., Schmidhuber, J.: Long short-term memory. Neural Comput. **9**(8), 1735–1780 (1997)
15. Pei, W., Ge, T., Chang, B.: Max-margin tensor neural network for Chinese word segmentation. In: Proceedings of the 52nd Annual Meeting of the Association for Computational Linguistics (Volume 1: Long Papers), vol. 1, pp. 293–303 (2014)
16. Qiu, X., Huang, X.: Convolutional neural tensor network architecture for community-based question answering. In: IJCAI, pp. 1305–1311 (2015)
17. Yang, Y., Yih, W., Meek, C.: WikiQA: a challenge dataset for open-domain question answering. In: EMNLP, pp. 2013–2018 (2015)
18. Wang, M., Smith, N.A., Mitamura, T.: What is the jeopardy model? A quasi-synchronous grammar for QA. In: EMNLP-CoNLL, vol. 7, pp. 22–32 (2007)
19. Cui, Y., Chen, Z., Wei, S., Wang, S., Liu, T., Hu, G.: Attention-over-attention neural networks for reading comprehension. arXiv preprint arXiv:1607.04423 (2016)
20. Pennington, J., Socher, R., Manning, C.: GloVe: global vectors for word representation. In: Proceedings of the 2014 Conference on Empirical Methods in Natural Language Processing (EMNLP), pp. 1532–1543 (2014)
21. Hermann, K.M., et al.: Teaching machines to read and comprehend. In: Advances in Neural Information Processing Systems, pp. 1693–1701 (2015)

Labeling Information Enhancement for Multi-label Learning with Low-Rank Subspace

An Tao[1(✉)], Ning Xu[2,3], and Xin Geng[2,3]

[1] School of Information Science and Engineering, Southeast University, Nanjing, China
taoan@seu.edu.cn

[2] School of Computer Science and Engineering, Southeast University, Nanjing, China
{xning,xgeng}@seu.edu.cn

[3] Key Laboratory of Computer Network and Information Integration, Southeast University, Ministry of Education, Nanjing, China

Abstract. In multi-label learning, each training example is represented by an instance while associated with multiple class labels simultaneously. Most existing approaches make use of multi-label training examples by utilizing the logical labeling information, i.e., one class label is either fully relevant or irrelevant to the instance. In this paper, a novel multi-label learning approach is proposed which aims to enhance the labeling information by extending logical labels into numerical labels. Firstly, a stacked matrix is constructed where the feature and the logical label matrix are placed vertically. Secondly, the labeling information is enhanced by leveraging the underlying low-rank structure in the stacked matrix. Thirdly, the multi-label predictive model is induced by the learning procedure from training examples with numerical labels. Extensive comparative studies clearly validate the advantage of the proposed method against the state-of-the-art multi-label learning approaches.

Keywords: Multi-label learning · Label enhancement · Low-rank

1 Introduction

In multi-label learning, there are multiple labels associated to the same instance simultaneously [1,2]. In more formal terms, let $\mathcal{X} = \mathbb{R}^d$ denote the d-dimentional feature space and $\mathcal{Y} = [y_1, \ldots, y_t]$ denote the label set with t possible labels. Given a training set $\mathcal{D} = \{(\boldsymbol{x}_i, \boldsymbol{y}_i) | 1 \leq i \leq n\}$, where $\boldsymbol{x}_i \in \mathcal{X}$ is the feature vector and $\boldsymbol{y}_i \in \{0, 1\}^t$ is the label vector, the task of traditional multi-label learning is to learn a model built from the feature space to the label space. During the past decade, multi-label learning has been applied successfully to learn data with rich semantics, e.g. text [3,4], image [5,6], audio [7,8], video [9], etc.

X. Geng and B.-H. Kang (Eds.): PRICAI 2018, LNAI 11012, pp. 671–683, 2018.
https://doi.org/10.1007/978-3-319-97304-3_51

(a)

(b)

Fig. 1. Two natural scene image examples which are both described by the label set $\mathcal{Y} = \{sky, water, cloud, beach, plant, house\}$ in different value.

The accessible labeling information of multi-label training example is categorical, i.e. each class label $\boldsymbol{y}_i$ is regarded to be either relevant or irrelevant for instance $\boldsymbol{x}_i$. Such label $\boldsymbol{y}_i$ is called *logical label*. Nonetheless, recent studies show that categorical labeling information is actually a simplification of the rich semantics encoded by multi-label training examples [10]. In order to enhance the labeling information, the logical label should be extended to be numerical. This new label is called *numerical label*, which carries more semantic information and describes the instance more comprehensively. An example is shown in Fig. 1. Figure 1(a) and (b) are both annotated with the label set $\mathcal{Y}$=\{*sky*, *water*, *cloud*, *beach*, *plant*, *house*\}. In order to specify the numerical label, we let the sign of the numerical label denotes whether the label is relevant or irrelevant to the corresponding instance, and let the absolute numerical value denote the degree to which the label describes the instance. To reflect the labeling information with numerical labels, for the *within-instance label variance*, the related label *beach* in Fig. 1(b) should have larger value than the value of the related label *water*, because the former can describe the image more apparently than the latter. Similarly, for the *between-instance label variance*, the value of the related label *house* in Fig. 1(a) should be larger than the value of the same label in Fig. 1(b). The process of recovering numerical labels from logical labels can be called *label enhancement* (LE). LE can be seen as a data preprocessing step which aims to facilitate in learning a better model from the feature space to the label space.

To enhance the labeling information of multi-label examples, we first construct a stacked matrix where the feature and the logical label matrix are placed vertically. Then we assume that the stacked matrix belongs to an underlying low-rank subspace [11,12]. The stacked matrix is therefore an underlying low-rank matrix.

Based on the above assumption, we propose an efficient multi-label method named LIEML, i.e., *Labeling Information Enhancement for Multi-label Learning*. The basic strategy of LIEML is to enhance the labeling information of multi-label examples by leveraging the underlying low-rank structure in the stacked matrix.

Specifically, we minimize the rank of the stacked matrix until obtaining the lowest rank. In order to prevent the values in the stacked matrix from deviating the original values too much, we add two functions on the feature and the label portion of the stacked matrix respectively. The numerical labels are then obtained from the label portion of the stacked matrix. After that, the desired multi-label predictive model is learned from training examples with numerical labels based on tailored multivariate regression techniques. Experimental studies across a wide range of benchmark data sets show that LIEML achieves highly competitive performance against other state-of-the-art multi-label learning approaches.

The rest of this paper is organized as follows. First, existing work related to our proposed approach is discussed in Sect. 2. Then, the details of LIEML are proposed in Sect. 3. After that, the results of comparative studies are reported in Sect. 4. Finally, conclusions are drawn in Sect. 5.

2 Related Work

Existing multi-label approaches can be roughly grouped into three categories based on the thought of *order of label correlations* [2]. The first-order approaches which assume independence among class labels are the simplest ones [13,14]. Then the multi-label classification becomes a series of binary classification problems. On the contrary, second-order approaches consider the correlations between pairs of class labels [15,16], and the high-order approaches consider the correlations among label subsets or all the class labels [17]. The approaches above all treat the label as the logcial label, representing whether the label is fully relevant or irrelevant to the corresponding instance. In contrast, LIEML enhances the labeling information by transforming logical label to numerical label.

There have been some multi-label works which transform the logical label space to the numerical label space. For example, [18] tries to reduce the computational effort by seeking the principle correlations between labels, especially for the data sets with large numbers of labels. The bases of the numerical space are the combinations of the logical label vectors. Another work [19] projects the feature space and the label space to a new space where the correlation between the projections of the two spaces are maximized. In both cases, the dimensionality of the label space is reduced. However, the meaning of each dimension still remains in LIEML.

Recently, there are also some attempts which aim to facilitate multi-label predictive model induction by manipulating the feature space. In [20], label propagation is conducted over the fully-connected affinity graph specified over the feature space. In [10], the manifold structure of feature space is characterized by the weighted k-nearest neighbor graph defined over training examples. Different to those approaches, LIEML recovers numerical label by exploiting the structure of the stacked matrix via low-rank assumption.

3 The LIEML Algorithm

The learning procedure of LIEML consists of two steps, including label enhancement and predictive model induction. Technical details of these steps are scrutinized as follows.

3.1 Label Enhancement

As shown in Sect. 1, the training set of multi-label learning can be expressed as $\mathcal{D} = \{(\boldsymbol{x}_i, \boldsymbol{y}_i)|1 \leq i \leq n\}$. Given any instance $\boldsymbol{x}_i \in \mathbb{R}^d$ and the logical label vector $\boldsymbol{y}_i \in \{-1, 1\}^t$, we use $\boldsymbol{u}_i \in \mathbb{R}^t$ to denote the numerical label vector. Note that here we use -1 instead of 0 in the logical label vector to represent irrelevant to the instance.

The goal of LE is to recover the numerical labels from the logical labels in $\mathcal{D}$. To solve the problem, we consider the linear model

$$\boldsymbol{u}_i = \boldsymbol{W}^\top \boldsymbol{x}_i + \boldsymbol{b}, \tag{1}$$

where $\boldsymbol{W} = [\boldsymbol{w}^1, \ldots, \boldsymbol{w}^t]$ is a weight matrix and $\boldsymbol{b} \in \mathbb{R}^t$ is a bias vector. For convenient describing, we set $\hat{\boldsymbol{W}} = [\boldsymbol{W}^\top, \boldsymbol{b}]$. Then the Eq. 1 becomes

$$\boldsymbol{U} = \hat{\boldsymbol{W}}[\boldsymbol{X}; \boldsymbol{1}^\top]. \tag{2}$$

As shown in Sect. 1, we construct a stacked matrix $\boldsymbol{Z} = [\boldsymbol{Y}; \boldsymbol{X}; \boldsymbol{1}^\top]$ and assume that $\boldsymbol{Z}$ is an underlying low-rank matrix, i.e., $\text{rank}(Z) \ll \min(d+t+1, n)$. This assumption succeeds in many component analysis techniques, e.g., principal component analysis (PCA) and Fisher's linear discriminant analysis (FLDA). Because of our model in Eq. 2, an all-1 row is added in $\boldsymbol{Z}$. After minimizing the rank of $\boldsymbol{Z}$, we gain the numerical label matrix $\boldsymbol{U}$ from the position of $\boldsymbol{Y}$ in $\boldsymbol{Z}$. The optimization problem of LE in this paper becomes

$$\begin{aligned} \underset{Z \in \mathbb{R}^{(t+d+1)\times n}}{\text{argmin}} \quad & L(\boldsymbol{Z}) + R(\boldsymbol{Z}) \\ \text{s.t.} \quad & z_{(t+d+1)\cdot} = \boldsymbol{1}^\top. \end{aligned} \tag{3}$$

In order to prevent the label values in $\boldsymbol{Z}$ from deviating the original values too much, for L we choose the logistic loss function as

$$L(\boldsymbol{Z}) = \frac{\lambda}{tn} \sum_{i=1}^{t} \sum_{j=1}^{n} \log(1 + e^{-y_{ij} z_{ij}}), \tag{4}$$

where λ is a positive trade-off weight.

Because rank($\boldsymbol{Z}$) is non-convex and difficult to optimize, we relax rank($\boldsymbol{Z}$) with the convex nuclear norm $\|\boldsymbol{Z}\|_*$. Considering the feature values should not deviate from the orignal values too much, we choose the squared function on the position of $\boldsymbol{X}$ in $\boldsymbol{Z}$. This leads to the following R which we wish to minimize

$$R(\boldsymbol{Z}) = \mu\|\boldsymbol{Z}\|_* + \frac{1}{dn}\sum_{i=1}^{d}\sum_{j=1}^{n}\frac{1}{2}(z_{(i+t)j} - x_{ij})^2, \tag{5}$$

where μ is a positive trade-off weight.

Formulating the LE problem into an optimization framework over Eqs. 4 and 5, the target function T_1 is yielded as

$$T_1(\boldsymbol{Z}) = \frac{\lambda}{tn}\sum_{i=1}^{t}\sum_{j=1}^{n}\log(1+e^{-y_{ij}z_{ij}}) + \mu\|\boldsymbol{Z}\|_* + \frac{1}{dn}\sum_{i=1}^{d}\sum_{j=1}^{n}\frac{1}{2}(z_{(i+t)j} - x_{ij})^2. \tag{6}$$

To optimize the Eq. 6, we modify the Fixed Point Continuation (FPC) method [21], which is to alternate between the gradient descent $\boldsymbol{A}^k = \boldsymbol{Z}^k - \tau g(\boldsymbol{Z}^k)$ and the shrinkage $\boldsymbol{Z}^{k+1} = S_{\tau\mu}(\boldsymbol{A}^k)$. For the gradient descent, τ is a step size whose choice will be discussed next, and $g(\boldsymbol{Z}^k)$ is the matrix gradient of the logistic loss function and the squared function in Eq. 3. We define $g(\boldsymbol{Z}^k)$ as

$$g(\boldsymbol{z}_{ij}) = \begin{cases} \frac{\lambda}{tn}\frac{-y_{ij}}{1+e^{y_{ij}z_{ij}}}, & i \le t \\ \frac{1}{dn}(z_{ij} - x_{(i-t)j}), & t < i \le t+d \\ 0, & i = t+d+1 \end{cases}. \tag{7}$$

For the shrinkage, $S_{\tau\mu}(\cdot)$ is a matrix shrinkage operator. Let $\boldsymbol{A}^k = \boldsymbol{U}\boldsymbol{\Lambda}\boldsymbol{V}^\top$ be the SVD of $\boldsymbol{\Lambda}^k$. Then $S_{\tau\mu}(\boldsymbol{A}^k) = \boldsymbol{U}\max(\boldsymbol{\Lambda} - \tau\mu, 0)\boldsymbol{V}^\top$, which reduces the nuclear norm.

To improve the speed of convergence, we begin with a large value μ_1 for μ, and determine the sequence value as $\mu_{k+1} = \max(\mu_k\eta_\mu, \mu_{min})$, $k = 1, ..., L-1$, through a decay parameter η_μ. The sequence is ended with the smallest value μ_L which is equal to μ_{min}.

3.2 Predictive Model Induction

We build the learning model through an adapted regressor based on MSVR [10]. Similar to MSVR, we generalize the 1-D SVR to solve the multi-dimensional case. In addition, our regressor not only concerns the distance between the predicted and the real values, but also the sign consistency of them. The target funciton T_2 we wish to minimize is

$$T_2(\boldsymbol{\Theta}, \boldsymbol{m}) = \frac{1}{2}\sum_{j=1}^{t}\|\boldsymbol{\theta}_j\|^2 + \gamma_1\sum_{i=1}^{n}\Omega_1(r_i) + \gamma_2\sum_{i=1}^{n}\sum_{j=1}^{t}\Omega_2(q_{ij}), \tag{8}$$

where $r_i = \|\boldsymbol{e}_i\| = \sqrt{\boldsymbol{e}_i^\top\boldsymbol{e}_i}$, $\boldsymbol{e}_i = \boldsymbol{u}_i - \varphi(\boldsymbol{x}_i)^\top\boldsymbol{\Theta} - \boldsymbol{m}$, $q_{ij} = y_{ij}(\varphi(\boldsymbol{x}_i)^\top\boldsymbol{\theta}_j + m_j)$, $\boldsymbol{\Theta} = [\boldsymbol{\theta}_1, \ldots, \boldsymbol{\theta}_t]$, $\boldsymbol{m} = [m_1, \ldots, m_t]$. $\varphi(\boldsymbol{x})$ is a nonlinear transformation of $\boldsymbol{x}$ to a higher dimensional feature space.

To consider all dimensions into a unique restriction and yield a single support vector for all dimensions, we set Ω_1 as

$$\Omega_1(r) = \begin{cases} 0, & r < \varepsilon \\ r^2 - 2r\varepsilon + \varepsilon^2, & r \geq \varepsilon \end{cases}. \tag{9}$$

This will create an insensitive zone determined by ε around the estimate, i.e., the value of r less than ε will be ignored.

To make the signs of the numerical label and the logical label as same as possible, we set Ω_2 as

$$\Omega_2(q) = -q\sigma(-q) = \begin{cases} 0, & q > 0 \\ -q, & q \leq 0 \end{cases}, \tag{10}$$

where $\sigma(q)$ is an activation function where the value will be equal to 0 if q is negative, otherwise equal to 1. For the meaning of Eq. 10, if the signs of the predicted numerical label and the logical label are different, the result of Eq. 10 will be positive, otherwise zero.

To minimize $T_2(\boldsymbol{\Theta}; \boldsymbol{m})$, we use an iterative quasi-Newton method called Iterative Re-Weighted Least Square (IRWLS) [22]. Firstly, we approximate $T_2(\boldsymbol{\Theta}; \boldsymbol{m})$ by its first order Taylor expansion at the solution of the current k-th iteration, denoted by $\boldsymbol{\Theta}^{(k)}$ and $\boldsymbol{m}^{(k)}$

$$\Omega_1'(r_i) = \Omega_1(r_i^{(k)}) + \left.\frac{d\Omega_1(r)}{dr}\right|_{r_i^{(k)}} \frac{(\boldsymbol{e}_i^{(k)})^\top}{r_i^{(k)}} \left(\boldsymbol{e}_i - \boldsymbol{e}_i^{(k)}\right), \tag{11}$$

where $\boldsymbol{e}_i^{(k)}$ and $r_i^{(k)}$ are calculated from $\boldsymbol{\Theta}^{(k)}$ and $\boldsymbol{m}^{(k)}$. Then a quadratic approximation is further constructed

$$\begin{aligned} \Omega_1''(r_i) &= \Omega_1(r_i^{(k)}) + \left.\frac{d\Omega_1(r)}{dr}\right|_{r_i^{(k)}} \frac{r_i^2 - (r_i^{(k)})^2}{2r_i^{(k)}} \\ &= \frac{1}{2}a_i r_i^2 + \nu, \end{aligned} \tag{12}$$

where

$$a_i = \frac{1}{r_i^{(k)}} \left.\frac{d\Omega_1(r)}{dr}\right|_{r_i^{(k)}} = \begin{cases} 0, & r_i^{(k)} < \varepsilon \\ \frac{2\left(r_i^{(k)} - \varepsilon\right)}{r_i^{(k)}}, & r_i^{(k)} \geq \varepsilon \end{cases}, \tag{13}$$

and ν is a constant term that does not depend on either $\boldsymbol{\Theta}^{(k)}$ or $\boldsymbol{m}^{(k)}$. Combining Eqs. 8, 10 and 12 can get

$$T_2''(\boldsymbol{\Theta}, \boldsymbol{m}) = \frac{1}{2}\sum_{j=1}^{t} \|\boldsymbol{\theta}_j\|^2 + \frac{1}{2}\gamma_1 \sum_{i=1}^{n} a_i r_i^2 + \gamma_2 \sum_{i=1}^{n}\sum_{j=1}^{t} q_{ij}\sigma(-q_{ij}) + \nu. \tag{14}$$

Algorithm 1. LIEML

Input: The training set $\mathcal{D} = \{(\boldsymbol{x}_i, \boldsymbol{y}_i)|1 \leq i \leq n\}$, parameters μ_{min}, η_μ, λ, γ_1, γ_2, step size τ, convergence criterion ε;
Output: Model parameters $\boldsymbol{\beta}$ and $\boldsymbol{m}$;

Initial the stacked matrix $\boldsymbol{Z}^{(0)}$;
Determin $\mu_1 > \mu_2 > \cdots > \mu_L = \mu_{min} > 0$;
for *each* $\mu \leftarrow \mu_1, \mu_2, ..., \mu_L$ **do**
  $k \leftarrow 0$;
  repeat
    Compute $\boldsymbol{A}^{(k)} \leftarrow \boldsymbol{Z}^{(k)} - \tau g(\boldsymbol{Z}^{(k)})$;
    Compute SVD of $\boldsymbol{U}^{(k)}\boldsymbol{\Lambda}^{(k)}(\boldsymbol{V}^{(k)})^\top \leftarrow \boldsymbol{A}^{(k)}$;
    Compute $\boldsymbol{Z}^{(k+1)} \leftarrow \boldsymbol{U}^{(k)}\max(\boldsymbol{\Lambda}^{(k)} - \tau\mu, 0)(\boldsymbol{V}^{(k)})^\top$;
    Project $\boldsymbol{Z}^{(k+1)}$ to feasible region $z_{(t+d+1)\cdot} \leftarrow \mathbf{1}^\top$;
    $k \leftarrow k + 1$;
  until $|T_1(\boldsymbol{Z}^{(k)}) - T_1(\boldsymbol{Z}^{(k-1)})| < \varepsilon$;
end
$\boldsymbol{U} \leftarrow z_{(1:t)\cdot}$;
Initial the model parameter $\boldsymbol{\beta}^{(0)}$ and $\boldsymbol{m}^{(0)}$;
Compute target function $T_2(\boldsymbol{\beta}^{(0)}, \boldsymbol{m}^{(0)})$ by Eq. 8;
$k \leftarrow 0$;
repeat
  Compute the descending directions $\boldsymbol{\beta}'$ and $\boldsymbol{m}'$ by Eq. 15;
  repeat
    Compute the model parameter $\boldsymbol{\beta}^{(k+1)}$ through a line search algorithm combining $\boldsymbol{\beta}^{(k)}$ and $\boldsymbol{\beta}'$;
    Compute the model parameter $\mathbf{m}^{(k+1)}$ through a line search algorithm combining $\mathbf{m}^{(k)}$ and $\mathbf{m}'$;
    Compute $T_2(\boldsymbol{\beta}^{(k+1)}, \boldsymbol{m}^{(k+1)})$ by Eq. 8;
  until $T_2(\boldsymbol{\beta}^{(k+1)}, \boldsymbol{m}^{(k+1)}) < T_2(\boldsymbol{\beta}^{(k)}, \boldsymbol{m}^{(k)})$;
  $k \leftarrow k + 1$;
until $|T_2(\boldsymbol{\beta}^{(k)}, \boldsymbol{m}^{(k)}) - T_2(\boldsymbol{\beta}^{(k-1)}, \boldsymbol{m}^{(k-1)})| < \varepsilon$;

The optimum of this piecewise quadratic problem can be integrated as solving a system of linear equations for $j = 1, ..., t$

$$\begin{bmatrix} \gamma_1\boldsymbol{\Phi}^\top\boldsymbol{D}_a\boldsymbol{\Phi} + \boldsymbol{I} & \gamma_1\boldsymbol{\Phi}^\top\boldsymbol{a} \\ \gamma_1\boldsymbol{a}^\top\boldsymbol{\Phi} & \gamma_1\mathbf{1}^\top\boldsymbol{a} \end{bmatrix} \begin{bmatrix} \boldsymbol{\theta}'_j \\ m'_j \end{bmatrix} = \begin{bmatrix} \gamma_1\boldsymbol{\Phi}^\top\boldsymbol{D}_a\boldsymbol{u}_j + \gamma_2\boldsymbol{\Phi}^\top\boldsymbol{D}_j\boldsymbol{y}_j \\ \gamma_1\boldsymbol{a}^\top\boldsymbol{u}_j + \gamma_2(\boldsymbol{\sigma}_j)^\top\boldsymbol{y}_j \end{bmatrix}, \tag{15}$$

where $\boldsymbol{\Phi} = [\varphi(\boldsymbol{x}_1), ..., \varphi(\boldsymbol{x}_n)]^\top$, $\boldsymbol{a} = [a_1, ..., a_n]^\top$, $(\boldsymbol{D}_a)_{ik} = a_i\delta_{ik}$ (δ_{ik} is the Kronecker's delta function), $(\boldsymbol{D}_j)_{ik} = \sigma(-q_{ij})\delta_{ik}$, $\boldsymbol{\sigma}_j = [\sigma(-q_{1j}), ..., \sigma(-q_{nj})]^\top$, $\boldsymbol{y}_j = [y_{1j}, ..., y_{nj}]^\top$. Then, the direction of the optimal solution ($\boldsymbol{\Theta}'$ and $\boldsymbol{m}'$) of Eq. 15 is used as the descending direction for the optimization of $T_2(\boldsymbol{\Theta}; \boldsymbol{m})$, and the solution for the next iteration ($\boldsymbol{\Theta}^{(k+1)}$ and $\boldsymbol{m}^{(k+1)}$) is obtained via a line search algorithm along this direction.

Table 1. Attributes of the benchmark multi-label data sets

Datasets	$\|S\|$	$dim(S)$	$L(S)$	$F(S)$	$LCard(S)$	$LDen(S)$	$DL(S)$	$PDL(S)$	Domain
cal500	502	68	174	numeric	26.044	0.150	502	1.000	audio
emotion	593	72	6	numeric	1.868	0.311	27	0.046	audio
medical	978	1449	45	nominal	1.245	0.028	94	0.096	text
llog	1460	1004	75	nominal	1.180	0.016	304	0.208	text
enron	1702	1001	53	nominal	3.378	0.064	753	0.442	text
image	2000	294	5	numeric	1.236	0.247	20	0.010	image
scene	2407	294	5	numeric	1.074	0.179	15	0.006	image
yeast	2417	103	14	numeric	4.237	0.303	198	0.082	biology
slashdot	3782	1079	22	nominal	1.181	0.054	156	0.041	text
corel5k	5000	499	374	nominal	3.522	0.009	3175	0.635	image

According to the representor's theorem [23], under fairly general conditions, a learning problem can be expressed as a linear combination of the training examples in the feature space, i.e., $\boldsymbol{\theta}^j = \sum_i \varphi(\boldsymbol{x}_i)\boldsymbol{\beta}_j = \boldsymbol{\Phi}\boldsymbol{\beta}_j$. If we replace this expression into Eq. 15, it will generate the inner product $< \varphi(\boldsymbol{x}_i), \varphi(\boldsymbol{x}_j) >$, and then the kernel trick can be applied. After that the line search algorithm can be expressed in terms of $\boldsymbol{\beta}_j$ and m_j. Therefore the target function can be renamed as $T_2(\boldsymbol{\beta}, \boldsymbol{m})$. The pseudocode of LIEML is given in Algorithm 1.

4 Experiments

4.1 Experiment Configuration

Data Sets. A total of ten benchmark multi-label data sets[1] are employed for performance evaluation. Table 1 summarizes detailed characteristics of the real data sets, which are roughly organized in ascending order of the number of examples $|S|$. As shown in Table 1, the ten data sets cover a broad range of cases with diversified multi-label properties and thus serve as a solid basis for thorough comparative studies. For each multi-label data set S, we use $|S|$, $dim(S)$, $L(S)$, and $F(S)$ to represent its number of examples, number of features, number of class labels and feature type respectively. In addition, several multi-label statistics [24] are further used to characterize properties of the data set, including label cardinality $LCard(S)$, label density $LDen(S)$, distinct label sets $DL(S)$, and proportion of distinct label sets $PDL(S)$. Detailed definitions on these properties can be found in [24].

Comparing Algorithms. In this paper, we choose to compare the performance of LIEML against six well-established multi-label learning algorithms: BR [13], CLR [16], ECC [24], RAKEL [25], LP [20], and ML^2 [10].

[1] The data sets can be downloaded from: http://meka.sourceforge.net/#datasets and http://mulan.sourceforge.net/datasets.html.

Table 2. Performance of each comparing algorithm (mean±std.) on the benchmark multi-label data sets.

Comparing algorithm	*Ranking-loss* ↓				
	cal500	emotion	medical	llog	enron
LIEML	**0.177±0.002(1)**	0.221±0.011(2)	**0.026±0.005(1)**	0.144±0.008(2)	**0.076±0.002(1)**
BR	0.258±0.003(6)	0.233±0.016(6)	0.091±0.005(5)	0.328±0.007(6)	0.312±0.009(7)
CLK	0.239±0.026(5)	0.222±0.014(3)	0.123±0.026(7)	0.190±0.015(5)	0.089±0.002(2)
ECC	0.205±0.004(4)	0.227±0.017(4)	0.032±0.007(2)	0.154±0.009(3)	0.120±0.004(5)
RAKEL	0.444±0.005(7)	0.254±0.020(7)	0.095±0.033(6)	0.412±0.010(7)	0.241±0.005(6)
LP	0.181±0.003(2)	**0.182±0.012(1)**	0.034±0.006(4)	**0.125±0.005(1)**	0.091±0.003(4)
ML^2	0.188±0.002(3)	0.231±0.012(5)	0.032±0.005(2)	0.158±0.005(4)	0.090±0.012(3)
Comparing algorithm	***Ranking-loss* ↓**				
	image	scene	yeast	slashdot	corel5k
LIEML	**0.143±0.006(1)**	0.065±0.003(2)	0.170±0.002(2)	**0.093±0.002(1)**	0.121±0.002(2)
BR	0.314±0.014(7)	0.229±0.010(7)	0.190±0.004(4)	0.240±0.008(6)	0.416±0.003(6)
CLK	0.294±0.009(5)	0.127±0.003(4)	0.198±0.003(6)	0.260±0.007(7)	**0.114±0.002(1)**
ECC	0.276±0.005(4)	0.151±0.005(5)	0.190±0.003(4)	0.123±0.004(3)	0.292±0.003(5)
RAKEL	0.311±0.010(6)	0.205±0.008(6)	0.245±0.004(7)	0.190±0.005(5)	0.627±0.004(7)
LP	0.181±0.008(3)	0.087±0.006(3)	0.174±0.004(3)	0.132±0.005(4)	0.145±0.002(3)
ML^2	**0.143±0.007(1)**	**0.064±0.003(1)**	**0.168±0.003(1)**	0.095±0.003(2)	0.163±0.003(4)
Comparing algorithm	***One-error* ↓**				
	cal500	emotion	medical	llog	enron
LIEML	**0.119±0.014(1)**	0.350±0.023(2)	**0.166±0.011(1)**	0.766±0.020(3)	**0.225±0.011(1)**
BR	0.921±0.025(7)	0.375±0.027(6)	0.297±0.036(6)	0.884±0.011(6)	0.648±0.019(7)
CLK	0.331±0.111(6)	0.356±0.030(5)	0.688±0.143(7)	0.900±0.019(7)	0.376±0.017(4)
ECC	0.191±0.021(4)	0.353±0.040(4)	0.182±0.019(3)	0.785±0.009(4)	0.424±0.013(6)
RAKEL	0.286±0.039(5)	0.392±0.035(7)	0.208±0.071(4)	0.838±0.014(5)	0.412±0.016(5)
LP	0.120±0.015(2)	**0.303±0.027(1)**	0.213±0.021(5)	0.748±0.011(2)	0.311±0.013(3)
ML^2	0.141±0.016(3)	0.352±0.021(3)	0.179±0.019(2)	**0.683±0.018(1)**	0.258±0.090(2)
Comparing algorithm	***One-error* ↓**				
	image	scene	yeast	slashdot	corel5k
LIEML	**0.271±0.010(1)**	0.197±0.006(2)	**0.226±0.009(1)**	0.387±0.009(2)	0.650±0.006(2)
BR	0.538±0.019(7)	0.475±0.014(7)	0.285±0.008(7)	0.734±0.017(6)	0.919±0.006(7)
CLK	0.514±0.014(5)	0.371±0.008(4)	0.270±0.007(6)	0.979±0.003(7)	0.721±0.007(4)
ECC	0.486±0.018(4)	0.373±0.008(5)	0.256±0.007(5)	0.481±0.014(4)	0.699±0.006(3)
RAKEL	0.515±0.017(6)	0.444±0.012(6)	0.251±0.008(4)	0.453±0.005(3)	0.819±0.010(6)
LP	0.353±0.017(3)	0.270±0.016(3)	0.241±0.011(3)	0.558±0.009(5)	0.755±0.005(5)
ML^2	0.272±0.009(2)	**0.194±0.008(1)**	0.228±0.009(2)	**0.382±0.009(1)**	**0.647±0.007(1)**

For LIEML, the first value μ_1 for μ is set to $\sigma\eta_\mu$, where σ is the largest singular value of Z and the decay parameter η_μ is set to 0.25. The last value μ_{min} for μ is set to 10^{-5}. The parameter λ is chosen among $\{10^{-1}, 1, 10, 10^2\}$. The step size τ is set to $\min(\frac{3.8tn}{\lambda}, dn)$. The parameters γ_1 and γ_2 are set to 1 and 0.1 respectively. The convergence criterion ε is set to 10^{-5}. The kernel function in LIEML is radial basis function (RBF). The four algorithms, including BR, CLR, ECC, and RAKEL, are operated on the MULAN multi-label learning package. The base classifier for the four algorithms is logistic regression model. The ensemble size for ECC is set to 30, and for RAKEL is set to $2t$ with $k = 3$. The parameter α in LP is set to 0.5. The number of neighbors K for ML^2 is set to $t + 1$.

Table 3. Performance of each comparing algorithm (mean±std.) on the benchmark multi-label data sets.

Comparing algorithm	*Hamming-loss* ↓				
	cal500	emotion	medical	llog	enron
LIEML	**0.136±0.001(1)**	0.251±0.006(3)	0.015±0.001(3)	**0.015±0.000(1)**	**0.047±0.001(1)**
BR	0.214±0.004(7)	0.265±0.013(5)	0.022±0.003(5)	0.052±0.003(7)	0.105±0.003(7)
CLK	0.165±0.005(5)	0.270±0.011(7)	0.024±0.002(6)	0.019±0.002(5)	0.072±0.002(6)
ECC	0.146±0.002(4)	0.254±0.013(4)	0.013±0.001(2)	0.016±0.000(2)	0.064±0.001(5)
RAKEL	0.138±0.002(2)	0.269±0.011(6)	**0.010±0.003(1)**	0.017±0.001(4)	0.058±0.001(3)
LP	0.167±0.004(6)	**0.223±0.007(1)**	0.017±0.001(4)	0.016±0.000(2)	0.063±0.003(4)
ML^2	0.138±0.002(2)	0.243±0.010(2)	0.283±0.027(7)	0.021±0.001(6)	0.051±0.001(2)

Comparing algorithm	*Hamming-loss* ↓				
	image	scene	yeast	slashdot	corel5k
LIEML	0.160±0.003(2)	0.083±0.002(2)	**0.195±0.003(1)**	**0.040±0.001(1)**	**0.009±0.000(1)**
BR	0.287±0.008(6)	0.184±0.005(7)	0.219±0.003(6)	0.130±0.003(7)	0.027±0.000(7)
CLK	0.305±0.005(7)	0.181±0.004(6)	0.222±0.002(7)	0.058±0.001(5)	0.011±0.001(3)
ECC	0.244±0.005(4)	0.133±0.002(4)	0.216±0.002(5)	0.049±0.001(4)	0.015±0.001(5)
RAKEL	0.286±0.007(5)	0.171±0.005(5)	0.202±0.003(3)	0.048±0.001(3)	0.012±0.001(4)
LP	0.190±0.005(3)	0.127±0.005(3)	0.214±0.004(4)	0.060±0.002(6)	0.024±0.000(6)
ML^2	**0.156±0.004(1)**	**0.076±0.003(1)**	0.196±0.003(2)	0.043±0.001(2)	0.010±0.001(2)

Comparing algorithm	*Coverage* ↓				
	cal500	emotion	medical	llog	enron
LIEML	**0.744±0.007(1)**	0.347±0.010(2)	**0.041±0.006(1)**	**0.149±0.007(1)**	**0.226±0.006(1)**
BR	0.852±0.014(6)	0.363±0.015(6)	0.118±0.007(6)	0.377±0.008(6)	0.601±0.014(7)
CLK	0.794±0.010(5)	0.351±0.016(3)	0.143±0.030(7)	0.225±0.016(5)	0.243±0.006(3)
ECC	0.788±0.008(4)	0.356±0.013(4)	0.048±0.009(2)	0.192±0.010(4)	0.300±0.009(5)
RAKEL	0.971±0.001(7)	0.381±0.019(7)	0.117±0.040(5)	0.459±0.011(7)	0.523±0.008(6)
LP	0.747±0.007(2)	**0.318±0.031(1)**	0.052±0.001(4)	0.159±0.006(2)	0.242±0.005(2)
ML^2	0.780±0.008(3)	0.357±0.009(5)	0.048±0.008(2)	0.162±0.008(3)	0.256±0.017(4)

Comparing algorithm	*Coverage* ↓				
	image	scene	yeast	slashdot	corel5k
LIEML	**0.168±0.006(1)**	**0.068±0.003(1)**	0.454±0.004(2)	**0.109±0.002(1)**	0.276±0.004(2)
BR	0.301±0.012(7)	0.207±0.009(7)	0.474±0.005(4)	0.259±0.009(6)	0.758±0.003(6)
CLK	0.286±0.008(5)	0.120±0.007(3)	0.492±0.006(6)	0.272±0.007(7)	**0.267±0.004(1)**
ECC	0.272±0.005(4)	0.141±0.004(4)	0.476±0.004(5)	0.139±0.004(3)	0.562±0.007(5)
RAKEL	0.298±0.010(6)	0.186±0.006(6)	0.558±0.006(7)	0.212±0.005(5)	0.886±0.004(7)
LP	0.198±0.007(3)	0.171±0.009(5)	**0.451±0.005(1)**	0.148±0.005(4)	0.328±0.005(3)
ML^2	**0.168±0.007(1)**	**0.067±0.003(1)**	0.454±0.004(2)	0.112±0.003(2)	0.372±0.006(4)

Evaluation Metrics. We use five evaluation metrics widely-used in multi-label learning in this paper, i.e., *Ranking-loss*, *One-error*, *Hamming-loss*, *Coverage*, and *Average precision* [2]. For all the five multi-label metrics, their values vary between [0, 1]. Furthermore, for average precision, the larger the values the better the performance. While for the other four metrics, the smaller the values the better the performance. These metrics serve as good indicators for comprehensive comparative studies as they evaluate the performance of the learned models from various aspects.

4.2 Experimental Results

Tables 2, 3, and 4 report the detailed experimental results of each comparing algorithm on the benchmark multi-label data sets. On each data set, 50% examples are randomly sampled without replacement to form the training set, and the

Table 4. Performance of each comparing algorithm (mean±std.) on the benchmark multi-label data sets.

Comparing algorithm	*Average precision* ↑				
	cal500	emotion	medical	llog	enron
LIEML	**0.512±0.003(1)**	0.745±0.011(2)	**0.872±0.011(1)**	0.347±0.014(3)	**0.698±0.008(1)**
BR	0.300±0.005(7)	0.730±0.015(6)	0.762±0.022(5)	0.215±0.009(5)	0.381±0.009(7)
CLK	0.395±0.042(5)	0.742±0.016(3)	0.400±0.062(7)	0.194±0.018(7)	0.610±0.008(4)
ECC	0.463±0.006(4)	0.740±0.021(4)	0.860±0.015(3)	0.342±0.009(4)	0.559±0.008(5)
RAKEL	0.353±0.006(6)	0.717±0.023(7)	0.700±0.234(6)	0.197±0.013(6)	0.539±0.006(6)
LP	0.496±0.005(3)	**0.779±0.012(1)**	0.837±0.018(4)	0.390±0.009(2)	0.661±0.007(3)
ML^2	0.501±0.003(2)	0.737±0.013(5)	0.865±0.014(2)	**0.405±0.013(1)**	0.681±0.053(2)
Comparing algorithm	*Average precision* ↑				
	image	scene	yeast	slashdot	corel5k
LIEML	**0.824±0.006(1)**	0.884±0.004(2)	**0.766±0.005(1)**	0.708±0.006(2)	**0.305±0.003(1)**
BR	0.649±0.012(7)	0.692±0.010(7)	0.734±0.004(5)	0.427±0.014(6)	0.123±0.003(6)
CLK	0.666±0.008(5)	0.778±0.004(4)	0.730±0.003(6)	0.250±0.007(7)	0.274±0.002(3)
ECC	0.685±0.008(4)	0.766±0.005(5)	0.741±0.004(4)	0.628±0.009(3)	0.264±0.003(4)
RAKEL	0.661±0.010(6)	0.713±0.008(6)	0.720±0.005(7)	0.617±0.004(4)	0.122±0.004(7)
LP	0.775±0.009(3)	0.842±0.009(3)	0.753±0.006(3)	0.579±0.009(5)	0.241±0.002(5)
ML^2	**0.824±0.006(1)**	**0.885±0.004(1)**	0.765±0.005(2)	**0.711±0.005(1)**	0.297±0.002(2)

rest 50% examples are used to form the test set. The sampling process is repeated for ten times, and the average predictive performance across ten training/testing trials are recorded. For each evaluation metric, ↓ indicates the smaller the better while ↑ indicates the larger the better. The best performance among the seven comparing algorithms is shown in boldface.

From the result tables we can see, across all the evaluation metrics, LIEML ranks 1*st* in the most cases. Note that ML^2 ranks 1*st* in the second most cases, and the number of cases where LIEML ranks 1*st* is 1.73% larger than the number of cases where ML^2 ranks 1*st*. Thus LIEML achieves rather competitive performance against ML^2. Because the model of LE in LIEML is linear, but nonlinear in ML^2, it is uneasy for LIEML to beat ML^2 with the less efficient linear way. Apart from ML^2, LIEML obviously outdistances the other five well-established multi-label learning algorithms. Therefore, the results of the experiment validate the effectiveness of our LIEML algorithm for multi-label learning.

5 Conclusion

This paper proposes a novel multi-label learning method named LIEML, which enhances the labeling information by extending logical labels into numerical labels. We first construct a stacked matrix where the feature and the label matrix are placed vertically. Then, we enhance the labeling information by leveraging the underlying low-rank structure in the stacked matrix. After that, we induce the multi-label predictive model by the learning procedure from training examples with numerical labels. Experimental results clearly validate the advantage of LIEML against the state-of-the-art multi-label learning approaches. In the future, we will explore if there exist better ways to make use of the labeling information for multi-label learning.

Acknowledgements. This research was supported by the National Key Research & Development Plan of China (No. 2017YFB1002801), the National Science Foundation of China (61622203), the Jiangsu Natural Science Funds for Distinguished Young Scholar (BK20140022), the Collaborative Innovation Center of Novel Software Technology and Industrialization, and the Collaborative Innovation Center of Wireless Communications Technology.

References

1. Tsoumakas, G., Katakis, I., Vlahavas, I.: Mining multi-label data. In: Maimon, O., Rokach, L. (eds.) Data Mining and Knowledge Discovery Handbook, pp. 667–685. Springer, Boston (2009). https://doi.org/10.1007/978-0-387-09823-4_34
2. Zhang, M.-L., Zhou, Z.-H.: A review on multi-label learning algorithms. IEEE Trans. Knowl. Data Eng. **26**(8), 1819–1837 (2014)
3. Rubin, T., Chambers, A., Smyth, P., Steyvers, M.: Statistical topic models for multi-label document classification. Mach. Learn. **88**(1–2), 157–208 (2012)
4. Yang, B., Sun, J.-T., Wang, T., Chen, Z.: Effective multilabel active learning for text classification. In: Proceedings of 15th ACM SIGKDD International Conference on Knowledge Discovery and Data Mining, New York, NY, pp. 917–926 (2009)
5. Cabral, R., Torre, F., Costeira, J., Bernardino, A.: Matrix completion for multi-label image classification. In: Proceedings of 24th International Conference on Neural Information Processing Systems, Granada, Spain, pp. 190–198 (2011)
6. Wang, H., Huang, H., Ding, C.: Image annotation using multi-label correlated green's function. In: Proceedings of 12th IEEE International Conference on Computer Vision, Kyoto, Japan, pp. 2029–2034 (2009)
7. Lo, H.-Y., Wang, J.-C., Wang, H.-M., Lin, S.-D.: Costsensitive multi-label learning for audio tag annotation and retrieval. IEEE Trans. Multimedia **13**(3), 518–529 (2011)
8. Sanden, C., Zhang, J.-Z.: Enhancing multi-label music genre classification through ensemble techniques. In: Proceedings of 34th ACM SIGIR Conference on Research and Development in Information Retrieval, New York, NY, pp. 705–714 (2011)
9. Wang, J., Zhao, Y., Wu, X., Hua, X.-S.: A transductive multi-label learning approach for video concept detection. Pattern Recogn. **44**(10–11), 2274–2286 (2011)
10. Hou, P., Geng, X., Zhang, M.-L.: Multi-label manifold learning. In: Proceedings of 30th AAAI Conference on Artificial Intelligence, Phoenix, AZ, pp. 1680–1686 (2016)
11. Liu, G., Lin, Z.-C., Yang, S.-C., Sun, J., Yu, Y., Ma, Y.: Robust recovery of subspace structures by low-rank representation. IEEE Trans. Pattern Anal. Mach. Intel. **35**(1), 171–184 (2013)
12. Eriksson, B., Balzano, L., Nowak, R.: High-rank matrix completion. In: Proceedings of 15th International Conference on Artificial Intelligence Statistics, La Palma, Canary Islands, vol. 20, pp. 373–381 (2012)
13. Boutell, M., Luo, J., Shen, X., Brown, C.: Learning multi-label scene classification. Pattern Recogn. **37**(9), 1757–1771 (2004)
14. Zhang, M.-L., Zhou, Z.-H.: ML-KNN: a lazy learning approach to multi-label learning. Pattern Recogn. **40**(7), 2038–2048 (2007)
15. Elisseeff, A., Weston, J.: A kernel method for multilabelled classification. In: Proceedings of Advance Neural Information Processing Systems 14, Vancouver, Canada, pp. 681–687 (2001)

16. Frnkranz, J., Hllermeier, E., Menca, E., Brinker, K.: Multilabel classification via calibrated label ranking. Mach. Learn. **73**(2), 133–153 (2008)
17. Tsoumakas, G., Katakis, I., Vlahavas, I.: Random k-labelsets for multilabel classification. IEEE Trans. Knowl. Data Eng. **23**(7), 1079–1089 (2011)
18. Tai, F., Lin, H.-T.: Multilabel classification with principal label space transformation. Neural Comput. **24**(9), 2508–2542 (2012)
19. Sun, L., Ji, S., Ye, J.: Canonical correlation analysis for multilabel classification: a least-squares formulation, extensions, and analysis. IEEE Trans. Pattern Anal. Mach. Intel. **33**(1), 194–200 (2011)
20. Li, Y.-K., Zhang, M.-L., Geng, X.: Leveraging implicit relative labeling-importance information for effective multi-label learning. In: Proceedings of 15th IEEE International Conference on Data Mining, Atlantic City, NJ, pp. 251–260 (2015)
21. Ma, S.-Q., Goldfarb, D., Chen, L.-F.: Fixed point and bregman iterative methods for matrix rank minimization. Math. Programm. **128**(1–2), 321–353 (2011)
22. Pérez-Cruz, F., Vázquez, A., Alarcón-Diana, P., Artés-Rodríguez, A.: An IRWLS procedure for SVR. In: 10th European Conference on Signal Processing, Tampere, Finland, pp. 1–4 (2000)
23. Schlkopf, B., Smola, A.: Learning with Kernels. The MIT Press, Berlin (2001)
24. Read, J., Pfahringer, B., Holmes, G., Frank, E.: Classifier chains for multi-label classification. Mach. Learn. **85**(3), 333–359 (2011)
25. Tsoumakas, G., Katakis, I., Vlahavas, I.: Random klabelsets for multilabel classification. IEEE Trans. Knowl. Data Eng. **23**(7), 1079–1089 (2011)

Deep Coordinated Textual and Visual Network for Sentiment-Oriented Cross-Modal Retrieval

Jiamei Fu[1,2], Dongyu She[2], Xingxu Yao[2], Yuxiang Zhang[1], and Jufeng Yang[2(✉)]

[1] College of Computer Science and Technology, Civil Aviation University of China, Tianjin, China
[2] College of Computer and Control Engineering, Nankai University, Tianjin, China
yangjufeng@nankai.edu.cn

Abstract. Cross-modal retrieval has attracted more and more attention recently, which enables people to retrieve desired information efficiently from a large amount of multimedia data. Most methods on cross-modal retrieval only focus on aligning the objects in image and text, while sentiment alignment is also essential for facilitating various applications, *e.g.*, entertainment, advertisement, *etc.* This paper studies the problem of retrieving visual sentiment concepts with a goal to extract sentiment-oriented information from social multimedia content, *i.e.*, sentiment oriented cross-media retrieval. Such problem is inherently challenging due to the subjective and ambiguity characteristics of the adjectives like "sad" and "awesome". Thus, we focus on modeling visual sentiment concepts with adjective-noun pairs, *e.g.*, "sad dog" and "awesome flower", where associating adjectives with concrete objects makes the concepts more tractable. This paper proposes a deep coordinated textural and visual network with two branches to learn a joint semantic embedding space for both images and texts. The visual branch is based on a convolutional neural network (CNN) pre-trained on a large dataset, which is optimized with the classification loss. The textual branch is added on the fully-connected layer providing supervision of the textual semantic space. In order to learn the coordinated representation for different modalities, the multi-task loss function is optimized during the end-to-end training process. We have conducted extensive experiments on a subset of the large-scale VSO dataset. The results show that the proposed model is able to retrieval sentiment-oriented data, which performs favorably against the state-of-the-art methods.

Keywords: Cross-modal retrieval · Visual sentiment analysis
Convolutional neural network

J. Fu and D. She—The two authors contributed equally to this paper.

X. Geng and B.-H. Kang (Eds.): PRICAI 2018, LNAI 11012, pp. 684–696, 2018.
https://doi.org/10.1007/978-3-319-97304-3_52

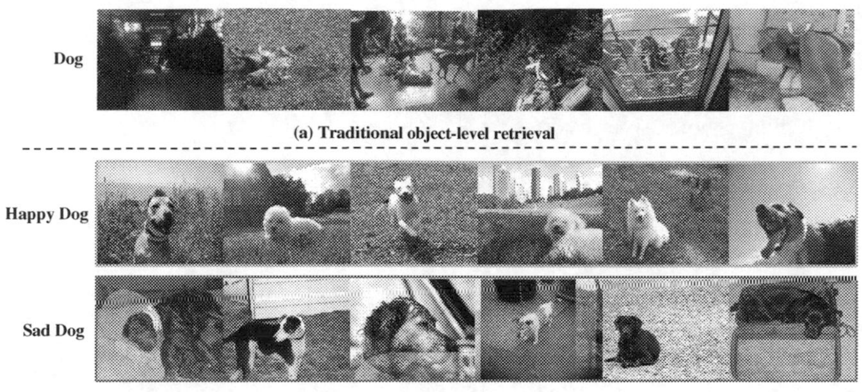

Fig. 1. Some examples from the VSO dataset [7]. The traditional cross-modal retrieval task focuses on the object-level alignment (a), while this work focuses the sentiment-oriented retrieval task (b).

1 Introduction

With the advance of social media, more and more people tend to share experiences and opinions on the social networks, *e.g.*, Flickr, Twitter and Instagram, *etc.* Generally, user-generated contents include multimedia data, *e.g.*, texts, images and videos, which have experienced tremendous growth in recent years. Cross-modal retrieval therefore emerges as the research topic and has attracted much attention [1–3], which aims to retrieve relevant data of another modality given one modality of data as the query. The existing methods mainly focus on aligning the objects in image and text, while computational sentiment understanding of such media data is of great importance for applications, *e.g.*, affective computing [4], opinion mining [5], entertainment [6], *etc.* This paper studies the problem of retrieving visual sentiment concepts with a goal to extract sentiment-oriented information from social multimedia content, referred as *sentiment oriented cross-modal retrieval.*

Numerous methods mainly focus on learning separate representation and projecting different modalities to a common space for similarity measure, which can be divided to two types: traditional and deep learning based methods. The first is to learn projections in the traditional frameworks, *e.g.*, canonical correlation analysis (CCA) [1], which cannot capture the complex cross-modal correlation. Recently, deep learning has achieved great progress in single-modal scenario, *e.g.*, image classification [8], object detection [9]. There are several methods [10,11] that utilize the ability of deep neural network to model complex cross-modal correlation of the object. While modeling the concrete visual concepts (*i.e.*, nouns) has been widely studied, there is little work that model the affective visual concepts. Such problem is inherently challenging due to the subjective and ambiguity characteristics of the adjectives like "sad" and "awesome". Thus, we focus on modeling visual sentiment concepts with adjective-noun pairs (ANP), *e.g.*, "sad dog" and "awesome flower", where associating adjectives with concrete objects makes the concepts more tractable. Thus, different from traditional object-level retrieval task, *sentiment-oriented cross-modal retrieval task* aims to retrieval images when given ANP queries with sentiment alignment and vice versa as shown in Fig. 1.

In order to address this problem, this paper proposes deep coordinated textual and visual network to learn a sentiment semantic embedding space for both images and texts. In specific, the visual branch is based on a convolutional neural network (CNN) pre-trained on a large dataset, *i.e.*, ImageNet [12], which is optimized with the classification loss. The textual branch is added on the fully-connected layer providing supervision of the textual semantic space by employing the semantic regularization constraint. In order to learn the coordinated representation for different modalities, the multi-task loss function is optimized during the end-to-end training process. Extensive experiments have been conducted on a subset of the large-scale VSO dataset [7]. The results show that the proposed model is able to retrieval sentiment-oriented data, which performs favorable against the state-of-the-art methods.

2 Related Work

In this section, we focus on reviewing the related approaches for cross-modal retrieval ranging from traditional methods [3,13,14] to deep learning based methods [15,34].

2.1 Traditional Methods

Canonical correlation analysis is widely used for model multimodal data and extended to variable types [3,13,14], which aims to learn a common space along with two modalities of data. For example, Rasiwasia *et al.* [1] propose a two-stage method to combine category information with CCA and learn a semantic space to measure the similarity of different features between two modalities. Li *et al.* [16] propose cross-modal factor analysis (CFA) to learn the pairwise cross-modal correlation, which attempts to minimize the Frobenius norm between pairwise data. CCA is unsupervised that does not need the category labels, while some researchers try to apply semi-supervised learning and graph regularization into cross-modal common representation learning. For example, Zhai *et al.* [17] propose joint representation learning (JRL) to utilize graph to model each modality of data to a common space and further learn semantic representation in an semi-supervised model. Joint graph regularized heterogeneous metric Learning (JGRHML) is proposed to learn the project matrices by adopting metric learning and graph regularization [19]. Wang *et al.* [18] utilize multimodal graph regularization on the projected data with an iterative algorithm to preserve inter-modality and intra-modality relationships. In addition, multi-view CCA [13] is proposed to project visual and textual features to the common space and combine a third view tolearn high-level semantic and multi-label CCA [20] is developed

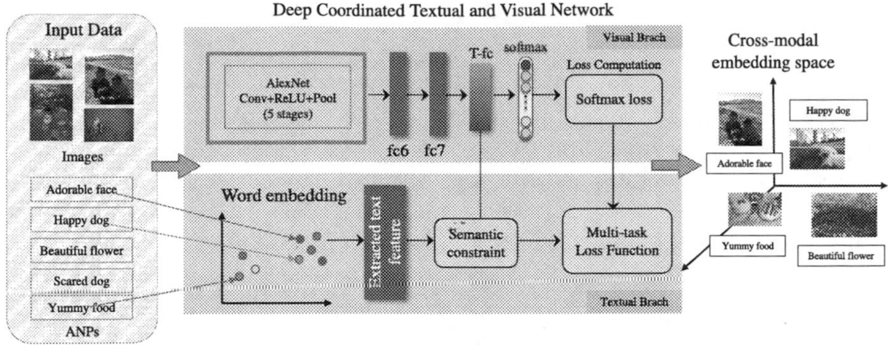

Fig. 2. Illustration of the proposed deep coordinated textual and visual network. Given the images and the corresponding ANP, we employ two branches and represent the different modalities in the joint feature embedding space. The multi-task loss is optimized for the cross-modal representation learning.

to address the problem of cross-modal retrieval when data has multiple labels and incorporate such information to learn the subspace.

2.2 Deep Learning Based Methods

Deep learning has shown the strong ability to extract the representation of texts and images, which has achieved state-of-the-art performance in various related tasks, *e.g.*, object detection [16,32,33] and visual sentiment prediction [29,30] and image retrieval [31]. Srivastava *et al.* [34] propose multimodal deep belief network (DBN) to utilize two separate DBNs to model image and text and then employ a joint RBM to learn common representation. Ngiam *et al.* [15] attempt to extend RBM to model data of multiple modalities based on deep auto-encoder network, named bimodal autoencoders. Correspondence autoencoder (Corr-AE) [21] is proposed to learn separate representation and then jointly learn the correlation with two subnetworks by minimizing error of combination of representation learning between different modalities. Peng *et al.* [2,22] propose cross-media multiple deep networks (CMDN) to jointly learn the intra-modality and inter-modality correlation with two separate networks and then apply hierarchical learning to model correlation between different modalities. Liu *et al.* [27] propose a framework to map features of cross-media data to an common semantic space and model the similarity of data. Some researchers also try to combine DNN with CCA, namely deep canonical correlation analysis (DCCA) [10,23], which use two separate subnetworks to learn non-linear representation and design the correlation constraints to maximize the total correlation.

3 Methodology

As illustrated in Fig. 2, we develop a deep framework including two branches, *i.e.*, visual branch and textual branch, which can be used to learn non-linear and complex representation for images and texts. In addition, we employ the classification loss and semantic constraint as the multi-task optimization function, which learns the cross-modal representation during the end-to-end training. The detailed construction is illustrated in the following section.

3.1 Visual Branch

Different from the traditional object recognition task that images of the same categorization often share highly-similar appearance patterns, visual sentiment analysis are usually involved with great intra-class variance. With the sentiment supervision, it is challenging to learn a mapping function from the low-level image features to high-level semantic space due to the "affective gap" [24]. Recently, CNN has the ability to extract high-level semantic representation from images, which has achieved state-of-the-art performance in the visual recognition tasks. To utilize the high-level features to guide the sentiment representation learning, we employ the AlexNet [12] as the basic model, which is composed of five convolutional layers and three fully-connected layers. The adopted AlexNet architecture consists of more than 60 million parameters, which is hard to optimize from scratch with the limited amount of affective data. Considering the good results achieved by previous work with transfer learning [25], we initialize the weights in each layer but the last one with the parameters from the pre-trained model on the ImageNet dataset [26].

As a supervised learning approach, the fine-tuned model is adopted to learn a function $f : \chi \rightarrow y$, from a collection of affective training examples $\{(x_n, y_n, s_n)\}_{n=1}^{N}$, where N is the size of the training set, x_n is the affective image, y_n and s_n is the associated ANP label and text. During each training epoch, each image is resized into 256×256 pixels and CNN crops $227 \times 227 \times 3$ patches from each image as input. We use the output from the penultimate layer as the feature $\mathbf{d}_n$ of each patch, the fine-tuning of the last layer is done by maximizing the following log likelihood function:

$$L_{cls} = \sum_{n=1}^{N} \sum_{c \epsilon y} \prod (y_n = c) \log p(y_n = c | \mathbf{d}_n, \mathbf{w}_c) \tag{1}$$

where $\mathbf{W} = \{\mathbf{w}_c\}_{c \epsilon y}$ is the set of model parameters, and $\prod(x) = 1$ if x is true. The sentiment probability $p(y_n = c|\mathbf{d}_n, \mathbf{w}_c)$ can be defined by

$$p(y_n = c|\mathbf{d}_n, \mathbf{w}_c) = \frac{exp(\mathbf{w}_c^T \mathbf{d}_n)}{\sum_{c' \epsilon y} exp(\mathbf{w}_{c'}^T \mathbf{d}_n)} \tag{2}$$

Since the category number of affective dataset is not equal to that of ImageNet, the c-way fc8 classification layer is changed to the class number required by the sentiment dataset, which can produce a probability distribution over the emotional class labels.

3.2 Textual Branch

In order to learn the joint embedding space for image and text modalities, we propose to add the textual branch in the deep model. Given the ANP consisting of adjective and noun word, we first employ the word2vec model to generate textual embedding, which is trained on a large news dataset [2]. The input is denoted as the word sequence $s = <s^{(1)}, s^{(2)}>$, where each word can be represented by a k-dimensional real-valued vector using the word2vec model. For words that do not found in the dictionary of word2vec, we initialize the word vectors randomly. In this work, we use the fixed-length word2vec word embeddings and set $k = 300$ empirically. Thus, the textual embedding of the input ANP can be denoted by

$$\mathbf{v} = [\text{word2vec}(s^{(1)}), \text{word2vec}(s^{(2)})], \tag{3}$$

where $[\cdot]$ denotes the concatenation operation and $\mathbf{v} \in \mathbb{R}^{2k}$.

To facilitate the textual learning process, we insert a fully connected layer T_fc into the middle between fc7 layer and fc8 layer. Similar to the fully-connected layer in CNN, ReLU is utilized as the nonlinear activation function for such fully-connected layer. We add a semantic regularization constraints into the network providing supervision to the semantic space, which is denoted by:

$$L_{sem} = \sum_{n=1}^{N} (||f_{W_T}^{(T)} x_n - \mathbf{v_n}||^2), \tag{4}$$

where $f_{W_T}^{(T)}$ is the output from the T_fc layer of the proposed network.

3.3 Coordinated Feature Learning

To address the problem of cross-modal embedding space learning, we consider the multi-task loss to optimize the correspondence between semantic representation of image and text with the corresponding label vector. Thus, our loss function to be minimized is integrated with two types of losses, denoted as:

$$L = L_{cls}(x, y) + L_{sem}(x, s), \tag{5}$$

where L_{cls} and L_{sem} denote the classification loss and semantic regularization constraint, respectively. The proposed network can thus be optimized with stochastic gradient descent (SGD) in an end-to-end manner. By this way, the semantic representation of pairs of image and text are well consistent, which benefits the alignment between the sentiment in the different modalities.

Based on the trained model, the cross-modality retrieval of a given image can be summarized as follows. For each test image, we first generate the $2k$-dimensional T_fc features as the textual embedding of the sample. To search for an ANP which has a similar emotion as a given query image, we determine the nearest neighbors in terms of the feature representation according to the Euclidean distance, and vice versa.

Table 1. The ANPs with six most popular nouns from the VSO dataset. We use these ANPs to collect images to form our dataset for sentiment-related retrieval task.

Adjective	Noun
Bad, broken, clean, crazy, damaged, dirty, expensive, fancy, hot, lonely, safe, tiny, ugly	Car
Adorable, aggressive, cute, dirty, faithful, fluffy, friendly, funny, happy, lonely, muddy, playful, sad, scared, shy, silly, sleepy, smiling, tiny, tired, wet	Dog
Adorable, cute, fancy, gorgeous, pretty, sexy, traditional	Dress
Adorable, angry, attractive, chubby, clean, crazy, crying, cute, dirty, dumb, excited, funny, grumpy, handsome, hilarious, innocent, mad, pretty, scared, silly, sleepy, sweet, tired, ugly, weird, worried	Face
Beautiful, dry, dying, favorite, fragile, golden, little, prickly, smelly, strange, stunning, sunny, tiny, wild	Flower
Colorful, delicious, dry, excellent, fancy, favorite, greasy, great, hot, natural, super, tasty, yummy	Food

4 Experiment

4.1 Dataset

For the sentiment-oriented cross-modal retrieval, we collect a subset of the large-scale VSO dataset that contains millions of images by querying Flickr with 1553 adjective and noun pairs (ANPs) following [28]. We only select the ANPs related to six most popular nouns, *i.e.*, car, dog, face, dress, flower and food, which are frequently occurred and more detectable in the social media. Such nouns are also associated with different adjectives to form 94 ANPs that show various sentiments, as shown in Table 1. If our method can effectively address the retrieval task on this subset, we can easily extend the work to cover more multimedia data. A total of 36,175 pairs of images and texts are finally collected as our dataset in this paper. Some example ANPs are shown in Fig. 3.

4.2 Experiment Settings

For the text modality, we use a publicly available word embeddings [2] to represent these ANPs, which has been pre-trained on large amount of words from Google News using the continuous bag-of-words model. We randomly split the dataset into 80% and 20% for training and testing set, respectively. The learning rates of the convolutional layers and the last fully-connected layer are initialized as 0.001 and 0.001, respectively. We employ stochastic gradient descent (SGD) to train the deep network using batches of 256, which ensures one batch to cover the whole 94 categories. We implement our framework based on AlexNet [12]. All our experiments are carried out on one NVIDIA GTX 1080 GPU with 32 GB CPU memory.

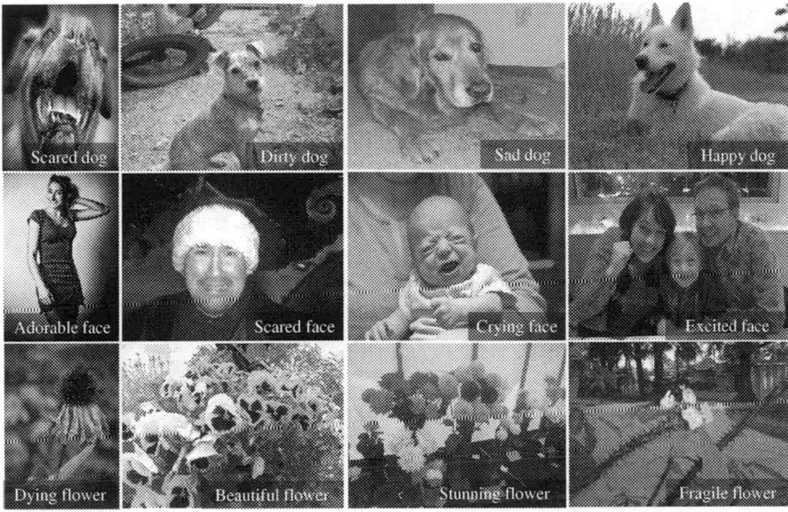

Fig. 3. Some examples of image-ANP pairs from the collected dataset.

4.3 Baseline

We evaluate our method against the other methods, including *correlation matching* (CM), *semantic matching* (SM), *semnatic correlation matching* (SCM) [1]. CM depends on subspace learning to model correlation between image and text subspaces. SM first abstracts the multi-modal data to a high-level representation, which aims to learn the correlation between the text and image by subspace learning. SCM combines subspace and semantic modeling and utilize logistic regression to maximize correlated subspaces. We also compare the performance of different combination of text feature and visual feature for these methods on this dataset. For visual features, we attempt to compare the hand-craft feature, such as GIST feature and MPEG-7 feature, and deep feature. In this paper, we utilize AlexNet to extract deep visual feature. And we use the public available code with default parameters to extract the GIST visual feature, which results in a 512-dimensional feature vector.

4.4 Evaluation Metrics

To evaluate the effectiveness of our proposed approach, two cross-modal retrieval tasks are conducted: Image as the query to retrieval text and Text as the query to retrieval images. And we also report the average results in two tasks. Following [19], we report the average recall of the gold item at position 10 of the ranked list (R@10), and precision at position 10 of the ranked list (P@10), for cross-modal retrieval tasks. In addition, we compute the F-score by the formulation:

$$F\text{-}score = \frac{2 \times PR}{P + R} \tag{6}$$

Table 2. Cross-modal retrieval performance on the subset of VSO dataset. We evaluate several baselines for cross-modal retrieval, including SM, CM, SCM with different features. Note the GIST, MPEG_7 represents the hand-craft visual feature, and deep feature represent feature extracted from the CNN pre-trained on ImageNet.

Method	Image → Text				Text → Image				Average			
	P@10	R@10	F-score	MAP	P@10	R@10	F-score	MAP	P@10	R@10	F-score	MAP
CM-GIST	0.0428	0.0052	0.0093	0.1308	0.0840	0.0070	0.0129	0.0569	0.0634	0.0061	0.0111	0.0939
CM-MPEG_7	0.0524	0.0054	0.0098	0.1476	0.0989	0.0076	0.0141	0.0689	0.0757	0.0065	0.0120	0.1082
CM-Deep	0.0783	0.0086	0.0155	0.2010	0.1629	0.0106	0.0199	0.1066	0.1206	0.0096	0.0178	0.1538
SM-GIST	0.1049	0.0057	0.0110	0.1673	0.1494	0.0110	0.0204	0.0615	0.1272	0.0084	0.0157	0.1144
SM-MPEG_7	0.1329	0.0065	0.0124	0.1952	0.1525	0.0138	0.0253	0.0769	0.1427	0.0101	0.0189	0.1361
SM-Deep	0.2062	**0.0170**	**0.0314**	0.2811	0.2692	0.0157	0.0297	0.1370	0.2377	**0.0164**	**0.0306**	0.2091
SCM-GIST	0.1024	0.0052	0.0099	0.1646	0.1283	0.0087	0.0163	0.0623	0.1154	0.0139	0.0248	0.1134
SCM-MPEG_7	0.1216	0.0061	0.0116	0.1878	0.1229	0.0090	0.0168	0.0775	0.1223	0.0076	0.0143	0.1327
SCM-Deep	0.1767	0.0089	0.0169	0.2562	0.2036	0.0130	0.0244	0.1285	0.1902	0.0110	0.0208	0.1924
Ours	**0.2250**	0.0118	0.0224	**0.3064**	**0.2781**	**0.0177**	**0.0333**	**0.1897**	**0.2516**	0.0144	0.0272	**0.2481**

The mean average precision (MAP) is used to evaluate the overall performance of approaches for cross-media retrieval task. To compute MAP, we first evaluate the average precision (AP) of a set of R retrieved sets by

$$AP = \frac{1}{R}\sum_{k=1}^{N}\frac{R_k}{k} \times rel_k, \tag{7}$$

where R is the number of relevant items in the retrieved set N, R_k denotes the precision of the top k retrieved results, and $rel_k = 1$ when the k-th retrieved item is relevant and otherwise 0. The MAP is the average value of the AP values over all queries in the query set. The larger MAP indicate better performance.

4.5 Results Analysis

In order to illustrate the effectiveness of our method, we report comparative results with other methods on the dataset in Table 2. As is shown, when we utilize the same method, such as SCM, deep feature improve mAP by 9% compared with hand-craft features, *i.e.*, MPEG_7 feature. When using SM, deep feature outperforms the GIST feature by about 12% in image retrieval text task on mAP. We can conclude that deep visual feature combined with the traditional methods improve the retrieval performance against the hand-craft features, *i.e.*, GIST feature and MPEG_7 feature. It also can be seen that SM outperform CM and SCM, for example, SM improve mAP about 8% compared with CM and 3% against SCM when using deep visual feature and text word2vec feature. Our framework performs favorably against all the baseline methods on all evaluate metrics. For example, our method improves mAP about 2% compared with SM-Deep, 10% compared with CM-Deep in image retrieval text task. Because our framework can optimize both subnetworks simultaneously, *i.e.*, textual network and visual network, to further learn two representation in an end-to-end manner. The two networks can be boosted in the training process of the framework.

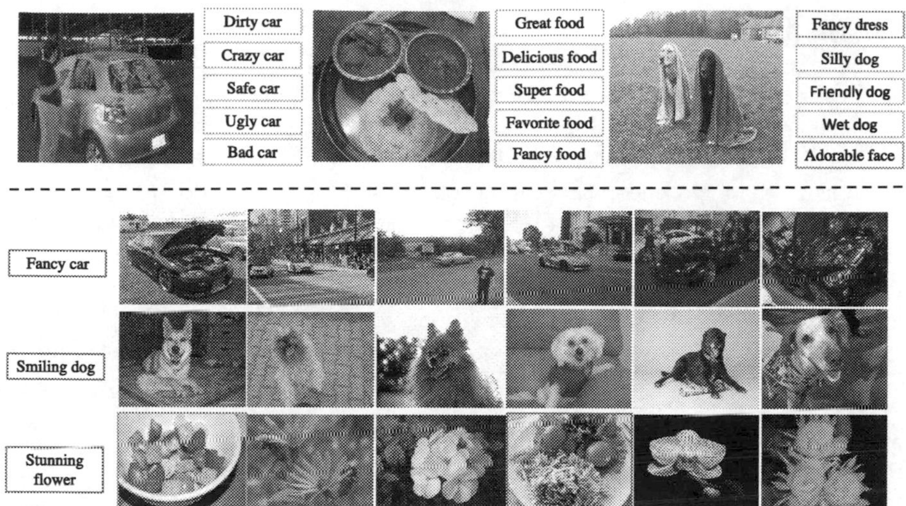

Fig. 4. Several correct and failure retrieved results of our method on the dataset. In the top line, *i.e.*, cases of image query text, the correct related and false ANP is marked with green and red. In the cases of text query images, the first two line show our top-6 retrieval results. While some image retrieved by 'stunning flower' is false, with red border. (Color figure online)

Thus, we draw the following conclusions: First, the deep visual feature can represent that image feature more effectively compared with the traditional feature. Second, the fine-tuned feature on the affective image dataset can represent the visual modality related to sentiment to further improve performance.

4.6 Visualization

To qualitatively evaluate our proposed approach, we visualize some example results, *i.e.*, image retrieved by text query and text retrieved by image query. We show our cross-modal retrieval example results in Fig. 4. In the cases of image query texts, the retrieved ANP is related to object and sentiment in image. For example, for 'dirty car' queries, the first retrieved image is completely corresponding to the image. While other ANP is related to objects 'car'. The right is failure result, which demonstrates that the color of dog is similar to the cloth and confuse the model to return the false results. While the correct result occurs in the fourth position. As is shown, in the cases of text query images, *i.e.*, the first line, our approach retrieval the correct images in top-6. And the false retrieved image with red border. Although the top-1 retrieved example does not have the same ANP label, such image has the related sentiment, *e.g.*, stunning flower. But our approach still achieves good performance on cross-modal retrieval task and can effectively retrieval sentiment-related and object-alignment results.

5 Conclusion

In this work, we introduce a novel problem in the field of cross-modal retrieval, *i.e.*, sentiment oriented cross-media retrieval. Different from traditional task, we focus on the problem of retrieving visual sentiment concepts in affective image and retrieving image according to the emotional text. To address this problem, we propose a deep coordinated neural network combines two branches, i.e. visual and textual branches, which is optimized with a multi-task loss function for the cross-modal representation learning. The experiments on the subset of VSO dataset demonstrate that our method can efficiently establish the correspondence between different modalities, i.e., image and text, and further improve the retrieval performance.

Acknowledgments. This work was partially supported by grants from the NSFC (No. U1533104), the Natural Science Foundation of Tianjin, China (No. 18JCYBJC15400), and the Open Project Program of the National Laboratory of Pattern Recognition (NLPR).

References

1. Rasiwasia, N., et al.: A new approach to cross-modal multimedia retrieval. In: Proceedings of the 18th ACM International Conference on Multimedia, pp. 251–260. ACM, New York (2010)
2. Mikolov, T., Sutskever, I., Chen, K., Corrado, G.S., Dean, J.: Distributed representations of words and phrases and their compositionality. In: Advances in Neural Information Processing Systems, pp. 3111–3119 (2013)
3. Pereira, J.C., et al.: On the role of correlation and abstraction in cross-modal multimedia retrieval. IEEE Trans. Pattern Anal. Mach. Intell. **36**(3), 521–535 (2014)
4. Joshi, D., et al.: Aesthetics and emotions in images. IEEE Sig. Process. Mag. **28**(5), 94–115 (2011)
5. Truong, Q.T., Lauw, H.W.: Visual sentiment analysis for review images with item-oriented and user-oriented CNN. In: Proceedings of the 2017 ACM on Multimedia Conference, pp. 1274–1282. ACM (2017)
6. Jia, J., Wu, S., Wang, X., Hu, P., Cai, L., Tang, J.: Can we understand van Gogh's mood?: learning to infer affects from images in social networks. In: Proceedings of the 20th ACM International Conference on Multimedia, pp. 857–860. ACM (2012)
7. Sharif Razavian, A., Azizpour, H., Sullivan, J., Carlsson, S.: CNN features off-the-shelf: an astounding baseline for recognition. In: Proceedings of the IEEE Conference on Computer Vision and Pattern Recognition Workshops, pp. 806–813 (2014)
8. Simonyan, K., Zisserman, A.: Very deep convolutional networks for large-scale image recognition. arXiv preprint arXiv:1409.1556. (2014)
9. Girshick, R., Donahue, J., Darrell, T., Malik, J.: Rich feature hierarchies for accurate object detection and semantic segmentation. In: Proceedings of the IEEE Conference on Computer Vision and Pattern Recognition, pp. 580–587 (2014)
10. Andrew, G., Arora, R., Bilmes, J., Livescu, K.: Deep canonical correlation analysis. In: International Conference on Machine Learning, pp. 1247–1255 (2013)
11. Wang, W., Yang, X., Ooi, B.C., Zhang, D., Zhuang, Y.: Effective deep learning-based multi-modal retrieval. VLDB J. **25**(1), 79–101 (2016)

12. Krizhevsky, A., Sutskever, I., Hinton, G.E.: ImageNet classification with deep convolutional neural networks. In: Advances in Neural Information Processing Systems, pp. 1097–1105 (2012)
13. Gong, Y., Ke, Q., Isard, M., Lazebnik, S.: A multi-view embedding space for modeling internet images, tags, and their semantics. Int. J. Comput. Vis. **106**(2), 210–233 (2014)
14. Klein, B., Lev, G., Sadeh, G., Wolf, L.: Associating neural word embeddings with deep image representations using fisher vectors. In: Proceedings of the IEEE Conference on Computer Vision and Pattern Recognition, pp. 4437–4446 (2015)
15. Ngiam, J., Khosla, A., Kim, M., Nam, J., Lee, H., Ng, A.Y.: Multimodal deep learning. In: 28th International Conference on Machine Learning, pp. 689–696 (2011)
16. Li, D., Dimitrova, N., Li, M., Sethi, I.K.: Multimedia content processing through cross-modal association. In: Proceedings of the Eleventh ACM International Conference on Multimedia, pp. 604 611. ACM (2003)
17. Zhai, X., Peng, Y., Xiao, J.: Learning cross-media joint representation with sparse and semisupervised regularization. IEEE Trans. Circuits Syst. Video Technol. **24**(6), 965–978 (2014)
18. Wang, K., He, R., Wang, L., Wang, W., Tan, T.: Joint feature selection and subspace learning for cross-modal retrieval. IEEE Trans. Pattern Anal. Mach. Intell. **38**(10), 2010–2023 (2016)
19. Zhai, X., Peng, Y., Xiao, J.: Heterogeneous metric learning with joint graph regularization for cross-media retrieval. In: Association for the Advancement of Artificial Intelligence (2013)
20. Ranjan, V., Rasiwasia, N., Jawahar, C.V.: Multi-label cross-modal retrieval. In: IEEE International Conference on Computer Vision, pp. 4094–4102 (2015)
21. Feng, F., Wang, X., Li, R.: Cross-modal retrieval with correspondence autoencoder. In: 22nd ACM International Conference on Multimedia, pp. 7–16 (2014)
22. Peng, Y., Huang, X., Qi, J.: Cross-media shared representation by hierarchical learning with multiple deep networks. In: 25th International Joint Conference on Artificial Intelligence, pp. 3846–3853 (2016)
23. Yan, F., Mikolajczyk, K.: Deep correlation for matching images and text. In: IEEE Conference on Computer Vision and Pattern Recognition, pp. 3441–3450 (2015)
24. Machajdik, J., Hanbury, A.: Affective image classification using features inspired by psychology and art theory. In: 18th ACM International Conference on Multimedia, pp. 83–92. ACM (2010)
25. You, Q., Luo, J., Jin, H., Yang, J.: Building a large scale dataset for image emotion recognition: the fine print and the benchmark. In: Association for the Advancement of Artificial Intelligence, pp. 308–314 (2016)
26. Deng, J., Dong, W., Socher, R., Li, L.J., Li, K., Fei-Fei, L.: ImageNet: a large-scale hierarchical image database. In: IEEE Conference on Computer Vision and Pattern Recognition, pp. 248–255 (2009)
27. Liu, T., Zhao, Y., Wei, S., Wei, Y., Liao, L.: Enhanced isomorphic semantic representation for cross-media retrieval. In: IEEE International Conference on Multimedia and Expo, pp. 967–972 (2017)
28. Chen, T., Yu, F.X., Chen, J., Cui, Y., Chen, Y.Y., Chang, S.F.: Object-based visual sentiment concept analysis and application. In: Proceedings of the 22nd ACM International Conference on Multimedia, pp. 367–376. ACM (2014)
29. Yang, J., Sun, M., Sun, X.: Learning visual sentiment distributions via augmented conditional probability neural network. In: The Association for the Advancement of Artificial Intelligence, pp. 224–230 (2017)

30. Yang, J., She, D., Sun, M.: Joint image emotion classification and distribution learning via deep convolutional neural network. In: Proceedings of the 26th International Joint Conference on Artificial Intelligence, pp. 3266–3272 (2017)
31. Yang, J., She, D., Lai, Y., Yang, M.H.: Retrieving and classifying affective images via deep metric learning. In: The Association for the Advancement of Artificial Intelligence (2018)
32. Yang, J., She, D., Sun, M., Cheng, M.M., Rosin, P., Wang, L.: Visual sentiment prediction based on automatic discovery of affective regions. IEEE Trans. Multimed. **PP**(99), 1 (2018)
33. Yang, J., She, D., Lai, Y.K., Rosin, P.L., Yang, M.H.: Weakly supervised coupled networks for visual sentiment analysis. In: IEEE Conference on Computer Vision and Pattern Recognition (2018)
34. Srivastava, N., Salakhutdinov, R.R.: Multimodal learning with deep boltzmann machines. In: Advances in Neural Information Processing Systems, pp. 2222–2230 (2012)

A New Context-Based Clustering Framework for Categorical Data

Thanh-Phu Nguyen(✉), Duy-Tai Dinh, and Van-Nam Huynh

School of Knowledge Science, Japan Advanced Institute of Science and Technology, 1-1 Asahidai, Nomi, Ishikawa 923-1292, Japan
{ntphu,taidinh,huynh}@jaist.ac.jp

Abstract. Clustering is a fundamental task that has been utilized in many scientific fields, especially in machine learning and data mining. In clustering, dissimilarity measures play a key role in formulating clusters. For handling categorical values, the simple matching method is usually used for quantifying their dissimilarity. However, this method cannot capture the hidden semantic information that can be inferred from relationships among categories. In this paper, we propose a new clustering framework for categorical data that is capable of integrating not only the distributions of categories but also their mutual relationship information into the pattern proximity evaluation process of the clustering task. The effectiveness of the proposed clustering algorithm is proven by a comparative study conducted on existing clustering methods for categorical data.

Keywords: Clustering task · Categorical data
Dissimilarity measure · Unsupervised learning

1 Introduction

Clustering is a common method that is widely used in a variety of fields. Clustering groups data into clusters. For each cluster, objects in the same cluster are similar between themselves and dissimilar to objects in other clusters [1]. Clustering techniques can be classified into two main classes: hierarchical clustering and partitional clustering [2]. In fact, partitional methods have shown their effectiveness for solving clustering problems with scalability. Among them, the k-means [3] is probably the most well-known and widely used method. However, one inherent limitation of this approach is its data type constraint, as the k-means technically can only work with numerical data type.

During the last decade or so, several attempts have been made in order to remove the numeric data only limitation of k-means to make it applicable to clustering for categorical data. Particularly, some k-means like methods for categorical data have been proposed such as k-modes [4], k-representatives [5], k-centers [6] and k-means like clustering algorithm [7]. Although these algorithms

X. Geng and B.-H. Kang (Eds.): PRICAI 2018, LNAI 11012, pp. 697–709, 2018.
https://doi.org/10.1007/978-3-319-97304-3_53

use a similar clustering fashion to the k-means algorithm, they are different in defining cluster mean or dissimilarity measure for categorical data.

Furthermore, measures to quantify the dissimilarity (similarity) for categorical values are still not well-understood because there is no coherent metric available between categorical values thus far. Several methods have been proposed for encoding categorical data as numerical values such as dummy coding (or indicator coding) [8,9]. Particularly, they use binary values to indicate whether a categorical value is absent or present in a data record. However, by treating each category as an independent variable in that way, many important features and characteristics of categorical data type such as the distribution of categories or their relationships may not be taken into account.

Moreover, the significance of considering those information in order to quantify the dissimilarity between categorical data has been proven by several previous studies [7,10]. Especially, in the field of clustering with categorical data, most previous works have unfortunately neglected the semantic information potentially inferred from relationships among categories. In this research, we propose a new clustering algorithm that is able to integrate those kinds of information into the clustering process for categorical data.

Generally, the key contribution of this work is threefold:

- First, we extend an existing measure for categorical data to a new dissimilarity measure that is suitable for solving our problem. The measure is based on the conditional probability of correlated attributes values to include the mutual relationship between categorical attributes.
- Then, we propose a new categorical clustering algorithm that takes account of the semantic relationships between categories into the dissimilarity measure.
- Finally, we carry out an extensive experimental evaluation on benchmark data sets from UCI Machine Learning Repository [11] to evaluate the performance of our proposed algorithm with other existing methods in term of clustering quality.

The rest of this paper is organized as follows. In the Sect. 2, related work is reviewed. In the Sect. 3, a new clustering algorithm for categorical data is proposed. Next, the Sect. 4 describes an experimental evaluation. Finally, the Sect. 5 draws a conclusion.

2 Related Work

The conventional k-means algorithm [3] is one of the most often used clustering algorithms. It has some important properties: its computational complexity is linearly proportional to the size of datasets, it often terminates at a local optimum, its performance is dependent on the initialization of the centers [12]. However, working only on numerical data restricts some applications of the k-means algorithm. Specifically, it cannot process directly categorical data - a popular data type in many real life applications nowadays.

To address this limitation, several k-means like methods have been proposed for clustering task with categorical data. In 1997, Huang proposed k-modes and k-prototypes algorithms [4,13,14]. The k-modes [4] uses the simple matching measure to quantify the dissimilarity between categorical objects. It uses the modes to represent clusters, and a frequency-based method to update modes in the clustering process. The mode of a cluster is a data point whose attribute values are assigned by the most frequent values of the attribute's domain set appearing in the cluster. The k-modes first selects k initial modes (one for each cluster) from a data set X. Then, it allocates each object in X to a cluster whose mode is the nearest to that object based on the simple matching dissimilarity measure, and updates the mode of the cluster after each allocation. Next, it retests the dissimilarity of objects against the current modes after all objects have been allocated to clusters. Finally, it repeats the assignment step until no object has changed clusters after a full cycle test of the whole data set X.

The k-prototypes [13] is a combination of k-means and k-modes approaches to cluster objects with mixed numeric and categorical attributes. The k-prototypes can be divided into three steps: initial prototype selection, initial allocation and re-allocation. The first process randomly selects k objects as the initial prototypes for clusters. The second process assigns each object to a cluster and updates the cluster prototype after each assignment. The reallocation process updates prototypes for both the previous and current clusters of the object. Consequently, it iterates reallocation process until all objects are assigned to clusters and no object has changed clusters.

In 2004, San et al. proposed a k-means like algorithm named k-representatives [5]. The k-representatives applies the Cartesian product and union operations for the formation of cluster centers based on the notion of means in the numerical setting. In addition, it uses the dissimilarity based on the relative frequencies of categorical values within the cluster and the simple matching measure between categorical values. The algorithmic structure of k-representatives is formed in the same way as the k-modes [4].

Recently, Chen and Wang proposed a kernel-density-based clustering algorithm named k-centers [6]. The k-centers uses kernel density estimation method to define the mean of a categorical data set as a statistical center of the set. It incorporates a new feature weighting in which each attribute is automatically assigned with a weight to measure its individual contribution for the clusters. More recently, Nguyen and Huynh proposed the k-means like clustering framework [7]. This method extends k-representatives by replacing the simple matching measure with an information theoretic-based dissimilarity measure and adding a new concept of cluster centers.

3 The Proposed Clustering Algorithm

In this section, we propose a new clustering algorithm, namely $RICS$, that can integrate the mutual relationship information between categorical attributes into the clustering process. Details of the proposed algorithm are presented in two parts. The first part refers to significant elements of a k-means like clustering algorithm. The second part introduces a new dissimilarity measure for categorical data. Before going into the details of the clustering algorithm, we first introduce some notations that will be used in the rest of this paper.

3.1 Notations

Given a categorical data set X that contains n instances described by d attributes. The notations used in the rest of this paper are presented in the following.

- An attribute of X is denoted by A_j, $j \in \{1, \ldots, d\}$. For each A_j, its domain is denoted by $dom(A_j)$. Moreover, each value of A_j is denoted as a_l (or simply a) with $l \in \{1, \ldots, |dom(A_j)|\}$.
- An instance of X is presented as a vector $x = [x_1, \ldots, x_d]$ where the value of x at an attribute A_j is denoted as x_j, $j \in \{1, \ldots, d\}$.
- The frequency of $a_l \in dom(A_j)$ is denoted as $P(a_l)$ and calculated by

$$P(a_l) = \frac{count(A_j = a_l|X)}{|X|} \tag{1}$$

similarly, for $a_l \in dom(A_j)$ and $a_{l'} \in dom(A_{j'})$ we have

$$P(a_l, a_{l'}) = \frac{count((A_j = a_l) \text{ and } (A_{j'} = a_{l'})|X)}{|X|} \tag{2}$$

3.2 *k*-Means Like Clustering Framework

The clustering method proposed in this paper basically follows the k-means like clustering scheme as studied in [7]. Specifically, it still reserves the general procedure of the k-means but includes a modified concept of cluster centers based on the work of Chen and Wang [6] and a weighting method for each categorical attribute as well.

3.2.1 Representation of Cluster Centers

Let $C = \{C_1, \ldots, C_k\}$ be the set of k clusters of X, for any two different clusters C_i and $C_{i'}$ we have

$$C_i \cap C_{i'} = \emptyset \text{ if } i \neq i' \text{and } X = \bigcup_{i=1}^{k} C_i \tag{3}$$

Furthermore, for each cluster C_i, the center of C_i is defined as

$$V_i = [v_{i1}, \ldots, v_{ij}, \ldots, v_{id}] \tag{4}$$

where v_{ij} is a probability distribution on the domain of an attribute A_j that is estimated by a kernel density estimation function K.

$$v_{ij} = [p(a_1), \ldots, p(a_{|dom(A_j)|})] \tag{5}$$

where

$$p(a_l) = \sum_{a \in dom(A_j)} f_i(a) K(a|\lambda_j) \tag{6}$$

with $f_i(a)$ is the frequency probability of an attribute value a in the cluster V_i.

$$f_i(a) = \frac{count(A_j = a|V_i)}{|V_i|} \tag{7}$$

Moreover, consider σ_{ij} as the set that contains all available values of attribute A_j that exist in cluster V_i

$$\sigma_{ij} = \{a, a \in dom(A_j)|V_i\} \tag{8}$$

then the kernel function $K(a|\lambda_j)$ to estimate the probability of those attribute values in cluster V_i is defined as

$$K(a|\lambda_j) = \begin{cases} 1 - \frac{|\sigma_{ij}|-1}{|\sigma_{ij}|}\lambda_j & \text{if } a = a_l \\ \frac{1}{|\sigma_{ij}|}\lambda_j & \text{if } a \neq a_l \end{cases} \tag{9}$$

where λ_j is the smoothing parameter for C_j and has the value range of $[0, 1]$. In order to select the best parameter λ_j, the least squares cross validation (LSCV) method [6] is utilized. In the case $a \notin \sigma_{ij}$, $K(a|\lambda_j)$ value is set to 0.

Finally, from (4)–(6), we have the general formulation to compare the dissimilarity between a data instance $x \in X$ and a cluster center V_i described as below.

$$D(x, V_i) = \sum_{j=1}^{d} d(x_j, v_{ij}) = \sum_{j=1}^{d} \sum_{a \in dom(A_j)} p(a) \times dis(x_j, a) \tag{10}$$

where $dis(x_j, a)$ is the measure to quantify the dissimilarity between two values of an attribute A_j. Detailed information about this measure will be described in Subsect. 3.3.

3.2.2 Weighting Scheme for Categorical Attributes

A weighting model is also applied for categorical attributes as studied in [15]. Generally, a larger weight is set to attributes that have a smaller sum of within cluster distances and vice versa. More details of this method could be found in [15].

Consequently, we have a vector of weights $W = [w_1, \ldots, w_d]$ that is assigned to each attribute where each $w_j \leq 1$ and $\sum_{j=1}^{d} w_j = 1$.

Then, the weighted dissimilarity measure between a data instance x and a cluster center V_i could be defined as

$$D_w(x, V_i) = \sum_{j=1}^{d} w_j \times d(x_j, v_{ij}) \tag{11}$$

Based on these definitions, the clustering algorithm now aims to minimize the following objective function:

$$J(U, V, W) = \sum_{i=1}^{k} \sum_{g=1}^{n} \sum_{j=1}^{d} u_{i,g} \times w_j \times d(x_j, v_{ij}) \tag{12}$$

subject to

$$\begin{cases} \sum_{i=1}^{k} u_{i,g} = 1 & 1 \leq g \leq n \\ u_{i,g} \in \{0,1\} & 1 \leq g \leq n,\ 1 \leq i \leq k \\ \sum_{j=1}^{d} w_j = 1 & 0 \leq w_j \leq 1 \end{cases} \tag{13}$$

where $U = [u_{i,g}]_{n \times k}$ is the partition matrix. The algorithm for the k-means like clustering framework is described in Algorithm 1.

Algorithm 1. k-means like clustering framework [7]

Input: Data set $X = \{x_1, ..., x_n\}$
Output: Optimized clusters $C = \{C_1, ..., C_k\}$
1: Initialize centers for k clusters $V = [V_1, ..., V_k]$.
2: Initialize weights $W = [w_1, ..., w_d]$ and set $\lambda = 0$ for each attribute.
3: ***do***
4: Keep V and W fixed, generate U to minimize the distances between objects and cluster centers using Eq. (11).
5: Keep U fixed, update V using Eq. (5) and Eq. (6).
6: Generate W using formulas from [15].
7: ***while*** partitions still change.

3.3 A Context-Based Dissimilarity Measure for Categorical Data

In order to quantify the dissimilarity between categorical values, we extend the similarity measure proposed in [16] that could be able to integrate not only the distribution of categories but also their mutual relationship information. Specifically, the dissimilarity measure considers the amount of information to describe the appearances of pairs of attribute values rather than single values only. However, instead of considering all possible cases, only pairs of attributes that are highly correlated with each other are selected.

3.3.1 Correlation Analysis for Categorical Attributes

For the purpose of selecting highly correlated attribute pairs, the interdependence redundancy measure proposed by Au et al. [17] is adopted to quantify the dependency degree between each pair of attributes. Specifically, the interdependence redundancy value between two attributes A_j and $A_{j'}$ is computed as in the following formula.

$$R(A_j, A_{j'}) = \frac{I(A_j, A_{j'})}{H(A_j, A_{j'})} \tag{14}$$

where $I(A_j, A_{j'})$ denotes the mutual information [18] between attribute A_j and $A_{j'}$ and $H(A_j, A_{j'})$ is their joint entropy value. We have the formulas for those measures as the followings.

$$I(A_j, A_{j'}) = \sum_{p=1}^{|dom(A_j)|} \sum_{q=1}^{|dom(A_{j'})|} P(a_{jp}, a_{j'q}) * \log \frac{P(a_{jp}, a_{j'q})}{P(a_{jp}) * P(a_{j'q})} \tag{15}$$

$$H(A_j, A_{j'}) = - \sum_{p=1}^{|dom(A_j)|} \sum_{q=1}^{|dom(A_{j'})|} P(a_{jp}, a_{j'q}) * \log P(a_{jp}, a_{j'q}) \tag{16}$$

According to Au et al. [17], the interdependency redundancy measure has the value range of $[0, 1]$. A large value of R implies a high degree of dependency between attributes.

For each attribute A_j, in order to select its highly correlated attributes, a relation set is defined and denoted as S_j. Specifically, S_j contains attributes whose the associated interdependency redundancy values with A_j are larger than a specific threshold γ.

$$S_j = \{A_{j'} | R(A_j, A_{j'}) > \gamma, 1 \leq j, j' \leq d\} \tag{17}$$

3.3.2 New Dissimilarity Measure for Categorical Data

For integrating the relationship information that is contained in the set S_j, the conditional probability of correlated attributes values is utilized to include the mutual relationships between categorical attributes. In particular, to quantify the similarity between categorical values of attribute A_j, the following measure is implemented.

$$sim(x_j, x'_j) = \sum_{A_{j'} \in S_j} \sum_{a \in dom(A_{j'})} \frac{1}{|S_j|} \times \frac{1}{|dom(A_{j'})|} \times \frac{2 \times \log P(\{x_j, x'_j\}|a)}{\log P(x_j|a) + \log P(x'_j|a)} \tag{18}$$

It could be easily seen that the similarity measure in Eq. (18) have the value range of $[0, 1]$. Specifically, when x_j and x'_j are identical, their similarity degree is equal to 1. Then, the dissimilarity measure between two values of an attribute that is used in Eq. (10) could be defined as below.

$$dis(x_j, x'_j) = 1 - sim(x_j, x'_j) \tag{19}$$

The extended dissimilarity measure defined in Eq. (19) satisfies the following conditions:

1. $dis(x_j, x'_j) \geq 0$ for each x_j, x'_j with $j \in \{1, \ldots, d\}$
2. $dis(x_j, x_j) = 0$ with $\forall j \in \{1, \ldots, d\}$
3. $dis(x_j, x'_j) = dis(x'_j, x_j)$ for each x_j, x'_j with $j \in \{1, \ldots, d\}$.

For reducing the computational time of the proposed algorithm, the relation set of each attribute is generated in advance. Moreover, the dissimilarity between attribute values is also precomputed and cached in a multi-dimensional matrix for later used. Finally, details of the *RICS* algorithm are described in the Algorithm 2.

Algorithm 2. *RICS* clustering method

Input: Data set $X = \{x_1, ..., x_n\}$
Output: Optimized clusters $C = \{C_1, ..., C_k\}$
Generate relation set S_j for all attributes A_j using Eq. (14)-(17).
Precompute dissimilarity value $dis(a_l, a_{l'})$ for all $a_l, a_{l'} \in dom(A_j)$ with $j \in \{1, ..., d\}$ using Eq. (18), (19).
Initialize centers for k clusters $V = [V_1, ..., V_k]$.
Initialize weights $W = [w_1, ..., w_d]$ and set $\lambda = 0$ for each attribute.
do
  Keep V and W fixed, generate U to minimize the distances between objects and cluster centers using Eq. (11).
  Keep U fixed, update V using Eq. (5) and Eq. (6).
  Generate W using formulas from [15].
while partitions still change.

4 Experimental Evaluation

To evaluate the efficiency of the newly proposed algorithm, we conduct a comparative experiment on commonly used clustering methods for categorical data. Specifically, we contrast our new proposed clustering framework *RICS* with the implementation of k-modes [4], k-representatives [5] and k-means like clustering framework [7]. Furthermore, for each algorithm, we run 300 times per dataset. For the threshold value γ, it is practically found that with $\gamma = 0.1$ we could achieve general good results. Also, the value of parameter k is set equal to the number of classes in each dataset. The final results for three evaluation metrics are calculated by averaging the results of 300 running times.

4.1 Testing Datasets

Datasets for the experiment are selected from the UCI Machine Learning Repository [11]. The chosen 14 datasets contain not only categorical attributes but also integer and real values. For those numerical values, a discretization tool of Weka [19] is utilized for discretizing numerical values into equal intervals which are, in turn, treated as categorical values. In addition, the average dependency degree of each dataset is computed by averaging the interdependency redundancy values of all distinct pairs of attributes based on Eq. (14). Main characteristics of selected datasets are summarized in Table 1.

4.2 Clustering Quality Evaluation

In this research, in order to take advantages of class information in the original datasets, we take the same approach as [7] by utilizing the following supervised

Table 1. Main characteristics of 14 datasets from UCI

Dataset	Inst.	Attr.	Classes	Data types	Avg. dependency degree
Soybean	307	35	19	Categorical	0.153
Hayes-roth	160	5	3	Categorical	0.113
Wine	178	13	3	Integer, Real	0.089
Voting-records	435	16	2	Categorical	0.085
Dermatology	366	33	6	Categorical, integer	0.052
Breast cancer	286	9	2	Categorical	0.027
Post-operative	90	8	3	Categorical, integer	0.014
Chess	3196	36	2	Categorical, integer	0.010
Tictactoe	958	9	2	Categorical	0.006
Splice	3190	61	3	Categorical	0.003
Car	1728	6	4	Categorical	0
Lenses	24	4	3	Categorical	0
Nursery	12960	8	5	Categorical	0
Balance-scale	625	4	3	Categorical	0

evaluation metrics for assessing clustering results: Purity, Normalized Mutual Information (NMI) and Adjusted Rand Index (ARI).

In particular, let us denote $C = \{C_1, \ldots, C_J\}$ as a partition of the dataset that is generated by the clustering algorithm, and $P = \{P_1, \ldots, P_I\}$ is the partition which is inferred by the original class information. The total number of objects in the dataset is denoted by n.

Purity Metric. To compute purity value of a clustering result, firstly, each cluster is assigned to the class which is most frequent in the cluster. Then, the accuracy of this assignment is measured by counting the number of correctly assigned objects and dividing by the number of objects in the dataset. It is also worth noting that the purity metric could be significantly effected by the existence of imbalanced classes.

$$Purity(C, P) = \frac{1}{n} \sum_{j} \max_{i} |C_j \cap P_i| \tag{20}$$

NMI Metric. The NMI metric provides an information that is independent from the number of clusters [20]. This measure takes its maximum value when the clustering partition matches completely the original partition. NMI is computed as the average mutual information between any pair of clusters and classes.

$$NMI(C,P) = \frac{\sum_{i=1}^{I}\sum_{j=1}^{J}|C_j \cap P_i|\log\frac{n|C_j \cap P_i|}{|C_j||P_i|}}{\sqrt{\sum_{j=1}^{J}|C_j|\log\frac{|C_j|}{n}\sum_{i=1}^{I}|P_i|\log\frac{|P_i|}{n}}} \tag{21}$$

ARI Metric. The third metric is the Adjusted Rand Index [21]. Let a be the number of object pairs belonging to the same cluster in C and to the same class in P. This metric captures the deviation of a from its expected value corresponding to the hypothetical value of a obtained when C and P are two random, independent partitions.

The expected value of a is denoted as $E[a]$ and computed by:

$$E[a] = \frac{\pi(C)\pi(P)}{N(N-1)/2} \tag{22}$$

where $\pi(C)$ and $\pi(P)$ denote respectively the number of object pairs from the same clusters in C and from the same class in P. The maximum value for a is defined as:

$$max(a) = \frac{1}{2}(\pi(C) + \pi(P)) \tag{23}$$

The agreement between C and P can be estimated by the adjusted rand index as follows:

$$ARI(C,P) = \frac{a - E[a]}{max(a) - E[a]} \tag{24}$$

when $ARI(C,P) = 1$, we have identical partitions.

4.3 Experimental Results

From the results in Tables 2, 3 and 4, there is no best method for all of the testing datasets. However, we could see that the proposed clustering framework $RICS$ has achieved relatively good results comparing with other methods. Specifically, it performs effectively with highly correlated datasets such as soybean, hayes-roth, wine and dermatology. Moreover, the average results in all three tables show that our proposed framework has the best average results.

It is also worth noting that if we take a glance at the purity results in Table 2, the k-modes appears to outperform k-representatives and k-means like clustering method, and has a good performance when compared to $RICS$. However, when we make a more detailed inspection of the NMI and ARI results, it could be seen that k-modes actually has poor performances regarding those two more significant standards, while $RICS$ is still the one that has most of the best results over the total of 14 datasets.

Table 2. Purity results for categorical datasets

Data sets	RICS	k-means like framework	k-representatives	k-modes
Soybean	**0.7176**	0.7142	0.7152	0.6099
Hayes-roth	0.3954	0.3953	0.3998	**0.4079**
Wine	**0.9397**	0.9214	0.9380	0.7707
Voting-records	**0.8770**	0.8760	0.8764	0.8581
Dermatology	0.8560	0.8506	**0.8593**	0.7116
Breast-cancer	**0.7028**	**0.7028**	**0.7028**	**0.7028**
Post-operative	**0.7111**	**0.7111**	**0.7111**	**0.7111**
Chess	0.5223	0.5225	0.5222	**0.5761**
Tictactoe	0.6534	0.6534	0.6534	**0.6558**
Splice	**0.7586**	0.7572	0.6159	0.5188
Car	**0.7150**	0.7059	0.7046	0.7004
Lenses	0.6999	0.6981	**0.7018**	0.6446
Nursery	0.4449	0.4502	0.4324	**0.4704**
Balance-scale	0.5779	**0.5787**	0.5761	0.5496
Average	**0.6837**	0.6812	0.6721	0.6348

Table 3. NMI results for categorical datasets

Data sets	RICS	k-means like framework	k-representatives	k-modes
Soybean	0.7517	0.7473	**0.7545**	0.6069
Hayes-roth	0.0041	0.0038	0.0011	**0.0050**
Wine	0.7893	0.7580	**0.7941**	0.4252
Voting-records	**0.5055**	0.5002	0.4990	0.4359
Dermatology	**0.8551**	0.8512	**0.8551**	0.5735
Breast-cancer	**0.0041**	0.0040	0.0018	0.0038
Post-operative	0.0146	0.0140	0.0198	**0.0243**
Chess	0.0006	0.0007	0.0002	**0.0187**
Tictactoe	0.0346	**0.0393**	0.0087	0.0206
Splice	**0.4620**	0.4592	0.2820	0.0473
Car	**0.1435**	0.1234	0.1213	0.0475
Lenses	**0.3444**	0.3442	0.3432	0.1880
Nursery	0.0947	**0.1038**	0.0855	0.0601
Balance-scale	0.0485	**0.0491**	0.0474	0.0313
Average	**0.2895**	0.2856	0.2724	0.1777

Table 4. ARI results for categorical datasets

Data sets	RICS	k-means like framework	k-representatives	k-modes
Soybean	0.4642	0.4655	**0.4754**	0.3748
Hayes-roth	**−0.0102**	−0.0105	−0.0138	−0.0111
Wine	**0.8200**	0.7721	0.8145	0.4287
Voting-records	0.5642	0.5644	**0.5658**	0.5119
Dermatology	**0.7494**	0.7421	0.7389	0.5503
Breast-cancer	0.0018	0.0015	−0.0030	**0.0020**
Post-operative	**−0.0105**	−0.0113	−0.0110	−0.0178
Chess	−0.0001	0.0001	−0.0003	**0.0238**
Tictactoe	0.0325	**0.0380**	0.0218	0.0247
Splice	**0.3927**	0.3900	0.2021	0.0289
Car	0.0555	**0.0598**	0.0537	0.0239
Lenses	**0.2108**	0.2075	0.1835	0.0596
Nursery	0.0578	**0.0637**	0.0559	0.0506
Balance-scale	0.0507	**0.0522**	0.0505	0.0323
Average	**0.2413**	0.2382	0.2239	0.1487

5 Conclusion

In this paper, we have proposed a new clustering method for categorical data that could be able to integrate not only the distributions of categories but also their relationship information into the quantification of dissimilarity between data objects. The experiments have shown that the proposed clustering algorithm *RICS* has a competitive performance when compared to other popular used clustering methods for categorical data. For the future work, we are planning to extend *RICS* so that it could be used to solve the problem of clustering with mixed numeric and categorical datasets.

References

1. Berkhin, P.: A survey of clustering data mining techniques. In: Kogan, J., Nicholas, C., Teboulle, M. (eds.) Grouping Multidimensional Data, pp. 25–71. Springer, Heidelberg (2006). https://doi.org/10.1007/3-540-28349-8_2
2. Jain, A.K., Murty, M.N., Flynn, P.J.: Data clustering: a review. ACM Comput. Surv. (CSUR) **31**(3), 264–323 (1999)
3. MacQueen, J.: Some methods for classification and analysis of multivariate observations. The Regents of the University of California (1967)
4. Huang, Z.: Extensions to the k-means algorithm for clustering large data sets with categorical values. Data Min. Knowl. Discov. **2**(3), 283–304 (1998)
5. San, O.M., Huynh, V.N., Nakamori, Y.: An alternative extension of the k-means algorithm for clustering categorical data. Int. J. Appl. Math. Comput. Sci. **14**, 241–247 (2004)

6. Chen, L., Wang, S.: Central clustering of categorical data with automated feature weighting. In: Twenty-Third International Joint Conference on Artificial Intelligence (2013)
7. Nguyen, T.-H.T., Huynh, V.-N.: A k-means-like algorithm for clustering categorical data using an information theoretic-based dissimilarity measure. In: Gyssens, M., Simari, G. (eds.) FoIKS 2016. LNCS, vol. 9616, pp. 115–130. Springer, Cham (2016). https://doi.org/10.1007/978-3-319-30024-5_7
8. Cohen, J., Cohen, P.: Applied Multiple Regression/Correlation Analysis for the Behavioral Sciences. L. Erlbaum Associates, Hillsdale (1983)
9. Ralambondrainy, H.: A conceptual version of the K-means algorithm. Pattern Recogn. Lett. **16**(11), 1147–1157 (1995)
10. Ienco, D., Pensa, R.G., Meo, R.: From context to distance: learning dissimilarity for categorical data clustering. ACM Trans. Knowl. Discov. Data **6**(1), 1:1–1:25 (2012)
11. Lichman, M.: UCI machine learning repository (2013). http://archive.ics.uci.edu/ml
12. Gan, G., Ma, C., Wu, J.: Data Clustering: Theory, Algorithms, and Applications, vol. 20. SIAM, Philadelphia (2007)
13. Huang, Z.: Clustering large data sets with mixed numeric and categorical values. In: Proceedings of the 1st Pacific-Asia Conference on Knowledge Discovery and Data Mining (PAKDD), pp. 21–34. Citeseer (1997)
14. Huang, Z.: A fast clustering algorithm to cluster very large categorical data sets in data mining. In. In Research Issues on Data Mining and Knowledge Discovery, pp. 1–8 (1997)
15. Huang, J.Z., Ng, M.K., Rong, H., Li, Z.: Automated variable weighting in k-means type clustering. IEEE Trans. Pattern Anal. Mach. Intell. **27**(5), 657–668 (2005)
16. Nguyen, T.-P., Ryoke, M., Huynh, V.-N.: A new context-based similarity measure for categorical data using information theory. In: Huynh, V.-N., Inuiguchi, M., Tran, D.H., Denoeux, T. (eds.) IUKM 2018. LNCS (LNAI), vol. 10758, pp. 114–125. Springer, Cham (2018). https://doi.org/10.1007/978-3-319-75429-1_10
17. Au, W.H., Chan, K.C.C., Wong, A.K.C., Wang, Y.: Attribute clustering for grouping, selection, and classification of gene expression data. IEEE/ACM Trans. Comput. Biol. Bioinf. **2**(2), 83–101 (2005)
18. MacKay, D.J.C.: Information Theory Inference and Learning Algorithms. Cambridge University Press, New York (2002)
19. Hall, M.A., Holmes, G.: Benchmarking attribute selection techniques for discrete class data mining. IEEE Trans. Knowl. Data Eng. **15**(6), 1437–1447 (2003)
20. Strehl, A., Ghosh, J.: Cluster ensembles a knowledge reuse framework for combining multiple partitions. J. Mach. Learn. Res. **3**, 583–617 (2003)
21. Hubert, L., Arabie, P.: Comparing partitions. J. Classif. **2**(1), 193–218 (1985)

TypicFace: Dynamic Margin Cosine Loss for Deep Face Recognition

Lei Li[✉], Heng Luo, Lei Zhang, Qing Xu, and Hao Ning

The Visual Defence Intelligence Network, Suzhou 215332, China
stone2002hm@gmail.com

Abstract. The performance of face recognition under the open-set protocol is heavily influenced by the discrimination of facial features. However, the Softmax loss, which has been widely used in deep CNN, usually lacks the power to discriminate those features. To address this problem, several loss functions have been proposed recently. All these refined algorithms share the same intuition: maximizing inter-class boundary and minimizing intra-class variance. In this paper we present a novel loss function, namely TypicFace, which separates the face features of an individual into two portions: the typical feature and the atypical feature. Discrimination is strengthened on the typical part and weakened on the atypical one relatively, which is more intuitive. More importantly, our experiments on Label Face in the Wild (LFW) [4] and BLUFR [5] show that TypicFace consistently performs better than the current state-of-the-art methods using the same network architecture and training dataset.

Keywords: Face recognition · Face verification · Loss function

1 Introduction

Face recognition, as one of the most common computer vision tasks, usually includes two sub-tasks: face verification and face identification, while face verification performs the comparison on a pair of faces to decide whether they're derived from the same individual or not, and face identification identifies a particular face from a gallery of faces. Both of the tasks could be divided into three steps which are face detection, feature extraction and classification, respectively.

In terms of testing protocol, face recognition can be evaluated under closed-set or open-set setting. For closed-set protocol, all testing identities are predefined in training set. Therefore, closed-set face recognition can be well addressed as a classification problem, where features are expected to be separable. For open-set protocol, the testing identities are usually disjoint from the training set, which makes problem more challenging yet close to practice. Since it is impossible to classify faces to known identities in training set, we need to map faces to a discriminative feature space. In this scenario, face identification can be viewed as performing face verification between the probe face and all identities in the gallery. Open-set face recognition is essentially a metric learning problem, where the key is to learn discriminative large-margin features. Desired features for open-set face recognition are expected to satisfy the criterion that the maximal intra-class distance is smaller than the minimal inter-class distance under a

X. Geng and B.-H. Kang (Eds.): PRICAI 2018, LNAI 11012, pp. 710–718, 2018.
https://doi.org/10.1007/978-3-319-97304-3_54

certain metric space. However, learning features with this criterion is generally difficult because of the intrinsically large intra-class variation and high inter-class similarity [7] that faces exhibit.

Deep CNN is able to extract clean high-level features, which makes it possible to achieve superior performance with relatively simple classification network: usually, multilayer perceptron networks followed by a softmax layer [8, 9]. But none of CNN-based approaches are capable to effectively formulate the aforementioned criterion with softmax loss functions. In recent studies [1–3], it was learned that traditional softmax is insufficient to maximize the discrimination ability in classification. The softmax loss is typically adept in separating different classes, but not good at making features of the same class compact. To address this, several loss functions are proposed based on the same intuition: maximizing inter-class variance or/and minimizing intra-class variance. In [6] a regularization term was added to penalize the feature-to-center distance. In [1–3] the softmax loss was modified by pushing the classification boundary closer to the weight vector of each class.

In this paper, we follow the intuition that in [3]. Beyond that, the TypicFace makes the classification boundary varies as the angular distance between feature vector and the weight vector varies. The reason will be shown in Sect. 3.4.

Experiment on LFW [4] and BLUFR [5] shows that our loss function with the same network architecture achieves better results than the current state-of-the-art approaches.

2 Related Work

2.1 Normalization Approaches

Normalization has been studied in recent deep face recognition tasks. [10] normalizes the weights by replacing the inner product with cosine similarity in softmax loss. [11] applies the L2 constraint on features to embed faces in normalized space. Note that normalization on feature vectors or weights vectors achieves much lower intra-class angular variability by concentrating more on the angle variability during training. Hence the angles between identities can be well optimized. The aforementioned A-Softmax [2] and AM-Softmax [3] also adopts normalization approaches in feature learning.

2.2 Softmax-Based Loss Functions

In CNN, softmax is one of the most commonly used components which benefits from its simplicity and relatively excellent performance except it does not explicitly encourage discriminative learning of features. Liu et al. [1] proposed a large margin softmax (L-Softmax) which has improved feature discrimination by adding angular constraint to each individual. Angular softmax (A-Softmax) [2] behaves better than L-Softmax by normalizing the weights to focusing more attention on the angular variability. The softmax loss was reformulated to cosine loss while normalizing both features and weight vectors to remove radial variation in [3]. By introducing a cosine margin term m to further maximize decision margin in angular space, it achieves better performance on a series recognition benchmarks [4, 5] under the open-set protocol.

3 From Softmax to TypicFace

3.1 Softmax

The formulation of the original softmax loss is given by:

$$L_S = \frac{1}{N}\sum_{i=1}^{N} - \log p_i = \frac{1}{N}\sum_{i=1}^{N} - \log \frac{e^{f_{y_i}}}{\sum_{j=1}^{C} e^{f_j}}$$

Where p_i denotes the posterior probability of x_i being correctly classified. The N is the number of training samples and C is the number of classes. The f_j is usually formulated as activation of a fully connected layer with weight vector W_j and bias b_j. We fix the $b_j = 0$ for simplicity, and as a result f_j is given by:

$$f_j = W_j^T x = \|W_j\| \|x\| \cos\theta_j$$

Where θ_j is the angle between W_j and x. This formula suggests that both norms and angles contribute to the posterior probability. Note the red areas of Fig. 1 indicate the overlapping of decision margin with softmax under angular coordinate system.

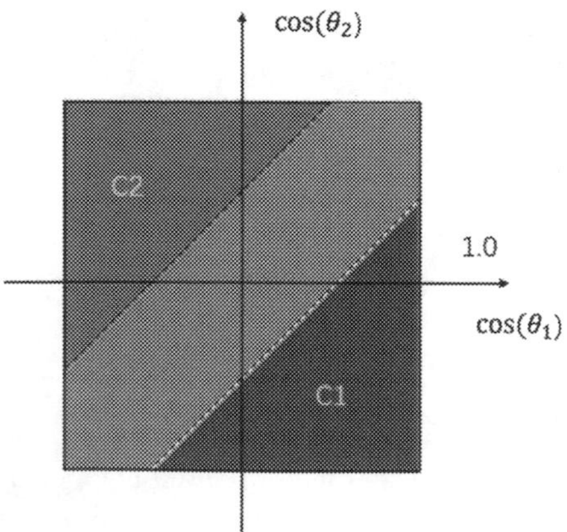

Fig. 1. The decision margin for softmax for two classes classification

3.2 A-Softmax [2]

The weight vectors could be normalized into an unit vector (making $\|W_j\|$ to be 1) and then the target log value is transformed from $\|x\| \cos\theta_j$ to $\|x\|\varphi(\theta_j)$. in [2],

$$L_{AS} = \frac{1}{N}\sum_{i=1}^{N} -\log \frac{e^{\|x\|\varphi(\theta_{y_i})}}{e^{\|x\|\varphi(\theta_{y_i})} + \sum_{j=1, j\neq y_i}^{C} e^{\|x\|\cos(\theta_j)}}$$

Where the $\varphi(\theta_{y_i})$ is usually a piece-wise function defined as:

$$\varphi(\theta_{y_i}) = \frac{(-1)^k \cos(m\theta) - 2k + \lambda\cos\theta}{1+\lambda}, \quad \theta \in \left[\frac{k\pi}{m}, \frac{(k+1)\pi}{m}\right]$$

Where m is usually an integer larger than 1 and λ is a hyperparameter to control how hard the classification boundary should be pushed. During training, the λ is annealing from $1,000$ to a small value to make the angular space of each class become more and more compact. In the experiments, it was set the minimum value of λ to be 5 and m = 4, which is approximately equivalent to m = 1.5.

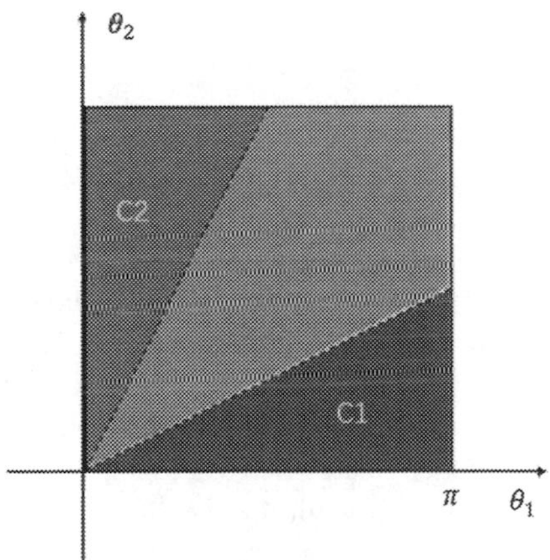

Fig. 2. The decision margin for A-Softmax [2] for two classes classification

3.3 AM-Softmax [3]

In [3], the angular margin m is removed to the outside of $\cos\theta$, and normalize the feature vectors (making $\|x\|$ to be s), thus they propose the additive margin loss function:

$$L_{AMS} = \frac{1}{N}\sum_{i=1}^{N} -\log \frac{e^{s(\cos(\theta_{y_i})-m)}}{e^{s(\cos(\theta_{y_i})-m)} + \sum_{j=1, j\neq y_i}^{C} e^{s\cos(\theta_j)}}$$

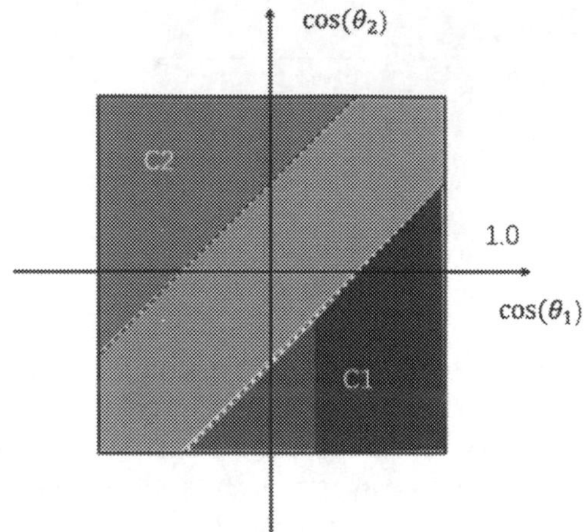

Fig. 3. The decision margin for AM-Softmax [3] for two classes classification

3.4 TypicFace (Proposed)

As a shortage of A-Softmax, when θ reduces, the margin between the features belong to the two classes becomes smaller. And it vanishes completely when $\theta = 0$ as shown in Fig. 2, which is harmful to the face recognition under the open-set protocol.

Potential improvement could be made to AM-Softmax, while the author keeps an invariant boundary between classes (shown in Fig. 3), indicating all features within an individual are equally treated with discrimination. To improve that, we start from a more intuitive assumption. Take class 1 in Fig. 3 for example (marked as blue), features within the class are separated into two portions: the typical feature (marked as dark blue in Fig. 3) and the atypical feature (marked as light blue in Fig. 3). The typical feature has a smaller angular distance with the weight vector of the class, indicating it has a higher similarity with that vector. Therefore, the typical feature is what exactly makes the class unique among all the individuals, and it should have a centralized distribution. Comparatively, with a bigger angular distance, the atypical feature has a lower similarity with the weight vector of the class. Therefore, it is reasonable that the atypical one with a diffuse distribution is responsible for the connections between other individuals, i.e. the similarity.

Based on the assumption, to well identify an individual, two portions of features aforementioned should be treated differently with discrimination. Higher discrimination is demanded for the typical feature. More precisely, as the angular distance between the typical feature and the weight vector of the class reduces, indicating the feature becomes more typical, more compactness is applied on it (marked as the red area in Fig. 5). Meanwhile the atypical feature requires a different strategy, which is as the angular distance enlarges, indicating the more atypical feature it is, we loosen the distribution of that feature (marked as the purple area in Fig. 5).

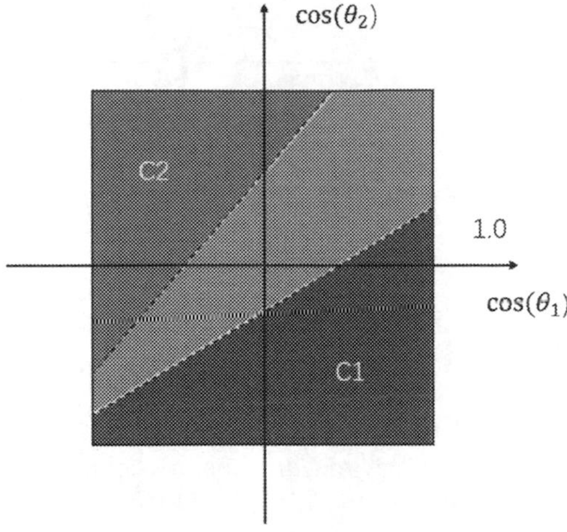

Fig. 4. The decision margin for TypicFace for two classes classification

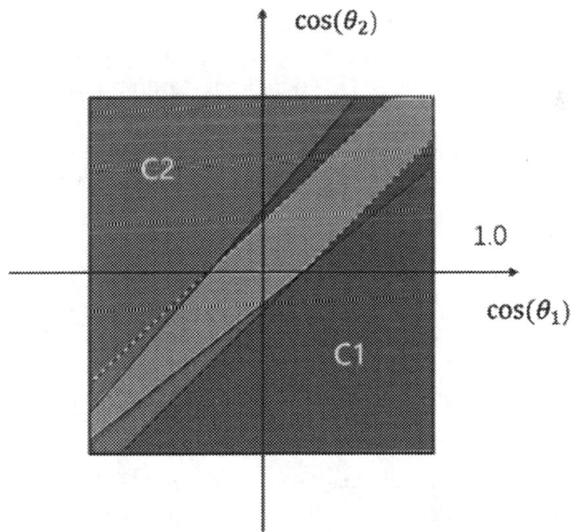

Fig. 5. The comparison of decision margin between AM-softmax [3] and TypicFace for two classes classification. The dashed line represents decision boundary of AM-softmax [3] while the solid one represents the decision boundary of TypicFace. Reduced feature distribution is marked as red color in the figure, due to the compression from AM-softmax [3] to TypicFace; where the purple portion is on account of widened feature distribution from AM-softmax [3] to TypicFace.

Based on the conclusion above, we introduce the other hyperparameter d ($d \in [0, 1]$), which determine the variance of the margin. So we have:

$$L_{TypicFace} = \frac{1}{N}\sum\nolimits_{i=1}^{N} -\log\frac{e^{s\cdot d(\cos(\theta_{y_i})-m)}}{e^{s\cdot d(\cos(\theta_{y_i})-m)} + \sum\nolimits_{j=1,j\neq y_i}^{C} e^{s(\cos(\theta_j))}}, \text{ d } \in [0,1]$$

And the Fig. 4 shows the classification boundary as well as the margin.

4 Periments

4.1 Implementation Details

Setting. Our function is implemented using Caffe framework [12]. We follow all the experimental settings from [2, 3], including the image resolution, preprocessing method and the network structure. Specifically MTCNN [13] was used to detect faces and facial landmarks in images. Then the faces are aligned according to the detected landmarks. The aligned face images are of size 112×96, and are normalized by subtracting 128 and dividing 128. Our network structure follows the specification in [2, 3], which is a modified ResNet [14] with 20 layers that is adapted to face recognition.

Training. All the networks are trained from scratch. We set the weight decay parameter to be 5e−4. The batch size is 256 and the learning rate begins with 0.1 and is divided by 10 at 16K, 24K and 28K iterations. The training is finished at 30K iteration. During training, we only use image mirror to do the augmentation. We train our model on a small training dataset, which is the publicly available CASIA-WebFace [15].

Dataset Overlap Removal. The dataset we use for training is CASIA-Webface [15], which contains 494,414 training images from 10,575 identities. To perform open-set evaluations, we remove the overlapped identities between training dataset (CASIS-Webface [15]) and testing datasets (LFW [4], BLUFR [5]) by using the cleaned dataset of CASIA-Webface [15] provided by [3]. To be rigorous, all the experiments in this paper are based on the cleaned dataset and use the same network architecture for every compared method.

Testing. We extract the deep features from the output of the FC1 layer. For all experiments the final representation of testing face is obtained by concatenating its original face features and its horizontally flipped features. The score (metric) is computed by the consine distance of two features. The nearest neighbor classifier and thresholding are used for face identification and verification, respectively.

4.2 Experiments on LFW [4] and BLUFR [5]

LFW dataset [4] includes 13,233 face images from 5749 different identities, containing faces with large variation in pose, expression and illuminations. We follow the unrestricted with labeled outside data protocol [16]. The performance of our method are evaluated on 6,000 face pairs from LFW. The results are given in Table 1. We refer the results in [3]. As shown in Table 1, the proposed TypicFace achieves the state-of-the-

Table 1. Performance on modified ResNet-20 with various loss functions.

Loss function	m	d	LFW [4] 6,000 pairs	BLUFR [5] VR@FAR = 0.1%	BLUFR [5] DIR@FAR = 1%
A-Softmax	~1.5	–	99.08%	97.06%	81.93%
AM-Softmax	0.25	–	99.13%	97.13%	81.42%
	0.30	–	99.08%	97.56%	84.02%
	0.35	–	98.98%	97.69%	84.82%
	0.40	–	99.17%	97.71%	84.51%
TypicFace	0.25	0.825	99.20%	**97.82%**	85.73%
	0.30	0.875	99.25%	97.79%	**85.71%**
	0.35	0.925	**99.32%**	97.72%	84.48%
	0.40	0.90	99.27%	97.73%	85.01%

art result of 99.32% on LFW 6,000 pairs. What is worth mentioning is it's outperform the AM-Softmax, which means the assumption we proposed in 4.4 is more reasonable.

The BLUFR [5] is a benchmark protocol based on LFW database for large-scale unconstrained face recognition under both verification and open-set identification scenarios, which is focus on low FARs. As shown in Table 1, the proposed TypicFace also achieves the state-of-the on it.

5 Conclusions

We proposed a novel approach named TypicFace to guide the deep CNNs to learn dynamically and intuitively discriminative features by manipulating the cosine margin between decision boundaries, for boosting the performance of deep face recognition. Our loss function is built upon the previous margin schemes [2, 3], but it is more reasonable. Comprehensive experiments show that our loss function performs better than A-Softmax [2], AM-Softmax [3] on LFW [4] and BLUFR [5].

6 Future Work

The assumption herein separates feature distribution of an individual into two parts, typical and atypical, which are treated differently. To categories those two feature distribution, the points on the intersection between boundary of AM-Softmax and TypicFace play an import role, and that would be the spot of future discovery. As for atypical distribution, it can be applied in unsupervised learning (e.g.: cluster and etc.) to increase the accuracy of refined similarity.

References

1. Liu, W., Wen, Y., Yu, Z., et al.: Large-margin softmax loss for convolutional neural networks, pp. 507–516 (2016)
2. Liu, W., Wen, Y., Yu, Z., et al.: SphereFace: deep hypersphere embedding for face recognition, pp. 6738–6746 (2017)
3. Wang, H., Wang, Y., Zhou, Z., et al.: AM-softmax: large margin cosine loss for deep face recognition (2018)
4. Huang, G.B., Mattar, M., Berg, T., et al.: Labeled faces in the wild: a database for studying face recognition in unconstrained environments (2007)
5. Liao, S., Lei, Z., Yi, D., et al.: A benchmark study of large-scale unconstrained face recognition. In: IEEE International Joint Conference on Biometrics, pp. 1–8. IEEE (2014)
6. Wen, Y., Zhang, K., Li, Z., Qiao, Yu.: A discriminative feature learning approach for deep face recognition. In: Leibe, B., Matas, J., Sebe, N., Welling, M. (eds.) ECCV 2016. LNCS, vol. 9911, pp. 499–515. Springer, Cham (2016). https://doi.org/10.1007/978-3-319-46478-7_31
7. Ross, A., Jain, A.K.: Multimodal biometrics: an overview. In: 2004 European Signal Processing Conference, pp. 1221–1224. IEEE (2010)
8. Taigman, Y., Yang, M., Ranzato, M., et al.: DeepFace: closing the gap to human-level performance in face verification. In: IEEE Conference on Computer Vision and Pattern Recognition, pp. 1701–1708. IEEE Computer Society (2014)
9. Sun, Y., Wang, X., Tang, X.: Deep learning face representation from predicting 10,000 classes. In: IEEE Conference on Computer Vision and Pattern Recognition, pp. 1891–1898. IEEE Computer Society (2014)
10. Wang, F., Xiang, X., Cheng, J., et al.: NormFace: L2 hypersphere embedding for face verification (2017)
11. Ranjan, R., Castillo, C.D., Chellappa, R.: L2-constrained softmax loss for discriminative face verification (2017)
12. Jia, Y., Shelhamer, E., Donahue, J., et al.: Caffe: convolutional architecture for fast feature embedding. In: ACM International Conference on Multimedia, pp. 675–678. ACM (2014)
13. Zhang, K., Zhang, Z., Li, Z., et al.: Joint face detection and alignment using multitask cascaded convolutional networks. IEEE Sig. Process. Lett. **23**(10), 1499–1503 (2016)
14. He, K., Zhang, X., Ren, S., et al.: Deep residual learning for image recognition. In: IEEE Conference on Computer Vision and Pattern Recognition, pp. 770–778. IEEE Computer Society (2016)
15. Yi, D., Lei, Z., Liao, S., Li, S.Z.: Learning face representation from scratch. arXiv preprint arXiv:1411.7923, 28 November 2014
16. Huang, G.B., Learned-Miller, E.: Labeled faces in the wild: updates and new reporting procedures. Department of Computer Science, University of Massachusetts Amherst, Amherst, MA, USA, Technical Report, pp. 1–7 (2014)

Semi-supervised Feature Selection Based on Logistic I-RELIEF for Multi-classification

Baige Tang[1] and Li Zhang[1,2](✉)

[1] School of Computer Science and Technology & Joint International Research Laboratory of Machine Learning and Neuromorphic Computing, Soochow University, Suzhou 215006, Jiangsu, China
bgtang@stu.suda.edu.cn, zhangliml@suda.edu.cn

[2] Provincial Key Laboratory for Computer Information Processing Technology, Soochow University, Suzhou 215006, Jiangsu, China

Abstract. The semi-supervised Logistic I-RELIEF (SLIR) algorithm has been proposed for feature selection, which can handle both labeled and unlabeled data to perform feature selection. However, SLIR can only deal with binary problems. To remedy it, this paper presents a multi-classification semi-supervised Logistic I-RELIEF (MSLIR) algorithm for feature selection. Based on SLIR, MSLIR designs a novel scheme to calculate the margin vectors of unlabeled samples. Experimental results demonstrate the efficiency and effectiveness of our algorithm.

Keywords: Logistic I-RELIEF · Feature selection
Multi-classification · Semi-supervised · Margin vector

1 Introduction

High-dimensional data, such as DNA microarray data, medical data, and satellite remote sensing data, may contain irrelevant information, which generally exists in machine learning and pattern recognition. It is meaningful to use feature selection or feature extraction as a pre-processing way for reducing the negative influence of irrelevant data. Feature selection, as a dimensionality reduction technology makes great contributions to saving storage space and reducing the computational cost. Therefore, feature selection is widely applied to many learning tasks.

Feature selection methods can be categorized into three groups: supervised, unsupervised and semi-supervised methods. Supervised feature selection methods include RELIEF-based methods [1–3], Fisher criterion-based methods [4,5], etc. RELIEF is one of the most effective feature selection algorithms, which finds a weight vector for features by maximizing the margin between the differences of given samples and their nearest neighbors in two classes. The features with larger weights could be selected to perform classification tasks. The variants of RELIEF have been proposed, such as Logistic I-RELIEF (LIR) [1] and

X. Geng and B.-H. Kang (Eds.): PRICAI 2018, LNAI 11012, pp. 719–731, 2018.
https://doi.org/10.1007/978-3-319-97304-3_55

RELIEF-F [3]. Supervised feature selection methods require a large amount of labeled data which is hard to obtain. It is difficult for supervised feature selection methods to choose features that are distinguishable from few labeled data in the training dataset. Therefore, many unsupervised feature selection methods have been proposed [6–8], which can effectively utilize unlabeled data. However, these methods ignore the information contained in labeled data, so they cannot identify the discriminative features well [7].

The semi-supervised feature selection methods can achieve better performance since they make full use of the labeled and unlabeled data. Common methods include the clustering-based method [9], locality sensitive-based method [10], local discriminative information-based method [11], semi-supervised Logistic I-RELIEF method (SLIR) [12], forward method [13,14], multi-objective optimization method [15], spectral analysis method [16], and so on. This paper focuses on the RELIEF-based methods. In SLIR, labeled data are used to maximize the distance between samples in different classes, while the unlabeled data samples are used to extract the geometric structure in a data space [12]. SLIR is the first and successful variant of RELIEF in semi-supervised learning. However, SLIR can only deal with binary problems and cannot effectively solve the multi-class problems.

To solve this issue, we propose a multi-classification semi-supervised Logistic I-RELIEF (MSLIR) algorithm for feature selection based on SLIR. Under the semi-supervised learning framework, RELIEF-based methods need to consider how to compute the margin vector of an unlabeled sample. MSLIR designs a novel scheme to calculate the margin vectors of unlabeled samples for multi-classification problems.

The rest of paper is arranged as follows. Section 2 briefly introduces related work include Logistic I-RELIEF and semi-supervised Logistic I-RELIEF. We propose multi-classification semi-supervised Logistic I-RELIEF algorithm in Sect. 3. Experimental results are presented in Sect. 4. The paper is concluded in Sect. 5.

2 Related Work

This section mainly introduces two algorithms: LIR and SLIR, where SLIR is an extended algorithm of LIR.

2.1 Logistic I-RELIEF

In I-RELIEF, neighbors of a given sample in the original feature space is inconsistent with the nearest neighbors in the weighted feature space, so LIR proposes a new probabilistic model to calculate the distance between samples and their neighbors.

A assume that the input dataset is $D = \{(\mathbf{x}_n, y_n)\}_{n=1}^{N} \subset R^I \times \{+1, -1\}$, where $\mathbf{x}_n$ is a labeled sample and y_n is its label, I is the number of original features, and N is the number of samples. Here, we discuss the binary problem: $+1$ and -1 represent positive and negative classes, respectively.

The optimization problem of LIR can be described as:

$$\min_{\mathbf{w}} \sum_{n=1}^{N} \log(1+\exp(-\mathbf{w}^T\mathbf{z}_n)) + \lambda\|\mathbf{w}\|_1$$
$$s.t. \quad \mathbf{w} \geq 0 \tag{1}$$

where $\|\cdot\|_1$ is the 1-norm, $\mathbf{w}$ is the feature weight vector which represents the importance of features, $\lambda \geq 0$ is a regularization parameter to avoid overfitting, and $\mathbf{z}_n$ is the margin vector of the sample $\mathbf{x}_n$ which can be written as follows:

$$\mathbf{z}_n = \sum_{\mathbf{x}_i \in M_n} P(\mathbf{x}_i = NM(\mathbf{x}_n)|\mathbf{w})|\mathbf{x}_n - \mathbf{x}_i| - \sum_{\mathbf{x}_i \in H_n} P(\mathbf{x}_i = NH(\mathbf{x}_n)|\mathbf{w})|\mathbf{x}_n - \mathbf{x}_i| \tag{2}$$

where $M_n = \{\mathbf{x}_i|(\mathbf{x}_i, y_i) \in D, y_i \neq y_n, i = 1, \ldots, N\}$, $H_n = \{\mathbf{x}_i|(\mathbf{x}_i, y_i) \in D, y_i = y_n, i = 1, \ldots, N\}$, $P(\mathbf{x}_i = NM(\mathbf{x}_n)|\mathbf{w})$ and $P(\mathbf{x}_i = NH(\mathbf{x}_n)|\mathbf{w})$ are the probabilities that the sample $\mathbf{x}_i$ is the nearest miss and the nearest hit of $\mathbf{x}_n$, respectively, $NM(\mathbf{x}_n)$ represents the nearest miss of sample $\mathbf{x}_n$ and $NH(\mathbf{x}_n)$ represents the nearest hit of sample $\mathbf{x}_n$.

2.2 Semi-supervised Logistic I-RELIEF

On the basis of Logistic I-RELIEF algorithm, Sun et al. [12] extended Logistic I-RELIEF to semi-supervised learning. Due to the introduction of unlabeled samples, the calculation for the margin vectors of unlabeled samples needs to be revised.

We are given a labeled sample set $D_l = \{(\mathbf{x}_i^l, y_i^l)\}_{i=1}^L (y_i \in \{\pm 1\})$ and an unlabeled sample set $D_u = \{\mathbf{x}_i^u\}_{i=1}^U$. For a given labeled sample $\mathbf{x}^l$ and unlabeled sample $\mathbf{x}^u$, let their margin vector be $\mathbf{z}^l$ and $\mathbf{z}^u$, respectively. Since $\mathbf{x}^l$ is a labeled sample, its margin vector $\mathbf{z}^l$ can be computed as Eq. (2). Fortunately, $\mathbf{z}^u$ has the same absolute value, regardless of which class the sample $\mathbf{x}^u$ belongs to. Therefore, $\mathbf{z}^u$ can use the same way of computing $\mathbf{z}_n$. SLIR can be cast into the following optimization problem:

$$\min_{\mathbf{w}} \|\mathbf{w}\|_1 + \alpha \sum_{i=1}^{L} \log(1+\exp(-\mathbf{w}^T\mathbf{z}_i^l)) + \beta \sum_{i=1}^{U} \exp(-(\mathbf{w}^T\mathbf{z}_i^u)^2/\delta)$$
$$s.t. \quad \mathbf{w} \geq 0 \tag{3}$$

where δ is the kernel width, $\mathbf{z}_i^l$ is margin vector of sample $\mathbf{x}_i^l$, $\mathbf{z}_i^u$ is margin vector of sample $\mathbf{x}_i^u$, α and β represent the contribution of labeled and unlabeled samples to the cost function (3), respectively. Then (3) can be solved by using the gradient descent method.

3 Semi-supervised Logistic I-RELIEF for Multi-classification

SLIR can only deal with bianry problems. To solve this issue, we propose the MSLIR algorithm for multi-classification based on SLIR. Given a labeled sample set $D_l = \{(\mathbf{x}_i^l, y_i^l)\}_{i=1}^L$ with $y_i^l \in \{1, 2, \ldots, c\}$ and the class number c, and an unlabeled sample set $D_u = \{\mathbf{x}_i^u\}_{i=1}^U$, the goal of MSLIR is to find feature weights for multi-classification tasks under the semi-supervised situation. There are $L+U$ samples in total ($L \ll U$). MSLIR designs a novel scheme to calculate the margin vectors of unlabeled samples, based on which MSLIR can be formulated as an optimization problem similar to SLIR. In the following, we discuss MSLIR in detail.

3.1 Calculation of Margin Vectors

MSLIR requires to calculate margin vector for each sample including labeled and unlabeled one. The margin vector $\mathbf{z}_i^l$ of the labeled sample $\mathbf{x}_i^l$ can be expressed as follows:

$$\mathbf{z}_i^l = \sum_{\mathbf{x}_k^l \in M_i} P(\mathbf{x}_k^l = NM(\mathbf{x}_i^l)|\mathbf{w})|\mathbf{x}_i^l - \mathbf{x}_k^l| - \sum_{\mathbf{x}_k^l \in H_i} P(\mathbf{x}_k^l = NH(\mathbf{x}_i^l)|\mathbf{w})|\mathbf{x}_i^l - \mathbf{x}_k^l| \tag{4}$$

where the set $M_i = \{\mathbf{x}_k^l|(\mathbf{x}_k^l, y_k^l) \in D_l, y_k^l \neq y_i^l, i = 1, \ldots, L, y_i^l = \{1, \ldots, c\}\}$ contains all labeled samples that have different labels from $\mathbf{x}_i^l$, the set $H_i = \{\mathbf{x}_k^l|(\mathbf{x}_k^l, y_k^l) \in D_l, y_k^l = y_i^l, i = 1, \ldots, L\}$ contains all labeled samples that have the same labels as $\mathbf{x}_i^l$.

For the multi-classification problem, the sample $\mathbf{x}_i^u$ in the data set D_u may belong to any class, hence, the calculation of the margin vectors of unlabeled samples needs to be redefined. Suppose that we assign a temporary label to the unlabeled sample $\mathbf{x}_i^u$. Then we can calculate the candidate margin vector $(\mathbf{z}_i^u)^j$ of the unlabeled sample $\mathbf{x}_i^u$ with the assigned label j as follows:

$$(\mathbf{z}_i^u)^j = \sum_{\mathbf{x}_k^l \in \overline{M}_i^j, y_k \neq j} P(\mathbf{x}_k^l = NM^j(\mathbf{x}_i^u)|\mathbf{w})|\mathbf{x}_i^u - \mathbf{x}_k^l| - \sum_{\mathbf{x}_k^l \in \overline{H}_i^j, y_k = j} P(\mathbf{x}_k^l = NH^j(\mathbf{x}_i^u)|\mathbf{w})|\mathbf{x}_i^u - \mathbf{x}_k^l| \tag{5}$$

where $\overline{M}_i^j = \{\mathbf{x}_k^l|(\mathbf{x}_k^l, y_k^l) \in D_l, y_k^l \neq j, k = 1, \ldots, L, j = 1, \ldots, c\}$ is the sample set that contains all labeled samples whose label is not equal to j, and $\overline{H}_i^j = \{\mathbf{x}_k^l|(\mathbf{x}_k^l, y_k^l) \in D_l, y_k^l = j, k = 1, \ldots, L\}$ is the sample set that contains all labeled samples whose label is equal to j.

Which is the possible margin vector of the sample $\mathbf{x}_i^u$ among the c candidate margin vectors? Without any apriori information, we consider the candidate margin vector which has the greatest inner product with the feature weight vector $\mathbf{w}$ as the possible one. Then $\mathbf{z}_i^u$ can be determined by:

$$\mathbf{z}_i^u = \arg \max_{j=1,\ldots,c} \mathbf{w}^T (\mathbf{z}_i^u)^j \tag{6}$$

3.2 Optimization Problem and Algorithm Description

After the margin vectors of labeled and unlabeled samples are defined, MSLIR is to solve the following optimization problem:

$$\begin{aligned} \min_{\mathbf{w}} \ & \|\mathbf{w}\|_1 + \alpha \sum_{i=1}^{L} \log(1 + \exp(-\mathbf{w}^T \mathbf{z}_i^l)) \\ & + \beta \sum_{i=1}^{U} \log(1 + \exp(-\mathbf{w}^T \mathbf{z}_i^u)) \\ s.t. \quad & \mathbf{w} \geq 0 \end{aligned} \tag{7}$$

where $\alpha \geq 0$ and $\beta \geq 0$ are the regularization parameters that control the importance of labeled and unlabeled samples, respectively. By comparing (3) and (7), we find that there are two differences between them. First, the calculation way of $\mathbf{z}_i^u$ is different. In (3), calculating $\mathbf{z}_i^u$ does not consider the label of $\mathbf{x}_i^u$. Contrary, the calculation of $\mathbf{z}_i^u$ takes into account the possible label of $\mathbf{x}_i^u$. Second, (7) uses the same logical regression form for both labeled and unlabeled samples to ensure the symmetry of labeled and unlabeled samples.

In order to facilitate calculation, we convert the optimization problem (7) to an unconstraint optimization problem. Let $\mathbf{w} = [v_1^2, \ldots, v_I^2]^T$ and $\mathbf{v} = [v_1, \ldots, v_I]$. The optimization formula (7) can be rewritten as:

$$\begin{aligned} \min_{\mathbf{v}} J = & \|\mathbf{v}\|_2^2 + \alpha \sum_{i=1}^{L} \log(1 + \exp(-\sum_{d=1}^{I} v_d^2 z_{id}^l)) \\ & + \beta \sum_{i=1}^{U} \log(1 + \exp(-\sum_{d=1}^{I} v_d^2 z_{id}^u)) \end{aligned} \tag{8}$$

where $\mathbf{z}_i^l = [z_{i1}^l, \ldots, z_{iI}^l]$. In order to solve formula (8), we use the gradient descent method. The derivation of J to $\mathbf{v}$ can be written as follows:

$$\begin{aligned} \frac{\partial J}{\partial v_k} = & 2v_k - \alpha \sum_{i=1}^{L} \frac{\exp(-\sum_{d=1}^{I} v_d^2 z_{id}^l)(2v_k z_{ik}^l)}{1 + \exp(-\sum_{d=1}^{I} v_d^2 z_{id}^l)} \\ & - \beta \sum_{i=1}^{U} \frac{\exp(-\sum_{d=1}^{I} v_d^2 z_{id}^u)(2v_k z_{ik}^u)}{1 + \exp(-\sum_{d=1}^{I} v_d^2 z_{id}^u)} \end{aligned} \tag{9}$$

Let $Q_1 = \sum_{i=1}^{L} \frac{\exp(-\sum_{d=1}^{I} v_d^2 z_{id}^l)(v_k z_{ik}^l)}{1+\exp(-\sum_{d=1}^{I} v_d^2 z_{id}^l)}$ and $Q_2 = \sum_{i=1}^{U} \frac{\exp(-\sum_{d=1}^{I} v_d^2 z_{id}^u)(v_k z_{ik}^u)}{1+\exp(-\sum_{d=1}^{I} v_d^2 z_{id}^u)}$, the update formulation for each dimension can be described as:

$$v_k \leftarrow v_k - \eta(v_k - \alpha Q_1 - \beta Q_2) \tag{10}$$

Algorithm 1. MSLIR

Input: Labeled dataset $D_l = \{(\mathbf{x}_i^l, y_i^l)\}_{i=1}^L \subset R^I \times \{1, 2, \ldots, c\}$; unlabeled dataset $D_u = \{\mathbf{x}_i^u\}_{i=1}^U \subset R^I$, regularization parameters α and β, the iteration number T, and the stop criterion θ.
Output: Feature weight $\mathbf{w}$.

begin
  Initialization: Set $\mathbf{w}_{(0)} = [1, 1, \ldots, 1]^T, t = 1, \rho = 1$;
  while $t \leq T$ && $\rho > \theta$ **do**
    Compute $\mathbf{z}_i^l$ by (4), $i = 1, \ldots, L$;
    Compute $(\mathbf{z}_i^u)^j$ by (5), $j = 1, \ldots, c$ and find $\mathbf{z}_i^u$ by (6), $i = 1, \ldots, U$;
    Solve formula (7) using the gradient descent method to find $\mathbf{v}$;
    Compute $\mathbf{w}_{(t)} = [v_1^2, \ldots, v_I^2]^T$;
    $\rho = \|\mathbf{w}_{(t)} - \mathbf{w}_{(t-1)}\|$;
    $t = t + 1$;
  end
  $\mathbf{w} = \mathbf{w}_{(t)}$;
  Output $\mathbf{w}$.
end

where η is the learning rate. The pseudo-code of MSLIR is shown in Algorithm 1. The algorithm alternatively modifies the weight vector until convergence.

The computational complexity of MSLIR includes three parts: the calculation of the margin vectors for both labeled and unlabeled samples, and the solution to the optimization problem (8). In MSLIR, the computational complexity of solving (8) and calculating the margin vectors for labeled samples are identical to SLIR. The computational complexity of calculating the margin vectors for unlabeled samples is $O(cdLU)$ in MSLIR. For the same task, SLIR has the computational complexity of $O(dLU)$. In a nutshell, MSLIR has a compared complexity with SLIR.

4 Experiments

In this section, we evaluate the performance of the proposed MSLIR algorithm on one artificial dataset and eight UCI datasets [17]. The compared methods include LIR, SLIR and RELEIF-F. In each dataset, we added 100 irrelevant features to each sample, which are independently sampled from zero-mean, unit-variance Gaussian distribution, then we normalize these irrelevant features with the original data. All the experiments are implement in MATLAB R2013a on a PC with an Inter Core I5 processor with 4 GB RAM.

4.1 Artificial Dataset

We conduct experiments on the "ThreeCircles" dataset to verify the ability of the proposed algorithm in feature selection. There are 3 classes in the "ThreeCircles"

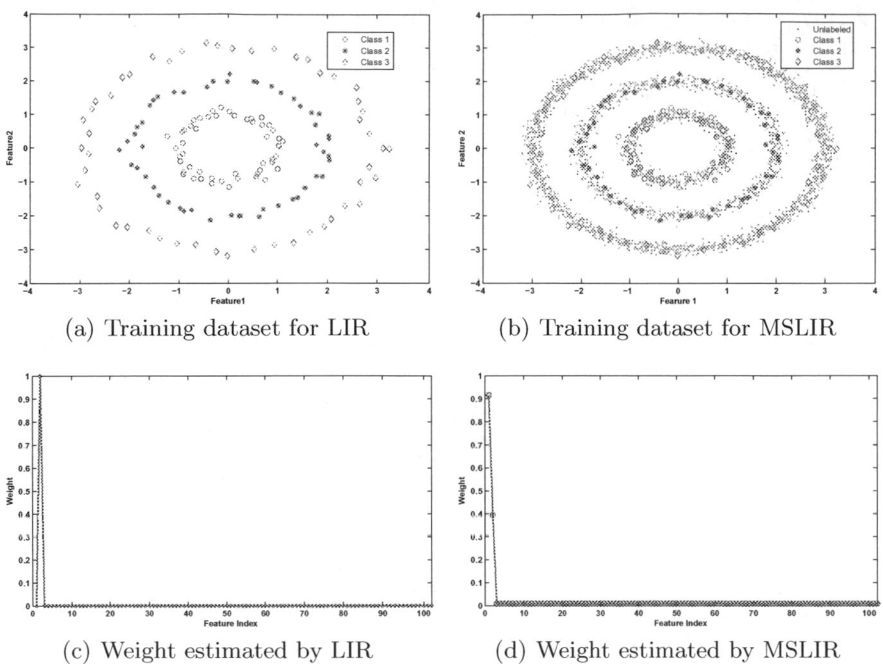

(a) Training dataset for LIR (b) Training dataset for MSLIR

(c) Weight estimated by LIR (d) Weight estimated by MSLIR

Fig. 1. "ThreeCircles" dataset (a) training dataset for LIR, (b) training dataset for MSLIR, feature weights estimated by (c) LIR and (d) MSLIR.

dataset, as shown in Fig. 1(a) and (b). In Fig. 1(a), each class has 51 labeled samples. In Fig. 1(b), each class also has 51 labeled samples as Fig. 1(a), and additionally 3450 unlabeled ones. LIR and MSLIR are conducted to compare the performance in feature selection. In MSLIR, let regularization parameters $\alpha = 6$ and $\beta = 3$. Let kernel width $\delta = 8$ for MSLIR and LIR.

In Fig. 1(c), LIR fails to identify the useful feature since the weight of the first feature is equal to zero. Figure 1(d) shows that the first two features selected by MSLIR has the highest weights and the weights of other noisy features are nearly zero. The results in Fig. 1(c) and (d) indicate that MSLIR can successfully identify the first two useful features using labeled and unlabeled data.

4.2 UCI Datasets

In this section, we use eight UCI datasets to verify the performance of algorithms. The eight UCI datasets include Wine, Vehicle, Yeast, Iris, Wdbc, Heart, Pima and Sonar datasets, of which the first four datasets are multi-class ones, and the rest are two-class ones. The datasets are randomly divided into independent training and test subsets, where training subsets contain labeled and unlabeled data. Semi-supervised methods use both labeled and unlabeled data, and supervised methods only use labeled data. The data information is summarized in Table 1, where "#Training" and "#Test" represent the number of

Table 1. Information of four UCI datasets.

Data sets	#Training		#Test	#Feature	#Class
	#Labeled	#Unlabeled			
Wine	10	40	128	13(100)	3
Vehicle	30	170	646	18(100)	4
Yeast	178	250	1056	8(100)	10
Iris	20	30	100	4(100)	3
Heart	40	130	100	13(100)	2
Wdbc	20	149	400	30(100)	2
Pima	20	148	600	8(100)	2
Sonar	20	38	150	61(100)	2

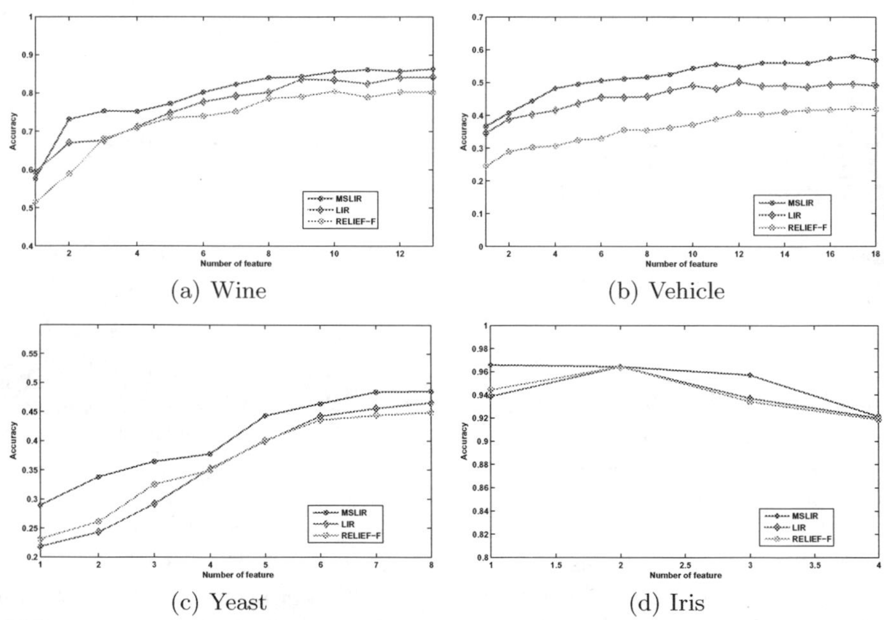

Fig. 2. Classification accuracy of MSLIR, RELIEF-F and LIR on UCI datasets, (a) Wine, (b) Vehicle, (c) Yeast and (d) Iris.

training samples and test samples, respectively. The total number of "#Labeled" and "#Unlabeled" data is equal to the number of training samples. "#Feature" represents the dimension of dataset.

The classifier utilized in our experiments is support vector machine (SVM). The Gaussian kernel parameter and regularization parameter of SVM are determined by the grid search method, where both parameters vary from 2^{-10} to 2^{10}.

Multi-classification Datasets. We compare the proposed feature selection algorithm with RELIEF-F and LIR, which both are supervised algorithms for solving multi-classification problems. We use the cross-validation method to select parameter α and β in MSLIR. The regularization parameter and learning rate in LIR follow the setting in [1]: $\lambda = 10$ and $\eta = 0.03$. Experiments are implemented on the Wine, Vehicle, Yeast and Iris datasets, each of which is randomly partitioned 10 times. We report the average results. The curves of the average classification accuracy vs. the n top-ranked features are shown in Fig. 2, where n is the original feature dimension of datasets. In Fig. 2(a), (b) and (c), the classification accuracy of the three algorithms also gradually increases as the number of selected features increases, which indicates that the useful features are gradually found. We can see that SMLIR is always better than LIR and RELIEF-F, which may indicate LIR and RELIEF-F algorithms contain noise features. In Fig. 2(d), MSLIR achieves the best classification accuracy when one feature is used, and LIR and RELIEF-F need two features. Obviously, MSLIR has a significantly higher performance than the other two algorithms. The best average accuracy and the corresponding standard deviation are given in Table 2. We can observe that MSLIR has a great improvement on Wine and Vehicle datasets.

Table 2. Classification accuracy and standard deviations (%) of SVM using features selected by MSLIR, LIR and RELIEF-F

Data sets	MSLIR	LIR	RELIEF-F
Wine	**88.59** $\pm$ 9.07	84.14 $\pm$ 6.38	82.11 $\pm$ 8.62
Vehicle	**57.97** $\pm$ 4.62	50.22 $\pm$ 9.11	42.11 $\pm$ 10.69
Yeast	**48.55** $\pm$ 14.17	46.59 $\pm$ 14.95	44.91 $\pm$ 17.41
Iris	**96.57** $\pm$ 1.21	96.43 $\pm$ 1.21	96.43 $\pm$ 1.21

In Fig. 3, we give the feature weights of the three algorithms on the Wine dataset. We can observe that MSLIR correctly selects relevant features, while LIR assigns higher weights to some irrelevant features, and RELEIF-F fails to identify noise data. In summary, MSLIR can handle feature selection problems for multi-classification under the semi-supervised framework. The supervised approaches do not remove the noise features well with few labeled data. Because of the introduction of unlabeled data, MSLIR can effectively eliminate noise features.

Binary Classification Datasets. We conduct experiments to compare MSLIR with SLIR and prove that MSLIR is also suitable for binary problems. SLIR is a semi-supervised feature selection method for solving binary problems. In MSLIR, the way of parameter setting is the same as the multi-classification case. The parameters α and β are determined by the cross-validation method in SLIR. Experiments are implemented on the Heart, Wdbc, Pima and Sonar datasets,

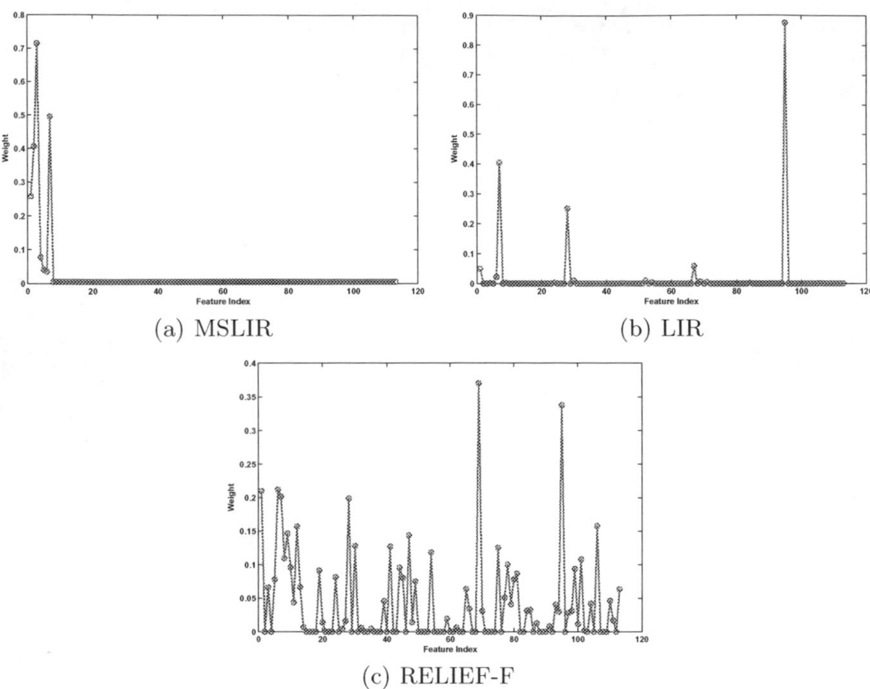

Fig. 3. Feature weights obtained by (a) MSLIR, (b) LIR and (c) RELIEF-F on the Wine dataset

each of which is randomly divided 10 times and the average accuracy is taken as the final results.

The results are shown in Fig. 4. In Figs. 4(a) and (c), we can observe that classification accuracy of MSLIR and SLIR are steady. However, MSLIR is much better than SLIR, which indicates MSLIR does not choose noise features. Figure 4(b) shows that SMLIR reaches the best accuracy when the number of features is 6, and SLIR when the number of features is 25, which implies that MSLIR chooses few features to reach the better accuracy. The best average classification accuracy and corresponding standard deviations are listed in Table 3. Compared to

Table 3. Classification accuracy and standard deviations (%) of SVM using features selected by MSLIR and SLIR

Data sets	MSLIR	SLIR
Heart	**83.1** $\pm$ 3.93	79.9 $\pm$ 4.04
Wdbc	**90.65** $\pm$ 3.15	86.8 $\pm$ 5.14
Pima	**69.17** $\pm$ 3.90	66.9 $\pm$ 3.25
Sonar	**70.13** $\pm$ 5.44	67.33 $\pm$ 8.38

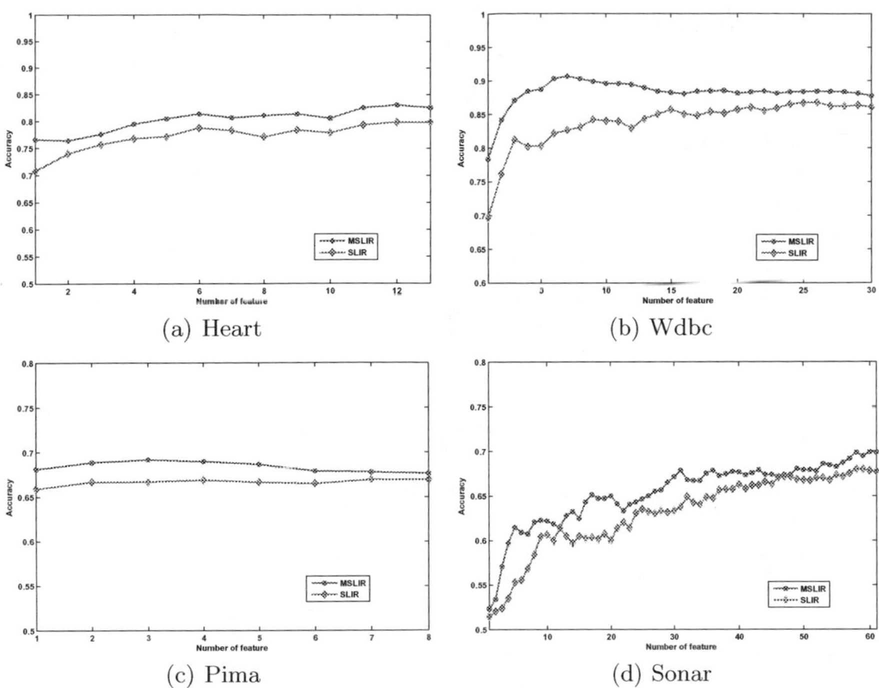

Fig. 4. Classification accuracy of MSLIR and SLIR on UCI datasets, (a) Heart, (b) Wdbc, (c) Pima and (d) Sonar.

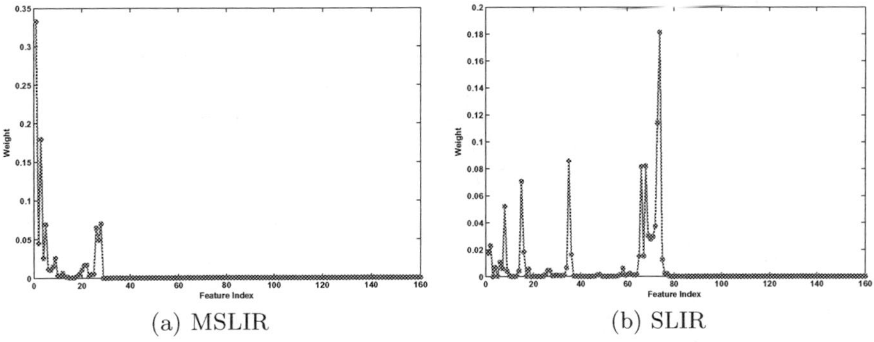

Fig. 5. Feature weights obtained by (a) MSLIR and (b) SLIR on the Sonar dataset

SLIR, the accuracy of MSLIR is improved 3.2%, 3.85%, 2.27% and 2.80% on Heart, Wdbc, Pima and Sonar datasets, respectively.

Figure 5 shows the distribution of feature weights on the Sonar dataset, we can see that MSLIR selects relevant features, while SLIR evaluates noise features higher weights and fails to distinguish relevant features.

Compared to SLIR, MSLIR can effectively solve the binary problems, and improve the classification accuracy.

5 Conclusion

In this paper, we propose MSLIR based on SLIR. MSLIR overcomes the drawback of SLIR, which can make full use of unlabeled information to select relevant features on multi-class of data. The results on one artificial dataset demonstrate that MSLIR can effectively handle noise data. When dealing with multi-class classification tasks, MSLIR can extract effective features under the semi-supervised framework compared to supervised methods. For binary classification problems, MSLIR can achieve better performance than SLIR despite the fact that both methods are semi-supervised learning ones.

Acknowledgement. This work was supported in part by the National Natural Science Foundation of China under Grants No. 61373093, No. 61402310, No. 61672364 and No. 61672365, by the Soochow Scholar Project of Soochow University, by the Six Talent Peak Project of Jiangsu Province of China.

References

1. Sun, Y.: Iterative RELIEF for feature weighting: algorithms, theories, and applications. IEEE Trans. Pattern Anal. Mach. Intell. **29**, 1035–1051 (2007)
2. Kira, K., Rendell, L.A.: The feature selection problem: traditional methods and a new algorithm. In: Tenth National Conference on Artificial Intelligence, pp. 129–134 (1992)
3. Kononenko, I.: Estimating attributes: analysis and extensions of RELIEF. In: Bergadano, F., De Raedt, L. (eds.) ECML 1994. LNCS, vol. 784, pp. 171–182. Springer, Heidelberg (1994). https://doi.org/10.1007/3-540-57868-4_57
4. Cheng, Z., Zhang, Y., Fan, X., Zhu, B.: Study on discriminant matrices of commonly used fisher discriminant functions. Acta Automatica Sin. **36**(10), 1361–1370 (2010)
5. Chen, L.F., Liao, H.Y.M., Ko, M.T., Lin, J.C., Yu, G.J.: A new LDA based face recognition system which can solve the small sample size problem. Pattern Recognit. **33**(10), 1713–1726 (2000)
6. Mitra, P., Murthy, C.A., Pal, S.K.: Unsupervised feature selection using feature similarity. IEEE Trans. Pattern Anal. Mach. Intell. **24**(3), 301–312 (2002)
7. He, X., Cai, D., Niyogi, P.: Laplacian score for feature selection. In: International Conference on Neural Information Processing Systems, vol. 18, pp. 507–514 (2005)
8. Bishop, C.M.: Pattern Recognition and Machine Learning. Springer, New York (2006)
9. Quinzn, I., Sotoca, J.M., Pla, F.: Clustering-based feature selection in semi-supervised problems. In: International Conference on Intelligent Systems Design and Application, pp. 535–540 (2009)
10. Zhao, J., Lu, K., He, X.: Locality sensitive semi-supervised feature selection. Neurocomputing **71**(10), 1842–1849 (2008)
11. Zeng, Z., Wang, X.D., Zhang, J., Wu, Q.: Semi-supervised feature selection based on local discriminative information. Neurocomputing **173**(P1), 102–109 (2016)

12. Cheng, Y., Cai, Y., Sun, Y., Li, J.: Semi-supervised feature selection under the Logistic I-RELIEF framework. In: International Conference on Pattern Recognition, pp. 1–4 (2008)
13. Ren, J., Qiu, Z., Fan, W., Cheng, H., Yu, P.S.: Forward semi-supervised feature selection. In: Washio, T., Suzuki, E., Ting, K.M., Inokuchi, A. (eds.) PAKDD 2008. LNCS (LNAI), vol. 5012, pp. 970–976. Springer, Heidelberg (2008). https://doi.org/10.1007/978-3-540-68125-0_101
14. Wang, B., Jia, Y., Yang, S.: Forward semi-supervised feature selection based on relevant set correlation. Int. Conf. Comput. Sci. Softw. Eng. **4**, 210–213 (2008)
15. Handl, J., Knowles, J.: Semi-supervised feature selection via multi-objective optimization. In: International Joint Conference on Neural Networks, pp. 3319–3326 (2006)
16. Zhao, Z., Liu, H.: Semi-supervised feature selection via spectral analysis. In: SIAM International Conference on Data Mining, SIAM-2007, SIAM, Minneapolis, Minnesota, USA, pp. 641–646 (2007)
17. UCI Machine Learning Repository. http://archive.ics.uci.edu/ml/datasets.html

Genetic Programming for Feature Selection and Feature Construction in Skin Cancer Image Classification

Qurrat Ul Ain(✉), Bing Xue, Harith Al-Sahaf, and Mengjie Zhang

Victoria University of Wellington, P.O. Box 600, Wellington 6140, New Zealand
{Qurrat.Ul.Ain,Bing.Xue,Harith.Al-Sahaf,Mengjie.Zhang}@ecs.vuw.ac.nz

Abstract. The incidence of skin cancer, particularly, malignant melanoma, continues to increase worldwide. If such a cancer is not treated at an early stage, it can be fatal. A computer system based on image processing and computer vision techniques, having good diagnostic ability, can provide a quantitative evaluation of these skin cancer cites called skin lesions. The size of a medical image is usually large and therefore requires reduction in dimensionality before being processed by a classification algorithm. Feature selection and construction are effective techniques in reducing the dimensionality while improving classification performance. This work develops a novel genetic programming (GP) based two-stage approach to feature selection and feature construction for skin cancer image classification. Local binary pattern is used to extract gray and colour features from the dermoscopy images. The results of our proposed method have shown that the GP selected and constructed features have promising ability to improve the performance of commonly used classification algorithms. In comparison with using the full set of available features, the GP selected and constructed features have shown significantly better or comparable performance in most cases. Furthermore, the analysis of the evolved feature sets demonstrates the insights of skin cancer properties and validates the feature selection ability of GP to distinguish between benign and malignant cancer images.

Keywords: Genetic programming · Image classification
Dimensionality reduction · Feature selection · Feature construction

1 Introduction

Melanoma is the most serious type of skin cancer, which spreads rapidly to other parts of the body if left untreated. Hence, early detection is essential, as the estimated 5-year survival rate for melanoma decreases from over 99% if detected in earliest stages to about 14% if detected in later stages [7]. New Zealand has the highest melanoma incidence rate in the world having more than 4000 new cases each year. Since this cancer is visible on the skin, it is potentially detectable at a very early stage that can lead to earlier more effective treatment. New computer

X. Geng and B.-H. Kang (Eds.): PRICAI 2018, LNAI 11012, pp. 732–745, 2018.
https://doi.org/10.1007/978-3-319-97304-3_56

vision technologies not only allow earlier detection of melanoma, but also reduces the large number of needless, costly and painful biopsy procedures [6]. This work develops a computational method which may allow medical practitioners and patients to adequately track skin lesions and detect cancer earlier.

A powerful way to achieve skin cancer detection via computer vision is to use dermoscopy images, and form the task as a binary image classification problem, i.e., *benign* and *malignant* classes of images [22]. For skin cancer classification, important characteristics for distinguishing between different cancer types, are based on dermoscopy criteria, specifically, Asymmetry, Border, Colour, and Diameter (ABCD) rule [20], and 7-point check-list method [4] (Asymmetry, Pigment network, Dots/Globules, Streaks, Regression areas, Blue-whitish veil and presence of Colours; white, red, light-brown, dark-brown, blue-gray, black). These are the key medical properties that help dermatologists for classification of various types of cancer. The dermosopic images are huge in size, whereas the relevant information about the disease is confined in a limited number of pixels or features in these images. Hence, there is a need for dimensionality reduction which aims at reducing the number of features and selecting only prominent features having good discriminating ability between classes. This helps reduce computation time as well as increase performance and interpretability of the commonly used classification algorithms. Moreover, in order to find which salient texture patterns or image features in these images are the cause behind a particular cancer type, interpretable methods are required to provide insights of these critical features.

Genetic Programming (GP) is an evolutionary computation (EC) algorithm based on Darwinian principles of biological evolution and natural selection [11]. GP automatically explores the solution space to evolve a computer program (model/solution), often represented by a tree-like structure, for a given problem [11]. GP has the ability to perform implicit feature selection by selecting prominent features at its terminal (leaf) nodes and the goodness of the evolved program is evaluated by a fitness measure [2]. Feature selection (FS) selects a subset of original features while feature construction (FC) creates a new feature(s) from the original set of features [21]. FC involves transforming a given set of input features to generate a new set of more powerful features [17]. FS and FC both can help improve performance by selecting relevant features and constructing new high-level features. Hence, FS and FC are good tools not only to improve performance, but also to reduce the dimensionality and hence provide features which take less computation time while being processed by the classification algorithm. Moreover the medical practitioners are interested in finding the cause of a disease, and a system is highly recommended to have such causal information. With the property of GP evolved programs being interpretable, giving information about which features are prominent in constructing new high-level features, the medical practitioners can gain deep understanding of which specific texture patterns and colour variations are the cause of the disease. However, there is limited work done to FS and FC in dermoscopy image classification.

Goals: This work develops a new FS and FC method using GP for skin cancer image classification problems. Different from most existing methods, the proposed method aims at constructing features only using the GP-selected features, which can have the ability to construct more informative features as compared to construct features from all of the original features. GP-selected and GP-selected-constructed features will be applied with common machine learning algorithms for classification. This work aims to address the following questions:

- Which features get selected by GP during the evolutionary process to achieve better classification performance and why?
- Whether GP can construct informative feature from GP-selected features that improve the performance of common classification algorithms for the task of skin cancer image classification?
- Whether GP-selected-constructed features provide better discriminating ability while using colour features or gray-scale features?
- How well this new method works as compared to other existing method?
- While analyzing the pixel-based texture patterns, how the GP-selected features can help identify those patterns which are prominent in effectively contributing to the classification performance?

2 Background

2.1 Related Work

Over the last two decades, several computer-aided diagnostic (CAD) systems [7] have been developed to help medical practitioners distinguish between *benign* and *malignant* skin lesions [1,8,22]. Zortea et al. [22] developed a CAD tool based on a camera with attached dermatoscope, and compared its performance to three experienced dermatologists. The system extracts features related to the asymmetry, colour, border, geometry, and texture of skin lesions, computed from automatically segmented images. With a dataset of 206 skin lesions, the classifier (quadratic discriminant analysis) provided competitive sensitivity (86%) and specificity (52%) compared to the most accurate dermatologist. *Sensitivity* is the accuracy of correctly classified diseased instances and *specificity* is the accuracy of correctly classified non-disease instances.

Abuzaghleh et al. [1] proposed a non-invasive real-time automated skin lesion system for the early detection and prevention of melanoma. This system has two components: (1) a real-time alert to help the users prevent skin burn measured by an equation, and (2) an automated image analysis module capable of capturing and classifying the lesion images. The second module includes image acquisition, hair removal, lesion segmentation, feature extraction, and classification. The method used the standard overall classification accuracy (i.e. the number of correctly classified instances divided by the total number of instances) as a fitness measure which is not suitable for an imbalance dataset [19]. Esteva et al. [7] demonstrated the classification of skin lesions using convolutional neural network (CNN) trained from images, using only pixels and class labels. The CNN

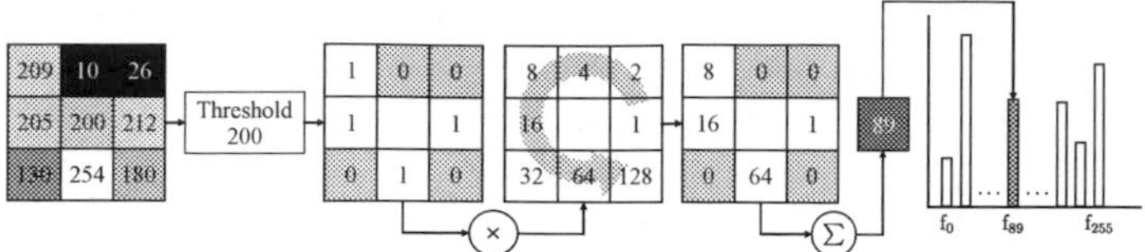

Fig. 1. The LBP process.

was trained using thousands of images, from 2,032 different classes and its performance is tested against 21 dermatologists on biopsy-proven clinical images. The CNN method outperformed all the experts, demonstrating artificial intelligence being capable of classifying skin cancer with a level of competence comparable to dermatologists. Generally, the performance of CNN is primarily constrained by data and can only classify well provided sufficient training examples which leads to long computation time and requires huge computing resources.

Menegola et al. [15] demonstrated transfer learning for automated melanoma screening using deep neural network (DNN). One of the key limitation of using pre-trained DNN is that the images must be resized to match the architecture. In [7,15], the images are resized to a smaller size distorting the aspect ratio, which badly effects the texture patterns important to discriminate between classes. In [3], GP has been utilized to automatically evolve a classifier for binary skin cancer image classification based on domain specific features provided by the dermatologists and texture features extracted by local binary patterns. The experiment results and analysis of the evolved programs confirmed the ability of GP for feature selection. Motivated by this feature selection ability, we will use GP as a feature selection and feature construction method in our current work.

Despite extensive research in investigating the diverse presentations and physical characteristics of skin cancer, the clinical diagnostic accuracy remains suboptimal. Skin lesion classification is a very challenging problem for several reasons including relatively poor contrast between the skin and lesion areas, variations in skin tone, presence of artefacts (hairs, ink, gel bubbles, date markers, ruler marks, etc.), non-uniform lighting, physical location of the lesion and most importantly variations in the lesion itself in terms of shape, size, colour, texture and location in the image frame [16]. While designing a robust skin cancer image classification algorithm, these factors must be considered which makes this task harder as compared to other image classification problems.

2.2 Local Binary Patterns

Local binary patterns (LBP) is a dense image descriptor developed by Ojala et al. [18] that has been extensively used for feature extraction in a wide range of computer vision tasks. LBP scans the image in a pixel-by-pixel fashion using a sliding window of fixed radius. The central pixel value is computed based on the intensity values of neighbouring pixels lying on the radius as depicted in Fig. 1. It then generates a histogram (i.e. feature vector) based on the computed values. The LBP operator is defined as:

$$LBP_{p,r} = \sum_{i=0}^{p-1} S(v_i - v_c)2^i \tag{1}$$

where p is the number of neighbouring pixels, r is the radius, v_i and v_c are the intensity values of the ith neighbour and central pixel, respectively. $S(x)$ returns 0 if $x < 0$ and 1 otherwise. The value computed from the above expression is assigned to central pixel and corresponding bin of histogram is incremented by 1. The value of tth bin of a histogram H computed on an image of size $m \times n$ as:

$$H(t) = \sum_{i=0}^{m-1} \sum_{j=0}^{n-1} (LBP_{p,r}(V_{i,j}) = t) \tag{2}$$

where the value of t ranges from 0 to $T - 1$, T is the maximum number of bins in the histogram, and $V_{i,j}$ is the value of the pixel at coordinate (i, j). Moreover, there are two kinds of LBP codes: *uniform* and *non-uniform*. A code is uniform if circularly it does not have more than two bitwise transitions from 0 to 1 or 1 to 0. For example, the codes 00111000, 00001111, and 10000001 are uniform, whilst the codes 00110110, 01001110, and 01010100 are non-uniform. Uniform codes detect various texture primitives such as corners, edges, line ends, dark spots and flat regions in images. Using only uniform codes, the size of the feature vector can be reduced from 2^p bins to $p(p-1) + 3$ bins, simply by combining non-uniform codes. In dermoscopy images, uniform codes help in detection of streaks (line ends) and blobs space (flat regions) which may help improve performance.

3 The Proposed Method

The proposed GP method is described in this section. It consists of two stages; one for feature selection (stage-1) and second for feature construction (stage-2). The overall structure is depicted in Figs. 2 and 3. First the images are converted to feature vectors by using LBP as discussed in Sect. 2.2. Then these features are fed into GP method. GP has the ability of implicit feature selection during its evolutionary process, since not all the features are used as the leaf nodes of a GP tree. The leaf nodes of a GP tree are the selected features. With the help of genetic operators, such as crossover and mutation, GP evolves a classifier/GP tree including informative features. These selected features usually have high discriminating ability between classes. After performing GP for multiple runs, i.e. 10, the features appearing in the best individual (evolved tree) having highest performance on training data are selected.

The selected features which are obtained from stage-1 are used as the input to stage-2 for feature construction. Here again after the 10 individual GP runs, the evolved individual/tree having the highest performance on the training data is selected. The evolved tree is the one constructed feature which will be used along with GP-selected features (computed after stage-1) for classification. To this end, we have the selected features (outcome of stage-1) and a constructed feature (outcome of stage-2). These selected and constructed features are concatenated to form the final feature vector, which will be given to the classification method.

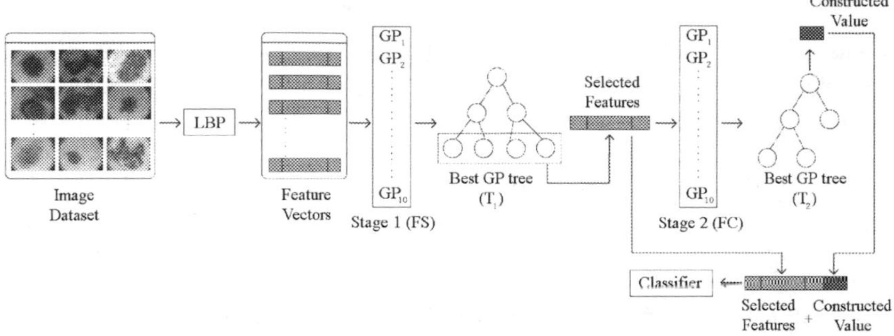

Fig. 2. Training process: training images are first converted to feature vectors using LBP which are given to GP method for feature selection (stage-1). Among the 10 GP runs, the best GP tree having highest performance is selected. Features appearing in this GP tree are called GP-selected features which are then given to GP method for feature construction (stage-2). Again among the 10 GP runs, the best performing GP tree is selected which is called GP-constructed feature. A new feature vector having GP-selected and GP-constructed feature is formed which is given to the classifier.

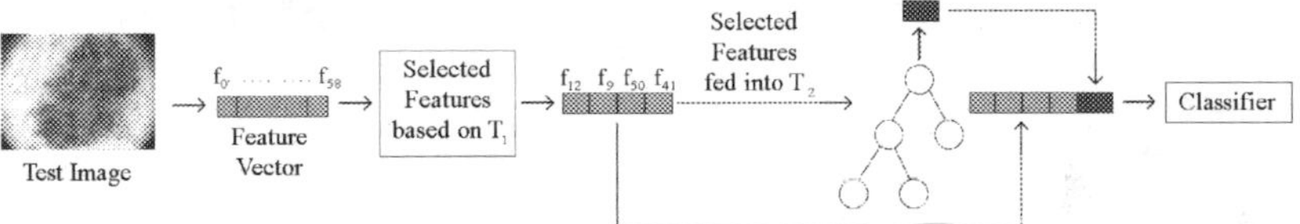

Fig. 3. Test process: each test image is converted to a feature vector using LBP (here features from f_0 to f_{58} represents 59 LBP$_{gray}$ features. Based on best GP tree (T_1), evolved on training data in stage-1, some of the features are selected (e.g. f_{12}, f_9, f_{50}, f_{41}). These feature values are fed into the best GP tree (T_2) evolved on training data in stage-2 to get GP-constructed feature value for each test image. GP-selected and GP-constructed features make the final feature vector to be given to the classifier.

In order to deal with FS bias and FC bias issues, the dataset is divided into 10 folds where 9 folds are used for training and 1 fold for testing, such that only training folds are used for FS and FC and the test fold remain unseen during the learning process. The method used for FS and FC using the training data to evolve selected features (outcome of stage-1) and to evolve constructed feature (outcome of stage-2) is illustrated in Fig. 2. For getting the transformed feature vectors for the test instances, the method illustrated in Fig. 3 has been adopted in this work.

3.1 Fitness Function

Having (very) different number of instances in different classes is commonly referred as a class imbalance problem. In this case, the use of the standard overall classification accuracy, defined as the ratio ($N_{\text{correct}}/N_{\text{total}}$) between correctly classified instances (N_{correct}) and total number of instances (N_{total}), is inappropriate. Alternatively, the balanced classification accuracy has been used as a good measure for imbalance classification problems [19], since it gives equal importance to both classes without any bias. Therefore, we adopted it as the fitness function in this study, which is given in Eq. (3):

$$Fitness = \frac{1}{2}\left(\frac{TP}{TP+FN} + \frac{TN}{TN+FP}\right) \tag{3}$$

where TP, TN, FP, and FN refers to true positive, true negative, false positive, and false negative, respectively, where *malignant* is the positive class and *benign* is the negative class.

3.2 Terminal Set and Function Set

The terminal set consists of uniform LBP features. Gray-level LBP features (referred as LBP_{gray}) are a total of 59 features and colour LBP features (referred as LBP_{rgb}) are 177 features. For computing LBP_{rgb}, a colour image is converted to its red, green and blue channel images and then LBP features are extracted from each of them. Hence there are a total of 177 (= 59 LBP features × 3 channels) LBP_{rgb} features. The value of the ith feature is indicated as Fi. The window size of 3×3 pixels and a radius of 1 pixel ($\text{LBP}_{8,1}$) is used.

The function set consists of four arithmetic operators, two trigonometric functions and one conditional operator, which are $\{add, sub, mul, div, sin, cos, if\}$. The first three arithmetic operators and the two trignometric operators have the same arithmetic and trigonometric meaning. However, division is protected that returns 0 when divided by 0. The *if* operator takes four inputs and returns the third if the first is greater than the second; otherwise, it returns the fourth.

4 Experiment Design

4.1 Dataset

A dataset of dermoscopy images namely PH^2 [14] gathered at Pedro Hispano Hospital Portugal, is used in the experiments. Dermoscopy is a non-invasive technique that allows microscopic visualization of inner skin morphological structures not visible to the naked eye [13]. Such images are rich enough to investigate them for presence/absence of skin cancer. The images are 8-bit RGB (red, green and blue) color images. The dataset includes 200 images which belong to three classes: common nevi (80 instances), atypical nevi (80 instances), and melanomas (40 instances). In dermatology, common nevi refers to non-disease lesion, atypical nevi refers to a currently non-disease lesion, but has chances to develop malignancy at a later stage, and melanoma is the diseased lesion. For our experiments focusing on binary classification, 80 common nevi and 80 atypical nevi are used as "*benign*" class, and 40 *melanoma* are used as "*malignant*" class. Samples of the two classes are presented in Fig. 4.

 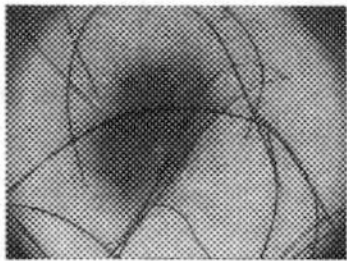  

Fig. 4. Some dermoscopy images: *benign* lesions (first two), and melanomas (last two).

Table 1. Parameter settings of the GP method.

Parameter	Value	Parameter	Value
Generations	50	Initial population	Ramped half-and-half
Population size	1024	Selection type	Tournament
Crossover rate	0.80	Tournament size	7
Mutation rate	0.19	Tree minimum depth	2
Elitism rate	0.01	Tree maximum depth	8

For performing the experiments, *10-fold cross validation* is used. The dataset is divided into ten folds such that nine folds are used for training and one fold for test. In our experiments features are selected and constructed using nine (training) folds and the last (test) fold remains unseen during this FS and FC processes in order to avoid FS and FC biases. This process is repeated ten times for all the different combinations of folds and the results are reported as mean and standard deviation of the fitness value. All the folds are randomly selected but are ensured that the ratio of instances of each class in each fold is the same as in the original dataset.

4.2 GP Parameters

The GP parameters are listed in Table 1. For generating the initial population, "Ramped half-and-half" method is used and the population size is set to 1024. Tournament selection with size 7 is applied to pick good individuals for producing new generations while maintaining population diversity. During the evolutionary process, the percentages for producing new individuals through crossover, mutation and elitism are 0.8, 0.19 and 0.01, respectively. The depth of the trees ranges between 2 and 8. After reaching a maximum of 50 generations, the evolutionary process stops unless a perfect individual with accuracy 100% is found.

For stage-1, the number of individual GP runs is 10. Among these 10 evolved trees, the one having highest performance on the training data is selected and the features appearing in that tree (GP-selected features) are used as input to stage-2 for feature construction. Here in stage-2, GP runs for 10 times and evolves trees. Again the best performing tree among the 10 evolved trees on the training data is selected as the constructed feature. The above procedure is repeated 30 times to get 30 sets of selected and constructed features. Note that the test folds remain unseen during both stages in order to avoid FS and FC biases. In one set of experiments, the random seeds for each of the 10 runs are all different. The implementation of GP method is done using the Evolutionary Computing Java-based (ECJ) package version 23 [12].

4.3 Methods for Classification

To check the performance of the feature sets obtained from GP on the test set, six classification methods are applied: Naïve Bayes (NB), k-Nearest Neighbor (k-NN) where $k = 1$ (the closest neighbor), Support Vector Machines (SVM), Decision Trees (J48), Random Forest (RF), and Multilayer Perceptron (MLP). The implementations of all these methods are taken from the commonly used Waikato Environment for Knowledge Analysis (WEKA) package [9]. In a study [10] on kernel functions in SVM, it has been shown that non-linear kernel can achieve similar or better performance than linear kernel. Hence, a Radial basis Function (RBF) kernel is used instead of the default linear kernel in WEKA. For MLP, the learning rate, momentum, training epochs and number of hidden layers are set to 0.1, 0.2, 60, and 20, respectively. These parameters are specified empirically as they gave the best performance amongst other settings.

5 Results and Discussions

5.1 Overall Results

The results of the two experiments using LBP_{gray} and LBP_{rgb} are presented in Table 2. Vertically, the table comprises of two blocks where first corresponds to the results of using LBP_{gray} features and second shows results of LBP_{rgb} features. Horizontally, the table consists of 7 columns where first lists the classification algorithm, second and third show respectively the training and test performances using all features represented by "*All*". The rest of the columns show training and test performances using GP-selected, and GP-selected-constructed features. The values of the results using all features is the mean and standard deviation of applying 10-folds cross validation to the dataset. For "GP-selected" and "GP-selected-constructed" columns, the training (Fig. 2) and test (Fig. 3) processes are repeated 30 times, hence we get 30 accuracies for each classifier which are represented as mean and standard deviation ($\bar{x} \pm s$) in Table 2. For making a clear comparison between using different feature-sets, the results are also tested using *Wilcoxon signed-rank test* with a significance level of 5%. The statistical test has been applied on the test results to check which feature-set has better ability to discriminate between *benign* and *malignant* classes. The symbols "+", "–" and "=" are used to represent significantly better, significantly worse and not significantly different performance, respectively, of the two features-sets (GP-selected and GP-selected-constructed) in comparison with all features. For example, in LBP_{rgb} block the test performance of SVM using GP-selected features is represented as "76.42 ± 1.35+" where the "+" sign represents that GP-selected features have significantly outperformed all features.

Table 2. The accuracy (%) on the training and test set using all features, GP-selected features, and GP-selected-constructed features (results are represented in terms of mean accuracy and standard deviation ($\bar{x} \pm s$)).

		All (59 feature)		GP-selected (28.26 feature)		GP-selected-constructed (29.26 feature)	
		Training	Test	Training	Test	Training	Test
LBP_{gray}	NB	71.63 ± 2.97	63.44 ± 12.2	72.12 ± 0.89	65.75 ± 1.71+	74.32 ± 1.46	65.71 ± 2.46+
	SVM	89.93 ± 1.36	70.94 ± 11.9	80.79 ± 1.50	70.29 ± 1.67−	84.11 ± 1.79	70.94 ± 2.55=
	KNN	100.0 ± 0.00	71.25 ± 9.46	100.0 ± 0.00	67.76 ± 1.94−	100.0 ± 0.00	67.55 ± 1.99−
	J48	88.89 ± 8.68	61.56 ± 13.7	85.07 ± 2.79	62.94 ± 2.69+	92.03 ± 1.73	64.84 ± 3.55+
	RF	100.0 ± 0.00	62.81 ± 10.2	100.0 ± 0.00	64.17 ± 1.48+	100.0 ± 0.00	65.97 ± 2.02+
	MLP	74.44 ± 1.53	67.81 ± 8.62	69.76 ± 1.69	66.16 ± 2.15−	73.81 ± 2.04	67.33 ± 2.29=
		(177 feature)		(34.89 feature)		(35.95 feature)	
		Training	Test	Training	Test	Training	Test
LBP_{rgb}	NB	79.10 ± 1.62	76.25 ± 8.75	78.19 ± 0.75	76.04 ± 1.81=	79.82 ± 0.96	76.21 ± 1.91=
	SVM	100.0 ± 0.00	75.00 ± 13.6	85.29 ± 1.14	76.42 ± 1.35+	87.59 ± 1.44	75.77 ± 2.41=
	KNN	100.0 ± 0.00	74.69 ± 13.7	100.0 ± 0.00	73.31 ± 1.88−	100.0 ± 0.00	73.31 ± 1.88−
	J48	90.87 ± 8.31	73.13 ± 9.60	83.22 ± 1.59	73.39 ± 1.96=	92.08 ± 1.17	72.74 ± 2.84=
	RF	100.0 ± 0.00	75.94 ± 9.79	100.0 ± 0.00	75.34 ± 1.47−	100.0 ± 0.00	75.53 ± 1.72=
	MLP	84.13 ± 1.69	76.88 ± 10.1	80.32 ± 0.62	**78.17 ± 0.83**+	82.55 ± 1.08	**77.54 ± 1.67**+

Analysing the effect of dimensionality reduction, it has been seen that while using LBP_{gray} features (59 in total), GP selects only half of the features (around 28) in its tree having tree depth of 8. Here the number of features is 28.26 computed as average number of features appeared in 30 evolved GP trees. In case of LBP_{rgb}, the reduction in number of features is significant (from 177 to around 35). Except k-NN, all the classification algorithms have achieved either better or comparable performance for classifying skin cancer images. This shows that GP with its feature selection ability, has pushed most of the classification algorithms achieve good classification performance even with reduced number of features. Moreover, the feature constructed by GP-selected features are more powerful in creating good training models as compared to feature constructed by all set of features. This is evident when comparing GP-selected and GP-selected-constructed results. Our method allows GP to perform implicit feature selection twice during each stage, which helps improve the classification performance.

Variation in colour of *malignant* melanoma is a major discriminative aspect for dermatologists [5] which is validated by the results as well. Comparing the results of gray features and colour features, colour features have shown better performance in almost all cases. According to the overall results, MLP achieved the highest performance, i.e., 78.17% ± 0.83, which is comparatively well enough as compared to the state-of-the-art method [5] having 84.3% balanced accuracy on the same dataset and same fitness measure, considering overhead of preprocessing and manual segmentation, which requires human expertise in [5].

5.2 Analysis of the Evolved Features

To see why the GP-selected-constructed features can achieve good performance, we show a good GP tree (Fig. 5) among the 10 GP runs after stage-2 having

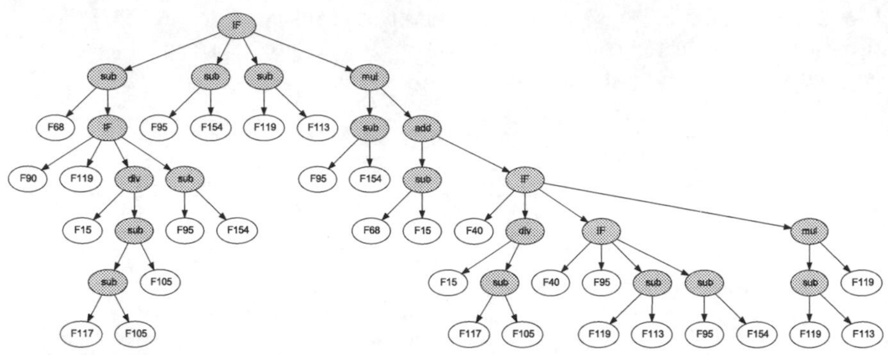

Fig. 5. A good evolved GP tree after stage-2 having 90.63% accuracy on training data.

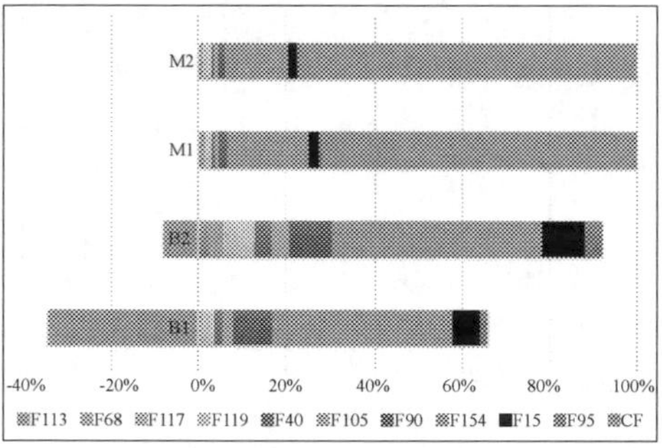

Fig. 6. Bar chart showing the values of different selected features after stage-1 and value of constructed feature "CF" after stage-2.

90.63% accuracy on the training set. This tree is taken from LBP_{rgb} experiments where the total number of features is 177. In the figure, gray nodes represent functions and white nodes represent terminals. Note that for constructing this tree, features selected by a tree in stage-1 are used only and not the whole feature set. Hence, employing feature selection twice. This tree is constructed from ten LBP_{rgb} features appeared in a tree in stage-1, which are F15, F40, F68, F90, F95, F105, F113, F117, F119, and F154. The values of these 10 selected features (after stage-1) and the constructed feature (after stage-2) are plotted in a bar chart shown in Fig. 6. For analysis of the selected feature, we take the simple example of features F15 and F154. As an example, we take the values of these features for only two instances from each class. The bar plot shows that the values of F15 (shown in black) and F154 (shown in green) for the *benign* instances (B1 and B2) are high as compared to values for *malignant* instances (M1 and M2). Hence, by combining these GP-selected features, the constructed feature divides instances of the two classes into two completely separate intervals as shown by blue colour in Fig. 6. Therefore, using these powerful GP-selected-constructed features from the selected features, the common classification algorithms become able to achieve better discrimination between the *benign* and *malignant* classes, resulting in improved classification performance.

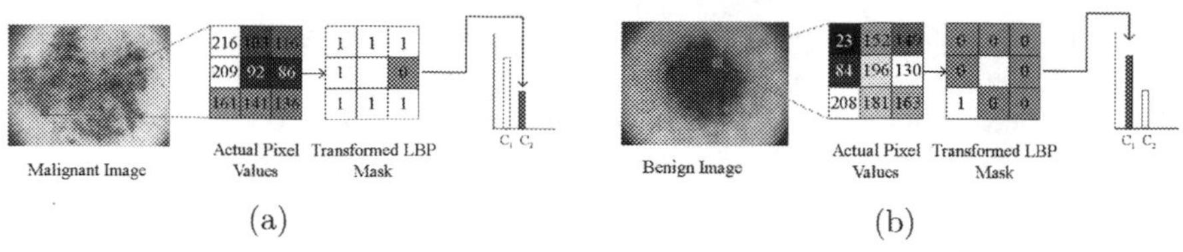

Fig. 7. Feature analysis (a) *Malignant*, and (b) *Benign*.

We further analyse the LBP texture pattern of these two features F15 and F154 to match skin cancer image properties like streaks and blobs. Figure 7(a) shows the extracted 3×3 window for F15, its transformed LBP mask and the histogram showing the given pattern added to the *malignant* class bin represented as C_2. This mask shows presence of line ends in the image, which matches the presence of streaks in *malignant* images. According to the bar chart, this value is less for *malignant* images and high for *benign* images, which helps our method to distinguish between the two classes effectively. Similarly, Fig. 7(b) shows the extracted 3×3 window for F154, its transformed LBP mask and the histogram showing the given pattern added to the *benign* class bin represented as C_1. This mask shows the presence of corners in an image. Its value for the *malignant* class is lower as compared to the *benign* class. This maps to the structure of the *benign* and *malignant* lesions. The *benign* lesions are often a confined dense structure having less variation in colour, however *malignant* lesions have often sparse structure, spreading over a larger region with no defined boundary and varying colour (refer to Figs. 4 and 7 for a visual illustration).

6 Conclusions

Motivated by the powerful ability of GP in feature selection and feature construction, we developed a GP based two-stage method for feature selection (stage-1) and feature construction (stage-2) for the task of skin cancer image classification. The GP selected and constructed features together have shown powerful ability to help common classification algorithms achieve better performance as compared to using the full set of features. Our method constructed new features from GP selected features, hence using the feature selection ability twice, resulting in more powerful constructed features. Using these GP selected and constructed features, the classification algorithms have shown to provide effective solutions for the real-world cancer detection problem. The results have also shown that colour features have more potential to distinguish between *benign* and *malignant* skin lesions as compared to gray features. We further analysed the GP selected features and GP constructed features to get into the insights of skin cancer properties. It has been found that the LBP patterns can be mapped to skin cancer properties, explaining the contribution of the selected features towards their distinguishing behaviour. In the future, we would like to investigate the effect of employing preprocessing techniques to remove noise from the images.

We are also interested to further investigate the classification performance of our method by using a different dataset and also focus on the computation time to make it effective for real-world applications like skin cancer diagnosis.

References

1. Abuzaghleh, O., Barkana, B.D., Faezipour, M.: Noninvasive real-time automated skin lesion analysis system for melanoma early detection and prevention. IEEE J. Transl. Eng. Health Med. **3**, 1–12 (2015)
2. Ahmed, S., Zhang, M., Peng, L.: Enhanced feature selection for biomarker discovery in LC-MS data using GP. In: Proceedings of the 2013 IEEE Congress on Evolutionary Computation, pp. 584–591. IEEE (2013)
3. Ain, Q.U., Xue, B., Al-Sahaf, H., Zhang, M.: Genetic programming for skin cancer detection in dermoscopic images. In: Proceedings of the 2017 Congress on Evolutionary Computation, pp. 2420–2427. IEEE (2017)
4. Argenziano, G., Fabbrocini, G., Carli, P., De Giorgi, V., Sammarco, E., Delfino, M.: Epiluminescence microscopy for the diagnosis of doubtful melanocytic skin lesions: comparison of the ABCD rule of dermatoscopy and a new 7-point checklist based on pattern analysis. Arch. Dermatol. **134**(12), 1563–1570 (1998)
5. Barata, C., Marques, J.S., Celebi, M.E.: Improving dermoscopy image analysis using color constancy. In: Proceedings of the 2014 IEEE International Conference on Image Processing, pp. 3527–3531. IEEE (2014)
6. Carli, P., et al.: Addition of dermoscopy to conventional naked-eye examination in melanoma screening: a randomized study. J. Am. Acad. Dermatol. **50**(5), 683–689 (2004)
7. Esteva, A., et al.: Dermatologist-level classification of skin cancer with deep neural networks. Nature **542**(7639), 115–118 (2017)
8. Ferris, L.K., et al.: Computer-aided classification of melanocytic lesions using dermoscopic images. J. Am. Acad. Dermatol. **73**(5), 769–776 (2015)
9. Hall, M., Frank, E., Holmes, G., Pfahringer, B., Reutemann, P., Witten, I.H.: The WEKA data mining software: an update. SIGKDD Expl. Newslett. **11**(1), 10–18 (2009)
10. Keerthi, S.S., Lin, C.J.: Asymptotic behaviors of support vector machines with Gaussian kernel. Neural Comput. **15**(7), 1667–1689 (2003)
11. Koza, J.R.: Genetic programming: on the programming of computers by means of natural selection. Stat. Comput. **1**, 87–112 (1992)
12. Luke, S.: Essentials of Metaheuristics, 2nd edn. Lulu, Abu Dhabi (2013). http://cs.gmu.edu/sean/book/metaheuristics/
13. Marghoob, A.A., Malvehy, J., Braun, R.P.: An Atlas of Dermoscopy. CRC Press, Boca Raton (2012)
14. Mendonça, T., Ferreira, P.M., Marques, J.S., Marcal, A.R.S., Rozeira, J.: PH2-a dermoscopic image database for research and benchmarking. In: Proceedings of the 35th Annual International Conference of the IEEE Engineering in Medicine and Biology Society, pp. 5437–5440. IEEE (2013)
15. Menegola, A., Fornaciali, M., Pires, R., Bittencourt, F.V., Avila, S., Valle, E.: Knowledge transfer for melanoma screening with deep learning. arXiv preprint arXiv:1703.07479 (2017)
16. Mishra, N.K., Celebi, M.E.: An overview of melanoma detection in dermoscopy images using image processing and machine learning. arXiv preprint arXiv:1601.07843 (2016)

17. Neshatian, K., Zhang, M., Andreae, P.: A filter approach to multiple feature construction for symbolic learning classifiers using genetic programming. IEEE Trans. Evol. Comput. **16**(5), 645–661 (2012)
18. Ojala, T., Pietikäinen, M., Harwood, D.: A comparative study of texture measures with classification based on featured distributions. Pattern Recogn. **29**(1), 51–59 (1996)
19. Patterson, G., Zhang, M.: Fitness functions in genetic programming for classification with unbalanced data. In: Orgun, M.A., Thornton, J. (eds.) AI 2007. LNCS (LNAI), vol. 4830, pp. 769–775. Springer, Heidelberg (2007). https://doi.org/10.1007/978-3-540-76928-6_90
20. Stolz, W., et al.: ABCD rule of dermatoscopy: a new practical method for early recognition of malignant-melanoma. Eur. J. Dermatol. **4**(7), 521–527 (1994)
21. Xue, B., Zhang, M., Browne, W.N., Yao, X.: A survey on evolutionary computation approaches to feature selection. IEEE Trans. Evol. Comput. **20**(4), 606–626 (2016)
22. Zortea, M.: Performance of a dermoscopy-based computer vision system for the diagnosis of pigmented skin lesions compared with visual evaluation by experienced dermatologists. Artif. Intell. Med. **60**(1), 13–26 (2014)

Unsupervised Stereo Matching with Occlusion-Aware Loss

Ningqi Luo[1(✉)], Chengxi Yang[2], Wenxiu Sun[2], and Binheng Song[1]

[1] Graduate School at Shenzhen, Tsinghua University, Shenzhen, China
lnq16@mails.tsinghua.edu.cn

[2] SenseTime Group Limited, Hongkong, China
{yangchengxi,sunwenxiu}@sensetime.com

Abstract. Deep learning methods have shown very promising results for regressing dense disparity maps directly from stereo image pairs. However, apart from a few public datasets such as Kitti, the ground-truth disparity needed for supervised training is hardly available. In this paper, we propose an unsupervised stereo matching approach with a novel occlusion-aware reconstruction loss. Together with smoothness loss and left-right consistency loss to enforce the disparity smoothness and correctness, the deep neural network can be well trained without requiring any ground-truth disparity data. To verify the effectiveness of the proposed method, we train and test our approach without ground-truth disparity data. Competitive results can be achieved on the public datasets (Kitti Stereo 2012, Kitti Stereo 2015, Cityscape) and our self-collected driving dataset that contains diverse driving scenario compared to the public datasets.

Keywords: Stereo matching · Unsupervised · Occlusion-aware Driving scenario

1 Introduction

The accurate estimation of disparity maps is the key to a large variety of computer vision tasks, such as autonomous driving, 3D reconstruction and many others. Given a rectified stereo pair, disparity map can be estimated by computing relative horizontal displacement of pixels between left and right images. That is, for an arbitrary pixel (x, y) in left image, the disparity d is estimated by finding the correspondence pixel $(x - d, y)$ in the right image.

Due to the recent advances in Convolutional Neural Networks (CNNs), the deep learning approach has surpassed the classical approaches in stereo matching, especially at very challenging datasets such as Kitti Stereo 2012 or Kitti Stereo 2015. Although inspiring performances are reported by deep learning approaches MatchNet [1], CRL [2], DispNet [3], and GC-Net [4], they are still required to follow a well-established stereo matching pipeline for correspondence matching and optimization to achieve state-of-the-art accuracy. End-to-end disparity regression from stereo pairs is achievable with the ground-breaking work

X. Geng and B.-H. Kang (Eds.): PRICAI 2018, LNAI 11012, pp. 746–758, 2018.
https://doi.org/10.1007/978-3-319-97304-3_57

of DispNet [3], which incorporates all the necessary blocks, including correspondence matching, optimization/refinement into a single CNN. The end-to-end approach also speeds up the computation considerably. However, a large amount of image pairs with ground-truth disparities (*i.e.*, tens of thousands) are required during training, rather than patch pairs as used in MatchNet [1]. Yet, such large amount of data is barely available in existing dataset. To handle this problem, they train the end-to-end network firstly on a generated synthetic dataset, then fine-tuned on the targeted dataset with few ground-truth disparities available for improved performance. However, for practical scenarios without ground-truth disparities, the performance of pre-trained model may deteriorate substantially.

(a) Stereo 2012 (b) Stereo 2015 (c) Cityscapes (d) Our dataset

Fig. 1. Our results on Kitti Stereo 2012, Stereo 2015, Cityscapes and our dataset. From top to bottom: left image, occlusion map and disparity map.

To tackle the lack of ground-truth problem and inspired by the classical stereo matching approach, we intend to train the CNN in an unsupervised way. And as reported in Xu and Jia [5], one of the main challenges of stereo matching is matching ambiguities occurred at object boundaries. When taking the ground truth occlusion information into optimization, very accurate disparity estimation can be achieved. This indicates that partial occlusion is one major element that affects stereo matching. Thus, appropriate occlusion detection and handling becomes important. In this paper, we propose to identify the occlusion area explicitly and construct an occlusion-aware reconstruction loss during training. In addition, to correctly regress the disparities at the occluded areas, we infer those disparities by enforcing the smoothness constraints on the predicted disparity, based on the observation that high quality disparities may turn out to be piece-wise smooth. Enforcing smoothness helps propagating the predictions from non-occluded areas with low reconstruction loss to occluded areas with a constant high reconstruction loss. Left-right disparity consistency loss is further introduced for improving the correctness of estimated disparities. The effectiveness of our unsupervised approach is demonstrated by quantitative evaluation on Kitti Stereo 2012 [6] and Kitti Stereo 2015 [7], and qualitative evaluation on Cityscapes [8] and our self-collected dataset. The first row of Fig. 1 shows sample images of the four evaluated datasets. The second row of Fig. 1 shows the detected occlusion area. The last row of Fig. 1 shows the predicted disparities of our proposed approach, without using the ground-truth disparities during training.

Our paper is structured as follows. We review related works in Sect. 2. Then we elaborate our proposed unsupervised framework with occlusion-aware loss in Sect. 3. In Sects. 4 and 5, experimentation and conclusions are presented respectively.

2 Related Work

Estimating a dense disparity map from a stereo image pair is a long-lasting problem that has been studied for decades. In this section, we review related stereo matching schemes and deep learning techniques.

Classical Stereo Matching Methods. Stereo algorithms, including *local* and *global* methods, generally perform a subset of the following four steps [9]: (1) matching cost computation; (2) cost aggregation; (3) disparity computation or optimization; and (4) disparity refinement. Local and window-based methods [10,11] aggregate the matching cost by summing or average over a support region and then perform a local winner-take-all (WTA) optimization at each pixel. In contrast, global methods such as graph cut [12] and belief propagation [13,14] treat disparity assignment as an optimization problem to minimize a global energy function for all disparity values. Although local methods can be very fast, global approaches are in general more effective. A good trade-off between accuracy and execution time is a method called Semi-Global Matching (SGM) [15] which aggregates matching cost radiometrically in several directions. Additionally, NLCA [16] and ST [17] present a tree-based cost aggregation method which computing the (1) to (3) steps by constructing a minimum spanning tree (MST). To further improve the accuracy of the estimated disparity, refinement steps are often adopted. Rhemann et al. [18] and Yang [19] refine disparity by mutual consistency check. Graphical models such as MRF [20] and CRF [21,22] are also widely used for post disparity refinement.

Supervised Deep Learning for Stereo Matching. CNN-based approaches estimate disparities reflecting part or all of the aforementioned four steps. These approaches can be roughly divided into matching cost learning, regularity learning and end-to-end disparity learning. In contrast to hand-crafted matching cost metrics, MatchNet [1] extracts features from a pair of patches followed by a decision module for measuring similarity. Zbontar et al. [23] formulates pairwise matching as a binary classification problem to determine if two patches match. Luo et al. [24] proposed to learn a probability distribution over all disparity values. The second category learns the regularization. Based on the observation that disparity images are generally piecewise smooth, Menze et al. [25] applied adaptive smoothness constraints using texture and edge information for a dense stereo estimation. By discovering locally inconsistent labeled pixels, Gidaris et al. [26]

proposed the detection, replacement, refinement framework. The last category formulates stereo matching as a supervised regression task. Learned in an end-to-end framework, DispNet [3], FlowNet [27,28], GC-Net [4] and CRL [2] directly computes the per-pixel disparity of stereo pairs. They achieve state-of-the-art matching results on stereo benchmark.

Unsupervised Deep Learning for Stereo Matching. Recently, deep neural network based schemes incorporating view reconstruction losses have been applied to compute disparity map, which do not require ground truth depth map. Spatial Transform Networks [29] is a typical way to perform image reconstruction, as did in Monodepth [30–32]. Close to Monodepth in spirit, Zhou et al. [33] proposed iterative unsupervised training framework consists of disparity prediction, confidence map estimation, training data selection based on novel view synthesis. With this framework, [33] is suitable for matching data for different scenarios. Very recently SsSMNet [34] designed a symmetrical neural network which is able to generate disparity maps for both left and right images at once, and is self-adaptive with disparity left-right consistency. These unsupervised training networks require a very limited amount of training data that has ground truth disparities.

3 Proposed Scheme

This section illustrates the framework of our unsupervised scheme for stereo matching, the architecture of our neural network, the detection of occlusion map, and the loss functions for occlusion handling.

3.1 Framework

Our stereo matching network f is an end-to-end trainable framework taking left image I_l and right image I_r as input, and produces disparity maps D_l with $f(I_l, I_r)$. Given I_r and estimated D_l, the new left image can be reconstructed using backward warping $I_l^{'} = warp(D_l, I_r)$. Cause of deviation between estimated D_l and ground truth D_l^*, there are differences between I_l and $I_l^{'}$. Thus, we use reconstruction error as an evaluation of estimated D_l. Considering causes of occlusion area in stereo images, we calculate occlusion maps U, and optimize D_l by minimizing the matching cost of I_l and $I_l^{'}$ on non-occluded area. Additionally, disparity smoothness loss and left-right consistency loss are also constraints in our scheme. Using combination of three loss functions, f can be well trained without requiring any ground truth disparity data.

3.2 Neural Network Architecture

Our neural network architecture is illustrated in Fig. 2. The neural network takes stereo images as input, as shown in Fig. 2a, followed by two convolution layers

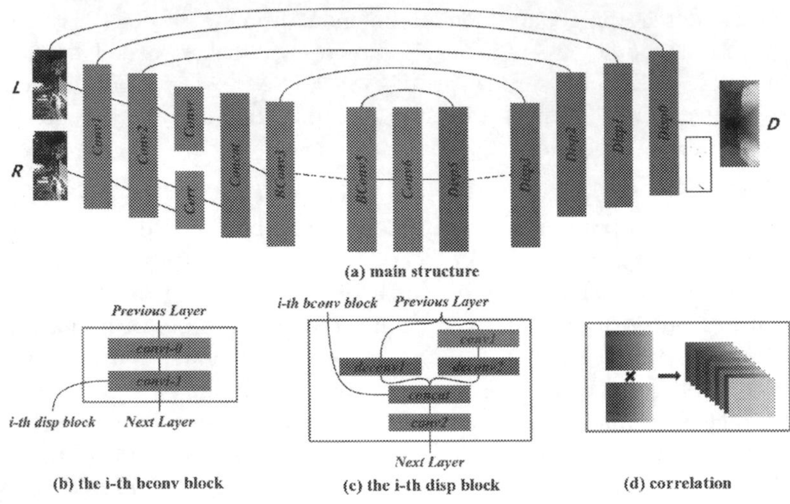

Fig. 2. Architecture of our neural network. (Color figure online)

where left and right input share weights. Deep features extracted from convolution layers traverse at different disparity levels, and are crossed assembled to a stack in the correlation block. Crossed features combine with the deep feature of left input in the concatenation layer (green-yellow), followed by a series of down-sampling (orange) and up-sampling (green) processes. We pack repeated parts of these processes into bconv-block and disp-block, as shown in Fig. 2b and c. The final disparity map is extracted from the block disp0, and an occlusion map is acquired at the same time (Table 1).

Correlation block, as shown in Fig. 2d, produces a crossed feature which consists of left and right input at different disparity levels. In this block, right feature map J_r traverses in a preset disparity range from M toward N, and left feature map J_l is copied $N - M + 1$ times. The crossed feature is constructed with $\left[[J_r^n \circ J_l]^{N-M+1}\right]$ where $\circ$ is the Hadamard product and n is disparity level range from M to N. The ith disp-block connects with both previous disp-block and the ith convolution layer where i is from 0 to 5. From block disp0 to block disp5, full disparity map and five subsampled disparity maps at different scales are produced. All of them are constrained by well-designed loss functions with different weights.

3.3 Occlusion Map

Appropriate occlusion detection and handling is important for stereo matching. Contiguous objects A and B in the left image share the same horizontal line. Suppose the right object B is closer than A, the right-side marginal zone of A is a potential occlusion area in the right image, which means it could not match any area in right image or be reconstructed from the right image. In our view synthesis based stereo matching scheme, we analysis the cause of occlusion area

Table 1. Details of our neural network. Where $a[i] = [16, 32, 64, 128, 256, 512]$, $b[i] = [1, 2, 4, 8, 16, 32, 64]$, $c[i] = [20, 97, 193, 385, 769, 1025]$ and $K = N - M + 1$.

Name	Layer setting	Output dimension
Input	$\frac{input}{255}$	$H \times W \times 3$
Conv1	$7 \times 7, 64, 2$	$\frac{1}{2}H \times \frac{1}{2}W \times 64$
Conv2	$5 \times 5, 128, 2$	$\frac{1}{4}H \times \frac{1}{4}W \times 128$
Corr	concat left and shifted right	$\frac{1}{4}H \times \frac{1}{4}W \times K$
Convr	$1 \times 1, 64, 1$	$\frac{1}{4}H \times \frac{1}{4}W \times 64$
Concat	concat Corr and Convr	$\frac{1}{4}H \times \frac{1}{4}W \times (K + 64)$
conv3-1	$5 \times 5, 256, 2$	$\frac{1}{8}H \times \frac{1}{8}W \times 256$
conv3-2	$3 \times 3, 256, 1$	$\frac{1}{8}H \times \frac{1}{8}W \times 256$
conv4-1	$3 \times 3, 512, 2$	$\frac{1}{16}H \times \frac{1}{16}W \times 512$
conv4-2	$3 \times 3, 512, 1$	$\frac{1}{16}H \times \frac{1}{16}W \times 512$
conv5-1	$3 \times 3, 512, 2$	$\frac{1}{32}H \times \frac{1}{32}W \times 512$
conv5-2	$3 \times 3, 512, 1$	$\frac{1}{32}H \times \frac{1}{32}W \times 512$
conv6-1	$3 \times 3, 1024, 2$	$\frac{1}{64}H \times \frac{1}{64}W \times 1024$
conv6-2	$3 \times 3, 1024, 1$	$\frac{1}{64}H \times \frac{1}{64}W \times 1024$
DispBlock-i		
conv1	$3 \times 3, a[i], 1$	$\frac{1}{b[i+1]}H \times \frac{1}{b[i+1]}W \times a[i]$
deconv1	$4 \times 4, a[i], 1$	$\frac{1}{b[i]}H \times \frac{1}{b[i]}W \times a[i]$
deconv2	$4 \times 4, 1, 1$	$\frac{1}{b[i]}H \times \frac{1}{b[i]}W \times 1$
concat	concat convi-2, deconv1, deconv2	$\frac{1}{b[i]}H \times \frac{1}{b[i]}W \times c[i]$
conv2	$3 \times 3, 1, 1$	$\frac{1}{b[i]}H \times \frac{1}{b[i]}W \times 1$
Output	DispBlock-1-conv2	$H \times W \times 1$

in stereo images, and calculate occlusion maps for occlusion-aware reconstruction loss. We compute the occlusion map of left input as

$$U_{ij} = S_{k=1}^{K}\big(\mathcal{T}(D_{ij} - D_{ij+k} + k)\big) \tag{1}$$

where

$$\mathcal{T}(x) = \begin{cases} 1 & x > 0 \\ 0 & x \le 0 \end{cases} \tag{2}$$

$$S_{k=1}^{K}(x_k) = x_1 \wedge x_2 \wedge \cdots \wedge x_K \tag{3}$$

The occlusion map U calculated in (1) is a 2D binary matrix filled with 0 and 1 where 0 means occlusion area. For an arbitrary single point at the ith line and j^{th} column of left disparity map, as shown in Fig. 3, we compare this point (i, j) with K points on the right side respectively. We make a judgment that (i, j) might be covered by $(i, j + k)$ if $D_{ij} - D_{ij+k} + k$ is negative where $k \in [1, K]$. Considering all K judgments, we set U_{ij} negative if any comparison is negative or

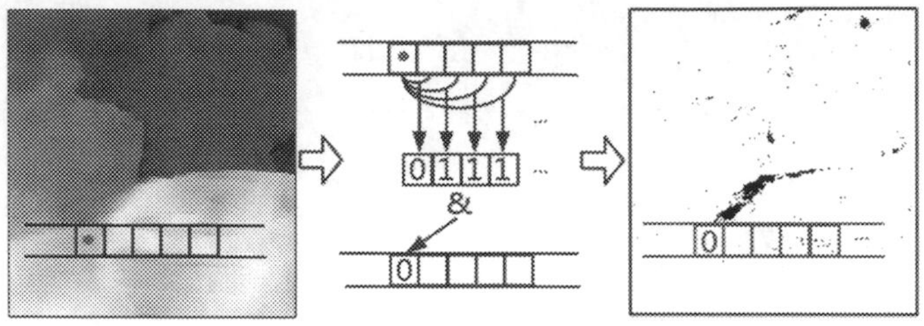

Fig. 3. Process of computing an occlusion map.

else positive. For efficiency, we calculate the whole occlusion map by computing matrix difference of traversed disparity maps on different disparity levels.

3.4 Loss Functions

The total loss $\mathcal{L}$ in our scheme is a combination of three main terms,

$$\mathcal{L} = \omega_r U(\mathcal{L}_r) + \omega_s \mathcal{L}_s + \omega_c \mathcal{L}_c \tag{4}$$

where $\mathcal{L}_r$ is reconstruction loss which encourages the reconstructed image to appear similar to the corresponding input, $U(\mathcal{L}_r)$ is the reconstruction loss with occlusion-aware module $U(\cdot)$, $\mathcal{L}_s$ is a disparity smoothness loss, $\mathcal{L}_c$ is disparity left-right consistency loss. ω_r, ω_s and ω_c are weights of $U(\mathcal{L}_r)$, $\mathcal{L}_s$ and $\mathcal{L}_c$ respectively.

Reconstruction Loss. To evaluate the similarity between reconstructed and reference images, we use structural similarity index measurement (SSIM) and L1 difference. $\mathcal{L}_r$ is designed as

$$\mathcal{L}_r = \frac{1}{hw} \sum_{i=1}^{h} \sum_{j=1}^{w} \mathcal{L}_{r_{ij}} \tag{5}$$

$$\mathcal{L}_{r_{ij}} = \alpha \frac{1 - SSIM(I_{ij}, I'_{ij})}{2} + (1-\alpha) \|\nabla I_{ij} - \nabla I'_{ij}\| \tag{6}$$

where h and w are height and width of input images, equilibrium coefficient $\alpha \in (0, 1)$, ∇I and $\nabla I'$ are gradients of reference image I and reconstructed image I'. We calculate the matching costs of each pairwise pixels between left and right input using Eq. (6), and average them with (5).

Occlusion area in left image could not match any area in right image or be reconstructed from right image. Considering of this situation, we apply occlusion-aware module at reconstruction loss. With the occlusion map U described in Sect. 3.2, the reconstruction losses of occlusion areas (0 in U) are set as average matching cost of all non-occluded areas.

$$v = \frac{\|U \circ P\|_1}{\|U\|_1} \tag{7}$$

$$U(\mathcal{L}_r) = \frac{1}{hw}\|U \circ P + v(\mathbf{1} - U)\|_1 \tag{8}$$

where $\circ$ is the Hadamard product, U is the binary matrix calculated in Sect. 3.2, P is a matrix consist of $\mathcal{L}_{r_{ij}}$ and matrix $\mathbf{1}$ is filled with 1. All these three matrix are $h \times w$. Note that $\|\cdot\|_1$ is entry-wise matrix 1-norm which calculates the sum of all elements in the matrix, due to all elements in U and other matrices of intermediate processes are positive. The average matching cost v of non-occluded area is acquired in (7). Then we use $v(\mathbf{1}-U)$ as loss of occlusion area. Combined with the loss $U \circ P$ of non-occluded area, the occlusion-aware reconstruction loss of all $h \times w$ elements is calculated in (8). Comparison of naive reconstruction loss $\mathcal{L}_r$ and occlusion-aware reconstruction loss $U(\mathcal{L}_r)$ in Sect. 4.3 shows that proposed occlusion-aware module $U(\cdot)$ improve our scheme.

Disparity Smoothness Loss. We assume that the disparity maps are locally smooth and depth discontinuities often occur with large image gradients. We use an L1 penalty on the disparity gradients ∇D and weight it with image gradients ∇I. The edge-aware smoothness loss is designed as

$$\mathcal{L}_s = \frac{1}{hw}\sum_{i=1}^{h}\sum_{j=1}^{w}|\nabla_x D_{ij}|e^{-|\nabla_x^2 I_{ij}|} + |\nabla_y D_{ij}|e^{-|\nabla_y^2 I_{ij}|} \tag{9}$$

where ∇x and ∇y are gradients of images in horizontal and vertical directions. The weight term $e^{-|\nabla^2 I|}$ restricts locally abrupt changes in D if the corresponding areas of I are smooth in the color space.

Left-Right Consistency Loss. Left-right disparity consistency is used in the stereo matching schemes, such as symmetrically neural network SsSMNet [34] which generate disparity maps for both left and right images at the same time. Our neural network only produces disparity maps of left images directly. To acquire disparity maps of right images, we first horizontally flip stereo images $\overrightarrow{I_l}$ and $\overrightarrow{I_r}$ to $\overleftarrow{I_l}$ and $\overleftarrow{I_r}$ respectively. The disparity map $\overleftarrow{D_r}$ can be calculated by forward computaion $f(\overleftarrow{I_r}, \overrightarrow{I_l})$ with our neural network. Finally, the disparity map $\overrightarrow{D_r}$ of right image is acquired by horizontally flipping $\overleftarrow{D_r}$. To ensure coherence of estimated left-view and right-view disparity maps D_l and D_r, we use an L1 penalty on left-right disparity consistency as

$$\mathcal{L}_c = \frac{1}{hw}\sum_{i=1}^{h}\sum_{j=1}^{w}|D^l_{ij} - D^r_{ij-D^l_{ij}}| \tag{10}$$

For an arbitrary point (i, j) in D^l, the correspondence is found at $(i, j - D^l_{ij})$ in D^r. We use L1 penalty on the deviation of disparities between the pairwise points, followed by computing average loss of all $h \times w$ elements.

With occlusion-aware reconstruction loss, disparity smoothness loss and left-right consistency loss discussed above, the deep neural network can be well trained without ground-truth disparity data.

4 Experiment

In this section, we illustrate experiment setting, compare our scheme with related works, and analysis the performance of proposed occlusion-aware reconstruction loss.

4.1 Setup

There are four driving datasets we used in our experiment: Kitti Stereo 2012 [6] and Kitti Stereo 2015 [7] supply ground truth disparities, Cityscapes [8] and our self-collected dataset do not. Kitti Stereo 2012 consists of 194 training pairs and 195 testing pairs. The qualities in Kitti Stereo 2015 are both 200. 1500 training and 1500 testing stereo images in Cityscapes are used. The same amount of images in our self-collected dataset come into use.

Parameters in our scheme are set as follow. Range of disparity levels $[M, N]$ in correlation layer is $[-10, 70]$. Maximum searching bias K for computing occlusion map is 30. Weights of losses ω_r, ω_s, ω_c and α are 28.8, 3.2, 0.32 and 0.98 respectively. The shape $h \times w$ of both input stereo images and output disparity maps is 448×1472. In order to uniform input shape, we resize stereo images using bilinear sampling. And we resize output disparity maps to the raw shape of corresponding images using the nearest sampling. Our scheme is implemented in TensorFlow framework [35].

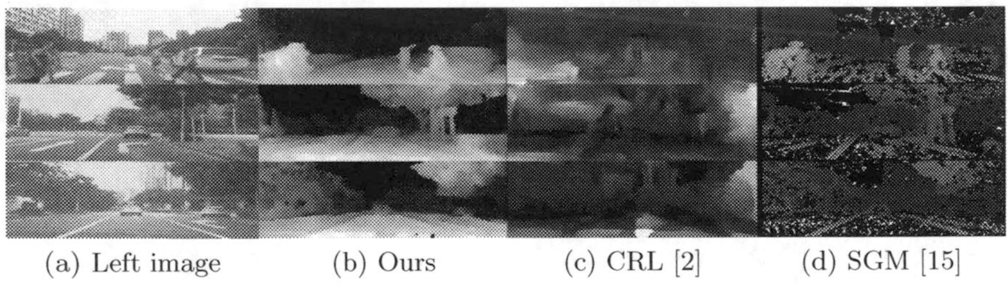

(a) Left image (b) Ours (c) CRL [2] (d) SGM [15]

Fig. 4. Results on our dataset. From left to right: left image, our result, results of supervised deep learning CRL [2] and classical method SGM [15].

4.2 Comparisons

We compare our scheme with supervised deep learning models [2,3], classical stereo matching methods [15,36], and unsupervised deep learning models [30,33]. Evaluation on Kitti stereo benchmark is shown in Table 2. The indexes avg-noc (px) and avg-all (px) in Stereo 2012 are average disparity error in non-occluded and total area. Stereo 2015 considers a pixel to be correctly estimated if the disparity error is $< 3px$. The indexes D1-noc and D1-all are used to show the percentage of stereo disparity outliers. Lower is better in Table 2.

Table 2. Comparisons of our method and related works. [2,3] are supervised deep learning models, [15,36] are classical stereo matching methods, [30,33] and ours are unsupervised deep learning models.

Method	Kitti				Time cost
	Stereo 2012		Stereo 2015		
	Avg-noc	Avg-all	D1-noc	D1-all	avg(s)
CRL [2]	0.9	1.0	**2.45**	**2.67**	0.47
DispNetC [3]	0.9	1.0	4.32	4.34	**0.06**
SGM [15]	1.2	1.3	4.86	6.29	**5**
Displets [36]	0.7	0.8	**3.00**	**3.43**	265
MonoDepth [30]	0.9	0.9	9.08	9.19	0.63
Zhou et al. [33]	-	-	6.81	7.29	0.39
Ours	1.1	1.2	**6.31**	**6.63**	**0.22**

Supervised learning method CRL [2] ranks top on Kitti Stereo 2015 benchmark. But [2] does not produce similarly fine disparity maps for our self-collected dataset without ground truth, as shown in Fig. 4. Classical stereo matching methods [15,36] cost much more time than deep learning schemes. MonoDepth [30] and very recently Zhou et al. [33] are unsupervised deep learning models. They could efficiently product fine disparity maps after unsupervised training. Comparison shows that our method achieves the smallest error and the least time cost on Stereo 2015 among unsupervised deep learning methods.

Table 3. Comparisons of reconstruction losses.

With occlusion map	Stereo 2012		Stereo 2015		Cityscapes		Our dataset	
	Avg-noc	Avg-all	D1-noc	D1-all	SSIM	L1	SSIM	L1
Yes	1.07	1.20	6.31	6.63	0.5645	18.31	0.5734	24.81
No	1.19	1.32	6.59	6.78	0.5635	18.37	0.5707	24.83

4.3 Effect of Occlusion-Aware Reconstruction Loss

To verify the effectiveness of the proposed occlusion-aware reconstruction loss, we identically train two models except for reconstruction loss (with or without occlusion-aware module). The qualitative comparisons on Kitti Stereo 2012, Stereo 2015, Cityscapes, and our dataset are shown in Table 3.

Evaluations on Kitti Stereo 2012 and 2015 with ground truth data show that our occlusion-aware model decreases 10% average pixel error (Avg-all) and 2% quantity of outliers (D1-all) compared to the model without occlusion-aware module. To quantify performance of reconstruction losses on Cityscapes and our dataset which do not supply ground truth disparities, the comparison focuses on evaluation of view synthesis. With stereo images and corresponding disparity maps produced by two models, we reconstruct new left images using backward warping. SSIM (higher is better) and L1 difference (lower is better) between reconstructed and reference images are used to evaluate predicted disparity maps. Our occlusion-aware scheme achieves higher SSIM and lower L1 difference than the scheme without occlusion-aware module. Meanwhile, the average time costs of two models in the test are the same, 0.22 s for each pairwise input. Computing occlusion maps for the occlusion-aware reconstruction loss is only needed in the process of neural network training. Contrast tests on Kitti, Cityscapes and our self-collected dataset show that the proposed occlusion-aware reconstruction loss has a catalytic role in our unsupervised stereo matching scheme.

We have successfully applied occlusion-aware module at reconstruction loss. Further, this reusable module may produce similarly satisfying results with disparity smoothness loss and left-right consistency loss. These need more discussions and experiments.

5 Conclusion

We have constructed a CNN-based neural network which is able to learn to produce dense disparity maps directly from the stereo inputs. After unsupervised training with occlusion-aware reconstruction loss, disparity smoothness loss and left-right consistency loss, our model is able to produce fine disparity maps. We compare our scheme with related works. Comparisons show that our scheme achieves the smallest error and the least time cost on Kitti Stereo benchmark among unsupervised deep learning methods. Experiments on Kitti, Cityscapes and our self-collected driving dataset verify the effectiveness of proposed occlusion-aware module on reconstruction loss. We will further evaluate the performance of this reusable module with other loss functions.

References

1. Han, X., Leung, T., Jia, Y., Sukthankar, R., Berg, A.C.: MatchNet: unifying feature and metric learning for patch-based matching. In: CVPR (2015)
2. Pang, J., Sun, W., Ren, J.S., Yang, C., Yan, Q.: Cascade residual learning: a two-stage convolutional neural network for stereo matching. In: ICCVW (2017)
3. Mayer, N., et al.: A large dataset to train convolutional networks for disparity, optical flow, and scene flow estimation. In: CVPR (2016)
4. Kendall, A., et al. Bry, A.: End-to-end learning of geometry and context for deep stereo regression. In: arXiv preprint arXiv:1703.04309 (2017)
5. Xu, L., Jia, J.: Stereo matching: an outlier confidence approach. In: Forsyth, D., Torr, P., Zisserman, A. (eds.) ECCV 2008. LNCS, vol. 5305, pp. 775–787. Springer, Heidelberg (2008). https://doi.org/10.1007/978-3-540-88693-8_57
6. Geiger, A., Lenz, P., Urtasun, R.: Are we ready for autonomous driving? The KITTI vision benchmark suite. In: CVPR (2012)
7. Menze, M., Geiger, A.: Object scence flow for autonomous vehicles. In: CVPR (2015)

8. Cordts, M., et al.: The Cityscapes dataset for semantic urban scene understanding. In: CVPR (2016)
9. Scharstein, D., Szeliski, R.: A taxonomy and evaluation of dense two-frame stereo correspondence algorithms. IJCV **47**(1–3), 7–42 (2002)
10. Scharstein, D., Szeliski, R.: Stereo matching with nonlinear diffusionD. IJCV **28**(2), 155–174 (1998)
11. Yoon, K.J., Kweon, I.S.: Adaptive support-weight approach for correspondence search. TPAMI **28**(4), 650–656 (2006)
12. Kolmogorov, V., Zabih, R.: Computing visual correspondence with occlusions via graph cuts. In: ICCV (2001)
13. Klaus, A., Sormanm, M., Karner, K.: Segment-based stereo matching using belief propagation and a self-adapting dissimilarity measure. In: ICPR (2006)
14. Yang, Q., Wang, L., Yang, R., Stewénius, H., Nistér, D.: Stereo matching with color-weighted correlation, hierarchical belief propagation and occlusion handling. TPAMI **31**(3), 492–504 (2009)
15. Hirschmuller, H.: Stereo processing by semiglobal matching and mutual information. TPAMI **30**(2), 328–341 (2008)
16. Yang, Q.: A non-local cost aggregation method for stereo matching. In: CVPR (2012)
17. Mei, X., Sun, X., Dong, W., Wang, H., Zhang, X.: Segment-tree based cost aggregation for stereo matching. In: CVPR (2013)
18. Rhemann, C., Hosni, A., Bleyer, M., Rother, C., Gelautz, M.: Fast cost volume filtering for visual correspondence and beyond. In: CVPR (2011)
19. Yang, Q.: Stereo matching using tree filtering. TPAMI **37**(4), 834–846 (2015)
20. Zhang, L., Seitz, S.M.: Estimating optimal parameters for MRF stereo from a single image pair. TPAMI **29**(2), 331–342 (2007)
21. Scharstein, D., Pal, C.: Learning conditional random fields for stereo. In: CVPR (2007)
22. Li, Y., Huttenlocher, D.P.: Learning for stereo vision using the structured support vector machine. In: CVPR (2008)
23. Zbontar, J., LeCun, Y.: Stereo matching by training a convolutional neural network to compare image patches. JMLR **17**(1), 2287–2318 (2016)
24. Luo, W., Schwing, A.G., Urtasun, R.: Efficient deep learning for stereo matching. In: CVPR (2016)
25. Menze, M., Geiger, A.: Object scene flow for autonomous vehicles. In: CVPR (2015)
26. Gidaris, S., Komodakis, N.: Detect, replace, refine: deep structured prediction for pixel wise labeling. In: CVPR (2017)
27. Fischer, P., et al.: FlowNet: Learning optical flow with convolutional networks. In: ICCV (2015)
28. Ilg, E., Mayer, N., Saikia, T., Keuper, M., Dosovitskiy, A., Brox, T.: FlowNet 2.0: evolution of optical flow estimation with deep networks. In: CVPR (2017)
29. Jaderberg, M., Simonyan, K., Zisserman, A., Kavukcuoglu, K.: Spatial transformer networks. arXiv preprint arXiv:1506.02025 (2015)
30. Godard, C., Mac Aodha, O., Brostow, G.J.: Unsupervised monocular depth estimation with left-right consistency. In: CVPR (2017)
31. Garg, R., B.G., V.K., Carneiro, G., Reid, I.: Unsupervised CNN for Single view depth estimation: geometry to the rescue. In: Leibe, B., Matas, J., Sebe, N., Welling, M. (eds.) ECCV 2016. LNCS, vol. 9912, pp. 740–756. Springer, Cham (2016). https://doi.org/10.1007/978-3-319-46484-8_45
32. Zhou, T., Brown, M., Snavely, N., Lowe, D.: Unsupervised learning of depth and ego-motion from video. In: CVPR (2017)

33. Zhou, C., Zhang, H., Shen, X., Jia, J.: Unsupervised learning of stereo matching. In: ICCV (2017)
34. Zhong, Y., Dai, Y., Li, H.: Self-supervised learning for stereo matching with self-improving ability. arXiv preprint arXiv:1709.00930 (2017)
35. Abadi, M., et al.: TensorFlow: large-scale machine learning on heterogeneous distributed systems. arXiv preprint arXiv:1603.04467 (2016)
36. Guney, F., Geiger, A.: Displets: resolving stereo ambiguities using object knowledge. In: CVPR (2015)

Siamese Network Based Features Fusion for Adaptive Visual Tracking

Dongyan Guo[1], Weixuan Zhao[1], Ying Cui[1,2(✉)], Zhenhua Wang[1], Shengyong Chen[1], and Jian Zhang[3]

[1] College of Computer Science and Technology, Zhejiang University of Technology, Hangzhou 310023, China
cuiying@zjut.edu.cn

[2] Key Laboratory of Intelligent Perception and Systems for High-Dimensional Information of Ministry of Education, Nanjing University of Science and Technology, Nanjing 210094, China

[3] Global Big Data Technologies Centre, University of Technology Sydney, Sydney 2007, Australia

Abstract. Visual object tracking is a popular but challenging problem in computer vision. The main challenge is the lack of priori knowledge of the tracking target, which may be only supervised of a bounding box given in the first frame. Besides, the tracking suffers from many influences as scale variations, deformations, partial occlusions and motion blur, *etc.* To solve such a challenging problem, a suitable tracking framework is demanded to adopt different tracking scenes. This paper presents a novel approach for robust visual object tracking by multiple features fusion in the Siamese Network. Hand-crafted appearance features and CNN features are combined to mutually compensate for their shortages and enhance the advantages. The proposed network is processed as follows. Firstly, different features are extracted from the tracking frames. Secondly, the extracted features are employed via Correlation Filter respectively to learn corresponding templates, which are used to generate response maps respectively. And finally, the multiple response maps are fused to get a better response map, which can help to locate the target location more accurately. Comprehensive experiments are conducted on three benchmarks: Temple-Color, OTB50 and UAV123. Experimental results demonstrate that the proposed approach achieves state-of-the-art performance on these benchmarks.

Keywords: Deep learning · Siamese Network · Object tracking Feature fusion

1 Introduction

Visual object tracking is one of the hotspots in computer vision. Object tracking is widely employed in many real-world visual applications, such as autonomous driving, video surveillance, human-computer interaction, *etc.* The task of object

X. Geng and B.-H. Kang (Eds.): PRICAI 2018, LNAI 11012, pp. 759–771, 2018.
https://doi.org/10.1007/978-3-319-97304-3_58

tracking is estimating the trajectory of an object in an image sequence. However, the only knowledge about the object is that the target location in the first frame. The lack of priori knowledge makes the task challenging. Besides, the problem is challenged from many influences such as illumination variations, scale variations, non-rigid deformations, fast motion, background clutters, motion blur and occlusions.

In recent years, correlation filter based methods have shown excellent performance on object tracking benchmarks [30]. However, most of these methods only use hand-crafted appearance features to present the tracking target, which cannot get satisfactory performance in some scene applications like occlusions [6,7,31], background clutters [2,19,31], *etc.* In the process of object tracking, most of the existing adaptive model based approaches which update the model continuously through the tracking process can achieve better performance [2,6,11,24]. The target information in later frames can make the adaptive model become more accurate. However, in the other side, the model may be updated with some negative information such as target losing. With the accumulation of these small negative errors, the performance of the model become worse. Finally, these small errors may lead to model drift and target lost.

Fig. 1. A qualitative comparison of our approach with other three state-of-the-art approaches on three example sequences. It is shown the three sequences results: Motor Rolling (top row), Soccer (middle row) and skating2 (bottom row). These example sequences include these cases: scale variation, occlusion, deformation, fast motion, out-of-plane rotation, in-plane rotation and background clutters. Our approach achieves superior results in these scenarios.

Deep neural networks can train powerful models with large numbers of labeled training samples. When enough priori knowledge of the target is obtained, the deep neural networks can achieve excellent performance in many application scenes. However, the lack of priori knowledge about the target is the main challenge for training deep neural networks in object tracking task.

Moreover, the training of deep neural networks is time consuming for real time on-line training and tracking.

A possible way to solve the above problems is to train the deep neural networks model offline. Some existing works adapt a pre-trained model for the target to get CNN (Convolutional Neural Network) features [8,10,22]. Though the pre-trained model bypass the online learning problem, its fixed metric prevents the learning strategy from exploiting the sense-specific cues which is important for discrimination. Some approaches use Siamese CNN architecture, which is a non-online adaptation network [3,5,14,18,26]. Siamese CNN is trained offline but have excellent performance in discriminating whether or not the same object in two image patches. According to some research works, combining on-line learning method with pre-trained CNN features has obtained successful improvement. For example, with deep integration of CNN and correlation filter, some investigators take the correlation filter as a network layer [27].

However, it is difficult to achieve satisfactory tracking results with single feature for both on-line and off-line learning strategy. Each feature has its own disadvantages. To overcome the shortcoming, combining different features is a good way to apply in the object tracking task. For example, HOG (Histogram of Orientation Gradient) presents the oriented gradients histograms for an image and it is also a general feature which has employed in many state-of-the-art methods [2,6,7,16]. Those trackers achieve excellent performance in scenarios with little deformation and occlusions. But the HOG features based method has its drawbacks, for example, it is sensitive to large deformation. The trackers perform poorly when the object change rapidly. However, the CNN features are powerful in image representations, it is not sensitive to deformation. It turns out that as long as there are enough diverse training samples, the CNN features can achieve excellent performance even in scenarios with large object variations and background clutters. The one shortcoming is that if the training samples are not enough and lacking some kinds of scenes, the performance of CNN will drop very fast.

A key issue in general object tracking is designing general object descriptors to describe object discriminatively with any class. In this paper, we propose a Siamese Network framework that combines the CNN features with hand-crafted appearance feature for adaptive robust object tracking and achieve excellent performance (see Fig. 1). The features fused in this paper are CNNs and HOGs. Moreover, our network can not only fuse CNN and HOG features, but also integrate CNN features with more features. In the network, we apply the Correlation Filter to generate a discriminative template for CNN and HOG features respectively, which can be used to get CNN and HOG response maps. Thousands of parameters have been trained through the Siamese Network framework to improve the CNN and HOG features fusion results. The improvement is beneficial to the tracking performance. The architecture of our network is shown in Fig. 2. In general, the network architecture we proposed can be divided into three parts. The feature extraction layer are utilized to extract different features from the training samples and testing samples. The training image is an image patch of the previous frame that contains the tracking target. The test image is the current frame to be searched of. The template generation layer utilize the features extracted from the training image to generate the corresponding template. The corresponding response maps can be obtained by the convolution of the feature maps and the discriminative templates. And finally, the multiple response maps are fused by fusion layer to generate the final response. The final response map help to locate the target location more accurately. Experimental results show that our approach is a robust general tracker, and achieves state-of-the-art performance on multiple benchmarks. Code is avaliable online[1].

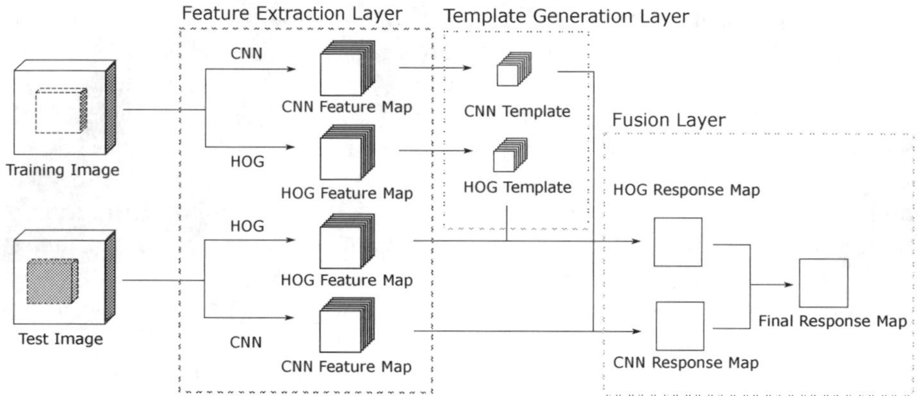

Fig. 2. The architecture of our proposed network.

2 Related Work

The mainstream object tracking methods can be divided into two categories—generative [1,21,25] or discriminative [13,15,32] approaches. Generative model approaches use the statistical models or templates to describe the object. The generative model approaches consist of Kalman filtering, Particle filter, mean-shift and so on. Discriminative model approaches use the machine learning to train classifier by taking the object as the positive samples and the background as the negative samples. And then, use the classifier to find the optimal region of target frame by frame. The Support Vector Machine (SVM) is a classical machine learning algorithm used in discriminative model approaches. Many approaches like Struck tracker [13] employ haar features and structured SVM to achieve the tracking task.

The Discriminative Correlation Filters (CF) is an outstanding method of discriminative model approaches. In recent years, these trackers have been employed in the CF and achieved excellent performance on tracking bechmarks. The MOOSE tracker [4] is the work of Bolme et al. which is the first tracker that

[1] https://github.com/neednieming/SNBFF.

used the CF. These trackers like CSK [15] and MOOSE use the raw pixels combined with CF to estimate the trajectory of an object. However, these methods could not take advantage of image features, and tracking performance is extremely limited. With the help of HOG features, KCF/DCF [16] improve the tracking results. But the HOG is sensitive to deformation while the tracker CN [11] demonstrates that the color feature is robustness to deformation. In any case, it is difficult to achieve satisfactory tracking results with single feature. With the development of deep learning, the method based on deep learning is developing rapidly in the visual object tracking. Recent works have focused on learning universal object descriptors to achieve tracking task. These methods [3,5,14,18,26,27] are based on the Siamese CNN architecture. The network is trained offline, so it can take advantage of information present in numerous training images. The GOTURN tracker [14] based on this architecture can run 100FPS in GPU mode. However, the performance of this method is not satisfactory. End-to-end representation learning method SiameseFC [3] and CFNet [27] get excellent performance in aspects of speed and results. The network we designed combines different features to improve the generality of the tracker, and achieves state-of-the-art performance on multiple benchmarks.

The method of combining multiple estimates can improve tracking results. The Staple [2] tracker combines HOG and color histogram together to make up for the defect of the two features, so it can make the tracker robust to deformation. The tracker in [28] use a factorial HMM to combine the results of five independent trackers. The MEEM [31] tracker stores a collection of past models. For each frame, the tracker can obtain an evaluation result equal to the number of storage models. Using the loss entropy function, an optimal one is selected from these results. Our approach differs from these approaches in that (a) our approach based on a deep neural network architecture is a end-to-end method. (b) A deep integration of different features are achieved in our network by training correlation weights, and these features can describe the object more elaborate. (c) We add a fusion layer in the network to fuse different response maps. The output of the fusion layer can help to locate the target more accurate.

3 The Proposed Approach

We briefly introduce our proposed network framework in Sect. 3.1. And then, the usage of the Correlation Filter to generate CNN and HOG template is explained in Sect. 3.2 and the fusion approach is presented in Sect. 3.3. In the last, we illustrate the use of the fusion model for object tracking in Sect. 3.4.

3.1 Siamese Network Framework

The starting point of this paper is to design a network to combine different features more compact. The CFNet [27] uses the CNN features for visual object tracking and get state-of-the-art performance in the OTB benchmarks [29,30].

However, using the CNN features should face a key problem, if the training samples are not enough and lack some scenes, the CNN features may not achieve satisfactory tracking results in some scenes which are not contained in the training samples. We find that combining the CNN with HOG can improve the universal property of the tracker.

The network we proposed is used to fuse the response map of features. The input of the network is pairs of image patches (x', y'). The image x' represents the object of interest in the x_{th} frame of an image sequence and the object is in the middle of the image x'. Moreover, the image y' represents the object search area in the $x + 1_{th}$ frame of an image sequence and the size of y' is larger than x'. The y' is extracted from $x + 1_{th}$ frame based on the object location in the x_{th} frame.

HOG and CNN features are extracted from the two inputs respectively. Here we utilize the fuction f_c and f_h to extract CNN and HOG features from an image respectively. The parameters used in feature extraction function f are trained by our proposed network. A pair of image patches can yield four feature maps (two CNN feature maps $f_c(x')$, $f_c(y')$ and two HOG feature maps $f_h(x')$, $f_h(y')$) which can get two response maps after cross-correlated operation:

$$g_c(x', y') = f_c(x') \star f_c(y') \tag{1}$$

$$g_h(x', y') = f_h(x') \star f_h(y') \tag{2}$$

Equation 1 gets the CNN feature response map while Eq. 2 gets the HOG feature response map. In order to get a better response map, it is necessary to fuse the CNN response map and HOG response map.

$$g(x', y') = M_\rho(g_c, g_h) \tag{3}$$

Here, the maximum value of the response map $g(x', y')$ is related to the center of the target. The function M is used to represent the fusion approach and the ρ is the learnable parameters. More details about the function M will be explained in Sect. 3.3.

To obtain the model, the network is trained offline. The training image samples of the network are millions of random pair (x'_i, y'_i). Each image pair has a spatial map of label information which is composed of $\{-1, 1\}$. The label is represented whether the pixel point is belonging to the ground truth or not.

$$L_i(r, c) = \begin{cases} -1, & \textit{not belong to ground truth} \\ 1, & \textit{belong to ground truth} \end{cases} \tag{4}$$

Here, r and c represent the row number and col number of the spatial map. The purpose of the network training is minimizing the element-wise logistic loss function ℓ:

$$\arg\min \sum_i \ell(g(x', y'), L_i) \tag{5}$$

3.2 Correlation Filter

The Correlation Filter is an algorithm to train a liner template for discriminating the relationship of image and image transformation. The problem of solving the correlation filter template is equivalent to solving the ridge regression problem. In the following, the correlation filter template is denoted as w, $x \in \mathbb{R}^{m \times m \times K}$ is a K-channel feature image, $y \in \mathbb{R}^{m \times m}$ is the desired response map. In our network, the CNN and HOG feature maps of training image x' are all belong to feature image x. Under a least-squares Correlation Filter formulation, the problem can be represented as:

$$\arg\min_{w} \|w \star x - y\|^2 \tag{6}$$

where symbol $\star$ denotes the circular cross-correlation. To avoid overfitting, we should add the quadratic regularization into Eq. 6 and get:

$$\arg\min_{w} \|w \star x - y\|^2 + \lambda \|w\|^2 \tag{7}$$

To solve the problem, and obtain the optimal template w, we set and expand $F(w)$,

$$\begin{aligned} F(w) &= \|w \star x - y\|^2 + \lambda \|w\|^2 \\ &= (w \star x - y)^T (w \star x - y) + \lambda w^T w \end{aligned} \tag{8}$$

The optimal template w can then obtained by solving the equation $\frac{d(F(w))}{dw} = 0$,

$$w = \frac{y}{x \star x + \lambda} \star x \tag{9}$$

It is time-consuming to solve Eq. 9 in time domain. To avoid the problem, we can make fast Fourier transform for Eq. 9,

$$\hat{w} = \frac{\hat{y}^* \circ \hat{x}}{(\hat{x}^* \circ \hat{x}) + \lambda} \tag{10}$$

where $\hat{w}$ represents the value of w in the frequency domain, the x^* denotes conjugation and the symbol $\circ$ denotes the element-wise multiplication. And introducing inverse fast Fourier transform $\hat{w}$ can get the optimal template w.

3.3 Feature Fusion

In Sect. 3.1, we briefly introduce our proposed network framework, the feature extraction layer of the network can extract features from pairs of image patches (x', y'). These features can obtain two response maps by correlation filter operation. In order to make better use of these response maps, set different weights, and fuse these together to obtain a new response map. The fusion approach can make full use of the advantages of the two features and make up for the deficiency between the two features, therefore the tracking performance could be improved. In Sect. 3.2, the feature templates are obtained through correlation filter, therefore Eqs. 1 and 2 can be represented as:

$$g_c(x', y') = w(f_c(x')) \star f_c(y') \tag{11}$$

$$g_h(x', y') = w(f_h(x')) \star f_h(y') \tag{12}$$

where the function $w(x)$ is represented to get the optimal template w. The fusion approach can use the Eq. 13 to represent,

$$m(x', y') = \sum_{d=1}^{D} g_d(x', y') * k_d \tag{13}$$

where D is the amount of features, k_d is the fusion kernal which trained by our network.

In the last, in order to make the response map more suitable for logistic regression, the scale and bias are added into $m(x', y')$ to get the function $M(x', y')$,

$$M(x', y') = sm(x', y') + b \tag{14}$$

In order to make the fusion result become better, all the parameters are trained through the network.

3.4 Visual Object Tracking Algorithm

The network needs a pair of image patches as input. The input of the model consists of the target region in the previous frame and the search region in the current region. The search region is extracted as a sub-window centred at the previously estimated position which size is four times of the object. The output of the model is the fusion response map. The maximum value of the response is corresponding to the center of the object.

Although the model is trained offline, we find that the updating strategies using online learning can improve the experimental results. When a pair of image patches is inputted to the model, two new template $w(f_c(x'))$ and $w(f_h(x'))$ are obtained. The approach fuses new feature template with old feature template is shown in Eq. 15,

$$\begin{aligned} Temp_{c,new} &= (1 - \eta_c)Temp_{c,pre} + \eta_c w(f_c(x')), \\ Temp_{h,new} &= (1 - \eta_h)Temp_{h,pre} + \eta_c w(f_h(x')). \end{aligned} \tag{15}$$

where the parameter η represents the learning rate of the template in online tracking.

4 Experiments

We evaluate our proposed network by performing contrast experiments on three benchmarks: Temple-Color [20], UAV123 [23], and OTB50 [29,30]. The fundamental purpose of our experiments is to evaluate the effect of using our network to train parameters for feature fusion during training. First, we compare the effects of different convolutional layer depths on the tracking performance. And then, we compare our approach with some state-of-the-art trackers on benchmarks. Bounding box overlap ratio and center location error are two metrics to evaluate the trackers. The bounding box overlap ratio is defined to measure the bounding boxes overlap of ground truth R_{gt} and the tracker's predict result R_t.

$$S(\sigma_{over}) = \frac{R_{gt} \cap R_t}{R_{gt} \cup R_t} \geq \sigma_{over} \tag{16}$$

The center location error is defined as the bounding box center Euclidean distance between ground truth P_{gt} and the trackers predict result P_t.

$$P(\sigma_{succ}) = \|P_{gt} - Pt\| \leq \sigma_{succ} \tag{17}$$

4.1 Evaluation of Different Convolutional Layer Depths

In this part, we use the bounding box overlap ratio to evaluate the trackers. The success plot is calculated as the percentage of frames with an intersection-over-union (IOU) overlap exceeding a threshold. The Temple-Color is the validation dataset in this part. Since we can only get the model of CFNet [27] using Conv-1, Conv-2 and Conv-5, our approach uses the same convolutional layers to do comparison. The results are shown in Fig. 3. In Fig. 3, we can find that the result of our approach is better than CFNet. It proves that the combination of the CNN and HOG features improves the performance of the tracker. To show the tracking results of HOG fused with varying convolutional layers, we choose the results when the overlap threshold is 0.5. The results are shown in Fig. 4. In Fig. 4, we find that the Conv-2 can achieve better results, when more convolutional layers are added it seems to be redundant.

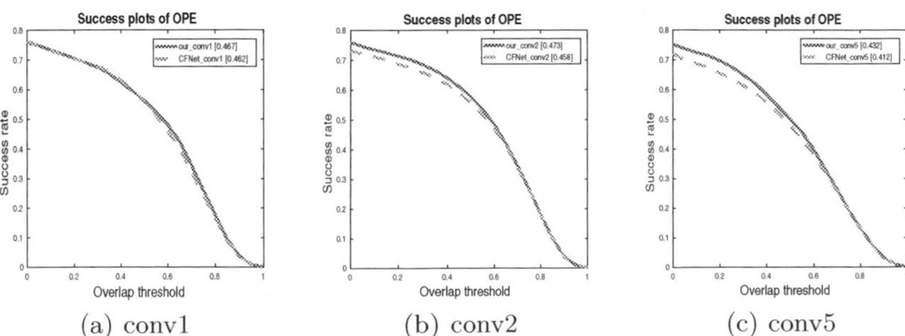

(a) conv1 (b) conv2 (c) conv5

Fig. 3. Success rates of rectangle overlap for different convolutional layers on the validation dataset temple-color.

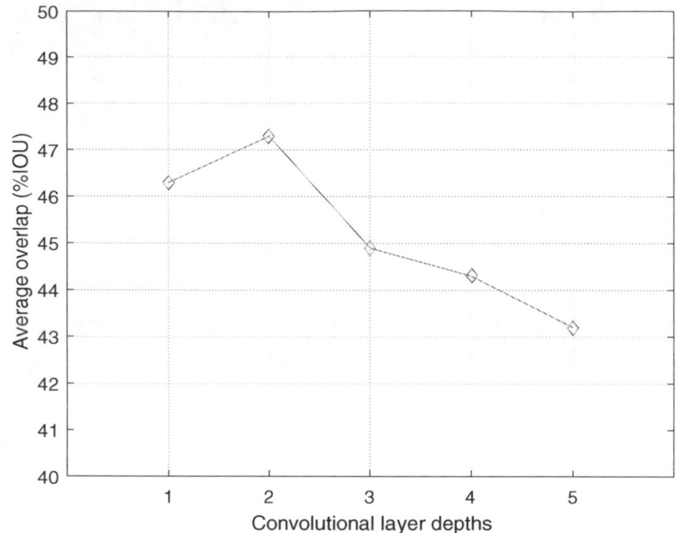

Fig. 4. The accuracy with different convolutional layer depths of our approach.

4.2 Comparisons with State-of-the-Art Methods

We compare our proposed approach with 13 state-of-the-art trackers: KCF [16], Staple [2], SAMF [19], SiameFC [3], CFNet [27], MEEM [31], SRDCF [9], DSST [6], DAT [24], ACT [11], TGPR [12], KCFDP [17] and fDSST [7]. Our experiments are using success plot and precision plot. The comparisons are done on the benchmarks UVA123 and OTB50, detailed as follows.

UAV123: UAV123 is a very large dataset which is captured from low-altitude UAVs. The dataset consists of sequences from an aerial viewpoint, containing a total of 123 video sequences and more than 110K frames. Figures 5(a), (b) show the results of precision and success rate respectively. Among the comparison with the Siamese Network based approach, SiameseFC and CFNet provide the best results with AUC scores of 47.8% and 47.6% respectively. Our approach provides a better performance with an AUC score of 49.7%.

OTB50: OTB2013, OTB50 and OTB100 are commonly used OTB datasets in comparative experiments. OTB50 is the most challenging dataset of these OTB datasets, so the experiment only compare in the OTB50. The dataset contains 50 video sequences. Figures 5(c), (d) show the results of precision and success rate respectively. Figure 5 show that our approach achieves state-of-the-art results on UAV123 and OTB50 datasets. Compared with SRDCF, employing hand-crafted features, our approach achieve a better performance with an AUC score of 55.1%. Compared with the deep features trackers SiameseFC and CFNet, our approach also achieves a better performance.

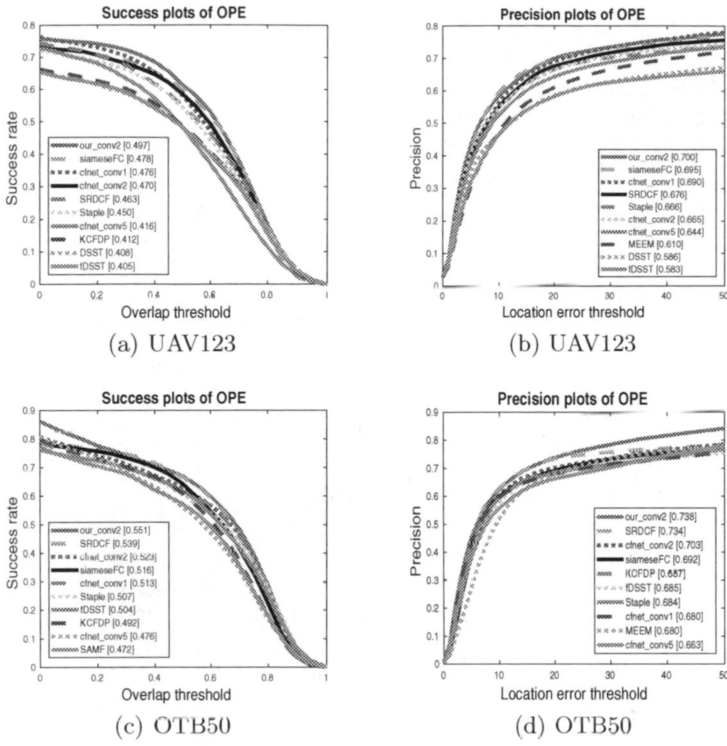

Fig. 5. Success plots on the UAV-123 (a) and OTB50 (c) datasets. Precision plots on the UAV123 (b) and OTB50 (d) datasets. The score of each tracker is shown in the legend. Our approach achieves state-of-the-art performance in all datasets. For clarity, only the results of top 10 trackers are shown in the legend.

5 Conclusion

In this paper, we propose a novel approach based on Siamese Network for robust visual object tracking. The training of the network model makes up the defect of different features in the tracking effect. Our feature fusion network improves the generality of the tracker, achieves excellent performance in scenes with fast motion, motion blur, background clutters and so on. Furthermore, our approach achieves the state-of-the-art performance on UAV123, OTB50 and Temple-Color. It also shows that the deep network model is trained with a large amount of data has a good application prospect in the object tracking, and the work based on Siamese Network is worthy for further study.

Acknowledgments. This work was supported in part by Natural Science Foundation of Zhejiang Province (LQ18F030013, LQ18F030014, LQ16F030007) and Innovation Foundation from Key Laboratory of Intelligent Perception and Systems for High-Dimensional Information of Ministry of Education (JYB201706).

References

1. Bao, C., Wu, Y., Ling, H., Ji, H.: Real time robust L1 tracker using accelerated proximal gradient approach. In: CVPR (2012)
2. Bertinetto, L., Valmadre, J., Golodetz, S., Miksik, O., Torr, P.H.: Staple: complementary learners for real-time tracking. In: CVPR (2016)
3. Bertinetto, L., Valmadre, J., Henriques, J.F., Vedaldi, A., Torr, P.H.S.: Fully-convolutional siamese networks for object tracking. In: Hua, G., Jégou, H. (eds.) ECCV 2016. LNCS, vol. 9914, pp. 850–865. Springer, Cham (2016). https://doi.org/10.1007/978-3-319-48881-3_56
4. Bolme, D.S., Beveridge, J.R., Draper, B.A., Lui, Y.M.: Visual object tracking using adaptive correlation filters. In: CVPR (2010)
5. Chen, K., Tao, W.: Once for all: a two-flow convolutional neural network for visual tracking. TCSVT **PP**(99), 1 (2017)
6. Danelljan, M., Häger, G., Khan, F., Felsberg, M.: Accurate scale estimation for robust visual tracking. In: BMVC (2014)
7. Danelljan, M., Häger, G., Khan, F.S., Felsberg, M.: Discriminative scale space tracking. PAMI **39**(8), 1561–1575 (2017)
8. Danelljan, M., Hager, G., Shahbaz Khan, F., Felsberg, M.: Convolutional features for correlation filter based visual tracking. In: ICCV Workshops (2015)
9. Danelljan, M., Hager, G., Shahbaz Khan, F., Felsberg, M.: Learning spatially regularized correlation filters for visual tracking. In: CVPR (2015)
10. Danelljan, M., Robinson, A., Shahbaz Khan, F., Felsberg, M.: Beyond correlation filters: learning continuous convolution operators for visual tracking. In: Leibe, B., Matas, J., Sebe, N., Welling, M. (eds.) ECCV 2016. LNCS, vol. 9909, pp. 472–488. Springer, Cham (2016). https://doi.org/10.1007/978-3-319-46454-1_29
11. Danelljan, M., Shahbaz Khan, F., Felsberg, M., Van de Weijer, J.: Adaptive color attributes for real-time visual tracking. In: CVPR (2014)
12. Gao, J., Ling, H., Hu, W., Xing, J.: Transfer learning based visual tracking with Gaussian processes regression. In: Fleet, D., Pajdla, T., Schiele, B., Tuytelaars, T. (eds.) ECCV 2014. LNCS, vol. 8691, pp. 188–203. Springer, Cham (2014). https://doi.org/10.1007/978-3-319-10578-9_13
13. Hare, S., et al.: Struck: structured output tracking with kernels. PAMI **38**(10), 2096–2109 (2016)
14. Held, D., Thrun, S., Savarese, S.: Learning to track at 100 FPS with deep regression networks. In: Leibe, B., Matas, J., Sebe, N., Welling, M. (eds.) ECCV 2016. LNCS, vol. 9905, pp. 749–765. Springer, Cham (2016). https://doi.org/10.1007/978-3-319-46448-0_45
15. Henriques, J.F., Caseiro, R., Martins, P., Batista, J.: Exploiting the circulant structure of tracking-by-detection with kernels. In: Fitzgibbon, A., Lazebnik, S., Perona, P., Sato, Y., Schmid, C. (eds.) ECCV 2012. LNCS, vol. 7575, pp. 702–715. Springer, Heidelberg (2012). https://doi.org/10.1007/978-3-642-33765-9_50
16. Henriques, J.F., Caseiro, R., Martins, P., Batista, J.: High-speed tracking with kernelized correlation filters. PAMI **37**(3), 583–596 (2015)
17. Huang, D., Luo, L., Wen, M., Chen, Z., Zhang, C.: Enable scale and aspect ratio adaptability in visual tracking with detection proposals. In: BMVC (2015)
18. Leal-Taixé, L., Canton-Ferrer, C., Schindler, K.: Learning by tracking: Siamese CNN for robust target association. In: CVPR Workshops (2016)

19. Li, Y., Zhu, J.: A scale adaptive kernel correlation filter tracker with feature integration. In: Agapito, L., Bronstein, M.M., Rother, C. (eds.) ECCV 2014. LNCS, vol. 8926, pp. 254–265. Springer, Cham (2015). https://doi.org/10.1007/978-3-319-16181-5_18
20. Liang, P., Blasch, E., Ling, H.: Encoding color information for visual tracking: algorithms and benchmark. TIP **24**(12), 5630–5644 (2015)
21. Liu, B., Huang, J., Kulikowski, C., Yang, L.: Robust visual tracking using local sparse appearance model and K-selection. PAMI **35**(12), 2968–2981 (2013)
22. Ma, C., Huang, J.B., Yang, X., Yang, M.H.: Hierarchical convolutional features for visual tracking. In: ICCV (2015)
23. Mueller, M., Smith, N., Ghanem, B.: A benchmark and simulator for UAV tracking. In: Leibe, B., Matas, J., Sebe, N., Welling, M. (eds.) ECCV 2016. LNCS, vol. 9905, pp. 445–461. Springer, Cham (2016). https://doi.org/10.1007/978-3-319-46448-0_27
24. Possegger, H., Mauthner, T., Bischof, H.: In defense of color-based model-free tracking. In: CVPR (2015)
25. Sevilla-Lara, L., Learned-Miller, E.: Distribution fields for tracking. In: CVPR (2012)
26. Tao, R., Gavves, E., Smeulders, A.W.: Siamese instance search for tracking. In: CVPR (2016)
27. Valmadre, J., Bertinetto, L., Henriques, J.F., Vedaldi, A., Torr, P.H.: End-to-end representation learning for correlation filter based tracking. In: CVPR (2017)
28. Wang, N., Yeung, D.Y.: Ensemble-based tracking: aggregating crowdsourced structured time series data. In: ICML (2014)
29. Wu, Y., Lim, J., Yang, M.H.: Online object tracking: a benchmark. In: CVPR (2013)
30. Wu, Y., Lim, J., Yang, M.H.: Object tracking benchmark. PAMI **37**(9), 1834–1848 (2015)
31. Zhang, J., Ma, S., Sclaroff, S.: MEEM: robust tracking via multiple experts using entropy minimization. In: Fleet, D., Pajdla, T., Schiele, B., Tuytelaars, T. (eds.) ECCV 2014. LNCS, vol. 8694, pp. 188–203. Springer, Cham (2014). https://doi.org/10.1007/978-3-319-10599-4_13
32. Zhang, K., Zhang, L., Yang, M.-H.: Real-time compressive tracking. In: Fitzgibbon, A., Lazebnik, S., Perona, P., Sato, Y., Schmid, C. (eds.) ECCV 2012. LNCS, vol. 7574, pp. 864–877. Springer, Heidelberg (2012). https://doi.org/10.1007/978-3-642-33712-3_62

ANNC: AUC-Based Feature Selection by Maximizing Nearest Neighbor Complementarity

Xuemeng Jiang[1], Jun Wang[2], Jinmao Wei[1(✉)], Jianhua Ruan[3], and Gang Yu[1]

[1] College of Computer and Control Engineering, Nankai University, Tianjin 300071, China
2120160412@mail.nankai.edu.cn, {weijm,yugang}@nankai.edu.cn

[2] College of Mathematics and Statistics Science, Ludong University, Shandong 264025, China
junwang@mail.nankai.edu.cn

[3] Department of Computer Science, University of Texas, San Antonio, TX, USA
Jianhua.Ruan@utsa.edu

Abstract. Feature selection is crucial for dimension reduction. Dozens of approaches employ the area under ROC curve, i.e., AUC, to evaluate features, and have shown their attractiveness in finding discriminative targets. However, feature complementarity for jointly discriminating classes is generally improperly handled by these approaches. In a recent approach to deal with such issues, feature complementarity was evaluated by computing the difference between the neighbors of each instance in different feature dimensions. This local-learning based approach introduces a distinctive way to determine how a feature is complementarily discriminative given another. Nevertheless, neighbor information is usually sensitive to noises. Furthermore, evaluating merely one-side information of nearest misses will definitely neglect the impacts of nearest hits on feature complementarity. In this paper, we propose to integrate all-side local-learning based complementarity into an AUC-based approach, dubbed ANNC, to evaluate pairwise features by scrutinizing their comprehensive misclassification information in terms of both k-nearest misses and k-nearest hits. This strategy contributes to capture complementary features that collaborate with each other to achieve remarkable recognition performance. Extensive experiments on openly available benchmarks demonstrate the effectiveness of the new approach under various metrics.

Keywords: Feature selection · AUC · Nearest neighbors
Feature complementarity · All-side recognition

1 Introduction

In a variety of machine learning fields, such as text classification, image retrieval, disease diagnosis, and so forth, samples are described by an enormous number

X. Geng and B.-H. Kang (Eds.): PRICAI 2018, LNAI 11012, pp. 772–785, 2018.
https://doi.org/10.1007/978-3-319-97304-3_59

of features [1–4]. High-dimensional data suffers learning difficulties both in time and space consumptions [5]. Furthermore, redundant and noisy features that pervasively exist in the original space deteriorate the generalization capabilities and learning performance of the algorithms [6,7]. As such, feature selection has been taken as an essential technology in machine learning and become more important in recent years. It aims at choosing a subset of features to give a compact and accurate representation for the original learning target and construct a reduced recognition space [8].

Dozens of correlation measurements have been utilized as evaluation criteria in feature selection. Among these criteria, the area under ROC (Receiver Operating Characteristic) curve, i.e., AUC, has shown its striking performance, especially in some complicated learning scenarios, e.g., class-imbalanced feature selection. This attributes to the distinct properties of AUC, such as independence from the decision threshold, invariance to prior probability distributions, and so forth. The statistical property of AUC can directly reflect how well a feature distinguishes the target, and thus, AUC has been used in selecting discriminative features in many state-of-the-art feature selection works [9–14]. FAST [9] directly takes the sum of the area under ROC curve as AUC score to determine feature relevance with target classes. As a variant, pAUC, which corresponds to a confined range under ROC curve, is used to select features in the literature [10]. MDFS [11] focuses on multi-class problems and achieve excellent performance in the multi-class learning tasks. A complicated issue for these representative AUC-based approaches is that the selected features are correlated with each other, which substantially deteriorates the recognition performance of the newly built feature subspace. Therefore, several approaches have been proposed to solve this problem, such as FROC [12], ARCO [13], and so forth. FROC measures feature redundancy through the area between ROC curves with Markov blanket analysis, and ARCO alleviates feature redundancy via Spearman's rank correlation coefficient.

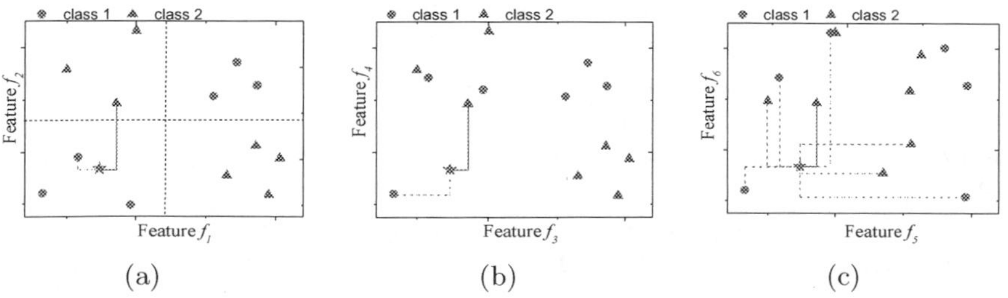

Fig. 1. Distributions of binary-class instances in pairwise feature spaces: the nearest hit and nearest miss of the red star instance are captured through Manhattan distance measure.

The aforementioned works have shown attractive selection performance in practice. However, feature complementarity that is important for determining the global recognition performance of the selected feature subset is improperly handled by these approaches. To further illustrate this issue, instance distributions in pairwise feature spaces are depicted in Fig. 1. As shown in Fig. 1(a), it is apparent that both two features possess poor predictive performance if they are individually taken as a classifier. That is, the binary-class instances cannot be correctly recognized whenever projected along f_1 or along f_2. Yet all of these instances can be correctly classified in the pairwise feature space constituted by f_1 and f_2, due to their strong complementarity. This complementarity information is critical for determining the joint recognition performance of two features, but being overlooked by most existing AUC-based feature selection approaches.

A recently proposed approach named AVC [14] endeavors to evaluate feature complementarity by measuring the extra-class separability in pairwise feature space, which can clearly find the complementarity of the two features in Fig. 1(a). By investigating we find that, AVC argues that three feature combinations in Fig. 1 achieve identical recognition performance for the red star instance, due to its consistent recognition situation when being observed merely through its 1-nearest miss (i.e., the blue triangle instance that is connected with the red star instance through a solid line). However, it is clear that f_1 and f_2 should be prior selected to construct the reduced feature space, in which all of the binary-class instances can be correctly recognized. This selection decision can be easily drawn if the intra-class correlation is simultaneously analyzed with the extra-class separation. Moreover, only considering 1-nearest neighbor is not robust for determining feature complementarity, which is also clearly demonstrated in Figs. 1(b) and (c). That is, the analysis concerning 1-nearest hit and 1-nearest miss yields the conclusion that the discriminative ability of unifying f_3 and f_4 is identical to that of unifying f_5 and f_6. Actually, we can observe that the union of f_3 and f_4 is relatively superior to the union of f_5 and f_6, because the binary-class instances are more difficult to be partitioned in the latter feature space than in the former feature space. As such, we state that the all-side recognition situation, in which k-nearest misses as well as k-nearest hits are considered simultaneously, should be examined when measuring feature complementarity.

In view of the above analysis, a new approach, dubbed AUC-based Feature Selection by Maximizing Nearest Neighbor Complementarity (ANNC), is proposed in this paper. ANNC captures the optimal features with maximal recognition complementarity through examining their all-side recognition situations. Specifically, for each misclassified instance, its k-nearest hits and k-nearest misses are comprehensively analyzed under the measurement of Manhattan distance in the subspace constructed by pairwise features. Additionally, ANNC optimizes the parameter k, i.e., the number of nearest neighbors, in the manner of discussing instance density, rather than cautiously tuning its value by multiple experiments.

The remainder of this paper is organized as follows: in Sect. 2, we propose ANNC and give its detailed theoretic analysis and optimization algorithm. Experimental evaluations regarding the selection performance between ANNC and five state-of-the-art feature selection approaches are conducted in Sect. 3. Finally, conclusion is drawn in Sect. 4.

2 Feature Selection Based on AUC by Maximizing Nearest Neighbor Complementarity (ANNC)

2.1 Feature Complementarity in ANNC

An explicit way of assessing the discriminative performance of a feature is to directly take it as an individual classifier, whose evaluation score can be calculated by AUC [15] as

$$AUC = \frac{1}{n_0 n_1}\left[\sum_{x \in C^+} r(x) - \frac{1}{2} n_0 (n_0 + 1)\right], \tag{1}$$

where $r(x)$ denotes the rank of instance x, C^+ represents the positive class, and n_0 and n_1 represent the numbers of positive instances and negative instances. If a positive instance ranks lower than a negative instance, there exists a misclassified instance.

The misclassification instances in pairwise feature space can be categorized into two groups. That is, the common misclassified instances shared by two features and the misclassified instances unshared by two features. The common misclassified instances are critical in feature evaluation with more instructive information. The corresponding features are complementary for their classification abilities if this kind of instances can be correctly recognized in pairwise feature space. In other words, their performance outperforms their individual performance when being combined as an union. Thus, the common misclassified instances in ANNC are defined as follows:

Definition 1 (Common Misclassified Instance Subset). *The common misclassified instance subset of features f_i and f_j is defined as*

$$\Omega_{ij} = \bigcap_{l=i,j} S_l \quad \underset{l=i,j}{S_l} = \left\{x_m \left| r(x_m) < n_1, x_m \in C^+ \vee r(x_m) > n_1, x_m \in C^- \right.\right\}, \tag{2}$$

where S_l is the misclassified instance subset of feature f_l, $r(x_m)$ is the rank of instance x_m on f_l, n_1 is the number of negative instances, C^+ and C^- respectively represent the positive class and the negative class.

In order to measure whether the common misclassified instance x_m can be correctly recognized in pairwise feature subspace, we consider x_m as a representative point for its neighboring region. In this work, Manhattan distance is used as the distance measure, which has been widely used in margin distance calculation [16]. For determining, if two features are complementary with each other, we need to satisfy the following two goals:

(1) Neighbors from the same class are closely situated around x_m, in this subspace; and simultaneously,
(2) Neighbors from different classes are far away from x_m.

This is a widely held belief that both kinds of correlations play near-identical roles in feature evaluation [17]. On consideration of this principle, we measure the correlation of the common misclassified instance x_m with its nearest hits and its nearest misses as follows:

$$b_{ij}^{m} = \frac{1}{k}\sum\nolimits_{p=1}^{k} \left\| x_m, M_p^m \right\|, w_{ij}^{m} = \frac{1}{k}\sum\nolimits_{p=1}^{k} \left\| x_m, H_p^m \right\|, x_m \in \Omega_{ij}, \quad (3)$$

where k denotes the number of nearest neighbors, M_p^m represents the pth nearest miss of x_m in the feature space of f_i and f_j, and H_p^m denotes its pth nearest hit. Note that $\|x_m, I\|$ is the Manhattan distance between two involved variables.

Definition 2 (Feature Complementarity). *The pairwise complementarity between features f_i and f_j is defined as*

$$Com\left(f_i, f_j\right) = \frac{1}{|\Omega_{ij}|}\sum\nolimits_{x_m \in \Omega_{ij}} \left(b_{ij}^{m} - w_{ij}^{m}\right), \quad (4)$$

According to Definition 2, the feature combination that "pulls" x_m close to its intra-class instances and "pushes" x_m away from its extra-class instances is highly scored. It means that in this case, the common misclassified instances possess high probabilities of being correctly recognized on the pairwise feature space. It is seen that, ANNC examines the all-side complementarity, i.e., the comprehensive observation information of the common misclassified instances, and thereby is capable of selecting complementary features with joint classification abilities.

As to the multi-class issue, it can be divided into multiple binary-class recognition subproblems. A complicated problem is that the nearest miss information extracted from different classes should be unequally weighted when analyzing the misclassification information of features. For instance, the nearest miss of x_r from a quite distant class makes less sense for determining the misclassification situation than that from a relatively close class. Therefore, we only focus on the nearest misses from the k closest classes in feature evaluation. Suppose $S_{l_1,l_2}\left(f_i\right)$ represents the misclassified instance set of f_i with respect to the classes l_1 and l_2. Then, we unifies its misclassified instance subsets in all of the binary-class subproblems as follows:

$$MS\left(f_i\right) = \bigcup_{1 \le l_1 \le l_2 \le q} S_{l_1,l_2}(f_i), \quad (5)$$

where q is the number of the binary-class subproblems.

2.2 Procedure of ANNC

A top-k feature selection approach pursues the top-ranked features that are strongly relevant to classes, and hence, the informative but also highly redundant features are selected [18]. In ANNC, we consider both feature relevance and feature complementarity, in order to find highly discriminative as well as highly complementary features. The selection framework of ANNC is illustrated in Fig. 2. We define $Cor(f_i, f_j)$ to represent a weighted linear combination of these two feature relationships as follows:

$$Cor(f_i, f_j) = \alpha \cdot Com\,(f_i, f_j) + (1 - \alpha) \cdot auc,\ auc = 2\max\{AUC(f_i), AUC(f_j)\}, \tag{6}$$

where $\alpha \in [0, 1]$ is a loading coefficient, and $Com\,(f_i, f_j)$ is the pairwise feature complementarity given in Definition 2. $Cor(f_i, f_j)$ is obtained by balancing the importance of feature relevance and feature complementarity in feature evaluation. For example, suppose $\alpha = 0.5$, and then, a high $Cor(f_i, f_j)$ indicates at least one feature in the feature combination is strongly predictive for classes, and meanwhile, f_i and f_j are complementary with each other. If α is larger than 0.5, $Cor(f_i, f_j)$ pays more attention on feature complementarity. In this situation, highly complementary but not highly relevant features are preferred.

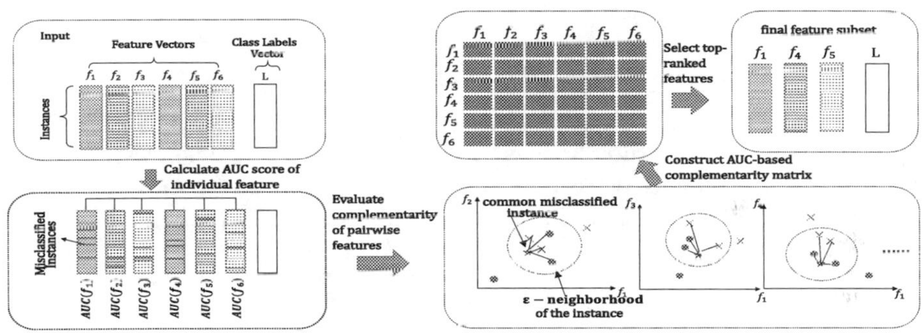

Fig. 2. Selection framework of ANNC.

The procedure of ANNC is illustrated in Algorithm 1. To select t^* features from the original feature set with size m, ANNC first picks out the feature with largest AUC. Then, each candidate feature is evaluated according to its E_i in line 7, and the one with highest score is selected. As to the time consumption, suppose the training data set contains n instances, then the time complexity of calculating AUC is $O\,(mn \log n)$ in line 2. To select the top-t features in line 3 costs $O(mlogt)$ time. In lines 5 to 8, to calculate $Cor(f_i', f_j^*)$ for a pair of features takes $O(kn \log n)$, and this iteration is repeated for tt^* times. Commonly, the number of the candidate features, i.e., t, k, and the number of the selected features, i.e., t^*, are much smaller than m and n. Therefore, the total time complexity of ANNC is approximately equal to $O\,(mn \log n + m \log t)$.

2.3 Evaluation of K

As aforementioned, ANNC observes the k-nearest neighbors of the common misclassified instances in feature evaluation because neighbor information is usually

Algorithm 1. ANNC algorithm

input: F,$F^* = \emptyset$,α, ε
t//number of the candidate features, t^*//number of the selected features
output: $F^* = \{f_1^*, f_2^*, ..., f_{t^*}^*\}$;
begin
calculate $AUC(f_i)$ for each feature f_i (i=1,...,m) in F with Eq. (1);
select the top-t features with maximal AUC to construct F';
$f_1^* = \arg\max_{f_i \in F}\{AUC(f_i)\}$, $F^* = F^* \bigcup \{f_1^*\}$, $F' = F' \setminus \{f_1^*\}$;
for $k = 2$ to t^* **do**,
    for f_i' in $|F'|$ **do**,
        calculate $E_i = \frac{1}{|F^*|}\sum_{f_j^* \in F^*} Cor(f_i', f_j^*)$ according to Eq. (6);
    end for
    $f_k^* = \arg\max_{f_i' \in F'}\{E_i\}$, $F^* = F^* \cup \{f_k^*\}$, $F' = F' \setminus \{f_k^*\}$;
end for;
return F*;
end;

sensitive to noises. In this paper, we solve this problem via a density-based technology. For each common misclassified instance, we define a neighborhood region and calculate the instance density within this region. Intuitively, an equal k value is adopted for the regions with the same instance density. To properly determine the instance density, we give two definitions as follows:

Definition 3 (ε-Neighborhood). *The neighborhood of the common misclassified instance x_m within the region with radius ε is calculated as*

$$N_\varepsilon(x_m) = \{x_t \,|dis(x_m, x_t) \le \varepsilon, x_t \in X\}, \tag{7}$$

where $dis(\cdot,\cdot)$ is the Euclidean distance between two involved instances, and X is the instance set.

Definition 4 (Density Region). *Suppose $|N_\varepsilon(x_m)|$ is the ε-neighborhood density of x_m. Then,*

$|N_\varepsilon(x_m)| = \theta$, x_m is in the uniform-density region;
$|N_\varepsilon(x_m)| > \theta$, x_m is in the high-density region;
$|N_\varepsilon(x_m)| < \theta$, x_m is in the low-density region.

where θ is a predefined threshold.

According to Definitions 3 and 4, ε and θ are closely correlated with each other. θ can be measured as the average density of the common misclassified instances in the ε -neighborhood region, which is estimated as

$$D_\varepsilon(X) = \frac{1}{|X|}\sum_{i=1}^{|X|}|N_\varepsilon(x_i)|. \tag{8}$$

Then, we can set $\theta = D_\varepsilon(X)$. Commonly, $k < \sqrt{n}$, where n is the total number of instances in data sets. For those instances in the high-density region, it is better to consider more neighbors, and thus, we can constrain $k \in (\theta, \sqrt{n})$. For those in the low-density region, we consider fewer neighbors and constrain $k \in (0, \theta)$. In practice, we can adopt the median of the corresponding intervals as k value.

3 Experiments

This section compares ANNC with five state-of-the-art feature selection approaches, i.e., FAST [9], ARCO [13], AVC [14], ReliefF [19], and Inf-FS [20]. Among them, FAST, ARCO, and AVC are the AUC-based approaches. ReliefF is a widely used feature selection approach that adopts nearest neighbor rule in its feature evaluation like ANNC. Inf-FS is a recently proposed approach that employs graph theory to perform infinite feature selection. It beats some popular selection approaches through an extensive empirical evaluation. Thus, we also take ReliefF and Inf-FS as baselines and compare their selection performance with ANNC. In the following experiments, the number of the nearest neighbors in ReliefF is set to 3, and the loading coefficient in Inf-FS is fixed to 0.5. For ANNC, we optimize α in Eq. (7) by cross-validation strategy and ε is set to 0.4.

3.1 Exp. 1: Noisy Feature Test

In this subsection, we mainly test the performance of the compared approaches in selecting optimal features from irrelevant noisy features. Iris data set, which is a well-known UCI [21] data set, is used as the benchmark. It contains 150 instances that are characterized by 4 numerical features and classified into 3 groups. Noisy features drawn from Gaussian distributions are added to Iris, and their number increases from 100 to 500 in the interval of 50. The compared approaches evaluate and rank features according to their criteria, and the average ranks of the original four features on the ranking lists are recorded to test the robustness of each approach to noisy situations. Note that the original four features in Iris are relevant to the target classes, and the other ones are noisy features that are weakly relevant or irrelevant to classes. Thus, a small value of the average ranks, i.e., relatively high ranks of the original four features, indicates robust performance under conditions of high noise. The experimental results are shown in Fig. 3.

It is demonstrated from Fig. 3 that ANNC outperforms the five baselines when the number of noisy features increases. ReliefF also performs well, although inferior to our ANNC, which attributes to its top-k selection strategy and ignorance about feature complementarity. Note that AVC, which also considers feature complementarity, shows unpromising performance in this noisy test. AVC merely analyzes the one-side recognition information in feature evaluation, and this kind of information is insufficient for finding the really significant features. In general, the experimental results imply that the k-nearest neighbor rule works well in feature evaluation, even in noisy circumstance. ANNC can be expected to select the significant features from high noisy subsets.

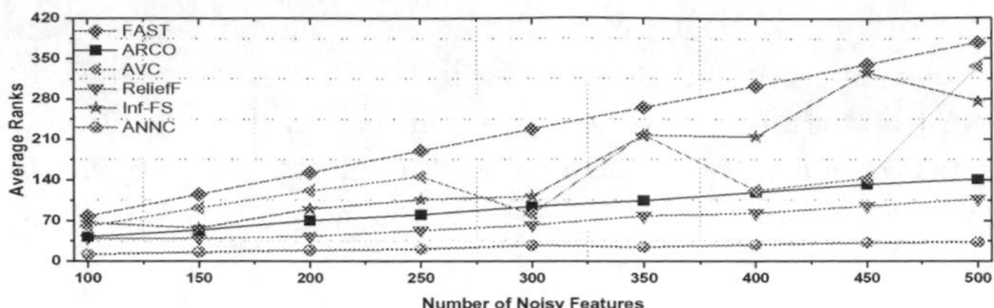

Fig. 3. Average ranks of the relevant features selected by the compared approaches (the lower of the ranks, the better.)

Table 1. Benchmark data sets

Data set	♯Features	♯Instances	♯Classes	Source
Urban Land Cover (ULC)	148	168	9	UCI
Musk (Version 1)	168	476	2	UCI
MADELON (MLN)	500	4400	2	UCI
Colon (COL)	2000	62	2	Microarray
SRBCT (SRT)	2309	83	4	Microarray
Leukemia-3c (LEU)	7130	72	3	Microarray
Carcinom (CAR)	9182	174	11	Microarray
TCGA-KIRC (KIR)	20502	606	2	DNA-seq
GLI-85 (GLI)	22283	85	2	Microarray
Breast Cancer (BRC)	22481	97	2	Microarray

3.2 Exp. 2: Classification Performance

Ten groups of public data sets in Table 1 are used to evaluate the recognition performance of the selected features in this subsection. They include three groups of UCI data sets, six groups of microarray expression data sets [22], and one group of DNA-seq data set, and all of them are normalized with standard variances. These datasets have been taken as benchmarks in many previous feature selection works [23–25]. Three classifiers are built with the selected features, i.e., Support Vector Machine (SVM) classifier, Naive Bayes (NB) classifier, and 1-Nearest Neighbor (1-NN) classifier, and 10-fold cross validations are conducted. The number of the selected features sequentially increases from 5 to 100 in the interval of 5. That is, the compared approaches respectively select 20 groups of feature subsets whose sizes increase from 5 to 100 for comparison. The average classification accuracies of three classifiers across the selected feature subsets are recorded in Table 2.

To further illustrate the classification, the variations of average classification accuracies of the three classifiers on six benchmark data sets in Table 1 are depicted in Fig. 4. It is shown from Table 2 and Fig. 4 that compared with the baselines, the features selected by ANNC are more predictive for the recognition

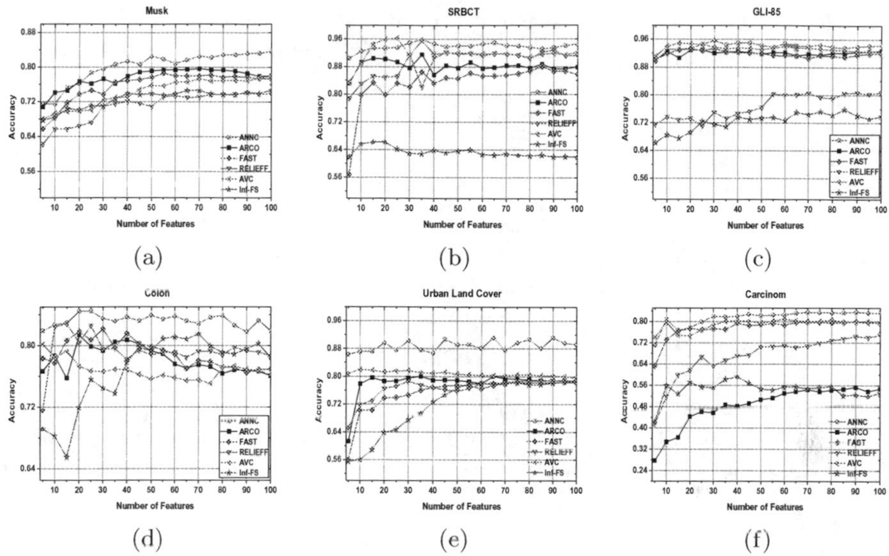

Fig. 4. Average classification accuracy of the 1-NN classifier, SVM classifier and NB classifier.

targets. Concerning the average classification accuracies, it reveals that the SVM classifier and 1-NN classifier are superior to the NB classifier. Yet it should be pointed out that this phenomenon is not general on some single data sets. For instance, on the data sets of *SRT* and *GLI*, a majority of the compared approaches perform better on the NB classifier than on the SVM classifier and 1-NN classifier. Generally speaking, it follows from Table 2 that ANNC performs comparable or superior to the other feature selection approaches across different classifiers.

To comprehensively evaluate the selection performance of the compared approaches, we utilize some other metrics, i.e., AUC and Balanced Error Rate (BER), as shown in Fig. 5. Note that statistical tests are important and will be added in the future work. In the figure, the average AUC and BER across all of the benchmark data sets are represented by boxes, which describe the median values and lower and upper quartiles of the corresponding evaluation metrics. Additionally, minimal, mean, and maximal values are represented by red crossbars. As illustrated in Fig. 5, ANNC dominates the performance of the baselines in most cases. Notice that four AUC-based approaches, i.e., ANNC, FAST, ARCO, and AVC, are significantly more competitive than ReliefF and Inf-FS under the metric of AUC (except for FAST on the 1-NN classifier). FAST, which exploits a top-k selection strategy and just selects the most relevant features, is relatively inferior to the other three AUC-based approaches, as shown in Fig. 5. This is in some sense coincident with the observation reported in [14].

Table 2. Average classification accuracy (mean ± std.) of the selected features (in percentage): 10-fold cross-validation is conducted, and the best results are highlighted in bold.

Dataset	FAST	ARCO	AVC	ReliefF	Inf-FS	ANNC
(a) SVM classification accuracy						
ULC	71.18±0.05	75.71 ± 0.03	79.90 ± 0.01	73.46 ± 0.04	68.60 ± 0.10	**91.91 ± 0.02**
Musk	75.26 ± 0.13	74.41 ± 0.16	71.66 ± 0.29	61.00 ± 0.21	73.91 ± 0.03	**85.31 ± 0.05**
MLN	62.08 ± 0.04	62.00 ± 0.01	61.69 ± 0.06	60.99 ± 0.04	61.07 ± 0.36	**71.78 ± 0.17**
COL	72.04 ± 0.14	94.64 ± 0.14	93.59 ± 0.17	86.19 ± 0.19	63.50 ± 0.13	**96.35 ± 0.17**
SRT	81.87 ± 0.42	83.47 ± 0.34	90.03 ± 0.5	64.31 ± 0.2	67.02 ± 0.66	**94.75 ± 0.10**
LEU	94.34 ± 0.61	**98.61 ± 0.74**	94.75 ± 0.88	97.22 ± 0.76	69.30 ± 0.24	98.14 ± 0.56
CAR	64.46 ± 0.50	51.51 ± 0.20	**68.06 ± 0.54**	63.90 ± 0.22	48.43 ± 0.18	67.19 ± 0.05
KIR	**98.90 ± 0.90**	95.11 ± 0.80	97.75 ± 0.74	83.27 ± 0.16	78.43 ± 0.18	98.00 ± 0.90
GLI	91.18 ± 0.07	90.87 ± 0.15	92.93 ± 0.07	69.42 ± 0.50	69.39 ± 0.01	**93.57 ± 0.14**
BRC	54.25 ± 0.10	73.87 ± 0.10	76.24 ± 0.12	53.92 ± 0.27	61.57 ± 0.41	**79.76 ± 0.13**
Avg.	*76.62*	*80.02*	*82.66*	*71.37*	*66.12*	***87.67***
(b) NB classification accuracy						
ULC	80.93 ± 0.4	82.83 ± 0.32	81.75 ± 0.10	79.07 ± 0.26	72.99 ± 0.10	**87.06 ± 0.29**
Musk	71.40 ± 0.46	**75.41 ± 0.30**	70.65 ± 0.36	67.76 ± 0.39	68.58 ± 0.04	74.54 ± 0.21
MLN	61.16 ± 0.08	61.50 ± 0.01	**61.99 ± 0.07**	61.80 ± 0.04	60.00 ± 0.30	61.20 ± 0.08
COL	79.47 ± 0.20	80.75 ± 0.20	78.29 ± 0.23	83.52 ± 0.30	64.57 ± 0.28	**83.73 ± 0.14**
SRT	65.14 ± 0.46	97.73 ± 0.20	98.07 ± 0.20	94.24 ± 0.18	65.81 ± 0.18	**98.90 ± 0.23**
LEU	55.86 ± 0.30	95.83 ± 0.30	96.18 ± 1.13	83.05 ± 0.19	80.90 ± 0.42	**96.29 ± 0.14**
CAR	80.09 ± 0.25	55.30 ± 0.70	80.10 ± 0.30	61.13 ± 0.80	54.08 ± 0.66	**80.84 ± 0.36**
KIR	97.65 ± 0.14	96.35 ± 0.40	97.70 ± 0.60	92.29 ± 0.39	84.08 ± 0.66	**98.23 ± 0.14**
GLI	92.87 ± 0.12	93.46 ± 0.15	**94.18 ± 0.13**	83.47 ± 0.05	72.36 ± 0.30	93.37 ± 0.10
BRC	77.01 ± 0.50	73.82 ± 0.90	74.92 ± 0.60	69.57 ± 0.20	61.63 ± 0.40	**79.65 ± 0.10**
Avg.	*76.16*	*81.29*	*83.38*	*77.58*	*68.44*	***85.48***
(c) 1-NN classification accuracy						
ULC	74.85 ± 0.3	77.22 ± 0.32	80.59 ± 0.11	78.17 ± 0.15	74.90 ± 0.04	**87.91 ± 0.23**
Musk	81.29 ± 0.39	83.00 ± 0.21	80.48 ± 0.30	**84.64 ± 0.36**	80.82 ± 0.24	81.07 ± 0.3
MLN	66.68 ± 0.67	55.10 ± 0.20	65.80 ± 0.44	**72.77 ± 0.52**	64.87 ± 0.32	67.74 ± 0.63
COL	79.47 ± 0.23	80.76 ± 0.21	78.29 ± 0.23	81.52 ± 0.36	61.09 ± 0.40	**81.73 ± 0.14**
SRT	65.51 ± 0.50	92.68 ± 0.16	92.18 ± 0.16	92.91 ± 0.42	75.31 ± 0.28	**92.90 ± 0.10**
LEU	57.33 ± 0.45	93.74 ± 0.28	95.89 ± 0.19	86.77 ± 0.39	80.93 ± 0.82	**96.81 ± 0.12**
CAR	89.04 ± 0.05	59.24 ± 0.12	89.12 ± 0.41	76.67 ± 0.11	60.08 ± 0.10	**89.16 ± 0.05**
KIR	98.49 ± 0.30	96.64 ± 0.12	98.10 ± 0.91	94.10 ± 0.60	85.08 ± ± 0.10	**98.79 ± 0.02**
GLI	91.41 ± 0.26	91.81 ± 0.15	92.96 ± 0.12	78.21 ± 0.48	74.68 ± 0.45	**94.59 ± 0.11**
BRC	77.01 ± 0.05	76.65 ± 0.10	71.54 ± 0.10	69.57 ± 0.20	57.82 ± 0.70	**77.65 ± 0.09**
Avg.	*78.15*	*80.68*	*84.49*	*81.52*	*71.56*	***86.90***

3.3 Exp. 3: Evaluation of α

The coefficient α in Eq. (6) balances the importance of feature relevance and feature complementarity. We optimize α by cross-validation in the aforementioned experiments. In this subsection, we analyze the effects of α on the selection performance of ANNC.

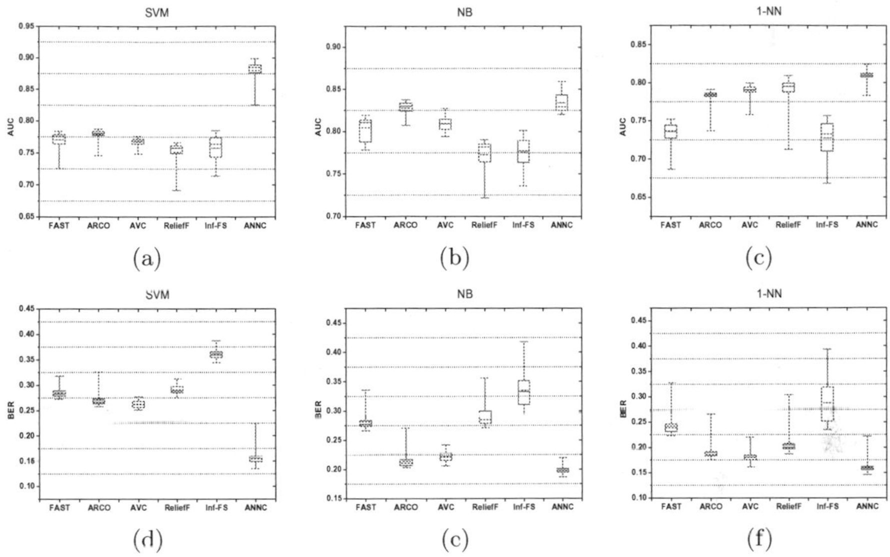

Fig. 5. Averaged AUC (the upper three subfigures) and BER (the lower three subfigures) of three classifiers across all of the benchmark data sets.

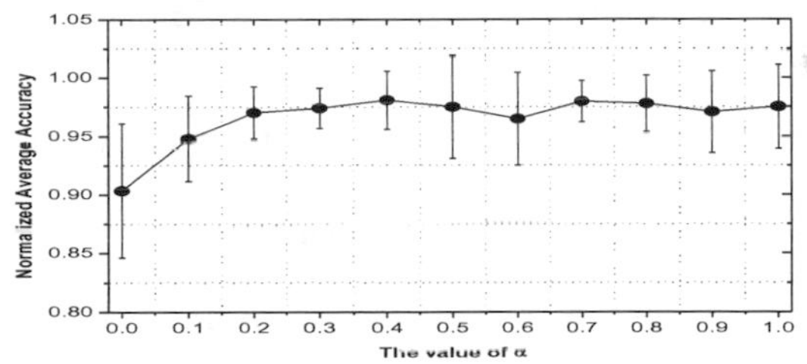

Fig. 6. Variation of the normalized average SVM accuracy when α increases.

ANNC selects 50 features on each benchmark data set in Table 1 and employs these features to build the SVM classifier. In the feature selection process, α is varied in the interval [0,1] at 0.1 step. The SVM accuracies with different α values on each data set are normalized by the maximum performance and averaged across the benchmarks. A normalized score close to 1 indicates that with the features selected by ANNC under this parameter configuration, SVM reaches its best performance. Figure 6 illustrates the variation of SVM accuracy of ANNC with different α. We can observe that when $\alpha = 0$ (i.e., only AUC is considered), the recognition performance is relatively low, due to the existence of a large number of redundant features. Another observation is that through the analysis of the error bars, the best combination of feature relevance and feature complementarity appears at $\alpha = 0.7$. It validates the effectiveness of considering feature complementarity in feature selection from another aspect.

4 Conclusion

In this paper, we propose a novel AUC-based feature selection approach on the basis of feature complementarity with k-nearest neighbor rule, dubbed ANNC. Specifically, the all-side recognition situations of pairwise features are analyzed to measure their complementarity via investigating the k-nearest neighbors of the common misclassified instances. By this way, ANNC is expected to find the significant features that are complementary with each other in recognizing target classes. The empirical evaluation under various measurement metrics validates the effectiveness of ANNC in selecting informative features and achieving high classification performance.

Acknowledgments. This work was supported in part by the National Natural Science Foundation of China under Grant No. 61772288, the Science Foundation of Tianjin China under Grant No. 18JCZDJC30900.

References

1. Guyon, I., Elisseeff, A.: An introduction to variable and feature selection. J. Mach. Learn. Res. **3**, 1157–1182 (2003)
2. Nie, F., Zhu, W., Li, X.: Unsupervised feature selection with structured graph optimization. In: Proceeding of the 30th AAAI, pp. 1302–1308 (2016)
3. Barbu, A., She, Y., Ding, L., et al.: Feature selection with annealing for computer vision and big data learning. IEEE Trans. Pattern Anal. Mach. Intell. **39**(2), 272–286 (2017)
4. Wang, H., Zhang, P., Zhu, X., et al.: Incremental subgraph feature selection for graph classification. IEEE Trans. Knowl. Data Eng. **29**(1), 128–142 (2017)
5. Li, J., Liu, H.: Challenges of feature selection for big data analytics. IEEE Intell. Syst. **32**(2), 9–15 (2017)
6. Tang, J., Alelyani, S., Liu, H.: Feature selection for classification: a review. In: Data Classification: Algorithms and Applications. CRC Press, CA (2014)
7. Zhao, Z., Wang, L., Liu, H., Ye, J.: On similarity preserving feature selection. IEEE Trans. Knowl. Data Eng. **25**(3), 619–632 (2013)
8. Jiang, L.X., Zhang, H., Cai, Z.H.: Discriminatively improving Naive Bayes by evolutionary feature selection. Rom. J. Inf. Sci. Technol. **9**(3), 163–174 (2006)
9. Chen, X., Wasikowski, M.: FAST: a roc-based feature selection metric for small samples and imbalanced data classification problems. In: Proceeding of the 14th ACM SIGKDD International Conference on KDD, pp. 124–132 (2008)
10. Wang, Z., Chang, Y.C.: Marker selection via maximizing the partial area under the ROC curve of linear risk scores. Biostatistics **12**(2), 369–385 (2011)
11. Wang, R., Tang, K.: Feature selection for MAUC-oriented classification systems. Neurocomputing **89**, 39–54 (2012)
12. Mamitsuka, H.: Selecting features in microarray classification using ROC curves. Pattern Recogn. **39**(12), 2393–2404 (2006)
13. Wang, R., Tang, K.: Feature selection for maximizing the area under the ROC curve. In: Proceeding of ICDMW 2009, pp. 400–405 (2009)
14. Sun, L., Wang, J., Wei, J.: AVC: selecting discriminative features on basis of AUC by maximizing variable complementarity. BMC Bioinf. **18**(3), 73–89 (2017)

15. Hand, D.J., Till, R.J.: A simple generalisation of the area under the ROC curve for multiple class classification problems. Mach. Learn. **45**(2), 171–186 (2001)
16. Sun, Y., Todorovic, S., Goodison, S.: Local-learning-based feature selection for high-dimensional data analysis. IEEE Trans. Pattern Anal. Mach. Intell. **32**(9), 1610–1626 (2010)
17. Liu, Y., Tang, F., Zeng, Z.: Feature selection based on dependency margin. IEEE Trans. Cybern. **45**(6), 1209–1221 (2015)
18. Wang, J., Wei, J.M., Yang, Z., Wang, S.Q.: Feature selection by maximizing independent classification information. IEEE Trans. Knowl. Data Eng. **29**(4), 828–841 (2017)
19. Robnik-Šikonja, M., Kononenko, I.: Theoretical and empirical analysis of ReliefF and RReliefF. Mach. Learn. **53**(1–2), 23–69 (2003)
20. Roffo, G., Melzi, S., Cristani, M.: Infinite feature selection. In: Proceedings of the IEEE ICCV 2015, pp. 4202–4210 (2015)
21. Bache, K., Lichman, M.: UCI machine learning repository. http://archive.ics.uci.edu/ml
22. Van't Veer, L.J., Dai, H., Van De Vijver, M.J., et al.: Gene expression profiling predicts clinical outcome of breast cancer. Nature **415**(6871), 530–536 (2002)
23. Liu, X.W., Wang, L., Zhang, J., Yin, J.P., Liu, H.: Global and local structure preservation for feature selection. IEEE Trans. Neural Netw. Learn. Syst. **25**(6), 1083–1095 (2014)
24. Xu, J.L., Nie, F.P., Han, J.W.: Feature selection via scaling factor integrated multi-class support vector machines. In: Proceeding of the 26th IJCAI, pp. 1302–1308 (2017)
25. Jiang, L.X., Cai, Z.H., Zhang, H., Wang, D.H.: Not so greedy: randomly selected naive Bayes. Expert Syst. Appl. **39**(6), 11022–11028 (2012)

Prediction of Nash Bargaining Solution in Negotiation Dialogue

Kosui Iwasa[1(✉)] and Katsuhide Fujita[2(✉)]

[1] Graduate School of Engineering, Tokyo University of Agriculture and Technology, Tokyo, Japan
iwasaKosui@gmail.com
[2] Institute of Engineering, Tokyo University of Agriculture and Technology, Tokyo, Japan
katfuji@cc.tuat.ac.jp

Abstract. There are several studies that focus on the support systems that can be used for human-human negotiations. However, existing automated agent-agent negotiation systems require the participants to set utility functions manually. Additionally, a method to predict the utility functions from the negotiation dialogues in natural language and to find a bargaining solution has not been proposed yet. By developing such a method, the existing research related to automated negotiations can be utilized for the negotiation dialogues in real-life situations. Therefore, we propose a method to predict the utility function of each agent and Nash bargaining solution only from the negotiation dialogues using gated recurrent units (GRUs) [4] with attention [3]. We demonstrate that the rate of Nash bargaining solution that was obtained by using our method outperforms the rate that was obtained while humans were negotiating.

Keywords: Automated negotiation · Natural language processing Recurrent neural networks

1 Introduction

Improving the degree of agreement between participants in human-human negotiations is useful for economic or political activities. Therefore, there are several studies that are related to the analysis of negotiations majorly based on the game theory [15]. The degree of agreement generally comprises fairness and the utilities that are involved for each participant during the negotiations. From this viewpoint, there are several proposed conditions that final agreements should satisfy. In particular, Nash [16] proposed Nash bargaining solution. Kalai proposed Kalai-Smorodinsky bargaining solution [10] and Egalitarian bargaining solution [9]. Furthermore, automated negotiations are expected to support or act on human negotiations to ensure fairness and total utilities for each participant [6]. For example, Automated Negotiating Agents Competition (ANAC) [8] has been conducted to design and implement an intelligent negotiating agent for

X. Geng and B.-H. Kang (Eds.): PRICAI 2018, LNAI 11012, pp. 786–796, 2018.
https://doi.org/10.1007/978-3-319-97304-3_60

maximizing social welfare over the course of multi-issue negotiations. However, the existing studies have two problems. First, though agents in these existing studies consider the utility functions to be well-known and well-defined, it is difficult to manually describe the details related to the preferences of participants in real-life negotiations. Secondly, in order to utilize the existing research for supporting people negotiating, it forces the people to negotiate in a limited protocol, not in natural language. Also, methods for predicting the utility functions using the negotiation dialogues in natural language and for determining the bargaining solution have not been proposed yet. Therefore, it is not feasible to apply existing studies to support human-human negotiations.

Meanwhile, in the field of natural language processing, the applications of methods based on recurrent neural networks (RNNs) are remarkable. Because recurrent neural networks (RNNs) and their extension methods act as a form of language models which can flexibly express the meaning, they are extensively used for dialogue systems [18], machine translation [4], sentiment classification [20], and so on. Therefore, we assume that RNNs can also predict the utility functions of each participant.

This paper proposes a method for predicting Nash bargaining solution in multi-issue negotiations among humans based on natural language conversations. Because our method predicts the utility functions for each participant, all participants have to do is to talk in few turns to enable our method to determine the bid that acts as Nash bargaining solution. We propose the method to predict Nash bargaining solution through the following steps:

1. Encode a negotiation dialogue in natural language by using Attention based GRUs.
2. Predict utility functions for each participant.
3. Find Nash bargaining solution in the negotiation by exhaustive search and propose it to participants.

The rest of this paper is organized as follows: Sect. 2 describes related works. Section 3 shows the definition of negotiations in this paper. Section 4 explains our proposed method. Section 5 evaluates solutions our method recommends against solutions that human-human negotiation or previous work concludes. Section 6 describes conclusions.

2 Related Work

2.1 Automated Negotiation (Agent-Agent Negotiation)

The ANAC [8] has been conducted annually since 2010 and consists of two sections as follows.

- **average individual utilities:** Agents compete to maximize their own individual utilities in negotiations.
- **average social welfares:** Agents compete to maximize social welfare that they produce in negotiations.

The competition was based on the GENIUS environment, which is a general environment for negotiation with intelligent multipurpose usage simulation [13]. By analyzing the results of ANAC, the stream of strategies of ANAC and important factors for developing the competition have been demonstrated. Baarslag et al. [1] presented an in-depth analysis of the ANAC in 2011. The study analyzes different strategies using the classification of agents with respect to their concessional behavior based on a set of standard benchmark strategies and empirical game theory (EGT) to investigate the robustness of the strategies. It also exhibits that the most adaptive negotiation strategies, while being robust across different opponents, are not necessarily those that can win the competition. Furthermore, our EGT analysis also highlights the importance of considering metrics.

Although this protocol is clear and easy enough for computers, it is too simple for humans, who mainly negotiate in natural language dialogue. Thus, negotiation protocols which do not mainly use natural languages are not suitable for human-human negotiation support systems. Concessional behavior based on a set of standard benchmark strategies and empirical game theory (EGT) to investigate the robustness of the strategies. It also exhibits that the most adaptive negotiation strategies, while being robust across different opponents, are not necessarily those that can win the competition. Furthermore, our EGT analysis also highlights the importance of considering metrics.

Kawaguchi et al. [11] proposed a strategy to compromise on the estimated maximum value that was based on the estimated maximum utility. These studies have significantly contributed to bilateral multi-issue closed negotiation. Fujita [5] proposed a compromising strategy for adjusting the speed of making agreements using the conflict mode and focused on multi-time negotiations.

Recently, some studies focused on the divided components of the negotiation strategies in the alternating offering protocol: proposals, responses, and opponent modeling. Effective strategies can be achieved by combining the strategies of top agents in competitions depending on the opponent's strategies and negotiation environments. Nowadays, many of the sophisticated agent strategies comprise a fixed set of modules. Therefore, the studies for proposing negotiation strategies that focus on the modules are observed to be both important and influential. Baarslag et al. [2] focused on the acceptance dilemma wherein accepting a current offer may be suboptimal because better offers may still be presented. However, a delay in acceptance may prevent an agreement from being reached, resulting in a break off with zero gains for either party. This study proposed new acceptance conditions and investigated correlations between the properties of the negotiation environment and the efficacy of acceptance conditions. Highly-accurate individually and socially efficient opponent preference modeling in bilateral multi-issue negotiations has also been analyzed [22]. Shinohara et al. [17] proposed preliminary works that are related to privacy issues in negotiation; however, the evaluations of this study are not sufficient to demonstrate the effectiveness of the proposed method. Besides, the automated negotiations are applied to human-agent negotiations [14] and game-playing [7].

Although this protocol is clear and easy enough for computers, it is too simple for humans who mainly use natural language dialogue to negotiate. Thus, negotiation protocols that do not use natural languages are not suitable for human negotiation support systems. Furthermore, to simulate human negotiation in automated negotiations and to support the negotiation, participants must define their own utility functions. It is troublesome, and there is reduced significantly to support the negotiations using these systems.

2.2 Negotiation Agent for Negotiation Dialogues in Natural Language

Lewis et al. [12] proposed an end-to-end negotiator for human-agent negotiation dialogue in natural language. The negotiator aims to maximize its own utilities. The model comprises four GRUs: a dialogue encoder, a speech generator, and two solution generators (bidirectional GRUs). Furthermore, the authors trained the negotiator through reinforcement learning.

However, the method exhibits two limitations that affect its application in supporting negotiations among humans. First, concerning social welfare and individual utilities, the result of negotiations between the negotiator and a human is inferior to that obtained by the negotiations among humans. Second, participants must define their own utility function to enable the agent to act as a negotiator.

2.3 Recurrent Neural Networks (RNNs) for Natural Language Processing

In the field of natural language processing, RNNs are extensively used for several purposes. Cho et al. [4] proposed an RNN-based machine translation method, which obtained a higher bilingual evaluation understudy (BLEU) score than that obtained by prior popular methods. Sordoni et al. [18] proposed an end-to-end dialogue system based on RNNs. Bahdanau et al. [3] proposed a machine translation method using bidirectional RNNs with attention. When attention-based RNNs generate a token, the models can focus on the input words that are related to the output word. Therefore, it is inferred that the model is fit to focus on the words that are related to the preference of the agent.

3 Problem Definition

We focus on multi-issue dialogue negotiations in which utility spaces are linear. Further, there is no dependency between issues in such negotiations. We assume that two agents $\boldsymbol{A} = \{a_1, a_2\}$ participate in a negotiation. Participants negotiate to determine the *option* that should be adopted for each *issue*. An issue i comprises options $\boldsymbol{O^i} = \{x | x \in \mathbb{N} \cap Min(i) \leq x \leq Max(i)\}$, which are integers within the range according to the issue $[Min\,(i)\,, Max\,(i)]$. Furthermore, each issue has a weight $w_i, \sum_{i \in \boldsymbol{I}} w_i = 1$ for each agent. A bid is a set of options for each issue. It is called *bid.* All the bids in a negotiation are denoted by a Cartesian product of options belonging to each issue in the negotiation. *Utility function* $U_a(\boldsymbol{B})$ returns a reward according to a bid $\boldsymbol{B}$ and the preference of an agent a. The purpose of negotiation for an agent a is to maximize the utility function $U_a(\boldsymbol{B})$ that is given as follows:

$$U_a(\boldsymbol{B}) = \sum_{i \in \boldsymbol{I}} w_i^a \cdot O_i, \tag{1}$$

where $\boldsymbol{I}$ represents a set of issues, and $\boldsymbol{B}_a = \{O_i | i \in \boldsymbol{I}\}$ represents a set of bids for agent a.

Negotiation dialogues are conducted by participants talking in English alternately. After the predetermined turns have passed, each participant offers a bid or refuses agreement. If the participants accept an agreement, they receive rewards following the formed bid and their own utility functions. Otherwise, they receive no rewards. We assumed that the maximum utility each participant can earn is equal.

Our objective is to predict Nash bargaining solution. Nash bargaining solution is a bid that maximizes the product of utilities for each participant. It can be defined as follows:

$$arg\ max_B \prod_{a \in \boldsymbol{A}} U_a(B) \tag{2}$$

Additionally, Nash bargaining solution satisfies Pareto optimality in this problem.

4 Prediction of Nash Bargaining Solution

We estimate the weights of each issue for each participant and search for Nash bargaining solution through exhaustive search based on the estimated weights. A linear utility function prediction problem can be solved by estimating weights of each issue. For example, in a negotiation in which people divide multiple types of items and in which utilities are linearly dependent on the number and the importance of each item, predicting a reward is equal to predicting the weight of each item. Furthermore, although an exhaustive search has computational complexity $O(N^I)$, it is not a serious problem because it takes little time to calculate the reward of each draft, and there are few issues and options in the negotiation problems we assume.

First, before a dialogue is encoded, we add tokens to the head of utterances in order to identify who has spoken: <TGT> is added to prediction target participant, and <OTHERS> are added to the others (Fig. 1).

Further, we encode a dialogue using RNNs (Fig. 2). To encode a dialogue for predicting the utility functions, we apply bidirectional N-layers GRUs. We also apply dropout [19] for each layer. A bidirectional RNN comprises two RNNs. The first RNN processes in the forward direction, whereas the second RNN processes

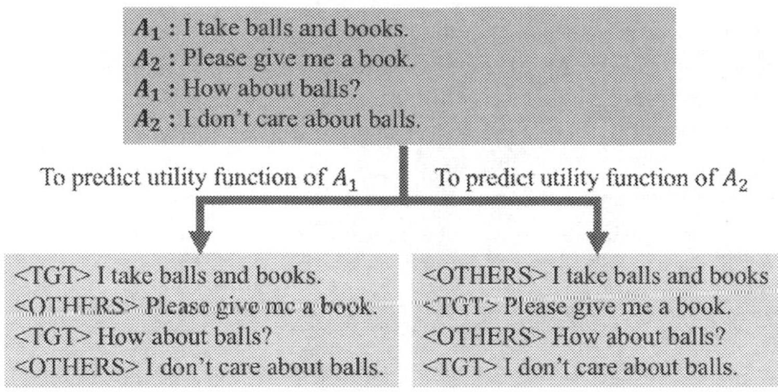

Fig. 1. Preprocessing to predict the utility function for each participant

in the backward direction. The outputs from each RNN are further concatenated. A bidirectional RNN enables the embedding of forward and backward information in a sequence. GRUs and long short-term memory (LSTMs) are the expansion of RNNs that enable the training of long-term dependencies. To focus on more important aspects of this study, we use GRUs, which exhibit a simpler architecture than that of LSTMs.

$$h_t^{f,1} = GRU^f(h_{t-1}^{f,1}, Ex_t) \tag{3}$$

$$h_t^{b,1} = GRU^b(h_{t+1}^{b,1}, Ex_t) \tag{4}$$

$$h_t^1 = [h_t^{f,N}, h_t^{b,N}] \tag{5}$$

$$h_t^{f,n} = GRU^f(h_{t-1}^{f,n}, h_t^{n-1}) \tag{6}$$

$$h_t^{b,n} = GRU^b(h_{t+1}^{b,n}, h_t^{n-1}) \tag{7}$$

$$h_t = [h_t^{f,N}, h_t^{b,N}] \tag{8}$$

Third, we convert the encoded token vectors to a dialogue-context vector with attention. Like fillers and prepositions, some of the words that are spoken are not necessary to determine the issue that is important for an agent. Therefore, we only need to focus on a few words, which demonstrates whether the agent cares about a particular issue. Thus, we apply an attention mechanism, which focuses on a particular part of the given information. Setting weights α_t for each sequence using the softmax activation, an attention mechanism, gives us the sum of the weighted sequences h^α.

$$\alpha_t = \frac{exp(W^\alpha \cdot h_t)}{\sum_{t'} exp(W^\alpha \cdot h_t')} \tag{9}$$

$$h_t^\alpha = h_t \cdot \alpha_t \tag{10}$$

$$h^\alpha = \sum_t h_t^\alpha \tag{11}$$

Fourth, we predict the issue weights $\boldsymbol{W_I} = \{w_i | i \in \boldsymbol{I}\}$ using a completely connected layer which is inputted dialogue embedding and softmax activation. We use a mean square error as loss function.

$$w'_i = W^i \cdot h^\alpha + b_i \tag{12}$$

$$w_i = \frac{exp(w'_i)}{\sum_{i \in \boldsymbol{I}} exp(w'_i)} \tag{13}$$

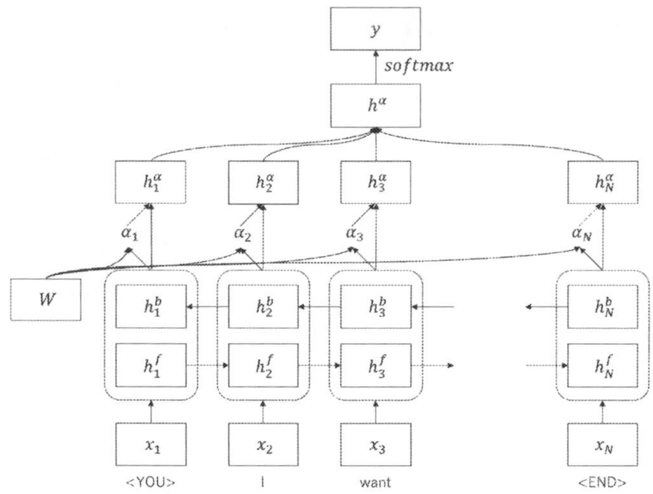

Fig. 2. Utility function prediction model

Finally, using the estimated issue weights for each participant, we search for Nash bargaining solution by performing an exhaustive search. We consider the set of options that maximize the utility of each participant as the predicted Nash bargaining solution.

5 Evaluation

5.1 Experimental Settings

We use the multi-issue bargaining dataset that was released by Facebook AI research for the evaluation [12]. To the best of our knowledge, this is the only open source of data related to the negotiation among participants in the English language; further, there are multiple issues with each dialogue scenario exhibiting a different utility space. In addition, the utility spaces are well-defined.

In this dataset, two humans negotiate in English and divide books, hats, and balls. In total, there are 5 to 7 items, and at least one item exists for each item type. Besides, each agent assigns a different score for each item type. First, they talk by taking turns within ten turns. When agents believe that they have already built a consensus, the agents should say "<selection>," which indicates that it is the end of the negotiation dialogue and that it is time for both agents to suggest a bid. A bid depicts the number of items that an agent receives for each item type. Finally, if there is no contradiction between the bids, agents receive utilities according to the number of each item that they have received and the weights of each item type. Otherwise, they can receive no reward. According to the item types $\boldsymbol{S} = \{book, ball, hat\}$, the number of items for each type $N_s (s \in \boldsymbol{S})$, and the score of an item type $score(s, a)$ for an agent a, the following requirement is satisfied.

$$\sum_{s \in \boldsymbol{S}} N_s \cdot score(s, a) = 10 \tag{14}$$

In addition, a score for each item type is non-zero for at least one agent, and the scores of some item types are non-zero for both the users. The two constraints make it impossible that all the agents will receive a maximum reward. Thus, these constraints are intended to make these negotiations competitive.

To apply our method, we consider i_s to as a problem to determine the number of items s that are received by the agent whose utility function is predicted. Similarly, we consider the weight $w^a_{i_s}$ of issue i_s for an agent a as the normalized score $score(s, a)$ of an item s. The normalization can be processed as follows:

$$w^a_{i_s} = \frac{score(s, a)}{\sum_{s' \in \boldsymbol{S}} score(s', a)} \tag{15}$$

The loss function was the mean square error, and the gradient method was RMSprop (learning rate $= 10^{-3}$, rho $= 0.9$, epsilon $= 10^{-7}$, decay $= 0.0$) for which the parameters are observed to comprise the default value of Hinton et al. [21]. The number of GRU layers is 3. In GRUs, the number of units is 256, the activation function is *tanh*, the dropout rate in hidden layers is 0.5, and the dropout rate in input layer is 0.2. The learning ran 20 for epochs.

5.2 Experimental Results

Prediction of Issue Weights. We first demonstrate our results by predicting issue weights. We applied 10-fold cross-validation to evaluate the performance of our method. A Spearman's rank correlation coefficient means the estimation accuracy of the ordinal utility model and a general accuracy means the estimation accuracy of the cardinal utility model. We obtained a Spearman's rank correlation coefficient between our results and the ground truths of **61%** and an accuracy of **70%** for the optimal essential issue prediction. Therefore, our proposed method can predict the issue weights of each agent, almost accurately. This result indicates that our proposed method can predict the important elements of the preference of each agent from the negotiation dialogues in natural language.

Prediction of Nash Bargaining Solution. We evaluate our proposed method using the percentage of Pareto optimal solutions against the results of negotiation among humans, which are included in the dataset. The results with 10-fold cross-validation are evaluated using the following measures.

- **% Nash bargaining.** The percentage of solutions that satisfies Nash bargaining solution in all the negotiations.
- **% Pareto optimal.** The percentage of solutions that satisfies Pareto optimal solutions in all the negotiations.
- **Nash product.** The product of utilities in each agent. The Nash bargaining solution maximizes the product of surplus utilities, which is called as the Nash product.
- **Social welfare.** The sum of utilities in each agent.

Table 1. A comparison of the percentage of Nash bargaining solution and Pareto optimal solution between ours and humans.

	% Nash bargaining	% Pareto optimal
Ours	**46.5**	**68.6**
Humans	44.7	63.8

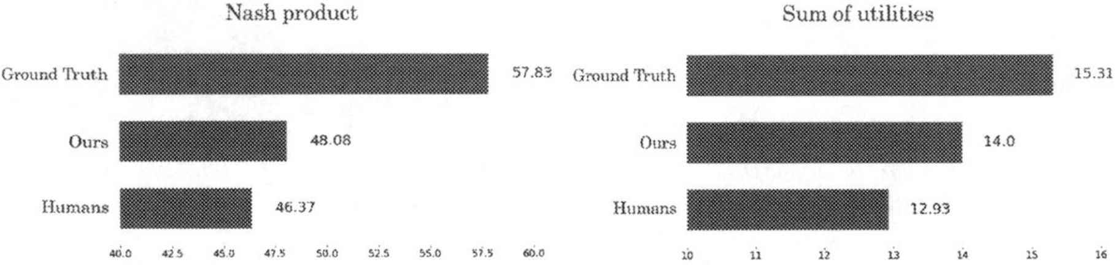

Fig. 3. Results of the theoretical maximum, our method, and humans. We demonstrate the comparison of the product of utilities in the left figure and the sum of utilities in the right figure.

Table 1 presents a comparison between our method and a method in which humans use the rate of Nash bargaining solution and Pareto optimal solutions. Figure 3 demonstrates the results that were compared with the product and sum of utilities. In addition, Lewis et al. [12] indicated in their paper that their end-to-end negotiator obtained 82.4% in the rate of Pareto optimal within **agreed** negotiations, which constitute 57.2% of all negotiations. So that, their negotiator obtained 47.2% in the rate of Pareto optimal within **all** negotiations. Considering these results and the existing work, our proposed method acquired state-of-the-art Pareto optimal bid suggestion in the dataset. Furthermore, our proposed method obtained more social welfare and Nash product than the way in which each participant suggests a bid and tries to form an agreement.

6 Conclusion

This paper presented a method for predicting Nash bargaining solution for negotiation dialogues. Although automated negotiations in agent-agent negotiations require that participants should manually define their utility functions for supporting negotiations among humans, our method does not incorporate such a requirement for supporting negotiations. Our method can estimate Nash bargaining solution simply by participants talking. Furthermore, our method comprises two processes: (1) predicting utility functions for each user from dialogues using attention-based GRUs; (2) finding a solution that satisfies the definition of Nash bargaining solution using exhaustive search. We demonstrated that the social welfare of the solutions that were searched using our method outperforms the social welfare of the solutions that were obtained based on negotiations among humans.

In future studies, we will prepare a dataset for negotiating dialogues in which the utility functions are nonlinear and in which the options in each issue will affect the options in other issues to incorporate more realistic settings. Additionally, it is also important to explore a model that can predict the utility function in a more direct manner. Furthermore, through multitasking learning, we will be able to develop a model that can learn a general method for predicting the utility functions from negotiations in different domains.

Acknowledgements. This work was supported by JST CREST Grant Number JPMJCR15E1, Japan.

References

1. Baarslag, T., et al.: Evaluating practical negotiating agents: results and analysis of the 2011 international competition. Artif. Intell. J. (AIJ) **198**, 73–103 (2013)
2. Baarslag, T., Hindriks, K.V.: Accepting optimally in automated negotiation with incomplete information. In: Proceedings of the 12th International Conference on Autonomous Agents and Multi-Agent Systems, AAMAS 2013, pp. 715–722 (2013)
3. Bahdanau, D., Cho, K., Bengio, Y.: Neural machine translation by jointly learning to align and translate. arXiv preprint arXiv:1409.0473 (2014)
4. Cho, K., et al.: Learning phrase representations using RNN encoder-decoder for statistical machine translation. arXiv preprint arXiv:1406.1078 (2014)
5. Fujita, K.: Compromising adjustment strategy based on TKI conflict mode for multi-times bilateral closed negotiations. Comput. Intell. **34**, 85–103 (2017). https://doi.org/10.1111/coin.12107
6. Jennings, N.R., Faratin, P., Lomuscio, A.R., Parsons, S., Wooldridge, M.J., Sierra, C.: Automated negotiation: prospects, methods and challenges. Group Decis. Negot. **10**(2), 199–215 (2001)
7. Jonge, D.D., Zhang, D.: Automated negotiations for general game playing. In: Proceedings of the 16th Conference on Autonomous Agents and Multi-Agent Systems, AAMAS 2017, pp. 371–379 (2017)
8. Jonker, C.M., Aydogan, R., Baarslag, T., Fujita, K., Ito, T., Hindriks, K.V.: Automated negotiating agents competition (ANAC). In: AAAI, pp. 5070–5072 (2017)

9. Kalai, E.: Proportional solutions to bargaining situations: interpersonal utility comparisons. Discussion Papers 179. Center for Mathematical Studies in Economics and Management Science, Northwestern University, March 1977. https://ideas.repec.org/p/nwu/cmsems/179.html
10. Kalai, E., Smorodinsky, M.: Other solutions to Nash's bargaining problem. Econometrica **43**(3), 513–518 (1975). http://www.jstor.org/stable/1914280
11. Kawaguchi, S., Fujita, K., Ito, T.: Compromising strategy based on estimated maximum utility for automated negotiation agents competition (ANAC-10). In: Mehrotra, K.G., Mohan, C.K., Oh, J.C., Varshney, P.K., Ali, M. (eds.) IEA/AIE 2011. LNCS, vol. 6704, pp. 501–510. Springer, Heidelberg (2011). https://doi.org/10.1007/978-3-642-21827-9_51
12. Lewis, M., Yarats, D., Dauphin, Y.N., Parikh, D., Batra, D.: Deal or no deal? End-to-end learning for negotiation dialogues. CoRR abs/1706.05125 (2017). http://arxiv.org/abs/1706.05125
13. Lin, R., Kraus, S., Baarslag, T., Tykhonov, D., Hindriks, K., Jonker, C.M.: Genius: an integrated environment for supporting the design of generic automated negotiators. Comput. Intell. **30**, 48–70 (2012). https://doi.org/10.1111/j.1467-8640.2012.00463.x
14. Mell, J., Gratch, J.: Grumpy & Pinocchio: answering human-agent negotiation questions through realistic agent design. In: Proceedings of the 16th Conference on Autonomous Agents and Multi-Agent Systems, AAMAS 2017, pp. 401–409 (2017)
15. Nash, J.F., et al.: Equilibrium points in n-person games. Proc. Nat. Acad. Sci. **36**(1), 48–49 (1950)
16. Nash Jr., J.F.: The bargaining problem. Econometrica: J. Econ. Soc. 155–162 (1950)
17. Shinohara, H., Fujita, K.: Alternating offers protocol considering fair privacy for multilateral closed negotiation. In: An, B., Bazzan, A., Leite, J., Villata, S., van der Torre, L. (eds.) PRIMA 2017. LNCS, vol. 10621, pp. 533–541. Springer, Cham (2017). https://doi.org/10.1007/978-3-319-69131-2_36
18. Sordoni, A., et al.: A neural network approach to context-sensitive generation of conversational responses. In: Proceedings of the 2015 Conference of the NAACL-HLT, pp. 196–205 (2015)
19. Srivastava, N., Hinton, G., Krizhevsky, A., Sutskever, I., Salakhutdinov, R.: Dropout: a simple way to prevent neural networks from overfitting. J. Mach. Learn. Res. **15**(1), 1929–1958 (2014)
20. Tang, D., Qin, B., Liu, T.: Document modeling with gated recurrent neural network for sentiment classification. In: Proceedings of the 2015 Conference on Empirical Methods in Natural Language Processing, pp. 1422–1432 (2015)
21. Tieleman, T., Hinton, G.: Lecture 6.5—RmsProp: divide the gradient by a running average of its recent magnitude. COURSERA: Neural Netw. Mach. Learn. **4**, 26–31 (2012)
22. Zafari, F., Mofakham, F.N.: POPPONENT: highly accurate, individually and socially efficient opponent preference model in bilateral multi issue negotiations. In: Proceedings of the Twenty-Sixth International Joint Conference on Artificial Intelligence, IJCAI 2017, pp. 5100–5104 (2017)

Joint Residual Pyramid for Depth Map Super-Resolution

Yi Xiao[1], Xiang Cao[1], Yan Zheng[2(✉)], and Xianyi Zhu[1]

[1] College of Computer Science and Electronic Engineering, Hunan University, Changsha, Hunan, China
yixiao_csee@hnu.edu.cn

[2] College of Electrical and Information Engineering, Hunan University, Changsha, Hunan, China
yanzheng@hnu.edu.cn

Abstract. High-resolution (HR) depth map can be better inferred from a low-resolution (LR) one with the guidance of an additional HR texture map of the same scene. Recently, deep neural networks with large receptive fields are shown to benefit applications such as image completion. Our insight is that super resolution (SR) is similar to image completion, where only parts of the depth values are precisely known. However, large receptive fields in general will increase the depth and the number of parameters of the network, which may cause degradation and large memory consumption. To solve these problems, we adapt the convolutional neural pyramid (CNP) structure by introducing residual block and linear interpolation layer, and adopt the CNP in the joint super-resolution framework. We call this convolutional neural model joint residual pyramid (JRP). Our JRP model consists of three sub-networks, two convolutional neural residual pyramids concatenated by a normal convolutional neural network. The convolutional neural residual pyramids extract information from large receptive fields of the depth map and guidance map, while the convolutional neural network effectively transfers useful structures of the guidance image to the depth image. Experimental results show that our model outperforms existing state-of-the-art algorithms not only on data pairs of RGB/depth images, but also on other data pairs like color/saliency and color-scribbles/colorized images.

Keywords: Deep learning · Neural convolutional pyramid
Joint super-resolution · Residual block

The work is supported by the National Key Research and Development Program of China(Grant Num: 2018YFB0203900), NSFC from PRC (Grant Num.: 61502158), Hunan NSF (Grant Num.: 2017JJ3042, 2018JJ3067), and China Postdoctoral Foundation (Grant Num.: 2016M590740).

X. Geng and B.-H. Kang (Eds.): PRICAI 2018, LNAI 11012, pp. 797–810, 2018.
https://doi.org/10.1007/978-3-319-97304-3_61

1 Introduction

Acquiring accurate, high quality and High Resolution (HR) depth information is especially important for many applications of vision related tasks, such as 3D reconstruction, virtual reality, robot vision and 3DTV. While high quality texture images can be easy acquired by a simple color camera, depth data of HR is hard to acquire. Generally speaking, depth acquisition methods can be divided into stereo matching based methods, laser scanning based methods and range sensing based methods.

Stereo matching based methods obtain depth information by correspondence matching and triangulating two or multiple texture images. However, the performance of these methods are dramatically affected by the occlusion and distributions of textures [25]. Also, high resolution results require high computational costs. Laser scanning based methods can acquire high quality depth maps, but its slice-by-slice scanning process is rather time-consuming and infeasible in dynamic scenes. In contrast, range sensing based methods which use depth sensors, such as time-of-fight (TOF) camera and Microsoft Kinect, can be used in a dynamic environment. However, the acquired depth maps are of low resolution (512×424 for Kinect 2.0).

In order to solve this problem, researchers have made a lot of efforts to improve the resolution of Low Resolution (LR) depth maps. Joint or guided image filtering methods [10,14], which take an extra HR texture image as a reference or guidance, have achieved great success in recent years. The main idea of joint filtering is to transfer the structural information in the HR reference image to the up-sampled depth image, so that the missing information of the depth image are restored as much as possible. However, it is ambiguous to determine which parts should be preserved and which parts should be smoothed. Ham *et al.* took into account the structures in both target and guidance image instead of unilaterally transferring the structures of RGB image to the depth image [8]. However, the hand-crafted objective functions used in [8] may not reflect natural image priors well. Recently, joint deep convolutional neural networks (JDCNNs) [13,18] were proposed by combining the joint filtering and deep convolutional neural networks (CNNs). They showed better performances than classical methods in depth map super resolution.

As pointed out by Shen *et al.*, large receipt fields in deep CNN model can significantly benefit applications such as noise suppression and image completion [27]. Our insight is that super resolution is similar to noise suppression and image completion, where only parts of the depth values are precisely known. Therefore, increasing the receipt fields in the JDCNN model may also improve the performance of the network. Unfortunately, large receptive fields in general will increase both the depth and the number of parameters of the network. Deeper network model may make the network hard to train and degrades the performance of the network (called the degradation problem) [9]. Also, since the JDCNN model has two branches, the increase of parameters will consume a large number of memory in the training.

To solve these problems, we adopt the convolutional neural pyramid (CNP) structure model, which can efficiently increase the receptive field without significantly increasing the number of parameters of the network [27], for joint depth map super-resolution. To relieve the degradation problem, we further introduce residual block [9] and linear interpolation block into the CNP model, resulting our final convolutional neural network model, joint residual pyramid (JRP), which enables large receipt fields without significantly increasing the computational costs and memory costs. Our JRP model mainly consists of three subnetworks, where two convolutional neural residual pyramids (CNRPs) are concatenated by a CNN. The two CNRPs are designed to extract information from large receptive fields, while the CNN model is designed to transfer the useful structures of the guidance images to the up-sampled target image. The flowchart of our JRP model is shown in Fig. 1. To verify the performance of our model, we tested our model with several types of data pairs, including RGB/depth images, color/saliency images, and color-scribbles/colorized images. Experimental results on several benchmark data sets show that our method outperforms the existing state-of-the-art algorithms without significantly sacrificing computation efficiency and memory space.

The contributions of this paper are three-fold:

(1) we adopt the convolutional neural pyramid structure in the joint depth super-resolution framework to efficiently increase the receptive field;
(2) we introduce the residual block and linear interpolation block and propose the novel JRP model to improve the performances of network;
(3) we apply our model in several applications and get state-of-the-art performances without significantly increasing computation efficiency and memory space.

2 Background and Related Work

Generally speaking, depth map SR methods can be classified into local-based, global-based and CNN-based methods.

2.1 Local-Based Methods

In local-based depth map Super Resolution (SR) methods, each value in the SR image is given by the weighted average of its neighboring pixels in the LR depth map and guidance image [10,14,19,20,32]. Yang *et al.* proposed to use a HR color map as a reference to iteratively refine LR depth maps [32]. Kopf *et al.* proposed a joint bilateral upsampling (JBU) procedure that considered both the depth map smoothness and the color map similarity [14], but it may cause unwanted gradient reversal artifacts. To solve this problem, He *et al.* used local linear transform of the guidance image to product filtering output [10]. Liu *et al.* proposed utilizing geodesic distances to upsample LR depth map with a registered HR color image [19]. Lu and Forsyth used the relationship between image segmentation boundaries and depth boundaries to reconstruct HR depth map [20].

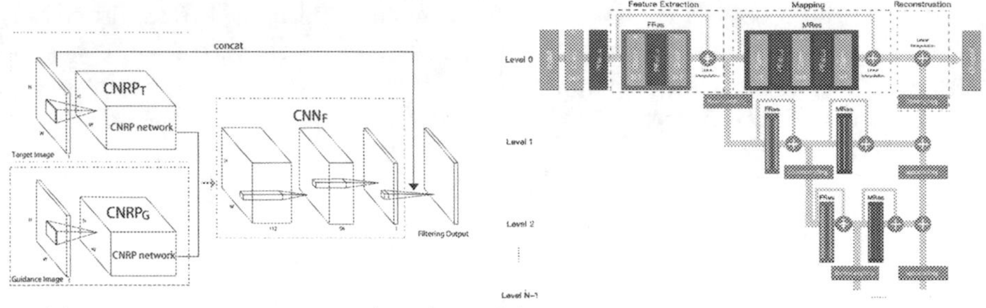

(a) Joint Residual Pyramid (JRP) (b) Convolutional Neural Residual Pyramid (CNRP)

Fig. 1. The network architecture of our model. (a) Joint pyramid residual network model. Our model consists of three sub-network: CNRP_T, CNRP_G and CNN_F. CNRP_T and CNRP_G extract feature maps from the target and guidance images, respectively. CNN_F concatenate the feature maps from CNRP_G and CNRP_T and reconstruct the desired output. (b) Convolution neural residual pyramid. Each residual pyramid level includes feature extracting part, mapping part and reconstructing part. The CNRP can enlarge the receptive fields without sacrificing computational efficiency.

2.2 Global-Based Methods

In contrast, global-based depth map SR methods [1,4,7,8,16,23,31] restore the SR image by solving an optimizing problem with certain regression terms. Diebel *et al.* combined LR depth maps with registered HR camera maps to reconstruct HR depth maps, which may cause over-smooth depth map [4]. To maintain sharp depth boundaries and prevent depth bleeding during propagation, Park *et al.* combined several weighting factors together with nonlocal means filtering [23]. Given a database of training patches [1], Aodha *et al.* inferred the HR map from a single LR map. Ferstl *et al.* especially formulated SR as a global energy optimization problem using Total Generalized Variation (TGV) regularization [7]. Yang *et al.* proposed an adaptive color-guided autoregressive model to construct a unified depth recovery framework [31]. Ham *et al.* fused appropriate structures of static and dynamic color maps to reconstruct HR depth maps [8]. Lei *et al.* considered view synthesis quality to reconstruct SR depth maps [16].

2.3 CNN-Based Methods

Convolutional neural networks (CNNs) have achieved great success in high-level computer vision [15]. They were used to solve some low-level vision, such image SR [5,13,18,24]. Existing CNN-based methods take either one or two image as inputs. Dong *et al.* proposed an end-to-end SR convolution neural network (SRCNN) for single image SR [5]. Ren *et al.* fused different individual networks to construct a super resolution system [24]. Joint deep convolutional neural networks [13,18], taking the depth image and guidance images as inputs, were proposed to simulate a joint filter. Hui *et al.* proposed a multi-scale guided convolutional network (MSG-Net) for depth map super resolution. Li *et al.* proposed a deep convolution network to perform joint filtering [18]. The model consists of three sub-networks. The first two CNNs extract informative features from both target and guidance images in parallel. The third CNN then concatenates the feature responses to selectively transfer common structures and re-construct the filtered output [18]. In contrast, our model uses two joint convolutional neural pyramids [27] enhanced with residual blocks [9] and linear interpolation blocks as feature extractors. In addition, we concatenate the target image by a skip-connection [12] at the end of our model to improve the flow of information and gradients throughout the network.

3 Proposed Method

3.1 Overview

As illustrated in Fig. 1(a), our joint residual pyramid (JRP) network is composed of three sub-networks, two convolutional neural residual pyramid networks (CNRP_T, CNRP_G) followed by a normal CNN (CNN_F). CNRP_T and CNRP_G concurrently extract the informative features from large receptive fields in the target and guidance images. Their output feature maps are then concatenated and feeded to CNN_F, which transfers useful structures from the guidance image to the target image. In order to improve the flow of information and gradients throughout the network [12], the target image is concatenated with the output of CNN_F and then convolved to produce the final SR image.

3.2 Convolutional Neural Residual Pyramid Network

Large receptive fields are essential for many low-level vision tasks such as image SR and suppressing noise. Pyramid structure can greatly enlarge the receptive fields without significantly sacrificing computation efficiency and memory space. We adapt the idea of the CNP model [27] into our joint framework. Since deep structure often incurs the degradation problem, which makes the network hard to train and degrades the performances, we further introduce the residual shortcut connections and linear interpolation layer in the our model, resulting a convolutional neural residual pyramid (CNRP). Each CNRP level includes feature extraction block, non-linear mapping block and reconstruction block, two residual shortcut connections associated with two corresponding linear interpolation layers, as illustrated in Fig. 1(b). In the following, we will introduce each block in more detail.

Feature Extraction Block: We apply convolution layers to extract image features. The feature extraction block in level L_i, consisting of Conv-PReLU-Conv layers with kernel size 3×3, takes the down-sampled feature maps from the feature extraction part in L_{i-1} (except L_0, whose inputs are the 56-channel feature maps of the target image or the guidance image generated by a Conv-PReLU layer with kernel size 3×3) and outputs 56-channel feature maps. The output feature maps are feeded to not only the non-linear mapping block in the same level, but also to the feature extraction block in level L_{i+1}. Since the feature extraction in higher levels receives recursively down-sampled feature maps, it can extract information from larger recept fields with a fixed kernel size. The down-sampling operation is performed by a max pooling layer.

Nonlinear Mapping Block: Motivated by [6], the nonlinear mapping block is designed to contain a shrinking layer, a nonlinear mapping layer and an expanding layer. The shrinking layer is a convolution layer with kernel size 1×1, which save computational cost by reducing the 56-channel feature maps to 12-channel feature maps. The non-linear mapping layer with kernel size 3×3 further exacts features from the shrunk maps and output 12-channel feature maps. The expanding layer uses a convolution layer with kernel size 1×1 and expands the 12-channel feature maps to 56-channel feature maps to get more information. PReLU rectification is applied after each layer.

Residual Shortcut Connection: Motivated by the ResNet [9], we introduce residual shortcut connection to relieve the degradation problem. In each CNRP level, we add two residual shortcut connection as shown in Fig. 1(b). The first connection is to connect the inputs and outputs of the feature extraction block, while the second one is to connect the inputs and outputs of the non-linear mapping block.

Linear Interpolation Layer: In previous work such as [9], element-wise summation is usually used to fuse the feature maps from the residual shortcut connections and the main branches. In contrast, we introduce an element-wise linear interpolation layer to fuse the feature maps from the shortcut connections and the blocks. The way of our interpolation can choose the best weighting factor from different branches by training, which is shown to improve the performance in our experiments Sect. 4.3. Suppose the feature maps from the shortcut connection and the main branch are x_1 and x_2, respectively, the element-wise linear interpolation y is given by

$$\mathrm{y} = \alpha x_1 + (1 - \alpha) x_2 \tag{1}$$

where α is a coefficient to be learned in the training.

Reconstruction Part: The reconstruction part in level L_i fuses not only the feature maps from the nonlinear mapping part in the same level, but also the up-sampled feature maps from the reconstruction part in level L_{i+1}. We also use the linear interpolation layer (Eq. (1)) to fuse the feature maps from different levels. The up-sampling operation is performed by a deconvolution layer of stride 2 with kernel size 5×5. Since features from level L_{i+1} with larger recept fields are recursively fused to level L_i, the final reconstruction part in level L_0 will obtain features of a large recept field.

3.3 Joint SR Network

The features extracted from the target image and the guidance image by CNRP_T and CNRP_G should be fused appropriately to increase the resolution of the target image. To achieve this task, a sub-network CNN_F is designed to concatenate the output feature maps of CNRP_T and CNRP_G (112 channels in total). The CNN_F consists of three convolution layers of kernel size 3×3. The first convolution layer outputs 56-channel feature maps; the second layer outputs a 1-channel map; the third layer outputs the final SR image. A PReLU layer is applied after the first convolution layer. In order to better guide the training, the target image is skip connected as the input of the third convolution layer, which is shown to improve the performance in the experiments.

3.4 Loss Function

Pixel-wise loss functions such as mean squared error (MSE) tend to deal with inherently blurry predictions [22]. In order to sharpen the image prediction and improve perceptual qualities, we introduce the gradient loss function (GDL). The GDL compute the gradient difference of ground truth image I^{HR} and prediction image $\phi_\theta\left(I^{LR}\right)$ using the Sobel operator. So our loss function include two parts: MSE and GDL. The MSE for N training samples is given by

$$l_{mse} = \frac{1}{N}\left\|I^{HR} - \phi_\theta\left(I^{LR}\right)\right\|_2^2 \tag{2}$$

where ϕ denotes our JRP model and θ is the set of parameters. The GDL for N training samples is given by

$$\begin{aligned} l_{grad} = \frac{1}{N}(&\left\|\nabla_x\left(I^{HR}\right) - \nabla_x\left(\phi_\theta\left(I^{LR}\right)\right)\right\|_2^2 + \left\|\nabla_y\left(I^{HR}\right) - \nabla_y\left(\phi_\theta\left(I^{LR}\right)\right)\right\|_2^2 + \\ &\sqrt{\|\nabla_x(I^{HR}) - \nabla_x(\phi_\theta(I^{LR}))\|_2^2 + \|\nabla_y(I^{HR}) - \nabla_y(\phi_\theta(I^{LR}))\|_2^2 + \lambda}), \end{aligned} \tag{3}$$

where ∇_x and ∇_y denotes the gradient in horizontal and vertical direction, respectively; λ is a constant, which is set to 0.01 in our experiment. In the experiment, we find that the GDL in this form is more stable than normal gradient loss functions in the training.

We also tried pre-trained 19 layers VGG [29] loss function [2] to train our network as comparative experiments. The qualitative and quantitative comparison of different loss functions will be discussed in the experiments Sect. 4.3.

4 Experiments and Applications

4.1 Training Settings

We implement our network in Tensorflow on an NVIDIA GeForce GTX 1080Ti graphics card. We collect 1449 RGB/D image pairs from NYU data set [28], 1000 RGB/D image pairs for training and 449 RGB/D image pairs for testing. We augment the training data by clip, rotation and mirror and generate 160,000 training patch pairs of size 128 × 128. The batch size is set to 20. The network is trained with 100,000 steps and the initial learning rate is 1e−3, which decays by 0.8 times per 10000 steps. We train our network for joint image SR. We get the low-resolution target image from a ground-truth image using nearest-neighbor down-sampling. When our JRP model is trained with the augmented RGB/D data pairs, it can be directly applied to several different joint image SR tasks, including depth map SR, chromaticity map SR and saliency map SR. In experiments, we provide the average root mean squared errors (RMSEs) of test data set, except for the visual results, to evaluate the results.

Table 1. Time (second) of each 100 steps with batch size 1, network parameters (million), RMSEs and memory consumption (MB) analysis in terms of different sizes of receptive fields (RF). The RMSE of 39 and 83 Layers is missing, because our GPU memory does not allow 39 and 83 layers in training with batch size of 20.

RF	Our CNRP					Single-level CNN [18]				
	Levels	Time	Mem.	Paras.	RMSE	Layers	Time	Mem.	Paras.	RMSE
9	0	2.14	56	0.20	9.17	6	2.14	56	0.20	9.17
20	1	3.00	74.25	0.50	6.94	10	2.67	81	0.62	6.95
42	2	3.51	78.81	0.79	6.38	21	5.31	158	1.24	21.81
78	3	3.98	79.85	1.09	6.19	39	9.69	284	2.26	–
166	4	4.42	80.24	1.39	6.36	83	20.47	592	4.74	–

4.2 Pyramid Levels vs. Performance

Since the number of pyramid levels N in our JRP model will affect the performance of our network, we test the impact of N on 16× joint depth map SR using the data set of Lu [21]. As shown in Table 1, the performance (RMSE) of JRP increases as the pyramid level N becomes larger until the receptive field of level $N = 4$ exceeds the training image resolution. Therefore, we set $N = 3$ in all our experiments. We also compare the recept field, runtime, memory consumption, number of parameters and performance of our JRP model with those of the single-level CNN model [18] (corresponding to level 0 of our model) as shown in Table 1. To increase the recept field of the model in [18], we increase the number of convolution layers. As shown in Table 1, our JRP model can enlarge the receptive fields and produce better results without significantly sacrificing computational efficiency.

4.3 Loss Functions and Network Structures

We then evaluate the loss functions and network structures proposed in Sect. 3.2 with Lu data sets [21] for 16× depth map SR. As show in Table 2, our loss function with MSE and GDL achieves the best performance compared other combination of loss functions such as MSE, MSE + VGG, and MSE + GDL + VGG. In addition, network structure is also important to the quality of SR. Thanks to the proposed residual blocks and linear interpolation blocks in our JRP model, the average RMSE values of the test images reduce 0.2 for 16× SR as shown in Table 3.

Table 2. Numerical comparisons of different loss functions for depth map 16 × SR.

Loss function	MSE	MSE + VGG	MSE + VGG + GDL	MSE + GDL
RMSE	6.35	6.23	6.41	6.19

Table 3. Comparisons of different network structures for depth map 16× SR.

Methods	No residual connection	No linear interpolation	No residual connection & No linear interpolation	JRP
RMSE	6.34	6.37	6.39	6.19

4.4 Depth Map SR

We compare our JRP model with several state-of-the-art methods, including local-based methods [10,14], global-based method [8], and CNN-based method [18]. We first provide the visual comparisons with several state-of-art SR methods in Fig. 2. It is observed that the results of He [10] and Li [18] are over smoothed (Fig. 2(d) and (e)). The JBU [14] and Ham [8] approaches transfer erroneous details (Fig. 2(f) and (g)). In contrast, the SR depth maps reconstructed by our JRP model are sharper and has less artifacts than the other methods (Fig. 2(h)).

We also provide a numerical comparison with the state-of-the-art SR methods using the average RMSEs in Table 4. The four benchmark test data sets include: (1) 30 RGB/depth hole-filled pairs from Middlebury data sets [11,26], (2) Lu data sets [21] contains 6 RGB/depth pairs captured by ASUS Xtion Pro, (3) the 449 RGB/D testing pairs in NYU v2 data sets [28], (4) 299 RGB-D image pairs from align_kv2 sub-folder obtained by the Kinect V2 sensor in SUN RGB/D data sets [30].

The RMSE values are computed from the code packages with suggested parameters provided by the authors. As shown in the Table 4, our JRP model achieves the state-of-the-art performance, especially for Middlebury [11,26], Lu [21] and NYU [28] data sets. For the Sun data set, our results are comparable to the best results in the 2× SR case. Thanks to the large recept field provided by our JRP model, our results obviously outperform the other methods in 4×, 8× and 16× SR.

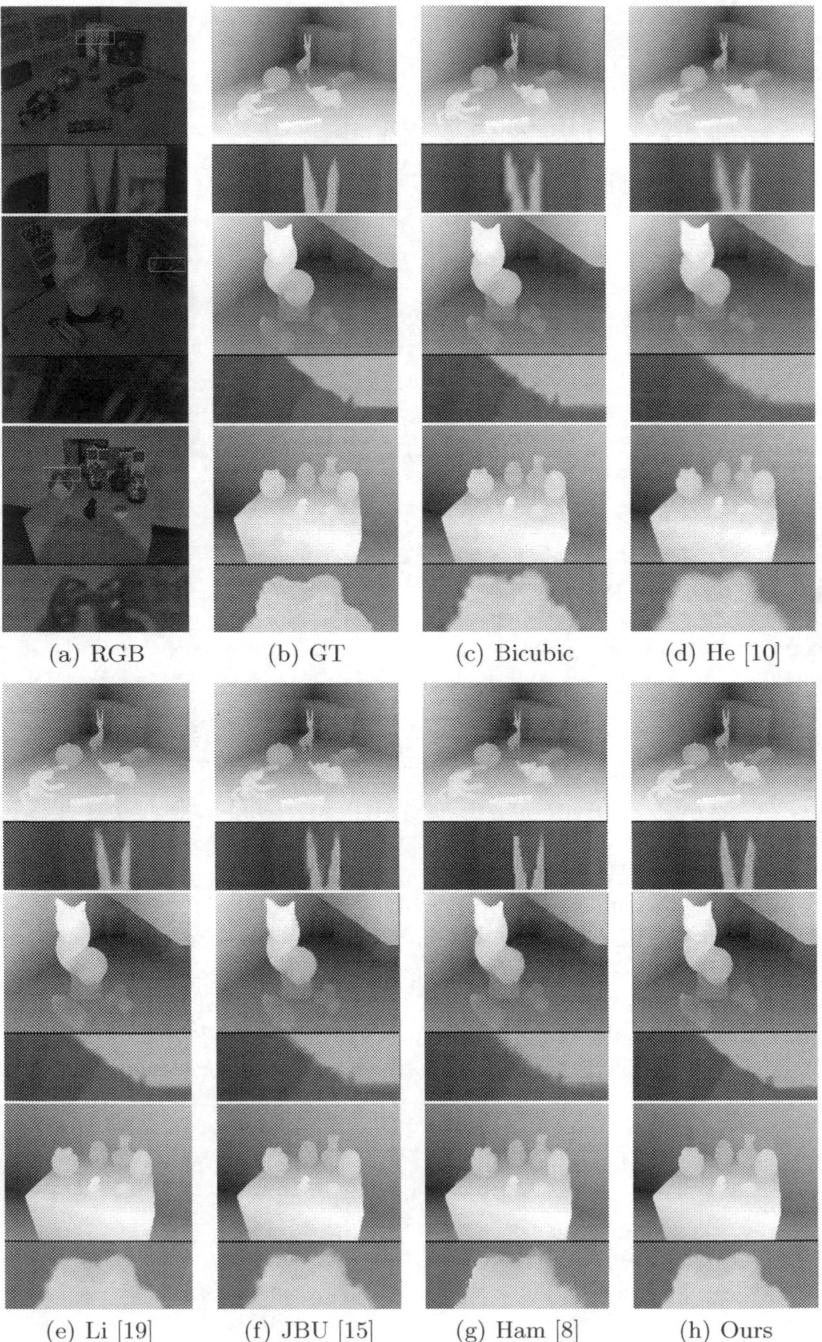
(a) RGB (b) GT (c) Bicubic (d) He [10]
(e) Li [19] (f) JBU [15] (g) Ham [8] (h) Ours

Fig. 2. Visual comparisons of depth map SR results (4×).

Table 4. Average RMSE comparison of depth map SR on the four benchmark datesets. We map depth values into the range [0, 255] for each data set. Bold Values indicate the best performance and underscored values indicate the second best.

Methods	Middlebury [11,26]				Lu [21]				NYU [28]				SUN [30]			
	2×	4×	8×	16×	2×	4×	8×	16×	2×	4×	8×	16×	2×	4×	8×	16×
Bicubic	1.97	4.45	7.59	11.88	2.16	5.08	9.22	14.27	2.11	4.51	7.85	12.36	2.44	3.89	5.62	8.05
Kopf [14]	1.41	2.44	3.82	<u>6.12</u>	1.39	2.99	5.06	<u>7.51</u>	<u>1.22</u>	2.30	4.60	7.23	**1.74**	<u>2.73</u>	<u>3.85</u>	<u>5.72</u>
He [10]	2.43	4.10	7.26	11.71	3.03	4.89	8.85	14.10	2.31	4.10	7.53	12.20	2.43	3.56	5.40	7.96
Li [18]	<u>1.28</u>	<u>2.14</u>	<u>3.63</u>	6.13	<u>1.24</u>	<u>2.55</u>	<u>4.71</u>	7.66	1.30	<u>2.00</u>	<u>3.41</u>	<u>5.07</u>	<u>1.75</u>	3.25	5.04	7.56
Ham [8]	1.91	3.15	5.01	8.81	2.40	4.61	7.50	11.49	1.63	3.01	7.20	11.00	2.13	3.35	5.19	7.75
Ours	**1.12**	**1.84**	**3.09**	**5.41**	**0.86**	**1.92**	**3.75**	**6.19**	**0.96**	**1.54**	**2.99**	**4.91**	1.77	**2.71**	**3.53**	**5.07**

4.5 Chromaticity Map SR

We apply our model to chromaticity map SR. The test data are six color-scribbles/colorized image pairs provided by the authors of [17]. We first compute the LR map by down-sampling the colorized image and use it as the target image. We then use the HR color-scribbles map as guidance image to construct the output HR Chromaticity map.

Figure 3 shows the visual comparisons with the method of Bicubic, He [10] and Li [18]. Our results show more faithful edges and less color bleeding artifacts (3(f)). We also provide the qualitative evaluations in Table 5. We use the colorized image as the ground truth and calculate the RMSE values. The RMSE values in Table 5 show that our results best approximate the ground truth.

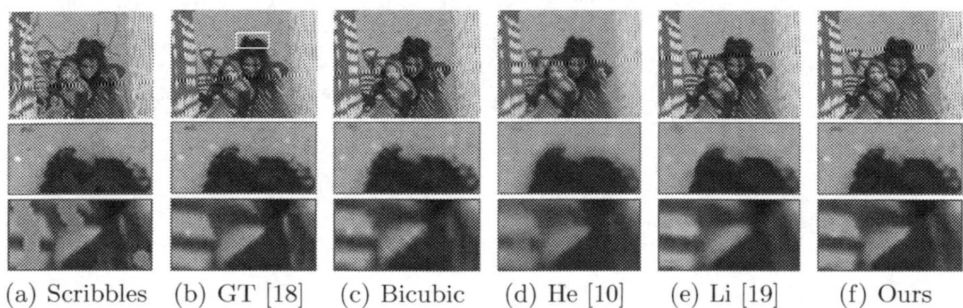

(a) Scribbles (b) GT [18] (c) Bicubic (d) He [10] (e) Li [19] (f) Ours

Fig. 3. Visual comparisons of chromaticity map SR results (2×).

4.6 Saliency Map SR

We also apply our trained JRP model in saliency map SR. We random collect eight color/saliency map pairs from MSRA10K salient object database [3] in the test. We use nearest-neighbor down-sampling to get the LR saliency map and use HR color map as the guidance image. We compare our results with those of Bicubic, He [10] and Li [18]. Visual comparison in Fig. 4 and numerical

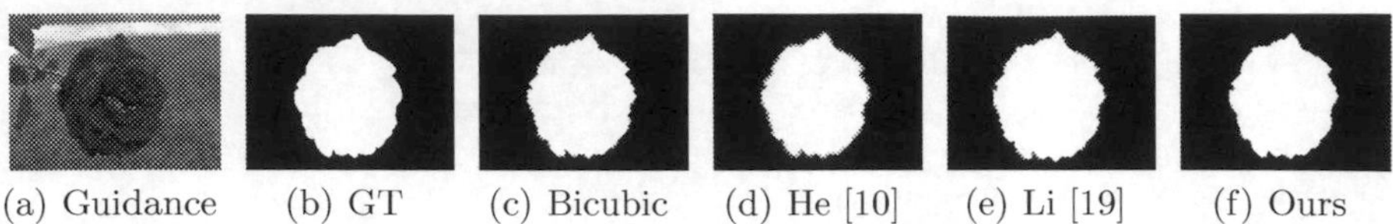

(a) Guidance (b) GT (c) Bicubic (d) He [10] (e) Li [19] (f) Ours

Fig. 4. Visual comparisons of saliency map SR results (4×).

Table 5. Average RMSE comparisons of different methods for chromaticity map SR and saliency map SR.

Methods	Bicubic	He [10]	Li [18]	Ours
2× Chromaticity	10.91	11.18	9.72	**6.93**
4× Chromaticity	20.54	17.99	14.18	**12.75**
2× Saliency	14.08	14.99	12.29	**10.64**
4× Saliency	23.05	21.08	18.27	**15.14**

comparison in Table 5 show that our results can better reconstruct image content by better transferring useful structure from the guidance image to the target image.

5 Conclusion and Future Work

We have proposed a joint convolution residual pyramid for joint image SR. Our model can enable large receptive fields and transfer useful structures from the guidance image to enhance the resolution of the target image. Experimental results verified the performance of method on joint depth map SR, chromaticity map SR and saliency map SR. In the future, we would like to apply our model on more applications.

References

1. Mac Aodha, O., Campbell, N.D.F., Nair, A., Brostow, G.J.: Patch based synthesis for single depth image super-resolution. In: Fitzgibbon, A., Lazebnik, S., Perona, P., Sato, Y., Schmid, C. (eds.) ECCV 2012. LNCS, vol. 7574, pp. 71–84. Springer, Heidelberg (2012). https://doi.org/10.1007/978-3-642-33712-3_6
2. Chen, Q., Koltun, V.: Photographic image synthesis with cascaded refinement networks. In: ICCV, pp. 1520–1529 (2017)
3. Cheng, M.M., Warrell, J., Lin, W.Y., Zheng, S., Vineet, V., Crook, N.: Efficient salient region detection with soft image abstraction. In: ICCV, pp. 1529–1536 (2013)
4. Diebel, J., Thrun, S.: An application of markov random fields to range sensing. In: NIPS, pp. 291–298 (2005)

5. Dong, C., Loy, C.C., He, K., Tang, X.: Learning a deep convolutional network for image super-resolution. In: Fleet, D., Pajdla, T., Schiele, B., Tuytelaars, T. (eds.) ECCV 2014. LNCS, vol. 8692, pp. 184–199. Springer, Cham (2014). https://doi.org/10.1007/978-3-319-10593-2_13
6. Dong, C., Loy, C.C., Tang, X.: Accelerating the super-resolution convolutional neural network. arXiv abs/1608.00367 (2016). http://arxiv.org/abs/1608.00367
7. Ferstl, D., Reinbacher, C., Ranftl, R., Ruether, M., Bischof, H.: Image guided depth upsampling using anisotropic total generalized variation. In: ICCV, pp. 993–1000 (2013)
8. Ham, B., Cho, M., Ponce, J.: Robust image filtering using joint static and dynamic guidance. In: CVPR, pp. 4823–4831 (2015)
9. He, K., Zhang, X., Ren, S., Sun, J.: Deep residual learning for image recognition. In: CVPR, pp. 770–778 (2016)
10. He, K., Sun, J., Tang, X.: Guided image filtering. In: ECCV, pp. 1–14 (2010)
11. Hirschmuller, H., Scharstein, D.: Evaluation of cost functions for stereo matching. In: CVPR, pp. 1–8 (2007)
12. Huang, G., Liu, Z., Weinberger, K.Q.: Densely connected convolutional networks. In: CVPR (2017)
13. Hui, T.-W., Loy, C.C., Tang, X.: Depth map super-resolution by deep multi-scale guidance. In: Leibe, B., Matas, J., Sebe, N., Welling, M. (eds.) ECCV 2016. LNCS, vol. 9907, pp. 353–369. Springer, Cham (2016). https://doi.org/10.1007/978-3-319-46487-9_22
14. Kopf, J., Cohen, M.F., Lischinski, D., Uyttendaele, M.: Joint bilateral upsampling. In: SIGGRAPH, p. 96 (2007)
15. Krizhevsky, A., Sutskever, I., Hinton, G.E.: Imagenet classification with deep convolutional neural networks. In: NIPS, pp. 1097–1105 (2012)
16. Lei, J., Li, L., Yue, H., Wu, F., Ling, N., Hou, C.: Depth map super-resolution considering view synthesis quality. TIP **26**(4), 1732 (2017)
17. Levin, A., Lischinski, D., Weiss, Y.: Colorization using optimization. In: SIGGRAPH, pp. 689–694 (2004)
18. Li, Y., Huang, J.-B., Ahuja, N., Yang, M.-H.: Deep joint image filtering. In: Leibe, B., Matas, J., Sebe, N., Welling, M. (eds.) ECCV 2016. LNCS, vol. 9908, pp. 154–169. Springer, Cham (2016). https://doi.org/10.1007/978-3-319-46493-0_10
19. Liu, M.Y., Tuzel, O., Taguchi, Y.: Joint geodesic upsampling of depth images. In: CVPR, pp. 169–176 (2013)
20. Lu, J., Forsyth, D.: Sparse depth super resolution. In: CVPR, pp. 2245–2253 (2015)
21. Lu, S., Ren, X., Liu, F.: Depth enhancement via low-rank matrix completion. In: CVPR, pp. 3390–3397 (2014)
22. Mathieu, M., Couprie, C., Lecun, Y.: Deep multi-scale video prediction beyond mean square error. In: ICLR (2016)
23. Park, J., Kim, H., Tai, Y.W., Brown, M.S., Kweon, I.: High quality depth map upsampling for 3D-TOF cameras. In: ICCV, pp. 1623–1630 (2011)
24. Ren, H., Elkhamy, M., Lee, J.: Image super resolution based on fusing multiple convolution neural networks. In: CVPR, pp. 1050–1057 (2017)
25. Scharstein, D., Szeliski, R.: A taxonomy and evaluation of dense two-frame stereo correspondence algorithms. IJCV **47**(1–3), 7–42 (2002)
26. Scharstein, D., Pal, C.: Learning conditional random fields for stereo. In: CVPR, pp. 1–8 (2007)
27. Shen, X., Chen, Y., Tao, X., Jia, J.: Convolutional neural pyramid for image processing. CoRR abs/1704.02071 (2017). http://arxiv.org/abs/1704.02071

28. Silberman, N., Hoiem, D., Kohli, P., Fergus, R.: Indoor segmentation and support inference from RGBD images. In: Fitzgibbon, A., Lazebnik, S., Perona, P., Sato, Y., Schmid, C. (eds.) ECCV 2012. LNCS, vol. 7576, pp. 746–760. Springer, Heidelberg (2012). https://doi.org/10.1007/978-3-642-33715-4_54
29. Simonyan, K., Zisserman, A.: Very deep convolutional networks for large-scale image recognition. Computer Science (2014)
30. Song, S., Lichtenberg, S.P., Xiao, J.: Sun RGB-D: a RGB-D scene understanding benchmark suite. In: CVPR, pp. 567–576 (2015)
31. Yang, J., Ye, X., Li, K., Hou, C., Wang, Y.: Color-guided depth recovery from RGB-D data using an adaptive autoregressive model. TIP **23**(8), 3443–3458 (2014)
32. Yang, Q., Yang, R., Davis, J., Nister, D.: Spatial-depth super resolution for range images. In: CVPR, pp. 1–8 (2007)

Reading More Efficiently: Multi-sentence Summarization with a Dual Attention and Copy-Generator Network

Xi Zhang, Hua-ping Zhang(✉), and Lei Zhao

Beijing Institute of Technology, No. 5, Zhongguancun South Street, Haidian Distirct, Beijing 100081, China
{xi_zhang,kevinzhang,zhao_lei}@bit.edu.cn

Abstract. Sequence-to-sequence neural networks with attention have been widely used in text summarization as the amount of textual data has exploded in recent years. The traditional approach to automatic summarization is based only on word attention and most of them focus on generating a single sentence summarization. In this work, we propose a novel model with a dual attention that considers both sentence and word information and then generates a multi-sentence summarization word by word. Additionally, we enhance our model with a copy-generator network to solve the out-of-vocabulary (OOV) problem. The model shows significant performance gains on the CNN/DailyMail corpus compared with the baseline model. Experimental results demonstrate that our method can obtain ROUGE-1 points of 37.48, ROUGE-2 points of 16.40 and ROUGE-L points of 34.36. Our work shows that several features of our proposed model contribute to further improvements in performance.

Keywords: Text summarization · Dual attention
Copy-generator network

1 Introduction

The growth in the amount of available textual information available - news, blogs, chats, reports, essays, etc. - has been explosive in recent years. As a result, the extraction of important content (i.e., salient ideas) from such a large body of source material has become an urgent need. Automatic text summarization provides an efficient solution through the generation of short summaries containing the main information from articles and excerpts.

There are two primary approaches to the task: extractive and abstractive. Extractive methods determine the most important sentences in the source text and then compose the summary. Abstractive methods apply advanced natural

This work was supported by National Natural Science Foundation of China (61772075).

X. Geng and B.-H. Kang (Eds.): PRICAI 2018, LNAI 11012, pp. 811–823, 2018.
https://doi.org/10.1007/978-3-319-97304-3_62

language processing algorithms to generate more concise abstracts using techniques such as transposition, synonymous substitution, sentence abbreviation, and so on. Abstractive methods generate new text, to the point of rephrasing and using words not present in the original text, producing output that more closely resembles human summaries. Because of the difficulty and uncertainty of abstractive summarization, early works proposed using extractive methods [4,14]. These methods reduced the task of the summary to identifying the most important sentences in the document, which is a task of sorting sentences. With the development of deep neural networks, abstractive summarization has advanced with it and achieved good results. Bahdanau *et al.* [1] first used a model called sequence to sequence in machine translation, using an encoding-decoding framework to encode the input sentence as an abstractive representation and then to decode an output sentence according to the encoded information. This method was soon applied to many areas of natural language processing, including speech recognition [3] and video captioning [21]. Rush *et al.*'s [17] neural attention model used enhanced training to generate a sentence representing the whole article. Much of the work on summarization has focused on producing a single sentence summary [2,25]. However, single sentence summaries are often inadequate, especially for users navigating a large number of headlines. In 2016, Nallapati *et al.* [12] proposed an English multi-sentence summarization data set. Multiple sentence summarization introduces other challenges, including the requirement for more abstraction and better handling of repeated sentences, but is ultimately more useful. In this paper, we pursue multiple sentence summarization using a novel model which inspired by the recent success of application neural networks. We construct our model with a bi-directional LSTM encoder and a dual attention-based decoder, as described in Sect. 3.2. To solve the out-of-vocabulary (OOV) words problem and improve the accuracy, we add a copy-generator network to enable the duplication of words from the original text or the generation the new words as needed.

To test the effectiveness of our method, we ran extensive comparisons with basic sequence to sequence attention models and abstractive methods. The main contributions of this paper are: (1) We conduct our experiment with sequence-to-sequence with attention using a multi-sentence data set. (2) We have presented a dual attention model and copy-generator network for multi-sentence summarization. (3) Our model progressively builds document vectors by aggregating important words vector to sentences vectors and then aggregating important sentences vectors to document vectors. And this idea can be used in multiple documents summarization. Section 4.4 describes the results of our tests demonstrating that our approach outperforms the baseline model by a high ROUGE points.

2 Related Work

Most of the early work on abstractive summarization focused on single sentence summarization, also known as sentence compression. However, single sentence summarization is inadequate for many uses. In particular, the information in many sources cannot be reduced to a single sentence. Nallapati *et al.* [12] modified the DeepMind question-answer dataset (Hermann *et al.* [9]) for use with summarization, added the CNN/Daily Mail dataset, proposed a new dataset consisting of multi-sentence summaries, and provided the first abstractive baselines for further research.

And then, there has been some work on multi-sentence summarization. See *et al.* [18] proposed a novel architecture that augmented the standard sequence to sequence attentional model in two orthogonal ways. Paulus *et al.* [15] introduced a neural network model with a novel intra-attention method that monitored the input and continuously generated output separately along with a new training method that combined standard supervised word prediction and reinforcement learning (RL). Nallapati *et al.* [11] presented two novel and contrasting architectures using Recurrent Neural Network (RNN) for extractive summarization of documents. Then, Nallapati *et al.* [10] presented SummaRuNNer, an RNN-based sequence model for extractive summarization of documents and showed that it achieved comparable or better performance compared to state-of-the-art methods.

The mechanism of attention may have been considered early, but the concept was first proposed formally in 2014. A paper by Dzmitry *et al.* [1] referred to the attention mechanism through alignment learning and translation. Numerous articles about attention emerged afterward. Wang *et al.* [23] introduced the application of a single attention model in the field of news recommendation and screening. Ren *et al.* [16] described the use of the hierarchical attention model to extract abstracts from articles. Tong *et al.* [20] described how to use the hierarchical attention model to help generate rock descriptions. In 2017, Nam *et al.* [13] proposed dual attention networks (DANs) which jointly leverage visual and textual attention mechanisms to capture fine-grained interplay between vision and language. Seo *et al.* [19] described the use of a dual attention model for a recommendation system.

The problem of rare and unknown words is an important issue that influences the performance of many NLP systems, including both traditional count-based and deep learning models. Vinyals *et al.* [22] introduced a new neural architecture to learn the conditional probability of an output sequence with elements that are discrete tokens corresponding to positions in an input sequence, called a Pointer Net (Ptr-Net). The architecture used attention as a pointer to select a member of the input sequence as the output. After that, the pointer network has been used to create hybrid approaches for Neural Machine Translation (NMT) (Gülçehre *et al.* [8]). Gu *et al.* [7] incorporated copying into the sequence to sequence learning model and proposed a new model called CopyNet that used an encoder-decoder structure. Zeng *et al.* [24] have proposed a simple copy mechanism that exploits very small vocabularies and handles out-of-vocabulary words. Unlike them, our pointer network also considers sentence information.

3 Models

In this section, we first describe the sequence to sequence attention model that serves as our baseline and then propose a dual attention model for summarization. Finally, we describe the added copy-generator machine.

3.1 Sequence to Sequence Text Summarization

The model structure that we used as our baseline is shown in the following figure. Dzmitry Bahdanau *et al.* [1] observed that the fixed-length vector representation would limit the performance of the encoder-decoder architecture (Fig. 1).

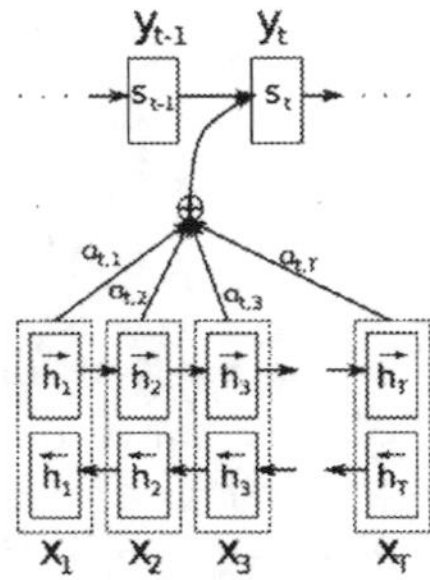

Fig. 1. Example of attention model. We made improvements to enable the model to find the contributing input sub-sequence automatically when outputting a single word.

The encoder here is a bi-directional RNN. We define the conditional probability as $P(y_i|y_1, y_2, ..., y_{i-1}, x) = g(y_{i-1}, s_i, c_i)$. The implicit state s_i is calculated as $s_i = f(s_{i-1}, y_{i-1}, c_i)$. The context vector calculation formula is

$$c_i = \sum_{j=1}^{T_x} \alpha_{ij} h_j \quad (1)$$

The weight parameter is

$$\alpha_{ij} = \frac{exp^{e_{ij}}}{\sum_{k=1}^{T_x} exp(e_{ik})} \quad (2)$$

where $e_{ij} = activation(s_{i-1}, h_j)$ is an "alignment model" used to characterize the matching degree between the jth position of the input sequence and the ith position of the output sequence and h_j indicates the combination of bi-directional RNN hidden states such that $h_j = [h_j^L; h_j^R]$. According to the characteristics of the RNN sequence, h_j contains more information in the neighborhood window of the sequence. α_{ij} is the normalized form of e_{ij} and c_i is the geometric mean calculating this information for all positions in the input sequence. In the author's article, this effect is referred to as an "attention mechanism".

3.2 Dual Attention

The following figure shows a diagram of the model. This model has two inputs: the word sequence provided to the word encoder network and the sentences sequence in the article provided to the sentence network. Then we can get a final vocabulary distribution (Fig. 2).

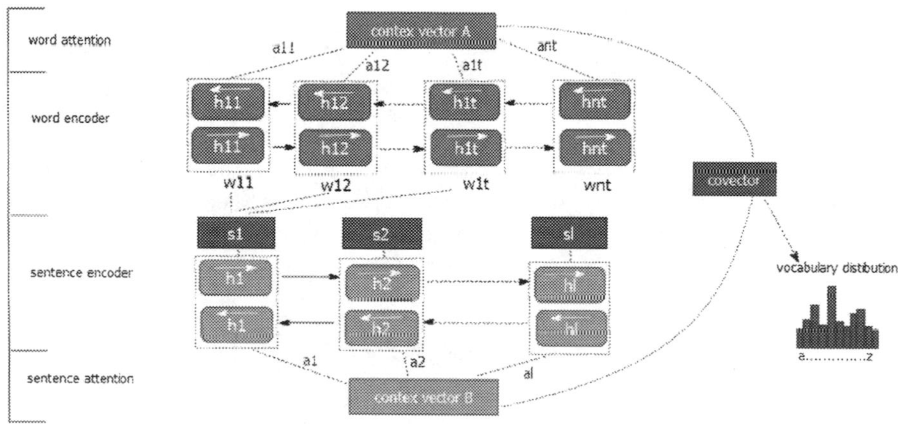

Fig. 2. Example of dual attention model. The two attentions are used together for the summarization, with the output of the dual attention model representing a concatenation.

The dual attention model is a parallel model unlike the basic attention model mentioned previously. The "dual attention" consists of word attention (w-Attn) and sentence attention (s-Attn). w-Attn identifies attractive keywords in the sliding window (based on keywords in the summarization preferences, such as "who", "where", "what" *et al.*). s-Attn analyzes the text for importance. As an example assume that a document has l sentences s_i with each sentence containing t words. w_{it} with $t\epsilon[1,t]$ represents the words in the ith sentence. The proposed model projects the raw document into a vector representation. In the following paragraphs, we present how we construct the dual structure using sentence and word level attention.

Word Encoder. Given a sentence with words w_{it}, $t\epsilon[0,t]$, we first embed the words into vectors through an embedding matrix W_e, $x_{it} = W_e w_{it}$. We use a bi-directional LSTM to obtain word annotations that incorporate contextual information from both directions of the words. The bi-directional LSTM contains the forward LSTM $\underset{f}{\rightarrow}$ that reads the sentence w_{i1} from w_{i1} to w_{it} and a backward LSTM$\underset{f}{\leftarrow}$ that reads from w_{it} to w_{i1}, described as:

$$x_{it} = W_e w_{it}, t \epsilon [1, t]$$
$$\overrightarrow{h_{it}} = \overrightarrow{LSTM}(x_{it}), t \epsilon [1, t],$$
$$\overleftarrow{h_{it}} = \overleftarrow{LSTM}(x_{it}), t \epsilon [t, 1],$$

We obtain an annotation for a given word w_{it} by concatenating the forward hidden state $\overrightarrow{h_{it}}$ and backward hidden state $h_{it} = [\overrightarrow{h_{it}}, \overleftarrow{h_{it}}]$, which summarizes the entire sentence centered around w_{it}. Note that we use word embeddings directly. For a more complete model we could use a LSTM to obtain word vectors directly from characters.

Word Attention. Not all words contribute equally to the representation of a sentence's meaning. Hence, we introduce an attention mechanism to extract words that are important to the meaning of the sentence and aggregate the representation of those informative words to form a context vector A. This done according to the following:

$$u_{it} = tanh(W_w h_{it} + b_w) \tag{3}$$

$$\alpha_{it} = \frac{exp(u_{it}^T u_w)}{\sum_t exp(u_{it}^T u_w)} \tag{4}$$

$$A = \sum_t \alpha_{it} h_{it} \tag{5}$$

We measure the importance of the word based on the similarity of u_{it} with a word level context vector u_w and the normalized importance weight α_{it} obtained through a softmax function. After that, we compute the context vector A (we abuse the notation here) as a weighted sum of the word annotations. The context vector u_w can be understood as a high level representation of a fixed query "What is the informative word" over the words. The word context vector u_w is randomly initialized and jointly learned during the training process.

Sentence Encoder. Given a sentence vector s_i, we can get sentence vectors $[w_{i1}, x_{i2}...x_{it}]$. We use a bidirectional LSTM to encode the sentences:

$$\overrightarrow{h_i} = \overrightarrow{LSTM}(s_i), t \epsilon [1, l],$$
$$\overleftarrow{h_i} = \overleftarrow{LSTM}(s_i), t \epsilon [l, 1],$$

We obtain the sentence vectors in a similar way. We concatenate h_i and h_j to produce an annotation of a sentence i, i.e., $h_i = [\overrightarrow{h_i}, \overleftarrow{h_i}]$. h_i summarizes the neighboring sentences around sentence i but still focuses on sentence i.

Sentence Attention. To prioritize sentences that are clues to the correct classification of a document, we again use an attention mechanism and introduce a sentence level context vector to measure the importance of the sentences. This yields

$$u_i = tanh(W_s h_i + b_s) \tag{6}$$

$$\alpha_i = \frac{exp(u_i^T u_s)}{\sum_i exp(u_i^T u_s)} \tag{7}$$

$$B = \sum_i \alpha_i h_i \tag{8}$$

where B is the vector that summarizes all the information of all the sentences in a document. Similarly, the sentence-level context vector can be randomly initialized and jointly learned during the training process. Then, we can get the covector $[A, B]$ that contains the information of two aspects. We can get vocabulary distribution $P_{vocab}(w)$

$$P_{vocab}(w) = softmax(V_0(V[[A, B], c_t] + b) + b_0) \tag{9}$$

where V, V_0, b and b_0 are learnable parameters. c_t is the decoder state. $P_{vocab}(w)$ is a probability distribution over all words in the vocabulary, and provides us with our nal distribution from which to predict words w.

3.3 Copy-Generator Network

In the copy-generator model depicted in Fig. 3, the attention distribution and covector $[A, B]$ are calculated as described in Sect. 3.2.

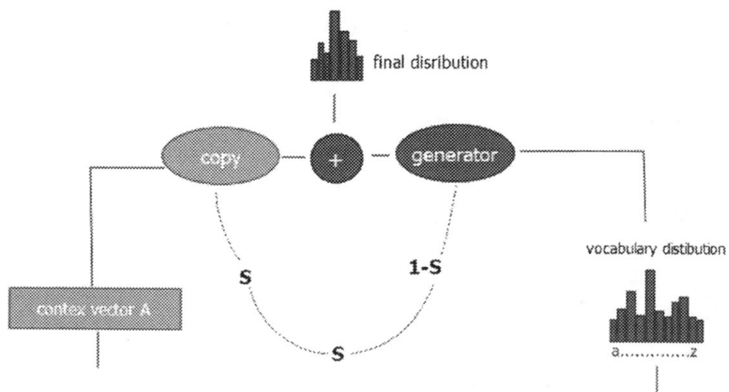

Fig. 3. Example of copy-generator. Our copy-generator network is a hybrid between our baseline and a pointer network (Vinyals *et al.* [22]), as it allows both the copying of words via pointers and the generation of words from a fixed vocabulary.

In addition, the generation probability $S_{gen} \in [0,1]$ for timestep t is calculated from the covector $[A,B]_t$, the decoder state c_t, and the decoder input w_t such that

$$S_{gen} = \sigma(w_{[A,B]}^T[A,B]_t + w_c^T c_t + w_w^T w_t + b) \tag{10}$$

where the vectors $w_{[A,B]}$, w_c, w_w and scalar b are learnable parameters and σ is the sigmoid function. Next, S_{gen} is used as a soft switch to choose between *generating* a word from the vocabulary by sampling from the vocabulary distribution, or *copying* a word from the input sequence by sampling from the word attention distribution a_{it}^t.

$$S(w) = S_{gen}P_{vocab}(w) + (1 - S_{gen})\sum[a_{it}^t] \tag{11}$$

Note that if w is an out-of-vocabulary (OOV) word, then $P_{vocab}(w)$ is zero; similarly if w does not appear in the source document, then $\sum[a_{it}^t]$ is zero. The ability to produce OOV words is one of the primary advantages of copy-generator models. In contrast, models such as our baseline are restricted to their pre-set vocabulary.

4 Experiments

In this section we describe the corpora we used, the evaluation metric, and implementation details of our approach along with the results of our tests.

4.1 Dataset

For our experiments, we used the CNN/DailyMail corpus originally constructed by (Hermann *et al.* [9]) for the task of passage-based answering of questions, and re-purposed for the task of document summarization as proposed in (Nallapati *et al.* [12]) for abstractive summarization. This corpus contains 286,817 training pairs, 13,368 validation pairs, and 11,487 test pairs. Nallapati *et al.* [12] provides the corpus scripts. The source contains online news articles (781 tokens on average) paired with multi-sentence summaries (3.75 sentences or 56 tokens on average). The story archives are available from the official websites for both CNN and the Daily Mail.

4.2 Evaluation Metric

We used the standard ROUGE metric [6] to evaluate our work. ROUGE measures the quality of the summary by computing overlapping lexical units, such as unigram, bigram, trigram, and longest common subsequence (LCS). It is the standard evaluation metric for DUC shared tasks and popular for summarization evaluation also. Following previous works, we used ROUGE-1 (unigram), ROUGE-2 (bigram), and ROUGE-L (LCS) as the evaluation metrics in our reported experimental results.

4.3 Implementation Details

Model Parameters. We initialized model parameters randomly using a Gaussian distribution. Our experiments were conducted with tensorflow, 256-dimensional hidden-units and 128-dimensional word embedding. We set the word embedding size to 128 and all LSTM hidden state sizes to 256. The word embeddings were learned from scratch during training. We used Adagrad (Duchi *et al.* [5]) as our optimizing algorithm or the hyperparameters of the Adam optimizer. We set learning rate to 0.15 and the initial accumulator value to 0.1.

Computational Costs. We trained all our models on two *Titan X* GPUs with a batch size of 16. Training required 8439 MB of GPU memory and several seconds for one training step, saving checkpoints to path. The summary generation process was reasonably fast with a throughput of about 20 summaries per second on a single GPU using a batch size of 1.

Beam Search. We used a beam search to generate multiple summary candidates to obtain better results. To avoid favoring shorter outputs, we averaged the ranking score along the beam path by dividing it by the number of generated words. We set the beam size to 4 both to decode quickly and to receive improved results.

4.4 Results

We first compared our dual attention model with the baseline model. The basic sequence to sequence model with attention using the LSTM for the encoder and decoder both. With just a simple attention in the model, the algorithm cannot capture structure information from the source text. For our dual attention model, we uses a bi-directional LSTM cell encoder and a single LSTM decoder. Our dual-level encoder has a parallel level structure, giving it a natural application to the text summarization task. We first trained both the baseline and dual attention models for 50,000 iterations (about 2 epochs). Training took about 12 h for the 50k vocabulary model.

Table 1. ROUGE F_1 scores on the test set.

Model	Rouge		
	1	*2*	*L*
seq2seq+attn	13.75	1.43	12.79
seq2seq+dual attn	14.77	1.53	13.71

Our results are given in Table 1. We evaluated our models with the standard ROUGE metric, reporting the F1 scores for ROUGE-1, ROUGE-2 and ROUGE-L (which respectively measure the word overlap, bigram overlap, and longest common sequence between the reference summary and the summary to be evaluated). We obtained our ROUGE scores using the pyrouge package. All of our ROUGE scores have a 95% confidence interval of at most ±0.25 as reported by the official ROUGE script. According to Table 1, it can be seen that our dual attention model has a small improvement compared with the simple sequence to sequence baseline model. Our model outperformed the baseline by 2 ROUGE points.

Table 2. ROUGE F_1 scores on the test set

Model	Rouge		
	1	*2*	*L*
seq2seq+attn	33.63	13.35	30.98
abstractive model(nallapi)	35.46	13.30	32.65
dual attn+copy-generate	37.48	16.40	34.36

Table 3. Examples of source document

Source document
real madrid fell to a lacklustre 1-0 defeat at the hands of athletic bilbao saturday , potentially handing the la liga advantage to arch rival barcelona . a stunning header from aritz aduriz shortly before half time was enough to win the day for an organized and impressive bilbao *(...)* gareth bale struck a post with an extraordinary shot from close to the halfway line as full time approached while arduriz almost doubled bilbao 's lead with another headed chance late on . the result means second placed barca can now take top spot should it win at home to mid-table rayo vallecano sunday *(...)*

After the first test, we added the copy-generator machine to our dual attention model. We trained both our baseline models for about 600,000 iterations (33 epochs), similar to the 35 epochs required by Nallapati *et al.* 's [12] best model. Training took about 6 days for the 50k vocabulary. We trained our copy-generator model about 38,4274 training iterations (21.5 epochs). Notably, the copy-generator model made much quicker progress in the early phases of training.

Our model made obvious improvements compared with the simple sequence to sequence baseline model as shown in Table 2. And compared with Nallapati *et al.* 's [12], our model, performance on ROUGE-1 increased by approximately 4 points, on ROUGE-2 by approximately 3 points, and on ROUGE-L by approximately 3 points.

Table 3 shows the source documents. Result shown in the Table 4, example from the CNN/Daily Mail test dataset showing the outputs of our models. The baseline model appears to struggle with the rare word. In addition, the baseline model can't reproduce out-of-vocabulary words (such as bundesliga bilbao in

Table 4. Examples of summmarizations

Reference summary
real madrid slump to defeat against athletic bilbao.solitary goal from aritz aduriz enough to give the basques victory. bayern munich continue bundesliga domination.
seq2seq+attn
real madrid beat athletic UNK 1-0 at rayo vallecano to go top of UNK.real madrid beat barcelona 1-0 at home to rayo vallecano on sunday .real are now without a win in two league games at rayo vallecano.
dual attn
real madrid beat rayo vallecano 3-1 at the bernabeu on sunday. real madrid 's cristiano ronaldo scores twice as real madrid beat UNK 4-1 in the champions league on sunday. real madrid beat osasuna 2-0 at the bottom of the UNK .
dual attn+copy generator
real madrid beat athletic bilbao 1-0 at the hands of athletic bilbao. gareth bale scores a stunning header from aritz aduriz. real are now without a win in two league games while real are now up to eighth.

Table 4). Our dual attention model seems better. After added the copy-generator net work, the OOV problem is solved. It is accurate but repeats itself.

5 Conclusion

In this paper, we have presented a dual attention model and copy-generator network for multi-sentence summarization. Experimental results demonstrate that our designed model performs significantly better than previous methods. But there also a lot of repeated words's problem. And we only conducted experiments on English data sets. There is no Chinese multi-sentence summarization data set yet. Our next work may build Chinese multi-sentence summarization data sets.

References

1. Bahdanau, D., Cho, K., Bengio, Y.: Neural machine translation by jointly learning to align and translate. CoRR abs/1409.0473 (2014). http://arxiv.org/abs/1409.0473
2. Chopra, S., Auli, M., Rush, A.M.: Abstractive sentence summarization with attentive recurrent neural networks. In: The 2016 Conference of the North American Chapter of the Association for Computational Linguistics: Human Language Technologies, NAACL HLT 2016, San Diego, California, USA, 12–17 June 2016, pp. 93–98 (2016). http://aclweb.org/anthology/N/N16/N16-1012.pdf
3. Chorowski, J., Bahdanau, D., Serdyuk, D., Cho, K., Bengio, Y.: Attention-based models for speech recognition. In: Advances in Neural Information Processing Systems 28: Annual Conference on Neural Information Processing Systems 2015, 7–12 December 2015, Montreal, Quebec, Canada, pp. 577–585 (2015). http://papers.nips.cc/paper/5847-attention-based-models-for-speech-recognition

4. Dorr, B., Zajic, D., Schwartz, R.: Hedge trimmer: a parse-and-trim approach to headline generation. In: Proceedings of the HLT-NAACL 2003 on Text Summarization Workshop, vol. 5, pp. 1–8. Association for Computational Linguistics (2003)
5. Duchi, J.C., Hazan, E., Singer, Y.: Adaptive subgradient methods for online learning and stochastic optimization. J. Mach. Learn. Res. **12**, 2121–2159 (2011)
6. Flick, C.: Rouge: a package for automatic evaluation of summaries. In: The Workshop on Text Summarization Branches Out, p. 10 (2004)
7. Gu, J., Lu, Z., Li, H., Li, V.O.K.: Incorporating copying mechanism in sequence-to-sequence learning. In: Proceedings of the 54th Annual Meeting of the Association for Computational Linguistics, ACL 2016, 7–12 August 2016, Berlin, Germany, Volume 1: Long Papers (2016). http://aclweb.org/anthology/P/P16/P16-1154.pdf
8. Gülçehre, Ç., Ahn, S., Nallapati, R., Zhou, B., Bengio, Y.: Pointing the unknown words. In: Proceedings of the 54th Annual Meeting of the Association for Computational Linguistics, ACL 2016, 7–12 August 2016, Berlin, Germany, Volume 1: Long Papers (2016). http://aclweb.org/anthology/P/P16/P16-1014.pdf
9. Hermann, K.M., Kociský, T., Grefenstette, E., Espeholt, L., Kay, W., Suleyman, M., Blunsom, P.: Teaching machines to read and comprehend. In: Advances in Neural Information Processing Systems 28: Annual Conference on Neural Information Processing Systems 2015, 7–12 December 2015, Montreal, Quebec, Canada, pp. 1693–1701 (2015). http://papers.nips.cc/paper/5945-teaching-machines-to-read-and-comprehend
10. Nallapati, R., Zhai, F., Zhou, B.: Summarunner: a recurrent neural network based sequence model for extractive summarization of documents. In: Proceedings of the Thirty-First AAAI Conference on Artificial Intelligence, 4–9 February 2017, San Francisco, California, USA, pp. 3075–3081 (2017). http://aaai.org/ocs/index.php/AAAI/AAAI17/paper/view/14636
11. Nallapati, R., Zhou, B., Ma, M.: Classify or select: neural architectures for extractive document summarization. CoRR abs/1611.04244 (2016). http://arxiv.org/abs/1611.04244
12. Nallapati, R., Zhou, B., dos Santos, C.N., Gülçehre, Ç., Xiang, B.: Abstractive text summarization using sequence-to-sequence RNNs and beyond. In: Proceedings of the 20th SIGNLL Conference on Computational Natural Language Learning, CoNLL 2016, Berlin, Germany, 11–12 August 2016, pp. 280–290 (2016). http://aclweb.org/anthology/K/K16/K16-1028.pdf
13. Nam, H., Ha, J., Kim, J.: Dual attention networks for multimodal reasoning and matching. In: 2017 IEEE Conference on Computer Vision and Pattern Recognition, CVPR 2017, Honolulu, HI, USA, 21–26 July 2017, pp. 2156–2164 (2017). https://doi.org/10.1109/CVPR.2017.232,
14. Neto, J.L., Freitas, A.A., Kaestner, C.A.A.: Automatic text summarization using a machine learning approach. In: Bittencourt, G., Ramalho, G.L. (eds.) SBIA 2002. LNCS (LNAI), vol. 2507, pp. 205–215. Springer, Heidelberg (2002). https://doi.org/10.1007/3-540-36127-8_20
15. Paulus, R., Xiong, C., Socher, R.: A deep reinforced model for abstractive summarization. CoRR abs/1705.04304 (2017). http://arxiv.org/abs/1705.04304
16. Ren, P., Chen, Z., Ren, Z., Wei, F., Ma, J., de Rijke, M.: Leveraging contextual sentence relations for extractive summarization using a neural attention model. In: Proceedings of the 40th International ACM SIGIR Conference on Research and Development in Information Retrieval, Shinjuku, Tokyo, Japan, 7–11 August 2017, pp. 95–104 (2017). https://doi.org/10.1145/3077136.3080792

17. Rush, A.M., Chopra, S., Weston, J.: A neural attention model for abstractive sentence summarization. In: EMNLP, pp. 379–389. The Association for Computational Linguistics (2015)
18. See, A., Liu, P.J., Manning, C.D.: Get to the point: summarization with pointer-generator networks. In: Proceedings of the 55th Annual Meeting of the Association for Computational Linguistics, ACL 2017, Vancouver, Canada, 30 July–4 August, Volume 1: Long Papers, pp. 1073–1083 (2017). https://doi.org/10.18653/v1/P17-1099
19. Seo, S., Huang, J., Yang, H., Liu, Y.: Interpretable convolutional neural networks with dual local and global attention for review rating prediction. In: Proceedings of the Eleventh ACM Conference on Recommender Systems, RecSys 2017, Como, Italy, 27–31 August 2017, pp. 297–305 (2017). https://doi.org/10.1145/3109859.3109890
20. Tong, B., et al.: Learning to generate rock descriptions from multivariate well logs with hierarchical attention. In: Proceedings of the 23rd ACM SIGKDD International Conference on Knowledge Discovery and Data Mining, Halifax, NS, Canada, 13–17 August 2017, pp. 2031–2040 (2017). https://doi.org/10.1145/3097983.3098132
21. Venugopalan, S., Xu, H., Donahue, J., Rohrbach, M., Mooney, R.J., Saenko, K.: Translating videos to natural language using deep recurrent neural networks. In: The 2015 Conference of the North American Chapter of the Association for Computational Linguistics: Human Language Technologies, NAACL HLT 2015, Denver, Colorado, USA, 31 May–5 June 2015, pp. 1494–1504 (2015). http://aclweb.org/anthology/N/N15/N15-1173.pdf
22. Vinyals, O., Fortunato, M., Jaitly, N.: Pointer networks. In: Advances in Neural Information Processing Systems 28: Annual Conference on Neural Information Processing Systems 2015, 7–12 December 2015, Montreal, Quebec, Canada, pp. 2692–2700 (2015). http://papers.nips.cc/paper/5866-pointer-networks
23. Wang, X., et al.: Dynamic attention deep model for article recommendation by learning human editors' demonstration. In: Proceedings of the 23rd ACM SIGKDD International Conference on Knowledge Discovery and Data Mining, Halifax, NS, Canada, 13–17 August 2017, pp. 2051–2059 (2017). https://doi.org/10.1145/3097983.3098096
24. Zeng, W., Luo, W., Fidler, S., Urtasun, R.: Efficient summarization with read-again and copy mechanism. CoRR abs/1611.03382 (2016). http://arxiv.org/abs/1611.03382
25. Zhou, Q., Yang, N., Wei, F., Zhou, M.: Selective encoding for abstractive sentence summarization. In: Proceedings of the 55th Annual Meeting of the Association for Computational Linguistics, ACL 2017, Vancouver, Canada, 30 July–4 August, Volume 1: Long Papers, pp. 1095–1104 (2017). https://doi.org/10.18653/v1/P17-1101

Staged Generative Adversarial Networks with Adversarial-Boundary

Zhifan Li, Dandan Song[(✉)], and Lejian Liao

Beijing Engineering Research Center of High Volume Language Information Processing and Cloud Computing Applications, Beijing Key Laboratory of Intelligent Information Technology, School of Computer Science and Technology, Beijing Institute of Technology, Beijing 100081, China
{lizhifan,sdd,liaolj}@bit.edu.cn

Abstract. Generative Adversarial Networks (GANs) provide a novel way to learn disentangled representations. However, it is still challenging for them to generate convincing images. In this paper we introduce a novel *Adversarial-Boundary Staged Generative Adversarial Networks* (ABS-GAN) to generate more realistic images. ABS-GAN improves image quality from two aspects. On one hand, the complete training process is separated into two stages. The Stage-I generator is trained for decreasing the Earth-Mover distance between real and generated distributions. The Stage-II generator aims at explicitly reducing the distance further based on the Stage-I generator. On the other hand, the discriminator is treated as a projector from image to scalar. The discriminator tries to make the boundary between real and generated distributions clear in scalar space. Thus the generator synthesizes more realistic images, thanks to the extra adversarial boundary information. We conduct experiments on real-world datasets (CIFAR-10, STL-10, CelebA) to show the performance of our ABS-GAN. Comparisons with baseline model on benchmark datasets demonstrate that the proposed method achieves excellent improvement in producing convincing images in a simple way.

Keywords: StageGAN · Adversarial-boundary · ABS-GAN

1 Introduction

Generative Adversarial Networks (GANs) [5] are novel methods for unsupervised and semi-supervised learning. With adversarial generator and discriminator, GANs cast generative process into a minimax game. The generator is trained for producing realistic images while the discriminator attempts to distinguish generated images from real ones. The main advantage of GANs is that they can represent all distributions, even if the distribution can not be quantified, whereas methods based on Markov chains require that the distribution have specific mathematical form.

X. Geng and B.-H. Kang (Eds.): PRICAI 2018, LNAI 11012, pp. 824–836, 2018.
https://doi.org/10.1007/978-3-319-97304-3_63

GANs have shown promising results in numerous challenging tasks, such as realistic image generation [6,8], image manipulation [26], text-to-image synthesis [16,25], information retrieval [22] and text generation [24].

Despite of the great success, there are several obstacles for current GAN models to overcome. It is still challenging to generate convincing images on datasets with high variability, e.g., CIFAR-10. Most GAN variants attempt to improve image quality at the cost of making generator and discriminator more and more complicated.

We argue that there exists two different ways to improve the generated image quality. On one hand, it's a natural idea to train a better generator directly. On the other hand, we can also aim at training a better discriminator, and get a better generator, due to the adversarial training process.

In this paper, we introduce novel methods to generate better images from this two aspects. To directly train a better generator, we first separate the complete training process into two stages. The Stage-I generator is trained for decreasing Earth-Mover distance [1] between real and generated distributions. The Stage-II generator aims at explicitly reducing the distance further based on the Stage-I generator. Then we treat the discriminator as a projector from image space to scalar space. We encourage the discriminator to make the boundary between real and generated distribution clear in scalar space. Thanks to the adversarial training process, we also get a better generator. We conduct experiments on real-world datasets (CIFAR-10, STL-10, CelebA) to demonstrate both qualitative and quantitative performance of our proposed model.

The rest of this paper is organized as follows. In Sect. 2, we review several recent works related to ours. In Sect. 3, we introduce notations and the preliminary GAN models. We then derive Staged Generative Adversarial Networks (StageGAN) in Sect. 4.1 and Adversarial-Boundary Generative Adversarial Networks (AB-GAN) in Sect. 4.2. As a combined result, we introduce the eventual Adversarial-Boundary Staged Generative Adversarial Networks (ABS-GAN) in Sect. 4.3. To demonstrate the improvement of our models, we present both qualitative and quantitative results in Sect. 5. Finally we conclude the paper and discuss the future work in Sect. 6.

2 Related Works

GANs [5] provide a new way to learn representations even without quantifying the distribution. However, the original GAN is trained by MLP and only succeeds in generate convincing grayscale images on MNIST. Since convolutional neural networks (CNNs) play more and more important roles in computer vision task [7,19,20], Radford et al. [15] proposed DCGAN to bridge the gap between CNNs and GANs. With several techniques, such as batch normalization and LeakyReLU, DCGAN generates more realistic images than ever before. However, it still suffers from training instability and mode collapse.

Arjovsky et al. [1,2] proved that it was Jensen-Shannon divergence that made GANs training unstable. Alternatively, they proposed Earth-Mover (EM) distance, which has better theoretical properties than the original. Furthermore, they derived Wasserstein GANs (WGAN) to cure the main training problems of GANs thoroughly. Gulrajani et al. [6] proposed WGAN-GP that replaced weight clipping with gradient penalty. WGAN-GP succeeds in training with deep 101-layer ResNet [7] and synthesizes attractive images on several challenging datasets. Petzka et al. [14] improved WGAN-GP by using a weaker regularization term to enforce the Lipschitz constraint.

Class label information has been proven very helpful in improving the generated image quality. Mirza et al. [12] proposed Conditional GAN by concatenating class labels and feature maps. For the first time, GAN could produce samples with specific class. Odena et al. [13] devised AC-GAN by adding an auxiliary classifier. During training, AC-GAN explicitly assigned each generated sample a specific label as its target class.

Besides these models with exactly one generator and one discriminator, there are several GAN variants using more generators or discriminators. D2GAN [21] has two discriminator and one generator. One discriminator rewards high scores for samples from real distribution whilst another discriminator, conversely, favoring data from the generated distribution, and the generator produces data to fool both two discriminators. MAD-GAN [4] incorporates multiple generators capable of generating samples from high probability modes, which enforces different generators to generate samples from diverse modes.

Instead of one complete training process, GANs can also be trained in several stages. When processing text-to-image synthesis task, Zhang et al. [25] proposed a novel StackGAN to decompose the hard problem into more manageable subproblems through a sketch-refinement process. Stage-I GAN sketches the primitive shape and basic colors of the object conditioned on the given text descriptions. Stage-II GAN corrects the defects in Stage-I results and completes details of the object by reading the text description again, yielding higher resolution images with better image quality. In short, the Stage-II GAN is trained to refine the results from the Stage-I GAN. To our knowledge, it was the first time to separate GAN training process into several sub-stages. Contrary to StackGAN, we adopt same networks for each stage and none of them are well-designed, making our ABS-GAN simpler but more general.

3 Preliminaries

3.1 Generative Adversarial Networks

Generative Adversarial Networks [5] learns a distribution p_g simulating the real distribution p_r. The generator G is a neural network transforming random noise $z \sim p_z$ into images, while the discriminator D is a standard binary classifier outputing the probability that x comes from true distribution.

The generator and discriminator play the following minmax game:

$$\min_G \max_D \ \mathbb{E}_{x \sim p_r} [\log D(x)] + \mathbb{E}_{z \sim p_z} [\log (1 - D(G(z)))] \tag{1}$$

With the $-\log D$ trick, the generator attempts to minimize:

$$-\ \mathbb{E}_{z\sim p_z}\left[\log D\left(G\left(z\right)\right)\right] \tag{2}$$

If given enough capacity and training time, p_g will converge to a good estimator of p_r, where the discriminator cannot tell generated images from real ones. At that time, the training process stopped and we got the perfect generator, theoretically. However, GAN models suffer from training instability and model collapse in practice.

3.2 AC-GAN

GAN can produce samples with more variability, if taking both noise z and class label c into consideration. Odena et al. [13] proposed AC-GAN to synthesize more convincing images. AC-GAN is a class conditional GAN [12], but with an auxiliary classifier that is tasked with reconstructing class labels. They assign each sample a target label, and the auxiliary classifier tries to maximize the probability that x is classified into target class.

Besides the loss functions in original GAN, the discriminator and generator in AC-GAN also maximize the following softmax entropy:

$$\mathbb{E}_x\left[-\sum_{i=1}^{K} y_i \log p_i\right] \tag{3}$$

where y is the real distribution of x's target label, and p is the output label distribution from auxiliary classifier.

3.3 WGANs

Arjovsky et al. [1,2] proved that GAN got unstable because it tried to minimizing Jensen-Shannon distance between distributions, which is not a good metric when distributions are nearly non-overlapping. They proposed EM distance and derived WGAN under K-Lipschitz constraint. In their work, weight clipping is used to satisfy K-Lipschitz continuity: $\nabla_x D(x) \leq K$.

From WGAN on, the discriminator D is also called critic, because it outputs a real value rather than a probability.

And the minmax game between generator and critic is given as:

$$\min_G \max_D\ \mathbb{E}_{x\sim p_r}\left[D\left(x\right)\right] - \mathbb{E}_{z\sim p_z}\left[D\left(G\left(z\right)\right)\right] \tag{4}$$

Gulrajani et al. [6] pointed the drawbacks of weight clipping in critic and proposed WGAN-GP that meet 1-Lipschitz constraint by gradient penalty.

The minmax game in WGAN-GP becomes:

$$\min_G \max_D\ \mathbb{E}_{x\sim p_r}\left[D\left(x\right)\right] - \mathbb{E}_{\tilde{x}\sim p_g}\left[D\left(\tilde{x}\right)\right] + \lambda \mathbb{E}_{\hat{x}\sim p_{\hat{x}}}\left[\left(||\nabla_{\hat{x}} D(\hat{x}) - 1||_2\right)^2\right] \tag{5}$$

where $\hat{x}$ is sampled from the straight line between x and $\tilde{x}$, and λ controls the importance of gradient penalty item respect to original EM loss.

Under unsupervised settings, WGAN-GP directly optimizes EM distance. For supervised learning, it also maximizes the softmax entropy from AC-GAN.

4 Methods

4.1 StageGAN

We divide the complete training process into two stages. In Stage-I, the generator G_1 aims at decreasing the EM distance as WGAN-GP does. We use the same loss function with WGAN-GP for both generator G_1 and critic D_1. In Stage-II, the generator G_2 is trained not only for reducing the EM distance further, but also generating better images than G_1. It is natural to investigate how to define "better" between G_1 and G_2.

We first introduce some important notations. With p_{G_1}, p_{G_2} being the distribution generated by G_1, G_2 respectively, let EMD_1 denote the distance between p_r and p_{G_1}, EMD_2 denote the distance between the p_r and p_{G_2}.

As Arjovsky et al. [2] pointed out, under 1-Lipschitz constraint, the EM distance between p_G and p_r is:

$$EMD = \mathbb{E}_{x \sim p_r}\left[D\left(x\right)\right] - \mathbb{E}_{x \sim p_G}\left[D\left(x\right)\right] \tag{6}$$

We can encourage G_2 to generate better images than G_1 by adding the following constraint on G_2:

$$EMD_2 < EMD_1 \tag{7}$$

With relaxing constraint and enough training iterations, the target constraint is equivalent to:

$$\max_{G_2} \; EMD_1 - EMD_2 \tag{8}$$

In WGANs, EM distance is measured by the critic D. Since we have two critics, it is necessary to make a better choice between them.

If D_2 is selected as the public critic to measure the closer distribution distance, then EMD_1 and EMD_2 are given as:

$$EMD_1 = \mathbb{E}_{x \sim p_r}\left[D_2\left(x\right)\right] - \mathbb{E}_{x \sim p_{G_1}}\left[D_2\left(x\right)\right] \tag{9}$$

$$EMD_2 = \mathbb{E}_{x \sim p_r}\left[D_2\left(x\right)\right] - \mathbb{E}_{x \sim p_{G_2}}\left[D_2\left(x\right)\right] \tag{10}$$

When training G_2, both p_r and p_{G_1} are constraints. Substitute Eqs. 9 and 10 into Eq. 8 and ignore constant terms, we get the following target function:

$$\max_{G_2} \; \mathbb{E}_{x \sim p_{G_2}}\left[D_2\left(x\right)\right] \tag{11}$$

Since it is exactly the loss function of G_2 in original WGANs, we argue that it makes no contribution to StageGAN when compared with WGANs.

Alternatively, if we choose D_1 as the public critic, then EMD_1 and EMD_2 are calculated as:

$$EMD_1 = \mathbb{E}_{x \sim p_r}\left[D_1\left(x\right)\right] - \mathbb{E}_{x \sim p_{G_1}}\left[D_1\left(x\right)\right] \tag{12}$$

$$EMD_2 = \mathbb{E}_{x \sim p_r}\left[D_1\left(x\right)\right] - \mathbb{E}_{x \sim p_{G_2}}\left[D_1\left(x\right)\right] \tag{13}$$

Based on the fact that p_{G_1} and p_r are constants for G_2, we substitute Eqs. 12 and 13 into Eq. 8 and get a more reasonable loss function:

$$\max_{G_2} \mathbb{E}_{x\sim p_{G_2}}\left[D_1(x)\right] \tag{14}$$

Since we train D_1 in Stage-I with standard WGAN-GP, we believe that D_1 is a relatively good critic for measuring the distance between distributions.

Taking the original EM loss function into consideration, G_2 minimizes:

$$\min_{G_2} -\alpha\, \mathbb{E}_{x\sim p_{G_2}}\left[D_1(x)\right] - \beta\, \mathbb{E}_{x\sim p_{G_2}}\left[D_2(x)\right] \tag{15}$$

where α and β adjust the importance between gradients from D_1 and D_2.

To make training process simple, we first train G_1 and D_1 in Stage-I. Then we fix G_1 and D_1 and only train G_2 and D_2 adversarially in Stage-II. In this way, we derive another explanation for Eq. 15. Gradients from both historical critic D_1 and current critic D_2 provide guidance for updating G_2. Inspired by this, we can treat the softmax entropy in the same way when training StageGAN under supervised settings.

Note that we only attempt to encourage G_2 to generate better images, thus the loss function of D_1, D_2 and G_1 are same with WGAN-GP. They are given as:

$$\min_{G_1} -\mathbb{E}_{x\sim p_{G_1}}\left[D_1(x)\right] \tag{16}$$

$$\max_{D_1} \mathbb{E}_{x\sim p_r}\left[D_1(x)\right] - \mathbb{E}_{\tilde{x}\sim p_{G_1}}\left[D_1(\tilde{x})\right] + \lambda \mathbb{E}_{\hat{x}\sim p_{\hat{x}}}\left[\left(||\nabla_{\hat{x}} D_1(\hat{x}) - 1||_2\right)^2\right] \tag{17}$$

$$\max_{D_2} \mathbb{E}_{x\sim p_r}\left[D_2(x)\right] - \mathbb{E}_{\tilde{x}\sim p_{G_2}}\left[D_2(\tilde{x})\right] + \lambda \mathbb{E}_{\hat{x}\sim p_{\hat{x}}}\left[\left(||\nabla_{\hat{x}} D_2(\hat{x}) - 1||_2\right)^2\right] \tag{18}$$

To make training process economical, we use same network architecture at both stage. Before Stage-II starts, we copy parameters from the well-trained D_1, G_1 to D_2, G_2. Since G_1 makes no contribution to Stage-II except providing initial parameters for G_2, it is enough to use only one generator from beginning to end. That is, we train the same generator at both stages.

To make training process stable, we need ensure the transition from Stage-I to Stage-II be smooth enough. In other words, the loss function of D_1 and D_2 should be identical when Stage-II begins. From the loss function, we can see that D_1 and D_2 have the same loss already at the beginning of Stage-II, because D_2 and G_2 are inherited from D_1 and G_1. To stabilize generator, we add constraint $\alpha + \beta = 1$ to G_2. When Stage-II begins, the loss function of G_1 and G_2 are identical, since D_1 is equivalent to D_2 already.

Eventually, G_2 minimizes:

$$\min_{G_2} -\alpha\, \mathbb{E}_{x\sim p_{G_2}}\left[D_1(x)\right] - (1-\alpha)\cdot \mathbb{E}_{x\sim p_{G_2}}\left[D_2(x)\right] \tag{19}$$

4.2 AB-GAN

The critic can be seen as a projector from image space to scalar space or 1-D axis, since it takes an image as input and outputs a scalar. Because EM distance between real and generated distribution is always positive and the critic is trained for maximizing this EM distance, we believe that the critic attempts to project real images into the positive direction of the 1-D axis and to project generative images into the negative direction of the 1-D axis (Fig. 1).

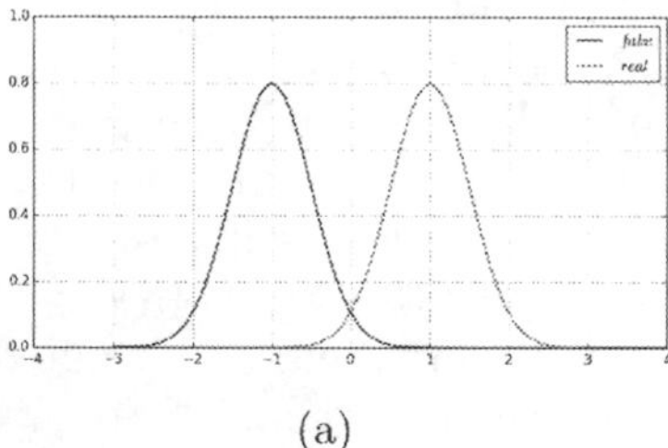

(a)

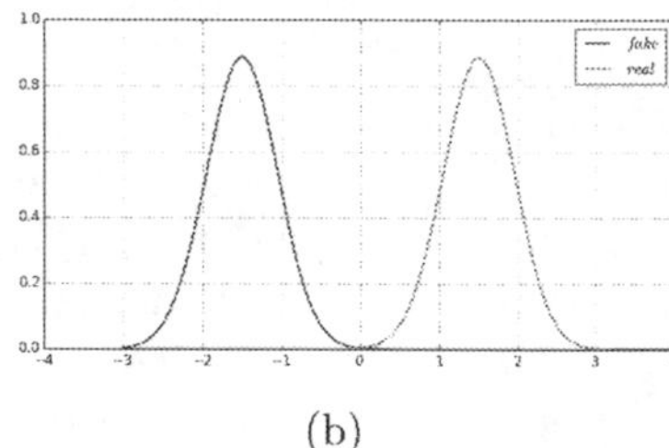

(b)

Fig. 1. The critic projects real (in green) and generative (in blue) images into 1-D axis. (a) Critics in WGANs ignore the overlapping boundary. (b) With adversarial boundary, AB-GAN separates the overlapping regions. Distributions may be any form, and gaussian is only used for illustrating overlapping. (Color figure online)

In original WGANs, the critic tries to maximize the distance between the mean values of two projection area. However, if the projection areas overlap to some extent, the critic can be confused near the boundary. When critic has trouble in distinguishing generated samples from real ones, the training process tends to be stopped unexpectedly. Since what we want is a wiser critic, the boundary between projection area should be clear enough. To satisfy this constraint, we need maximize the lower bound of projection area of real distribution and minimize the upper bound of generated distribution. Thus we append the following item to critic's EM loss:

$$\max\{\min_{x\sim p_r} D(x)\} + \min\{\max_{x\sim p_g} D(x)\} \tag{20}$$

To balance the adversarial training process between generator and critic, an extra item is also added to generator's loss:

$$\max\{\max_{x\sim p_g} D(x)\} \tag{21}$$

Note that the adversarial boundary loss is only used for helping improving WGAN performance. To encourage WGANs to pay more attention to the original EM loss, we use a hyper-parameter δ to control the importance of boundary loss.

4.3 ABS-GAN

StageGAN improves GAN performance by forcing the generator to produce better images explicitly and directly, while AB-GAN does in an indirect way, since we intend to train a clever critic at the beginning. In other words, this two methods promote GAN models from different aspects. Putting them together, we can get Adversarial-Boundary Staged Generative Adversarial Networks easily.

In ABS-GAN, the boundary loss are given as:

$$\max_{G_j}\{\max_{x \sim p_{G_j}} D_j(x)\} \tag{22}$$

$$\max_{D_j}\{\min_{x \sim p_r} D_j(x)\} + \min_{D_j}\{\max_{x \sim p_{G_j}} D_j(x)\} \tag{23}$$

where G_j and D_j are generator and critic in Stage-jth respectively.

5 Experiments

To investigate the performance of our ABS-GAN on image generation task, we conduct experiments on three benchmark datasets: CIFAR-10 [10], STL-10 [3] and CelebA [11].

We use WGAN-GP [6] as our baseline. In all experiments, as WGAN-GP did, we set hyper-parameter $\lambda = 10$. Besides, we fix our new hyper-parameter $\alpha = 0.2$ and $\delta = 0.1$. On each dataset, we compare our StageGAN, AB-GAN and ABS-GAN with baseline and other popular models.

For quantitative evaluation, we adopt Inception score proposed in [18]. This metric rewards good and varied images in the same batch, and is well-correlated with human judgment. As [18] did, we select 10 partitions of 50,000 randomly generated samples to compute the Inception scores.

For qualitative comparison, we present generated samples by our model. Instead of cherry-picked, all sample images are generated during training process.

5.1 CIFAR-10

CIFAR-10 contains 50,000 32×32 color images in 10 classes: airplane, automobile, bird, cat, deer, dog, frog, horse, ship, and truck.

On CIFAR-10, we use WGAN-GP with ResNet designed by [6] for fair comparison. We use Adam optimizer [9] with learning rate of 0.0002, the first-order momentum of 0 and the second-order momentum of 0.9. Instead of decaying learning rate in each stage, we decay learning rate to 0 during the whole training process. The results are detailed in Tables 1, 2 and Fig. 2.

For StageGAN, the Stage-II generator reduces the EM distance further based on the Stage-I generator, thus the generated distribution is closer to the real ones. This is consistent with the Inception score.

For AB-GAN, the critic tries to separate the projection boundary. The generator is trained more sufficiently, thanks to the extra update information from critic. This is also supported by the Inception score.

Since StageGAN and AB-GAN generate better image from different aspects, it is easily to put them together. After combination, ABS-GAN improves image quality further, under both unsupervised and supervised settings.

Table 1. Unsupervised inception scores on CIFAR-10

Method	Score
DFM [23]	7.72 ± 0.13
WGAN-GP [6]	7.86 ± 0.07
AB-GAN (ours)	7.95 ± 0.11
WGAN-LP [14]	8.02 ± 0.08
StageGAN (ours)	8.02 ± 0.13
ABS-GAN (ours)	$\mathbf{8.05 \pm 0.09}$

Table 2. Supervised Inception scores on CIFAR-10

Method	Score
Improved GAN [18]	8.09 ± 0.07
AC-GAN [13]	8.25 ± 0.07
WGAN-GP [6]	8.42 ± 0.10
StageGAN (ours)	8.52 ± 0.11
AB-GAN (ours)	8.55 ± 0.11
ABS-GAN (ours)	$\mathbf{8.61 \pm 0.10}$

5.2 STL-10

STL-10 is a more diverse dataset than CIFAR-10, consisting of 100,000 96×96 color images subsampled from ImageNet [17]. For the lack of label information, STL-10 is mainly used for unsupervised learning.

To compare with other methods, we rescale the STL-10 images down to 48×48 as [23]. We use a slightly-modified version of WGAN-GP with ResNet. The only difference is that we adjust the feature size in generator and critic, since WGAN-GP with ResNet is designed for CIFAR-10 with 32×32 resolution. We use Adam optimizer and the same settings with CIFAR-10. Experiment results are given in Table 3 and Fig. 3.

On STL-10, StageGAN, AB-GAN and ABS-GAN improve image quality in the same way with CIFAR-10. In addition, we train our model on the 32×32 resolution of STL-10 and achieve a score of 8.65, with 8.39 of WGAN-GP for comparison. This demonstrates ABS-GAN can generate better images than WGAN-GP under different resolutions.

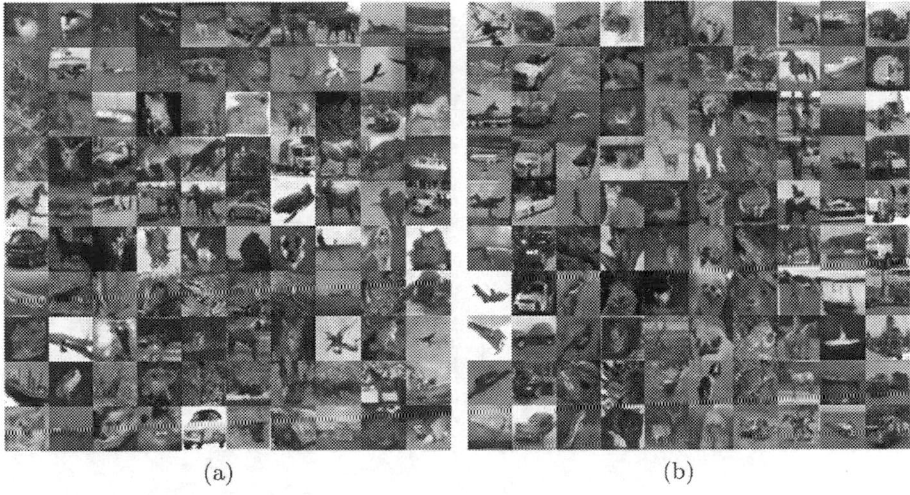

(a) (b)

Fig. 2. Generated samples by our ABS-GAN on CIFAR-10: (a) Generated samples by unsupervised model and (b) generated samples by supervised model. Each column corresponds to one class in the CIFAR-10 dataset.

Fig. 3. Generated samples by our ABS-GAN on STL-10.

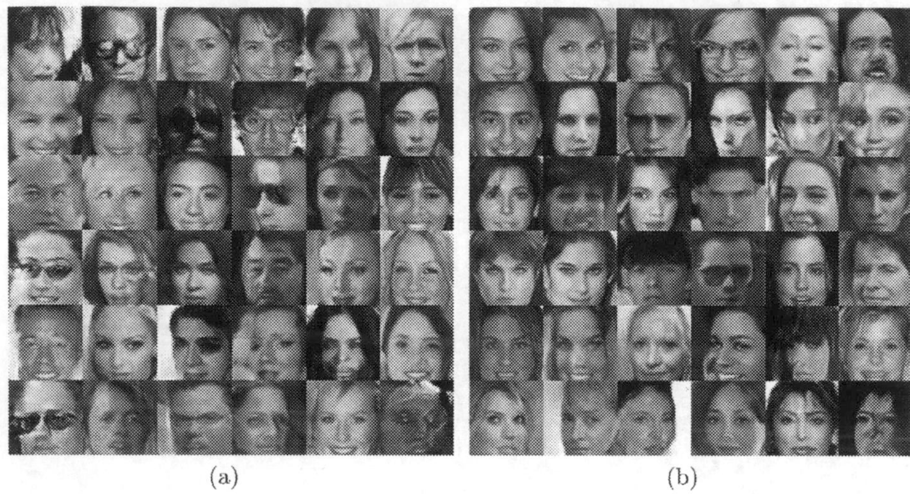

Fig. 4. Generated samples on CelebA: (a) Generated samples by WGAN-GP and (b) generated samples by our ABS-GAN. Both models are trained without ResNet.

Table 3. Unsupervised inception scores on STL-10

Method	Score
DFM [23]	8.51 ± 0.13
WGAN-GP [6]	9.05 ± 0.12
StageGAN (ours)	9.30 ± 0.13
AB-GAN (ours)	9.39 ± 0.11
ABS-GAN (ours)	$\mathbf{9.46 \pm 0.12}$

5.3 CelebA

CelebA is a large-scale face attributes dataset with more than 200,000 218×172 celebrity images, each with 40 attribute annotations. The images in this dataset cover large pose variations and background clutter.

On CelebA, we use the standard DCGAN designed by [15], but train models with EM loss. We use Adam optimizer with learning rate of 0.0002 and the first-order of momentum of 0.5. Again, we decay learning rate to 0 gradually during the whole training process.

As DCGAN, we preprocess dataset images by center-cropping to get 64×64 inputs. We first train the standard WGAN-GP on CelebA. Then we test our StageGAN, AB-GAN and ABS-GAN under same settings.

Inception score is an unsuitable metric on datasets with low variability, e.g., CelebA, since celebrity images only belong to two class: man and woman. For qualitative comparison, we present the generated samples by WGAN-GP and

ABS-GAN in Fig. 4. Experiments on CelebA without ResNet suggest ABS-GAN outperforms WGAN-GP on different architectures.

6 Conclusion and Future Work

In this paper, we introduce StageGAN to improve image quality by reducing EM distance explicitly and AB-GAN to train a better critic, providing extra information for generator training. Putting them together, we derive ABS-GAN. Experiments on CIFAR-10, STL-10 and CelebA demonstrate its performance.

We use the standard WGAN-GP and DCGAN network to train ABS-GAN without fine-tuning or complexing the existing architecture. And we use the same hyper-parameters in all experiments. All those show that ABS-GAN can be trained in a simple and stable way.

Since ABS-GAN is derived from unsupervised learning and EM distance, a future direction of this work is to make full use of label information to improve ABS-GAN performance in supervised learning further.

Acknowledgments. This work was supported by National Key Research and Development Program of China (Grant No. 2016YFB1000902), National Program on Key Basic Research Project (973 Program, Grant No. 2013CB329600), and National Natural Science Foundation of China (Grant No. 61472040).

References

1. Arjovsky, M., Bottou, L.: Towards principled methods for training generative adversarial networks (2017)
2. Arjovsky, M., Chintala, S., Bottou, L.: Wasserstein GAN (2017)
3. Coates, A., Ng, A.Y., Lee, H.: An analysis of single-layer networks in unsupervised feature learning. J. Mach. Learn. Res. **15**, 215–223 (2011)
4. Ghosh, A., Kulharia, V., Namboodiri, V., Torr, P.H.S., Dokania, P.K.: Multi-agent diverse generative adversarial networks (2017)
5. Goodfellow, I.J., et al.: Generative adversarial networks. In: Advances in Neural Information Processing Systems, vol. 3, pp. 2672–2680 (2014)
6. Gulrajani, I., Ahmed, F., Arjovsky, M., Dumoulin, V., Courville, A.: Improved training of Wasserstein GANs (2017)
7. He, K., Zhang, X., Ren, S., Sun, J.: Deep residual learning for image recognition, pp. 770–778 (2015)
8. Huang, R., Zhang, S., Li, T., He, R.: Beyond face rotation: global and local perception GAN for photorealistic and identity preserving frontal view synthesis, pp. 2458–2467 (2017)
9. Kingma, D., Ba, J.: Adam: a method for stochastic optimization. Computer Science (2014)
10. Krizhevsky, A.: Learning multiple layers of features from tiny images (2009)
11. Liu, Z., Luo, P., Wang, X., Tang, X.: Deep learning face attributes in the wild, pp. 3730–3738 (2014)
12. Mirza, M., Osindero, S.: Conditional generative adversarial nets. Computer Science, pp. 2672–2680 (2014)

13. Odena, A., Olah, C., Shlens, J.: Conditional image synthesis with auxiliary classifier GANs (2016)
14. Petzka, H., Fischer, A., Lukovnicov, D.: On the regularization of Wasserstein GANs (2017)
15. Radford, A., Metz, L., Chintala, S.: Unsupervised representation learning with deep convolutional generative adversarial networks. Computer Science (2015)
16. Reed, S., Akata, Z., Yan, X., Logeswaran, L., Schiele, B., Lee, H.: Generative adversarial text to image synthesis, pp. 1060–1069 (2016)
17. Russakovsky, O., et al.: Imagenet large scale visual recognition challenge. Int. J. Comput. Vis. **115**(3), 211–252 (2015)
18. Salimans, T., Goodfellow, I., Zaremba, W., Cheung, V., Radford, A., Chen, X.: Improved techniques for training GANs (2016)
19. Simonyan, K., Zisserman, A.: Very deep convolutional networks for large-scale image recognition. Computer Science (2014)
20. Szegedy, C., et al.: Going deeper with convolutions, pp. 1–9 (2014)
21. Tu, D.N., Le, T., Vu, H., Phung, D.: Dual discriminator generative adversarial nets (2017)
22. Wang, J., et al.: IRGAN: a minimax game for unifying generative and discriminative information retrieval models (2017)
23. Warde-Farley, D., Bengio, Y.: Improving generative adversarial networks with denoising feature matching (2016)
24. Yu, L., Zhang, W., Wang, J., Yu, Y.: SeqGAN: sequence generative adversarial nets with policy gradient (2016)
25. Zhang, H., et al.: StackGAN: text to photo-realistic image synthesis with stacked generative adversarial networks, pp. 5908–5916 (2016)
26. Zhu, J.Y., Park, T., Isola, P., Efros, A.A.: Unpaired image-to-image translation using cycle-consistent adversarial networks, pp. 2242–2251 (2017)

Semi-supervised DenPeak Clustering with Pairwise Constraints

Yazhou Ren[1(✉)], Xiaohui Hu[1], Ke Shi[1], Guoxian Yu[2], Dezhong Yao[3], and Zenglin Xu[1]

[1] SMILE Lab, School of Computer Science and Engineering, University of Electronic Science and Technology of China, Chengdu, China
yazhou.ren@uestc.edu.cn

[2] School of Computer and Information Science, Southwest University, Chongqing, China

[3] Key Laboratory for NeuroInformation of Ministry of Education, School of Life Science and Technology, University of Electronic Science and Technology of China, Chengdu, China

Abstract. Density-based clustering is an important class of approaches to data clustering due to good performance. Among this class of approaches, DenPeak is an effective density-based clustering method that can automatically find the number of clusters and find arbitrary-shape clusters in relative easy scenarios. However, in many situations, it is usually hard for DenPeak to find an appropriate number of clusters without supervision or prior knowledge. In addition, DenPeak often fails to find local structures of each cluster since it assigns only one center to each cluster. To address these problems, we introduce a novel semi-supervised DenPeak clustering (SSDC) method by introducing pairwise constraints or side information to guide the cluster process. These pairwise constraints or side information improve the clustering performance by explicitly indicating the affiliated cluster of data samples in each pair. Concretely, SSDC firstly generates a relatively large number of temporary clusters, and then merges them with the assistance of samples' pairwise constraints and temporary clusters' adjacent information. The proposed SSDC can significantly improve the performance of DenPeak. Its superiority to state-of-the-art clustering methods has been empirically demonstrated on both artificial and real data sets.

Keywords: Semi-supervised clustering · DenPeak
Density-based clustering · Pairwise constraints

1 Introduction

Clustering partitions unlabeled points into several groups so that points in the same group are more similar to each other than to those in other groups. It is a fundamental unsupervised technique which is widely used in big data analysis, pattern recognition, computer vision, and artificial intelligence [27]. Traditional

X. Geng and B.-H. Kang (Eds.): PRICAI 2018, LNAI 11012, pp. 837–850, 2018.
https://doi.org/10.1007/978-3-319-97304-3_64

clustering algorithms include k-means [16], mean shift clustering [6,19,21], hierarchical clustering algorithm [14], non-negative matrix factorization based clustering [12,13], consensus clustering [18,20], etc. Recently, the density-based clustering algorithms have gained a lot of interests because they can find arbitrary-shape clusters without specifying the number of clusters. Over the past decades, a number of density-based clustering algorithms have been proposed, such as DBSCAN [8], OPTICS [2], DenPeak [23], etc.

Among the existing density-based clustering algorithms, DenPeak is one of the most popular ones. DenPeak greatly simplifies the laborious hyper-parameter tuning process involved in others. The calculation of DenPeak is elegant and easily-explicable; there is no kernel mapping, eigen-problems or multi-exemplar optimization [9]. Specifically, there are four steps in DenPeak: (1) It calculates the global density ρ for all the data points; (2) It computes distance δ which is measured by the minimum distance between a point and any other points with higher density; (3) It selects points with high ρ and δ values as cluster centers. (4) Each of the remaining points are assigned to the same cluster as its nearest neighbor of higher density.

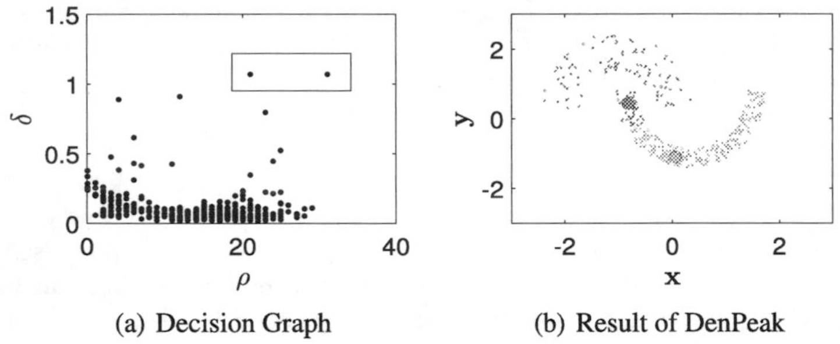

Fig. 1. Results of DenPeak on Jain.

Despite its great success, DenPeak still has two main inherent drawbacks: (1) In real clustering tasks, it is hard to choose an appropriate number of clusters. (2) DenPeak assigns the highest-density center to each cluster, ignoring the fact that multiple centers can coexist in a cluster. DenPeak suffers from the information loss of local structures. A demonstration is described in Fig. 1, which shows the decision graph and the corresponding result of DenPeak. We can find from Fig. 1(a) that a number of points have high ρ and δ values and can be considered as centers. We actually can not make sure how many cluster centers should be selected without prior knowledge. Suppose we are told to choose two cluster centers, which are included by a box in Fig. 1(a). The clustering result of DenPeak is still not satisfied due to the information loss of local structures, as shown in Fig. 1(b). Here, data points are colored according to the cluster center to which they are assigned.

From another perspective, semi-supervised clustering, which is accepted as an improving generalization method in machine learning, has produced a wide range of influence [22,28,29]. It typically makes use of side information of some instances, such as pairwise constraints to attain more accurate division of data. There are two types of pairwise constraints, i.e., must-link and cannot-link constraints. Must-link means that two instances are known to be in the same cluster in advance, while cannot-link indicates the corresponding two instances belong to different clusters [9]. By integrating this information, semi-supervised clustering can be used to gain better quality of the clustering results and more effective computation performance by speeding up convergence and preventing the formation of empty clusters [4]. Apparently, the original DenPeak is not able to make use of the pairwise constraints to guide the clustering process.

The advantages of semi-supervised clustering motivate us to introduce pairwise constraints to address the drawbacks of DenPeak. In fact, there is already a semi-supervised algorithm based on DenPeak, namely SDenPeak, has already been proposed [9]. SDenPeak is an extended variant of DenPeak, which utilizes pairwise constraints to improve the clustering performance. However, although this algorithm partially enhances the original unsupervised version, it does not make full use of pairwise constraints in the clustering process and fails to remove the number of clusters as a prerequisite.

To address this, in this work we propose a novel semi-supervised DenPeak clustering (SSDC) approach, which utilizes must-link and cannot-link constraints to improve the clustering quality of DenPeak. The key idea of SSDC is to firstly choose a relatively large number of temporary cluster centers, and then adequately use must-link constraints and adjacent information to guide the clustering process and ensure none of cannot-link constraints is violated.

The contributions of this paper are three-fold:

(1) The proposed SSDC adequately makes use of pairwise constraints and adjacent information to significantly improve the performance of DenPeak.
(2) SSDC is robust to the number of temporary clusters and can automatically find the number of clusters without human intervention.
(3) SSDC inherits the advantages of DenPeak, such as ease of understanding, explanation, and implementation.

2 Related Work

A lot of density-based clustering algorithms have been proposed. Density-based spatial clustering of applications with noise (DBSCAN) seeks to clustering large and noisy data sets [8]. DBSCAN introduces the concept of neighborhood, a sphere containing a minimum number of data points [24]. The idea of dense neighborhood has motivated other density-based clustering algorithms, including DENCLUE [11], OPTICS [2], DESCRY [1], DenPeak [23] and some other related methods [7,10,15,17]. OPTICS identifies the clustering structure by ordering points and reachable distances [25].

Among the existing algorithms, DenPeak is one of the most popular density-based clustering methods. DenPeak [23] assumes that high density appears around a cluster's center and low density exists on the margins. At the same time, the distance between cluster centers is relatively larger. It combines both density and distance for discovering non-spherical shaped clusters and makes significant improvement in choosing clusters as well as outlier elimination. However, DenPeak has drawbacks that it might be hard to choose an appropriate number of clusters and it typically fail when multiple modes/centers exist in a cluster. To address these issues, in this paper we propose a novel semi-supervised DenPeak clustering approach, namely SSDC, which significantly improves its original unsupervised version.

Traditional clustering methods are usually unsupervised. However, in real clustering tasks, some prior knowledge such as pairwise constraints are know in advance. To make use of such prior knowledge, many semi-supervised clustering algorithms have been proposed in the past several decades, e.g., constrained k-means [26], PCKmeans [3], C-DBSCAN [24], SDenPeak [9], etc.

SDenPeak is an extended variant of DenPeak by utilizing must-link and cannot-link constraints to guide the clustering procedure. The key idea of SDenPeak is to search for the optimal data partition to ensure that none of the specified constraints are violated [9]. SDenPeak is able to generate more satisfactory clustering results on some targeting data sets than its original unsupervised version. However, it needs to specify the number of clusters as prior knowledge, which is not known in real clustering problems.

3 Our Method

This section elucidates the proposed semi-supervised DenPeak clustering with pairwise constraints (SSDC). Let $\mathcal{X} = \{x_1, x_2, \ldots, x_n\}$ be the data set, where n is the number of points. The set of initial must-link constraints is denoted by $ML = \{(x_i, x_j) : x_i \text{ and } x_j \text{ belong to the same cluster}\}$ and the set of cannot-link constraints is $CL = \{(x_i, x_j) : x_i \text{ and } x_j \text{ belong to different clusters}\}$, $1 \leq i, j \leq n$. The aim of SSDC is to partition $\mathcal{X}$ into an appropriate number of disjoint clusters with the help of the abovementioned pairwise constraints. In general, SSDC contains two key steps, i.e., generating and merging temporary clusters.

3.1 Generating Temporary Clusters

The underlying assumption of DenPeak is that cluster centers own high density while the margins have low density. DenPeak also assumes a large distance between any two cluster centers [23]. SSDC incorporates two fundamental concepts in DenPeak: local density ρ and minimum distance δ from points of higher density. Local density ρ_i of data point x_i is defined as [23]:

$$\rho_i = \sum_j \chi(d_{ij} - d_c) \tag{1}$$

where $\chi(x) = 1$ if $x < 0$ and $\chi(x) = 0$ otherwise, d_{ij} is the distance[1] between points x_i and x_j, and d_c is a predefined parameter as the cutoff distance.

[1] Euclidean distance is used in this paper.

Intuitively, ρ_i is equal to the number of points whose distances to x_i is less than d_c. δ_i of point x_i is defined as [23]:

$$\delta_i = \min_{j:\rho_j > \rho_i} (d_{ij}) \tag{2}$$

δ_i represents the minimum distance between x_i and any other points with higher density than x_i.

In unsupervised DenPeak, those data points with high ρ and δ values are selected as cluster centers. However, it is really hard for DenPeak to choose a suitable number of clusters in real clustering tasks because usually a number of points with high ρ and δ values can be considered as candidates of centers. Even the number of clusters is given as prior knowledge, it is still hard for DenPeak to choose the right cluster centers. Furthermore, a cluster only has one center, may leading to loss of local information. We will demonstrate this by experimental results on synthetic data in Sect. 4.

Different from DenPeak, our SSDC selects a relatively large number of temporary cluster centers in the beginning. This typically guarantees that every local density area is represented by a cluster. In fact, there are often several centers/modes (those multiple points with both high δ and ρ values) that exist in one cluster. SSDC selects all this kind of points as temporary cluster centers. Concretely, we develop two approaches: (1) In order to facilitate the demonstration, we manually choose from the decision graph. We use this method when demonstrating two-dimensional artificial data sets. (2) For real data sets, we compute the $\gamma = \rho \times \delta$ values of all the points and choose the k largest ones. k is the number of temporary clusters and is typically much larger than the true number of clusters.

After temporary cluster centers have been found, each remaining point is assigned to the same cluster as its nearest neighbor of higher density, as done in DenPeak. During this procedure, we use cannot-link constraints to guide the assignment. Specifically, if a point x_i has any cannot-link constraints with other points in the cluster which x_i is assigned to, we split this cluster into two temporary clusters, whose centers are the two points with the two largest $\gamma = \rho \times \delta$ values in the corresponding cluster. Note that if this operation happens, the final number of temporary clusters is larger than k. This ends until all the cannot-link constraints are not violated, then a set of temporary clusters (which can be also named by "local clusters") can be obtained.

3.2 Merging Temporary Clusters

Since the temporary clusters are generally more than actual number of clusters, SSDC then merges temporary clusters. When merging these clusters, we take both samples' must-link constraints and temporary clusters' adjacent information into account, under the premise that none of the clusters violates any cannot-link constraint. By progressively merging these local clusters, SSDC is able to find clusters of arbitrary clusters.

(a) Merging Temporary Clusters with Must-Link Constraints

Definition 1. *(Constraint matrix) Constraint matrix is a $n \times n$ matrix, each entity V_{ij} of which is defined as follows:*

$$V_{ij} = \begin{cases} 1 & if\,(x_i, x_j) \in ML \\ -1 & if\,(x_i, x_j) \in CL \\ 0 & otherwise \end{cases} \tag{3}$$

Obviously, $V_{ij} = V_{ji}, 1 \leq i, j \leq n$.

Definition 2. *(Connectivity) For two temporary clusters C_1 and C_2, if they satisfy the following condition:*

$$\exists x_i \in C_1\, and\, \exists x_j \in C_2, V_{ij} = 1 \tag{4}$$

we say that there exists connectivity between C_1 and C_2, or these two clusters are connectable.

In this step, SSDC enforces the must-link constraints. If two temporary clusters are connectable, SSDC considers merging them. To be specific, SSDC processes each must-link constraint in turn. For any pair of points x_i and x_j satisfying $V_{ij} = 1$, if x_i and x_j are not in the same temporary cluster, we find the two temporary clusters that contain x_i and x_j. If none of cannot-link constraints is violated in the union of these two temporary clusters, we merge them. As a result, when this step stops, none of cannot-link constraints is violated in each of the new generated clusters.

(b) Merging Adjacent Temporary Clusters

Definition 3. *(Cluster distance) Distance between two clusters is defined as the shortest pairwise distance between the two clusters. Formally, clustering distance between C_1 and C_2, which is denoted by $d(C_1, C_2)$, is defined as follows:*

$$d(C_1, C_2) = \min_{x_i \in C_1, x_j \in C_2} d_{ij} \tag{5}$$

If $d(C_1, C_2) < d_c$ (d_c is the parameter used in the definition of local density, as shown in Eq. (1)), we call C_1 and C_2 are adjacent clusters, or call C_1 and C_2 are adjacent to each other.

In this step, SSDC firstly calculates all the cluster distances and finds all pairs of adjacent clusters. Then, SSDC checks in turn whether the union of each pair of adjacent clusters violates cannot-link constraints. If not, the corresponding two clusters are merged, otherwise the merge operation is abandoned in order to ensure that all the cannot-link constraints are satisfied.

When merging steps (a) and (b) are done, l disjoint clusters $\{C_1, C_2, \ldots, C_l\}$ are obtained and the final clustering result is given. The pseudo-code of SSDC is summarized in Algorithm 1. SSDC improves the performance of DenPeak by considering both the pairwise constraints and adjacent information. None of cannot-link constraints is violated in the final clustering result of SSDC. The corresponding conclusion is shown in Theorem 1.

Algorithm 1. The SSDC Algorithm.

Input: Data set $\mathcal{X}$; Sets of pairwise constraints ML and CL; The number of temporary cluster centers k.
Output: The final clustering result.

Step 1 $\rightarrow$ Generating temporary clusters
for each point x_i in $\mathcal{X}$ **do**
    Compute ρ_i and δ_i according to Eqs. (1) and (2).
    Compute $\gamma_i = \rho_i \times \delta_i$.
end for
Select points with the k largest γ values as temporary cluster centers.
Assign the remaining points and obtain temporary clusters $C = \{C_1, \ldots, C_k\}$.
while any temporary cluster violates cannot-link constraints **do**
    Find the temporary cluster that violates the constraints, namely C_i.
    Split C_i into two new temporary clusters.
    Update temporary clusters C.
end while
Step 2a $\rightarrow$ Merging temporary clusters with must-link constraints
while $\exists i, j$, C_i and C_j are connectable and $C_i \cup C_j$ does not violate cannot-link constraints **do**
    Merge C_i and C_j.
end while
Step 2b $\rightarrow$ Merging adjacent temporary clusters
while $\exists i, j$, C_i and C_j are adjacent and $C_i \cup C_j$ does not violate cannot-link constraints **do**
    Merge C_i and C_j.
end while
Final l disjoint clusters $\{C_1, C_2, \ldots, C_l\}$ are obtained and are returned as the final clustering result.

Theorem 1. *$\forall$ final cluster $C_i, i = 1, 2, \ldots, l$, $\forall$ two data points x_j, $x_k \in C_i$, $V_{jk} \neq -1$.*

Proof. When generating temporary clusters, if any temporary cluster contains cannot-link constraints, spilt the cluster. When merging temporary clusters, if two temporary clusters satisfy must-link constraints or they are adjacent clusters, but violate cannot-link constraints, then abandon the merge operation. As a result, none of the cannot-link constraints are violated in the final clustering result.

4 Experiments

4.1 Experimental Setup

We test our SSDC and the comparing clustering methods on two synthetic data sets[2] and eleven real data sets. We choose normalized mutual information (NMI)

[2] http://cs.joensuu.fi/sipu/datasets/.

and adjusted rand index (ARI) which are widely used measurements to evaluate the performance of clustering methods. The real data sets used in our experiments include Chainlink[3], CinC (CinC_ECG_torso), Diatom (DiatomSizeReduction)[4], YaleB (Yale Face Database B)[5], COIL20 (the first three classes are used in the experiments)[6], Lymphoma, and Srbct[7]. CNAE-9, Protein, LetterDOQ (letters 'D', 'O', and 'Q' are chosen for experiments), and Optdigits are all UCL data sets[8]. Table 1 demonstrates the characteristics of those real data sets. Each feature of each data set is normalized to have zero mean value and unit variance.

Table 1. The real data sets used in the experiments.

Data	#points	#features	#classes
Chainlink	1000	3	2
CinC	1420	1639	4
CNAE-9	1080	856	9
COIL20	216	1024	3
Diatom	322	345	4
LetterDOQ	450	16	3
Lymphoma	62	4026	3
Optdigits	1797	64	10
Protein	67	20	3
Srbct	63	2308	4
YaleB	2414	1024	38

The following methods are tested in our experiments:

- k-means: k-means clustering [16].
- DBSCAN: Density-based spatial clustering of applications with noise [8].
- DenPeak: Clustering by fast search and find of density peaks [23].
- COP-KM (COP-Kmeans): Constrained k-means [26].
- PC-KM (PCKmeans): Pairwise constrained clustering [3].
- SDenPeak: Semi-supervised version of DenPeak [9].
- FOSC: Framework for optimal selection of clusters [5].
- SSDC-1: The proposed SSDC with $\sqrt{n}$ initial temporary clusters[9].
- SSDC-2: The proposed SSDC with $\frac{\sqrt{n}}{2}$ initial temporary clusters.

[3] https://rdrr.io/cran/diffusionMap/man/Chainlink.html.

[4] www.cs.ucr.edu/~eamonn/time_series_data/.

[5] http://cvc.cs.yale.edu/cvc/projects/yalefaces/yalefaces.html.

[6] http://www.cs.columbia.edu/CAVE/software/softlib/coil-20.php.

[7] http://csse.szu.edu.cn/staff/zhuzx/Datasets.html.

[8] https://archive.ics.uci.edu/ml/datasets.html.

[9] In real clustering tasks, $\sqrt{n}$ is typically larger than the true number of clusters. Thus, we set the initial number of temporary clusters to $\sqrt{n}$ and $\frac{\sqrt{n}}{2}$ to test the performance of SSDC.

k-means, DBSCAN, and DenPeak are unsupervised clustering methods, while all the other comparing clustering algorithms are semi-supervised. In the experiments, DenPeak, SSDC and SDenPeak need parameter d_c. For fair comparison, we set d_c in the same way for these three methods. Concretely, we sort distances between data points with any other points in an ascending order and select the value in the $3\% \times n$ position as d_c. For DBSCAN, we set the number of points in a neighborhood of a point $MinPts$ to 4. The 4-th nearest neighbor distances of all points are computed and the neighborhood's radius Eps is set to the median of those values. There are two types of pairwise constraints in data sets. We select pairs of data points randomly and check the labels of each pair: if two data points have same label, we generate a must-link constraint; if two data points have different labels, we generate a cannot-link constraint. For each data set, we perform 20 independent runs with different sets of pairwise constraints and report the average results. We use t-test to assess the statistical significance of the results at 5% significance level.

4.2 Results on Synthetic Data Sets

We conduct experiments on two synthetic data sets, i.e., Jain and Flame to test the performance of SSDC. We plot the decision graph, initial, and final result of

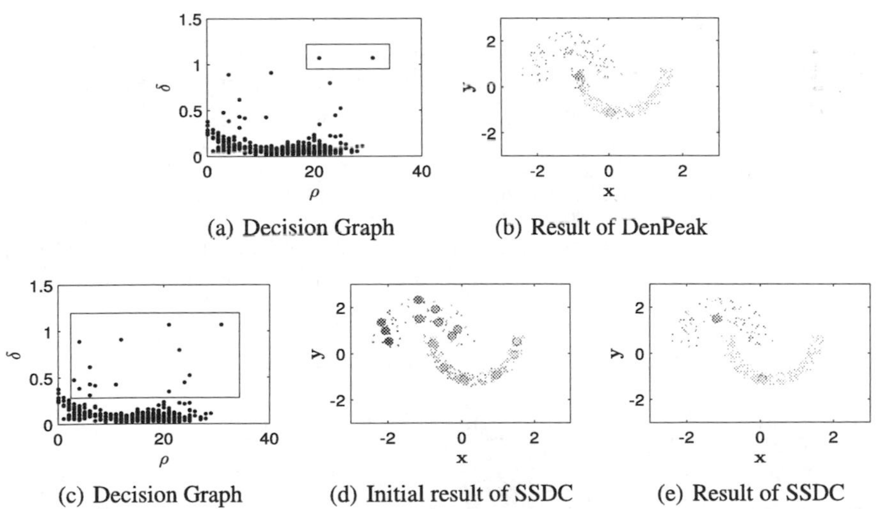

Fig. 2. The Jain data set has 373 points, 2 features and 2 classes. (a) The points in the black box in the decision graph are selected as clustering centers for DenPeak. (b) Different clusters are represented by different colors, and each cluster center is highlighted. Data points are assigned to the cluster center with the same color. (c) Those selected points (in the box) are temporary cluster centers for SSDC. (d) The initial result of temporary clusters. (e) The final result of SSDC. In DenPeak algorithm, we choose 2 cluster centers in decision graph, while we choose 15 points with relatively large ρ and δ values for SSDC. As shown, DenPeak can not provide satisfactory result and SSDC achieves the perfect performance. (Color figure online)

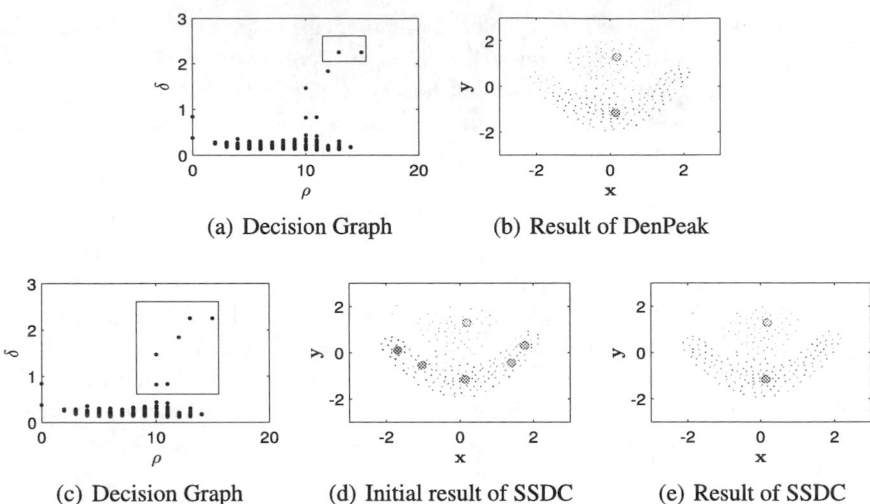

Fig. 3. The Flame data set has 240 points, 2 features and 2 classes. In DenPeak algorithm, we choose 2 clusters in decision graph, while we choose 6 centers with relatively large ρ and δ values for SSDC. It is shown that even given the real number of clusters, DenPeak still performs worse than SSDC. (Color figure online)

SSDC. In order to compare SSDC with DenPeak, we also show the decision graph and clustering result of DenPeak. For SSDC, the number of pairwise constraints is set to $0.5 \times n$. The corresponding results and analysis are given in Figs. 2 and 3.

4.3 Results on Real Data Sets

In this section, we evaluate the performance of the proposed algorithm and the comparing methods on real data sets. Tables 2 and 3 show the mean values of

Table 2. Results on real data sets (ARI, %).

Data	k-means	DBSCAN	DenPeak	COP-KM	PC-KM	SDenPeak	FOSC	SSDC-1	SSDC-2
Chainlink	7.62	7.25	7.86	72.69	6.56	55.95	**100.00**	**100.00**	**100.00**
CinC	15.29	44.54	34.08	7.46	15.06	37.70	49.74	**82.45**	**85.80**
CNAE-9	0.79	1.63	12.62	10.15	2.82	4.99	1.63	**24.27**	**23.91**
COIL20	37.78	70.42	27.77	54.99	49.81	52.77	84.40	**95.86**	**92.09**
Diatom	66.24	55.07	59.18	72.22	63.14	74.66	44.17	79.17	**84.33**
LetterDOQ	3.77	4.38	17.09	5.58	4.46	12.03	6.70	**18.31**	**18.40**
Lymphoma	45.17	49.76	65.64	49.41	50.20	**76.55**	67.44	**73.39**	71.59
Optdigits	44.45	34.49	55.85	50.25	46.73	43.03	26.16	56.63	**58.90**
Protein	**20.90**	2.38	12.23	12.48	19.86	12.90	13.36	**20.54**	18.36
Srbct	15.10	-2.08	13.84	17.44	13.35	24.71	8.85	**28.58**	**29.33**
YaleB	1.76	1.20	4.70	1.97	**15.96**	10.19	0.73	**15.96**	**15.90**

Table 3. Results on real data sets (NMI, %).

Data	k-means	DBSCAN	DenPeak	COP-KM	PC-KM	SDenPeak	FOSC	SSDC-1	SSDC-2
Chainlink	10.54	40.28	45.74	78.83	6.33	48.83	**100.00**	**100.00**	**100.00**
CinC	23.43	61.78	66.87	10.03	23.01	49.58	61.36	87.20	**90.67**
CNAE-9	10.76	3.83	46.97	26.98	9.61	25.47	4.51	**55.12**	**54.80**
COIL20	43.84	76.10	59.41	60.94	73.74	55.34	84.89	**96.48**	**94.06**
Diatom	73.93	66.18	67.15	66.05	70.09	77.85	63.47	82.45	**86.33**
LetterDOQ	5.72	14.01	37.25	6.09	5.52	18.10	32.91	**40.93**	**40.53**
Lymphoma	59.02	**66.59**	56.31	42.93	58.44	64.71	66.26	65.16	63.52
Optdigits	60.14	60.18	72.70	59.49	61.91	66.23	60.86	73.93	**74.74**
Protein	**35.22**	15.38	31.91	28.21	33.92	25.09	24.29	**36.16**	34.32
Srbct	28.60	6.69	40.04	37.78	27.42	39.27	27.02	53.88	**54.32**
YaleB	14.77	17.14	31.23	14.96	14.26	44.46	36.26	**53.61**	**53.36**

ARI and NMI for 20 trails with $0.5 \times n$ pairs of constraints, respectively. In each row, we highlight the best and comparable results in boldface. We can see that SSDC-1 performs comparably with SSDC-2 in most of cases, indicating that different choices of the number of initial temporary clusters does not significantly affect the clustering performance of SSDC.

Another observation obtained from Tables 2 and 3 is that SSDC-1 and SSDC-2 achieve the best performance in most of time. Though some algorithms lead the performance on some data sets, such as DBSCAN performs the best on Lymphoma with NMI, our SSDC-1 still achieves comparably best performance with ARI. Overall, SSDC generally outperforms the other comparing methods.

4.4 Sensitivity Analysis

To study the impact of the number of constraints on the performance of SSDC, we vary the number of constraints from 0 to n (the number of data points) with an interval of $10\% \times n$. We show the performance of SSDC and report the results of k-means, DBSCAN, DenPeak, and SDenPeak as references. To save space, we only plot the NMI values of six real data sets in Fig. 4. In all figures, the horizontal axis depicts the number of constraints, e.g., a value of 5 means $50\% \times n$ pairwise constraints are used. The vertical axis shows the NMI values. As the number of constraints grows, SSDC generally performs better. When enough prior information has been captured, its performance becomes stable. It can be also found that SSDC performs better than other algorithms in most of time.

4.5 Time Complexity Analysis

The time complexity of generating temporary cluster is $O(n^2 + k \times n + k \times n_c)$, where n, $k < n$, n_c denote the number of data points, the number of temporary clusters, and the number of cannot-link constraints, respectively. In real machine learning tasks, the semi-supervised information is typically limited and thus $O(n_c) = O(n)$ and $O(n_m) = O(n)$ generally hold, where n_m is the number of must-link constraints. Thus, the complexity of generating temporary cluster is $O(n^2)$, which is the same as DenPeak. Compared with DenPeak, the main additional operations of SSDC are in the merging step. Thus, the time complexity of SSDC is higher than DenPeak. However, the gap between the running time of these two methods is not large in real clustering tasks. Due to limited space, we only report the running time of DenPeak and SSDC-2 on the first nine tested data sets, as shown in Table 4. It can be seen from Table 4 that the running time of SSDC is slightly larger than that of DenPeak.

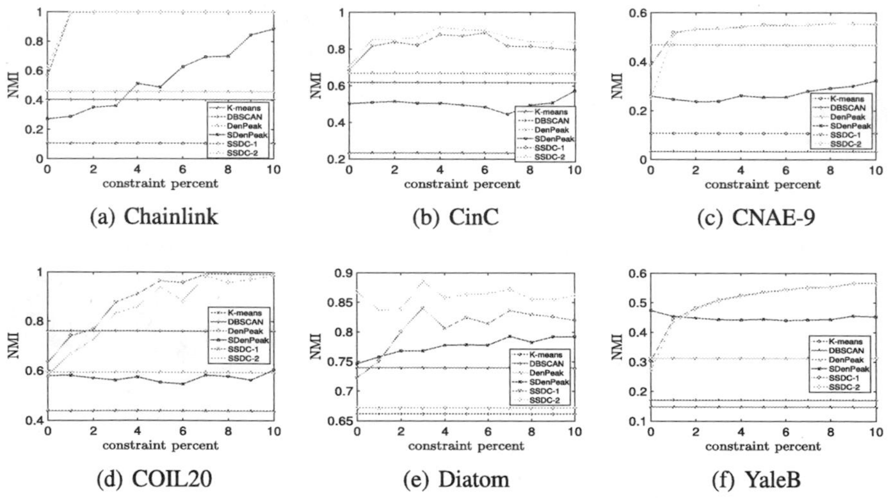

Fig. 4. Sensitivity analysis of the number of constraints (NMI).

Table 4. The running time (seconds) of DenPeak and SSDC.

Data	Chainlink	CinC	CNAE-9	COIL20	Diatom	LetterDOQ	Lymphoma	Optdigits	Protein
DenPeak	4.0	8.2	7.0	0.3	0.5	0.9	0.1	18.6	0.1
SSDC-2	5.8	14.2	12.5	0.4	0.8	1.3	0.1	26.0	0.1

5 Conclusion and Future Work

In this paper, we propose a novel semi-supervised DenPeak clustering (SSDC). SSDC adequately makes use of must-link and cannot-link constraints to enhance the clustering performance of DenPeak. SSDC discovers clusters of arbitrary shapes by firstly generating temporary local clusters and then merging them with pairwise constraints and adjacent information. Experiments on both synthetic and real-world data sets demonstrate the effectiveness of SSDC. To extend the proposed framework to hierarchical density-based clustering is an interesting future work.

Acknowledgments. This paper was in part supported by Grants from the Natural Science Foundation of China (No. 61572111), a Project funded by China Postdoctoral Science Foundation (No. 2016M602674), a 985 Project of UESTC (No. A1098531023601041), and two Fundamental Research Funds for the Central Universities of China (Nos. ZYGX2016J078 and ZYGX2016Z003).

References

1. Angiulli, F., Pizzuti, C., Ruffolo, M.: DESCRY: a density based clustering algorithm for very large data sets. In: Yang, Z.R., Yin, H., Everson, R.M. (eds.) IDEAL 2004. LNCS, vol. 3177, pp. 203–210. Springer, Heidelberg (2004). https://doi.org/10.1007/978-3-540-28651-6_30
2. Ankerst, M., Breunig, M.M., Kriegel, H.P., Sander, J.: OPTICS: ordering points to identify the clustering structure. In: ACM SIGMOD, pp. 49–60. ACM (1999)
3. Basu, S., Banerjee, A., Mooney, R.J.: Active semi-supervision for pairwise constrained clustering. In: SIAM International Conference on Data Mining, pp. 333–344 (2004)
4. Bradley, P., Bennett, K., Demiriz, A.: Constrained k-means clustering, pp. 1–8. Microsoft Research, Redmond (2000)
5. Campello, R.J.G.B., Moulavi, D., Zimek, A., Sander, J.: A framework for semi-supervised and unsupervised optimal extraction of clusters from hierarchies. Data Min. Knowl. Discov. **27**(3), 344–371 (2013)
6. Comaniciu, D., Meer, P.: Mean shift: a robust approach toward feature space analysis. IEEE Trans. Pattern Anal. Mach. Intell. **24**(5), 603–619 (2002)
7. Du, Q., Dong, Z., Huang, C., Ren, F.: Density-based clustering with geographical background constraints using a semantic expression model. ISPRS Int. J. Geo-Inf. **5**(5), 72 (2016)
8. Ester, M., Kriegel, H.P., Sander, J., Xu, X., et al.: A density-based algorithm for discovering clusters in large spatial databases with noise. In: Proceedings of the 2nd International Conference on Knowledge Discovery and Data Mining, pp. 226–231 (1996)
9. Fan, W.Q., Wang, C.D., Lai, J.H.: SDenPeak: semi-supervised nonlinear clustering based on density and distance. In: Proceedings of 2016 IEEE Second International Conference on Big Data Computing Service and Applications, pp. 269–275. IEEE (2016)
10. Gu, Y., Ye, X., Zhang, F., Du, Z., Liu, R., Yu, L.: A parallel varied density-based clustering algorithm with optimized data partition. J. Spat. Sci. **63**, 1–22 (2017)
11. Hinneburg, A., Keim, D.A., et al.: An efficient approach to clustering in large multimedia databases with noise. In: KDD 1998, pp. 58–65 (1998)
12. Huang, S., Ren, Y., Xu, Z.: Robust multi-view data clustering with multi-view capped-norm k-means. Neurocomputing (2018). https://doi.org/10.1016/j.neucom.2018.05.072

13. Huang, S., Wang, H., Li, T., Li, T., Xu, Z.: Robust graph regularized nonnegative matrix factorization for clustering. Data Min. Knowl. Discov. **32**(2), 483–503 (2018)
14. Jain, A.K., Murty, M.N., Flynn, P.J.: Data clustering: a review. ACM Comput. Surv. **31**(3), 264–323 (1999)
15. Lv, Y., et al.: An efficient and scalable density-based clustering algorithm for datasets with complex structures. Neurocomputing **171**, 9–22 (2016)
16. MacQueen, J.: Some methods for classification and analysis of multivariate observations. In: Proceedings of the 5th Berkeley Symposium on Mathematical Statistics and Probability, pp. 281–297. University of California Press (1967)
17. Mai, S.T., He, X., Feng, J., Plant, C., Böhm, C.: Anytime density-based clustering of complex data. Knowl. Inf. Syst. **45**(2), 319–355 (2015)
18. Ren, Y., Domeniconi, C., Zhang, G., Yu, G.: Weighted-object ensemble clustering. In: Proceedings of the IEEE International Conference on Data Mining, pp. 627–636. IEEE (2013)
19. Ren, Y., Domeniconi, C., Zhang, G., Yu, G.: A weighted adaptive mean shift clustering algorithm. In: SIAM International Conference on Data Mining, pp. 794–802 (2014)
20. Ren, Y., Domeniconi, C., Zhang, G., Yu, G.: Weighted-object ensemble clustering: methods and analysis. Knowl. Inf. Syst. **51**(2), 661–689 (2017)
21. Ren, Y., Kamath, U., Domeniconi, C., Zhang, G.: Boosted mean shift clustering. In: Calders, T., Esposito, F., Hüllermeier, E., Meo, R. (eds.) ECML PKDD 2014. LNCS (LNAI), vol. 8725, pp. 646–661. Springer, Heidelberg (2014). https://doi.org/10.1007/978-3-662-44851-9_41
22. Ren, Y., Zhang, G., Yu, G.: Random subspace based semi-supervised feature selection. In: International Conference on Machine Learning and Cybernetics, pp. 113–118 (2011)
23. Rodriguez, A., Laio, A.: Clustering by fast search and find of density peaks. Science **344**(6191), 1492–1496 (2014)
24. Ruiz, C., Spiliopoulou, M., Menasalvas, E.: C-DBSCAN: density-based clustering with constraints. In: An, A., Stefanowski, J., Ramanna, S., Butz, C.J., Pedrycz, W., Wang, G. (eds.) RSFDGrC 2007. LNCS (LNAI), vol. 4482, pp. 216–223. Springer, Heidelberg (2007). https://doi.org/10.1007/978-3-540-72530-5_25
25. Ruiz, C., Spiliopoulou, M., Menasalvas, E.: Density-based semi-supervised clustering. Data Min. Knowl. Discov. **21**(3), 345–370 (2010)
26. Wagstaff, K., Cardie, C., Rogers, S., Schrödl, S., et al.: Constrained k-means clustering with background knowledge. In: ICML, pp. 577–584 (2001)
27. Xu, R., Wunsch, D.: Survey of clustering algorithms. IEEE Trans. Neural Netw. **16**(3), 645–678 (2005)
28. Yu, Y., Yu, G., Chen, X., Ren, Y.: Semi-supervised multi-label linear discriminant analysis. In: Liu, D., Xie, S., Li, Y., Zhao, D., El-Alfy, E.S. (eds.) ICONIP 2017. LNCS, vol. 10634, pp. 688–698. Springer, Cham (2017)
29. Zhu, X.: Semi-supervised learning literature survey. Technical report 1530, Computer Sciences, University of Wisconsin-Madison (2005)

A Novel Convolutional Neural Network for Statutes Recommendation

Chuanyi Li[1,2], Jingjing Ye[2], Jidong Ge[1,2(✉)], Li Kong[2], Haiyang Hu[1,3], and Bin Luo[1,2]

[1] State Key Laboratory for Novel Software Technology, Nanjing University, Nanjing, China
lcynju@126.com, gjdnju@163.com

[2] Software Institute, Nanjing University, Nanjing, China

[3] School of Computer Science and Technology, Hangzhou Dianzi University, Hangzhou, China

Abstract. In recent years, statutes recommendation has been a popular research subject of artificial intelligence in legal domain. However, the existing statutes recommendation systems are more oriented to professionals, such as judges and lawyers, and are not suitable for general public who have no legal knowledge and cannot independently extract key points. We use deep learning to solve the ambiguity and variability of general public's linguistic expressions about cases. We propose a novel Convolutional Neural Network (CNN) architecture to obtain the relations between statutes and cases. Unlike previous works, in order to utilize the semantics of statutes, we also put statute content as model input besides case description. Moreover, different from the *Top-k* method, the numbers of statutes recommended by our model varies among cases. In addition, all the features of the case statements and statute contents are extracted automatically without any human intervention. So, the approach for training the model can be easily applied in different types of cases and laws. Experiments results on the juridical document corpus of the proposed CNN model surpass those of previous neural network competitors.

Keywords: Statutes recommendation · Convolutional Neural Network
Natural Language Processing

1 Introduction

As artificial intelligence is applied in more and more applications, courthouses are starting to focus on intelligent judges. Robot judges, robot legal consultants and other products are emerging. Statutes recommendation is an important part of judicative intelligence. Because statutes are the support of case verdicts. If we can predict the statutes accurately, we can get the trends of verdicts to some extent. What's more, recommending proper statutes for cases is quite useful for all roles involved in legal cases, such as judges, lawyers and interested parties. It can help the judges to process the cases more effectively and efficiently. It can also impel lawyers to find more references so as to defend better. For people without professional legal knowledge,

X. Geng and B.-H. Kang (Eds.): PRICAI 2018, LNAI 11012, pp. 851–863, 2018.
https://doi.org/10.1007/978-3-319-97304-3_65

statutes recommendation is much more helpful. It is hard for them to find proper statutes without the assistance of professionals. Seeking advice from law firms costs much time and money. A system which can recommend proper statutes according to given case descriptions will benefit them a lot.

There have been a few studies on statutes prediction or recommendation (Kim et al. 2016; Chen and Chi 2010; Chou and Hsing 2010; Conrad and Schilder 2007; Moens 2001). However, most of them focused on retrieving or classifying statutes based on keywords, which are difficult to use for people without professional legal knowledge. The recent improvement made by Liu et al. (2015) considers to retrieve relevant statutes from a query sentence using daily customary terms. Liu et al. (2015) implemented a system to classify user query by Support Vector Machine (SVM). The accuracy of this model largely depends on the quality of the input query sentences. However, key points of a case cannot always be summarized within a proper chief query sentence especially by non-professional users. They may describe a case by some facts which are irrelevant to the final judgment. Besides, the model always returns a fixed number (e.g., 5 or 10) of statutes for any case, although the number of statutes cited by cases varies a lot, which is from one to even over twenty. This is also a potential limitation of most of existing statutes recommendation systems. Furthermore, the adopted multi classification strategy is sensitive to the category distribution of training samples, and categories imbalance may lead to the deviation of model. The classifier model is more inclined to recommend popular statues and ignore the infrequent statutes directly. But popular statutes are usually universal to many cases. For example, the 64-th article in *Civil Procedure Law of the People's Republic of China* reads: "当事人对自己提出的主张，有责任提供证据……" (It is the duty of a party to an action to provide evidence in support of his allegations…[1]). These popular statutes are usually not the crucial statutes which affect the judgement of cases. The users pay more attention to the statutes which are closely related to the cases. Lastly, most of existing systems do not use the statutes' semantic information to extract the case features more accurately. They just regard statutes as labels.

In this paper, we propose a statutes recommendation framework based on a novel CNN model to overcome existing problems. There are three key features of the pro-posed framework:

1. One of the inputs is plaintiff claiming segment using daily customary terms. It is the case description submitted to the court by the plaintiff, which does not contain many professional legal terms. This ensures the usability of system for general public. At the same time, it is the only information that judges and lawyers can get before hold hearings.
2. Statute contents are also treated as the inputs of the model. This is beneficial to highlight the crucial features of cases and reduce the weight of irrelevant information. It can also assist us in finding statutes more relevant to cases.
3. The statutes predicting problem is formalized as a binary classification task: determine whether the statute is suitable for the case according to the given text

[1] The English version of Civil Procedure Law of the People's Republic of China, http://www.npc.gov.cn/englishnpc/Law/2007-12/12/content_1383880.htm.

couple of statute and case. Compared to the pervious classifying model which only extracts the features of cases, the goal of our CNN model is to capture the semantic relations between case description and the reference statutes.

The flow chart of the model is shown in Fig. 1. If the number of candidate statutes is k, we should run this classifier model for k times. So, the numbers of recommended statutes will not affect each other. In real applications, we can limit the number of candidate statutes to a reasonable number by restraining the cause of cases or requesting user select law scope.

The rest of this paper is organized as follows. Section 2 presents the research background, including recommender systems (RS), CNN and related techniques, as well as discussion of the motivation of proposing a novel CNN model for predicting statutes. Section 3 introduces the proposed CNN architecture in detail. The experiments and results are presented in Sect. 4. Section 5 concludes the paper.

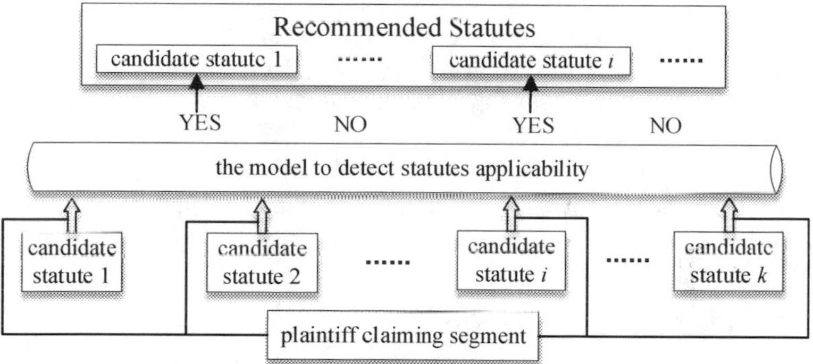

Fig. 1. The flow chart of the statutes recommendation model

2 Background

2.1 Recommender System

Recommender Systems are software tools to assist users in finding useful information quickly. The term first appeared in the 1990s (William et al. 1995; Shardanand et al. 1995; Resnick et al. 1994). Unlike the search engine, the recommender systems don't require the user to provide clear requirements. They analyze the users' historical behaviors and model the users' interests so as to recommend information that meets users' demands. Nowadays, recommender systems are applied in a diversity of fields including music, books, finance, law etc. The recommender system algorithms can be mainly classified into three categories: collaborative filtering, content-based filtering and hybrid methods.

In the scene of statutes recommendation, each case needs to be recommended only once. They don't have behavior histories. Every recommendation is faced to a "new user". In the early stage of the study, we have tried the filtering based on the neighborhood. We found out the similar cases through the case features and used the similar cases' statutes as the recommended statutes. But, unfortunately, the result of the experiment was bad. We analyzed the data set and found that the case statements of the same case cause are pretty similar. For example, the statement of a divorce case is "原告李娟诉称，2001年6月，原、被告经人介绍相识。后于2002年3月10日登记结婚。婚后未有子女。由于双方婚前缺乏了解，婚后感情不和，经常为生活琐事生气，夫妻感情已经完全破裂。现请求依法判令解除原、被告的婚姻关系。" (The plaintiff Li Juan said that, the plaintiff and the defendant introduced to each other in June 2001, and then they got married in March 10, 2002. There is no child after marriage. Due to the lack of understanding before marriage, they are on bad terms and always argue for trivial matters after marriage. The affection between husband and wife is shattered entirely. Now the plaintiff askes the court to release the marriage relationship between the plaintiff and the defendant.) The statement of another case is almost the same except for having a son and a daughter after marriage. The intersection of statutes cited by the two cases is empty. Obviously, whether having a child or not is a key point. But it is very difficult for machine to learn key elements from a large number of similar parts. We can list the key points manually, but the cost is too high. Just for divorce cases, there are also many key points such as family violence, property disputes, paramour, bigamy and so on. For thousands of case causes, the workload is too heavy.

So, we decide to adopt content-based filtering. We add statute features as inputs in order to highlight the key parts in the case statements. We predict by analyzing the relationship between case statements and statute contents.

2.2 Convolutional Neural Network

CNN model has its success on fields like computer vision (Neverova et al. 2014), speech recognition (Deng et al. 2013) and natural language processing (Collobert and Weston 2008). A filter with width m can learn to recognize specific n-grams of texts where n is less than or equal to the filter width m. What's more, the position of n-grams hardly influences the meaning of the sentence. So, pooling operation which owns a property of local translation invariance can help to capture features more effectively. Previous studies have shown that CNN model has a good performance on text classification, sentiment analysis, and text similarity (Kim 2014; Kalchbrenner et al. 2014; He et al. 2015). Accordingly, we attempt to use a CNN model to recommend statutes for cases.

2.3 Attention Mechanism

Attention mechanism was first widely used in computer vision (Mnih et al. 2014), and was extended to machine translation in Natural Language Processing (NLP) field by Bahdanau et al. (2015). It is used to find out the words in the source language related to the generated word in the target language. As a result, translating as well as aligning will be done at the same time. Attention mechanism can observably improve the accuracy of the translation. It is similar to statutes recommendation since we want to find out the key words of case statements related to the statute, just like the alignment in machine translation. Inspired by attention mechanism, we adopt a correlation matrix to measure semantic similarity between statutes and cases in our model.

2.4 Word Vectors

Word vectors generated by neural network language model were proposed by Bengio et al. in 2003. Word vectors are used to reconstruct the representation of words into form of vectors. Compared to TF-IDF, it has a nice property that semantical close words are likewise close in Euclidean or cosine distance. This model is suitable for various languages, including Chinese. In our experiment, we used word vectors to represent words in lower dimensional vector space. We constructed multiple correlation matrices by using different distance measurements.

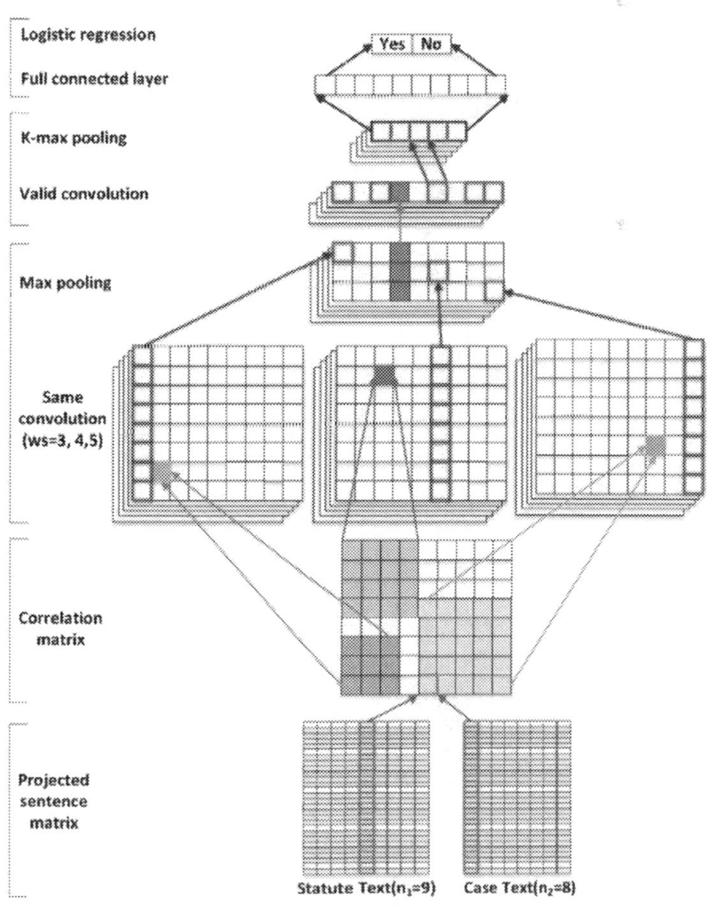

Fig. 2. The CNN architecture to judge whether the statute is suitable for certain case

3 The Proposed CNN Structure

In this section, we describe our model which is shown in Fig. 2. The model is used to judge whether the statute is suitable for certain case by means of measuring semantic relations between the statute and the basic situation of the case.

3.1 Correlation Matrix

We combine case statements and statute contents at the first layer of the network in order to capture their relations. Our inputs are pairs of texts, which have distinct lengths. Let S^1 represents the statute text and S^2 represents the case text. An embedding layer which can be fine-tuned during training will project each word of the text to a q-dimensional word vector. Suppose that S_i^1 responds to the vector of the i-th word in S^1, then the dot correlation matrix $M^{dot} \in R^{n_1 \times n_2}$ can be represented as

$$M_{ij}^{dot} = S_i^1 \cdot S_j^2, \tag{1}$$

where n_1 is the length of S^1 and n_2 is the length of S^2. There are other alternative correlation matrices, for example, Euclidean correlation matrix M^{Euc}, shown in Eq. (2) and Manchester correlation matrix M^{Man}, shown in Eq. (3).

$$M_{ij}^{Euc} = \sum\nolimits_{d=1}^{q} \left(S_{i,d}^1 - S_{j,d}^2\right)^2 \tag{2}$$

$$M_{ij}^{Man} = \sum\nolimits_{d=1}^{q} \left|S_{i,d}^1 - S_{j,d}^2\right| \tag{3}$$

Here $S_{i,d}^1$ means the d-th dimension of S_i^1. We can also use multiply matrices by concentrating them into multi-channel, which can improve performance slightly, but do harm to efficiency.

3.2 Convolution

The convolution operation at the first convolution layer of the network is convolving a matrix of weights $W_c \in R^{ws \times ws \times c}$ with correlation matrices mentioned above, where ws is the window size and c is the number of correlation matrices we applied. We use Same Convolution (Fukushima and Neocognitron 1982) with zero padding to control the kernel width and the size of the output independently and gain the output of the same size with different window sizes. After that, each value in the output matrix should be added to a bias and perform an operation of a nonlinear function, such as ReLU.

A feature map can be seen as extracting a certain feature of the input. We use multiple feature maps so that we can gather different kinds of text features, which is helpful to improve the system performance.

Denoting the number of feature maps as f_s, the output of Same Convolution has size $n_1 \times n_2 \times f_s$. We pick up the maximum value over dimension n_2 through a max-overtime pooling operation (Collobert et al. 2011). The resulting matrix has dimensions $n_1 \times f_s$.

We apply multiply window sizes with same filter map size and concentrate the outputs together. We denote the generating matrix as O^s whose dimensions are $n_1 \times g \times f_s$, where g is the number of distinct window sizes. Then, we convolute weights U $\in R^{1 \times g \times f_s}$ with O^s at the second convolution layer. Similarly, there are more than one feature maps and each feature map has a bias term and a nonlinear function. However, we use Valid Convolution (Fukushima and Neocognitron 1982) without zero padding rather than Same Convolution this time.

3.3 *K*-max Pooling

Please notice that the number of input neurons at the full connected layer is fixed, but the lengths of S^1 and S^2 vary considerably. In order to solve the problem of variable text lengths, we use Kalchbrenner et al. (2014)'s *k*-max pooling to project sentences of distinct lengths to the same size. Unlike max pooling, it selects *k* top values from each dimension rather than one. As a result, it avoids the loss of features. For example, max pooling can't distinguish whether a valuable feature occurs one or multiple times in a single row.

3.4 Full Connection

The output matrix of *k*-max pooling layer will be flattened to a vector v as the input of full connected layer. Then, the vector v will be multiplied with weights W_f and be added to a scalar b_f. The result will be operated by sigmoid function to get the probability whether the statute is suitable to the case. It can be formulated as

$$y = \sigma\left(W_f v + b_f\right). \quad (4)$$

The whole operation can also be seen as a logistic regression.

We train the network by minimizing the cross-entropy loss between the predicted and expected distributions. We also employ dropout and L2 regularization on the weight and bias vectors at the penultimate layer to prevent overfitting.

4 Experiments and Results

4.1 Datasets

We selected 13000 juridical documents of divorce cases randomly from China Judgment Documents Repository as the whole cases data set. The *juridical document* is a summary of the case, written by the judge after the completion of the trial. It includes the basic situation of the case, the parties, the evidences, the judgment result, the trial and analysis process and so on. It is used to document a case. Except for confidential cases, the juridical document is open to all, so it has high readability. We picked up the contents of plaintiff claiming segment as case statements. The data set was randomly split into 4936 training, 1737 development and 6327 testing.

Unlike English, Chinese has the characteristics of continuous writing without blank characters. If the computer can't obtain the exact boundary of words, it is difficult to gain the semantic information contained in the text (Lai et al. 2013). So, word segment is a common data preprocessing operation in Chinese language processing. Nowadays, there are many excellent word segment tools, such as ANSJ, JIEBA, ICTCLAS, SCWS, LTP, NLPIR and so on. We used ANSJ to segment texts. ANSJ owns four segment patterns: base mode, precise mode, index mode and NLP mode. In this paper, we chose the NLP mode to segment word. Because it is the most accuracy mode and it supports digit recognition, name recognition, organization recognition and new word detection.

After word segment, we removed the following characters to filter out irrelevant interferential words.

- Words of time, place, people name, organization name were ignored.
- Prepositions and conjunctions were removed since their major function is to connect the grammatical structure, not to express semantic.
- We also removed non-Chinese characters and single character words since a Chinese word usually consists of at least two characters.
- The words appeared over 10000 times or less than 5 times in the whole corpus were discarded. We can't identify one case from all the cases through frequent words since most of case statements have these words. We also can't gather a group of cases cited the same statute by rare words since most of case statements don't own these words. So, both the frequent words and the rare words can't be-come the case features.
- Furthermore, we make a constraint that each word should only occur once in every 5-gram of the text. If there are more than one, only the first will be kept. Because we found that the beginning of a sentence in plaintiff claiming is often the repeat of last sentence. For example, "2003年7月，两人经人介绍相识。两人相识后，于2005年5月20日登记结婚。" (In July 2003, the plaintiff and the defendant introduced to each other. After acquainted with each other, they married in May 20, 2005.). The reason of choosing number 5 is that the max window size of our CNN model is 5.

The length of case statement inputs varies from 10 to 317. The cases distribution based on the length of preprocessed case statements is shown in Table 1.

Table 1. The cases distribution based on the length of preprocessed case statements.

Dataset	10–19	20–29	30–39	40–49	50–59	60–69	70–79	80–89	≥ 90
Training	731	1346	996	704	418	245	127	82	287
Test	975	1696	1421	940	535	282	230	116	132

We only chose the whole 50 statutes in *Marriage Law of the People's Republic of China* as the candidate statutes since statutes in the same law are more similar and confusing. For example, the following three statutes in *Marriage Law of the People's Republic of China*[2] are quite analogous.

- 第三条 禁止包办、买卖婚姻和其他干涉婚姻自由的行为。禁止借婚姻索取财物。禁止重婚。禁止有配偶者与他人同居。禁止家庭暴力。禁止家庭成员间的虐待和遗弃。(Article 3 Marriage upon arbitrary decision by any third party, mercenary marriage and any other acts of interference in the freedom of marriage shall be prohibited. The exaction of money or gifts in connection with marriage shall be prohibited. Bigamy shall be prohibited. Anyone who has a spouse shall be prohibited to cohabit with another person of the opposite sex. Family violence shall be prohibited. Maltreatment and desertion of one family member by another shall be prohibited.)
- 第十条 有下列情形之一的，婚姻无效：（一）重婚的；（二）有禁止结婚的亲属关系的；（三）婚前患有医学上认为不应当结婚的疾病，婚后尚未治愈的；（四）未到法定婚龄的。(Article 10 The marriage shall be invalid if: (1) either of the married parties commits bigamy; (2) there is the prohibited degree of kinship between the married parties; (3) before marriage either of the parties is suffering from a disease which is regarded by medical science as rending a person unfit for marriage and which has not yet been cured after marriage; or (4) one of the married parties has not reached the statutory age for marriage.)
- 第四十六条 有下列情形之一，导致离婚的，无过错方有权请求损害赔偿：(一)重婚的；（二）有配偶者与他人同居的；（三）实施家庭暴力的；（四）虐待、遗弃家庭成员的。(Article 46 Where one of the following circumstances leads to divorce, the unerring party shall have the right to claim compensation: (1) bigamy is committed; (2) one party who has a spouse cohabits with another person of the opposite sex; (3) family violence is committed; or (4) a family member is maltreated or abandoned.)

If the model can choose proper statutes from these similar statutes, it should be easier to distinguish less similar statutes and get better results. If you want to get the statute contents of the whole laws, you may pay to the courts or the law agencies who own the law database. The statute contents were preprocessed as the same as case statements. The length of statute inputs varies from 3 to 55. The cases distribution based on the number of quoted statutes is shown in Table 2.

Table 2. The cases distribution based on the number of quoted statutes.

Dataset	1	2	3	4	5	6	7	8	9
Training	2839	739	738	400	157	42	14	5	2
Test	3596	1003	944	483	217	65	15	4	0

[2] The English version of Marriage Law of the People's Republic of China, http://www.npc.gov.cn/englishnpc/Law/2007-12/13/content_1384064.htm.

The distribution of the positive and negative classes is extremely unbalanced, since statutes unquoted by a case are far more than quoted. In order to avoid the negative class shift, we randomly selected four unquoted statutes as negative samples for each positive sample. The cited frequency of the statute determines the probability of the selection. The training sample format is (statute content, case statement, 1) for positive sample and (statute content, case statement, 0) for negative sample.

4.2 Pre-trained Word Vectors

Pre-training word vectors from a large corpus is a common method in natural language processing. It can improve performance in the absence of a large supervised training set (Collobert et al. 2011; Socher et al. 2011; Iyyer et al. 2014).

We trained the word vectors from all the juridical documents of cases happened in 2015 and 2016, totally 2000000 pieces. We used the full text of the juridical documents, rather than plaintiff claiming segment. We still selected ANSJ as the word segmentation tool and adopted the NLP mode. We removed all the non-Chinese characters and single character words. The vectors have dimensionality of 200 and were trained using the continuous bag-of-words architecture (Le and Mikolov 2014). Words not included in the set of pre-trained words are initialized to be mean of all word vectors.

4.3 Training

Training is done through stochastic gradient descent over shuffled mini-batches of size 64 with the Adagrad update rule (Duchi et al. 2011).

We use rectified linear units as the activation function. Filter window sizes of Same Convolution are 3, 4, 5 and each has 128 feature maps while Valid Convolution has 256 feature maps. Dropout rate is 0.5, L2 regularization weight is 5×10^{-4}, and learning rate is 10^{-3}.

We chose two approaches as contrasts. The one is the CNN model proposed by Kim (2014) which has been proved to be one of the best models on text classification. The case statements are inputs and the statute labels are outputs. We consider each candidate statute as a label, so the number of output neurons is 50. We choose the top-2 statutes as a recommendation. Since the network cannot handle the inputs with random lengths, we regard the largest text length in the training set as the fixed text length. If the length of the input is smaller than that, pad with <unk>. If it is larger than that, it will be truncated.

The other contract model is the CNN model proposed by He et al. (2015) which has superior performance on text similarity. Both case statements and statute contents are inputs while outputs are binary classes. Notice that it cannot handle the inputs with random lengths, too. Text should be padded or truncated to a fixed length as above.

4.4 Results

In this paper, we use precision, recall and F1-score to measure the model performance. Precision is a measure of the correctness of the recommendation. It is defined as:

$$Precision = \frac{1}{N}\sum\frac{R}{T}, \tag{5}$$

where N denotes the total number of cases, R denotes the number of statutes which are predicted right, T denotes the total number of statutes which are recommended. Recall is a measure of the coverage of the recommendation. The formula is as follows:

$$Recall = \frac{1}{N}\sum\frac{R}{S}, \tag{6}$$

where S is the number of statutes which are actually cited. Precision and recall are mutual condition. For one extreme example, if we recommend all candidate statutes, the recall will be 100% and the precision will be quite low. So, we can use F1-score as a compromise. F1-score is the harmonic mean of precision and recall. It is defined as:

$$F1\text{-}score = \frac{2 \times Precision \times Recall}{Precision + Recall} \tag{7}$$

Table 3 shows the experiment results on divorce cases. Our model outperforms the other systems. Via the results of Kim's CNN model and ours, it embodies the key insight that the semantic information of statute contents is beneficial to identifying statutes applicability, which is agreed with our expectation. The possible reason for surpassing the approach of He et al. (2015) is that we put the case statements and statute contents together at the first layer of CNN model while He et al. (2015) associates them until the last full connected layer.

Table 3. Experiment results on divorce cases.

Model	Precision	Recall	F1 score
Kim 2014	0.6321	0.8090	0.7069
He et al. 2015	0.8749	0.7023	0.7791
Ours	0.9359	0.7173	0.8121

5 Conclusion

In this paper, we presented a novel CNN model for statutes recommendation. We use word2vec to express the semantic meaning of the text. We combine statute contents and case statements at the first layer of the network. Then we obtain the relations between these two texts through the convolution of different kernel sizes and k-max pooling. In the end, whether the statute is used in the case or not is computed by the full connection layer. Experiments show that the model has good performance.

In future work, we will dedicate to make the proposed model achieve the ability to judge the applicability of new-released statutes, since the exiting statutes recommendation frameworks based on classification techniques cannot meet the demand. Besides, we will try to mine associative statute rules to optimize the outputs of our CNN model.

Acknowledgment. This work was supported by the National Key R&D Program of China (2016YFC0800803), the National Natural Science Foundation of China (No. 61572162, 61572251, 61702144), the Natural Science Foundation of Jiangsu Province (No. BK20131277), the Zhejiang Provincial Key Science and Technology Project Foundation (NO. 2018C01012), the Zhejiang Provincial National Science Foundation of China (No. LQ17F020003), and the Fundamental Research Funds for the Central Universities.

References

Kim, W., Lee, Y., Kim, D., Won, M., Jung, H.: Ontology-based model of law retrieval system for R&D projects. In: Proceedings of the 18th Annual International Conference on Electronic Commerce: e-Commerce in Smart Connected World, pp. 1–6 (2016)

Chen, C., Chi, J.Y.P.: Use text mining to generate the draft of indictment for prosecutor. In: Proceedings of the 2010 Pacific Asia Conference on Information Systems (PACIS), pp. 706–712 (2010)

Chou, S.C., Hsing, T.P.: Text mining technique for Chinese written judgment of criminal case. In: IEEE Intelligence and Security Informatics Conference, pp. 113–125 (2010)

Conrad, J.G., Schilder, F.: Opinion mining in legal blogs. In: Proceedings of the 11th International Conference on Artificial Intelligence and Law (ICAIL), pp. 231–236 (2007)

Moens, M.F.: Innovative techniques for legal text retrieval. In: Proceedings of the 5th International Conference on Artificial Intelligence and Law, pp. 29–57 (2001)

Liu, Y., Chen, Y., Ho, W.: Predicting associated statutes for legal problems. Inf. Process. Manag. **51**, 194–211 (2015)

Hill, W.C., Stead, L., Rosenstein, M., Furnas, G.W.: Recommending and evaluating Choices in a virtual community of use. In: The Proceedings of the 1995 International Conference of Human-Computer Interaction (CHI), pp. 194–201 (1995)

Shardanand, U., Maes, P.: Social information filtering: algorithms for automating "Word of Mouth". In: The Proceedings of the 1995 International Conference of Human-Computer Interaction (CHI), pp. 210–217 (1995)

Resnick, P., Iacovou, N., Suchak, M., Bergstrom, P., Riedl, J.: GroupLens: an open architecture for collaborative filtering of netnews (CSCW), pp. 175–186 (1994)

Neverova, N., Wolf, C., Taylor, G.W., Nebout, F.: Multi-scale deep learning for gesture detection and localization. In: Agapito, L., Bronstein, M.M., Rother, C. (eds.) ECCV 2014. LNCS, vol. 8925, pp. 474–490. Springer, Cham (2014). https://doi.org/10.1007/978-3-319-16178-5_33

Deng, L., Hinton, G., Kingsbury, B.: New types of deep neural network learning for speech recognition and related applications: an overview. In: Proceedings of 2013 IEEE International Conference on Acoustics, Speech and Signal Processing (ICASSP), pp. 8599–8603 (2013)

Collobert, R., Weston, J.: A unified architecture for natural language processing: deep neural networks with multitask learning. In: Proceedings of the 25th International Conference on Machine Learning, pp. 160–167 (2008)

Kim, Y.: Convolutional neural networks for sentence classification. In: Proceedings of the 2014 Conference on Empirical Methods in Natural Language Processing, pp. 1746–1751 (2014)

Kalchbrenner, N., Grefenstette, E., Blunsom, P.: A convolutional neural network for modelling sentences. In: Proceedings of the 52nd Annual Meeting of the Association for Computational Linguistics, pp. 655–665 (2014)

He, H., Gimpel, K., Lin, J.: Multi-perspective sentence similarity modeling with convolutional neural networks. In: Proceedings of the 2015 Conference on Empirical Methods in Natural Language Processing, pp. 1576–1586 (2015)

Mnih, V., Heess, N., Graves, A., Kavukcuoglu, K.: Recurrent models of visual attention. In Proceedings of the 2014 Annual Conference on Neural Information Processing Systems (NIPS), pp. 2204–2212 (2014)

Bahdanau, D., Cho, K., Bengio, Y.: Neural machine translation by jointly learning to align and translate. In: Proceedings of the 2015 International Conference on Learning Representations (ICLR), pp. 1–15 (2015)

Bengio, Y., Ducharme, R., Vincent, P., Jauvin, C.: A neural probabilistic language model. J. Mach. Learn. Res. **2003**(3), 1137–1155 (2003)

Fukushima, K., Neocognitron, S.M.: A new algorithm for pattern recognition tolerant of deformations and shifts in position. Pattern Recogn. **15**(6), 455–469 (1982)

Collobert, R., Weston, J., Bottou, L., Karlen, M., Kavukcuglu, K., Kuksa, P.: Natural language processing (almost) from scratch. J. Mach. Learn. Res. **12**, 2493–2537 (2011)

Lai, S., Xu, L., Chen, Y., Liu, K., Zhao, J.: Chinese word segment based on character representation learning. J. Chin. Inf. Process. **2013**(5), 8–14 (2013)

Socher, R., Pennington, J., Huang, E., Ng, A., Manning, C.: Semi-supervised recursive autoencoders for predicting sentiment distributions. In: Proceedings of the 2011 International Conference on Empirical Methods in Natural Language (EMNLP), pp. 151–161 (2011)

Iyyer, M., Enns, P., Boyd-Graber, J., Resnik, P.: Political ideology detection using recursive neural networks. In: Proceedings of the 2014 Annual Meeting of the Association for Computational Linguistics (ACL), pp. 1113–1122 (2014)

Le, Q., Mikolov, T.: Distributed represenations of sentences and documents. In: Proceedings of the 2014 International Conference on Machine Learning (ICML), pp. 1188–1196 (2014)

Duchi, J., Hazan, E., Singer, Y.: Adaptive subgradient methods for online learning and stochastic optimization. J. Mach. Learn. Res. **12**, 2121–2159 (2011)

Towards Understanding User Requests in AI Bots

Oanh Thi Tran[1,2(✉)] and Tho Chi Luong[2]

[1] International School, Vietnam National University, Hanoi Xuan Thuy, Cau Giay, Hanoi, Vietnam
oanhtt@isvnu.vn

[2] FPT Technology Research Institute, Duy Tan, Cau Giay, Hanoi, Vietnam
tholc2@fpt.com.vn

Abstract. This paper presents the task of deeply analyzing user requests: the situation in ordering bots where users input an utterance, the bots would hopefully extract its full product descriptions and then parse them to recognize each product information (PI). This information is useful to help bots better understand user requests, and act upon a much wider range of actions. We model it as a two-layer sequence labeling problem and apply CRFs to solve the task. We investigate two different feature settings, which are manually designed and automatically learnt from neural models of LSTM and CNN, to build good CRF models. In designing features, we propose additional ones based on Brown clustering to enhance the performance of CRF models. To verify the effectiveness, we build a corpus in the retail domain to conduct extensive experiments. The results show that automatically learnt features are very effective and commonly yield better performance than manually designed features. In both settings, adding the information of tags in one layer can also boost the performance of the other layer. Overall, we achieve the best performance with the F-measure of 93.08% in recognizing full product descriptions, and the F-measure of 92.97% in recognizing PI. To our knowledge, this is the first attempt towards understanding user utterances in the context of building Vietnamese ordering bots.

Keywords: Ordering chatbots · Understanding user requests
Product information · Neural models

1 Introduction

Chatbots are changing the way companies engage with their customers. Many companies are jumping on this growing trend to give customers more accessibility to merchants, offer consumers a variety of options, etc. Most real chatbots often allow users to execute a single task through a conversational interface. A challenge to building such chatbots is the ability to understand user requests in sophisticated natural languages. Let us take a bot as an example, one that only does one thing - orders takeout. When someone states a task he want to

X. Geng and B.-H. Kang (Eds.): PRICAI 2018, LNAI 11012, pp. 864–877, 2018.
https://doi.org/10.1007/978-3-319-97304-3_66

complete via the message '*ship me a cup of tea please*', the bot would hopefully recognize the ordering command '*ship*'[1] and the full product description '*a cup of tea*', then analyze that content to extract its PI[2] ('*a* (amount = 1) *cup* (unit of measurement) of *tea* (product name)'). Understanding user requests allows our bots to response and act upon a much wider range of actions, or even ask the user for any missing value until bots understand and acknowledge the request (e.g. if the user did not mention product attributes or product quantities, bots would provide a response with appropriate information or direction to understand user needs (*hot coffee* or *ice coffee*, or what size (*large, medium, or small*) the user would like to order); if the chosen product is not found, bots would ask users to choose available alternative products; or if the requested product is relevant, then bots would confirm and automatically add that order into his shopping cart, etc.). This makes our bots smarter and seem more human, and thus more engaging. Such systems usually consist of three key steps as shown in Fig. 1. This figure also presents another complicated example of user utterances.

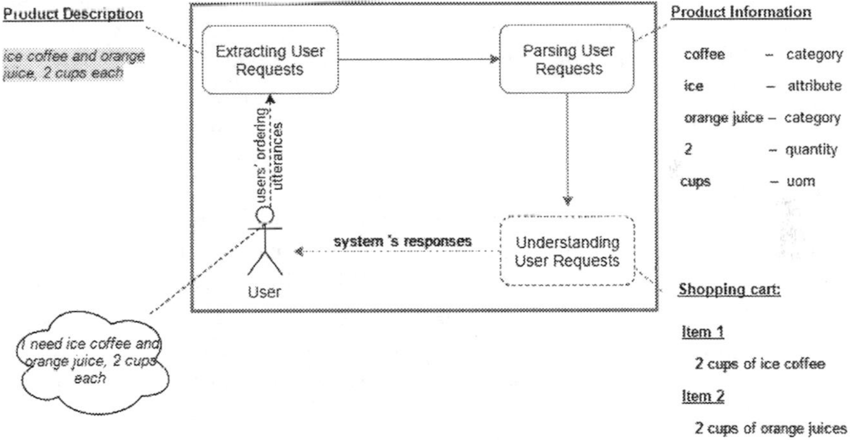

Fig. 1. A framework for analyzing users' requests.

1. *Extracting user requests*: Each incoming request will be analyzed to extract full product descriptions which customers wish to order.
2. *Parsing user requests*: This step parses those product descriptions to map each text fragment into a basic PI. This information will be helpful for AI bots in automatically determining users' desired products.
3. *Understanding user requests*: To help our bots better understand ordering contents, we need a further step to associate PI into complete items.

[1] via another intent detection module.

[2] Selling online requires companies to collect clear basic PI that consumers can actually understand. Without PI, e.g. the name of the product, price and product category, the product could not be found and sold online at all.

In this paper, we concentrate on the first two steps. These are important and challenging problems requiring the value of understanding texts because:

- A product description can be mentioned in different ways (*2 large cups of coffee*, *coffee 2 cups of large size*, *coffee give me two cups*, etc.).
- Product descriptions and some PI are typically long (i.e. containing more than four words).
- Variations in product names, spelling errors, error typos, abbreviations, teen-code languages, etc. are quite common in social data like this.
- Many utterances are complicated and hence more difficult to analyze (e.g case *1c* in Sect. 4.1).

There have been some studies on processing user requests in chatbots [9, 14, 19–21]. The most common technique used is the information retrieval (IR) method. The method could find the most similar question to respond to users the paired answer [9, 20] or using keyword matching or rule-based methods [14] to somewhat catch up the idea about user desires. Unfortunately, using hand-crafted matching rules is cost-consuming, requires domain experts, and cannot handle with ambiguity. To overcome these drawbacks, some researches [6, 21] proposed to detect which products customers are mentioning by extensively exploiting some external data resources such as search logs and community sites. However, this method could not be used to extract many types of PI (as in this work). Moreover, these resources may be intractable in many cases due to unavailability or difficulty to collect.

To our knowledge, there has no public research about deeply analyzing user requests to support online ordering of customers, especially for Vietnamese. In this paper, therefore, we focus on studying and building an intelligent module to equip our AI bots with the ability to understand what users have requested. To achieve this goal, we formulate the task as a two-layer sequence labeling task and apply CRFs [10] to solve the task. We investigate two feature settings to build good CRFs models, which are manually designed and automatically learnt from neural models of LSTM [7] and CNN [12]. In designing features, we propose additional ones based on Brown clustering [5] to enhance the performance of CRF models. In both setting, we also propose adding the information of tags in one layer to boost the performance of the other layer. To verify the effectiveness of the proposed method, we also build a corpus in the domain of drinks ordering to conduct different experiments. In conclusion, our paper makes the following contributions:

1. Proposing a framework for solving the task of understanding user requests in online shopping contexts.
2. Introducing an annotated corpus about user requests in the retail domains of ordering drinks in Vietnam.
3. Showing the effectiveness of the proposed method by conducting extensive experiments.

The rest of this paper is organized as follows. Section 2 presents some related work. Section 3 describes our solution to extract and parse user requests. In

Sect. 4, we show the process of building corpus, setting up experiments, and experimental results using different settings. Some errors are listed in Sect. 5. Finally, we conclude the paper and point out some future work in Sect. 6.

2 Related Work

To understand and response users, current chatbots mostly use IR techniques [9,16,20]. That is given a question, the approach retrieves the most similar question in existing question-answer (FAQ) pairs and takes the paired answer as a response. This technique is usually applied to build open-domain chatbots (e.g. serving chit-chat), or answer FAQs in a given domain. For examples, Britxey et al. [4] built a bot answering a wide variety of sexual health questions on HIV/AIDS.

In e-commerce domains, there existed several researches on analyzing user utterances using IR techniques. For example, Cui et al. [6] selected the best answer from existing data sources within the page (including PI, question answering datasets, and customer reviews) to support chit-chat, answer information, and give comments about a given product. Yan et al. [21] presented a general solution towards building task-oriented dialogue systems for online shopping, aiming to assist online customers in completing various purchase-related tasks, such as searching products and answering questions. To detect which product a customer is asking, the system matched the question to basic PI using DSSM model [8]. Unfortunately, these studies do not support customers to perform ordering online, and their external data resources are not always tractable.

For Vietnamese, to our knowledge there was very little work about this topic [14,19]. Ngo et al. [14] used a MaxEnt classifier to classify applications and a conjunction matching method to identify actions. Designing that matching is cost-consuming, requires domain experts, and cannot handle with ambiguity (especially with the variation of languages in informal speeches). In this work, they focused on processing simple questions which are usually easier to analyze to support users completing some tasks using mobile phones.

Despite the popularity and improved techniques, chatbots still face various challenges in understanding user requests, processing them to generate an appropriate response, especially in ordering chatbots. Users can give requests in a variety of ways, and conversation styles also vary from person to person. Therefore, to enhance experiences of human in ordering online products, in this paper, we focus on analyzing user requests to help bots better understand human effectively. The proposed method does not use extra external resources and also does not suffer from drawbacks of rule-based approaches.

3 A Proposed Approach to Analyze User Requests

3.1 Analyzing User Requests as a Two-Layer Sequence Labeling Task

The problem can be stated as follows: Given a user utterance in the form of a natural language $X = \{x_1, x_2, \ldots, x_n\}$, x_i is the ith word. The model would extract its full product descriptions and then recognize PI inside them. PI commonly includes categories, brands, attributes, extra-attributes, packsizes, numbers, and uoms as described as follows:

- *Category*: Product types having particular shared characteristics, e.g. in the drinks domain, we may have categories of *coffee*, *tea*, *juice*, etc.
- *Brand*: A variation of products, e.g we may have different types of juice such as *orange juice*, *lemon juice*, etc.
- *Attribute*: More details about products, e.g. *hot* or *cold*.
- *Extra-attribute*: Some remarks about products, e.g. *little sugar* or *lots of ice*.
- *Packsize*: Product sizes provided such as *small*, *medium*, and *large*.
- *Number*: Product quantities that customers want to order.
- *Uom*: the standard packing unit of measurement.

To solve this task, we model it as a two-layer sequence labeling problem. In layer 1, product descriptions are considered as entities. In layer 2, each PI is considered as a sub-entity. One example of annotating the ordering utterance is given in Fig. 2 using the IOB2 [17] notation. Every token which is a start token of an entity is labeled as a B-label. An I-label is assigned to a token if it is inside an entity. Other words that do not belong to any entity are labeled as an O-label. The word 'label' was replaced with the type of a specific entity.

WORDS	LEVEL-1 (top entities)	LEVEL-2 (sub-entities)
cho *(give)*	O	O
mình *(me)*	O	O
hai *(two)*	B_PRODUCT	B_number
cốc *(cups)*	I_PRODUCT	B_uom
café *(coffee)*	I_PRODUCT	B_category
đen *(black)*	I_PRODUCT	B-brand
đá *(ice)*	I_PRODUCT	B-attribute
nhé *(please)*	O	O

Fig. 2. An example of user requests in the IOB notation.

3.2 A Proposed Models for Solving the Sequence Labeling Task

A fast and effective strategy to label each word is to use its own features to predict labels independently. Each PI usually consists of several consecutive words, so it is beneficial to model labels jointly. Sequence labeling is the best solution by making the optimal label for a given element dependent on the choices of nearby elements. For this, we use CRFs [10] which are widely applied, and yield state-of-the-art results in many NLP tasks.

The conditional probability of a state sequence $S =< s_1, s_2, \ldots, s_T >$ given an observation sequence $O =< o_1, o_2, \ldots, o_T >$ is calculated as:

$$P(s|o) = \frac{1}{Z} exp(\sum_{t=1}^{T} \sum_{k} \lambda_k \times f_k(s_{t-1}, s_t, o, t)) \tag{1}$$

where $f_k(s_{t-1}, s_t, o, t)$ is a feature function (manually designed or automatically learnt from a neural model) whose weight λ_k is to be learned via training. To make all conditional probabilities sum up to 1, we must calculate the normalization factor Z over all state sequences:

$$Z = \sum_{s} exp(\sum_{t-1}^{T} \sum_{k} \lambda_k \times f_k(s_{t-1}, s_t, o, t)) \tag{2}$$

To build the strong model, CRFs need a good feature set. These features can be manually designed or automatically learnt through neural models. In this paper, we investigate these two methods.

Designing Feature Sets Manually. We use the following features which are commonly used in extracting entities [15] in general:

- Word unigram and word bigram[3]
- Prefixes: the first letters of tokens (up to four letters).
- Suffixes: the last letters of tokens (up to four letters).
- Word shape: token-level evidence for "being a particular entity" - orthographic evidence - *It expresses what does the word being tagged as a name look like?* - such as whether the token is a valid, first letter capitalized, etc.

For unigram and bigram, we consider the context of $[-2, -1, 0, 1, 2]$. It means that when extracting features f, we have $f[-2]$, $f[-1]$, $f[0]$, $f[1]$, and $f[2]$ for unigram; and $f[-2]f[-1]$, $f[-2]f[0]$, $f[0]f[1]$, and $f[1]f[2]$ for bigram.

To enhance the performance, in this paper, we propose using a new kind of features based on the Brown clustering algorithm. This feature has not been utilized in previous researches to recognize entities. The Brown clustering algorithm is a word clustering algorithm based on the mutual information of bigrams [5]. The input to the algorithm is a set of words and a text corpus. In the initial step, each word belongs to its own individual cluster. The algorithm then gradually groups clusters to build a hierarchical clustering of words. We use this word representation as features in our model.

Extracting Features Automatically Using Neural Models. Most state-of-the-art sequence labeling models rely heavily on hand-crafted features and domain-specific knowledge in order to learn effectively. In the past few years,

[3] part-of-speech labels are not used here because current Vietnamese pos taggers did not yield good performance on social media texts.

non-linear neural networks with as input distributed word representations have been broadly applied to NLP problems with great success. Specifically, LSTM [7] and CNN [12] have shown great success in modeling sequential data like speech recognition, POS tagging, and NER.

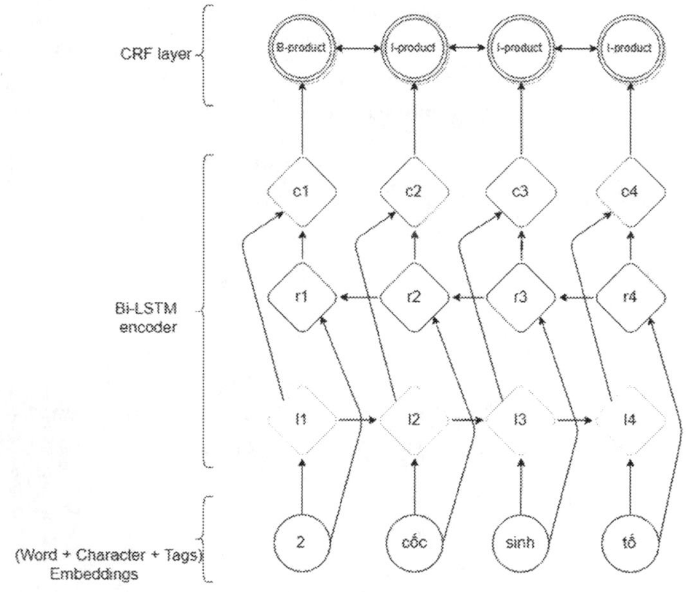

Fig. 3. A framework of using biLSTM-CRF.

In this paper, we also investigate these two neural models to automatically learn features for CRF models. These models use no language-specific resources beyond a small amount of supervised training data and unlabeled data.

biLSTM

This paper adapts the method of Lample et al. [11] which has the ability of capturing both orthographic evidence and distributional evidence. This method is able to obtain state-of-the-art NER performance in many languages without any hand-engineered features or gazetteers. In order to train a model, we use word embeddings, character embeddings. We also exploit tags of the other layer as additional features to train the model of a given layer. In the prediction phase, to predict tags of one layer, we must use trained models to predict tags of the other layer then use these tags as features to predict tags of that layer. Figure 3 illustrates the architecture of applying biLSTM-CRF for this task.

GRAM-CNN

biLSTM captures the information contained in whole sentences. However, LeCun et al. [12] argued that long sentences could contain information unrelated with the target entities, and hence, in domains with long sentences (which many user

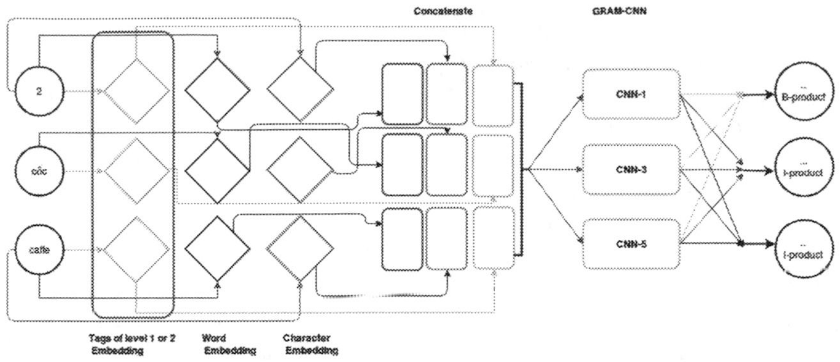

Fig. 4. A framework of using GRAM-CNN.

utterances belong to), the utilization of local information rather than whole sentences may help improve precision. Gram-CNN allows the model to extract local information between a target word and its neighbors, and hence leverages the local contexts based on n-gram character and word embeddings via CNN. Similar to biLSTM, we also use ground truth (or predicted) tags of one layer when training/testing the other model. The architecture of this approach is shown in Fig. 4 and undergoes through the following steps.

1. Generate the character, word and tags of the remaining layer embeddings.
2. Concatenate all embeddings into a combine vector.
3. Extract each word 's local features with several kernel sizes as the final representation of each word. The kernel size is equal to the size of a convolutional window across k tokens ($k = 1, 3, 5$). Suppose we are selecting a word indexed by i in a sentence from feature maps f_j convoluted by kernel size j.

$$O_i = tan\ h(f_j[i - j + 1 : i]) \tag{3}$$

4. Apply CRF to model labels jointly based on the output of GRAM-CNN.

4 Experiments

4.1 Building the Corpus

We collected raw input data from two resources:

- The history log of a famous Vietnamese restaurant.
- Asking three people to write other ordering utterances using their own informal speeches to enrich the corpus.

We also added other utterances having no ordering intents. The reason is that the intent detection module might not be perfect, so it could mis-classify some non-ordering-intent utterances as having ordering intents. Finally, we obtained 1070 raw utterances in the domain of ordering drinks. By observing, we realized that user utterances can be divided into one of the two following categories:

1. Utterances having ordering intents and each full product description inside them is clearly presented. We saw four sub-types of this group:
   (a) The PI is expressed in the order of *product_quantity, product_uom, product_category, product_attribute, product_extra_info, product_packsize.*
   (b) Special forms: the order of PI may be listed in an arbitrary form.
   (c) Utterances describe more than one product, and when clarifying their PI, users could group some common PI (e.g. *same sizes*) about several products instead of separately stating PI for each product (see one example in Fig. 1), etc.
2. Utterances without ordering intents are mis-classified into this process by intent detection modules, and they contain or do not contain PI inside them.

Then, we annotated that data at two levels using the label set listed in Sect. 3.1. Some statistics about the corpus are given in Table 1.

Table 1. Some statistics about the number of entities in the corpus.

Level	Types of PI	Quantities
1	product	1194
2	number	1322
	category	1231
	packsize	277
	attribute	641
	uom	131
	extra-attribute	670
	brand	664

4.2 Experimental Setups

We conducted 5-fold cross-validation tests. At each turn, we randomly left 20% training data as development sets for choosing best parameters. The system performance is evaluated using precision, recall, and the F_1 score as in many sequence labeling tasks [15]. In experiments, we exploited three available tools with some modifications to fit our contexts:

- CRF: use library of pyCRFsuite
- BiLSTM-CRF: https://github.com/glample/tagger
- Gram-CNN-CRF: https://github.com/valdersoul/GRAM-CNN

About word embeddings, we collected the raw data from Vietnamese newpapers (≈7 GB texts) to train the word vector model using Glove[4]. We fixed the

[4] https://github.com/standfordnlp/GloVe.

number of word embedding dimensions at 50, the number of character embedding dimensions at 25, and the number of dimensions for tags of layers at 10. To produce word representations, we used that plain text to conduct the Brown clustering algorithm to cluster words. We set the number of clusters at 200. For this task, we extracted features at 4-bit depth and 6-bit depth.

4.3 Experimental Results

Three types of experiments are performed. The first one is to verify the effectiveness of proposed features using Brown clustering. The second one is to make comparison between two feature settings, which are manually designed or automatically learnt from neural models. The last one is to demonstrate that whether using tags of one layer can boost the performance of the other layer or not.

Experiments Using Brown Clustering as Additional Features. Figure 5 indicated experiment results with/without using Brown clustering as features. It expressed that using Brown clustering was quite effective and overall improved the performance of systems in both two layers.

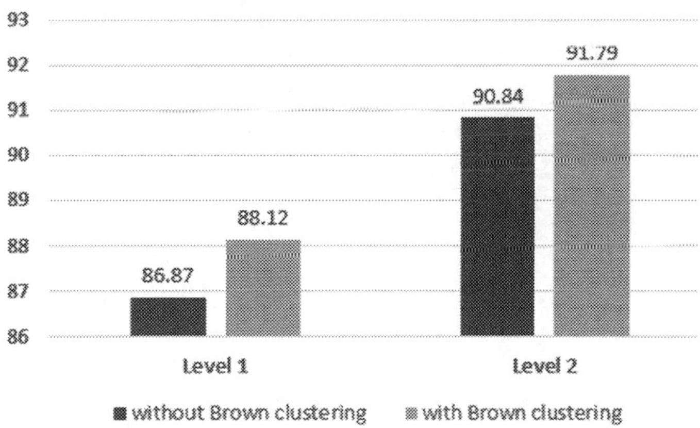

Fig. 5. Experimental results (F1 score) of using CRFs with/without Brown clustering as features.

Experiments on Comparing the Effectiveness of Two Feature Settings. For recognizing product descriptions in layer 1 (see Table 2), using CRFs produced the lowest performance with the F-measure of 88.12%. By using neural networks, we could boost the performance of the system. Specifically, in comparison to using CRFs, Gram-CNN-CRF and biLSTM-CRF improved the performance by 2.79% and 2.4%, respectively. Between these two neural models, GramCNN-CRF yielded a little bit higher performance than biLSTM-CRF.

For recognizing PI in layer 2, Gram-CNN also yielded the best performance with a F-measure of 93.08%, which is 1.29% higher than the second best system - CRFs. The lowest performing approach is biLSTM-CRF with the F-measure of 90.11%. Among PI, detecting some information (such as product-number, product-attribute) is easier than others (such as product-brand, product-extra-attribute).

In general, it can be said that automatically learning features using neural models yields better performance than manually designing them.

Table 2. Experimental results of two layers using CRFs, biLSTM-CRFs, and Gram-CNN-CRFs.

		CRF			biLSTM-CRF			Gram-CNN-CRF		
		P	R	F_1	P	R	F_1	P	R	F_1
Level 1	product_desc	87.36	88.9	88.12	89.71	91.35	90.52	90.6	91.24	**90.91**
Level 2	attribute	95.81	94.38	95.08	93.69	95.63	94.63	95.9	97.24	**95.8**
	brand	85.32	86.86	86.07	82.44	83.24	82.77	89.38	88.64	**88.98**
	category	90.23	90.63	90.42	86.24	88.45	87.32	91.44	91.9	**91.67**
	extra_attribute	87.43	87.78	**87.53**	87.89	86.76	87.26	88.83	86.24	87.39
	packsize	89.94	90.12	90.01	85.03	86.82	85.84	91.62	93.14	**92.36**
	number	96.07	94.67	95.36	95.24	95.35	95.28	95.88	95.92	**95.89**
	uom	89.61	93.53	91.48	88.8	91.73	90.16	92.12	92.33	**92.19**
	Averaged	91.6	91.98	91.79	89.39	90.86	90.11	92.95	93.21	**93.08**

Experiments on Adding Tags of One Layer in Predicting Other Layer. Table 3 shows experimental results of each layer by adding information about tags of the other layer. We observed a large performance increase in level 1. Specifically, when applying models of CRFs, and Gram-CNN-CRF, F-measures increased up to 89.02% and 92.97%, respectively. Using biLSTM-CRF slightly decreased the F-measure from 90.52% to 89.85%. This means that using the information about PI is quite effective in recognizing the whole product description. Conversely, the information of product description somewhat also increased the performance of detecting PI in level 2. There was a small improvement in F-measures using CRFs and biLSTM-CRF, however no change in the case of Gram-CNN-CRF. In general, the information about tags of each layer is beneficial to each other.

Table 3. Experimental results using tags of one layer as additional features in building models of the other layer

		CRF			biLSTM-CRF			Gram-CNN-CRF		
		P	R	F_1	P	R	F_1	P	R	F_1
Level 1	product_desc	89.16	88.88	89.02	89.04	90.68	89.85	92.10	93.86	**92.97**
Level 2	attribute	96.13	94.47	95.29	96.16	95.17	95.64	96.15	97.19	**96.66**
	brand	87.53	86.26	86.88	81.79	85.8	83.67	88.91	88.76	**88.79**
	category	90.48	89.45	89.96	88.27	88.81	88.54	92.45	93	**92.72**
	extra_attribute	88.31	87.32	87.65	84.01	83.06	83.49	87.18	89.13	**88.07**
	packsize	93.19	89.65	91.38	88.98	89.28	89.08	93.84	94.13	**93.97**
	number	96.87	94.53	95.68	97	96.15	**96.57**	96.18	96.44	96.3
	uom	89.1	92.41	90.7	91.06	93.76	**92.31**	90.68	92.48	91.52
	Averaged	92.35	91.42	91.88	90.94	91.75	91.34	93.11	93.12	**93.08**

Case	Error examples
1	... mười năm (đúng chính tả là *"mười lăm"*) .... *ten years (should be "fifteen")*
2	... sinh tố size S 1 vị việt quất ... *... smoothie size S with the flavour of biberry ...*
3	.... 1 cốc hazenut loại cốc to .... *... 1 cup of hazenut with the cup of large size ...*
4	... 2 bình chà hg vị nho .... *... 2 bottles of tea with grape flavor ...*

Fig. 6. Some error examples in the best system using Gram-CNN-CRF models.

5 Error Analysis

Observing the output of the best system, we saw some errors which can be classified into some of the following types:

- Spelling errors in a variety of ways as in case 1 (see Fig. 6), which lead the system only recognizes '*ten*' rather than '*fifteen*' as a number.
- Some categories are mis-recognized as attributes, and categories are mis-recognized as brands. For example, in case 4, the system mis-classified '*tea with grape flavor*' as a product category. The ground truth should be '*tea*' as a product category, and '*grape flavor*' as its brand.
- In some sentences, when referring attributes of a product, users occasionally add some extra descriptions in informal speeches (case 2, 3) which make our system could not handle (not learnt from training data).

6 Conclusion

In this paper, we described the task of deeply analyzing user requests. The main points are to extract full product descriptions and then parse them to recognize their PI. To solve the task, we modeled two layers of sequence labeling and then applied CRFs to build models. To build the strong model using CRFs, we tried two feature settings. Firstly, we manually designed good feature sets based on previous researches on NER tasks. Moreover, we also proposed additional features based on Brown clustering algorithm. These features were indeed helpful to boost the performance of CRFs models. Secondly, we investigated two powerful neural models to automatically learn features for CRF models. These models use no language-specific resources beyond a small amount of supervised training data and unlabeled data. To verify the effectiveness of the proposed models, we built a corpus in the retail domain. The experimental results showed that using automatically learnt features was very effective and commonly yielded better performance than manually designed features. In addition, the information about tags in one level was also helpful in recognizing entities in other level. Overall, we achieved the best performance with the F-measure of 93.08% in layer 1, and the F-measure of 92.97% in layer 2. This result is very promising to help bots better understand user requests.

In the future, we will investigate the third phase of the framework. We also intend to adapt the proposed method so that it can work well in other domains rather than the drinks ordering domain.

References

1. Bach, N.X., Minh, N.L., Oanh, T.T., Shimazu, A.: A two-phase framework for learning logical structures of paragraphs in legal articles. ACM Trans. Asian Lang. Inf. Process. (ACM TALIP) **12**(1), 1–32 (2013)
2. Bikel, D.M., Schwartz, R.L., Weischedel, R.M.: An algorithm that learns what's in a name. Mach. Learn. J. **34**(1–3), 211–231 (1999)
3. Borthwick: Maximum entropy approach to named entity recognition. Ph.D. thesis, New York University (1999)
4. Brixey, J., et al.: SHIHbot: a Facebook chatbot for sexual health information on HIV/AIDS. In: 18th Annual Meeting of the Special Interest Group on Discourse and Dialogue, pp. 370–373. Association for Computational Linguistics (2017)
5. Brown, P., deSouza, P., Mercer, R., Pietra, V., Lai, J.: Class-based n-gram models of natural language. J. Comput. Linguist. **18**(4), 467–479 (1992)
6. Cui, L., Huang, S., Wei, F., Tan, C., Duan, C., Zhou, M.: Superagent: a customer service chatbot for e-commerce websites. In: Proceedings of ACL 2017, System Demonstrations, pp. 97–102. Association for Computational Linguistics (2017)
7. Hochreiter, S., Schmidhuber, J.: Long short-term memory. J. Neural Comput. **9**(8), 1735–1780 (1997)
8. Huang, P.S., He, X., Gao, J.F., Deng, L., Acero, A., Heck, L.: Learning deep structured semantic models for web search using clickthrough data. In: Proceedings of the 22nd ACM International Conference on Information and Knowledge Management, pp. 2333–2338. ACM, New York (2013)
9. Ji, Z.J., Lu, Z.D., Li, H.: An information retrieval approach to short text conversation. arXiv:1408.6988 [cs.IR] (2014)
10. Lafferty, J.D., McCallum, A., Perera, F.C.N.: Conditional random fields: probabilistic models for segmenting and labeling sequence data. In: 18th International Conference on Machine Learning, pp. 282–289. Morgan Kaufmann Publishers Inc., San Francisco (2001)

11. Lample, G., Ballesteros, M., Subramanian, S., Kawakami, K., Dyer, C.: Neural architectures for named entity recognition. In: 2016 Conference of the North American Chapter of the Association for Computational Linguistics: Human Language Technologies, pp. 260–270. Association for Computational Linguistics, San Diego (2016)
12. LeCun, Y., Bengio, Y.: Convolutional networks for images, speech, and time series. In: The Handbook of Brain Theory and Neural Networks, pp. 255–258. MIT Press, Cambridge (1998)
13. Li, W., McCallum, A.: Rapid development of Hindi named entity recognition using conditional random fields and feature induction. ACM Trans. Asian Lang. Inf. Process. (TALIP) **2**(3), 290–294 (2003)
14. Ngo, T.-L., et al.: Identifying user intents in vietnamese spoken language commands and its application in smart mobile voice interaction. In: Nguyen, N.T., Trawiński, B., Fujita, H., Hong, T.-P. (eds.) ACIIDS 2016. LNCS (LNAI), vol. 9621, pp. 190–201. Springer, Heidelberg (2016). https://doi.org/10.1007/978-3-662-49381-6_19
15. Nguyen, C.T., Tran, T.O., Phan, X.H., Ha, Q.T.: Named entity recognition in Vietnamese free-text and web documents using conditional random fields. In: The 8th Conference on Some selection problems of Information Technology and Telecommunication, HaiPhong, Vietnam (2005)
16. Qiu, M., et al.: AliMe chat: a sequence to sequence and rerank based chatbot engine. In: Annual Meeting of the Association for Computational Linguistics (2017)
17. Sang, E.F., Veenstra, J.: Representing text chunks. In: Proceedings of the ninth conference on European chapter of the Association for Computational Linguistics, pp. 173–179. Association for Computational Linguistics (1999)
18. Sobhana, N.V., Mitra, P., Ghosh, S.K.: Conditional random field based named entity recognition in geological text. Int. J. Comput. Appl. **1**(3), 119–122 (2010)
19. Tran, P.-N., Ta, V.-D., Truong, Q.-T., Duong, Q.-V., Nguyen, T.-T., Phan, X.-H.: Named entity recognition for Vietnamese spoken texts and its application in smart mobile voice interaction. In: Nguyen, N.T., Trawiński, B., Fujita, H., Hong, T.-P. (eds.) ACIIDS 2016. LNCS (LNAI), vol. 9621, pp. 170–180. Springer, Heidelberg (2016). https://doi.org/10.1007/978-3-662-49381-6_17
20. Yan, Z., et al.: DocChat: an information retrieval approach for chatbot engines using unstructured documents. In: The Proceedings of ACL (2016)
21. Yan, Z., Duan, N., Chen, P., Zhou, M., Zhou, J., Li., Z.: Building task-oriented dialogue systems for online shopping. In: Proceedings of AAAI, pp. 4618–4626 (2017)
22. Zhu, Q., Li, X., Conesa, A., Pereira, C.: GRAM-CNN: a deep learning approach with local context for named entity recognition in biomedical text. J. Bioinform. 18 (2017)

A Deep Reinforced Training Method for Location-Based Image Captioning

Lei Zhao, Chunxia Zhang, Xi Zhang, Yating Hu(✉), and Zhendong Niu(✉)

School of Computer Science and Technology, Beijing Institute of Technology, 5 South Zhongguancun Street, Haidian District, Beijing, China
{zhao_lei,cxzhang,xi_zhang,00034490,zniu}@bit.edu.cn

Abstract. Neural encoder-decoder frameworks have been used extensively in image captioning. Recent research has shown that reinforcement learning can be utilized to train these frameworks directly on non-differentiable evaluation metrics. However, the captions generated by this method usually have limited grammaticality and readability. In this paper, we propose a novel model with the location-based mechanism which introduces the location information of each region in the image, and a combined training method that combines the cross entropy loss and reinforcement learning. We evaluate our model on four public benchmarks: Flickr8k, Flickr30k, MSCOCO and Image Chinese Captioning (ICC). Experimental results show that our model can improve the readability of the generated captions and outperforms the state-of-the-art methods across different evaluation metrics.

Keywords: Image captioning · Location-based mechanism
Combined training

1 Introduction

Being able to automatically generate a natural language description from an image is a very challenging task at the intersection of computer vision, natural language processing and artificial intelligence. This task, often referred to as image or visual captioning, forms the technical foundation of many important applications, such as semantic visual search, aid for visually impaired people and visual intelligence in chatting robots.

Inspired by the recent success of machine translation, researchers studied an end-to-end encoder-decoder framework for image captioning. Approaches following this framework generally encode an image as a single feature vector by convolutional neural networks (CNN), and then feed such vector into recurrent neural networks (RNN) to generate captions [4,8,30]. More recently in [34], the

This work was supported by the National Natural Science Foundation of China (No. 61370137) and the Ministry of Education China Mobile Research Foundation Project (No. 2016/2-7).

X. Geng and B.-H. Kang (Eds.): PRICAI 2018, LNAI 11012, pp. 878–890, 2018.
https://doi.org/10.1007/978-3-319-97304-3_67

researchers utilized an attention-based mechanism to learn where to focus in the image during caption generation. The attention-based mechanisms lead to better generalization, as these models can compose novel text descriptions based on the recognition of the global and local entities that comprise images.

The models above are usually trained to maximize the likelihood of the next ground-truth word given the previous ground-truth words. However, this method will lead to the "exposure bias" problem [22], since at the test time, the model uses previously generated words from the model distribution to predict the next word. The second problem is about the inconsistency between the optimizing function at training time and the evaluation metrics at test time. The training procedure attempts to lower the cross entropy loss, while the metrics used to evaluate a generated sentence are some discrete and non-differentiable NLP metrics, such as BLEU [20], ROUGE [13], CIDEr [28] and METEOR [3]. In order to solve these two problems, there are some works exploring the idea of incorporating the reinforcement learning into image captioning. For example, [25] proposed a self-critical sequence training algorithm which uses the reinforcement learning algorithm to optimize a particular evaluation metric.

Despite their better performance, the models above still have some shortcomings. Although directly optimizing the evaluation metric can apparently improve the scores of the metrics, the generated captions usually have limited grammaticality and readability [15]. However, using cross entropy loss to optimize the model can often generate more readable captions. So combing these two optimizing methods will effectively solve the readability issue of the reinforcement learning. In this paper, we present a new training method called combined training to the image captioning. We combine the cross entropy loss and the reinforcement learning algorithm together to optimize the model. Besides, the location information of each image region is important when encoding images into vectors and can improve the performance of the model. So we additionally add the location information of the image region and present a new location-based mechanism.

Overall, the main contributions of this paper are:

- We introduce the location information of each region in the image to image captioning and propose a new location-based mechanism.
- We combine the cross entropy loss and the reinforcement learning algorithm together to optimize the model which can not only improve the scores of the evaluation metrics but also generate more fluent and readable captions.
- We conduct a massive of experiments and comparisons with other methods. The results demonstrate that our model outperforms the state-of-the-art methods on Flickr8k [23], Flickr30k [36], MSCOCO [14] and Image Chinese Captioning (ICC) [32] datasets.

2 Related Work

Early approaches to image captioning can be roughly divided into two families. The first one is based on template matching [5,11,12]. These approaches start from detecting objects, actions and attributes in images and then fill them into a hand-designed and rigid sentence template. The captions generated by these approaches are not always fluent and expressive. The second family is grounded on retrieval based approaches, which first select a set of the visually similar images from a large database and then transfer the captions of retrieved images to fit the query image [7,19]. There is little flexibility to modify words based on the content of the query image, since they directly rely on captions of training images and cannot generate new captions.

Motivated by the recent success of sequence-to-sequence learning in machine translation [2,27], researchers proposed an end-to-end encoder-decoder framework for image captioning [4,8,18,30]. This framework usually uses the CNN as the encoder and the RNN as the decoder. The differences of various methods mainly lie in the types of CNN architectures and RNN based language models. For example, the vanilla RNN was used in [8,18], while the LSTM was used in [30]. The image feature vector was only fed into the RNN once at the first time step in [30], while it was used at each time step of the RNN in [18].

Recently, a large number of attention-based deep neural networks have been proposed for image captioning. For instance, [34] applied the attention mechanism in the image captioning task in which the decoder can function as the human's eye focusing its attention on different regions of the image at each time step. [35] proposed a semantic attention model which selectively attends to semantic concept regions by fusing the global image feature and the semantic attributes feature from an attribute detector. [17] presented an adaptive attention model with a visual sentinel to decide whether to attend to the image or to the visual sentinel. More recently, based on object detection, an up-down attention model was proposed in [1], which demonstrated a state-of-the-art performance on image captioning. However, the models above don't consider the location information of each region in the image which is essential for describing images.

More recently, researchers made efforts to incorporate reinforcement learning into the standard encoder-decoder framework to address the exposure bias and the non-differentiable metric issues. Specifically, [22] used the REINFORCE algorithm [31] and proposed a novel training method at sequence level directly optimizing the non-differentiable test metric. [16] applied the policy gradient algorithm in the training procedure for image captioning models, in which the words sampled from the current model at each time step were awarded with different future rewards via averaging the rewards of some Monte-Carlo samples. Self-critical sequence training (SCST) [25] adopted the policy gradient algorithm as well but the difference from [16] is that SCST just ran the LSTM forward process twice and obtained two sequences, one generated by running the inference algorithm at test time and the other sampled from the multinomial strategy. SCST made the reward of the sequence from the inference algorithm as a baseline to reduce the training variance. Although using the methods above can apparently improve the scores of the metrics, the generated captions usually have limited grammaticality and readability when compared with optimizing the cross entropy loss.

3 Methodology

We first give our encoder-decoder image captioning framework in Sect. 3.1. In Sect. 3.2, we introduce our location-based mechanism for image encoding. We describe the attention model of the decoder part in Sect. 3.3 and then present our combined training method in Sect. 3.4.

3.1 Encoder-Decoder Framework

We start by briefly describing the generic encoder-decoder image captioning framework [30,34]. Traditionally, given an image and the corresponding caption, CNN can be seen as an encoder to encode the input image and RNN functions as a decoder to generate the captions. As for our framework, the location-based mechanism described in Sect. 3.2 can be regarded as the encoder part in this work. And following the work in [1], we adopt two layers of attention-based LSTM to be the decoder. The overview of our framework is illustrated in Fig. 1.

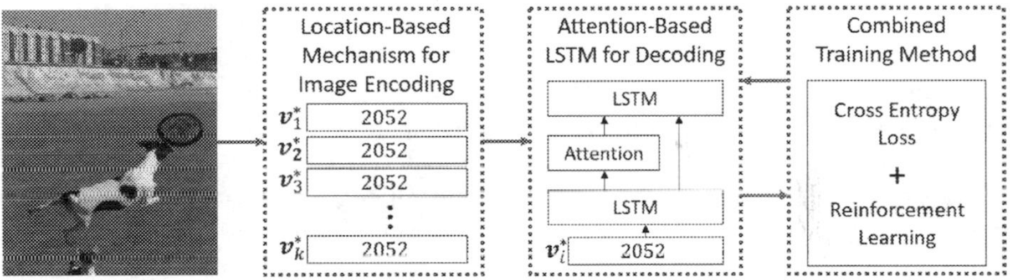

Fig. 1. Overview of our framework. Given an image, we use the location-based mechanism to encode it into a set of k image features and feed them into two layers of attention-based LSTM. During training, we employ the combined training method to optimize the model.

And in the following sections, we will refer to the operation of the LSTM over a single time step using the following notation:

$$\boldsymbol{h}_t = \text{LSTM}(\boldsymbol{x}_t, \boldsymbol{h}_{t-1}) \tag{1}$$

where $\boldsymbol{x}_t$ is the LSTM input vector and $\boldsymbol{h}_t$ is the LSTM output vector. Here we have neglected the propagation of memory cells for notational convenience.

3.2 Location-Based Mechanism for Image Encoding

As discussed in Sect. 1, the location information of the image region is essential for describing images. And in this work, we use the Faster R-CNN [24] to do object detection, and then concat the region feature and the region location to form the location-based embedding mechanism. Faster R-CNN is an object detection model designed to identify instances of objects belonging to certain classes and localize them with bounding boxes. Traditionally, given an image I, a deep CNN encodes it into a fixed-sized set of image features V through the spatial output layer. While in our method, we encode the image into a variably-sized set of k image features V^*, where each image feature encodes a salient region of the image.

Following the work in [1], we first initialize the Faster R-CNN with the ResNet-101 [6] pretrained for classification on ImageNet [26]. Then we train the model above on Visual Genome [29] data. The hyperparameters we use are the same as in [1]. After that, the location-based model is successfully pretrained.

Then we use the pretrained model to process the images in the experiment datasets. As a result, for each selected region i of the image, we can not only obtain the vector $\boldsymbol{v}_i$, which is defined as the mean-pooled convolutional feature from this region, but also obtain the concrete location $\boldsymbol{l}_i$ of this region. The dimension of $\boldsymbol{v}_i$ and $\boldsymbol{l}_i$ is 2048 and 4 respectively. Then, we concatenate the location information $\boldsymbol{l}_i$ and the feature vector $\boldsymbol{v}_i$ of the region to get the new feature representation $\boldsymbol{v}_i^*$ whose dimension D is 2052, given by:

$$\boldsymbol{v}_i^* = [\boldsymbol{v}_i, \boldsymbol{l}_i] \tag{2}$$

Using this method, only a relatively small number of k image region features are selected from a large number of possible configurations. And the selected image features not only contain visually salient objects of the image, but also contain the specific location information of each region. As a comparison, the selected image features are the more direct and richer representation of the image than the features extracted from the spatial output layer of a deep CNN. As for the number of regions per image k, we allow it to vary with the complexity of the image, up to a maximum of 100. Overall, given an image I, the location-based model can encode it into a set of k image features V^*, $V^* = \{\boldsymbol{v}_1^*, \ldots, \boldsymbol{v}_k^*\}$, $\boldsymbol{v}_i^* \in \mathbb{R}^D$.

3.3 Attention-Based LSTM for Decoding

Rather than utilizing a static representation of the image, attention models dynamically re-weight the input spatial features to focus on specific regions of the image. In this paper, we follow the work in [1] and use two layers of LSTM to achieve the attention model. The overall attention model is illustrated in Fig. 2.

The input vector to the first layer LSTM consists of the previous output of the second layer LSTM, concatenated with the mean-pooled image feature $\bar{\boldsymbol{v}}^* = \frac{1}{k}\sum_i \boldsymbol{v}_i^*$ and an encoding of the previously generated word, given by:

$$\boldsymbol{x}_t^1 = [\boldsymbol{h}_{t-1}^2, \bar{\boldsymbol{v}}^*, W_e \Pi_{\mathrm{t}}] \tag{3}$$

where $W_e \in \mathbb{R}^{E \times \Sigma}$ is a word embedding matrix for a vocabulary of size Σ, and Π_{t} is one-hot encoding of the input word at timestep t. The word embedding is learned from random initialization without pretraining.

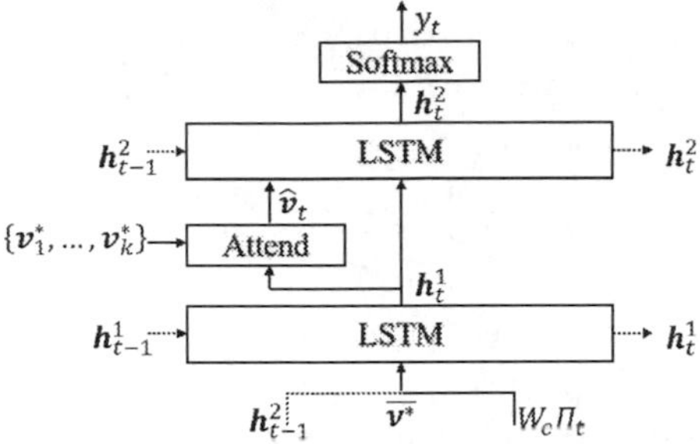

Fig. 2. Overview of the attention model. Two LSTM layers are used to selectively attend to spatial image features $\{v_1^*, \ldots, v_k^*\}$ generated by location-based model.

Given the output $\boldsymbol{h}_t^1$ of the first layer LSTM, at each time step t we generate a normalized attention weight $\alpha_{i,t}$ for each of the k image features $\boldsymbol{v}_i^*$ as follows:

$$a_{i,t} = \boldsymbol{w}_a^T \tanh\left(W_{va}\boldsymbol{v}_i^* + W_{ha}\boldsymbol{h}_t^1\right) \tag{4}$$

$$\boldsymbol{\alpha}_t = \mathrm{softmax}(\boldsymbol{a}_t) \tag{5}$$

where $W_{va} \in \mathbb{R}^{H\times V^*}$, $W_{ha} \in \mathbb{R}^{H\times M}$ and $\boldsymbol{w}_a \in \mathbb{R}^H$ are learned parameters. The attended image feature used as input to the second layer LSTM is calculated as a convex combination of all input features:

$$\hat{\boldsymbol{v}}_t = \sum_{i=1}^{K} \alpha_{i,t}\boldsymbol{v}_i^* \tag{6}$$

As for the second layer of LSTM, the input consists of the attended image feature, concatenated with the output of the first layer of LSTM, given by:

$$\boldsymbol{x}_t^2 = [\hat{\boldsymbol{v}}_t, \boldsymbol{h}_t^1] \tag{7}$$

At each timestep t, the conditional distribution over possible output words is given by:

$$p(y_t \mid y_1, \ldots, y_{t-1}) = \mathrm{softmax}(W_p\boldsymbol{h}_t^2 + \boldsymbol{b}_p) \tag{8}$$

where $W_p \in \mathbb{R}^{\Sigma\times M}$ and $\boldsymbol{b}_p \in \mathbb{R}^{\Sigma}$ are learned weights and biases.

3.4 Combined Training Method

In this section, we explore different kinds of ways to train our captioning model. And after comparing different training methods, we propose the combined training based on reinforcement learning for our captioning model.

Cross Entropy Loss. The most widely used method to train the encoder-decoder framework is to minimize the cross entropy loss (CE). We define

$y^* = \{y_1^*, y_2^*, \ldots, y_T^*\}$ as the ground-truth caption and our captioning model with parameters θ. The training objective is the minimization of the following loss:

$$L_{CE}(\theta) = -\sum_{t=1}^{T} \log\left(p_\theta(y_t^* \mid y_1^*, \ldots, y_{t-1}^*)\right) \tag{9}$$

However, minimizing L_{CE} will lead to two important problems. The first is called the "exposure bias" problem [22]. The model has the knowledge of the ground-truth caption during training while at the test time, the model uses previously generated words from the model to predict the next word. The second problem is the inconsistency between the optimizing function at training time and the evaluation metrics at test time. The training procedure attempts to minimize the cross entropy loss, while the metrics used to evaluate a generated caption are some discrete and non-differentiable NLP metrics such as CIDEr.

Reinforcement Learning. One way to solve these two problems is to incorporate the reinforcement learning to image captioning which maximizes the specific discrete metric instead of minimizing the cross entropy loss. In our model, we use the self-critical policy gradient training algorithm [25].

For this training algorithm, the model produces two different captions at each training iteration. The first is y^s, which is obtained by sampling from the $p_\theta(y_t^s \mid y_1^s, \ldots, y_{t-1}^s)$ probability distribution at each decoding time step. The second is the baseline output: $\hat{y}$, which is obtained by greedily decoding at each time step. Then we define r as the reward function for an output caption and we choose the CIDEr [28] to be the reward function. The training objective $L_{RL}(\theta)$ is the following formulation:

$$L_{RL}(\theta) = (r(\hat{y}) - r(y^s)) \sum_{t=1}^{T} \log\left(p_\theta(y_t^s \mid y_1^s, \ldots, y_{t-1}^s)\right) \tag{10}$$

We can see that if the sampled caption y^s obtains a higher reward than the baseline caption $\hat{y}$, minimizing L_{RL} is equivalent to maximizing the conditional likelihood of y^s.

Combined Training. Although directly optimizing the evaluation metric using reinforcement learning can apparently improve the scores of the metrics, the generated captions are usually not fluent and readable [15]. And human-readability is better captured by a language model. Since the training objective using cross entropy loss is essentially a conditional language model, calculating the probability of a token y_t based on the previously predicted caption $\{y_1, \ldots, y_{t-1}\}$, we hypothesize that it can assist the reinforcement learning algorithm to generate more natural captions. Finally we define a combined training (CT) method which combines the cross entropy loss and the reinforcement learning algorithm. Using the combined training method, we can combine the advantages of the cross entropy loss and the reinforcement learning algorithm, hence effectively solving the readability issues of the reinforcement learning as well as the exposure bias problem and the loss-evaluation mismatch problem of the cross entropy loss. The training objective $L_{CT}(\theta)$ is the following formulation:

$$L_{CT}(\theta) = \lambda L_{RL}(\theta) + (1 - \lambda) L_{CE}(\theta) \tag{11}$$

where λ is a scaling factor between $L_{RL}(\theta)$ and $L_{CE}(\theta)$. A similar method has been used in [33] for machine translation and in [21] for abstractive summarization, but it is the first time using the combined training method for image captioning to improve the readability of the captions.

4 Experiments

4.1 Datasets and Settings

We evaluate our proposed method on the popular Flickr8k [23], Flickr30k [36] and MSCOCO [14] datasets as well as the image Chinese captioning (ICC) [32] dataset. We report results using the COCO captioning evaluation tool[1], including BLEU [20], METEOR [3], ROUGE-L [13] and CIDEr [28].

Flickr8k, Flickr30k and MSCOCO contain 8,000, 31,783 and 123,287 images respectively and each image has five reference captions in English. To make the results comparable to others, we use the publicly available splits[2] of training, validating and testing sets for Flickr8k, Flickr30k and MSCOCO. We also follow the publicly available code [8] to preprocess the captions (*i.e.* building dictionaries, tokenizing the captions).

Image Chinese captioning (ICC) is the largest image captioning dataset whose captions are labeled in Chinese. The number of captions is 1,050,000 captions for 210,000 images in training, 150,000 captions for 30,000 images in validation and 150,000 captions for 30,000 images in testing. Since the standard testing set is not public, we merge the training and validation images and randomly split them into 220,000 images in training, 10,000 images in validation and 10,000 images in testing for offline evaluation. One difference is that we use the "Jieba" Chinese word segmentation module instead of the English tokenization module during preprocessing the captions.

4.2 Implementation Details

We set the size of hidden state M in each LSTM to 1024, the size of the hidden state H in attention layer to 512 and the size of word embedding E to 1024. We train all models with a batch size of 16 using ADAM [9] optimizer with a learning rate of 5×10^{-4} under CE loss and 5×10^{-5} under RL loss and CT loss. We use a $\lambda = 0.9924$ for the CT loss function. At test time, we use beam search of width 3 on all our models to generate captions.

[1] https://github.com/tylin/coco-caption.

[2] https://github.com/karpathy/neuraltalk.

4.3 Performance on Datasets

To test the effectiveness of the location-based mechanism and the combined training method, we conduct a series of experiments on the typical English (Flickr30k) and Chinese (ICC) datasets. We first run the model under CE loss with and without location information to validate the location-based mechanism and select the best performing architecture. Next we initialize the model with the best CE parameters and we compare the reinforcement learning using RL loss with our combined training method using CT loss. The results of these four models are listed in Table 1. We observe that the location-based mechanism can improve the performance apparently through comparing CE model with other three models. In addition, we can see that on all datasets, both the RL and CT models obtain much higher scores than the CE model, which verifies the effectiveness of reinforcement learning. And the CT model has the competitive performance in all metrics when compared with the RL model both in English and Chinese.

Table 1. Performance of our proposed models on Flickr30k and ICC datasets.

Dataset	Model	BLEU-1	BLEU-2	BLEU-3	BLEU-4	METEOR	ROUGE-L	CIDEr
Flickr30k	CE	0.680	0.501	0.360	0.255	0.201	0.463	0.540
	CE-location	0.684	0.503	0.362	0.259	0.205	0.468	0.543
	RL-location	0.715	0.527	0.378	0.270	0.206	**0.482**	**0.569**
	CT-location	**0.723**	**0.533**	**0.384**	**0.276**	**0.208**	**0.482**	0.567
ICC	CE	0.848	0.758	0.673	0.596	0.419	0.702	1.956
	CE-location	0.855	0.764	0.681	0.603	0.422	0.706	1.969
	RL-location	**0.868**	0.779	0.691	0.610	0.423	0.711	**2.091**
	CT-location	0.866	**0.782**	**0.692**	**0.613**	**0.427**	**0.713**	2.089

To verify the effectiveness of our proposed model, we also compare our CT model with several state-of-the-art methods on Flickr8k, Flickr30k and MSCOCO datasets. The comparison results are shown in Table 2. We can see that our CT-location model outperforms all the other models in all metrics on Flickr8k and Flickr30k datasets. As for MSCOCO dataset, our CT-location model achieves the best performance on BLEU-2, BLEU-3, BLEU-4, METEOR, ROUGE-L among all the models. When looking at other metrics, our model is also one of the best. The reason why our model does not beat Up-Down [1] in all metrics especially CIDEr is that we use the combined training method to improve the readability instead of directly optimizing CIDEr.

4.4 Qualitative Analysis

To better understand whether the combined training method improves the readability of the generated captions compared to reinforcement learning, we provide some quality examples of our models shown in Fig. 3. The captions of the top three images are in English and the bottom three are in Chinese. We also translate the Chinese captions into English for better understanding. For each language, the captions in the first and second rows are generated under the CE loss with and without location information. And the captions in the third and last rows are generated under the RL loss and CT loss respectively. So we can see that the RL and CT model can generate more descriptive captions than the CE model both in English and Chinese. For instance in image 2, the RL model and CT model can "see" the ball in the image, while the CE model only recognizes three dogs. Specifically, when comparing the RL and CT model, we find that RL model tends to generate ungrammatical phrases which lead to the readability issues of the captions. Taking the image 6 as an example, there exists the truncated sentence towards the end of the caption generated by the RL model. This confirms that optimizing for the discrete evaluation metric such as CIDEr with the reinforcement learning can be detrimental to the model quality. While, our CT model not only has the competitive performance in all metrics, but also can generate more fluent and readable captions, which demonstrates the usefulness and value of our combined training method for image captioning.

Table 2. Performance comparison of our proposed model with other models on Flickr8k, Flickr30k and MSCOCO datasets. (–) indicates unknown scores.

Dataset	Model	BLEU-1	BLEU-2	BLEU-3	BLEU-4	METEOR	ROUGE-L	CIDEr
Flickr8k	Google NIC [30]	0.630	0.410	0.270	–	–	–	–
	Log Bilinear [10]	0.656	0.424	0.277	0.177	0.173	–	–
	Toronto [34]	0.670	0.457	0.314	0.213	0.203	–	–
	CT-location	**0.712**	**0.527**	**0.376**	**0.260**	**0.216**	**0.498**	**0.640**
Flickr30k	Google NIC [30]	0.663	0.423	0.277	0.183	–	–	–
	Toronto [34]	0.669	0.439	0.296	0.199	0.185	–	–
	ATT-FCN [35]	0.647	0.460	0.324	0.230	0.189	–	–
	Adaptive [17]	0.677	0.494	0.354	0.251	0.204	–	0.531
	CT-location	**0.723**	**0.533**	**0.384**	**0.276**	**0.208**	**0.482**	**0.567**
MSCOCO	Google NIC [30]	0.666	0.451	0.304	0.203	–	–	–
	Toronto [34]	0.718	0.504	0.357	0.250	0.230	–	–
	ATT-FCN [35]	0.709	0.537	0.402	0.304	0.243	–	–
	Adaptive [17]	0.742	0.580	0.439	0.332	0.266	–	1.085
	SCST [25]	–	–	–	0.333	0.263	0.553	1.114
	Up-Down [1]	**0.798**	–	–	0.363	**0.277**	0.569	**1.201**
	CT-location	0.795	**0.623**	**0.478**	**0.365**	**0.277**	**0.570**	1.197

Fig. 3. Quality examples of our models.

5 Conclusion

In this paper, we presented the location-based mechanism and the combined training method to image captioning task. The location-based mechanism introduces the location information of the image regions which is essential for describing images and can assist the model to generate more descriptive captions. Besides, the combined training method combines the advantages of the cross entropy loss and the reinforcement learning algorithm, hence effectively solving the readability issues of the reinforcement learning and improving the grammaticality and readability of the generated captions. Experimental results on Flickr8k, Flickr30k, MSCOCO and ICC datasets and comparisons with state-of-the-art methods demonstrated the effectiveness of our proposed method both in English and Chinese.

References

1. Anderson, P., et al.: Bottom-up and top-down attention for image captioning and VQA. arXiv preprint arXiv:1707.07998 (2017)
2. Bahdanau, D., Cho, K., Bengio, Y.: Neural machine translation by jointly learning to align and translate. arXiv preprint arXiv:1409.0473 (2014)
3. Denkowski, M., Lavie, A.: Meteor universal: language specific translation evaluation for any target language. In: Proceedings of the Ninth Workshop on Statistical Machine Translation, pp. 376–380 (2014)
4. Donahue, J., et al.: Long-term recurrent convolutional networks for visual recognition and description. In: Proceedings of the IEEE Conference on Computer Vision and Pattern Recognition, pp. 2625–2634 (2015)
5. Farhadi, A., et al.: Every picture tells a story: generating sentences from images. In: Daniilidis, K., Maragos, P., Paragios, N. (eds.) ECCV 2010. LNCS, vol. 6314, pp. 15–29. Springer, Heidelberg (2010). https://doi.org/10.1007/978-3-642-15561-1_2
6. He, K., Zhang, X., Ren, S., Sun, J.: Deep residual learning for image recognition. In: Proceedings of the IEEE Conference on Computer Vision and Pattern Recognition, pp. 770–778 (2016)
7. Hodosh, M., Young, P., Hockenmaier, J.: Framing image description as a ranking task: data, models and evaluation metrics. J. Artif. Intell. Res. **47**, 853–899 (2013)
8. Karpathy, A., Fei-Fei, L.: Deep visual-semantic alignments for generating image descriptions. In: Proceedings of the IEEE Conference on Computer Vision and Pattern Recognition, pp. 3128–3137 (2015)
9. Kingma, D.P., Ba, J.: Adam: a method for stochastic optimization. arXiv preprint arXiv:1412.6980 (2014)
10. Kiros, R., Salakhutdinov, R., Zemel, R.: Multimodal neural language models. In: International Conference on Machine Learning, pp. 595–603 (2014)
11. Kulkarni, G., et al.: BabyTalk: understanding and generating simple image descriptions. IEEE Trans. Pattern Anal. Mach. Intell. **35**(12), 2891–2903 (2013)
12. Li, S., Kulkarni, G., Berg, T.L., Berg, A.C., Choi, Y.: Composing simple image descriptions using web-scale n-grams. In: Proceedings of the Fifteenth Conference on Computational Natural Language Learning, pp. 220–228. Association for Computational Linguistics (2011)
13. Lin, C.Y.: Rouge: a package for automatic evaluation of summaries. In: Text Summarization Branches Out (2004)
14. Lin, T.-Y., et al.: Microsoft COCO: common objects in context. In: Fleet, D., Pajdla, T., Schiele, B., Tuytelaars, T. (eds.) ECCV 2014. LNCS, vol. 8693, pp. 740–755. Springer, Cham (2014). https://doi.org/10.1007/978-3-319-10602-1_48
15. Liu, C.W., Lowe, R., Serban, I.V., Noseworthy, M., Charlin, L., Pineau, J.: How not to evaluate your dialogue system: an empirical study of unsupervised evaluation metrics for dialogue response generation. arXiv preprint arXiv:1603.08023 (2016)
16. Liu, S., Zhu, Z., Ye, N., Guadarrama, S., Murphy, K.: Optimization of image description metrics using policy gradient methods. arXiv preprint arXiv:1612.00370 (2016)
17. Lu, J., Xiong, C., Parikh, D., Socher, R.: Knowing when to look: adaptive attention via a visual sentinel for image captioning. In: Proceedings of the IEEE Conference on Computer Vision and Pattern Recognition, CVPR, vol. 6 (2017)
18. Mao, J., Xu, W., Yang, Y., Wang, J., Huang, Z., Yuille, A.: Deep captioning with multimodal recurrent neural networks (m-RNN). arXiv preprint arXiv:1412.6632 (2014)

19. Ordonez, V., Kulkarni, G., Berg, T.L.: Im2Text: describing images using 1 million captioned photographs. In: Advances in Neural Information Processing Systems, pp. 1143–1151 (2011)
20. Papineni, K., Roukos, S., Ward, T., Zhu, W.J.: BLEU: a method for automatic evaluation of machine translation. In: Proceedings of the 40th Annual Meeting on Association for Computational Linguistics, pp. 311–318. Association for Computational Linguistics (2002)
21. Paulus, R., Xiong, C., Socher, R.: A deep reinforced model for abstractive summarization. arXiv preprint arXiv:1705.04304 (2017)
22. Ranzato, M., Chopra, S., Auli, M., Zaremba, W.: Sequence level training with recurrent neural networks. arXiv preprint arXiv:1511.06732 (2015)
23. Rashtchian, C., Young, P., Hodosh, M., Hockenmaier, J.: Collecting image annotations using Amazon's Mechanical Turk. In: Proceedings of the NAACL HLT 2010 Workshop on Creating Speech and Language Data with Amazon's Mechanical Turk, pp. 139–147. Association for Computational Linguistics (2010)
24. Ren, S., He, K., Girshick, R., Sun, J.: Faster R-CNN: towards real-time object detection with region proposal networks. In: Advances in Neural Information Processing Systems, pp. 91–99 (2015)
25. Rennie, S.J., Marcheret, E., Mroueh, Y., Ross, J., Goel, V.: Self-critical sequence training for image captioning. arXiv preprint arXiv:1612.00563 (2016)
26. Russakovsky, O., et al.: Imagenet large scale visual recognition challenge. Int. J. Comput. Vis. **115**(3), 211–252 (2015)
27. Sutskever, I., Vinyals, O., Le, Q.V.: Sequence to sequence learning with neural networks. In: Advances in Neural Information Processing Systems, pp. 3104–3112 (2014)
28. Vedantam, R., Lawrence Zitnick, C., Parikh, D.: CIDEr: consensus-based image description evaluation. In: Proceedings of the IEEE Conference on Computer Vision and Pattern Recognition, pp. 4566–4575 (2015)
29. Vendrov, I., Kiros, R., Fidler, S., Urtasun, R.: Order-embeddings of images and language. arXiv preprint arXiv:1511.06361 (2015)
30. Vinyals, O., Toshev, A., Bengio, S., Erhan, D.: Show and tell: a neural image caption generator. In: 2015 IEEE Conference on Computer Vision and Pattern Recognition, CVPR, pp. 3156–3164. IEEE (2015)
31. Williams, R.J.: Simple statistical gradient-following algorithms for connectionist reinforcement learning. In: Sutton, R.S. (ed.) Reinforcement Learning. SECS, vol. 173, pp. 5–32. Springer, Boston (1992). https://doi.org/10.1007/978-1-4615-3618-5_2
32. Wu, J., et al.: AI challenger: a large-scale dataset for going deeper in image understanding. arXiv preprint arXiv:1711.06475 (2017)
33. Wu, Y., et al.: Google's neural machine translation system: bridging the gap between human and machine translation. arXiv preprint arXiv:1609.08144 (2016)
34. Xu, K., et al.: Show, attend and tell: neural image caption generation with visual attention. In: International Conference on Machine Learning, pp. 2048–2057 (2015)
35. You, Q., Jin, H., Wang, Z., Fang, C., Luo, J.: Image captioning with semantic attention. In: Proceedings of the IEEE Conference on Computer Vision and Pattern Recognition, pp. 4651–4659 (2016)
36. Young, P., Lai, A., Hodosh, M., Hockenmaier, J.: From image descriptions to visual denotations: new similarity metrics for semantic inference over event descriptions. Trans. Assoc. Comput. Linguist. **2**, 67–78 (2014)

Graph Stream Mining Based Anomalous Event Analysis

Meng Yang[1,2(✉)], Lida Rashidi[1,2], Sutharshan Rajasegarar[3,4], and Christopher Leckie[1,2]

[1] Data61 Victoria Research Laboratory, Melbourne, Australia
{myang3,lrashidi}@student.unimelb.edu.au

[2] School of Computing and Information Systems, The University of Melbourne, Melbourne, Australia
caleckie@unimelb.edu.au

[3] School of Information Technology, Deakin University, Geelong, Australia
srajas@deakin.edu.au

[4] Department of Electrical and Electronic Engineering, The University of Melbourne, Melbourne, Australia

Abstract. A major challenge in video surveillance is how to accurately detect anomalous behavioral patterns that may indicate public safety incidents. In this work, we address this challenge by proposing a novel architecture to translate the crowd status problem in videos into a graph stream analysis task. In particular, we integrate crowd density monitoring and graph stream mining to identify anomalous crowd behavior events. A real-time tracking algorithm is proposed for automatic identification of key regions in a scene, and at the same time, the pedestrian flow density between each pair of key regions is inferred over consecutive time intervals. These key regions are represented as the nodes of a graph, and the directional pedestrian density flow between regions is used as the edge weights in the graph. We then use Graph Edit Distance as the basis for a graph stream analysis approach, to detect time intervals of anomalous flow activity and to highlight the anomalous regions according to the heaviest subgraph. Based on the experimental evaluation on four real-world datasets and a benchmark dataset (UCSD), we observe that our proposed method achieves a high cross correlation coefficient (approximately 0.8) for all four real-world datasets, and 82% AUC with 28% EER for the UCSD datasets. Further, they all provide easily interpretable summaries of events using the heaviest subgraphs.

Keywords: Anomalous event detecting · Crowd density monitoring
Graph stream mining · Heaviest subgraphs · Video surveillance

1 Introduction

The need for detecting anomalous events in video surveillance has received ample attention in recent years. Existing methods used in automated video surveillance

X. Geng and B.-H. Kang (Eds.): PRICAI 2018, LNAI 11012, pp. 891–903, 2018.
https://doi.org/10.1007/978-3-319-97304-3_68

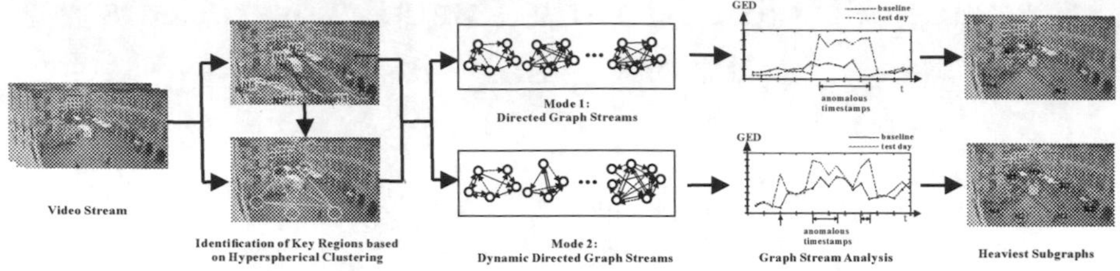

Fig. 1. The proposed monitoring system.

systems mainly model the statistics of the background, and then extract the dynamics and appearance of foreground objects, such as pedestrians and cars. Research in this area commonly follows the approach that normal patterns are first learned from training videos, and are then used to detect events that deviate from this representation. In order to address abnormal event detection, several methods have been proposed. For instance, the authors in [4] proposed a trajectory based method that uses a Multi-scale Histogram of Optical Flow (MHOF) as the extracted feature for joint sparsity model building, and this model is specially designed for multi-object anomaly detection. In terms of motion representation based approaches, Kim and Grauman [5] propose a method that models the optical flow patterns of crowd behavior with a mixture of probabilistic Principal Component Analysis (PCA). In [7], a joint model called the mixture of dynamic textures (MDT) is utilized for representing crowd behavior, and in [8], social force and other concepts are used as features to represent crowd behavior, and then these concepts are combined with a latent Dirichlet allocation (LDA) model for anomaly detection. Another category is deep model based approaches. For example, Xu et al. [9] proposed a deep learning architecture called Appearance and Motion DeepNet (AMDN), which captures and automatically learns appearance, motion and joint correlation features from video sequences for anomalous event detection. Feng et al. [11] proposed a framework that uses Stacked Denoising Auto-encoders (SDAEs) to capture short-term clues at first, followed by a sequence of recurrent neural networks in the form of Long Short-term Memory (LSTM) for learning long-term dependencies, in order to detect anomalous events.

Moreover, due to the complex nature of video stream analysis, it is difficult to use predefined rules to identify particular incidents and to characterize normal behavior patterns. Therefore, we focus on detecting anomalous incidents in videos from a statistical perspective. Specifically, we propose a novel framework that combines real-time tracking with graph mining to detect anomalous events in video streams by using a graph representation for each video image. We can then identify graph subsequences that are significantly different from the majority of graph subsequences. The first stage of our approach is to convert the video stream into a graph stream. A real-time method is used to extract the tracks of pedestrians. From these tracks we need to infer the nodes and links of our graph representation. This is achieved by clustering similar tracks, so that each cluster represents a significant crowd flow. The start and end coordinates of the cluster correspond to key regions in the scene, and are represented by nodes in the graph, while the cluster corresponds to a link between these nodes in the graph. At any point in time, the crowd density of the flow between each pair of key regions is used as the edge weight in the directed graph.

The second stage of our approach is to detect anomalous events from the inferred graph stream. A history of past graph streams is used as a baseline. New incoming graph streams are compared against baselines from the comparable time periods, in order to detect whether the current graph subsequence is anomalous. An important advantage of our graph representation is that users can be given an interpretable summary of the anomalous event based on the heaviest subgraph [14] during that event. Our proposed monitoring architecture is summarized in Fig. 1.

We begin by presenting the problem statement in the next section. Our methodology is given in Sect. 3, and in Sect. 4 we evaluate our approach on four real-world video datasets and a benchmark dataset UCSD Ped1. These results demonstrate the ability of our approach to accurately detect anomalous events, as well as identifying the anomalous regions or flows in the heaviest subgraph.

2 Problem Statement

As shown in Fig. 1, our proposed monitoring system consists of three tasks: automatically identifying the key regions, crowd density monitoring, and graph stream mining. The first two tasks are based on an improved multi-object Hungarian tracking algorithm. We denote the objects in a frame as $S = \{s_i, i = 1 \ldots s\}$, where s is the maximum number of objects. The important regions of a frame are denoted as nodes $N = \{n_i, i = 1 \ldots n\}$, where n is the maximum number of nodes. By using a multi-object tracking approach, we can count the number of people moving between every pair of nodes, denoted as $N_{ij} = \{n_{ij}, i, j \in [1 \ldots n]\}$ and $G_t = \{N_{ij}^t : i, j \in [1 \ldots n]\}$ represents the detected number of people moving between each pair of regions during the interval t. After the first two tasks, the crowd movement information is represented as a graph sequence, which is divided into several fixed length intervals $t = 1 \ldots T$. At the global level, the whole video stream can be represented as $G = \{G_t, t \in [1 \ldots T]\}$, where T is the maximum timestamp. At the local level, we can obtain a single time series for every flow $G = \{G_t^{ij}, t \in [1 \ldots T]\}$ Note that the number of people from Node i to Node j can be different from that of Node j to Node i. Finally, different graph analytics techniques can be applied to the graph stream to extract and characterize events in the video.

The task of automatically identifying key regions in the scene can be done in two modes. In Mode 1, we randomly select an interval Δ of the video as pre-training data. After obtaining the tracks of all moving pedestrians during $\Delta = 30\,\mathrm{min}$, we then use a hyperspherical clustering method to group similar tracks (as shown in Fig. 1). The start and end regions of these clusters are recognized as key regions. Then we perform crowd density monitoring between each pair of key regions, and the number of pedestrians is used as the weight of that edge of the graph. We normally collect data every $\delta = 3\,\text{min}$. Then the whole video stream can be analyzed as a sequence of directed graphs. In Mode 2, we perform automatic key region identification and crowd density monitoring at the same time, which means key regions need to be identified after each interval, so the locations and number of nodes are dynamic. Therefore, the whole video stream is analyzed as a dynamic directed graph sequence.

In this paper, we conduct the experiments on four real-world datasets by using Mode 1. In this case, we aim at analyzing the static directed graph sequence. Further, we test on the UCSD Ped1 dataset by using Mode 2, in which our dynamic graph representation can help depict the anomalous flow.

3 Methodology

In this section, we present our real-time multi-object monitoring algorithm, which comprises video pre-processing, object detection, and an improved Hungarian assignment based approach. We then present our hyperspherical clustering based approach for automatic identification of key regions, and the graph mining approach for anomalous event detection.

3.1 Pedestrian Monitoring

Video Pre-processing and Object Detection. The video data is first pre-processed using a two-dimensional Gaussian low-pass filter in order to eliminate high frequency noise. The parameters of the Gaussian filter are set as $\sigma = 0.5$ and the block size is 5 by 5. The parameters are chosen in such a way that it retains the low-frequency information and edge information in the filtered output.

The object detection algorithms currently available in the literature can be categorized into parametric and sample-based methods, which consider the pixel changes of objects or crowds. The basic parametric approach estimates the Probability Density Function (PDF) at every pixel coordinate, and uses this function to group background or foreground pixel values [15]. Given our focus on solving real-life scenarios, an important challenge is how to model complex crowded situations. Consequently, we use a sample-based algorithm ViBe [15] for object detection, which is a versatile random technique to estimate the background in video sequences. By aggregating previously observed values for each pixel location, a group of sample values are used for building the pixel model. When a new frame arrives, the model can be rapidly updated, while subtracting the moving objects.

Object Tracking. The Hungarian assignment algorithm [17] is used with the Kalman filter [16] to accurately perform multi-target (object) tracking. The basic scheme assigns an index to every visible object detected using ViBe from the previous step, where the index set is denoted as $Ind = \{ind_i : i = 1 \ldots I\}$, where I is the maximum number of detected moving objects in the current frame. Afterwards, these I objects are mapped to their new index set based on their predicted positions. The assignment problem is then converted to a function optimization problem. The Hungarian approach starts from a square penalty matrix C and it is based on the non-negative matrix C_0 with Eq. (1):

$$C_0 = (d_{ij}) \tag{1}$$

where d_{ij} denotes the matching error costs of state estimation e_i and measurement m_j using the Euclidean distance. If the number of estimation objects n_e is different from the number of visible objects n_m in the current frame, the matrix C_0 will not be the same as C. Therefore, the matrix C is generated by setting some rows or columns to zeros as shown in Eq. (2).

$$C = \begin{cases} \left[C_0 \; 0_{n_e \times (n_e - n_m)}\right] & n_e > n_m \\ C_0 & n_e = n_m \\ \begin{bmatrix} C_0 \\ 0_{n_e \times (n_e - n_m)} \end{bmatrix} & n_e < n_m \end{cases} \tag{2}$$

The objective function of the optimization assignment matrix X can be summarized as Eq. (3), where $X = [x_{ij}]$ is chosen to minimize the expression:

$$\sum_{i=1}^{n} \sum_{j=1}^{n} c_{ij} x_{ij} \tag{3}$$

where $x_{ij} = 1$ (e_i is assigned to m_j) and $x_{ij} = 0$ (otherwise). The term c_{ij} represents the cost associated with mapping estimated objects to actual objects in Eq. (3). In our implementation, we improve the Hungarian algorithm with blob matching (i.e., regions of connected pixels) and occlusion handling [18], which can better connect the current objects with accurate objects in the next frame. The depth model is used to make the tracks cleaner and more accurate, which is based on determining the depth of the tracked objects. First, the probability density function (4) is generated for the depth of pedestrians at each pixel from a set of training data. We use the first 20 frames of every pedestrian as the training data to generate the PDF, so that occlusion handling can then start from frame 21.

$$z_\varphi(D) = \sum_{\omega \in \Omega_\varphi} \delta(D - D_\omega) \tag{4}$$

where φ denotes image pixel that each object m_j occupies, $z_\varphi(D)$ is the observed depth histogram, Ω_φ is the set of blobs and $\delta(\cdot)$ is the Kronecker delta function. If there is an occlusion ω in pixel φ, $z_\varphi(D)$ is aggregated on the depth of the occlusion blob ω, and is represented as D_ω. The aggregation process is repeated 20 times by using the training data. As a result, a set of observed depth histograms $z_\varphi(D)$ can then be used to produce the activity map A_φ, as shown in (5):

$$A_\varphi = \sum_{D \in D_{\min}, D(i_\varphi)} z_\varphi(D) \tag{5}$$

When an occlusion occurs, the depth model of each object is used to assign an accurate position to these objects in the next frame, which can improve the accuracy and effectiveness of the multi-object tracking algorithm.

3.2 Graph Representation

After obtaining the trajectories from the above step, we need to construct our graph representation of the crowd movements from their trajectories. First, we need to automatically identify the key regions of the scene, which correspond to the nodes of the graph. Then key regions are identified by clustering the trajectories using a hyperspherical clustering algorithm [19,20], so that the start and end regions of these clustered trajectories represent the nodes of the graph. Our approach has three main steps: fixed-width clustering, merging clusters and merging key regions. The overall procedure is shown in Fig. 2.

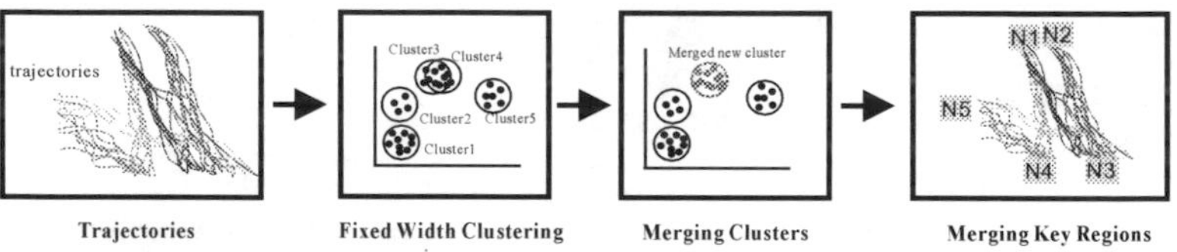

Fig. 2. The process of automatic identification of key regions.

Step 1: Fixed-Width Clustering. Consider a trajectory set represented as $T = \{t_i : i = 1 \dots n\}$, Fixed width clustering starts with the first cluster being centered on the first track t_1, with a fixed cluster width of ω. Then, for the next trajectory vector t_i, we compute the Euclidean distance d_i between t_i and the centroid of the nearest cluster c_r. The way to calculate the distance between two trajectories is proposed in [20]. If $d_i \leq \omega$, then the current track vector t_i is added to cluster c_r and the centroid of this cluster is updated as the mean value of all the vectors in it. On the other hand, if $d_i \geq \omega$, the current trajectory vector t_i forms a new cluster c_f and the centroid of t_i forms the centroid of c_f. This process is repeated until all the trajectory vectors have been considered.

Step 2: Merging Clusters. After detecting all possible clusters, we need to identify the similar clusters that can be merged together. Therefore, we used fixed-width cluster merging as our second step. Based on the cluster set $C = \{c_r : r = 1 \dots N_c\}$ that we obtained from the previous step, where N_c is the number of clusters, we merge two clusters c_i and c_j when the distance between the centroids of these two clusters is smaller than a threshold τ. This process is repeated until there remain no pair of clusters that can be merged.

Step 3: Merging Key Regions. The start and end locations of the (trajectory) clusters obtained from the previous step are recognized as the key regions, which are then used as nodes of the graph. However, there are possibilities for multiple clusters with similar start and end points, yet with different paths. Therefore, we need to merge the start and points, i.e., key regions, of these clusters together as our third step. If the distance between two key regions is smaller than a region merging threshold τ_k, then these two key regions are merged into a new region.

Finally, all of the key regions are represented as nodes in the graph. The crowd density between each pair of key regions is used as the edge weights of the graph. In this way, the video stream can be succinctly represented as a sequence of graph adjacency matrices.

3.3 Anomaly Detection

Our aim is to find the timestamps of the start and end of each anomalous event in our video sequence. Our architecture is used to analyze the video data from a set of weekdays, so that the resulting average graph stream can be used as the baseline. Then we test a new incoming video to infer if the graph series of the new test video is significantly different from the average graph sequence of the corresponding baseline. If so, then this episode is identified as anomalous. In this paper, we utilize Graph Edit Distance (GED) [12] with single variable Cumulative Sum (CUSUM) [13] to perform this graph stream analysis. GED is often used to measure the distances between two graphs. CUSUM monitors the mean value of a process based on a time series of data, in order to detect change points that correspond to the start and end timestamps of abnormal episodes. When the CUSUM test is applied to the sequence of GED values, we can detect abnormal episodes.

In experiment one, the monitoring interval we choose is $\delta = 3\,\text{min}$, and the user defined parameters h and k will affect the performance of the CUSUM, which are set to be 4 and 0.4, respectively [13]. To build the baseline graph stream for the weekdays $G^{baseline} = \{G_t^{baseline}, t \in [1 \dots T]\}$ we use the graph sequences that we obtained from Monday to Thursday $\{G^{day}\}_{day \in [Mon,Tue,Wed,Thu]} = \{G_t^{day}, t \subset [1 \dots T]\}$. Each time stamp of the baseline stream is computed as the average of these four weekdays $G_t^{baseline} = \frac{\sum_{day \in [Mon,Tue,Wed,Thu]} G_t^{day}}{4}$, where $t \in [1 \dots T]$. To elaborate, the edge weights of each $G_t^{baseline}$ is the average value of the edge weights from the mentioned four days for the time stamp t. Now, we can test the behavior of any given day based on the constructed baseline. For instance, given the Friday graph stream $G^{Fri} = \{G_t^{Fri}, t \in [1 \dots T]\}$, we need to calculate to what extent its behavior deviates from that of the baseline. To measure the dissimilarity between G^{Fri} and $G^{Baseline}$, we compute the time series of GEDs between the two graphs as shown in Eqs. (6) and (7). Thereafter, we apply a single variable CUSUM to detect the time stamps and consequently episodes where an anomalous event has occurred.

$$GED\left(G^{Fri}, G^{baseline}\right) = \left\{GED\left(G_t^{Fri}, G_t^{Baseline}\right), t \in [1 \dots T]\right\} \tag{6}$$

$$\begin{aligned} &GED\left(G_t^{Fri}, G_t^{Baseline}\right) = \\ &sqrt\left(\sum_{i=1}^{n}\sum_{j=1}^{n}\left(N_{ij}^{Fri} - N_{ij}^{Baseline}\right)^2 + \left(N_{ji}^{Fri} - N_{ji}^{Baseline}\right)^2\right) \end{aligned} \tag{7}$$

In experiment two, we consider Mode 2 of our framework, in which automatically identifies key regions in a dynamic manner, so the monitoring interval we choose is small: $\delta = 25$ frames. The user defined parameters h and k are set to be 6 and 0.4, respectively. Because the datasets we used in experiment two are a benchmark dataset, we take training dataset as the baseline and the test dataset as the test data. Like Eqs. (6) and (7), we measure the dissimilarity between G^{test} and $G^{Baseline}$. Therefore, the outlier score δ that is calculated by (8) is used for anomaly detection.

$$\delta = GED\left(G^{test}, G^{baseline}\right) - \rho \tag{8}$$

where ρ is the offset. We perform anomalous event detection and evaluation at the frame-level in the next section. At first, we define normal video frames as the frames with no anomalies. Therefore, a frame is defined as normal ($\Psi = 1$) or anomalous ($\Psi = 0$) as follows:

$$\Psi = \begin{cases} 1, & \delta < \eta \\ 0, & \text{otherwise} \end{cases} \tag{9}$$

where η is a user-defined threshold, and is chosen based on empirical evaluation. By changing η, ROC curves are created that can be used as our evaluation criteria.

Once we have identified an anomalous episode, we can also use our graph representation to identify the anomalous flows in the scene. This is done by extracting the heaviest subgraph (the subgraph with larger link weights) in the episode [14], which can show the main flows that contributed to the anomaly. For example, consider the graph shown in Fig. 3a, which has nodes A, B, C, D and E with edges $\{(A,B)(B,A)(A,C)(C,A)\ldots(E,D)\}$. The weight of each edge is the number of pedestrians moving from one node to another and the mean value of the weight is calculated as the measurement standard. The weights that are larger than the mean value are included in the heaviest subgraph. The heaviest subgraph of our example graph is illustrated in Fig. 3c.

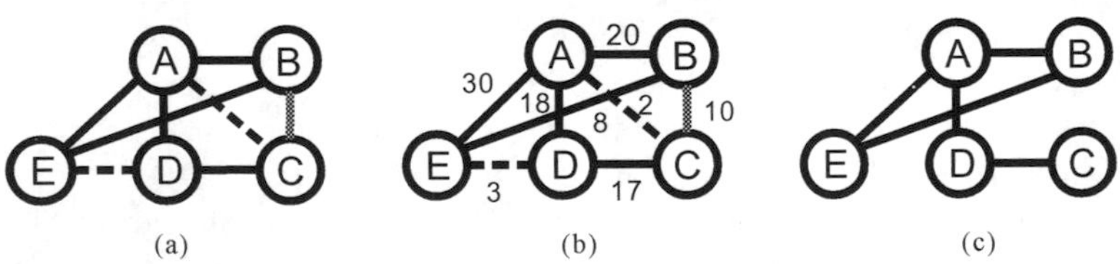

Fig. 3. An example of determining the heaviest subgraph. (a) The original graph. (b) Graph with weights. (c) The heaviest subgraph.

4 Results and Discussion

4.1 Datasets and Experimental Setup

In this section, we conduct an experimental evaluation on four real-world video datasets: (1) Mulhouse: Place de la Rpublique Camera (https://myearthcam.com/orelli), (2) Lausanne: Place de la Palud Camera (http://worldcams.tv/cities/lausanne-place-de-la-palud), (3) Rijeka: the HNK Ivana pl. Zajca Camera (https://rijeka.livecamcroa-tia.com/rijeka07.html) and (4) Edinburgh Royal

Mile Camera (https://worldcams.tv/cities/edinburgh-royal-mile). Further, we apply our framework on the UCSD Ped1 dataset (http://www.svcl.ucsd.edu/projects/anomaly/dataset.htm) and evaluate the performance at the frame-level. We assume that these cameras are all well calibrated. Sample images are shown in Figs. 4 and 5.

Our tracking algorithm is implemented in Visual Studio 2015 with OpenCV 3.0.0. The graph stream analysis and evaluation method are implemented in Matlab 2013b. The computer used is Windows 7 (64 bit) with a 4 GB NVIDIA graphics card (NVIDIA NVS 315 HD) and a multi-core Intel® i7 - 4790 CPU running at 3.6 GHz with 16 GB RAM.

4.2 Quantitative Analysis and Evaluation on Real-World Datasets

For each dataset, we collect the video data from Monday to Thursday, and take two hours (11 am–1 pm) of each day as the baseline. We then analyze the heaviest subgraph of these anomalous events.

In Dataset1, time intervals 11–17 and 28–37 are identified as anomalous. The heaviest subgraph for interval 11–17 is shown in Fig. 4a. In Dataset2, time intervals 21–23 and 27–36 are identified as anomalous, and the heaviest subgraph corresponding to the first interval is shown in Fig. 4b. In Dataset3, time intervals 17–18, 25 and 33–34 are anomalous, and their heaviest subgraph is shown in Fig. 4c. In terms of Dataset4, time intervals 4–6, 15–23 and 30 are anomalous, and their heaviest subgraph is shown in Fig. 4d.

Fig. 4. The heaviest subgraphs for anomalous timestamps (a) Dataset1 Mulhouse: Place de la Rpublique Camera. (b) Dataset2 Lausanne: Place de la Palud Camera. (c) Dataset3 Rijeka: the HNK Ivana pl. Zajca Camera. (d) Dataset4 Edinburgh Royal Mile Camera.

As shown in Fig. 4b, the subgraph corresponds to the time intervals 21–23 of the Dataset2 time series. This means there are significant changes that happened among these nodes as shown in the subgraph. Compared with the ordinary subgraph, the edges N24 and N13 are eliminated, which illustrates the pedestrian density from Node 2 to Node 4 and from Node 1 to Node 3 is dramatically decreased.

We then evaluate the detected anomalous time series using the cross correlation coefficient (CCC), which determines the correlation between the ground truth and the outcome of the proposed methods. Cross-correlation is often used as a measure of similarity between two signals [21]. This can be considered as our accuracy measure. If the coefficient is closer to 1, the performance is better. The evaluation results of our proposed methods on the four datasets are given in Table 1.

Table 1. Evaluation result on four datasets.

Datasets	CCC
Mulhouse: Place de la Rpublique Camera	0.792
Lausanne: Place de la Palud Camera	0.832
Rijeka: the HNK Ivana pl. Zajca Camera	0.817
Edinburgh Royal Mile Camera	0.803

As shown in Table 1, our method achieves the best performance on Dataset2, Lausanne: Place de la Palud Camera, which has a 0.832 cross correlation coefficient, followed by a Rijeka: the HNK Ivana pl. Zajca Camera (Dataset3), Edinburgh Royal Mile Camera (Dataset4), and Mulhouse: Place de la Rpublique Camera (Dataset1). The evaluation result is around 0.80. In general, these evaluation results demonstrate that our monitoring system can be used in real-world scenarios.

4.3 Quantitative Analysis and Evaluation on UCSD Datasets

In the second experiment, we apply our framework on the UCSD Ped1 Test001-005, Test006-010, and Test011-015 datasets and evaluate the performance at the frame-level. This provides a basis for comparison with existing methods.

A frame-level anomalous event is defined such that if a person in a frame is detected as an anomaly, then this frame will be labeled as anomalous [1]. A true positive means that the ground-truth of a detected anomaly is also abnormal. On the other hand, if it is actually a normal frame, this detection is identified as a false positive. We conducted experiments on the UCSD Test001-005, Test006-010, and Test011-015 datasets, and the frame-level detection results are shown in Fig. 5a. The x-coordinate is the false positive rate (FPR) and the y-coordinate is the true positive rate (TPR).

We use ROC curves as our evaluation criteria. Each ROC curve is produced by changing the user-defined threshold parameter in Eq. (9). Next, we use two quantitative indexes, the Area under the ROC Curve (AUC) and Equal Error Rate (EER) to analyze the results. AUC is the area under the ROC curve and EER is the value of the ratio of misclassified items, which means the FPR equals the miss rate. The FPR is defined as FPR = 1-TPR. As shown in Fig. 5a, the AUC and EER value for Test001-005, Test006-010, and Test011-015 is 84.2%, 78.2%, 83.7% and 31%, 27.1%, 27%. We then analyze the heaviest subgraph as shown in Fig. 5b, which indicate the anomalous flows.

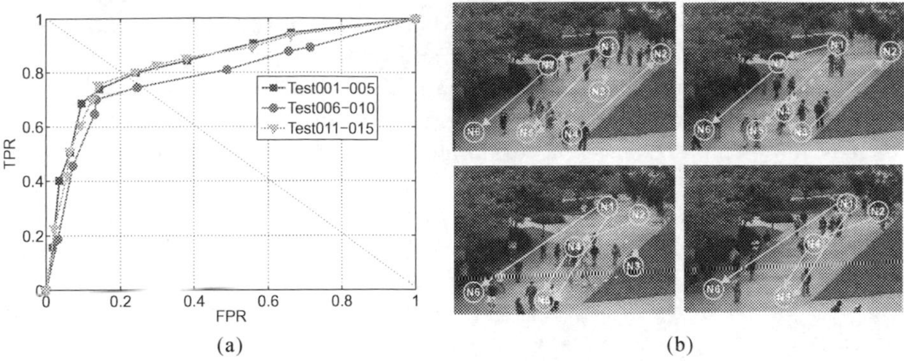

Fig. 5. (a) ROC curves, and (b) the example heaviest subgraphs for anomalous frames in the UCSD Ped1 datasets.

Table 2. Comparison with existing methods in terms of AUC and EER on UCSD Ped1 datasets.

Algorithm	Frame-level	
	AUC	EER
Sparse reconstruction [2]	19.0%	86.0%
Adam [3]	64.9%	38.0%
MPPCA [5]	67.0%	40.0%
SF-MPPCA [6]	76.9%	32.0%
MDT [7]	81.8%	25.0%
SF [10]	76.8%	31.0%
H-MDT [1]	-	17.8%
Our method	**82.1%**	**28.3%**

We take the average AUC and EER of these four test datasets and compare with other existing methods in Table 2. It shows that our approach outperforms most of the existing state-of-the-art (SOTA) methods, and it is competitive with the best baseline [7].

4.4 Discussion

For experiment 1, in terms of performance, the cross correlation coefficient varies from 0.79 to 0.83 over all the datasets. The variation is due to the fact that the complexity of each scene is different, which can affect the performance of real-time tracking. For example, compare the Lausanne: Place de la Palud Camera (Dataset2) and Edinburgh Royal Mile Camera (Dataset4), as shown in Fig. 4b and d, the former can achieve better performance because the size of pedestrians varies over the field of view. For experiment 2, we conduct quantitative analysis and evaluation on a benchmark dataset UCSD. As the ROC curves shown in Fig. 5a, UCSD Ped1 Test001-005, Test006-010, and Test011-015 datasets all achieve competitive AUC and EER. Generally, the evaluation shows that our method achieves reasonable accuracy and interpretable results on all of the datasets. Moreover, it is important to note that our approach is unsupervised, which is important in surveillance applications with a large number of video streams.

Our future work involves detecting anomalous events in the video data simultaneously from several video streams. This requires simultaneous clustering based on the similarity of the change points across these streams.

5 Conclusions

In this paper, we propose an anomalous timestamps monitoring architecture, which includes pedestrian movement tracking and graph mining analysis components. In detail, a real-time tracking algorithm is proposed for automatic identification of key regions in the scene, and at the same time, the pedestrian flow density between each pair of key regions during a sequence of consecutive time intervals is monitored. These key regions are recognized as the nodes of a graph, and the directional pedestrian density is used as the edge weights of the graph. Therefore, the whole video stream is analyzed as a time series of directed graphs. We then analyze the graph series by using a graph mining approach. In order to demonstrate that our system can be used in real-world scenarios, we conduct the experiment on four real-world datasets. We aim at monitoring the anomalous events in a video, using previous graph time series as a baseline. If the graph time series is different from the baseline, our proposed monitoring system detects the timestamps of the anomalous event. Further, it can help users interpret the event by highlighting which regions or flows are anomalous based on heaviest subgraph during the event. The evaluation reveals that our proposed method can successfully detect the anomalous timestamps in all datasets. Moreover, we conduct quantitative analysis and evaluation on a benchmark dataset (UCSD) against existing state-of-the-art (SOTA) methods. The AUC and EER are 82.1% and 28.3%, respectively. It shows that our approach is either comparable or outperforms most previous SOTA methods. In addition to the accuracy of our algorithm, it is able to produce interpretable results.

References

1. Li, W., Mahadevan, V., Vasconcelos, N.: Anomaly detection and localization in crowded scenes. IEEE Trans. Pattern Anal. Mach. Intell. **36**, 18–32 (2014)
2. Cong, Y., Yuan, J., Liu, J.: Sparse reconstruction cost for abnormal event detection. In: IEEE CVPR, pp. 3449–3456 (2011)
3. Adam, A., Rivlin, E., Shimshoni, I., Reinitz, D.: Robust real-time unusual event detection using multiple fixed-location monitors. IEEE Trans. Pattern Anal. Mach. Intell. **30**, 555–560 (2008)
4. Mo, X., Monga, V., Bala, R., Fan, Z.: Adaptive sparse representations for video anomaly detection. IEEE Trans. Circuits Syst. Video Technol. **24**, 631–645 (2014)

5. Kim, J., Grauman, K.: Observe locally, infer globally: a space-time MRF for detecting abnormal activities with incremental updates. In: IEEE CVPR, pp. 2921–2928 (2009)
6. Roshtkhari, M.J., Levine, M.D.: Online dominant and anomalous behavior detection in videos. In: IEEE CVPR, pp. 2611–2618 (2013)
7. Mahadevan, V., Li, W., Bhalodia, V., Vasconcelos, N.: Anomaly detection in crowded scenes. In: IEEE CVPR, pp. 1975–1981 (2010)
8. Mehran, R., Oyama, A., Shah, M.: Abnormal crowd behavior detection using social force model. In: IEEE CVPR, pp. 935–942 (2009)
9. Xu, D., Ricci, E., Yan, Y., Song, J., Sebe, N.: Learning deep representations of appearance and motion for anomalous event detection. arXiv preprint arXiv:1510.01553 (2015)
10. Reddy, V., Sanderson, C., Lovell, B.C.: Improved anomaly detection in crowded scenes via cell-based analysis of foreground speed, size and texture. In: IEEE CVPRW. IEEE (2011)
11. Feng, Y., Yuan, Y., Lu, X.: Deep representation for abnormal event detection in crowded scenes. In: Proceedings of the ACM Multimedia Conference, pp. 591–595 (2016)
12. Gao, X., Xiao, B., Tao, D., Li, X.: A survey of graph edit distance. Pattern Anal. Appl. **13**, 113–129 (2010)
13. Basseville, M., Nikiforov, I.V.: Detection of Abrupt Changes: Theory and Application, vol. 104. Prentice Hall, Englewood Cliffs (1993)
14. Bogdanov, P., Mongiov, M., Singh, A.K.: Mining heavy subgraphs in time-evolving networks. In: IEEE ICDM, pp. 81–90 (2011)
15. Barnich, O., Van Droogenbroeck, M.: ViBe: a powerful random technique to estimate the background in video sequences. In: IEEE ICASSP, pp. 945–948 (2009)
16. Cuevas, E., Zaldivar, D., Rojas, R.: Kalman filter for vision tracking. Technical report B, Fachbereich Mathematikund Informatik, Freie Universitat Berlin (2005)
17. Ltteke, F., Zhang, X., Franke, J.: Implementation of the Hungarian method for object tracking on a camera monitored transportation system. In: 7th German Conference on VDE, pp. 1–6 (2012)
18. Greenhill, D., Renno, J., Orwell, J., Jones, G.A.: Occlusion analysis: learning and utilising depth maps in object tracking. Image Vis. Comput. **26**, 430–441 (2008)
19. Rajasegarar, S., Leckie, C., Palaniswami, M.: Hyperspherical cluster based distributed anomaly detection in wireless sensor networks. J. Parallel Distrib. Comput. **74**, 1833–1847 (2014)
20. Yang, M., Rajasegarar, S., Rao, A.S., Leckie, C., Palaniswami, M.: Anomalous behavior detection in crowded scenes using clustering and spatio-temporal features. In: Shi, Z., Vadera, S., Li, G. (eds.) IIP 2016. IAICT, vol. 486, pp. 132–141. Springer, Cham (2016). https://doi.org/10.1007/978-3-319-48390-0_14
21. Kennedy, H.L.: A new statistical measure of signal similarity. In: Information, Decision and Control, pp. 112–117 (2007)

Nonlinearized Relevance Propagation

Quexuan Zhang(✉) and Yukio Ohsawa

School of Engineering, The University of Tokyo,
Hongo 7-3-1, Bunkyo, Tokyo 113-8654, Japan
kokhin.cheung@gmail.com, ohsawa@sys.t.u-tokyo.ac.jp
http://www.panda.sys.t.u-tokyo.ac.jp/

Abstract. We propose nonlinearized relevance propagation (NRP), an improved method of exploring deep neural networks (DNN). This method derives from well-known layer-wise relevance propagation (LRP), which employs a linear process to explain a DNN model's outputs ordinarily. Although the nonlinear functions are widely used by most of the neural network models, to the best of our knowledge, they have not been employed in the LRP for DNN models. In this paper, we apply NRP to the attentive pooling answer selection model and compare the performance of NRP to sensitivity analysis (SA) and LRP of the linear setting. The result shows exploiting nonlinear functions in LRP can help inputs retain more information of importance than SA. The contribution of this work is extending the use of relevance propagation in understanding inner workings of complicated DNN models.

Keywords: Relevance propagation · Nonlinear function
Deep learning · Answer selection

1 Introduction

In recent years, application of deep learning spreads rapidly in computer vision (CV) and natural language processing (NLP). Though deep neural network (DNN) models have been proven to be extremely powerful at lots of tasks, due to the stigma around the black box, many users are craving the interpretability of them. For those desires, several methods have come out [10]. Layer-wise relevance propagation (LRP), which is used for explaining classifier decisions in CV initially [3], is attracting diverse attentions [1,7,8]. Recently, not limited to the application to support vector machine and convolutional neural network (CNN), it is exercised to recurrent neural network (RNN) models in NLP as well [2,5].

Answer selection is a crucial question answering (QA) task, in which, given a question q and an answer candidate pool $\boldsymbol{a}$ for this question, the system must return the correct answers or rank the candidates in a meaningful order. There have been many answer selection applications, *e.g.* answer recommendation in QA web service and virtual assistants. As deep learning become increasingly

Supported by JST CREST JPMJCR1304, JSPS Kakenhi JP 16H01836, JP 16K1242.

X. Geng and B.-H. Kang (Eds.): PRICAI 2018, LNAI 11012, pp. 904–914, 2018.
https://doi.org/10.1007/978-3-319-97304-3_69

popular, CNN and RNN have been exploited in answer selection [6,16,17,19]. Some of those methods have cross-layer connections such as attentive pooling (AP) and gated units [4,14,20]. Also, most of the answer selection systems use the cosine similarities between paired representations of questions and answers to make selection decisions. Another work endeavored to aid analysis of attention-based answer selection models by visualizing attention weights [12,13].

Without regard to CNN or RNN, DNN models include nonlinear transformations, *e.g.* sigmoid function, hyperbolic tangent function and rectified linear unit (ReLU), to augment the representation capability of themselves. Aiming to handle the relevance propagation for complex DNN models, we provide nonlinearized relevance propagation (NRP) which uses nonlinear functions to boost the performance in LRP.

We organize the work as follows. In Sect. 2 we describe the background and previous approaches. In Sect. 3 we present the details of the proposed methods and apply it to a bidirectional LSTM (biLSTM) based AP answer selection model as an example. Experimental settings and results are discussed in Sect. 4. Finally, Sect. 5 concludes our work.

2 Previous Work

Given an input $\boldsymbol{x}$ with d dimensions of feature, a DNN model encode it to an output responding to an actual concept. We can describe the model as a function f, while the output is $f(\boldsymbol{x})$. For each feature x_i, we ask for an approach to finding a relevance score R_i indicating how important the feature x_i is in contributing to $f(\boldsymbol{x})$.

2.1 Sensitivity Analysis

Sensitivity analysis (SA) is a gradient-based method for the purpose [21], which is defined as

$$R_i = \left(\frac{\partial}{\partial x_i} f\left(\boldsymbol{x}\right) \right)^2 . \tag{1}$$

We can obtain the partial derivatives of each feature by using the chain rule and backpropagation algorithms, which is also a common technique to train a DNN model.

2.2 Layer-Wise Relevance Propagation and $\alpha\beta$-rule

Layer-wise relevance propagation leverages value decomposition to resolve the output into relevance scores, and then propagate the scores backward to the inputs layer-by-layer conservatively. Between a network layer l and the successive layer $l+1$, LRP keeps the consistence of relevance scores across layers by

$$\sum_j R_{j \leftarrow k}^{(l)} = R_k^{(l+1)} \tag{2}$$

and

$$R_j^{(l)} = \sum_k R_{j \leftarrow k}^{(l+1)}, \tag{3}$$

with j and k the indices for neurons of the two layers. $R_{j \leftarrow k}$ indicates the propagated relevance score from neuron k to neuron j when they have a connection. Since $\sum_j R_j^{(l)} = \sum_j \sum_k R_{j \leftarrow k}^{(l+1)} = \sum_k \sum_j R_{j \leftarrow k}^{(l)} = \sum_k R_k^{(l+1)}$, we can get the formulation of relevance conservation for a DNN model:

$$\sum_{i=1}^{d} R_i^{(0)} = \cdots = \sum_j R_j^{(l)} = \sum_k R_k^{(l+1)} = \cdots = f(\boldsymbol{x}). \tag{4}$$

Most layers of DNN models can be described as

$$\begin{aligned} c_{jk} &= a_j w_{jk} \\ c_k &= \sum_j c_{jk} + b_k \\ a_k &= \sigma\left(c_k\right), \end{aligned} \tag{5}$$

where a_j is an input neuron, c_k denotes a linear connection from all (a_j)s to neuron a_k with weights $(w_{jk})s$ and a bias b_k, and σ is a nonlinear activation function.

With Taylor decomposition strategy [3], the typical usage for such DNN layers is the linear $\alpha\beta$-rule, which is given by

$$R_{j \leftarrow k} = \left[\alpha \left(\frac{c_{jk}^{+}}{\sum_j c_{jk}^{+} + b_k^{+}}\right) + \beta \left(\frac{c_{jk}^{-}}{\sum_j c_{jk}^{-} + b_k^{-}}\right)\right] R_k. \tag{6}$$

Here, $(\cdot)^{+}$ and $(\cdot)^{-}$ denote the positive and negative parts of c_{jk} and $b_k$respectively, and the parameters α and β satisfy the constraints $\alpha + \beta = 1$ and $\alpha > 0$ for the conservation of relevance. The practical choices of the parameters are $\alpha = 1, \beta = 0$ and $\alpha = 2, \beta = -1$. Introducing small stabilizers can avoid division by zero.

2.3 Special Relevance Propagation Rules

There have been lots of work utilizing LRP to analyze DNN models with special layers which cannot be characterized as Eq. (5) [10]. Two of them are very related to this work.

Ding *et al.* [5] applied LRP to a biLSTM-based sequence-to-sequence model for visualization of neural machine translation. For element-wise multiplication,*e.g.* $a_k^{(l+1)} = a_j{}^{(l)} \cdot a_j'{}^{(l)}$, this work defined a relevance propagation rule:

$$R_{j \leftarrow k} = \frac{a_j}{a_j + a_j'} R_k. \tag{7}$$

Arras *et al.* [2] exploited SA and LRP to elucidate RNN-based text sentiment classification. There was a special rule addressing relevance propagation through gates in RNN models. A gate weight w_j^g is often calculated by Eq. (5) with sigmoid activation. For $a_k = w_j^g \cdot a_j$, the propagation strategy was

$$R_{j \leftarrow k} = R_k. \tag{8}$$

3 Proposed Methods

In this section, we present the reasons of using nonlinearized relevance propagation. Then we define the propagation rules conducting NRP and exercise them to an attentive pooling answer selection model.

3.1 Nonlinear Functions

Despite the fact that conventional LRP passes the relevance scores for DNN in a linear way [3,15], we believe that nonlinearizing the relevance scores is of use in explaining DNN models. The reasons show as follows.

Decomposition Rules for Special Layers. As mentioned in Sect. 2.3, there are various layers designed for DNN models. The relevance propagation rules for those layers are defined by each practical application. Those rules may not meet the Taylor decomposition framework [10] and produce some relevance errors. One example is the attention pooling network [14]. This model uses a soft alignment [18] to compute pooling weights, from where it is hard to propagate the relevance scores back to the inputs.

Relevance Errors Accumulation. Following the last point, if some neurons receive wrong relevant information, the other neurons in lower layers will cumulate the errors. This phenomenon may be prominent in very in-depth models, especially in RNN-based networks.

Effect of Nonlinear Functions. An appropriate nonlinearizer can make the value distribution approximate to a certain real value subspace. We expect that this attribute can help the inputs receive constructive information of relevance from the output side.

3.2 Propagation Rules

Let h be an arbitrary function in the following. We rewrite the Eq. (6) for further calculation.

Definition 1. *Improved $\alpha\beta$-rule.*

$$R_{j \leftarrow k} = \left[\alpha \left(\frac{h\left(c_{jk}^{+}\right)}{\sum_j h\left(c_{jk}^{+}\right) + h\left(b_k^{+}\right)} \right) + \beta \left(\frac{h\left(c_{jk}^{-}\right)}{\sum_j h\left(c_{jk}^{-}\right) + h\left(b_k^{-}\right)} \right) \right] R_k, \tag{9}$$

where $\alpha + \beta = 1$ and $\alpha > 0$.

We can introduce a nonlinear function to h in Eq. (9) for NRP. The nonlinearization chosen to use in $\alpha\beta$-rule must keep the monotonicity of the original $(\cdot)^+$ and $(\cdot)^-$ parts, *e.g.* hyperbolic tangent $\tanh(x)$ and error function $\text{erf}(x)$. Also, we can opt for positive semidefinite axial symmetry functions, *e.g.* square function $h(x) = x^2$. Furthermore, we can compose the absolute value operation and some monotonic functions as the nonlinearizer, *e.g.* $h(x) = \sqrt{|x|}$ or $h(x) = \log(|x| + 1)$. Besides, we construct value masks to avoid windfall relevance to the zero-neurons, *i.e.*, $h(0) = 0$, when using some nonlinear functions over the origin, such as $h(x) = \exp(|x|)$, $h(x) = \text{sigmoid}(|x|)$ and hyperbolic cosine $\cosh(x)$.

We find that the propagation rule defined in [2] does not conserve the relevance scores if the signs of the two elements are different. Therefore, we provide a conservational version as follow.

Definition 2. *Improved relevance propagation rule for element-wise multiplication following the $\alpha\beta$-rule.*

$$R_{j\leftarrow k} = \begin{cases} \frac{a_j}{a_j + a'_j} R_k & \textit{if } a_j > 0, a'_j > 0 \textit{ or } a_j < 0, a'_j < 0 \\ \alpha R_k & \textit{for } a_k \leftarrow a_j \textit{ if } a_j > 0, a'_j < 0 \\ \beta R_k & \textit{for } a_k \leftarrow a_j \textit{ if } a_j < 0, a'_j > 0 \end{cases} \tag{10}$$

3.3 Application to Attentive Pooling Network

According to the model definition in [17], an attentive pooling network (APN) can be described as follows. Given two token sequences $q = (t_1 \cdots t_m \cdots t_M)$ and $a = (t_1 \cdots t_n \cdots t_N)$ as a question and one of its candidate answers, $Q = [Q_{sm}]$ and $A = [A_{sn}]$ are two matrices denoting the representations of q and a output by the biLSTM layers. A biLSTM layer has S hidden neurons, *i.e.*, the index $s = 1, \cdots, S/2$ for one direction. Succeeding the biLSTM layers, there is a bilinear connection of Q and A without bias for the soft alignment matrix G. Through max-pooling along the question and answer sequences over G, we can obtain two importance vectors (v_m^q) and (v_n^a). Applying the softmax function to (v_m^q) and (v_n^a), we get two pooling weight vectors (w_m^q) and (w_n^a). The pooling results of q and a are $\boldsymbol{p}^q = (p_s^q) = [Q_{sm}](w_m^q)$ and $\boldsymbol{p}^a = (p_s^a) = [A_{sn}](w_n^q)$. In the output layer, the function $\text{cossim}(q, a) = (\sum_s p_s^q p_s^a)/(\|\boldsymbol{p}^q\|\|\boldsymbol{p}^a\|)$ calculates how much the candidate answer is related to the question. Now, we show the implement in our experiments.

From the Output Layer to the Pooling Results. The relevance propagation starts from the output layer. The model's output function mentioned above can be considered as a linear connection of $(p_s^q p_s^a)$s to the output with the same weight $(\|\boldsymbol{p}^q\|\|\boldsymbol{p}^a\|)^{-1}$. We initially set the output's relevance score R^o to 1 and apply original $\alpha\beta$-rule Eq. (6) to divide the relevance into $(R_s^{p\leftarrow o})s$ for each $p_s^q p_s^a$. Then, we use Eq. (10) to partition each $R_s^{p\leftarrow o}$ into $R_s^{q\leftarrow p}$ and $R_s^{a\leftarrow p}$ for each p_s^q and p_s^a respectively.

From Attentive Pooling Layers to LSTM Layers. From the linear connection $p_s^q = \sum_m Q_{sm} w_m^q$ and $p_s^a = \sum_n A_{sn} w_n^a$, we employ Eq. (9) with function h for the division of the relevance scores $R_s^{q \leftarrow p}$ and $R_s^{a \leftarrow p}$ into $(R_{sm}^{Q \leftarrow q})$s and $(R_{sn}^{A \leftarrow a})$s for each Q_{sm} and A_{sn}.

From LSTM Layers to Tokens. As this routine is the same for questions and answers, we take an answer a for example. Let vector $\boldsymbol{e}_n$ be the word embedding of the token t_n, and vector (g_{sn}) be the LSTM cell memory neurons at t_n. The LSTM cell state at t_n is vector (z_{sn}), and $z_{sn} = i_{sn} \cdot g_{sn} + f_{sn} \cdot z_{s,n-1}$ where i and f are input gates and forget gates. In the cell state calculation at t_1, we define $z_{s,0} = 0$. For the sake of convenience, we omit the index symbol s when referring to one hidden neuron in the following.

For the forward LSTM layers, starting with t_N, we follow the propagation rule for gates defined in Eq. (8) to transmit the hidden output A_N's relevance score $R_N^{A \leftarrow a}$ to z_N directly. Then by using Eq. (6), we separate the relevance score of z_N into $R_N^{z_{N-1} \leftarrow z}$ and $R_N^{g \leftarrow z}$. $R_N^{z_{N-1} \leftarrow z}$ is fed into the relevance score of z_{N-1}, while $R_N^{g \leftarrow z}$ is for g_N. Next, we reuse Eq. (6) upon $\boldsymbol{e}_N$ and A_{N-1} with their respective cell memory weights and biases to calculate t_N's relevance score $R_N^{t \leftarrow g}$ and a feeding score $R_{N-1}^{A \leftarrow g}$. Then we sum up $R_{N-1}^{A \leftarrow a}$ and $R_{N-1}^{A \leftarrow g}$ as the relevance score of t_{N-1}'s hidden output A_{N-1} for the next backward propagation. By repeating this procedure until to t_1, we can obtain the forward relevance scores $(R_{sn}^{t \leftarrow g})$s for t_n. After that, we operate the similar approach to get the relevance scores $(\widetilde{R}_{sn}^{t \leftarrow g})$s for t_n in the reverse order. Finally, we sum up all the $(R_{sn}^{t \leftarrow g})$s and $(\widetilde{R}_{sn}^{t \leftarrow g})$s along the hidden neurons for the relevance score of t_n.

4 Experiments

In this section we report the details of experiments and the results by comparing our method to SA and the original LRP framework.

4.1 Dataset and Preprocessing

In our experiments, we exploit the nfL6: Yahoo non-factoid question dataset[1]. This dataset contains 87,361 samples in 21 categories, where each question has a ground truth answer and one or more than one negative answers. However, the ground truth data may have duplicates in the negative lists for the same questions, and accordingly we have to remove them. Besides, we clean the URLs in sentences and split each content into tokens by using spaCy[2].

Rather than using the whole dataset as training data, we pick up three categories, *Computer & Internet*, *Health* and *Society & Culture*, as three subsets. We split them into training sets, development sets and test sets by 8:1:1 in the original orders respectively.

[1] https://ciir.cs.umass.edu/downloads/nfL6/.
[2] https://spacy.io.

4.2 Model Setup

We implement the APN models for each subset with Adam optimizers [9] and 100 dimensions Glove embeddings [11] in Pytorch[3]. The embedding weights update during the training. We also set a 9 epochs patience for the early stopping. The accuracy is calculated by

$$Acc = \frac{|\{q|\text{cossim}(q, a_{\text{truth}}) > \text{cossim}(q, a_{\text{neg}})_{\max}\}|}{|\boldsymbol{q}|}. \tag{11}$$

The hyper-parameters and the result states of selected models show in Table 1.

Table 1. Hyper-parameters and result states of the selected models.

Parameters or states	*Computer & Internet*	*Health*	*Society & Culture*
Margin [17]	2		
Dropout	0.5		
Batch size	16		
L2 regularization coef.	1.0×10^{-5}		
Hidden size	100	120	100
Epoch	6th	6th	15th
Average loss	0.1213	0.1625	0.1518
Acc. on dev. (#samples)	0.6015 (1222)	0.4626 (1070)	0.3445 (865)
Acc. on test (#samples)	0.5724 (1223)	0.4654 (1070)	0.2763 (865)

4.3 Validation of Relevance

We exploit the token deleting method proposed by [3] to validate the result of our methods quantitatively. We fix the question inputs and the maximum similarity scores with the negative answers, and choose the ground truth data with token lengths greater or equal to 10 for the experiments. Deleting a token denotes setting the token's embedding weights to $\mathbf{0}$ in the following.

According to the relevance scores provided by different methods, we perform two experiments on development sets and test sets. The first one is deleting tokens form 1 to 5 in descending order of the relevance scores and testing how **low** the accuracies will be for true positive data (TP). The second experiment is similar, but we delete words in ascending order of the relevance scores to observe how **high** the accuracies become for false positive samples (FP). Tables 2 and 3 show the results at deleting 1 token and 5 tokens by different choices of function h, parameter α for each data subset.

From the results, we can observe that applying nonlinear functions in LRP helps the inputs recall more important information than the baseline. Especially, the results for *Society & Culture* are sharp in Experiment 1, and all the tests with $\alpha = 2$ are far better than SA.

[3] http://pytorch.org.

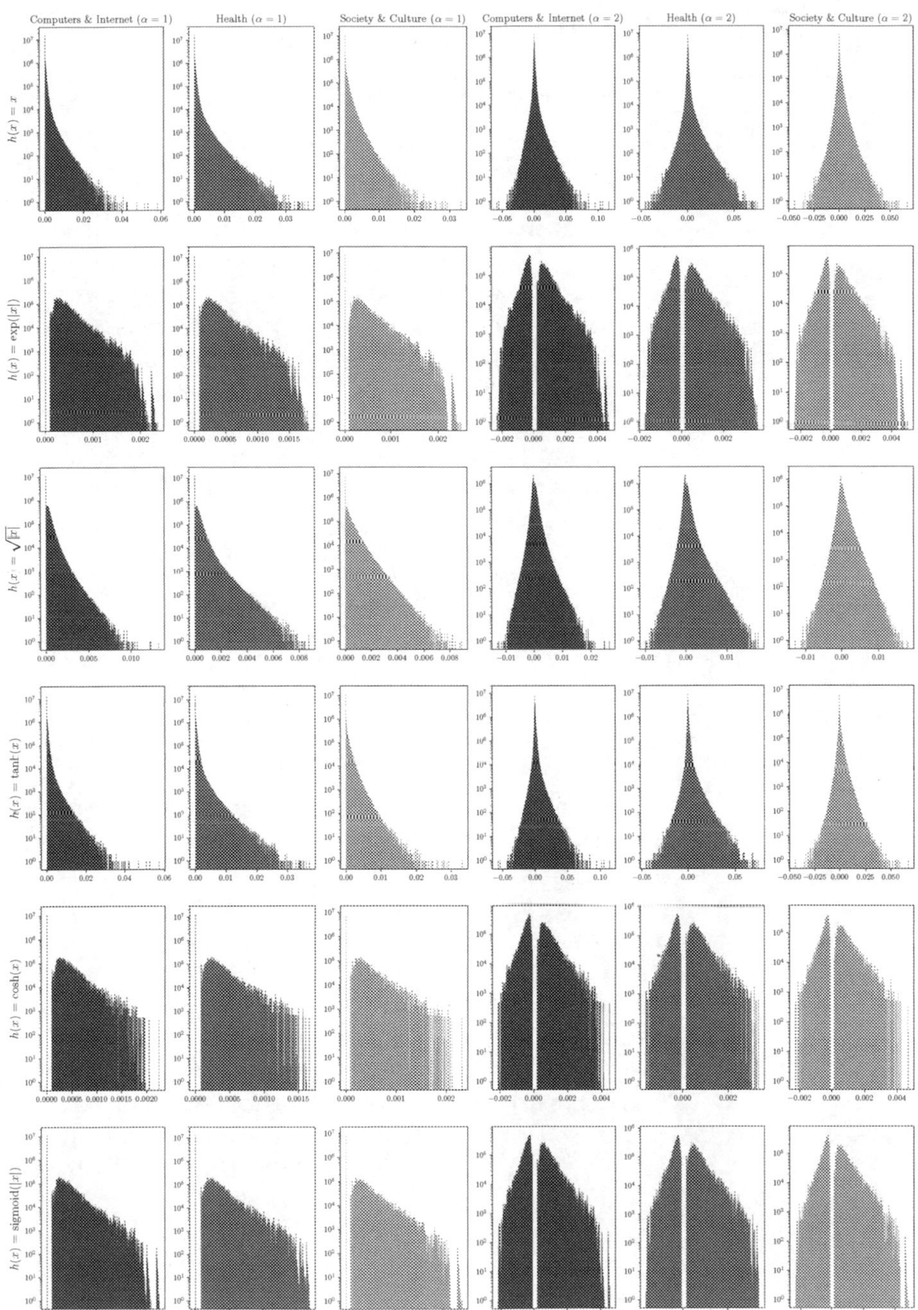

Fig. 1. The value distributions of the coefficients to propagate the relevance scores from attentive pooling layers to biLSTM output layers upon ground truth data. The number of bins in each histogram is 400.

Table 2. The results for Experiment 1. The bold values are the best scores in the columns.

Settings		*Computer & Internet*		*Health*		*Society & Culture*	
Acc@#(tokens deleted)		1	5	1	5	1	5
SA		0.83275	0.50523	0.90131	0.61732	0.89944	0.80074
$h(x) = x$	$\alpha = 1$	0.83275	0.54495	0.89829	0.58912	0.89758	0.69088
$h(x) = \exp(\|x\|)$	$\alpha = 1$	**0.82927**	**0.49617**	0.89527	0.56999	0.81192	**0.34451**
$h(x) = \sqrt{\|x\|}$	$\alpha = 1$	0.83136	0.53659	0.89728	**0.55690**	0.86778	0.61266
$h(x) = \tanh(x)$	$\alpha = 1$	0.83345	0.54495	0.89829	0.58912	0.89758	0.69088
$h(x) = \cosh(x)$	$\alpha = 1$	**0.82927**	**0.49617**	0.89527	0.56999	**0.81006**	**0.34451**
$h(x) = \text{sigmoid}(\|x\|)$	$\alpha = 1$	**0.82927**	**0.49617**	0.89527	0.56999	0.81192	**0.34451**
$h(x) = x$	$\alpha = 2$	0.95679	0.87944	0.89527	0.67372	0.88827	0.69646
$h(x) = \exp(\|x\|)$	$\alpha = 2$	0.93798	0.84808	**0.87513**	0.65559	0.88268	0.67784
$h(x) = \sqrt{\|x\|}$	$\alpha = 2$	0.95331	0.86760	0.88419	0.67170	0.88082	0.67412
$h(x) = \tanh(x)$	$\alpha = 2$	0.95679	0.87944	0.89527	0.67372	0.88827	0.69832
$h(x) = \cosh(x)$	$\alpha = 2$	0.93868	0.84739	0.87613	0.65257	0.88082	0.67039
$h(x) = \text{sigmoid}(\|x\|)$	$\alpha = 2$	0.93798	0.84739	**0.87513**	0.65458	0.88082	0.67225
#(TP with#tokens $\geq$ 10)		1435		993		537	

Table 3. The results for experiment 2. The bold values are the best scores in the columns.

Settings		*Computer & Internet*		*Health*		*Society & Culture*	
Acc@#(tokens deleted)		1	5	1	5	1	5
SA		0.01287	0.06436	0.00436	0.02964	0.01174	0.03772
$h(x) = x$	$\alpha = 1$	0.00396	0.04257	0.00349	0.01569	0.00168	0.03437
$h(x) = \exp(\|x\|)$	$\alpha = 1$	0.00099	0.03861	0.00349	0.01831	0.00419	0.04778
$h(x) = \sqrt{\|x\|}$	$\alpha = 1$	0.00198	0.03465	0.00436	0.01569	0.00168	0.04107
$h(x) = \tanh(x)$	$\alpha = 1$	0.00396	0.04158	0.00349	0.01569	0.00168	0.03437
$h(x) = \cosh(x)$	$\alpha = 1$	0.00099	0.03762	0.00349	0.01918	0.00419	0.04862
$h(x) = \text{sigmoid}(\|x\|)$	$\alpha = 1$	0.00099	0.03861	0.00349	0.01831	0.00419	0.04778
$h(x) = x$	$\alpha = 2$	0.05347	0.05545	0.09939	**0.10462**	0.06035	0.08550
$h(x) = \exp(\|x\|)$	$\alpha = 2$	0.05446	0.07030	0.07149	0.08195	0.04946	0.07712
$h(x) = \sqrt{\|x\|}$	$\alpha = 2$	**0.05743**	0.05842	**0.10201**	0.09154	**0.06119**	**0.09053**
$h(x) = \tanh(x)$	$\alpha = 2$	0.05347	0.05644	0.09939	**0.10462**	0.06035	0.08550
$h(x) = \cosh(x)$	$\alpha = 2$	0.05545	**0.07129**	0.07149	0.08282	0.04946	0.07460
$h(x) = \text{sigmoid}(\|x\|)$	$\alpha = 2$	0.05446	**0.07129**	0.07149	0.08282	0.04946	0.07628
#(FP with#tokens $\geq$ 10)		1010		1147		1193	

To discuss the above results, we plot the distributions of the coefficients to allocate relevance scores by applying Eq. (9) upon ground truth's $(A_{sn}w_n^a)$s in Fig. 1. We can see that the difference in the results between the linear setting and $\tanh(x)$ is small because their outputs are almost identical under the $(A_{sn}w_n^a)$s' range. When operating $h(x) = \exp(|x|)$, $\cosh(x)$ and $h(x) = \text{sigmoid}(|x|)$, we can relax the value distribution to scatter the relevance information into other neurons. Though the relaxation ability of $h(x) = \sqrt{|x|}$ is not competitive, it balances the influences of positive and negative inputs in the $\alpha = 2$ situation.

5 Conclusion

In the paper, we proposed an improved approach to propagating the relevance for model understanding. The experiments showed that applying nonlinear functions to the LRP process can help the inputs receive more meaningful information of importance than SA. However, this work does not elucidate the way of selecting optimized nonlinear functions. It needs more work to practice in the future.

References

1. Arras, L., Horn, F., Montavon, G., Müller, K.R., Samek, W.: What is relevant in a text document?: an interpretable machine learning approach. PLoS ONE **12**(8), e0181142 (2017). https://doi.org/10.1371/journal.pone.0181142
2. Arras, L., Montavon, G., Müller, K.R., Samek, W.: Explaining recurrent neural network predictions in sentiment analysis, pp. 159–168 (2017). http://arxiv.org/abs/1706.07206
3. Bach, S., Binder, A., Montavon, G., Klauschen, F., Müller, K.R., Samek, W.: On pixel-wise explanations for non-linear classifier decisions by layer-wise relevance propagation. PLoS ONE **10**(7), 1–46 (2015). https://doi.org/10.1371/journal.pone.0130140
4. Bachrach, Y., et al.: An attention mechanism for answer selection using a combined global and local view, pp. 1–8, July 2017. http://arxiv.org/abs/1707.01378
5. Ding, Y., Liu, Y., Luan, H., Sun, M.: Visualizing and understanding neural machine translation. In: Proceedings of the 55th Annual Meeting of the Association for Computational Linguistics (Volume 1: Long Papers), pp. 1150–1159 (2017). https://doi.org/10.18653/v1/P17-1106, http://aclweb.org/anthology/P17-1106
6. Feng, M., Xiang, B., Glass, M.R., Wang, L., Zhou, B.: Applying deep learning to answer selection: a study and an open task. In: ASRU 2015 - Proceedings 2015 IEEE Workshop on Automatic Speech Recognition and Understanding, pp. 813–820 (2016). https://doi.org/10.1109/ASRU.2015.7404872
7. Horn, F., Arras, L., Montavon, G., Müller, K.R., Samek, W.: Discovering topics in text datasets by visualizing relevant words, pp. 1–10 (2017). http://arxiv.org/abs/1707.06100
8. Kanter, J.M., Veeramachaneni, K.: Deep feature synthesis: towards automating data science endeavors. In: Proceedings of the 2015 IEEE International Conference on Data Science and Advanced Analytics, DSAA 2015 (2015). https://doi.org/10.1109/DSAA.2015.7344858, http://arxiv.org/abs/1708.08296
9. Kingma, D.P., Ba, J.: Adam: a method for stochastic optimization. In: 2017 IEEE International Conference on Consumer Electronics ICCE 2017, pp. 434–435, December 2014. https://doi.org/10.1109/ICCE.2017.7889386, http://arxiv.org/abs/1412.6980
10. Montavon, G., Samek, W., Müller, K.R.: Methods for interpreting and understanding deep neural networks. Digit. Sig. Process. A Rev. J. **73**, 1–15 (2018). https://doi.org/10.1016/j.dsp.2017.10.011

11. Pennington, J., Socher, R., Manning, C.: Glove: global vectors for word representation. In: Proceedings of the 2014 Conference on Empirical Methods in Natural Language Processing (EMNLP), pp. 1532–1543 (2014). https://doi.org/10.3115/v1/D14-1162, http://aclweb.org/anthology/D14-1162
12. Rücklé, A., Gurevych, I.: End-to-end non-factoid question answering with an interactive visualization of neural attention weights. In: Proceedings of the 55th Annual Meeting of the Association for Computational Linguistics-System Demonstrations (ACL), pp. 19–24 (2017). https://doi.org/10.18653/v1/P17-4004, https://www.informatik.tu-darmstadt.de/fileadmin/user_upload/Group_UKP/publikationen/2017/2017_ACL_AR_End2End_QA.pdf
13. Rücklé, A., Gurevych, I.: Representation learning for answer selection with LSTM-based importance weighting. In: Proceedings of the 12th International Conference on Computational Semantics (IWCS 2017) (2017). (to appear). http://www.aclweb.org/anthology/W17-6935
14. dos Santos, C., Tan, M., Xiang, B., Zhou, B.: Attentive Pooling Networks (CV) (2016). http://arxiv.org/abs/1602.03609
15. Shrikumar, A., Greenside, P., Kundaje, A.: Learning Important Features Through Propagating Activation Differences (2017). http://arxiv.org/abs/1704.02685
16. Tan, M., dos Santos, C., Xiang, B., Zhou, B.: LSTM-based deep learning models for non-factoid answer selection, vol. 1, pp. 1–11 (2015). http://arxiv.org/abs/1511.04108
17. Tan, M., dos Santos, C., Xiang, B., Zhou, B.: Improved representation learning for question answer matching. In: Proceedings of the 54th Annual Meeting of the Association for Computational Linguistics (Volume 1: Long Papers), pp. 464–473 (2016). https://doi.org/10.18653/v1/P16-1044, http://aclweb.org/anthology/P16-1044
18. Vinyals, O., Kaiser, L., Koo, T., Petrov, S., Sutskever, I., Hinton, G.: Grammar as a foreign language, pp. 1–15 (2014). https://doi.org/10.1146/annurev.neuro.26.041002.131047, http://arxiv.org/abs/1412.7449
19. Wang, B., Liu, K., Zhao, J.: Inner attention based recurrent neural networks for answer selection. In: Proceedings of the 54th Annual Meeting of the Association for Computational Linguistics (Volume 1: Long Papers), pp. 1288–1297 (2016). https://doi.org/10.18653/v1/P16-1122, http://aclweb.org/anthology/P16-1122
20. Wu, W., Wang, H., Li, S.: Bi-directional gated memory networks for answer selection. In: Sun, M., Wang, X., Chang, B., Xiong, D. (eds.) CCL/NLP-NABD -2017. LNCS (LNAI), vol. 10565, pp. 251–262. Springer, Cham (2017). https://doi.org/10.1007/978-3-319-69005-6_21
21. Zurada, J., Malinowski, A., Cloete, I.: Sensitivity analysis for minimization of input data dimension for feedforward neural network. In: Proceedings of IEEE International Symposium on Circuits and Systems - ISCAS 1994 6, pp. 447–450. https://doi.org/10.1109/ISCAS.1994.409622, http://ieeexplore.ieee.org/document/409622/

Online Personalized Next-Item Recommendation via Long Short Term Preference Learning

Yingpeng Du, Hongzhi Liu(✉), Yuanhang Qu, and Zhonghai Wu

School of Software and Microelectronics, Peking University, Beijing, People's Republic of China
{dyp1993,liuhz,qu_yh,wuzh}@pku.edu.cn

Abstract. Precise prediction of users' next choices in time is critical for users' satisfaction and platforms' benefit. A user's next choice heavily depends on the user's long-term preference and recent actions. However, existing methods either (1) ignore the long-term personalized preference or the recent sequential actions of users, or (2) can't update the model in time when receiving users' new action information. To solve these problems, we propose an online personalized next-item recommendation method via long short term preference learning. The proposed method integrates the information of users' long-term personalized preference and short-term sequential actions to predict the next choices. The trained model could be updated online via an extra preference transition matrix. Experimental results on our real-world datasets show that the proposed method consistently outperforms several state-of-the-art methods.

Keywords: Personalized recommendation · Sequential patterns
Online update · Collaborative filtering · Next-item prediction

1 Introduction

Recommender Systems (RSs) provide users with personalized recommendations based on their past feedback, which help to deal with information overloading on the Internet [1]. For instance, RSs behind websites (e.g. Amazon) help users explore what they may like from millions of items, which improves users' satisfaction and business profits.

In spite of many successful algorithms in RSs, capturing dynamic user preference over time is still a great challenge in RSs. The main challenge comes from two sides: WHEN and HOW should RSs change user's preference profile. First, good RSs should react to user's behavior instantly, so it should update user's preference when receiving new action information. Second, good RSs should explore the sequential feedback and account for the basic taste of users [16]. Therefore, we integrate the information of users' long-term personalized preference and short-term sequential actions. For instance, suppose a user browse

X. Geng and B.-H. Kang (Eds.): PRICAI 2018, LNAI 11012, pp. 915–927, 2018.
https://doi.org/10.1007/978-3-319-97304-3_70

Amazon for shopping: she first puts a mobile phone into cart, then the next choice may be protective shell according short-term preference, good RSs should recommend the red protective shell as long-term preference indicates she is a fan of red. When she puts the protective shell into cart, RS should recommend the protective film then. The dynamic RS should keep updating and make next-item recommendation until the shopping is over.

The existing next-item RS can be roughly divided into pattern-based and model-based ones. Pattern-based methods [4,19] are straightforward solution to next-item recommendation, they capture associations between elements (e.g. users, items, timestamp) then make recommendation based on them. However, they tend to recommend popular items rather than suitable but newly-released one due to the lower support measure of them.

Model-based methods capture dynamic preference in two ways. One class of methods [5,6,10,11,13] updates users' preference by retraining with the whole users' behavior including new feedback. But they neglect the sequential information as treating whole purchase history equally. For instance, they make no difference whether phone or protective shell is purchased firstly. The other class of methods [15,16,18] models the sequential patterns mostly relying on Markov chains or Recurrent Neural Networks (RNN). However, they recommend the next item based on successive disjoint basket and session. The basket (session) results in the constant users' preference in a certain period, which can't update the model in time when receiving users' new action information.

In addition, RSs require the fast updating and response for instant feedback. Models relying on retraining [5,6,10,11,13] and network [18] don't work well because of their long computational time for updating. In this paper, we put up with a updating strategy with pretraining the preference transition matrix for fast updating requirement.

In this paper, we propose a model-based method that integrates the information of users' long-term personalized preference and short-term sequential actions to predict the next choices. The long-term preference indicates the basic taste of users, while the short-term preference models users' current taste based on an extra preference transition matrix, which can be pretrained for fast updating requirement.

The main contributions of this paper include:

1. We integrate the information of users' long-term personalized preference and short-term sequential actions to predict the next choices. Sequential patterns analysis is modeled effectively.
2. Our model shows the lower time complexity in both training and updating phase, which scales well for real-world applications.
3. Experiment shows our model consistently outperforms state-of-the-art model-based methods with both parameters learning and updating phase on four real-world datasets.

The rest of this paper is organized as follows. Section 2 reviews some related work. Section 3 formulates the problem and describes the proposed long and short term preference and learning algorithm. Empirical evaluation of the proposed algorithm and comparison with other state-of-the-art algorithms are presented in Sect. 4. Finally, Sect. 5 concludes the paper.

2 Related Work

Capturing dynamic user preference over time is a great challenge in RSs. The existing work can be roughly divided into pattern-based and model-based ones.

Pattern-based methods are straightforward solution to next-item recommendation, which capture associations between elements then makes recommendation based on them. Choi et al. [4] combine implicit collaborative filtering and sequential patterns analysis to calculate the support of item from subsequence. Xiang et al. [19] build up the user-item-time graphs to learn relation rules between different users and items for temporal recommendation. Although their methods are effective and simple, the newly-released items are easy to be omitted due to the lower support measure of them [17].

Model-based methods capture dynamic preference in two ways. One class of model-based methods captures dynamic preference by retraining whole past feedback as well as new feedback. Rendle et al. [13] put up with an online-update process to profile new-user/item. Devooght et al. [5] propose a line search implicit Matrix Factorization (MF) method with dynamic data. As a recent work by He et al. [6] has present an element-wise Alternating Least Squares (eALS) technique based algorithm, which has a popularity-aware weighting scheme and speeds up the optimization with a low complexity model. Matuszyk et al. [10,11] put forward to a selective forgetting strategy based on sliding window and fading factors technique [8]. However, their models neglect the sequential information as they treat whole purchase history equally.

The other class of model-based methods mainly bases on Markov chains or RNN to model sequential feedback, using successive disjoint basket and session to make next-item recommendation. Rendle et al. [15] propose a factorized personalized Markov Chains (MC) algorithm (FPMC) bringing both MC and MF approaches together. Wang et al. [16] put up with a hierarchical representation model (LHR) to learn the complicated interactions among different factors by nonlinear operations. Yu et al. [18] appeal to Dynamic Recurrent Network to model global sequential features among all sequential baskets of a user. However, the basket or session assumes the constant users' preference in a certain period, which makes it harder to response the users' instant feedback.

What's more, some work needs to incorporates contextual information (e.g. position, weather, etc.). Cheng et al. [3] predict where user would go next by resorting to near position of users. Wang et al. [16] combine transaction and contextual information to predict the next choice of users. However, the contextual information is not widespread and hard to collect.

3 Long-Term and Short-Term Matrix Factorization

In this section, we first formulate the problem of personalized next-item RSs, then introduce main idea of our model. We come up with the training and updating algorithm for our model. Finally, we compare the time complexity of all methods.

3.1 Problem Definition

The task in this paper is to profile the dynamic taste of user and make the appropriate recommendation over time. Let U and V denote the total users and items, respectively, and m, n be the number of users and items. All users have a series of chronological feedback of items. For a particular user u, the historical feedback list $R(u)$ is composed of feedback in time order: $R(u) = ({i_1}^{t_1}, {i_2}^{t_2}, \ldots, {i_k}^{t_k}, {i_{k+1}}^{t_{k+1}}, \ldots)$, where ${i_1}^{t_1}$ means user u have feedback with item i_1 at time t_1 and $t_k \leq t_{k+1}$. We denote $R = \{R(u)|u \in U\}$ as all users' feedback.

Different from traditional RSs which only rank the unpurchased items for the active user u, we need to rank all items for user u at time t_i, because the same item may be purchased multiple times by a user at different time.

3.2 Long- and Short-Term Preference Model (LSPM)

Previous work constructs a single matrix to profile users' preference [5–7, 13, 16]. In this paper, we profile users' preference by two different matrices. The former matrix $\mathbf{W} = \mathbb{R}^{m \times d}$ aims to profile users' long-term preference and the later matrix $\mathbf{Y} = \mathbb{R}^{n \times d}$ contributes to construct short-term preference. And $\mathbf{H} = \mathbb{R}^{n \times d}$ profiles items' properties. Notice that d is the dimension of latent space and $\mathbf{W}$, $\mathbf{Y}$, $\mathbf{H}$ are model parameters to be learned by LSPM. The model parameters can also be regarded as latent factors, modeling the non-observed preference of users and properties of items [14]. Denote vectors w_i, y_i and h_i as the i-th row of $\mathbf{W}$, $\mathbf{Y}$ and $\mathbf{H}$. In our model, we assume the preference (denoted as p_{ut}) for user u at time t can be expressed as the combination of long-term preference (w_u) and short-term preference (s_{ut}) at time t. Therefore, the dynamic preference of user u at time t is as follow:

$$p_{ut} = w_u + \alpha s_{ut}$$

where α is the weight of short preference. The long preference w_u is not time relevant. For the short-term preference, we only take the recent k (called window size) items feedback for a particular user u at the time t. Inspired by the fading latent factors of [10, 11], we assign the smaller weight for the older feedback items on short-term preference.

$$s_{ut} = \sum_{l=1}^{k} y_{L^k(u,t)(l)} * D_k(l)$$

where $L^k(u,t) \subset R(u)$ denote the recent k items feedback at the time t for a particular user u, the list $D_k = (1/l|l = 1, \cdots, k)$. Let the $D_k(l)$ and $L^k(u,t)(l)$ be the l-th element of D_k and $L^k(u,t)$.

The estimator for user u likes item i at time t is formulated as follow:

$$r_{ui}^t = p_{ut}^\top \cdot h_i = (w_u + \alpha \sum_{l=1}^{k} y_{L^k(u,t)(l)} * D_k(l))^\top \cdot h_i$$

By implementing $\hat{x}_{uij}^t = r_{ui}^t - r_{uj}^t$ into BPR scheme [9,14,15], we get the loss function:

$$\begin{aligned}
\text{LSPM-opt:=} & \sum_{(u,i,j)\in D_s^t} ln\sigma(\hat{x}_{uij}^t) - \lambda_\theta||\theta||^2 \\
= & \sum_{(u,i,j)\in D_s^t} ln\sigma(p_{ut}^\top \cdot h_i - p_{ut}^\top \cdot h_j) - \lambda_\theta||\theta||^2 \\
= & \sum_{(u,i,j)\in D_s^t} ln\sigma[(w_u + \alpha \sum_{l=1}^{k} y_{L^k(u,i)(l)} * D_k(l))^\top \cdot (h_i - h_j)] - \lambda_\theta||\theta||^2
\end{aligned}$$

where $D_s^t = \{(u,i,j)\}$ means that user u purchased item i but not yet purchased item j at time t, and θ means all parameters need to learn. $||\cdot||^2$ is $L2$ norm and λ_θ is the regularization coefficient. In real-world scenario when a new rating comes in, the long-term preference stays stable, while the short-term preference changes with respect to new feedback.

3.3 Parameters Learning

As the loss function is differentiable, we choose gradient descent based algorithms for maximization naturally. However, we have $O(|U||V|)$ training triples in D_s^t, computing the full gradient in each update step is not feasible. As a result, we appeal to Stochastic Gradient Descent (SGD) [2] to maximize the objective function BPR-opt. [14] points out item-wise or user-wise full cycles sampling will lead to poor convergence as there are so many consecutive updates on the same user-item pair. We choose user-item pairs (u, i^t) randomly where $i^t \in R(u)$, then sample the item j not purchased yet by user u at time t. The gradients of objective function BPR-opt with respect to vectors $\boldsymbol{\theta}$ are calculated as follows:

$$\begin{aligned}
\frac{\partial BPR-opt}{\partial \boldsymbol{\theta}} &= \sum_{(u,i,j)\in D_s} \frac{\partial}{\partial \boldsymbol{\theta}} ln\sigma(\hat{x}_{uij}) - \lambda_\theta \frac{\partial}{\partial \boldsymbol{\theta}}||\boldsymbol{\theta}||^2 \\
&\propto \sum_{(u,i,j)\in D_s} \frac{-e^{-\hat{x}_{uij}}}{1+e^{-\hat{x}_{uij}}} \frac{\partial}{\partial \boldsymbol{\theta}} \hat{x}_{uij} - \lambda_\theta \boldsymbol{\theta}
\end{aligned} \tag{1}$$

By applying SGD, we sample a triple $(u,i,j) \in D_S^t$ to update the model. The derivatives of every model parameter $\boldsymbol{\theta}$ show as follow and the pseudocode of our model for parameters learning is shown in Algorithm 1.

$$\frac{\partial}{\partial \boldsymbol{\theta}} \hat{x}^t_{uij} = \begin{cases} (h_{if} - h_{jf}), & \text{if } \boldsymbol{\theta} = w_{uf}; \\ (w_u f + \alpha \sum\limits_{l=1}^{k} y_{L^k(u,i)(l)f} * D_k(l)), & \text{if } \boldsymbol{\theta} = h_{if}; \\ -(w_u f + \alpha \sum\limits_{l=1}^{k} y_{L^k(u,i)(l)f} * D_k(l)), & \text{if } \boldsymbol{\theta} = h_{jf}; \\ \alpha D_k(l) * (h_{if} - h_{jf}), & \text{if } \boldsymbol{\theta} \in \{y_{lf} | l \in L^k(u,t)\}; \\ 0, & \text{otherwise} \end{cases} \tag{2}$$

Algorithm 1. LSPM Parameters Learning Algorithm

Input: All users' feedback R, Dimension of latent factor d, Window size k, Sample number N, Short preference weight α.
Output: Latent matrices $\mathbf{W}$, $\mathbf{Y}$, $\mathbf{H}$ and u's preference p_{ut} at time t.

```
    Initialization:
    Randomly initialize the parameters W = R^{m×d}, Y = R^{n×d} and H = R^{n×d};
    Training:
    repeat
        for (t = 0; t < N; t = t + 1) do
            Sample (u, i, j) ∈ D_S and find L^k(u, i);
            for (f = 0; f < d; f = f + 1) do
                Update θ_f ← θ_f + lr ∂BPR−opt/∂θ_f based on (1),(2) ;
            end for
        end for
    until convergence
    Calculate p_ut = w_u + Σ_{l=1}^{k} y_{L^k(u,t)(l)} * D_k(l);
```

Time Complexity. In Algorithm 1, updating one sample takes $O(d)$ time. Thus, one iteration takes $O(|R|d)$ time, where $|R|$ is the number of all users' feedback. Table 1 summarizes the time complexity of other state-of-the-art MF algorithms. LSPM, HRM and BPR are the most efficient algorithms, which are sample-based methods. The rest algorithms are the whole-data based method, such as ALS, eALS, RCD, which show the higher time complexity.

Table 1. Time complexity of implicit MF methods offline.

Algorithm	Time complexity
ALS (Hu et al. [7])	$O((m+n)d^3 + \|R\|d^2)$
RCD (Devooght et al. [5])	$O((m+n)d^2 + \|R\|d)$
eALS (He et al. [6])	$O((m+n)d^2 + \|R\|d)$
BPR (Rendle et al. [14])	$O(\|R\|d)$
HRM (Wang et al. [16])	$O(\|R\|d)$
LSPM	$O(\|R\|d)$

3.4 Updating Strategy

After parameters learning process, we learn the parameters for our model, which denoted as $\hat{W}, \hat{Y}, \hat{H}$. In real-world scenario, when a new feedback comes in, we are supposed to update the model parameters. As our model can learn the sequential patterns, we do not need to retrain the users' and items' latent factors as the previous work [5,6,10,11,13] does. We only need to update users' and items' latent factors then reconstruct user's preference. Empirically, study shows that 5–10 samples updating for new interaction is sufficient to get good results. Algorithm 2 summarizes the incremental learning strategy for our model.

Algorithm 2. LSPM Updating Learning Algorithm

Input: $\hat{\mathbf{W}}$, $\hat{\mathbf{Y}}$, $\hat{\mathbf{H}}$, new iteraction (u, i), time t;
Output: Refreshed Latent Matrices **W**, **Y** and **H**; **Training:**

for $(t = 0; t < SampleNum; t = t + 1)$ **do**
  Sample $(u, i, j) \in D_S^t$;
  for $(f = 0; f < d; f = f + 1)$ **do**
    Update $\theta_f \leftarrow \theta_f + \alpha \frac{\partial BPR-opt}{\partial \theta_f}$ based on (1),(2) ;
  end for
end for
return W, **Y** and **H**;

Time Complexity. The updating for a new interaction (u, i) can be done in $O(k)$ time for LSPM, while $O(d^2 + (|R(u)| + |R(i)|)d)$ for whole-data based methods RCD, eALS and $O((|R(u)| + |R(i)|)d)$ for Sample-based method BPR.

4 Experiment

4.1 Experimental Setup

Datasets:
We experimented with four publicly data sets with the timestamp: Yelp, MovieLens100k, Last.fm, Netflix. The characteristics of the four datasets are summarized in Table 2. Those data sets have been widely used to evaluate recommendation algorithms. We follow the common practice [6,14–16] to remove the user or item if it has less than 10 interactions for MovieLens and Netflix and 5 interactions for Last.fm, which is relatively sparse.

Baseline:
We compare our model with the following state-of-the-art methods:

- **RCD** [5]**:** This is a line search implicit MF method with dynamic data, which is suitable for online learning.

Table 2. Description of the experimental data sets

Dataset	Feedback	User	Item	Density
Yelp	731,671	25,677	25,815	0.11%
Netflix	998,539	6,040	3,260	5.07%
MovieLens	97,953	943	1,152	9.02%
Last.fm	54,519	922	5,572	1.06%

- **eALS** [6]**:** This is the state-of-the-art implicit MF method that has the same time complexity with RCD. It proposes a popularity-aware weighting scheme to differentiate different unobserved items.
- **BPR** [13,14]**:** This is a sample-based algorithm that maximizes the distance between implicit feedbacks and the unobserved. We adopt [13] for online incremental learning.
- **HRM** [16]**:** This is a sample-based algorithm to learn the complicated interactions among different factors by nonlinear operations. It models sequential patterns by the heirachical structure.

Parameter Settings: Experiments indicate that setting short preference weight α as 1 and window size as 5 shows good performance for our model. For the sample-based method, we set learn rating lr as 0.05 for fast learning speeding in parameters learning and updating phase except 0.01 for denser data set MovieLens. For regularization, we set λ as 0.01 for all methods for a fair comparison.

For the whole-data based method, we tune parameters based on authors' implementation if it exists, otherwise we tune to their best.

4.2 Leave-One-Out Protocol

Although some protocols [7,12,14] split the data into train set and test set randomly, they destroy the sequential patterns of them. RSs should make recommendation at the current time. Consequently, we use leave-one-out evaluation to test our model, which the last interaction is held out for prediction while the rest data is used for training process. Thus, it only evaluates model's capability for providing one-shot recommendation. We rank 100 items that are likely to be liked for a particular user per time. To assess the ranking list, we adopt Hit Ratio (HR), Normalized Discounted Cumulative Gain (NDCG) and Precision (PREC). The first measures the fact whether ground-truth item is contained in the ranking list, while the other focus on the position of hit.

Comparison with Whole-Data based MF Methods:

In this part, we compare the performance of LSPM with other whole-data based MF methods. Figure 1 shows the prediction of different whole-data based model with varying d. It shows that LSPM outperforms other models consistently, which shows the priority of our algorithm. All algorithms show the same trend as

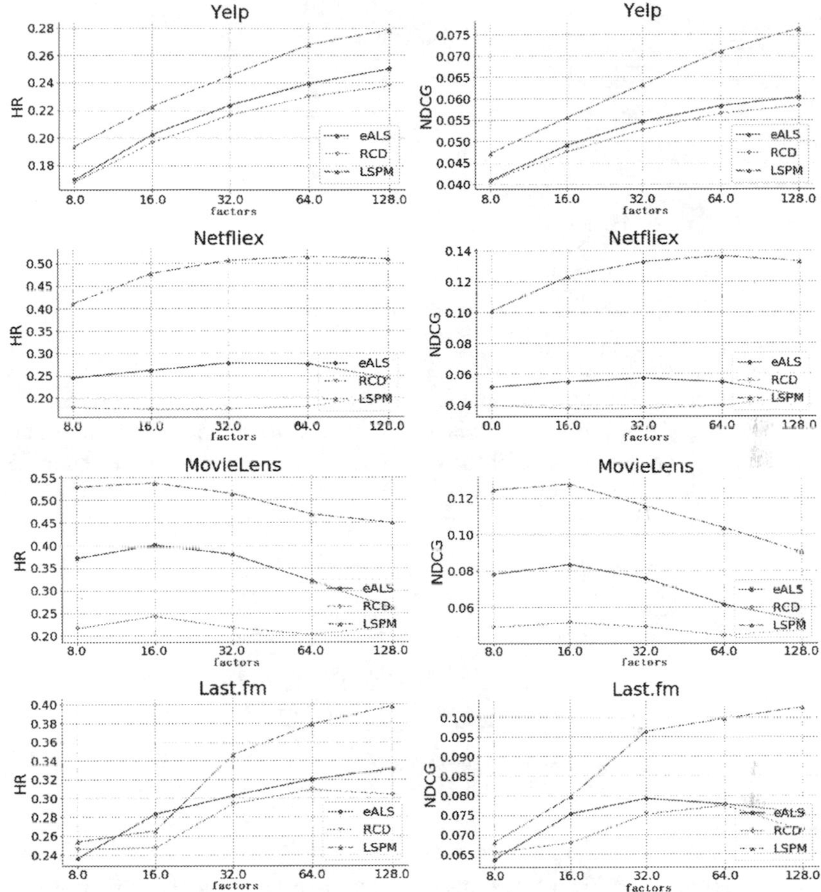

Fig. 1. Comparison with the whole-data based MF across Factors.

the d rises up except for MovieLens, as larger factors enhance the representation of models. For the sake of preventing overfitting, we don't test larger d for those models. Compared with the best performance of baseline algorithms, the improvements of LSPM are up to 11.44%, 109.22%, 73.05%, 20.31% for HR and 26.69%, 190.39%, 71.34%, 35.76% for NDCG with the four datasets (Yelp, Netflix, MovieLens, Last.fm) respectively. Our model not only hits the ground-truth items with high accuracy but also assigns it the aheader position. We believe the priority of our model comes from chronological structure of datasets, we explain it in latter part.

Compare Sample-Based MF Methods (BPR):
In this part, we compare our model with sample-based methods, which share same time complexity. We adopt the same regularization rate 0.01 for a fair comparison. Notice that we only run our model for 100 iterations, which are

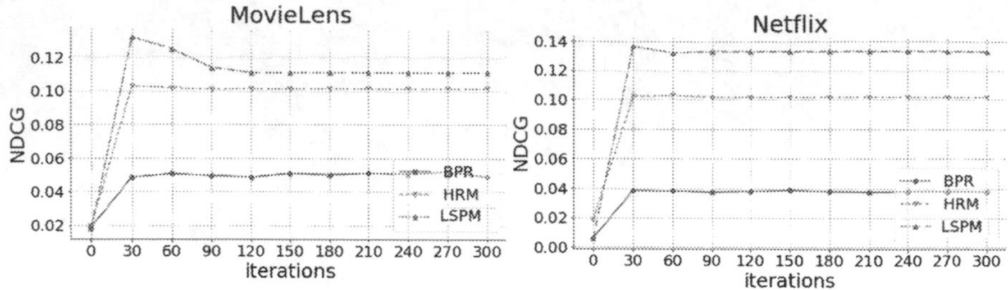

Fig. 2. Comparison with sample-based MF methods in each iteration.

enough to converge. Figure 2 plots the performance (NDCG) of our model, HRM and BPR in each iteration. As no basket for yelp and little baskets for Last.fm, we only test those algorithms with MovieLens and Netflix. It shows that LSPM achieves the high accuracy and fast convergence.

Table 3. The average variance for different datasets

Dataset	S_c	S_r	S_c/S_r
Yelp	0.0118	0.0094	1.2553
Netflix	2.1589	0.5791	3.7280
MovieLens	0.7959	0.3491	2.2798
Last.fm	0.0413	0.0303	1.3630

Sequential Patterns for Datasets: We explore the structure of datasets in this part. We assume that the feedback items with the closer timestamp is more similar with each other, known as sequential patterns, which tends to cluster the items with closer timestamp. We sample interactions (u, i) from R and record the particular items with two different rules. The first rule records the closer timestamp interactions for a particular user while the second rule records randomly. Then we calculate the average variance for all items for two methods, which is denoted as S_c and S_r. The higher S_c/S_r means the more evident structure of sequential patterns. The experiment shows in Table 3. We find the more evident structure for Netflix, MovieLens than Yelp and Last.fm, which explains why our model and HRM preform so good in former datasets.

4.3 Updating Protocol

We create the real-world scenario by stimulating the dynamic data stream. We sort all interactions chronologically, then reserve the first 90% interactions as the train set and hold the last 10% for testing. We first learn parameters by train set, and then test the new interaction from the hold-out data one by one and update our model correspondingly. Therefore the data from test set is not only test example but also training example. In this phase, we also adopt HR, NDCG and PREC for ranking list assessing.

As HRM has to rely on next-basket prediction, we only compare LSPM with next-item RSs for updating protocol, which can be divided into whole-data based MF methods RCD, eALS and sample-based method BPR.

Table 4. Performance improvement of CPML over baseline algorithms

Dataset	Method	HR	NDCG	PREC
Yelp	eALS	0.2311	0.0577	0.0209
	RCD	0.2233	0.0547	0.0190
	BPR	0.1908	0.0458	0.0153
	LSPM	**0.2542**	**0.0676**	**0.0275**
	Improve.	**10.00%**	**17.16%**	**31.58%**
Netflix	eALS	0.1049	0.0212	0.0047
	RCD	0.1217	0.0245	0.0052
	BPR	0.0414	0.0075	0.0011
	LSPM	**0.3531**	**0.0827**	**0.0252**
	Improve.	**190.14%**	**237.55%**	**384.62%**
MovieLens	eALS	0.2258	0.0442	0.0083
	RCD	0.2789	0.0627	0.0187
	BPR	0.2399	0.0473	0.0092
	LSPM	**0.4273**	**0.0981**	**0.0290**
	Improve.	**53.21%**	**56.46%**	**55.08%**
Last.fm	eALS	0.1686	0.0376	0.0103
	RCD	0.1383	0.0298	0.0073
	BPR	0.1339	0.0264	0.0068
	LSPM	**0.1882**	**0.0463**	**0.0157**
	Improve.	**11.63%**	**23.14%**	**52.43%**

With the test data inflows chronologically, we show average performance evolution of all model in Table 4. It shows that LSPM consistently outperforms all baseline models evidently by both measurements. What's more, same as leave-one-out evaluation, LSPM has the larger improvement for NDCG than HR, which means our model tends to predict high quality items.

4.4 Parameter Analysis

In this part, we explore how window size k and short preference weight α influence our model. We test them in leave-one-out protocol. Figure 3 left part shows the prediction of LSPM model with varying window size. The prediction accuracy rises first and then drops as k increases, because too large/small k results in

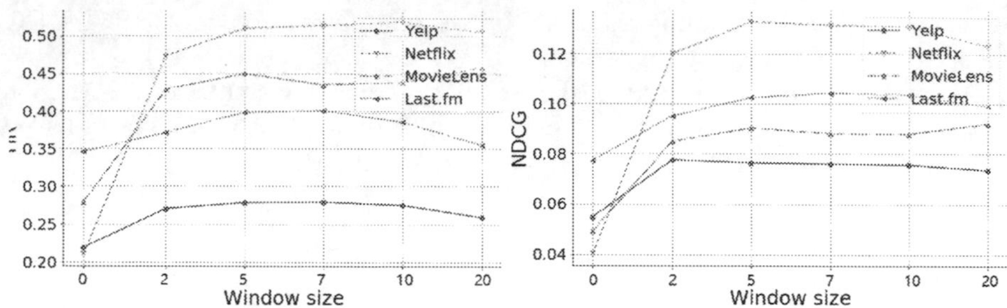

Fig. 3. Performance of LSPM across Window Size and short preference weight.

less/over memory for short preference. When $k = 5$ LSPM shows both high accuracy and efficiency. Figure 3 right part shows the prediction of LSPM model with preference weight α. When $\alpha = 1$ LSPM shows the high accuracy. In addition, the data sets (e.g. Netflix, MovieLens) with more evident sequential patterns structure show more significant improvement by incorporating short preference.

5 Conclusion

In this paper, we propose a method that integrates the information of users' long-term personalized preference and short-term sequential actions to predict the next choices. To learn sequential patterns, we resort to an extra preference transition matrix with forgetting strategy, which contributes to low time complexity and high accuracy. Extensive experiments demonstrate the promise of our approach in comparison with the state-of-the-art algorithms for next-item RSs.

Acknowledgement. This work was partially sponsored by National Key R&D Program of China (Grant No. 2017YFB10 020 02) and PKU-Tencent joint research Lab.

References

1. Bobadilla, J., Ortega, F., Hernando, A., et al.: Recommender systems survey. Knowl.-Based Syst. **46**, 109–132 (2013)
2. Burges, C., Shaked, T., Renshaw, E., et al.: Learning to rank using gradient descent. In: Proceedings of the 22nd International Conference on Machine Learning, pp. 89–96. ACM (2005)
3. Cheng, C., Yang, H., Lyu, M.R., et al.: Where you like to go next: successive point-of-interest recommendation. In: IJCAI, vol. 13, pp. 2605–2611 (2013)
4. Choi, K., Yoo, D., Kim, G., et al.: A hybrid online-product recommendation system: combining implicit rating-based collaborative filtering and sequential pattern analysis. Electron. Commer. Res. Appl. **11**(4), 309–317 (2012)
5. Devooght, R., Kourtellis, N., Mantrach, A.: Dynamic matrix factorization with priors on unknown values. In: Proceedings of the 21th ACM SIGKDD International Conference on Knowledge Discovery and Data Mining, pp. 189–198. ACM (2015)

6. He, X., Zhang, H., Kan, M.Y., et al.: Fast matrix factorization for online recommendation with implicit feedback. In: Proceedings of the 39th International ACM SIGIR Conference on Research and Development in Information Retrieval, pp. 549–558. ACM (2016)
7. Hu, Y., Koren, Y., Volinsky, C.: Collaborative filtering for implicit feedback datasets. In: Proceedings of 8th IEEE International Conference on Data Mining (ICDM 2008), pp. 263–272 (2008)
8. Vinagre, J., Jorge, A.M.: Forgetting mechanisms for scalable collaborative filtering. J. Braz. Comput. Soc. **18**(4), 271–282 (2012)
9. Liu, H., Wu, Z., Zhang, X.: CPLR: collaborative pairwise learning to rank for personalized recommendation. Knowl.-Based Syst. **148**, 31–40 (2018)
10. Matuszyk, P., Spiliopoulou, M.: Selective forgetting for incremental matrix factorization in recommender systems. In: Džeroski, S., Panov, P., Kocev, D., Todorovski, L. (eds.) DS 2014. LNCS (LNAI), vol. 8777, pp. 204–215. Springer, Cham (2014). https://doi.org/10.1007/978-3-319-11812-3_18
11. Matuszyk, P., Vinagre, J., Spiliopoulou, M., et al.: Forgetting techniques for stream-based matrix factorization in recommender systems. Knowl. Inf. Syst. **55**(2), 275–304 (2018)
12. Pan, R., Zhou, Y., Cao, B., et al.: One-class collaborative filtering. In: Eighth IEEE International Conference on Data Mining, ICDM 2008 IEEE, pp. 502–511. IEEE (2008)
13. Rendle, S., Schmidt-Thieme, L.: Online-updating regularized kernel matrix factorization models for large-scale recommender systems. In: Proceedings of the 2008 ACM Conference on Recommender Systems, pp. 251–258. ACM (2008)
14. Rendle, S., Freudenthaler, C., Gantner, Z., Thieme, L.S.: BPR: Bayesian personalized ranking from implicit feedback. In: Proceedings of the 25th Conference on Uncertainty in Artificial Intelligence (UAI 2009), pp. 452–461 (2009)
15. Rendle, S., Freudenthaler, C., Schmidt-Thieme, L.: Factorizing personalized Markov chains for next-basket recommendation. In: Proceedings of the 19th International Conference on World Wide Web, pp. 811–820. ACM (2010)
16. Wang, P., Guo, J., Lan, Y., et al.: Learning hierarchical representation model for next-basket recommendation. In: Proceedings of the 38th International ACM SIGIR Conference on Research and Development in Information Retrieval, pp. 403–412. ACM (2015)
17. Wang, S., Hu, L., Cao, L.: Perceiving the next choice with comprehensive transaction embeddings for online recommendation. In: Ceci, M., Hollmén, J., Todorovski, L., Vens, C., Džeroski, S. (eds.) ECML PKDD 2017. LNCS (LNAI), vol. 10535, pp. 285–302. Springer, Cham (2017). https://doi.org/10.1007/978-3-319-71246-8_18
18. Yu, F., Liu, Q., Wu, S., et al.: A dynamic recurrent model for next basket recommendation. In: International ACM SIGIR Conference on Research and Development in Information Retrieval, pp. 729–732. ACM (2016)
19. Xiang, L., Yuan, Q., Zhao, S., et al.: Temporal recommendation on graphs via long-and short-term preference fusion. In: Proceedings of the 16th ACM SIGKDD International Conference on Knowledge Discovery and Data Mining, pp. 723–732. ACM (2010)

Enhancing Artificial Bee Colony Algorithm with Superior Information Learning

Xinyu Zhou(✉), Yunan Liu, Mingwen Wang, and Jianyi Wan

School of Computer and Information Engineering,
Jiangxi Normal University, Nanchang 330022, China
xyzhou@whu.edu.cn

Abstract. Artificial bee colony (ABC) algorithm has attracted much attention for its good performance and simple structure in recent years. However, its solution search equation does well in exploration but badly in exploitation, which may result in slow convergence rate for complex optimization problems. To address this defect, many ABC variants have been developed based on utilizing the global best individual or the group of elite individuals. Although the utilization of such good individuals is indeed beneficial to enhance the exploitation, it may also run the risk of causing the algorithm too greedy. In this paper, we proposed a modified ABC algorithm with superior information learning (SIL) strategy for achieving a better balance between the exploration and exploitation abilities. In the proposed SIL strategy, the individuals are expected to learn superior information from an exemplar which has better fitness value than the individuals themselves. The exemplar is no longer acted by the global best individual or the elite group. The proposed SIL strategy is designed to utilize the valuable information of good individuals while without losing the diversity. In the experiments, 22 well-known test functions and six state-of-the-art ABC variants are used. The comparison results showed that our approach significantly accelerate the convergence rate, and has better or at least comparable performance than the competitors on most of the test functions.

Keywords: Artificial bee colony · Superior information learning
Neighborhood search

1 Introduction

Artificial bee colony (ABC) algorithm, first proposed by Karaboga in 2005 [1], is one of the most popular swarm intelligence algorithms, which has attracted much attention for its good performance and simple structure in recent years. The ABC algorithm simulates the intelligence foraging behavior of honeybees, and it has been successfully applied to solve variant real-world optimization problems. However, some researchers pointed out that ABC tends to suffer from slow convergence rate when dealing with complex optimization problems. The possible main reason is that its solution search equation does well in exploration but badly in exploitation. Therefore, how to modify the solution search equation for the better exploitation ability is the key of enhancing the performance of ABC.

X. Geng and B.-H. Kang (Eds.): PRICAI 2018, LNAI 11012, pp. 928–940, 2018.
https://doi.org/10.1007/978-3-319-97304-3_71

Following the line of modifying the solution search equation, many ABC variants have been developed in the last few years. Among these ABC variants, most of them focused on utilizing the global best individual or the group of elite individuals. Zhu et al. [2] proposed a modified solution search equation based on the inspiration of particle swarm optimization (PSO). In the proposed search equation, the information of the global best individual is incorporated. Be inspired by the mutation strategies of differential evolution (DE), Gao et al. [3] proposed a modified ABC (MABC) algorithm based on their new search equation, i.e., ABC/best/1. Recently, Zhou et al. [4] developed an improved MABC variant by introducing a global neighborhood search (NS) operator. The NS operator aims to search the vicinity of the global best individual for enhancing the exploitation ability. Yu et al. [5] designed an adaptive greedy position update strategy with elite group in their proposed AABC algorithm. Based on the elite group, Cui et al. [6] proposed a novel ABC algorithm with depth-first search framework and elite-guided search equation (DFSABC-elite), in which the global best individual is used as well. Very recently, inspired by the DFSABC-elite algorithm, Kong et al. [7] proposed a novel ABC algorithm based on elite group guidance and the combined breadth-depth search strategy, in which a modified neighborhood search equation is designed by utilizing the elite group.

There is no doubt that the information of the global best individual or the elite group is indeed beneficial to enhance the exploitation. However, if the mechanism of utilizing the information is not well designed, it may also run the risk of causing the algorithm too greedy. Because the global best individual or the elite group has significant impact on other individuals, if it is trapped by local optimum, the other individuals would tend to converge to the same position quickly. Therefore, how to effectively utilize the valuable information of good individuals without losing diversity is a challenging research topic. In this paper, we propose a modified ABC algorithm with superior information learning strategy (abbreviated as SILABC). In the SILABC, the proposed SIL strategy is designed to utilize the valuable information of good individuals. Be different from some of the above mentioned ABC variants, in the SIL strategy, the good individual is no longer acted by the global best individual or the elite group, instead it is a randomly chosen individual through a neighborhood search operator. To validate the performance of our approach, 22 well-known test functions are used in the experiments, and six recently proposed ABC variants are included for comparison. The experimental results showed that our approach can achieve better or at least comparable performance than the competitors on most of the test functions.

2 Related Work

2.1 The Basic ABC Algorithm

In ABC, the entire working process was divided into four phases: initialization phase, employed bee phase, onlooker bee phase, and scout bee phase. In initialization phase, let $X_i = \{X_{i,1}, X_{i,2}, \ldots, X_{i,D}\}$ represent the ith food source (solution) with the population size N and the dimension D. The initial population is generated according to Eq. (1).

$$x_{i,j} = x_{min,j} + rand(0,1)\left(x_{max,j} - x_{min,j}\right) \tag{1}$$

where i = 1, 2, …, N, j = 1, 2, …, D. $x_{\min,j}$ and $x_{\max,j}$ are the lower and upper bounds on the jth dimension, respectively. And *rand(0, 1)* is a random number from 0 to 1 for the dimension j. Moreover, the fitness value of each food source is calculated by Eq. (2).

$$fit_i = \begin{cases} \frac{1}{1+f(x_i)} & \text{if}(f(x_i) \geq 0) \\ 1 + abs(f(x_i)) & \text{otherwise} \end{cases} \tag{2}$$

where fit_i is the fitness value of food source X_i, and $f(X_i)$ is the objective function value of X_i.

In employed bee phase, the bees adopt the following search equation to generate a candidate solution V_i from the parent individual X_i.

$$v_{i,j} = x_{i,j} + \emptyset_{i,j}\left(x_{i,j} - x_{k,j}\right) \tag{3}$$

where $v_{i,j}$ is the jth dimension of new food source V_i; $\emptyset_{i,j}$ is a random number in the range [−1, 1]; k is randomly chosen from {1, 2, …, N} and has to be different from the selected i; $i \in$ {1, 2, …, N} and $j \in$ {1, 2, …, D}.

After each employed bee finishes its search task, each onlooker bees selects a food source to perform exploitation according to the selection probability p, which is calculated as follows:

$$p_i = \frac{fit_i}{\sum_{j=1}^{SN} fit_j} \tag{4}$$

where fit_i is the fitness value of solution X_i, which is proportional to the nectar amount of the ith food source. By this probabilistic selection method, the onlooker bees would continue to select part of the food sources for further exploitation using the same solution search equation shown in Eq. (3).

In the last phase, scout bee phase, if a food source cannot be further improved for at least *limit* times, it is considered to be exhausted. In ABC, *limit* is the only one single specific control parameter needed to be tuned. For the scout bee, the Eq. (1) is used to generate a new food source to replace the abandoned.

2.2 The MABC-NS Algorithm

To enhance the exploitation of ABC, Gao et al. [3] proposed a modified search equation ABC/best/1 based on the inspiration of the DE mutation strategy (DE/best/1). Meanwhile, the search equation of ABC is retained, and a selective probability is introduced in MABC. The ABC/best/1 solution search equation is devised as follows:

$$v_{i,j} = x_{best,j} + \emptyset_{i,j}\left(x_{r1,j} - x_{r2,j}\right) \tag{5}$$

where x_{best} is the best food source in the current population; $\emptyset_{i,j}$ is a random number in the range [−1, 1]; the indices $r1$ and $r2$ are mutually exclusive integers randomly chosen from $\{1, 2, \ldots, N\}$; It is noted that if an individual bursts out of the search space by any search equations, the individual will be anew generated by Eq. (1).

In researches of the recent years, the neighborhood information of the solution is used to solve complex optimization problems, because basic ABC and its variants often suffer from the problem of premature convergence. Therefore, different neighborhood search operators have been designed, and they also have shown superior performance in some EAs [4, 8–10]. It is used to enhance exploitation in MABC-NS by Zhou [4] that an efficient global neighborhood search (NS) operator for improving particle swarm optimization (PSO) algorithm presented by Wang [10]. The global neighborhood search operator make a trial individual TX_i be generated by the following equation:

$$TX_i = r_1 \cdot X_i + r_2 \cdot \text{gbest} + r_3 \cdot (X_a - X_b) \tag{6}$$

where r_1, r_2, and r_3 are three mutually exclusive numbers distributed randomly in (0, 1), and they have to accord with the condition: $r_1 + r_2 + r_3 = 1$; *gbest* is the global best solution of the entire population; *a* and *b* are two indexes of the randomly selected food sources, and they have to different from *i*. According to Eq. (6), we found that the TX_i actually included multi-individual information which consists of partial content of X_i, *gbest*, X_a and X_b. This setting is useful for accelerating the convergence of the algorithm. A clear explanation of the operator of global NS is presented in Fig. 1.

As illustrated in Fig. 1, all blue circles make up the population, and the red circle is the global best solution. The area covered by the red lines is the available search area where the trial individual is generated by Eq. (6). The NS strategy is helpful to solve multimodal problems. Individuals are located at different regions. Therefore, if the current individual falls into local minima, individuals in other regions may pull the trapped individual forward. It was noted in [4] that the complete and detailed implementation of MABC-NS algorithm.

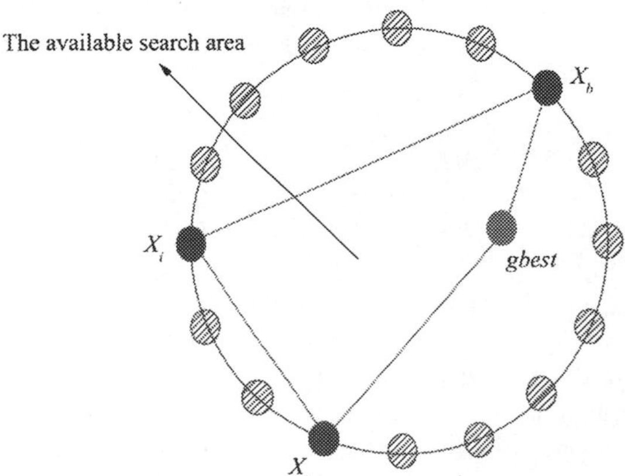

Fig. 1. The global neighborhood search operator (Color figure online)

3 Our Approach

3.1 Superior Information Learning (SIL) Strategy

From the description in the Sect. 1, it can be observed that the utilization of good individuals is beneficial to enhance the exploitation of ABC. Because the good individuals usually locate in the vicinity of the global optimum, thus they may contain valuable information for search. Following this line, we still attempt to utilize good individuals in the SIL strategy for better exploitation. However, there exists an issue that the algorithm would become too greedy if good individuals are limited to the global best individual or a few elite individuals. Because the global best individual or the elite individuals have significant impact on other individuals, if they are trapped by local optimum, the other individuals would also tend to converge to the same position quickly. To tackle this problem, we redefine the concept of good individuals in the SIL strategy. In fact, as for the idea of utilizing good individuals for search, two related problems would emerge: (1) Which individuals can be considered as good individuals? (2) How to utilize these good individuals?

For the first problem, we redefine the concept of good individuals which is no longer acted by the global best individual or the elite individuals. In contrast, for a given individual *TX*, if there exists any individual *X* of which fitness value is worse than that of *TX*, the individual *TX* can be considered as a good individual for the individual *X*. By making this simple modification on the concept of good individuals, except for the worst individual in the population, each individual get the chance of becoming an exemplar to provide superior information for other individuals to learn.

For the second problem, Meng et al. [11] proposed the crisscross optimization (CSO) algorithm which consists of three parts: horizontal crossover, vertical crossover and competitive operator. And we researched that the vertical crossover is applied to enhance the exploration performance of PSO variant [12] in 2017. In this paper, we propose SIL strategy inspirited from the horizontal crossover.

In the original horizontal crossover, the population is divided into two equal parts. And then two individual X_{i} and X_{k} are taken out without repeating from the parts to exchange respective information (whether good or bad) on all dimensions by Eqs. (7) and (8). The information exchange based on general individual information appears to be extremely passive.

$$cs_{i,j} = r_1 \cdot x_{i,j} + (1 - r_1) \cdot x_{k,j} + c_1 \cdot \left(x_{i,j} - x_{k,j}\right) \tag{7}$$

$$cs_{k,j} = r_2 \cdot x_{k,j} + (1 - r_2) \cdot x_{i,j} + c_2 \cdot \left(x_{k,j} - x_{i,j}\right) \tag{8}$$

where $cs_{\mathrm{i,j}}$ and $cs_{\mathrm{k,j}}$ are the crossover solutions of corresponding individuals on *j*th dimension, respectively; r_1 and r_2 are uniformly generated random values within (0, 1); c_1 and c_2 are uniformly generated values within (−1, 1);

Unlike the original horizontal crossover, the newly proposed strategy is very proactive. Whenever an individual has good enough information, it has the learning probability *p* to share this information with other individual or others. In other words, the good information will spread rapidly across the population and other individuals, as learners, will learn the information if they need. It is noted that SIL strategy is a one-way process which the exemplar will only provide the superior information to any individual which needs it and will not learn any information. Therefore, the learning equation of SIL strategy is as follows:

$$lx_{obj,j} = r \cdot x_{i,j} + (1 - r) \cdot x_{obj,j} + c \cdot \left(x_{i,j} - x_{obj,j}\right) \tag{9}$$

where X_i is the sharer of the good information; X_{obj} is the receiver; LX_{obj} is the learning solution; *obj* is an index of the learner; *r* is called learning coefficient and is a uniformly random value between 0 and 1; *c* is called acceleration coefficient which uniformly distributed random value between −1 and 1.

In theory, the superior information can be integrated into any individual of the population and help them to search new better solutions. But actually, not all individuals need the information. For example, the solution quality of some individuals is better than the exemplar's. Such individuals often have superior information, and they are suitable as learning exemplars rather than information recipients or learners. The superior information is spread downward. The procedure of the SIL strategy is illustrated in Algorithm 1. In that, *FEs* is the number of used fitness function evaluations, and *MaxFEs*, as the terminal condition, is the maximal number of fitness function evaluations.

It can be observed from Algorithm 1 that we restricted both the input and output of the superior information. In the input, only the information from better individuals will be learned. And only worse individuals than exemplar will become learner of the superior information.

It can be found that we introduced the probability *p* to control execution of SIL for reducing redundancy of learning resources in SIL. It is obvious that a bigger probability can make the same superior information be fully utilized (accelerate the convergence) and a lower can make individuals have more chances to learn different superior information (increase the diversity of the population). In this paper, the probability *p* is set 1 for maximizing utilization ratio of the superior information.

Algorithm 1 The procedure of the SIL strategy

```
Input the individual X_i of the information;
FOR obj = 1 to N
    IF obj != i THEN
      IF the X_i is better than X_obj AND rand(0,1) < p THEN
        Generate a new learning solution LX_obj according Eq. (9);
        Calculate the fitness value of LX_obj;
        FEs = FEs + 1;
        IF the LX_obj is better than its parent X_obj THEN
          Replace X_obj with LX_obj;
        END IF
      END IF
    END IF
END FOR
```

Algorithm 2 The procedure of SILABC

```
Randomly initialize N solutions { X_i | i = 1,2,... , N } in the population by Eq. (1);
Calculate fitness value of each solution;
FEs = N;
WHILE FEs < MaxFEs
   FOR i = 1 to N
      Generate a new candidate solution V_i according to Eq. (3);
      Calculate the fitness value of V_i;
      FEs = FEs + 1;
      IF the V_i is better than its parent X_i THEN
         Replace X_i with V_i;
      END IF
   END FOR
   /* The global neighborhood search operator */
   FOR i = 1 to N
      IF rand(0,1) < P_ns THEN
         Generate a trial solution TX_i according to Eq. (6);
         FEs = FEs + 1;
         /* The superior information learning strategy */
         IF the TX_i is better than its parent X_i THEN
            Replace X_i with TX_i;
            Perform SIL strategy according to Algorithm 1;
         END IF
      END IF
   END FOR
END WHILE
```

3.2 SILABC Algorithm

As we all know, good guiding information can improve the search effectiveness. There is much superior information which is of high quality and includes multi-individual information, as learning exemplar, in population after performing NS operator. The superior information can be diffused throughout the population and be fully learned by the SIL strategy. In this section, we proposed the SILABC algorithm.

Specifically, whenever the NS operation is performed, the new trial solution included multi-individual information is generated. If the fitness value of the trial solution is better than its parent solution, the multi-individual information just will be superior information and will be spread throughout the population to be learned via the SIL strategy. Such information is superior and well suited to guide the search for better solutions. The detailed procedure of the SILABC is illustrated in Algorithm 2.

4 Experimental Results

4.1 Benchmark Functions and Parameter Settings

There are 22 well-known benchmark functions with dimension $D = 30$ used in the following experiments. These test function, which their names and search ranges listed in Table 1, are also widely used in other work [3, 8, 10, 13]. Among them, F01−F04 and F08−F11 are continuous unimodal functions. F05 is the Rosenbrock function which is unimodal for D = 2 and 3 but is multimodal in high dimension cases. F06 is a discontinuous step function, and F07 is a noisy quartic function. The remaining ones are multimodal function and all of the functions have the same global optimum zero.

For the parameter settings, we follow the original settings of MABC-NS [4], i.e. $N = 75$. What's more, the termination condition only is the maximum number of function evaluation (*MaxFEs*) which is set to 5000 * D. For maximizing learning of the superior information, the learning probability p is set 1. Finally, each algorithm will be conducted 25 times independent run for all test functions, and the mean value and standard deviation (mean ± std) are recorded.

Table 1. The 22 benchmark functions used in the experiments

Func.	Name	Search range	Func.	Name	Search range
F01	Sphere	[−100, 100]	F12	Schwefel 2.26	[−500, 500]
F02	Schwefel 2.22	[−10, 10]	F13	Rastrigin	[−5.12, 5.12]
F03	Schwefel 1.2	[−100, 100]	F14	Ackley	[−32, 32]
F04	Schwefel 2.21	[−100, 100]	F15	Griewank	[−600, 600]
F05	Rosenbrock	[−30, 30]	F16	penalized 1	[−50, 50]
F06	Step	[−100, 100]	F17	penalized 2	[−50, 50]
F07	Quartic with noise	[−1.28, 1.28]	F18	NCRastrigin	[−5.12, 5.12]
F08	Elliptic	[−100, 100]	F19	Alpine	[−10, 10]
F09	SumSquare	[−10, 10]	F20	Levy	[−10, 10]
F10	SumPower	[−1, 1]	F21	Bohachevsky_2	[−100, 100]
F11	Exponential	[−1.28, 1.28]	F22	Weierstrass	[−0.5, 0.5]

4.2 Effectiveness of the Proposed Approach

In order to validate the effectiveness of our proposed approach and the capability of accelerating convergence, SILABC is compared with ABC, MABC and MABC-NS on 22 benchmark functions with 30 dimensions. The algorithm parameters of ABC, MABC and MABC-NS take the recommended empirical values stated in the previous sections. And the paired Wilcoxon signed-rank test is used to compare the significance among four algorithms. The signs "†", "‡" and "≈"indicate our approach is better than, worse than and similar to its competitor according to the Wilcoxon signed-ranked test at $\alpha = 0.05$, respectively. In the last row, the overall performance is summarized as *w*/*l*/*t*, which denotes that our approach wins on *w* functions, lose on *l* functions and ties on *t* functions. The detailed experimental results are shown in Table 2.

As can be seen from Table 2, SILABC has better performance on 22 benchmark functions. SILABC can find the optimum on F06, F10, F11, F13, F15, F18, F21 and F22, and new local optimal solutions on F14 and F19. In contrast, SILABC can find the optimal solutions only on F10, but other algorithms cannot. In addition, we present the convergence curves of the above four algorithms on six representative test functions in Fig. 2.

It can be seen form Fig. 2 that although four involved ABC variants have the same or near solutions on the test functions but SILABC has amazing convergence speed and converges much faster than ABC, MABC and MABC-NS on F01, F10, F13, F14 and F19. The experiment showed that the proposed approach can effectively speed up convergence rate of SILABC and help individuals quickly locate the optimal region.

Table 2. Comparative results of ABC, MABC and MABC-NS at $D = 30$

Func.	ABC	MABC	MABC-NS	SILABC
	Mean ± Std	Mean ± Std	Mean ± Std	Mean ± Std
F01	3.57E−10 ± 2.13E−10†	1.02E−25 ± 6.65E−26†	1.52E−81 ± 3.01E−81†	2.28E−174 ± 0.00E+00
F02	1.04E−06 ± 3.37E−07†	4.12E−14 ± 1.18E−14†	6.00E−42 ± 4.28E−42†	4.12E−94 ± 1.49E−93
F03	6.98E+03 ± 1.70E−03†	1.69E+04 ± 2.03E+03†	1.42E−58 ± 6.25E−58‡	3.08E−34 ± 1.00E−33
F04	3.07E+01 ± 4.26E+00†	1.24E+01 ± 1.71E+00†	6.74E−31 ± 7.12E−31†	1.08E−53 ± 2.52E−53
F05	6.34E−01 ± 7.13E−01‡	2.99E+00 ± 2.64E+00‡	2.79E+01 ± 2.50E−01≈	2.80E+01 ± 1.03E−01
F06	0.00E+00 ± 0.00E+00≈	0.00E+00 ± 0.00E+00≈	0.00E+00 ± 0.00E+00≈	0.00E+00 ± 0.00E+00
F07	1.75E−01 ± 4.76E−02†	3.44E−02 ± 8.03E−03†	1.76E−04 ± 1.07E−04≈	1.61E−04 ± 1.01E−04
F08	9.24E−05 ± 4.22E−05†	1.09E−22 ± 5.75E−23†	5.30E−78 ± 1.66E−77†	6.20E−170 ± 0.00E+00
F09	1.01E−11 ± 7.41E−12†	1.12E−26 ± 8.68E−27†	9.17E−83 ± 2.23E−82†	4.64E−178 ± 0.00E+00
F10	2.69E−11 ± 1.05E−10†	7.71E−27 ± 1.56E−26†	2.03E−72 ± 4.83E−72†	0.00E+00 ± 0.00E+00
F11	6.84E−07 ± 6.35E−07†	7.23E−07 ± 6.68E−07†	0.00E+00 ± 0.00E+00≈	0.00E+00 ± ± 0.00E+00
F12	3.82E−04 ± 1.09E−08≈	3.82E−04 ± 4.93E−13≈	3.82E−04 ± 4.93E−13≈	3.82E−04 ± 3.56E−13
F13	6.03E−06 ± 2.74E−04†	0.00E+00 ± 0.00E+00≈	0.00E+00 ± 0.00E+00≈	0.00E+00 ± 0.00E+00
F14	3.55E−06 ± 1.18E−06†	5.77E−13 ± 2.02E−13†	1.87E−15 ± 4.27E−15†	4.44E−16 ± 0.00E+00
F15	1.77E−08 ± 2.53E−09†	3.75E−14 ± 1.78E−13†	0.00E+00 ± 0.00E+00≈	0.00E+00 ± 0.00E+00
F16	6.38E−12 ± 3.65E−12†	7.00E−28 ± 4.04E−28†	7.14E−31 ± 7.61E−31≈	9.37E−30 ± 3.82E−29
F17	5.10E−10 ± 2.34E−10†	1.44E−26 ± 7.15E−27‡	1.67E−29 ± 1.33E−29‡	1.52E−02 ± 2.76E−02
F18	0.00E+00 ± 0.00E+00‡	0.00E+00 ± 0.00E+00≈	0.00E+00 ± 0.00E+00≈	0.00E+00 ± 0.00E+00
F19	7.90E−05 ± 2.66E−05†	1.13E−12 ± 1.45E−12†	1.34E−42 ± 1.37E−42†	4.46E−96 ± 6.67E−96
F20	2.94E−08 ± 5.65E−08†	8.23E−25 ± 4.72E−25†	5.32E−28 ± 5.86E−28≈	3.93E−27 ± 9.68E−27
F21	5.74E−08 ± 8.34E−08†	0.00E+00 ± 0.00E+00≈	0.00E+00 ± 0.00E+00≈	0.00E+00 ± 0.00E+00
F22	3.94E−04 ± 7.41E−05†	1.42E−14 ± .23E−15†	0.00E+00 ± 0.00E+00≈	0.00E+00 ± 0.00E+00
w/*l*/*t*	20/1/1	15/2/5	8/2/12	–

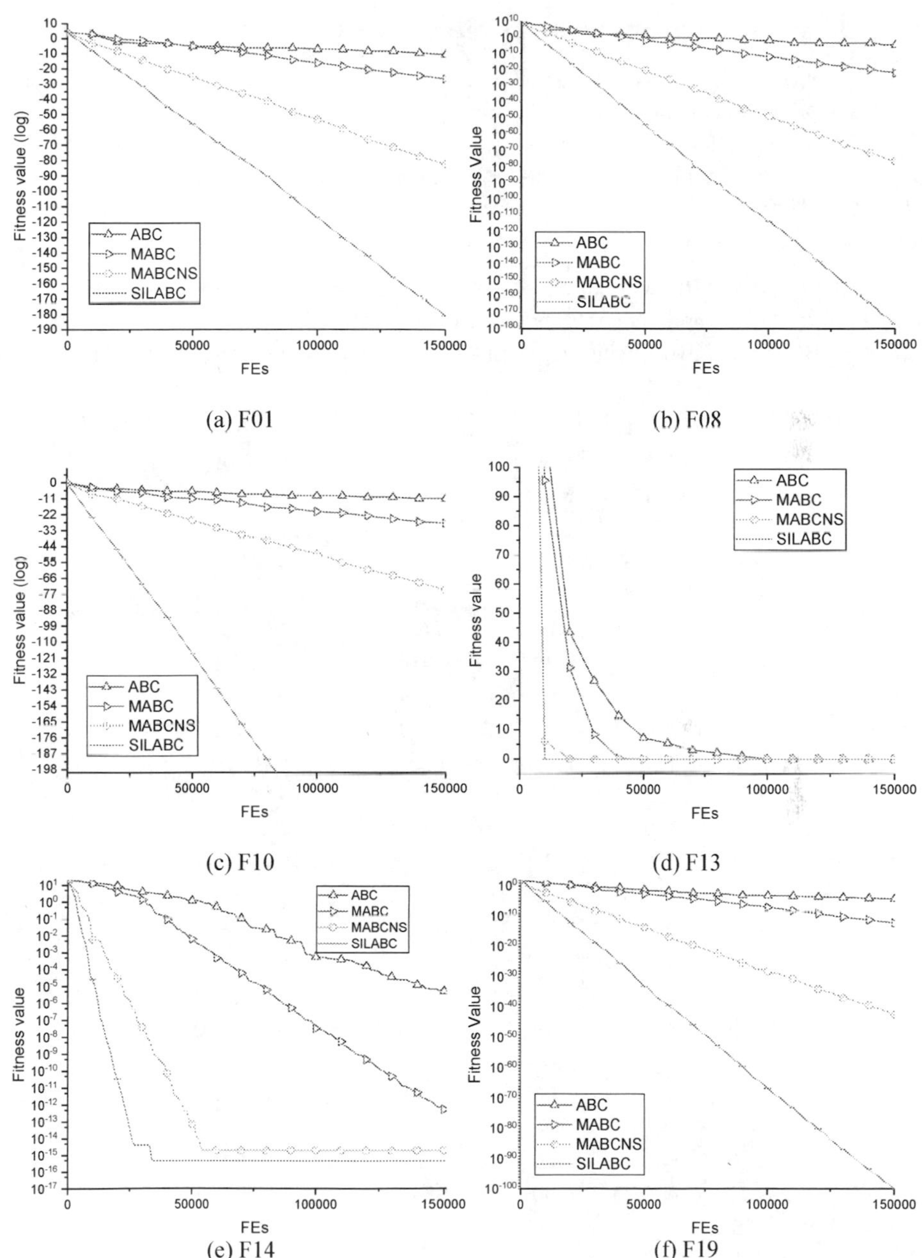

Fig. 2. The convergence curves of ABC, MABC, MABC-NS and SILABC on some representative functions at $D = 30$

4.3 Comparison with Several up-to-Date ABC Variants

In this section, SILABC is compared with three up-to-date ABC variants on 22 test functions with dimensions $D = 30$. To make a fair comparison, for all the compared algorithms, parameter settings are in accordance with the best settings except the population size N and the termination condition $MaxFEs$ which are $N = 75$ and $MaxFEs = 5000 * D$, respectively. These three compared ABC variants are listed as follows:

- AABC (2016): ABC with an adaptive greedy position update strategy [5].
- ABCG (2018): improved ABC based on the gravity model [14].
- DFSABC-elite (2016): using depth-first search and elite-guided search [6].

Table 3. Comparative results of AABC, ABCG and DFSABC-elite at $D = 30$

Func.	AABC	ABCG	DFSABC-elite	SILABC
	Mean	Mean	Mean	Mean
F01	1.93E−24†	1.55E−26†	1.16E−57†	2.28E−174
F02	4.13E−13†	1.11E−15†	7.73E−30†	4.12E−94
F03	9.87E+03†	3.02E+03†	4.25E+03†	3.08E−34
F04	2.16E+01†	1.32E−01†	3.67E−01†	1.08E−53
F05	9.48E−01‡	4.20E+01$^{\approx}$	5.16E−01‡	2.80E+01
F06	0.00E+00$^{\approx}$	0.00E+00$^{\approx}$	0.00E+00$^{\approx}$	0.00E+00
F07	9.76E−02†	1.21E−02†	1.31E−02†	1.61E−04
F08	3.91E−20†	5.93E−18†	1.07E−53†	6.20E−170
F09	3.34E−25†	2.81E−14†	2.51E−58†	4.64E−178
F10	1.38E−19†	2.80E−56†	1.88E−40†	0.00E+00
F11	1.51E−06†	7.91E−06†	2.69E−06†	0.00E+00
F12	3.82E−04$^{\approx}$	3.82E−04$^{\approx}$	3.82E−04$^{\approx}$	3.82E−04
F13	0.00E+00$^{\approx}$	0.00E+00$^{\approx}$	0.00E+00$^{\approx}$	0.00E+00
F14	1.40E−12†	3.87E−14†	2.73E−14†	4.44E−16
F15	4.91E−14†	0.00E+00$^{\approx}$	0.00E+00$^{\approx}$	0.00E+00
F16	1.32E−26†	2.99E−26†	1.57E−32‡	9.37E−30
F17	2.68E−25‡	2.09E−25‡	1.35E−32‡	1.52E−02
F18	0.00E+00$^{\approx}$	0.00E+00$^{\approx}$	0.00E+00$^{\approx}$	0.00E+00
F19	2.06E−10†	1.98E−03†	1.38E−16†	4.46E−96
F20	2.66E−16†	4.10E−24†	1.35E−31‡	3.93E−27
F21	0.00E+00$^{\approx}$	0.00E+00$^{\approx}$	0.00E+00$^{\approx}$	0.00E+00
F22	2.19E−14†	0.00E+00$^{\approx}$	0.00E+00$^{\approx}$	0.00E+00
w/l/t	15/2/5	13/1/8	11/4/7	-

The final results are given in Table 3. In the same way, to compare the significance between tow algorithms, the paired Wilcoxon signed-rank test is used and the last row summarizes the comparison results. From the Table 3, it can be seen that our approach is better than the involved three algorithms on most of benchmark functions, and this also illustrates SILABC has a significantly powerful convergence capability.

5 Conclusion

In this work, the novel superior information learning strategy for learning superior information based on neighborhood search was presented and it was integrated into MABC-NS to evolve a new ABC variant, called SILABC. The individuals are expected to learn superior information from an exemplar which has better fitness value than the individuals themselves. In order to improve the efficiency and reduce the search redundancy of the strategy, we have simply restricted the input of information and object of output. Finally, comparisons have been conducted 22 well-known benchmark functions. The experimental results demonstrated that SILABC surpass compared algorithms on the majority of benchmark functions in terms of solution accuracy, convergence speed.

In our future work, we will investigate further that the effect of the value of the learning probability p on the stability of its mother algorithm and how to determinate value of the probability p. And the new information learning strategy will be embedded in other ABC variants or some other non-ABC methods. In addition, we will conduct comprehensive comparisons of SILABC with other EAs.

Acknowledgments. This work is supported by the National Natural Science Foundation of China (Nos. 61603163, 61462045 and 61562042) and the Science and Technology Foundation of Jiangxi Province (No. 20151BAB217007).

References

1. Karaboga, D.: An idea based on honey bee swarm for numerical optimization. Erciyes University, Kayseri (2005)
2. Zhu, G., Kwong, S.: Gbest-guided artificial bee colony algorithm for numerical function optimization. Appl. Math. Comput. **217**(7), 3166–3173 (2010)
3. Gao, W., Liu, S.: A modified artificial bee colony algorithm. Comput. Oper. Res. **39**(3), 687–697 (2012)
4. Zhou, X., Wang, H., Wang, M., Wan, J.: Enhancing the modified artificial bee colony algorithm with neighborhood search. Soft. Comput. **21**(10), 2733–2743 (2017)
5. Yu, W., Zhan, Z., Zhang, J.: Artificial bee colony algorithm with an adaptive greedy position update strategy. Soft. Comput. **22**(2), 437–451 (2018)
6. Cui, L., et al.: A novel artificial bee colony algorithm with depth-first search framework and elite-guided search equation. Inf. Sci. **367–368**, 1012–1044 (2016)
7. Kong, D., Chang, T., Dai, W., Wang, Q., Sun, H.: An improved artificial bee colony algorithm based on elite group guidance and combined breadth-depth search strategy. Inf. Sci. **442–443**, 54–71 (2018)
8. Das, S., Abraham, A., Chakraborty, U.K., Konar, A.: Differential evolution using a neighborhood-based mutation operator. IEEE Trans. Evol. Comput. **13**(3), 526–553 (2009)
9. Gao, W., Chan, F.T.S., Huang, L., Liu, S.: Bare bones artificial bee colony algorithm with parameter adaptation and fitness-based neighborhood. Inf. Sci. **316**, 180–200 (2015)
10. Wang, H., Sun, H., Li, C., Rahnamayan, S., Pan, J.: Diversity enhanced particle swarm optimization with neighborhood search. Inf. Sci. **223**(2), 119–135 (2013)
11. Meng, A., Chen, Y., Yin, H., Chen, S.: Crisscross optimization algorithm and its application. Knowl.-Based Syst. **67**, 218–229 (2014)

12. Yu, X., Liu, Y., Feng, X., Chen, G.: Enhanced comprehensive learning particle swarm optimization with exemplar evolution. In: Shi, Y., et al. (eds.) SEAL 2017. LNCS, vol. 10593, pp. 929–938. Springer, Cham (2017). https://doi.org/10.1007/978-3-319-68759-9_76
13. Wang, H., Wu, Z., Rahnamayan, S., Sun, H., Liu, Y., Pan, J.: Multi-strategy ensemble artificial bee colony algorithm. Inf. Sci. **279**(9), 587–603 (2014)
14. Xiang, W.L., Meng, X.L., Li, Y.Z., He, R.C., An, M.Q.: An improved artificial bee colony algorithm based on the gravity model. Inf. Sci. **429**, 49–71 (2018)

Robust Factorization Machines for Credit Default Prediction

Weijian Ni[1], Tong Liu[1(✉)], Qingtian Zeng[1], Xianke Zhang[1], Hua Duan[1], and Nengfu Xie[2]

[1] College of Computer Science and Engineering, Shandong University of Science and Technology, Qingdao, China
niweijian@gmail.com, liu_tongtong@foxmail.com, qt_zeng@163.com, zhangxianke@sdust.edu.cn, huaduan59@163.com

[2] Agricultural Information Institute, Chinese Academy of Agricultural Sciences, Beijing, China
xienengfu@caas.cn

Abstract. Credit default prediction is a topic of great importance in lending industry. Just like many real-world applications, the dataset in the task is often class-imbalanced and noisy, degrading the performance of most machine learning methods. In this paper, we propose an extension of Factorization Machines, named RobustFM, to address the problem of class-imbalance and noisiness in the credit default prediction task. The proposed RobustFM employs a smoothed asymmetric Ramp loss function, into which truncation and hinge parameters are introduced to facilitate noise tolerance and imbalanced learning. Experimental results on several real credit datasets show that RobustFM significantly outperforms state-of-the-art methods in terms of F-measure.

Keywords: Factorization machines · Ramp loss
Imbalanced classification · Credit default prediction

1 Introduction

Credit default, generally refers to failure to pay interest or principal on a loan when due, is a primary potential source of risk in lending business. Distinguishing credit applicants with high default risk from credit-worthy ones has been identified as a crucial issue for risk management in financial institutions. Over the last decades, researchers and practitioners have sought to develop credit models using modern machine learning techniques [1] for their ability to model complex multivariate functions without rigorous assumptions for the input data.

Despite encouraging successes in recent studies, accurate predictive analysis of credit default through using machine learning techniques is by no means a trivial task. Many of the challenges stem from the fact that the data in the task, i.e., samples of credit applicants, is generally imbalanced and noisy. Defaults, which are often of more focused interests in the credit default prediction task,

X. Geng and B.-H. Kang (Eds.): PRICAI 2018, LNAI 11012, pp. 941–953, 2018.
https://doi.org/10.1007/978-3-319-97304-3_72

would only hit a small segment of credit customers in a real credit business [2]. This results in a heavily skewed class distribution of credit data. In addition, credit data is collected from loan records of financial institutions; however, due to privacy issues, system malfunctions or even human error, historical loan records are often incomplete or erroneous, making the credit data noisy. Therefore, in order to facilitate responsible decision-making for credit granting, the problems of class-imbalance and noisiness in credit data should be fully addressed.

Factorization machines (FM), proposed by Rendle [3] in the context of recommendation system, is a novel predictive model that maps a number of predictor variables to some target. The advantages FM offers over traditional classification approaches is that it provides a principled way to model second-order (up to arbitrary order in theory) variable interactions in linear complexity. FM has shown great promise in a number of prediction tasks, such as context-aware recommendation [4,5] and click-through rate prediction [6–8]. However, the potential of exploiting FM in credit risk evaluation has been little investigated so far. We argue that FM is powerful in credit default prediction task for at least the following reasons. First, for the task of credit default prediction, the combinations of predictor variables (e.g., family, age, and salary), usually much more discriminative than single ones, can be naturally modeled through variable interactions in FM. Second, FM embeds features into a low-rank latent space such that variable interactions can be estimated under high sparsity; thus FM can be viewed as a favored formulism for tackling sparse credit data.

In this work, we explore the use of FM for credit default prediction, with an emphasis on the class-imbalanced and noisy natural of credit data. We incorporate a new non-convex loss function into the learning process of FM and give rise to a novel **Robust F**actorization **M**achines (RobustFM) model that enhances FM for prediction under class-imbalance and noisiness settings. The new non-convex loss function is essentially a smoothed asymmetric Ramp loss [9] with additional degrees of freedom to tolerate the noise and imbalanced class distribution of credit data. Unlike convex loss functions used in traditional FM, the new loss function is upper bounded so as to enhance the robustness of the learning procedure. Furthermore, asymmetric margins are introduced to push learning towards achieving a larger margin on the rare class (defaulters).

The rest of the paper is organized as follows. In Sect. 2, we present preliminaries of this work, including Credit Default Prediction and Factorization Machines. We then present the details of the proposed RobustFM in Sect. 3. Experiment results are shown in Sect. 4. Finally, we review related work and conclude the paper in Sects. 5 and 6, respectively.

2 Preliminary

2.1 Credit Default Prediction

In point view of machine learning, the credit default prediction task is generally formalized as binary classification. Formally, each credit applicant is represented by a set of features (e.g., applicant's age, monthly income, education, employment and loan purpose), denoted as $\mathbf{x} \in \mathbb{R}^d$, where d is the number of features. Each credit applicant belongs to either of the two classes with a label $y \in \{+1, -1\}$. In this work, we use $+1$ and -1 to denote credit applicants with high default risk (hereafter, bad applicants) and low default risk (hereafter, good applicants), respectively.

Given a training set $D = D^{(+)} \cup D^{(-)} \in \mathbb{R}^d \times \{+1, -1\}$, in which $D^{(+)}$ and $D^{(-)}$ denote a set of historical bad and good credit applicants, respectively. In general, $|D^{(+)}| < |D^{(-)}|$. The goal of credit default prediction is to learn a function $f : \mathbb{R}^d \mapsto \{+1, -1\}$, which is capable of classifying a new credit applicant into one of the two classes.

2.2 Factorization Machines

Factorization Machines (FM) takes as input a real valued vector $\mathbf{x} \in \mathbb{R}^d$, and estimates the target by modelling pairwise interactions of sparse features using low-rank latent factors. The model equation of FM is formulated as:

$$\hat{y}(\mathbf{x}; \Theta) = w_0 + \sum_{j=1}^{d} w_j x_j + \sum_{j=1}^{d} \sum_{j'=j+1}^{d} \langle \mathbf{v}_j, \mathbf{v}_{j'} \rangle x_j x_{j'} \tag{1}$$

where the parameters Θ have to be estimated are:

$$w_0 \in \mathbb{R}; \quad \mathbf{w} \in \mathbb{R}^d; \quad \mathbf{V} = (\mathbf{v}_1, \cdots, \mathbf{v}_d) \in \mathbb{R}^{pd}$$

In Eq. 1, the first two items on the right-hand-side are linear combinations of each features with weights w_j $(1 \leq j \leq d)$ and global bias w_0, and the last item on the right-hand-side is pairwise feature interactions using a factorized weighting schema $\hat{w}_{jj'} = \langle \mathbf{v}_j, \mathbf{v}_{j'} \rangle = \sum_{k=1}^{p} v_{jk} \cdot v_{j'k}$, where $\mathbf{v}_j$ is factor vector of the j-th feature. Feature factors in FM are commonly said to be low-rank, due to $p \ll d$.

In addition to theoretical soundness of low-rank feature factorization, FM is also practically efficient for its linear prediction time complexity. Computing pairwise feature interaction directly requires time complexity of $O(d^2)$; however, it has been shown that the pairwise feature interaction in FM can be computed in $O(pd)$ using the equivalent formulation of Eq. 1 [3]:

$$\hat{y}(\mathbf{x}; \Theta) = w_0 + \sum_{j=1}^{d} w_j x_j + \frac{1}{2} \sum_{k=1}^{p} \left(\left(\sum_{j=1}^{d} v_{jk} x_j \right)^2 - \sum_{j=1}^{d} v_{jk}^2 x_j^2 \right) \tag{2}$$

The model parameters Θ of FM can be estimated through minimizing empirical risk over training set D, together with regularization of parameters:

$$\mathcal{O}_D(\Theta) = \frac{1}{|D|} \sum_{(\mathbf{x},y) \in D} \ell \left(y, \hat{y}(\mathbf{x}; \Theta) \right) + \sum_{\theta \in \Theta} \lambda_\theta \theta^2 \tag{3}$$

where $\ell(y, \hat{y})$ is the loss function to evaluate the disagreement of the prediction value $\hat{y}$ with the actual label y. Without confusion, we sometimes use $\hat{y}$ to represent the prediction $\hat{y}(\mathbf{x}; \Theta)$ in the rest of the paper.

For binary classification, the most widely adopted loss function in FM is Logistic loss:

$$\ell_{\text{logit}}(y, \hat{y}) = \ln\left(1 + e^{-y\hat{y}}\right)$$

Despite effectiveness in various prediction tasks, FM still suffers from the curse of learning from imbalanced and noisy data. When the one class vastly outnumbers others, the learning objective in Eq. 3 can be dominated by instances from the major class. As such, FM tends to be overwhelmed by the major class, ignoring the minor, yet important ones, which is bad applicants in credit default prediction task. Furthermore, the Logistic loss, as convex loss functions, gives high penalties to those misclassified samples far from the origin, increasing the chances of outliers having a considerable contribution to the global loss. Thus the parameters estimated through optimizing Eq. 3 may be inevitably biased by outliers in noisy datasets, leading to a suboptimal predictive model that attempts to account for these outliers.

In this work, instead of Logistic loss, we incorporate into FM a new smoothed asymmetric Ramp loss allowing for class-dependent and up-bounded penalties for misclassified instances. This results in *RobustFM*, a new extension of FM that addresses imbalanced and noisy class distribution simultaneously, greatly improving the accuracy of credit default prediction under real-world scenarios.

3 Smooth Asymmetric Ramp Loss

Ramp loss, a non-convex loss function proposed by Collobert [9], is essentially a "truncated" version of Hinge loss used in support vector machines:

$$\ell_{\text{R}}(y, \hat{y}; \gamma) = \begin{cases} 1 - \gamma & \text{if } y\hat{y} < \gamma \\ 1 - y\hat{y} & \text{if } \gamma \leq y\hat{y} \leq 1 \\ 0 & \text{if } y\hat{y} > 1 \end{cases}$$

Intuitively, Ramp loss is constructed by flattening Hinge loss when the so-called functional margin $y\hat{y}$ smaller than a predefined parameter $\gamma < 0$. In other words, a fixed non-zero penalty $1 - \gamma$, rather than linear penalty $1 - y\hat{y}$ in Hinge loss, is applied to the samples mistakenly predicted far away from the origin (i.e., $y\hat{y} < \gamma$).

Studies have proven Ramp loss's superiority over Hinge loss in terms of robustness to noisy labels [10, 11]. However, Ramp loss applies a unified penalty, either $1-\gamma$ or $1-y\hat{y}$, to all samples no matter to which class they belong. Similar as Logistic loss and Hinge loss, the empirical risk based on Ramp loss will be dominated by negative instances if the class distribution is highly imbalanced. Ramp loss thus still suffering from imbalanced class distribution.

One way to address the class-imbalance problem is to apply class-dependent penalties to the training errors. We introduce new parameters in Ramp loss to control the degree of penalty for positive and negative classes, and construct an **asymmetric Ramp (aRamp) loss**:

$$\ell_{\mathrm{aR}}(y,\hat{y};\gamma,\tau^{(+)},\tau^{(-)}) = \begin{cases} \tau^{(y)} - \gamma & \text{if } y\hat{y} < \gamma \\ \tau^{(y)} - y\hat{y} & \text{if } \gamma \le y\hat{y} \le \tau^{(y)} \\ 0 & \text{if } y\hat{y} > \tau^{(y)} \end{cases} \quad (y \in \{+1,-1\})$$

There are three parameters in asymmetric Ramp loss: γ ($\gamma < 0$) is truncation parameter that decides the point to flatten the loss function; $\tau^{(+)}$ and $\tau^{(-)}$ are the hinge parameters for false negative and false positive errors, respectively. In general, $\tau^{(+)} > \tau^{(-)} \ge 1$, since false negative error is considered more serious than false positive error in imbalanced classification problems.

One should note that the asymmetric Ramp loss is not differentiable at the truncation point ($y\hat{y} = \gamma$) and the hinge points ($y\hat{y} = \tau^{(y)}$), whereas smoothness is a desired property for gradient-based optimization techniques, e.g., stochastic gradient descent and alternating coordinate descent, which have been widely used for training FM. Motivated by the smoothing mechanism adopted in designing Huber loss [12], we make use of smooth quadratic function to approximate the asymmetric Ramp loss at the non-smooth points. More specifically, we derive a **smooth asymmetric Ramp (saRamp) loss** as follows:

$$\ell_{\mathrm{saR}}(y,\hat{y};\gamma,\tau^{(+)},\tau^{(-)},\delta) = \begin{cases} \tau^{(y)} - \gamma & \text{if } y\hat{y} < \gamma - \delta \\ \tau^{(y)} - y\hat{y} - \dfrac{(\gamma + \delta - y\hat{y})^2}{4\delta} & \text{if } \gamma - \delta \le y\hat{y} \le \gamma + \delta \\ \tau^{(y)} - y\hat{y} & \text{if } \gamma + \delta < y\hat{y} < \tau^{(y)} - \delta \\ \dfrac{(\tau^{(y)} + \delta - y\hat{y})^2}{4\delta} & \text{if } \tau^{(y)} - \delta \le y\hat{y} \le \tau^{(y)} + \delta \\ 0 & \text{if } y\hat{y} > \tau^{(y)} + \delta \end{cases}$$

The saRamp loss is quadratic for small interval around the truncation point $[\gamma - \delta, \gamma + \delta]$ and the hinge point $[\tau^{(y)} - \delta, \tau^{(y)} + \delta]$, and linear for other values. Figure 1 illustrates the aRamp loss and saRamp loss with different interval length δ. It is easy to verify that $\lim_{\delta \to 0} \ell_{\mathrm{saR}}(y,\hat{y};\gamma,\tau^{(+)},\tau^{(-)},\delta) = \ell_{\mathrm{aR}}(y,\hat{y};\gamma,\tau^{(+)},\tau^{(-)})$. We omit the proof due to brevity. In practice, we set $\delta = 0.1$. Without ambiguity, we briefly denote saRamp loss $\ell_{\mathrm{saR}}(y,\hat{y};\gamma,\tau^{(+)},\tau^{(-)},\delta)$ as $\ell_{\mathrm{saR}}(y,\hat{y})$ hereafter.

The derivative of the saRamp loss w.r.t. the functional margin can be easily derived as follows:

$$\frac{\partial \ell_{\mathrm{saR}}(y,\hat{y})}{\partial (y\hat{y})} = \begin{cases} 0 & \text{if } y\hat{y} < \gamma - \delta \\ \dfrac{\gamma + \delta - y\hat{y}}{2\delta} - 1 & \text{if } \gamma - \delta \le y\hat{y} \le \gamma + \delta \\ -1 & \text{if } \gamma + \delta < y\hat{y} < \tau^{(y)} - \delta \\ -\dfrac{\tau^{(y)} + \delta - y\hat{y}}{2\delta} & \text{if } \tau^{(y)} - \delta \le y\hat{y} \le \tau^{(y)} + \delta \\ 0 & \text{if } y\hat{y} > \tau^{(y)} + \delta \end{cases} \tag{4}$$

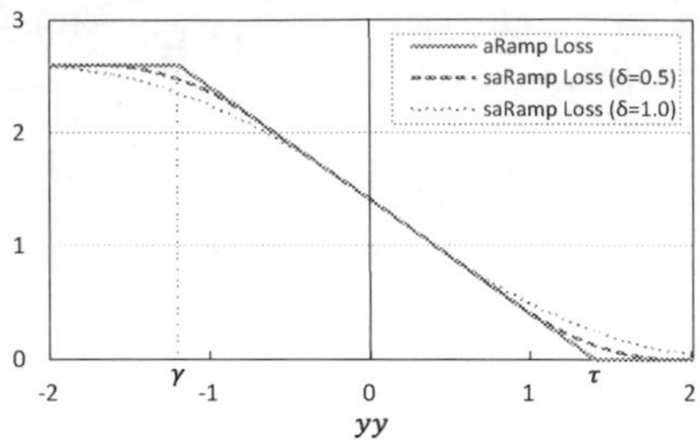

Fig. 1. Asymmetric Ramp loss and smooth asymmetric Ramp loss

4 Parameter Estimation

To solve the highly non-convex problem in Eq. 3 in a large scale, iterative optimization methods are usually preferred, due to the simplicity nature and flexibility in the choices of loss function. In this work, we employ Stochastic Gradient Descent (SGD), one of the most popular optimization method in factorization models, to estimate the parameters of RobustFM. Simply put, SGD updates parameters iteratively until convergence. In each iteration, an instance $(\mathbf{x}, y)$ is randomly drawn for training data D, and the update is performed towards the direction of negative gradient of the objective w.r.t. each parameter $\theta \in \Theta$:

$$\theta^{(t)} = \theta^{(t-1)} - \eta \cdot \left(\frac{\partial \mathcal{O}_{\{(\mathbf{x},y)\}}(\Theta^{(t-1)})}{\partial \theta} \right) \tag{5}$$

where $\eta > 0$ is the learning rate of gradient descendent.

Plugging the learning objective Eq. 3 into Eq. 5, we derive the parameter updating formula:

$$\theta^{(t)} = \theta^{(t-1)} - \eta \cdot \left(\frac{\partial \ell_{\mathrm{saR}}(y, \hat{y}(\mathbf{x}; \Theta^{(t-1)}))}{\partial \theta} + 2\lambda_\theta \theta^{(t-1)} \right)$$

Applying the chain rule to Eq. 4 yields the derivative of the saRamp loss w.r.t. model parameters:

$$\begin{aligned} \frac{\partial \ell_{\mathrm{saR}}(y, \hat{y})}{\partial \theta} &= \frac{\partial \ell_{\mathrm{saR}}(y, \hat{y})}{\partial (y\hat{y})} \cdot \frac{\partial (y\hat{y})}{\partial \theta} \\ &= \begin{cases} y \cdot \left(\frac{\gamma + \delta - y\hat{y}}{2\delta} - 1 \right) \cdot \frac{\partial \hat{y}}{\partial \theta} & \text{If } \gamma - \delta \leq y\hat{y} \leq \gamma + \delta \\ -y \cdot \frac{\partial \hat{y}}{\partial \theta} & \text{If } \gamma + \delta < y\hat{y} < \tau^{(y)} - \delta \\ -y \cdot \frac{\tau^{(y)} + \delta - y\hat{y}}{2\delta} \cdot \frac{\partial \hat{y}}{\partial \theta} & \text{If } \tau^{(y)} - \delta \leq y\hat{y} \leq \tau^{(y)} + \delta \\ 0 & \text{Otherwise} \end{cases} \end{aligned}$$

where $\frac{\partial \hat{y}}{\partial \theta}$ is the partial derivatives of model equation of FM w.r.t. each parameters. According to Eq. 2, it can be written as follows:

$$\frac{\partial \hat{y}}{\partial w_0} = 1$$
$$\frac{\partial \hat{y}}{\partial w_j} = x_j \ (1 \le j \le d)$$
$$\frac{\partial \hat{y}}{\partial v_{jk}} = x_j \sum_{j' \ne j} v_{j'k} x_{j'} \ (1 \le j \le d, 1 \le k \le p)$$

Given the above equations, the parameter estimation procedure for RobustFM is summarized in Algorithm 1. Note that, for each instance, the runtime complexity of Algorithm 1 remains the same as traditional FM, i.e., $O(p \cdot N_0(\mathbf{x}))$ where $N_0(\mathbf{x})$ denotes the number of non-zero features of the instance. Even so, the learning procedure of RobustFM is more computational efficient than that of traditional FM, because Algorithm 1 only iterates over the instances with non-zero gradient (line 5) whereas all instances in training data are to be handled in each iterations of traditional FM learning procedure.

Algorithm 1. ParaEstimate

Input: Training set D
Output: Model parameters Θ

1: Initial model parameters: $w_0 \leftarrow 0$; $\mathbf{w} \leftarrow (0, \cdots, 0)$; $\mathbf{V} \sim \mathcal{N}(0, 0.1)$;
2: **repeat**
3:     **for** $(\mathbf{x}, y) \in D$ **do**
4:         Predict current instance as $\hat{y}(\mathbf{x}; \Theta)$
5:         **if** $\gamma - \delta < y \cdot \hat{y}(\mathbf{x}; \Theta) < \tau^{(y)} + \delta$ **then**
6:             Update w_0, $\mathbf{w}$ and $\mathbf{V}$ according to Eq. 5.
7:         **end if**
8:     **end for**
9: **until** convergence

5 Experiments

5.1 Experimental Settings

Datasets. Several real-world credit datasets, including four public datasets and one private dataset, are used for empirical evaluation of the proposed RobustFM. A summary of the five datasets is illustrated in Table 1.

Australian, *German* and *Taiwan* are public credit datasets available from UCI Machine Learning Repository that have been widely used in the literature. *SomeCredit* is the dataset of Kaggle competition *Give Me Some Credit* that aims to predict the probability of future financial distress of loan borrowers. Besides these public datasets, we used a private dataset, denoted as *SD-RCB*, in this experiment. The dataset is sourced from a regional bank of China which provides micro-credit services to self-employed workers and farmer households.

In total, more than 50 thousands historical credit records are collected from the credit scoring system of the bank. The attributes of each credit records include custom demographics, credit application information, historical repayment behavior, and etc.

From Table 1, it has to be noted that the number of defaulters is always less than that of non-defaulters in all these datasets, and the default rate is even less than 10% in *SomeCredit* and *SD-RCB*, the two large-scale real-world credit datasets. This provides practical evidence of class-imbalance problem in real-world credit default prediction tasks.

Table 1. Statistics of credit datasets

Dataset	#samples	#attributes	Default rate (%)
Australian[a]	690	14	44.5
German[b]	1,000	20	30.0
Taiwan[c]	30,000	23	22.1
SomeCredit[d]	150,000	10	6.7
SD-RCB	54,893	46	9.2

[a]http://archive.ics.uci.edu/ml/datasets/statlog+(australian+credit+approval)
[b]https://archive.ics.uci.edu/ml/datasets/statlog+(german+credit+data)
[c]https://archive.ics.uci.edu/ml/datasets/default+of+credit+card+clients
[d]https://www.kaggle.com/c/GiveMeSomeCredit

Evaluation Measures. In order to compare the performance among different approaches, we employ the following three types of measures in this experiment:

- Accuracy (*Acc*). Accuracy aims to evaluate the correctness of categorical predictions: $Acc = \frac{1}{N}\sum_{i=1}^{N}\mathbb{I}_{[y_i \neq \mathrm{sgn}(\hat{y}_i)]}$
- Brier Score (*BS*). Most classifiers give probabilistic predictions $\hat{y} = \hat{p}(\pm 1|\mathbf{x})$, rather than category predictions $\hat{y} = \pm 1$, making Accuracy calculated in an unnatural way – a categorical prediction can be only inferred by assigning a manually-tuned threshold to raw predictions. Unlike Accuracy, Brier Score aims to evaluate the correctness of the raw probabilistic predictions: $BS = \frac{1}{N}\sum_{i=1}^{N}(y_i - \hat{p}(y_i|\mathbf{x}_i))^2$
- Precision (*Pre*), Recall (*Rec*) and F-measure (F_1). One important shortage of *Acc* and *BS* is that a classifier is evaluated without taking into account the variations between classes. However, in the credit default prediction tasks, the correctness of predictions on defaulters is much more important than that on non-defaulters. We thus employ three performance measures: Precision, Recall and F-measure. Essentially, Precision and Recall measure the type-I error (non-defaulter classified as defaulter) and the type-II error (defaulter classified

as non-defaulter), respectively, and F-measure is the harmonic average of Precision and Recall.

Baselines. To verify the advantage of the proposed RobustFM, we compare it with several state-of-the-art credit default prediction models. First, the most widely used classification techniques in the task of credit default prediction [1], including logistic regression (LR), neural networks (NN) and support vector machines (SVM), are selected as baselines. Second, the traditional FM, as well as its extensions with traditional Hinge loss and Ramp loss, are applied to the task of credit default prediction and selected as baselines.

5.2 Performance Evaluation

In this experiment, five-fold cross validation is performed on each dataset and the average performance on the five folds is reported. Table 2 presents the experimental results and comparisons on each dataset.

It can be seen from Table 2 that the proposed RobustFM, compared to baseline methods, achieves the highest F_1 score on all the five datasets. We perform statistical significance test to check whether the improvements are significant. More specifically, paired t-tests is applied on the predicted results obtained by RobustFM and the nearest counterpart. The results indicate that the improvements of RobustFM are significant with p-value ≤ 0.05 on datasets *German* and *Taiwan* and p-value ≤ 0.01 on datasets *SomeCredit* and *SD-RCB*, marked with single and double asterisks in Table 2, respectively. In fact, the imbalanced ratio of the datasets *SomeCredit* and *SD-RCB* is much higher than that of others. The comparison results prove the effectiveness of RobustFM in dealing with imbalanced data, especially with high imbalanced ratio and large size.

From Table 2, we have the following more observations:

i. Besides F_1, RobustFM achieves the highest *Recall* on four of the five datasets. This is in fact favored in real-world credit default prediction tasks in which missing a true defaulter in predictions is typically perceived as a more severe error than misclassifying a non-defaulter as a defaulter.
ii. Achieving highest F_1 doesn't necessarily result in highest *Accuracy* and *BS*. As a matter of fact, RobustFM only achieves the highest *Accuracy* on dataset *Australian* which is a rather balanced dataset of small size. However, it is well recognized that *Accuracy* is not suitable for evaluating performances on class-imbalanced setting.
iii. Among all the baselines, FM-based methods (FM, FM_{Hinge}, and FM_{Ramp}) perform better than most traditional methods (LR, NN, and SVM) in terms of almost all performance measures. This result coincides with the findings of previous studies on FM from a variety of tasks such as click-through rate prediction and context-aware recommendation, and further verifies our intuition of the advantages of FM when applying to the credit prediction tasks described before.

Table 2. Prediction performance of each approaches

Dataset	Methods	$Acc(\%)$	BS	$Pre(\%)$	$Rec(\%)$	$F_1(\%)$
Australian	LR	68.84	0.2976	72.10	88.25	79.34
	NN	67.97	0.2443	**73.00**	83.76	78.00
	SVM	67.97	0.2488	68.14	99.15	80.77
	FM	70.69	0.2166	72.34	89.47	80.00
	FM-Hinge	70.68	0.2325	71.43	92.10	80.45
	FM-Ramp	72.41	0.2153	72.92	92.11	81.39
	RobustFM	**73.28**	**0.2114**	72.73	**94.74**	**82.29**
German	LR	**75.70**	**0.2902**	**62.18**	49.33	54.89
	NN	75.30	0.3004	60.56	51.67	55.63
	SVM	72.50	0.3464	53.70	59.67	56.52
	FM	74.85	0.3477	53.85	60.87	57.14
	FM-Hinge	71.86	0.4123	49.15	63.04	55.24
	FM-Ramp	74.25	0.4327	52.63	65.22	58.25
	RobustFM	70.66	0.3681	48.06	**80.43**	**60.17***
Taiwanese	LR	80.73	0.2688	63.51	30.76	41.38
	NN	81.06	0.2622	62.73	35.97	45.64
	SVM	79.73	0.2812	58.61	38.16	44.94
	FM	**81.96**	0.1668	**65.48**	35.67	46.18
	FM-Hinge	81.14	**0.1628**	58.60	44.61	50.65
	FM-Ramp	81.26	0.1932	59.18	43.96	50.45
	RobustFM	77.78	0.1932	48.95	**55.58**	**52.06***
SomeCredit	LR	93.59	0.2002	55.49	19.29	28.62
	NN	93.43	0.2004	52.18	18.30	26.99
	SVM	93.58	0.1645	**55.78**	17.43	26.52
	FM	93.76	0.1469	53.17	23.16	32.26
	FM-Hinge	93.67	**0.1238**	55.45	21.25	30.73
	FM-Ramp	**93.96**	0.1513	54.74	24.14	33.50
	RobustFM	93.24	0.1611	47.20	**34.21**	**39.67****
SD-RCB	LR	52.38	0.5850	**67.82**	15.81	23.55
	NN	55.09	0.4426	55.90	13.35	20.19
	SVM	67.86	0.4209	53.19	16.49	24.41
	FM	90.19	0.2989	37.37	20.73	26.67
	FM-Hinge	**91.37**	**0.1764**	49.71	24.09	32.45
	FM-Ramp	85.83	0.3373	26.85	**37.54**	31.31
	RobustFM	88.62	0.2561	34.07	34.45	**34.26****

5.3 Hyper-parameter Study

Compared with traditional FM, there are two additional hyper-parameters: γ and $\tau^{(+)}$[1]. Experiments are performed to study how the prediction performance of RobustFM is affected by these parameters. More specifically, by fixing one of the parameters, we vary the other one and record the prediction performance in terms of *Precision*, *Recall* and F_1 (see Fig. 2(a) and (b)). Due to space limitation, only the results on the dataset *SomeCredit* are reported, and the results on other datasets are similar.

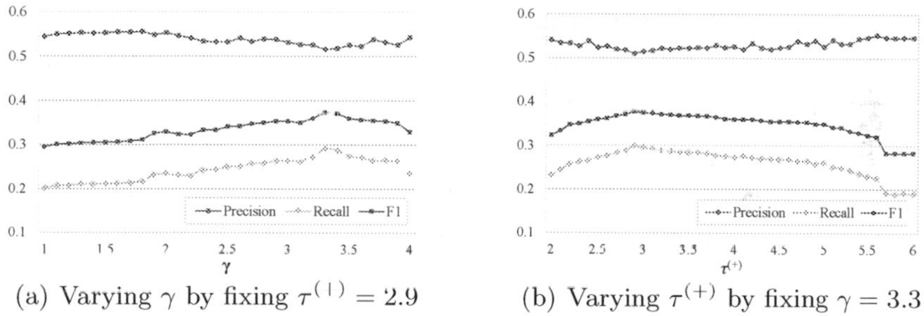

(a) Varying γ by fixing $\tau^{(+)} = 2.9$ (b) Varying $\tau^{(+)}$ by fixing $\gamma = 3.3$

Fig. 2. The effects of hyper-parameters

To choose the truncation parameter γ, one may typically start from a number slightly smaller than 0 and then decrease γ to tune the level of learning insensitivity of RobustFM. From Fig. 2(a), it can be seen that the prediction performance of RobustFM varies slightly when $\gamma \in (2, 4)$ and the optimal F_1 score is achieved around $\gamma = 3.3$. When γ is getting smaller and smaller, the robustness of RobustFM is reduced, causing performance to degrade as depicted in Fig. 2(a). Similarly, to choose the margin parameter $\tau^{(+)}$, one may typically start from a number slightly larger than 1.0 and increase $\tau^{(+)}$. While $\tau^{(+)}$ is increasing, the classification hyperplane is moving towards to the major class. This process can be illustrated in Fig. 2 in which the *Recall* increases constantly as $\tau^{(+)}$ increases from 2.0 to 3.0. From Fig. 2(b), it also can be seen that the prediction performance of RobustFM varies slightly when $\tau^{(+)} \in (2, 5)$ and the optimal F_1 score is achieved around $\tau^{(+)} = 2.9$. Overall, these experiments indicate that the proposed RobustFM performs quite steadily with wide-range values of truncation parameter and margin parameter.

6 Related Work

Credit default prediction has long been a central concern of financial risk management research. More recently, emerging machine learning techniques, instead

[1] In practice, the negative margin parameter $\tau^{(-)}$ is usually set as 1, thus $\tau^{(+)}$ can be just viewed as the relative positive margin.

of simple statistical methods, have been widely applied in the literature. Extensive studies have already demonstrated that machine learning techniques outperform classical statistical methods on various credit risk evaluation tasks. Until recently, almost all of the popular machine learning algorithms, e.g., support vector machines [13,14], decision tree [15] and neural networks [16,17] have been employed to construct credit risk model. Recent studies show that ensemble method that integrates predictions of several individual classifiers is a promising approach for credit risk modeling. A number of ensemble strategies have been proposed to construct more powerful credit risk models [18–20].

The class-imbalance problem in credit data has drawn attention in the literature. Several experimental studies have shown that most machine learning algorithms (e.g., decision tree, neural networks, and etc) perform significantly worse on imbalanced credit datasets [21,22]. Recently, A few studies have tried to tackling the class-imbalance problem in credit data by developing specific feature selection and ensemble strategies [23].

7 Conclusion and Future Work

In this paper, we propose a novel approach *RobustFM* for the credit default prediction task. Compared with existing machine learning based credit risk models, the main advantage of RobustFM is to address the issues of class-imbalance and noisiness in the credit data simultaneously. We demonstrate RobustFM's effectiveness on credit default prediction task via experimental evaluations on several real credit application datasets. It can be concluded that the proposed RobustFM is a worthwhile choice for the credit default prediction task.

Several issues could be considered for future work. For example, there are additional hyper-parameters in RobustFM that need to be tuned to yield good predictions. Further study should be continued to apply automated machine learning techniques to derive the optimal hyper-parameters automatically.

Acknowledgement. This work is partially supported by Natural Science Foundation of China (61602278, 71704096, 61472229 and 31671588), Sci. & Tech. Development Fund of Shandong Province (2016ZDJS02A11, 2014GGX101035 and ZR2017MF027), the Taishan Scholar Climbing Program of Shandong Province, and SDUST Research Fund (2015TDJH102).

References

1. Lessmann, S., Baesens, B., Seow, H.-V., Thomas, L.C.: Benchmarking state-of-the-art classification algorithms for credit scoring: an update of research. Eur. J. Oper. Res. **247**(1), 124–136 (2015)
2. Pluto, K., Tasche, D.: Estimating probabilities of default for low default portfolios. In: Engelmann, B., Rauhmeier, R. (eds.) The Basel II Risk Parameters, pp. 75–101. Springer, Heidelberg (2011). https://doi.org/10.1007/978-3-642-16114-8_5
3. Rendle, S.: Factorization machines with libFM. ACM Trans. Intell. Syst. Technol. (TIST) **3**(3), 57 (2012)

4. Wang, S., Li, C., Zhao, K., Chen, H.: Learning to context-aware recommend with hierarchical factorization machines. Inf. Sci. **409**, 121–138 (2017)
5. Rendle, S., Gantner, Z., Freudenthaler, C., Schmidt-Thieme, L.: Fast context-aware recommendations with factorization machines. In: Proceedings of the 34th ACM SIGIR, pp. 635–644 (2011)
6. Juan, Y., Zhuang, Y., Chin, W.-S., Lin, C.-J.: Field-aware factorization machines for CTR prediction. In: Proceedings of the 10th ACM RecSys, pp. 43–50 (2016)
7. Pan, Z., Chen, E., Liu, Q., Xu, T., et al.: Sparse factorization machines for click-through rate prediction. In: Proceedings of the 16th IEEE ICDM, pp. 400–409 (2016)
8. Guo, H., Tang, R., Ye, Y., Li, Z., He, X.: DeepFM: a factorization-machine based neural network for CTR prediction. arXiv preprint arXiv:1703.04247
9. Collobert, R., Sinz, F., Weston, J., Bottou, L.: Trading convexity for scalability. In: Proceedings of the 23rd ICML, pp. 201–208 (2006)
10. Ghosh, A., Kumar, H., Sastry, P.: Robust loss functions under label noise for deep neural networks. In: Proceedings of the 31th AAAI, pp. 1919–1925 (2017)
11. Cevikalp, H., Franc, V.: Large-scale robust transductive support vector machines. Neurocomputing **235**, 199–209 (2017)
12. Zhang, T.: Solving large scale linear prediction problems using stochastic gradient descent algorithms. In: Proceedings of the 21th ICML, p. 116 (2004)
13. Hens, A.B., Tiwari, M.K.: Computational time reduction for credit scoring: an integrated approach based on support vector machine and stratified sampling method. Expert Syst. Appl. **39**(8), 6774–6781 (2012)
14. Danenas, P., Garsva, G.: Selection of support vector machines based classifiers for credit risk domain. Expert Syst. Appl. **42**(6), 3194–3204 (2015)
15. Nie, G., Rowe, W., Zhang, L., Tian, Y., Shi, Y.: Credit card churn forecasting by logistic regression and decision tree. Expert Syst. Appl. **38**(12), 15273–15285 (2011)
16. Lisboa, P.J., et al.: Partial logistic artificial neural network for competing risks regularized with automatic relevance determination. IEEE Trans. Neural Netw. **20**(9), 1403–1416 (2009)
17. Marcano-Cedeno, A., Marin-De-La-Barcena, A., Jiménez-Trillo, J., Pinuela, J., Andina, D.: Artificial metaplasticity neural network applied to credit scoring. Int. J. Neural Syst. **21**(04), 311–317 (2011)
18. Ala'raj, M., Abbod, M.F.: A new hybrid ensemble credit scoring model based on classifiers consensus system approach. Expert Syst. Appl. **64**, 36–55 (2016)
19. Xiao, H., Xiao, Z., Wang, Y.: Ensemble classification based on supervised clustering for credit scoring. Appl. Soft Comput. **43**, 73–86 (2016)
20. Xia, Y., Liu, C., Li, Y., Liu, N.: A boosted decision tree approach using bayesian hyper-parameter optimization for credit scoring. Expert Syst. Appl. **78**, 225–241 (2017)
21. Louzada, F., Ferreira-Silva, P.H., Diniz, C.A.: On the impact of disproportional samples in credit scoring models: an application to a Brazilian bank data. Expert Syst. Appl. **39**(9), 8071–8078 (2012)
22. Brown, I., Mues, C.: An experimental comparison of classification algorithms for imbalanced credit scoring data sets. Expert Syst. Appl. **39**(3), 3446–3453 (2012)
23. Sun, J., Lang, J., Fujita, H., Li, H.: Imbalanced enterprise credit evaluation with DTE-SBD: decision tree ensemble based on SMOTE and bagging with differentiated sampling rates. Inf. Sci. **425**, 76–91 (2018)

Multi-label Active Learning with Conditional Bernoulli Mixtures

Junyu Chen, Shiliang Sun, and Jing Zhao(✉)

Department of Computer Science and Technology, East China Normal University, 3663 North Zhongshan Road, Shanghai 200062, People's Republic of China
juaychen@gmail.com, {slsun,jzhao}@cs.ecnu.edu.cn

Abstract. Multi-label learning is an important machine learning task. In multi-label classification tasks, the label space is larger than the traditional single-label classification, and annotations of multi-label instances are typically more time-consuming or expensive to obtain. Thus, it is necessary to take advantage of active learning to solve this problem. In this paper, we present three active learning methods with the conditional Bernoulli mixture (CBM) model for multi-label classification. The first two methods utilize the least confidence and approximated entropy as the selection criteria to pick the most informative instances, respectively. Particularly, an efficient approximated calculation via dynamic programming is developed to compute the approximated entropy. The third method is based on the cluster information from the CBM, which implicitly takes the advantage of the label correlations. Finally, we demonstrate the effectiveness of the proposed methods through experiments on both synthetic and real-world datasets.

Keywords: Active learning · Multi-label classification
Machine learning

1 Introduction

Multi-label classification is an important machine learning task and has been used in many aspects of the applications. For many real-world data, one object can be assigned into multiple categories, and the category number of the object is not fixed. This kind of problem is often called multi-label classification. For example, in educational text categorization, the educational news could cover several topics such as preschool, primary school, high school and university. In music information retrieval, a piece of symphony could convey various message such as blue, jazz and classical music. Formally, let $\mathcal{X}$ denote the instance space and $\mathcal{Y} = \{y^1, y^2, \ldots, y^l\}$ denote the label space, the task of multi-label learning is to learn a function $h : \mathcal{X} \rightarrow \mathcal{P}(\mathcal{Y})$ from the training set $\mathcal{D} = \{(\boldsymbol{x}_i, \boldsymbol{y}_i)\}$, where the power set $\mathcal{P}(\mathcal{Y})$ is the set of all subsets of $\mathcal{Y}$, including the empty set $\emptyset$ and $\mathcal{Y}$ itself. Early multi-label learning mainly focuses on the problem of

J. Chen and S. Sun—The authors contributed equally to this work.

X. Geng and B.-H. Kang (Eds.): PRICAI 2018, LNAI 11012, pp. 954–967, 2018.
https://doi.org/10.1007/978-3-319-97304-3_73

multi-label text categorization [1–3]. During the past decade, multi-label learning has gradually attracted significant attentions from machine learning and related communities, and has been widely applied to diverse problems such as image automatic annotation [4], web mining [5], tag recommendation [6,7] etc.

Early researchers on multi-label classification attempt to tackle the task as some well-established learning scenarios. The binary relevance (BR) method decomposes the multi-label learning problem into several independent binary classification problems, where each binary classification problem corresponds to a possible label in the label space [4,8,9]. One advantage of the BR method is that the algorithm is easy to implement. The disadvantage is that it ignores the dependence among labels so that the individual label predictions can often be conflicting. For example, in image tagging tasks, an image may be tagged as a cat but not an animal when using the BR method. For dealing with this problem, the power set (PS) method treats each label subset as a class and trains it as a multi-class learning problem [10]. As a consequence, it would be restricted to predicting the label subsets only seen in the training set, and would not predict the labels unseen. Another disadvantage is that the method is often infeasible for the exponential number of labels sets. Recently, the conditional Bernoulli mixtures (CBM) [11] was proposed to be a state-of-the-art multi-label learning method. It is a probabilistic model, which can construct dependencies between labels appropriately.

Given a powerful multi-label learning method, another key point to obtain good performance is to have enough training data or necessary training data. In supervised learning, labeling data is inevitable and tedious. Especially for multi-label learning, the labeling process is much more expensive and time-consuming than single-label problems. Specifically, in the single-label cases, a human annotator only needs to identify a single category to complete labeling, whereas in the multi-label cases, the annotator must consider all the possible labels for each instance, even if the resulting labels are sparse. Thus, if we cannot access the labeled data as many as possible, we can choose the instances to label as necessary as possible. Active learning is to make appropriate instance selection strategies, which aims to choose the most informative instances to obtain the best classification performance. Our work focuses on developing effective active learning methods based on the CBM for solving multi-label learning problems.

There is some existing work on active learning. For example, Gaussian process with manifold-preserving graph reduction (MPGR)-based active leaning (GPMAL) and support vector machine (SVM)-based margin sampling active learning (SVMMAL) are two kinds of active learning methods for binary classification, which provide two kinds of basic guidelines for further research [12]. The GPMAL first applies the MPGR to select a subset and then employs the prediction mean and prediction variance of GP to reselect the most informative instances from the subset. The SVMMAL selects the instances according to the distances from the points to the classification boundary. Besides binary classification active learning methods, some multi-label active learning methods were also developed. Bin-Min [13] was proposed to use the one-versus-all strategy for multi-label classification with SVM as the base classifier and select the most uncertain instances from the unlabeled set. The mean max loss (MML) or 1DAL strategy [14] selected the instances which had the maximum mean loss value over the predicted classes. In this method, one SVM was trained for each label, and a threshold cutting method was used to decide the target labels. The overall loss value was averaged over the labels. This strategy selected instances only according to the sample correlations, and it did not take advantage of the label correlations. 2DAL [15] considered both relationships between samples and between labels, in which sample-label pairs are chosen to minimize the multi-label Bayesian error bound. More recently, some multi-label active learning methods based on label ranking models were also developed [16–18].

Despite the excellent performance of active learning algorithms, there are still some shortcomings that we should not omit. For example, in the process of active selection, we usually take all the unlabeled instances into account without considering the structural information and spatial diversity among them. This will lead to a result that in the same area there are more than one point to be selected, and thus it is possible to produce redundancy which can decrease the classification accuracy. This phenomenon is also called sampling bias. We will develop effective active learning methods based on CBM with additional sampling bias correction procedure. In addition, In order to avoid the influence of noisy points and simultaneously consider the space connectivity among instances, we introduce a method called cluster-based entropy (CBE) based on CBM. By using CBM, we can construct several clusters which can represent the global distribution structure using fewer instances. This can eliminate the influence of noisy points and promote the selection quality.

In this paper, we propose three principled multi-label active learning methods based on the CBM. The first two multi-label active learning strategies are based on the least confidence and approximated entropy, respectively. The third strategy is made according to the CBE. We evaluate our methods on both the synthetic data and real-world data. The promising experimental results demonstrate the effectiveness of the proposed multi-label active learning methods, and the detailed performance difference among the three proposed methods are also analyzed to give guidance for later researchers.

2 Bernoulli Mixtures and Conditional Bernoulli Mixtures

Bernoulli Mixtures (BM) is a classical model for multi-dimensional binary variable density estimation, where the learnability is realized by assuming independence of variables within each mixture component. Thus, each component density is simply a product of Bernoulli densities, and the overall model has the form

$$p(\boldsymbol{y}) = \sum_{k=1}^{K} \pi_k \prod_{l=1}^{L} Bern(y_l; \mu_{lk}), \tag{1}$$

where μ_{lk} represents the parameters of the lth Bernoulli distribution in the kth component. BM provides an effective approach to model the dependency among different binary variables but with the formulation that is easy to compute.

For multi-label learning, the analysis in [19] depicts that labels could be conditionally independent given input features. With this assumption, conditional Bernoulli mixtures (CBM) [11] extends the BM with both mixture coefficients and Bernoulli distributions conditional on $\boldsymbol{x}$. The distribution of the labels conditional on the input is expressed as

$$p(\boldsymbol{y}|\boldsymbol{x}) = \sum_{k=1}^{K} \pi_k(\boldsymbol{x};\alpha_k) \prod_{l=1}^{L} Bern(y_l|\boldsymbol{x};\beta_{kl}), \tag{2}$$

where α_k represents the parameters of function $\pi_k(\cdot)$, and β_{kl} represents the parameters of the lth Bernoulli distribution in the kth component.

The structure of CBM is similar to mixture of experts (ME) [20], where a gate function divides the input space into disjoint regions probabilistically, and an expert model generates the output for their region. We can view CBM as a multi-label extension of mixture of experts with a particular factorization of labels inside each expert. Thus, CBM tackles the multi-label problem as a multi-class problem and several binary problems. The categorical distribution $\pi_k(\boldsymbol{x};\alpha_k)$ also called gating function assigns each instance $\boldsymbol{x}$ to the kth component with probability $\pi_k(\boldsymbol{x};\alpha_k)$, which divides the input space into several regions such that each region only contains conditional independent labels. The gating function $\pi_k(\boldsymbol{x};\alpha_k)$ can be instantiated by any multi-class classifier which provides probabilistic estimate, such as multinomial logistic regression, and the label prediction function $Bern(y^l|\boldsymbol{x})$ can be instantiated by any binary classifier with probabilistic outputs.

In addition, the prediction of CBM is a notable problem, as making the optimal prediction in terms of subset accuracy requires finding the most probable label subset $\boldsymbol{y}^* = \arg\max_{\boldsymbol{y}} p(\boldsymbol{y}|\boldsymbol{x})$. There are 2^L label subset candidates, and it is intractable to evaluate the probability for each of them. Many multi-label methods suffer from this intractability for exact inference. CBM [11] uses the ancestor sampling strategy for the prediction, where the component index k according to the mixture coefficient $\pi_k(\boldsymbol{x};\alpha_k)$ is first sampled, and then each label y_l is independently sampled with probability $Bern(y_l|\boldsymbol{x};\beta_{kl})$. The procedure can be repeated multiple times to generate a set of $\boldsymbol{y}$ candidates, from which we pick the most frequent one. Sampling is easy to implement, but does not guarantee that the predicted $\boldsymbol{y}$ is the global optimal.

3 Methods

3.1 Learning Framework

In order to select queries, an active learner must have a way of assessing how informative each instance is. Let $\boldsymbol{x}^*$ be the most informative instance according to some query strategy $\phi(\boldsymbol{x})$, which is a function used to evaluate each instance $\boldsymbol{x}$ in the unlabeled pool $\mathcal{U}$. Moreover, let $\mathcal{X} = \mathbb{R}^d$ denote the d-dimensional instance space and $\mathcal{Y} = \{y^1 \dots y^l\}$ denote the label space, the task of multi-label learning is to learn a function $h : \mathcal{X} \rightarrow \mathcal{P}(\mathcal{Y})$, where the power set $\mathcal{P}(\mathcal{Y})$ is the set of all subsets of $\mathcal{Y}$ including the empty set and $\mathcal{Y}$ itself.

In many real-world learning problems, lots of unlabeled data are collected at once, and we assume that there is a small set of labeled data $\mathcal{L}$ and a large pool of unlabeled data $\mathcal{U}$. We query a batch of data from unlabeled pool and add them to the labeled set. The overall active learning procedure is described in Algorithm 1.

Algorithm 1. Pool-based active learning.

Input: Labeled set $\mathcal{L}$, unlabeled set $\mathcal{U}$, batch size B and informative function $\phi(\boldsymbol{x})$

repeat
  Train classifier $\mathcal{C}$ with labeled set $\mathcal{L}$.
  for $b = 1 \dots B$ **do**
    Query the most informative instance $\boldsymbol{x}_b{}^* = \arg\max_{\boldsymbol{x} \in \mathcal{U}} \phi(\boldsymbol{x})$.
    Labeled set $\mathcal{L} = \mathcal{L} \cup (\boldsymbol{x}_b{}^*, \boldsymbol{y}_b^*)$.
    Unlabeled set $\mathcal{U} = \mathcal{U} \setminus \boldsymbol{x}_b{}^*$.
  end for
until Enough instances are queried

3.2 Selection Criteria

In this section, we will introduce three criteria to select a bunch of informative instances, in which the instance uncertainty or label dependence are considered.

Maximize Least Confidence (LC). For problems with multiple labels, an intuitive selection strategy is to query the instance whose prediction has the least confident:

$$\phi^{LC}(\boldsymbol{x}) = 1 - \arg\max_{y \in \mathcal{P}(\mathcal{Y})} p(\boldsymbol{y}|\boldsymbol{x}). \tag{3}$$

This approach queries the instance for which the current model has the least confidence in its most likely label. However, this criterion only considers information about the most probable label and throws away information about the rest of labels.

Maximize Approximate Entropy (AE). Another uncertainty-based measure of informativeness is entropy [21]. For a discrete random variable X, the entropy is given by

$$H(X) = -\sum_X p(X) \ln p(X). \tag{4}$$

In active learning, we wish to employ the entropy of our model's prediction distribution over its labels. Thus, we have

$$\phi^E(\boldsymbol{x}) = -\sum_{y\in\mathcal{P}(\mathcal{Y})} p(\boldsymbol{y}|\boldsymbol{x}) \ln p(\boldsymbol{y}|\boldsymbol{x}). \tag{5}$$

However, the number of possible labels grows exponentially with the element number of $\mathcal{Y}$. Empirically, only a few labels contribute to the entropy, and the probabilities for the rest of labels are almost zero which can be ignored. Note that $\lim_{p\to 0} p \ln p = 0$, and we shall take $p(\boldsymbol{y}|\boldsymbol{x}) \ln p(\boldsymbol{y}|\boldsymbol{x}) = 0$. Thus, we have the form of approximate entropy as

$$\phi^{AE}(\boldsymbol{x}) = -\sum\nolimits_{y\in\mathcal{N}(\mathcal{Y})} p(\boldsymbol{y}|\boldsymbol{x}) \ln p(\boldsymbol{y}|\boldsymbol{x}) \le \phi^E(\boldsymbol{x}), \tag{6}$$

where $\mathcal{N}(\mathcal{Y}) = \{\boldsymbol{y}_1, \ldots, \boldsymbol{y}_N\}$ is the set of the N most possible labels in the power set. It is worth noting that the number N here is not a fixed number, which indicates a threshold making sure that the sum of probabilities in most possible labels $\sum_{i=1}^{N} p(\boldsymbol{y}_i|\boldsymbol{x})$ is very close to 1. In addition, $\phi^{AE}(\boldsymbol{x})$ is the lower bound of $\phi^E(\boldsymbol{x})$, and it will become a tighter bound as $\sum_{i=1}^{N} p(\boldsymbol{y}_i|\boldsymbol{x})$ is closer to 1. Inspired by the dynamic programming prediction method in CBM [11], we present an algorithm for finding the labels with higher probabilities, and calculate the approximate entropy to measure the uncertainty.

To calculate the approximate entropy for $p(\boldsymbol{y}|\boldsymbol{x})$, we need to find the labels with higher probability $p(\boldsymbol{y}|\boldsymbol{x})$. There must exist a component k for which the component probability $\prod_{l=1}^{L} Bern(y_l; \mu_k)$ is high. Thus, we can drop those labels with lower probabilities in each component. We iterate on finding the next label $\boldsymbol{y}$ with the highest probability and add it to the label set until the reset subset candidates will never produce a high probability. The overall procedure is described in Algorithm 2.

Maximize Cluster-Based Entropy (CBE). The two strategies mentioned above only consider the instance uncertainty and do not take advantages of the label correlations. Taking advantages of the simplicity of CBM, we can implicitly capture label correlations rather than directly model such correlations. The labels for the data point $\boldsymbol{x}$ whose mixing coefficients in some components account for a particular proportion often contain correlations. We can verify it by computing the following covariance matrix.

$$\begin{aligned} Cov[\boldsymbol{y}|\boldsymbol{x}] &= \sum_{k=1}^{K} \pi_k [\boldsymbol{\Sigma}_k + \boldsymbol{\mu}_k \boldsymbol{\mu}_k^\top] - E[\boldsymbol{y}|\boldsymbol{x}] E[\boldsymbol{y}|\boldsymbol{x}]^\top \\ &= \sum_{k=1}^{K} \pi_k \boldsymbol{\Sigma}_k + \sum_{k=1}^{K} \pi_k (1-\pi_k) \boldsymbol{\mu}_k \boldsymbol{\mu}_k^\top - \sum_{i<j} \pi_i \pi_j \boldsymbol{\mu}_i \boldsymbol{\mu}_j^\top, \end{aligned} \tag{7}$$

where $E[\boldsymbol{y}|\boldsymbol{x}] = \sum_{k=1}^{K} \pi_k \boldsymbol{\mu}_k$, $\boldsymbol{\Sigma}_k = \mathrm{diag}\{\mu_{lk}(1-\mu_{lk})\}$. Because $\boldsymbol{\Sigma}_k$ is a diagonal matrix, the non-diagonal elements come from the rest part in Eq. (7). Those

Algorithm 2. Approximate Entropy Calculation by Dynamic Programming

Input: Trained CBM model $\mathcal{C}$ and corresponding parameters $\boldsymbol{\pi}, \boldsymbol{\mu}$.

Initialize candidate component set $\mathcal{S} = \{1, 2, \ldots, K\}$, label set $\mathcal{N}(\mathcal{Y})$ and maximum marginal probability M
for $k = 1, 2, \ldots, K$ **do**
  Initialize the maximum component probability G_k.
end for
while $\mathcal{S} \neq \emptyset$ **do**
  for $k \in \mathcal{S}$ **do**
    Find the next highest probability label $\boldsymbol{y}$ unseen in $\mathcal{N}(\mathcal{Y})$ in component k.
    Add label $\boldsymbol{y}$ and corresponding $p(\boldsymbol{y}|\boldsymbol{x})$ to the label set $\mathcal{N}(\mathcal{Y})$.
    Let $p = \sum_{m=1}^{K} \pi_m \prod_{l=1}^{L} Bern(y_l; \mu_m)$ and $q = \prod_{l=1}^{L} Bern(y_l; \mu_k)$.
    if $p > M$ **then**
      Set $M = p$.
    end if
    if $\pi_k q \leq M/K$ or $\pi_k q + \sum_{m \neq k} \pi_m G_m \leq M$ **then**
      Remove k from $\mathcal{S}$.
    end if
  end for
end while
Calculate the approximate entropy $\phi = -\sum_{\boldsymbol{y} \in \mathcal{N}(\mathcal{Y})} p(\boldsymbol{y}|\boldsymbol{x}) \ln p(\boldsymbol{y}|\boldsymbol{x})$

Output: The approximate entropy ϕ.

data points only belonging to a single component can be considered as having no dependent labels. Accordingly, we can calculate the entropy of probabilistic gating functions to model such correlations. In order to take account of both least confidence and label correlation and avoid introducing new parameters, we start with the points with highest entropy of $\pi_k(\boldsymbol{x})$ from each clusters, respectively. Then, we reselect the least confident points from each cluster and add those to the labeled set. This method also considers the cluster information and prevents the selected data point far away from the underlying distribution.

3.3 Sampling Bias Correction

In the analysis of [22], the labeled points are always not the representatives of the underlying distribution, because in the setting of active learning, querying the unlabeled point closest to the boundary (or most uncertain, or most likely to decrease overall uncertainty) is very easy to be far away from the underlying distribution due to the presence of noise.

Sampling bias is also one of the most fundamental challenge posed by active learning. LC and AE methods are unable to handle such problem. In this paper, we present a random heuristic method to solve it. Specifically, we equivalently divide the instances in the unlabeled set up into several clusters, and select the most uncertain instance from each cluster and add them to the labeled set. With the benefit of CBM, CBE method inherently contains clustering information and prevents the selected data point far away from the underlying distribution.

4 Experiments

In this section, we present the evaluation on a synthetic dataset and a real-world dataset. We compared the following approaches in our experiments:

- **Random,** the baseline using random selection strategy.
- **LC,** the active learning method based on the strategy of maximizing least confidence.
- **AE,** the active learning method based on the strategy of maximizing approximate entropy.
- **CBE,** the active learning method based on the strategy of maximizing cluster-based entropy.

4.1 Experimental Setting

In our experiments, we split the training set and testing set once, randomly select some labeled data point from the training set and let the rest of it become the unlabeled set. We proceed to randomly select the labeled set as the starting training size for ten times and record the average result. CBM is used to train a multi-label classifier for all the comparing active learning methods, in which the gating function $\pi_k(\boldsymbol{z}|\boldsymbol{x};\alpha_k)$ is instantiated by multinomial logistic regression and $Bern(y^l|\boldsymbol{x},\boldsymbol{z};\beta_k)$ is instantiated by logistic regression. We set the number of components to $K = 30$ and the variance of Gaussian prior to $\sigma = 10$. As a baseline, the method of random selection is performed. The real-world dataset used in our experiments is available from the Mulan[1].

We use two metrics to measure the performance of our methods, hamming loss and F1 score. The definitions are as follows.

- Hamming loss:

$$\frac{1}{NL}\sum_{n=1}^{N}\sum_{l=1}^{L}\mathbf{XOR}(\boldsymbol{y}_{nl},\boldsymbol{y}_{nl}{}^{*}),$$

  where **XOR** is exclusive (or exclusive disjunction) operation that outputs true only when inputs differ. In practice we substitute true value for one. Hamming loss evaluates the fraction of misclassified instance-label pairs, i.e. a relevant label is missed or an irrelevant is predicted.
- F1 Score:

$$F1 = 2 \times \frac{precision \times recall}{precision + recall}.$$

  The F1 score can be interpreted as a weighted average of the precision and recall, where an F1 score reaches its best value at 1 and worst score at 0. In our experimental settings, we use micro-F1 metric, which counts the total true positives, false negatives and false positives for each label.

[1] http://mulan.sourceforge.net/datasets-mlc.html.

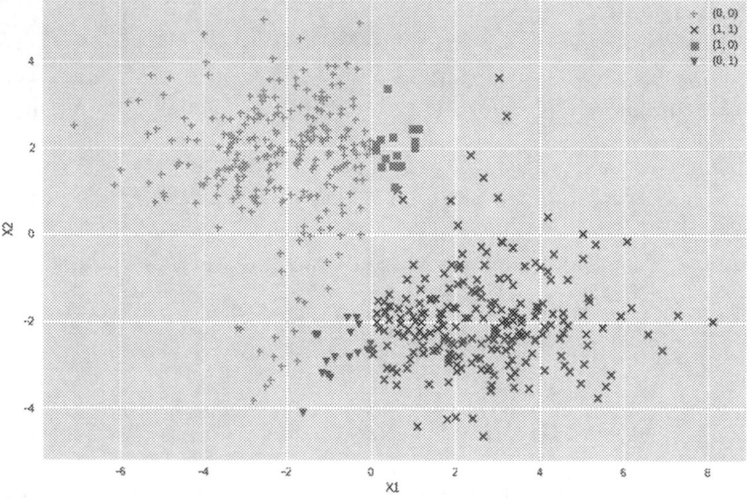

Fig. 1. The distribution of the synthetic 500 instances, where the two labels are rendered with different colors and markers, and the data are linear separable with two linear decision boundaries ($x_1 = 0$ and $x_2 = \sqrt{3}x_1$). (Color figure online)

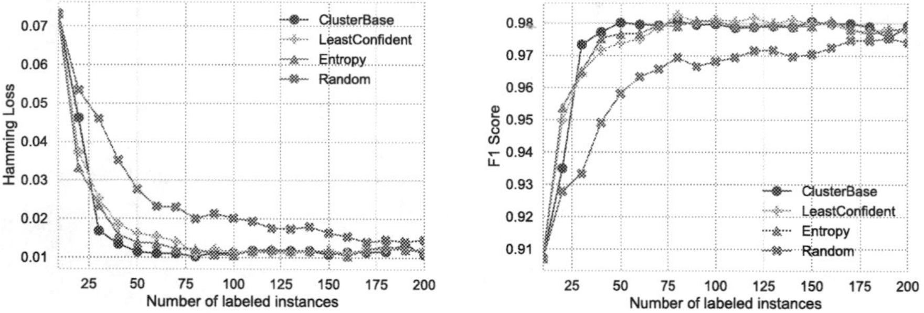

Fig. 2. The average results over 10 runs regarding hamming loss and F1 score on the synthetic dataset.

4.2 Datasets and Results

Synthetic Dataset. We first consider a simple synthetic dataset with a two-dimensional input $\boldsymbol{x} = (x_1, x_2)$ which are sampled from a mixture of Gaussian distributions with two components. The mean of the two Gaussian distributions lies in the second quadrant and the fourth quadrant, respectively. The two labels y_1, y_2 are as follows. The first label is set to one for positive values of x_1, and to zero for negative values, i.e., $y_1 = [x_1 > 0]$. The second label is defined in the same way, but the decision boundary ($x_1 = 0$) is rotated by an angle $\alpha = \pi/3$. The two decision boundaries partition the input space into four regions. It is a two-label classification problem on this dataset. We generate 500 example from the mixture of Gaussian distributions, and we use 250 examples as the

Table 1. Performance in terms of F1 score on the synthetic dataset.

# of selected instances	CBE	AE	LC	RND
20	93.49 ± 2.33	$\mathbf{95.37 \pm 1.83}$	94.99 ± 1.2	92.79 ± 1.56
30	$\mathbf{97.33 \pm 1.77}$	96.49 ± 1.85	96.44 ± 1.8	93.33 ± 1.61
40	$\mathbf{97.72 \pm 0.85}$	97.53 ± 0.94	97.17 ± 1.41	94.91 ± 1.89
50	$\mathbf{98.01 \pm 0.34}$	97.67 ± 0.46	97.37 ± 1.53	95.81 ± 1.64
60	$\mathbf{97.96 \pm 0.18}$	97.68 ± 0.61	97.51 ± 1.09	96.33 ± 1.95
70	$\mathbf{97.93 \pm 0.18}$	97.93 ± 0.82	97.85 ± 0.95	96.57 ± 1.58

Table 2. Performance in terms of hamming loss on the synthetic dataset.

# of selected instances	CBE	AE	LC	RND
20	4.62 ± 1.59	$\mathbf{3.32 \pm 0.94}$	3.72 ± 1.22	5.34 ± 1.68
30	$\mathbf{1.68 \pm 1.09}$	2.34 ± 1.26	2.52 ± 1.25	4.60 ± 1.51
40	$\mathbf{1.34 \pm 0.44}$	1.58 ± 0.62	1.84 ± 0.90	3.52 ± 1.14
50	$\mathbf{1.14 \pm 0.23}$	1.38 ± 0.26	1.62 ± 1.02	2.76 ± 0.99
60	$\mathbf{1.10 \pm 0.17}$	1.36 ± 0.51	1.54 ± 0.78	2.32 ± 1.13
70	$\mathbf{1.10 \pm 0.14}$	1.22 ± 0.61	1.42 ± 0.59	2.30 ± 0.91

training set, 250 examples as the test set. Figure 1 depicts the distribution of the generated data. In the beginning, we randomly select five examples as the labeled set and the rest of examples as the unlabeled set. Figure 2 shows the average results over ten runs regarding F1 score and hamming loss. Tables 1 and 2 compares the performance on F1 score and hamming loss after selecting 10 unlabeled instances each time, showing the mean and standard deviation of ten-time experiments. The proposed CBE strategy outperforms the other strategies on the whole.

According to Fig. 2, we find that CBE obtains slight improvement while the other two methods make a big step at the first selection. It is because that at the beginning the classifier with inadequate data cannot capture the label correlations. CBM overtakes other methods and demonstrates its superiority after the second selection. According to Tables 1 and 2, it is worthwhile to mention that AE and CBE are more stable than LC, which have lower standard deviation. This is attributed to the integrated consideration of all label combinations in AE and the additional cluster information in CBE.

Scene Dataset. We also consider the real-world dataset for evaluation. SCENE is an multi-label image dataset which has 6 labels (beach, sunset, fall foliage, field, mountain, urban). The features are extracted after conversion from raw images to LUV space and are divided into 49 blocks using a 7×7 grid. We compute the first and second moments (mean and variance) of each band,

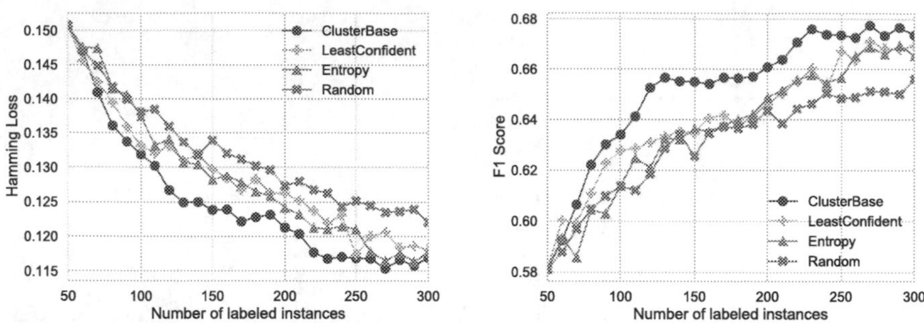

Fig. 3. The average results over 10 runs regarding hamming loss and F1 score on the SCENE dataset.

Table 3. Performance in terms of F1 score on the SCENE dataset.

# of selected instances	CBE	AE	LC	RND
70	**60.64 ± 3.84**	58.58 ± 4.08	59.94 ± 3.14	59.69 ± 4.05
90	**63.02 ± 2.72**	60.28 ± 3.52	62.27 ± 3.76	60.98 ± 2.66
110	**64.12 ± 2.10**	62.48 ± 1.89	62.86 ± 4.24	61.20 ± 1.81
130	**65.66 ± 2.20**	63.25 ± 2.21	63.33 ± 3.24	62.85 ± 1.74
150	**65.51 ± 1.38**	63.65 ± 1.63	63.47 ± 3.24	62.55 ± 2.48
170	**65.67 ± 2.03**	63.79 ± 2.44	64.18 ± 2.35	63.71 ± 2.60
190	**65.70 ± 2.74**	64.21 ± 3.19	64.11 ± 1.22	63.82 ± 2.57
210	**66.37 ± 1.50**	65.16 ± 2.57	65.02 ± 1.52	63.84 ± 2.27
230	**67.60 ± 0.81**	65.77 ± 1.50	66.03 ± 1.76	64.63 ± 2.89
250	**67.36 ± 1.75**	65.67 ± 2.72	66.72 ± 1.39	64.84 ± 2.41
270	**67.75 ± 2.38**	66.89 ± 2.18	67.10 ± 1.09	65.13 ± 1.95
290	**67.66 ± 2.36**	66.96 ± 1.53	66.80 ± 1.28	65.02 ± 2.93

corresponding to a low-resolution image and computationally inexpensive texture features, respectively. The result is a $49 \times 2 \times 3 = 294$-dimensional feature vector per image. We use the default training/test split set for the dataset. In the beginning, we randomly select 80 examples as the labeled set and the rest of examples as the unlabeled set. The experiments are repeated for 10 times and the average results are reported in Fig. 3. The classifier achieves high performance with much fewer iterations by our proposed active learning approach. Tables 3 and 4 compares the performance on F1 score and Hamming loss after selecting 20 unlabeled instances each time. Seen from the over trends of the curve, the proposed cluster-based entropy strategy outperforms the other strategies.

According to the Fig. 3, we find that CBE obtains slight improvement at the start again and overtakes other methods after more iterations and CBE is the most efficient method among them. Being different from the one in synthetic dataset, the report in scene dataset shows that LC is more effective than AE

Table 4. Performance in terms of hamming loss on the SCENE dataset.

# of selected instances	CBE	AE	LC	RND
70	**14.09 ± 1.19**	14.74 ± 1.31	14.25 ± 1.03	14.48 ± 1.41
90	**13.37 ± 0.80**	14.06 ± 1.26	13.60 ± 1.19	13.99 ± 0.94
110	**13.02 ± 0.84**	13.32 ± 0.69	13.20 ± 1.37	13.84 ± 0.74
130	**12.49 ± 0.76**	13.07 ± 0.68	13.10 ± 1.02	13.37 ± 0.69
150	**12.38 ± 0.35**	12.82 ± 0.55	12.97 ± 1.01	13.39 ± 0.90
170	**12.22 ± 0.57**	12.78 ± 0.77	12.67 ± 0.76	13.12 ± 0.65
190	**12.31 ± 0.76**	12.59 ± 1.10	12.63 ± 0.44	12.96 ± 0.66
210	**12.04 ± 0.36**	12.32 ± 0.81	12.52 ± 0.60	12.80 ± 0.66
230	**11.68 ± 0.30**	12.11 ± 0.47	12.20 ± 0.61	12.63 ± 0.85
250	**11.69 ± 0.53**	12.10 ± 0.97	11.74 ± 0.49	12.52 ± 0.66
270	**11.54 ± 0.77**	11.65 ± 0.73	12.06 ± 0.54	12.35 ± 0.57
290	**11.58 ± 0.75**	11.64 ± 0.55	11.86 ± 0.63	12.39 ± 0.88

and encounter some difficulties at the beginning. It is because the entropy can be inaccurate when the label space is very large and the classifier is not well developed. In general, the CBE is the most effective and stable method among the three methods.

4.3 Discussion

From the above two experiments, we observe that the proposed CBE strategy has a slight improvement at the beginning compared to other two methods but has a more significant improvement after several iterations. This phenomenon can be attributed to the fact that at the beginning the classifier with inadequate data cannot capture the label correlations. After several iterations, the classifier has constructed label dependence to a certain extent and is more likely to select such informative instances that contain more than one label. Therefore, it is reasonable to employ the least confidence or the entropy strategy at the start and shift to the cluster-based entropy strategy when the classifier has captured label dependence. The combining method may boost the performance, and the conjecture also need more experiments to verify. Besides, it also needs a strategy to find the appropriate time to shift. Finally, for most cases, we observe that CBE is comparable to AE and LC, which means that the performance of CBE is more stable.

5 Conclusion and Future Work

In this paper, we present three active learning algorithms for multi-label classification with CBM. It utilizes least confidence, approximated entropy and cluster-based entropy as the uncertainty measure to pick the most informative data points. Experimental results on synthetic and real-world datasets show that our methods outperform random selection. In the future, we plan to perform theoretical analysis on the methods and extend our work to multiview multi-label active learning [23–25].

Acknowledgments. This work is supported by the National Natural Science Foundation of China under Project 61673179 and Shanghai Sailing Program.

References

1. McCallum, A.: Multi-label text classification with a mixture model trained by EM. In: AAAI Workshop on Text Learning, pp. 1–7 (1999)
2. Schapire, R.E., Singer, Y.: Boostexter: a boosting-based system for text categorization. Mach. Learn. **39**(2–3), 135–168 (2000)
3. Ueda, N., Saito, K.: Parametric mixture models for multi-labeled text. In: Advances in Neural Information Processing Systems, pp. 737–744 (2003)
4. Boutell, M.R., Luo, J., Shen, X., Brown, C.M.: Learning multi-label scene classification. Pattern Recogn. **37**(9), 1757–1771 (2004)
5. Kazawa, H., Izumitani, T., Taira, H., Maeda, E.: Maximal margin labeling for multi-topic text categorization. In: Advances in Neural Information Processing Systems, pp. 649–656 (2005)
6. Katakis, I., Tsoumakas, G., Vlahavas, I.: Multilabel text classification for automated tag suggestion. In: Proceedings of the ECML/PKDD, pp. 1–9 (2008)
7. Song, Y., Zhang, L., Giles, C.L.: A sparse Gaussian processes classification framework for fast tag suggestions. In: Proceedings of the 17th ACM Conference on Information and Knowledge Management, pp. 93–102 (2008)
8. Joachims, T.: Text categorization with support vector machines: learning with many relevant features. In: Nédellec, C., Rouveirol, C. (eds.) ECML 1998. LNCS, vol. 1398, pp. 137–142. Springer, Heidelberg (1998). https://doi.org/10.1007/BFb0026683
9. Lewis, D.D., Yang, Y., Rose, T.G., Li, F.: RCV1: a new benchmark collection for text categorization research. J. Mach. Learn. Res. **5**(4), 361–397 (2004)
10. Tsoumakas, G., Katakis, I.: Multi-label classification: an overview. Int. J. Data Warehous. Min. **3**(3), 1–13 (2007)
11. Li, C., Wang, B., Pavlu, V., Aslam, J.: Conditional Bernoulli mixtures for multi-label classification. In: Proceedings of the International Conference on Machine Learning, pp. 2482–2491 (2016)
12. Zhou, J., Sun, S.: Gaussian process versus margin sampling active learning. Neurocomputing **167**, 122–131 (2015)
13. Brinker, K.: On active learning in multi-label classification. In: Spiliopoulou, M., Kruse, R., Borgelt, C., Nürnberger, A., Gaul, W. (eds.) From Data and Information Analysis to Knowledge Engineering, pp. 206–213. Springer, Berlin (2006). https://doi.org/10.1007/3-540-31314-1_24
14. Li, X., Wang, L., Sung, E.: Multilabel SVM active learning for image classification. In: Proceedings of the International Conference on Image Processing, pp. 2207–2210 (2004)
15. Qi, G.J., Hua, X.S., Rui, Y., Tang, J., Zhang, H.J.: Two-dimensional active learning for image classification. In: Computer Vision and Pattern Recognition, pp. 1–8 (2008)

16. Huang, S., Zhou, Z.: Active query driven by uncertainty and diversity for incremental multi-label learning. In: IEEE 13th International Conference on Data Mining, pp. 1079–1084 (2013)
17. Huang, S., Chen, S., Zhou, Z.: Multi-label active learning: query type matters. In: International Joint Conference on Artificial Intelligence, pp. 946–952 (2015)
18. Gao, N., Huang, S., Chen, S.: Multi-label active learning by model guided distribution matching. Front. Comput. Sci. **10**(5), 845–855 (2016)
19. Dembczyński, K., Waegeman, W., Cheng, W., Hüllermeier, E.: On label dependence and loss minimization in multi-label classification. Mach. Learn. **88**(1–2), 5–45 (2012)
20. Jordan, M.I., Jacobs, R.A.: Hierarchical mixtures of experts and the EM algorithm. Neural Comput. **6**(2), 181–214 (1994)
21. Shannon, C.E.: A mathematical theory of communication. Bell Syst. Tech. J. **27**(3), 379–423 (1948)
22. Dasgupta, S., Hsu, D.: Hierarchical sampling for active learning. In: Proceedings of the International Conference on Machine Learning, pp. 208–215 (2008)
23. Sun, S.: A survey of multi-view machine learning. Neural Comput. Appl. **23**, 2031–2038 (2013)
24. Zhao, J., Xie, X., Xu, X., Sun, S.: Multi-view learning overview: recent progress and new challenges. Inf. Fusion **38**, 43–54 (2017)
25. Sun, S., Shawe-Taylor, J., Mao, L.: PAC-Bayes analysis of multi-view learning. Inf. Fusion **35**, 117–131 (2017)

Investigating the Dynamic Decision Mechanisms of Users' Relevance Judgment for Information Retrieval via Log Analysis

Yi Su[1], Jingfei Li[2(✉)], Dawei Song[3,4(✉)], Pengqing Zhang[1], and Yazhou Zhang[1]

[1] School of Computer Science and Technology, Tianjin University, No. 135 Yaguan Road, Jinnan District, Tianjin 300350, People's Republic of China

[2] National Computer Network Emergency Response Technical Team, Coordination Center of China, No. 3A Yumin Road, Chaoyang District, Beijing 100020, People's Republic of China

jingfeili@tju.edu.cn

[3] School of Computer Science and Technology, Beijing Institute of Technology, No. 5 South Zhongguancun Street, Haidian District, Beijing 100081, People's Republic of China

dawei.song2010@gmail.com

[4] School of Computing and Communications, The Open University, Walton Hall, Milton Keynes MK7 6AA, UK

Abstract. Measuring relevance of documents with respect to a user's query is at the heart of information retrieval (IR), where the user's relevance judgment criteria have been recognized as multi-dimensional. A set of relevance dimensions that are considered as critical factors in document relevance judgment have been investigated, such as topicality, novelty, and reliability. However, most existing work focuses on individual relevance dimensions, yet neglecting how different dimensions would interact with each other to influence the overall relevance judgment in real-world search scenarios. This paper aims at an initial step to fill the gap. Specifically, we divide 7 relevance dimensions in an enriched Multidimensional User Relevance Model (MURM) into three categories according to three main requirements for document relevance, i.e., document content requirement, document quality requirement and personalization requirement. We then exploit the Learning to Rank framework to conduct document ranking experiments on a query log dataset from a prominent search engine. The experimental results indicate the existence of an order effect between different dimensions, and suggest that considering different dimensions across categories in different orders for document relevance judgment could lead to distinct search results. Our findings provide valuable insights to build more intelligent and user-centric information retrieval systems, and potentially benefit other natural language processing tasks that involve decision making from multiple perspectives.

Keywords: Information retrieval · User relevance dimensions
Order effect

X. Geng and B.-H. Kang (Eds.): PRICAI 2018, LNAI 11012, pp. 968–979, 2018.
https://doi.org/10.1007/978-3-319-97304-3_74

1 Introduction

Information Retrieval (IR) is an area closely related to natural language processing (NLP) and artificial intelligence (AI). It aims to provide users with relevant search results satisfying their information needs. For this purpose, substantial prior work attempted to develop system-centered information retrieval algorithms, which mainly focus on content matching between documents and user input queries. However, the user's information seeking process turns out to be a far more complex cognition and decision making process beyond simple one-off content matching. The user's information need is often dynamic and uncertain. The user's criteria for determining the relevance of a document with respect to the information need in her/his mind can involve various different decision perspectives or relevance dimensions (e.g., topical similarity, novelty, reliability), which may dynamically evolve during the information seeking process. Therefore, how to effectively integrate these multiple perspectives into the existing system-oriented frameworks is an important yet challenging problem in IR and related NLP and AI tasks.

The core issue of leveraging human factors in IR is how humans perceive and judge the relevance of documents (In short, user relevance judgment). It has been studied from cognitive and psychological perspectives. Various previous studies on user relevance attempted to identify and define critical relevance criteria. For instance, the so-called Maxims of Conversation [1,2] proposed by Grice was based on principles that dealt specifically with communication: information, truth, relevance and clarity. Many subsequent researches were based on [1,2]. A representative work was the Multidimensional User Relevance Model (MURM) proposed by Xu and Chen [3], which included five relevance dimensions: topicality, novelty, understandability, reliability and scope. While MURM had been shown effective in IR tasks, it did not explicitly describe the user's search interests and habits, which were considered as important in personalized IR [4,5]. To address this limitation, Li et al. [4] later proposed an enriched MURM with two additional personalized dimensions, i.e., interest and habit, resulting a total number of 7 relevance dimensions. However, In [4], all the seven relevance dimensions were investigated and tested individually, without considering their combinations and complex interactions.

We believe it is inadequate to consider only one criterion when judging the relevance of a document, as in the user's information seeking journey, the user's cognitive states related to those dimensions would interact with each other and evolve dynamically. For example, a user may be initially interested in documents that are topically similar to the query. After clicking on and reading some retrieved documents, the user may become more interested in finding those documents that are more authoritative and convincing. Studying such interactions between relevance dimensions will help us better understand the dynamics of relevance dimensions throughout the whole retrieval process, but also provide inspirations for other natural language processing tasks, such as automatic dialogue analysis, question answering, where a decision making process from multiple perspectives is involved. However, in the current literature, there is a lack of systematic investigations and proper methodology to tackle this issue, especially in realistic information seeking settings.

In this paper, we focus on investigating the dynamic interactions among relevance dimensions in the enriched MURM for document relevance judgment. The main contributions are as follows:

(1) We divide the dimensions into three categories according to three key types of requirement for document relevance, i.e., document content requirement; document quality requirement and personalization requirement. (2) We propose two main research questions and corresponding hypotheses with regard to the three categories. (3) We exploit the learning-to-rank framework to conduct document ranking experiments using features extracted from a real user query log dataset from a major search engine.

An in-depth analysis of the experimental results reveals a series of interesting findings about how different relevance dimensions interfere with each other and generate an impact on the final document relevance score.

2 Related Work

2.1 The Enriched Multidimensional User Relevance Model

Many empirical studies have been done in the literatures to identify relevance criteria or factors that could affect users' perceptions of relevance [5–7]. While a large number of factors have been proposed, they overlap largely. Based on established theories of psychology and communication [1,2], e.g., Grice's maxims on human communication, and substantial previous studies [8–11], Xu and Chen [3] proposed five relevance dimensions that could affect the users' relevance judgment on the retrieved documents, including topicality, novelty, understandability, reliability and scope. This framework was named as Multidimensional User Relevance Model (MURM). The confirmatory analysis in their work suggested that topicality and novelty were two major underlying dimensions of relevance. In terms of understandability, reliability and scope, the findings showed that they exerted relatively less influences than topicality and novelty.

Furthermore, Li et al. [4] pointed out that the original MURM model could not explicitly formulate the user's search interests and habits, which were critical in the personalized relevance judgment [4,5]. Consequently, an enriched MURM was proposed, with two additional user-oriented dimensions, i.e., habit and interest [4]. The enriched MURM contained 7 dimensions, which were topicality, novelty, reliability, understandability, scope, interest and habit. Each dimension was associated with a set of computable features. In total, there were 33 computable features for all dimensions, most of which could be extracted from user query logs. Document ranking experiments were conducted on a subset of Bing's query logs, from which some interesting observations were made. For example, the experimental results suggested that the ranking model trained with the topicality dimension, which had long been seen as the most important factor for relevance judgment in classical search systems, surprisingly gained the lowest performance in the Bing log dataset, while the model trained with the reliability dimension performed the best. However, Li et al. defined the relevance dimensions and trained the ranking model with each dimension individually, without taking into account the combination of multiple dimensions. The user's relevance decision making in real information seeking scenarios often involves multiple dimensions interacting with each other to influence the final relevance judgment, and such interaction is also dynamic. Therefore, the complex and dynamic interaction of relevance dimensions needs to be studied and captured, in order to design and develop more intelligent IR systems that are compatible to human cognitive information processing.

2.2 Interaction Between Relevance Dimensions

To understand how humans perceive and judge the relevance of documents, there have been studies on the causes that could have effects on the dynamic evolution of the users' relevance judgment. Xu and Wang [14] studied a set of mechanisms that could lead to the order effect [15–17] in relevance judgments, including the learning effect, sub-need scheduling effect and cursoriness effect. The empirical study illustrated these three mechanisms. However, a rather artificial experimental setting was adopted in their work. For example, they studied only one search session, with one topic and one corpus, which limited the generalizability of findings.

Bruza and Chang [18] examined whether relevance dimensions interacted via an order effect. They aimed to detect if there existed an order effect between certain relevance dimensions and if a quantum inspired model based on incompatible decision perspectives could be a valid explanation for the order effect. They performed a crowdsourced study through Amazon's Mechanical Turk platform. The experimental results suggested that the interactions between dimensions could be detected in a majority of queries and some decisions with respect to specific dimensions of relevance, and such interaction could be explained with an incompatible decision based on the quantum model. However, the sample size in the study was too small to reflect the universality of the phenomenon. Moreover, the crowdsourced study involved some uncontrolled factors, which might affect the experiment results.

3 Research Questions and Experimental Design

In Sect. 2, we have reviewed the related work on MURM and dynamic relevance judgment. To gain further insights about inter-dimension interactions, in this paper, we categorize the seven relevance dimensions of the enriched MURM into three categories according to three main requirements for relevance decision about a document.

Document relevance is regarded as a subjective, multidimensional, dynamic and measureable concept [19]. As far as we know, there was no agreement on factors beyond topicality [5–7,20]. In fact, topicality was identified as the basic condition of relevance [11]. Xu and Chen [3] suggested that topicality and novelty were two major underlying dimensions of relevance. As a consequence, we categorize topicality and novelty as the document content requirement which is a fundamental criterion of the document relevance. According to Li et al. [4], the interest and habit were defined mainly to depict users' personalized behavioral characteristics, which were relatively less relevant to the document content features. Thus we identify the interest and habit dimensions as the personalization requirement. Finally, we identify the remaining dimensions, i.e., understandability, scope and reliability, as the document quality requirement, since they are defined to measure the additional features of documents besides the basic content requirement.

3.1 Research Questions and Corresponding Hypotheses

In this paper we will use above categorization, and investigate the interactions between relevance dimensions across categories. We propose two research questions and corresponding hypotheses, which are tested through system experiments.

Question 1: Does there really exist an order effect between different relevance dimensions?

We adopt the view that the information seeking is a dynamic and multi-staged information exploration process, in which the user's cognitive state corresponding to the relevance criteria keeps evolving with respect to the user's interaction with the documents [7]. Suppose users only pay attention to two relevance dimensions (e.g., topicality and reliability) for their information need, then how would they consider these two dimensions when they are judging one document? Do they first make judgment based on one relevance dimension and then the other, or just take into consideration these two dimensions simultaneously? If the order effect in relevance judgment does exist, how would it affect the relevance degree of the document?

In this paper, assuming that users tend to do stepwise judgment, we are more interested in the order effect between dimensions from different requirement categories, where the order effects might be more significant.

Hypothesis 1: There exist general order effects between different relevance dimensions from different requirement categories, but to different extents, some would be more significant while some might be less. And such order effects will have an effect on the document relevance judgment.

Question 2: How would the different consideration steps of requirement categories affect the document relevance degree?

As mentioned above, the information seeking is a multi-staged process [7]. Users may give attention to certain kind of information need within a period of time, and the attention may evolve as time goes by. For this reason, we assume that users do stepwise relevance judgment on a document. For example, some users may focus on document content first then followed by quality, and finally personal searching styles, while some others may care about document quality primarily, then followed by personal preferences and document content.

Here we would like to investigate how would the relevance degree of a document dynamically change with different requirement categories considered step by step, and if different orders of consideration will lead to different final relevance degree of the document.

Hypothesis 2: Different consideration orders of requirement categories could lead to different performances of the corresponding ranking models, and the dynamic performance trends in every step would vary from model to model.

3.2 Experimental Design

Li et al. [4] defined 33 computable features in the enriched MURM. In this paper, we exploit the learning-to-rank algorithm [21] to learn ranking models from these computable features and carry out document ranking experiments. We will explore the dynamics among the relevance dimensions through model performance evaluations.

Dataset
We conduct the document ranking experiments in the real search scenes. Compared with the user studies and simulation experiments, the experimental results from real search engines are more convincing, and could be regarded as a consequence of user cognitive states to some extent.

The first set of experiments are conducted on a subset of query log data, which includes 1166 randomly sampled users, collected from the Bing search engine during the period from July 1 to July 31, 2012. In the log, each query is followed by an originally ranked document list returned by the search engine. There are 540258 queries and 474553 clicks in total, among all the clicks there are 359902 SAT-Clicks (Li adopted the SAT-Click criteria as an indication of relevance and assign each retrieved document with a corresponding relevance degree. Specifically, degree 0 is assigned to the unclicked documents, 1 to the clicked but not SAT-Click documents and 2 to the SAT-Click documents).

Experimental Procedure
To test the first research question, we design a set of experiment procedures:

1. Test if $Effect(M_{ab}) = Effect(M_{ba})$
   Where a and b denote two different relevance dimensions, note that they are from different requirement sets. For example, a denotes topicality from the content requirement set and b denotes reliability from the quality requirement set. M_{ab} is the learning-to-rank ranking model trained with features of dimension a and b together, where the features' positions of dimension a are in front of dimension b, M_{ba} is just reversed. $Effect(M_{ab})$ represents the evaluation value of M_{ab} and the same as $Effect(M_{ba})$. The evaluation metric we adopt is NDCG@N (N = 10, ALL).
   The purpose of procedure 1 is to check if the performance of the model would be affected by the positions of features during the training process.

2. Test if $\mathit{Effect}(M_{a,b}) = \mathit{Effect}(M_{ab})$
   In this procedure, we perform stepwise training. First, we use the features of dimension a to train the model, and do the first re-ranking operation to get the preliminary ranking scores. Besides the scores of the testing dataset, we can also use the trained model to get the first ranking scores of the documents from training and validation dataset, and treat them as additional features of the documents. Second, we use these additional features as well as the features of dimension b to train the model once again and perform the second re-ranking. $\mathit{Effect}(M_{a,b})$ represents the final evaluation value of this stepwise trained model, and $\mathit{Effect}(M_{ab})$ is just the same meaning as that in procedure 1. By this way we get the performance of the model which considers different dimensions sequentially.
   Procedure 2 aims to check if the stepwise trained model has different performance from the model with all features trained together at once (in Procedure 1). If the results are different, it would suggest that considering different relevance in order could have an impact on the document relevance judgment.
3. Test if $\mathit{Effect}(M_{a,b}) = \mathit{Effect}(M_{b,a})$
   In this part, we get the model $M_{b,a}$ by similar training procedure as $M_{a,b}$, the only difference is the training order of the dimension a and b. Then we observe if the performances of these two models are the same. If the results are different, it would lead support to existence of the order effect between these two dimensions.

To investigate the second research question, we design the following experiment procedures:

1. Choose one requirement set A to train the model, and get the first stage scores of the documents.
2. Use the features of dimensions from another requirement set B as well as the additional feature, i.e., the normalized scores of training and validation dataset got in the first stage, to train the model again and get the second stage scores of the documents.
3. Use the features of the dimensions in the last requirement set C and new additional feature, i.e., the normalized scores of training and validation dataset calculated in procedure 2, to train the model. By this way we could get a model that trained with all requirements sequentially, and get final scores of the documents.
4. Evaluate those models and compare their performances in different stages, in order to get the dynamic trends of the performances with different requirement consideration orders.

4 Experimental Results and Analysis

4.1 Order Effects Between Dimensions

Table 1 gives the NDCG@10 values of models trained with possible dimension pairs in different requirement sets. The term ‘Dimension Pairs’ means all the possible dimension pairs between different requirement sets. The term $\mathit{Effect}(M_{a,b})$

means the performance of the model $M_{a,b}$ where the dimension orders are consistent with the orders shown in 'Dimension Pairs', and *Effect*($M_{b,a}$) is just in the reversed dimension order. For example, for the pair 'Topicality-Reliability', $M_{a,b}$ means the training order of the dimension is topicality first and then reliability. $M_{b,a}$ is just similar except the training order. *Effect*(M_{ab}) and *Effect*(M_{ba}) are the performances of the models trained with features of topicality and reliability together. $\Delta 1$ is the difference value of the performances between *Effect*($M_{a,b}$) and *Effect*($M_{b,a}$), $\Delta 2$ is the difference value between *Effect*(M_{ab}) and the higher one between *Effect*($M_{a,b}$) and *Effect*($M_{b,a}$).

With regard to the proposed research questions, the experimental results have shown some interesting phenomena.

The experimental results suggest that for all the dimension pairs, *Effect*(M_{ab}) = *Effect*(M_{ba}), as shown in Table 1. This is critical because it means the positions of the features have no influence on the model training process. As a consequence, we can choose either of them to do further comparisons with other experimental results.

One significant result we find from Table 1 is that for all dimension pairs except 'Interest-Reliability', the models trained stepwise perform worse than the models trained with features together at once. This result leads to some valuable implications. We regard the latter as the common way of consideration in IR system design, since it assumes users consider all the dimensions simultaneously and equally. While as above mentioned, the information seeking is a staged process, users are more intended to focus on some specific information needs primarily, and might shift their attention to other information needs after the first relevance judgment stage. For this reason we treat the models trained stepwise as the cases of practical situations. The conclusion can be drew that the stepwise consideration of different dimension orders could affect the perfor-

Table 1. Performances of models trained in different dimension pairs (NDCG@10)

Dimension pairs	*Effect*($M_{a,b}$)	*Effect*($M_{b,a}$)	*Effect*(M_{ab})	*Effect*(M_{ba})	$\Delta 1$	$\Delta 2$
Topicality-Reliability	80.42	80.54	80.62	80.62	**−0.12**†	**0.08**†
Topicality-Scope	57.20	57.35	58.68	58.68	**−0.15**†	**1.33**†
Topicality-Understandability	59.17	59.14	59.76	59.76	0.03	**0.59**†
Novelty-Reliability	67.43	67.66	68.11	68.11	**−0.23**†	**0.45**†
Novelty-Scope	67.82	67.76	69.56	69.56	**0.06**†	**1.74**†
Novelty-Understandability	80.90	80.80	81.12	81.12	0.10	**0.22**†
Habit-Novelty	72.04	71.65	73.09	73.09	**0.39**†	**1.05**†
Habit-Topicality	66.52	66.56	67.04	67.04	−0.04	**0.48**†
Interest-Novelty	71.04	70.15	71.53	71.53	**0.89**†	**0.49**†
Interest-Topicality	69.22	63.76	69.52	69.52	**5.46**†	**0.30**†
Habit-Reliability	80.86	80.84	81.11	81.11	0.02	**0.25**†
Habit-Scope	66.95	66.89	67.60	67.60	0.06	**0.65**†
Habit-Understandability	67.44	67.50	67.87	67.87	−0.06	**0.37**†
Interest-Reliability	80.49	80.82	80.63	80.63	**−0.33**†	**−0.19**†
Interest-Scope	68.80	68.77	68.91	68.91	0.03	**0.11**†
Interest-Understandability	69.26	68.84	69.80	69.80	**0.42**†	**0.54**†

The value in boldface with a † means a statistically-significant difference. (%)

mances of models, and it has provided us an alternative direction on improving the information retrieval systems, i.e., the designers should take this discrepancy into consideration.

In terms of the order effects, unlike $Effect(M_{ab})$ and $Effect(M_{ba})$, we can find from Table 1 that for all dimension pairs, $Effect(M_{a,b}) \neq Effect(M_{b,a})$, and the difference value varies from dimension pairs. This result gives support to our Hypothesis 1 effectively. 6 out of 16 values in $\Delta 1$ are negative, which means the models trained first with dimension a and after dimension b perform worse than the opposite.

4.2 Sequential Effects in Document Relevance Judgment

With regard to Question 2, Table 2 presents different performances of models which consider different orders of the requirement sets. We also draw some valuable conclusions from the table.

We can infer from Table 2 that for NDCG@10, the model performs best when we first consider the document quality requirement, then the personalization requirement, and document content last. It performs worst when the sequence becomes to content, quality and then personalization. While differently, for NDCG@ALL, the model performs best in the case that we consider the document content requirement preliminary, then the document quality and the personalization requirement last. This discrepancy indicates that when users mainly focus on relatively more relevant documents, the qualities of the documents and their own personalized preferences might be more attractive, which is also consistent with our actual life. But from the perspective of overall range, users still tend to treat the document contents as the primary consideration, i.e., whether the retrieved documents could satisfy their requirement on the topicality and novelty information needs.

Furthermore, we observe the differences between models in which the first requirement set are the same. It can be found that for both NDCG@10 and NDCG@ALL, the difference value is biggest when we first consider the document content requirement, while the discrepancies of the remaining two groups are very small. That indicates when document content are first considered, the different consideration orders of document quality and personalization requirement could

Table 2. Performances of models trained with different requirement set orders (%)

Requirement order	NDCG@10	NDCG@ALL	Δ
R_c, R_q, R_p	80.65	82.22	1.57
R_c, R_p, R_q	81.05	81.75	0.7
R_q, R_c, R_p	81.25	81.95	0.7
R_q, R_p, R_c	81.29	81.97	0.68
R_p, R_c, R_q	81.00	81.73	0.73
R_p, R_q, R_c	80.81	81.52	0.71

have an impact on the search result. Besides, the NDCG@10 and NDCG@ALL of the model trained with all of the dimension features are 82.69% and 83.31% respectively, both higher than the models trained stepwise. This comparison is also in line with the above mentioned result on dimension pairs.

4.3 A Further Study on TREC Session Track Task

Besides the experiments on Bing query logs, we also conduct similar experiments on the session tracks of TREC 2013 and 2014. There are 87 assessed session tasks in TREC 2013, and 100 in TREC 2014. We combine them and carry out 5-fold cross validation to gain an average evaluation result for all tasks.

The experimental results also confirm the existence of order effects between different dimensions, and give support to our hypothesis. Table 3 presents us with the average performances of models trained with different requirement set orders. It can be found from the table that for NDCG@10, the model trained in the sequence of quality, personalization and content performs best, which is consistent with the result in Table 2, besides, it also performs best for NDCG@ALL. Another interesting thing is that the difference is biggest between two models which consider personalization requirement set first, different from that in Table 1.

Figure 1 provides the average performances in different stages of the 6 models. We surprisingly find that at the first stage, models considering document content requirement get lowest performance, and the differences between the remaining models at first stage are relatively small, with personalization requirement consideration slightly higher. Moreover, there exist some similarities among the four models in which the personalization requirement is not the first consideration. The promoting effects of the performance come to the greatest when the models take into consideration the personalization requirement. This phenomenon suggests that the personalization information could be a capable factor in improving the discriminations of the search results. The model in sequence of document quality, personalization and document content performs best, and we can draw the implication from the result that high quality and exact personalization are more attractive and competitive for the relevance degree of documents than simply content matching.

Table 3. Average performances of models in different requirement set orders (%)

Requirement order	NDCG@10	NDCG@ALL	Δ
R_c, R_q, R_p	22.62	18.35	−4.27
R_c, R_p, R_q	23.17	18.59	−4.58
R_q, R_c, R_p	23.58	18.71	−4.87
R_q, R_p, R_c	23.89	18.86	−5.03
R_p, R_c, R_q	22.59	18.14	−4.45
R_p, R_q, R_c	23.72	18.61	−5.11

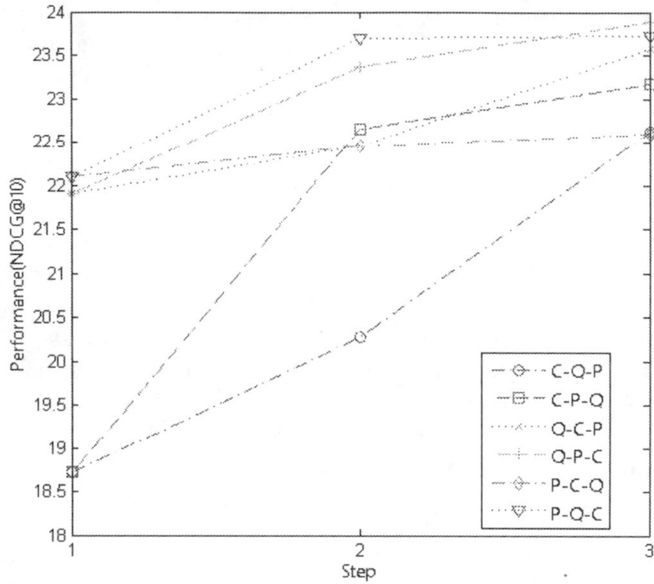

Fig. 1. Average performances in different stages of models on session track (%)

5 Conclusion

In this paper, we have investigated some dynamic decision mechanisms in users' document relevance judgment based on the enriched Multidimensional User Relevance Model. For well-directed study, we divide the 7 relevance dimensions of the enriched MURM into 3 categories. Then we propose two main questions and corresponding hypotheses, and adopt system experiments to test them. The experimental results give support to the existence of order effects between different dimensions, and also suggest that different sequences of requirement considerations would lead to different performances of the models. This work could provide instructions and directions for more intelligent IR system designs, and also foundations for further researches on multidimensional user relevance.

Acknowledgment. This work is supported in part by the Chinese National Program on Key Basic Research Project (973 Program, grant No. 2014CB744604, 2013CB329304), the Chinese 863 Program (grant No. 2015AA015403), the Natural Science Foundation of China (grant No. U1636203, 61272265, 61402324), the Tianjin Research Program of Application Foundation and Advanced Technology (grant no. 15JCQNJC41700), and the European Union's Horizon 2020 research and innovation programme under the Marie Skłodowska-Curie grant agreement No. 721321.

References

1. Grice, H.P.: Logic and conversation. Syntax Semant. **3**, 41–58 (1975)
2. Grice, H.P.: Studies in the Way of Words. Harvard University Press, Cambridge (1989)

3. Xu, Y., Chen, Z.: Relevance judgment-what do information consumers consider beyond topicality? J. Am. Soc. Inform. Sci. Technol. **57**(7), 961–973 (2006)
4. Li, J., Zhang, P., Song, D., Wu, Y.: Understanding an enriched multidimensional user relevance model by analyzing query logs. J. Assoc. Inf. Sci. Technol. **68**(12), 2743–2754 (2017)
5. Schamber, L., Bateman, J.: User criteria in relevance evaluation: toward development of a measurement scale. In: Proceedings of the 59th Annual Meeting of the American Society for Information Science, vol. 33, pp. 218–225. Information Today, Medford (1996)
6. Hirsh, S.G.: Children's relevance criteria and information seeking on electronic resources. J. Am. Soc. Inf. Sci. **50**(14), 1265–1283 (1999)
7. Wang, P., Soergel, D.: A cognitive model of document use during a research project: study I. Document selection. J. Am. Soc. Inf. Sci. **49**(2), 115–133 (1998)
8. Cattell, R.B.: Personality and Motivation: Structure and Measurement. World Book Co., Oxford (1975)
9. Petty, R., Priester, J., Wegender, D.: Cognitive processes in attitude change. In: Wyer, R., Srull, T. (eds.) Handbook of Social Cognition, pp. 69–142. Erlbaum, Hillsdale (1994)
10. Maron, M.E.: On indexing, retrieval and the meaning of about. J. Am. Soc. Inf. Sci. **28**(1), 38–43 (1977)
11. Greisdorf, H.: Relevance thresholds: a multi-stage predictive model of how users evaluate information. Inf. Process. Manag. **39**, 403–423 (2003)
12. Bennett, P.N., et al.: Modeling the impact of short and long-term behavior on search personalization. In: Proceedings of the 35th International ACM SIGIR Conference on Research and Development in Information Retrieval, pp. 185–194. ACM, Portland (2012)
13. Dou, Z., Song, R., Wen, J.R.: A large-scale evaluation and analysis of personalized search strategies. In: Proceedings of the 16th International Conference on World Wide Web, pp. 581–590. ACM, Banff (2007)
14. Xu, Y., Wang, D.: Order effect in relevance judgment. J. Assoc. Inf. Sci. Technol. **59**(8), 1264–1275 (2008)
15. Eisenberg, M., Barry, C.L.: Order effects: a study of the possible influence of presentation order on user judgments of document relevance. J. Am. Soc. Inf. Sci. **39**(5), 292–300 (1988)
16. Purgailis Parker, L.M., Johnson, R.E.: Does order of presentation affect users' judgment of documents? J. Am. Soc. Inf. Sci. **41**(7), 493–494 (1990)
17. Huang, M., Wang, H.: The influence of document presentation order and number of documents judged on users' judgments of relevance. J. Am. Soc. Inf. Sci. Technol. **55**(11), 970–979 (2004)
18. Bruza, P., Chang, V.: Perceptions of document relevance. Front. Psychol. **5**(5), 612 (2014)
19. Schamber, L., Eisenberg, M.B., Nilan, M.S.: A re-examination of relevance: toward a dynamic, situational definition. Inf. Process. Manag. **26**(6), 755–776 (1990)
20. Bateman, J.: Changes in relevance criteria: a longitudinal study. In: Proceedings of the 61st Annual Meeting of the American Society for Information Science, vol. 35, pp. 23–32. Springer, Pittsburgh (1998)
21. Burges, C.J.: From ranknet to lambdarank to lambdamart: an overview. Learning **11**, 223–581 (2010)

A Correlation-Aware ML-kNN Algorithm for Customer Value Modeling in Online Shopping

Yuan Zhuang[1], Xiaolin Li[1], Yue Sun[1], and Xiangdong He[2(✉)]

[1] School of Management, Nanjing University, Nanjing 210093, Jiangsu, China
[2] Network and Information Center, Nanjing University, Nanjing 210093, Jiangsu, China
hexd@nju.edu.cn

Abstract. For online retailers, it is necessary to select a relatively small set of valuable customers, so as to guide the marketing efforts and increase the profits. Drawing on prior literatures, the repeat purchase, the price sensitivity and the brand loyalty are always viewed as important labels of profitable customers. And the three labels are highly correlated. However, prior researches mostly investigated the three labels separately. Correlations between each pair of the three labels are not taken into consideration. Therefore, this work proposes a correlation-aware multi-label kNN algorithm (CAML-kNN) to model the customer value based on the three labels, as well as to capture the latent correlations among them by generating a super-set of correlated labels. Besides, we also conduct extensive experiments with the real-world data to validate the algorithm's effectiveness in segmenting customers and profiling the customer value. With the proposed algorithm, we can help retailers generate customer segments accurately, and pave the way for successful target marketing.

Keywords: Customer value modeling · Multi-label · Correlation aware

1 Introduction

The popularity of online shopping has brought on intense competitions and made online retailers nowadays more difficult to expand the market. In online shopping, customers are more sensitive to price changes and less likely to keep loyal on one brand than off-line customers [4]. Thus, it is necessary for retailers to provide quality services for customers, so as to increase the revenues. However, retailers' marketing resources are always limited. Identifying specific customers is needed to concentrate the efforts on a few key customers, so that the promotion of the brand can be more cost-effective [19].

This research was supported by the National Science Foundation of China (NSFC) via the grant numbers: 61773199, 71732002, as well as the Philosophy and Social Science Foundation of the Higher Education Institutions of Jiangsu Province, China (2017SJB0006).

X. Geng and B.-H. Kang (Eds.): PRICAI 2018, LNAI 11012, pp. 980–992, 2018.
https://doi.org/10.1007/978-3-319-97304-3_75

The customer segments to target on should have high utilities, and then the marketing efforts can be concentrated in a rational way. As the profitability of customers has become increasingly pivotal in business, it is essential to allocate marketing resources to the customer groups that can be cultivated the most efficiently by the firm. To this end, this study proposes to develop a model that enables a firm to supercharge its profits by customizing its responses to distinct profitable customers. Drawing on prior literatures, a large number of researchers have put effort into identifying the key labels of profitable customers. Among these literatures, the repeat purchase, the price sensitivity and the brand loyalty are highlighted.

To profile the three labels, we have studied large-scale product transaction events in an Alibaba B2C platform. The extracted transaction records show that, in practice, the three labels can be highly correlated. For instance, customers more sensitive to price changes may be less likely to keep loyal on one brand. And with high brand loyalty, customers can be easily retained and ultimately promoted to purchase repeatedly. However, prior researches mostly investigated the three labels separately. That is, the correlations between each pair of the three labels are not taken into consideration. In this paper, the proposed model not only profiles the repeat purchase, the price sensitivity and the brand loyalty, but also the correlations among the three labels.

Along these lines, this paper develops a multi-label kNN algorithm (ML-kNN) to model the customer value based on the information of the three labels, as well as to capture the latent correlations among them by generating a super-set of correlated labels. The proposed algorithm is named as the correlation aware multi-label kNN algorithm (CAML-kNN). In the proposed algorithm, we first extract customers' repeat purchase records and thereby profile the first label. Then, we employ a standard K-means algorithm on customers' attributes related to the price and payment to profile the second label. Third, the brand loyalty label is a latent state that can not be directly observed. A traditional research in [13] reported a RMF model that customers' brand loyalty can be quantified with three indexes:

- *Recency:* the last time of the customer's consumption;
- *Frequency:* the frequency of the customer's consumption;
- *Monetary:* the total amount of the customer's consumption.

Thus, in this paper, a RMF model is employed to generate the three indexes and then quantify the brand loyalty with a standard K-means algorithm.

With the proposed algorithm, we can segment customers as 8 groups in terms of each pair of the three labels ($2 \times 2 \times 2$). Based on the 8 groups, we can help online retailers find out profitable customers, rationally formulate different marketing strategies, and thereby allocate marketing resources to maximize the sales and profits. Besides, we also conduct extensive experiments over a real-world data set. Data collected from the Taobao platform provides strong support for the effectiveness of the proposed algorithm in segmenting customers and profiling the customer value. The experimental results validate that the proposed algorithm outperforms other baseline algorithms.

2 Research Background

The related work can be categorized as: (i) customer value modeling; (ii) RFM model; and (iii) multi-label learning.

2.1 Customer Value Modeling

Retailers' marketing resources are always limited. Thus, it is necessary for a retailer to identify a relatively small set of valuable customers, so as to guide the marketing efforts, and as a result to increase the profits [25]. Customer identification plays an important role in customer relationship management with specific customers.

In this context, a large number of studies have been conducted to profiling the individual customer value [21]. The work in [29] explored the consumer behavior patterns and marketing strategies by integrating the neural network and association rules. Researchers also found that the social influence is of great importance to figure out the profitable users for social marketing [20]. Jacobs, et al. [15] developed a model by introducing the links among quality, customer satisfaction, loyalty, and profitability. Awuah et al. [1] argued that the repeat and regular purchase from end users can make the firm profitable. The work in [10, 22] revealed that customers of different price sensitivity have different requirements for products and the brand reputation. And researchers in [11] tested the mediating role of the brand loyalty in the relationship between the consumer value and the purchase intention. Along these lines, in this paper, we propose to model the customer value based on three labels: (i) repeat purchase; (ii) price sensitivity; and (iii) brand loyalty.

2.2 RFM Model

The RFM model is a classical quantitative model which is widely used in user segmentation. According to the RFM model in [13], the customer loyalty for one retailer can be quantified with three indexes: (i) *Recency:* the last time of the consumer consumption; (ii) *Frequency:* the frequency of the consumer consumption; and (iii) *Monetary:* the total amount of the consumer consumption. In particular, the *Recency* value indicates the interval between the consumer's last transaction time and the current transaction time, which is in negative correlation with the possibility of the consumer loyalty. The *Frequency* value is in positive correlation with the consumer loyalty. And customers of high *Monetary* are the core customers that likely to bring the most profits to the retailers. The RFM model is successfully adopted in many domains to label the brand loyal consumer, such as retail [6], banking [12], and e-commerce [16, 17].

Prior work has developed extensive novel models to segment users by combining the RFM model with the data mining technology. For instance, Liu et al. [18] employed a weighted RFM model to segment customers, and then utilized association rules to make recommendations for different consumer segments. Cheng et al. [7] proposed a classification method for the customer retrieval based on the RFM model and the rough set theory. Chiang et al. [8] presented a RFMDR model based on the RFM model to identify valuable customers. And the work in [26] introduced the data mining technology and a RFM model to analyze customers' values for a veterinary hospital.

2.3 Multi-label Learning

Over the past decade, the multi-label learning has been widely used in various domains, such as scene recognition [2], gene functional classification [9], text classification [5,24], and feature selection [28].

In terms of correlations among the labels, the multi-label learning algorithms can be divided into three categories [32]. The first category is the first-order multi-label learning algorithm. These algorithms decompose the multi-label learning problem into several single labeling classification problems. The correlations among the labels are not taken into account [31]. The second category is the second-order multi-label learning algorithm. These algorithms introduce the latent information of correlations among the labels to build a multi-labels learning system. However, only pairwise relations between labels will be considered [3,30]. As for the third category is the high-order multi-label learning algorithm. These algorithms consider high-order relations among labels, such as influences from all other labels [27], or connections among random subsets of labels [23].

The basic ML-kNN algorithm is a first-order multi-label learning [31], based on the standard k-nearest neighbor (kNN) algorithm. Many relative researches have focused on revising and optimizing this algorithm [14]. Despite the wide use in multi-label learning domain, the ML-kNN algorithm is weak at in dealing with the category imbalance and the correlation information among labels. That is, the correlations among labels are not addressed in the basic ML-kNN.

3 CAML-kNN Model

In this paper, we propose a correlation-aware multi-label kNN algorithm (CAML-kNN). Main notations used in this paper are shown in Table 1. The proposed algorithm models the customer value based on three labels: (i) repeat purchase (labeling customers having repurchase behaviors); (ii) price-sensitivity (labeling price sensitive customers); and (iii) brand loyalty (labeling loyal customers).

3.1 The Basic ML-kNN Model

The basic ML-kNN algorithm finds out k nearest observed neighbors of unobserved instances, and then predicts the label sets of unobserved instances according to their neighbors' label sets, based on the maximum a posteriori (MAP) principle.

Consider a set of m instances $T = \{t_1, \ldots, t_m\}$ and n labels $L = \{l_1, \ldots, l_n\}$, where t_i is the i-th instance in T and l_u is the u-th label in L. And $Y = \{Y_1, \ldots, Y_m\}$ is the label sets of individual instances, where Y_i denotes the label

Table 1. Symbol table

Notation	Description
t_i	The i-th instance $\in T = \{t_1, \ldots, t_m\}$
l_u	The u-th label $\in L = \{l_1, \ldots, l_n\}$
Y_i	The label set of instance t_i
y_i	The n-length label vector of instance t_i
N_i	The set of instance t_i's K nearest neighbors
C_i	The known label sets of N_i
$H_{i,u}$	The event that instance t_i has label l_u
A	The super-sets for labels L
s	The number of instances estimated to have label l_u
S_u	The total number of the smaller class
B_u	The total number of the larger class
W_u	The imposed weight of the u-th label

set of instance t_i. In addition, consider a n-length label vector y_i for instance t_i, where $y_i(u)$ takes the value of 1 if $l_u \in Y_i$ and 0 otherwise. Given the set of instance t_i's k nearest neighbors (kNNs) N_i, we can calculate a overall membership counting vector C_i [31] to represent the known label sets of N_i, where:

$$C_i(u) = \sum_{j \in N_i} y_j(u) \tag{1}$$

Here, $C_i(u)$ is the number of instances having the label l_u among the kNNs of t_i. Then we obtain the estimation of the label vector y_i for instance t_i with the maximum a posteriori (MAP) principle. To be specific, the u-th element $\hat{y}_i(u)$ in the n-length estimation vector $\hat{y}_i$ is given by:

$$\begin{aligned} \hat{y}_i(u) &= Pr\{\frac{P(H_{i,u}|E^{l_u}_{C_i(u)})}{P(\neg H_{i,u}|E^{l_u}_{C_i(u)})} > 0.5\} \\ &= Pr\{\frac{P(H_{i,u})P(E^{l_u}_{C_i(u)}|H_{i,u})}{P(\neg H_{i,u})P(E^{l_u}_{C_i(u)}|\neg H_{i,u})} > 0.5\}; \end{aligned} \tag{2}$$

Here, $H_{i,u}$ denotes the event that instance t_i has label l_u, while $\neg H_{i,u}$ denotes the event that instance t_i does not have label l_u. And $E^{l_u}_{C_i(u)}$ denotes the event that there are exactly $C_i(u)$ instances having label l_u among N_i. The threshold is artificially set as 0.5, since consumers having labels are always more representative than others among the kNNs.

As a lazy learning algorithm, the basic ML-kNN algorithm is a multi-label learning algorithm with relative less time cost. In addition, the basic ML-kNN algorithm can hardly be affected by redundant attributes or irrelevant attributes in the estimating process.

3.2 Model Development

In this paper, the proposed correlation-aware multi-label kNN algorithm revises the basic ML-kNN algorithm by addressing the correlation information among labels. The proposed algorithm aims at dealing with the issue that label l_u may be correlated with label l_v. That is, the fact that instance t_i has label l_u may affect the possibility that t_i has label l_v. To deal with this problem, we let A be the super-sets for labels. The formula of the n-length estimation vector $\hat{y}_i$ is given by:

$$\hat{y}_i(u) = Pr\{\frac{P(H_{i,u}|E^{l_u}_{A_i(u)})P(E^{l_u}_{C_i(u)}|H_{i,u})}{P(\neg H_{i,u}|E^{l_u}_{A_i(u)})P(E^{l_u}_{C_i(u)}|\neg H_{i,u})} > 0.5\} \tag{3}$$

Here, $H_{i,u}$ denotes the event that instance t_i has label l_u. And we let $A = \{A_1, A_2, \ldots, A_i, \ldots, A_m\}$, here $A_i(u)$ is the set of all the labels (excluding l_u) of instances in N_i having label l_u. Thereby, $E^{l_u}_{A_i(u)}$ is the event that the labels in $A_i(u)$ are exactly the labels correlated with label l_u based on N_i.

To be specific, if an instance has both label l_u and label l_v, the two labels may be correlated, and we name the two labels as correlated-potential labels. Similarly, we initialize the correlated-potential label set $A_{i,u}$ for label l_u and instance t_i, based on all the labels (excluding l_u) of instances having label l_u in N_i. That is, label l_u's correlated-potential label set is the collection of all the other labels related to the same instance set with l_u in N_i. Based on all the labels, we obtain the correlated-potential label set A_i for instance t_i. Then, if $\hat{y}_i(u) = 0$, that is instance t_i is predicted to not have label l_u, we will remove labels in $A_{i,u}$. Subsequently, we can obtain the final super-set of correlated label set A_i for instance t_i, and thereby we can obtain the super-set of correlated label set A for all the instances. In this way, we take into account the correlations among labels to improve the prediction accuracy.

Besides, the issue of class-imbalance is also considered by imposing weights on the data set. The class-imbalance is the issue that the total number of one class in the data set is far less than the total number of another class. For instance, customers of high loyalty may occupy a rather small share among all the customers. Specifically, we set the total number of the smaller class as S_u, and the total number of the other class as B_u. Here, u represents the u-th label. Thus, the imposed weight W_u of the u-th label is given by:

$$W_u = \frac{B_u}{S_u} \tag{4}$$

4 Experimental Results

In this section, based on a real-world transaction data set, two experiments are conducted to evaluate the performances of the proposed algorithm: (i) experiments on customer labeling; and (ii) experiments on multi-labeling learning.

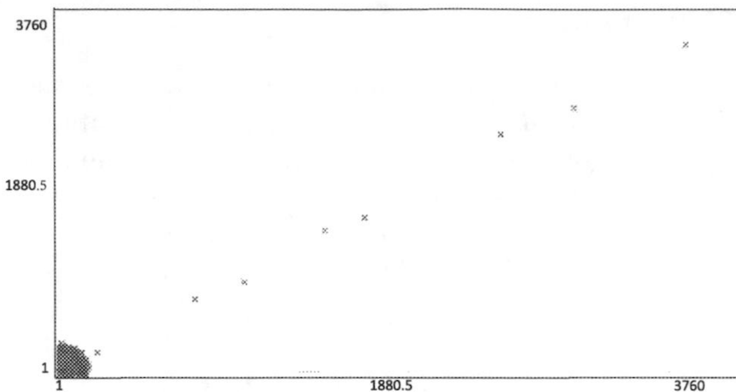

Fig. 1. Abnormal detection

4.1 The Experimental Data

The data set used to calibrate and validate the model is the purchase records of one online cosmetics retailer in Taobao, the largest B2C platform in China. This data set consists of 10 attributes from July 7, 2004 to July 7, 2014. In particular, attributes we used in this paper include: customerno, total_fee, discount_fee, adjust_fee, num , payment, refund_fee, price, title, and trade_from. The specific descriptions of these attributes are shown in Table 2.

Table 2. Data description

Data sources	Description	Data sources	Description
customerno	ID of the consumer	payment	payment of the order
total_fee	total payment of the order	refund_fee	refund fee of order
discount_fee	discount amount of the order	price	price of the product
adjust_fee	adjust fee of the order	title	name of the product
num	number of items in the order	trade_from	Trade sources

Besides, we also detected the abnormal records based on consumers' total order amounts, as can be seen in Fig. 1. Some customers' total order amounts are considerably higher than others'. In this case, this paper regarded these customers as abnormal customers that can be removed and not taken into account. Finally, 41,729 customers' records are kept for experiments.

4.2 Experiments on Customer Labeling

Based on our proposed correlation-aware multi-label kNN algorithm (CAML-kNN), we profiled with three labels: (i) repeat purchase; (ii) price sensitivity; and (iii) brand loyalty, to classify and find out profitable customers.

Table 3. Extraction on the price-sensitivity label

Metric	Description
Pay_sum	Cumulative consumption fee
Dis_sum	Cumulative discount amount
Buy_num	Cumulative consumption amount
Dis_num	Cumulative discount fee

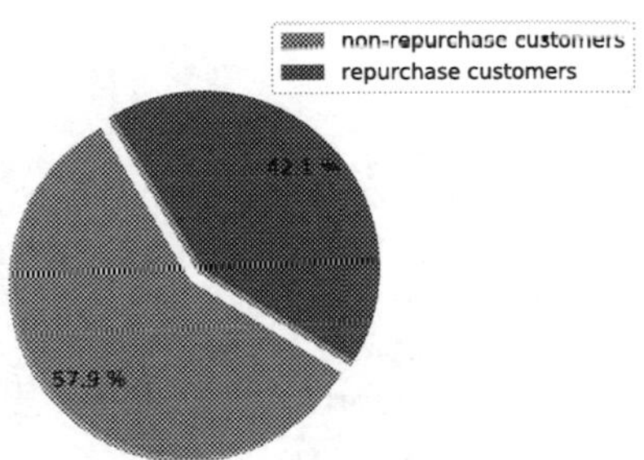

Fig. 2. Repurchase customers

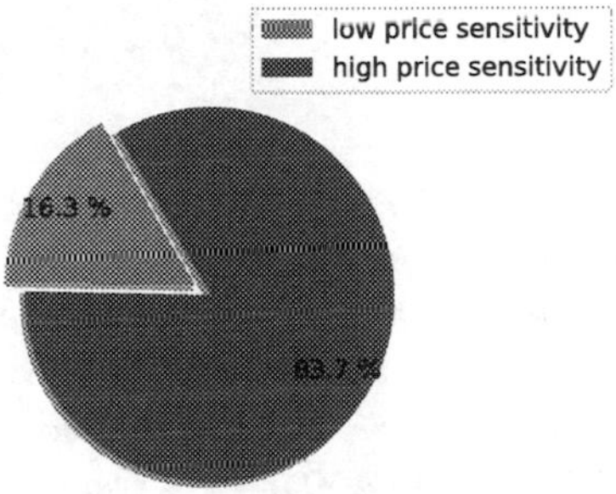

Fig. 3. Price-sensitive customers

Specifically, we first regarded customers placing more than one orders on the target retailer as customers of the repeat-purchase label. As shown in Fig. 2, customers ever placing more than one orders account for 42.13% among all the customers. That is, a relatively high proportion of customers has chosen the same retailer more than once. It can be inferred that it is feasible for retailers to retain and further strengthen the relationship with repeat-purchase customers by conducting promotions or sending text messages.

Then, we profiled the price sensitivity label by calculating two ratios: (i) $sum\_ratio = Dis\_sum/Pay\_sum$; and (ii) $num\_ratio = Dis\_num/Pay\_num$, based on the extracted indexes in Table 3. Then we normalized the six attributes and conducted the k-means algorithm to classify and label customers. As we can see in Fig. 3, low price-sensitive customers only account for 16.29% among all the customers, that is, the proportion of high price-sensitive customers is up to 83.71%. It can be inferred that most customers always prefer products with discounts and can easily switch their choices. And low price-sensitive customers have the potential to be the stable and profitable customers, appropriate actions should be taken on to retain them.

Table 4. Extraction on the brand loyalty label

Metric	Description
Recency	The interval between the latest and the second latest consumption
Frequency	Cumulative consumption amount
Monetary	Cumulative consumption fee

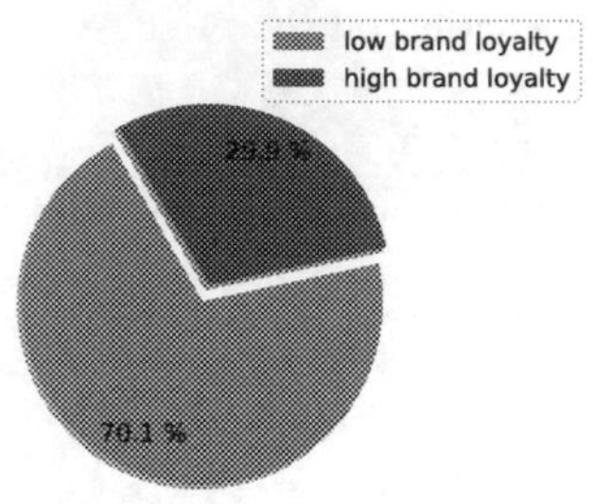

Fig. 4. Brand-loyal customers

Third, we adopted a RMF model and extracted the three indexes: (i) *Recency*; (ii) *Frequency*; and (iii) *Monetary*, as shown in Table 4. And likewise, we normalized the three indexes and conducted the k-means method to find out the brand-loyal customers. Besides, in practice, for different product types, the weights of the indexes in the RMF model are different. In this paper, we attached more weights on the number of orders (*Frequency*). As can be seen in Fig. 4 and Table 5, we obtained two customer clusters. Customers in *Cluster*0 account for 70.09% of all the customers, while the total payments and ordering frequencies of customers in *Cluster*0 are far less than those in *Cluster*1. It can be inferred that customers in *Cluster*0 are normal customers, the characteristics of which are in line with most online customers. And customers in *Cluster*1 are loyal customers that retailers should attach greater attention to and provide customized service for.

Table 5. Statistics of the RMF model

Metric	Average value (data set)	Average value (Cluster 0)	Average value (Cluster 1)
Number	42,806	30,002	12,804
Recency	0	−0.0031	0.0446
Frequency	0	−0.0067	0.0951
Monetary	25.0469	22.4231	62.4784

To sum up, based on the three labels we extracted, retailers can classify customers as $8(2 \times 2 \times 2)$ groups and develop according marketing strategies. For instance, for customers of high repurchases, low price sensitivity and high brand loyalty, retailers can mark them as the most profitable customers and provide them with the customized service. As for customers of high repurchases, high price sensitivity and low brand loyalty, retailers can push more promotion notifications to them to stimulate their consumption and improve their conversion rates to loyal customers.

4.3 Evaluation Metrics on Multi-label Learning

In this paper, five metrics will be used to evaluate the performances of the proposed algorithm in multi-label learning.

- **Hamming Loss:** The Hamming Loss value is a metric to examine the misclassification of each single sample. The smaller the value is, the higher the accuracy of the model's prediction tends to be. The formula for the Hamming Loss is as follows:

$$hloss(y_i, \hat{y}_i) = \frac{1}{|T|} \sum_{i-1}^{|T|} \frac{xor(y_i, \hat{y}_i)}{|L|} \tag{5}$$

  Here, $|T|$ denotes the test data set size, $|L|$ denotes the label set size, y_i and $\hat{y}_i$ donate the actual value and the predicted result of instance t_i's label set. Besides, the function xor denotes the number of different elements across y_i and $\hat{y}_i$.
- **One-Error:** The One-Error metric is used to address the importance of the customers' most typical labels. The smaller the value is, the higher the accuracy of the model's prediction tends to be. The formula of the One-Error is shown below:

$$One\text{-}Error(y_i, \hat{y}_i) - \frac{1}{|T|} \sum_{i-1}^{|T|} [argmaxrank(\hat{y}_i) \notin y_i] \tag{6}$$

  Here, the function $argmaxrank$ denotes the top-rank labels in instance t_i's predicted label set. And $argmaxrank(\hat{y}_i) \notin y_i$ denotes the number of the predicted top-rank labels not in the actual label set.
- **Coverage:** The Coverage metric is used to measure the model's ability in finding out all the actual labels of customer i. The smaller the value is, the higher the accuracy of the model's prediction tends to be. The formula of the Coverage is shown below:

$$Coverage(y_i, \hat{y}_i) = \frac{1}{|T|} \sum_{i-1}^{|T|} [maxrank(y_i, \hat{y}_i) - 1] \tag{7}$$

  Here, the function $maxrank(y_i, \hat{y}_i)$ denotes the minimum subset size containing all the labels in the actual label set, from the sorting predicted label set.
- **Ranking Loss:** The Ranking Loss metric is used to investigate the occurrence of sort errors in the predicted label set. The smaller the value is, the higher the accuracy of the model's prediction tends to be. The formula of the Ranking Loss is shown as follows:

$$RankingLoss(y_i, \hat{y}_i) = \frac{1}{|T|} \sum_{i-1}^{|T|} \frac{|\{(l_u, l_v) | rank(y_i, l_u) \geq rank(\hat{y}_i, l_v)\}|}{|y_i||\hat{y}_i|} \tag{8}$$

Here, $(l_u, l_v) \in y_i \times \hat{y}_i$, the function $rank(y_i, l_u)$ denotes the rank of the label l_i in the actual label set y_i.

- **Average Precision:** The Average Precision metric examines the ability of ensuring that the label preceding the actual relevant labels is still the actual relevant label. The higher the value is, the higher the accuracy of the model's prediction tends to be. The formula of the Average Precision is shown as follows:

$$Ave\_Precision(y_i, \hat{y}_i) = \frac{1}{|T|} \sum_{i-1}^{|T|} \sum_{l_u \in y_i} \frac{|\{l_v | rank(\hat{y}_i, l_v) \geq rank(y_i, l_u)\}|}{|y_i| rank(y_i, l_u)} \tag{9}$$

Here, $l_v \in y_i$, the function $rank(y_i, l_u)$ denotes the rank of the label l_u in the actual label set y_i.

4.4 Experiments on Multi-label Learning

In this section, we conducted experiments and compared the performances of the proposed correlation-aware multi-label kNN algorithm (CAML-kNN) with the basic ML-KNN algorithm, a BR algorithm with multi-label learning, and a MLNB algorithm. The results are shown in Figs. 5 and 6.

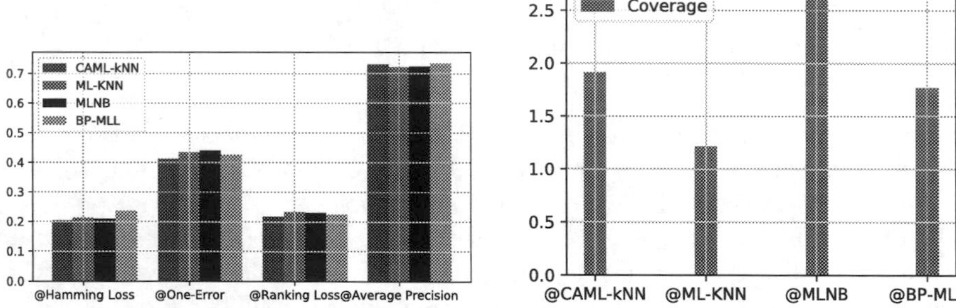

Fig. 5. Model performances comparison A **Fig. 6.** Model performances comparison B

Here, a better algorithm is viewed as the algorithm with higher Average Precision value, and lower Hamming Loss value, One-Error value, Coverage value and Ranking Loss value. It is obvious that the proposed algorithm outperforms other three algorithms at most of the metrics (Hamming Loss; One-Error; and Ranking Loss). These three metrics all reflect the models' ability in ruling out the incorrect or irrelevant labels. That is, by introducing the category weights and the correlation information among labels, the proposed algorithm is better at avoiding the misclassification of individual labels. Besides, the relevant labels are more likely to be ranked higher than irrelevant labels based on the proposed algorithm. However, the proposed algorithm is weak at finding out all the relevant labels. As shown in Fig. 5, the Coverage value of the CAML-kNN algorithm ranks the third among the four algorithms. That is, labels weakly related with customers can hardly be found by the CAML-kNN.

5 Conclusion

In this paper, we obtained further insights into the consumer value modeling by segmenting customers in terms of three labels: (i) repeat purchase; (ii) price sensitivity; and (iii) brand loyalty. To be specific, we proposed a correlation-aware multi-label kNN algorithm (CAML-kNN) to take the correlation information among labels into consideration, by generating a super-set of correlated labels. Besides, we introduced the k-means algorithm and a RMF model to quantify the latent price sensitivity label and brand loyalty label. In this way, we can segment customers as 8 groups and find the characteristics and distributions of each group. The proposed algorithm can help retailers identify customers of the most profitability to taken on target marketing. It is also demonstrated in experiments that the proposed algorithm performs better than other baseline algorithms at most of the metrics.

References

1. Awuah, G.B., Reinert, V.: Small firms' use of their business relationships to cope with increased competition. Int. Acad. Bus. Econ. **12**(2) (2012)
2. Boutell, M.R., Luo, J., Shen, X., Brown, C.M.: Learning multi-label scene classification. Pattern Recogn. **37**(9), 1757–1771 (2004)
3. Brinker, K.: Multilabel classification via calibrated label ranking. Mach. Learn. **73**(2), 133–153 (2008)
4. Brynjolfsson, E., Smith, M.D.: Frictionless commerce? A comparison of internet and conventional retailers. INFORMS (2000)
5. Chen, W., Yan, J., Zhang, B., Chen, Z., Yang, Q.: Document transformation for multi-label feature selection in text categorization. In: IEEE International Conference on Data Mining, pp. 451–456 (2007)
6. Chen, Y.L., Hu, Y.H.: Constraint-based sequential pattern mining: the consideration of recency and compactness. Decis. Support Syst. **42**(2), 1203–1215 (2006)
7. Cheng, C.H., Chen, Y.S.: Classifying the segmentation of customer value via RFM model and RS theory. Expert Syst. Appl. **36**(3), 4176–4184 (2009)
8. Chiang, W.Y.: To mine association rules of customer values via a data mining procedure with improved model: an empirical case study. Expert Syst. Appl. **38**(3), 1716–1722 (2011)
9. Elisseeff, A., Weston, J.: A kernel method for multi-labelled classification. In: International Conference on Neural Information Processing Systems: Natural and Synthetic, pp. 681–687 (2001)
10. Erdem, T., Swait, J., Louviere, J.: The impact of brand credibility on consumer price sensitivity. Int. J. Res. Mark. **19**(1), 1–19 (2002)
11. Ghanbari, M., Yasemi, M., Abasi, E., Ozturk, I.: The intermediate role of brand loyalty in the relationship between consumer value and purchase intention (case study: Consumers of Snowa household appliances in Kermanshah city). Int. Rev. Manag. Mark. (2017)
12. Hsieh, N.C.: An integrated data mining and behavioral scoring model for analyzing bank customers. Expert Syst. Appl. **27**(4), 623–633 (2004)
13. Hughes, A.M.: Strategic Database Marketing: The Masterplan for Starting and Managing a Profitable, Custom-Based Marketing Program. Quorum Books (2000). (Ed. by, A.M. Hughes)

14. Ivasic-Kos, M., Pobar, M., Ribaric, S.: Two-tier image annotation model based on a multi-label classifier and fuzzy-knowledge representation scheme. Pattern Recogn. **52**, 287–305 (2016)
15. Jacobs, F.A., Johnston, W., Kotchetova, N.: Customer profitability: prospective vs. retrospective approaches in a business-to-business setting. Ind. Mark. Manag. **30**(4), 353–363 (2001)
16. Li, Y.M., Lin, C.H., Lai, C.Y.: Identifying influential reviewers for word-of-mouth marketing. Electron. Commer. Res. Appl. **9**, 294–304 (2010)
17. Liu, D.R., Lai, C.H., Lee, W.J.: A hybrid of sequential rules and collaborative filtering for product recommendation. Inf. Sci. **179**(20), 3505–3519 (2009)
18. Liu, D.R., Shih, Y.Y.: Integrating AHP and data mining for product recommendation based on customer lifetime value. Inf. Manag. **42**, 387–400 (2005)
19. Liu, L., Yang, Z., Benslimane, Y.: Conducting efficient and cost-effective targeted marketing using data mining techniques. In: Intelligent Systems, pp. 102–106 (2014)
20. Ma, G., Liu, Q., Wu, L., Chen, E.: Identifying hesitant and interested customers for targeted social marketing. In: Pacific-Asia Conference on Knowledge Discovery and Data Mining, pp. 576–590 (2015)
21. Ngai, E.W.T., Xiu, L., Chau, D.C.K.: Application of data mining techniques in customer relationship management: a literature review and classification. Expert Syst. Appl. **36**(2), 2592–2602 (2009)
22. Petrick, J.F.: Segmenting cruise passengers with price sensitivity. Tour. Manag. **26**(5), 753–762 (2005)
23. Read, J., Pfahringer, B., Holmes, G.: Multi-label classification using ensembles of pruned sets. In: Eighth IEEE International Conference on Data Mining, pp. 995–1000 (2009)
24. Schapire, R.E., Singer, Y.: BoosTexter: A Boosting-Based System for Text Categorization. Kluwer Academic Publishers, Dordrecht (2000)
25. Wang, Y., Wu, L., Wu, Z., Chen, E., Liu, Q.: Selecting valuable customers for merchants in e-commerce platforms. In: IEEE International Conference on Data Mining, pp. 1281–1286 (2017)
26. Wei, J.T., Lin, S.Y., Yang, Y.Z., Wu, H.H.: Applying data mining and RFM model to analyze customers' values of a veterinary hospital. In: International Symposium on Computer, Consumer and Control, pp. 481–484 (2016)
27. Yan, R., Tesic, J., Smith, J.R.: Model-shared subspace boosting for multi-label classification. In: ACM SIGKDD International Conference on Knowledge Discovery and Data Mining, pp. 834–843 (2007)
28. Yan, Y., et al.: Multi-label learning with label-specific feature selection. In: International Conference on Neural Information Processing, pp. 305–315 (2017)
29. ZekićSušac, M., Has, A.: Data mining as support to knowledge management in marketing. Bus. Syst. Res. J. **6**(2), 18–30 (2015)
30. Zhang, M.L., Zhou, Z.H.: Multilabel neural networks with applications to functional genomics and text categorization. IEEE Trans. Knowl. Data Eng. **18**(10), 1338–1351 (2006)
31. Zhang, M.L., Zhou, Z.H.: ML-kNN: a lazy learning approach to multi-label learning. Pattern Recogn. **40**(7), 2038–2048 (2007)
32. Zhang, M.L., Zhou, Z.H.: A review on multi-label learning algorithms. IEEE Trans. Knowl. Data Eng. **26**(8), 1819–1837 (2014)

Binary Collaborative Filtering Ensemble

Yujia Zhang[1], Jun Wu[1(✉)], and Haishuai Wang[2]

[1] School of Computer and Information Technology, Beijing Jiaotong University, Beijing 100044, China
{zhangyujia,wuj}@bjtu.edu.cn

[2] Department of Biomedical Informatics, Harvard University, Boston, MA 02115, USA
HaishuaiWang@hms.harvard.edu

Abstract. We address the efficiency problem of Collaborative Filtering (CF) in the context of large user and item spaces. A promising solution is to hash users and items with binary codes, and then make recommendation in a Hamming space. However, existing CF hashing methods mainly concentrate on modeling the user-item affinity, yet ignore the user-user and item-item affinities. Such manner results in a large encoding loss and deteriorates the recommendation accuracy subsequently. Towards this end, we propose a Binary Collaborative Filtering Ensemble (BCFE) framework which ensembles three popularly used CF methods to preserve the user-item, user-user and item-item affinities in the Hamming space simultaneously. In order to avoid a time-consuming computation of the user-user and item-item affinity matrices, an anchor approximation solution is employed by BCFE through subspace clustering. Specifically, we devise a Discretization-like Bit-wise Gradient Descend (DBGD) optimization algorithm that incorporates the binary quantization into the learning stage and updates binary codes in a bit-by-bit way. Such a discretization-like algorithm can yield more high-quality binary codes comparing with the popular "two-stage" CF hashing schemes, and is much simpler than the rigorous discrete optimization. Extensive experiments on three real-world datasets show that our BCFE approach significantly outperforms state-of-the-art CF hashing techniques.

Keywords: Recommender systems · Collaborative filtering
Anchor representation · Learning to hash

1 Introduction

With the thrift of Web services like Amazon, Facebook and Flickr, the need for recommender systems is occurring more and more frequently in our daily life. However, the ever-growing scales of users and items within these Web services make today's recommendation more challenging than ever before. Consequently, how to design an efficient recommender system scaling well with large user and item spaces has been a matter concerned by both academia and industry.

X. Geng and B.-H. Kang (Eds.): PRICAI 2018, LNAI 11012, pp. 993–1004, 2018.
https://doi.org/10.1007/978-3-319-97304-3_76

It is out of question that Collaborative filtering (CF) is the most widely adopted and successful recommendation technique. The primary areas of CF are neighborhood methods and latent factor models. Neighborhood methods mainly concentrate on calculating the user-user similarity [8] or the item-item similarity [9] to predict the preferences between users and items, while latent factor models (e.g. matrix factorization [4]) directly model user-item similarity in a low-dimensional latent vector space shared by users and items, and then the prediction for user-item ratings can be estimated by inner products between the corresponding user and item vectors. Essentially, recommendation by CF can be viewed as a similarity search problem, i.e., seeking the top-K 'similar' items which are queried by a given user. When the size of users or items is large, similarity search will be a critical efficiency bottleneck of various recommender systems.

Hashing is a promising approach to tackle fast similarity search [14]. By encoding high dimensionality data into compact binary codes, hashing makes efficient in-memory similarity calculation of massive data feasible. Recently, there has appeared several works [2,6,16–18] to bring the advance of hashing into CF for higher recommendation efficiency. However, those works mainly focus on modeling the user-item affinity in the Hamming space, and ignore the user-user and item-item affinities in the original vector space. We argue that such manner oversimplifies the original data geometry in the continuous vector space, resulting in a large encoding loss in the Hamming space. Subsequently the inaccurate binary codes of users and items will inevitably deteriorate the recommendation performance.

In this paper, we propose a Binary Collaborative Filtering Ensemble (BCFE) approach that integrates the merits of both latent factor model and neighborhood methods into a unified formulation, aiming at preserving the user-item affinity in the Hamming space while saving the original user-user and item-item affinities in the vector space. In this way, the original data geometry in the vector space is preserved as much as possible, and thus BCFE could make up for the encoding loss in the Hamming space to some degree. Furthermore, in order to avoid a time-consuming computation of user-user and item-item affinity matrices in the original vector space, we adopt an anchor approximate strategy to accelerate the training process. Concretely, we cluster users and items in a low-dimensional latent space obtained by regular matrix factorization, and then choose the cluster centroids as anchors. As a result, we can replace the user-user/item-item affinity with the user-anchor/item-anchor affinity, which can reduce the time complexity from square to sub-linear. In particular, we devise a Discretization-like Bit-wise Gradient Descend (DBGD) optimization algorithm, which integrates the binary quantization into training and could update the binary codes in a bit-by-bit way. It is similar to the discrete optimization externally, yet much simpler than it. To a great extent, our DBGD algorithm could reduce the encoding loss because each bit of the codes is optimal, and it is much faster than the optimization methods used by the regular "two-stage" CF hashing schemes, e.g. Gradient Descend.

The rest of this paper is organized as follows. In Sect. 2, we elaborate the BCFE formulation and corresponding DBGD solution. Section 3 reports on the experiments. Section 4 reviews the related work. Finally, Sect. 5 concludes this paper and raises several problems for future works.

2 The Proposed BCFE Approach

In this section, we will elaborate our BCFE approach which is to learn informative binary codes for users and items by ensembling three canonical CF techniques. At first, let us start with some necessary preliminaries, and then illustrate the problem formulation and corresponding solution.

2.1 Preliminaries

Let $\mathcal{U} = \{u_1, \cdots, u_m\}$ be a set with m users, and $\mathcal{I} = \{i_1, \cdots, i_n\}$ denotes a set with n items. All interactions associating $\mathcal{U}$ with $\mathcal{I}$ can be represented by a User-Item (UI) rating matrix $\mathbf{R} \in [0,1]^{m \times n}$ whose element r_{ui} indicates the rating of user u scored on item i[1]. CF aims at factorizing $\mathbf{R}$ into a user latent-feature matrix $\mathbf{P} \in \mathbb{R}^{f \times m}$ and a item latent-feature matrix $\mathbf{Q} \in \mathbb{R}^{f \times n}$, where $f \ll min\{m, n\}$ is the feature dimension, and $\hat{\mathbf{R}} = \mathbf{P}^T\mathbf{Q}$ is expected to recovery the observed ratings as well as predict the unobserved ones. In this way, both users and items are mapped into a joint a low-dimensional latent space where the user-item similarity (or preference) is estimated by vector inner product. Formally, suppose $\mathbf{p}_u \in \mathbb{R}^f$ (the u-th column of $\mathbf{P}$) and $\mathbf{q}_i \in \mathbb{R}^f$ (the i-th column of $\mathbf{Q}$) are the user-specific and item-specific feature vectors, the rating of user u for item i is approximated by $\hat{r}_{ui} = \mathbf{p}_u^T\mathbf{q}_i$. A typical cost function of CF can be defined as

$$\underset{\mathbf{P},\mathbf{Q}}{\arg\min} \sum_{(u,i)\in\Omega} (r_{ui} - \mathbf{p}_u^T\mathbf{q}_i)^2 + \lambda(\|\mathbf{P}\|_F^2 + \|\mathbf{Q}\|_F^2) \tag{1}$$

where Ω is a set of the index of observed entries, and $\lambda > 0$ is a free parameter. The first term of Eq. (1) is a fitting term that ensures the learned $\hat{\mathbf{r}}_{ui}$ to be consistent with the observed ratings, and the second term is the regularizer that is to alleviate model overfitting. In general, Eq. (1) can be solved by stochastic gradient decent (SGD) or alternating least squares (ALS) [4].

After we obtained the optimized user and item feature vectors, recommendation is then reduced to a similarity search problem. Concretely, given a 'quer' user $\mathbf{p}_u$, we recommend items by ranking the predicted ratings $\mathbf{Q}^T\mathbf{p}_u \in \mathbb{R}^n$. However, when n is large, such similarity search is apparently an efficiency bottleneck for practical recommender systems. Towards this end, in the next subsection we will study how to conduct similarity search in a hamming space efficiently.

[1] Without loss of generality, we rescale all ratings in the interval $[0, 1]$.

2.2 Problem Formulation

Our BCFE approach is devised based on an intuition that a 'good' CF-hasher should preserve the user-item, user-user and item-item similarities in the Hamming space simultaneously, in order to maintain the original data geometry in the continuous vector space as much as possible. Denote $\mathbf{B} = [\mathbf{b}_1 \cdots \mathbf{b}_m] \in \{\pm 1\}^{f \times m}$ and $\mathbf{D} = [\mathbf{d}_1 \cdots \mathbf{d}_n] \in \{\pm 1\}^{f \times n}$ respectively as the f-length user and item binary codes, the problem of our BCFE is formulated as

$$\arg\min_{\mathbf{B},\mathbf{D}} \mathcal{F} = \mathcal{L} + \mathcal{S} + \mathcal{R} \tag{2}$$

where $\mathcal{L}$, $\mathcal{S}$ and $\mathcal{R}$ denote the loss, smoothness and regularization terms, respectively.

Loss term is defined as a squared loss on observed ratings

$$\mathcal{L}(\mathbf{b}_u, \mathbf{d}_i) = \sum_{(u,i)\in\Omega} (r_{ui} - sim_H(\mathbf{b}_u, \mathbf{d}_i))^2 \tag{3}$$

where $sim_H(\mathbf{b}_u, \mathbf{d}_i) = \frac{1}{2} + \frac{1}{2f}\mathbf{b}_u^T \mathbf{d}_i$ denotes the Hamming similarity between $\mathbf{b}_u$ and $\mathbf{d}_i$ defined by Zhou and Zha [18].

The smoothness term is defined on two kNN graphs

$$\begin{aligned}\mathcal{S}(\mathbf{b}_u, \mathbf{d}_i) = &\sum_u \sum_{v\in\mathcal{N}_u} W_{uv}^{\mathcal{U}} \|\mathbf{b}_u - \mathbf{b}_v\|^2 \\ &+ \sum_i \sum_{j\in\mathcal{N}_i} W_{ij}^{\mathcal{I}} \|\mathbf{d}_i - \mathbf{d}_j\|^2\end{aligned} \tag{4}$$

where $W_{uv}^{\mathcal{U}}$ (or $W_{ij}^{\mathcal{I}}$) is the similarity between user u and v (or item i and j), and $\mathcal{N}_u$ (or $\mathcal{N}_i$) denotes the set of nearest neighbors of the user u (or item i), both of which are measured or determined in the original continuous space.

The regularization term is defined as

$$\mathcal{R}(\mathbf{B}, \mathbf{D}) = \|\mathbf{B1}\|^2 + \|\mathbf{D1}\|^2 \tag{5}$$

where $\mathbf{1} = [1 \cdots 1]^T$. The effect of Eq. (5) is to make the binary codes be balanced, i.e., each bit of the binary codes has equal chance to be 1 or -1, which is different from the L2 regularization used in Eq. (1).

It is worth noting that a process of nearest neighbor search is required in Eq. (4), which might be very time-consuming when the user/item space is large. Inspired by the idea of anchor approximation used in the large scale machine learning [5,7], we hope to find a few anchors for users/items, and each anchor approximately represents a group of similar users/items. For a user/item, we only need to take its anchor into consideration, rather than all of its nearest neighbors. In details, we apply K-means algorithm to $\{\mathbf{p}_u\}_{u=1}^m$ and $\{\mathbf{q}_i\}_{i=1}^n$ which can be deemed as the low-dimensional and compact representations of users and items in comparison to the high-dimensional and sparse ones of original UI matrix. In other words, we actually adopt a subspace clustering solution to group users and items, which is benefit to yielding high-quality clusters [11]. After we obtain a few user/item clusters, the centroid of each cluster could be regarded as the anchor of the users/items within a same cluster, because the centroid is a natural approximate representation of the users/items belonging to a same cluster. Considering this, we redefine smoothness term as

$$\mathcal{S}(\mathbf{b}_u, \mathbf{d}_i) = \sum_u \|\mathbf{b}_u - \mathbf{c}_u^p\|^2 + \sum_i \|\mathbf{d}_i - \mathbf{c}_i^q\|^2 \tag{6}$$

where $\mathbf{c}_u^p$ (or $\mathbf{c}_i^q$) is the centroid of the cluster which includes user u (or item i). Given a data collection with n instances. Searching k_1 nearest neighbors for all instances is with the complexity of $\mathcal{O}(k_1 n^2)$. In contrast, clustering all instances into k_2 groups is with the complexity of $\mathcal{O}(k_2 tn)$, where t is the iteration runs needed for K-means algorithm convergence. In general, k_1, k_2 and t are much smaller than n, so the complexity of kNN search and K-means can be approximated by $\mathcal{O}(n^2)$ and $\mathcal{O}(n)$ respectively. In other words, we successfully reduce the complexity of smoothness term from square to linear.

In summary, we simplify the original BCFE in Eq. (2) as

$$\begin{aligned}\arg\min_{\mathbf{B},\mathbf{D}} \mathcal{F} = & \sum_{(u,i)\in\Omega} (r_{ui} - \frac{1}{2} - \frac{1}{2f}\mathbf{b}_u^T\mathbf{d}_i)^2 \\ & + \alpha \sum_u \|\mathbf{b}_u - \mathbf{c}_u^p\|^2 + \beta \sum_i \|\mathbf{d}_i - \mathbf{c}_i^q\|^2 \\ & + \lambda(\|\mathbf{B1}\|^2 + \|\mathbf{D1}\|^2)\end{aligned} \tag{7}$$

where $\alpha > 0$, $\beta > 0$ and $\lambda > 0$ are three tuning parameters. The first term is to model the user-item affinity (users' preference), and the second and third terms are respectively to preserve the user-user and item-item affinities. In essence, the three terms carry on the spirits of the matrix factorization, user-based and item-based methods, respectively. From another angle, our approach is an ensemble of the three popularly used CF techniques. Next, we will introduce an efficient solution for the optimization problem in Eq. (7).

2.3 Solution

Most notably, the BCFE problem in Eq. (7) is defined in the hamming space, which makes it difficult to optimize in general. A widely used approach is to relax the optimization problem by discarding the discrete constraints and then rounding off or rotating the obtained continues solutions to binary codes, so often called 'two-stage' approach. Differently, inspired by [10,16], we hope to integrate the quantization into the optimization process to get the binary codes bit-by-bit, aiming to diminish the accumulated quantization deviations originating from traditional 'two-stage' approach.

To facilitate optimization, we relax the solution space $\{\pm1\}^f$ to a continuous interval $[-1,+1]^f$ at first. Then, different from previous 'two-stage' methods, we

Algorithm 1. The DBGD Algorithm

Initialization : $t = 0, \gamma_t = 0.01, \mathbf{b}_u, \mathbf{d}_i \in \mathbb{R}^{f \times m}$ by Eq. (1)
while $t \leq T$ **do**
  repeat
    for $k = 1$ to f **do**
      Update $b_{uk}^{(t+1)} = b_{uk}^{(t)} - \gamma_t \frac{\partial \mathcal{F}}{\partial b_{uk}^{(t)}}$;
      $b_{uk} = sgn(b_{uk}^{(t+1)})$;
      Update $d_{ik}^{(t+1)} = d_{ik}^{(t)} - \gamma_t \frac{\partial \mathcal{F}}{\partial d_{ik}^{(t)}}$;
      $d_{ik} = sgn(d_{ik}^{(t+1)})$;
    end for
  until There is no more change for each bit of $\mathbf{b}_u$ and $\mathbf{d}_i$
  if $\mathcal{F}(\mathbf{b}_u^{(t+1)}, \mathbf{d}_i^{(t+1)}) < \mathcal{F}(\mathbf{b}_u^{(t)}, \mathbf{d}_i^{(t)})$ **then**
    $\gamma_{t+1} = 2\gamma_t$;
  else if $\mathbf{b}_u^{(t+1)} = \mathbf{b}_u^{(t)}$, $\mathbf{d}_i^{(t+1)} = \mathbf{d}_i^{(t)}$ **then**
    $\gamma_{t+1} = \gamma_t/2$;
  end if
  $t = t + 1$;
end while

merge the binary quantization into a dimension-wise gradient descend process, which optimizes the objective variable dimension by dimension. After gaining a one-dimensional result, we directly use $sgn(\cdot)$ function to get a binary bit of objective variable. And in the next iteration, for a binary code, we still use gradient descend to update it, which could make the difference between real and binary values as small as possible. In other words, it is an interaction process between real and binary values, so the quantization loss could be decreased to the most extent. Such processing is similar to discrete optimization in form, so we term it as the Discretization-like Bit-wise Gradient Descend (DBGD) algorithm. In essence, DBGD is a coordinate descend style solution, and thus it can converges very fast.

Denote b_{uk} (d_{ik}) as the k-th bit of $\mathbf{b}_u$ ($\mathbf{d}_i$) and $\mathbf{b}_{u\bar{k}}$ ($\mathbf{d}_{i\bar{k}}$) as the rest codes excluding b_{uk} (d_{ik}). After relaxing the problem, we use DBGD method to update b_{uk} (d_{ik}) while fixing $\mathbf{b}_{u\bar{k}}$ ($\mathbf{d}_{i\bar{k}}$). The partial derivatives of Eq. (7) with respect to b_{uk} and d_{ik} can be expressed as follows:

$$\frac{\partial \mathcal{F}}{\partial b_{uk}} = -\frac{1}{f}\sum_i (r_{ui} - \frac{1}{2} - \frac{1}{2f}\mathbf{b}_u{}^T\mathbf{d}_i)d_{ik} + 2\alpha(b_{uk} - c_{uk}^p) + 2\lambda\sum_{u'} b_{u'k} \tag{8}$$

$$\frac{\partial \mathcal{F}}{\partial d_{ik}} = -\frac{1}{f}\sum_i (r_{ui} - \frac{1}{2} - \frac{1}{2f}\mathbf{b}_u{}^T\mathbf{d}_i)b_{uk} + 2\beta(d_{ik} - c_{ik}^q) + 2\lambda\sum_{i'} d_{i'k} \tag{9}$$

We summarize DBGD in Algorithm 1, where $\lambda_t > 0$ is a learning rate used in the t-th iteration, and T iterations in total. Note that we initialize $\mathbf{b}_u$ and $\mathbf{d}_i$ by solving the regular CF problem in Eq. (1), in order to speed up the algorithm convergence.

3 Experimental Analysis

In this section, we first introduce some necessary preparations for experiments, and then present the experimental results of our approach compared with several other state-of-the-art recommendation methods.

3.1 Experimental Setup

We utilize three real word datasets to evaluate the performance of our proposed methods. Table 1 gives the statistics of these datasets.

Table 1. Statistics of datasets

Datasets	users\items\ratings	Density
MovieLens-100k	943\1682\100000	6.30%
MovieLens-1M	6040\3952\1000209	2.81%
Douban	2964\39695\894888	0.76%

The ratings of all datasets are integers ranging from 1(bad) to 5(good). For all datasets, we select 80% of the whole ratings for training and 20% for testing, on which α, β, λ in Eq. (2) are tuned. We generate 5 splits of datasets randomly and report the averaged performance with all parameters are tuned. Moreover, we exclude all ratings in training stage and use only testing data to calculate NDCG@10.

Our goal is to evaluate the preference accurate preserved ability of the gained binary representations. Recently, there has emerged a lot of studies [12,15] which consider that recommendation problem is better treated as a learning to rank problem. Because of that, we choose NDCG (Normalized Discounted Cumulative Gain) [3] as our evaluation metric, which has been widely used to evaluate the quality of rankings. We use NDCG@10 as an evaluation in our experiments to confirm the recommendation accuracy.

Hamming ranking and hashtable lookup are two search protocols that focus on different aspects of hashing codes. Compared with hashtable lookup, hamming ranking can provide a better measurement of the learned hamming space because it linearly scans the whole data. Therefore, in our experiments, we adopt hamming ranking as our search protocol. Hamming ranking ranks items according to their hamming similarities to the target user. Although the search complexity is linear, hamming similarities can be calculated by fast bit operations. We use code length within $\{10, 15, 20, 25, 30, 35\}$.

We compare the proposed BCFE approach with several state-of-the-art methods enumerated as follows.

- **BCCF** [18]**:** This method is a "two-stage" Binary Code learning method for CF. First, it imposes a balanced code regularization; then, it applies a binary quantization to the real-valued representation.

- **PPH** [17]**:** This is also a "two-stage" learning method. At the relaxation stage, it adopts a constant feature norm constraint to obtain the maximum ratings. At the quantization stage, it quantizes the latent representations into (b-2)-bit phase codes and 2-bit magnitude codes, which can reduce the quantization loss to some degree.
- **DCF** [16]**:** This method can directly learn user-item binary codes via discrete optimization.
- **RHPLSHCF** [1]**:** LSH is a classic representation for data-independent methods. This is a LSH method based on random hyperplane projection. We simply use it on the original UI rating matrix to get the binary codes.

Moreover, to verify the usefulness of our DBGD learning algorithm, a variant of BCFE, termed as BCFE-GD, is also included in the comparison. BCFE-GD is almost the same with BCFE, except for the former employs regular GD optimization and median binary quantization. For convenience, we treat median quantization as all the compared "two-stage" methods' quantization method.

Because we use the regular MF's result to select anchor representations, for convenience, instead of random initialization, we also use MF' results as our BCFE's initialization. The parameters are turned via 5-fold cross validation and grid search technique. We set the parameters $\alpha = 0.3$, $\beta = 0.3$, $\lambda = 0.02$ for the three datasets. The suitable user and item cluster centroids are (25,50), (46,62), (35,100) for MovieLens-100k, MovieLens-1M and Douban separately.

3.2 Result Analysis

At first, we compare the performance of our BCFE approach with several state-of-the-art methods. The corresponding quantitative results are shown in Fig. 1. From experimental results, some interesting observations are revealed. First, all data-dependent CF hashing methods outperform the data-independent CF hashing method RHPLSHCF. This observation is consistent with the result observed from the traditional hash experiments conducted in information retrieval. Second, the performance of PPH and DCF are not stable to all the datasets, especially on MovieLens-1M and Douban. One possible reason is that both of them only pay attention on the user-item similarity, which may cause their methods are sensitive to the datasets. Also, the binary codes produced by PPH are imbalanced, which aggravates the instability of algorithm. In contrast, BCFE has stable performance on all three datasets because it takes user-item, user-user and item-item similarities into consideration simultaneously. Third, BCFE considerably outperforms all the state-of-the-arts and even better than DCF which directly learns the binary codes without relaxation. This is due to that BCFE utilizes more information from original space, and thus it produces high quality binary codes. It is worth noting that BCFE achieves better performance by using only 10 bits and NDCG@10 rises steadily when the code length becomes larger. This suggests that BCFE can reduce a huge amount of memory and time cost compared with other methods.

Furthermore, in order to verify whether the DBGD algorithm is benefit or not, we compare BCFE with its variant BCFE-GD. Due to the lack of space, we

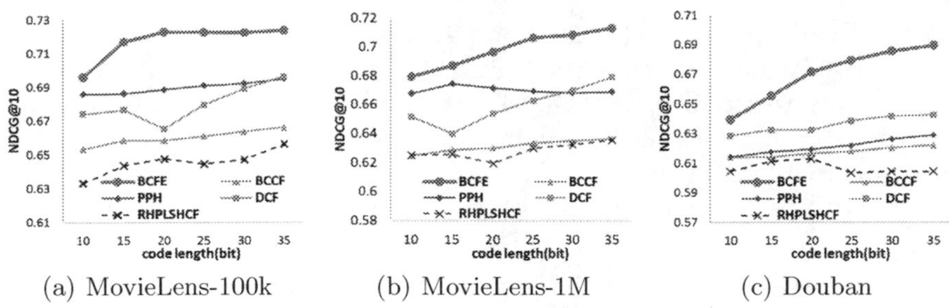

(a) MovieLens-100k (b) MovieLens-1M (c) Douban

Fig. 1. The performance of BCFE on MovieLens-100k, MovieLens-1M and Douban datasets compared with several existing methods.

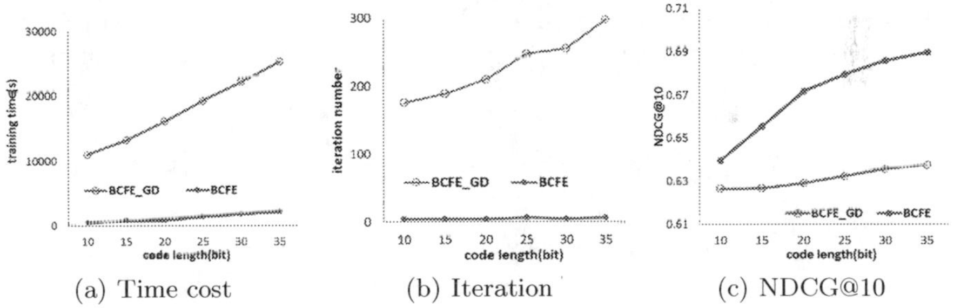

(a) Time cost (b) Iteration (c) NDCG@10

Fig. 2. Time cost, iterations and recommendation performance of BCFE-GD and BCFE on MovieLens-100k.

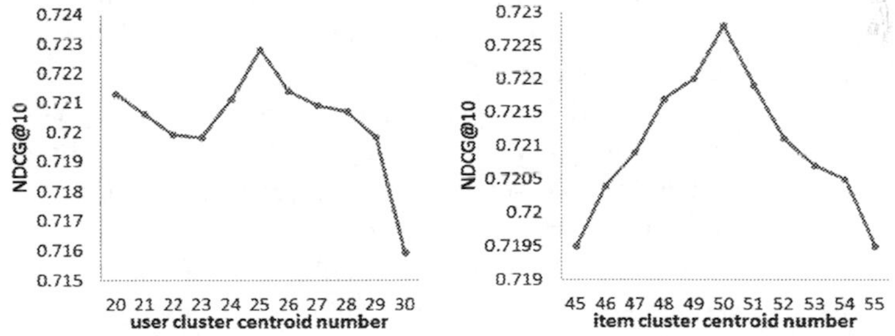

Fig. 3. Recommendation performance of BCFE with respect to the user cluster centroid number and item cluster centroid number on MovieLens-100k.

only show the experimental results on MovieLens-100k. As shown in Fig. 2(a) and (b), we can observe that the training time cost and iteration numbers of BCFE is much less than BCFE-GD. BCFE-GD uses GD to get the optimal whole relaxed codes, which makes the training process is time-consuming and slow to converge. DBGD learning algorithm accelerates the convergency of training that is due to the integration of binary quantization stage. The procedure of BCFE usually converges with less than 10 iterations. With the accurate solution for each bit, the whole optimization is very efficient and thus can easily scale to massive data. As shown in Fig. 2(c), we present the performance measured by NDCG@10 under different optimization methods. We can found that BCFE significantly outperforms BCFE-GD. The reason is that BCFE aims at getting the optimal bit that could make each bit carry more information as much as possible, while BCFE-GD gets the optimal whole relaxed representation and needs a quantization process after learning stage resulting in cause more quantization loss.

At last, we investigate the impact of the numbers of user cluster centroid and item cluster centroid for the proposed method. We report the performance of BCFE measured by NDCG@10 with respect to different numbers of user cluster centroid and item cluster centroid in Fig. 3. From Fig. 1, we can see that the performance measured by NDCG@10 first increases and then decreases in most cases, which indicates that a good number of user/item cluster centroid can enhance the learning process and thus improves the accuracy of learnt binary codes.

4 Related Work

This paper mainly concentrates on CF hashing, so we only review recent advanced hashing-based recommendation approaches. CF hashing aims at improving the efficiency of recommender system. The efficiency of recommendation actually consists of two dimensions, i.e. the efficiency of preference modeling and the efficiency of preference prediction. The former has been extensively studied, among which parallel computing is most popular. CF hashing focuses on the efficiency of preference prediction, which attracts much less attention, although it is as important as modeling.

As a pioneer work, CF-Budget [2] applied LSH to generate hash codes of Google news users based on an item-sharing similarity. Yet it mainly focused on reducing storage cost rather than discussing recommendation speedup. Zhou and Zha [18] applied Iterative Quantization for generating binary code from rotated continuous user and item representation, and achieved the amazing 110 times recommendation speedup. Zhang et al. [17] argued that inner product is not a proper similarity for hashing. Instead, they proposed to regularize the user and item representations to compute their cosine similarities, and then quantized them by respectively thresholding their magnitudes and phases. The aforementioned CF hashing methods obtained the hash codes for users and items through two independent steps, i.e., relaxed user-item feature learning and binary quantization. To avoid the quantization error, Zhang et al. [16] directly learned binary codes for users and items, which could yield more high-quality binary codes.

5 Conclusions

In this paper, we have proposed a Binary Collaborative Filtering Ensemble (BCFE) approach for making recommendations efficiently. In sharp contrast to existing CF hashing methods which only pay attention on user-item affinity in a Hamming space, besides this, our BCFE approach also takes user-user and item-item affinities into consideration. Moreover, in order to avoid a time-consuming KNN search, we also develop an anchor approximate mechanism to accelerate the BCFE training. For the better accuracy and fast convergency, we propose Discretization-like Bit-wise Gradient Descend (DBGD) algorithm which could make each bit of the binary codes optimal and accelerate the iteration. Through extensive experiments, we demonstrate that our BCFE can achieve better performance than several state-of-the-arts and it has better convergency and stability meanwhile.

To our best knowledge, this work is one of only a few pioneering studies on learning to hash solution to CF ensemble. As moving forward, we are going to study more sophisticated solutions to find better anchor representation as well as extend our BCFE solution to the problem of recommendation with evolving social networks [13].

Acknowledgments. The authors would like to thank the anonymous reviewers for their constructive suggestions. This work was supported in part by the 'Natural Science Foundation of China' #61671048 and the 'Research Foundation for Talents of Beijing Jiaotong University' #2015RC008.

References

1. Charikar, M.S.: Similarity estimation techniques from rounding algorithms. In: Proceedings of ACM Symposium on Theory of Computing, pp. 380–388 (2002)
2. Karatzoglou, A., Smola, A.J., Weimer, M.: Collaborative filtering on a budget. In: AISTAT, pp. 389–396 (2011)
3. Keklinen, J.: Binary and graded relevance in IR evaluations comparison of the effects on ranking of IR systems. Inf. Process. Manag. **41**(5), 1019–1033 (2005)
4. Koren, Y., Bell, R., Volinsky, C.: Matrix factorization techniques for recommender systems. Computer **42**(8), 30–37 (2009)
5. Liu, L., Shao, L., Shen, F., Yu, M.: Discretely coding semantic rank orders for supervised image hashing. In: CVPR, pp. 5140–5149 (2017)
6. Liu, X., He, J., Deng, C., Lang, B.: Collaborative hashing. In: CVPR, pp. 2147–2154 (2014)
7. Qin, J., et al.: Binary coding for partial action analysis with limited observation ratios. In: CVPR, pp. 6728–6737 (2017)
8. Resnick, P., Iacovou, N., Suchak, M., Bergstrom, P., Riedl, J.: GroupLens: an open architecture for collaborative filtering of netnews. In: ACM Conference on Computer Supported Cooperative Work, pp. 175–186 (1994)
9. Sarwar, B., Karypis, G., Konstan, J., Riedl, J.: Item-based collaborative filtering recommendation algorithms. In: International Conference on World Wide Web, pp. 285–295 (2001)
10. Shen, F., Shen, C., Liu, W., Shen, H.T.: Supervised discrete hashing. In: CVPR, pp. 37–45 (2015)
11. Vidal, R.: Subspace clustering. IEEE Sig. Process. Mag. **28**(2), 52–68 (2011)
12. Volkovs, M., Zemel, R.S.: Collaborative ranking with 17 parameters. In: NIPS (2012)

13. Wang, H., et al.: Incremental subgraph feature selection for graph classification. IEEE Trans. Knowl. Data Eng. **29**(1), 128–142 (2017)
14. Wang, J., Liu, W., Kumar, S., Chang, S.: Learning to hash for indexing big dataa survey. Proc. IEEE **104**(1), 34–57 (2015)
15. Weimer, M., Karatzoglou, A.: Maximum margin matrix factorization for collaborative ranking. In: NIPS, pp. 1–8 (2007)
16. Zhang, H., Shen, F., Liu, W., He, X., Luan, H., Chua, T.S.: Discrete collaborative filtering. In: SIGIR, pp. 325–334 (2016)
17. Zhang, Z., Wang, Q., Ruan, L., Si, L.: Preference preserving hashing for efficient recommendation. In: SIGIR, pp. 183–192 (2014)
18. Zhou, K., Zha, H.: Learning binary codes for collaborative filtering. In: KDD, pp. 498–506 (2012)

Social Collaborative Filtering Ensemble

Honglei Zhang[1], Gangdu Liu[2], and Jun Wu[1(✉)]

[1] School of Computer and Information Technology, Beijing Jiaotong University, Beijing 100044, China
{16120453,wuj}@bjtu.edu.cn

[2] School of Civil and Transportation Engineering, Beijing University of Civil Engineering and Architecture, Beijing 100044, China
15398518@bjtu.edu.cn

Abstract. Collaborative filtering (CF) technique plays an important role in generating personalized recommendations, but its performance is challenged by the problems of data sparsity and cold start. Besides, different CF methods have their own advantages, so another tough issue is how to exploit the complementary properties of different methods. In this paper, we propose a general framework to ensemble three popularly used CF methods, termed as TriCF, aiming to further elevate recommendation accuracy. In order to alleviate the data sparsity problem, we incorporate social information into TriCF by graph embedding, denoted as SoTriCF. In particular, a mapping from social domain to rating domain is built by a neural network model, which can enhance the cold-start users' latent representation learned from rating data. Extensive experiments on three real-world datasets show that the proposed approaches achieve significant improvements over state-of-the-art methods.

Keywords: Recommender systems · Collaborative filtering
Social network · Latent representation

1 Introduction

Recommender systems, which are capable of reaching the equilibrium between information producers and consumers, are now ubiquitous online. Collaborative filtering (CF) is the most successful and widely used recommendation technique, and numerous CF algorithms emerged in last two decades. Roughly speaking, such algorithms can be grouped into two categories, neighborhood methods and latent factor models. Neighborhood-based methods focus on finding the nearest neighbors of the active user [21] or target item [23], and make prediction based on the ratings from these neighbors. Latent factor models [12] primarily center on embedding both users and items into a common latent subspace, and then

This work was performed when the second author was a joint-training student of Beijing University of Civil Engineering and Architecture (BUCEA) and Beijing Jiaotong University (BJTU) from 2015 to 2018.

X. Geng and B.-H. Kang (Eds.): PRICAI 2018, LNAI 11012, pp. 1005–1017, 2018.
https://doi.org/10.1007/978-3-319-97304-3_77

the prediction can be estimated by inner products between user and item latent factors. As demonstrated by [2], however, none of them is always dominant in various recommendation scenarios, and the performance of a CF algorithm is related to various factors, such as the number of users/items, and the density level of the user-item rating matrix. Hence, for further improve recommender systems, we need to integrate the merits of different CF approaches.

It is well-known that CF methods have to confront the problems of data sparsity and cold start. In recent years, in addition to the rating data, a large number of recommendation scenarios have emerged in which various additional information sources are available [24], e.g. the social relationships among users [25]. A few studies have demonstrated that incorporating such social information into CF algorithms is helpful to elevate the recommendation accuracy and to alleviate the problems of data sparsity and cold start [8,10,15–17]. However, such improvement is limited, because existing social recommender systems ignore a phenomenon that the social data is also very sparse, even though it is complementary to the rating data. In other words, dealing with the social sparsity is as important as the rating sparsity to establish a high-performance social recommender system.

In this paper, we intend to solve the problems mentioned above, by proposing the SoTriCF approach that integrates the merits of three popularly used CF methods to improve the recommendation accuracy. Moreover, SoTriCF encodes the social connections among users into low-dimensional and compact vectors, and takes that as side-information to enhance the CF ensembling, such that the sparsity of rating data and social data are jointly addressed. Specifically, we design a method to latent representation mapping based on a neural network model, which can enhance the latent representation of cold-start users learned from rating data using their social latent representations. The experimental analysis on three datasets shows that our SoTriCF approach outperforms other state-of-the-art methods.

The rest of this paper is organized as follows. Section 2 reviews the related work. Section 3 presents the proposed SoTriCF approach. Section 4 reports on the experiments. Finally, Sect. 5 concludes this paper and raises several problems for future works.

2 Related Work

In this section, we briefly classify related work into three dimensions, i.e. collaborative filtering, social recommendation, and graph embedding.

Collaborative filtering (CF) is a family of algorithms widely used in recommendation systems. Neighborhood-based methods and latent factor models, can be differentiated depending on how the rating data are processed. Neighborhood-based methods use a certain similarity measure to select users (or items) that are similar to the active user (or the target item). Then, the prediction is calculated from the ratings of these neighbors. It can be further divided into user-based and item-based on the basis of whether the process of seeking neighbors is focused on similar users [21] or items [23]. Latent factor models aim at factorizing the user-item rating matrix, and use the factorized user-specific and item-specific matrices to make further missing data prediction [11,12,18,19]. Different CF methods have their own advantages and are applicable to different scenarios, so it is natural to ensemble them for better prediction performance. Koren [11] presented an integrated model that combines latent factor model and item-based CF, however, which is very memory-consuming. In this paper, we try to ensemble three widely-used CF methods, i.e. the user-based CF, item-based CF, and matrix factorization (MF), through a unified formulation in a more efficient way.

Due to the potential value of social relations in recommender systems, social recommendation has attracted increasing attention in recent years. Existing social recommendation methods can be roughly categorized into three types [25], i.e., Regularization methods, Ensemble methods and Co-factorization methods. Regularization methods focus on a users's preference should be similar to that of their social friends [10,17]. The basic idea of Ensemble methods is that the predicted rating for a given user is a combination of ratings from the user and their social network [15]. In Co-factorization methods, the underlying assumption is that the user should share the same user preference in the rating space and the social space [8]. However, similar to the rating data, the social data is also very sparse, which is one of challenges we tackle in this paper.

Furthermore, our approach is also related to graph embedding technique, which embeds complex social relations into a low-dimensional vector space. Such low-dimensional representation is much more denser than the traditional graph representation, so graph embedding is a potential solution to alleviating the sparsity of social network. Existing graph embedding methods can be broadly divided into three types, factorization based methods [3,22], random walk based methods [5,20] and deep learning based methods [26]. For comprehensive review of graph embedding, please refer to [4]. Recently, Zhang et al. [30] first extracted a implicit social network based on the affinity calculated from the user-item rating matrix, and then incorporated such social information into matrix factorization by graph embedding. However, an early empirical study [14] had demonstrated that the explicit social connection is more effective than the implicit social relationship inferred from rating data to enhance the recommendation accuracy. Hence the improvement made by [30] is limited. Differently, we try to exploit the explicit social connections by graph embedding to enhance the CF ensembling, aiming at addressing the sparsity of rating data and social data jointly.

3 The Proposed SoTriCF Approach

In this section, we will elaborate our SoTriCF approach whose framework is shown in Fig. 1. It consists of three main modules. The first module is a latent factor model that incorporates the merits of three popularly-used CF methods into a unified formulation, and is learned based on both rating data and social data. The second module is a graph embedding model which embeds social network into a low-dimensional vector space, in order to alleviate the sparsity

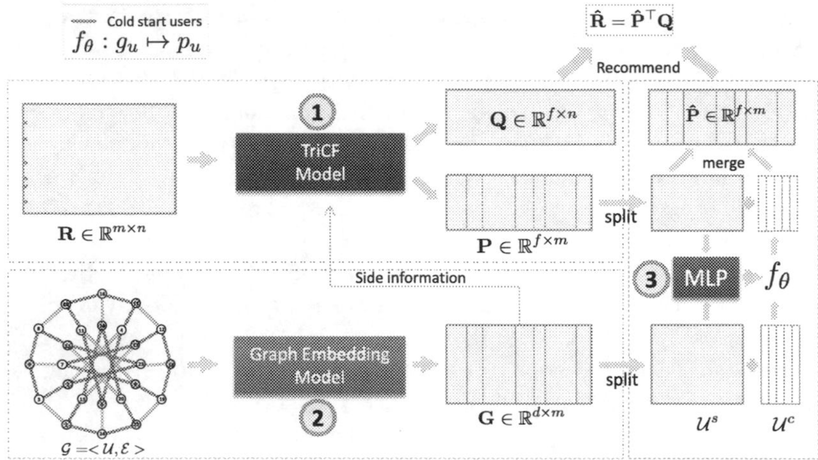

Fig. 1. Framework of our SoTriCF approach.

of social data. The last one is a Multi-Layer Perceptron (MLP) model that is to build a nonlinear mapping from the users social latent representation to rating latent representation (detailed in Sect. 3.4). Using such mapping, the cold-start users identified from the rating data can be enhanced by their social information.

3.1 Preliminaries

Let $\mathcal{U} = \{u_1, \cdots, u_m\}$ be a set with m users, and $\mathcal{I} = \{i_1, \cdots, i_n\}$ denote a set with n items. All interactions associating $\mathcal{U}$ with $\mathcal{I}$ can be represented by a user-item rating matrix $\mathbf{R} \in \{1, 2, 3, 4, 5\}^{m \times n}$ whose element r_{ui} indicates the rating of user u scored on item i. Furthermore, we define $\mathcal{I}_u \in \mathcal{I}$ be the set of items rated by a certain user u, and $\mathcal{U}_i \in \mathcal{U}$ denotes the set of users who have rated a certain item i. We also define $\mathcal{G} = <\mathcal{U}, \mathcal{E}>$ as the social network among users, where $\mathcal{E} = \{e_{uv}\}$ is a set of edge recording the friend relationship between users, and $\mathcal{F}_u \in \mathcal{U}$ denotes the set of friends of user u.

An efficient and effective solution to recommender systems is the MF models that factorize the user-item rating matrix, and utilize the factorized user and item vectors to predict missing data. Let $\mathbf{p}_u$ be the user-specific latent vector and $\mathbf{q}_i$ be the item-specific latent vector. For better modeling the user-item interaction, we take the biases of users and items into consideration, where μ denotes the overall average rating, b_u and b_i indicate the deviations of user u and item i, respectively. A typical cost function can be defined as

$$\min_{\mathbf{p}_u, \mathbf{q}_i, b_u, b_i} \frac{1}{2} \sum\nolimits_{(u,i) \in \Omega} [\, (r_{ui} - \mu - b_u - b_i - \mathbf{p}_u^T \mathbf{q}_i)^2 + \gamma(\|\mathbf{p}_u\|^2 + \|\mathbf{q}_i\|^2 + b_u^2 + b_i^2) \,] \tag{1}$$

where Ω is a set of the index of observed entries, and $\gamma > 0$ is a free parameter. The first term of Eq. (1) is a fitting term that ensures the learned $\hat{\mathbf{r}}_{ui}$ to be consistent with the observed ratings, and the second term is the regularizer that is to alleviate model overfitting.

Another promising solution is neighborhood-based methods which use similarity measures to identify a neighborhood of the active user (or target item), and then calculate the prediction using the ratings from these neighbor users (or items). For example, the user-based method is to predict the unobserved rating r_{ui} by averaging the observed ratings from the neighbors of the user u

$$\hat{r}_{ui} = \bar{r}_u + \frac{\sum_{v \in \mathcal{N}_u \wedge i \in \mathcal{I}_v} S_{uv}(r_{vi} - \bar{r}_v)}{\sum_{v \in \mathcal{N}_u} S_{uv}} \tag{2}$$

where $\mathcal{N}_u$ denotes the user u's neighbors, and S_{uv} is the similarity between user u and v, which can be calculated by Pearson Correlation Coefficient (PCC) [1]

$$S_{uv} = \frac{\sum_{i \in \mathcal{I}_u \cap \mathcal{I}_v} (r_{ui} - \bar{r}_u)(r_{vi} - \bar{r}_v)}{\sqrt{\sum_{i \in \mathcal{I}_u \cap \mathcal{I}_v} (r_{ui} - \bar{r}_u)^2} \sqrt{\sum_{i \in \mathcal{I}_u \cap \mathcal{I}_v} (r_{vi} - \bar{r}_v)^2}}. \tag{3}$$

Likewise, the item-based method is to predict the unobserved rating r_{ui} by averaging the observed ratings from the neighbors of the item i

$$\hat{r}_{ui} = \frac{\sum_{j \in \mathcal{N}_i \cap \mathcal{I}_u} S_{ij} r_{uj}}{\sum_{j \in \mathcal{N}_i \cap \mathcal{I}_u} S_{ij}} \tag{4}$$

where $\mathcal{N}_i$ denotes a set of item i's neighbors, and S_{ij} is the similarity between item i and j, which can be also calculated by PCC

$$S_{ij} = \frac{\sum_{u \in \mathcal{U}_i \cap \mathcal{U}_j} (r_{ui} - \bar{r}_u)(r_{uj} - r_u)}{\sqrt{\sum_{u \in \mathcal{U}_i \cap \mathcal{U}_j} (r_{ui} - \bar{r}_u)^2} \sqrt{\sum_{u \in \mathcal{U}_i \cap \mathcal{U}_j} (r_{uj} - \bar{r}_u)^2}}. \tag{5}$$

An empirical study demonstrates that none of CF methods is dominant in all recommendation tasks, even though MF models achieves slightly better performance in most cases. Considering this, in the next subsection, we will ensemble the three CF methods mentioned above for higher prediction accuracy.

3.2 Ensembling Three CF Methods

A 'good' CF solution should maintain the user-user affinity and the item-item affinity when it model the users' preference in a common subspace of users and items, such that the data geometry in the original space could be preserved as much as possible. Based on this intuition, we propose the TriCF method by extending the regular MF formulation Eq. (1) by adding the smoothness terms of users and items

$$\min_{\mathbf{p}_u,\mathbf{q}_i,b_u,b_i} \frac{1}{2}\sum\nolimits_{(u,i)\in\Omega} [\, (r_{ui} - \mu - b_u - b_i - \mathbf{p}_u^T\mathbf{q}_i)^2$$
$$+ \quad \alpha \sum_{v\in\mathcal{N}_u} S_{uv}\|\mathbf{p}_u - \mathbf{p}_v\|^2$$
$$+ \quad \beta \sum_{j\in\mathcal{N}_i} S_{ij}\|\mathbf{q}_i - \mathbf{q}_j\|^2$$
$$+ \quad \gamma(\|\mathbf{p}_u\|^2 + \|\mathbf{q}_i\|^2 + b_u^2 + b_i^2)\,] \tag{6}$$

where $\alpha > 0$ and $\beta > 0$. The second and third terms of Eq. (6) are user smoothness and item smoothness respectively, and S_{uv} and S_{ij} can be calculated by Eqs. (3) and (5) respectively.

It is noting that the two smoothness terms in Eq. (6) follow the spirit of the user-based method (Eq. (2)) and the item-based method (Eq. (4)). This is motivated by the assumption that if two users impose similar ratings on some items, they will have similar rating behaviors on the remaining items. Likewise, if two items are rated similarly by a portion of the users, they will still be rated similarly by the remaining users. By adding the user and item smoothness terms into the regular MF formulation, our TriCF can collaboratively exploit the merits of both latent factor models and neighborhood-based methods.

It is well-known that the performance of CF methods is often limited by the sparsity inherent in the rating data, and thus we will study the solution to incorporating social signal into TriCF formulation in the next subsection.

3.3 Exploiting Social Signal in TriCF

To exploit the social signal, we further extend the TriCF formulation by introducing a social smoothness term. As a result, we further change Eq. (6) to

$$\min_{\mathbf{p}_u,\mathbf{q}_i,b_u,b_i} \mathcal{L} = \frac{1}{2}\sum\nolimits_{(u,i)\in\Omega} \{\, (r_{ui} - \mu - b_u - b_i - \mathbf{p}_u^T\mathbf{q}_i)^2$$
$$+\alpha\left[\lambda \sum_{v\in\mathcal{N}_u} S_{uv}\|\mathbf{p}_u - \mathbf{p}_v\|^2 + (1-\lambda)\sum_{v\in\mathcal{F}_u} S_{uv}^{\mathcal{N}}\|\mathbf{p}_u - \mathbf{p}_v\|^2\right]$$
$$+\beta \sum_{j\in\mathcal{N}_i} S_{ij}\|\mathbf{q}_i - \mathbf{q}_j\|^2$$
$$+\gamma(\|\mathbf{p}_u\|^2 + \|\mathbf{q}_i\|^2 + b_u^2 + b_i^2)\, \} \tag{7}$$

where $\lambda > 0$, and $S_{uv}^{\mathcal{N}}$ is the social similarity estimated from social connections. Now we have two user smoothness terms, which are from rating data and social data respectively.

A local minimum of the objective function given by Eq. (7) can be found by performing gradient descent or statistic gradient descent in variables $\mathbf{p}_u$, $\mathbf{q}_i$, b_u and b_i,

$$\frac{\partial \mathcal{L}}{\partial \mathbf{p}_u} = \sum_{i \in I_u} e_{ui} \cdot \mathbf{q}_i + \alpha(\lambda \sum_{v \in \mathcal{N}_u} S_{uv}(\mathbf{p}_u - \mathbf{p}_v) + (1-\lambda) \sum_{v \in \mathcal{F}_u} S^{\mathcal{N}}_{uv}(\mathbf{p}_u - \mathbf{p}_v)) + \gamma \mathbf{p}_u \tag{8}$$

$$\frac{\partial \mathcal{L}}{\partial \mathbf{q}_i} = \sum_{u \in U_i} e_{ui} \cdot \mathbf{p}_u + \beta \sum_{j \in \mathcal{N}_i} S_{ij}(\mathbf{q}_i - \mathbf{q}_j) + \gamma \mathbf{q}_i \tag{9}$$

$$\frac{\partial \mathcal{L}}{\partial b_u} = \sum_{i \in I_u} e_{ui} + \gamma b_u \tag{10}$$

$$\frac{\partial \mathcal{L}}{\partial b_i} = \sum_{u \in U_i} e_{ui} + \gamma b_i \tag{11}$$

where $e_{ui} = \hat{r}_{ui} - r_{ui}$ indicates the prediction error for user u on item i.

Given the social network, we can compute $S^{\mathcal{N}}_{uv}$ based on the network structure, as done in the link prediction study [13]. However, social data is also very sparse. To this end, we advocate to use graph embedding technique, which can embed social network into a low-dimensional and compact vector space. In such space, each user node is represented by a low-dimensional vector, and thus the sparsity problem can be alleviated to some degree.

Let $\mathbf{g}_u \in \mathbb{R}^d$ and $\mathbf{g}_v \in \mathbb{R}^d$ be two latent representation learned by DeepWalk, more details of which can be found in [20]. Given $\mathbf{g}_u$ and $\mathbf{g}_v$, we can calculate $S^{\mathcal{N}}_{uv}$ by a Gaussian kernel

$$S^{\mathcal{N}}_{uv} = \exp\left(-\frac{\|\mathbf{g}_u - \mathbf{g}_v\|^2}{\sigma^2}\right) \tag{12}$$

where σ is a scale parameter that can be tuned by a local scaling technique, the effectiveness of which has been verified by spectrum clustering [29] and manifold ranking [28].

As mentioned before, the problem of cold-start users is one of challenges for CF technique, and it is desirable to improve the experience of the cold-start users who rate very few items. Hence we will study the solution to enriching cold-start users using social signal in the next subsection.

3.4 Enhancing the Latent Representation of Cold-Start Users

For any user u, we can learn two latent representations $\mathbf{p}_u \in \mathbb{R}^f$ and $\mathbf{g}_u \in \mathbb{R}^d$ from rating data and social data respectively. We refer to the rating domain as the target domain and the social domain as the source domain. Our solution to enhancing cold-start users is based on an intuition that there is a potential relation between the two domains, and we aim to build a mapping to capture this potential relation. With such mapping, we can improve the representation of a cold-start user learned from the target domain using its another representation learned from the source domain. As demonstrated by [9], any continuous mapping can be realized by a neural network with one hidden layer, which can capture the more complex relationship than linear transformation. So we apply a multi-layer perceptron (MLP) model to construct the mapping from the source domain to the target domain.

In order to guarantee its robustness to noise caused by data sparsity in rating data and social data, only the entities with sufficient data in both domains are used to learn the mapping function. As is common practice, we define users that rated less than five items as cold-start users in rating domain and users that have less than four friends as cold-start users in social domain. Let $\mathcal{U}_{cs}$ and $\mathcal{U}_{ct}$ denote the sets of cold-start users identified from the source domain and the target domain respectively. It worth noting that the users in $\mathcal{U}_{cs} \cap \mathcal{U}_{ct}$ are not useful to representation mapping, because their $\mathbf{p}_u$s and $\mathbf{g}_u$s are unreliable. Fortunately, in most datasets used for social recommendation we observed that very few users are in $\mathcal{U}_{cs} \cap \mathcal{U}_{ct}$. We define $\mathcal{U}_{train} = (\mathcal{U} \setminus \mathcal{U}_{cs}) \cap (\mathcal{U} \setminus \mathcal{U}_{ct})$ as the training user set and $\mathcal{U}_{test} = \{u | u \notin \mathcal{U}_{cs} \wedge u \in \mathcal{U}_{ct}\}$ as the testing user set. The users in $\mathcal{U}_{train}$ are not 'cold-start' in both domains and used to learn the mapping function, while the users in $\mathcal{U}_{test}$ are not 'cold-start' in the source domain yet 'cold-start' in the target domain because we only pay attention on the target domain.

Given the training user set $\{< \mathbf{g}_u, \mathbf{p}_u >, u \in \mathcal{U}_{train}\}$, we can learn a MLP model $f_\theta : \mathbb{R}^d \mapsto \mathbb{R}^f$, where $\mathbf{g}_u$ is the input representation (feature) and $\mathbf{p}_u$ is the output representation (label). Based on such mapping function, for a user $v \in \mathcal{U}_{test}$, we can take its reliable social representation $\mathbf{g}_v$ as input, and obtain its improved rating representation by $\hat{\mathbf{p}}_v = f_\theta(\mathbf{g}_v)$. At last, the recommendation on the cold-start users is made using their improved rating representations.

4 Experimental Analysis

In this section, we first introduce some necessary preparations for experiments, and then present the experimental results of our approach compared with several other state-of-the-art recommendation methods.

4.1 Experimental Setup

We employ three datasets (FilmTrust, Douban and Ciao) which are publicly available on the web to make our experiments reproducible. FilmTrust is a small-scale dataset [7]. In this dataset, 95% of users rated no more than 50 items, in which 15% of users are cold-start users. Moreover, the social data is sparse as well, and the average number of friends per user is only 1.22. Douban is a medium-scale dataset [17]. In this dataset, the number of items is far more than that of users and each user has 12.07 friends in average. Ciao is a large-scale dataset [6]. In such dataset, 90% of users rated less than 50 items, in which 8% of users are cold-start users. The social density of this dataset is only 0.04% around and the average amount of each users friends is 15.16. A more detailed statistics about these three datasets are summarized in Tables 1 and 2, in terms of rating information and social information respectively.

Table 1. Statistics of three datasets about ratings data.

Datasets	Users	Items	Ratings	Avg.Num.Ratings per user	Avg.Num.Ratings per item	Density
FilmTrust	1,508	2,071	35,497	23.54	17.14	1.136%
Douban	2,963	39,694	894,887	301.9	22.54	0.760%
Ciao	7,375	105,114	284,086	38.52	2.66	0.037%

Table 2. Statistics of three datasets about social data.

Datasets	Followers	Followees	Links	Avg.Num.Friends per User	Density
FilmTrust	609	732	1,853	1.23	0.415%
Douban	2,745	2,741	35,771	12.07	0.475%
Ciao	6,792	7,297	111,781	15.16	0.225%

We utilize two metrics to measure the prediction accuracy, root mean square error (RMSE) and mean absolute error (MAE), defined as

$$RMSE = \sqrt{\frac{\sum_{(u,i)\in\mathcal{T}}(r_{ui} - \hat{r}_{ui})^2}{|\mathcal{T}|}}, \; MAE = \frac{\sum_{(u,i)\in\mathcal{T}}|r_{ui} - \hat{r}_{ui}|}{|\mathcal{T}|}$$

where $\mathcal{T}$ denotes the testing set and $|\bullet|$ is the number of a set. The smaller RMSE and MAE values are, the better prediction performance is.

We compare the proposed TriCF and SoTriCF approaches with a number of related existing methods. The compared methods are enumerated as follows, where the first two methods are used in the traditional recommendation scenarios, and the last five methods are designed for the social recommendation tasks.

- **PMF:** A canonical latent factor model which factorizes both users and items in a common subspace [18].
- **SVD++:** A latent factor model which models the biases of users and items, and incorporates the user implicit feedback into matrix factorization formulation [11].
- **SoRec:** A matrix factorization model with social regularization [16].
- **RSTE:** An ensemble method which combines a basic matrix factorization model with a social-based neighbor model [15].
- **SocialMF:** A social model which forces on the preference of a user to be closer to the average of their social friends [10].
- **SoReg:** A social model which forces on the preference closeness of two connected users in social network controlled by similarity based on ratings data [17].
- **TrustSVD:** A extended method of SVD++, which incorporates both rating implicit feedback and social implicit feedback into formulation [8].

For all the compared methods, we adopt the parameter configuration as described in previous works or by experimental selection for the best results. The parameters are tuned via 5-fold cross validation and grid search technique, and for our approach, we set the parameters $\lambda = 0.3$ for FilmTrust and Ciao, $\lambda = 0.5$ for Douban; and $\alpha = 0.002$, $\beta = 0.001$, $\gamma = 0.05$ for the three datasets. We set $f = 10$ to learn the latent representation of users and items, and $d = 30$ to learn the node representation in graph embedding.

Table 3. Performance of our SoTriCF approaches with several existing methods.

Datasets	Filmtrust		Douban		Ciao	
Metrics	RMSE Improve	MAE Improve	RMSE Improve	MAE Improve	RMSE Improve	MAE Improve
PMF	0.87869 7.99%	0.66427 6.21%	0.78625 2.91%	0.62643 3.10%	1.02434 4.83%	0.78124 3.84%
SVD++	0.86800 6.85%	0.64954 4.09%	0.84862 10.04%	0.65794 7.74%	1.03408 5.72%	0.76056 4.15%
TriCF	**0.83321** 2.96%	**0.64779** 3.83%	**0.77969** 2.09%	**0.62257** 2.50%	**0.99524** 2.04%	**0.75676** 3.67%
SoRec	0.83923 3.66%	0.64388 3.24%	0.90601 15.74%	0.69780 13.01%	1.13637 14.21%	0.83797 13.00%
RSTE	0.84654 4.49%	0.65970 5.56%	0.81357 6.17%	0.63896 5.00%	1.00414 2.91%	0.76473 4.67%
SocialMF	0.84782 4.64%	0.65727 5.21%	0.79398 3.85%	0.62561 2.97%	0.99508 2.03%	0.74941 2.72%
SoReg	0.83114 2.72%	0.64120 2.84%	0.78006 2.14%	0.61729 1.67%	0.99506 2.03%	0.75176 3.02%
TrustSVD	0.84404 4.21%	0.65178 4.42%	0.79347 3.79%	0.62555 2.96%	1.03295 5.62%	0.75903 3.95%
SoTriCF	**0.80851**	**0.62300**	**0.76340**	**0.60701**	**0.97490**	**0.72902**

4.2 Result Analysis

At first, we compare performance of our TriCF and SoTriCF approaches with several existing methods. The corresponding quantitative results are shown in Table 3, and column 'Improve' indicates the relative improvements that our TriCF and SoTriCF achieve relative to their basic models respectively. From experimental results, the following interesting observations are revealed.

- By comparing the three CF methods for regular recommendation, our TriCF approach outperforms the two baselines PMF and SVD++, which verfies the benefit of ensembling latent factor models and neighborhood methods. It is

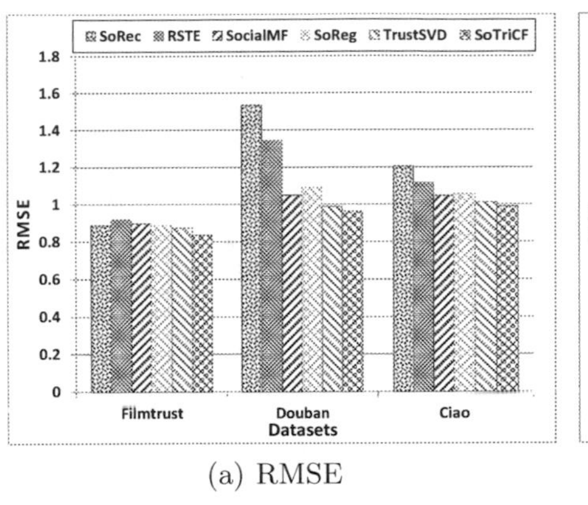

(a) RMSE

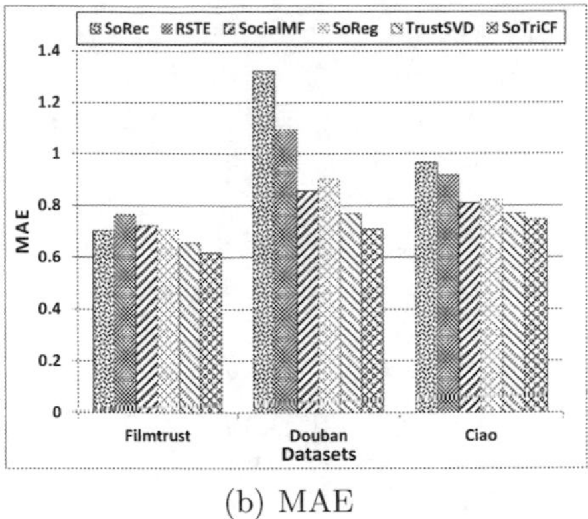

(b) MAE

Fig. 2. The performance comparisons for social recommendation on cold-start users.

worth noting that the performance of SVD++ is not as excellent as that reported in [11], because the implicit feedback signal is not available in the three datasets used in our experiments.

- In most cases, the performance of social CF methods is better than the regular CF methods. This observation reveals that the social signal is an effective compensation to the rating signal, which is consistent with previous studies [8,10,15–17].
- In comparison of the six social CF methods, our SoTriCF achieves the best performance on all datasets. The main difference between our SoTriCF approach and other five social CF methods is that SoTriCF exploits the social signal in a low-dimension embedding space of social network, while the other five methods exploit the social signal directly. It well demonstrates that adopting graph embedding is beneficial to alleviate the sparsity of original social signal. That is, the motivation of this work is empirically verified.

Furthermore, we investigate the performance of various social CF methods on cold-start users to verify whether our representation mapping solution to cold-start users is effective or not. Experimental results of RMSE and MAE for social recommendation task on cold-start users are presented in Fig. 2(a) and (b). From the results, we can observe that the RMSE and MAE values generated by our method are much smaller than those generated by other comparison methods in all datasets. This confirms that our approach can consistently generate better results than the state-of-the-art social recommendation methods in the case of cold start.

5 Conclusions

In this work, we have proposed a SoTriCF approach that ensembles three popularly used CF methods within a unified learning formulation. To well handle the sparsity inherent in both rating data and social data, we exploit the social information in CF ensemble by graph embedding. In order to alleviate the cold start problem, we also developed a solution to latent representation mapping from social domain and rating domain based on a neural network model, which can enhance the cold-start users latent representation learned from rating data using their social information. Experimental study has validated the superiority of the proposed approaches in comparison to state-of-the-art methods.

In the future, we will extend our SoTriCF approach by incorporating more side-information, in order to further improve its prediction performance. Moreover, inspired by the evolving graph mining technique [27], another extension of this work is to develop the online version of SoTriCF to take the social data stream into consideration.

Acknowledgments. The authors would like to thank the anonymous reviewers for their constructive suggestions. This work was supported in part by the 'Natural Science Foundation of China' #61671048 and the 'Research Foundation for Talents of Beijing Jiaotong University' #2015RC008.

References

1. Breese, J.S., Heckerman, D., Kadie, C.: Empirical analysis of predictive algorithms for collaborative filtering. In: UAI, pp. 43–52 (1998)
2. Cacheda, F., Carneiro, V., Fernández, D., Formoso, V.: Comparison of collaborative filtering algorithms: limitations of current techniques and proposals for scalable, high-performance recommender systems. ACM Trans. Web **5**(1), 2 (2011)
3. Cao, S., Lu, W., Xu, Q.: Grarep: learning graph representations with global structural information. In: CIKM, pp. 891–900 (2015)
4. Goyal, P., Ferrara, E.: Graph embedding techniques, applications, and performance: a survey. Knowl.-Based Syst. **151**, 78–94 (2018)
5. Grover, A., Leskovec, J.: node2vec: scalable feature learning for networks. In: SIGKDD, pp. 855–864 (2016)
6. Guo, G., Zhang, J., Thalmann, D., Yorke-Smith, N.: ETAF: an extended trust antecedents framework for trust prediction. In: ASONAM, pp. 540–547 (2014)
7. Guo, G., Zhang, J., Yorke-Smith, N.: A novel Bayesian similarity measure for recommender systems. In: IJCAI, pp. 2619–2625 (2013)
8. Guo, G., Zhang, J., Yorke-Smith, N.: TrustSVD: collaborative filtering with both the explicit and implicit influence of user trust and of item ratings. In: AAAI, pp. 123–129 (2015)
9. Hornik, K., Stinchcombe, M., White, H.: Multilayer feedforward networks are universal approximators. Neural Netw. **2**(5), 359–366 (1989)
10. Jamali, M., Ester, M.: A matrix factorization technique with trust propagation for recommendation in social networks. In: RecSys, pp. 135–142 (2010)
11. Koren, Y.: Factorization meets the neighborhood: a multifaceted collaborative filtering model. In: SIGKDD, pp. 426–434 (2008)
12. Koren, Y., Bell, R., Volinsky, C.: Matrix factorization techniques for recommender systems. Computer **42**(8), 30–37 (2009)
13. Lü, L., Zhou, T.: Link prediction in complex networks: a survey. Phys. A Stat. Mech. Appl. **390**(6), 1150–1170 (2011)

14. Ma, H.: An experimental study on implicit social recommendation. In: SIGIR, pp. 73–82 (2013)
15. Ma, H., King, I., Lyu, M.R.: Learning to recommend with social trust ensemble. In: SIGIR, pp. 203–210 (2009)
16. Ma, H., Yang, H., Lyu, M.R., King, I.: SoRec: social recommendation using probabilistic matrix factorization. In: CIKM, pp. 931–940 (2008)
17. Ma, H., Zhou, D., Liu, C., Lyu, M.R., King, I.: Recommender systems with social regularization. In: WSDM, pp. 287–296 (2011)
18. Mnih, A., Salakhutdinov, R.R.: Probabilistic matrix factorization. In: NIPS, pp. 1257–1264 (2008)
19. Paterek, A.: Improving regularized singular value decomposition for collaborative filtering. In: SIGKDD, vol. 2007, pp. 5–8 (2007)
20. Perozzi, B., Al-Rfou, R., Skiena, S.: Deepwalk: online learning of social representations. In: SIGKDD, pp. 701–710 (2014)
21. Resnick, P., Iacovou, N., Suchak, M., Bergstrom, P., Riedl, J.: GroupLens: an open architecture for collaborative filtering of netnews. In: CSCW, pp. 175–186 (1994)
22. Roweis, S.T., Saul, L.K.: Nonlinear dimensionality reduction by locally linear embedding. Science **290**(5500), 2323–2326 (2000)
23. Sarwar, B., Karypis, G., Konstan, J., Riedl, J.: Item-based collaborative filtering recommendation algorithms. In: WWW, pp. 285–295 (2001)
24. Shi, Y., Larson, M., Hanjalic, A.: Collaborative filtering beyond the user-item matrix: a survey of the state of the art and future challenges. ACM. Comput. Surv. **47**(1), 3 (2014)
25. Tang, J., Hu, X., Liu, H.: Social recommendation: a review. Soc. Netw. Anal. Min. **3**(4), 1113–1133 (2013)
26. Wang, D., Cui, P., Zhu, W.: Structural deep network embedding. In: SIGKDD, pp. 1225–1234 (2016)
27. Wang, H., et al.: Incremental subgraph feature selection for graph classification. IEEE Trans. Knowl. Data Eng. **29**(1), 128–142 (2017)
28. Wu, J., Li, Y., Feng, S., Shen, H.: A self-immunizing manifold ranking for image retrieval. In: Pei, J., Tseng, V.S., Cao, L., Motoda, H., Xu, G. (eds.) PAKDD 2013. LNCS (LNAI), vol. 7819, pp. 426–436. Springer, Heidelberg (2013). https://doi.org/10.1007/978-3-642-37456-2_36
29. Zelnik-Manor, L., Perona, P.: Self-tuning spectral clustering. In: NIPS, pp. 1601–1608 (2005)
30. Zhang, C., Yu, L., Wang, Y., Shah, C., Zhang, X.: Collaborative user network embedding for social recommender systems. In: SDM, pp. 381–389 (2017)

High-Performance OCR on Packing Boxes in Industry Based on Deep Learning

Fei Chen[1], Bo Li[1(✉)], Rong Dong[2], and Peng Zhao[2]

[1] School of Electronic Science and Engineering, Nanjing University, Nanjing, China
liboee@nju.edu.cn

[2] Nanjing Huichuan Image Vision Technology Co. Ltd., Nanjing, China

Abstract. OCR is a historic but still challenging task, especially in industry conditions where it demands very high computational efficiency and accuracy. In this work, a high-performance OCR method based on deep learning is proposed. First, the region of character string is segmented using semantic segmentation network, and the tilt angle of the string is corrected so that the system is adaptive to character rotation. Then the intervals between adjacent characters are recognized by a column-classification network so that characters in the same string are well separated. Finally, each region of separated character is fed to an image-classification network to ensure a high-accuracy recognition. Different from existing networks which carry out tasks of location and classification simultaneously, in the proposed framework three different networks including the semantic segmentation network, the column classification network and the image-classification network are independent. Each of them is dedicated to its own classification task so that the classification accuracy is best. Another advantage of this framework is that it is convenient to do data augmentation. Different from traditional OCR algorithm based on deep learning, which mainly need a large number of labeled samples, the proposed algorithm only needs 100 training samples with the size of 640 * 480 to achieve an accuracy of 99.92%, moreover, the whole detection process requires only about 78 ms per image on average.

Keywords: OCR · Column-classification network · Deep learning

1 Introduction

The rapid development of computer vision and the Internet have brought forth tremendous new products and services, which have triggered huge demand for practical vision techniques. OCR on packing boxes, affording a way to determine whether the optical character is correct directly in the industry, which is obviously among the most pressing techniques. Consequently, OCR on packing boxes have attracted much attention from both computer vision community and industrial community.

Though extensively studied in the past decade, detecting and reading characters on packing boxes in industry are still difficult tasks. The major challenges stem from three aspects: (1) Various interference factors, such as noise, distortion, low contrast, non-uniform illumination will have a bad impact on the optical character recognition

X. Geng and B.-H. Kang (Eds.): PRICAI 2018, LNAI 11012, pp. 1018–1030, 2018.
https://doi.org/10.1007/978-3-319-97304-3_78

(2) Different optical characters have different fonts, colors, scales and directions, the algorithm must have strong generalization performance. (3) Compared with the character recognition in natural scene, in order to be spread the industry, the algorithm has higher requirements for accuracy and time-consuming. What's more, the small sample training must be done.

In this paper, we propose the idea of region detection and character recognition to perform the optical character recognition on packing boxes. There are two main types of character regions detection algorithms: feature extraction based on sliding windows, classification and MSER [1] (Maximally Stable Extremal Regions), SWT [2] (Strokc Width Transform) algorithm based on connected component analysis. The former has been eliminated due to its bad performance to accurately detect the regions of the slanted characters. The latter has become the mainstream of character regions detection because of its insensitivity to the changes of character scale, orientation, and font. However, under the harsh conditions of fuzzy, imbalanced illumination, low resolution, low contrast, connected component analysis can't guarantee a better detection performance.

In terms of single-line character recognition, the mainstream recognition method is CRNN (CNN+RNN) [3] algorithm. However, the number of training samples required for the CRNN [3] is too high, so it is not suitable to be performed in the industry. Segmentation and recognition is another idea of single-line character recognition. However, the segmentation algorithm based on vertical projection [4] or connected component analysis [5] relies too much on the choice of the threshold, which can't guarantee good segmentation performance in the case of non-uniform illumination and low-contrast.

Our proposed algorithm including region detection and character recognition has shown excellent performance in some difficult cases which are shown in Fig. 1. For example, Fig. 1a and b: characters are obscure and low-contrast. Fig 1c: the character '2' and '0' are stuck together. These cases above can't be effectively solved by traditional methods.

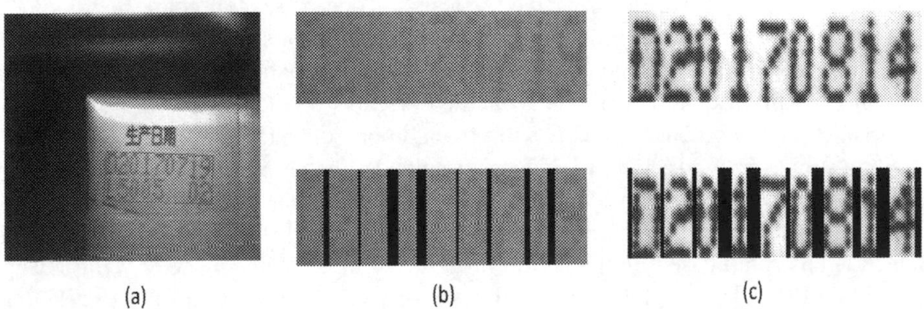

Fig. 1. Detection examples of the proposed method

Finally, the experimental results on a variety of packing boxes datasets show that the algorithm in this paper is more effective than traditional algorithms. The region detection and character recognition algorithms both have better adaptability and accuracy.

The core contribution of this work are character region detection and character recognition, which achieve state-of-the-art performance on our packing boxes datasets. Moreover, the algorithm we proposed only needs 100 training pictures to achieve an accuracy of 99.92%, which takes 62 ms for one picture. In summary, the accuracy, time-consuming, sample numbers and training complexity all meet the requirements of the industry.

2 Relative Work

In recent years, the community has witnessed a surge of research efforts on optical character recognition. A rich body of novel ideas and effective methods have been proposed. In this section, we focus on works that are most relevant to the proposed algorithm.

Optical Character Recognition on packing boxes generally involves two steps, the character regions detection and the character recognition.

The region detection algorithm can be specifically divided into traditional algorithm and deep learning algorithm. The traditional algorithm can be further divided into two types: Sliding-window and connected component analysis. Sliding-window methods have been very popular in the field of scene text detection. Such methods make use of the texture or local structure property of text and scan all possible positions and scales in the image. However, this method has high requirements on the classifier [6–8], which is required to be able to cope with various forms of fonts and backgrounds, what's worse, sliding window can't detect the character regions with direction accurately. Usually connected component analysis method uses the color, brightness, edge information of the character to separate character region from non-character region by clustering. SWT [2] and MSER [1] are two representative component-based methods for character regions detection, which constitute the basis of a lot of subsequent works. These algorithms assume that characters consist of one or several connected components and utilize this property to seek individual characters or strokes. These algorithms obtained excellent performance on a variety of standard datasets. However, the performance of the MSER [1] depends on the selection of the threshold, causing the generalization performance is not well. In addition, the printing ink doesn't have obvious strokes in industry, SWT [2] is not suitable for the punctate structure.

The region detection algorithm based on deep learning can also be divided into two categories, which are based on the region proposal and segmentation. The earliest detection algorithm based on the region proposal is an article published by Bai Xiang et al. in CVPR 2015 [9]. The detection effect is very good. The basic idea is to design a template with symmetry based on the similarity of the structure of the text line itself, then scan the image at different scales and obtain a symmetrical center point through its response. After obtaining the symmetry center point, a bounding box is obtained through the height and connectivity of the text, finally CNN is used for subsequent processing. The work of the Qiao Yu research group on ECCV2016 [10] is very new. They take some blocks on the VGG [21] feature map and calculate the score for each block. In the process of calculating the score, the context information is taken into account, then the text features of each row are input into the BLSTM (Bidirectional Long Short-term Memory) model to better determine the score of the text. This method solves the problem of the direction changing in the text to some extends. Prof. Jin Lianwen's work on CVPR 2017 [11] puts forward an important point: When you create a proposal, regressing an arbitrary polygon is better than regressing a rectangular box. Based on the detection framework of SSD [14] (Single Shot MultiBox Detector), they add the process of returning to the bounding box and the matching process to the network structure, which achieve better recognition results and take into account the speed.

Another region detection algorithm is based on the idea of segmentation. Bai Xiang et al.'s work on CVPR 2016 [12] saw the text line as a target that needs to be segmented to obtain a salience map of the text, then combine with other features to get efficient text detection region. Recently some methods used segmentation and bounding box regression at the same time to detect scene text. An article on CVPR 2017 [13] optimize and accelerate PVANet [15] to get the output including fractional edge scores, regression of rotated bounding boxes and polygon bounding boxes, those improvements get good results.

The detection model is divided into two categories according to whether or not the characters are divided. The commonly used method of single-line character detection is the CRNN [3] model proposed by Bai Xiang et al. in 2015. It combines the advantages of CNN (Convolutional Neural Network) learning directly from the original image and RNN (Recurrent Neural Network) outputing sequences. Faster-RCNN [16] and SSD [14] are another detection method. The basic idea is to regard the single character as an independent target. However, Faster-RCNN [16] and SSD [14] output the target category and position at the same time, which increases the training difficulty and the coupling of the network, making the detection accuracy and time impossible to be obtained at the same time. Moreover, the above two types of detection methods require a large number of labeled samples for training, Therefore, under the condition of insufficient samples, CRNN [3], Faster-RCNN [16] or SSD [14] is not suitable to be used.

Segmentation and recognition is another detection method. Generally, before segmentation, we need to do some preprocessing work. For example, the median filter, the histogram equalization and the inflation etc., the segmentation algorithm can be divided into two types of vertical projection [4] and connected component analysis [5]. By calculating the sum of each column from left to right, the vertical projection [4] sets the column whose sum is 0 to background. The simplest way of connected component analysis [5] is to find the minimum coverage rectangle directly in each contour of the binary image. However, the segmentation algorithms above need to do threshold binarization firstly. There are large number of types of packing boxes which have different fonts and orientations. To make matters worse, sometimes, the character regions are blurry and low-contrast, making it difficult to find a suitable threshold to distinguish from the character regions and complex backgrounds.

3 Ours Method

In this section, the proposal algorithm of this paper will be introduced in detail. The character recognition process of this paper is divided into three parts: region detection, segmentation and classification, which is shown in Fig. 2, the region detection algorithm is U-net [17] segmentation+proposal extraction+correction, and the segmentation algorithm uses the convolutional neural network to classify the column of the single-line characters. This is a breakthrough and improvement of the traditional segmentation algorithm. Finally, we use ZF network [18] to identify a single code character.

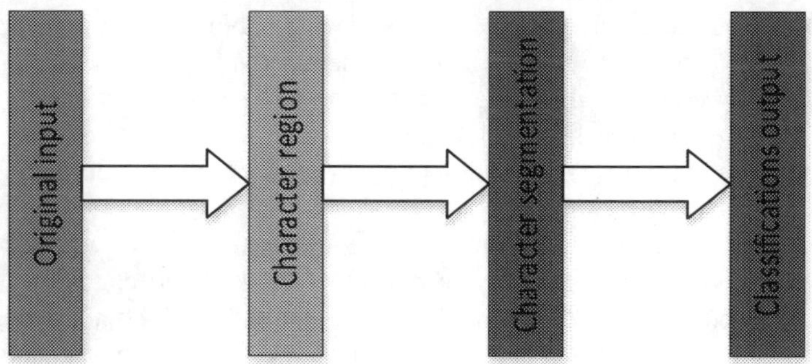

Fig. 2. The character recognition process of this paper

3.1 Character Regions Detection

The primary goal of the character recognition on packing is to locate the character regions. In this paper, we use the U-net [17] to locate the region of the characters whose main advantage is the U-net can accurately detect the region of the sloping characters when the character regions are blurred or low-contrast. Moreover, the training sample is small, the speed of training and detection is very fast, the output of the U-net [17] is a binary map, then we use the rotation rectangle to extract the proposal from the binary map, then the final step is to correct the rotated rectangle.

U-net. U-net [17] is a widely used network in the field of medical image processing. Compared with FCN [19] (Fully Convolutional Networks), there is a large change in the network structure. In the up-sampling phase, the up-sampling layer introduces its own convolution layer in addition to the layers of the encoding features. what's more, U-net [17] only needs one training process, which is better than FCN [19].

Region Detection and Direction Correction. The output of U-net [17] is a binary map. In this paper we regard the white pixel as the region of the characters. The next step is to locate the region from the original image according to the binary map. Here, we propose the region as a rotated rectangle, and directly extract the minimum enclosing rectangle of the white pixel, Finally, a simple affine transformation is used to correct the direction.

3.2 Column Classification

The column classification algorithm based on deep learning proposed in this paper has a better segmentation performance for the complex cases, for example, the characters are obscure, low-contrast or stuck together. In the single-line character recognition, the essence of the segmentation is to judge each column belongs to the foreground or the background. However, some traditional segmentation algorithms such as vertical projection [4] and connected-component analysis [5] are extremely dependent on the choice of the threshold, what's worse, sometimes we can't find a suitable threshold to distinguish between background and foreground. Therefore, the two algorithms above often don't have a satisfactory segmentation performance for some difficult cases. In this paper we propose a segmentation algorithm based on deep learning to learn the potential features of each column. Then we classify based on the features of each column.

The structure of column classification network is as followed (Fig. 3):

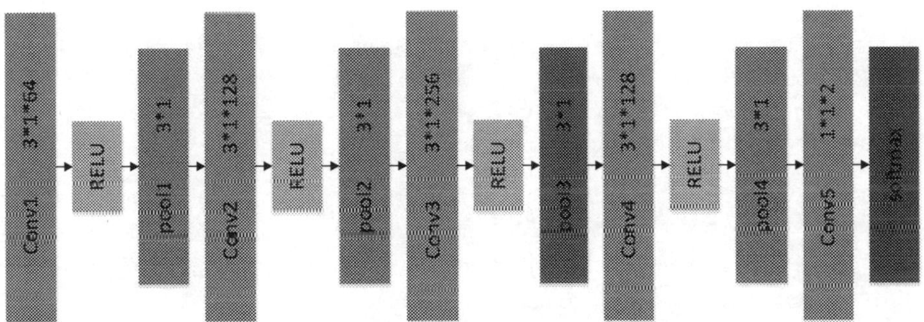

Fig. 3. The structure of column classification network

As we can see, the column classification network only requires the input pictures have a fixed length of height. That is to say, when the input size is W * H * C, the output size is W * 1 * 1. The sizes of kernels are both 3 * 1 in convolution and pooling layers. As we all know, in convolutional neural network, each convolution and pooling operation is a feature extraction of the upper layer. Then we use softmax function to classify each column from the feature of the last layer. Finally, the experiments on varieties of packing boxes show that the column classification network achieves better segmentation performance than traditional algorithms.

3.3 Single Character Recognition

Data Augmentation. The outstanding feature of the deep learning algorithm is the large requirements for the datasets. When the number of given datasets is not enough, data augmentation is needed. Common methods of data augmentation include adding noise, adjusting contrast and perspective transformation, etc. In this paper we also use a random step method to increase the number of trainings for single character recognition network. We use a sliding window to slide in single-line characters when the IOU (intersection over union) of the sliding window and the single character is greater than 0.9, we mark it a positive sample, and mark the position of the sliding window the category of the single character.

ZF-net. ZF-net [18] is the champion of ILSVRC (ImageNet Large Scale Visual Recognition Challenge) in 2013. On the basis of AlexNet [20], there are many fine adjustments. For example, using RELU activation function, cross-entropy cost function, replacing the original big filters with multi-layers small filters and so on. Afterwards, more and more better network frameworks are designed, such as VGG [21], GoogleNet [22], ResNet [23], etc. However, their network structures are more complicated and the number of layers is larger. It is not necessary to use such a complex network in a simple single character recognition.

4 Experiments

All the experiments in this article are performed under the win10 (2.4 GHz 4-core CPU, 8G RAM, NVIDIA GeForce GTX 1080Ti GPU) operating system. The convolutional neural network is built based on MXNET and the algorithm is implemented with C++ and python programming languages.

4.1 Dataset and Evaluation Protocol

In this paper, we evaluate the proposed algorithm on various of packing boxes and follow the standard evaluation protocols in this field.

Datasets: The datasets, with the size of 640 * 480, used in our proposal algorithm are shown in Fig. 4. Each kind of packing boxes has different backgrounds and fonts, in this paper, we use 100 samples for training and 1000 labeled samples for testing.

Fig. 4. Four kinds of packing boxes used in our experiment

Evaluation Protocol: In this paper, we use different performance evaluation protocols to evaluate the region detection, column classification, and characters recognition algorithms on packing boxes. The first is the IOU (intersection over union), which refers to the overlap ratio of the prediction and the ground truth, in region detection experiments, we consider it a positive proposal when the IOU is larger than 0.9, otherwise, it's a negative proposal. For the classification of two categories, there are three important metrics in performance assessment: precision, recall and F1-measure. Precision measures the ratio between true positives and all detections, while recall measures the ratio true positives and all true samples that should be detected. F1-measure, as an overall, single indicator of algorithm performance, is the harmonic mean of precision and recall. For multiple classification problems, we use accuracy to evaluate their performance. Accuracy refers to the proportion between correctly predicted samples and the total number of samples.

4.2 Experimental Results

Region Detection. Figure 5 shows an example of region detection results of the algorithm on the packing boxes datasets. It can be seen that thc proposed algorithm shows great detection performance.

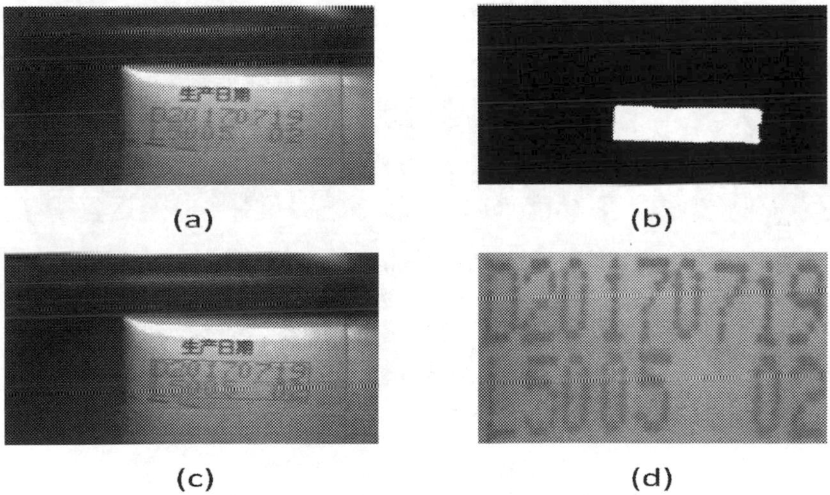

Fig. 5. The region detection results of the algorithm on the packing boxes datasets, (a) Input image. (b) The result of the U-net. (c) Extract the rotated rectangle from the (b). (d) Correct the rotated rectangle.

The performances of the proposed algorithm as well as other methods on the packing boxes dataset are shown in Table 1.

The proposed algorithm achieves an F1-measure of 1.0, outperforming other methods. Compared to the MSER [1] and SWT [2], the recall of our algorithm (1.0) is much higher than that of 0.964 and 0.958, what's more, the IOU of our algorithm confirms the effectiveness of our algorithm, especially its advantage in handling various challenging cases such as fuzzy and low-contrast. Finally, the time for U-net [17] +proposal extraction is only 40 ms, which is much better than the 100 ms for MSER [1] +proposal extraction and the 130 ms for SWT [2] +proposal extraction.

Table 1. Performances of different algorithms evaluated on the packing boxes dataset.

	Precision	Recall	F1-measure	IOU	Time
MSER [1] +proposal extraction	100%	96.4%	1.018	0.932	100 ms
SWT [2] +proposal extraction	100%	95.8%	1.022	0.904	130 ms
U-net [17] +proposal extraction	100%	100%	1.000	0.988	20 ms

Column Classification. Due to the accuracy of region detection and the consistency of the upper and lower line of characters, the two lines of characters can be obtained by intercepting the corrected picture from the middle. Figure 6 shows the experimental results of the column classification algorithm in this paper:

Fig. 6. The results of the column classification algorithm

In the column classification network, we use a kernel with the size of 3 * 1 in convolution and pooling layers. The following Table 2 shows the classification performance of different size of the kernels.

Table 2. Performances of different kernel scale evaluated on the column classification

Size(convolution +pooling)	Precision	Recall	F1-measure
3 * 3 + 3 * 3	93.62%	92.74%	1.0732
3 * 3 + 3 * 1	96.32%	94.68%	1.0472
3 * 1 + 3 * 1	99.92%	99.94%	1.0007

From the table, we can see that the kernels with 3 * 1 scale in convolution and pooling layers are superior to the traditional 3 * 3 scale convolution kernels and 3 * 3 scale pooling kernels regardless of the precision or recall. In fact, in terms of the column classification, the data in each column is a separate sample, the 3 * 3 scale convolution kernel fuses the neighborhood information of each column, thus destroying the independence of the original data and increases the complexity of the data. On the other hand, the number of samples was discarded excessively with a 3 * 3 scale kernel in pooling layers, making the final fineness inconsistent with that of the original sample, thus failing to achieve optimal segmentation performance.

The Table 3 above shows the segmentation performances of the segmentation algorithm in 2000 single-line character pictures, and compared with the segmentation results of the vertical projection [4] and connected component analysis [5]. The column classification network uses 200 training pictures, and the training time is 20 min, vertical projection and [4] connected-domain analysis [5] use OTSU (the low threshold and the high threshold) for Threshold, here we consider the columns belonging to the characters to be positive samples.

Table 3. Performances of different algorithms evaluated on the column classification

Method	Precision	Recall	F1-measure	Time
Vertical projection [4] (OTSU-low)	90.48%	98.24%	1.0615	4 ms
Vertical projection [4] (OTSU-high)	98.36%	88.62%	1.0725	4 ms
Connected component analysis [5] (OTSU-low)	92.28%	96.46%	1.0601	5 ms
Connected component analysis [5] (OTSU-high)	98.58%	86.34%	1.0863	5 ms
Column classification	99.92%	99.94%	1.0007	2 ms

It can be seen that the column classification algorithm is superior to the vertical projection and connected component analysis algorithms in F1–measure (1.0007) and time consuming (2 ms), what's more, the vertical projection [4] and connected component analysis [5] algorithms show an opposite increase in precision and recall in the high and low threshold, which shows that the choice of the threshold has a great effect on the performance of the segmentation. When the character regions are fuzzy, low-contrast or stuck together, the vertical projection and connected component analysis algorithms based on threshold show poor segmentation performance. Figure 7 shows the threshold results of single-line characters whose characters are low-contrast or stuck together. It can be seen that we can't find a suitable threshold to separate the characters from the background. Therefore, vertical projection and connected component analysis cannot perform well when the characters are fuzzy, low contrast or stuck together.

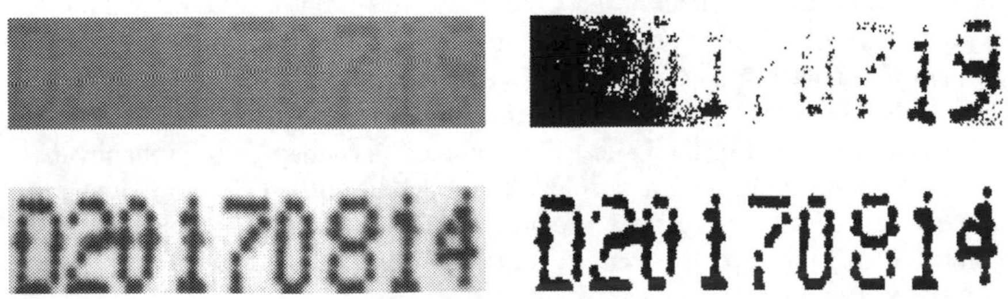

Fig. 7. The threshold results of single-line characters whose characters are low-contrast or stuck together.

Character Recognition. The following Table 4 is the classification result of our proposed algorithm. We also compare with other defection algorithms such as Faster-RCNN [16], SSD [14] and CRNN [3] model. In terms of the training number, the algorithm proposed only needs 100 training samples, however, Faster-RCNN [16], SSD [14] and CRNN [3] models can't be trained to converge with 100 samples. In order to compare the detection performance of the four algorithms, in this paper, we use 2000 samples to train Faster-RCNN [16] and SSD [14], and 6000 pictures to train CRNN [3] to ensure that each network is trained to the best condition.

Table 4. Performances of different algorithms evaluated on the character recognition

Method	Accuracy	Time
U-net [17] +proposal extraction +Faster-RCNN [16]	99.90%	120 ms
U-net [17] +proposal extraction +SSD [14]	96.86%	62 ms
U-net [17] +proposal extraction +CRNN [3]	99.96%	50 ms
U-net [17] +proposal extraction +column classification +ZF-net [18]	99.92%	64 ms

The Faster-RCNN [16] has a higher precision of 99.90% in the detection algorithm, but its time-consuming is the highest among the four algorithms, what's worse, the training process is tedious and complex. SSD [14] has. a less time-consuming, but the accuracy is only 96.86%. CRNN [3] is the best detection algorithm from the accuracy and the time-consuming, but its demand for data is too large, which requires 6000 training samples. so it is not suitable to be used in the industry. The algorithm we proposed has an accuracy of 99.92%, better than Faster-RCNN [16] and SSD [14], in addition, it only takes 64 ms, meeting the requirement of real-time detection in the industry, Last but not least, the proposed algorithm achieves the goal of small samples training with only 100 training samples. The 99.92% accuracy and 64 ms time-consuming all meet the requirements of the industry. Therefore, it is suitable to be used in the industry.

5 Discussion

In this section, we will discuss two topics about the optical character recognition algorithm proposed in this paper. The one is the extraction of the characters' region, due to the great segmentation effect of the U-net [17], we simply regard that the minimum enclosing rectangle of the white pixel is the region of the characters, this is a wrong assumption when the result of the U-net [17] is terrible, a better solution is to change the output of the U-net [17], turning the classification problem into regression problem, which means the output of the U-net [17] is not a binary map but a probabilistic heat map. The value of each pixel represents the probability that the pixel belongs to the characters' region. Then we extract a rotated rectangle which has a highest score from the probabilistic heat map by searching, the score of the rotated rectangle is the sum of the pixel's value within the rotated rectangle from the probabilistic heat map.

The other topic is the column classification network, in the proposed algorithm three different networks including the semantic segmentation network, the column classification network and the image-classification network are independent. Each of them is dedicated to its own classification task so that the classification accuracy is best. However, which component plays a major role towards the optical character recognition? From the three experiments of the Sect. 4.2, comparing with semantic segmentation network and image-classification network, the column classification network has the most obvious improvement in their own classification task. In addition, the results of the character segmentation not only depend on the outputs of the column classification network, but also rely on the prior information such as the width of the character and the background, which contributes a better segmentation performance.

6 Conclusion

In this paper, we have presented a novel algorithm for optical character recognition on packing boxes in industry. The proposed algorithm based on deep learning includes three parts: region detection, column classification and character recognition. Different from traditional deep learning algorithms which require a large amount of labeled samples, the algorithm proposed only need 100 training samples with a size of 640 * 480 to achieve a satisfactory accuracy of 99.92%, what's more, the whole recognition process requires only 78 ms. The core contribution of the proposed algorithm is a column classification network, the using of the kernels of 3 * 1 scale makes it perform well especially in some complex situations than traditional segmentation algorithm, like vertical projection [4] and connected component analysis [5]. The experiments on the datasets of packing boxes in industry demonstrate that the proposed algorithm outperforms other competing methods in the literature.

Acknowledgement. This work is partially supported by the Key Project supported by Shenzhen Joint Funds of the National Natural Science Foundation of China (Grant No. U1613217).

References

1. Endicott, J., Spitzer, R.L., Fleiss, J.L.: Mental status examination record (MSER): reliability and validity. Compr. Psychiatry **16**(3), 285–301 (1975)
2. Epshtein, B., Ofek, E., Wexler, Y.: Detecting text in natural scenes with stroke width transform. In: Computer Vision and Pattern Recognition, pp. 2963–2970. IEEE (2010)
3. Gers, F.A., Schmidhuber, E.: LSTM recurrent networks learn simple context-free and context-sensitive languages. IEEE Trans. Neural Netw. **12**(6), 1333–1340 (2001)
4. Xia, H., Liao, D.: The study of license plate character segmentation algorithm based on vetical projection. In: International Conference on Consumer Electronics, Communications and Networks, pp. 4583–4586. IEEE (2011)
5. Khandelwal, A., Choudhury, P., Sarkar, R., Basu, S., Nasipuri, M., Das, N.: Text line segmentation for unconstrained handwritten document images using neighborhood connected component analysis. In: Chaudhury, S., Mitra, S., Murthy, C.A., Sastry, P.S., Pal, S.K. (eds.) PReMI 2009. LNCS, vol. 5909, pp. 369–374. Springer, Heidelberg (2009). https://doi.org/10.1007/978-3-642-11164-8_60

6. Zhu, J., Zou, H., Rosset, S., et al.: Multi-class AdaBoost. Stat. Interface **2**(3), 349–360 (2009)
7. Joachims, T.: Making large-scale SVM learning practical. Technische Universität Dortmund, Sonderforschungsbereich 475: Komplexitätsreduktion in multivariaten Datenstrukturen, pp. 499–526 (1999)
8. Pinkus, A.: Approximation theory of the MLP model in neural networks. Acta Numer. **8**, 143–195 (1999)
9. Zhang, Z., Shen, W., Yao, C., et al.: Symmetry-based text line detection in natural scenes. In: IEEE Conference on Computer Vision and Pattern Recognition, pp. 2558–2567. IEEE Computer Society (2015)
10. Tian, Z., et al.: Detecting text in natural image with connectionist text proposal network. In: Leibe, B., Matas, J., Sebe, N., Welling, M. (eds.) ECCV 2016. LNCS, vol. 9912. Springer, Cham (2016). https://doi.org/10.1007/978-3-319-46484-8
11. Liu, Y., Jin, L.: Deep matching prior network: Toward tighter multi-oriented text detection. arXiv preprint arXiv:1703.01425 (2017)
12. Zhang, Z., et al.: Multi-oriented text detection with fully convolutional networks. In: Proceedings of the IEEE Conference on Computer Vision and Pattern Recognition (2016)
13. He, W., et al.: Deep Direct Regression for Multi-Oriented Scene Text Detection. arXiv preprint arXiv:1703.08289 (2017)
14. Liu, W., et al.: SSD: single shot multibox detector. In: Leibe, B., Matas, J., Sebe, N., Welling, M. (eds.) ECCV 2016. LNCS, vol. 9905, pp. 21–37. Springer, Cham (2016). https://doi.org/10.1007/978-3-319-46448-0_2
15. Hong, S., Roh, B., Kim, K.H., et al.: PVANet: lightweight deep neural networks for real-time object detection. arXiv preprint arXiv:1611.08588 (2016)
16. Ren, S., He, K., Girshick, R., et al.: Faster R-CNN: towards real-time object detection with region proposal networks. In: International Conference on Neural Information Processing Systems, pp. 91–99. MIT Press (2015)
17. Ronneberger, O., Fischer, P., Brox, T.: U-Net: convolutional networks for biomedical image segmentation. In: Navab, N., Hornegger, J., Wells, W.M., Frangi, A.F. (eds.) MICCAI 2015. LNCS, vol. 9351, pp. 234–241. Springer, Cham (2015). https://doi.org/10.1007/978-3-319-24574-4_28
18. Zeiler, M.D., Fergus, R.: Visualizing and understanding convolutional networks. In: Fleet, D., Pajdla, T., Schiele, B., Tuytelaars, T. (eds.) ECCV 2014. LNCS, vol. 8689, pp. 818–833. Springer, Cham (2014). https://doi.org/10.1007/978-3-319-10590-1_53
19. Long, J., Shelhamer, E., Darrell, T.: Fully convolutional networks for semantic segmentation. In: Proceedings of the IEEE Conference on Computer Vision and Pattern Recognition (2015)
20. Krizhevsky, A., Sutskever, I., Hinton, G.E.: ImageNet classification with deep convolutional neural networks. In: International Conference on Neural Information Processing Systems, pp. 1097–1105. Curran Associates Inc. (2012)
21. Simonyan, K., Zisserman, A.: Very deep convolutional networks for large-scale image recognition. Comput. Sci. (2014)
22. Szegedy, C., Liu, W., Jia, Y., et al.: Going deeper with convolutions. In: Proceedings of the IEEE Conference on Computer Vision and Pattern Recognition, pp. 1–9 (2015)
23. He, K., Zhang, X., Ren, S., et al.: Deep residual learning for image recognition. In: Proceedings of the IEEE Conference on Computer Vision and Pattern Recognition, pp. 770–778 (2016)

An Implementation of Large-Scale Holonic Multi-agent Society Simulator and Agent Behavior Model

Takayuki Ito[1(✉)], Takanobu Otsuka[1], Teruyoshi Imaeda[1], and Rafik Hadfi[2]

[1] Nagoya Institute of Technology, Gokiso, Showa-ku, Nagoya 466-8555, Japan
{ito.takayuki,otsuka.takanobu,imaeda.yoshiteru}@nitech.ac.jp
[2] Monash University, Clayton, Australia
rafik.hadfi@monash.edu

Abstract. This paper presents a large-scale multiagent simulator that can simulate any complex urban environment and demonstrates its implementation on a distributed computing environment. We focus on society simulation, in particular traffic and crowd simulations, within any geographic area on earth. We adopt an multi-agent based approach for the different behaviors of the vehicles, drivers, and pedestrians. The proposed driving behavioral models can realistically emulate driving behaviors of humans. The resulting simulator succeeds to simulate at least more than 50,000 vehicles on the one server with a visualization.

Keywords: Multi-agent simulation · Society simulator
Large-scale traffic simulation · Driving behavior modeling

1 Introduction

Multiagent simulation has been studied very widely and it has been focused as an alternative way to simulate complex systems. The main goal of a multiagent simulation is to model the real world in terms of autonomous agents that can purposely interact with their external environment [8,13,21]. An agent can basically gather information from the environment using sensors, while attempting to execute its objectives using effectors [18].

The traditional simulations, like the weather simulator, depend on the simple physical equations, and calculate the huge set of them and their relations. Then the result will represent some predication based on the past values for the physical equations. This kind of physical simulation would be valuable when we can represent a complex system as the set of physical equations, like weathers, ocean currents, chemical reactions, etc.

However, the complex systems based human activities, like economy, traffic, crowd moving, etc., can not be represented based on only simple physical equations. Rather we need to build behavior models for each entity in the simulation.

X. Geng and B.-H. Kang (Eds.): PRICAI 2018, LNAI 11012, pp. 1031–1043, 2018.
https://doi.org/10.1007/978-3-319-97304-3_79

For example, in a traffic simulation, we need to simulate ordinal drivers' behaviors while simulating senior drivers' behaviors so that we can design the future city traffic systems including senior drivers.

In this paper, we present an implementation of a large-scale multiagent society simulator. The vision and aim of this society simulator is to simulate all entities in a society. The entities includes pedestrians, cars, bikes, weathers, infrastructures like signals. Therefore, we propose an holonic multi-agent architecture for this vision. We recognize this vision is very ideal. Thus, we started from a society which include cars, pedestrians (crowds), and some weather information. Also, to this end, our implementation architecture is quite scalable so that one computer can simulator at least 50,000 agents that can be cars, pedestrians and also other entities.

Our architecture follows a multilayered (*holonic*) scheme in the sense that it has a self-organizing property in the way different parts of the simulation are autonomously handled [7,14]. Holonic multiagent systems [2,6] are a rational and practical way for a recursive modeling of autonomous agents which allows a dynamic reorganization of the whole system. This kind of simulator can become a testbed for general-purpose computational intelligence and can be used for the benchmarking of routing algorithms.

There are a lot of multiagent traffic simulators [3,19]. However, in general, these simulators do not assume to simulate the whole society. For example, MATSim [1] is a populer trafic simulator but it is not possible that MATSim simulates the whole society.

Each layer processes a particular aspect of the simulation through the interactions of its internal elements. A layer will therefore be represented by a complex network of interacting agents that can communicate within that layer and possibly with other layers. The idea behind this simulation architecture is to adopt a holonic multiagent architecture coupled to a behavioral-based agent simulation. This is in fact a way to refine both the microscopic and the macroscopic aspects found in many traffic simulators.

The availability of data collected via sensors and smartphones allows us to better model human and driver behaviors. For example, this allows for the analysis of driver behaviors and the its decision-making mechanisms [5,12,16,17]. As a result, we can build large-scale simulations by embedding the social interactions and by elaborating sophisticated human behavior models [10]. The resulting multiagent social simulation [4] is well-suited to any social context.

To model drivers and pedestrians, we conducted several experiments to gather real drivers' behaviors and also pedestrians/crowd's behaviors in cooperation with real world organizations in Nagoya city, Japan. To model drivers, we created an smartphone application that can gather driving data with location and moving data using GPS. Here, we succeeded to model kind and rough handling behaviors.

To model pedestrians, we gather crowd walking data in the train station in Nagoya area. Here we succeeded to resolve a real-world problem on privacy preserving. Namely, we developed a methodology to gather only crowd behaviour without getting any identification and also any identifiable information. But because of the page limitation, we omit this for this paper.

This paper presents an implementation of a large-scale multiagent society simulator. It is the current results of this project while the whole project is on-going. Section 2 presents an holonic architecture of our society simulator. Section 3 shows agent behavior modeling, in particular drivers and crowds. Section 4 shows the details of the implementation of our society simulator and some discussions. Section 5 concludes this paper as a summary.

2 Conceptual Architecture: A Large-Scale Holonic Multi-agent Simulator

2.1 Outline [13,14]

Our idea is to represent the whole complex system as a superposition of layers, organized as a pipeline, shown in Fig. 1. Each layer operates autonomously with all its internal threads, agents, graphical objects, etc. The holonic aspect resides in the fact that the content of each layer is a hierarchy in itself and that all the components of the layers can interact according to the dynamics of the simulation. For instance, the vehicles (Vehicles layer) are driven by drivers (Drivers layer) according to traffic lights (Synch layer), while interacting with routes, map, sensors and possibly pedestrians (Walkers). The whole is affected by the weather layer that embodies the physical conditions (precipitations) that affect the whole system.

We note that the layers should be as independent as possible so that the complexity of the simulation does not affect the communication between the different layers. Additionally, there should be a separation between the vehicles and the map in the sense that the way the vehicles navigate their space should not be specific to one particular Geographic Information System (GIS). In the following we adopt OpenStreetMap [9] as referential.

2.2 The Architecture

The architecture of the simulator is illustrated in Fig. 1. As mentioned in the previous section, we should lower the coupling between the layers of the simulator. Specifically, there should be independence between the actual simulation (**Behavior Models** and **Physical Engine**) and the corresponding OpenStreetMap rendering. This is important when the renderer is complex, that is, when we are not only rendering vehicles, but rendering pedestrians, weather data, snow, etc. This separation obeys the Dependency Inversion Principle in the sense that physical simulation acts as a high-level, abstract, objective, mathematical representation of the phenomena we want to simulate, while the OpenStreetMap rendering is one possible way of rendering the simulation. The renderer could easily be exchanged by another one. In the following, we provide a brief description of the components of the architecture.

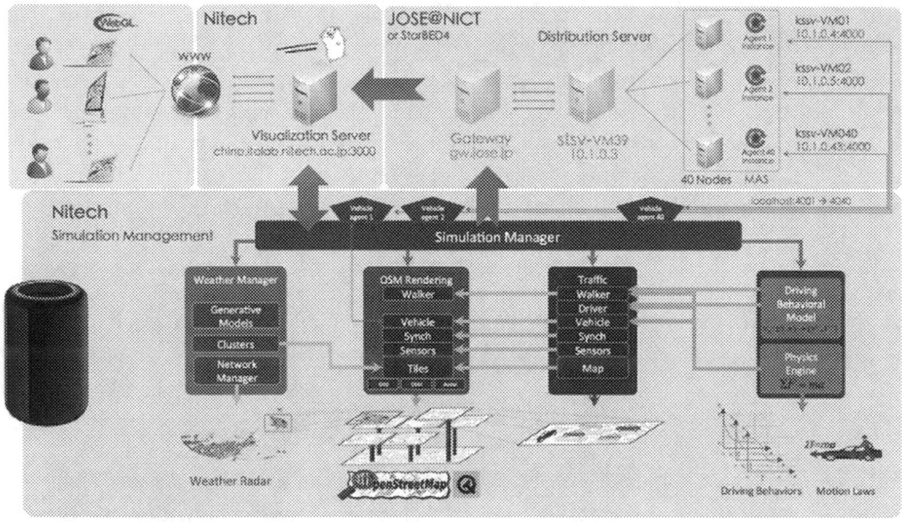

Fig. 1. Pipeline multiagent architecture of the simulator

Physics Engine and Behavioral Models. The Physics Engine component provides an approximate simulation of the physics that underly traffic, motion and the interactions between the agents. This component performs the simulation in real-time before rendering the result. The Behavioral Models describe the scenarios that govern the motion of the vehicles and the pedestrians.

Traffic Tier. The traffic tier is composed of 5 classes of agents. Firstly, pedestrians are implemented as artificial agents that perform random walks. In particular, an agent performs mobility generation within a closed polygon, or as a random itinerary on the map. Additionally, such agents can predict collisions with other agents. Secondly, a vehicle is driven by an agent (driver) that can also perform collision detection, traffic lights and lanes assessment. Thirdly, a vehicle is in fact an agent that modulates the forces acting on a graphical vehicle object. Such forces include the acceleration, direction, location, friction, velocity, and breaking. Fourthly, we distinguish a set of agents that update and synchronize the states of the traffic lights according to three time intervals. Finally, a sensor network is built on top of the map and allows the detections of the vehicles motion.

Weather Manager. The weather simulation is in fact the generation of precipitation as if it is detected by a Weather Surveillance Radar (WSR). Additionally, it is possible to download this data in real-time and render it directly onto the map. The weather radars are capable of detecting the motion of rain droplets in addition to the intensity of the precipitation. Both types of data can be analyzed to determine the structure of storms and their potential to cause severe weather.

The simulation of the weather is a mapping between a precipitation vector field onto the geographic tiles, represented as weather clusters. This mapping is computed dynamically since the tiles are loaded as a function of the simulation location.

OpenStreetMap Rendering. The rendering of the geographic map relies on downloading and updating a hierarchy of OpenStreetMap tiles. Such tiles correspond to a specific area of the map and are loaded dynamically, depending on where the simulation is being run. Herein, we use two different maps. The first map (core map) is assigned to the physics engine and is used to run the simulation in real-time so that the result is later rendered onto the second map. The second map represents a real-world referential (OpenStreetMap in our case). The mapping from the core map to the OpenStreetMap map converts absolute references into latitude/longitude references. This conversion is required since it is difficult to manipulate latitudes and longitudes within a small area due to floating-point inaccuracies (E.g. manipulating vectors with latitudes in {136.892649, 136.909015, 136.909011}).

3 Behavior Modeling

3.1 Driver Behavior Modeling

We propose the speed model and the cornering model as a driver behavior model. There could be the other characteristics for such a driver model. However, we selected speed and cornering as the most important features that characterise the behavior of drivers.

Figure 2 show the speed model. The left of Fig. 2 shows the definitions of straight paths and cornering paths while the right of it shows the parameters of this model.

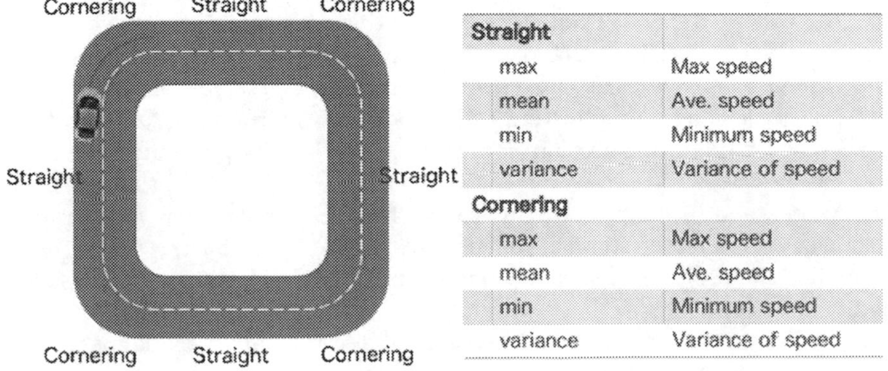

Straight	
max	Max speed
mean	Ave. speed
min	Minimum speed
variance	Variance of speed
Cornering	
max	Max speed
mean	Ave. speed
min	Minimum speed
variance	Variance of speed

Fig. 2. The speed model

The cornering model is defined as a relation between steering angle x and speed $f(x)$ in cornering situations. We gathered real driving data from the experiments, and fitted the nonlinear function (1) to the data.

$$f(x) = \frac{a}{(x+c)^k} + b \tag{1}$$

a, b, c and k are the parameters decided by data-fitting.

Figure 3 shows the cornering model. The left picture in Fig. 3 shows the real driving track and the real curve route while the right picture shows the result of fitting the data with the function (1).

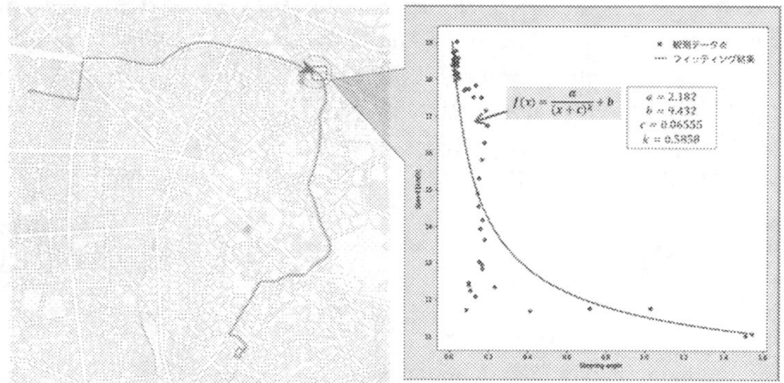

Fig. 3. Cornering model

3.2 Extracting Model Parameters from Driving Data

In our experiment, we employed the sensing values of **GNSS**, **triaxial acceleration** and **electronic compass**.

As a preparation, we deduce a regression function that predicts the amount of accelerations (stepping pedals), breaks, and staring angles from acceleration data and speed data. To deduce a regression function, we use 4 h driving data set provided by Udacity [20]. Also, we use a support vector machine.

As data cleaning, (1) adjusting GNSS position information, (2) calculating GNSS speed, (3) filtering acceleration values, (4) calculating gravity vector from acceleration values, (5) predicting the position of smartphone in the car coordinate system, and (6) alignment: translating from acceleration values into values in the car coordinate system. In particular, in (5), based on the vector in (4), we predict the position of smart phone in a car, and we use this result for the alignment in (6).

After data cleaning, adjusting steering values, calculating model parameters in car speed model and cornering model.

Model Construction Based on Real Data. In the experiments, we gathers sensing values of **GNSS**, **triaxial acceleration** and **electronic compass** with our logger application that can work on iPhone we developed in Fig. 4.

User Interface

Put a smartphone in a car

Fig. 4. Smartphone application

Based on the related work [11], smart phones are fixed at the car or the human body, and we set the IMU sampling rate 10[sps]. In the data gathering, 7 drivers logged their driving behaviour in 7 days, under the normal daily driving situations. Table 1 presents a part of the car speed models obtained by this data gathering.

In Table 1, in cornering situations, subjects A, B, C, E, and F drive at low average speed (10–20 [km/h]) while subject D drive at faster average speed (20–30 [km/h]). Thus, we succeeded to extract the model parameters that present characteristics of each subject.

Figure 5 shows cornering models we obtained. We succeeded to extract a variety of cornering models that are different from each others. Thus it can be said that we succeeded to extract the cornering model that presents characteristics of each driver.

4 Distributed Implementation

4.1 Distributed Simulator

Figure 6 shows the whole picture of the proposed architecture. The proposed architecture mainly consists of the following two parts: (1) the simulation part for distributed simulation on the distributed computing environment shown at the bottom of Fig. 6. This part employs the city maps to realize routes for traffic. (2) The visualization part to visualize the simulation results shown at the top of Fig. 6.

Table 1. Car speed model parameters obtained by the experiment (Kind: S = Straight, C = Cornering, Scale: km/h)

Subject	Kind	Mean [km/h]	Variance [km/h]
A	S	50.5350	101.8474
A	C	**14.4522**	377.2569
B	S	45.3546	35.7092
B	C	**18.6872**	383.7020
C	S	47.5319	104.5713
C	C	**14.8029**	423.4410
D	S	55.5247	218.2258
D	C	**30.2854**	686.2202
E	S	46.3676	29.8947
E	C	**15.7417**	71.3720
F	S	46.3676	29.8947
F	C	**15.7417**	71.3720

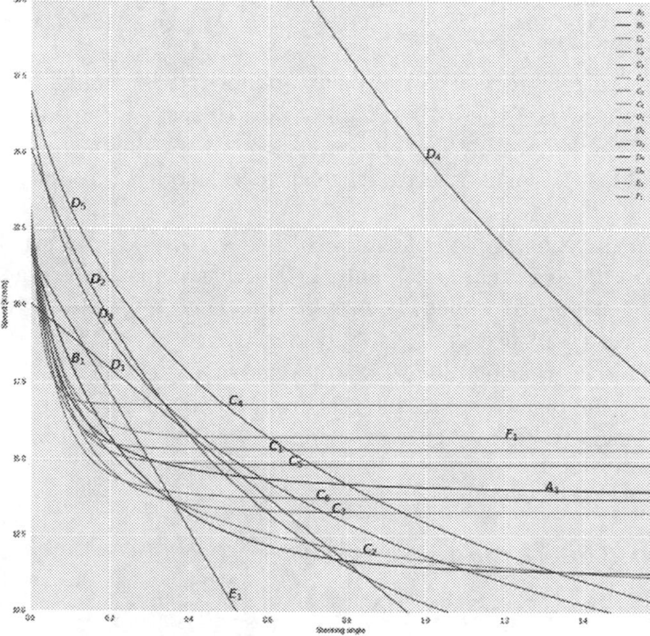

Fig. 5. Cornering models obtained

In the simulation part, there are a simulation manager and simulation nodes (=servers). The simulation manager manages simulation nodes while simulation nodes compute the real simulation for their assigned area. The whole simulated

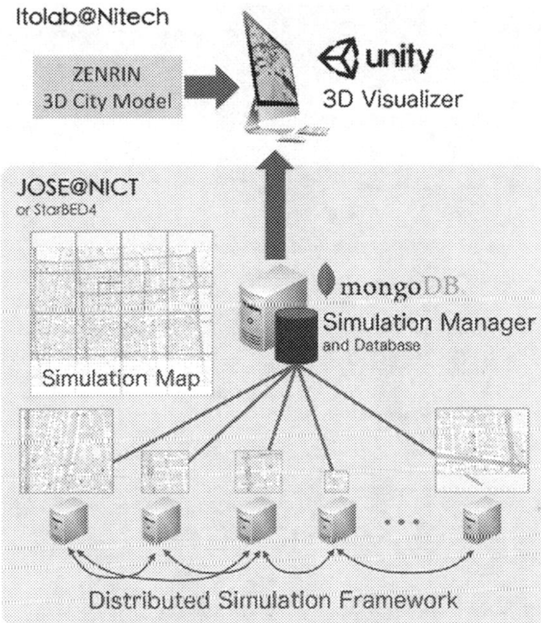

Fig. 6. Distributed architecture

area is divided into several areas in grid as shown in Fig. 6. One gird/arc is assigned to one simulation node. The size of each area is dynamically controlled by a method inspired from the Voronoi computing method which has been widely employed in the online game engine (For example, [15]) in order to efficiently distribute the cost of computation. Voronoi computing method reduces the computational cost for each area based on area partitioning by the Voronoi diagram. If an area has many agents, the size of that area tend to be small while it tends to be larger if there are less agents.

In simulation, agent's position is updated based on its behaviour model. The simulation manager send a message to all the simulation nodes synchronously. Then, all of the simulation node computes the behaviors of all agents in its assigned area, and send the information back to the simulation manager. To update the position of an agent, we require information of its vicinity. Thus, if an agent locates at the edge of an area, the adjacent areas exchange these information.

We use C# as the programming languages with Mongo DB as the fast data base. We defined our original data format to represent city maps, which can be converted from many standard map formats, like Zenrin map in Japan. Our data format is based on XML in Fig. 7.

Figure 8 shows a simple visualization of simulation of around 50000 cars in the north are of Nagoya city in Japan. Each car has its own behavior model and the entire movements are quite smooth in our simulation environment.

Fig. 7. Our map data

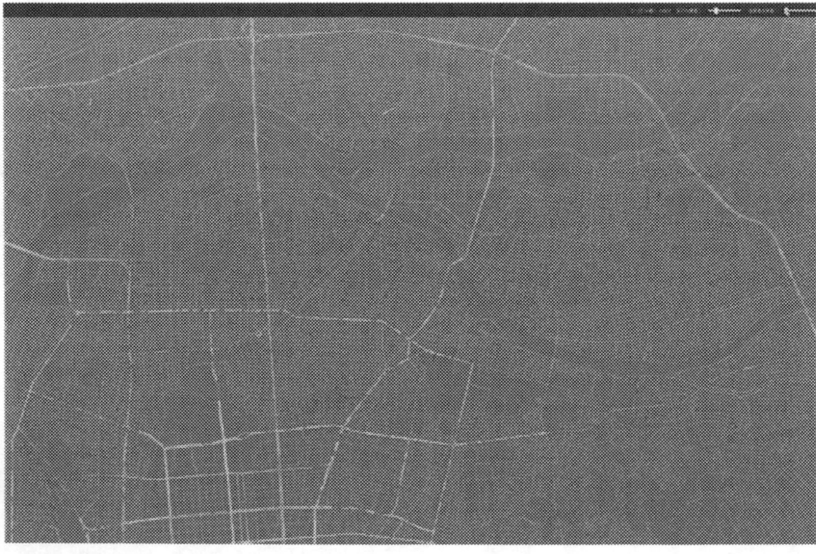

Fig. 8. A simulation of around 50000 cars in the north area of Nagoya city in Japan

4.2 3D Visualization

We believe that 3D visualization is required in order to explanation and accountability. For example, when a local-government tries to build a future city plan, they have to explain the plan to civilian so that civilian can understand it intuitively as like they are facing it. In this sense, 3D visualization is the most preferable way. We implemented the 3D visualization function by using the Unity which has been widely employed by the developers of 3D online games. Unity provides super efficient platform to realize 3D visualizations. Our simulator firstly produces the result of simulations by using the distributed simulator, and then 3D visualization system can re-produce the 3D-simulation from the recorded results of simulations. Figure 9 shows our 3D visualization system.

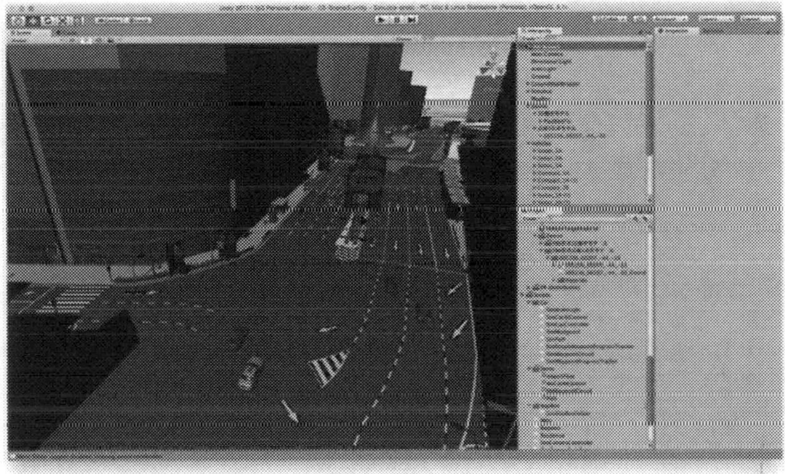

Fig. 9. 3D viewer

5 Conclusions

This paper presents an implementation of large-scale multiagent society simulators. In particular, this paper focuses on traffic simulation and behavior model for drivers. The proposed architecture effectively distribute the burden for computation by using the Voronoi algorithm, which has been focused in online games. Also, we employ holonic architecture where a simulator has several layers so that each layer can be independently modeled. For example, one layer can manage traffic while another layer can manage pedestrian. We gathered driving data by using smartphone application we implemented. Then we fitted a model to the data and obtained several driving behaviors. We also conducted to gather pedestrian data in a large scale. Here, we developed a novel way to gather crowd behavior data without obtaining any identifications for each civilian. It is of importance because the privacy is the top priority in Japan. However, because of the limit of space, we omit the details of the methodology. In the current implementation, we succeeded to move around 50,000 agents on the single server, and it is sufficient to simulate a large part of city. Currently, we are hardly working toward to realize a more sophisticated simulation for a society that includes cars, pedestrians, and weather.

References

1. Horni, A., Nagel, K., Axhausen, K.W.: The Multi-Agent Transport Simulation MATSim. Ubiquity Press, London (2016)
2. Abdoos, M., Mozayani, N., Bazzan, A.L.: Holonic multi-agent system for traffic signals control. Eng. Appl. Artif. Intell. **26**(5), 1575–1587 (2013)
3. Donieca, A., Mandiaub, R., Piechowiak, S., Espié, S.: A behavioral multi-agent model for road traffic simulation. Eng. Appl. Artif. Intell. **21**, 1443–1454 (2008)
4. Davidsson, P.: Multi agent based simulation: beyond social simulation. In: Moss, S., Davidsson, P. (eds.) MABS 2000. LNCS (LNAI), vol. 1979, pp. 97–107. Springer, Heidelberg (2000). https://doi.org/10.1007/3-540-44561-7_7
5. Dia, H.: An agent-based approach to modelling driver route choice behaviour under the influence of real-time information. Transp. Res. Part C: Emerg. Technol. **10**(5–6), 331–349 (2002)
6. Fischer, K., Schillo, M., Siekmann, J.: Holonic multiagent systems: a foundation for the organisation of multiagent systems. In: Mařík, V., McFarlane, D., Valckenaers, P. (eds.) HoloMAS 2003. LNCS (LNAI), vol. 2744, pp. 71–80. Springer, Heidelberg (2003). https://doi.org/10.1007/978-3-540-45185-3_7
7. Georgiadis, I., Magee, J., Kramer, J.: Self-organising software architectures for distributed systems. In: Proceedings of the First Workshop on Self-Healing Systems, pp. 33–38. ACM (2002)
8. Hadfi, R., Tokuda, S., Ito, T.: Traffic simulation in urban networks using stochastic cell transmission model. Comput. Intell. **33**(4), 826–842 (2017). https://doi.org/10.1111/coin.12115
9. Haklay, M.M., Weber, P.: OpenStreetMap: user-generated street maps. IEEE Pervasive Comput. **7**(4), 12–18 (2008)
10. Hattori, H., Nakajima, Y., Yamane, S.: Massive multiagent-based urban traffic simulation with fine-grained behavior models (2011)
11. Wahlstom, J., Skog, I., Händel, P.: Smartphone-based vehicle telematics: a ten-year anniversary. IEEE Trans. Intell. Trans. Syst. b **18**, 2802–2825 (2017)
12. Nagel, K., Marchal, F.: Computational methods for multi-agent simulations of travel behaviour. In: Proceedings of International Association for Travel Behavior Research (IATBR), Lucerne, Switzerland (2003)
13. Hadfi, R., Ito, T.: Multilayered multiagent system for traffic simulation: (demonstration). In: Proceedings of the 2016 International Conference on Autonomous Agents and Multiagent Systems, Richland, SC, pp. 1474–1476. International Foundation for Autonomous Agents and Multiagent Systems (2016)
14. Hadfi, R., Hayashi, M., Ito, T: A pipeline multiagent architecture for road traffic simulation. In: Proceedings of ITS World Congress 2017 (2016)
15. Ricci, L., Genovali, L., Guidi, B.: HyVVE: a Voronoi based hybrid architecture for massively multiplayer on-line games. In: 2013 International Conference on Data Communication Networking (DCNET), pp. 1–9, July 2013
16. Rossetti, R.J., Bordini, R.H., Bazzan, A.L., Bampi, S., Liu, R., Van Vliet, D.: Using BDI agents to improve driver modelling in a commuter scenario. Transp. Res. Part C: Emerg. Technol. **10**(5–6), 373–398 (2002)

17. Rossetti, R.J., Liu, R., Cybis, H.B., Bampi, S.: A multi-agent demand model. In: Proceedings of the 13th Mini-Euro Conference and the 9th Meeting of the Euro Working Group Transportation, pp. 193–198, Bari, Italy (2002)
18. Russell, S., Norvig, P.: Artificial Intelligence: A Modern Approach (1995)
19. Tranouez, P., Daudé, E., Langlois, P.: A multiagent urban traffic simulation. CoRR abs/1201.5472 (2012)
20. Udacity: Udacity. public driving dataset. https://www.udacity.com/self-driving-car. Accessed 17 Nov 2017
21. Wooldridge, M., Jennings, N.R.: Intelligent agents: theory and practice. Knowl. Eng. Rev. **10**(02), 115–152 (1995)

Establishing Connections in a Social Network

Radial Versus Medial Centrality Indices

Yanni Tang[1], Jiamou Liu[2(✉)], Wu Chen[1(✉)], and Zhuoxing Zhang[1]

[1] College of Computer and Information Science, Southwest University, Chongqing, China
chenwu@swu.edu.cn

[2] The University of Auckland, Auckland, New Zealand
jiamou.liu@auckland.ac.nz

Abstract. The extent to which a node occupies a central position in a social network amounts to a crucial indicator of personal influence. Few works address the mechanisms that would allow an individual to integrate into a network, and even fewer examine the correlation between this process and various notions of centrality. In this paper, we tackle this problem by focusing on the process in which a newcomer joins a network through building connections and gains centrality. We provide three efficient heuristics that build edges between the newcomer and existing members of a social network and compare their performances in terms of three centrality metrics. We perform experiments on random graphs generated by two synthetic network models and four real-world networks. Not only our heuristics considerably outperform the random benchmark algorithm, but the results also reveal some new insights that are related to centrality and network topology. In particular, the results distinguish between measures along two dimensions: the first concerns with the number of centers in a network, and the second concerns with the type of involvement of a node in the network.

Keywords: Social network · Edge establishment · Centrality
Radial and medial centrality

1 Introduction

Centrality measures the extent to which a node integrates into a network and forms an important basis of social network modeling and simulation. The notion has been used to represent crucial traits such as structural holes [10], influence [8], and cohesion [6,12]. Generally speaking, higher centrality nodes in a network have wider access to information flow and thus better exposure to news, opportunities and skill sets. Imagine a graduate student who participates an academic

This work was supported by the Major Project of National Social Science of China (14ZDB016).

X. Geng and B.-H. Kang (Eds.): PRICAI 2018, LNAI 11012, pp. 1044–1057, 2018.
https://doi.org/10.1007/978-3-319-97304-3_80

conference for the first time. As it takes time and effort to know another person, it is important to calculate beforehand who she should establish link with so that she can embed herself well in the academic community. While myriad centrality notions have been used in a network context, few works paid attention to the mechanism of creating social ties for an individual to gain centrality, even fewer studied such mechanism by bringing multiple centrality metrics into consideration. More specifically, the problem of *social network building* takes a graph-centric view of a social network and demands an algorithmic analysis of the process in which a node – a so-called newcomer – joins an existing network by creating new edges, hoping to become a central node. This paper aims to explore this problem along three dimensions of considerations.

The first dimension refers to the interplay between strong and weak ties. As Granovetter stated in his seminal work [7], weak ties emerge between distinct closed groups and enable the diffusion of knowledge across communities. They provide brokerage and define structural resilience of the network. On the other hand, strong ties exist between individuals who are within close proximity of each other and share common neighbors. Effective network building procedure would naturally rely on a balance between both types of ties.

The second dimension refers to the centrality measure which, as pointed out by Borgatti and Everett, is an attribute that indicates how a node plays a part in the cohesion of the network [1]. Namely, a "walk structure" contains nodes in the network and how they reach each other. Here, a "walk" is referred to as a type of engagement between nodes. Centrality is revealed from the role of each node in the walk structure. This defines a typology that puts various centrality metrics into perspective.

The third dimension refers to the meso-level structural property of the social network. A core/periphery structure combines a highly-connected, dense core, and loosely-knitted sparse periphery and amounts to a prevalent meso-level property of social networks. A unimodal network is one that contains exactly one such center, whereas a multimodel network is one that contains multiple centers, in which case, the network would consists of several distinct cores. As argued in [1], radial centrality is appropriate mostly for unimodel networks. We expect that our work on network integration would reflect this fact and distinguish between different types of network topologies.

Contribution. This paper's novelty lies in designing and evaluating new algorithmic solutions that can merge a newcomer into a network efficiently. Instead of picking a single centrality metric as the objective, we use three well-known centrality metrics and place special attention on contrasting radial with medial centrality. (1) We propose three new heuristics for this problem. The first heuristic (MaxEig) iteratively links nodes with the highest eigenvector centrality. The second heuristic (Express) builds links between the newcomer and nodes with high degree and those that are far from them; the aim here is to construct bridges that cut cross multiple clusters, while utilizing the core/periphery structure of the network. The third heuristic (Community) relies on a community detection algorithm to compute dense substructures in the network and link the newcomer with nodes within each community. (2) We implement these heuristics and compare them with a random benchmark algorithm. Our experiments are carried out over networks of various size generated using two random network models: a scale-free network model and a small-world network model. We also test the algorithms on four real-world social networks. In all experiments our heuristics significantly outperform the random benchmark algorithm. (3) The results of our experiments clearly distinguish the radial and the medial heuristics. Over scale-free networks, the last two heuristics (Express and Community) outperform the first heuristic (MaxEig) in general for the radial centralities (i.e., closeness and eigenvector centralities), while MaxEig is better for the betweenness centrality. On the other hand, MaxEig performs slightly ahead on the small-world networks which do not exhibit a strong core/periphery structure.

Related Work. Many works targeted at vital node selection, i.e., locating a set of individuals whose collective positional advantage (e.g. influence or centrality) is maximized [13]. Influence maximization problem is an important instance of this problem which can be facilitated by maximizing centrality [2]. Crescenzi et al. demonstrates that maximizing closeness centrality for a newcomer is NP-hard [3]. Puzis et al. looks for groups of nodes with the highest group betweenness centrality and proved that this problem is also NP-hard [17]. This paper investigates the problem of embedding a node into a network through establishing ties, which is related but clearly different from centrality maximization.

Social network integration refers to the process that merges two network into a single entity through establishing edges. Moskvina and Liu initiated this problem in [14]. Through a series of works, they've studied strategies to establish edges between two networks to minimize the diameter of the resulting network [15,16]. The authors also studied the problem of adding edges to place the newcomer at the Jordan center, which consists of all nodes with the smallest eccentricity [14]. Social network building is a restriction of social network integration and focuses on the case when one of the component network consists of a single node. Yan et. al. investigated social building in a dynamic network [19,20]. Our work differs from the above as we, instead of focusing solely on closeness centrality, combine a number of centrality metrics and use a unifying typology to our analysis.

2 A Typology of Centrality

We view a *social network* as an unweighted, undirected, connected graph $G = (V, E)$ where V is a set of nodes and E is a set of edges on V. An undirected edge that connects node u to node v is denoted as uv. A *path* (of length k) is defined as a sequence of nodes $u_0, u_1, \ldots, u_k$ where $u_iu_{i+1} \in E$ for any $0 \leq i < k$. The *distance* between u and v, denoted by $d(u, v)$, is the length of a shortest path from u to v. The *neighborhood* of u is defined as $N(u) := \{v \mid uv \in E\}$, while the h*-neighborhood* of u is defined as $N_h(u) := \{v \mid d(u, v) \leq h\}$. The study of social networks focuses on some important structural features [4]. A network is either *unimodal* which means that it contains a single core/periphery substructure, or *multimodal* which means that it contains multiple cores.

Centrality is a function $c\colon V \to \mathbb{R}$ that expresses in a certain sense how much any node v is engaged with the rest of the network; a higher $c(v)$ would denote a higher level of engagement and that v would sit more towards the "center" of the network. On the other hand, a lower $c(v)$ would imply less involvement of v with others and thus v sits towards the "periphery" of the network. Borgatti and Everett classify centrality notions by the different roles in which a node plays in its engagement with the network [1]. We illustrate this classification as follows:

- The first type of centrality aims to capture the extent to which a node interacts with others. For example, a central node should play a significant role in disseminating information. Messages that are sent out from a more central node is more likely to reach other nodes. In other words, the centrality of a node v expresses a form of "dyadic cohesiveness" between v and other nodes. Here, v acts as the initiator of the engagement. Thus we call this form of centrality *radial centrality*.
- The second type of centrality aims to capture the extend to which a node mediates between others. For example, a central node should bridge between multiple parties in a social network to allow information to pass through. In this sense, a central node acts as an information gatekeeper. We call this form of centrality *medial centrality*.

More formally we make the following definitions. Given a network $G = (V, E)$, a *dyadic walk structure* is defined as a matrix $W\colon V^2 \to \mathbb{R}$ where $W(x, y)$ denotes a form of "engagement" that node x has with node y.

Definition 1. *Let W be a dyadic walk structure. A* radial centrality *based on W is $c_{\mathsf{r},W}\colon V \to \mathbb{R}$ such that for every node $x \in V$,*

$$c_{\mathsf{r},W}(x) = \sum_{y \in V} W(x, y).$$

As an example, let $A\colon V^2 \to \mathbb{N}$ be the adjacency matrix of the graph G. The *degree* is simply the radial centrality based on A, i.e. $C_{Deg}(v) = c_{\mathsf{r},A}(v)$ for any node $v \in V$ [9]. In our work we use two prominent radial centrality metrics.

Closeness Centrality. Let $D\colon V^2 \to \mathbb{R}$ be the *length matrix* defined by $D(x, y) = \frac{1}{(n-1)d(x,y)}$. The *closeness centrality* is the radial centrality based on D, i.e., $C_{Cls}(v) = c_{\mathsf{r},D}(v)$. In other words, $C_{Cls}(v)$ is the average among the reciprocal of distances between v and all other nodes.

Eigenvector Centrality. Let $R\colon V^2 \to \mathbb{R}$ be the *volume matrix* defined by $R(x, y) = \lim_{i\to\infty}(\frac{1}{\lambda}(A + I))^i$ where λ is the dominant eigenvalue of E. This limit exists by the Perron-Frobenius theorem. Intuitively, $R(x, y)$ expresses a discounted number of paths (with possible repeated nodes) of length k ad infinitum between x and y. The *eigenvector centrality* is the radial centrality based on R, i.e., $C_{Eig}(v) = c_{\mathsf{r},R}(v)$.

A *triadic walk structure* of a graph $G = (V, E)$ is a tensor $U : V^3 \to \mathbb{R}$ where $U(x, y, z)$ evaluates a form of x's "intermediation" between nodes y and z.

Definition 2. *Let U be a triadic walk structure. A* medial centrality *based on U is $c_{\mathsf{m},U} : V \to \mathbb{R}$ such that for every node $x \in V$, $c_{\mathsf{m},U}(x) = \sum_{y\in V}\sum_{z\in V} U(x, y, z)$.*

For example, define $T : V^3 \to \{0, 1\}$ such that $T(x, y, z) = 1$ if and only if x, y, z are mutually connected by edges. The medial centrality based on T gives $c_{\mathsf{m},T}(x)$ equal to the number of closed triads that x is involved in. Betweenness centrality is one of the most mentioned medial centrality.

Betweenness Centrality. Let σ_{xy} refer to the total number of shortest paths starting from node x to node y, and let $\sigma_{xy}(v)$ refer to the number of shortest paths between x and y while going through node v. Let the tensor $B : V^3 \to \mathbb{Z}$ be defined by $B(x, y, z) = \frac{\sigma_{yz}(x)}{\sigma_{yz}}$ if x, y, u are pairwise-distinct; and $B(x, y, z) = 0$ otherwise. Then the *betweenness centrality* is simply the medial centrality based on B. This notion measures the "fraction of shortest paths going through a given node" and captures global information as it depends on the shortest paths of potentially distant nodes [5]. Formally, it is given by the definition of:

$$C_{Btw}(u) = \sum_{s\neq u\neq t} \frac{\sigma_{st}(u)}{\sigma_{st}} \tag{1}$$

The medial centralities are regarded as fundamentally different from the radial counterparts [1]. For example, in a multimodal network (which contains multiple centers), minimizing the average distance between a node and all other nodes would not reveal either center of the graph, but rather, it outputs a node in the periphery region between centers.

Network Building Problem. Throughout we use u to denote a *newcomer* node and $G = (V, E)$ a network where $u \notin V$. The node u is interested in establish connections with nodes in V in order to maximize its centrality in the resulting merged network. More formally, we define the following operation:

Definition 3. *Given a network $G = (V, E)$, a newcomer node $u \notin V$, and a subset $S \subseteq V$ of nodes, we use $E_S(u)$ to denote the set of edges $\{uv \mid v \in S\}$. Define $G \oplus E_S(u)$ as the resulting merged network $(V \cup \{u\}, E \cup E_S(u))$.*

We put a constraint that bounds the number of new connections to be created. Thus the *network building problem* takes as input a network G and a natural number $k \in \mathbb{N}$. The output will be a set S of k edges so that u will achieve high closeness, eigenvector and betweenness centrality in the merged network $G \oplus E_S(u)$. Our next goal is to propose algorithms to solve this problem.

3 Algorithms for the Network Building Problem

The network building problem presented above amounts to a multi-objective optimization with three objective functions. Any solutions for this problem will not only rely on the network topology, but also on which centrality metric that we specifically target on. We present three algorithms for the network building problem which are based on different intuitions about the centrality metrics and the network topology. Each algorithm takes a network $G = (V, E)$ and $k \in \mathbb{N}$ as input and aims to compute a set of k nodes $S = \{v_1, \ldots, v_k\}$. Metrics are calculated for the resulting graph $G \oplus E_S(u)$. To pick each v_i, the algorithm maintains a set U of *uncovered nodes* and picks nodes from U iteratively. The starting configuration is $U = V$ and the procedure repeats until $U = \varnothing$ or k nodes have been picked.

MaxEig Algorithm. The first algorithm is a heuristic that is based on the idea of maximizing the centrality of the node whom u is connected to. This is an "eager" approach where the newcomer aims to build links with those who are highly interactive with others. This algorithm iteratively selects the node with the highest eigenvector centrality and creates an edge between the newcomer and the selected node. To ensure that no two selected nodes are near one another, the nodes inside the h-neighborhood of the selected node are disqualified from ever becoming a selected node, where $h = \ln(r)$ where r is the radius of the graph. This process repeats until all k iterations have completed or until no more nodes are qualified to become selected nodes. As eigenvector centrality, being a radial centrality metric, is appropriate only for unimodal networks, we expect that this algorithm to have good outcome for graphs with a single core. Algorithm 1 describes the selection process in this strategy.

Algorithm 1. MaxEig

```
Input: G(V, E), u, k ∈ ℕ
  U := V; i := 0
  while (U ≠ ∅) and i < k do
      Find v ⊂ U with maximum C_Eig(v_i)
      U ← U \ N_ln(r)(u)                         ▷ r is the graph radius
      Create an edge between u and v
      i := i + 1
  end while
```

Express Algorithm. The second algorithm is developed around the notion of *brokerage* [14]. A broker is a node that sits between diverse regions of the network and acts as "fast-track" channels between separate regions in the network. Edges between brokers and other nodes are typically weak ties (i.e., bridges) who share little common neighbors. The algorithm aims to convert the newcomer into a broker by finding distant nodes and linking each of them to the newcomer. It begins by finding a node with the highest degree centrality. Then the algorithm finds a node which is furthest away from the starting node. An edge is created between the starting node and the newcomer, followed by another edge created between the newcomer and the finishing node. The neighborhoods of both selected nodes are removed from the uncovered set to ensure that the next pair of selected nodes is sufficiently distant from the already selected nodes. Algorithm 2 describes the selection process in this algorithm.

Algorithm 2. Express

Input:$G(V, E), u, k \in \mathbb{N}$
  $U := V; i := 0$
  while $(U \neq \varnothing)$ and $i < k$ **do**
    Find $v_1 \in U$ with maximum $C_{Deg}(v_1)$
    Find $v_2 \in U$ with maximum $d(v_1, v_2)$
    $U \leftarrow U \setminus N(u); U \leftarrow U \setminus N(v)$
    Create an edge between uv_1 and an edge uv_2
    $i := i + 1$
  end while

Community Algorithm. The third algorithm is based on the assumption that the network is multimodal; When the network contains several core/periphery substructures, the newcomer would integrate well into the network if it establishes ties to bridge all centers in the network. A prevalent property of a complex network is that it would contain a collection of densely connected communities [11]. Intuitively, by identifying the community structure of the network and find central nodes in the communities, we would be able to identify multiple centers of the network. Thus the goal of designing the Community algorithm is to reflect the performance of medial centrality on multimodel networks. Community algorithm proceeds by utilizing betweenness centrality.

Algorithm 3. Community

Input:$G(V, E), u, k \in \mathbb{N}$
  $U := V$
  Divide G into k communities using an existing community detection algorithm
  for every community **do**
    Find $v \in U$ with maximum $C_{Btw}(v)$
    Create an edge between u and v
  end for

4 Experiment and Analysis

Datasets. We run our algorithms over two random graph models and four real-world networks. This is done to provide a well-rounded analysis on the performance and behaviour of the algorithms created.

Generated Graphs. To ensure that we produce results that are compatible and comparable to that of similar papers within the field, we generate two established types of random graphs, namely Barabàsi-Albert (BA)'s scale-free network model and Watts-Strogatz (WS)'s small-world model. Each model produces graphs of eight different sizes; starting at graphs with 250 nodes, and increasing node count by 250, until reaching graphs with a cardinality of 2000 nodes. For each graph size, the generators created a set of 20 graphs, so that the results found from each algorithm could be averaged. In total we generate 160 graphs for each model which amounts to a total of 320 synthetic networks. In our experiments we check the centrality gained by the newcomer when the number of edges established is $k \leq 10$; This value is empirically obtained given the size of the networks (which range from 2000 to 20000). The BA model generates scale-free graphs whose degree distribution follows an asymptomatic power law. The WS model produced graphs which emulate small-world networks. These graphs have high levels of clustering and low average path lengths. While the WS graphs were being generated, they had a base degree of six and a rewire probability of 0.1. This ensured that the graphs that were produced had a clustering coefficient which was high enough that the nodes grouped into cliques, while still being low enough to be considered realistic.

Real-World Graphs. We also select four real-world social networks. The sizes of the graphs varied from $\approx 6,000$ to 20000 nodes. All of these graphs originated from social networking sites such as Facebook, AnyBeat and Google+. Table 1 shows their attributes and references.

Table 1. Details of the real-world social networks. The table lists for each dataset the number of nodes, clustering coefficient, edge:node ratio, number of communities and the maximum modularity, as obtained by the classical Louvain method for community detection based on modularity maximization.

Name	#Nodes	Clus coef.	E/N	#Community	Modularity
soc-Anybeat [18]	12644	0.227	5.3	41	0.43
socfb-American75 [18]	6386	0.24	34.1	10	0.42
socfb-BC17 [18]	11509	0.21	42.31	7	0.55
soc-Gplus [18]	23628	0.218	1.66	33	0.74

Results and Evaluation. To measure the performance of our algorithms and observe to what extent these positional advantages are achieved, the effectiveness of the algorithms will be measured using the three types of centrality metrics of the newcomer in the resulting network. At the same time, a random algorithm is included as a benchmark to compare the other algorithms against. It was implemented to select k nodes at random from the network, and created edges between the newcomer and those selected nodes.

Observation 1. We observe the centrality of the newcomer during the execution of the algorithms across 10 iterations of edge creation. See Figs. 1 and 2.

Here we use synthetic networks with 2000 nodes, and the results are averaged across all 20 variations. In all cases, our three algorithms significantly outperform the benchmark algorithm.

For BA graph (Fig. 1), Community results in the steepest growth on closeness and eigenvector centrality in comparison to the other three algorithms. This advantage, however, is not present in terms of betweenness. In retrospect, the dichotomy between radial versus medial centralities asserts that they captures different roles in which a node plays in its engagement with the network [1]. As BA networks resemble unimodal networks which have single center, we would expect the algorithms behaves differently on BA networks. Indeed, our results demonstrates a clear contrast between radial centrality (closeness and eigenvector) and medial centrality (betweenness).

From WS graph (Fig. 2), Community and MaxEig algorithms are equally matched in improving newcomer's three types of centrality. This may be indicating that WS graphs do not exhibit a clear single-center structure and are not unimodal networks. So no obvious difference between radical centrality and medial centrality are observed.

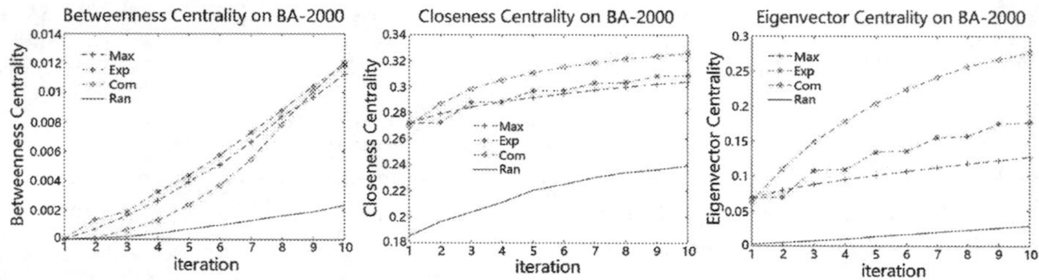

Fig. 1. Betweenness(left), closeness(center) and eigenvector(right) centrality of newcomer on BA graphs with 2000 nodes over 10 iterations

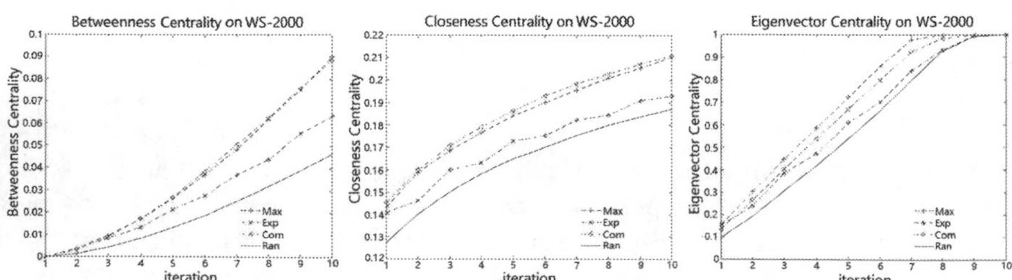

Fig. 2. Betweenness(left), closeness(center) and eigenvector(right) centrality of newcomer on WS graphs with 2000 nodes over 10 iterations

Observation 2. We observe the three types of centrality of the newcomer after 10 iterations. The results are in Fig. 3 and are averaged across 20 variations for each graph size to compensate for any irregularities. On all cases in both BA and WS graphs, the random benchmark algorithm performed the worst in comparison to our three counterparts. In terms of performance, Community algorithm appears to have the best results on average in BA graphs. Although for betweenness centrality, it fluctuates when the graph size is relatively small, and gradually improves as the graph becomes larger. The results, once again, show the difference of radial centrality and medial centrality on BA networks: The curves of closeness and eigenvector centrality very much align with each other, with Community being consistently the best performing algorithm. Moreover, the betweenness curves have very different performance rank of the algorithms. On the other hand, MaxEig algorithm is slightly better than Community algorithm in WS graphs. But the advantage of Community algorithm becomes evident in increasing eigenvector centrality.

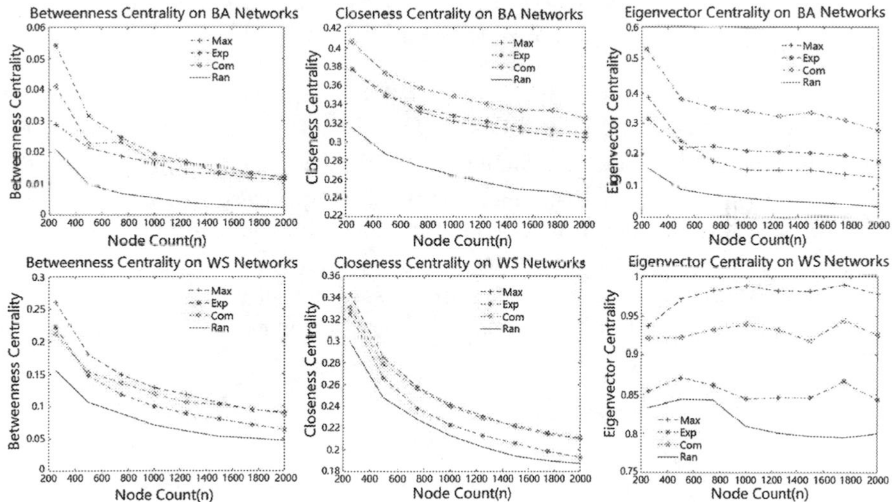

Fig. 3. Betweenness(left), closeness(center) and eigenvector(right) of newcomer on different BA(top) and WS(bottom) graphs sizes after 10 iterations

Observation 3. We also observe the centrality of the newcomer after 10 iterations on four real-world graphs. The results are shown in Fig. 4. Community algorithm performs better than others on improving newcomer's betweenness centrality. The maximum improvement is 541 times that of the random algorithm. MaxEig improves the newcomer's eigenvector centrality the most and the maximum improvement is 27 times that of random algorithm. The three algorithms are comparable in terms of closeness centrality.

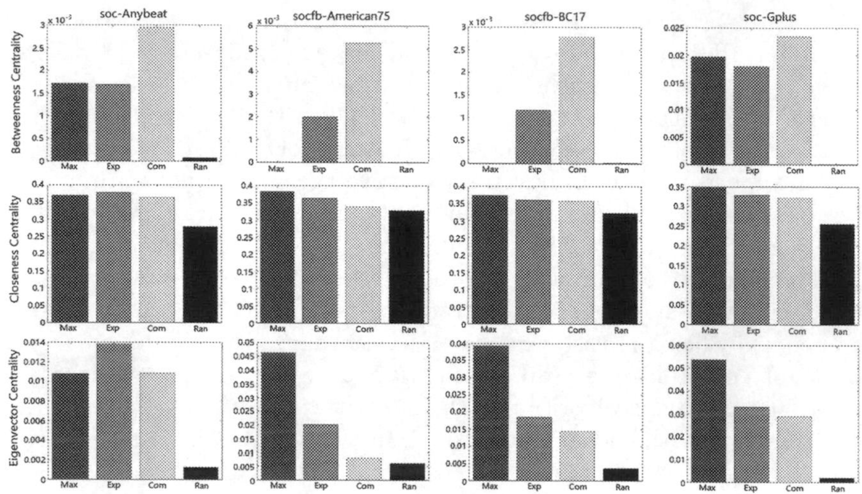

Fig. 4. Betweenness(top), closeness(center) and eigenvector(bottom) of newcomer on soc-Anybeat, socfb-American75, socfb-BC17, soc-Gplus after 10 iterations

We use radar diagrams to better contrast the three types of centrality on the networks in Figs. 5 and 6. To make the differences among results stand out, we normalize these metrics: define normalized$(C(u))) := \frac{C(u)}{\max(C(u))}$, where $C \in \{C_{Btw}, C_{Cls}, C_{Eig}\}$, and the max operation is applied on the results of the centrality over all four algorithms. Therefore the values in the diagrams do not indicate the true centrality, but rather how the results are compared across the algorithms. Figure 5 shows the results in three different number of iterations. On BA graph with 2000 nodes, Community has better performance in improv-

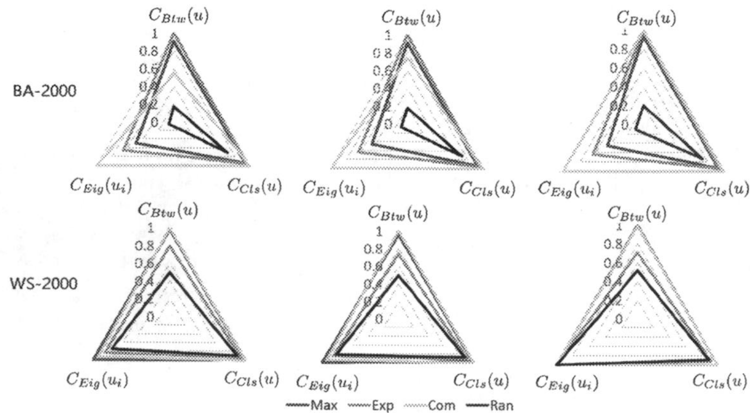

Fig. 5. Radar diagram of BA(top) and WS(bottom) graph with 2000 nodes after 5 (left), 7 (center), and 10 iterations(right)

ing closeness centrality and eigenvector centrality. Community gives the highest eigenvector centrality but relatively low betweenness centrality, while Express improves betweenness and closeness centrality the most. This is remarkable given that Community is aimed at improving medial centrality while MaxEig targets at the radial centrality. On WS graphs, Community and MaxEig algorithms lead to very similar increase in all types of centrality. Community has good performance in improving betweenness centrality and closeness centrality. On real-word graphs, three algorithms also have decent performance on closeness centrality.

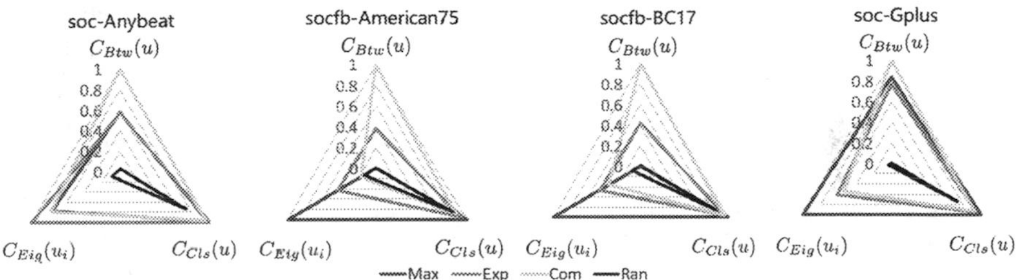

Fig. 6. Radar diagram of the four real-world networks 10 iterations

5 Conclusion and Future Work

This paper amounts to one of the first efforts that address link creation within the framework of multiple centrality maximization. In particular, we focus on a dichotomy between radial and medial centrality [1]. The radial (closeness and eigenvector) and medial (betweenness) centrality differ by the roles in which individuals engage with the network. Our experiments demonstrate their fundamental differences. We introduces three new algorithms that create edges for a newcomer. In all cases, our algorithms significantly outperform the random benchmark algorithm: Community achieves up to 541 times improvement in betweenness that of the benchmark over a network of >20000 nodes, while MaxEig achieves up to 27 times improvement in eigenvector centrality that of the benchmark. The results also contrast between BA and WS graphs and gives insight over the differences between unimodal and multimodal networks.

Clearly, our results should be strengthened by running the algorithms on more network instances for further correlation between centrality and structural features of the network. We also should consider more notions of centrality, such as GPI power, geodesic k-path centrality, disjoint k-path centrality, Katz's measure of centrality [1]. An interesting question would be to inquiry a new centrality metric that combines radial and medial centrality. The current scope of the paper only covers the situation of a newcomer merging into an existing network that is static. Naturally, one improvement that is immediately apparent would be extending this algorithm to accommodate for inputs where the network is a dynamic entity.

References

1. Borgatti, S.P., Everett, M.G.: A graph-theoretic perspective on centrality. Soc. Netw. **28**(4), 466–484 (2006)
2. Chen, W., Wang, Y., Yang, S.: Efficient influence maximization in social networks. In: ACM SIGKDD International Conference on Knowledge Discovery and Data Mining, pp. 199–208 (2009)
3. Crescenzi, P., D'Angelo, G., Severini, L., Velaj, Y.: Greedily Improving Our Own Centrality in A Network. In: Bampis, E. (ed.) SEA 2015. LNCS, vol. 9125, pp. 43–55. Springer, Cham (2015). https://doi.org/10.1007/978-3-319-20086-6_4
4. Csima, B.F., Khoussainov, B., Liu, J.: Computable categoricity of graphs with finite components. In: Beckmann, A., Dimitracopoulos, C., Löwe, B. (eds.) CiE 2008. LNCS, vol. 5028, pp. 139–148. Springer, Heidelberg (2008). https://doi.org/10.1007/978-3-540-69407-6_15
5. Freeman, L.C.: A set of measures of centrality based on betweenness. Sociometry **40**(1), 35–41 (1977)
6. Gargiulo, M., Benassi, M.: Trapped in your own net? Network cohesion, structural holes, and the adaptation of social capital. Organ. Sci. **11**(2), 183–196 (2000)
7. Granovetter, M.S.: The strength of weak ties. Am. J. Sociol. **78**(6), 1360–1380 (1973)
8. Kempe, D., Kleinberg, J., Tardos, E.: Maximizing the spread of influence through a social network. In ACM SIGKDD International Conference on Knowledge Discovery and Data Mining, pp. 137–146 (2003)
9. Khoussainov, B., Liu, J., Khaliq, I.: A dynamic algorithm for reachability games played on trees. In: Královič, R., Niwiński, D. (eds.) MFCS 2009. LNCS, vol. 5734, pp. 477–488. Springer, Heidelberg (2009). https://doi.org/10.1007/978-3-642-03816-7_41
10. Kleinberg, J., Suri, S., Wexler, T.: Strategic network formation with structural holes. ACM SIGecom Exch. **7**(3), 11 (2008)
11. Liu, J., Wei, Z.: Community detection based on graph dynamical systems with asynchronous runs. In: Computing and Networking (CANDAR) Second International Symposium on 2014, pp. 463–469. IEEE (2014)
12. Liu, J., Wei, Z.: Network, popularity and social cohesion: a game-theoretic approach. In: AAAI, pp. 600–606 (2017)
13. Lü, L., Chen, D., Ren, X.L., Zhang, Q.M., Zhang, Y.C., Zhou, T.: Vital nodes identification in complex networks. Physics reports, vol. 650, pp. 1–63 (2016)
14. Moskvina, A., Liu, J.: How to build your network? A structural analysis. In: Proceedings of IJCAI 2016 (2016)
15. Moskvina, A., Liu, J.: Integrating networks of equipotent nodes. In: Nguyen, H.T.T., Snasel, V. (eds.) CSoNet 2016. LNCS, vol. 9795, pp. 39–50. Springer, Cham (2016). https://doi.org/10.1007/978-3-319-42345-6_4
16. Moskvina, A., Liu, J.: Togetherness: an algorithmic approach to network integration. In: IEEE/ACM International Conference on Advances in Social Networks Analysis and Mining 2017, pp. 223–230 (2016)
17. Puzis, R., Zilberman, P., Elovici, Y., Dolev, S., Brandes, U.: Heuristics for speeding up betweenness centrality computation. In: Privacy, Security, Risk and Trust, pp. 302–311 (2012)
18. Rossi, R., Ahmed, K.: The network data repository with interactive graph analytics and visualization. In: Proceedings of the Twenty-Ninth AAAI Conference on Artificial Intelligence (2015)

19. Yan, B., Chen, Y., Liu, J.: Dynamic relationship building: exploitation versus exploration on a social network. In: Bouguettaya, A., et al. (eds.) WISE 2017. LNCS, vol. 10569, pp. 75–90. Springer, Cham (2017). https://doi.org/10.1007/978-3-319-68783-4_6
20. Yan, B., Liu, Y., Liu, J., Cai, Y., Su, H., Zheng, H.: From the periphery to the center: information brokerage in an evolving network. arXiv preprint arXiv:1805.00751 (2018)

Gradient Hyperalignment for Multi-subject fMRI Data Alignment

Tonglin Xu, Muhammad Yousefnezhad, and Daoqiang Zhang(✉)

College of Computer Science and Technology,
Nanjing University of Aeronautics and Astronautics, Nanjing 211106, China
dqzhang@nuaa.edu.cn

Abstract. Multi-subject fMRI data analysis is an interesting and challenging problem in human brain decoding studies. The inherent anatomical and functional variability across subjects make it necessary to do both anatomical and functional alignment before classification analysis. Besides, when it comes to big data, time complexity becomes a problem that cannot be ignored. This paper proposes Gradient Hyperalignment (Gradient-HA) as a gradient-based functional alignment method that is suitable for multi-subject fMRI datasets with large amounts of samples and voxels. The advantage of Gradient-HA is that it can solve independence and high dimension problems by using Independent Component Analysis (ICA) and Stochastic Gradient Ascent (SGA). Validation using multi-classification tasks on big data demonstrates that Gradient-HA method has less time complexity and better or comparable performance compared with other state-of-the-art functional alignment methods.

Keywords: Hyperalignment · Gradient · ICA · Brain decoding
Classification

1 Introduction

Functional Magnetic Resonance Imaging (fMRI) is a widely used neuroimaging method [1]. In fact, fMRI allows us to understand the information that a brain region represents and how that information is encoded, rather than just knowing what a brain region does [2]. Many modern human brain fMRI studies require the use of multiple subject data, which is important for assessing the generalization and validity of the findings of the experiments across subjects [3]. Besides, multiple subject data is better than single subject data because only one subject may carry a large amount of noise [4]. However, since different subject's spatial response patterns are different, one challenging problem in multi-subject analysis is that the analysis requires credible functional alignments and anatomical alignments between neural activities in different subjects, which can greatly improve the performance of classification models shown in previous studies [1–6]. In general, there are two types of alignment, anatomical alignment and functional alignment, both of which can work together. Anatomical alignment is the most common alignment method for fMRI imaging. It is based on anatomical features and it uses structural MRI images such as Talairach alignment [7]. However, this method can only produce limited accuracy because the size, shape, and

X. Geng and B.-H. Kang (Eds.): PRICAI 2018, LNAI 11012, pp. 1058–1068, 2018.
https://doi.org/10.1007/978-3-319-97304-3_81

anatomical location of functional loci vary from subject to subject [8, 9]. It is well known that the anatomical and functional topography are different among different subjects and anatomical alignment is not sufficient to align the functional topography. Therefore, functional alignment is used to align the brain neural responses across subjects.

Hyperalignment (HA) is the most popular and effective functional alignment method known as 'anatomy free' [6]. Haxby et al. [6] first proposed HA to extract shared features across subjects then map different subjects to a common space. By using hyperalignment, the accuracy of multivariate pattern (MVP) classification is greatly improved in contrast with anatomical alignments and other functional alignments. Mathematically, hyperalignment can be explained by Canonical Correlation Analysis (CCA). According to this, Xu et al. [10] proposed Regularized Hyperalignment (RHA) to show that regularized approaches can be transformed into basic hyperalignment problems. In another approach, Chen et al. [5] developed SVD-Hyperalignment algorithm which employs a joint Singular Value Decomposition (SVD) of response matrices to reduce the dimensionality of the data. Then, hyperalignment is performed in the lower dimensional feature space. Further, Chen et al. [4] proposed Shared Response Model (SRM), which is a contrast to the methods where the number of features equals the number of voxels. In addition, Guntupalli et al. [11] developed SearchLight (SL) hyperalignment algorithm in contrast with regions of interest (ROI) hyperalignment algorithm, which can capture fine-scale topographies. In order to extend linear representation of fMRI responses to a nonlinear embedding space, Lorbert et al. [12] proposed Kernel Hyperalignment (KHA). Besides, Chen et al. [13] designed a multi-layer convolutional auto encoder (CAE) for multi-subject, whole brain, spatially local, fMRI data aggregation, which is also a nonlinear functional alignment model. CAE model is based on SRM and uses Searchlight algorithm to preserve spatial locality. Similarly, Zhang et al. [14] proposed a searchlight based shared response model to identify shared information in small contiguous regions. They combined Independent Component Analysis (ICA) and searchlight to solve SRM problem.

In conclusion, all the works above tried to find a better solution for HA. The main challenge is that when applying these methods to big data, the runtime is high. As is known to all, the dimensionality of multi-subject fMRI data is very high. Therefore, previous fMRI analysis often selects a subset of voxels within ROI, or selects a subset of principal components of the ROI. However, sometimes the number of voxels selected in ROI is also very large. As a result, spatial complexity and time complexity are two important criterions for the evaluation of hyperalignment algorithms. Another question is whether the voxels or features found by above methods are independent? Indeed, independence as a guiding principle to select features is very effective. If the components are statistically independent, this means that the value of any one of the components gives no information on the values of the other components [15].

As the main contribution of this paper, we propose a novel gradient approach, which is called Gradient Hyperalignment (Gradient-HA), in order to solve the independence, high dimension problems in fMRI analysis. Indeed, Gradient-HA employs ICA and uses Stochastic Gradient Ascent (SGA) for optimization [15]. Consequently, Gradient-HA generates low runtime on large datasets, and the training data is not referenced when Gradient-HA computes the functional alignment for a new subject. The proposed method is related to SR-ICA [14]. Indeed, the main difference between Gradient-HA and the SR-ICA is that SR-ICA is an SRM problem but Gradient-HA solves the HA problem.

The rest of this paper is organized as follows: In Sect. 2, this study briefly introduces the HA method. Then, Gradient-HA is proposed in Sect. 3. Experimental results are reported in Sect. 4. And finally, this paper presents conclusion and points out some future works in Sect. 5.

2 Hyperalignment

Preprocessed fMRI time-series data for S subjects can be denoted by $X_i \in \mathbb{R}^{T \times V}, i = 1 : S$, where V denotes the number of voxels, T denotes the number of time points in units of TRs (Time of Repetition). In most fMRI studies, the number of voxels is more than the number of time points, so the matrix X_i and the voxel correlation map $X_i^T X_j$ may not be full rank. Since the data was collected when all subjects were presented with the same, time synchronized stimuli, the temporal alignment can be omitted. In other word, the same time point is considered to represent the same stimuli for all subjects. However, multi-subject data is not spatially aligned. For spatial alignment, we need a metric to measure it. We generally expect that the k-th column of X_i has a larger correlation with the k-th column of X_j, so Inter-Subject Correlation (ISC) is a useful metric which can be defined for two different subjects as follows [2, 3, 5, 10, 16]:

$$\mathrm{ISC}\left(X_i, X_j\right) = (1/v)\mathrm{tr}\left(X_i^T X_j\right) \tag{1}$$

If X_i are column-wise standardized (each column has zero mean and unit variance), the ISC lies in $[-1, +1]$ with large values of ISC indicating better alignment [3, 10, 16].

The HA problem is based on (1), which can be formulated as:

$$\max_{R_{i=1:S}, R_{j=1:S}} \sum\nolimits_{i<j} \mathrm{ISC}\left(X_i R_i, X_j R_j\right) \tag{2}$$

where $R_i \in \mathbb{R}^{V \times V}$ is the HA solution for i-th subject, which can be seen as the orthogonal transformations of the rows of X_i and this common "rotation" of the rows preserves the geometry of the temporal trajectory of the data. To avoid overfitting, we put constraints on R_i, $R_i^T R_i = I$, where I is the identity matrix. This leads to the basic HA problem [3, 5, 10, 16]:

$$\min_{R_i, R_j} \sum\nolimits_{i<j} \left\| X_i R_i - X_j R_j \right\|_F^2 \tag{3}$$

$$\text{subject to } R_i^T R_i = I$$

In order to solve (3), we can change (3) to another formulation:

$$\min_{R_i,G} \sum_{i=1}^{S} \|X_i R_i - G\|_F^2 \tag{4}$$

$$\text{subject to } R_i^T R_i = I$$

where $G = S^{-1} \sum_{j=1}^{S} X_j R_j$ is the HA template. The formulation (3) and (4) are equivalent because we have the identity [18]:

$$\sum_{i<j} \|X_i R_i - X_j R_j\|_F^2 = S \sum_{i=1}^{S} \|X_i R_i - G\|_F^2 \tag{5}$$

Indeed, the HA template (G) can be used for functional alignment in the test data before classification. Most of the previous studies used CCA for finding this template.

3 Gradient Hyperalignment

As we mentioned above, we are trying to propose an algorithm to find independent features and has less time complexity on big data. On the one hand, in order to solve the independence problem, we use independent component analysis (ICA) algorithm to obtain the independent features. On the other hand, in order to solve the time complexity problem, we try to use stochastic gradient algorithm to improve the time complexity of the algorithm. Indeed, we will demonstrate in the following that the objective function of ICA and HA are equal to some extent, so we can get the solution of HA by calculating the solution of ICA. Besides, stochastic gradient algorithm is one of the effective algorithms to solve ICA. In a nutshell, our proposed algorithm, Gradient-HA, is implemented by calculating the solution of ICA using stochastic gradient algorithm.

The standard ICA is a generative model, which tries to find a process of mixing independent components that can generate the observed data. ICA can be measured by non-gaussianity, likelihood, mutual information or tensorial methods. Using our notation, given data $X_i^T \in \mathbb{R}^{V \times T}$, ICA can be formulated as follows [14, 15]:

$$X_i^T = A_i Y \tag{6}$$

where $A_i \in \mathbb{R}^{V \times V}$ is the mixing matrix, $Y \in \mathbb{R}^{V \times T}$ is the independent components matrix.

Obviously, Eq. (6) is equivalent to:

$$B_i X_i^T = Y \tag{7}$$

where $B_i \in \mathbb{R}^{V \times V}$ is the inverse of A_i.

To solve ICA problem, we get the following optimization problem:

$$\min_{B_i, Y} \sum_{i=1}^{M} \left\| X_i B_i^T - Y^T \right\|_F^2 \quad (8)$$

$$\text{subject to } B_i^T B_i = I$$

Compare (8) and (4), by letting $B_i^T = R_i, Y^T = G$, we can see that ICA problem can be used to solve HA problem. In other words, we can use ICA instead of CCA to find HA template (G).

Algorithm 1: Gradient Hyperalignment

Input: Data $\mathbf{X_i}, \mathbf{i = 1, \ldots, S}$, number of features **f**, convergence threshold $\boldsymbol{\tau}$, max iteration **N**, number of subjects **S**, learning rates $\boldsymbol{\mu}$, batch_size **b**.

Output: $\mathbf{R_i}$, **G**

Method:

1. Center the data to make its mean zero.
2. Randomly initialize matrices $\mathbf{R_i}$.
3. Randomly select **b** rows of matrices $\mathbf{X_i}, \mathbf{R_i}$ as new $\mathbf{X_i}, \mathbf{R_i}$.
4. Compute $\mathbf{G} = {}^{1}/_{\mathbf{S}} \sum_{\mathbf{i}}^{\mathbf{S}} \mathbf{X_i R_i}$ according to (4).
5. Update the separating matrix according to (13).

$$\mathbf{R_i} \leftarrow \mathbf{R_i} + \boldsymbol{\mu} \mathbf{X_i^T} \boldsymbol{g}(\mathbf{G})$$
$$\textbf{where } \boldsymbol{g}(\mathbf{G}) = \boldsymbol{tanh}\,(\mathbf{G})$$

6. If not converged, go back to step 3.

3.1 Optimization

In this section, we propose an effective approach for optimizing the ICA objective function by using negentropy and stochastic gradient ascent (SGA) [15].

In order to optimize (8), one solution is to calculate the gradient of (8) and use stochastic gradient descent (SGD) algorithm. However, there are two unknown variables, B_i and Y, in (8), so it is difficult to calculate the gradient. Besides, by calculating the gradient of (8) directly cannot guarantee the independence of the features in Y^T. A basic principle in ICA is that non-gaussian is independent [15]. Therefore, instead of calculating the gradient of (8) directly, we choose to maximize the non-gaussianity of Y^T. For simplicity, we choose to use the notation in (4) instead of (8) here, so we will use R_i and G instead of B_i^T and Y^T in the following.

One way to measure non-gaussianity is by negentropy, so we choose to maximize negentropy instead of maximize nongaussian directly. Negentropy of G can be denoted by J(G), which is defined as follows:

$$J(G) = H\left(G_{gauss}\right) - H(G) \quad (9)$$

where G_{gauss} is a gaussian random variable of the same correlation (and covariance) matrix as G, $H(\cdot)$ is the differential entropy defined as follows:

$$H(G) = -\int p_G(\eta) \log p_G(\eta) d\eta \tag{10}$$

where $p_G(\eta)$ is the density of G.

In practice, we only need the approximation of negentropy. By using approximation, we get the following formula [15]:

$$J(G) \propto [E\{f(G)\} - E\{f(v)\}]^2 \tag{11}$$

where v is a gaussian random variable, $f(\cdot)$ is a nonquadratic function, e.g. *logcosh*. E is the expectation. Then we can calculate the gradient of J(G):

Table 1. Accuracy of Gradient-HA method and other state-of-the-art methods

Algorithm	DS105	DS107	DS232
Linear-SVM	0.1427 ± 0.0074	0.2583 ± 0.0128	**0.3158 ± 0.0365**
ICA	0.1222 ± 0.0082	0.2471 ± 0.0124	0.2534 ± 0.0126
PCA	0.1247 ± 0.0164	0.2454 ± 0.0083	0.2538 ± 0.0083
SRM	0.2125 ± 0.0500	0.4624 ± 0.0167	0.2534 ± 0.0235
SR-ICA	0.2137 ± 0.0568	0.3387 ± 0.0287	0.2532 ± 0.0111
Gradient-HA	**0.2765 ± 0.0009**	**0.5088 ± 0.0199**	0.2584 ± 0.0151

$$\Delta R_i \propto E\left\{X_i^T g(G)\right\} \tag{12}$$

where the function $g(\cdot)$ is the derivative of the function $f(\cdot)$, e.g. *tanh*. For SGA, we can ignore *E* here. Then the gradient of J(G) can be represented as follows:

$$\Delta R_i \propto X_i^T g(G) \tag{13}$$

Since we have calculated the gradient of J(G), we can use SGA to optimize it. In order to apply this algorithm to big data, we use a batch of the time points instead of whole time points. In this way, the accuracy of the final results is fine, and by changing the batch size, we can improve the accuracy.

4 Experiments

In this section, we will report the results of the experiments. As a baseline classification model, we use linear-SVM algorithm to generate multi-class classification results [17]. All datasets are separately preprocessed by FSL 5.0.10 (https://fsl.fmrib.ox.ac.uk), i.e. slice timing, anatomical alignment, normalization, smoothing. Regions of Interest (ROI) are also denoted by employing the main reference of each dataset. In addition, leave-one-subject-out cross-validation is utilized for partitioning datasets to the training set and testing set. Different functional alignment methods are employed for functional aligning and generating the general template (G). Then the mapped neural activities are used to generate the classification model. The performance of the proposed method is compared with the linear-SVM algorithm as the baseline, where the features are used after anatomical alignment without applying any hyperalignment mapping. Further, performances of the standard ICA, PCA, SRM [4] and SR-ICA [14] are reported as state-of-the-arts functional alignment methods.

4.1 Task Analysis

This paper utilizes three datasets, shared by Open fMRI (https://openfmri.org), for running empirical studies. As the first dataset, "Visual Object Recognition" (DS105) includes S = 6 subjects. It also contains K = 8 categories of visual stimuli, i.e. gray-scale images of faces, houses, cats, bottles, scissors, shoes, chairs, and scrambles (nonsense patterns). As the second dataset, "Word and Object Processing" (DS107) includes S = 48 subjects. It contains K = 4 categories of visual stimuli, i.e. words, objects, scrambles, consonants. As the last dataset, "Adjudicating between face-coding models with individual-face fMRI responses" (DS232) includes S = 10 subjects. It contains K = 4 categories of visual stimuli, i.e. objects, scrambled, faces and places. As Table 1 demonstrates, the performance of classification analysis without functional alignment methods is significantly low except for DS232. We get the results in Table 1 when the number of features selected is equal to the number of time points. However, for the basic algorithm linear-SVM we use the whole voxels and get the best result in DS232. Compared with other functional alignment methods, Table 1 shows that the proposed algorithm has generated better performance because it provided a better embedded space in order to align neural activities.

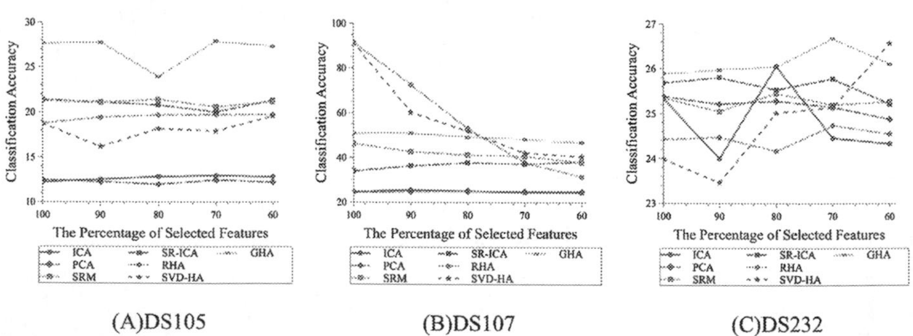

Fig. 1. Classification by using feature selection

4.2 Classification by Using Feature Selection

In this section, we will analyze the performance of classification results by selecting different feature (or voxel) numbers on DS105, DS107 and DS232. In fact, the algorithm will have less time complexity when choosing fewer features. Further, we want to test whether fewer features can still guarantee or even improve the classification accuracy. In general, the number of voxels per subject in fMRI data is much larger than the number of time points. For ICA, when the number of time points is smaller than the number of features, we cannot obtain enough information to calculate all the independent components. Therefore, we believe that when the number of selected features is exactly equal to the number of time points in each subject, it is sufficient to obtain enough information to ensure the classification accuracy. Besides, we further reduce the number of features so that it is lower than the number of time points to test how the classification accuracy changes when fewer features are selected. In this experiment, the performance of the proposed method is compared with ICA, PCA, SRM [4], SR-ICA [14], SVD-HA [5], RHA [10] as the state-of-the-art HA techniques, which can apply feature selection before generating a classification model. After applying functional alignment methods on fMRI data, we then use linear-SVM as the classification model for generating multi-classification results.

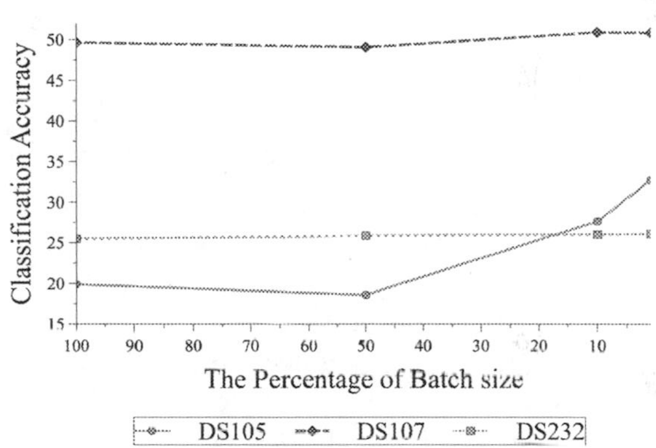

Fig. 2. Classification by selecting different percentage of batch size

Figure 1 illustrates the classification accuracy when the number of selected features varies from 100% to 60% of the number of time points (see Fig. 1). For simplicity, we use GHA to represent our Gradient-HA method in all figures. As is shown in the figure, the performance of the proposed method is better in comparison with the other methods in most of the cases due to its better feature representation. For DS107, the performance of RHA and SVD-HA is better than all of the other methods. Since the number of voxels in DS107 is small, RHA and SVD-HA can provide acceptable performance on DS107. However, these methods cannot generate suitable accuracy for high-dimensional datasets such as DS105, or DS232.

4.3 Classification by Changing the Batch Size

In this section, we will analyze the classification results by selecting different batch sizes. The point where our method is different from other methods is that our method can choose different batch sizes. When running the Gradient-HA method, we randomly use some small patches of the time points instead of using all time points. One of primary reason for selecting the batch size is reducing the program memory footprint and runtime. Like feature analysis, we also use three datasets DS105, DS107 and DS232. Since the number of time points in the three datasets are different, we do not select the same batch size for all three datasets here. Instead, we select the batch size according to the number of time points, which varies from 100% to 1% of the number of time points in each dataset. Since the other methods cannot select batch size, we just compare the results with our proposed method itself. The experimental results are shown in Fig. 2. As we can see in the figure, when selecting the smaller batch size, the performance of Gradient-HA is robust and even improved for DS105. Therefore, we can use only a few time points when running Gradient-HA algorithm in big data. Thus, we can save a lot of time in this way.

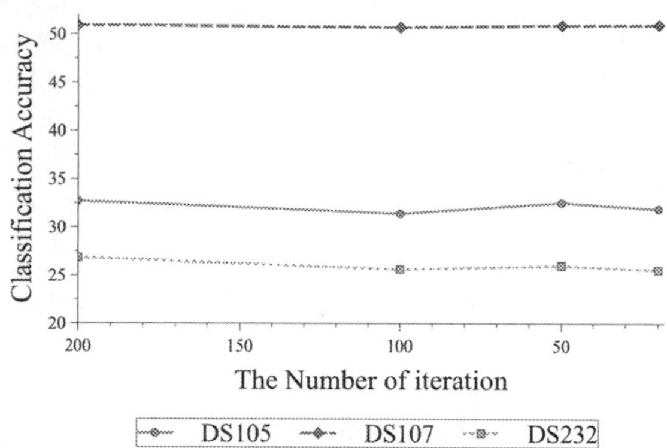

Fig. 3. Classification by selecting different iteration

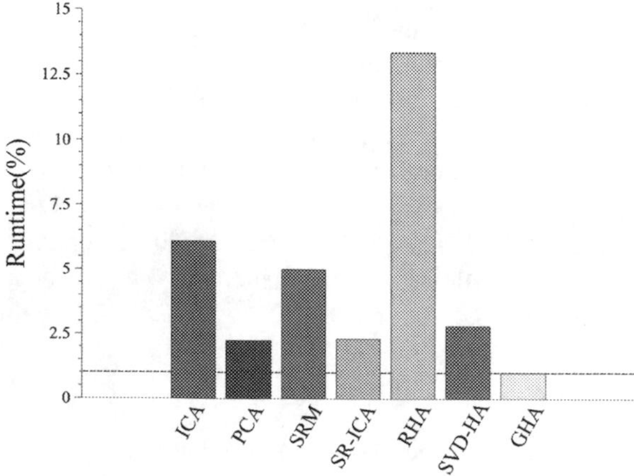

Fig. 4. Runtime analysis

4.4 Classification by Changing the Iterations

In this section, we will analyze the classification results by selecting different iterations. A major problem encountered in the functional alignment when applied to big data is that the algorithm does not converge or it converges very slowly. Therefore, it is necessary to set a maximum number of iterations when running the algorithm. And it is significant to design experiments to study the effect of different iterations on the classification accuracy of the algorithm. When classification accuracy of the algorithm no longer rises or even decreases, the iterating can be stopped to reduce the runtime of the program. Figure 3 shows the performance of our method when setting different iterations (see Fig. 3). As we can see, when selecting fewer iterations, the accuracy decreases slowly, so we do not need to run too many iterations when using Gradient-HA method.

4.5 Runtime Analysis

The main advantage of the proposed algorithm is that it solves the high time complexity problem in functional alignment methods when applied to big data. The above analysis shows that our algorithm reduces the runtime through feature selection, stochastic gradient ascent and iteration number setting. In this section, we compare the mean runtime of our algorithm with that of other algorithms. The results are generated by calculating the mean runtime on DS105, DS107 and DS232. Figure 4 shows the runtime results in comparison with other functional alignment methods, where the runtime of other methods is scaled based on our Gradient-HA method (see Fig. 4). As this figure demonstrated, the proposed method generates the best runtime, which proves that our method is effective and works well. Further, RHA method generates the worst runtime because it uses SVD too many times when calculating the HA solution.

5 Conclusion

This paper proposes a gradient-based functional alignment algorithm in order to apply hyperalignment to multi-subject fMRI big data. The Gradient-HA algorithm solves the hyperalignment problem by calculating the solution of ICA using stochastic gradient ascent. This algorithm can solve the problem of fMRI data with multiple subjects, a large number of samples and plenty of voxels. We also design experiments to show how Gradient-HA can be used for post-alignment classification. The results of the experiments show that our method is better than many other state-of-the-art functional alignment algorithms regarding classification accuracy and runtime. Therefore, our method has more advantages than the general functional alignment methods on big data. In the future work, we can apply Gradient-HA to more bigger datasets, and extra optimize the gradient algorithm to obtain higher accuracy and faster runtime.

Acknowledgments. This work was supported in part by the National Natural Science Foundation of China (61473149, 61422204, and 61732006).

References

1. Logothetis, N.K.: The neural basis of the blood–oxygen–level–dependent functional magnetic resonance imaging signal. Philos. Trans. R. Soc. Lond. **357**(1424), 1003 (2002)
2. Haxby, J.V., Connolly, A.C., Guntupalli, J.S.: Decoding neural representational spaces using multivariate pattern analysis. Ann. Rev. Neurosci. **37**(37), 435–456 (2014)
3. Yousefnezhad, M., Zhang, D.: Local discriminant hyperalignment for multi-subject fMRI data alignment. In: 34th AAAI Conference on Artificial Intelligence, pp. 59–61, San Francisco, USA (2017)
4. Chen, P.H., Chen, J., Yeshurun, Y., Hasson, U., Haxby, J.V., Ramadge, P.J.: A reduced-dimension fMRI shared response model. In: 28th Advances in Neural Information Processing Systems, Canada, pp. 460–468 (2015)
5. Chen, P.H., Guntupalli, J.S., Haxby, J.V., Ramadge, P.J.: Joint SVD-Hyperalignment for multi-subject FMRI data alignment. In: 24th IEEE International Workshop on Machine Learning for Signal Processing, France, pp. 1–6 (2014)
6. Haxby, J.V., Guntupalli, J.S., Connolly, A.C., et al.: A common, high-dimensional model of the representational space in human ventral temporal cortex. Neuron **72**(2), 404–416 (2011)
7. Laitinen, L.: Co-planar stereotaxic atlas of the human brain: 3-dimensional proportional system: an approach to cerebral imaging. Clin. Neurol. Neurosurg. **91**(3), 277–278 (1989)
8. Watson, J.D.R., Myers, R., Frackowiak, R.S., et al.: Area V5 of the human brain: evidence from a combined study using positron emission tomography and magnetic resonance imaging. Cereb. Cortex **3**(2), 79–94 (1993)
9. Rademacher, J., Caviness, V.S., Steinmetz, H., et al.: Topographical variation of the human primary cortices: implications for neuroimaging, brain mapping, and neurobiology. Cereb. Cortex **3**(4), 313–329 (1993)
10. Xu, H., Lorbert, A., Ramadge, P.J., Guntupalli, J.S., Haxby, J.V.: Regularized hyperalignment of multi-set fMRI data. In: IEEE Statistical Signal Processing Workshop, USA, pp. 229–232 (2012)
11. Guntupalli, J.S., Hanke, M., Halchenko, Y.O., et al.: A model of representational spaces in human cortex. Cereb. Cortex **26**(6), 2919–2934 (2016)
12. Lorbert, A., Ramadge, P.J.: Kernel hyperalignment. In: 25th Advances in Neural Information Processing Systems, Harveys, pp. 1790–1798 (2012)
13. Chen, P.H., et al.: A convolutional autoencoder for multi-subject fMRI data aggregation. In: 29th Workshop of Representation Learning in Artificial and Biological Neural Networks, Barcelona (2016)
14. Zhang, H., Chen, P.H., et al.: A searchlight factor model approach for locating shared information in multi-subject fMRI analysis. arXiv preprint arXiv:1609.09432 (2016)
15. Hyvärinen, A., Karhunen, J., Oja, E.: Independent Component Analysis, 7th edn. Wiley, New York (2001)
16. Yousefnezhad, M., Zhang, D.: Deep Hyperalignment. In: Conference on Neural Information Processing Systems, USA (2017)
17. Smola, A.J., Schölkopf, B.: A tutorial on support vector regression. Stat. Comput. **14**(3), 199–222 (2004)
18. Gower, J.C., Dijksterhuis, G.B.: Procrustes Problems, 1st edn. Oxford University Press, Oxford (2004)

Node Based Row-Filter Convolutional Neural Network for Brain Network Classification

Bingcheng Mao, Jiashuang Huang, and Daoqiang Zhang(✉)

College of Computer Science and Technology,
Nanjing University of Aeronautics and Astronautics, Nanjing 211106, China
dqzhang@nuaa.edu.cn

Abstract. Brain network plays an important role in the diagnosis of brain diseases. Recently, applying convolutional neural networks (CNNs) in brain network has attracted great interests. Although traditional convolution can capture all the nearest neighbors of a point in Euclidean space, it may miss the nearest neighbors of the node in the graph (i.e., in topological space). Hence, how to design a meaningful convolutional operator is a major challenge for brain network classification. Accordingly, in this paper, we propose a node based row-filter convolutional neural network, named NRF-CNN, for brain network classification. The proposed NRF-CNN can learn the high-order representation for brain network without losing important structure information. Specifically, we first introduce the concept of node neighbor within one step. Then, we define a novel row-filter convolutional operator, which can effectively capture local pattern of graph by applying a row scanning on adjacent matrix. Next, we adopt a structure preserved pooling to enrich the node representation by multiply input adjacent matrix and the node representation. Further, we stack several row-filter convolutional layers and structure preserved pooling layers to capture feature representation with more complex information. Finally, we fuse all features learned from each layer by linear weighting. To evaluate the effectiveness of our approach, we compare it with state-of-the-art methods in brain network classification on three real brain network datasets. The experimental results demonstrate that our approach outperforms the others, showing better capacity in capturing meaningful and discriminative representations for brain networks.

Keywords: Brain network · Graph · Node based Row-Filter Convolutional neural network

1 Introduction

Brain network plays an important role in the diagnosis of brain disease. In general, brain network is represented as graph where nodes and edges denote brain regions and connections between pairs of regions, respectively [1]. Usually, these brain networks are constructed from neuroimaging data, e.g., resting-state functional magnetic resonance image (fMRI). Connections of brain network have been proved to be associated with many brain diseases because the structural changes in the brain network usually

X. Geng and B.-H. Kang (Eds.): PRICAI 2018, LNAI 11012, pp. 1069–1080, 2018.
https://doi.org/10.1007/978-3-319-97304-3_82

precede the clinical symptoms that doctors can diagnoses [2]. Hence, analyzing brain network would be useful for early detection and treatment of brain diseases.

Many methods have been proposed for brain network classification over the last decades. A common method is to analyze the brain network in vector space by transforming structural data into vectors, such as complex network based methods and connection weights based methods. Obviously, it is inappropriate for the brain network analysis because these methods do not consider the graph structure information. To overcome this problem, Fei et al. [3] proposed a subnetwork-based method, which can preserve structure information by utilizing the most frequent subgraphs mined from brain networks. However, these methods only focus on the simple spatial similarity in graphs. To find more complex information in brain networks, Verma and Zhang used eigenvalue-decomposition in standard graph Laplacian to find basis with which the graph can be transformed into a spectrum based vector representation [6]. But this method is not flexible due to the calculation of Laplacian matrix for every graph and hard to obtain a meaningful representation related to the original node because they are analyzed in spectral space.

Deep neural network (DNN) has achieved great success in many tasks [7]. In order to use its powerful learning ability, many researchers have proposed deep learning based methods in graph learning [8–10]. However, these methods cannot be applied to brain network classification directly because social network or molecular network usually has different label information on each node while brain network has its own overall label. In order to use DNN in brain network properly, another property should be considered. The property is that brain network has much low-order to high-order structural information and effective use of this information can greatly help our classification [4]. According to this, convolutional neural network (CNN) is a good approach in most of the DNN methods, because CNN can identify simple structures and then use these simple structures to identify more complex structures. For example, in face recognition, they first find representations of the human eye, mouth and other small organs in the first few convolutional layers, and then constitute the entire face in the last few convolutional layers. However, the convolution designed for pictures is usually not suitable on the brain network because the locality of graph data is different from traditional Euclidean grid structure data. In Euclidean grid structure data, one point's neighbors are those points lying around it. Differently, this property is not always valid in graph data. As is shown in Fig. 1, nodes c, d and e are close in the graph Fig. 1(a) and they are neighbors in Fig. 1(b). However, they are not neighbors in Fig. 1(c) although Figs. 1(b) and 1(c) represent the same graph Fig. 1(a). Therefore, Wang et al. [11, 12] proposed graph reordering to make the edges more closely in adjacent matrix. It can alleviate the situation but it is not guaranteed that we can capture all the local nodes with a grid convolutional filter. On the other hand, many methods [6, 13] have good performance in classification but they are hard to detect the lesion region which is very helpful to understand the disease. Therefore, our goal is to define a suitable convolution filter that can not only find local structures but also help identify disease areas.

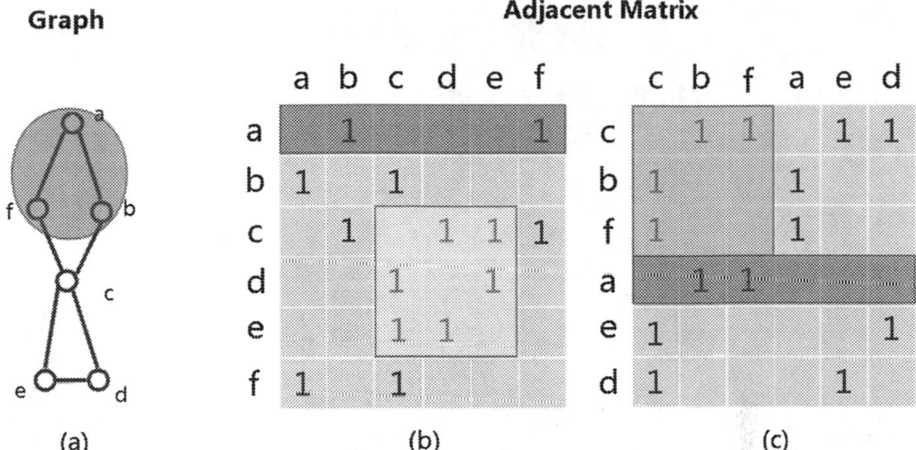

Fig. 1. Local pattern on graph. Adjacent matrix (b) and (c) are the same presentation of graph (a). Row based local pattern is stable but square grid local pattern is changed when adjacent matrix changed.

To address the above challenges, we propose a node based row-filter convolution neural network named NRF-CNN in this paper. Specifically, we use NRF-CNN to capture the brain network's local information based on the graph and learn the graph representation in the highly ordered and non-linear latent space. To solve the issue of non-Euclidean structure with graph data, we define a row convolutional filter based on graph node so that the activation of the convolution will not change even if the node index is changed. In addition, we use a linear mapping to enrich the node output without losing of structure information. To overcome the limited quantity of datasets, we use random disturbance to get more training data. Results on three real world datasets show that NRF-CNN not only improves the accuracy of classification, but also can get the disease-related brain area.

2 Method

2.1 Architecture of NRF-CNN

Figure 2 illustrates the architecture of our NRF-CNN. The adjacent matrix is fed into initial row-filter convolutional layer. Next, several structure preserved pooling layers and row-filter convolutional layers are alternately stacked. Then, outputs of all pooling layers and the last convolutional layer are fused for the fully connected layer. Finally, the result of classification can be acquired after softmax layer.

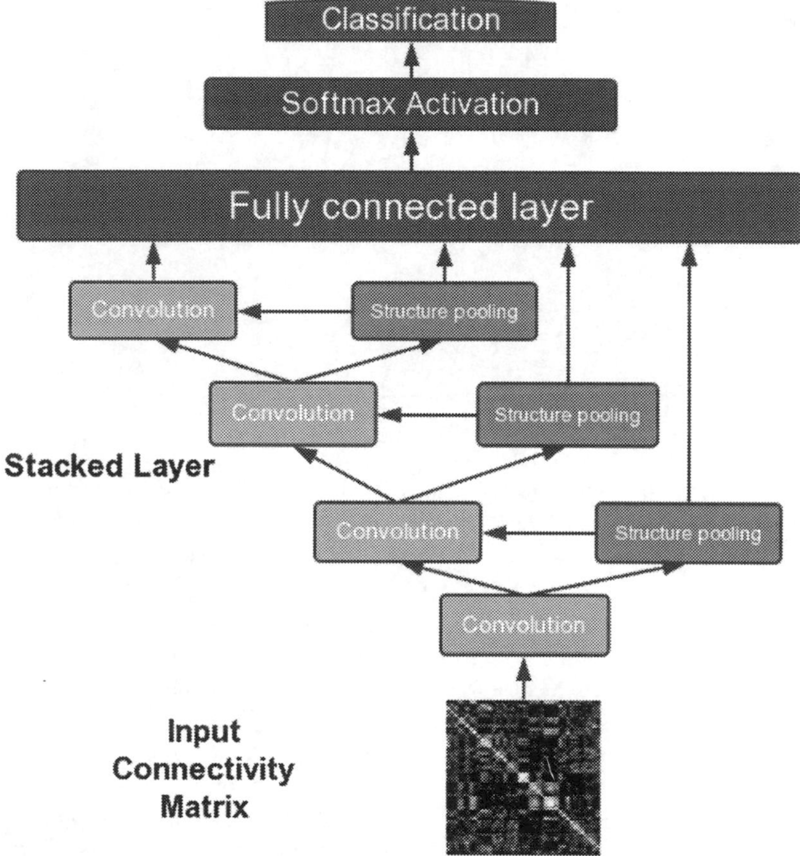

Fig. 2. The architecture of node based row-filter convolutional neural network.

2.2 Definition of Graph Local Pattern

For a graph $G = (V, E, W)$, where V is node set with $|V| = \mathrm{N}$ and $E \subseteq V \times V$ is the set of edges connecting nodes, W is the connectivity weight matrix associate with each edge. We construct locality of G based on node v, then all the other nodes can be its neighbor with N steps in a connected graph. We only focus on these nodes within a step of V. This local pattern is stable for the node index in the adjacency matrix and Fig. 1 shows the condition. Therefore, it is meaningful to grid convolution with which the {c, d, e} node set can be captured on the right adjacent matrix but the left adjacent matrix does not contain this pattern. For our definition, the local pattern does not change when the adjacent matrix changed.

2.3 Node Based Row-Filter Convolution

Following the aforementioned concept, we can define our node based row-filter convolution. For every hidden node in neural network, we have:

$$O^l_{i,m} = f^l\left(\sum_{j=1}^{M^{l-1}} A^l_{i,j} w^{l,m}_j + b^{l,m}\right) \tag{1}$$

where $i \in \{1, 2, 3, \ldots, N\}, m \in \{1, 2, 3, \ldots, M^l\}$, $A^l \in \mathbb{R}^{N \times M^{l-1}}$ is the input of l-th layer ($M^0 = N$ is the first layer input dimension), subscript i, j is A's row and column index; $w^{l,m} \in \mathbb{R}^{1 \times M^l}$ is the m-th filter weights at l-th layer, subscript j is w's element index; $b^{l,m}$ is m-th bias at l-th layer; f^l is activation function at l-th layer. N is the node number of brain network, M^{l-1} and M^l represent the $(l-1)$-th and l-th filter number respectively. $O^l \in \mathbb{R}^{N \times M^l}$ is the output map at l-th layer. With one filter, we can get an activation vector where each element associates with each node. Then we can get M^l different feature vectors by applying M^l different filters (e.g., $w^{l,m}$).

2.4 Structure Preserved Pooling

To capture high-order features from brain network, we stack several convolutional layers. It is noted that when we get a feature map after one layer's convolution, each column represents node's non-linear signal with one specific filter. We use a linear mapping to combine these non-linear signals. After convolution at l-th layer, we have:

$$S^l = O^l \in \mathbb{R}^{N \times M^l} \tag{2}$$

S^l is the activation matrix, each column $s_j \in \mathbb{R}^{N \times 1}$ is node's represent vector with j-th filter at l-th layer. Then we can apply a transformation in s with transform matrix P:

$$r^l_j = P^l s^l_j \tag{3}$$

Combine all features s, we can get the matrix form:

$$R^l = \frac{P^l S^l}{\rho} \tag{4}$$

$R^l \in \mathbb{R}^{N \times M^l}$ is the mapped activation matrix. ρ is the regular item to control the magnitude. The next problem is how to define the transform matrix P. In fact, we have the adjacency matrix A for every graph. Row of A is node's relation with other nodes. Column of S is the convolutional signal with each brain node. So when we apply inner product with row of A and column of S, signal vector constant with graph structure can be enhanced while the others will be weakened. We add the graph structure information in each pooling layer so that the structure information will not decline so much with the stacking of convolutional layers (Fig. 3).

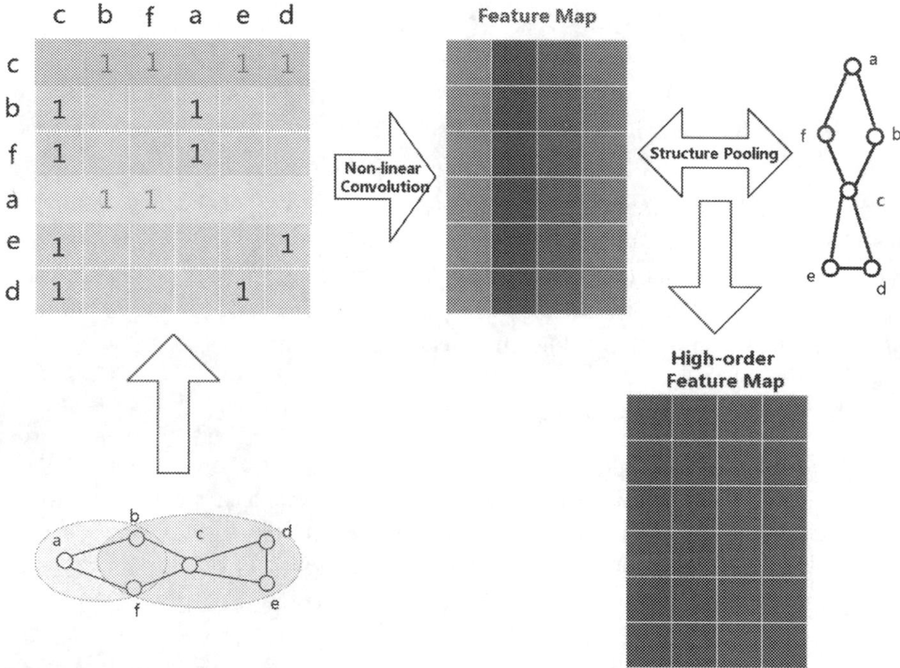

Fig. 3. Illustration of node based row-filter convolution and structure preserved pooling. A graph is presented as an adjacent matrix, then row-filter convolution is applied to capture the non-linear features. Different colors in feature map mean features captured by different row-filter. We get concentrated features by multiply convolutional signals with input adjacency matrix.

2.5 Feature Fusion with Different Layers

The features from different convolutional layers reflect various graph information, which are becoming more and more comprehensive with the layer stacking. We can take advantage of all the information by combining the features together. In this paper, we use these combined features as the input of convolutional layers. The input of l-th layer can be written as:

$$A^l = S^{l-1} + \sum_{j=1}^{K_l} \lambda_j R^j \tag{5}$$

where S^{l-1} is the output at ($l-1$)-th layer, R^j is the structure preserved pooling outputs at j-th layer, λ_j is the combination coefficient, and K_l is the fusion number of feature map. In our implementation, we choose the feature map of previous layer for every hidden layer and use the outputs of all pooling layers and the last convolutional layer for the fully connected layer.

3 Experiments

3.1 Data Collection

In our experiments, we evaluate the proposed methods on three brain disease datasets, which are Schizophrenia (SZ), Autism Spectrum Disorder (ASD) and single center schizophrenia (s-SZ) contains 773, 468 and 200 subjects respectively. The first two datasets are from different centers, e.g., different hospitals or different scanning machines. These datasets are downloaded from the International Neuroimaging Data-Sharing Initiative (INDI). Data information and preprocess can be found in the website [14].

3.2 Compared Methods

In this paper, we also compare our NRF-CNN method to state-of-the-art methods for brain network classification. The compared methods are described in detail below.

Support vector machine (SVM): In this method, we transform the adjacent matrix into a vector then use the default parameters in our implementation with the code in python package of sklearn [5].

Frequent subgraph mining (FSM): It is a widely used method in graph mining. We set the subgraph node number of four then get an indicator vector by search the top-100 frequent subgraph for every brain network. With the representation, we use linear SVM for brain network classification. It is a representation of traditional graph mining method [3].

Family of graph spectral distances (FGSD): Verma and Zhang [6] proposed a graph representation method with the graph spectral distance and graph spectrum. We use the code they provided and treat this as a representative of the spectrum method. We use the default parameters they given in our implementation.

Convolutional neural network (CNN): It is the traditional convolution neural network with convolutional layer, pooling layer, non-linear and fully connected layer stacked. We set 3×3 convolution filter, 2×2 pooling filter, ReLU activation function, cross-entropy loss and Adam optimizer for our CNN experiment [9].

Structural deep brain network mining (SDBN): Wang et al. [9] proposed a CNN method with the graph node index reordering. It is a better way to mining information in graph than traditional CNN because after the node index reordering, some big edge weights will lie on a square grid which is better for CNN. The parameter settings are the same as their paper's.

3.3 Experiment Setting

Figure 2 shows our architecture of NRF-CNN. Specifically, activation function is sigmoid activation function. Our main optimization goal is cross-entropy loss. All the weights are initialized by a Gaussian distribution with zero mean and 0.1variance. We applied l2-norm on all the neural network weights for the purpose of reducing the risk of overfitting. The dropout is also added after the fully connected layer with the rate of 0.5. We apply Adam optimizer to optimize our loss because it is better than traditional gradient descent. We perform 5-fold (each fold 3 training sets, 1 test set and 1 validation set.) cross-validation on balanced datasets and report the average results. We stop our training when the validation loss is minimal. The number of convolution filters is set to 90, 75, 60, 60 for each layer, and the number of hidden nodes in fully connected layer is set as the same number of brain network regions. All the codes are implemented in Tensorflow.

Table 1. Average accuracy performances of the compared methods (%).

Data set	Method					
	SVM	FSM	FGSD	CNN	SDBN	NRF-CNN
SZ-773	64.31	65.12	53.14	65.26	67.14	**73.42**
ASD-468	60.68	62.13	53.41	61.67	61.23	**69.71**
sSZ-200	72.37	68.29	61.07	65.27	71.36	**77.20**

3.4 Performance on Brain Disease Classification Problem

Table 1 lists the results of brain disease classification with six methods in three datasets. It is obviously that the performance of our approach is better than other methods. Specifically, the proposed method yields a classification accuracy of 73.42%, 69.71%, 77.2% in SZ, ASD, sSZ datasets. The classification accuracy of FGSD method is obviously worse than others because it is designed for unweighted graph, which may lose information in weighted brain network. FSM does not achieve a good accuracy because it is hard to search all subgraphs with an exponential process. For CNN and SDBN methods, their performances are similar with FSM, which means the local pattern they defined is not sufficient. Our approach is better than these because we use a more meaningful local filter which can capture all the neighbor information of one node. SVM method does not contain the structure information of brain network, but its performance is not bad, which means there are non-structural features in brain network. In our method, all features are used by row-filter convolutional layers and structure information is used by structure preserved pooling layers. Therefore, our approach has the best performance in brain network classification compared with these methods.

3.5 Performance with Data Augmentation

We also use data augmentation to improve the classification performance. Data augmentation can be implemented by disturbing data in the training data. Specially, we randomly set 3% edge weights in brain network to be zero, which means the edges are removed. In this way, some brain networks may change from connected graph to non-connected graph. We can learn from Fig. 4(b) that when we add augmented data to our training set, the test accuracy can be improved. It is worth noting that the training accuracy for augmented data is extremely lower than normal samples even if small number of edges has been removed. This may be because the graph is divided into several subgraphs that are not connected to each other. Obviously, our model can capture these small but important changes in the brain network by considering all connections of a node. What's more, the accuracy of augmented data is also increasing although the edges are different each time when they are randomly removed. This means that our model can capture the overall structure by subgraphs.

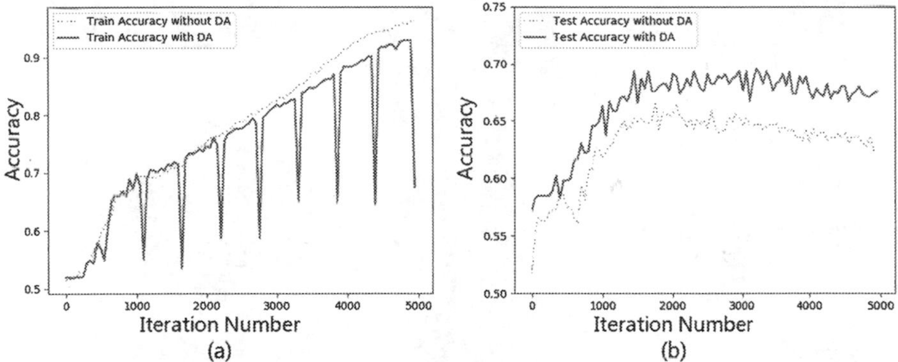

Fig. 4. Comparison of accuracy after using data augmentation. (a) Is train accuracy and (b) is test accuracy. The test accuracy can be improved while train accuracy will be reduced by using data augmentation.

3.6 Lesion Detection of Brain Region

Based on the weights of the fully connected layer, we can identify the brain regions associated with disease. Specially, we summarize the absolute weights of the first fully connected layer for each brain network region, and think these value represent the discriminant power. Figure 5 shows the correlation between brain regions and autism. Besides, we can locate the most relevant brain regions including Thalamus, Ftontal_Mid, Temporal_Sup, and Temporal_Mid, which have been proved to be related to autism in other previous work.

3.7 Feature Representations from Different Layers

In order to prove that our model can learn the discriminant features, we visualize feature representations from different layers into two-dimensional space by t-SNE method. Specially, 42 test ASD subjects including 21 patients and 21 normal controls are fed into our trained NRF-CNN model and then different representations from different layers are captured. From Fig. 6, we can see that the representations are becoming more and more distinguishable with two categories. Figure 6(a) is the input representation, and all the subjects are mixed together. Interestingly, we can see from Fig. 6(b) that after one layer's transformation, different categories have the trend to separate.

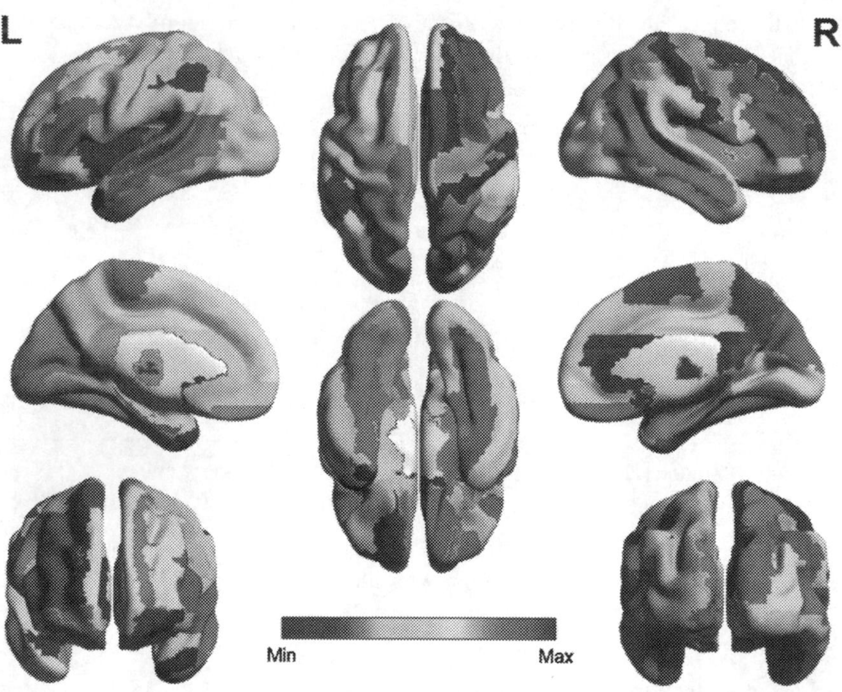

Fig. 5. Correlation learned by NRF-CNN between brain regions and autism. Red brain areas are more discriminatory while blues are more irrelevant with autism. (Color figure online)

Then in the next layer, patients are almost lying on the half of the figure in Fig. 6(c). Figure 6(d) shows the fully connected layer's representation, and it is obviously that two categories are put on both sides. Figure 6(c) shows that our model has the tendency to learn the patient representation first, which means our model focuses more on the unusual pattern in brain network.

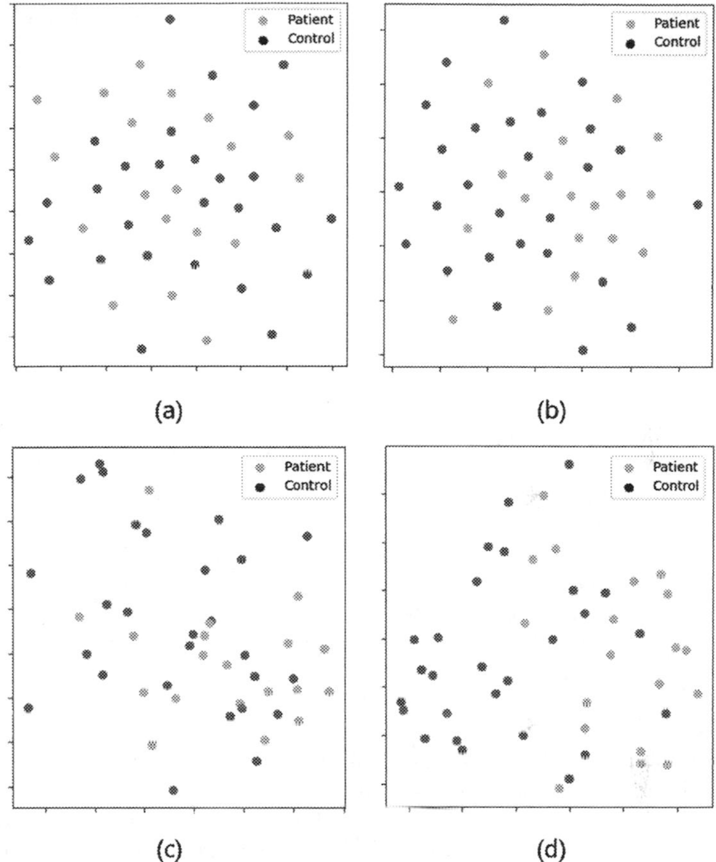

Fig. 6. ASD test subjects' features captured from different layers and these features are embedded to two-dimensional space using the t-SNE method (with 42 samples). (a) Is the input matrix, (b) is the first layer's output, (c) is the second layer's output, (d) is the fully connected layer's feature.

4 Conclusion

In this paper, a node based row-filter convolutional neural networks, named NRF-CNN, is proposed to classify the brain disease and learn the meaningful representations for brain networks. First, we define a node local pattern on adjacent matrix then we propose a row-filter convolutional operator to replace the grid convolutional operator in traditional CNNs. Second, we define a pooling operator with original input and convoluted output, which can preserve node information and graph structure information. Third, we fuse all the features from first hidden layer to last hidden layer, by which all the low and high order information can be fused. Our experiments show that NRF-CNN is better than other widely used methods in brain network classification.

Acknowledgements. This work was supported in part by the National Natural Science Foundation of China (61473149, 61422204, and 61732006).

References

1. Rubinov, M., Sporns, O.: Complex network measures of brain connectivity: uses and interpretations. Neuroimage **52**(3), 1059–1069 (2010)
2. Jie, B., Zhang, D., Wee, C.Y., Shen, D.: Topological graph kernel on multiple thresholded functional connectivity networks for mild cognitive impairment classification. Hum. Brain Mapp. **35**(7), 2876 (2014)
3. Fei, F., Jie, B., Zhang, D.: Frequent and discriminative subnetwork mining for mild cognitive impairment classification. Brain Connect. **4**(5), 347–360 (2014)
4. Rubinov, M., et al.: Small-world properties of nonlinear brain activity in schizophrenia. Hum. Brain Mapp. **30**(2), 403–416 (2009)
5. Sacchet, M.D., Prasad, G., Foland-Ross, L.C., Thompson, P.M., Gotlib, I.H.: Support vector machine classification of major depressive disorder using diffusion-weighted neuroimaging and graph theory. Front. Psychiatry **6**, 21 (2015)
6. Verma, S., Zhang, Z.L.: Hunt for the unique, stable, sparse and fast feature learning on graphs. In: Advances in Neural Information Processing Systems, pp. 87–97 (2017)
7. LeCun, Y., Bengio, Y., Hinton, G.: Deep learning. Nature **521**(7553), 436–444 (2015)
8. Atwood, J., Towsley, D.: Diffusion-convolutional neural networks. In: Advances in Neural Information Processing Systems, pp. 1993–2001 (2016)
9. Bruna, J., Zaremba, W., Szlam, A., LeCun, Y.: Spectral networks and locally connected networks on graphs. arXiv preprint arXiv:1312.6203 (2013)
10. Duvenaud, D.K., et al.: Convolutional networks on graphs for learning molecular fingerprints. In: Advances in Neural Information Processing Systems, pp. 2224–2232 (2015)
11. Wang, S., He, L., Cao, B., Lu, C.T., Yu, P.S., Ragin, A.B.: Structural deep brain network mining. In: Proceedings of the 23rd ACM SIGKDD International Conference on Knowledge Discovery and Data Mining, pp. 475–484. ACM (2017)
12. Luo, Z., Liu, L., Yin, J., Li, Y., Wu, Z.: Deep learning of graphs with Ngram convolutional neural networks. IEEE Trans. Knowl. Data Eng. **29**(10), 2125–2139 (2017)
13. Defferrard, M., Bresson, X., Vandergheynst, P.: Convolutional neural networks on graphs with fast localized spectral filtering. In: Advances in Neural Information Processing Systems, pp. 3844–3852 (2016)
14. INDI Homepage. http://fcon_1000.projects.nitrc.org/. Accessed 12 Nov 2017

Author Index

Printed in the United States
By Bookmasters